ARCHAEOLOGICAL GAZETTEER
OF AFGHANISTAN

ARCHAEOLOGICAL GAZETTEER OF AFGHANISTAN

Revised Edition

Warwick Ball

OXFORD

UNIVERSITY PRESS

OXFORD

UNIVERSITY PRESS

Great Clarendon Street, Oxford, OX2 6DP,
United Kingdom

Oxford University Press is a department of the University of Oxford.
It furthers the University's objective of excellence in research, scholarship,
and education by publishing worldwide. Oxford is a registered trade mark of
Oxford University Press in the UK and in certain other countries

First published in French by Editions
Recherche sur les civilisations, A.D.P.F. 1982
Revised edition published in 2019

Impression: 1

Published in the United States of America by Oxford University Press
198 Madison Avenue, New York, NY 10016, United States of America

British Library Cataloguing in Publication Data
Data available

Library of Congress Control Number: 2018953895

ISBN 978–0–19–927758–2

Printed and bound by
CPI Group (UK) Ltd, Croydon, CR0 4YY

To the memory of Jean-Claude Gardin

NOTE ON TRANSLITERATION

1. Persian/Dari: The system that was recommended for the pre-1979 journal *Iran* has been adopted, with the following simplifications:

z ض s ث t ط z ظ s ص h ح ʿ ع

2. Pashto/Pukhtu: A standardised system has been formulated by the International Centre for Pashto Sudies in Kabul, but to minimise the use of diacritical marks I have used the same system as for Persian, with the following simplifications for the additional letters:

n ن n ن r ر r ن t ن oy نی e ی dz خ ts خ g ک x ش

3. Turkish/Uzbek/Turkmen: In general I have transliterated from the version written in Arabic script using the same system as for Persian. In some cases, however, I have used the modern Latinised Turkish form when it is more familiar, e.g. Effendi Tepe, Toprakkale.

4. Baluch, Brahui, Nuristani, Wakhi, etc.: Transliterated from the version written in Arabic script, when known. Otherwise, as it occurs by the modern user.

5. Other non-Latin scripts: For Russian the system used by the British Library has been adopted. For Japanese, as transcribed in the Japanese publications cited.

In general, diacritical marks have been avoided for the sake of simplicity, with the exception of the macron over long vowels: ā, ī, ū, etc. Whenever a particular spelling is in more common usage than its correctly transcribed form, this has been used, e.g. Begram instead of Bagram, Surkh Kotal instead of Surkh Kutal, Kandahār instead of Qandahār, Tillya Tepe instead of Tila Tapa, etc. If the original language form of a name is not known or cannot otherwise be checked, macrons are omitted.

Although I have attempted to adhere to these forms as much as possible, many inconsistencies inevitably occur. In many cases—such as place names recorded by 19th-century travellers—the original forms are not known.

ABBREVIATIONS USED IN THE TEXT

ABC	Afghan Boundary Commission
ACHCO	Afghan Cultural Heritage Consulting Organization
AIA	Afghan Institute of Archaeology
AKTC	Aga Khan Trust for Culture
AMNH	American Museum of Natural History
ASI	Archaeological Survey of India
AUFS	American Universities Field Staff
BIAS	British Institute of Afghan Studies
BIPS	British Institute of Persian Studies
BM	British Museum
CNRS	Centre National de la Recherche Scientifique
DACAAR	Danish Committee for Aid to Afghan Refugees
DAAD	Deutscher Akademischer Austausch-Dienst
DAFA	Délégation Archéologique Française en Afghanistan
DAI	Deutsches Archëologisches Institut
HSA	Historical Society of Afghanistan
IsIAO	Istituto Italiano per l'Africa e l'Oriente
IsMEO	Istituto Italiano per il Medio ed'Estremo Oriente
ROM	Royal Ontario Museum
SAC	Seistan Arbitration Commission
SOAS	School for Oriental and African Studies

CHRONOLOGICAL TABLE

PERIODS

Lower Palaeolithic

Middle Palaeolithic 50,000–30,000 BC.

Upper Palaeolithic 15,000–10,000 BC.

Epi-Palaeolithic 10,000–8000 BC.

Neolithic 8000–4000 BC.

Bronze Age 4000–1500 BC.

Iron Age 1500–700 BC.

Achaemenid c.530–330 BC.

Seleucid c.330–185 BC in Seistan, 330–250 BC in the remainder of the country.

Mauryan c.275–185 BC in Jalālābād, Ghazni, Kandahār, and Bust areas only.

Graeco-Bactrian c.250–110 BC in Balkh and Badakhshān areas, 250–160 BC in Herat, Bādghīs, and Kābul areas, 185–110 BC in the remainder of the country.

Parthian c.160 BC–AD 225 in Herat and Bādghīs areas, 155 BC–AD 20 in Seistan, and 155–90 BC in Kandahār and Bust areas.

Indo-Greek c.155–90 BC in Kābul, Jalālābād, and Ghazni areas only.

Saka c.90 BC–AD 2 in Kābul, Jalālābād, Ghazni, Kandahār, and Bust areas only.

Early Kushan c.110 BC–AD 75 in Balkh and Badakhshān areas only.

Indo-Parthian c. AD 20–225 in Kandahār, Bust, and Seistan areas, AD 20–75 in Kābul, Jalālābād, and Ghazni areas.

Great Kushan c. AD 75–225 in Balkh, Badakhshān, Kābul, Jalālābād, and Ghazni areas only.

Early Sasanian c.275–345 in Balkh, Badakhshān, Kābul, and Jalālābād areas, 275–450 in all other areas.

Kushano-Sasanian c.345–425 in Balkh and Badakhshān and 345–450 in Kābul and Jalālābād areas.

Hunnic groups c.475–565 in Balkh and Badakhshān, 450–535 in Kābul, Jalālābād, Ghazni, and Kandahār areas, and 485–565 in Bādghīs.

Later Sasanian c.450–650 in Herat, Bust, and Seistan, 565–650 in Bādghīs, Balkh, and Badakhshān, and 535–650 in the remainder of the country.

Turk Khanates c.650–875 in Balkh, Badakhshān, and Bāmiyān areas, 650–820 in Bāghdīs.

Umayyad-Abbasid c.650–800 in Seistan and 650–820 in Herat.

Turki Shahi c.650–850 in Kābul, Jalālābād, Ghazni, and Kandahār areas. 650–800 in Bust area.

Tang Eastern Wakhan only.

Tahirid c.820–75 in Herat and Bādghīs areas only.

Saffarid c.860–920 in Bust and Seistan, 875–900 in Kandahār area.

Samanid c.875–1000 in Herat, Bādghīs, Balkh, and Badakhshān areas, 900–980 in Kandahār area, and 910–1000 in Bust and Seistan areas.

Hindu Shahi c.875–1000 in Jalālābād, 875–980 in Kābul, and 875–960 in Ghazni area.

Ghaznavid *c.*960–1150 in Ghazni, 980–1150 in Kābul and Kandahār areas, 1000–1150 in Jalālābād, Bust, and Seistan areas, and 1000–1050 in Herat, Bādghīs, Balkh, and Badakhshān areas.

Seljuk *c.*1050–1150 in Herat, Bāghdīs, Balkh, and Badakhshān areas only.

Ghurid *c.*1150–1220.

Kart *c.*1245–1350 in Herat and Bādghīs only.

Kayani *c.*1260–1380 in Bust and Seistan areas only.

Chaghatai *c.*1330–1380 in Balkh, Badakhshān, Kābul, Jalālābād, Ghazni, and Kandahār areas, 1350–1380 in Herat and Bādghīs areas.

Timurid *c.*1380–1500.

REGIONAL/CHRONOLOGICAL CHART FOR THE HISTORICAL PERIODS

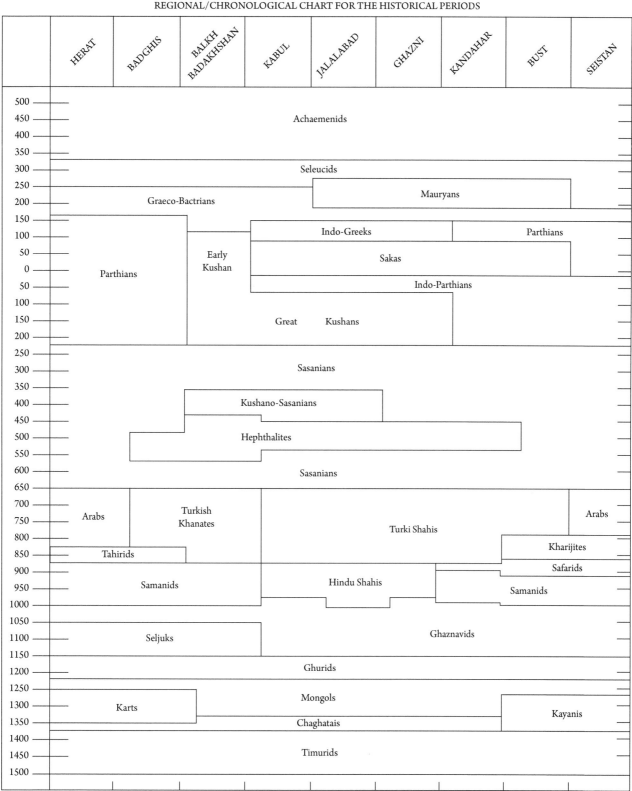

ACKNOWLEDGEMENTS

This work developed out of my *Archaeological Gazetteer of Afghanistan/Catalogue des sites archéologiques d'Afghanistan*, originally published in 1982. The original was made possible through the support of the Délégation Archéologique Française d'Afghanistan, the Centre National de la Recherche Scientifique, the Direction Générale des Relations Culturelles du Ministère des Affaires Étrangères (France), the British Academy, and the British Institute of Afghan Studies.

Over the many years since then a great many individuals have helped in the making of the present work. In addition to those acknowledged in the original edition, I would like to thank Osmund Bopearachchi, Elizabeth Errington, John Falconer, Anna Filigenzi, Henri-Paul Francfort, Ana Rosa Rodríguez García, Frantz Grenet, Norman Hammond, Jolyon Leslie, Bertille Lyonnet, John Macginnis, Rachel Mairs, Mike Mantia, Philippe Marquis, Lolita Nehru, François Neuville, Bernard O'Kane, Lore Sander, Nicholas Sims-Williams, and David Thomas who have offered advice, information, and material generally, although all errors are entirely my own. Part of the work of preparation was carried out with the aid of a grant from the Gerald Avery Wainwright Fund of the University of Oxford.

The original work was long before electronic versions existed, so when embarking upon the update, the original edition was entirely retyped by Rose Paterson, enabling me to work on it digitally. Elizabeth Willcox translated all of the French entries in the original edition especially for the new one. William Trousdale, formerly of the Smithsonian Institution, generously supplied a large amount of new unpublished information from his Helmand-Sistan surveys of the 1970s, with further input more recently from him and his colleague Mitchell Allen working on the material. Paul Bucherer-Dietschi of the Afghanistan Institute in Bubendorf, Switzerland, allowed me the use of the bibliographical classification system he had developed specially for the Institute, as well as access to the incomparable library there. Oliver Ball and Wendy Ball painstakingly copy-edited and correlated major draft sections of the work, saving me from many an error and inconsistency, but are in no way responsible for errors that crept in since.

Hilary O'Shea, Classics and Archaeology Editor at Oxford University Press, supported the project with enthusiasm right from the beginning, and I greatly regret that unforeseen delays at my end prevented her from seeing it through press before her retirement in 2014. I would like to thank both her and her successor at the Press, Charlotte Loveridge, together with Jenny King and all production and design staff at OUP, for their patience and for seeing this long delayed work through press.

In 2016 Gil Stein and Emily Hammer of the Afghan Heritage Mapping Partnership (AHMP) at the Oriental Institute, University of Chicago, kindly invited me to Chicago to meet with their mapping team and discuss sharing information of mutual interest. The AHMP team then generously supplied me with updated coordinates of the Catalogue entries based upon their high-resolution satellite images. The team also generated an entirely new set of maps, both the period maps and the regional maps, from the satellite images especially for this edition. The corrected coordinates and maps were generated at the Oriental Institute's CAMEL (Center for Ancient Middle Eastern Landscapes) lab. The coordinate data research team was led by Emily Hammer (former director of the OI CAMEL lab), CAMEL lab acting director Anthony Lauricella and Rebecca Seifried; special thanks are due to Gwendolyn Kristy, Shaheen Chaudry, Elise Macarthur, Oren Siegel, and Michael Johnson. The maps were designed and produced by AHMP-Chicago Project Manager Kathryn Franklin and Emily Boak. I owe an enormous thanks to the entire team in Chicago for their meticulousness and generosity in making this happen.

I owe more thanks than I can possibly express to Jonathan L. Lee who, over more than forty years, has given unstintingly of his own unsurpassed knowledge of Afghanistan in support of this project. As will be obvious in the following pages, a huge amount of invaluable information is due to the records he made over his many field trips there, often in remote parts of the country visited by few, if any, other researchers. Indeed, many of the more important discoveries, such as the Ghulbiyan painting and the Rag-i Bibi relief, to name just two of a large number, are due to him.

The original edition included a very large amount of previously unpublished material, mainly by Jean-Claude Gardin and Bertille Lyonnet from their surveys in eastern Bactria. Gardin also secured funding both for my research and for the eventual publication in the *Éditions Recherche sur les civilisations* series. He further made available a substantial body of other unpublished material from both the DAFA archives and its pottery collections, the latter studied and dated by Gardin and Lyonnet specially for inclusion in the *Gazetteer*. The archival material included the then unpublished surveys of the Hindu Kush fortifications by Marc Le Berre. Without all this unpublished material, the original *Gazetteer*, as well as its current incarnation, would be considerably less. Although most of this work has since been published elsewhere (Le Berre 1987; Lyonnet 1997; Gardin 1998), it was decided to include all the site information here in English translation in order to make it more available to a wider audience.

Above all therefore, I owe an enormous debt to the late Jean-Claude Gardin whose initial support and encouragement of this project right at the beginning turned it into more than a mere card index. It is deeply regretted that he could not see the current project through to its end. Without his generosity, guidance, and vision, this work would not exist. Dedicating it to his memory is the least that can be done to repay my debt to a great scholar and friend.

Warwick Ball

Scottish Borders 2018

CONTENTS

LIST OF FIGURES

Numbers refer to site catalogue numbers.

LIST OF MAPS

The maps were specially generated for the Gazetteer at the University of Chicago-Oriental Institute's Center for Ancient Middle Eastern Landscapes (CAMEL) lab using satellite imagery. The coordinate data research team was led by Emily Hammer (former director of the OI CAMEL lab), CAMEL lab acting director Tony Lauricella and Rebecca Seifried. The maps were designed and produced by Afghan Heritage Mapping Project Manager Kathryn Franklin and Emily Boak.

Introduction

The background to the present work lies in the exciting archaeological climate of Afghanistan in the 1970s. Increasing numbers of foreign archaeological missions were engaged in fieldwork: following on from the pioneering work of the Délégation Archéologique Française en Afghanistan (DAFA) since 1922, British, German, Italian, Japanese, Soviet, and US missions were undertaking active research, as well as the Afghans themselves under the auspices of the Afghan Institute of Archaeology. The latest to establish a permanent presence in Kabul was the British Institute of Afghan Studies, in 1972. To keep abreast of these activities, in 1979 work on compiling a simple card-index file of archaeological sites in Afghanistan was begun for the library of the British Institute. It was designed as a quick, working reference guide to the major sites for the use of researchers who needed further information on a particular site or sites, modelled on those indexes existing at the time in the British School of Archaeology at Athens and the Institute of Archaeology at London University. The value of such a guide soon became apparent, and it was decided to expand this index into a full catalogue encompassing as many of the sites and monuments as possible that could be found from published sources. As such, all known sites, whether they were simply unidentified mounds observed in passing or major monumental and excavated sites, could be referred to quickly and a comprehensive list of publications dealing with each site be consulted, in tandem with expanding the Institute library. In its loose, unbound form it was designed not only to be consulted for reference but also to be constantly enlarged, updated, and improved by its users.

As a result of expanding the index into a more comprehensive catalogue, it was suggested that a second version be prepared for publication as a gazetteer, and the original work was conceived. At the same time several colleagues offered to contribute their own unpublished field material for inclusion in the *Gazetteer* as a means of publishing sites hitherto accessible only in private archives. Chief of these were Jean-Claude Gardin and Bertille Lyonnet, who had recently completed their eastern Bactria surveys. It was also suggested that various miscellaneous sites that had been sporadically recorded over the years but not published, be also included. These sites are often only noticed in passing and their recording therefore is usually not important or systematic enough to form separate publications, and so are consequently shelved and forgotten. Again, the instigator was primarily Jean-Claude Gardin, who accordingly made available such material from the DAFA archives and its pottery collections. Such data, while probably unpublishable independently, is still valuable information: including it in such a general compendium is perhaps the only way of making known what would otherwise remain forgotten in storage; it does at least prevent needless repetition of fieldwork in the future. With the inclusion of all this new material the project became a more ambitious undertaking with a two-fold aim: first, as a channel for combining the existing knowledge of the sites in a simple, easily referable form; and second, as a pooling of resources of other researchers, combining new material with that already existing to make our archaeological picture of Afghanistan as complete and up-to-date as possible. Thus, the original *Archaeological Gazetteer of Afghanistan* was born, appearing in 1982. The present work is an updated and expanded version on this.

At the same time, the original concept of a card catalogue to be maintained and administered at the British Institute of Afghan Studies was regarded as an ongoing project parallel to the *Gazetteer*. It was envisaged that discoveries of additional sites and new publications would be added, as well as older discoveries and publications omitted in the original edition, so that it would gradually expand and become a general repository for the archaeology of Afghanistan, free to users. As part of this process it was also envisaged that a *Gazetteer Supplement* be published every few years as new material warranted.

Such are brave statements of intent! The closure of the British Institute of Afghan Studies in 1983, together with my own departure to research and professional activities unrelated to Afghanistan soon afterwards, rendered both the maintenance of a card catalogue and the publication of *Supplements* impracticable. Most of all, the complete halt of any field research in Afghanistan seemed to render it pointless.

However, this does not—or should not—mean that research must cease, and in the first edition of the *Gazetteer* I wrote that the enforced halt in fieldwork is an excellent opportunity for a long overdue reassessment and general stock-taking, with all field-work completed in the past finally getting published. Much too can be achieved by re-examining and correlating past investigations, without the need for field-work. With the hindsight provided by this, more fresh avenues for research should open up than would otherwise have been possible, and one can perhaps hope that Afghan studies will enter a period of consolidation, rather than grind to a halt.

Of course, history has taken its course and there has been great destruction of cultural heritage in Afghanistan—most notoriously the National Museum and the Bāmiyān Buddhas—and this has been well enough publicised not to require reiterating here. In the light of this, it is all the more encouraging to look back over the almost four decades since the beginning of the project of 'reassessment and general stock-taking' at what has been achieved. Major fieldwork projects have been published, many of them of work carried out up to fifty years ago: the ongoing Aï Khanoum publications, Bāmiyān, Dilbarjīn, the Eastern Bactria Surveys, Herat, the Hindukush surveys, Kandahār, Shahr-i Zohak, Short-ughaï, Surkh Kotal, and Tillya Tepe—the list is by no means exhaustive. Important works of synthesis and discussion have also appeared on archaeology, art, architecture, numismatics, religion, prehistory, Graeco-Bactria, the Kushans, and historical studies generally, to list just some of the main areas.

In addition to the very solid achievements in publication listed above, there have been important new archaeological discoveries as well in the intervening years. Major discoveries such as the Rabātak inscription of Kanishka, for example, has considerably enhanced our understanding of Kushan history. An astonishing two more *tons* of coins have been added to the already large quantities from Mīr Zakah. The Ghulbiyān painting was one of the most important additions to the corpus of Central Asian painting in fifty years. There have been discoveries since of more paintings at Chehel Burj in Bāmiyān Province, another Greek inscription from Kandahār, another Bactrian inscription at Tang-i Safidak, a vast archive of Bactrian documents from northern Afghanistan providing incomparable new historical information on much of the first millennium AD, Aramaic documents probably from Balkh providing information on the last days of the Achaemenids and Alexander's invasion, extensive new Buddhist monastic 'cities' at Kharwar and Mes Aynak, a Ghurid period city revealed at the Minaret of Jam, a major new stupa-monastery complex at Killigān near Bāmiyān, new excavations at more stupa-monastery complexes at Tepe Nārenj and Qol-i Tūt in Kābul that flourished well into the Islamic period, possible Graeco-Bactrian and Kushan temples at Tepe Zargarān at Balkh, as well as numerous other objects, sites, and monuments. These discoveries foreshadow greater ones still to come.

With the reopening of Afghanistan to international researchers in the early 2000s—particularly the reopening of the DAFA in 2002 together with the return of German, Italian, Japanese, US, and other missions—the time felt ripe for a reissue of the *Gazetteer*, with a new preface to bring it up to date. Accordingly, this was discussed with Jean-Claude Gardin and François Neuville of the Éditions Recherche sur les civilisations in 2002, to appear in 2003. On further consideration, particularly in the light of the new discoveries and publications since the first edition, it was decided that a completely new expanded and updated edition would be more valuable than simply a reissue, which would obviously take longer to produce. The ERC decided that it would be unable to go ahead with such an expanded version, and so proposals were taken to Oxford University Press, who accepted the new and longer project.

Since then, world-wide interest in Afghanistan's cultural heritage has been accelerating. The exhibition showcasing the National Museum's treasures that toured the world between 2007 and 2014 attracted huge public attention. In its wake came numerous scholarly publications, conferences, and cultural initiatives. The Balkh Art and Cultural Heritage Project initiated in Oxford in 2011, the Oriental Institute–National Museum Partnership Project initiated in Kabul and Chicago in 2014, and the European Society for Afghan Studies initiated in St Petersburg in 2017 is a small sample of the many and increasing number of such initiatives. The years 2016 and 2017 saw at least ten international conferences, workshops, and other scholarly activities either focusing directly on Afghanistan or relating to it. The number of publications since 2000 listed in this bibliography is a reflection of such interest.

At the time of going to press the output of new studies shows no sign of abating. A new scholarly journal, *Afghanistan*, the journal of the American Institute of Afghanistan Studies, has appeared with two issues a year, the first in April 2018. The imminent publications of the German Archaeological Institute surveys of the Herat region in the 2000s, as well as the Smithsonian Helmand-Sistan surveys in the 1970s, will substantially increase the number of sites recorded in this volume. The ongoing work of the Afghan Heritage Mapping Partnership at the Oriental Institute, University of Chicago, using high-resolution satellite imagery is mapping more previously unrecorded sites than ever before that will increase by many times again the number of recorded sites. The complete archaeological archive of the late Klaus Fischer covering his activities in Afghanistan from the 1950s to the 1970s has been deposited in the Afghanistan Institut in Bubenthal, Switzerland, awaiting study. Clearly, this current edition, like the previous, can only be viewed as interim.

ARRANGEMENT OF THE MATERIAL

Periods Covered

The time span ranges from the earliest known period (Lower Palaeolithic in the case of Afghanistan), to the Timurid. The Timurids are used as a terminus because after this period virtually every modern town and even many large villages would qualify as a 'site'. This would make the work much too top heavy and would in any case cover ground more adequately covered in modern studies. It is regrettable however, that due to this rule many important late monuments, such as the Bāgh-i Bābur in Kābul or Takht-i Pul near Mazār-i Sharīf, without which no study of Islamic architecture in Afghanistan is complete, are left out. One must however, stop somewhere, otherwise there would be no reason for not including twentieth-century monuments such as the Dārulāmān palace.

That being so, a large number of sites recorded in the catalogue might well be post-Timurid. These are the many sites recorded in passing—usually by nineteenth-century observers—merely as 'fort' or 'ruins' or similar designation. They are included here, however, as being at least worthy of investigation: in the case of many such remains in Ghūr or Bāmiyān, for example, such remains proved when investigated to be major pre-Mongol defensive systems. Also of an indeterminate date are the large number of uninvestigated remains that are merely recorded on maps with a 'ruins' symbol as a result of aerial surveys. See, for example, the large number of such 'ruins' on Map 75 which might be nothing more than abandoned villages of comparatively recent date. There is only a single recorded site on this map, 57, an 'ancient' lead and zinc mine, which suggests that the surrounding 'ruins' are at least worthy of investigation. Map 79 has a similarly dense scatter or 'ruins' known only from their designation as such on the 1:100,000 maps as a result of aerial surveys. Recorded sites on this map, however, include dates ranging from the Bronze Age and Hellenistic to Sasanian and Shahi.

Of a completely separate category are those monuments that have been redated since the first edition of the *Gazetteer*. A re-examination of the material from the eastern Bactria surveys, for example, revealed more Bronze Age sites than were initially recognised,[1] enhancing considerably the recently identified 'Oxus Civilisation'. A notable example of redating is the Shrine of Khwāja Abu Nasr Parsa at Balkh, formerly celebrated as probably the best known 'Timurid' monument in Afghanistan, but more recently redated to the Shaibanid period in the sixteenth century.[2] It would be a mistake, however, to remove it from the catalogue, if only to keep the debate open.

[1] Lyonnet 1997. [2] O'Kane 2000.

Site Catalogue

All sites are listed by alphabetical order. This might not always be ideal: a listing by region or according to date, for example, might be more relevant for a researcher interested in a specific region or period. However, modern regional boundaries do not necessarily reflect historic reality, historic boundaries even less so, and in all cases can move and have done so: Greek Bactria, for example, does not correspond to, say, medieval Takhāristān and still less modern administrative boundaries. The starting point for researchers interested in a specific region would be the regional maps, and they would then consult the sites shown there by site number. Listing by period is even less practical: interpretation of dates change, and multi-period sites would result in needless repetition of site entries. The starting point here for researchers therefore would be the period maps or, better, the chronological index in Appendix 1.

An alphabetical listing therefore is the most practical. However, even this presents problems. To begin with, it became apparent when preparing this new edition that at many specialist conferences and publications, sites and monuments were often being referred to by their *Gazetteer* Site Catalogue numbers rather than their names: the site numbers in other words have become standard. Of course, this has the advantage that references to the original *Gazetteer* in publications before the new edition appeared will remain valid for the new edition (unlike page number references). But it also requires the names and the order in which they occur remain fixed in stone and unchanged, even where names in the original might have been misspelt or mistaken. The site of Haibak, for example, is more correctly spelt Aibak, but moving it from 'H' to 'A' would have required renumbering the entire sequence. Similarly, the Abbasid mosque at Balkh is in the Catalogue as Haji Piyada, but Haji Piyada is a modern unrelated grave adjacent to the mosque: the actual name of the mosque is Noh Gunbad.

The fixed alphabetical order proved more problematical when attempting to add 'new' sites in the update: maintaining the order would require complete renumbering (and renumbering yet again in any theoretical future edition). A number-letter system *might* have been a solution in maintaining the numerical system: the insertion of the five 'new' sites Qal'a-i Chara, Qal'a-i Chashma Khūni, Qal'a-i Chingiz, Qal'a-i Chulakai, and Qal'a-i Dahān-i Nau Jūi after Site 839 Qal'a-i Chigini *could* be numbered 839a, 839b, 839c, and so forth, or in a decimal system 839.1, 839.2, 839.3, albeit clumsily in both cases. But a future record of a site occurring after 839b or 839.2 would have to be 839b-a or 839.2.1 or similar aberrations. Reluctantly, therefore, it was decided to put all newly recorded sites into a separate Supplement, beginning with 2000 to clearly differentiate from the main catalogue, where the new sites are included in alphabetical order as cross-references. Hence, the above sites are 2185, 2186,

2123, 2187, and 2188. It was further agreed with the Afghan Heritage Mapping Partnership at the Oriental Institute, University of Chicago, embarking upon their own site numbering system for sites located by satellite imagery, that they would use the *Gazetteer* site numbers for previously recorded sites, but begin with 3000 for their newly located ones.

The site catalogue therefore is divided into two: Site Catalogue and Site Catalogue Supplement. Each site entry follows the same format: name, location, date, description, collection, fieldwork, and sources. The entries are arranged in alphabetical order according to the name of the site, and numbered consecutively, the site numbers being used for ease of cross-referencing. Where alternative names for a site exist (for example, Nād-i 'Ali or Bina-i Kai) the one in commonest usage is given as the heading of the entry (i.e. Nād-i 'Ali) with the alternatives appearing as a cross-reference. The only exceptions to this are when the commoner name is inaccurate and misleading. For example, the cave complex on the north of the Kābul River near Jalālābād commonly known as Bāsawal, is strictly speaking called Chakanūr; Bāsawal is *another* site opposite the caves on the south bank. Similarly the 'Qundūz Hoard' in fact came from the site of Khisht Tepe, ninety kilometres *north-west* of Qundūz; Qundūz is an entirely separate site altogether, unrelated to the Hoard. However, when a commoner name, although strictly speaking inaccurate, does not mislead, it has been retained it for convention's sake. For example, the Seljuk minaret of Daulatābād is actually located in the village of Zādiyān fourteen kilometres *north-east* of the village of Daulatābād; but Zādiyān is a major site in its own right, unrelated to the Daulatābād minaret. Although incorrect, therefore, it is widely published as Daulatābād and so maintained under that name in the catalogue, but given a separate site number to clearly differentiate it from Zādiyān, with the judicious use of cross-referencing to make it clear. These variations on site names have often led to past confusion and needless repetition of work: for example, in Takhār Province, Fischer's Pasha Khāna, Kohl's Rustam Tepe, and Gardin and Lyonnet's Khusti Qishlaq or Dorāhi all refer to the one site. In choosing which name to use, the name under which it is first published is generally chosen, but not invariably: in the example just cited, it was first published as Pasha Khāna by Fischer, but its definitive publication is that which occurs here by Gardin and Lyonnet, so Khusti Qishlaq is given as its Catalogue name. Undoubtedly mistakes and inconsistencies will be found, but as always, a liberal use of cross-referencing will hopefully eliminate confusion. The pinpointing of most site locations by the Chicago Mapping Project will further eliminate such apparent contradictions.

Other place name problems arise from the different languages used. There are the obvious Persian versus Pashto versions, Sabzavār or Shindand, for example, Fīl Khāna or Pīl Khāna. But more problems arise if a place name arrives into Latin script via a non-Afghan language altogether. A site in northern Afghanistan, for example, was recorded by Japanese archaeologists as Chār, but it was only on locating it on a map where it was recognised that the correct name was Chāl; the Japanese language having no sign for 'L'. More distortions come via Russian, which has no letter for 'H', so 'Kh' is substituted (for example 'Shakhri' for 'Shahr-i') or occasionally (and more bafflingly for a non-philologist) 'G'. Hence, 'Gerat' for 'Herat'.[3] A particular case is the site known by its Turkish/ Uzbek name of Tilla Tepe, 'treasure mound' in northern Afghanistan, which should actually be transcribed as *Tila Tapa* (تپه طلا in Dari). This arrived into English as the slightly distorted 'Tillya' when 'Tilla' was transcribed into Russian as 'Тиля' by its Soviet excavators because of the final Russian '-я' or '-ya'—a neat example of the pitfalls of trilingual footwork. However, the strictly speaking inaccurate 'Tillya' has entered universal usage when applied to this now famous site and treasure. The official transliteration system of the modern republic of Tajikistan can result in similar distortions, such as 'Somoni' for Samanid.

In most cases each entry refers to just one site, although natural groupings of several sites are often lumped together, for example, Safid Dagh and Surkh Dagh are included under Nād-i 'Ali, again with their separate names appearing as cross-references. This again sometimes leads to clumsiness: for example, Tepe Shutur, although excavated and published separately from the other Hadda sites of Bagh Gai, Deh Ghundi, Tepe Kalan, and others in the central nucleus, is included with these under the Hadda entry, while Chakhil-i Ghundi and Prates, although published together with the other Hadda sites, are located some distance away from the central Hadda nucleus and so appear as separate entries. Conversely, Bust and Lashkāri Bāzar, although one vast site stretching continuously for some seven kilometres, are published separately for convenience. Also, many of the sites in eastern Bactria have been lumped together under one entry, not so much because of natural groupings but more because such a large number of sites have been recorded there that to give each one a separate entry would result in the overall site pattern becoming too weighted towards eastern Bactria. Hence, the approximately 1,600 entries recorded in fact represent a total of some 2,100 individual sites. In general, sites within one kilometre of each other are lumped together, those further than a kilometre are separate. The system is at best a compromise, at worst inconsistent, alleviated by extensive use of cross-referencing and the listing of alternative names.

All sites were located originally on the 1:100,000 maps, so coordinates and location descriptions given in the Catalogue are as accurate as the original sources allowed, except when otherwise stated. In the various sources I have used, descriptions of the whereabouts of a particular site can sometimes be vague and misleading in the extreme. In particular,

---

[3] Which my Word program insists on 'correcting' to 'Great' and 'Heart'; perhaps it was designed by a Herati.

sites might be recorded under one name in the nineteenth century and then recorded under an entirely different name a century later, resulting two separate sites being misleadingly recorded. Masson's Kuh-i Bacha, for example, was originally identified with Ghundi Paisa, a site on the Begram plain where sherds were collected and stored by the DAFA. It has since been reidentified with Shotorak, although there is still uncertainty. Locating such sites therefore often required hours of scanning many maps in turn, and occasionally a restrained use of intelligent guesswork before a site could be located and placed on a map. Thankfully, the Afghan Heritage Mapping Partnership at the Oriental Institute, University of Chicago, relocated most of the sites more accurately in this edition from satellite imagery, occasionally in quite different places from my original locations. I have therefore given the Chicago coordinates when known, but kept my original coordinates; I have taken the Chicago coordinates however as definitive, and it is these locations that are on the new maps in this edition.

When known, dates both in year and historical period are given for each site, together with the evidence for that date (ceramic, numismatic, stylistic, and so forth). In practice, this amounts to only some two-thirds of the entries; those sites known only from early travellers' observations are usually undated. Even many of the dates that we do have—again, particularly those assigned to sites recorded some time ago—are unreliable, while many more are so broad as to be almost meaningless, for example, the vague classifications of 'pre-historic', 'pre-Islamic', or 'Islamic', or that much abused term 'Kushano-Sasanian'. The dates given in the sources I have drawn my information from however, I have used, even if they are suspect or too broad, except when a minor correction is needed for the sake of consistency: for example, if a site in western Afghanistan has been described as Kushan, I have corrected it to Parthian. In giving the dates in historical names as well (Iron Age, Kushan, etc.) it is with the reservation that such labels are often both facile and controversial, but are useful if only for the sake of convenience. For the palaeolithic periods the terms Lower, Middle, Upper, and Epi- (or Late) Palaeolithic have been adopted rather than the terms Levaloisian, Mesolithic, and so forth, in line with Richard S. Davis's argument.[4] The terms Neolithic, Bronze Age, and Iron Age follow conventional practice, but the terms for the historical periods are complex. I have invariably used the terms in their strict historical sense rather than their art style sense: for example, a site in Seistan may produce objects of a Kushano-Sasanian art style but it would nonetheless be Sasanian. The complexities arrive because the territory now covered by Afghanistan in the past belonged to different places at different times, so that first-century BC sites, for example, might be

Parthian in the west, Kushan in the north, and Saka in the east, while sites on the borders of these divisions could be any of these designations. Periods of only a brief span as far as Afghanistan is concerned, such as the Khwarazm-shahi or Ghuzz Turk, have mostly been omitted, perhaps wrongly, except where it may be exceptionally interesting or significant: for example, Kansīr in Badakhshan, which is thought to be Tang Chinese. For some multi-period sites that have a continual, uninterrupted occupation extending over a long time, such as Kandahār—sites which, although multi-period, are in effect one long single period—just the main periods have been listed for the sake of brevity, with the minor periods being assumed. The chronological table is an attempt at simplifying and systematising this complex regional/chronological terminology for the historical periods.

Descriptions in the main are kept to a minimum. The exceptions are previously unpublished sites, where the description needs to be detailed enough to meet the demands of a first publication. Some descriptions are very brief indeed and inadequate even for the needs of the *Gazetteer*, but this just reflects the inadequacy—or even complete lack—of the published descriptions from which they are drawn. In many cases more attention is given to the lesser known sites or to those drawn from publications that are obscure or difficult to find, in the belief that they deserve more notice than has previously been given. For the major excavated and/or monumental sites, such as Bāmiyān or Herat, descriptions are kept to the minimum, enough to form a framework on which to hang a bibliography and act as a guide to further reading. Since such sites deserve—and indeed have—whole volumes in themselves, it is beyond the scope to contribute more in an authoritative sense.

Plans of as many sites and monuments as possible are included, in practice amounting to little more than 10 per cent. Most have been redrawn from existing published plans to a standard format. Photographs, unfortunately in many cases, are not included, partly because of expense but mainly because of the impracticality of creating a photographic record of even the main sites.

When collections—usually sherds but also coins, sculptures, and other objects—have been made from a site, the location of that collection, if known, is given. This is necessarily very incomplete, as a complete survey is impossible. In any case, when a collection is reported to have been made from a particular site, mention is rarely made where it is subsequently housed. It can usually be assumed however, that collections made from official surveys and excavations over the past fifty years are housed—at least in part—in the National Museum of Afghanistan and/or in the Afghan Institute of Archaeology, despite the upheavals that that museum has undergone.

Details of the survey or excavation of each site are also given, unless a site has simply been noticed in passing and not recorded as a result of any systematic investigation.

[4] Davis 1978: 37.

Generally just the dates of fieldwork, the name of the person in charge, and the institutions—if any—which sponsored the fieldwork are given, together with the type of investigation: usually excavation or survey. Unless otherwise qualified (for example, geological survey), all surveys can be assumed to be archaeological.

Bibliography

Each site, unless published here for the first time, has its own list of source references. The list is as far as feasible comprehensive, giving both primary and secondary works. Book reviews are generally not included, unless they are important discussions in themselves. Except in a very few cases, online sources are not given, as they would run into tens of thousands, if not millions, and can in many cases be both transient and unreliable. In some cases, particularly those sites with a rich art or architecture, the list of references can exceed a hundred, and the entry is mainly bibliographical. However, I have been selective when sites have produced artistic, literary, or other works: references to Bactrian manuscripts that originated (probably) from Rui are included under that site, but references to Persian manuscripts that originated at Herat are not; references to the find spots of coin hoards (such as Mir Zakah) are included, but not to the places where they were produced (such as Balkh, known from mint marks). All references I have examined personally (if superficially), either in libraries and collections, or online if they have been uploaded or (increasingly) if they are from published journals that have online versions; I have not simply copied references over from other publications or sources. All annotations consequently are my own.

In the first edition it could be claimed with some confidence that the bibliography was comprehensive; in the more than thirty years since, such a claim is no longer possible, such is the huge flood of information that has appeared even in a relatively small subject such as Afghan archaeology. I have tried to give priority, therefore, just to primary publications, with secondary discussions given less priority. A further limitation has been accessibility: with my policy of only citing publications viewed personally, many important publications are necessarily omitted, but hopefully not too many. A few days in the outstanding library of the Afghanistan Institut in 2016 filled many a gap (it houses, for example, most relevant major Japanese publications). Without such limitations, the work would be endless.

Unlike in the original edition, the full bibliography is listed alphabetically. However, each title is also listed in the original subject classifications separately in abbreviated (author-date) form so as to retain its value as an independent bibliography. This classification system is based on the 'Afghanistan-Thesaurus' by the Foundation Bibliotheca Afghanica, Bubendorf, Switzerland. This was developed in the 1980s by Afghan and European specialists specifically for Afghan Studies. It has been slightly modified for the present use.

In theory all works that describe Afghan archaeological sites, however briefly and however aside from the main subject of the work, have been consulted. This includes—apart from the obvious archaeological reports—numismatic and epigraphic studies, art histories, picture books, travel books, intelligence records, geographical surveys, gazetteers, and generally any work of a topographical nature, so that the Bibliography reflects a far wider range of subjects than those purely archaeological—over 2,100 titles, more than the total number of entries they refer to (and nearly 50 per cent more than the original edition). Indeed, it is often the non-archaeological books that are the greatest sources for archaeological sites. Chief amongst these are the nineteenth-century travellers' reports, which are often marked by acute observation and energy. Particular mention must be made here of the five-volume *Records of the Intelligence Party, Afghan Boundary Commission*, together with its affiliated series of *Route Reports*, printed in Simla as secret Government of India documents between 1887 and 1891. Rarely have so able a body of observers and topographers been gathered together for one project, and the records they produced are perhaps the most invaluable sources ever compiled for Afghan studies in general.

Notable has been the huge increase in numismatic studies that have appeared since the first edition. However, large numbers of the coin discoveries on which these are based are unprovenanced and cannot be associated with any particular site, so the present selection is just a fraction of the studies that have appeared. The same can be said for many other accidental discoveries, although where possible I have attempted to include as many as possible by linking them—however tenuously—with a particular site. Many—but not all—of the Bactrian documents, for example, *probably* came from somewhere in or near Rui, so I have included the bibliography for them under that name. Or to give another example, a hoard of Hunnic coins discovered somewhere ten kilometres north of Kabul has been included under the entry for Kabul.

Maps

In the original edition, all site plans and drawings were in a separate atlas section along with the maps. These now are incorporated into the site catalogue, appearing with the site descriptions they illustrate. Because these have been removed the maps have been renumbered, but a concordance with the old map numbers is given for ease of cross-referencing with the old edition.

Maps here are now in two sections: period maps and regional maps. The original period maps were based on the 1:1,000,000 Operational Navigation Charts, Nos. G6, H7, and H8, published by the Defense Mapping Agency Aerospace

Center, Missouri. These contain all of the main dated sites and are an attempt to depict Afghanistan throughout the various periods, from Palaeolithic through to Timurid. Any attempt at interpreting historical patterns or densities from these maps however would be fallacious, and simply reflect the state of our knowledge of those periods. The concentration of Achaemenid sites in eastern Bactria, for example, does not necessarily mean that there were more Achaemenid settlements there than elsewhere in Afghanistan, it simply means that that area has been more intensively surveyed than perhaps other areas. The new period maps have been generated by the Afghan Heritage Mapping Partnership at the Oriental Institute, University of Chicago, modelled on those in the original edition.

The regional maps were originally based on the 1:100,000 stereo-topographic maps of 1960 and 1968, prepared from aerial surveys in the late 1950s by teams from the United States and Soviet Union for the Ministry of Mines of Afghanistan. Information has also been taken from the old Survey of India and British War Office Quarter Inch and One Inch scale maps, which, being based on ground surveys, are generally better for place names although not as accurate for geographical detail. Various other miscellaneous maps have also been used. All the 1:100,000 series were redrawn specially for the original edition. An entirely new set of regional maps were generated by the Afghan Heritage Mapping Partnership at the Oriental Institute, University of Chicago, based on satellite imagery specially for this edition. They follow in general the sequence and coverage of the maps in the original edition. However, new larger scale maps were generated for areas of particular site density, such as parts of eastern Bactria and the areas around Kābul and Jalālābād, and given new map number designations. Maps in the original edition that were numbered decimally are now given individual map numbers.

Every site is located on these maps and identified by its site number and occasionally by name. In addition to the sites mentioned in the text, all other features of archaeological interest, such as mounds, ruins, towers, and caves, are also marked. The maps therefore are not only meant as an illustration to the Site Catalogue, but are also meant as a guide to further field research.

Other Sections

In addition to the main sections and divisions discussed above, there are several smaller sections aimed at facilitating the use of the *Gazetteer*.

Appendix 1 lists all of the dated sites from the Catalogue in chronological order.

Appendix 2 lists collections in museums and institutions that house study material from Afghanistan. This list is unfortunately far from complete, but still hopefully serves as a guide. Unfortunately, many collections abroad contain unprovenanced material, so cannot be included.

Appendix 3 is a chronological list of archaeological fieldwork carried out in Afghanistan, from 1833 to the present. It acts as a summary of archaeological research, indicates what has been achieved and by whom, and hopefully a guide to future research.

Appendix 4 is a subject index, listing all specialised subjects that a researcher might wish to follow up in the Site Catalogue. Each heading is followed by the site numbers where that subject may be found. Notable are the large numbers of entries for fortifications (of all types), which far outweigh any other subject. The fact that there are so many fortifications is at least a reflection of the nature of Afghanistan and its history.

Appendix 5 is a glossary of terms, mainly geographical, commonly found in the place names in the text.

It is these concordances outside the main Catalogue that provide the user with keys for accessing particular areas of research and making the fullest use of the work. All sections are extensively cross-referenced so that it is possible to go directly to any site or sites in the Catalogue of particular interest.

Limitations

Perhaps the greatest limitation is that it simply stops at the modern borders of Afghanistan, borders which, by and large, are irrelevant for the periods in question. In no place do the modern borders follow natural boundaries—even the Oxus, like any major river such as the Nile or Indus, is hardly a boundary, but serves rather to bind cultural groups than separate them. Not only the much vaunted Durand line but *every* single border of Afghanistan divides ethnic, linguistic, cultural, historical, and geographic units; all Afghan ethnicities, with the exception of the Hazaras, are to be found outside Afghanistan as well. Much of the information compiled here, therefore, must be regarded as incomplete, and usually represents only a part (often a small part) of a picture that encompasses a far wider area.

THE MAKING OF A GAZETTEER: A RETROSPECTIVE JOURNEY

The nearly forty years that this project has been in the making have seen profound changes—revolutions even—in the processes of writing, research, production, and publication, and it might be worth recording some of the processes which form almost as much an archaeological record as the accounts of the sites themselves do. The original site catalogue was recorded in the late 1970s on mimeographed sheets of foolscap kept in alphabetical order in ring-binders, with each title in the bibliography recorded on a card index. Both the mimeographed catalogue and the card index were then typed up on an antiquated second-hand portable typewriter with a non-qwerty keyboard (I still keep it as an historical curiosity in our attic), macrons laboriously inserted manually by back-tracking and over-printing a dash above the vowels; copies were made with carbon paper and any mistakes corrected with 'Tippex' fluid. The period maps were made by covering the entire floor of the ballroom in the British Embassy residency in Kabul with the complete set of 1:100,000 maps of Afghanistan (a carpet which I suspect no other ballroom in the world has experienced), tracing off by pencil all features of geographical and archaeological interest onto tracing paper, and inserting all site locations based solely on the descriptions given in the original sources. These were then scaled down according to site density, and retraced onto Permatrace using Rapidographs and Letraset, with mistakes corrected by razor blade. The entire manuscript was then sent—by post—to the publisher, eventually to be returned first as galley-proofs and later as page-proofs.

The advent of computers and the internet has since rendered such processes obsolete (and one observes their passing with mixed feelings). No electronic version of either the original manuscript or the published volumes existed. With the decision in 2003 to bring out a complete revision, the first task therefore was to create a digital version from which to work. At the time, optical character recognition (OCR) systems were still in their infancy, particularly for recognising diacritical marks and unfamiliar proper names, so it was decided to have the entire book retyped from scratch by a professional typist. Years later again I discovered I could have saved my money: most of the Catalogue could be downloaded for free from the internet, mainly from a US military website. I am acknowledged, am flattered, but was never consulted.

The original bibliography was made possible mainly due to the magnificent library of the DAFA in Kabul. No longer having access to that library—nor indeed to any library that specialised in the archaeology of Afghanistan—presented problems in updating the bibliography. To some extent a few days in the superb library of the Afghanistan Institut in Switzerland made up for this (probably the best library in the world outside Afghanistan for Afghan studies). But once again the internet has revolutionised library research, with online journals and countless specialised websites such as Academia or JSTOR making it possible to consult publications from one's computer. Other websites make it possible to purchase volumes that are not on the internet at the click of a mouse. The ready accessibility of so much material however, comes with its own drawbacks: the more that is available the less that can be absorbed.

The original site drawings had been redrawn professionally from the original sources, and converting them into digital images simply a matter of scanning to appropriate resolution. This, however, could not be done for the period or regional maps, as so much more data had to be added. No longer having access to the original 1:100,000 maps or the British Embassy ballroom (which burnt down many years ago) nor indeed any convenient ballroom, for a long time I simply ignored the problem hoping it would go away (rather like a toothache or that ugly sound under the bonnet of one's car). Here, however, the Oriental Institute at the University of Chicago came to the rescue with their generous offer to generate an entirely new set of maps based on their high-resolution satellite images. The satellite images they receive from the State Department, which originate of course with the US military. A debt repaid—with interest.

Warwick Ball

Scottish Borders 2018

Site Catalogue

1. ĀBAKA
Including TEPE QURSI.

Original: Lat. 36° 40′ N, long. 69° 05′ E. Map 32.
Revised:
36.67036828, 69.08306909 / 36° 40′ 13.32581484′ N, 69° 04′ 59.04872580′ E (A).
36.66240767, 69.08194706 / 36° 39′ 44.66762028′ N, 69° 04′ 55.00940412′ E (B).
36.66071134, 69.06931547 / 36° 39′ 38.56083732′ N, 69° 04′ 09.53568336′ E (C).
Qundūz Province. 4 km from the central crossroads of Khānābād, on the Qundūz road, the tepes are located 800–1000 m to the south of this road. Mounds A and B correspond to tepes of 5 m and 4 m on the 1:100,000 map near the village of Abaka, mound C to the tepe of 4 m indicated to the north-east of the village Michin Khel.

Dates: Hunnic-Turk period, 5th–9th cent. (A, B); some Islamic sherds on C (ceramic).

Description: (A) Rounded mound, cut into by fields (diam. 30 m, height 5 m); in the cuts visible on the west side, jars in place at the present ground level, containing charcoal, plaster, burnt clay, above an ashy deposit (without traces of bones); 400 m to the south-south-east, a similar, smaller but higher mound (diam. 20 m, height 6–7 m). (B) Tepe Qursi: east–west oblong mound (50–30 m), flat top (6–7 m). (C) Square platform (30 × 30 m), oriented north–south, flat top (6 m); in the cuts visible at the north-west angle, at the present ground level, long superimposed burnt layers (alternating ash and clay). Mounds B and C are undermined by the rice fields, like A.

Collection: National Museum/AIA—sherds.

Fieldwork: 1978 Gardin et al., CNRS—survey.

Sources:
1. Site information by J.-C. Gardin.
2. Gardin and Lyonnet 1978–9: pl. VII—nos. 425–18.
3. Lyonnet 1997: figs 39, 49, 68, 69—nos. 425–18.
4. Gardin 1998: 77—nos. 425–18.

2. ĀB BAKHSH-I BĀLĀ

Original: Lat. 30° 17′ N, long. 61° 30′ E. approx. Map 94.
Revised: 30.2901773 N, 61.4879459 E / 30° 17′ 24.63826884 N, 61° 29′ 16.60525512 E.
Nīmrūz Province. In the Rūd-i Bīyābān c.2 km north-east of Gina and 2 km north-west of Tarākun; 1 km west of Ab Bahhsh-i Pā'īn.

Date: Parthian/Indo-Parthian, 200 BC–AD 200 (ceramic).

Description: A mound 40 m square and 7 m high.

Collection: AMNH—sherds.

Fieldwork: 1951 Fairservis, AMNH—survey.

Source: Fairservis 1961: 63—mention as Site RB 24.

3. ĀB BAKHSH-I PĀ'ĪN

Original: Lat. 30° 17′ N, long. 61° 30′ E. approx. Map 94.
Revised: 30.27773445 N, 61.48449892 E / 30° 16′ 39.84400920 N, 61° 29′ 04.19612892 E.
Nīmrūz Province. In the Rūd-i Bīyābān c.3 km north-east of Gina and 2 km north of Tarākun.

Date: Sasanian, AD 200–700 (ceramic).

Description: A large, heavily eroded mound, 20 m high, with the remains of a building on top. It is surrounded by several smaller mounds.

Collection: AMNH—sherds.

Fieldwork: 1951 Fairservis, AMNH—survey.

Source: Fairservis 1961: 63—brief description as Site RB 25.

ABBĀSĀBĀD. See 2000 ABBĀSĀBĀD in Supplement.

ĀBDĀN. See 868 QAL'A-I MUHAMMAD KHĀN TEPE.

ABDULĀBĀD. See 2001 ABDULĀBĀD in Supplement.

4. ABDULKHĒL

Original: Lat. 34° 31′ N, long. 70° 34′ E. Map 67.
Revised: 34.51980053 N, 70.5566484 E /
34° 31′ 11.28189828 N, 70° 33′ 23.93425512 E.
Nangahār Province. On the west bank of the Kūnar c.21 km
north-east of Jalālābād on the road to Islāmpūr.

Date: Sasanian/Hunnic, AD 3rd–6th cent. (stylistic).

Description: Remains of a fairly large stupa of poor construction, stylistically similar to the 'third class' stupas of
Hadda. There was no trace of any decoration or plaster, and
had been robbed.

Fieldwork: 1834 Masson — survey.

Sources:
1. Masson 1842, 2: 275 — brief description.
2. Errington 2017a: 160 — the Masson collection and archive relating to the site.

ABDUL TEPE. See 14 AGHA MAZĀR-I WALI TEPE.

ĀB-I ISTĀDĀ. See 345 GAZKAI.

ĀB-I RASŪL DĀD. See 2002 ĀB-I RASŪL DĀD in
Supplement.

5. ABRAU, south-west
   Including TEPE KASHKARI.

Original: Lat. 36° 24–40′ N, long. 69° 21–35′ E. Map 37.
Revised:
36.3992912 N, 69.36438318 E/
36° 23′ 57.44832072 N, 69° 21′ 51.77943720 E (A).
36.39313114 N, 69.36556924 E /
36° 23′ 35.27209500 N, 69° 21′ 56.04925608 E (B).
Takhār Province. 3.5 km north-east of Ishkamīsh, by the
Samandau-Chal road. Tepe A is located 500 m west of this
road, 100 m south of a stream from the spring called Kashkari; the hamlet of Abrau is 500 m to the north-east. (B) The
tepes of group B are situated around the spring itself, on the
edge of the road.

Dates: Hunnic-Turk, 5th–9th cent. (A); pre-Mongol
Islamic, 10th–13th cent. (A, B) (ceramic).

Description: (A) Tepe Kashkari (from the name of the
above spring): octagonal site (180 × 180 m), with irregular
sides, including: (a) a more or less square high central
mound (60 × 60 m at the base), steep slopes, flattened top
(15 × 15 m) dominating the plain by 11 m; (b) an 'Enclosure'
marked by a high octagonal embankment 3 m on average
above the plain; (c) a narrow interior strip of land (c.40 m),
on a slope towards the centre, raised in relation to the level

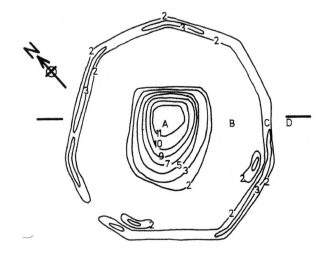

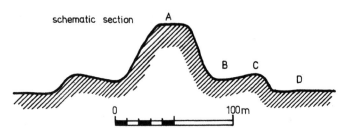

schematic section

5 Abrau, south-west (J.-C. Gardin).

of the plain (c.2 m); very few or no irregularities on the
surface, except for the two interior angles, south side.
A depression in the south-west marks perhaps an access
to the raised strip. Some of these features do not agree with
the first interpretation of the site as a fortified place (cf.
Gardin and Lyonnet 1978–9: pl. XI). (B) 500 m from A, in
the south-east sector, several small rounded mounds (diam.
20 to 40 m, height 2 m) next to the Kashkari spring, on the
west side of the Ishkamīsh road; another larger one (diam.
80 m), is located 300 m south of this spring, on the east side
of the road. The sherds (Islamic) are found not only on these
mounds, but also in the surrounding fields (*lalmī*), as well as
on all the zone between A and B.

Collection: National Museum/AIA — sherds.

Fieldwork:
1. 1960 Hayashi and Sahara, University of Kyoto — survey.
2. 1978 Gardin *et al.*, CNRS — survey.

Sources:
1. Site information by J.-C. Gardin.
2. Hayashi and Sahara 1962: 76 — photo, and description of
   the site in Japanese.
3. Gardin and Lyonnet 1978–9: pl. XI — nos. 376–80.
4. Lyonnet 1997–8: figs 68, 69 — nos. 376–80.
5. Gardin 1998: 99 — nos. 376–380.

6. ĀBRAU, north-west

Original: Lat. 36° 25' N, long. 69° 21' E. Map 37.
Revised: 36.40900136 N, 69.35666212 E /
36° 24' 32.40489564 N, 69° 21' 23.98363632 E.
Takhār Province. 3.5 km north-east of Ishkamīsh, at about
the middle of the plain in relation to the mountains which
bound it to the east and west; the tepes are accessed by a
track to the left of the Ishkamīsh to Samandau road, at the
level of the village of Qandahāriyā. The nearest hamlet is
however, Abrau, 1.3 km to the south-east.

Dates: Hellenistic, 3rd–1st cent. BC; Kushan, 1st–4th cent.;
some Islamic sherds (ceramic).

Description: Two mounds 50 m apart (diam. 60 m, height
2 and 3 m), in a north-west/south-east line, and a smaller
third one (diam. 30 m, height 1 m) 300 m to the west. *Lalmī*
cultivation on the mounds and in the surrounding fields.
The sherds of the Hellenistic period come from the highest
of these three mounds (3 m), in the north-west.

Collection: National Museum/AIA—sherds.

Fieldwork: 1978 Gardin *et al.*, CNRS—survey.

Sources:
1. Site information by J.-C. Gardin.
2. Gardin and Lyonnet 1997–8: pl. XI—no. 382.
3. Lyonnet 1997: figs 68, 69—no. 382.
4. Gardin 1998: 100—no. 382.

7. ABRU-I DUKHTĀRĀN

Lat. 34° 12' N, long. 63° 02' E. Map 53.
Herat Province. In the Tagau Ishiān near Kaughan in Obeh
district, near the village of ʿAlibāzīd.

Description: Remains of an ancient masonry aqueduct in
the gorge.

Fieldwork: 1885 Merk, ABC—topographical survey.

Sources:
1. Merk 1891: 228—mention.
2. Gazetteer 1975: III. 12—mention.

8. ABU HURAIRA

See also 520 KAM PIRAK, 814 PIT QAL'A TEPE,
1188 TEPE ZĀDIYĀN, 1245 ZĀDIYĀN, 2053 DAU-
LATĀBĀD in Supplement, and 2281 ZĀDIYĀN
KĀFIR QAL'A in Supplement.

Original: Lat. 37° 03' N, long. 66° 57' E. Map 27.
Revised: 37.04610682 N, 66.94468865 E /
37° 02' 45.98455884 N, 66° 56' 40.87912308 E.
Balkh Province. 2 km north of Zādiyān near Daulatābād.
42 km north-west of Balkh.

Dates: Ghaznavid/Seljuk, 1000–50 (stylistic).

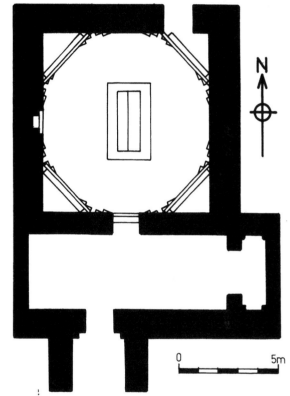

8 Abu Huraira—shrine (after Pugachenkova 1975).

Description: Approximately 500 m to the south of Zādiyān
Kāfir Qal'a citadel (see separate entry) is the mausoleum or
khāniqāh of Abu Huraira. It has an *īwān* entrance opening
onto an octagonal dome-chamber with simple arched
squinches, containing a cenotaph and mihrab. Construction
is of pakhsa blocks alternating with mud-bricks.

Fieldwork: 1972–4 Pugachenkova, Af/Sov. Mission—
survey of mausoleum.

Sources:
1. Pugachenkova 1975—description and plan of mausoleum.
2. Pugachenkova 1978: 31–3—brief but full description of
the mausoleum.

9. ADĪNA MASJĪD

Original: Lat. 36° 53′ N, long. 66° 42′ E. Map 26.
Revised: 36.89120124 N, 66.70405555 E /
36° 53′ 28.32448020 N, 66° 42′ 14.59999728 E.
Balkh Province. 24 km north-west of Balkh, just to the south-west of the road to Kilift.

Description: Ruins of an old baked brick caravanserai (still standing in the 19th cent.), known as Abdullah Khāni Rabāt, which is said to have been once decorated in glazed tiles. The settlement, which now lies to the north of the paved road, in the past lay on the old caravan route between Balkh and Āqcha. It appears all trace of this caravanserai has disappeared. The settlement is an important centre for local Sufis and contains a number of mosques (with *khāniqāhs*) all of which are probably post-Timurid.

Fieldwork:
1. 1886 Peacocke, ABC—topographical survey.
2. 1996 Jonathan L. Lee—reconnaissance.

Sources:
1. Additional site information by Jonathan L. Lee (photographs in archives).
2. Peacocke 1887: 319—mention.
3. Gazetteer 1979: IV. 42—mention.

10. ADĪNAPŪR

Lat. 34° 24′ N, long. 70° 13′ E. Map 65.
Laghmān Province. In the hills, 2 km to the north-west of Bālābāgh, on the north bank of the Surkh Rūd, 24 km west of Jalālābād.

Description: An extensive area of ruined fortifications and mounds. Some artificial caves with triangular openings are cut into the hills.

Fieldwork: 1834 Masson—survey.

Sources:
1. Masson 1833a: 10—brief description.
2. Masson 1840: 38—mention.
3. Masson 1842: ii. 183 and iii. 186–7—mention.
4. Errington 2017a: 138 and 2017b: 16, 18, 20–1—the Masson collection and archive relating to the site.

11. ĀDIR

Lat. 35° 49N, long. 64° 35′ E. Map 45.
Fāryāb Province. On the side of the mountains 5 km south east of Almār, in the area south-west of Maimanā.

Description: Local reports of life-size petroglyphs of sheep and cows.

Source: Site information by Jonathan L. Lee.

12. ADIRĀ

Original: Lat. 35° 15′ N, long. 66° 09′ E. Map 47.
Revised: 35° 15′ 26.816″ N, 66° 8′ 58.444″ E.
Balkh Province. On the road from Nayak to Sar-i Pul, just up the Ismaidān River.

Description: A ruined mud-brick fort in poor preservations, similar to Kushk-i Agha Bahār (no. 658).

Source: Maricq and Wiet 1959: 84—mention.

13. ADRASKĀN RŪD
See also 2057 DEH SABZ.

Original: Lat. 33° 38′ N, long. 62° 16′ E. Map 70.
Revised: 33.64267536 N, 62.26487524 E /
33° 38′ 33.63130644 N, 62° 15′ 53.55087588 E.
Herat Province. 80 km south of Herat, 300 m west of the Shindand road, south of the Adraskān Rūd, after crossing this river.

Dates: Achamenid, 6th–4th cent. BC; Partho-Sasanian, 1st–4th cent.; pre-Mongol Islamic, 10th–13th cent. (ceramic).

Description: Small quadrangular platform (60 × 60 m), height 5 m, at edge of the river; ruins of a brick caravanserai.

Collection: National Museum/AIA—sherds.

Fieldwork:
1. 1885–6 ABC—topographical exploration.
2. 1952 Le Berre-Gardin, DAFA—survey.
3. 1968–78 Kruglikova, Soviet-Afghan Mission—survey.

Sources:
1. DAFA archives: unpublished report by M. Le Berre 1952, Tepe Herat-Shindand6.
2. Maitland et al. 1887: 80—mention ruins of an old fort and caravanserai.
3. Peacocke 1887: 213—mentions two small ruined baked brick forts.
4. Amir Khan and Shahzada Taimus, 1888a: 137—mention.
5. Gazetteer 1975: III. 14—mention.
6. Gaibov et al. 2010: 112—mention that the platform had disappeared by 1970 (Site K150).

AGAKURU. See 134 BISH KA'IK.

14. AGHA MAZAR-I WALI TEPE
Including ABDUL TEPE

Original: Lat. 36° 49′ N, long. 66° 28′ E. Map 25.
Revised: 36.80993238 N, 66.45912692 E /
36° 48′ 35.75657052 N, 66° 27′ 32.85692496 E.
Jauzjān Province. 31 km south-east of Āqcha. South of the Balkh road, and east of the village of Fazilābād.

Description: Mound of circular form, diam. about 120 m, height 8 m, occupied by a *zīyārat* and a cemetery in its southern part. From Fazilābād other tepes maybe seen, one to the south and the other to the east (Abdul Tepe).

Fieldwork: 1948 Le Berre, DAFA—survey.

Source: DAFA archives: unpublished report by M. Le Berre, 1948, tépé P. 26.

15. ĀHANGARĀN, Ghūr

Original: Lat. 34° 28′ N, long. 65° 04′ E. Map 55.
Revised: 34.47499596 N, 65.0622859 E /
34° 28′ 29.98546644 N, 65° 03′ 44.22924504 E.
Ghūr Province. On the south bank of the Harī Rūd, 22 km west-south-west of Chakhcharān.

Dates: Sasanian, 3rd–6th cent. (ceramic); Ghurid, 12th cent. (documentary).

Description: Remains of a citadel on an earthern mound in the middle of the valley, 60 m from the river bank. It consists of inner and outer defences, reinforced by towers. Construction is of mud on a stone foundation. In the vicinity are four small mounds and a wide scatter of sherds. Traces of saltpetre have been detected in the walls.

Fieldwork:
1. 1885 Maitland and Talbot.
2. 1946 Kohzad, HAS—survey.
3. 1960 Fischer, DAAD—survey.
4. 1965 Leshnik, Heidelberg University—sondage.

Sources:
1. Maitland 1888a: 379—brief description of fort.
2. Le Strange 1905: 417—summary of the historical references.
3. Kohzad 1951–4, 8/4: 59–60—brief description.
4. Leshnik 1967—detailed description and drawings of the pottery series.
5. Fischer 1969: 343—brief summary.
6. Kluyver 2000: 6—description.

16. ĀHANGARĀN, Surkhāb

Original: Lat. 35° 03′ N, long. 68° 04′–68° 05′ E. Map 58.
Revised: 35.0587394 N, 68.08294674 E /
35° 03′ 31.46182308 N, 68° 04′ 58.60827948 E.
Baghlān Province. Chārikār to Dūshi road by the Shībar Pass, Surkhāb valley: in the side valley of Darra-i-Āhangarān.

Date: Turk, 7th–10th cent. (ceramic).

Description: Remains of a fortress dominated by a central trefoil shaped 'keep' in the form of three joined circular towers standing up to 20 m in height (Ruin 3). The walls are pierced by narrow slits, and the upper parts of the exterior decorated with an impressed zig-zag pattern. There is an outer enceinte to the south-west surrounded by a lower wall reinforced with semi-circular buttresses. Construction is of mud-bricks on stone foundations throughout. Nearby is a ruined tower of the same construction (Ruin 1), decorated on the exterior with impressed triangles. The interior has 'Sasanian' style semi-circular squinches.

Collections: National Museum/AIA—sherds.

Fieldwork: 1974–5 Le Berre, DAFA—survey.

Source: Le Berre 1987: 55–8, plates 12, 60–6—itinerary A2, Dara-i-Āhangarān, ruins 1 to 3; detailed description, plans and photographs.

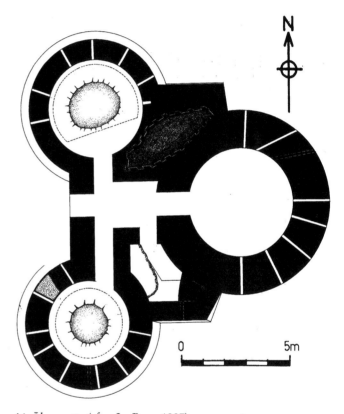

16   Āhangarān (after Le Berre 1987).

17. ĀHIN PUSH TEPE

Original: Lat. 34° 24–40′ N, long. 70° 27–45′ E. approx. Map 66.
Revised: 34.40969686 N, 70.44652748 E /
34° 24′ 34.90868664 N, 70° 26′ 47.49891180 E.
Nangahār Province. *C.*2 km south of Jalālābād, on a hill just to the west of the road to Hadda.

Date: Kushan, 2nd cent. (numismatic).

Description: A large stupa-monastery complex with later Islamic refortification, consisting of a square enclosure surrounding a central stupa. The stupa has now disappeared and its exact location is unknown. It had a drum of 17 m diameter resting on a platform 35 m square with a second platform below the first, like at Guldarra. There was an exterior decorative frieze of 'Indo-Corinthian' pilasters, and construction throughout was of diaper masonry. Remains of colossal figures were found in the excavations, and inside the stupa was found a gold reliquary set with stones and 20 gold Roman and Kushan coins.

Collection: BM—stupa deposits.

Fieldwork:
1. 1834 Masson—survey.
2. 1879 Amesbury and Simpson, Indian Army—excavations.

Sources:
1. Masson 1841: 100—mention.
2. Fergusson 1876: 93—discusses the stupa and date.
3. Cunningham 1879—description and illustrations of the coins; drawings of the stupa.
4. Hoernle 1879—detailed catalogue and discussion of the gold coins.
5. Simpson 1879a: 227–8—summary of excavations.
6. Simpson 1879b—brief account of the excavation.
7. Swinnerton 1879: 198—brief description of the remains.
8. Simpson 1879–80: 44–5 and 48–51—brief report and drawings of the excavations.
9. Leach 1880: 46—mentions the excavations.
10. Simpson 1881: 200–2—brief description of the excavations.
11. Cunningham 1889: 278—briefly discusses the significance of the Roman coins.
12. Cunningham 1892: 49—refers to the Roman coins in a discussion of the date of the Kushan coins.
13. Foucher 1942–7, 1: 152—brief discussion.
14. Mac Dowall 1968c: 143—discusses the Roman coins as evidence for dating the early reign of Huvishka.
15. Narain 1968: 227—refers to the Roman coins for confirming Kushan chronology.
16. Mizuno 1971: 115—mention.
17. Mac Dowall and Taddei 1978b: 247—mentions the Roman coins.
18. Errington and Fabrègues in Errington and Cribb 1992: 176–7—discuss the stupa deposits.

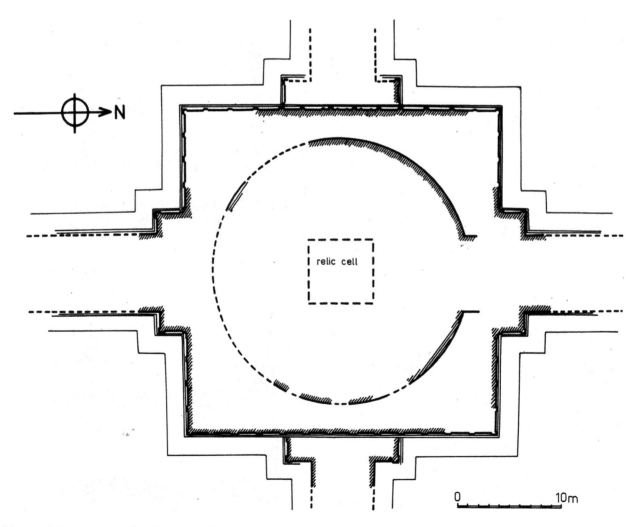

relic cell

0 _____ 10m

17 Āhin Push Tepe—stupa (after Simpson 1879–80).

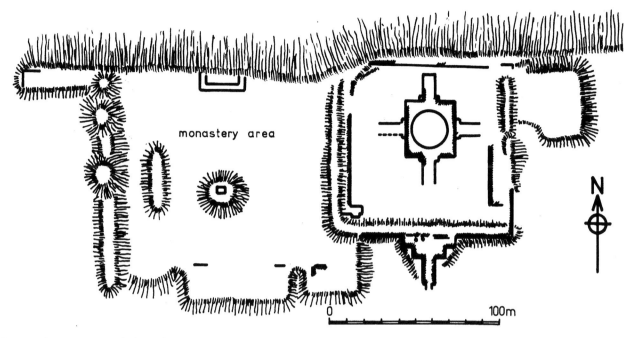

17 Āhin Push Tepe—general plan (after Simpson 1879–80).

19. Jongeward et al. 2012—catalogue and discussion of the reliquaries.
20. Errington 2017a: 156–9 and 2017b: 34, 36, 108, 116—the Masson collection and archive relating to the site.

AHMADĀBĀD. See **2003 AHMADĀBĀD** in Supplement.
AIBAK. See **407 HAIBAK.**

18. AÏ KHANOUM
Or BARBARAH.

Original: Lat. 37° 09–15' N, long. 69° 25–41' E. Map 34.
Revised: 37.16584363 N, 69.41154633 E /
37° 09' 57.03708312 N, 69° 24' 41.56677216 E.
Takhār Province. At the confluence of the Kokcha and the Āmū Daryā Rivers near Khwāja Ghar, c. 100 km north-east of Qunduz.

Dates: Bronze Age, 3rd–2nd mill.; Seleucid, 4th–3rd cent. BC; Graeco-Bactrian, 3rd–2nd cent. BC. (C-14, ceramic, epigraphic, stylistic).

Description: A predominately single-period urban site in a naturally fortified position, surrounded by defensive walls and, in places, a ditch. The lower town consists of three distinctive parts: (A) a habitation area to the south, (B) an administration area that includes a palace in the middle, and (C) an almost empty area in the north, with a main street connecting all three. The upper town has a necropolis and an acropolis. Construction is of mud-brick throughout, with columns and some thresholds in stone. Finds include sculptures, terracottas, coins, jewellery, Greek inscriptions, ivory throne fragments, a complete iron suit of armour, and two sundials. In the vicinity are remains of many canals.

During the 1990s the site was deliberately targeted for systematic pillaging, when most of it was destroyed.

Fieldwork:
1. 1964 Schlumberger, DAFA—survey.
2. 1965–78 Bernard, DAFA—excavations.
3. 1974–6 Gardin et al., CNRS—survey of surrounding plain.

Sources:
1. Rawlinson 1872: 509—mentions Barbarah as a Buddhist site.
2. Wood 1872: 259–60—describes a visit to the acropolis in 1838 and the ancient canal system on the plain.
3. Koshkaki 1923–4: 403—mentions remains.
4. Ramachandran and Sharma 1956: 126—describe a limestone architectural fragment in the governor's residence in Baghlān that may have come from Aï Khanoum.
5. Schlumberger 1965—preliminary report on the site.
6. Schlumberger and Bernard 1965—report on the discovery and the first sondages, with a description of the ceramics and other finds.
7. Bernard 1966—brief summary of the first season and the implications for Graeco-Bactrian archaeology.
8. Bernard 1967a—interim report on the second season: the administrative quarter, the temple of Heroōn, the capitals, and the sculpture.
9. Bernard 1967b—summary of excavations to date and description of the architecture and decoration.

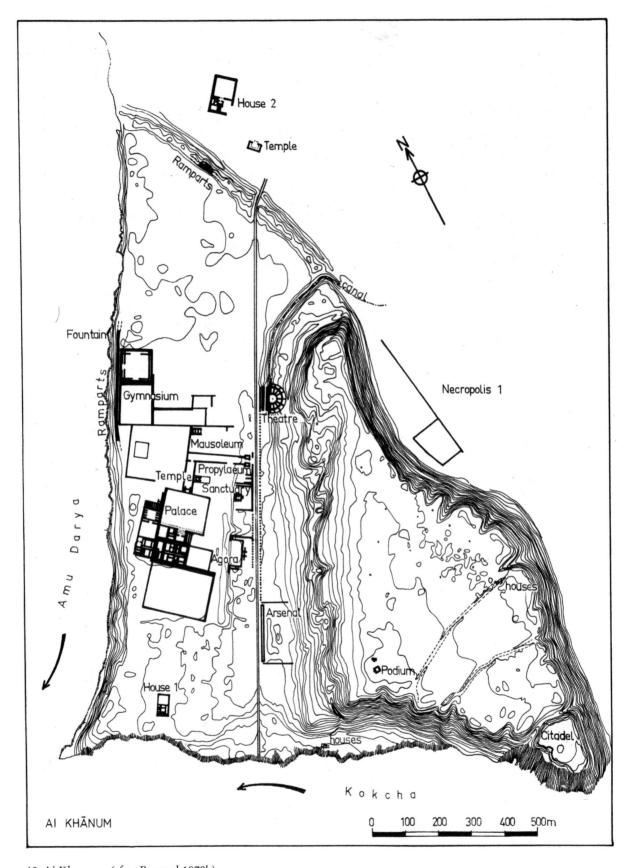

House 2

Temple

N

Ramparts

canal

Fountain

Necropolis 1

Ramparts

Gymnasium

Theatre

Amu Darya

Mausoleum

Propylaeum

Temple

Sanctuary

Palace

Agora

houses

Arsenal

Podium

House 1

houses

Citadel

Kokcha

AI KHĀNUM

0   100   200   300   400   500m

18 Ai Khanoum (after Bernard 1979b).

10. Schlumberger 1967—discusses Hellenism in Afghanistan in the light of recent discoveries at Aï Khanoum.
11. Bernard 1968a—interim report on the third season: the administrative quarter, a private house, and the gymnasium.
12. Bernard 1968b—full description and stylistic discussion of the Corinthian capitals from the administrative quarter.
13. Robert 1968—text, translation, and linguistic discussion of two Greek inscriptions.
14. Wheeler 1968: 70–87—discussion of the site and the legacy of Alexander.
15. Bernard 1969b—interim report on the fourth season: the administrative quarter, the private house, the acropolis, the stepped temple, and the sculpture.
16. Kuwayama 1969—examination of the column bases in relation to those south of the Hindu Kush.
17. Bernard 1970a—interim report on the fifth season: the administrative quarter, the private house, the stepped temple, column bases, the Cybele medallion, and the coins.
18. Bernard 1970b—stylistic discussion of ivory objects from Aï Khanoum and Nysa.
19. Gardin 1970—brief summary of the pottery.
20. Schlumberger 1970: 26–31—brief account of the site and the sculpture in a chapter on the Greek Macedonian epoch.
21. Bernard 1971a—short note on the non-Hellenistic aspects of the architecture and the finds.
22. Bernard 1971b—interim report on the 1970 season: the administrative quarter, the capitals, the ostracon, and the inscriptions.
23. Gardin 1971—interim report and type series on the ceramics from 1970.
24. Nāsir 1971—brief summary in Persian of the excavations.
25. Bernard 1972a—interim report on the 1971 season: the necropolis, the stepped temple, the administrative quarter, and ostracon.
26. Bernard 1972b—stylistic discussion of the columns and capitals.
27. Taddei 1972b—discusses some of the art-historical problems.
28. Audouin and Bernard 1973—description, photos, and detailed inventory of the Indian and Graeco-Bactrian coin hoard found in 1970.
29. Bernard 1973a—interim report on the 1972 season: the necropolis, the central temple, and the administrative quarter.
30. Bernard 1973b—general introduction to the excavations and the site.
31. Bernard 1973c—description of the construction materials: mud-brick, baked brick, stone, wood, and stucco.
32. Bernard 1973d—chronological conclusion and chart.

33. Bernard 1973e—report on the sculpture.
34. Bernard 1973f—general background and summary of the site.
35. Bernard, Gouin, and Le Berre 1973—detailed description of the southern half of the administrative quarter.
36. Bernard and Le Berre 1973—detailed description of the northern half of the administrative quarter.
37. Bernard, Le Berre, and Stucki 1973—description of the Temenos of Kineas.
38. De Lapparent and Desparmet 1973—brief geological analysis of the region.
39. Dupree 1973: 289–94—summary and assessment of the site.
40. Francfort 1973—discussion of the heart motif found in some of the objects from Aï Khanoum.
41. Gardin 1973—pottery type series and brief discussion.
42. Gouin 1973b—catalogue and brief report on the small finds—mostly arrow heads and bone objects.
43. Humayun 1973—historical background and legends associated with the name of Aï Khanoum.
44. Leriche 1973—discussion of the archaeology of Central Asia.
45. Le Rider 1973—description and photos of the coins.
46. Staviski 1973—discusses links between the capitals from Aï Khanoum and elsewhere.
47. Audouin and Bernard 1974—full description and typological analysis of the coins, with historical conclusions.
48. Bernard 1974a—interim report on the ninth and tenth seasons: the manor, the administration quarter, the stepped temple, the ramparts, and the sculpture.
49. Bernard 1974b—description of the site and finds and discussion as a Greek colony.
50. Dupree, N. H. et al. 1974—describe the inscription on display in the National Museum.
51. Lawn 1974—lists the results of nine C-14 tests on samples from the site.
52. Leriche 1974a—discussion of the beginnings of Graeco-Bactrian culture.
53. Leriche 1974b—full description and discussion of the defences, with reference to other Helenistic fortifications in Central Asia.
54. Pugachenkova 1974a—refers to Aï Khanoum in a wider discussion of Bactrian art and architecture.
55. Pugachenkova 1974b—discussion of Bactrian religion, based on evidence from Aï Khanoum and elsewhere.
56. Bernard 1975a—interim report on the 1974 season: the administrative quarter, the mausoleum, the gymnasium, and the pottery.
57. Bernard 1975b—note on the historical and archaeological significance of the coin hoard.
58. Gardin 1975—brief summary of the pottery from the 1974 season.

59. Petitot-Biehler 1975—detailed inventory and photos of the coin hoard found in 1973.

60. Balīka 1976—brief summary in Pashto of the site.

61. Bernard 1976a—interim report on the eleventh season: the administrative quarter, the gymnasium, the extramural temple, the ramparts, the fountain, and the theatre.

62. Bernard 1976b—discussion of the non-Hellenistic aspects of the architecture.

63. Bernard and Liger 1976—full report on the 1974 season's excavation at the administrative quarter.

64. Francfort 1976a: 105–13—detailed study of the fortifications.

65. Francfort and Liger 1976—full report on the 1974 season's excavation at the underground tomb.

66. Gardin and Gentelle 1976—preliminary results of the 1974 season's survey of the Aï Khanoum plain.

67. Gardin and Lyonnet 1976—interim report on the pottery and its chronology from the 1974 season.

68. Leriche 1976—discussion of the history of the fortifications.

69. Veuve and Liger 1976—report on the 1974 season's excavations at the gymnasium.

70. Bernard 1977a—brief outline of the oriental influences on Bactrian architecture.

71. Bernard 1977b—general background and summary of the site.

72. Davary 1977—lists the inscriptions and gives a bibliography for them.

73. Dupree, N. H. 1977: 431–44—good detailed guide to the site and the finds.

74. Francfort 1977—discussion of the houses excavated at the site and comparisons with similar types in Central Asia.

75. Gardin 1977—describes in detail the problems and methodology involved in the survey of the plain.

76. Gentele 1977—discusses the ancient irrigation systems on the plain and their modern derivations.

77. Pollack 1977a—discusses the Cybele medallion from the stepped temple, with background on the cult of Cybele.

78. Pollack 1977c—discusses the Tomb of Kineas and its background.

79. Staviski 1977—discusses Aï Khanoum as the Bactrian antecedant of the Kushans.

80. Bernard 1978a—an historical geography of Aï Khanoum and the plain combining the results of excavation and survey with written sources from Achaemenid to modern times.

81. Bernard 1978b—general background and description of the architecture.

82. Bernard 1978c—interim report on the twelfth and thirteenth seasons: the gymnasium, the fountain, the theatre, the propylaea, the palace, an inscription, and the houses.

83. Berthoud 1978—metallurgical and mineralogical analysis of some samples from a workshop.

84. Gentelle 1978—results of a geomorphological and hydrological survey of the Aï Khanoum plain.

85. Janin 1978—analysis of a sundial.

86. Mac Dowall and Taddei 1978a: 218–30—description of some of the monuments and finds.

87. Sultan 1978—discussion of the Hellenistic influences on the architecture.

88. Gardin and Lyonnet 1978–9—discuss the excavations and consequent survey of the hinterland.

89. Bernard 1979a—interim report on the 1978 season: the gymnasium, the theatre, the acropolis, the propylaea, the agora, the arsenal, and the palace.

90. Bernard 1979b—general summary of the site.

91. Bernard 1979c—discussion of the financial practices and the results of the 1978 season.

92. Francfort 1979a: 23–6—lists the site and discusses the general characteristics of Hellenistic fortifications.

93. Gardin and Gentelle 1979—discussion of the irrigation systems of the Aï Khanoum plain and the former prosperity and abandonment.

94. Guillaume 1979—detailed study of the propylaea.

95. Leriche and Thoraval 1979—detailed report on the excavation of the fountain.

96. Liger 1979—detailed analysis of the urban development and town planning.

97. Pugachenkova 1979a—discusses the principles of town planning, the fortifications, and the religious architecture.

98. Rapin 1979—detailed analysis of the excavations and architecture of the treasury with a catalogue of the finds.

99. Azizi 1980—describes the results of the hydrological survey of the Aï Khanoum plain.

100. Bernard 1980a—interim report on the 1978 season: the propylaea, the gymnasium, the palace, the arsenal, and the acropolis.

101. Bernard, Grenet, and Rapin 1980—discussion of the inscription in an unknown language on a silver ingot.

102. Bernard and Rapin 1980—report on the 1978 season's excavation of the palace treasury.

103. Fussman 1980: 36–8—discusses new evidence from Aï Khanoum for the era of Eucratides and the date of Kanishka.

104. Garczynski 1980—report on the 1978 season's excavations at the Doric court in the palace.

105. Gardin 1980—describes in general terms the area survey.

106. Grenet 1980b—describes the discovery of possible Zoroastrian burials at the site.

107. Grenet, Liger, and de Valence 1980—report on the 1978 season's excavations at the arsenal, with a detailed study of the armour.

108. Guillaume, Liger, and de Valence 1980—report on the 1978 season's excavations at the propylaea.
109. Leriche, Rougeulle, and Ghassouli 1980—report on the 1978 season's excavations at the fortifications.
110. Rohr 1980—detailed description and discussion of the significance of the second sundial.
111. Thoraval 1980—report on the 1978 season's excavations at the south side of the palace.
112. Veuve and Liger 1980—report on the 1978 season's excavations at the gymnasium.
113. Veuve, Liger, and de Valence 1980—report on the 1978 season's excavation of the public building on the main street.
114. Bernard 1982a—general summary in English of the excavations.
115. Bernard 1982b—general description of the results.
116. Veuve 1982—definitive publication of the sundials.
117. Rapin 1983—detailed study of economic texts from the treasury: inventory, texts, translation, and discussion on light shed on the economy and administration of the city.
118. Grenet 1983—discusses the Iranian proper names occurring in the treasury texts and the implications for early Zoroastrianism.
119. Guillaume 1983—fully illustrated detailed final report on the background, excavations, architecture, date, and descent of the propylaea.
120. Rapin 1983—inscriptions from the treasury.
121. Francfort 1984a—final report on the finds from the Temple of the Indented Niches.
122. Grenet 1984: 67–75—discusses the funerary architecture and practices it represents.
123. Sedov 1984—uses the pottery for dating sites on the opposite bank of the Āmū Daryā.
124. Bernard and Guillaume 1985—final report on the coins.
125. Leriche 1986—final report on the ramparts.
126. Colledge 1987—discusses the interaction of Greek architecture with local styles.
127. Guillaume and Rougeulle 1987—final report on the small finds.
128. Veuve 1987—final report on the gymnasium.
129. Gentelle 1989—full report on the ancient irrigation and hydrology of the area.
130. Guillaume 1991: 25–196—catalogue of the Graeco-Bactrian and Indian coins.
131. Rapin 1992—final report on the treasury.
132. Fussman 1996—critique of the excavations and the literature to date.
133. Mustamandi 1997—discusses the impact of Aï Khanoum on Gandharan art generally.
134. Lyonnet 1998—archaeological evidence for the end of the site.
135. Bopearachchi 2001—discusses a sculpture head, probably of Demetrius I, found in 1998.
136. Bernard, Besenval, and Jarrige 2002—notes on the looting of the site.
137. Bopearachchi 2002: 14—describes a Heracles statue illicitly excavated.
138. Bernard 2003—brief introduction to the site.
139. Rapin et al. 2003—exhibition catalogue of some of the objects.
140. Tissot 2006: 23–48—National Museum catalogue details and photos.
141. Cambon and Jarrige 2006, 2007—general overview and catalogue of objects in a touring exhibition.
142. Bopearachchi 2007—compares an acrolith from Takal Bala with sculpture from Aï Khanoum.
143. Lecuyet 2007—account of CGI reconstruction of the site.
144. Wightman 2007: 694–5—discusses the Temple of Indented Niches in context of Central Asian fire and water cults.
145. Hiebert 2008—general overview and catalogue of objects in a touring exhibition.
146. Mairs 2008—discusses the evidence from the site for Greek ethnic identity in Bactria.
147. Ball 2008: 68–70, 104–5, 248–51—summary.
148. Lerner 2010—argues for a later date for the abandonment.
149. Martinez-Sève 2010—argues that the Temple of Indented Niches continued in local use after the end of the Graeco-Bactrian kingdom.
150. Lerner 2011—a study of the economic inscriptions and coins arguing for a later abandonment of the site.
151. Mairs 2011b: 26–9—annotated guide to the main publications.
152. Shenkar 2011: 126–30—discussion of the Iranian elements of the temple architecture, postulating a syncretic Zeus Belos-Ahura Mazda cult.
153. Holt 2012b—discusses the numismatic eveidence for the abandonment of the site.
154. Rougemont 2012a: 200–55—full texts, translations, and discussions of all Greek inscriptions.
155. Rougemont 2012b—discusses the importance of the Greek inscriptions.
156. Lecuyot 2013—final report on the houses.
157. Mairs 2013—discusses the Temple with Indented Niches as evidence for cultural identity at the site.
158. Francfort et al. 2014—fiftieth-anniversary booklet on the excavations and discoveries by members of the team.
159. Mairs 2014a—detailed discussion of the site and its broad Hellenistic Central Asian context.
160. Mairs 2014b—discusses the Achaemenid origins of the site.

161. Martinez-Sève 2014—the spatial development and organization of the city, arguing that it was designed as a royal city from the beginning.
162. Francfort 2015—discusses a Bronze Age figurine and other material found on the citadel.
163. Kritt 2015: chapter 6—discusses the implications of a recently discovered Seleucid coin probably from Aï Khanoum.
164. Mairs 2015—discusses Greek names for evidence of the identity and origin of the colonisers.
165. Martinez-Sève 2015—general summary of the site and its chronology.
166. Laurecella et al. 2017—Aï Khanoum as a case study for using high resolution satellite imagery for monitoring site looting over time.

19. AINAK

Or MES AYNAK.
Including GUL HAMID, KAFIRIAT TEPE, SHĀH TEPE, TEPE WALI BABA.

Original: Lat. 34° 17–28' N, long. 69° 18–30' E. Map 65.
Revised: 34.26972709 N, 69.30810864 E /
34° 16' 11.01753408 N, 69° 18' 29.19109932 E.
Lōgar Province. In the mountainous area *c.*15 km due east of Gūmarān on the Lōgar River, turning eastwards off the Kābul-Gardēz road at Kulubkhēl.

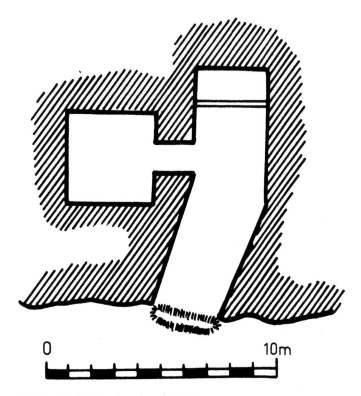

0   10m

19 Ainak (after Berthoud et al. 1977).

Dates: Saka, 2nd cent. BC–AD 1st cent. (C-14); Kushan, 2nd–4th cent.; Hunnic-Turki Shahi, 5th–9th cent. (ceramic).

Description: A vast urban site covering approximately a thousand hectares. On the flanks of the hill are diaper masonry terrace walls and there are remains of mud-brick structures lower down marking the remains of a substantial monastic settlement and associated town. Excavations have revealed several Buddhist monasteries, substantial Buddhist sculpture and paintings, and gold and semi-precious objects.

There is a large artificial cave 25 m long and up to 8 m high to the west of the modern settlement, with more ancient excavations to the east. Traces of an ancient copper mine, partly covered over by modern workings, consisting of many large heaps of slag, charcoal, and other signs of metalworking life everywhere.

Fieldwork:
1. 1977 CNRS—geological survey.
2. 2009–14 AIA and international teams—excavations.

Sources:
1. Gardin and Lyonnet, chronological study, 1980, of unpublished pottery from DAFA surveys.
2. Fussman and Le Berre 1976: 101–2—brief description.
3. Berthoud et al. 1977: 12–15—description of the geology and detailed description and sketch of the mine workings.
4. Paiman 2010—report on the painted Buddhist wall paintings and sculptures.
5. Engel 2011—richly illustrated general account of the site and excavations.
6. Marquis 2013—brief account of the excavations.
7. Thomalsky et al. 2013—discussion of metalworking at the site.
8. Baumer 2014: 75–7—breif description of the excavations and photos of some of the sculpture.
9. Faticoni 2014—discussion of a late 4th-century metal and precious stone treasure from the site.
10. Bloch 2015—brief account of the excavations with photos of the site and finds.
11. Khairzada 2015—summary of the excavations.

AIRATĀN. See 408 HAIRATĀN.

20. AJAMANDĀNĀ TEPE

Original: Lat. 36° 41' N, long. 68° 48' E. Map 32.
Revised: 36.6844376 N, 68.80910372 E /
36° 41' 03.97534452 N, 68° 48' 32.77339740 E.
Qundūz Province. 1 km north of Dūrman Tepe, 7 km south-west of Qundūz.

Date: Kushano-Sasanian, 4th–5th cent. (stylistic).

Description: A mound 4 m high. A column base, 31.5 cm diam., was found reused in a modern house nearby.

Fieldwork: 1963 Mizuno, Kyoto University — survey.

Source: Mizuno and Odani 1968: 47 and 105 — mention the site and illustrate the column base.

21. AKAM
Or DARRA-I JŪANDĀN or HAKAN.

Lat. 36° 13' N, long. 68° 04' E. Map 30
Samangān Province. 8 km south of Haibak, in the north wall of the Haibak River gorge.

Description: An artificial cave with an elliptical opening, high up in the cliff face.

Fieldwork: 1960 Hayashi and Sahara, Kyoto University — survey.

Sources:
1. Yavorski 1885: 105 — mention.
2. Hayashi and Sahara 1962: 42 — photo and brief description in Japanese.

22. AKHTACHI

Lat. 35° 04' N, long. 69° 49' E. Map 42.
Herat Province. On the Rūd-i Hazāra, *c*.12 km east of Gulrān and 12 km north-west of Tutakchi.

Description: Some ruins.

Source: Gazetteer 1975: III. 17 — mention.

23. ĀKHUNDZĀDA

Original: Lat. 31° 19' N, long. 65° 56' E. Maps 89, 99.
Revised: 31.3555802 N, 65.92950159 E /
31° 21' 20.08870668 N, 65° 55' 46.20572112 E.
Kandahār Province. Near Takhta Pul, 35 km south-east of Kandahār, 1 km to the south-west of the road to Spīn Baldak.

Dates: Indo-Parthian, 1st–3rd cent.; Ghaznavid, 11th–12th cent. (ceramic).

Description: A large ruined mud-brick caravanserai and deserted hamlet of late date. Immediately to the west, towards the desert, is a thick scatter of sherds and building debris stretching for several hundred metres, and three large, probably artificial, mounds.

Fieldwork: 1951 Casal, DAFA — survey.

Sources:
1. Site description by Warwick Ball.
2. Gardin and Lyonnet, chronological study, 1980, of unpublished pottery from DAFA surveys.

ĀKHUNDZĀDA TEPE. See **1160 TEPE ĀHINGARĀN.**

24. AKRAM QAL'A

Original: Lat. 31° 15' N, long. 64° 13' E. approx. Map 97.
Revised: 31.26127044 N, 64.22115646 E /
31° 15' 40.57360020 N, 64° 13' 16.16325600 E.
Helmand Province. On the right bank of the Helmand between Bust and Hazārjuft.

Dates: Bronze Age, 3rd mill. BC; Indo-Parthian, 1st–3rd cent. (ceramic).

Description: An artificial mound.

Fieldwork: 1966 Hammond, Cambridge University — survey.

Sources:
1. Hammond 1970: 449 — lists site (1) and gives photo. Description of the pottery types and general discussion of the survey results.
2. Besenval and Francfort 1994: 11 — reinterprets Hammond's Type 10 'cord marked' ware as Harappan.

25. ALA' CHAUPĀN
Or ALĪ CHAUPĀN.

Original: Lat. 36° 43' N, long. 67° 11' E. Map 27.
Revised: 36.71440965 N, 67.18421053 E /
36° 42' 51.87472236 N, 67° 11' 03.15790764 E.
Balkh Province. 5 km south-west of Mazār-i Sharīf to the south of the road to the airport (and now a part of Mazār suburbs).

Date: Kushan, AD 3rd cent.; Late Islamic (ceramic).

Description: Some dozen large mounds spread across the plain, with the remains of an extensive ancient irrigation system. Most have Islamic glazed sherds on top, but material as early as the 3rd century was also found. There is also an 18th-cent. *khānaqāh*.

Fieldwork: 1946 Wheeler, ASI — survey.

Sources:
1. Main site information by Jonathan L. Lee.
2. Shakur 1947: 54–5 — brief description.

26. ALAFSAFĪD

Lat. 35° 56' N, long. 66° 04' E. Maps 24, 47.
Jauzjān Province. On the edge of the river, region of Sar-i Pul, south-east of the village.

Date: Hunnic-Turk period, 5th–9th cent. (ceramic).

Description: None.

Collection: National Museum/AIA — sherds.

Source: Gardin and Lyonnet, chronological study, 1980, of unpublished pottery from DAFA surveys.

27. ALAYĀR
See also 1081 SHĪNIYA.

Lat. 34° 30' N, long. 65° 40' E. Map 55.
Ghūr Province. 4 km south of Shīniya, c.17 km west of
Daulatyār.

Description: Remains of many circular and square towers
on the hills around the village.

Fieldwork: 1946 Kohzad, HAS—survey.

Source: Kohzad 1951–4, 7/1: 50—mention.

ĀLCHĪN, Imām Sāhib. See **738 MULLĀH AFGHĀNI.**

28. ĀLCHĪN, QUNDŪZ.

Original: Lat. 36° 47' N, long. 68° 52'–68° 53' E. Map 32.
Revised:
36.78443588 N, 68.85955796 E/ 36° 47' 03.96915540 N,
68° 51' 34.40866644 E to
36.78493419 N, 68.88838571 E / 36° 47' 05.76307500 N,
68° 53' 18.18856068 E.
Qundūz Province. About 6 km north of Qundūz, by the
Qizil Qal'a road: (A) At the bridge over the canal which
crosses the village of Ālchīn in a west-north-west direction,
a road bordering the canal on the left bank leads to a tepe
located 700 m from the road, indicated on the 1:100,000
map as a mound 6 m high. (B) 1.6 km east of the same
bridge, a tepe corresponding to the mound of 7 m situated
on the 1:100,000 map south-east of Ālchīn; access is by a
road which leaves the Qundūz road 700 m south of the
bridge, towards the east.

Dates: Kushan, 1st–4th cent. and Hunnic-Turk, 5th–9th
cent.; a few Islamic sherds (ceramic).

Description: (A) Mound of irregular form, highly damaged
by cultivation; a quadrangular mass with sinuous sides
remains, of which a diagonal follows a north–south line
(40 × 30 m), with a flat top (4 m) in the north angle. (B)
Rectangular north-west/south-east mound (80 × 40), gently
sloping towards the south-west, but cut straight on the
three other sides; height 7 m, rising to 9 m in the south-
east angle. From the top, at about 2 km to the south-east, an
unsurveyed tepe of the same dimensions may be seen.

Collection: National Museum/AIA—sherds.

Fieldwork: 1978 Gardin et al., CNRS—survey.

Sources:
1. Site information by J.-C. Gardin.
2. Lyonnet 1978: 470, 489.
3. Gardin 1979: 79, nos. 470, 489.

29. ʿALIĀBĀD
Or QAL'A-I GIUBI or TAHARI TEPE.

Original: Lat. 36° 05–30' N, long. 68° 53–88' E. Map 32.

Revised: 36.50212339 N, 68.8927248 E / 36° 30' 07.64418888 N,
68° 53' 33.80928576 E.
Qundūz Province. On a bend in the river at the southern
end of the Qundūz plain, 26 km south of Qundūz to the
west of the road to Baghlān.

Dates: Bronze Age, 3rd–2nd mill. BC; Graeco-Bactrian,
3rd–2nd cent. BC; Kushan, 2nd cent. BC–AD 3rd cent.; Sasanian, 3rd–7th cent.; Turk, 7th–9th cent.; pre-Mongol
Islamic, 9th–13th cent. (ceramic).

Description: A huge fortified site in a strategic position
overlooking the Qundūz River. It is surrounded by massive
mud walls pierced by gateways, with a square fort to the
north by the river. The site stands on a natural hill further
built up by artificial deposits to a height of c.70 m. Ceramics
show an unbroken sequence from the Graeco-Bactrians to
the Mongol conquest. Surrounding the site are remains of a
canal system.

Fieldwork:
1. 1946 Wheeler, ASI—reconnaissance.
2. 1956 Ramachandran and Sharma, ASI—reconnaissance.
3. 1960 Fischer, DAAD—survey.
4. 1975 Kohl—survey.

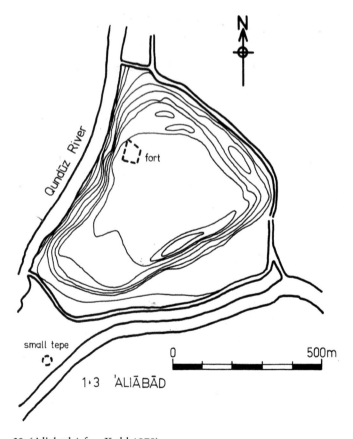

29 ʿAliābād (after Kohl 1978).

Sources:
1. Wheeler 1947: 61 – brief description.
2. Shakur 1947: 45 – brief description.
3. Caspani and Cagnacci 1951: 265 – mention.
4. Ramachandran and Sharma 1956: I. 25 – mention.
5. Fischer 1961a: 15 – description and photo.
6. Fischer 1969: 350 and pl. 24 – summary and aerial photo.
7. Kohl 1978: 68–71 – full description and assessment of the site, with a plan and photos of the site and sherds.

30. ʿALIGUL
Or CHAHĀRBĀGH 1, 2, and 3.

Lat. 30° 24' N, long. 70° 21' E. Map 66.
Nangahār Province. C.1 km west of the Chahārbāgh stupa and 2 km south-east of the Sultānpūr stupa, 1 km south-west of the village of ʿAligul and 9 km west of Jalālābād.

Date: Kushan, 1st–3rd cent. (architectural).

Description: Remains of a much-ruined stupa on a high base, with the remains of a monastery to the south. It is the western most stupa of the Chahārbāgh group. Inside were found only ashes. There are also remains of two more stupa-monastery complexes, which when opened also contained nothing.

Fieldwork:
1. 1834 Masson – excavation.
2. 1965 Mizuno, Kyoto University – survey.

Sources:
1. Masson 1841 102–3 – brief description as Topes 1–3.
2. Mizuno 1971: 119–120 – photos and brief description as Stupas 29–33.
3. Errington 2017a: 142–4 – the Masson collection and archive relating to the site.

31. ʿALI QUTAN

Original: Lat. 36° 23'–36° 24' N, long. 60° 19'–69° 20' E. Map 37.
Revised:
36.39739418 N, 69.31692662 E / 36° 23' 50.61904332 N, 69° 19' 00.93584244E (A).
36.3999357 N, 69.33860764 3E / 6° 23' 59.76852144 N, 69° 20' 18.98751552 E (B).
36.3958777 N, 69.30906192 E / 36° 23' 45.15970812 N, 69° 18, 32.62291920 E (C).
36.39209621 N, 69.33289203 E / 36° 23' 31.54633872 N, 69° 19' 58.41129648 E (D).
Takhār Province. Near Iskamish in the north-west sector, up to about 2 km from the town, in the direction of the different hamlets of Ali Qutan. The main group of tepes (A) lies 1.6 km to the north-west of the Ishkamīsh roundabout, in a straight line; a convenient landmark is the point where

the canal which crosses Ishkamīsh, coming from the south (sources of the Khwāja Bandi Kusha), divides into two branches, one continuing towards the north, the other branching towards the west; the tepes are situated between these two branches, not far from the fork. The other sites lie in a radius of less than 2 km: (B) to the north-east (1200 m), bordering the road which leads to the village of Ali Qutan; (C) to the west-north-west (1000 m), bordering the road which leads to Bad Guzar and Bangui; (D) to the south-east (1400 m), in the northern quarter of Ishkamīsh.

Dates: Hellenistic, 3rd–1st cent. BC (B); Kushan and Hunnic-Turk (1st–9th cent.); a few Islamic sherds (ceramic).

Description: (A) Two groups of two mounds 300 m apart, in a north-west/south-east line; the highest (6 m), round in form (diam. 100 m), is to the north-west; in the south-east, the largest of the two is square in form (30 × 30 m), oriented north–south, the top tiered in two levels, the highest to the east (3m). (B) Two rounded mounds (diam. 20 m, height 2 m), 100 m apart, degraded by ploughing; the surrounding fields also produce sherds, especially of the Hellenistic period. (C) square platform (20 × 20 m), low (0.8 m), depressed in the centre. (D) High mound (10 m), steep sides, damaged on all sides by houses; present surface of the base about 60 × 60 m. At *c*.1.5–2 m beneath the top surface, burnt layers visible in the sections, in almost all the circumference of the mound, and thick walls (80 cm) in *pakhsa*, oriented north–south and east–west; human bones in the shifted layers, on the west face.

Collection: National Museum/AIA – sherds.

Fieldwork: 1978 Gardin et al., CNRS – survey.

Sources:
1. Site information by J.-C. Gardin.
2. Gardin and Lyonnet 1978–9: pl. XI, nos. 368, 383–5.
3. Lyonnet 1997: figs 39, 68, 69 – nos. 368, 383–5.
4. Gardin 1998: 99, 100 – nos. 368, 383–5.

32. ʿALISAI

Lat. 34° 55' N, long 69° 44' E. Map 65.
Kāpisā Province. C. 20 km north-east of Tagau, between Nijrau and Sarubi.

Date: Kushan-Hunnic, 1st–6th cent. (architectural).

Description: Remains of a stupa.
Sources:
1. Masson, British Library MSS Eur. F63, F. 23 – sketch and brief description of stupa (I am grateful to Elizabeth Errington for bringing this to my attention).
2. Masson 1842: III. 165 and 169 – mention.
3. Foucher 1942: I, pl. XXIXc – photo of the stupa in 1928.
4. Fussman, Murad, and Ollivier 2008: pl. 96c – photo of the stupa.

33. 'ALISHANG

Original: Lat. 34° 42' N, long. 70° 09' E. Map 65.
Revised: 34.71033356 N, 70.14911075 E /
34° 42' 37.20083112 N, 70° 08' 56.79871260 E.
Laghmān Province. On the east bank of the 'Alishang
River, c.10 km north-west of its junction with the 'Alingar.

Date: Kushan—Hunnic, 1st–6th cent. (architectural).

Description: Many caves and mounds in the vicinity, and
the remains of an ancient fort. The caves are usually isolated
and not grouped, and contained nothing of note. The
mounds probably represent stupas, at least two stupa-
monastery complexes being recognised.

Fieldwork:
1. 1834 Masson—survey.
2. 1922 Foucher, DAFA—survey.

Sources:
1. Court 1837: 383–4—tentatively identifies the remains
   with Hellenistic Arigaeum.
2. Masson 1842: III. 292–3—brief description.
3. Foucher 1942–7: I. 150—brief description and photo.

ALLAH KĀRĪZ. See 2004 **ALLAH KĀRĪZ** in Supplement.

34. ALLAHNAZĀR

Lat. 34° 24–40' N, long. 70° 18–30' E. Map 65.
Nangahār Province. At the foot of the Safīd Kūh, 2 km
south of Sūltanpūr Ulyā, to the south of the road to
Gandamak.

Date: Kushan-Hunnic, 1st–6th cent. (architectural).

Description: About 30 caves cut into the side of a hill near a
spring. All are very small and eroded and some contain mud-
brick walls. On the top of the hill are the remains of a stupa
and enclosure.

Fieldwork: 1962 Mizuno, Kyoto University—survey.

Source: Mizuno 1971: 124—brief description with photos
and plan.

ALTAN JALAB. See 891 **QAL'A-I ZAFAR.**

35. ĀLTĪ KHWĀJA
Or ZĪYĀRAT-I ASĀB-I QĀF.

Lat. 35° 43' N, long. 63° 54' E. Maps 44, 45.
Faryāb Province. In the Hirak Valley on the Qal'a-i Nau-
Maimana road, 5.5 km south-south-east of Chahārshamba.

Description: An artificial cave a few metres up a ravine
opposite the village, known as the Zīyārat-i Āltī Khwāja

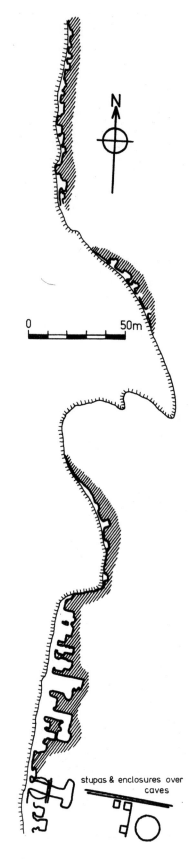

34 Allahnazār (after Mizuno 1971).

or Zīyārat-i Hazrat-i Asāb-i Qāf. It has a mud-brick doorway with a burial chamber some 10 m above the level of the entrance, lit by a shaft to the outside. The burial chamber traditionally contains six sleeping saints 2000 years old, presumably a reference to the account of the Seven Sleepers of Ephesus in the Qur'an. The cave is associated with the remains of a city to the south on a plateau below the Band-i Turkistān known as Shahr-i Dakianus (i.e. 'Decius') or Shahr-i Afsuz (i.e. 'Ephesus', possibly Takht-i Khātūn—see Site 1134).

In the vicinity of the cave are large numbers of mounds containing baked brick remains.

Fieldwork: 1886 Yate, Maitland, ABC—topographical survey.

Sources:
1. Grodekoff 1880: 144–5—mentions the cave and recounts a different legend.
2. Durand 1885: pl. 3.—sketch of exterior.
3. *Civ. and Military Gazette*, 2 Mar. 1886—description.
4. Maitland 1888b: 123—brief description.
5. Yate 1888: 151–2—recounts the legend surrounding the cave and mentions the remains.
6. Gazetteer 1907: II. 13—brief description.
7. Bruno 1962: 108—very brief description and photo.

36. ALTIN 1

Original: Lat. 36° 59' N, long. 66° 29' E. Map 25.
Revised: 36.98718369 N, 66.49083759 E /
36° 59' 13.86127608 N, 66° 29' 27.01533552 E.
Jauzjān Province. 1 km north of Altin 10, 30 km north-east of Āqcha.

Date: Achaemenid, 6th–4th cent. BC (ceramic).

Description: A fortified urban settlement, probably the administrative town for the Altin group of sites.

Fieldwork: 1972 Mustamandi and Sarianidi, Af/Sov. Mission—survey.

Source: Sarianidi 1977b: 102—mention.

37. ALTIN 10

Original: Lat. 36° 59' N, long. 66° 29' E. Map 25.
Revised: 36.98047257 N, 66.49691248 E /
36° 58' 49.70124408 N, 66° 29' 48.88492080 E.
Jauzjān Province. 30 km north-east of Āqcha, near the road from Balkh to Kilift.

Date: Achaemenid, 6th–4th cent. BC (ceramic).

Description: A large mound containing three structures, destroyed by fire. The first is a rectangular building, possibly a palace, measuring 80 × 55 m and divided into two porticoed courtyards. It had a roof supported by brick columns, and the end rooms of the porticos contained decorated niches. The

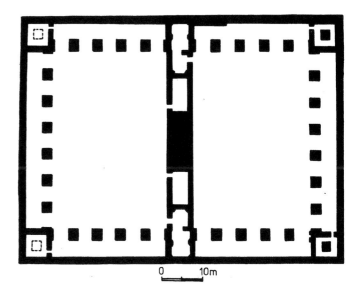

37 Altin 10—Palace I (after Kruglikova and Sarianidi 1976).

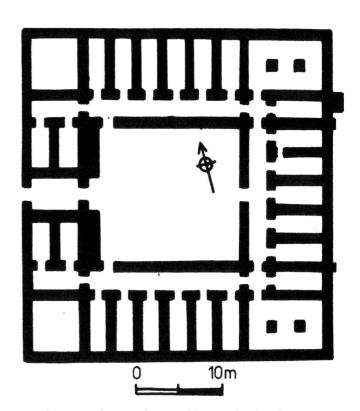

37 Altin 10—Palace II (after Kruglikova and Sarianidi 1976).

second structure, also possibly a palace, measured 36 m square and contained a courtyard with a pool in the centre. The rooms had white plastered surfaces, and amongst the finds were a heap of small, stepped clay altars. The third structure was not excavated.

Fieldwork: 1971–4 Kruglikova, Af/Sov. Mission—excavations.

Sources:
1. Kruglikova and Sarianidi 1976: 9–11—brief summary.
2. Kruglikova 1977c—very brief description of the palaces.
3. Sarianidi 1977b: 101–2—outline of the architecture.
4. Sarianidi 1977c: 121–8—description and discussion of the monumental architecture.
5. Mac Dowall and Taddei 1978a: 215—brief description.
6. Bernard and Francfort 1979: 121–2—summary of the site.

38. ALTIN DILYAR TEPE

Original: Lat. 37° 08–13' N, Long. 66° 46' E. Map 26.
Revised: 37.13722512 N, 66.76648715 E /
37° 08' 14.01044136 N, 66° 45' 59.35375440 E.
Balkh Province. In the dunes north of Balkh, 22 km south of the Āmū Daryā and 16 km north of Daulatābād.

Date: Achaemenid, 6th–4th cent. BC (ceramic).

Description: Remains of a circular walled town covering *c.*15 hectares, dominated by a central citadel, 28 m high. There is a 4 m wide aqueduct flowing northwards from the site.

Fieldwork:
1. 1886 Ata Muhammad, ABC—topographical survey.
2. 1974 Kruglikova and Mustamandi, Af/Sov. Mission—survey.
3. 2004 Fouache, Besanval, et al., DAFA—survey.

Sources:
1. Maitland 1888b: 274—mention
2. Kruglikova and Sarianidi 1976: 12, fig. 10—mention.

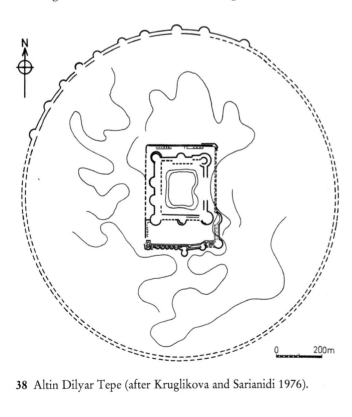

38 Altin Dilyar Tepe (after Kruglikova and Sarianidi 1976).

3. Francfort 1979a: 17–19—lists the site and discusses the general characteristics of Achaemenid fortifications.
4. Fouache, Besanval, et al.: 3423—mention the aqueduct.

AMARA KHĒL. See **283 DEH-I RAHMĀN.**

AMRĀN SĀHIB. See **1264 ZĪYĀRAT-I AMĪRĀN SĀHIB.**

AMRŪD. See **804 PASANG.**

39. ĀNA

Lat. 33° 25' N, long. 64° 22' E. Map 74.
Ghūr Province. 17 km south-east of Waras and 23 km south-west of Taiwāra.

Date: Ghurid, 12th–13th cent. (stylistic, geographical).

Description: Lines of square and round mud-brick towers and many other remains on both sides of the Āna Valley.

Fieldwork: 1946 Kohzad, HAS—survey.

Sources:
1. Fox 1943: 176—brief description.
2. Kohzad 1951–4, 9/2: 11—mention.
3. Fischer 1978a: 335, fig. 6.23—mention and photo.
4. Ball 2002: 34—mention.
5. Ball 2008: 151–2—summary.

ANDARĀB. See **105 BANŪ.**

40. ANDARĀBĪ
Including SHAUKUN TEPE.

Original: Lat. 36° 43' N, long. 69° 32' E. Map 36.
Revised: 36.71872162 N, 69.52840376 E /
36° 43' 07.39781616 N, 69° 31' 42.25353060 E.
Takhār Province. On the east bank of the Taluqān River, 1.8 km east-south-east of the bridge which crosses it near the town; the tepe is situated on the southern edge of the road which leads from the bridge towards the village of Andarābi.

Dates: Chalcolithic-Early Bronze Age, *c.*3500–2500 BC; Hunnic-Turk, 5th–9th cent.; some Islamic sherds (ceramic).

Description: Square platform (50 × 50 m) oriented about north–south, 2 m high, with traces of a wall on the north and east sides, and small hillocks (3 m) on the north-west and south-west angles. A depression in the middle of the south side possibly marks the location of a gate giving access to what would have been a caravanserai or a *qal'a* (the place-name, Shaukun Tepe, is associated with the memory of a period when it served as a halt for the night).

The tepe is today a cemetery; on the north face, cut straight down from the Taluqān track large jars containing human bones would have been found.

Collection: National Museum/AIA—sherds.

Fieldwork: 1978 Gardin et al., CNRS—survey

Sources:
1. Site information by J.-C. Gardin.
2. Lyonnet 1978: no. 404, fig. 7.
3. Gardin 1979: 74—no. 404.

41. ANDKHŪĪ

Original: Lat. 36° 57' N, long. 65° 07' E. Map 24.
Revised: 36.94856127 N, 65.11200108 E /
36° 56' 54.82056228 N, 65° 6' 43.20388116 E.
Faryāb Province. 138 km north of Maimana and 203 km west of Mazār-i Sharīf.

Dates: Sasanian, 3rd–7th cent. (stylistic); Timurid-Uzbek, 14th–17th cent. (epigraphic).

Description: In the north-west corner of the town are the remains of the Bālā Hisār, which is today still used as a military post. It forms an irregular polygon *c*.100 m in diameter, surrounded by a ditch, and probably dates from the Timurid period if not earlier.

In the ruins of the old town (north-west of the mid-20th century town) is the domed tomb and complex of Hazrat Ishān Bābā Walī which, in 1886, contained the date 787/1386. This does not appear to have survived and the present building appears to have little Timurid material and consists of an open courtyard surrounding a tank (*hauz*) dating from the late 19th to mid-20th century. In the early 1990s, the inscription was no longer in situ and was probably removed in the 1930s. In 1885 C. E. Yate recorded that Bābā Walī's shrine remains the most important shrine in Andkhūī.

To the south of the shrine of Bābā Walī is the shrine of Chahrda Ma'sūm. The double domed, baked brick building contains 14 ornate marble gravestones, including the graves of several women and children, dating from between 889/1484 (Yate writes 1472) to 984/1576. The graves are all members of a single extended clan of *shaikh*s, probably descendants of Sayyid Tāj al-Dīn of Andkhūī who was in turn a descendant of Sayyid Baraka (d. 1404), Timur Lang's spiritual adviser. According to Yate in 1885 there was a 'Kufic' inscription on the interior wall of this shrine. No such inscription remains today.

To the south-east of the tomb of Bābā Walī lie the fragmentary remains of a Timurid building, possibly the *madrasa* said to have been founded in the 15th century. Traces of blue glazed tilework can be seen on the exterior panelled façade of the structure which is in very poor condition.

In 1994 a small, bronze statuette of a female divinity (said to be of Anahita), in the possession of an antique dealer, was found in the vicinity of the town. Pre- and early Islamic pottery have also been found in the desert around the town. A relief depicting a Buddhist footprint was also found at Andkhūī.

Fieldwork:
1. 1885–6 Peacocke, Yate, ABC—topographical survey.
2. 1994–7 Lee—surveys.

Sources:
1. Site information by Jonathan L. Lee.
2. Durand 1885: II, pl. 12—sketch of the fort from the bazaar.
3. Peacocke 1887a: 93—brief description.
4. Yate 1888: 347–9—description of the town and some of the *zīyārats*, with translations of some of the inscriptions.
5. Le Strange 1905: 426—summary of the historical references.
6. Niedermeyer 1924—photographs of citadel and medieval bazaar (levelled during government replanning of the town in the 1940s).
7. Hayashi and Sahara 1962: 53 and 106—mention the Buddhist relief.
8. Gazetteer 1979: IV—brief mention of the shrine of Bābā Wali.
9. McChesney 1991b: 42–3—details of possible origin of graves at Chahrda Ma'sūm and mention of Timur and Bābā Wali.
10. Stuckert 1994—drawing of fortress.
11. Lee 1996: 24, 64—description of Chahrda Ma'sūm and mention of tombs.
12. Ball 2008: 153—summary.

42. ĀQCHA BĀLĀ HISĀR

Original: Lat. 36° 56' N, long. 66° 10' E. Maps 24, 25.
Revised: 36.92877273 N, 66.17657427 E /
36° 55' 43.58181540 N, 66° 10' 35.66737920 E.
Jauzjān Province. In the centre of the town of Aqchā, 96 km west of Mazār-i Sharīf.

Date: Graeco-Bactrian, 3rd–1st cent. (numismatic); Timurid, with 18th- and 19th-century additions (architectural).

Description: Circular mound crowned with an Islamic fortress situated in the northern and central part to the south of the modern town. It includes a monumental entrance flanked by half-towers, a courtyard, and several modern monuments. The citadel was levelled in the 1930s and little remains today of a once imposing fortress reputed to have been impregnable. 19th-century accounts of this fortress include references to a deep, water-filled ditch and steep sides. The citadel was one in a series of frontier defences guarding the approach to Balkh from the north-west. It is probably Chingizid but may well have Timurid elements. During the 18th–19th centuries the citadel played an important part in the internecine wars between various Uzbek rulers and the Durrani Afghans. In the south, a terreplein appears to mark the old site.

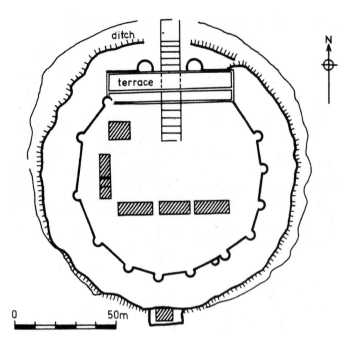

42 Aqcha Bālā Hisār—citadel (Marc Le Berre).

Fieldwork:
1. 1885 Peacocke ABC—reconnaissance.
2. 1946 Wheeler ASI—reconnaissance.
3. Le Berre, DAFA—survey.

Sources:
1. Le Berre, DAFA archives: unpublished 1948 report, tépé P. 9.
2. Peacocke 1887a: 105—brief description.
3. Wheeler 1947: 63—mention.
4. Caspani and Cagnazzi 1951: 244, fig. 236—mention and photo of Bālā Hisār.
5. Grötzbach 1976 and 1979—plan of new town of Āqcha with location of Bālā Hisār.
6. R. Stuckert 1994—sketch of fort just prior to demolition.
7. Lee 1996 (various)—history of fortress during Timurid and post-Timurid period.
8. Bopearachchi 2005—discussed a hoard of 48 Graeco-Bactrian coins found in or near Āqcha.

ANGURI. See 1084 SHIR-I HAIDAR.

43. ĀQ CHAPAR 1
See also 256 DASHLI.

Original: Lat. 37° 04' N, long. 66° 30' E. Map 25.
Revised: 37.07846745 N, 66.48795465 E /
37° 04' 42.48281316 N, 66° 29' 16.63673280 E.
Jauzjān Province. Part of the Dashli Oasis, 5 km south-east of Aq Chapar 2, 45 km north-east of Āqcha and 9 km east of the road to Kilift.

Date: Kushan, 1st BC–AD 3rd cent. (ceramic).

Description: A large, round or polyhedral monumental building, measuring 130 m in diameter. It is surrounded by a double ring of outer walls, with a gallery in between, pierced by embrasures and reinforced by salients measuring 4 m square.

Fieldwork: 1973 Sarianidi, af/Sov. Mission—survey.

Source: Sarianidi 1977b: 99–100—brief description of the architecture.

44. ĀQ CHAPAR 2
See also 256 DASHLI.

Lat. 37° 05' N, 66° 26' E. Map 25.
Jauzjān Province. Part of the Dashli Oasis, 3 km south of Dashli 3 and 3 km east of Dashli 1.5 km north-west of Āq Chapar 1.

Date: Iron Age, early 1st mill. BC (ceramic).

Description: A large round or polyhedral monument, similar in layout to Āq Chapar 1. It measures 170 m in diameter and is surrounded by a 1 m thick wall reinforced by 25–7 towers, each 4 m square.

Fieldwork: 1973 Sarianidi, Af/Sov. Mission—survey.

Source: Sarianidi 1977b: 99–100—brief description of the architecture.

45. ĀQ KAMAR

Lat. 35° 47' N, long. 65° 14' E. Map 46.
Faryāb Province. 6.5 km south of Bīlchirāgh on the eastern side of the Chashma Khwāb River gorge.

Description: Three artificial rock chambers cut into the grey siliceous limestone of the cliff face. They are partly ruined and each measure c.2.10 m square and have arched roofs.

Fieldwork: 1885–6 Amir Khan and Shahzada Taimus, Griesbach, ABC—topographical survey.

Sources:
1. Griesbach 1888b: 196—brief description.
2. Amir Khan and Shahzada Taimus 1888b: 231—mention.

ĀQĪNA. See 2005 ĀQĪNA in Supplement.

46. ĀQ KUPRUK
Including GHĀR-I ASB or DUKHTAR-I PĀD-SHĀH and GHĀR-I MĀR.

Lat. 36° 05' N, long. 66° 51' E. Map 47.
Balkh Province. Four sites alongside the Balkh River just to the north of the town of Āq Kupruk, in the hills c.77 km south of Mazār-i Sharīf.

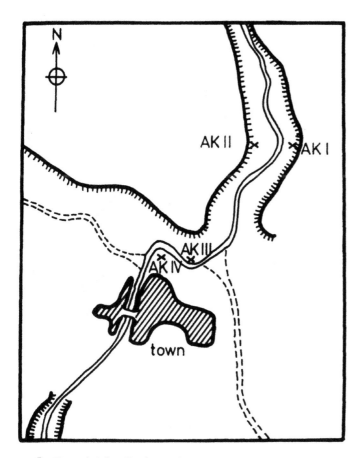

46 Āq Kupruk (after Davis 1978).

Dates: Epi-Palaeolithic, 20,000–15,000 BC; Aceramic Neolithic, 9000–5200 (C-14 lithic); Ceramic Neolithic, 5000–2000 BC; Iron Age/Achaemenid, 6th cent. BC; Kushan-Sasanian, 200–700 (C-14, lithic, ceramic).

Description: Āq Kupruk consists of four sites, numbered I, II, III, and IV. Āq Kupruk I, or Ghār-i Asb, is a rock shelter of the Kushan-Sasanian period, containing some fragmentary Buddhist frescos and some simple architecture. Āq Kupruk II, or Ghār-i Mār, is another rock shelter, probably the most productive of the three sites, producing material from all periods except the Kushan-Sasanian. About 10 per cent of the occupation area was excavated. Āq Kupruk III is an open-air site on the river terrace consisting of two periods, both in the Epi-Palaeolithic. In addition a fourth site, Āq Kupruk IV, was excavated briefly by McBurney nearer to the village, producing a 'Middle Mousterian' type of industry differing to that found by Dupree.

Finds included an extensive and sophisticated stone tool industry, very early stone sculpture, domesticated sheep and goat remains, fragments of beaten copper from the ceramic Neolithic, many projectile points, glass, terracotta, and simple jewellery.

Fieldwork:
1. 1959 Dupree, AUFS—survey.
2. 1960 Hayashi and Sahara, Kyoto University—survey.
3. 1962 and 1965 Dupree, AMNH—excavations.
4. 1971 McBurney, Cambridge University—sondage.

Sources:
1. Dupree 1960: 14—mentions the blade tools and Buddhist paintings.
2. Hayashi and Sahara 1962: 54–5 and 105—describe the frescos in Ghār-i Asb.
3. Dupree and Howe 1963: 3—mention.
4. Dupree 1964: 1–2—brief summary of the results of the 1962 excavations in Ghār-i Mār.
5. Dales 1965: 259—brief discussion of the chronology.
6. Dupree 1967: 8–27—a summary, with discussion on chronology and comparisons.
7. N. Dupree 1967: 23–9—brief description of the finds and the sequence.
8. Dupree 1968a—discussion and conjectures on the Epi-Palaeolithic stone head.
9. Dupree 1968b—good summary of the results.
10. Masson and Sarianidi 1969—discussion of the site in its wider chronological and regional context.
11. Fairservis 1971: 111–13—summary of the Ghār-i Mār sequence and results.
12. Brill 1972b—analysis of some glass from the 4th cent.
13. Caley 1972a—brief note on the metal fragments from Ghār-i Mār.
14. Caley 1972b—notes on some copper, bronze, and iron fragments.
15. Dupree 1972—tables summarizing the C-14 dates, the material and the stratigraphy.
16. Dupree and David 1972—full, well illustrated typologies and analyses of the stone and bone implements.
17. Dupree and Kolb 1972—preliminary report and general discussion of the pottery, with a catalogue of designs of the Iron Age.
18. Marshak 1972—very detailed study of the carved stone head and flat decorated stone.
19. McBurney 1972—mentions own work in the vicinity.
20. Perkins 1972—list and brief discussion of the plant remains.
21. Solem 1972—analysis and catalogue of the molluscs.
22. Dales 1973a: 124–5—very brief summary of the Epi-Palaeolithic and Neolithic levels.
23. Dupree 1973: 261–4 and 269–71—summary of the results for the prehistoric periods.
24. Davis 1974: 62–3 and 68–177—full description of the excavations and report on the Epi-Palaeolithic artefacts.
25. N. Dupree et al. 1974: 54–9—summary and description of the objects on display in the National Museum.
26. Shaffer 1976: 74—discussion of the protohistoric material in comparison with other material from Afghanistan.
27. Kolb 1977—brief summary of ceramic studies.
28. Davis 1978: 55–63—good, illustrated account of the Palaeolithic material.

29. Shaffer 1978b: 74–81 and 89–90—description of the protohistoric material and assessment of its importance.
30. Gupta 1979: I. 142 and II. 266–7—summary of the results and discussion of the lithic industry and its links in Central Asia.
31. Srivastava 1979b: 56—assesses the evidence from Aq Kupruk for the development of early society.
32. Zahir 1980—summary in Persian of the results.
33. Ball 2008: 43, 153—summary.
34. Tissot 2006: 10—National Museum catalogue details and photo.

47. ĀQ RABĀT
Including BAJGAH and SABZAK.

Original: Lat. 34° 56'–34° 57' N, long. 67° 39'–67° 40' E. Map 48.
Revised: 34.93084003 N, 67.65336505 E / 34° 55' 51.02411124 N, 67° 39' 12.11416200 E.
Bāmiyān Province. At the southern approach to the Āq Rabāt Pass leading from Bāmiyān to Saighān.

Date: Turk/pre-Mongol Islamic, 7th–13th cent. (architectural).

Description: Some extensive mud remains of fortifications on either side of the pass.

Fieldwork:
1. 1885 Maitland, ABC—topographical survey.
2. 1974–5 Le Berre, DAFA—survey.

Sources:
1. Masson 1839: 84—mention.
2. Masson 1842: II. 396—mention.
3. Maitland 1888b: 5—mention.
4. Le Berre 1987: 87, pl. 111b, c, d—brief description and photos; itinerary B2, Darra-i Sabzak, ruins 1 and 2.

48. ĀQ TEPE
Or NAWĀBĀD.

Original: Lat. 36° 52' N, long. 67° 06' E. Map 27.
Revised: 36.8680914 N, 67.09459729 E / 36° 52' 05.12905548 N, 67° 05' 40.55024472 E.
Balkh Province. 18.5 km north of Mazār-i Sharīf to the east of the road to Tāsh Guzar.

Description: A large, square mound, 8 m high.

Fieldwork: 1884–5 Peacocke, ABC—topographical survey.

Sources:
1. Peacocke 1887a: 303—mention.
2. Gazetteer 1979: IV. 53—mention.

49. ĀQ TEPE NAWARID

Original: Lat. 36° 48' N, long. 66° 39' E. Map 26.
Revised: 36.79582507 N, 66.65382413 E / 36° 47' 44.97026532 N, 66° 39' 13.76685324 E.
Balkh Province. 15 km south-east of Nimlik, 200 m south of the road to Balkh.

Date: Graeco-Bactrian, 3rd–2nd cent. BC (ceramic).

Description: Quadrangular enclosure (120×120 m), surrounded by a deep ditch and a wall; citadel (30×30 m) in the north-east angle (height 20 m). Many hillocks all around.

Fieldwork:
1. 1946 Wheeler, ASI—reconnaissance.
2. 1948 Le Berre, DAFA—survey.
3. 1960 Hayashi and Sahara, University of Kyoto—survey.

Sources:
1. Le Berre unpublished 1948 report, DAFA archives: tépé P. 42.
2. Shakur 1947: 68—mention.
3. Hayashi and Sahara 1962: 67—photo and brief description in Japanese.

50. ĀQ TEPE, QUNDŪZ

Original: Lat. 36° 59' N, long. 68° 34' E. Map 32.
Revised:
36.99189121 N, 68.55239921 E / 36° 59' 30.80835888 N, 68° 33' 08.63716428 E (B).
36.98744191 N, 68.55155476 E / 36° 59' 14.79085980 N, 68° 33' 05.59715328 E (A).
Qundūz Province. In the town of Āq Tepe, on the slopes that descend from the plateau of Chul-i Abdān towards the Qundūz River. (A) The largest tepe is 300 m north of the road that crosses Āq Gul in an east–west direction, between the two west branches of the canal of Char Gul which crosses this road; it corresponds to the mound of 6 m indicated on the 1:100,000 map in Āq Tepe. (B) A second tepe is located 600 m north-north-east of the preceding one.

Dates: Kushan; Kushano-Sasanian; Hunnic-Turk, 5th–9th cent.; a few Islamic sherds (ceramic).

Description: (A) Platform generally square in aspect (90×90 m, oriented according to an approximately north–south diagonal), strongly eroded in the south-west, and sloping towards the west, like the Āq Tepe plain itself, than which it is higher by 1 to 2 m. On this natural terreplein, undulations and sherds in the east sector. In the south-west, square mound (30×30), flat top (15×15 m), height 5 m in relation to the terreplein (north-east), 8 m in relation to the plain (south-west), with a lower adventitious embankment in the north-west (3 m). (B) rectangular mound oriented more or less east–west (60×50 m), summit surface highly undulating (height 2–3 m), earth loose; many fired bricks on the surface suggesting that the site could have been used at some point as a brickyard (one in activity exists near the Āq Tepe road, 500 m away). From the summit, a zīyārat may be seen to the west and 400 m to the north-north-west, a modern cemetery possibly established on a (non-surveyed) tepe.

Collections: National Museum/AIA—sherds.

Fieldwork:
1. 1975 Kohl—survey.
2. 1978 Gardin et al., CNRS—survey.

Sources:
1. Site information by J.-C. Gardin.
2. Kohl 1978: 68—mention and photo.
3. Gardin and Lyonnet 1997-8, 1978-9: pl. VI, nos. 501–2.
4. Lyonnet 1997: figs 68, 69—nos. 501, 502.
5. Gardin 1998: 85, nos. 501–2.

51. ĀQ TEPE, SALTUQ

Original: Lat. 36° 51' N, long. 66° 18' E. Map 25.
Revised: 36.84119127 N, 66.31773858 E /
36° 50' 28.28856660 N, 66° 19' 03.85890132 E.
Jauzjān Province. 16 km south-east of Āqcha, south of the Balkh road (c.2 km) and the village of Saltuq (c.800 m).

Description: Quadrangular enclosure (c.170 × 170 m), height 12 m, the south face is very degraded by erosion. No traces of a ditch, but a large enclosure wall. South of the tepe, an area of ruins; two tepes to the south-east.

Fieldwork: 1948 Le Berre, DAFA—survey.

Source: Le Berre, unpublished 1948 report, DAFA archives: tépé P. 19.

ARAB KAKUL. See 509 KAKUL.

ARAB TEPE. See 580 KHUSH GILDI.

52. ARAIRI

Lat. 31° 24' N, long. 62° 28' E. Map 85.
Nīmrūz Province. C.20 km south-west of Pul-i Ghurghuri, between the Khāsh Rūd and the road to Chakhānsūr.

Date: Mongol-Timurid, 13th–16th cent. (ceramic).

Description: Remains of a mud-brick building.

Source: Fischer et al. 1974-6: 32—mention as Ruin 6.

53. ARANJI
See also 256-9 DASHLI sites.

Original: Lat. 37° 01' N, long. 66° 27' E. Map 25.
Revised: 37.00980902 N, 66.45111219 E /
37° 00' 35.31245940 N, 66° 27' 04.00387032 E.

Jauzjān Province. 30 km north-east of Āqcha at the southern end of the Dashli Oasis, 10 km south-east of Dashli 1 and 2 km north of the village of Aranji.

Date: Late Bronze Age, 2nd millennium BC. (ceramic).

Description: Four small sites stretching east–west for 2.5 km and north–south for 1 km, comprising Dashli 28, 29, 34, and 35. Average size is c.200 × 150 m in area. The surface is covered in sherds, flints, and fragments of bronze.

Fieldwork: 1973 Sarianidi, Af/Sov. Mission—survey.

Source: Sarianidi 1977c—general discussion of the Dashli sites and material.

ARAP. See 674 LALMĪ BUZ.

54. ARCHĪ
Including QIZLA TEPE.

Original: Lat. 47° 02'–47° 03' N, long. 69° 13'–69° 14' E. Maps 31, 35.
Revised:
37.03401357 N, 69.2447628 E/ 37° 02' 02.44884660 N, 69° 14' 41.14607784 E (A).
37.03561047 N, 69.24245448 E / 37° 02' 08.19768804 N, 69° 14' 32.83613700 E (B).

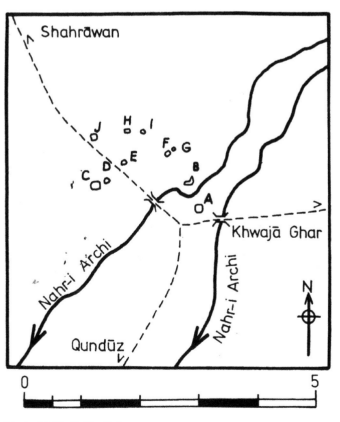

54 Archi (J.-C. Gardin).

37.03084214 N, 69.22398833 E / 37° 01' 51.03168924 N,
69° 13' 26.35799304 E (C).
37.04013523 N, 69.23205921 E /37° 02' 24.48684384 N,
69° 13' 55.41313908 E (E).
37.03996738 N, 69.23910559 E / 37° 02' 23.88257916 N,
69° 14' 20.78012292 E (F).
37.04047866 N, 69.23998656 E / 37° 02' 25.72316196 N,
69° 14' 23.95162068 E (G).
37.04637375 N, 69.23063884 E / 37° 02 46.94550000 N,
69° 13' 50.29983948 E (H).
37.04588676 N, 69.23393637 E / 37° 02 45.19234572 N,
69° 14' 02.17093416 E (I).
Qundūz Province. Group of 10 tepes north-west of the hotel
of Archī and on either side of the Archī road at Mullah Quli,
in an area of about 4 km²; see fig. A to J. The tepes H and
I correspond to the mounds of 8 m and 5 m indicated on the
1:100,000 map.

Dates: Achaemenid, 6th–4th cent. BC (A, B); Hellenistic,
3rd–1st cent. BC (A to F, I, J); Kushan, 1st–4th cent. (F to J);
pre-Mongol Islamic, 10th–13th cent. (A to H, J). (ceramic).

Description: Irregular quadrangular mounds, cut by farming
activities. The largest (A, B, C, D, F) measure 80 to 100 m per
side; the smallest (D, G to J) 40 to 50 m. The height varies:
c.2 m (D, E, J), 4 to 6 m (B, F, I), up to 8–10 m (A, C, G, H).
The top has in general the aspect of a wide platform, with a
depression in the centre; no strong slopes, except on B,
where the platform, 3 m high, is dominated in the south-
west by a mound of 6 m.

Collection: National Museum/AIA—sherds.

Fieldwork: 1977 Gardin et al. CNRS—survey.

Sources:
1. Site information by J.-C. Gardin.
2. Gardin and Lyonnet 1978–9: pl. IV, nos. 23 to 32.
3. Gardin 1980—describes in general terms the survey in
   the Archī area.
4. Gentelle 1989—full report on the ancient irrigation and
   hydrology of the area.
5. Lyonnet 1997: figs 25, 35, 39, 49, 68, 69—nos. 23–32.
6. Gardin 1998: 55–6, nos. 23–32.

55. ARŪKH, SOUTH

Lat. 31° 53' N, long. 65° 30' E. Map 89.
Kandahār Province. 3 km south of Mundigak. The tepe is
situated south of the village.

Dates: Partho-Sasanian, 1st–4th cent.; Sasano-Islamic, 5th–
9th cent.; pre-Mongol Islamic, 10th–13th cent. (ceramic).

Description: Square mound about 30 m per side, with gate
on the west face. An excavation authorized by the local
governor (digging of two galleries under the south wall of
the building) revealed walls in mud-brick and *pakhsa* resting
on natural soil.

The name is a corruption of Achaemenid *Harahuvatish*,
Greek *Arachosia*, Arabic *ar-Rūkhajj*, the name of the province in antiquity.

Collection: National Museum/AIA—sherds.

Fieldwork:
1. 1951 Casal, DAFA—survey.
2. 1974 Whitehouse, BIAS—survey.

Sources:
1. Casal: unpublished 1951 report, DAFA archives.
2. Ball 1996: 394—discussion of the name.

56. ARŪKH, WEST

Original: Lat. 31° 53' N, long. 65° 29' E. Map 89.
Revised: 31.89729263 N, 65.49056552 E /
31° 53' 50.25347664 N, 65° 29' 26.03588928 E.
Kandahār Province. In the Khākrīz Valley 3 km to the south of
Mundigak. The site is on the western side of Arūkh village.

Date: Late Islamic, undetermined (ceramic).

Description: An irregular group of low mounds, each *c*.400 m
across and 203 m high. The mounds could be house/
compound remains or rather scattered small settlements.
Probably a short-lived village site, possibly the predecessor
of the present-day settlement of Arūkh.

Fieldwork: 1974 Whitehouse, BIAS—survey.

Source: Site information by D. Whitehouse in unpublished
BIAS archive.

ASĀBĀD. See 773 NIJRAU.

57. ĀSAD QAL'A

Lat. 32° 06' N, long. 65° 31' E. Maps 75, 89.
Kandahār Province. On the main track from Kandahār to
Chura. The site is 2 km from the village.

Description: An ancient lead and zinc mine, consisting of a
shaft sunk 10 m into the vein.

Source: Berthoud et al. 1977: 809—brief description of the
geology and the workings.

ĀSHIQĀN WA 'ARIFĀN See **Supplement.**

ASHKINAK, Hāmūn. See 1073 SHAWĀL.

58. ASHKINAK, HELMAND
Or ISHKINAK or QAL'A-I JAN BEG.

Original: Lat. 30° 15' N, long. 62° 08' E. Map 95.

Revised: 30.24917437 N, 62.14242305 E /
30° 14' 57.02772264 N, 62° 08' 32.72298864 E.
Nīmrūz Province. On left (south) bank of Helmand, 5 miles west of Khijū (north bank according to Peacocke), 21 km east of Chahar Burjak.

Dates: Parthian, 1st–3rd cent.; Sasanian, 3rd–4th cent.; Ghaznavid (some), 11th–12th cent. (ceramic).

Description: An area of ruins dominated by the remains of a mud-brick fort. Much of the outer walls and inner keep, including some intact arches, was standing in the 1880s (Peacocke).

The name Ashkinak is now unknown; these ruins are known as Qal'a-i Jan Beg. Qal'a-i Jan Beg is on the south, rather than north, bank of the Helmand, as correctly stated in Gazetteer II. 140. I cannot account for the name Ashkinak; these ruins are not known by this name today. The site was most heavily occupied during Parthian and early Sasanian times, although there is evidence of occupation on a smaller scale during Ghaznavid times (Trousdale).

Fieldwork:
1. 1884 Peacocke, Maitland, ABC—topographical survey.
2. 1966, 1971–2 Trousdale, Smithsonian—survey.

Sources:
1. Additional information provided by W. Trousdale.
2. Bellew 1874: 209—mention.
3. Peacocke 1885a: 5—mention.
4. Maitland 1888a: 63—mention.
5. Peacocke 1887a: 18—brief description.
6. Gazetteer 1973: II. 25 and 140—brief description.

ASHRAF. See 263 DASHT-I LAJAM.

ASHRAK. See 370 GHUNDI SHĀH NASR.

59. ĀSNĀM

Original: Lat. 36° 35' N, long. 70° 51' E. Map 38.
Revised: 36.58553745 N, 70.84798986 E /
36° 35' 07.93480776 N, 70° 50' 52.76348556 E.
Badakhshān Province. On the south-east bank of the confluence of the Jūkhān and Kokcha Rivers, at the eastern entrance to the Āsnām Valley near Jurm.

Description: Remains of a settlement with stone walls up to 2 m high, enclosed by an outer fortification wall.

Fieldwork: 1975 Kohl—survey.

Source: Kohl 1978: 65—mention.

60. ASPAKI WATANI

Original: Lat. 36° 48' N, long. 66° 47' E. Map 26.
Revised: 36.80416675 N, 66.7907888 E / 36° 48' 15.00030108 N, 66° 47' 26.83966884 E.

Balkh Province. 11 km north-west of this town, 500 m north of tepes nos. 690 and 1227, on the other side of the same marshy arm.

Description: Rectangular platform measuring about 80 × 65 m, height 6 m, surrounded by a ditch which is now cultivated. No trace of construction is apparent.

Fieldwork: 1948 Le Berre, DAFA—survey.

Source: M. Le Berre: unpublished 1948 report, DAFA archives, tépé P. 5.

ASQALĀN. See 218 CHUL-I ABDĀN.

61. ĀSTĀNA TEPE

Original: Lat. 36° 42' N, long. 69° 50'–69° 51' E. Maps 37, 38.
Revised:
36.72760596 N, 69.85171547 E / 36° 43' 39.38145240 N, 69° 51' 6.17568156 E (A)
36.72148585 N, 69.84280946 E / 36° 43' 17.34905532 N, 69° 50' 34.11404736 E (C).
Takhār Province. 10 km south-west of Kalafgān, by the road which links this town to Tāluqān; tepe A is located near the first houses of Āstāna Tepe encountered when coming from Kalafgān, between these and the cliff of the deep torrent which flows a hundred metres to the north-west (Darya-i Shur).

Dates: Middle Bronze Age, *c.*2500–1500 BC (A); Hellenistic, 3rd–1st cent. BC (A); Kushan, 1st–4th cent. (A, B); pre-Mongol Islamic, 10th–13th cent. (ceramic).

Description: (A) On the terrace sloping towards the Darya-i Shur, large circular mound (diam. 80 m), 3 m high. (B) 700 m to the south-west, beneath the school of Āstāna Tepe, remains of a Kushan site visible in section in a nearby ravine, north side (jars in place). (C) 400 m further to the south-west, the road passes between two high natural mounds which overlook the same ravine, south side, just before its meeting with the Darya-i Shur; the slopes of these mounds were inhabited in the past, to judge by the many quern fragments and sherds scattered on them; they are today occupied by a cemetery.

Collections: National Museum/AIA—sherds.

Fieldwork: 1977 Gardin et al., CNRS—survey.

Sources:
1. Site information by J.-C. Gardin.
2. Gardin and Lyonnet 1978–9: pl. X, nos. 318–21.
3. Lyonnet 1997: Figs 13, 39, 49, 68, 69—nos 318–321.
4. Gardin 1998: 94—nos. 318–21.

ASYĀB-I BĀDĪ. See 2047 DARRA-I TAKHT in Supplement.

62. ĀSYĀ-I MURDYĀN

Original: Lat. 36° 53' N, long. 66° 30' E. Maps 25, 26.
Revised: 36.86501353 N, 66.50853625 E /
36° 51' 54.04869324 N, 66° 30' 30.73049964 E.
Jauzjān Province. 31 km south-east of Āqcha, north-west of the village of Nimlik, north of the Balkh road.

Description: Rectangular platform (*c.*70 × 37 m), height 2.50 m.

Fieldwork: 1948 Le Berre, DAFA — survey.

Source: M. Le Berre: unpublished 1948 report, DAFA archives, tépé P. 27.

63. ĀSYĀ-I QUNĀK
  Or SIĀH QANDŪQ.

Original: Lat. 36° 43' N, long. 66° 55' E. Map 27.
Revised: 36.72321121 N, 66.91513517 E /
36° 43' 23.56037364 N, 66° 54' 54.48661092 E.
Balkh Province. C.5 km south-east of Balkh, past Tepe Rustam.

Description: A very high, narrow circular mound of mud 18 m high, resembling a stupa. There are more ruins in the vicinity, including a 3 m high mound to the east.

Fieldwork:
1. 1924 Foucher, DAFA — survey.
2. 1960 Hayashi and Sahara, Kyoto University — survey.

Sources:
1. Yate 1888: 260 — mention.
2. Foucher 1942-7: I. 68 — mention and photo.
3. Hayashi and Sahara 1962: 59 and figs 60 and 163 — photos and brief summary in Japanese.

ATA KHĀN KHWĀJA. See **2006 ATA KHĀN KHWĀJA** in Supplement

AULIA TEPE. See **1225 UVLIA TEPE.**

AUPAR. See **350 GHANDAK.**

AUSAK. See **2007 AUSAK** in Supplement.

64. ĀWARZĀN

Original: Lat. 36° 40' N, long. 70° 11' E. Map 38.
Revised: 36.68258035 N, 70.20045868 E /
36° 40' 57.28927152 N, 70° 12' 01.65124260 E.
Badakhshān Province. On the west bank of the river in the Mashhad Valley, south of Kishm.

Date: Kushan, 1st cent. BC–AD 3rd cent. (ceramic).

Description: A steep-sided mound.

Fieldwork: 1975 Kohl — survey.

Source: Kohl 1978: 67 — mention.

65. AYATAN TEPE

Original: Lat. 36° 50' N, long. 67° 53' E. Map 29.
Revised: 36.83238123 N, 67.88703488 E /
36° 49' 56.57241432 N, 67° 53' 13.32555216 E.
Samangān Province. 21 km north-east of Tāshqurghān.

Dates: Bronze — beg. Iron, middle 2nd mill. to beg. 1st mill. BC; Achaemenid-Hellenistic, 6th–1st cent. BC; Kushan, 1st–3rd cent. (ceramic).

Description: Large low tepe; on the north side, square area defined by walls (about 60 × 60 m). Mud-bricks of the walls: 39 × 41 cm.

Collections: National Museum/AIA — sherds.

Fieldwork: 1969 Gouin, DAFA — survey.

Source: Gouin 1974, and unpublished report, site no. 35.

66. ĀZADĀN
  See also 428 HERAT.

Original: Lat. 34° 22' N, long. 62° 09' E. Maps 43, 52.
Revised: 34.36017645 N, 62.14822195 E /
34° 21' 36.63521172 N, 62° 08' 53.59902000 E.
Herat Province. 5 km north-west of Herat, *c.*2 km to the north of the road to Zindajān.

Date: Timurid, 15th cent. (epigraphic).

Description: The Shrine of 'Abd al-Walid, a complex consisting of a tomb, a mosque, an inn, and a cistern. The tomb is an original Kart structure with extensive modification under Amir 'Ali Shir Nawai and with extensive modern rebuilding. The mosque, although originally Timurid, was rebuilt in 1956. It still however contains the original grave of Nizam al-Mulk, which has an inscription in *suls* characters.

Fieldwork: 1978-9 Samizay, Kābul University/UNESCO — survey.

Sources:
1. Wolfe 1966: 26 — brief description.
2. Samizay 1981: 75-81 — summary with drawings and photos of the monument.
3. O'Kane 1987: 271-5 — detailed description.
4. Aalund 1990 — photos and plan of the monument.

AZĪZĀBĀD. See **2008 AZĪZĀBĀD** in Supplement.

BĀBĀ DARWĪSH. See **245 DARRA-I KŪR.**

BĀBĀ HATĪM. See **440 IMĀM SĀHIB.**

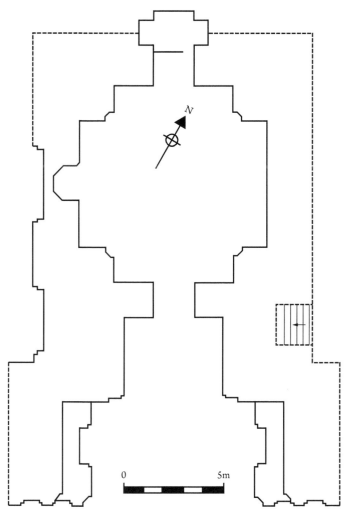

66 Azādān (after O'Kane 1987).

67. BĀBĀ KALĀ

Original: Lat. 34° 55' N, long. 70° 23' E. Map 65.
Revised: 34.92492956 N, 70.38145233 E /
34° 55' 29.74642212 N, 70° 22' 53.22838296 E.
Laghmān Province. On the west bank of the 'Alingār River,
north of Sundurwar.

Date: Hindu Shahi, 10th cent. (ceramic).

Description: Remains of stone walls on a hill.

Fieldwork: 1960–8 Fischer, DAAD—survey.

Source: Fischer 1969: 357—mention as Ruins G3 or G4.

BĀBA KUZAM. See 2009 **BĀBA KUZAM** in Supplement.

68. BĀBĀ QUSHQAR

Lat 36° 45' N, long. 67° 00' E. Map 27.
Balkh Province. 13 km east of Balkh, near Takhta Pul on the
road to Mazār-i Sharīf.

Description: A conspicuous walled mound.

Fieldwork: 1886 Maitland, ABC—topographical survey.

Source: Maitland 1888b: 181—mentions.

69. BĀBĀ RUSHNĀI
Or KHWĀJA RUSHNĀI.

Lat. 36° 45' N, long. 66° 53' E. Maps 26, 27.
Balkh Province. Near a small cemetery south-west of the
inner wall of ancient Balkh, just off the road to the village of
Deh-i Mirān.

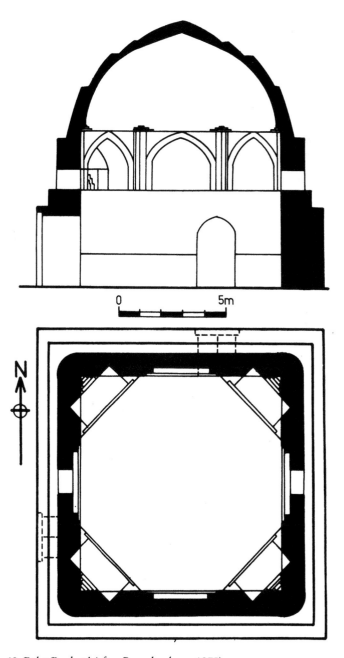

69 Bābā Rushnāi (after Pugachenkova 1975).

Dates: Ghaznavid, 1st half of 11th cent. (stylistic); Timurid, late 14th–15th cent. (epigraphic).

Description: A massive baked brick mausoleum with a shallow pointed dome. It has two entrances. Inside are the remains of a *suls* inscription recording the restoration of the building under the Timurids. There is a simple zone of transition of arched squinches.

Fieldwork: 1972–4 Pugachenkova, Af/Sov. Mission—survey.

Sources:

1. Pugachenkova 1975—architectural description and plan.
2. Pugachenkova 1978: 31—full description, plan, and elevation.
3. Mukhtarov 1980: 72–94—description and photo.
4. Golombek and Wilber 1988: 297—description of the Timurid restoration.
5. Hillenbrand 2000—discussion in the broader context of Ghaznavid and Ghurid architecture.

70. BĀD GUZAR

Original: Lat. 36° 25' N, long. 69° 20' E. Map 37.
36.44008361 N, 69.33177513 E / 36° 26' 24.30099744 N, 69° 19' 54.39047808 E to
36.42867652 N, 69.3283028 E / 36° 25' 43.23547956 N, 69° 19' 41.89006308 E.
Takhār Province. 5–6 km north-west of Ishkamīsh, west of the track which leads to Bangui by the valley of the Rūd-i Ishkamīsh, on the slopes of the hills where it heads toward the north; zone of many mounds, isolated or in groups of two or three; the northern and southern edges are marked by tepes of 4 m and 2 m, indicated respectively on the 1:100,000 map, west of the village of Bad Guzar.

Dates: Kushan, 1st–4th cent.; pre-Mongol Islamic, 10th–13th cent. (ceramic).

Description: These mounds are rounded and little eroded in spite of the cultivated fields (*lalmī*) surrounding them, sometimes up to the top; diam. 15 to 20 m, height 2 to 4 m. These are probably kurgans of the Kushan period, situated in a zone later occupied by a few farms, at the beginning of the Islamic period.

Collections: National Museum/AIA—sherds.

Fieldwork: 1978 Gardin et al., CNRS—survey.

Sources:

1. Site information by J.-C. Gardin.
2. Gardin and Lyonnet 1978–9: pl. XI, nos. 366–7.
3. Lyonnet 1978: fig. 49—nos. 366, 377.
4. Gardin 1979: 99—nos. 366–7.

71. BĀD-I ĀSYĀ, JAGHATŪ
See also 461 JAGHATŪ.

Lat. 33° 46' N, long. 68° 22' E. Map 80.

Ghazni Province. C.20 km north-west of Ghazni, on a mountain slope 1 km south of the site of Jaghatū.

Date: Turki Shahi, 7th–8th cent. (epigraphic).

Description: Remains of stone fortifications on the mountain slopes. On several rock faces there are also two late Bactrian cursive inscriptions and petroglyphs depicting goat, oxen, and human figures.

Fieldwork: 1958 Scerrato, IsMEO—survey.

Sources:

1. Humbach 1966–7: I. 104—brief analysis of the inscriptions.
2. Humbach 1967—brief epigraphical note.
3. Scerrato 1967—brief preliminary report on the remains.
4. Habibi 1969/70b: 11–19—photo and linguistic discussion of the inscriptions.
5. Habibi 1971: 56–7 and 138–9—photos of the inscriptions and discussion of the development of Afghan epigraphy.
6. Habibi 1974—summary of the inscriptions.
7. Davary 1977—lists the inscriptions and gives a bibliography.
8. Verardi 1977c: 119—brief summary of the site.
9. Mac Dowall and Taddei 1978b: 243–4—summary of the inscriptions.
10. Rahman 1979: 235–7—linguistic analysis of the inscriptions.
11. Verardi and Paparatti 2004: 91—briefly discuss the inscriptions.
12. Thomas 2015: 517—additional information from satellite imagery.

72. BĀD-I ĀSYĀ, KHANDŪD
See also 557 KHANDŪD.

Original: Lat. 36° 56' N, long. 72° 19' E. Map 39.
Revised: 36.93846983 N, 72.3272508 E / 36° 56' 18.49138548 N, 72° 19' 38.10286344 E.
Badakhshān Province. In Wakhān up a valley 1 km to the south of Khandūd.

Dates: ?Late Palaeolithic, 15,000–10,000 BC (stylistic); ?Kushan, 1st–3rd cent. (architectural).

Description: A stone platform, similar to Tup Khāna (Site 1204) with remains of mud-brick walls. There are also some petroglyphs of ibex and hunters nearby.

Source: Mouchet and Blanc 1972: 66–8—brief description.

73. BĀD-I SAH GHUNDĀI
Or TEPE AZAM QAL'A.

Original: Lat. 31° 36' N, long. 65° 51' E. Map 89.
Revised: 31.60500538 N, 65.85255132 E /
31° 36' 18.01935576 N, 65° 51' 09.18475956 E.

Kandahār Province. 14 km north-east of Kandahār, 1.5 km to the south of the road to Kābul.

Dates: Bronze Age, 2nd mill. BC; Hellenistic, 3rd–1st cent. BC; Partho-Sasanian, 1st–4th cent.; pre-Mongol Islamic, 10th–13th cent.; Timurid, 15th–16th cent. (ceramic).

Description: A large, roughly oval mound, 18 m high, 10 m long from north to south and with an area of 60 × 30 m on top. On the south and south-east side are low extensions, 2–3 m high, possibly a 'lower settlement' at the foot of the main mound. There is also a very small, low extension at the north and north-west end.

Fieldwork:
1. 1951 Casal, DAFA — survey.
2. 1966 Fischer, DAAD — survey.
3. 1974 Swiny and Whitehouse, BIAS — survey.

Sources:
1. Site information by S. Swiny and D. Whitehouse in unpublished BIAS archive.
2. Gardin and Lyonnet, chronological study of unpublished pottery from DAFA surveys.
3. Thompson 1964: 8 — mention.
4. Fischer 1967a: 151–2 — brief description and photos.
5. Fischer 1969: 338 — brief summary.

74. BĀDPASH

Original: Lat. 34° 37' N, long. 69° 53' E. Map 65.
Revised: 34.62259112 N, 69.8896622 E / 34° 37' 21.32804568 N, 69° 53' 22.78391100 E.
Laghmān Province. A hill just in the Dasht-i Shaitān in Tagau, between Gulbahār and Sarōbī.

Date: Kushan, 1st–3rd cent. (architectural).

Description: Remains of a stupa and monastery.

Source: Foucher 1942–7: I. 149 — mention.

75. BĀDQĀQ
Or BUTKĀK.

Original: Lat. 36° 05' N, long 64° 39' E. Map 24.
Revised: 36.10434744 N, 64.65742512 E / 36° 06' 15.65079372 N, 64° 39' 26.73044352 E.
Faryāb Province. Maimana district, 11 km upstream on the left bank of the Maimana River from its junction with the Qaisār River, c.28 km north of Maimana.

Description: A large, high mound with the remains of a fort on top.

Fieldwork: 1885–6 Maitland and Peacocke, ABC — topographical survey.

Sources:
1. Peacocke 1887a: 90 and 246 — mention.
2. Maitland 1888b: 155 — mention.

BAD SHĀŌ. See **479 JŪI NAU.**

76. BĀDURZĀI
Or BAHĀDURZĀI.

Original: Lat. 30° 11' N, long. 66° 02' E. Map 99.
Revised: 30.17471617 N, 66.01536622 E / 30° 10' 28.97820048 N, 66° 00' 55.31840928 E.
Kandahār Province. On the western side of the Shorawak Plain, c.100 km south of Spīn Baldak near the Pakistani border.

Description: A large mound with some ruins, including a ruined fort. There are many more artificial mounds on the plain.

Sources:
1. Campbell 1880: 621–2 — mention.
2. Gazetteer 1980: V. 73 — mention (Maitland).

BADWAN. See **1069 SHAMSHIR GHAR.**

BĀGH-I SHŪRSHŪR. See **2010 BĀGH-I SHŪR** in Supplement.

BĀGHA-I ZAGHIRAH. See **1019 SHĀH 'ALI.**

77. BĀGHAK
Or PUSHT-I GAU.

Original: Lat. 30° 09' N, long. 62° 30' E. Map 96.
Revised: 30.14893234 N, 62.55125461 E / 30° 08' 56.15643624 N, 62° 33' 04.51661112 E.
Nīmrūz Province. On the left (south) bank of the Helmand, 5.5 km west of Rūdbār.

Dates: Parthian-Sasanian, 1st–7th cent.; brief Tumurid, 14th cent. (ceramic).

Description: The name 'Bāghak' is not current. The ruins of a very large polygonal walled enclosure, with rooms around the interior of the walls, and a T-shaped architectural complex within, but with a vast amount of open ground. It is surrounded by several mounds and the remains of an ancient canal. Ruins of forts, villages, and canals and mounds along the valley for c.7 miles. There is heavy sherd cover of Parthian, Partho-Sasanian, and evidence of brief Timurid occupation. We found no evidence of Achaemenid occupation. The visible remains are largely Islamic, though elements of the plan are pre-Islamic.

Fieldwork:
1. 1884 Maitland, Peacocke, ABC — topographical survey.
2. 1966 Hammond, Cambridge University — survey.
3. 1966, 1971, 1978 Trousdale, Smithsonian — survey.

Sources:
1. Site information by W. Trousdale.
2. Bellew 1874: 206—mention.
3. Peacocke 1885a: 3—mention.
4. Maitland 1888a: 59—mention.
5. Peacocke 1887a: 17—mention.
6. Hammond 1970: 449—lists site (no. 29) with a general description of the pottery and discussion of the survey results.
7. Gazetteer 1973: II. 27—mention.

78. BĀGHAK-I BĀLĀ

Original: Lat. 30° 32' N, long. 61° 51' E. Map 93.
Revised: 30.50586057 N, 61.85724688 E /
30° 30' 21.09806640 N, 61° 51' 26.08876872 E.
Nīmrūz Province. 4 km south of Qal'a Fath, *c.*3 km to the east of the Helmand.

Date: Sasanian, 3rd–7th cent. (ceramic).

Description: A mound, with rectangular walls to the north.

Fieldwork: 1965–8 Fischer, DAAD—survey.

Source: Fischer 1969: 336—mention as Tepe D6.

79. BĀGH ARĀGH

Lat. 36° 45' N, long. 68° 40' E. Map 32.
Qundūz Province. C.19 km west of Qunduz near the left bank of the Qundūz River, 3 km south-east of Qush Tepe.

Date: Pre-Mongol Islamic, 10th–13th cent. (ceramic).

Description: Some mud-brick and baked brick ruins on the outskirts of the village. Some possible early Islamic coin hoards were allegedly found here.

Fieldwork: 1855, 60 Fischer, DAAD—survey.

Source: Fischer 1969: 350—very brief description.

80. BĀGH-I ĀSYĀ

Lat. 34° 35' N, long. 69° 14' E. approx. Map 61.
Kābul Province. Behind the Kābul airport, between Tara Khēl and the hill of Pāi Minār.

Dates: Hellenistic, 3rd–1st cent. BC; Kushan 1st–4th cent. (ceramic).

Description: None.

Collection: National Museum/AIA—sherds.

Source: Gardin and Lyonnet, 1980 study of unpublished ceramics from the DAFA surveys.

BĀGH GĀI. See **404 HADDA.**

81. BĀGH HINDŪ

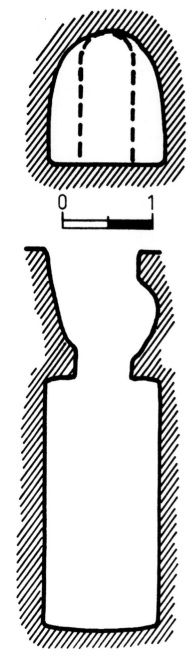

81 Bāgh Hindū (after Hayashi and Sahara 1962).

Lat. 36° 14–23' N, long. 68° 03–05' E. Map 30.
About 5 km south of Haibak on the east bank of the Tāshqurghān River, opposite and just upstream from Haibak Bālā Hisār.

Description: A single artificial cave high up in the cliff face. It has an elliptical arch opening, and is of uncertain date.

Fieldwork: 1960 Hayashi and Sahara, Kyoto University—survey.

Source: Hayashi and Sahara 1962: 42, figs 27 and 144—photo and description in Japanese.

82. BĀGH-I KHĀLĪL

Original: Lat. 31° 57' N. 65° 28' E. Map 89.
Revised: 31.97222131 N, 65.46845557 E /
31° 58' 19.99671780 N, 65° 28' 06.44004228 E.
Kandahār Province. In the Khākrīz Valley at the base of the foothills near Shāh Maqsūd, west of Chār Sang Tepe.

Description: Local reports of a mound. Not visited.

Source: Information by David Whitehouse from unpublished BIAS archive.

83. BĀGH-I MĪR

Original: Lat. 36° 41' N, long. 68° 57' E–68° 58' E. Map 32.
Revised:
36.68921648 N, 68.95167402 E / 36° 41' 21.17933880 N, 68° 57' 06.02647740 E (A).
36.68104107 N, 68.96297046 E / 36° 40' 51.74785344 N, 68° 57' 46.69364880 E (B).
Qundūz Province. About 10 km south-east of Qundūz, by the Khānābād road, *tepes in process of disappearing at the north-west (A) and south-east (B) extremities of the village of Bāgh-i Mir, on the edge of this road, north side; corresponding to the mounds of 6 m and 4 m indicated on the 1:100,000 map on the outskirts of this village.*

Dates: Middle Bronze, *c*.2500–1500 BC (B); Hellenistic (A); Kushan, 1st–4th cent. (B); pre-Mongol Islamic, 10th–13th (ceramic).

Description: (A) *Mound of irregular form (80 m north-west/-south-east × 40 m north-east/south-west), surrounded by little irrigation canals; very low in the south (1–2 m), a little higher in the north (3–4 m), at the present time protected from levelling by a cemetery. (B) Apparently intact platform (confirmed by locals), square (50 × 50), oriented north-east/-south-west; height 4–6 m, with culminating point at the north angle (8 m); protected by a cemetery and a zīyārat.*

The two mounds indicated on the 1:100,000 map 300 m to the north (height 7 m) and east (no measurement) of tepe A are in the process of disappearing (1978): low (1–2 m), narrow, unsurveyed platforms. The villagers confirm that several tepes of this region have recently been levelled by bulldozer to provide the earth necessary for the building of the Qundūz-Khānābād road.

Collections: National Museum/AIA—sherds.

Fieldwork: 1978 Gardin et al., CNRS—survey.

Sources:
1. Site information by J.-C. Gardin.
2. Gardin and Lyonnet 1978–9: pl. VII, nos. 431–2.
3. Lyonnet 1978: figs 13, 21–4, 39, 49, 68, 69—nos. 431, 432.
4. Gardin 1979: 78, nos. 431–2.

BĀGH-I MĪRI. See 674 LALMĪ BUZ.

84. BĀGH-I NAZĀRGĀH
See also 428 HERAT.

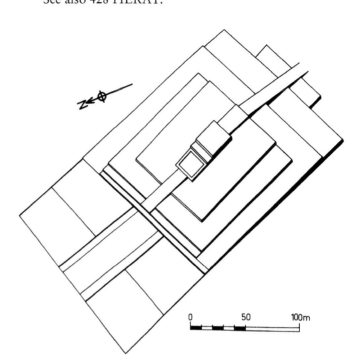

84 Bāgh-i Nazārgāh (W. Ball).

Lat. 34° 21' N, long. 62° 14' E., Map 52.
Herat Province. *C*.3 km north-east of Herat on the open ground between the edge of the cultivation and Gazurgāh.

Date: Timurid, 15th–16th cent. (ceramic).

Description: A series of immense artificial superimposed terraces covered in sherds and building debris, probably the remains of a Timurid monumental garden.

Fieldwork: 1977 Ball—survey.

Source: Ball 1981—detailed description and discussion.

85. BĀGH-I PUL GHUNDĀI

Original: Lat. 31° 37' N, long. 65° 34' E. Map 89.
Revised: 31.60969885 N, 65.56991766 E /
31° 36' 34.91587152 N, 65° 34' 11.70358140 E.
Kandahār Province. On the south side of the Kandahār-Herat road, 14 km west of Kandahār just east of the bridge over the Arghandāb.

Date: Bronze Age, 2nd–1st mill. BC (ceramic).

Description: A truncated conical mound, *c*.80–100 m diameter and 40 m high. There is a ledge on the north side, 5 m below the summit as though a platform had been made. It seems like a rock outcrop jacketed with earth and rubble to make a regular flat-topped mound. Little pottery, so probably not regular occupation. However, an irregular surface on the top suggests remains.

Fieldwork: 1974 Swiny and Whitehouse, BIAS—survey.

Source: Site information by S. Swiny and D. Whitehouse in unpublished BIAS archive.

BĀGH-I SŪFĪ. See 2179 QADER in Supplement.

86. BAGHLĀN SHAHR-I KUHNA
Or KUHNA QAL'A-YI BAGHLĀN. See also 689 LĪLĪ TEPE.

Original: Lat. 36° 13' N, long. 68° 49' E., Map 33.
Revised: 36.23890619 N, 68.78273839 E /
36° 14' 20.06227824 N, 68° 46' 57.85819104 E.
Baghlān Province. 11 km north-east of the new town, just to the east of the road to Qundūz.

Date: Kushan, 1st cent. BC–AD 3rd cent. (ceramic).

Description: A series of mounds and ruins extensively dug over with robber pits since 1992. As well as pottery, numerous ornaments, including gold ornaments (necklaces, earrings) as well as coins have been excavated.

Fieldwork: 1955–60 Fischer, DAAD—survey

Sources:
1. Site information by Jonathan L. Lee.
2. Fischer 1967a: 214—mention
3. Fischer 1969: 351–2—very brief summary.
4. Levi 1972: 131—brief description.

BĀGHSŪR. See 2010 BĀGH-I SHŪR in Supplement.

BĀGHSŪR. See 2263 TEPE BĀGH-I SŪR in Supplement.

BAGRĀM. See 122 BEGRAM.

87. BAGRĀMĪ

Lat. 34° 30' N, long. 69° 16' E. Map 61.
Kābul Province. 9 km east of Kābul, just to the south of the road to Latāband.

Description: Many mounds, the main one being a large, square mound, possibly representing the base and first stage of a stupa.

Sources:
1. Masson 1833a: 5—brief description.
2. Masson 1842: III. 163—mention.

88. BAHĀRAK, BADAKHSHĀN
See also 1037 SHAHR-I BARBAR, Badakhshān.

Lat. 37° 00' N, long. 70° 54' E. Map 38.
Badakhshān Province. 43 km east of Faizābād on the road to Ishkāshim.

Date: ?Late Palaeolithic, 15,000–10,000 BC (stylistic).

Description: Petroglyphs of ibex and hunters on some granite boulders.

Source: Dor 1976: 124—brief description and photos.

89. BAHĀRAK AND ŪCH ĀRIQ
Including CHAPAR QISHLAQ and KHWĀJA PAHLAWĀN.

Original: Lat. 36° 48'–36° 49' N, long. 69° 25'–69° 26' E. Maps 35, 36.
Revised:
36.80706425 N, 69.41158812 E / 36° 48' 25.43131620 N, 69° 24' 41.71723056 E (A).
36.81924061 N, 69.40751961 E / 36° 49' 09.26617836 N, 69° 24' 27.07057836 E (B).
36.82283616 N, 69.40957621 E / 36° 49' 22.21018968 N, 69° 24' 34.47435888 E (C).
36.81828171 N, 69.41417042 E / 36° 49' 05.81415708 N, 69° 24' 51.01351992 E (D).
Between 36.82415098 N, 69.41411906 E / 36° 49' 26.94352008 N, 69° 24' 50.82863364 E, 36.8207251 N, 69.41582585 E / 36° 49' 14.61035568 N, 69° 24' 56.97304632 E and 36.8230588 N, 69.41488754 E / 36° 49' 23.01169404 N, 69° 24' 53.59512888 E (E).
36.82577004 N, 69.41183424 E / 36° 49' 32.77212924 N, 69° 24' 42.60325068 E (F).
36.83869493 N, 69.3892623 E / 36° 50' 19.30173756 N, 69° 23' 21.34429512 E (end).
36.84602766 N, 69.38668798 E / 36° 50' 45.69957240 N, 69° 23' 12.07672548 E (end).
Takhār Province. Some 15 km from Tāluqān, by the road which follows the Rūd-i Shāhrawān, level with the villages of Bahārak and Ūch Āriq, to the west and east of the road: several small tepes dispersed over a zone of about 1200 m, at various distances from the road. On the west side: (A) at 800 m; near the school of Bahārak; (B) at 500 m, on the right bank of the canal called Badir, between Bahārak and Mullah Mimbar; (C) at 100 m, level with the latter village. On the east side: (D) at 20 m, not far south of the same Badir canal (at 200 m); (E.) 400 m north of this canal (at 300 m); (F) at 100 m, tepe called Chapar Qishlak, 1.2 km south of the point where the road crosses the canal which comes out of the village so named on the 1:100,000 map.

Dates: Beg. Iron Age, end 2nd–beg. 1st mill. BC (B, F); Achaemenid, 6th–4th cent. BC (A, B, F); Kushan and Hunnic-Turk, 1st–9th cent. (A, F); a few Islamic sherds on all the tepes (ceramic).

Description: These little tepes—and others, observed but not visited in the same zone—are all undermined by the advance of irrigated fields, so that their present form is not very significant, except perhaps for the first (A): apparently intact square platform, oriented north-east/south-west, 30 m per side, flat top (4 m). Mounds B and D are similar platforms, height 3 and 4 m; mounds C, E., F are smaller, rounded in form (diam. 15 to 20 m), same heights.

Other similar small tepes in the region of Khwāja Pahlawān, 2 km north-west of this zone, with sherds of the same periods.

Collections: National Museum/AIA—sherds.

Fieldwork: 1977 Gardin et al., CNRS—survey.

Sources:
1. Site information by J.-C. Gardin.
2. Gardin and Lyonnet 1978–9: pl. IX, nos. 255–8, 260–3.
3. Lyonnet 1997: figs 25, 35, 39, 49, 68, 69—nos. 255–8, 260–3.
4. Gardin 1998: 70, nos. 255–8, 260–3.

90. BĀHĪ

Lat. 34° 26' N, long. 70° 51' E. approx. Map 68.
Nangahār Province. At the first stage from Gūshta on the Kābul River towards Bajaur.

Description: Local reports of many caves and ancient remains.

Source: Masson 1842: I. 223—mention.

BAHRĀBĀD. See 111 BARNĀBĀD.

91. BĀIKHĀN QAL'A

Lat. 31° 16' N, long. 64° 15E approx. Map 97.
Helmand Province. On the west bank of the Helmand, between Bust and Hazārjuft.

Date: Sasanian, 3rd–7th cent. (ceramic).

Description: An artificial mound.

Fieldwork: 1966 Hammond, Cambridge University—survey.

Source: Hammond 1970: 449—lists site (No. 32) and discusses the pottery and general results of the survey.

92. BAIKTŪT

Original: Lat. 34° 33' N, long. 68° 56' E. Map 63.
Revised: 34.56599335 N, 68.94528179 E / 34° 33' 57.57607440 N, 68° 56' 43.01443572 E.
Kābul Province. 4 km south of Paghmān, *c.*20 km north-west of Kābul.

Date: Kushan, 1st–4th cent. (ceramic).

Description: Remains of a Buddhist complex.

Source: Caspani 1947b: 48—mention.

93. BAIZA
Or QASR-I GUL ANDAM.

Lat. 35° 46' N, long. 66° 39' E. Map 47.
Jauzjān Province. 30 km south of Zāri Bāzār on the left bank of the Amrakh stream.

Description: Ruins of a baked red-brick palace called Qasr-i Gul Andam, associated with a daughter of Jamshid. One gate was still standing in 1885. A few hundred metres to the east of the village is a group of mounds outlining a vast square, measuring 800–900 × 300 m, probably the remains of a fort. Much stone rubble around the fort, but no bricks.

Fieldwork: 1885 Sahibdad Khān, ABC—topographical survey.

Sources:
1. Sahibdād Khān 1888: 151—brief description.
2. Gazetteer 1979: IV. 62–3—brief description.

94. BĀJAURI TEPE GUDAMDAR
Including TEPE WĀKIL DIRĀZ KHĀN. See also 1224 UTĀQ.

Original: Lat. 37° 01'–37° 02' N, long. 69° 09'–69° 11' E. Maps 31, 32.
Revised:
37.03057876 N, 69.17224296 E / 37° 01' 50.08353132 N, 69° 10' 20.07465996 E (A).
37.03325317 N, 69.16744941 E / 37° 01' 59.71140588 N, 69° 10' 02.81786592 E (B).
37.01776242 N, 69.18785598 E / 37° 01' 03.94472856 N, 69° 11' 16.28151576 E (C).
Qundūz Province. About 6 km in a straight line west of Archi, 7–8 km by tracks across fields which lead from this town to the houses of Bājauri; none of the following three sites is indicated on the 1:100,000 map, but their present names and their location are well known to the inhabitants of Bājauri.

Dates: Achaemenid, 6th–4th cent. BC (B); Hellenistic, 3rd–1st cent. BC (A, B); Yuezhi (C); Kushan-Sasanian (B, C); Hunnic-Turk, 5th–9th cent. (A, C); pre-Mongol Islamic, 10th–13th cent. (C) (ceramic).

Description: (A) Tepe Gudamar: rectangular platform (100 × 80) oriented east–west, high part on the east side (*c.*10 m); suggests the plan of a farm, with a courtyard or garden in front of the main building. (B) 600 north-west of A, rectangular platform (70 × 30) oriented east–west, occupied by a modern cemetery ('qabristān-i Gudamdar'), high part in the west (1 m). (C) 700 m south-east of A, Tepe Wākiz Dirāz Khān: area of 300 × 300 m raised above the level of the plain, occupied in part by a cemetery and by modern houses, and covered by little mounds 2 to 6 m high; the general plan is hardly visible, the cultivated fields and modern constructions having already destroyed a part of the site.

Other traces of farms and hamlets such as A and B are present in the fields irrigated by the northern branches of the same Ārchī canal, up to the extremity of this canal, west of Dun Qishlaq (8 km north-west of Bājauri); the sherds recovered indicate the same chronological range as above.

Collections: National Museum/AIA—sherds.

Fieldwork: 1977 Gardin et al., CNRS—survey.

Sources:
1. Site information by J.-C. Gardin.
2. Gardin and Lyonnet 1978–9: pl. IV, nos. 65–7.
3. Lyonnet 1997: nos. 65–7.
4. Gardin 1998: 56–7, nos. 65–7.

BAJGAH. See 47 ĀQ RABĀT.

95. BAJGINA

Lat. 34° 31’ N, long. 65° 06’ E. Map 55.
Ghūr Province. On the right bank of the Harī Rūd 15 km west of Chachcharān.

Description: A small group of artificial caves, cut into the cliff face alongside the river. They are not monumental and contain no decoration, but probably served as a fort or refuge.

Source: N. Dupree 1977: 462—mention.

96. BĀLĀ KHĀNA, HELMAND

Lat 31° 40’ N, long. 64° 44’ E. Map 88.
Helmand Province. C.5 km from the right bank of the Arghandāb, c.40 km north of Bust.

Description: Remains of an old town and a fort or tower, on high ground.

Sources:
1. Bellew 1874: 165—mention.
2. Browne 1879—mention.
3. Gazetteer 1980: V. 79—mention.

97. BĀLA KHĀNA, JAGHŪRĪ
Or TEPE HISĀR.

Lat. 33° 12’ N, long. 67° 35’ E. Maps 78, 79.
Ghazni Province. In the Kūh-i Khūd Valley north-east of Jūghūr, immediately to the north of Hisār.

Description: A series of artificial caves, consisting mostly of cells with rectangular openings. The larger caves lower down are mostly filled in.

Fieldwork: 1975 Taddei and Verardi, IsMEO—survey.

Sources:
1. Verardi 1977a: 142—brief description.
2. Verardi and Paparatti 2004: 65–8—detailed description with drawings and photos.

98. BĀLĀ MURGHĀB
See also 477 JŪI KHWĀJA.

Original: Lat. 35° 35’ N, long. 63° 20’ E. Map 44.
Revised: 35.58146211 N, 63.33011579 E /
35° 34’ 53.26360248 N, 63° 19’ 48.41682744 E.
Bādghīs Province. 264 km north-east of Herat on the road to Mazār-i Sharīf.

Date: ?Early Islamic, 10th–13th cent. (documentary).

Description: A mound near the governor’s compound c.10 m high, surmounted by a modern fort. Remains of a bridge across the Murghāb River. Possibly the site of medieval Marv ar-Rūd.

Fieldwork: 1884 Maitland, ABC.

Sources:
1. Grodekoff 1880: 150—mentions extensive ruins in the vicinity.
2. A. C. Yate 1887: 202—brief description of the fort.
3. Maitland 1888a: 107—brief description. Mentions traces of bridges.
4. Le Strange 1905: 404–5—summary of the historical sources for Marv ar-Rūd.
5. Hamilton 1906: 142—brief description.
6. Caspani and Cagnacci 1951: 246 and figs 238 and 239—photo of the fort and brief discussion of Marv ar-Rūd.
7. Hussain 1954: 12—brief description of the site and long discussion of the historical geography of the area.
8. Sterling, ed. Lee 1991: 261—refers in 1828 to a statue cut in the ‘rocks of neighbouring mountains’ to the south-west of Bālā Murghāb.
9. Ball 2008: 154—summary.

99. BALKH
Including TAKHT-I RUSTAM, TEPE RUSTAM, and TEPE ZARGARĀN.
See also 410 HĀJI PIYĀDA and 2028 CHILSITŪN in Supplement.

Original: Lat. 36° 46’ N, long. 66° 54’ E. Map 27.
Revised: 36.76808564 N, 66.90115911 E /
36° 46’ 05.10829140 N, 66° 54’ 04.17278484 E.
Balkh Province. 21 km west of Mazār-i Sharīf.

Dates: Achaemenid 6th–4th cent. BC; Graeco-Bactrian, 3rd-mid-1st cent. BC; Kushan, 1st BC–AD 3rd cent.; Sasanian, 3rd–7th cent.; Turk, early Islamic, 7th–12th cent.;

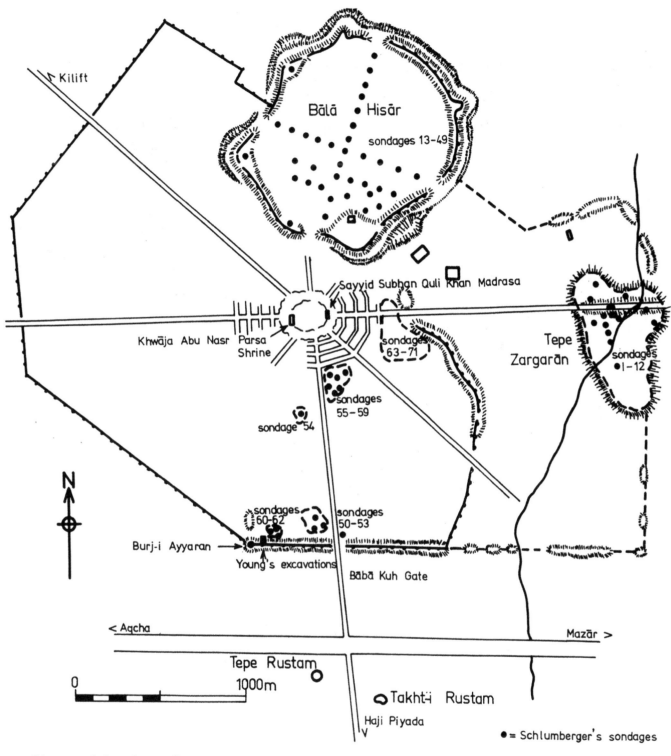

99 Balkh—general plan (after Gardin 1957).

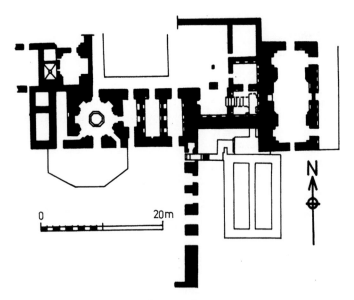

99 Balkh—Caravanserai (after Foucher 1942–7).

Timurid, 15th cent. (ceramic, numismatic, documentary, stylistic).

Description: A very large urban site enclosing an area of 11 km. It is surrounded by high defensive walls with a secondary fortified area, the Bālā Hisār, to the north. The main ancient site within the walls is Tepe Zargarān, an artificial mound with material dating from the Achaemenid period. The discovery of Classical column fragments in the early 21st century led to new excavations there, confirming its probable identification as the capital of the Graeco-Bactrian kingdom.

Later remains enclosed within the walls include the tiled 'Timurid' Shrine of Khwāja Abu Nasr Parsa dated 1460/61, and the 17th-century *Madrasa* of Sayyid Subhan Quli Khān, of which only one *iwān* remains with some tile decoration.

Just to the west of the road leading from the Aqchā Gate of Balkh are the ruins of a large mosque or temple consisting of a double row of detached round baked brick pillars surmounted by square caps for carrying a groined roof.

Extra-mural remains to the south include Takht-i Rustam, the mud remains of the Buddhist monastery of Nau Bahār, and Tepe Rustam, its associated stupa. There are also the remains of a stone-lined canal of the Kushan period.

In the early 2000s some 50 Aramaic documents on leather and wood were found almost certainly from Balkh, providing information on the last days of the Achaemenid Empire and the campaign of Alexander of Macedon in Bactria.

Collection: Khalili Collection, London—Aramaic documents.

Fieldwork:
 1. 1886 Peacocke, Yate, ABC—survey.
 2. 1924–5 Foucher, DAFA—sondages and survey.

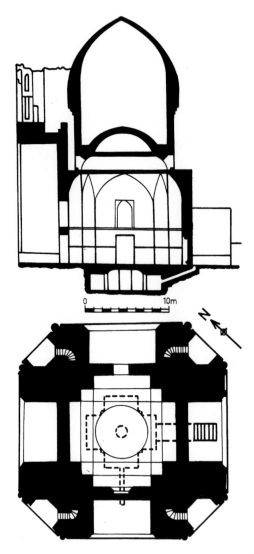

99 Balkh—Shrine of Khwāja Abu Nasr Parsa (after Pugachenkova 1970).

 3. 1935 Byron—survey of the shrine.
 4. 1946—Wheeler, ASI—reconnaissance.
 5. 1947–8 Schlumberger, DAFA—total of 59 sondages.
 6. 1953 Young, Univ. Mus., Univ. Penn.—excavation against south wall.
 7. 1955–6 Le Berre, DAFA—investigations of city walls.
 8. 1960 Hayashi and Sahara, Kyoto University—survey.
 9. 1974–5 Sengupta, Af/Ind Mission—restoration of the shrine.
 10. 2004–8 Besenval and Marquis, DAFA—excavations at the citadel and Tepe Zargarān.
 11. 2011–14 AKTC—conservation of main monuments.

Sources:
 1. Burnes 1834a: I. 237–42—description of the history and remains of the city, and of some of the coins collected.

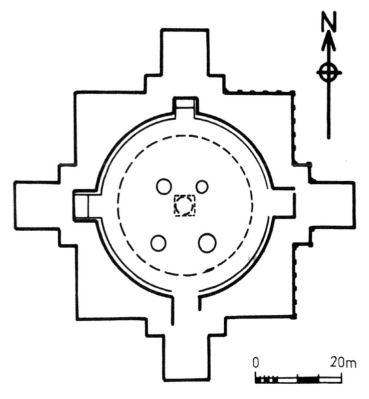

99 Balkh—Tepe Rustam (after Foucher 1942–47).

2. Jacquet 1836b: 249–50—description of a gold medallion of Mokadphises found by Honigberger.
3. Moorcroft and Trebeck 1841: 492–4—brief description of the remains.
4. Vambery 1864: 232–3—brief description of the remains.
5. Rawlinson 1872: 510–12—background to Buddhism at Balkh.
6. Holdich 1886: 9–10—brief description.
7. Peacocke 1887a: 322–4—brief description of the shrine and *madrasa*.
8. Maitland 1888b: 177–9—'Nothing of any particular interest in the place, and certainly nothing of any great antiquity'.
9. Yate 1888: 255–60—description of the remains, including Tepe and Takht-i Rustam.
10. Le Strange 1905: 420–2—summary of the historical sources.
11. Niedemeyer and Diez 1924: 45–9—and pls 198–213—summary and plan of the remains with photos of some buildings no longer extant.
12. Foucher 1931: 25–7—brief summary of the excavations.
13. Fouchet 1931: 131–3—some background with a note on the work of Foucher.
14. Byron 1935a—brief note and photos of the shrine.
15. Byron 1937: 285–6 and 296–7—description of the shrine.
16. Byron 1938: 1136–7—description and sketch plan of the shrine.
17. Foucher 1942–7: I. 55–121—reflections on the site, with description of the Islamic remains and the excavations. II. 373–7—brief summary and catalogue of the finds.
18. Schlumberger 1946—very brief report on the work of Foucher.
19. Caspani 1947a—background and tentative theories associated with Tepe and Takht-i Rustam.
20. Shakur 1947: 59–68—detailed description of the site and of two Hellenistic column bases found.
21. Wheeler 1947: 62–3—brief description and assessment.
22. Schlumberger 1948—summary of the results of the 1947 excavations.
23. Schlumberger 1949b—summary of the 1947 excavations with details of the stratigraphy.
24. Schlumberger 1949c—very brief summary of the 1947 excavations and disappointment at the results.
25. Deydier 1950: 203–4—summary and bibliography of the French work.
26. Kohzad 1953b: 9–10—summary of the French work.
27. Bivar 1954b—description and photos of two stone pedestals accidentally found and discussion on their possible use as fire altars.
28. Mandelshtam 1954—summary in Russian of the French work.
29. Young 1954: 52—mentions own sondage.
30. Wheeler 1954: 89–91—discusses archaeological strategy needed for excavating Balkh.
31. Young 1955—discusses at length the defences, topography, and urban development of Balkh, with a brief report on his own excavations.
32. Allchin 1957—refers to the site in a wider discussion of Bactrian chronology.
33. Gardin 1957a—typology in detail and conclusions on the ceramics.
34. Matson 1957: 12—very brief summary of the American excavations.
35. Schlumberger 1957b—introduction to the problems of archaeology at Balkh.
36. Buhler 1958b—brief general article on Hellenism at Balkh.
37. Hallade 1962a—discussion of Tepe Rustam and the development of Bactrian art.
38. Hayashi and Sahara 1962: 55–7—summary of the results of a survey of Tepe Zargarān and the Bālā Hisār.
39. Mizuno 1962—introduction to the Japanese survey.
40. Pugachenkova 1963: 166–8—description of the shrine.
41. Hansen 1964: 21–2—discusses the shrine and the need for its preservation.

42. Le Berre and Schlumberger 1964—description of the fortifications and the successive growth of the city, with a summary of the excavations and detailed analysis of the construction.
43. N. Dupree 1967a: 63–96—extensive historical background with descriptions of all remains.
44. Agrawala 1970: 6—discusses human figurines on some pottery handles excavated at Tepe Zargarān.
45. Anand 1970: 24–5—brief summary and photos of the Islamic remains.
46. Pugachenkova 1970: 33–7—full description and discussion of the shrine.
47. *Kabul Times* 1975—brief report on the restoration of the shrine.
48. Bulliet 1976—discusses the Nau Bahar monastery and its possible connections in Iran.
49. Cattenat and Gardin 1976—discuss the pottery and its links with Achaemenid pottery.
50. Fischer 1976: 131—discusses Tepe Rustam.
51. Francfort 1976a: 96–100—discussion and description of the fortifications.
52. Pugachenkova 1976a: 30 and 61—discusses the shrine.
53. Pugachenkova 1976b—architectural analysis of the city walls.
54. Staviski 1977—discusses Balkh and the Kishans of Bactria.
55. Francfort 1979a: 17–19 and 23–26—lists the site and discusses the general characteristics of Achaemenid and Hellenistic fortifications.
56. Pugachenkova 1979a: 18–31—discusses in detail the principles of town planning and fortifications.
57. Mukhtarov 1980—comprehensive study of the Timurid and later periods of Balkh.
58. Sarianidi 1981—discusses a group of bronze mirrors found at Balkh.
59. Grenet 1982: 157–9—discusses a 3rd–2nd cent. BC Margian terracotta figurine found in the Balkh oasis.
60. Golombek and Wilber 1988: 294–7—descriptions of the Timurid monuments.
61. McChesney 1991a—architecture of the Abu Nasr Parsa shrine.
62. Michaud and Barry 1996: pls 65, 69—colour photos of the shrine.
63. O'Kane 2000—argues that the Khwāja Parsa shrine is not Timurid but Uzbek.
64. Bernard, Besenval, and Jarrige 2002—summary of the new excavations at Tepe Zargarān.
65. Shaked 2003—preliminary report on the Aramaic documents.
66. Bernard, Besenval, and Marquis 2006—summary of previous French investigations and preliminary report on the new excavations at Tepe Zargarān.
67. Cambon and Jarrige 2006, 2007—illustrations of the new excavations at Balkh citadel and Corinthian columns from Tepe Zargaran.
68. Clarysse and Thompson 2007—discussion of two newly discovered Greek documents from Balkh.
69. Ball 2008: 52, 54, 60–1, 154–63—summary.
70. Besenval and Rassouli 2010—summary of excavations at Tepe Zargaran.
71. Naveh and Shaked 2012—full publication of the hoard of Achaemenid Aramaic administrative documents almost certainly from Balkh.
72. Azad 2013—a study of the medieval Muslim sacred places around Balkh and their relation to pre-Islamic Buddhist sites.
73. Henkelman and Folmer 2016—further discussion of the Aramaic documents.
74. Mairs 2016: 2038–43—discusses the Aramaic documents.
75. Jodidio et al. 2017: 250–303—reports on the Aga Khan Trust for Culture conservation work.

100. BĀMIYĀN
See also 330 FŪLĀDĪ, 508 KAKRAK, 1042 SHAHR-I GHULGHULA, and 1053 SHAHR-I ZUHAK.

Original: Lat. 34° 50' N, long. 67° 49E. Map 58.
Revised: 34.82934351 N, 67.81066016 E /
34° 49' 45.63662772 N, 67° 48' 38.37656520 E.
Bāmiyān Province. In the mountainous district of eastern central Afghanistan, 246 km by road west of Kābul.

Dates: ?Graeco-Bactrian, 2nd–1st cent. BC (numismatic); Kushan-Sasanian, 2nd–7th cent. (ceramic, stylistic); Turk-pre-Mongol Islamic, 7th–13th cent. (ceramic, architectural).

Description: An extensive area of remains along the foot of the cliffs bordering the north side of the valley. For a length of *c.*1800 m the cliff face is honeycombed with some 750 artificial caves, all forming a part of an extensive Buddhist monastic centre. Some are very large and elaborately decorated in sculptures and frescos. There are two large standing statues of Buddha, 53 m and 38 m high respectively, with a third seated Buddha between the two. At the foot of the cliffs many mounds cover structural remains, including a large stupa to the east of the 38 m Buddha and a series of Turk-Ghurid fortifications. Some Graeco-Bactrian coins were also excavated here in the 19th century.

In the 1990s part of a Buddhist library of manuscripts written on leaves, bark, and vellum consisting of many thousands of fragments were discovered in a cave near Bāmiyān and taken out of the country.

Excavations in the early 21st century at the foot of the great Buddhas uncovered remains of a significant *vihara*.

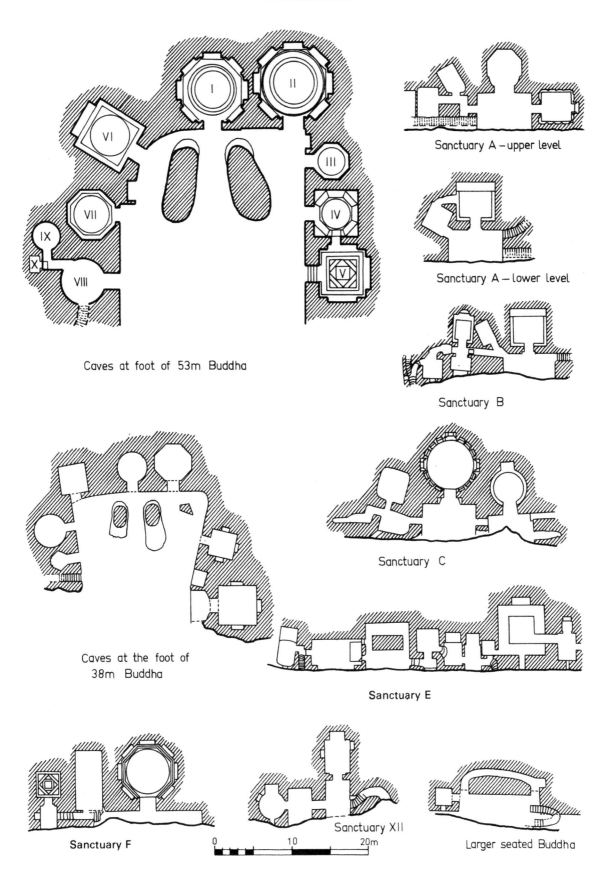

Caves at foot of 53m Buddha

Sanctuary A — upper level

Sanctuary A — lower level

Sanctuary B

Caves at the foot of 38m Buddha

Sanctuary C

Sanctuary E

Sanctuary F

Sanctuary XII

Larger seated Buddha

100 Bāmiyān—various caves (after Godard and Hackin 1928).

Collections:
1. National Museum, Kābul—objects from excavations.
2. Musée Guimet, Paris—paintings from the caves.
3. Schøyen Collection, Norway—Buddhist manuscripts.

Fieldwork:
1. 1885–6 Talbot, Maitland, Griesbach, ABC—survey.
2. 1922–6 Foucher, DAFA—survey.
3. 1923 Y. Godard, DAFA—survey.
4. 1924 Hackin, DAFA—survey.
5. 1930, 1933 Carl and Hackin, DAFA—excavations.
6. 1969 Kotera, Nagoya University—survey.
7. 1969–75 Sengupta, Af/Indian Mission—preservation of 38 m Buddha and associated shrines and frescos.
8. 1970 Kostka—photogrammetrical survey of 53 m Buddha.
9. 1974–5 Le Berre, DAFA—survey of fortifications.
10. 1974–8 Higuchi and Miyaji, Kyoto University—survey.
11. 2003–8—Tarzi, French Ministry of Foreign Affairs/National Geographic—excavations at the 'Eastern Monastery', 'Royal Monastery', and 'Royal Town'.

Sources:
1. Burnes 1833—description and sketch of two statues, with a conclusion that they were 'a caprice of some person of rank'.
2. Gerard 1833: 7–8—description of the 'Buts', noting their Hellenistic affinities.
3. Masson 1833b—description of the main cave groups, with drawings of the cliff face, some interiors, some frescos, and various decorative details.
4. Burnes 1834a: I. 183–8—description of the statues.
5. Burnes 1834b—general description and discussion of its possible associations.
6. Masson 1836b—describes a brief Pahlavi inscription in the large Buddha niche, which he ascribes Sasanian dating from AD 220.
7. Masson 1836d—brief description of the antiquities and tentative speculations as to their origins.
8. Jacquet 1837: 410–21—general discussion of the remains and their possible affinities.
9. Cunningham 1840—full descriptive catalogue of the Bactrian and two Sasanian coins found at Bāmiyān.
10. Hay 1840—brief description of some Graeco-Bactrian coins accidentally excavated.
11. Torrens 1840—numismatic discussion of the Graeco-Bactrian coins.
12. Moorcroft and Trebeck 1841: II. 387–93—describe the two Buddhas, the caves, and some of the frescos.
13. Cunningham 1842—illustrations and descriptions of some more Bactrian coins found at Bāmiyān.

14. Masson 1842: II. 382–8—description of the site and his own discoveries.
15. Eyre 1843: 361–6—description of some of the caves.
16. Lal 1846: 51–4—description of the remains with associated legends and stories.
17. Griffith 1847: 400–3—good description of the remains, including a stone and *pakhsa* stupa that still had intact reliefs.
18. Kaye 1879—brief description of the area, 'the idols of which I have little to say except that they are very large and very ugly'.
19. Yavorski 1885: 130–6 and 140–52—description of the statues and main caves with a very good summary of the history and sources.
20. Talbot et al. 1886—brief description and sketches of the principal remains, with architectural discussion by Simpson.
21. Griesbach 1888b: 212—briefly describes his own survey of the antiquities.
22. Maitland 1888a: 517–20—description and sketch of both Buddhas.
23. Simpson 1893: 103–5—briefly discusses the Buddhas and their classical origins.
24. Niedemeyer and Diez 1924: pls 215–19—photos of the remains.
25. Godard 1925a: 19–25—brief report on the initial work carried out by DAFA.
26. Buhot 1927—introduction to the site. Description of the sculptures, frescos, and architecture of the caves.
27. Pandit 1927—photos and summary of the French work.
28. Foucher 1928: 25—brief summary of the French work.
29. Godard and Hackin 1928—some background on the history and exploration of the site, with descriptions of the two Buddhas and the main caves and their decoration.
30. Goshal 1928: 21–3—discusses the remains as an extension of Indian culture.
31. Hackin 1928a—discusses a selected number of the statues and their influence through the draperies on Buddhist sculpture in India and Central Asia.
32. Matsumoto 1929—includes Bāmiyān in an examination of the different styles of Central Asian painting.
33. Grousset 1930—discusses the frescos.
34. Fabri 1931: 597–9—discussion of the hairstyle on one of the frescos and its place in the history of Indian costume.
35. Fouchet 1931: 121–3—some historical background and a general description.
36. Hackin 1932a—summary of the work of 1930.
37. Levi 1932: 1–13—linguistic discussion of some Sanskrit documents found at Bāmiyān.

38. Hackin 1933—summary of the results and description of the main caves.
39. Hackin and Bruhl 1933: 117–19—brief review of the work of Hackin and Carl.
40. Hackin and Carl 1933—description of new discoveries and of the 1930 excavations, with a full inventory of objects.
41. Hackin 1934—summary of the work carried out in 1930.
42. J. and R. Hackin 1934—visitor's guide to the site.
43. Hackin 1935a—discusses Bāmiyān as an extension of Sasanian art.
44. Gettens 1938—technical analysis of the materials used in the frescos.
45. Rowland 1938—study of a fresco of a representation of the sun god above the head of the 38 m Buddha.
46. Rowland and Coomaraswamy 1938: 40–70—some background, with illustrations, analyses, and comparisons of the main frescos.
47. Monod-Bruhl 1939: 103–10—description of the Bāmiyān exhibition in the Musée Guimet.
48. Yoshikawa 1941—outline of the architecture and art.
49. Foucher 1942–7: I. 129–35—describes briefly some of the remains and their historical background.
50. Kohzad 1944/45a—discusses the location of the temple mentioned by Huien Tsang and the excavation Cave G.
51. Kohzad 1944/45b—photos and description of a Sanskrit document found at Bāmiyān.
52. Yoshikawa 1944—summary of the French work.
53. Rowland 1946: 35–40—discussion of the frescos in the 38 m Buddha niche and their parallels.
54. Rowland 1947—description of the two Buddhas and the concepts they depict.
55. Zestovski 1948—description and sketches of the principal monuments.
56. Soper 1949–50: 264–5—briefly discusses the light symbolism and mithraic elements in the 53 m Buddha.
57. Deydier 1950: 178–90—summary and bibliography of the French work.
58. Kohzad 1950a—brief background and guide to the valley.
59. Bussagli 1953b—discussion of the classical influences on some of the frescos.
60. Kohzad 1953b: 7–8—summary of the site.
61. Rowland 1953: 104–9—description and discussion of the remains.
62. Mandelshtam 1954—brief discussion of the French work.
63. Kohzad 1955a—brief summary description of the site.
64. Kohzad 1955c: 21—summary of the site.

65. Kohzad 1955/56—guide to the main monuments and frescos with reprints of some of Zestovsky's drawings.
66. Fischer 1956—study of a fragmentary Jain image from Bāmiyān.
67. Frumkin 1957—brief discussion of Graeco-Buddhist art.
68. Makino 1957—discusses the location of the hypothetical reclining Buddha.
69. Buhler 1958a—brief description of the site.
70. Hackin 1959a—summary of the 1933 excavations in Groups J and K.
71. Ali 1961—general background from the point of view of cultural links with India.
72. Courtois 1961: 19–20 summary of the work to date.
73. Gullini 1961: pls 145–8—photos of the objects on display in the National Museum.
74. Gullini 1961—discusses some of the art-historical problems.
75. Rowland 1961—discussion of the iconographical concept of the bejewelled Buddha depicted in Cave 1.
76. Bruno 1962: 104–6—richly illustrated discussion of the conservation problems at Bāmiyān.
77. Bussagli 1962a: 43–4—outline of the art.
78. Hallade 1962b: 8–14—discussion of the art styles and their Indo-Iranian connections.
79. Mizuno 1962—introduction to the Japanese surveys at Bāmiyān.
80. Bussagli 1963: 36–40—discussion of the art of Bāmiyān.
81. Peter 1963—general description of the valley and of the rope used on the folds of the 53 m Buddha.
82. Pugachenkova 1963: 68–79—general summary of the site and art.
83. Scarcia 1963—discussion and translation of a medieval manuscript found in the Bāmiyān area.
84. Seckel 1964: 61–2—discussion of Bāmiyān in the context of the spread of Buddhism.
85. Yoshikawa 1964—illustrations and discussion of some Bāmiyān frescos exhibited in the Tokyo Museum.
86. Talbot Rice 1965: 162–9—brief summary of the art, with a discussion of the Sasanian elements.
87. Monod 1966: 364–9—descriptions of the objects on display in the Musée Guimet.
88. Rowland 1966a: 92–106—photos and brief introduction to the art.
89. Scarcia 1966—definitive reading of the text of the medieval manuscript.
90. N. Dupree 1967b—good general background and summary of the sources and good guide to all places of interest.

91. Auboyer 1968: pls 68–76—illustrates and discusses some of the frescos and architecture.

92. Hallade 1968: 155–8—discusses the development of an Irano-Buddhist style.

93. Hallade and Hinz 1968: pls 52 and 122–4—discussion and illustrations of the development of Gandharan art.

94. Auboyer 1969—well illustrated general article on the two Buddhas and associated frescos.

95. Anand 1971a—brief discussion on the cosmological symbolism of the Buddhas.

96. Anand 1971b—outline of the artistic antecedents of the standing Buddha.

97. N. Dupree 1971b—good, general summary of the two Buddhas and the caves.

98. Gazzola and Perrin 1971—results of a UNESCO study on the conservation and the problems caused by tourism.

99. Habibi 1971: 156—photo of one of the Sanskrit documents and discussion of the development of Afghan epigraphy.

100. Lal 1971—very brief introduction to the site and the Indian restoration project.

101. Rowland 1971—studies of a selected number of the paintings.

102. Rowland and Rice 1971: 34–41, pls 2, 3, 141–4—brief summary of the art and photos of the frescos on display in the National Museum.

103. Sengupta 1971—brief note on the technical problems involved in the preservation work.

104. Breshna 1972: 12–14—brief discussion of the statues and reconstruction of the faces.

105. Rowland 1972—discussion of the evidence of the Bāmiyān frescos for the development of a Central Asian style.

106. 2Sengupta 1972—description of the two Buddhas and associated shrines, and of the problems of their conservation.

107. Ushikawa 1972—briefly describes the photo-grammetrical survey of the 38 m Buddha.

108. Zander 1972: 568–70—describes the Italian plans for conservation at the site.

109. Lal 1973—brief note on the conservation work carried out in 1969–70 on the 38 m Buddha.

110. Sengupta 1973—brief but fully illustrated summary of the conservation work.

111. Shahrani 1973: 18–19—tentative reconstruction of the two Buddhas.

112. Tarzi 1973—discussion of the vase engravings in one of the caves.

113. Deshpande 1974—brief interim note on the structural and chemical work carried out in 1970–1 on the 38 m Buddha.

114. N. Dupree et al. 1974: 90–5—summary of the site and guide to the National Museum collection.

115. Fussman 1974a—report on the discovery of some new sculpture when restoring the 38 m Buddha.

116. Kostka 1974—description of the photo-grammetrical survey of the 53 m Buddha.

117. Rowland 1974: 82–106—detailed discussion, with comparisons and chronology, of the frescos and the concepts they represent.

118. Deshpande 1975a—discussion of the links through the frescos and sculpture with India.

119. Deshpande 1975b—summary of the structural and chemical preservation carried out on the 38 m Buddha in 1971–2.

120. Trousdale 1975: 71–85—discusses the scabbards depicted in some of the frescos.

121. Ball 1976—compares some of the sanctuaries with possible Mongol Buddhist remains in western Iran.

122. Gaulier et al. 1976—discussion of the religious iconography of the art.

123. Higuchi 1976—summary of the remains and the main styles.

124. Kuwayama 1976: 398–9—discusses the treatment of ribbons in some of the frescos.

125. Miyaji 1976b—divides the frescos into four basic styles and traces their influences.

126. H. Motamedi 1976—brief summary of the Kyoto University survey at Bāmiyān.

127. Sengupta 1976—report and photos on the completion of the restoration work on the 38 m Buddha.

128. Yoshikawa 1976—personal reminiscences and general guide to the site.

129. Zaryab 1976—discussion of Tarzi's theory on the location of the hypothetical reclining Buddha.

130. Tarzi 1977a—very full, richly illustrated descriptions of all the caves with discussion and artistic analysis of the sculpture.

131. Miyaji 1978—discusses some of the iconographical aspects of the art.

132. Sultan 1978—discussion of the Hellenistic aspects of the frescos.

133. Tarzi 1978—discussion of the links between the headdresses depicted in the frescos and those on the coins.

134. Kamāl 1979—analysis of the portraiture and construction techniques of the two statues.

135. Thapar 1979—brief report on the structural and chemical preservation carried out on the 38 m Buddha and associated frescos in 1973–4.

136. Miyaji 1980—discusses the second style recognized in the frescos and the results of the 1978 survey.

137. H. Motamedi 1980—background and source material for the site.

138. Stwodah 1980: 7—discusses the Sanskrit documents as the remains of an ancient library.

139. Higuchi 1983–4—very thorough photographic record and drawings of all paintings and caves (including Kakrak), together with a key to the cave numbering system. In Japanese, but summary and captions in English.

140. Le Berre 1987: 75–6, pls 96–7—itinerary B1, ruins 13–16; describes the medieval fortifications along the foot of the cliffs.

141. Klimburg-Salter 1989—attempts an integral approach: the art history related to contemporary literary and numismatic sources. Suggests Bāmiyān may have been a dynastic/religious capital for the Western Turk Empire.

142. Grenet 1994—discusses a painting in the 38 m Buddha and Zoroastrian iconography.

143. Higuchi and Barnes 1995—general summary of the Kyoto University work 1970–8.

144. Allon and Salomon 2000—publication of 250 fragmentary palm-leaf texts of the 2nd or 3rd century found at or near Bāmiyān.

145. Gilles 2000—discusses and illustrates the war damage.

146. Geoffroy-Schneiter 2001—photos of objects from the Musée Guimet.

147. Tissot and Darbois 2002—photos of objects from the Kābul Museum.

148. Kyoto University 2003—lavishly illustrated (in colour) the Japanese record of the paintings and cave numbering system (in Japanese).

149. Suzuki and Aoki 2004—general background, history of research, conservation and management issues.

150. *Asian Art* (Feb. 2005): 1—results of C-14 dating: 507 +/- 15 years for the 38 m Buddha and 551 +/- 15 years for the 53 m Buddha.

151. Odani 2005—redates the Buddhas to c. AD 400 based on comparative evidence from Basawal.

152. Suzuki and Aoki 2005—conference proceedings to discuss the site's importance and measures to be taken.

153. Klimburg-Salter 2006—discussion of the iconography of the paintings in the 38 m Buddha.

154. Maeda 2006—stylistic discussion of the paintings above the two great Buddhas.

155. Shoten 2006a—results of C-14 dating of the paintings to c. AD 650.

156. Shoten 2006b—analysis of the pigments and materials of the Buddha statues.

157. Omland 2006—discussion of the recovery and moral and legal issues surrounding the Buddhist manuscripts in the Schøyen Collection, Norway.

158. Tissot 2006: 107–15—National Museum catalogue details and photos.

159. N. Tarzi 2006—brief account of the search for the sleeping Buddha and excavations at the Eastern Monastery.

160. Maeda 2007—discusses the evidence of the paintings for ethnic origins of the people of Bāmiyān.

161. Momii and Seki 2007—chemical analysis of pigments in the paintings.

162. Taniguchi 2007—the issues of the conservation programme.

163. Klimburg-Salter 2008—emphasizes that Bāmiyān is part of an increase in Buddhist art in the first three centuries of Islam, perhaps as a result of the expansion of the Turk Empire in Central Asia.

164. Margottini 2009—UNESCO emergency measures to safeguard the remains of the Buddhas.

165. Petzet 2009—reports and recommendations for safeguarding and recording the fragments of the Buddhas.

166. Klimburg-Salter 2010—discusses the Buddhist centres of Bāmiyān, Kābul, and Ghazni as part of a complex Buddhist communications network in eastern Afghanistan between the 7th and 10th centuries.

167. Lin and Wheeler 2011—UNESCO recommendations for the preservation of the remains and landscape.

168. Sharma 2011—the Hariti iconography at Bāmiyān and comparisons throughout Asia.

169. Marguier 2012—the 2nd–9th and 10th–13th-century pottery from Tarzi's excavations.

170. Miyaji 2012—iconographical discussion of the Maitreya painting in the large Buddha niche.

171. Morgan 2012—general history and background, including an account of the destruction.

172. Tarzi 2012—detailed report of the excavation of the 'Eastern monastery', the 'royal monastery', and the 'royal town'.

173. Iwade and Shigeru 2013—architectural analysis of the cave architecture, richly illustrated in colour, based on the Japanese fieldwork.

174. Bouchenaki 2015—summary of the preservation plans for the giant Buddhas.

175. Petzet 2015—plans and recommendations for the preservation of the Buddha fragments.

176. Errington 2017a: 59–65—Masson's drawings and records of Bāmiyān.

177. Green 2017—discusses Bāmiyān and the establishment of pre-Taliban Afghan national identity.

101. BANĀDIR JUM'A KHĀN

Lat. 30° 43' N, long. 64° 06' E. Map 97.
Helmand Province. On the left bank of the Helmand, a few km south of the village of Banādir Jum'a Khān.

Dates: Achaemenid, 6th–4th cent. BC; Indo-Parthian, 1st–3rd cent.; Sasanian, 3rd–7th cent.; pre-Mongol Islamic, 7th–13th cent.; Timarid, 15th–16th cent. (ceramic).

Description: An area of level ground covered in sherds, but without any trace of buildings.

Fieldwork: 1966 Hammond, Cambridge University—survey.

Sources:
1. Bellew 1874: 189–90—mention.
2. Hammond 1970: 449—lists site (no. 37) and describes the pottery and general results of the survey.

BANĀQ. See 2011 BANĀQ in Supplement.

BAND-I DARRA-I BAND. See **2012 BAND-I DARRA-I BAND IN SUPPLEMENT.**

BAND-I RUSTAM. See 958 RŪDĪN.

102. BAND-I SARDA

Lat. 33° 17’ N, long. 68° 38’ E. Map 80.
Ghazni Province. 37 km south-east of Ghazni on the Jilga or Sarda River, just before the plain of Shilgar.

Date: Ghaznavid, 11–12th cent. (historical, geographical).

Description: An irrigation dam across the river. It was restored in the 20th century with Soviet aid for a large-scale irrigation project.

In the area mainly to the south and south-east of Band-i Sarda, between lat. 33° 10–22’ and long. 68° 25–40’, 31 separate sites have been recorded from satellite imagery, mainly mounds and ruins/enclosures.

Fieldwork: 1973 Balland, CNRS—hydrological survey.

Sources:
1. Broadfoot 1884: 351—mention.
2. Balland 1976—brief description and discussion of utilization.
3. Thomas 2015: 517—additional information from satellite imagery.

103. BAND-I SULTĀN

Original: Lat. 33° 45’ N, long. 68° 23’ E. Map 80.
Revised: 33.75870083 N, 68.37981522 E /
33° 45’ 31.32299304 N, 68° 22’ 47.33478264 E.
Ghazni Province. On the Ghazni River 23 km north of Ghazni, 8 km south of Jaghatū.

Date: Ghaznavid, 11th–12th cent. (historical, geographical).

Description: A rough stone dam 200 m long, 8 m high above water and 2 m thick. It has two sluice gates. It was restored in the early 16th century by Babur.

The ancient dam is now submerged as a result of a higher, second dam (built with German aid in the early 20th cent.) which was constructed downstream of the medieval dam.

During the breaching of this modern dam in 2004, the remains of the ancient dam were exposed but will disappear again on completion of a new section of dam, funded by the World Bank.

Fieldwork:
1. 1957 Bombaci and Scerrato, IsMEO—survey.
2. 1973 Balland, CNRS—hydrological survey.

Sources:
1. Additional information by Jonathan L. Lee (photographs in personal archives)
2. Vigne 1837: 775–6—very brief description.
3. Vigne 1840: 138–9—good description.
4. Broadfoot 1884: 346–7—fairly detailed description.
5. Fischer 1967a: 166—brief description.
6. Scerrato 1967: 12—very brief description.
7. Fischer 1969: 339—brief summary.
8. Balland 1976—brief description and photo, with a discussion of its utilization.
9. Thomas 2015: 517—additional information from satellite imagery.

104. BAND-I ZANAKHĀN

Lat. 33° 40’ N, long. 68° 36’ E. Map 80.
Ghazni Province. 20 km north-east of Ghazni, near the village of Zarak on the old caravan route to Logar.

Date: Ghaznavid, 11th–12th cent. (historical, geographical).

Description: A high stone dam used to irrigate the Dasht-i Kaiwān. It was ruined by the 16th century but restored in 1957–8.

Fieldwork: 1973 Balland, CNRS—hydrological survey.

Source:
1. Balland 1976—brief description and discussion of its utilization.
2. Thomas 2015: 517—additional information from satellite imagery.

105. BANŪ
Or ANDARĀB.

Original: Lat. 35° 37’ N, long. 69° 16’ E. Map 50.
Revised: 35.63711911 N, 69.26740404 E /
35° 38’ 13.62879240 N, 69° 16’ 02.65455264 E.
Baghlān Province. Immediately to the east of the Governor’s residence at Andarāb, c.70 km east of Dūshi.

Description: An easily defensible, strategic site of an ancient town, consisting of rubble foundations covering a semi-isolated alluvial plateau.

Fieldwork: 1922 Foucher, DAFA—survey.

Source: Foucher 1942–7: I. 136—brief description.

106. BĀRĀBĀD
Or BAHRĀBĀD or BAR RABĀT.

Original: Lat. 34° 27' N, long. 70° 25' E. Map 66.
Revised: 34.45397859 N, 70.41281656 E /
34° 27' 14.32291644 N, 70° 24' 46.13960304 E.
Nangahār Province. On the north bank of the Kābul River, 4 km west of Jalālābād and 4 km east of Fīl Khāna.

Dates: Saka/Indo-Parthian, 1st–2nd cent. (stylistic).

Description: A large stupa on a mound *c.*800 m from the river bank. It is decorated with a frieze of pilasters and blind arches, and contained a steatite reliquary and some crystal, but no coins. To the south-west is a monastery enclosure *c.*25 m square, and to the south-east is a second, smaller stupa 5.20 diam. and 6 m high.

There is also a series of caves in which was found a relief depicting a pair of feet surrounded by lotus leaves.

Collection: BM – stupa deposits.

Fieldwork:
1. 1833 Honigberger – excavation of stupa.
2. 1841 Pigou, Indian Army – excavation of caves.
3. 1965 Mizuno, Kyoto University – survey.

Sources:
1. Jacquet 1837: 425 and 433–40 – description of the stupa and finds.
2. Masson 1841: 88–9 – brief description.
3. Pigou 1841 – brief description of the work and sketch of the caves.
4. Mizuno 1971: 122–3 – brief description and photos.
5. Jongeward et al. 2012 – catalogue and discussion of the reliquaries.
6. Errington 2017a: 132–3 and 2017b: 30, 103, 112 – the Masson collection and archive relating to the site.

107. BARAK
Or BAHĀRAK.

Lat. 36° 58' N, long. 70° 52' E. Map 38.
Badakshān Province. On the east bank of the Kokcha, 45 km south of Faizābād. The site is just west of Barak.

Date: Late Islamic (ceramic).

Description: Site of an industrial settlement covered in baked bricks and metal slag.

Fieldwork: 1975 Kohl – survey.

Source: Kohl 1978: 65 – mention.

BĀRĀNĀBĀD. See 111 BĀRNĀBĀD.

108. BARANGTŪT

Original: Lat. 32° 24' N, long. 62° 04' E. Map 71.

Revised: 32.39591674 N, 62.07837739 E /
32° 23' 45.30026868 N, 62° 04' 42.15860760 E.
Farāh Province. In a cultivated valley north of the Farāh Rūd and about 4 km north-west of Farāh city.

Date: Bronze Age, possibly 3rd mill. BC (ceramic).

Description: The only one of many small mounds on which buff ware sherds and fragments of alabaster bowl were found.

Fieldwork:
1. 1949 De Cardi – survey.
2. 1950–1 Fairservis, AMNH – survey.

Sources:
1. Additional information by Beatrice De Cardi.
2. De Cardi 1950: 56 – mention.
3. Fairservis 1952: 31 – mention.
4. Fairservis 1961: 98 – mention.
5. A. Motamedi 1967: 32 – mentions De Cardi's survey.
6. Fairservis 1971: 116 – mention.

BARBARAH. See 18 AI KHĀNUM.

109. BARFAQ

Lat. 35° 20' N, long. 68° 08' E. Map 48.
Baghlān Province. Road from Chārikār to Dūshi by the Shībar Pass, in the Surkhāb valley: between Duāb-i Mikhzarīn and Talā.

Date: Turk and/or pre-Mongol Islamic, 7th–13th cent. (architectural).

Description: Ruins of a small fort high above the road in the form of a square with four circular towers at each corner. Construction is of mud-brick on stone footings.

Fieldwork: 1974–5 Le Berre, DAFA – survey.

Source: Le Berre 1987: 38–9 – itinerary A1, ruin 18; detailed description.

BĀRIK. See 1066 SHAKI NAUKA.

BARKAH. See 2013 BARKAH in Supplement.

110. BARKHAN-I ZĀDIYĀN

Lat. 37° 05' N, long. 66° 57' E. Map 27.
Balkh Province. In the dunes just to the north of Zādiyān, *c.*50 km north of Balkh.

Date: Epi-Palaeolithic, *c.*10,000 BC (lithic).

Description: Extensive surface site consisting of stone tools scattered over a wide area.

Fieldwork: 1975 Vinogradov, Af/Sov. Mission – survey.

Source: Vinogradov 1979: 15–20—general description of the survey with drawings of the material.

111. BĀRNĀBĀD
Or BĀRĀNĀBĀD.

Original: Lat. 34° 23' N, long. 61° 36' E. Map 51.
Revised: 34.38523112 N, 61.5917724 E /
34° 23' 06.83202336 N, 61° 35' 30.38063784 E.
Herat Province. On the south bank of the Harī Rūd 13 km north-east of Ghūriyān, in a small cemetery just outside the village of Bārnābād.

Date: Timurid, *c.*1495 (stylistic).

Description: The *Khāniqāh* of Khwāja Wahīd al-Dīn, consisting of an undecorated baked brick dome-chamber and a monumental portal.

Fieldwork:
1. 1975 O'Kane, BIPS—survey.
2. 1979 Samizay, Kābul University/UNESCO—survey.

Sources:
1. Seljuki 1967a: 147–8—description.
2. Herawi 1968—background and photo of the shrine.
3. *Kābul Times* 1979a—mentions repair work carried out.
4. Samizay 1981: 38–41—good description and plans of the monuments, with a note on the conservation needs.
5. Golombek and Wilber 1988: 297–8—description.
6. Aalund 1990—photo of the destroyed dome-chamber.

BAR RABĀT. See 106 BĀRĀBĀD.

112. BARRA KHĀNA

Lat. 34° 34' N, long. 65° 06' E. Map 55.
Ghūr Province. C.15 km north of the Harī Rūd on the road from Chakhcharān to Jam.

Description: A number of ruined towers on the hill tops. Illicit excavations in 2002 revealed spear heads, pots, and bronze bracelets, all from graves.

Sources:
1. N. Dupree 1977: 462—mention.
2. Stewart 2004: 183–4—mention.

113. BĀSAWAL
See also 163 CHAKANŪR.

Lat. 34° 15' N, long. 70° 52' E. Map 68.
Nangahār Province. On the south bank of the Kābul River, *c.*50 km east of Jalālābād, opposite the Chakanūr caves.

Description: An extensive scatter of sherds and other remains indicating an ancient site.

Sources:
1. Masson 1840: 32—mention.
2. Masson 1842: I and III. 168 and 248–9—mention.
3. Errington 2017a: 138–9 and 2017b: 11–12, 16, 18—the Masson collection and archive relating to the site.

114. BASHURA
See also 1234 WURSHAK.

Original: Lat. 33° 22' N, long. 64° 34' E. Maps 55, 74.
Revised: 33.34869103 N, 64.56690231 E /
33° 20' 55.28769684 N, 64° 34' 00.84831096 E.
Ghūr Province. 16 km from Yamān on the road to Zarnī via Kachi Gird and Wurshak.

Date: ?Ghurid, 12th–13th cent. (architectural, geographical).

Description: Ruins of many fortifications and other structures, with some more at the foot of the mountains to the south and east. They are said locally to be pre-Islamic.

Fieldwork: 1946 Kohzad, HSA—survey.

Source: Kohzad 1951–4, 9/1: 31–2—brief description.

115. BĀSIZ
Including QARA TEPE.

Original: Lat. 37° 10' N, long. 68° 46' E. Map 31.
Revised:
37.16732205 N, 68.77480719 E / 37° 10' 02.35937496 N, 68° 46' 29.30587428 E (A).
37.16814222 N, 68.77238836 E / 37° 10' 05.31197436 N, 68° 46' 20.59809600 E (B).
Qundūz Province. 12 km west of Imām Sāhib by the Qizil Qal'a road, 200–400 m south of this road; indicated as a tepe of 8 m on the 1:100,000 map.

Dates: Bronze, 1st half of 2nd mill. BC (A); Kushan and Kushan-Sasanian, 1st–6th cent.; a few Islamic sherds (ceramic).

Description: (A) Qara Tepe: oblong mound (150 × 100 m), oriented east–west, high (10–12 m), steep, except in the south-west part, which is gullied. The top is tabular, with a small hillock in the south-east, carrying a marker. In a cut of the gully, a wall made of superimposed beds of *pakhsa*, each a metre thick, with a pronounced receding slope, is visible: retaining wall? Elsewhere, traces of walls in long, thick (3.5–4 cm) mud-bricks. (B) About 300 m north-west of A, low platform (1m), oblong (50 × 20 m), deeply undermined by cultivation; many sherds in the neighbouring fields, as well as fragments of large, thick mud bricks (3.5 cm).

Collection: National Museum/AIA—sherds.

Fieldwork: 1977 Gardin et al., CNRS—survey.

Sources:
1. Site information by J.-C. Gardin.
2. Gardin and Lyonnet 1978–9: pl. V, nos. 120, 132.

3. Lyonnet 1997: figs 25, 49, 68 — nos. 120, 132.
4. Gardin 1998: 62, nos. 120, 132.

116. BATI KŪT
See also 735 MUHMAND DARRA.

Lat. 34° 15' N, long. 70° 44' E. Map 68.
Nangahār Province. 14 km west of Bäsawal, 3 km to the south of the road to Jalālābād from Tūrkhām.

Description: An extensive scatter of sherds stretching eastwards without a break as far as Mārkūh, marking the remains of an ancient settlement.

Sources:
1. Masson 1840: 32 — mention.
2. Masson 1842: I. 168 — mention.

117. BAYAK

Lat. 34° 15' N, long. 67° 35' E. Map 57.
Ghazni Province. In the Kūh-i Khūd Valley, between Hisār and Lalakhēl north-east of Jūghūr.

Description: A spectacular artificial cave complex, in two sides of a massif connected by a high vaulted passage. Many of the caves are inaccessible.

Fieldwork: 1974 Taddei and Verardi, IsMEO — survey.

Sources:
1. Taddei 1975: 546 — mention.
2. Verardi 1977a: 142 — brief description and photos.
3. Verardi and Paparatti 2004: 68–9 — detailed description with sketch and photos.

118. BĀYĀNI
Or KĀFIR QAL'A-I SAIGHĀN.

Original: Lat. 35° 12' N, long. 67° 47' E. Map 48.
Revised: 35.20290442 N, 67.78220849 E /
35° 12' 10.45592568 N, 67° 46' 55.95057084 E.
Bāmiyān Province. On the right bank of the Saighān River 15 km east of Saighān Alaqadari and 1 km north of the village of Bāyāni.

Date: Turk/pre-Mongol Islamic, 7th–13th cent. (architectural).

Description: Remains of a very large fort on a precipitous bluff of largely mud-brick construction on stone footings. There is a central 'keep' or 'donjon' at the highest point, with several towers connected by walls running down the slopes. Some impressed decoration in the walls. There are also some artificial caves at the bottom of the hill, with carved niches and benches, presumed Buddhist.

Fieldwork: 1974–5 Le Berre, DAFA — survey.

Sources:
1. Court 1837: 376–7 — tentatively identifies the remains with Alexandria Paropamisidae.
2. Masson 1839: 90 — mention.
3. Masson 1842: I. 405 — mention.
4. Yavorski 1885: 124 — mentions the fort and the caves.
5. Le Berre 1987: 58–9, pls 67, 68 — itinerary A1, Daryā-i Saighān, ruin 1; description and photographs of the fort.
6. Kluyver 2000: 2 — detailed description.

119. BĀZĀRAK
See also 780. NUQRI KHĀNA.

Lat. 35° 19' N, long. 69° 31' E. Map 50.
Parwān Province. In the Panjshīr Valley, c. 20 km north-east of Gulbahār.

Description: Ancient remains reported.

Source: Masson 1842: II. 168 — mention.

BĀZĀR GAI. See 2014. BĀZĀR GAI in Supplement.

120. BĀZĀR TEPE

Original: Lat. 35° 49' N, long. 64° 31' E. Map 45.
Revised: 35.8118463 N, 64.53210542 E / 35° 48' 42.64668072 N, 64° 31' 55.57949652 E.
Faryāb Province. 32 km south-west of Maimana on the road to Qaisār. The site is in a region called Qal'a-i Aghā Qasāb, between Jilgaldi and Qara Qūlī.

Description: Local reports of a low mound on the *dasht* c. 2 m in height, producing much glazed pottery.

Source: Information by Jonathan L. Lee.

121. BĀZITKHĒL
Or KUTPŪR 2. See also 469 JAMĀL KĀLA, 667 KUTPŪR.

Lat. 34° 27' N, long. 70° 20' E. Map 66.
Lāghman Province. C. 6 km south-west of Darunta between the Surkhāb River and the road. 1 km south of Kutpūr and 1 km north-east of Jamāl Kāla.

Date: Kushan AD 1st cent. (numismatic).

Description: Remains of a mud and stone stupa 33 m in diam. It is on a square platform and has a decorative frieze of pilasters. Condition is poor. Inside is a square chamber that contained a silver reliquary inside a steatite vase, a bulla with a Greek inscription, and several copper coins.

The stupa is surrounded by a scatter of sherds and building debris.

Collection: BM — stupa deposits.

Fieldwork:
1. 1833 Masson—excavations.
2. 1965 Mizuno, Kyoto University—survey.

Sources:
1. Masson 1841: 65–6—brief description of the stupa and contents as Kotpūr 2.
2. Wilson 1841: pl. V, figs 8–10—drawings of the coins.
3. Mizuno 1971: 119—description and photo of the present condition.
4. Jongeward et al. 2012—catalogue and discussion of the reliquaries.
5. Errington 2017a and 2017b—the Masson collection and archive relating to the site.

122. BEGRAM
Or BAGRĀM or KĀPĪSĀ. Including BURJ-I ABDULLAH.

Original: Lat. 34° 59' N, long. 69° 18–30' E. Map 64.
Revised: 34.99506819 N, 69.31075039 E /
34° 59' 42.24550056 N, 69° 18' 38.70141444 E.
Kāpīsā Province. Near the confluence of the Ghurband and Panjshīr Rivers, *c.*80 km north of Kābul.

Dates: Graeco-Bactrian, 3rd–2nd cent. BC; Indo-Greek-- Indo-Parthian, 2nd cent. BC–AD 1st cent.; Kushan, 1st–3rd cent.; Sasanian, 3rd–5th cent.; Turki/Hindu Shahi, 7th–10th cent.; Ghaznavid-Ghurid, 11th–13th cent. (numismatic).

Description: A very large urban site overlooking the river, consisting of a long fortified area made up of two walled enclosures: the Burj-i Abdullah to the north and the 'New royal city' to the south, where most of the excavations have taken place. There is in addition a third, purely urban area to the south of that. In the 19th century Begram was the site of extensive coin collecting, with a full range from Mauryan through to Ghurid being recovered. Between 1937 and 1946, the DAFA, in three campaigns of excavation, uncovered parts of the bazaar, the fortifications, the entrance, and the palace. It is most famous however for just two rooms (Nos. 10 and 13) in the palace which produced the vast treasure of ivories, stuccos, glassware, bronzes, and lacquers, dating from the 1st century BC to the beginning of 3rd century AD, originating from many parts of Asia.

A gold reliquary containing 23 gold Kushan and Roman coins was found probably in the vicinity of Begram sometime in or shortly before 2012.

Collections:
1. BM—coins collected by Masson.
2. National Museum—objects excavated by the DAFA.
3. Musée Guimet—objects excavated by the DAFA.

Fieldwork:
1. 1934–7 Masson—survey.
2. 1924 Hackin, DAFA—survey.
3. 1925 Barthoux, DAFA—survey.
4. 1937–40 Hackin, DAFA—excavations.
5. 1941–2 Ghirshman, DAFA—excavations.
6. 1946 Meunié, DAFA—excavations.
7. 1962–7 Mizuno, Kyoto University—survey.

Sources:
1. Masson 1834a—general observations on and illustrations of the main categories of coins.
2. Avdall 1836—brief description of the coins with the inscription *nanaia* and its possible identification with Anahita.
3. Jacquet 1836a—description of Masson's results.
4. Masson 1836a—description of the Begram region and notes on coin collecting during 1836. Discussion of the site as Alexandria ad Causacum.
5. Masson 1836c—summary of the results of collecting *c.*7000 coins.
6. Prinsep 1836a—detailed discussion of a selection of Masson's coins.
7. Prinsep 1836b—discussion of some 'Mithraic' coins from Masson's collection.
8. Jacquet 1837: 402–3—brief discussion of Masson's results.
9. Vigne 1837: 776–7—describes his own coin collecting at the site.
10. Chapman 1841—description of 20 bronze and precious stone seals found at Begram.
11. Wilson 1841: 11–12—summary of Masson's discoveries.
12. Masson 1842: III. 140–3 and 148–65—detailed description of the site and its geographical context, with a summary of his own work and assessment of the finds.
13. Cunningham 1846: 182–4—discusses the site in a reconstruction of the historical geography. Identifies the site as ancient Kartana.
14. Prinsep 1858: 352–9—discusses some new types of coins found by Masson.
15. Cunningham 1890: 123—refers to the Saka coins of Gondophares in Masson's collection.
16. Foucher 1928: 24–5—brief summary of the French survey.
17. Hackin 1933—summarises the results and main finds and traces the Hellenistic and Indian connections.
18. Konow 1935—linguistic analysis of a Kharoshthi bas-relief inscription.
19. Auboyer 1938: 217–20—summary of the finds.
20. Hackin 1938a: 1–6—summary of the excavations and finds.
21. Hackin 1938b—summary of the results.
22. Hackin 1938c: 2–7—summary of the work in 1937.
23. Kohzad 1938/39—long description in Persian of the objects and the implications of their find.
24. Foucher 1939a—discussion of two ivory plaques depicting a Buddhist legend.

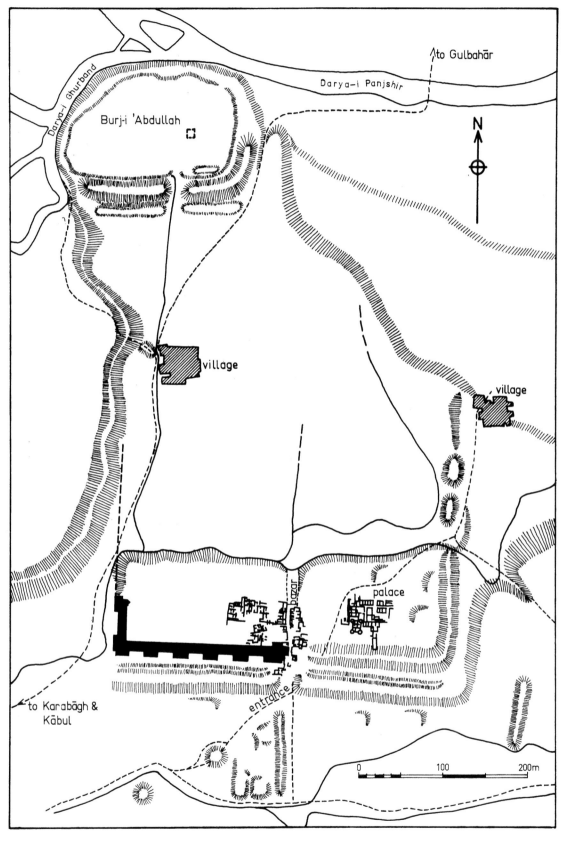

122 Begram—general plan (after Hackin 1939a, Ghirshman 1946, Hackin 1954a, and Meunié 1959).

25. Foucher 1939b—discusses its possible identification as Alexandria.
26. Hackin 1939a—background on the exploration of and some of the legends surrounding the site. Very summary description of the excavations and extensive catalogue and photos of the treasure.
27. Hackin 1939b—discusses two fragments of Syrian glassware from the treasure.
28. Hackin 1939c—summary of the 1939 excavations and finds with comparisons with Mathura.
29. Monod-Brühl 1939: 118–19—descriptions of some ivories, bronzes, and glassware on display in the Musée Guimet.
30. Tucci 1939—report on the discovery of the ivories and their artistic links in India.
31. Vogel 1939: 30–2—summary of the ivories.
32. Hackin 1939/40—summary and photos of the 1939 excavations.
33. Hackin 1940a—brief summary of the 1939 season and finds.
34. Hackin 1940b—brief report on the 1939 season.
35. Whitehead 1940–50—discusses many of the Indo-Greek coins found by Masson.
36. Yoshikawa 1941—summary of the finds and evaluation of their contribution to eastern art.
37. Schaeffer 1942—brief account of Hackin's work.
38. Foucher 1942–7: I. 140–2—description of the remains.
39. Ghirshman 1943–5—preliminary report with historical deductions of the 1941–2 excavations.
40. Yoshikawa 1944—summary of the site and general discussion of the objects.
41. Ghirshman 1946—full report on the architecture, ceramics, metal objects, figurines, and coins from the 1937–42 seasons, with a discussion on chronology and Kushan history in the light of Begram.
42. Hackin 1946—brief note on the discovery of the ivories.
43. Schlumberger 1947a: 15 and 17–18—discusses the implications of the discovery of the treasure.
44. Shakur 1947: 32–7—extensive description of the site and of coin finds dating to the pre-Mongol Islamic period.
45. Auboyer 1948—well-illustrated discussion of the ivories and the information they give on daily Indian life.
46. Bussagli 1949—brief discussion of Ghirshman's chronology for the Kushans.
47. Omar 1949—review of the excavations.
48. Schlumberger 1949b: 12–14—very brief summary of the results.
49. Wheeler 1949: 14–16—discusses the evidence of the glassware in terms of Romano-Buddhist connections.
50. Deydier 1949–50—discussion of a Kharoshthi relief inscription and its date.
51. Deydier 1950: 94–101—discussion with bibliography of the identification and importance of the finds.
52. Hackin 1951—report on the find of the treasure and discussion of the implications.
53. Lantier 1951—brief note on possible origins at Cologne for some of the glassware.
54. Hamelin 1952—fully illustrated study of the main examples of glassware from Begram.
55. Rogers 1952—discussion with comparisons of a late 1st-century ivory Sārdūla from Begram.
56. Auboyer 1953—discussion of one of the ivories that depicts a woman on a swing.
57. Bussagli 1953a—discusses the art from Begram and its relation to Indian aesthetics.
58. Curiel 1953: 124—refers to Sasanian coin finds.
59. Ghirshman 1953: 115–16—briefly describes the results of the latest work.
60. Kohzad 1953b: 4–5—summary of the site.
61. Kohzad 1953c—discusses the elephant symbolism at Begram.
62. Kohzad 1953d—discusses Begram as the summar capital of the Kushans.
63. Auboyer 1954—discusses aspects of daily life depicted on the ivories.
64. Eliséeff 1954—stylistic analysis of the Chinese lacquers.
65. Foucher 1954—discussion of a scene from a Buddhist legend depicted on two of the ivory plaques.
66. Hackin 1954a—general background to the finds with a note on the techniques used for removing the ivories.
67. Hackin 1954b—full descriptive catalogue of objects found.
68. Kurz 1954a—discussion and assessment of one of the more complex ivory plaques.
69. Kurz 1954b—detailed analysis with comparisons of the glassware and the Graeco-Roman plaster reliefs, and of the mythological scenes they depict.
70. Mandelshtam 1954—summary of the French excavations.
71. Meunié 1954—brief introduction to the excavations of Chantier 2.
72. Stern 1954—detailed stylistic analysis of the ivories with comparisons in India.
73. Adriani 1955—discussion of the seals and their place in Hellenistic art.
74. Kohzad 1955c: 35–9—discusses the cultural connections with the Roman world.
75. Wheeler 1955: 162–5—summary of the impact of Roman culture on the art of Begram.
76. Auboyer 1955–6—discussion of the different cultural contacts in Begram and the results of the 1937–9 excavations.

77. Bussagli 1955–6—discusses some of the religious aspects of Kushan art.
78. Kohzad 1956a—brief summary of the discoveries.
79. Ramachandran and Sharma 1956: II/2–II/23—summary of the Hindu iconography in the art.
80. Bussagli 1956–7: 156–7—discussion of the Hellenistic art at Begram.
81. Allchin 1957—discusses the chronology.
82. Frumkin 1957—brief discussion of the Graeco-Buddhist art.
83. Ghirshman 1957—discusses the evidence from Begram for Kushan chronology.
84. Carl 1959c—catalogue of the terracottas, stone objects, metal objects, sculptures, and coins from the bazaar.
85. L. Courtois 1959—discusses a ceramic jug and its stylistic implications.
86. Meunié 1959a—summary report on the excavations of the city gates and a brief note on the objects found.
87. Meunié 1959b—report on the excavations of the entrance to Begram.
88. Mac Dowall and Wilson 1960—discuss the evidence of the Apollodotus coins from Masson's collection.
89. Coarelli 1961—discusses a group of bronze busts.
90. J.-C. Courtois 1961: 20–2—summary of the work and discoveries.
91. Gullini 1961: pls 5–120—photos of the objects on display in the Kābul Museum.
92. Gullini 1961—discusses some of the art-historical problems.
93. Bussagli 1962a: 44–5—outline of the art.
94. Coarelli 1962—detailed study of some of the painted glass in the context of the Abrosian Iliad.
95. Roshan, ed. 1962—many photos of the objects on display in the National Museum.
96. Scerrato 1962b—discusses a Roman coin accidentally found at Begram.
97. Coarelli 1963—discussion of the glassware with comparisons in the West.
98. Pugachenkova 1963: 26–33—general summary.
99. Rowland 1964a—illustrates and discusses objects at a Tokyo Museum exhibition.
100. Talbot Rice 1965: 124–8—brief summary of the site and illustrations of some of the finds.
101. Monod 1966: 316–29—descriptions of the objects on display in the Musée Guimet.
102. Rowland 1966a: 22–64—introduction to the site and photos of many of the objects.
103. Barrett and Pinder-Wilson 1967–8—descriptions and photos of many of the objects.
104. Auboyer 1968: pls 8–37—illustrates and discusses many of the objects.
105. Dobbins 1968b—discussion of a dated Buddha image from Begram.
106. Hallade 1968—discussion of the evolution of Gandharan art.
107. Hallade and Hinz 1968: pls III, IV, 28–30, 49, and 132—discusses the place of Begram in the development of Gandharan art.
108. Mac Dowall 1968a (IV. 124)—discusses the incidence of Soter Megas coins in Masson's collection.
109. Maricq 1968—discusses the archaeological evidence from the excavations in support of an AD 78 date for Kanishka.
110. Mustamandi 1968c: 72–4—argues for the local manufacture of the stucco medallions.
111. Narain 1968: 211–13 and 228–30—evaluation of Begram II as evidence for a date for Kanishka.
112. Wheeler 1968: 91–4—summary of the site and the Indo-Greek legacy.
113. Azizi 1969/70b—a discussion of Achaemenid influences on the Begram sculpture.
114. Agrawala 1970: 4–6—discussion of the siren motif on a pottery handle from Begram.
115. Fussman 1970—linguistic analysis of some Kharoshthi inscriptions found in Ghrishman's excavations.
116. Auboyer 1971—discussion of some aspects of daily life revealed by the ivories.
117. Davidson 1971—discussion of new evidence for the dating of the ivories, equating them with Sanchi I, or 75–25 BC.
118. N. Dupree 1971a: 137–8—brief description of the site.
119. Mizuno 1971: 113–14—brief description of the site and report on the Japanese survey.
120. Rowland and Rice 1971: 11–21—brief summary of the site and photos of objects on display in the National Museum.
121. Scerrato 1971a—discussion of some bronze amulets from Begram, now in the British Museum.
122. Sivaramamurti 1971—discussion of the craftsmanship of the ivories.
123. Brill 1972a—results of a laboratory analysis of a glass fragment from Begram.
124. Davidson 1972—comparisons of the ivories with early Indian sculpture and argument for a 1st century BC date.
125. Tanabe 1973—re-examines the artistic value and chronology of the sculptures.
126. N. Dupree et al. 1974: 35–50—background to the site and treasures and guide to the National Museum exhibits.
127. Iourkevitch 1974—summary of the work carried out at Begram.
128. Kuwayama 1974b—reviews the architectural forms and ceramic types from Begram in a discussion of the dating evidence for Begram III, which he puts as 7th century.
129. Mac Dowall 1974: 249—discusses the evidence of Soter Megas coins in Masson's collection.
130. Deshpande 1975a—traces cultural links with India through the ivories.

131. Agrawala 1976—discuss a pottery vessel from Begram and its links with Mathura.
132. Azizi 1976—archaeological evidence for Kushan history.
133. Francfort 1976a: 93–6—discusses the fortifications.
134. Davary 1977—lists the inscriptions and gives a bibliography for them.
135. Tarzi 1977b—photos and summary of the treasure.
136. Sultan 1978—discusses Hellenistic influences in the art of Begram.
137. Francfort 1979a: 23–6—lists the site and discusses the general characteristics of fortifications in the Hellenistic period.
138. Srivastava 1979c—reviews the excavations.
139. Whitehouse 1989—discussion of the glass, with the suggested date of 2nd century AD for the concealment of the treasure.
140. Kuwayama 1991—discussion of the chronology for Begram III.
141. Delacour 1993—good reconstructed plan by Tissot.
142. Boardman in Errington and Cribb 1992: 112–14—describes some bronze busts from Begram.
143. Menninger 1996—detailed study of the glassware and plaster dishes.
144. Mustamandi 1997—discusses the impact of Begram on Gandharan art generally.
145. Bopearachchi 2000—discussion of a gilded silver Venus statue discovered in 1990 and now in a private collection.
146. Errington 2001—discusses the coins collected by Masson.
147. Geoffroy-Schneiter 2001—photos of objects from the Musée Guimet.
148. Tissot and Darbois 2002—photos of objects from the Kābul Museum.
149. Desbordes et al. 2003—exhibition catalogue of some of the ivories.
150. Dussubieux et al. 2003—analysis and exhibition catalogue of some of the glass.
151. Nehru 2004—new study of the ivories with reference to the art of Mathura and Bactria, with a broad 1st–2nd-century date.
152. Tissot 2006: 134–305—National Museum catalogue details and photos.
153. Cambon and Jarrige 2006, 2007—general discussion of the excavations and catalogue of ivories and glass in a touring exhibition.
154. Ball 2008: 80, 115, 174–5—summary.
155. Bopearachchi 2008: pls 15 and 16—illustrates two reliefs in private collections from the Begram area.
156. Kuwayama 2010—redates Begram III to the 6th–7th centuries.
157. Simpson 2011a—general introduction and catalogue of newly rediscovered ivories associated with a British Museum exhibition.
158. Zhang 2011—study of the Chinese lacquer, dated between 74 BC and AD 23.
159. Bopearachchi 2013—publication and discussion of a gold reliquary probably from Begram with Kushan and Roman gold coins.
160. Mairs 2012—discussion of the Egyptian glass in the context of Red Sea trade.
161. Mehendale 2012—discussion of the ivories, arguing that they were part of a collection for trade exchange rather than a royal treasure.
162. Passmore et al. 2012—detailed scientific analysis of a group of ivories.
163. Whitehouse 2012—discussion of the non-Roman origin of much of the glass, with a date in the early 2nd century for the deposition.
164. Ambers et al. 2014—account of the excavation, looting, recovery, scientific analysis, and conservation of the ivories.
165. Green 2017—discusses Begram and the establishment of pre-Taliban Afghan national identity.

123. BĪDISTĀN

Lat. 35° 50' N, long. 65° 54' E. Maps 24, 46.
Jauzjān Province. On the Sar-i Pul River *c.*10 km south of Jarghān, on the route from Sar-i Pul to Chiras.

Description: A small mound with some insignificant ruins on top, tentatively identified with Ferrier's 'Boudhi'.

Sources:
1. Ferrier 1857: 230—brief description.
2. Maricq and Wiet 1959: 74—mention.

124. BĪDMUSHKĪ
Or BĪD-I MUSHKĪN.

Lat. 34° 44' N, long. 66° 55' E. Map 47
Bāmiyān Province. On the Band-i Amīr River 5 km west of Yakaulang, to the north of the road to the present airport.

Date: Turk-pre-Mongol Islamic, 7th–13th century. (architectural, geographical, stylistic).

Description: Remains of a fortress consisting of several towers and traces of curtain walls. A second fortress is located on the north (right) bank of the Band-i Amīr river opposite Bīd-i Mushkīn.

Fieldwork:
1. 1970 Brett et al., Bristol University—survey.
2. 2002 Lee, Society for South Asian Studies—reconnaissance.

Sources:
1. Brett et al. 1970—map reference.
2. Lee 2006: 236—brief description, photographs in personal archives.

125. BĪDSAI
Or KŪH-I EL.

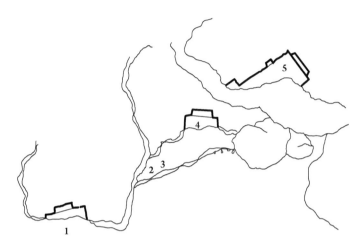

125 Bīdsai (after Verardi and Paparatti 2004).

Lat. 33° 09' N, long. 67° 06' E. Map 79.
Ghazni Province. In the Nāwa-i Qalandāri north of Tepe Sinaubar, in the Jāghūrī area south-west of Ghazni.

Date: Hunnic-Ghurid, 5th–13th cent. (stylistic—petroglyphs only).

Description: A large stone covered in petroglyphs depicting mostly ibex, with two human figures in combat. There is also a complex of artificial caves nearby in three groups. Cave 6 in Group A is a rectangular hall with an elliptical arch niche and platform at the end, approached by stairs from a lower level.

Fieldwork:
1. 1962 Bivar, SOAS—survey.
2. 1976 Taddei and Verardi. IsMEO—survey.

Sources:
1. Bivar 1971: 81–2—description, photo, and discussion of the petroglyphs.
2. Verardi 1977a: 150—mentions the caves.
3. Verardi and Paparatti 2004: 53–6—detailed description with drawings and photos.

126. BĪLCHIRĀGH

Lat. 35° 51' N, long. 65° 13' E. Maps 24, 46.
Faryāb Province. 1 km to the west of the town of Bīlchirāgh on the road to Maimana, on the north side of the entrance to the gorge.

Description: A series of caves dedicated to a saint. It was reported in the mid-1990s that a gold statuette had been found in the vicinity of this town.

Sources:
1. Additional information by Jonathan L. Lee.
2. Grodekoff 1880: 103–4—mention.

127. BĪMĀRĀN
Including SIĀH KUH A and B. See also 471. JĀNI TŪP.

Original: Lat. 34° 28–46' N, long. 70° 21–35' E. Map 66.
Revised: 34.45961078 N, 70.34591732 E /
34° 27' 34.59879540 N, 70° 20' 45.30236640 E.
Lāghmān Province. 11 km west of Jalālābād, at the foot of the Siāh Kūh on the Darūnta Plain.

Dates: Indo-Parthian, 1st cent.; Kushan, 1st–2nd cent. (numismatic, stylistic).

Description: Remains of four major stupas and at least two groups of votive stupas. The first is 38.40 m in circumference and in very dilapidated condition. It has a decorative frieze of blind arches and pilasters, and inside was a steatite vase and cover, both with Kharoshthi inscriptions, containing jewellery, coins, and a gold reliquary inset with rubies, depicting Buddha.

The second stupa, 43.90 m in circumference, lies in the centre of the village. It stands on a square platform and contained a steatite vase, jewellery, gold ornaments, and coins.

The third is 33 m in circumference and is surrounded by many mounds and two parallel lines of votive stupas. Inside was a silver reliquary, jewels, and coins.

The fourth is 43.90 m in circumference and is surrounded by extensive building debris. It contained nothing.

In addition to the stupas there is a complex of six artificial caves in the foothills to the north.

Collection: BM—reliquaries and other stupa deposits.

Fieldwork:
1. 1833 Honigberger—excavation.
2. 1834 Masson—excavation.
3. 1965 Mizuno, Kyoto University—survey.

Sources:
1. Masson 1841: 69–75 and 96—description of the stupas and discussion of the coins.
2. Wilson 1841: pls II, IV, VIII, and IX—drawings of the objects.
3. Cunningham 1854: 707–8—dates the inscription at 90 BC and discusses it as evidence for the Buddhist religion of the Sakas.
4. Prinsep 1858: 105–9—discusses the inscription.
5. Dowson 1863: 241–4—linguistic discussion of this and other inscriptions.

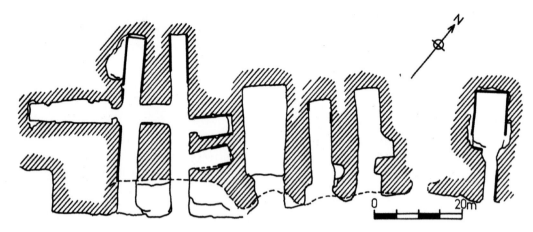

127 Bīmārān — caves (after Mizuno 1971).

6. Thomas 1863: 245, no. 24 — lists the inscription in a discussion of the Bactrian alphabet.

7. Senart 1890: 133–4 — linguistic discussion of some aspects of Dowson's translation of the inscription.

8. Partiger 1921 — text, translation, and analysis of the inscription.

9. Bachhofer 1925 — discusses the date of the reliquary.

10. Coomaraswamy 1926–7: 319 — concludes a late date for the reliquary in a discussion of the origin of the Buddha image.

11. Pandit 1927: 131 — photo of one of the stupas.

12. Bachhofer 1929: 75–7 and 94 — summary and discussion of the reliquary and the beginnings of Buddhist sculpture.

13. Konow 1929: 50–2 — summary of the site and transcription, translation, and analysis of the inscription.

14. Rowland 1936: 387–88 — discusses the gold reliquary as one of the first major examples of Gandharan art.

15. Gangoly 1937–8: 57–8 — discussion of the date of the reliquary in a history of the Buddha image.

16. Le May 1943 — discussion of the motifs depicted on the gold reliquary.

17. Van Lohuizen-de Leeuw 1949: 83–7, 93–6, and 101–3 — discusses the different evidence for the date of the gold reliquary.

18. Rowland 1953 — brief discussion of the evidence of the reliquary for dating Gandharan art.

19. Seckel 1964: 33 — photo of the reliquary and discussion of its Roman origins, dating it to AD 2nd/3rd century.

20. Bussagli 1968: 52–8 — considers the evidence of the reliquary for a date of Kanishka.

21. Dobbins 1968a — discusses the date of the gold reliquary.

22. Habibi 1971: 30–1 — discusses the inscription and the development of Afghan calligraphy.

23. Mizuno 1971: 117–18 and 123 — summary of a Masson's work and description of the present condition. Brief description of the caves and the mounds.

24. Mustamandi 1972 — discusses the origin of the eagle motif on the gold reliquary.

25. Davary 1977 — lists the inscription and gives a bibliography.

26. Mac Dowall and Taddei 1978a: 201 — summary of the inscription.

27. Kreitman in Errington and Cribb 1992: 186–92 — discusses the Stupa 2 deposits.

28. Carter 1997 — reappraisal of the reliquary.

29. Ball 2008: 113, 175–6 — summary.

30. Cribb 2017 — exhaustive discussion of the debates over the date of the reliquary.

31. Jongeward et al. 2012 — catalogue and discussion of the reliquaries.

32. Errington 2017a: 101–16 and 2017b: 19, 27–32, 42–51, 56–9, 79, 103, 108–17, 126 — the Masson collection and archive relating to the site.

BINA-I KAI. See 752 NĀD-I 'ALĪ.

128. BĪNĪ BĀDĀM

Lat. 34° 14' N, long. 68° 47' E. Map 60.
Wardak Province. To the west of the main Kābul road, just after the Maidān Valley c.70 km south of Kābul.

Description: Remains of a possible stupa.

Source: Raverty 1878: 692 — mention.

129. BĪNĪGĀH

Lat. 34° 28' N, long. 70° 33' E. Map 67.
Nangahār Province. On the west bank of the Kunār River, 15 km north-east of Jalālābād on the road to Islāmpūr.

Date: Kushan-Hunnic, 1st–6th cent. (architectural).

Description: Remains of a very small stupa on the hill.

Fieldwork: 1834 Masson—survey.

Sources:
1. Masson 1842: II. 275—mention.
2. Errington 2017a: 159–60—the Masson collection and archive relating to the site.

130. BĪN-I GAUGIR

Lat. 34° 14' N, 69° 10' E. Map 60.
Lōgar Province. 36 km south of Kābul, 5 km east of the Lōgar River.

Dates: Kushan and Hunnic-Turk, 1st–9th cent. (ceramic).

Description: None.

Collections: National Museum/AIA—sherds.

Source: Gardin and Lyonnet—1980 study of unpublished pottery from the DAFA surveys.

131. BĪNĪ MALAKH
Or RUSTĀQ I.

Lat. 37° 08' N, long. 69° 50' E. Maps 35, 38.
Takhār Province. On the north bank of the river 2 km east of Rustāq.

Date: Sasanian, 3rd–7th cent. (ceramic).

Description: A two-storied cave in a precipice.

Fieldwork: 1960–8 Fischer, Bonn University—survey.

Source: Fischer 1969: 352—mention as Rustāq I.

132. BĪRĀNA
See 1229 WARDAK.

133. BĪRĀNĪ

Original: Lat. 34° 27' N, long. 70° 22' E. Map 66.
Revised: 34.45946656 N, 70.36086614 E /
34° 27' 34.07962608 N, 70° 21' 39.11811876 E.
Laghmān Province. On the north-west bank of the junction of the Surkhāb and Kābul Rivers.

Description: A mound.

Fieldwork: 1834 Masson—survey.

Source: Masson 1841: 97—mention.

134. BĪSH KAʾIK
Including AGAKURU and TUNUK.

Original: Lat. 37° 10'–37° 11' N, long. 69° 45'–69° 46' E.
Map 35.
Revised:
37.16532227 N, 69.77678976 E / 37° 09' 55.16016480 N,
69° 46' 36.44314464 E (A).
37.17101242 N, 69.77422342 E / 37° 10' 15.64469688 N,
69° 46' 27.20431488 E (B).
37.18089581 N, 69.76236123 E / 37° 10' 51.22490880 N,
69° 45' 44.50041504 E (D).
37.18655543 N, 69.7557983 E / 37° 11' 11.59954332 N,
69° 45' 20.87388072 E (E).
Takhār Province. Not far from the village of Bīsh Kaʾik, 6 km north-west of Rustāq, several tepes spread along the edge of the road which leads to Chayāb, over 2.5 km: (A) at the crossing of the road with another road linking the hamlets of Tunuk and Agakuru, on the western edge of the road; (B) 500 m further, east side of the road, south of the village of Bīsh Kaʾik; (C) 700 m further, west side, at the exit of this village; (D) 800 m further, east side, a little before the road turns westward to cross the stream of Kāfir Qalʾa (no. 495); (E) further again (800 m), 200 m north of this elbow in the road, on a low terrace of the Rustāq River, which flows 600 m from there (to the north-east): this tepe is indicated on the 1:100,000 map as a mound of 2 m. The alignment of these mounds in relation to the road is probably due to the fact that it follows a crest of the curves of the level that ancient peoples appear to have chosen to live, on the slopes of the plain of Rustāq.

Dates: Achaemenid, 6th–4th BC (D, E); Hellenistic, 3rd–1st cent. BC (B, C, D); Kushan and Hunnic-Turk, 1st–9th cent. (B, E); pre-Mongol Islamic, 10th–13th cent.; and Timurid, 15th–16th cent. (all except B). (ceramic).

Description: (A) Small low hillock (diam. 20 m, height 1.5 m); the higher mound seen 400 m south-west of this point is natural. (B) Mound cut into a round shape by cultivated fields (diam. 30 m), flat square top (15 × 15 m, height 3 m; fragments of mud-bricks, 5 cm thick. (D) Mound eaten into by the road and by cultivation, 30 × 30 m, flat top, height 3 m. (E) Square platform (40 × 40 m) oriented parallel to the Rustāq River (north-north-west—south-south-east), and sloping towards it (south-west/north-east), like the terrace itself, which it dominates by 4 m; the high part of the tepe occupies the north-west quadrant.

Collection: National Museum/AIA—sherds.

Fieldwork: 1978 Gardin et al., CNRS—survey.

Sources:
1. Site information by J.-C. Gardin.
2. Gardin and Lyonnet 1978–9: pl. II—nos. 523–7.
3. Lyonnet 1997: figs 35, 39 49, 68, 69—nos. 523–7.
4. Gardin 1998: 92—nos. 523–7.

135. BĪSH KAPA
Or KADU KHUR.

Original: Lat. 36° 38'–36° 39' N, long. 69° 22' E. Map 36.
Revised:
Between 36.64490995 N, 69.36339009 E /
36° 38' 41.67580488 N, 69° 21' 48.20432868 E, 36.64199088 N,
69.36471437 E / 36° 38' 31.16717268 N, 69° 21' 52.97174712
E, 36.64165201 N, 69.36341931 E / 36° 38' 29.94725400 N,
69° 21' 48.30951060 E, and 36.64292852 N, 69.36360674 E /
36° 38' 34.54267092 N, 69° 21' 48.98426976 E (A).
Between 36.64642627 N, 69.36225189 E /
36° 38' 47.13456660 N, 69° 21' 44.10679716 E, 36.64703038 N,
69.36139511 E / 36° 38' 49.30937160 N, 69° 21' 41.02240572 E,
36.64773225 N, 69.36314321 E /
36° 38' 51.83610756 N, 69° 21' 47.31554628 E, and 36.6479218 N,
69.36072668 E / 36° 38' 52.51846452 N,
69° 21' 38.61604980 E (B).
Takhār Province. In the plain of Bīsh Kapa (or Kadu Khur),
2–3 km south-east of Bangui, two groups of tepes situated
on the more or less collapsed edge of a terrace of the Bangui
River (left bank), which has carved its bed a few hundred
metres from there, to the north-east. The first group is
located on the western edge of the Rūd-i Īshkamish, where
it joins the Bangui River (A); the second is at about 600 m
further to the north-west, on the same terrace edge (B).

Dates: Middle Bronze Age, c.2500–1500 BC (A); Beg. Iron,
end 2nd-beg. 1st mill. BC (B); Hellenistic, 3rd–1st cent. BC
(B); Kushan and Hunnic-Turk, 1st–9th cent. (A); some
Islamic sherds (A, B). (ceramic).

Description: (A) on the last elbow of the left bank of the
Rūd-i Īshkamish, three mounds close together, cut vertically by irrigated fields next to them (diam. 10 to 20 m,
height 2 to 4 m); 250 m to the north-west, three similar
mounds aligned north-east/south-west, of which the highest, strongly cut (12 × 12 m), still rises to 5 m (find of a bell-
shaped half column base in white limestone). (B) On the
edge of the road oriented south-west/north-east which
crosses the hamlet of Jalāyīr towards the Bangui River,

two parallel mounds, on the same collapsed terrace edge,
one to the left, the other to the right of the road (oriented
north-east/south-west, 80 × 25 to 40 m, flattened top,
height 2 to 5 m). 100 m lower down to the north-east, a
third mound, higher (up to 12 m), cut in two by the same
road; the two remaining hillocks are rounded (diam. 40 m),
flattened top.

Collection: National Museum/AIA—sherds.

Fieldwork: 1978 Gardin et al., CNRS—survey.

Sources:
1. Site information by J.-C. Gardin.
2. Gardin and Lyonnet 1978–9: pl. XI—nos. 354–61.
3. Lyonnet 1997: figs 13, 25, 35, 39, 49, 68, 69—nos.
   354–61.
4. Gardin 1998: 97—nos. 354–61.

136. BĪSH TAN TĒG, RŪD-I ĪSHKAMISH

Original: Lat. 36° 30'–36° 32' N, long. 69° 236' E. Map 37.
Revised:
36.52951164 N, 69.36927371 E / 36° 31' 46.24190652 N,
69° 22' 09.38536320 E (B).
36.49864778 N, 69.36213916 E / 36° 29' 55.13199540 N,
69° 21' 43.70099004 E (C).
Takhār Province. In the valley of the Rūd-i Īshkamish,
between Bangui and Īshkamish, at the level of the first
houses north of the village of Bīsh Tan Tēg: tepe A, clearly
visible from the Bangui to Īshkamish road, is located lower
down from this road, 200 m to the east, in the middle of
irrigated fields which occupy the bottom of the valley.

Dates: Achaemenid, 6th–4th cent. BC (A); Kushan, 1st–4th
cent. (A); Hunnic-Turk, 5th–9th cent. (B, C); pre-Mongol
Islamic, 10th–13th cent. (A). (ceramic).

Description: (A) Oblong mound north-east/south-west
(40 × 10 to 20 m), cut by cultivated fields, flattened top
(3 m); in the cuts of the north-east face, 1.5 m beneath the
top, thick ashy layers (40 cm), 6 m long. (B) 2.5 km to the

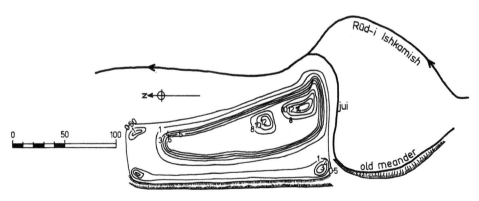

136 Bīsh Tan Tēg (J.-C. Gardin).

north, at the end of a line of hills on which the cemetery of the place called Madrasa is located, a little mound (50 × 20 m) overlooking by a dozen metres the gully of the same name. (C) 1 km south of A, 400 m east of the road, fortification dominating an old meander of the Rūd-i Īshkamish, covered today by the cemetery of Bīsh Tan Tēg. Rectangular north–south plan (200 × 50 m), with rampart and ditch on the north and west sides; the two other sides descend straight to the river. Bastions at the north-east, north-west, and south-west angles; citadel at the south-east angle, rising to 8 m above a terreplein which occupies two-thirds of the interior space, towards the north and towards the west.

Collection: National Museum/AIA — sherds.

Fieldwork: 1978 Gardin et al., CNRS — survey.

Sources:
1. Site information by J.-C. Gardin.
2. Gardin and Lyonnet 1978–9: pl. XI — nos. 363–5.
3. Lyonnet 1997: figs 25, 35, 49, 68, 69 — nos. 363–5.
4. Gardin 1998: 99 — nos. 363–5.

BIST. See 149 BUST.

137. BUGHI

Original: Lat. 36° 10’ N, long. 66° 05’ E. Maps 24, 47.
Revised: 36.16129004 N, 66.0909039 E / 36° 09’ 40.64413428 N, 66° 05’ 27.25403676 E.
Jauzjān Province. 20 km north-west of Sauzma Qal’a on the road to Sar-i Pul.

Description: A large artificial mound, with many more in the vicinity between 2 and 6 m high.

Fieldwork: 1885 Maitland, ABC — topographical survey.

Source: Maitland 1888b: 85 — mention.

138. BŪĪNA QARA

Original: Lat. 36° 19’ N, long. 66° 52’ E. Map 28.
Revised: 36.32186609 N, 66.90142291 E /
36° 19’ 18.71793984 N, 66° 54’ 05.12247420 E.
Balkh Province. C.65 km south of Mazār-i Sharīf on the road to Āq Kupruk, on the east bank of the Balkh River.

Date: Bronze Age, 3500–1500 BC (ceramic).

Description: A mound on the outskirts of the village, containing sherds with a superficial resemblance to those from Deh Morasi Ghundai and Mundigak.

Fieldwork: 1959 Dupree and Howe — survey.

Source: Dupree and Howe 1963: 2 — mention.

BUKSHOR. See 2010 in Supplement.

139. BŪLAQ URTA BUZ
Or DANGAR TEPE.

Lat. 36° 44’ N, long. 69° 34’ E. Map 36.
Takhār Province. In the houses of the place called Būlak Urta Buz, situated 3 km north-east of Tāluqān, on the left bank of the Gau Mulli canal which irrigates the foothills north of this town.

Dates: Hellenistic, 3rd–1st cent. BC; Kushan, 1st–4th cent.; a few Islamic sherds (ceramic).

Description: Dangar Tepe: oblong east–west mound (100 × 60 m), eroded on three sides north, west, south) by cotton fields; top flattened (4 m), with highest point in the east (6m), marked by a *zīyārat*.

Collection: National Museum/AIA — sherds.

Fieldwork: 1977 Gardin et al., CNRS — survey.

Sources:
1. Site information by J.-C. Gardin.
2. Gardin and Lyonnet 1978–9: pl. IX — no. 214.
3. Lyonnet 1997: figs 39, 49 — no. 214.
4. Gardin 1998: 69 — no. 214.

140. BULŪLA

Lat. 34° 53’ N, long. 68° 05’ E. Map 58.
Bāmiyān Province. At the western foot of the Shībar Pass, c.6 km east of the turnoff to Dūshi and 35 km east of Bāmiyān.

Description: Several caves and the remains of some ancient buildings.

Sources:
1. Masson 1839: 113 — mention.
2. Masson 1842: II. 447 — mention.

BUNYĀD KHĀN. See 2015 BUNYĀD KHĀN in Supplement.

141. BURAT TEPE
Including QARA TEPE.

Original: Lat. 36° 47’ N, long. 67° 30’–67° 31’ E. Map 29.
Revised:
36.77782372 N, 67.53171484 E / 36° 46’ 40.16539956 N, 67° 31’ 54.17342220 E (A).
36.78515113 N, 67.52907162 E / 36° 47’ 06.54406872 N, 67° 31’ 44.65782948 E (B).
36.78931818 N, 67.52440987 E / 36° 47’ 21.54543540 N, 67° 31’ 27.87554820 E (C).
36.78414089 N, 67.51656405 E / 36° 47’ 02.90719392 N, 67° 30’ 59.63058504 E (D).
Samangān Province. About 20 km north-west of Tāshqurghān, north of the road which links this town to Mazār-i

Sharīf (between the mileposts 386 km and 388 km, from Kābul): zone of tepes called Burat Tepe, extending to the north and to the west of the main one, called Qara Tepe (A).

Dates: Beg. Iron, end 2nd-beg. 1st mill. BC (A, B, C, D); Achaemenid, 6th–4th cent. BC; pre-Mongol Islamic, 10th–13th cent. (A); Timurid, 15th–16th cent. (A, D). (ceramic).

Description: (A) Oval east–west tepe (170 × 100 m), called Qara Tepe (height 6 m); steep slopes on the south side, excavation trench on the top; 0.6 km to the west-south-west, area of sherds with remains of potters' kilns. (B) Similar area and vestiges 1 km to the west-north-west of the preceding tepe; and little mounds of the same period (beg. Iron) in the north-north-west, at 0.7 and 1.5 km respectively. (C) Largest but low tepe 1.7 km north-west of tepe A, with probable remains of potters' kilns. (D) Small flattened tepe, 1.7 km west-north-west of tepe A, with potters' kilns.

Surface finds: besides the pottery, which was very abundant, objects in bronze and stone.

Excavations on sites A and B (two potters' kilns): in A, deep trench of 3 m, virgin soil not reached, remains of architecture (irregular wall in *pakhsa*).

Collections: DAFA and National Museum—pottery, objects in bronze (arrowheads, cloisonné seal), stone club, flint.

Fieldwork:
1. 1969 Gouin, DAFA—survey.
2. 1970, 1972 Gouin, DAFA—trenches on sites A and B.

Sources:
1. Gouin, unpublished report—sites no. 15 (A), 29 (C), 30 (A, potters' kilns), 31 (B), 32 (D), 33 and 46 (B, the two little mounds mentioned above).
2. Gouin 1973a: 86–95—summary and drawings of finds.
3. Gouin 1974: 169–77—description of site and of trench; 182–245—typology of pottery and commentary.

142. BURHANKHĀN

Original: Lat. 31° 14' N, long. 62° 07' E. Map 84.
Revised: 31.24797909 N, 62.09988539 E /
31° 14' 52.72470816 N, 62° 05' 59.58740724 E.
Nīmrūz Province. 9 km north-east of Chakhansūr, *c*.1 km north of the village of Burhankhān.

Dates: Sasanian, 3rd–7th cent.; early Islamic, 7th–13th cent. (ceramic).

Description: A low mound.

Fieldwork: 1960–70 Fischer, Bonn University—survey.

Source: Fischer et al. 1974–6: 41–2, pl. 190—mention and photo.

BURJ-I' ABDULLAH. See 122 BEGRAM.

143. BURJ-I GHUNDA
Or CHUNG-I DARĀZGU or DĪWĀL-I GHUNDA.

Lat. 31° 03' N, long. 62° 03' E. Map 92.
Nīmrūz Province. 15 km due south of Chakhānsūr, on the eastern edge of the Hāmūn between Sawal and Chīgīnī.

Date: Sasanian, 3rd–7th cent. (architectural, ceramic).

Description: A ruined, double-storeyed watch tower or dwelling tower, with some vaults still intact.

Fieldwork: 1960–70 Fischer, Bonn University—survey.

Sources:
1. Fischer 1966: 27—mention and photos.
2. Fischer 1967b—discusses the architectural affinities of the tower with Sasanian fire temples.
3. Fischer 1969: 335—brief summary.
4. Fischer 1970b: pls 32 and 35–7—photos of the remains.
5. Fischer 1973c: 142—mention.
6. Fischer et al. 1974–6: 37—mention.

BURJ-I GHUS KARI. See 2016 BURJ-I GHUS KARI in Supplement.

BURJ-I KEMRI. See 1087 SHĪWAKĪ.

BURJ-I SHAIKH SULAIMĀN. See 2017 BURJ-I SHAIKH SULAIMĀN in Supplement.

BURJ-I TĀJARMĪN. See 2018 BURJ-I TĀJARMĪN in Supplement.

144. BURJ-I LĀR

Lat. 31° 21' N, long. 62° 12' E. Map 84.
Nīmrūz Province. C.13 km to the east of Chapu and 10 km west of Kadah, in the area north-east of Chakhānsūr.

Dates: Early Islamic, 10th–13th cent.; Mongol-Timurid, 13th–16th cent. (ceramic).

Description: A hill with a watch tower on top.

Fieldwork:
1. 1903–5 Tate, SAC—survey.
2. 1960–70 Fischer, Bonn University—survey.

Sources:
1. Peacocke 1887a: 30—mention.
2. Tate 1910: 192—mention as a Zoroastrian *dakhma*.
3. Fischer et al. 1974–6: 51–2—summary and photos.

145. BURJ-I RŪD-I BĪYĀBĀN

Original: Lat. 30° 18' N, long. 61° 22' E. approximately. Map 94.
Revised: 30.29692628 N, 61.37318633 E /
30° 17' 48.93460656 N, 61° 22' 23.47078584 E.
Nīmrūz Province. In the Rūd-i Bīyābān 6 km south-east of Iran Border Post 20 and 11 km west of Gina. 2 km west of Burri.

Date: Sasanian, 3rd–7th cent. (ceramic).

Description: Remains of a watch tower and several smaller buildings. There is also a large mound, 40 × 25 m in area and 7 m in height, 300 m to the west.

Fieldwork: 1951 Fairservis, AMNH—survey.

Source: Fairservis 1961: 63—brief description as Sites RB 18 and 19.

146. BURJ-I SAMAD

Original: Lat. 30° 57' N, long, 62° 05' E. Map 92.
Revised: 30.94358584 N, 62.08065559 E /
30° 56' 36.90901716 N, 62° 04' 50.36012256 E.
Nīmrūz Province. 5.5 km south-west of Zīyārat-i Amīrān Sāhib, north-west of Chehel Burj.

Date: Early Islamic, 7th–13th cent. (ceramic).

Description: Remains of an isolated mud-brick tower.

Fieldwork: 1960–70 Fischer, Bonn University—survey.

Sources:
1. Fischer 1970a: fig. 12—photo.
2. Fischer 1970b: pl. 46—photo.
3. Fischer 1973c: 158—mention.
4. Fischer et al. 1974–6: 38—mention.

BURJ-I YAK. See **2019 BURJ-I YAK** in Supplement.

BURJ KĀFIR. See **651 KŪRRINDAR.**

147. BURRI

Original: Lat. 30° 18' N, Long. 61° 23' E. approximately. Map 94.
Revised: 30.29837393 N, 61.40762596 E /
30° 17' 54.14615772 N, 61° 24' 27.45345168 E.
Nīmrūz Province. On the south side of the Rūd-i Bīyābān, 8 km south-east of Iran Border Post 20 and 10 km west of Gina. 2 km east of Burj-i Rūd-i Bīyābān.

Dates: Iron Age, 1500–1200 BC; Sasanian, 3rd–7th cent. (ceramic).

Description: Ruins of a small rectangular fortress.

Fieldwork:
1. 1885 Merk, ABC—topographical survey.
2. 1951 Fairservis, AMNH—survey.

Sources:
1. Merk 1888: 27—mention
2. Fairservis 1961: 63—mention as RB 17.

148. BŪS-I SHĀN
Or PŪZA-I SHĀN or (correctly) PŪZA-I ĪSHĀN.

Lat. 36° 05' N, long. 68° 39' E. Map 33.
Baghlān Province. 6 km south of Baghlān on the road to Pul-i Khumri.

Dates: Hellenistic, 3rd–1st cent. BC; Kushan-Kushano-Sasanian, 1st–4th cent. (ceramic).

Description: Ruins of a small baked brick bridge and a fortress of large mud-bricks.

Fieldwork: 1955–60 Fischer, DAAD—survey.

Sources:
1. Gardin and Lyonnet, 1980 chronological study of unpublished pottery from DAFA surveys.
2. Additional information by Jonathan L. Lee 2002, correcting the name to Pūza-i Īshān (photos of site and bridge footing in personal archive).
3. J. C. Courtois 1961: 26—mention.
4. Fischer 1969: 350—mention.

149. BUST
Or BIST. See also **685 LASHKARI BĀZĀR.**

Original: Lat. 31° 30' N, long. 64° 21–35' E. Map 86.
Revised: 31.50316288 N, 64.35478881 E /
31° 30' 11.38636044 N, 64° 21' 17.23970268 E.
Helmand Province. 7 km south of Lashkargāh, at the confluence of the Arghandāb and Helmand Rivers.

Dates: Achaemenid, 6th–4th cent. BC. (epigraphic); Sasanian, 4th–7th cent. (ceramic, numismatic); Ghaznavid and Ghurid, 11th–13th cent. (architectural, ceramic, epigraphic, historical).

Description: Bust forms the southern end of the Lashkari Bāzār complex, and is dominated by an immense citadel on a mound of uncertain date surrounded by a high enclosure wall. High point of the citadel is toward the west, protecting the rest of the site from the prevailing wind, as is common elsewhere in the Helmand-Sistan region. On top of the citadel are the remains of many structures, both in mud and baked brick, most notable of which is a seven-storey galleried 'well' down through the middle.

At the foot of the citadel is a free-standing Ghurid arch, and outside the enclosure the most notable remains are a mud-brick, Ghaznavid palace and the probably later baked brick shrine of Ghiyyas al-Dīn or Shahzāda Sarbāz.

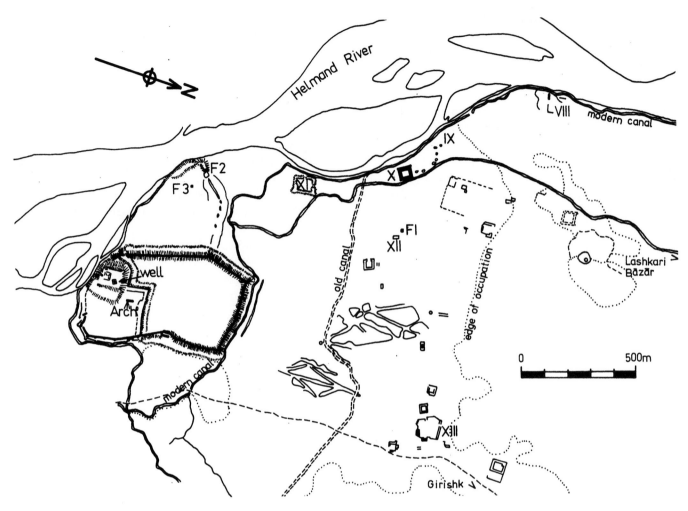

149 Bust—general plan (after Schlumberger and Sourdel-Thomine 1978).

There have been many important accidental finds from the site, including a collection of carved and inscribed bricks to the north of the citadel and a stone weight with an Old Persian cuneiform inscription found in the vicinity.

Fieldwork:
1. 1949 De Cardi—survey.
2. 1949–51 Schlumberger and Gardin, DAFA—excavations.
3. 1960, 1967 Trousdale, Smithsonian—survey.
4. 1976–7 Ajan, AIA—preservation of the arch.
5. 1976–8 Allen, Smithsonian Institution—survey.

Sources:
1. Bellew 1874: 172–7—detailed description of the citadel and of the excavation of some 'Sasanian fire-altar' coins.
2. Le Strange 1905: 344–5—summary of the historical sources.

3. Niedemeyer and Diez 1924: pls 136–7—photos and description of the citadel and arch before restoration, including remains (now gone) at the foot of the arch.
4. Pope 1935—brief architectural description of the arch with several of Hackin's photos.
5. Schroder 1938: 988–9—discusses the arch and its possible date.
6. Sourdel-Thomine 1956—analysis and translations of the decorated 12th/13th cent. inscriptions from the shrine.
7. Gardin 1963: 5–13—summary of the excavations and stratigraphy, with a typology and analysis of the pottery.
8. Pugachenkova 1963: 100–1—general summary of the remains.
9. Gnoli 1967: 78–9—discussion of possible Zoroastrian origins of Bust.

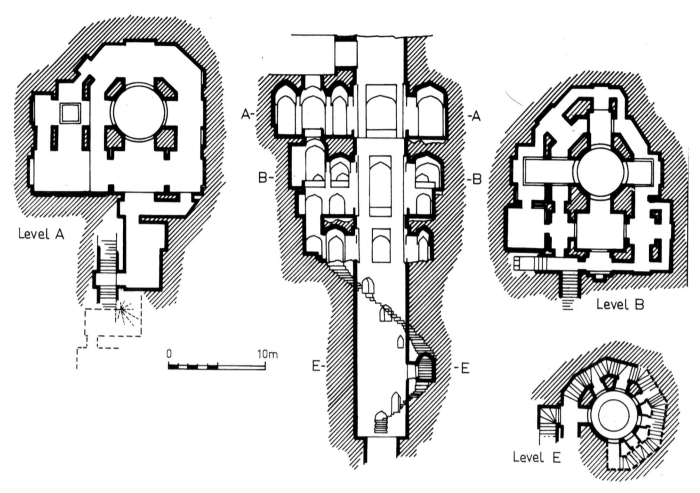

149 Bust—well (after Furughi 1981).

10. Hill and Grabar 1967: pls 152–62—photos of the arch, the palace, and the shrine.
11. Trousdale 1968—discusses the discovery of the cuneiform inscription.
12. Anand 1970: 21–2—brief summary and photos of the remains.
13. Crane and Trousdale 1972—photos and analysis of the inscribed decorated bricks.
14. Levi 1972: 253, n. 21—describes a Roman coin, probably found at Bust.
15. Davary 1975—photos of the architecture and historical/geographical background of the site in relation to other places mentioned in the sources.
16. *Kabul Times* 1976a—very brief report on the preservation of the arch.
17. N. Dupree 1977: 310–11—historical background and brief description.
18. *Kabul Times* 1977b—very brief report on the preservation of the arch.

19. Schlumberger 1978: 99—brief note on the archaeology of the site.
20. Schlumberger and Gardin—table of all sources that refer to Bust.
21. Sourdel-Thomine 1978: 63–8—stylistic and epigraphical analysis of the arch.
22. Crane 1979—description, drawings, analysis of decoration, and discussion of date (12th–early 13th cent.) of the Mausoleum of Ghiyath al-Dīn, or Shāhzāda Shaikh Husain ibn Shaikh Ibrahim. Mentions ruins of eight other tombs in vicinity.
23. Furughi 1981—report on the Afghan preservation work and detailed drawings of the well.
24. Klinkott 1983: 209–77—description of the fortifications.
25. Allen 1988–90—architectural notes on many of the standing remains, supplementing the French records of the site.
26. Hillenbrand 2000—discussion in the broader context of Ghaznavid and Ghurid architecture.
27. Ball 2008: 240–6—summary.

150. BUS TEPE

Original: Lat. 36° 48' N, long. 66° 36' E. Map 26.
Revised: 36.79968932 N, 66.60380556 E /
36° 47' 58.88153472 N, 66° 36' 13.70002248 E.
Jauzjān Province. 42 km east of Āqcha, 800 m south of the road to Balkh.

Description: A large, flat-topped, steep-sided rectangular mound, 100–50 m in area and 16 m in height. The base is surrounded by a ridge 3 m high and a ditch. There are no adjacent mounds.

Fieldwork:
1. 1938 Barger, ASI—survey.
2. 1946 Wheeler, ASI—reconnaissance.
3. 1948 Le Berre, DAFA—survey.

Sources:
1. M. Le Berre: unpublished 1948 report in DAFA Archives, Tépé P. 38.
2. Barger and Wright 1941: 55—brief description.
3. Shakur 1947: 68—mention.

BUTA KASHAN. See **927 QUCHI.**

BŪTGĀH. See **875 QAL'A-I QAISĀR.**

151. BUTKHĀK

Lat. 34° 40' N, long. 69° 22' E. Map 63.
Kābul Province. 17 km east of Kābul on the road to Jalālā-bād via the Lataband Pass.

Description: Some caves and some small mounds.

Source: Masson 1842: III. 175—mention.

152. BUZGHALAZ TEPE

Original: Lat. 36° 52' N, long. 66° 32' E. Maps 25, 26.
Revised:
36.86498507 N, 66.53964484 E / 36° 51' 53.94623760 N, 66° 32' 22.72141032 E (A).
36.8659521 N, 66.53364739 E / 36° 51' 57.42756612 N, 66° 32' 01.13061300 E (B).
Jauzjān Province. 250 m north of the village of Nimlik north of the road to Balkh.

Description: Two little tepes aligned east–west: (A) rectangular platform (50×40 m), height 5 m; (B) west of A, rectangular mound (120×50 m), 7 m high, very eroded. Between the two tepes stretches an undulating area, proof of ancient occupation. On the northern horizon, a dozen fairly large tepes.

Fieldwork: 1948 Le Berre, DAFA—survey.

Source: M. Le Berre: unpublished 1948 report in DAFA Archives, Tépés P. 30 and 31.

153. CHADUR TEPE

Lat. 36° 14' N, long. 66° 53' E. Map 28.
Balkh Province. On the west bank of the Balkh River, c.40 km south of Balkh just to the west of Qizil Kand.

Date: ?Bronze Age, 2nd mill. BC. (stylistic).

Description: A huge mound, the lowest layers of which are prehistoric. A possible Bronze Age dagger was found on the site.

Fieldwork:
1. 1885 Maitland, ABC—topographical survey.
2. 1966 Leshnik, Heidelberg University—survey.

Sources:
1. Maitland 1888b: 73—mention.
2. Bākhtār 1966: description.

154. CHĀGHAN SARĀĪ
Or CHĪGHA SARĀĪ. See also **706 MANGIR SAR** and **827 QĀDZYĀ.**

Lat. 34° 53' N, long. 71° 09' E. Map 68.
Kunār Province. At the confluence of the Pech and Kunār Rivers, c.100 km north-east of Jalālābād.

Date: Turki-Hindu Shahi, 8th–10th cent. (ceramic, stylistic).

Description: An extensive fortification system consisting of ramparts, towers, and buildings on a hill overlooking a Muslim cemetery. Incorporated into some of the graves are some ancient sculpture fragments, possibly from a shrine dedicated to a Shivaite linga cult in a medieval north-western Indian style.

Collection: National Museum.

Fieldwork:
1. 1947 and 54 Danish Anthropological Expedition.
2. 1959 Fischer, DAAD—survey.

Sources:
1. Holdich 1896—brief description of the fragmentary sculptures.
2. Holdich 1901: 250–1—brief description of the sculptures, attributing them to the Buddhists.
3. Holdich 1910: 130—mention.
4. Schiebe 1937: pl. 114—photo of one of the fragments.
5. Edelberg 1957—describes the remains and the sculptures.
6. Van Lohuizen-de Leeuw 1959—description of the remains and discussion of the associated Indian culture.
7. Edelberg 1960—brief note and photos of the sculptures, incorporating Van Lohuizen's research.
8. Fischer 1960: 10—mention.
9. Fischer 1961c—discuss the Hindu remains.

10. Fischer 1969: 357–9 — summary and aerial photos of the remains.
11. Tarzi 2000 — discussion of the schist sculptures.
12. Tissot 2006: 470 — National Museum catalogue details and photo.

155. CHAHĀRBĀGH
Or LAL QAL'A. See also 30 'ALIGUL, 727 MIRZA JAHĀNGĪR, 847 QAL'A-I HĀJI, and 1102 SIĀHSANG.

Original: Lat. 34° 24' N, long. 70° 22' E. Map 66.
Revised: 34.40249452 N, 70.35886867 E /
34° 24' 08.98028748 N, 70° 21' 31.92721776 E.
Nangahār Province. In the foothills *c.*2 km south of the village of Chahārbāgh, 9 km west of Jalālabād.

Date: Kushan, 1st cent. (numismatic).

Description: Remains of a stupa and associated monastery enclosure. Inside the stupa was a dome-chamber containing a steatite vase, a gold reliquary, and 28 'Indo-Saka' coins. There was also a tunnel continuing on underneath the stupa.

Collection: BM — stupa deposits.

Fieldwork:
1. 1934 Masson — excavation.
2. 1965 Mizuno, Kyoto University –survey.

Sources:
1. Jacquet 1837: 423–4 — general discussion of the finds.
2. Jacquet 1839 — general remarks on Masson's work.
3. Masson 1841: 103 — brief description of the stupa and contents as Tope 4.
4. Masson 1842: III. 154 — mention.
5. Ramachandran and Sharma 1956: I. 6 — mention.
6. Mizuno 1971: 120 and pls 34 and 35 — summary of Masson's work and photos of the present condition.
7. Mac Dowall and Taddei 1978b: 247 — mention the coins.
8. Ball 2008: 177 — summary.
9. Jongeward et al. 2012 — catalogue and discussion of the reliquaries.
10. Errington 2017a: 141–52 and 2017b: 19–20, 34–6, 42–7 — the Masson collection and archive relating to the site.

CHAHĀR BURJAK. See 2021 CHAHĀR BURJAK in Supplement.

CHAHĀR DARRA. See 2243 SHAHĀR KALĪL in Supplement.

156. CHAHĀR DARRACHA

Original: Lat. 36° 46'–36° 48' N, long. 68° 45'–68° 47' E. Map 32.

Revised: 36.7962864 N, 68.75658195 E / 36° 47' 46.63103028 N, 68° 45' 23.69503368 E.
Qundūz Province. Some 10 km north-west of Qundūz, on the road to Asqalān: (A) the first tepe on the west side of the road, at the level of the village of Chahār Darracha (corresponding to the mound of 3 m indicated on the 1:100,000 map); (B) a second mound 3.5 km to the north-west, east side of the road (at 200 m), on a small terrace overhang overlooking by 2–3 m the swampy edges of the Khānābād River, between the hamlet of Qal'acha and the village of Larkhabi.

Dates: Achaemenid, 6th–4th cent. BC (A); Kushan, 1st–4th cent. (A, B); some Islamic sherds on B (ceramic).

Description: (A) of the mound indicated on the map, only a small hillock of 10 × 10 m remains, height 3 m, cut both by the Asqalān road to the east and by cultivated fields on the west. (B) Triangular mound with two sides oriented about north–south and east–west (60 m), and a hypotenuse curved north-west/south-east, on the south side (85 m); top at the north-west angle (5 m), gradual slope towards the south-east.

Collection: National Museum/AIA — sherds.

Fieldwork: 1978 Gardin et al., CNRS — survey.

Sources:
1. Site information by J.-C. Gardin.
2. Gardin and Lyonnet 1978–9: pl. VII — nos. 491–2.
3. Lyonnet 1997: figs 25, 35, 49 — nos. 491–2.
4. Gardin 1998: 80 — nos. 491–2.

157. CHAHĀRDEH, FARĀH

Original: Lat. 32° 27' N, long. 62° 04' E. Map 71.
Revised: 32.46545454 N, 62.06927219 E /
32° 27' 55.63633140 N, 62° 04' 09.37986636 E.
Farāh Province. 10 km north-west of this town, east of the ruin of Shar-i Kuhna.

Dates: Achamenid, 6th–4th cent. BC; Partho-Sasanian, 1st–4th cent.; pre-Mongol Islamic, 10th–13th cent. (ceramic).

Description: Mound of circular form, surrounded by a ditch, with steep slopes highly eroded into gullies.

Collection: National Museum/AIA — sherds.

Fieldwork: 1952 Le Berre and Gardin, DAFA — survey.

Source: M. Le Berre: unpublished 1952 report in DAFA archives, tepe Shindand-Farah 6.

158. CHAHĀRDEH, NANGAHĀR
Or PĪR KĀMAL BĀBĀ ZĪYĀRAT.

Original: Lat. 34° 18' N, long. 70° 48' E. Map 68.
Revised: 34.30661077 N, 70.79328697 E /
34° 18' 23.79875436 N, 70° 47' 35.83307760 E.
Nangahār Province. On the south bank of the Kābul River, 10 km north-west of Bāsawal.

Date: Kushan-Hunnic, 1st–6th cent. (architectural).

Description: On top of a hill overlooking the plain are the remains of a stupa. It is in very bad condition, with most of the faces fallen away. Construction is of diaper masonry. On the north and south sides of the stupa are remains of a monastery, with some cells still discernible. On the north side is a high fortification wall, and in the surrounding hills are artificial caves.

Sources:
1. Simpson 1879–80: 41–2 — description.
2. Leach 1880: 43 — mention.
3. Gazetteer 1910: IV. 425 — mention.

CHAHĀR DIWĀL. See 2022 in Supplement.

CHAHĀR QISHLĀQ. See 738 MULLĀH AFGHĀNĪ.

CHAHĀR SHANBEH TEPE. See 2023 in Supplement.

159. CHAHĀR SHAKHLAK

Original: Lat. 30° 57' N, long. 62° 04' E. Map 92.
Revised: 30.94447547 N, 62.06824539 E /
30° 56' 40.11170244 N, 62° 04' 05.68340256 E.
Nīmrūz Province. 7.5 km south-west of Zīyārat-i Amīrān Sāhib, 3 km west of Burj-i Samad.

Date: Sasanian, 3rd–7th cent. (ceramic).

Description: Ruins of a mud fort.

Fieldwork: 1960–70 Fischer, Bonn University — survey.

Source: Fischer et al. 1974–6: 38 — mention.

160. CHAHĀR TŪT
    Or MIN BASHI or MIR 'ALI KHAL.

Original: Lat. 36° 40' N, long. 69° 06' E. Map 32.
Revised: 36.66190843 N, 69.10462414 E /
36° 39' 42.87036276 N, 069° 06' 16.64689716 E.
Qundūz Province. 3 km south–south-west of Khānābād, by the road to Aliābād; on the edge of the road to the west, in front of the old school of the village of Chahār Tūt.

Dates: Kushan, 1st–4th cent.; pre-Mongol Islamic, 10th–13th cent. (ceramic).

Description: Place-name Min Bashi, or Mir' Ali Khal: fortified site (100 × 100 m), presently occupied by a cemetery. General shape square (100 × 100 m), marked by the remains of the wall (height 3 m), with a citadel projecting on the west side, also square (40 × 40 m, height of walls 6 m). A depression in the middle of the east wall possibly indicates the location of a gate, facing the citadel, in an approximately east–west line (in fact slightly out of line:

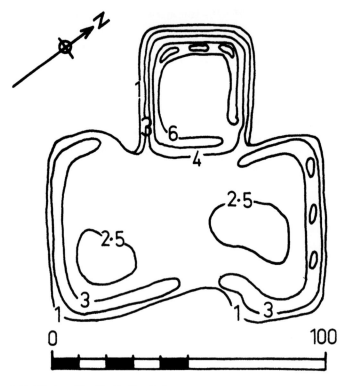

160   Chahār-Tūt (J.-C. Gardin).

west-north-west/east-south-east). The terreplein, *intra muros*, lies 1 to 2 m above the level of the plain, on the exterior; no recognizable structure is observable, but only two zones a little higher, in the north-east and south-east quadrants (separated by a road which crosses the site diagonally north-east/south-west), in relation to the lower part of the 'courtyard', to the west (1 m slope). Possible traces of redans on the north wall, but not convincing, as none are found on the other sides. In a cut of the north-east angle, over a length of 10 m, traces of a construction in mud-bricks 2 m high, on which rests an added earth talus.

Collection: National Museum/AIA — sherds;

Fieldwork: 1978 Gardin et al., CNRS — survey.

Sources:
1. Site information by J.-C. Gardin.
2. Gardin and Lyonnet 1978–9: pl. VII — no. 434.
3. Lyonnet 1997: fig. 49 — no. 434.
4. Gardin 1998: 78: 78 — no. 434.

CHAHIL. See 188 to 198 CHEHEL.

161. CHAI KHANJAR

Lat. 34° 59' N, long. 69° 36' E. Map 65.
Parwān Province. 2 km north-east of Mijrau Bāzār on the road from Gulbahār to Sarōbī.

Date: Kushan, 1st–3rd cent. (ceramic).

Description: A site consisting mainly of the surface scatter of plain red pottery with a hole dug by 'foreigners' (geologists?) in the back or mountain side.

Fieldwork: 1976 Kohl—survey.

Source: Information by P. L. Kohl.

162. CHĀ'ĪLA

Original: Lat. 36° 48' N, long. 68° 26' E. Map 36.
Revised:
36.79787983 N, 69.43317999 E / 36° 47' 52.36738728 N, 69° 25' 59.44797120 E (A).
36.80294319 N, 69.42636345 E / 36° 48' 10.59546708 N, 69° 25' 34.90842648 E (B).
Takhār Province. A dozen kilometres from Tāluqān, by the road which follows the Rūd-i Shāhrawān, at the level of the village of Cha'ila; the two tepes are on the north side of the road, one at 300 m (A), the other at 50 m (B). The first is located 500 m after the turn in the road at the passage of the Shuratu canal, coming from Tāluqān; the second is 700 m further, on the edge of the road.

Dates: Achaemenid, 6th–4th cent. BC (B); Hellenistic, 3rd–1st cent. BC (A, B); Kushan, 1st–4th cent. (B); pre-Mongol Islamic, 10th–13th cent. (ceramic).

Description: (A) Zone of mounds oriented north–south, separated by cultivated gullies (cotton): the visited tepe is the mound furthest to the west (80 × 50 m, height 5 m), occupied by a modern cemetery. (B) Conical mound (7 m) at the southern end of a low (2m) triangular platform, cut by cultivated fields (50 × 30 m).

Collection: National Museum/AIA—sherds.

Fieldwork: 1977 Gardin et al., CNRS—survey.

Sources:
1. Site information by J.-C. Gardin.
2. Gardin and Lyonnet 1978–9: pl. IX—nos. 252–3.
3. Lyonnet 1997: figs 25, 35, 39, 48—nos. 252–3.
4. Gardin 1998: 70—nos. 252–3.

163. CHAKANŪR, NANGAHĀR
Or BĀSAWAL.

Lat. 34° 17–28' N, long. 70° 53' E. Map 68.
Nangahār Province. On the north bank of the Kābul River opposite the town of Bāsawal, 50 km east of Jalālābād.

Date: Kushano-Sasanian, late 4th/early 5th cent. (stylistic).

Description: An artificial cave complex comprising some 150 chambers: assembly halls, cells, and circumambulatory *viharas*. In one chamber there are traces of a painting of Buddha. Outside some stone remains have been excavated, consisting of a possible assembly hall with five chapels. The finds included stucco statuary fragments and one Kharoshthi ostracron.

Collection: BM—excavated objects.

Fieldwork:
1. 1834 Masson—survey.
2. 1879 Swinnerton, Indian Army—survey.
3. 1965 Mizuno, Kyoto University—survey and excavation.

Sources:
1. Masson 1833a: 3—full description and sketch of the exterior of the caves and the environs.
2. Burnes 1834a: 121–2—brief description.
3. Masson 1840: 32—mention.
4. Moorcroft and Trebeck 1841: I. 356—mention
5. Masson 1842: II. 248–9—brief description.
6. Simpson 1882: 319–21—brief description.
7. Mizuno 1971: 101–11—description of the caves and summary report on the excavations, with many illustrations of both the site and the finds.
8. Davary 1977—mentions the inscription.
9. Errington 2017a: 138–9 and 2017b: 12, 16—the Masson collection and archive relating to the site.

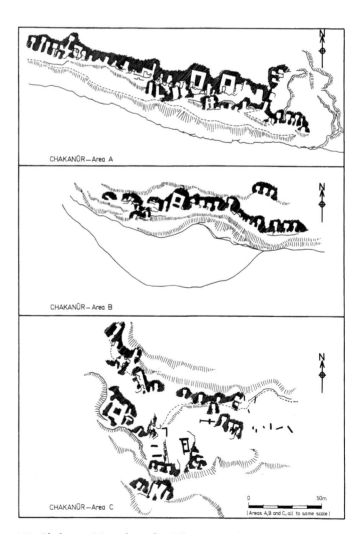

163 Chakanūr, Nangahār (after Mizuno 1971).

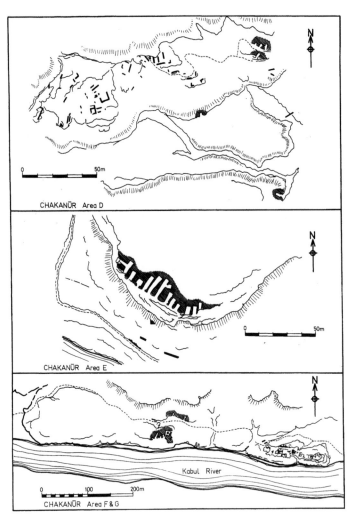

CHAKANŪR Area D

CHAKANŪR Area E

Kabul River

CHAKANŪR Area F & G

163 Continued

CHAKHĀNSŪR, Nīmrūz. See 2024 CHAKHĀNSŪR in Supplement.

164. CHAKHĀNSŪRAK
See also QAL'A-I NAU.

Original: Lat. 30° 59' N, long. 62° 05' E. Map 92.
Revised: 30.98991299 N, 62.07430466 E /
30° 59' 23.68676256 N, 62° 04' 27.49678860 E.
Nimrūz Province. 6 km due west of Zīyārat-i Amīran Sāhib, c.25 km south of Chakhānsūr.

Date: Mongol-Timurid, 13th–16th cent. (architectural, ceramic).

Description: Remains of a large ruined fortress (Fischer's Site 14). To the south are the remains of a series of pillars (Fischer's Site 13) with baked brick bases and mud-brick superstructures. They may have been parts of large enclosure walls.

Fieldwork:
1. 1936 Hackin and Meunié, DAFA—survey.
2. 1960–70 Fischer, Bonn University—survey.

Sources:
1. Sālnāma 1937/8: opp. 228—photos of the citadel.
2. Fischer 1971b: 44 and 46—description and photos.
3. Fischer 1973c: 146—map reference.
4. Fischer et al. 1974–8: 33—mention.

165. CHAKHIL-I GHUNDI
See also 404 HADDA.

Original: Lat. 34° 33–36' N, long. 70° 29–48' E. Map 67.

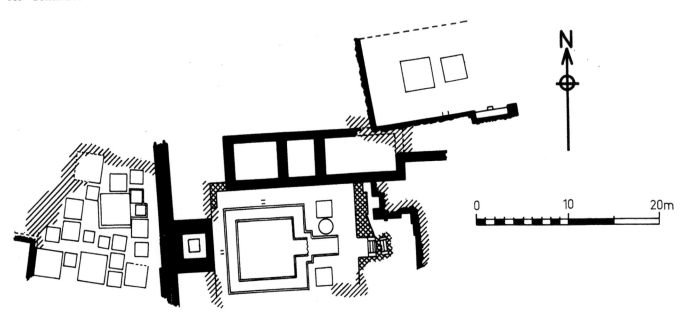

165 Chakhil-i Ghundi (after Barthoux 1933).

Revised: 34.36364875 N, 70.47641751 E /
34° 21' 49.13551188 N, 70° 28' 35.10304032 E.
Nangahār Province. 1.5 km north-east of the main Hadda complex, *c*.7 km south of Jalālābād.

Date: Kushan, Kushano-Sasanian, 2nd–5th cent. (stylistic).

Description: A stupa-monastery complex and associated habitation area, isolated on a small natural hill 17 m high. There was much stucco statuary and reliefs, with particularly elaborate façades on the votive stupas.

Collection: National Museum and Musée Guimet — objects from DAFA excavations.

Fieldwork: 1928 Barthoux, DAFA — excavations.

Source: Barthoux 1933a: 173–85 — description of the site and the art.

CHAKUR TEPE. See 450 ISHKILI.

166. CHĀL
Or CHĀR. Including KLOLA TEPE and TEMOR-SHO TEPE.

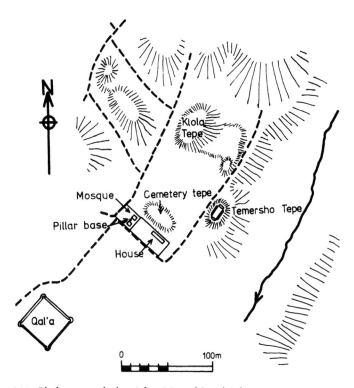

166 Chāl — general plan (after Hayashi and Sahara 1962).

Original: Lat. 36° 32–53' N, long. 69° 32–53' E. Map 37.
Revised: 36.52991327 N, 69.53929983 E /
36° 31' 47.68777416 N, 69° 32' 21.47937216 E.

Takhār Province. *C*.28 km north-east of Ishakamish on the route to Farkhar.

Description: In the mosque in the village is a reused column base of uncertain date. Nearby are two mounds, both small and irregular. Very few sherds, so no dating was possible.

Fieldwork: 1960 Hayashi and Sahara, Kyoto University — survey.

Source: Hayashi and Sahara 1962: 75–6 and 106 — plan of the area, brief description, and drawing of the column base.

CHALAP DALAN. See 188 CHEHEL ABDAL.

167. CHĀLGHŪR

Lat. 31° 32' N, long. 65° 33' E. Map 89.
Kandahār Province. 12 km east of Panjwāyī, 2 km west of Sa'id Qal'a Tepe.

Dates: Sasanian, 3rd–7th cent.; Turki Shahi–early Islamic, 8th–13th cent. (ceramic).

Description: None available.

Fieldwork: 1950–1 Fairservis, AMNH — survey.

Source: Fairservis 1971: 394 — mention (Khr–9).

CHĀMAN. See 1108 SPĪN BALDAK.

CHĀMAN-I HAUZURI. See 483 KĀBUL.

168. CHAMBĀRA

Original: Lat. 32° 50' N, long. 67° 49' E. Map 79.
Revised: 32.84336486 N, 67.83470014 E /
32° 50' 36.11349204 N, 67° 50' 04.92049752 E.
Ghazni Province. 5 km north-east of Muqqur, to the south-east of the main Kābul-Kandahār road.

Dates: Sasanian, 3rd–7th cent.; Turki Shahi–early Islamic, 8th–13th[h] cent. (ceramic).

Description: Several mounds.

Fieldwork:
1. 1966 Fischer, DAAD survey.
2. 1975 Taddei and Verardi, IsMEO — survey.

Sources:
1. Fischer 1967a: 165 — mention.
2. Fischer 1969: 339 — mention.
3. Verardi 1977a: 149 — mention.

CHAMBAR QAL'A. See 2025 in Supplement.

169. CHAM QAL'A, BAGHLĀN
Or SHAM QAL'A.

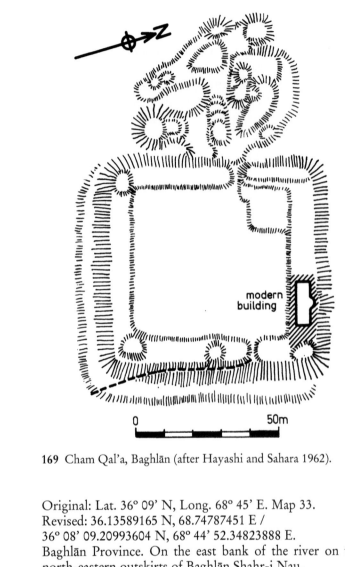

169 Cham Qal'a, Baghlān (after Hayashi and Sahara 1962).

Original: Lat. 36° 09' N, Long. 68° 45' E. Map 33.
Revised: 36.13589165 N, 68.74787451 E /
36° 08' 09.20993604 N, 68° 44' 52.34823888 E.
Baghlān Province. On the east bank of the river on the north-eastern outskirts of Baghlān Shahr-i Nau.

Dates: Kushan, 1st BC–AD 3rd cent. (stylistic). Hunnic-Turk, 5th–9th cent. (ceramic).

Description: A square fortification mound, *c.*50m square, with the remains of a gate or stupa on its north side. There is another mound to the west, possibly of a monastery.

From the site was an accidental discovery of Buddhist bas-reliefs and four limestone capitals from corner pilasters, with a lion-griffin motif.

This site has been extensively pillaged. In *c.*1996 monumental material from this site was being offered for sale in Balkh, including two of the finely carved capitals and pilasters.

Fieldwork:
1. 1946 Wheeler, ASI—reconnaissance.
2. 1960 Hayashi and Sahara, Kyoto University—survey.

Sources:
1. Gardin and Lyonnet, 1980 chronological study of unpublished pottery from DAFA surveys.
2. Additional information by Jonathan L. Lee, from a visit in 1998.
3. Shakur 1947: 44–5—brief description.
4. Caspani and Cagnacci 1951: 264—mention the site and finds.
5. Kohzad 1958/59: 26—mention.
6. J. C. Courtois 1961: 26—mention.
7. Hayashi and Sahara 1962: 67–8—summary in Japanese.
8. Dagens 1964a: 37–9—description of the capitals.
9. Rowland 1966a: 27—photo and brief introduction to one of the capitals.
10. Levi 1972: 130—brief description.
11. Staviski 1973—discussion of the typological links with other capitals from Central Asia.
12. N. Dupree et al. 1974: 12—description of the objects on display in the National Museum.
13. Tissot 2006: 95–6—National Museum catalogue details and photos.

170. CHANWAR

Lat. 33° 38' N, long. 69° 09' E approximately. Map 82.
Paktiyā Province. C.10 km north-west of Gardēz.

Date: Kushan-Sasanian, 1st–7th cent. (ceramic).

Description: Some ruins and a wide scatter of pottery. One sherd has a stamped motif of a Bactrian camel.

Fieldwork: 1966 Fischer, DAAD—survey.

Sources:
1. Fischer 1967a: 168—mention and photo of the sherd.
2. Fischer 1969: 341—brief summary and photo of sherds.

CHAPAR QISHLAQ. See **89 BAHĀRAK** and **ŪCH ĀRIQ.**

171. CHAPCHAL
See also 249 DARRA-I SŪF.

Lat. 36° 01' N, long. 67° 11' E. Maps 30, 47.
Balkh Province. In the Darra-i Sūf 19 km north-west of Qal'a-i Darra-i Sūf.

Description: A group of artificial caves, an extension of and similar to the main Darra-i Sūf series.

Fieldwork: 1886 Amir Khan, Griesbach, ABC—topographical surveys.

Sources:
1. Amir Khan 1888: 160—mention.
2. Griesbach 1888b: 204—mention.

CHAPU. See 558 KHARĀBA-I IDUKHĀN.

172. CHAQALAQ TEPE
Including PAIWAN TEPE.

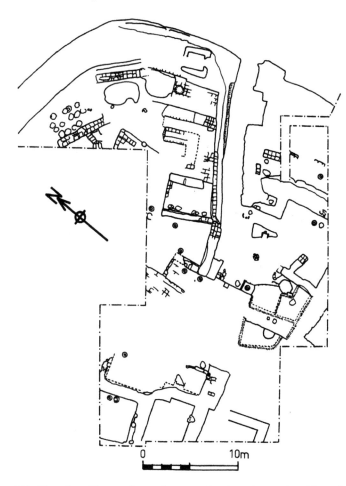

172 Chaqalaq Tepe—plan of upper levels (after Higuchi and Kuwayama 1970).

Original: Lat. 36° 39' N, long. 68° 50' E. Map 32.
Revised: 36.63177805 N, 68.83159444 E /
36° 37' 54.40099764 N, 68° 49' 53.73998040 E.
Qundūz Province. 11 km south of Qundūz, north of Cha-hār Deh, off the track to Tāshqurghān. 3 km south-east of Dūrman Tepe.

Dates: Graeco-Bactrian, 3rd–1st cent. BC. (stylistic); Kushan, 1st–3rd cent. (stylistic); Kushano-Sasanian, 4th–5th cent. (numismatic, stylistic); Turk, 7th–8th cent. (ceramic, numismatic).

Description: A fortified village surrounded by two enclosure walls. Excavations revealed about one-eighth of the upper area of the mound. Structures included a fragmentary stupa, and various irregular rooms. Finds included some limestone Buddhist sculptures and pillar bases, and 15 coins.

Adjacent is another very low mound called Paiwan Tepe.
Fieldwork: 1964, 1965, and 1967 Higuchi and Kuwayama, Kyoto University—excavations.
Sources:
1. Kuwayama 1969—examination of the pillar bases and amphorae, and their relation to the Hellenistic world.
2. Higuchi and Kuwayama 1970—fully illustrated summary report on the excavations, ceramics, coins, and other finds.
3. Higuchi 1972—very brief summary of the excavations and finds.
4. Higuchi 1974b: 117—very brief report.
5. Kuwayama 1974b—discusses the dating evidence for Chaqalaq III.
6. H. Motamedi 1975c: 252–5—summary of the excavations.
7. Tissot 2006: 102–4—National Museum catalogue details and photos.

CHĀR. See 166 CHĀL.

CHĀRBĀGH. See 2026 CHĀRBĀGH in Supplement.

173. CHĀR DARRA
Or MIRZA RAMAZAN TEPE. See also 313 EFENDI TEPE.

Original: Lat. 36° 44' N, long. 68° 44' E. Map 32.
Revised: 36.72643042 N, 68.72664583 E /
36° 43' 35.14950048 N, 68° 43' 35.92500132 E.
Qundūz Province. 12 km due west of Qundūz between Irganakh and the river.

Dates: Kushano–Sasanian, 1st–7th cent. (ceramic); Seljuk, 1048–73 (numismatic).

Description: A large, flat-topped mound, 25 × 20 m in area and 7 m in height. There are many more mounds in the vicinity containing mud-brick structures. In 1960 a hoard of 213 Ghaznavid and Seljuk gold dinars and some inlaid gold and silver jewellery was found at the site.

Collection: National Museum—coins.
Fieldwork:
1. 1955, 1960 Fischer, DAAD—survey.
2. 1960 Hayashi and Sahara, Kyoto University—survey.
Sources:
1. Hayashi and Sahara 1962: 73–4—photo and description in Japanese.
2. Sourdel-Thomine 1963–4—photos, inventory, and discussion of the coins.
3. Fischer 1969: 348—summary of the site.
4. Kalus 1979—discussion of this and other Islamic coin hoards in the National Museum.

174. CHĀR GALDAI

Original: Lat. 34° 69' N, long. 66° 36' E. Map 26.
Revised: 36.81998692 N, 66.60820644 E /
36° 49' 11.95289616 N, 66° 36' 29.54318256 E.
Balkh Province. 12 km east of Nimlik. North of the Balkh road, about 1 km south of the village of Dālbargān.

Description: Tepe of circular form (diam. *c.*80 m, height 14 m), surrounded by a ditch now filled with water. All around, a vast area of ruins.

Fieldwork: 1948 Le Berre, DAFA—survey.

Source: M. Le Berre: unpublished 1948 report, DAFA archives, tépé P. 37.

175. CHĀR GUL
Or KAR GUL.

Original: Lat. 36° 56' N, long. 68° 35' E. Map 32.
Revised: 36.93585045 N, 68.58714665 E /
36° 56' 09.06163764 N, 68° 35' 13.72793280 E.
Qundūz Province. In the village of Chār Gul, accessible by the track which follows the lower course of the Qundūz River, right bank, after its joining with the Khānābād River. The tepe is situated on the slopes which descend from the plateau of Chul-i Abdān towards the Qundūz River, 50 m north of a small overhang which circumvents the Yangi Araq canal, dug above the site on an older course.

Dates: Hunnic-Turk, 5th–9th cent.; pre-Mongol Islamic 10th–13th cent. (ceramic).

Description: Square platform, oriented north–south (40 × 40 m at the base), flat top, slightly depressed (30 × 30 m), height 5–6 m; slight overhang in the middle of the north-east and west sides, suggesting a redan, but not on the south (concave face, worn?).

Collection: National Museum/AIA—sherds.

Fieldwork:
1. 1975 Kohl—survey.
2. Gardin et al., CNRS—survey.

Sources:
1. Site information by J.-C. Gardin.
2. Kohl 1978: 68—brief description.
3. Gardin and Lyonnet 1978–9: pl. VI—no. 500.
4. Lyonnet 1997: figs 68, 69—no. 500.
5. Gardin 1998: 85—no. 500.

176. CHĀRIKĀR

Lat. 35° 01' N, long. 69° 10' E. Map 64.
Parwān Province. 63 km north of Kābul on the main road.

Dates: Indo-Greek, 2nd cent. BC; Kushano-Sasanian, 4th–5th cent. (numismatic).

Description: Several chance coin finds from here, mostly during the British occupation. There are also some fragments of steatite sculpture in a shrine.

Sources:
1. Masson 1842: III. 156—mentions the steatite.
2. Haughton 1948: 132—evaluation of the Haughton collection.
3. Jenkins 1959: 27—brief discussion of the Haughton collection.
4. Mac Dowall and Wilson 1960—discuss the evidence of the Apollodotus coins found.

177. CHARKHA
Or RABĀT-I CHIRKAH.

Original: Lat. 34° 26' N, long. 61° 37' E. Map 51.
Revised: 34.44353923 N, 61.60560319 E /
34° 26' 36.74123016 N, 61° 36' 20.17149876 E.
Herat Province. 66 km west of Herat on the road to Islām Qal'a, between Mamizak and Ruzanak.

Date: Timurid, 15th–16th cent. (ceramic).

Description: A ruined baked brick cistern and a scatter of baked bricks forming a vague square.

Fieldwork: 1977 Ball—survey.

Sources:
1. Maitland 1888a: 276—mentions ruined caravanserai.
2. Peacocke 1887a: 139—mention.

178. CHARKH-I FALAK

Original: Lat. 36° 45' N, long. 66° 57' E. Map 27.
Revised: 36.75380639 N, 66.9497149 E / 36° 45' 13.70300508 N, 66° 56' 58.97365584 E.
Balkh Province. 5 km east of Balkh on the old route to Mazār-i Sharīf.

Date: ?Sasanian, 3rd–7th cent. (architectural).

Description: Remains of a mud-brick stupa, consisting of a cylindrical drum resting on a square base. There are many more ruins stretching southwards.

Fieldwork:
1. 1922 Foucher, DAFA—survey.
2. 1946 Wheeler, ASI—reconnaissance.
3. 1956 Ramachandran and Sharma, ASI—reconnaissance.
4. 1960 Hayashi and Sahara, Kyoto University—survey.

Sources:
1. Maitland 1888b: 179—mention.
2. Foucher 1942–7: I. 59—mention.
3. Shakur 1947: 59—brief description.
4. Ramachandran and Sharma 1956: I. 22—mention.
5. M. N. Kohzad 1959: 1—mention.
6. Hayashi and Sahara 1962: 57, fig. 56—photo and summary in Japanese.

7. Melikian-Chirvani 1974: 5—mention as a 'Buddho-Muslim' site.

179. CHARKH-I LŌGAR

Original: Lat. 33° 48' N, long. 68° 57' E. Map 82.
Revised: 33.79697568 N, 68.94075869 E /
33° 47' 49.11244152 N, 68° 56' 26.73129732 E.
Lōgar Province. In the upper Lōgar Valley, c.12 km to the west of the Kābul-Gardēz road, c.80 km south of Kābul.

Date: Ghaznavid, 11th–12th cent. (stylistic).

Description: In the village is a modern mosque reusing an elaborately decorated wooden mihrab with a cusped horse-shoe arch niche head and wooden door, reported to have been brought from an earlier mosque in the village of Kachari, 3 km to the north.

Sources:
1. Bombaci 1959—very brief description.
2. Klimburg 1963: 34—very brief description.
3. Melikian-Chirvani 1977—photos with a short description and discussion.
4. Fischer 1978a: 313—description and photos.
5. Ball 2008: 178—summary.

180. CHĀR SANG TEPE
Or CHAHĀR SANG TEPE or SHAHR-I SANG.

Original: Lat. 31° 58' N, long. 65° 32' E. Map 89.
Revised: 31.96576897 N, 65.52301877 E /
31° 57' 56.76827868 N, 65° 31' 22.86757200 E.
Kandahār Province. In the Khākrīz Valley c.7 km north of Mundigak and 5 km east of Zīyārat-i Shāh Maqsūd.

Dates: Bronze Age, 2nd mill.BC; Hellenistic, 3rd–1st cent. BC; Indo-Parthian, 1st–4th cent.; pre-Mongol Islamic, 10th–13th cent. (ceramic).

Description: A medium sized circular mound c.100 m in diameter and 17 m in height. Eroded by a wadi or river on the north-eastern side.

Fieldwork:
1. 1951 Casal, DAFA—survey.
2. 1974 Swiny and Whitehouse, BIAS—survey.

Sources:
1. Site information by D. Whitehouse from unpublished report in BIAS archive.
2. Gardin and Lyonnet, 1980 chronological study of unpublished pottery from DAFA surveys.

181. CHĀSH BĀBĀ

Lat. 37° 29' N, long. 65° 45' E. Map 24.
Jauzjān Province. 4 km south of Khamiyāb on the Āmū Daryā.

Date: Neolithic, 8000–5000 BC (lithic).

Description: A high, isolated ridge with precipitous cliffs on the eastern and northern sides. On top is a surface scatter of stone tools.

Fieldwork: 1969 Vinogradov, Af/Sov. Mission—survey.

Source: Vinogradov 1979: 25—description and drawings of the material, with a photo of the ridge.

182. CHASHMA

Original: Lat. 36° 57'–36° 59' N, long. 69° 13'–69° 15' E. Maps 31, 35.
Revised:
Between 36.99562832 N, 69.25126819 E /
36° 59' 44.26196208 N, 69° 15' 04.56546636 E and
37.00224815 N, 69.25110329 E /
37° 00' 08.09333136 N, 69° 15' 03.97185264 E.
Qundūz Province. About 8 km south-south-west of Ārchī by the Qundūz road, forking at 5 km south-south-east to cross a bridge on the south branch of the Ārchī canal, to climb the terrace which edges the canal, south-east of the Ārchī plain. On all the surface of the terrace, up to the hills in the east and south, and up to the outskirts of the village of Wazīr Khān to the west, there are here and there areas of shallow undulations, covered in sherds which confirm the age of occupation on this plateau.

Dates: Hellenistic, 3rd–1st cent. BC; pre-Mongol Islamic, 10th–13th cent. (ceramic).

Description: Some ten sites have been surveyed; neither their exact situation, nor the description of each (the height of the undulations rarely reaches 1 m) are described here; retained only is the overall fact of the development of this zone of foothills in the Hellenistic period and in the first centuries of Islam, seen in the installation of particularly clever systems of irrigation (see Gardin and Lyonnet 1978–9).

Collection: National Museum/AIA—sherds.

Fieldwork: 1977 Gardin et al., CNRS—survey.

Sources:
1. Site information by J.-C. Gardin.
2. Gardin and Lyonnet 1978–9: pl. IV—nos. 48–58.
3. Lyonnet 1997: fig. 38—nos. 48–61.
4. Gardin 1998: 58—nos. 48–61.

183. CHASHMA-I KHŪNĪ

Lat. 33° 37' N, long. 64° 40' E. Maps 55, 74.
Ghūr Province. C.30 km north-east of Taiwāra, 1 km south-east of the road to Chakhcharān.

Date: Ghurid, 12th–13th cent. (stylistic).

Description: Remains of a large fort with many square towers. Construction is of mud on a stone foundation.

The walls contain elaborate plaster decoration of impressed triangles, floriations, and animal motifs.

Source: Klimburg 1960: 49–50 — photos and brief description of the remains.

184. CHASHMA-I MASHĀK

Original: Lat. 31° 57' N, long. 61° 46' E. Map 83.
Revised: 31.95853859 N, 61.76362069 E /
31° 57' 30.73891320 N, 61° 45' 49.03446888 E.
Nīmrūz Province. On the Farāh-Lāsh Juwain road, 31 km north of Lāsh Juwain.

Date: Early Islamic, 8th–13th cent. (ceramic).

Description: Some mud remains, probably of a caravanserai, with a depression marking a possible cistern.

Collection: National Museum — sherds.

Fieldwork: 1960–70 Fischer, Bonn University — survey.

Source: Fischer et al. 1974–6: 35 — mention.

185. CHASHMA-I OBEH
See also 2076 GHĀR-I KARŪKH in Supplement.

Lat. 34° 26' N, long. 63° 07' E. Map 53.
Herat Province. In the foothills of the Band-i Bādghīsāt 11 km north-west of Obeh, 107 km east of Herat.

Description: A series of thermal springs and a *zīyārat*, with several more graves and irregular stone constructions. Remains of a small settlement nearby.

(Note: the site catalogued under Chashma-i Obeh in the first edition was incorrect; that now appears as 2076 Ghār-i Karūkh in the Supplement.)

Fieldwork: 2005 Franke and Urban, DAI — survey.

Source: Franke and Urban 2006: 18 — brief description; fig. 23 — photo.

CHASHMA-I QAINAR. See 791 PAKHRAK.

186. CHASMA-I SHAFĀ
Or CHASHMA-I SHIFĀ.

Original: Lat. 36° 33' N, long. 66° 58' E. Map 28.
Revised: 36.55557885 N, 66.97305851 E /
36° 33' 20.08385064 N, 66° 58' 23.01063960 E.
Balkh Province. C.15 km south of Pul-i Imāmbukri, located on the northern exit of the Balkh Āb gorge as it breaks through the Alburz Hills on the Balkh-Āq Kupruk road.

Dates: Achaemenid, 6th–4th cent; Kushan, 1st–3rd cent; Kushano-Sasanian, 3rd–5th cent; Ghurid, 12th–13th cent (ceramic).

Description: The remains of a substantial city of the Achaemenid period has been recorded and some excavations carried out, possibly the site of ancient Zariaspa. Remains include a monumental fire temple that included a large limestone fire altar in the form of an inverted step-pyramid 2.10 m in height and with a top surface of 2.65 × 1.60. A hollow in the centre is believed to have been for the sacred fire. This is one of the oldest fire temples recorded, and has implications for the development of Zoroastrianism. Remains of an ancient fort on top of a hill. A domed baked brick structure on the left bank of the Balkh River, originally a shrine and bath house (*hammam*) built over a thermal spring (*shifā*, 'healing spring') which collapsed in the mid-1990s.

Fieldwork:
1. 1885 Maitland, ABC — topographical survey.
2. 1994, 2005 Lee — reconaissances.
3. 2008 Besenval and Marquis, DAFA — excavations.

Sources:
1. Additional information on the hammam by Jonathan L. Lee.
2. Maitland 1888b: 66 — mention.
3. Stuckert 1994: 94 — sketch of the Timurid buildings.
4. Besenval and Rassouli 2010 — brief description of the excavations.
5. Bendezu-Sarmiento and Marquis 2015: 105 — bird's-eye view of the site.

CHASHMA-I SHIR. See 1123 SURKH KOTAL.

187. CHĀYĀB
Or QAL'A-I BĪN.

Original: Lat. 37° 25' N, long. 69° 49' E. Maps 35, 38.
Revised: 37.39897952 N, 69.81080211 E /
37° 23' 56.32627992 N, 69° 48' 38.88760716 E.
Takhār Province. On the outskirts of the village of Chāyāb, on the western edge of the road which leads from the Chāyāb towards the north.

Dates: Pre-Mongol Islamic, 10th–13th cent.; Timurid and post-Timurid, 15th–17th cent. (ceramic).

Description: Qal' a-i Bīn: rectangular fortification (east–west, 40 × 30 m), flanked on the east by a small square citadel (20 × 20), in the continuation of the south side. The wall and the talus are preserved to a height of 6 m above ground level; a ditch 4 to 5 m wide surrounds all the construction, occupied today by small irrigation streams. Inside the rectangular enclosure, the ground surface is depressed: houses were built (ruins in the south-west), the land was cultivated. Access was probably through a gate situated in the east, by the north wall of the citadel. The top of the citadel (height 4 m) is flat, occupied by a house in the south-east angle; a natural cut in the east shows that the talus is in *pakhsa*, without the use of bricks. Other cuts in the north, as well as the supposed location of the gate (north-east), reveal thick layers of burnt rubble (charcoal, bricks, reddened earth), up to a metre beneath the present top of the rampart.

Collection: National Museum/AIA—sherds.

Fieldwork: 1978 Gardin et al. CNRS—survey.

Sources:
1. Site information by J.-C. Gardin.
2. Gardin and Lyonnet 1978–9: pl. II—no. 536.
3. Gardin 1998: 90—no. 536.

188. CHEHEL ABDAL
Or CHALAP DALAN.

Original: Lat. 33° 37' N, long. 64° 23' E. Maps 54, 55, 74.
Revised: 33.6244312 N, 64.45665777 E /
33° 37' 27.95230488 N, 64° 27' 23.96797344 E.
Ghūr Province. C.12 km due north of Taiwāra at the end of the Suri Valley.

Description: Remains of a citadel at the foot of the mountain of Chehel Abdal.

Fieldwork:
1. 1885 Imam Sharif, ABC—topographical survey.
2. 1946 Kohzad, HSA—survey.

Sources:
1. Holdich 1887: 26—mention.
2. Imam Sharif 1891a: 206—mention.
3. Kohzad 1951–4, 8/4: 63 and 65—mention.

189. CHEHEL BURJ, BĀMIYĀN
Or SHAHR-I BARBAR.

Original: Lat. 34° 55–59' N, long. 66° 23–37' E. Map 47.
Revised: 34.91789808 N, 66.61879461 E /
34° 55' 04.43308692 N, 66° 37' 07.66059780 E.
Bāmiyān Province. In the Band-i Amīr River Valley, 45 km north-west of Yakaulang.

Date: Turki Shahi (stylistic); Ghurid, 12th–13th cent. (architectural).

Description: Remains of a huge fortress commanding a fork in the road, consisting of three lines of walls completely surrounding a hill. The walls are reinforced by over more than 40 large towers up to 20 m high, and have loopholes in

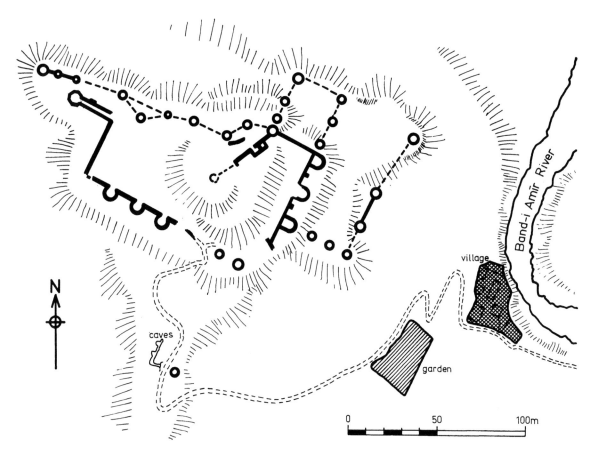

189 Chehel Burj, Bāmiyān (after Brett *et al.* 1970).

the form of long slits surmounted by three distinctive triangular openings. Construction is of mud-brick throughout on a stone foundation.

To the west are the possible remains of a small town or bazaar, enclosed by a wall. To the west and north-west are a number of artificial caves.

In 2000 wall paintings in the Sasanian style that appear to depict scenes from the *Shāh Nāma* (although they could have simply been court scenes or even religious motifs) were uncovered on the interior walls of the fortress, since badly damaged by looters.

Fieldwork:
1. 1885 Maitland, ABC—topographical survey.
2. 1970 Brett et al., Bristol University—survey.
3. 2000 Kluyver—survey.
4. 2002 Lee, Society for South Asian Studies—reconnaissance.

Sources:
1. Talbot et al. 1886: 330—fairly detailed description.
2. Maitland 1888a: 491–2—brief description.
3. Gazetteer 1910: IV. 91—brief description.
4. Holdich 1910: 257—mention.
5. Maricq and Wiet 1959: 84 and pls XV–XVI—brief mention and photos.
6. Brett et al. 1970: 34–6—detailed description with a plan and photos of the defences.
7. Francfort 1979a: 38—briefly describes the survival of Kushan military architecture in the fortifications.
8. Kluyver 2000: 2–4—detailed description of the paintings.
9. Lee 2006: 236–41—brief description of the fort and report on the paintings, with photos.
10. Ball 2008: 178—summary.

190. CHEHEL BURJ, SEISTAN

Original: Lat. 30° 56' N, long. 62° 07' E. Map 92.
Revised:
Between 30.94053274 N, 62.11289542 E /
30° 56' 25.91788164 N, 62° 06' 46.42350264 E,
30.93680197 N, 62.10894813 E / 30° 56' 12.48707760 N,
62° 06' 32.21325288 E,
30.93675628 N, 62.10649251 E / 30° 56' 12.32259324 N,
62° 06' 23.37304428 E,
30.93944419 N, 62.10614335 E / 30° 56' 21.99907032 N,
62° 06' 22.11607584 E and
30.94133307 N, 62.10228359 E / 30° 56' 28.79905200 N,
62° 06' 08.22093264 E.
Nīmrūz Province. 5 k m south of Zīyārat-i Amīrān Sāhib.

Dates: Indo-Parthian, 1st–3rd cent. (numismatic); Sasanian, 3rd–7th cent. (ceramic, stylistic); early Islamic, 7th–13th cent., and Mongol-Timurid, 13th–16th cent. (ceramic).

Description: An area of ruins consisting of: an immense medieval fortress (Fischer's Site 10) resting on a possibly

earlier mound; some very eroded pre-Islamic mud fortification walls forming a circle (Fischer's Site 11); a ruined square mud-brick tower with fortification walls and low mounds (Fischer's Site 9); and a line of fortifications to the north (Fischer's Site 12). The fortress consists of a courtyard *c.*170 m square surrounded by two-storey buildings and a gallery. The circular fortifications are covered in red spiral-burnished pottery, and in the early 20th century there were several chance finds of seals and Indo-Parthian coins.

Fieldwork:
1. 1903–5 Tate, SAC—survey.
2. 1936 Hackin and Meunié, DAFA—survey.
3. 1968 and 1970 Fischer, Bonn University—survey.

Sources:
1. Tate 1904: 667—mentions the seals.
2. McMahon 1906: 219—mention.
3. Tate 1910: 231–2—brief description and comparisons with Sar-o Tar.
4. Fischer 1969–70—photo of the remains.
5. Fischer 1970b: pl. 46—photo of the remains.
6. Fischer 1971a: pls 11 and 12—photos.
7. Fischer 1971b: 43–4—brief description with ground and aerial photos.
8. Fischer 1973c: 148—mention.
9. Fischer et al. 1974–6: 38—mention.
10. Klinkott 1982: 209–77—description of the fortifications.
11. Ball 2008: 179—summary.

CHEHEL DUKHTARĀN, Badakhshān. See 730 MUBARAK.

191. CHEHEL DUKHTARĀN, BALKH

Lat. 36° 43' N, long. 68° 56' E. Maps 37, 38.
Balkh Province. 3 km south-east of Balkh near Asyā-i Qunak on the road to Dehdādi.

Description: A large mound some 15 m high with traces of perimeter walls, ditch, and entrance way. An irregular mud-brick structure, possibly the remains of a stupa, located on the top of the mound covered by a modern shrine. Casual find of a Kushan coin (Vima Kadphises) was recovered from the site in 1978.

Fieldwork:
1. 1960 Hayashi and Sahara, Kyoto University—survey.
2. 1978 Lee—reconnaissance.

Sources:
1. Addional site information by Jonathan L. Lee.
2. Yate 1888: 260—brief description.
3. Foucher 1942–7: I. 69—mention.
4. Hayashi and Sahara 1962: 59 and fig. 69—photo and brief description in Japanese.

192. CHEHEL DUKHTARĀN, KĀBUL

Original: Lat. 34° 23' N, long. 69° 08' E approximately.
Map 62.
Revised: 34.38380732 N, 69.13359753 E /
34° 23' 01.70634300 N, 69° 08' 00.95111700 E.
Kābul Province. Just to the west of the main Kābul-Gardēz road, 48 km north of Pul-i Alam.

Dates: Kushan-Sasanian, 1st–7th cent.; Timurid, 15th–16th cent. (ceramic).

Description: Three mounds.

Sources:
1. Fischer 1967a: 167—mention.
2. Fischer 1969: 341—mention as Site A8.

193. CHEHEL DUKHTARĀN, KUSHK

Original: Lat. 35° 07' N, long. 62° 19' E. Map 43.
Revised: 35.11628237 N, 62.31795504 E /
35° 06' 58.61653956 N, 62° 19' 04.63814076 E.
Herat Province. On the east side of the Kushk River, 100 km north of Herat on the road to the Turmenistan border.

Description: A large cemetery and some baked brick ruins. There are also remains of a baked brick bridge over the Kushk Rūd.

Fieldwork: 1884–6 Maitland and Peacocke, ABC—topographical survey.

Sources:
1. Maitland 1888a: 170—brief description. Some more ruins to south.
2. Peacocke 1887a: 179–80, 270, 273, 376—brief descriptions.
3. Gazetteer 1975: III. 78—mention.

194. CHEHEL DUKHTARĀN, QUNDŪZ

See also 930. QUNDŪZ. Including QARAWAL TEPE and ZARKHARID-I SULTĀN.

Original: Lat. 36° 44' N, long. 68° 51' E. Map 32.
Revised:
36.74779697 N, 68.85779723 E / 36° 44' 52.06909848 N, 68° 51' 28.07001720 E (A).
36.75469782 N, 68.83558539 E / 36° 45' 16.91215452 N, 68° 50' 08.10738888 E (B).
36.73392194 N, 68.85224751 E / 36° 44' 02.11898436 N, 68° 51' 08.09102088 E (C).
Qundūz Province. Isolated tepes in the west sector of the Bālā Hisār of Qundūz, at less than 3 km. (A) 1 km to the west-north-west, on the edge of the Asqalān road, the first tepe corresponds to the mound of 3 m on the 1:100,000 map, 100 m north of this road. The second mound of 3 m

indicated towards the south-west, near the village of Qarawal Tepe, is no more than a hillock some 10 m in diameter, in the process of being erased by cultivation; not surveyed. (B) The second tepe is 1.9 km further, cut in two by the same road: cemetery of the neighbouring village of Zarkharīd-i Sultān, both sides of the road. (C) the third tepe is in a residential area north-west of Qundūz, Chehel Dukhtarān, 700 m south-west of the western end of the Bālā Hisār; also occupied by a cemetery.

Dates: Achaemenid, 6th–4th cent. BC; Kushan and Hunnic-Turk, 1st–9th cent.; Timurid, 15th–16th cent. (ceramic).

Description: (A) Oblong mound oriented about east–west (40 × 30 m), irregularly cut by cultivation, especially the west side (the sherds extend up to 50 m from the tepe, in the fields of maize and cotton); flat top (5m), tombs on the north face. (B) Oblong north–south mound (100 × 30 m, height 2.5 m), cut in two by the Qundūz road, and occupied today by a cemetery, on the two halves of the site; sherds are particularly abundant at the bottom of small canals which flow at the foot of the north mound. (C) High mound exploited as a source of clay, whose present shape, in plan, is that of a gourd oriented south-east/north-west (c.80 × 100 m), with the top in the south-east; two high points dominate the mound, one in the south-east (10 m, steep slopes), the other in the south-west (6 m, gentler slopes). In the cuts of the north-east face, large construction in *pakhsa*, 6 m high, surmounted by mud-bricks to a height of 2 m.

Collections: National Museum/AIA—sherds.

Fieldwork:
1. 1946 Wheeler, ASI—reconnaissance.
2. 1955, 1960 Fischer, DAAD—survey.
3. 1960 Hayashi and Sahara, University of Kyoto—survey.
4. 1978 Gardin et al., CNRS—survey.

Sources:
1. Site information by J.-C. Gardin.
2. Shakur 1947: 49—brief description
3. Caspani and Cagnacci 1951: 266—mention.
4. Fischer 1961a: 18—brief description and photo of Chehel Dukhtarān only.
5. Hayashi and Sahara 1962: 73, fig. 79—photo and description in Japanese of Chehel Dukhtarān only.
6. Fischer 1969: 349—brief summary.
7. Gardin and Lyonnet 1978–9: pl. VII—nos. 495–7.
8. Lyonnet 1997: figs 25, 35, 49, 68, 69—nos. 495–7.
9. Gardin 1998: 79—nos. 495–7.

195. CHEHEL GAZARI

Lat. 34° 06' N, long. 64° 32' E. Map 55.
Ghūr Province. 17 km west of Guzarpām on the road from Chakhcharān to Shahrak.

Date: Ghurid, 12th–13th cent. (architectural).

Description: A fortified area consisting of three conical towers.

Fieldwork:
1. 1884–5 Maitland and Talbot, ABC.
2. 1946 Kohzad, HSA—survey.

Sources:
1. Maitland 1888a: 372—mention in general terms. Notes strategic siting.
2. Trinkler 1928: 70—mention.
3. Kohzad 1951–4, 8/4: 62—mention.
4. Fischer 1978a: 335—mention.

CHEHELGHAR GHUNDAI. See 968 SA'ID QAL'A TEPE.

196. CHEHEL KAND

Lat. 37° 01' N, long. 73° 25' E. Map 40.
Badakhshān Province. In Wākhān, 4 km west of Sarhad towards Ptukh.

Description: Some petroglyphs and Persian graffiti on rocks to the north of the village.

Fieldwork: 1975 Gratzl et al.—survey.

Source: Gratzl et al. 1978: 334–6—description, drawings, and translations.

CHEHEL MAZĀR. See 208 CHILLA MAZĀR.

197. CHEHEL MIRĪZ

Original: Lat. 30° 14' N, long. 62° 08' E. Map 95.
Revised: 30.2292963 N, 62.14250818 E / 30° 13' 45.46667604 N, 62° 08' 33.02945916 E.
Nīmrūz Province. C.5 km east of Chahārburjak on the Helmand, opposite Ashkīnak.

Dates: Late Parthian-early Sasanian, 2nd–3rd cent. (ceramic).

Description: A round fort belonging to late Parthian and early Sasanian times. On the rolling *dasht* south of the Helmand, and close to an ancient canal paralleling the course of the river. Complex structure fills most of the area inside the walls.

Fieldwork:
1. 1884 Peacocke, Maitland, ABC—topographical survey.
2. 1971–4 Trousdale, Smithsonian—survey.

Sources:
1. Site information by W. Trousdale.
2. Peacocke 1885a: 4—mention.
3. Tate 1910: 148 and 241—mention.
4. Maitland 1888a: 63 and 64—mention.
5. Peacocke 1887a: 18—mention.

198. CHEHELTĀN

Lat. 34° 32' N, long. 68° 59' E. Map 63.
Kābul Province. In the centre of the plain, 13 km west of Kūt-i Sangi on the outskirts of Kābul.

Description: A very famous cave shrine, said to be the site of a pre-Buddhist sacred place.

Sources:
1. Masson 1842: II. 226—mention.
2. Caspani 1947b: 49—mention.
3. Lindberg 1949: 41—description.

199. CHICHAKTU
Or QAL'A-I ISFANDIAR.

Original: Lat. 35° 43' N, long. 64° 07' E. Map 45.
Revised: 35.71405631 N, 64.11011392 E /
35° 42' 50.60272392 N, 64° 06' 36.41009760 E.
Faryāb Province. On the south side of the valley 8 km west of Qaisar, on the Maimana-Bālā Murghāb road.

Description: Some ruins: site of a large city marked by about six large mounds.

Fieldwork: 1885 Maitland and Peacocke, ABC—topographical survey.

Sources:
1. Peacocke 1887a: 114 and 240—mention.
2. Maitland 1888b: 114—mention.

CHĪCHKA. See 917 QARLUQ.

CHIGHA SARĀĪ. See 154 CHAGHĀN SARĀĪ.

200. CHĪGĪNĪ 1

Lat. 30° 59' N, long. 62° 02' E. Map 92.
Nīmrūz Province. 23 km east of Zaranj, 1 km north-west of the road to Chakhānsūr.

Date: Timurid, 15th–16th cent. (ceramic).

Description: The remains of a house with an intact dome-chamber. Construction is of mud-brick with baked brick decoration.

Fieldwork: 1960–70 Fischer, Bonn University—survey.

Source: Fischer et al. 1974–6: pl. 114—photos.

201. CHĪGĪNĪ 2
See also 839 QAL'A-I CHĪGĪNĪ and 894 QAL'A-I ZARĪN.

Original: Lat. 31° 00' N, long. 62° 01' E. Map 92.

Revised: 30.99313998 N, 62.03707704 E /
30° 59' 35.30391108 N, 62° 02' 13.47736200 E.
Nīmrūz Province. On the edge of the Hāmūn 10 km
south-west of Qal'a-i Chigīnī and 25 km south of
Chakhānsur.

Date: Early Islamic, 8th–13th cent. (architectural).

Description: A deserted town containing several well-preserved houses. The most impressive one is a large *iwān* courtyard house, with a spacious vaulted *iwān* hall. The façade on either side of the hall is decorated in blind horseshoe arch decoration, the whole effect being very reminiscent of Ctesiphon (Fischer's Site 15).

Fieldwork:
  1. 1903–5 Tate, SAC — survey.
  2. 1936 Hackin and Meunié, DAFA — survey.
  3. 1970 Fischer, Bonn University — survey.

Sources:
  1. Tate 1910: 160 and 254 — brief description and photo.
  2. Hackin 1959c: figs 100–104 — photos of the remains.
  3. Fischer 1970a — photos of the remains.
  4. Fischer 1970b: pls 43–5 — photos of the remains.
  5. Fischer 1971a: 50 — brief description and photos.
  6. Fischer 1971b: 45 — photos and summary of its ruin type.
  7. Fischer 1972 — compares the *iwān* with Parthian origins.
  8. Behrens and Klinkott 1973 — architectural analysis of the *iwān* house and discussion of its typology.
  9. Fischer 1973c: 145 — mention.
  10. Fischer et al. 1974–6: 33 and pls 107–13 — mention and photos of the *iwān* house.
  11. Fischer 1978a: 378 — mention and photo.
  12. Klinkott 1982: 142–209 — description of the *iwān* houses.
  13. Ball 2008: 179 — summary.

CHILA GUR TEPE. See 968 SA'ID QAL'A TEPE.

CHILANG. See 2027 CHILANG in Supplement.

202. CHILIK-I QUL

Lat. 37° 08' N, long. 66° 10' E. Maps 24, 25.
Jauzjān Province. On the south edge of the dunes *c.*22 km north of Āqcha, 14 km east of Sayyidābād and 6–6.5 km north of the village of Chilik-i Qul.

Date: Neolithic, 7th–6th mill. BC (lithic).

Description: A surface site with a large number of stone tools scattered over an area of several kilometres.

Fieldwork: 1976 Vinogradov, Af/Sov. Mission — survey.

Source: Vinogradov 1979: 35 — general discussion of the lithic assemblage from the survey with comparisons in Soviet Central Asia (Sites 411–17).

203. CHILIK-I YALDASH

Lat. 37° 05' N, long. 66° 16' E. Maps 24, 25.
Jauzjān Province. On the southern edge of the dunes *c.*20 km north-east of Āqcha and 12 km west of the Dashli Oasis. 2.5–3 km north of the village of Chilik-i Yaldash.

Date: Neolithic, 7th–6th mill. BC (lithic).

Description: A surface site.

Fieldwork: 1976 Vinogradov, Af/Sov. Mission — survey.

Source: Vinogradov 1979: 32 — description and drawings of the material (Site 407).

204. CHILIK-I YASS KHĀN

Lat. 37° 06'–37° 07' N, long. 66° 14' E. Maps 24, 25.
Jauzjān Province. On the southern edge of the dunes 2 km north of the village of Chilik-i Yass Khān, *c.*20 km north-east of Āqcha and 15 km west of the Dashli Oasis.

Date: Neolithic, 7th–6th mill. BC (lithic).

Description: Two surface sites covering large areas *c.*1.5 km apart.

Fieldwork: 1976 Vinogradov, Af/Sov. Mission — survey.

Source: Vinogradov 1979: 32–5 — description and drawings of the material (Sites 409 and 410).

205. CHILIK SARDĀBA

Original: Lat. 36° 56' N, long. 66° 19' E. Maps 24, 25.
Revised: 36.93691751 N, 66.3159783 E / 36° 56' 12.90303312 N, 66° 18' 57.52186812 E.
Jauzjān Province. On the Nahr-i Fatehābād 13 km west of Āqcha and 2 km south of Fatehābād.

Description: Ruins of a large domed cistern and a large mound of baked bricks, probably the remains of a caravanserai.

Fieldwork: 1886 Peacocke, ABC — topographical survey.

Sources:
1. Peacocke 1887a: 332 — brief description.
2. Gazetteer 1979: IV. 164 — brief description.

CHILANG. See 2027 in Supplement.

206. CHILING

Lat. 30° 17' N, long. 61° 28' E. Map 94.
Nīmrūz Province. In the Rūd-i Bīyabān 2 km north-west of Gīna.

Dates: Sasanian, 3rd–7th cent.; early Islamic, 8th–13th cent. (ceramic).

Description: Remains of a small rectangular building measuring *c.*18 × 30 m on a silt bluff, similar to though smaller than Tarākūn.

Fieldwork:
1. 1885 Merk, ABC—topographical survey.
2. 1951 Fairservis, AMNH—survey.

Sources:
1. Merk 1888: 27—mention.
2. Fairservis 1961: 63—brief description (Site RB 22).

207. CHILING SHĀH MARDĀN

Original: Lat. 33° 24' N, long. 64° 18' E. Map 74.
Revised: 33.3974893 N, 64.28715283 E /
33° 23' 50.96148756 N, 64° 17' 13.75017468 E.
Ghūr Province. On a hill 18 km due south-west of Taiwāra, to the west of the road to Zarnī.

Description: A pointed peak containing some rough rock-cut steps leading to a shrine on the summit where 'Ali is said to have fasted for 40 days.

Fieldwork: 1885 Imam Sharif, ABC—topographical survey.

Sources:
1. Holdich 1886: 5—mention.
2. Holdich 1887: 26—mention.
3. Imam Sharif 1891a: 207—mention.
4. Gazetteer 1975: III. 89—mention.

208. CHILLA MAZĀR
Or CHEHEL MAZĀR. See also 220 DĀG-I NĀSIR.

Original: Lat. 36° 43' N, long. 68° 54' E. Map 32.
Revised:
36.71814388 N, 68.89929588 E / 36° 43' 05.31797160 N, 68° 53' 57.46517916 E (A).
36.71977976 N, 68.89981892 E / 36° 43' 11.20715328 N, 68° 53' 59.34811488 E (B).
Qundūz Province. At about 3 km from Qundūz, by the Khānābād road, two tepes, one situated at 400 m (A), the other at 500 m (B) north of this road, corresponding to the two mounds on the 1:100,000 map north of the village of Chilla Mazār, without an indication of altitude.

Dates: Achaemenid, 6th–4th cent. BC; Hunnic-Turk, 5th–9th cent. (A); Timurid, 15th–16th cent. (ceramic).

Description: (A) Square north–south platform (50 × 50m) cut back in the north by irrigated fields (a modern cemetery protects the mound on the other sides); flat top in the northern half (2–3 m), raised in the southern half by an east–west rectangular structure which reaches 6 m in the south-east angle (*zīyārat*). (B) Oblong north-west/south-east mound (50 × 15 × 20 m) on a cliff overlooking by about 15 m a meander of the canal called Nahr-i Gau Kush, to the north-east; the highest part is the northern half (flat top, 8 m above the cultivated fields) from which the land slopes to the south to the base of the mound at 2–3 m. The mound is cut back on the south-west side by cultivated fields, and on the south-east by the Nahr-i Gau Kush. In the cuts, on the south, a wall in *pakhsa* visible over some 20 m rests on burnt layers (alternating ashes and earth) which descend to 70 cm from the present ground surface; in the north, similar burnt layers 4 to 5 m high, containing bones, pebbles, mud-bricks, and sherds.

Collections: National Museum/AIA—sherds.

Fieldwork:
1. 1955, 1960 Fischer, DAAD—survey.
2. 1978 Gardin et al., CNRS—survey.

Sources:
1. Site information by J.-C. Gardin.
2. Fischer 1961a: 18—brief description.
3. Fischer 1966: 25–6—photo and commentary on the architecture of Sasanian style suggesting Indo-Iranian contacts.
4. Fischer 1969: 349—brief summary.
5. Gardin and Lyonnet 1978–9: pl. VII—nos. 426–7.
6. Lyonnet 1997: figs 25, 35, 69—nos. 426, 427.
7. Gardin 1998: 77—nos. 426–7.

CHILSITŪN. See **2028 CHILSITŪN** in Supplement.

CHIM QAL'A. See **2029 CHIM QAL'A, Jauzjān** and **2030 CHIM QAL'A, Baghlān** in Supplement.

209. CHIM QURGHĀN

Original: Lat. 37° 07' N, long. 69° 20' E. Maps 31, 35.
Revised: 37.11792011 N, 69.32728061 E /
37° 07' 04.51239132 N, 69° 19' 38.21019348 E.
Qundūz Province. 15 km from Khwāja Ghar on the Imām Sāhib road; on the edge of the road, north side, on the left bank of the Āmū Dāryā.

Dates: Iron Age, 1700–800 BC; Kushan and Hunnic-Turk, 1st–9th cent.; a few Islamic sherds. (ceramic).

Description: Semi-circular enclosure resting against a terrace of the Āmū Dāryā (left bank), diam. *c.*800 m, height 3–4 m, with a small citadel in the centre, dominating the river. The traces of interior constructions have been razed

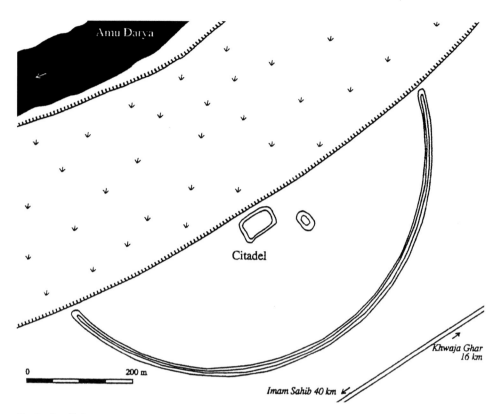

209 Chim Qurghān (J.-C. Gardin).

by cultivation, except for a mound in the east part, with jars in place which are still visible in the trenches of the bulldozer: the whole of the site served in 1977 as a source of material for repairing the nearby road.

Collection: National Museum/AIA—sherds.

Fieldwork: 1977 Gardin et al., CNRS—survey.

Sources:
1. Site information by J.-C. Gardin.
2. Gardin and Lyonnet 1978–9: pl. IV—no. 9.
3. Lyonnet 1997: figs 25, 35, 49, 68, 69—no. 9.
4. Gardin 1998: 55—no. 9.
5. Gardin 1995: 90–1—description and plan.

210. CHIM TEPE

Original: Lat. 36° 47' N, long. 68° 44' E. Map 32.
Revised: 36.77882043 N, 68.74590375 E /
36° 46' 43.75354044 N, 68° 44' 45.25348632 E.
Qundūz Province. About 13 km north-west of Qundūz, on the right bank of the Qundūz River, in the village of Chim Tepe. (A) The first tepe is the cemetery located at the entrance to the village, east side, 300 m north of a loop in the Qundūz River, on the slopes which dominate towards the east an old meander of this river (marshy zone below). (B) The second is 600 m further towards the west, 50 m south of the main street

of the village, on the edge of a terrace overlooking by some 10 m the same loop in the Qundūz River; a canal flows towards the north-west at the flank of this terrace.

Dates: Hellenistic, 3rd–1st cent. BC; Kushan, 1st–4th cent. (B); a few Islamic sherds (ceramic).

Description: (A) The development of the modern cemetery has erased or masked the possible traces of ancient structures; but sherds are abundant between the graves, over a surface of about a hectare. (B) Rectangular east–west mound (60 × 40 m), flat top, height 3 m in relation to the level of the terrace.

Collection: National Museum/AIA—sherds.

Fieldwork: 1978 Gardin et al., CNRS—survey.

Sources:
1. Site information by J.-C. Gardin.
2. Gardin and Lyonnet 1978–9: pl. VII—nos. 493 A, B.
3. Lyonnet 1997: figs 39, 49—no. 493.
4. Gardin 1998: 80—nos. 493 A, B.

211. CHĪNĪ KHĀN

Lat. 34° 45' N, long. 69° 10' E. Map 64.
Kābul Province. At the foot of the hills on the eastern side of the Kūh-i Dāman plain, 4 km east of Sara-i Khuja.

Description: An octagonal baked brick tomb, with a collapsed dome and four entrances. The inside walls have remains of relatively recent paintings and there is a gravestone dated 1211 AH. The building however appears much earlier. There is no mihrab.

Fieldwork:
1. 1834 Masson—survey.
2. 1925 Foucher, DAFA—survey.

Source:
1. Masson 1842: III. 145—brief description.
2. Foucher 1942–7: 144—mention.

CHĪN ZAI. See 674 LALM-I BUZ.

212. CHISHT

Lat. 34° 20' N, long. 63° 44' E. Map 54.
Herat Province. 17 km east of Obeh, in the valley of Tagau Chisht, on the road between Herat and Chakcharan.

Dates: Ghurid period, 12th cent. (architectural, decoration).

Description: Two monuments in brick, abundantly decorated, probably vestiges of a *madrasa* whose walls have disappeared. (A) One of them has a square plan (6.80 m per side), covered with a dome. Each interior face includes a wide niche covered by a pointed arch, of which the height almost reaches the drum of the dome, and flanked by two engaged columns. An octagonal plan is achieved through four pointed arches in the angles; the back of these arches is covered with 'little half-domes'. Where it springs above the drum, not high, the dome is an ellipse. A band of inscription in plaster, very well preserved, runs at the height of the column shafts, which have no capitals; another epigraphic band, of different moulding, decorates the arches. The south side is pierced by a door, the north and east sides by a wide bay; the east side also possesses a small opening in the wall of the drum.

The main façade, in the south, is laid with a geometric decoration in carefully cut and measured bricks, of which the upper part has completely disappeared. On each side of the door, a niche flanked by jambs; the east niche is surmounted by a slightly protruding pointed arch resting on two engaged colonnettes.

The whole is entirely covered by geometric decoration, except the upper part of the base of this niche, composed of a panel of inscription in one row. The west niche is less wide; the colonnettes are reduced to a slim quarter-circle without ornament. Its decoration is roughly similar to that of the east niche, but the panel inscription has two rows. The west jamb of this niche is reduced by half, and rests against the beginning of a wall perpendicular to the south façade, of which this is the only evidence.

(B) To the east of A, a monument also in fired bricks, of rectangular plan (8.11 × 5.60 m), entirely open on the south side, and partly covered by a dome resting on full walls, to the east and west, and on two arches, to the north and south. A mihrab is set at the centre of the west wall. The interior face of the arches is decorated with a geometric motif in bricks, edged by an ornate plaster moulding. This decoration stops on each side at a small epigraphic panel with one row. The drum of the dome is low, the spring of the dome perfectly round. The south arch carried by the jambs of which only a few fragments remain, carries a vertical epigraphic decoration of only one row.

The interior of the monument is well preserved, in spite of the collapse of the top of the dome. In the west wall, the mihrab has the form of a deep niche, of square plan at the base, covered by a protruding, raised arch; it is framed by a very full plaster decoration, which attempts to reproduce 'in lacework' the brick decoration of the interior face on the façade. On these two walls, at the base of the arches which support the dome, a moulded band surmounted by a sober decoration of shallow painted niches, topped by a protruding and raised pointed arch, which ties in with their flat ends. Each panel is composed of a central niche flanked on each side by a smaller niche, and surmounted by two others, very small. Each full face of the drum is also ornamented with two little niches.

Nothing else remains of this monument, but the north, east, and west walls show traces of prolongation in these three directions. The east wall is hollowed on the exterior with a niche that could be a second mihrab, of semi-cylindrical plan; its framing elements are destroyed.

Collection: National Museum/AIA—sherds.

Fieldwork:
1. 1885 Maitland, ABC—topographical exploration.
2. 1952 Le Berre and Gardin, DAFA—survey.
3. 1960 Le Berre, DAFA—architectural study.
4. 1978–9 Samizay, University of Kābul/UNESCO—survey.
5. 2005 Franke and Urban, DAI—survey.

Sources:
1. Site description unpublished report by M. Le Berre in DAFA archives.
2. Maitland 1888a: 351—brief description.
3. Le Strange 1905: 410–11—summary of the historical sources.
4. Niedemeyer and Diez 1924: 62 and pls 182–4—brief description and photos.
5. Kohzad 1951–4, 9/2: 20—brief description.
6. Maricq and Wiet 1959: 69–70—brief description.
7. Klimburg 1960: 50—photo and brief description.
8. Pugachenkova 1963: 98–9—general summary.
9. Hill 1966: 393–4—brief description.
10. Hill and Grabar 1967: pls 143–4—photos.
11. Seljuki 1967a: 153–7—photos and description (in Persian).
12. D. and J. Sourdel 1968: pls 78 and 189—photos and brief discussion.

MADRASA PLAN

MOSQUE PLAN

MADRASA SECTION

MOSQUE SECTION

0   10m

212 Chisht (after Samizay 1981).

13. Ghawwās 1969: 44—brief description.
14. Anand 1970: 24—brief summary and photos.
15. Hutt 1974: 170–1—brief discussion of the decoration.
16. N. Dupree 1977: 265–7—description and background.
17. *Kabul Times* 1979a—very brief report on the preservation work.
18. Rahīq 1979a—report on the conservation work carried out.
19. Samizay 1981: 16–19—description with illustrations of all remains, with a note on the conservation needs.
20. Aalund 1990: 13–15—brief assessment of conservation work required and photos.
21. Hillenbrand 2000—discussion in the broader context of Ghaznavid and Ghurid architecture.
22. Franke and Urban 2006: 5–8—detailed description with photos and plan of the *madrasa*.
23. Ball 2008: 120, 179–81—summary.
24. Abassi 2015: 218—photo of the new complete 'restoration' of the *madrasa* dome-chamber.

213. CHIT RABĀT KUHNA
Or KŪH-I CHATRĀBĀD.

Original: Lat. 36° 49' N, long. 67° 54' E. Map 29.
Revised: 36.81106552 N, 67.90892684 E /
36° 48' 39.83586624 N, 67° 54' 32.13661572 E.
Samangān Province. 24 km north-east of Tāshqurghān on the road to Khisht Tepe. The site is 13 km north-east of the village of Chit Rabāt.

Dates: Pre-Mongol Islamic, 10th–13th cent.; Timurid, 15th–16th cent. (ceramic).

Description: Considerable mud and mud-brick remains scattered about. Some are fortification walls, probably pre-dating the Uzbek invasion.

Fieldwork:
1. 1886 Maitland, ABC—topographical survey.
2. 1969 Gouin, DAFA—survey.

Sources:
1. Gouin, unpublished report in DAFA archives, site no. 34.
2. Gardin and Lyonnet: 1980 chronological study of unpublished pottery from DAFA surveys.
3. Maitland 1888b: 257—brief description.
4. Gazetteer 1979: IV. 166—brief description.

214. CHUBLUK TEPE

Lat. 37° 29' N, long. 65° 49' E. Map 24.
Jauzjān Province. On the banks of the Āmū Daryā 21 km north-west of Qarqīn, to the north of the road to Khāmiyāb.

Description: A long mound.

Fieldwork: 1886 Maitland, ABC—topographical survey.

Source: Maitland 1888b: 209—mention.

215. CHUGHA-I ULYĀ

Lat. 36° 44' N, long. 69° 12' E. Map 32.
Qundūz Province. About 10 km north-east of Khānābād, by the Tāluqān road: fork at Chugha-i Ulyā towards the bridge over the Tāluqān River which follows the old Tāluqān road, by the right bank. The site is located at the end of the steep spur which overlooks the river, at least 100 m south-east of the bridge.

Dates: Achaemenid, 6th–4th cent. BC; pre-Mongol Islamic, 10th–13th cent. (ceramic).

Description: No artificial mound is visible, but an area of sherds (50 × 50 m) on the flattened top of the spur (threshing floor), and in the lateral gullies. Remains of an older bridge oriented north-north-east, at least 100 m upstream.

Collection: National Museum/AIA—sherds.

Fieldwork: 1978 Gardin et al., CNRS—survey.

Source:
1. Site information by J.-C. Gardin.
2. Gardin and Lyonnet 1978–9: pl. VII—no. 446.
3. Lyonnet 1997: pl. VII—no. 446.
4. Gardin 1998: pl. VII—no. 446.

216. CHUGUR
Or CHOQOR.

Lat. 34° 37' N, long. 62° 05' E. Maps 43, 52.
Herat Province. 6.5 km south-west of Kush Rabāt, on the Galla Bid stream near Sinjidi.

Description: Reports of a ruined *rabāt* and the remains of a baked brick bridge.

Sources:
1. Maitland 1887c: 480—mention.
2. Gazetteer 1975: 81—mention.

217. CHŪLA

Original: Lat. 32° 44' N, long. 67° 50' E. Map 79.
Revised: 32.73276795 N, 67.83785272 E /
32° 43' 57.96461928 N, 67° 50' 16.26978588 E.
Ghazni Province. In a pass 12 km south-east of Muqqur on the road to Ab-i Istāda.

Date: Kushano-Sasanian, 1st–7th cent. (ceramic).

Description: Foundations of mud fortifications guarding the pass.

Fieldwork: 1966 Fischer, DAAD—survey.

Sources:

1. Fischer 1967a: 165—mention.
2. Fischer 1969: 340—brief summary (Site A3).

218. CHUL-I ABDĀN
Or ASQALĀN or DASHT-I ABDĀN or PUL-I ALCHIN.

Original: Lat. 36° 49' N, long. 68° 51' E. Map 32.
Revised: 36.81735363 N, 68.85291935 E /
36° 49' 02.47308348 N, 68° 51' 10.50966072 E.
Qundūz Province. 10 km north of Qundūz, by the road of Qizil Qal'a; after crossing the Khānābād River and the canal coming from the village of Baluch to the east, the road rises to a semi-desert plateau which extends to the west-north-west, above this canal (the Dasht-i Abdān). A tepe stands out on this plateau about 400 m west of the road, corresponding to the mound of 4 m on the 1:100,000 map, north of the village of Qungurāt; the mound of 3 m located 500 m from the preceding one, to the north-east, has disappeared, levelled by the recent construction of a large farm.

Dates: Bronze, end 3rd–beg. 2nd mill. BC; beg. Iron, end 2nd–beg. 1st mill. BC; Achaemenid, 6th–4th cent. BC; Hellenistic, 3rd–1st cent. BC (ceramic).

Description: Square mound, angles and sides rounded (30 × 30 m), flat top (4m), depressed in three points (clandestine excavations?). All around, over a radius of 100 m towards the north, the east and the south, area of habitation marked by low mounds (1–2 m) extending north-east and east–west, covered with sherds; these undulations extend further still, but are less evident (height less than 1 m), up to 300 m from the mound in the same directions. At this distance, to the east-north-east, there are traces of an ancient canal from the direction of the region of Baluch, which is discontinuous but certainly present over several kilometres towards the west-north-west, in the direction of Asqalān. Undulations similar to the preceding ones indicate areas of habitation, over all the extent of the Dasht-i Abdān (in Gardin and Lyonnet 1987–9 the beginnings of irrigation on this plateau, called the plateau of Asqalān, are dated to the pre-Hellenistic period: pp. 151–4, tables; the recent study of all the sherds collected on the Dasht-i Abdan, over some twenty sites, provides a date in the Bronze Age, in the second half of the 2nd millennium BC).

Collections: National Museum/AIA—sherds.

Fieldwork:

1. 1955, 1960 Fischer, DAAD—survey.
2. 1978 Gardin et al., CNRS—survey.

Sources:

1. Site information by J.-C. Gardin.
2. Fischer 1969: 350—mentioned as Tepe B 5.
3. Gardin and Lyonnet 1978–9: pl. VII—no. 471.

4. Lyonnet 1997: figs 13, 25, 35, 39—no. 471
5. Gardin 1998: 83—no. 471.

CHOR GUNBĀD. See **2031 CHOR GUNBĀD in Supplement.**

CHUNG-I DARAGZU. See **143 BURJ-I GHUNDA.**

CHURUK TEPE. See **2032 CHURUK TEPE in Supplement.**

DABAKH SAR. See **303 DUBAKH SAR.**

219. DAGHĀL-I DUKHTAR

Lat. 31° 23' N, long. 62° 28' E. Map 85.
Nīmrūz Province. C.20 km south-west of Pul-i Ghurghuri on the Khāsh Rūd, to the south of the road to Chakhānsur.

Date: Early Islamic, 8th–13th cent. (ceramic).

Description: Some ruins.

Fieldwork: 1960–70 Fischer, Bonn University—survey.

Source: Fischer et al. 1974–6: 32—mention (Ruin 7).

220. DĀG-I NĀSIR
See also 208 CHILLACHILLAA MAZĀR.

Original: Lat. 36° 42' N, long. 68° 54' E. Map 32.
Revised:
36.70874126 N, 68.90287347 E / 36° 42' 31.46851980 N, 68° 54' 10.34449020 E (A).
36.7117446 N, 68.90129488 E / 36° 42' 42.28056324 N, 68° 54' 04.66156260 E (A).
36.70674968 N, 68.8967749 E / 36° 42' 24.29883576 N, 068° 53' 48.38963208 E (B).
Qundūz Province. About 4 km from Qundūz, on the Khānābād road, several tepes in the process of disappearing between the road and the edge of the terrace which overlooks, 1 km to the south, the plain of Qundūz. The two highest correspond respectively to the mounds of 5 m (A) and 6 m (B) indicated on the 1:100,000 map, to the south-east and south-west of the village of Chilla Mazār.

Dates: Hunnic-Turk, 5th–9th cent.; Timurid, 15th–16th cent. (ceramic).

Description: (A) Oblong north-west/south-east mound (30 × 15 m), cut straight by irrigated fields; flat top (5 m); on all the perimeter, in the cuts, burnt layers appear from the present ground level up to a few centimetres from the top (alternating ashes and earth). 500 km to the north-north-west, on the edge of the Qundūz road (south side), oblong north–south mound (30 × 15 m), partly damaged by cultivation, flat top (3m). (B) Square north–south platform (20 × 20 m), undermined by cultivation, flat top (6 m); a local informant indicated the location, 100 m to the west, of a tepe which is today completely razed. 600 m to the south-south-east, on the edge of the terrace mentioned above (15 × 30 m above the plain of Qundūz), a small mound (diam. 20 m, height 5 m) and zones with sherds of the Kushan period.

Collection: National Museum/AIA — sherds.

Fieldwork: 1978 Gardin et al., CNRS — survey.

Sources:
1. Site information by J.-C. Gardin.
2. Gardin and Lyonnet 1978–9: pl. VII — nos. 422–5.
3. Lyonnet 1997: fig. 69 — nos. 422–5.
4. Gardin 1998: 77 — nos. 422–5.

DAHĀNA-I QISHLĀQ. See 981 SAMTI.

DAHĀNA KHUKKUSHTA. See 1075 SHĪBAR, west.

DAHĀNA KUTAK. See 1074 SHĪBAR, east.

221. DAHĀN-I ĀHANGARĀN

Lat. 34° 49' N, long. 67° 55' E. Map 58.
Bāmiyān Province. C.13 km east of Bāmiyān, opposite Tūpchi in the hills just to the north of the road to Shahr-i Zuhak.

Description: A few inaccessible caves.

Sources:
1. Masson 1839: 83 — mention.
2. Masson 1842: II. 379 — mention.

DAHĀN-I CHOQUR. See 2033 DAHĀN-I CHOQUR in Supplement.

222. DAHĀN-I DARRA
    See also 697 MAIMANA.

Lat. 35° 52' N, long. 64° 50' E. Map 24.
Faryāb Province. C.7 km south-east of Maimana on the road to Sar-i Hauz.

Description: Reports of a site where stone bowls and tools have been found.

Source: Report by Jonathan L. Lee.

DAHĀN-I GHŪRĪ. See 2034 DAHĀN-I GHŪRĪ in Supplement.

DAHĀN-I PALIZAK. See 820 PUL-I ZUHAK.

DAHĀN-I SAHRĀK. See 2035 DAHĀN-I SAHRĀK in Supplement.

DAHAN-I SHIR. See 1232 WAZĪRĀBĀD.

DAHĀN-I SIĀH BUMAK. See 2036 DAHĀN-I SIĀH BUMAK in Supplement.

DAHĀN-I TAMBURAK. See 2037. DAHĀN-I TAMBURAK in Supplement.

DAHĀN-I ZŪLFIQĀR. See 2038 DAHĀN-I ZŪLFIQĀR in Supplement.

223. DAI KUNDI

Lat. 34° 05' N, long. 66° 25' E. Map 56.
Ūruzgān Province. In the Hazārajat on the east bank of the Ab-i Baghāli Kundi, c.61 km south-west of Harkaul on the Panjau-Chakhcharān road.

Date: Turki-Hindu Shahi, 7th–10th cent. (stylistic).

Description: A bronze Hindu statue found at a site here.

Sources:
1. Gardiner 1853: 383–7 — a long, fanciful description of Hindu statuary in a cave near Dai Kundi.
2. Kohzad 1955b — photo of the statue on the front cover.

224. DAISHU
    Or DESHU. Including TANDURAK, MURTAZAH, KUHNA QAL'A.

Original: Lat. 30° 26' N, long. 63° 19' E. Map 98.
Revised: 30.43487874 N, 63.32804514 E /
30° 26' 05.56347444 N, 63° 19' 40.96251876 E.
Helmand Province. On the south bank of the Helmand, 12 km south-west of Malākhān and 13 km north of Khwāja 'Ali Bālā.

Dates: 1st mill BC, (C-14); Parthian, 1st–3rd cent. (architectural, ceramic); early Sasanian, 3rd–4th cent. (ceramic); Ghaznavid, 11th–12th cent. (ceramic).

Description: Extensive ruins of houses and towers, with a wide scatter of pottery. There are a number of ruins in the vicinity. The small square tower is called Tandurak, and is located on a bluff just south of the town. There is no clearly diagnostic ceramic near it. Within the town itself there is a single ruin of a fortified structure, a so-called 'dwelling tower' of Parthian period design, heavily rebuilt in Ghaznavid times.

It is called Murtazah. Within the flood plain to the north-west of the town are several tepes. The one closest to the town (approximately 1 km north-west) is known locally as Kuhna Qal'a. It is a rectangular mound *c.*35 × 77 m. The ceramic, much damaged by moisture and salts, is Parthian through early Sasanian. There are at least three other amorphous tepes in the flood plain between Deshu and Khwāja Ali Bālā. Preservation is poor. These unnamed tepes contained sherds belonging to the early 1st millennium BC (C-14). The tepes are likely still older as they are deeply buried in the aggrading Helmand flood plain. Alternatively, some of these may consist of poor, heavily salinated soil, periodically scraped into large mounds to expose less salty soil on the adjacent agricultural land in recent times. These 'false tepes' are characterised by a very light scatter of spalled sherds on, and adjacent to, the tepe and by regular shovel marks around their edges, a result of scraping the soil.

Fieldwork:
1. 1971–4 Trousdale, Smithsonian—survey.
2. 1975 Trousdale, Smithsonian—excavation.

Sources:
1. Site information by W. Trousdale.
2. Bellew 1874: 196—mention.

225. DAKDĪLA

Original: Lat. 30° 28' N, long. 61° 48' E. Map 93.
Revised: 30.47272377 N, 61.79803772 E /
30° 28' 21.80556408 N, 61° 47' 52.93577436 E.
Nīmrūz Province. On the west bank of the Helmand opposite Tirkuh, between Chahār Burjak and Qal'a-i Fath.

Date: Sasanian, 3rd–7th cent. (traditional).

Description: Ruins of a very high mud-brick fort on a small mound.

Fieldwork:
1. 1884 Peacocke, ABC—topographical survey.
2. 1903–5 Tate, SAC—survey.

Sources:
1. Smith 1876: 285—mention.
2. Peacocke 1885a: 7—mention.
3. Peacocke 1887a: 21—brief description.
4. Tate 1910: 101—photo and brief description.
5. Gazetteer 1973: II. 291—mention.

DAK-I MARI. See **2039 DAK-I MARI** in Supplement.

226. DAKKA

See also **518 KAMA DAKKA** and **675 LALPŪRA**.

Original: Lat. 34° 13' N, long. 71° 04' E. Map 68.
Revised: 34.23019525 N, 71.0289656 E / 34° 13' 48.70289892 N, 71° 01' 44.27616144 E.

Nangahār Province. On the south bank of the Kābul River opposite Lalpūra, *c.*12 km north-west of Tūrkhām on the Pakistan border.

Description: Many extensive ruins, including the remains of several forts and some caves.

Sources:
1. Raverty 1878: 43—mention.
2. Simpson 1882: 319—mentions the cave.

DALBARJĪN. See **295 DILBARJĪN**.

DALKHAK. See **2040 DALKHAK** in Supplement.

227. DA LŌY WYĀLA QAL'A

Original: Lat. 30° 36' N, long. 64° 00' E. approximately. Maps 97, 98.
Revised: 30.60606057 N, 64.01826867 E /
30° 36' 21.81805236 N, 64° 01' 05.76722568 E.
Helmand Province. On the east bank of the Helmand, *c.*3 km south-west of Gauharkhān.

Dates: Sasanian, 3rd–7th cent.; Samanid, 10th cent.; Ghaznavid, 11th–12th cent. (ceramic).

Description: An artificial mound.

Fieldwork: 1966 Hammond, Cambridge University—survey.

Source: Hammond 1970: 450—lists the site (no. 41) and discusses the pottery and general survey results.

DALWARJĪN. See **593 KHWĀJA GUL BARDAR**.

228. DAM, KŪRDŪ

Original: Lat. 30° 55' N, long. 62° 01' E. Map 92.
Revised: 30.91666471 N, 62.01509776 E /
30° 54' 59.99295024 N, 62° 00' 54.35195040 E.
Nīmrūz Province. In the desert on the edge of the dunes between Patanak and Kūrdū, 13.5 km south of Zīyārat-i Amīrān Sāhib.

Dates: Sasanian, 3rd–7th cent.; early Islamic, 8th–13th cent. (ceramic).

Description: A medieval mud-brick fortress (Fischer's Site 1) and a ruined hall with an elliptical barrel vault in a Partho-Sasanian style adjacent (Fischer's Site 2).

Fieldwork: 1960–70 Fischer, Bonn University—survey.

Sources:
1. Fischer 1970b: pls 51–4—photos of the remains.
2. Fischer 1971a: 43—photos and summary.
3. Fischer 1971b: 43—mention and photos.
4. Fischer 1973c: 145—mention.

229. DAM, SHAILA RŪD

Or KHAIMAH BARANG. See also 383 GUDAR-I SHAH.

Original: Lat. 29° 50' N, long. 61° 25' E. Map 94.
Revised: 29.83003745 N, 61.41899904 E /
29° 49' 48.13480452 N, 61° 25' 08.39653896 E.
Nīmrūz Province. On the south side of the Shaila Rūd on the edge of the Gaud-i Zirra, c.80 km due south-west of Chahar Burjak.

Date: Bronze Age, 4th–3rd mill. BC. (ceramic, C-14).

Description: A low natural hill with a Timurid period grave on top. The hill and the area around is covered in various prehistoric sherds, including 'basketware', greyware, and painted sherds.

'Dam', which means simply 'tepe', was taken from a published map. The site is called Khaimah Barang and was visited by members of the Seistan Arbitration Commission in 1904. The 4th millennium BC date is based on C-14 from the Smithsonian project.

Fieldwork:
1. 1904 Tate, SAC—survey.
2. 1968–71 Dales, University Museum Penn.—survey.
3. 1974 Trousdale, Smithsonian—survey.

Sources:
1. Addional information by W. Trousdale.
2. MacGregor 1882—brief notice.
3. Tate 1910: 133—general remarks on the signs of ancient habitation in the Gaud-i Zirreh.
4. Dales 1972: 36—brief description and a photo of the sherds.
5. Dales 1977c: 19—mention.
6. Ball 2008: 48, 181–2—summary.

230. DĀMAN-I DASHT

Original: Lat. 31° 38' N, long. 66° 08' E. Map 90.
Revised: 31.62997171 N, 66.15200637 E /
31° 37' 47.89814484 N, 66° 09' 07.22292660 E.
Kandahār Province. On the south bank of the Tarnak, c.10 km south of Zīyārat-i Akhundzāda between Kandahār and Shahr-i Sāfa.

Description: A huge artificial mound with a smaller mound on top, probably the remains of a fortress built in several stages.

Source: Masson 1842: II. 195—brief description.

DAMB. See 204. DAMB in Supplement.

DAMB KURUDI. Or **DAM-I KALAN.** See **2042 DAMB KURUDI** in Supplement.

DAMB-I RUSTAM. See **479 JŪI NAU.**

DAM-I DALĪL. See 2061 DIK-I DALĪL in Supplement.

DAM-I KALAN. See 2042 in DAMB KURUDI Supplement.

DAM-I MALIK KHAN. See **2043 DAM-I MALIK KHAN** in Supplement.

DAMĪR. See **723 MĪR BACHA KŪT.**

DA MULLĀ TEPE. See **444 ISHĀNĀN.**

DANGAR TEPE. See **139 BŪLAQ URTA BUZ.**

231. DANISTAMA

Lat. 35° 25–41' N, long. 68° 14–23' E. Map 48.
Baghlān Province. In the Surkhāb Valley 12 km north of Tāla, on the left bank of the river, 34 km from Dūāb-i Mīkhzarīn on the road to Dūshi.

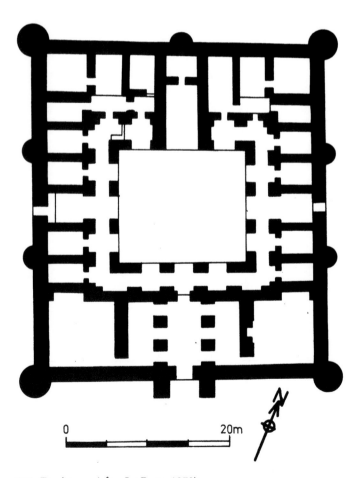

0   20m

231 Danistama (after Le Berre 1970).

Date: Ghaznavid-Ghurid, 11th–13th cent. (ceramic, stylistic).

Description: A mud-brick structure, possibly a *madrasa*, on a diaper masonry foundation. Fragments of elaborate stucco wall decoration were found, together with Ghaznavid slip-painted and Ghurid incised wares.

Fieldwork: 1960 Le Berre, DAFA—excavations.

Sources:
1. Fischer 1969: 345—mention as Tolo Barfaq II.
2. Le Berre 1970—summary report on the excavations and ceramics.
3. Fischer 1978a: 351–2—brief description and plan.
4. Hillenbrand 2000—discussion in the broader context of Ghaznavid and Ghurid architecture.
5. Ball 2008: 118, 182–3—summary.

DARAKHT-I TŪT. See 2044 DARAKHT-I TŪT in Supplement.

DARALI. See 239 DARRA-I 'ALI.

232. DARAUJI

Original: Lat. 33° 08' N, long. 62° 08' E. Map 70.
Revised: 33.10520199 N, 62.13211559 E /
33° 06' 18.72716076 N, 62° 07' 55.61612544 E.
Farāh Province. Along the road from Shindand to Farāh, at the place called Darauji, east bank of the Adraskan.

Description: Small conical tepe.

Fieldwork: 1952 Le Berre and Gardin, DAFA—survey.

Source: Le Berre: 1952 unpublished report, DAFA archives, tépé Shindand-Farah 1.

233. DARBAND, BĀMIYĀN
Including KĀFARI. See also 302 DŪĀB-I MIKHZARĪN, 1021 SHAHĪDĀN.

Original: Lat. 35° 17'–35° 18' N, long. 67° 54–67° 57' E. Map 48.
Bāmiyān Province. Road from Chārikār to Dūshi by the Shībar Pass, in the side valley of the Sūrkhab or Darya-i Kahmard (place-names Darband and Dasht-i Safid Kāfari), 12 km from Duāb-i Mikhzarīn.

Date: Turk and/or pre-Mongol Islamic period, 7th–13th cent. (architectural).

Description: Ruins of a substantial fortress on a hill, consisting of large numbers of towers linked by inner and outer walls. Above the main entrance, flanked by two towers, are two slits above which are impressed decorations in the form of triangles, with a further decoration in the form of a lozenze above. Construction is of mud-brick on stone

footings throughout. Several small forts and towers further downstream on either side of the river belong to the same defensive system guarding the route.

Fieldwork: 1974–5 Le Berre, DAFA—survey.

Source: Le Berre 1987: 64–5, pls 76–8—itinerary A2, Darya-i Kahmard, ruins 3a, 3b, 4, and 5; description and photos.

234. DARBAND, LŌGAR

Lat. 34° 17' N, long. 69° 21' E. Map 65.
Lōgar Province. 5 km east of Ainak in the foothills of the Sangdab Ghar.

Description: Remains of an ancient copper mine, consisting of heaps of copper slag and some excavations into the face of the vein for *c*.50 m. There is also some scatter of pottery.

Fieldwork: 1977 CNRS—geological survey.

Source: Berthoud et al. 1977: 15–16—description of the geology and the workings.

235. DARBAND-I JAUKAR

Original: Lat. 35° 41' N, long. 63° 22' E. Map 44.
Revised: 35.52249282 N, 63.371942 E / 35° 31' 20.97414084 N, 63° 22' 18.99120036 E.
Bādghīs Province. About 11 km south of Bālā Murghāb, on the steep slopes which dominate the river and sharply constrict the valley.

Description: On the left bank of the river, remains of towers on an outcrop. On the right bank, remains of walls and a monticule on a ridge. The construction is of stone blocks with lime mortar.

Fieldwork:
1. 1885 Maitland, ABC—topographical survey.
2. 1952 Le Berre and Gardin, DAFA—survey.

Sources:
1. M. Le Berre: unpublished 1952 report, DAFA archives.
2. Maitland 1888a: 205–6—mentions towers.
3. Vambery 1864: 262–3—mention.

236. DARGAH-I QAL'A-I PANJA
See also 873 QAL'A-I PANJA.

Lat. 36° 58' N, long. 72° 35' E. Map 39.
Badakhshān Province. In Wākhān, *c*.5.5 km up a valley south of Qal'a-i Panja.

Description: A series of granite boulders covered in petroglyphs depicting ibex and hunters. There is also a rough enclosure formed by rocks, and a scatter of pottery.

Source: Agresti 1970—brief description with a discussion of the date and function.

237. DARQAD

Lat. 37° 23' N, long. 69° 27' E. Map 34.
Takhār Province. An island in the bed of the Āmū Daryā at the northern end of the Ai Khānum plain.

Description: Some ruins seen from a distance but not visited.

Sources:
1. Lyonnet 1977: 21, fig. 2 — illustrates the importance of the Darqad ruins in connection with the Bronze Age settlement in the adjacent area of Shortughai.
2. Bernard 1978a: 53 — mention.

238. DARRA-I ĀHANGARĀN

Lat. 34° 46'–34° 48' N, long. 67° 55' E. Map 58.
Bāmiyān Province. One of the lateral valleys to the Bāmiyān Valley, towards the south. The site is 2.5 km up the valley.

Date: Turk and/or pre-Mongol Islamic period, 7th–13th cent. (architectural).

Description: Two badly eroded towers of mud-brick on stone footings, and the fragmentary remains of a third.

Fieldwork: 1974–5 Le Berre, DAFA — survey

Source: Le Berre 1987: 70–80, pl. 103 — brief description and photos

239. DARRA-I 'ALI
Or DARALI or QĀSH QAL'A.

Lat. 34° 39' N, long. 67° 02' E. Map 47.
Bāmiyān Province. In a small valley to the south of the Band-i Amīr River, c.24 km north-west of Band-i Amīr.

Dates: 5th–7th cent. (stylistic: caves); Ghurid (stylistic: fortress).

Description: Some 18 artificial caves cut into the sides of the valley, similar in style to the Bāmiyān caves. Some have traces of plaster. Above are the remains of a fortress.

Fieldwork:
1. 1885 Maitland, ABC — topographical survey.
2. 2002 Lee, Society for South Asian Studies — reconnaissance.

Sources:
1. Talbot et al. 1886: 331 — mention.
2. Lee 2006: 229–35 — brief description and photos.

240. DARRA-I CHAKMAKH

Lat. 36° 09' N, long. 66° 54' E. approximately. Map 47.
Balkh Province. An east–west valley running into the Balkh River 8 km south of Darra-i Dadil, in the Darra-i Sūf area west of Haibak.

Date: Middle Palaeolithic, 50, 000–30,000 BC (lithic).

Description: A surface site with many flint core tools and flake tools found, similar to Darra-i Dadil.

Sources:
1. Dupree and Howe 1963: 3 — mention.
2. N. Dupree 1967a: 149–50 — mention.

241. DARRA-I CHANGI
Or DARRA-I CHEHEL DUKHTARĀN.

Lat. 35° 50' N, long. 66° 40' E. approximately. Map 47.
Balkh Province. A small gorge coming into the Amrakh River from the east, c.2 km south of Wazān, midway between Zari and Bakhtagān.

Description: Ruins of 40 ancient forts, associated with legends of Jamshid, reported up the gorge.

Source: Sahibdad Khan 1888: 149–50 — mention.

242. DARRA-I DADIL

Lat. 36° 13' N, long. 66° 55' E. Maps 28, 47.
Balkh Province. A valley opening eastwards off the Balkh River c.16 km south of Buina Qara. The valley goes into the Darra-i Sūf area west of Haibak.

Date: Middle Palaeolithic, 50,000–30,000 BC (lithic).

Description: A surface site consisting of tens of thousands of flints scattered over the gravel terraces covering the valley floor. Of the 256 studied, 125 were clearly man-made, and they include cores, cleavers, five tupes of flakes, and scrapers. Typologically they appear early, and bear no comparisons with the Kara Kamar material.

Fieldwork: 1959 Dupree, AUFS — survey.

Sources:
1. Dupree 1960: 14 — mentions the discovery.
2. Dupree and Howe 1963: 2–12 — brief description, including classification and discussion of the material, but with no chronological conclusions.
3. N. Dupree 1967a: 28 — mention.
4. N. Dupree et al. 1974: 56 — description of the material displayed in the National Museum.

243. DARRA-I JAUZ

Lat. 35° 40' N, long. 65° 21' E. approximately. Map 46.
Faryāb Province. In the Darra-i Jauz, between Deh Mirān and Ghāl-i Namak, c.40 km south-east of Bīlchirāgh.

Description: Reports of a complex of artificial caves.

Source: Lee 1980 — mention from hearsay.

DARRA-I JUĀNDĀN. See 21 AKAM.

244. DARRA-I KALĀN

Lat. 36° 17' N, long. 67° 48' E. Map 30.
Samangān Province. C.13 km south-west of Kuk Jar, 15 km west of Haibak, and 20 km south-south-west of Kara Kamar.

Dates: Upper Palaeolithic, 15,000–10,000 BC; Epi-Palaeolithic, c.7500 BC (C-14, lithic).

Description: A rock shelter, technologically and chronologically similar to Āq Kupruk. The shelter is a very long, narrow one, in a wadi bed, and probably was used as a transit camp for hunters.

Fieldwork: 1965 Puglisi, IsMEO—excavations.

Sources:
1. Alessio et al. 1967: 360—summary of the C-14 samples.
2. Davis 1974: 63–4—description of the site and the lithic industry.
3. Davis 1978: 64—brief description.
4. Zāhir 1980—summary in Persian.

245. DARRA-I KŪR
Or BĀBĀ DARWĀSH.

Lat. 36° 47' N, long. 70° 00' E. Map 38.
Badakhshān Province. Just north-east of Kalafgān near the village of Chinār-i Gunjus Khān 63 km east of Tāluqān, on the road to Faizābād. The cave is high up on the side of the valley near the hamlet of Bābā Darwīsh.

Dates: Middle Palaeolithic, 50,000–30,000 BC (C-14, lithic); Late Neolithic/Bronze Age, c.220–1900 BC (C-14, ceramic, lithic).

Description: A rock shelter, well-stratified in silt deposits laid down by a stream. Approximately 8000 stone implements were recovered, of two basic types: flint and sickle blades, and large diabase points. Other finds included celts, scrapers, pounders, blades, simple jewellery, fauna (fish, rodent, horse, domesticated sheep and goat, onager), a fragment of a hominid right temporal bone, many bone implements and three fragments of tin bronze. Ceramics were mostly crude, black wares, sometimes decorated. The only architecture was 80 post-holes, suggestive of tents. The only burials were three articulated goat burials.

Fieldwork: 1966 Dupree, AMNH—excavations.

Sources:
1. Dupree and Howe 1963: 2—mention.
2. Dupree 1967: 12—mention.
3. Dupree 1968b—mention.
4. Dupree 1969—brief account of the excavations and of the find of the temporal bone.
5. Masson and Sarianidi 1969—discuss the site in its broader chronological and Near Eastern context.
6. Angel 1972—detailed examination of the temporal bone.
7. Caley 1972b: 45–6—notes on two bronze fragments.

8. Dupree 1972: 79—table summarizing the C-14 dates, stratigraphical associations, and material.
9. Dupree and Davis 1972: 34–5—brief note on the 'Goat Cult' Neolithic and later periods.
10. Dupree 1973: 260–1 and 265–6—brief summary of the results.
11. N. Dupree et al. 1974: 53 and 57—description of the objects on display in the National Museum.
12. Deshpande 1975a—traces ceramic links with India for the Bronze Age.
13. Shaffer 1976: 77—discusses briefly the Neolithic material.
14. Shaffer 1978b: 81–3—summary of the material.
15. Zāhir 1980—summary in Persian.
16. Ball 2008: 42, 44, 182—summary.

246. DARRA-I NĪĀZI

Lat. 34° 47' N, long. 70° 20' E. approximately. Map 65.
Laghmān Province. One of the southern valleys of the 'Alingār.

Description: Reports of ancient remains where a large treasure was found in the early 19th century.

Source: Masson 1842: III. 295—mention.

247. DARRA-I PARYĀNA

Lat. 34° 50' N, long. 70° 05' E. Map 65.
Laghmān Province. On the 'Alishang River adjacent to Kala Gush, 25 km from Tigarhi.

Date: Hindu Shahi, 9th–10th cent. (stylistic).

Description: Some rock-cut Hindu inscriptions, probably marking the Muslim conquest of the Laghmān Valley.

Fieldwork: 1925 Foucher, DAFA—survey.

Sources:
1. Foucher 1942–7: II. 386–7—description and photos.
2. Habibi 1971: 145—photo of the inscription and discussion of its place in the development of Afghan epigraphy.

DARRA-I SABZ. See **2045 DARRA-I SABZ in Supplement.**

DARRA-I SABZAK. See **2046 DARRA-I SABZAK in Supplement.**

248. DARRA-I SHĀKH

Original: Lat. 35° 37' N, long. 65° 13' E. Map 46.
Revised: 35.61627078 N, 65.2291234 E / 35° 36' 58.57480908 N, 65° 13' 44.84422488 E.
Faryāb Province. At a branch in the Shīrīn Tagau, c.35 km south of Bīlchīragh.

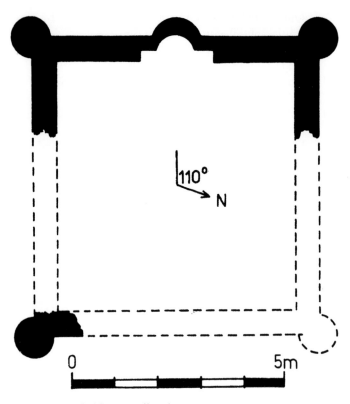

248 Darra-i Shākh (W. Ball and J. L. Lee).

Dates: Seljuk, 1st half of 12th cent. (stylistic); Ghurid, 13th cent. (ceramic, numismatic).

Description: An artificial mound encompassing a spur of rock near the settlement of the same name with brick and stone and mortar remains, probably the ruins of a citadel. Many objects have been found locally at the site, including five Khwarazmshahi coins dated AD 1200–20.

On top of a hill, 1.5 km north-west of the village, is the remains of a mosque, with its qibla wall still standing. It contains a mihrab with floral designs and a Kufic inscription in stucco.

It is reported locally that the mihrab of the Saljuq shrine has been looted and is no longer in situ. A hoard of some 500 bronze or copper coins, probably Khwarazmshahi, were discovered in the site in the 1980s. Other finds include a 'golden camel' weighing 1.5 kg and 50 cm high, which was sold to a dealer in Balkh.

Fieldwork:
1. 1978 Lee, BIAS—survey.
2. 1996 Lee—reconnaissance.

Sources:
1. Addional information on looting and finds by Jonathan L. Lee.
2. Lee 1980: 73–8—description of the remains and the coins.
3. Pinder-Wilson 1980—detailed description and art-historical analysis of the mihrab.

4. Hillenbrand 2000—discussion in the broader context of Ghaznavid and Ghurid architecture.

DARRA-I SHĀKH BĀBA. See 2097 JAR-I SHĀKH BĀBA in Supplement.

DARRA-I SHARWA. See 780 NUKRI KHĀNA.

249. DARRA-I SŪF
Or DARRA YUSŪF.
See also 171 CHAPCHAL and 2280 YŪSUF DARRA in Supplement.

Lat. 35° 58' N, long. 67° 14' E. Maps 30, 47.
Balkh Province. In the area west of Haibak. At the southern end of the Darr-i Sūf gorge, 13 km south-east of Chapchal and 6 km north-west of Dehi.

Description: Many artificial chambers cut out of the rock faces along the sides of the gorge, on several levels up to 130 m above river level. Those lower down are usually natural caves carrying some artificial touches. Some are quite large but often blocked by debris.

Fieldwork: 1885–6 Sahibdad Khan, Griesback, ABC—topographical survey.

Sources:
1. Griesbach 1888b: 204–5—brief description.
2. Sahibdad Khan 1888: 143—mention.
3. Gazetteer 1979: IV. 186–7—description.

DARRA-I TAKHT. See 2047 DARRA-I TAKHT in Supplement.

DARRA-I ZANG. See 893 QAL'A-I ZANGI.

250. DARŪNTA
See also 761 NANDARRA.

Lat. 34° 29' N, long. 70° 22' E. Map 66.
Laghmān Province. 12 km north-west of Jalālābād, to the west of the road to Kābul, above the Pul-i Darūnta.

Date: Mauryan, 3rd cent. BC (epigraphic).

Description: A fragmentary stone inscription found in 1932. It is a bilingual Aramaic and Prakit inscription from the 5th or 7th Pillar Edict of Ashoka.

There are also some artificial caves bordering the river.

Sources:
1. Holdich 1881a: 20—mentions the caves.
2. Birkeland 1938—discusses the text and drawns parallels with a Taxila inscription. Recognizes some words from an unknown language.

3. Foucher 1942–7: II. 384–5—brief description.
4. Altheim 1947—detailed study of the inscription, tentatively putting the unknown words as Avestan.
5. Henning 1949—linguistic analysis and translation of the inscription.
6. Caillat 1966—linguistic discussion on the occurrence of the word *shyty* in the Aramaic version.
7. Habibi 1971: 127—photo of the inscription.
8. Davary 1977—lists the inscription and gives a bibliography.
9. Mac Dowall and Taddei 1978a: 192—brief summary.
10. Itō 1979—discussion.
11. Davary 1981—discusses the Aramaic text.

251. DARWĀZA

Lat. 30° 46' N, long. 64° 12' E. approximately. Map 97.
Helmand Province. In the desert *c.*10 km east of the Helmand, *c.*13 km north-east of Safar.

Dates: Late Sasanian, 5th–7th cent.; Ghaznavid-Ghurid, 11th–13th cent. (ceramic).

Description: Some mounds and ruins.

Fieldwork: 1966 Hammond, Cambridge University—survey.

Source: Hammond 1970: 449–50—lists the site (nos. 4 and 33) and describes the pottery and general results of the survey.

252. DARWĀZA KAM

Original: Lat. 36° 47' N, long. 69° 00' E. Map 32.
Revised: 36.7788406 N, 69.0006206 E / 36° 46' 43.82615640 N, 69° 00' 02.23415748 E.
Qundūz Province. Midway between the villages of Darwāza Kam and Daulat Yār, towards the end of the canal called Kaghiz-i Payān, on the right bank of the Khānābād River; the site is 150 m east of this canal, at the location indicated as a natural mound on the 1:100,000 map.

Dates: Achaemenid, 6th–4th cent. BC; Hunnic-Turk, 5th–9th cent.; Timurid, 15th–16th cent. (ceramic).

Description: Tabular platform (80 × 60 m), 6 m high, of which the contours have been cut by the rice paddies which are expanding over the surrounding plain: two straight sides more or less T-shaped, to the south and the west, joined by a long rounded side, in the north-east (according to the villagers, the site formerly extended further in this north-east direction). No apparent structures on the top, which is more or less flat.

Collection: National Museum/AIA—sherds.

Fieldwork: 1978 Gardin et al., CNRS—survey.

Sources:
1. Site information by J.-C. Gardin.
2. Gardin and Lyonnet 1978–9: pl. VII—no. 445.

3. Lyonnet 1997: figs 25, 35, 69—no. 445.
4. Gardin 1998: 83—no. 445.

DARWĪSH ALI KUSA. See 2208 QAL'A-I QAZI in Supplement

253. DARWĪSH ANWAR KHĀN QAL'A

Original: Lat. 31° 03' N, long. 64° 12' E. Map 97.
Revised: 31.07085766 N, 64.19161838 E / 31° 04' 15.08757816 N, 64° 11' 29.82617412 E.
Helmand Province. On the left bank of the Helmand, 9 km south of Darwīshān.

Dates: Achaemenid, 6th–4th cent. BC; Indo-Parthian, 1st–3rd cent.; Sasanian, 3rd–7th cent.; Samanid-Ghaznavid, 10th–12th cent. (ceramic).

Description: A mound.

Fieldwork: 1966 Hammond, Cambridge University—survey.

Source: Hammond 1970: 449—lists site (no. 18) and describes the pottery and general survey results.

254. DARYĀBĀD

Original: Lat. 34° 32' N, long. 68° 57' E. approximately. Map 63.
Revised: 34.53738424 N, 68.95639345 E / 34° 32' 14.58326760 N, 68° 57' 23.01641352 E.
Kābul Province. Between Cheheltān and Sehgunbad, south of Paghmān.

Date: Kushan, 1st–4th cent. (ceramic).

Description: A rounded hill with a terrace wall and the remains of a stupa on its eastern side.

Source: Caspani 1947b: 49—mention.

255. DARZĀB

Original: Lat. 33° 14' N, long. 64° 25' E. Map 74.
Revised: 33.23820986 N, 64.41631147 E / 33° 14' 17.55549420 N, 64° 24' 58.72127544 E.
Ghūr Province. The first village in the Nīlī Valley 36 km from Yamān, north-east of Mahalla.

Date: Ghurid, 12th–13th cent. (architectural, geographical).

Description: Many ruins in the form of mounds at the foot of the hills to the south of the village. There are reports of a small brass statuette of a man on a tiger, a cast metal pot, and a Ghaznavid water container being found here.

Fieldwork: 1946 Kohzad, HAS—survey.

Source: Kohzad 1951–4, 9/1: 33—mention.

256. DASHLI 1
See also 43 ĀQ CHAPAR, 53 ARANJI, and 324
FARUK QAL'A.

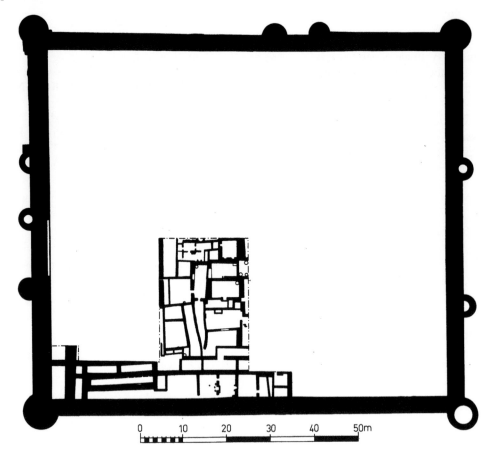

256 Dashli 1 (after Sarianidi 1971).

Original: Lat. 37° 05–08' N, long. 66° 24–40' E. Map 25.
Revised: 37.0861504 N, 66.402742 E / 37° 05' 10.14143964 N,
66° 24' 09.87118776 E.
Jauzjān Province. Part of the Dashli Oasis 38 km north-east
of Āqcha and 65 km north-west of Balkh, just to the east of
the Āqcha-Kilift road. 3 km south-west of Dashli 3.

Date: Late Bronze Age, last half of 2nd mill. BC (ceramic,
stylistic).

Description: A mound containing a large mud-brick fort
measuring 100 × 90 m, with walls up to 2 m high. There is
an associated settlement area measuring 150 × 120 m in area,
in two major building phases. Finds include bronze weapons and jewellery, with ceramics comparable to the greywares of Turkmenistan and north-eastern Iran. There were
two ritual goat burials, and inside the fort were some human
burials.

To the south, for some 2 km, are six more sites of the
same period, Dashli 2, 4, 5, 10, 11, and 12, each averaging
200 × 150 m in size and with a surface scatter of sherds,
flints, and bronze.

Fieldwork: 1969 Kruglikova and Sarianidi, Af/Sov.
Mission—excavations.

Sources:
1. Peacocke 1887a: 318—mentions ruins and mounds.
2. Kruglikova and Sarianidi 1971b: 11–13—brief, unillus-
   trated summary of the site.
3. Sarianidi 1971—brief report and photos of the excavations, and discussion of the cultural links.
4. Gouin 1974: 55–8—description and discussion of the
   ceramic tupes.
5. Sarianidi 1974a—preliminary report of the excavations.
6. Kruglikova and Sarianidi 1976—brief summary.
7. Sarianidi 1976—brief description of the excavations
   and extensive description and illustrations of the finds.
8. Shaffer 1976: 74–6—discusses briefly the architecture
   and material.
9. Biscione 1977—discusses the place of the Dashli Oasis
   in the growth of Central Asian urbanization.
10. Sarianidi 1977a—compares the ceramics and artefacts
    with those found in north-eastern Iran.

11. Sarianidi 1977c: 26–106—detailed discussion of the architecture, burials, ceramics, metal industry, and other finds.
12. Shaffer 1978b: 182–4—summary of the site and material.
13. Bernard and Francfort 1979: 139–48—summary and discussion of the new discoveries.
14. Francfort 1979a: 13–14—detailed description of the defences.
15. Gupta 1979, 2: 194–203—summary of the excavations and the results.
16. Srivastava 1979b: 57–9—discussion of Dashli and the development of early society.
17. Sarianidi 1979b—discusses a group of pottery cult dishes.
18. Kohl 1984: 161–5—brief summary.
19. Ligabue and Salvatore 1989—essays on the Bronze Age of Bactria, including summaries of the main discoveries of the Dashli sites.
20. Tissot 2006: 11—National Museum catalogue details and photos.
21. Ball 2008: 49–50, 183–6—summary.
22. Thomalsky et al. 2013—discussion of metalworking at the site.

257. DASHLI 3
See also 256 DASHLI 1.

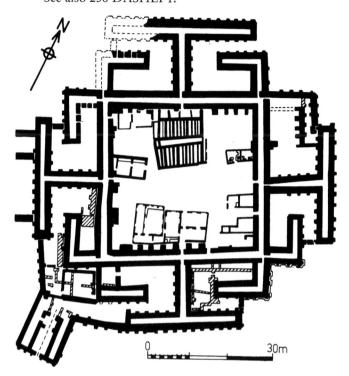

257 Dashli 3 (after Sarianidi 1977b).

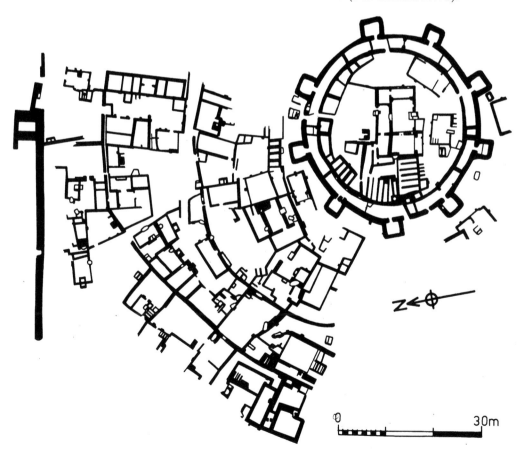

257 Dashli 3 (after Sarianidi 1977c).

Original: Lat. 37° 07–11' N, long. 66° 26–43' E. Map 25.
Revised: 37.10889197 N, 66.4198268 E / 37° 06' 32.01109776 N, 66° 25' 11.37649332 E.
Jauzjān Province. 65 km north-west of Balkh and 41 km north-east of Āqcha, just to the east of the road to Kilift. 3 km north-east of Dashli 1.

Dates: Late Bronze Age, 2300–1700 BC; Iron Age, 1700–800 BC (architectural, C-14, ceramic, stylistic).

Description: A hill with massive defences and associated lower settlement. In the lower settlement a large, circular building was excavated, possibly a temple with associated living quarters and storage areas. Next to it is another monumental building, probably a palace, with the exterior decorated with pilasters. At the edge of the site some burials were excavated, consisting of simple brick covered pits containing flexed burials and grave goods.

Finds include several complete pottery and stone vessels and some simple jewellery. Ceramics include greywares comparable to Turkmenistan and north-eastern Iran.

Fieldwork: 1969, 1974 Kruglikova and Sarianidi, Af/Sov. Mission — excavations.

Sources:
1. Sarianidi 1972b — discusses the Bronze Age material.
2. Sarianid 1974a — brief report.
3. Sarianidi 1974b — detailed report on the excavations in 1974.
4. Amiet 1977 — publishes a number of Bronze Age stone objects, figurines, bronzes, and jewellery that had been found clandestinely in the Dashli area.
5. Sarianidi 1977b: 97–110 — summary of the architecture and description and discussion of the finds.
6. Amiet 1978 — compares the finds from Dashli with some objects in the Louvre.
7. Jettmar 1978 — discusses bronze objects found in the Kābul bazaar and compares them with the Dashli material.
8. Sarianidi 1979b — discusses the cultural patterns and the Indo-Iranian connections.
9. Kohl 1984: 165–70 — description based on the Soviet publications.
10. Ball 2008: 49–50, 183–6 — summary.
11. Kohl 2007: chapter 5 — discusses the site in the context of the development of the Bronze Age in central Eurasia.

See also the bibliography for Dashli 1.

258. DASHLI, EAST

Original: Lat. 37° 04' N, long. 66° 31' E. Maps 25, 26.
Revised: 37.06688506 N, 66.52007086 E / 37° 04' 00.78619908 N, 66° 31' 12.25508520 E.
Jauzjān Province. The eastern end of the Dashli Oasis, 10 km east of Dashli 1 and 3–5 km north of Dilbarjān.

Date: Late Bronze Age, 2nd mill. BC (ceramic).

Description: Eight low mounds stretching north-west to south-east for c.3 km, comprising Dashli 17, 19, 20, 21, 22, 23, 24, and 25. Average size is 200 × 150 m in area. The surface is covered in sherds, flints, and bronzes.

Fieldwork: 1973 Sarianidi, Af/Sov. Mission — survey.

Source: Sarianidi 1977c — general discussion of the Dashli sites and material.
See also the bibliography for Dashli 1.

259. DASHLI, SOUTH

Original: Lat. 37° 03' N, long. 66° 26' E. Map 25.
Revised: 37.05564914 N, 66.43771333 E / 37° 03' 20.33689032 N, 66° 26' 15.76800600 E.
Jauzjān Province. The southern end of the Dashli Oasis, 6 km south of Dashli 1 and 4 km north of Aranji sites.

Dates: Late Bronze Age, 2nd mill. BC; Achaemenid, 6th–4th cent. BC (ceramic).

Description: A group of five low mounds, comprising Dashli 30–3 with Aq Chapar 12. Average size is 200 × 150 m in area, and there is a surface scatter of sherds, flint, and bronze.

Fieldwork: 1973 Sarianidi, Af/Sov. Mission — survey.

Source: Sarianidi 1977c — general discussion of the Dashli sites and material.
See also the bibliography for Dashli 1.

DASHT-I ABDĀN. See 218 CHUL-I ABDĀN.

260. DASHT-I ARCHĪ
See also 288 DEH NAHR-I JADĪD and 933 QŪNSAI.

Lat. 37° 01' N, long. 69° 13' E. Maps 31, 32.
Qundūz Province. 2 km south-west of Nawābād, c.53 km north of Khānābād.

Date: Sasanian, 3rd–7th cent. (ceramic).

Description: Remains of large circular and polygonal mud walls c.140 m across, with some ancient irrigation canals nearby.

Fieldwork: 1955–65 Fischer, DAAD — survey.

Source: Fischer 1969: 252 and 29–30 — aerial and ground photos, with a brief summary as Dasht-i Ārchī II.

261. DASHT-I BAGRĀM

Lat. 34° 26' N, long. 70° 25' E. Map 66.
Nangahār Province. 4 km west of Jalālābād, to the south of the road to Kābul.

Description: A large area of remains consisting of low mounds and sherds. Coins and other objects are often found.

Fieldwork: 1834 Masson—survey.

Source: Masson 1841: 99—mention.

DASHT-I BĀLĀ. See 321 FARKHAR.

DASHT-I BIYĀBĀN-I RAY MUHAMMAD. See 2048 DASHT-I BIYĀBĀN-I RAY MUHAMMAD in Supplement.

262. DASHT-I HAUZ

Lat. 31° 48' N, long. 61° 38' E. Map 83.
Nīmrūz Province. 11 km north of Lāsh Juwain, *c.*1 km to the west of the road to Farāh.

Date: Early Islamic, 8th–13th cent. (ceramic).

Description: A low mound, 50 × 30 m in area and 8 m in height.

Fieldwork: 1950 Fairservis, AMNH—survey.

Source: Fairservis 1961: 40—mentions the site and summarises the pottery (Site 15, Tell 2).

DASHT-I JALAUGĪRAK. See 2049 DASHT-I JALAU-GĪRAK in Supplement.

263. DASHT-I LAJAM
Including ASHRAF, TĀLĀ.

Original: Lat. 35° 23'–35° 25' N, long. 68° 14'–68° 16' E. Maps 48, 49.
Revised: 35.40464079 N, 68.26819261 E /
35° 24' 16.70683536 N, 68° 16' 05.49338484 E.
Baghlān Province. Road between Charikar and Dūshi by the Shībar Pass, in the valley of the Surkhāb: ruins of small forts or castles on the right bank of this river, downstream from Tālā (Dasht-i Lajam), and in the side valley of Ashraf (Kāfir Qal'a of the same name).

Dates: Turk, 7th–10th cent., and/or pre-Mongol Islamic, 11th–13th (architectural).

Description: Six very ruined mud-brick towers and small forts scattered across the valley, with a seventh (the Kāfir Qal'a of Dara-i Ashraf) in a side valley near the village of Khustgān). As none of these ruins produced any sherds, the chronological attribution is based only on the architectural observations of Le Berre.

Fieldwork: 1974–5 Le Berre, DAFA—survey.

Source: Le Berre 1987: 40–1 and 66, pls 38–40—itinerary A1, ruins 20 to 26; A2—Darra-i Ashraf, ruin 1; brief descriptions and photos.

264. DASHT-I MĪSHKUSHI

Lat. 31° 23' N, long. 61° 40' E. Map 83.
Nīmrūz Province. C.6 km north-west of Border Post 70 on the Lāsh Juwain-Chakhānsūr road.

Dates: Early Islamic, 8th–13th cent.; Mongol-Timurid, 13th–16th cent. (ceramic).

Description: A very large area of low mounds, each 25–30 m in height, stretching for some 2 km. The first group is a complex of 22 mounds stretching north–south, and the second group, to the south, consists of 35 mounds extending south-eastwards. Most are irregular, but some are square, suggesting buildings. The whole area is covered in sherds, glass, slag, and copper.

Fieldwork: 1950 Fairservis, AMNH—survey.

Source: Fairservis 1961: 41–2—description and summary of the finds (Sites 19 and 20, Tell Group 5).

265. DASHT-I NĀWAR
See also 877 QAL'A-I RUSTAM.

Lat. 33° 43' N, long. 67° 43' E. Map 78.
Ghanzi Province. On the north-western side of the lake, on the crest of the Kūh-i Qarabaya, *c.*60 km west of Ghazni.

Date: Kushan, 1st–2nd cent. (epigraphic).

Description: A series of rock-out inscriptions. The first is in the Bactrian language, and is from the reign of Ooemo in the year 279; the second is in middle Indian Kharoshthi from the reign of Rajatirajasa, also in the year 279; the third is in an unknown derived Kharoshthi script; the fourth is in Greek, and the fifth in Kharoshthi. The last two are in poor condition.

Sources:
1. Ahang 1968—very brief report on the discovery.
2. Fischer 1969: 342—mention.
3. Habibi 1969/70b: 49—mention and photo.
4. Habibi 1971: 57 and 140—photo and discussion of the inscription.
5. Fussman 1974c: 2–50—full description, linguistic analysis, and discussion of the inscriptions and other remains in the area.
6. Bivar 1976—discussion of the date of the inscriptions and review of Fussman's work. Confirmation of the date 125 or 128 as the date of Kanishka.
7. Davary and Humbach 1976—text, translation, and detailed commentary on the first inscription.
8. Davary 1977—lists the inscriptions and gives a bibliography.
9. Mac Dowall and Taddei 1978b: 238–40—brief description.
10. Sims-Williams and Cribb 1996: 80, 86—brief discussion of the Bactrian inscription.
11. Verardi and Paparatti 2004: 91—brief discussion of the inscription.
12. Ball 2008: 186—summary.

13. Sims-Williams 2008—some discussion of the inscription in the light of Rabatak.
14. Sims-Williams 2012b: 76–7—translation and discussion of the Bactrian inscription.

8. Zāhir 1980—brief summary in Persian.
9. Ball 2008: 186—summary.
10. Boulanger, Davis, and Glascock 2012—analysis of obsidian samples.

266. DASHT-I NĀWUR

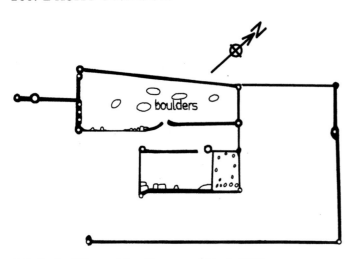

266 Dasht-i Nāwur (after Dupree and Davis 1976).

Lat. 33° 41' N, long. 67° 46' E. Map 78.
Ghazni Province. At the northern end of the lake, on and around Tepe Qādagak, *c.*60 km west of Ghazni.

Dates: ?Lower Palaeolithic; Middle Palaeolithic, 50,000–30,000 BC (lithic).

Description: A brackish lake measuring *c.*60 × 15 km. On the 'beaches' to the east and north are several Palaeolithic sites: Lower Palaeolithic on the east and Middle Palaeolithic on the north, which includes a large stone hill fortification and associated structures of uncertain date. The surface sites are covered in stone tools, 98 per cent of which are obsidian. These include cleavers, large scrapers, choppers, and microblades, some of which appear Lower Palaeolithic. The others bear similarities to the Darra-i Kūr industry.

Fieldwork: 1976 Dupree and Davis—survey.

Sources:
1. Fussman 1974c: 5—brief description of the hill fortification.
2. Dupree 1975—brief note and illustrations of the discovery.
3. Dupree 1976—short note and many photos on the material.
4. Dupree and Davis 1976—preliminary report with sketches and photos of the site and material.
5. Dupree and Davis 1977—full summary of the site and some of the material.
6. Davis 1978: 69–70—brief summary.
7. Bābak 1980—report in Persian of the discoveries.

267. DASHT-I QAL'A, LARWAND

Lat. 33° 02' N, long. 63° 50' E. Map 73.
Farāh Province. In the Larwand Valley 2 km north of Deh Tūrkān on the route from Mushkan to Parjuman.

Date: ?Ghurid, 12th–13th cent. (geographical, traditional).

Description: A small site in a commanding position on a bluff overlooking the Larwand River, now covered over by a village. Many objects are said to have been found here, including pottery, coins, and a monumental Ghurid inscription.

Fieldwork: 1977 Ball—survey.

Sources:
1. Ball 1990: 107—mention.
2. Ball 2002: 26—brief description.

268. DASHT-I QAL'A, NORTH

Original: Lat. 37° 09' N, long. 69° 28' E. Map 34.
Revised:
37.13547309 N, 69.48851328 E / 37° 08' 07.70311212 N, 69° 29' 18.64779900 E (A).

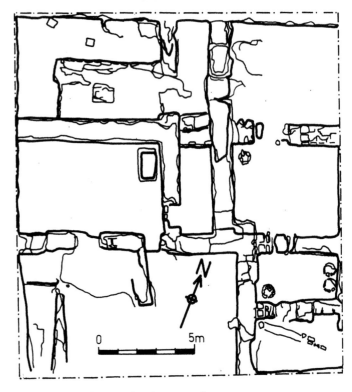

268 Dasht-i Qal'a, South (after Gentelle 1978).

37.13419236 N, 69.48801279 E / 37° 08' 03.09249600 N, 69° 29' 16.84605408 E (B).

Takhār Province. 500 m south-east of Dasht-i Qal'a.

Dates: Achaemenid, 6th–4th cent. BC; Kushan, 1st–4th cent. (ceramic).

Description: (A) Rectangular mound about 20 × 40 m. Trenches (6 × 4 and 4 × 4 m), architectural structures of mud-brick and Kushan material including a small pedestal; stratified Achaemenid material (one layer).

(B) Small neighbouring mound. Trench (5 × 5 m). Wall and Achaemenid material.

Collection: National Museum/AIA—objects.

Fieldwork: 1977 Francfort, DAFA—excavation.

Source:
1. Site information by H.-P. Francfort.
2. Gardin and Lyonnet 1978–9: pl. III—no. 106.
3. Lyonnet 1997: figs. 25, 35, 49—no. 106.
4. Gardin 1998: 42—no. 106.

269. DASHT-I QAL'A, SOUTH

Original: Lat. 37° 08–13' N, long. 69° 27–45' E. Map 34.
Revised: 37.14527407 N, 69.46105699 E / 37° 08' 42.98664372 N, 69° 27' 39.80515824 E.
Takhār Province. Near the preceding tepe (no. 268).

Date: Middle Bronze Age, *c*.2500–1500 BC; Hellenistic, 3rd–1st cent. BC (ceramic).

Description: Rural building preserved over 16.80 × 17.45 m. Three stratigraphic layers. Identified architectural structures: 'kitchen' with hearths, bathroom, silos. Material discovered: pottery, weighing devices, querns.

Collection: National Museum/AIA—objects.

Fieldwork: 1977 Francfort, DAFA—excavation.

Sources:
1. Site information by H.-P. Francfort.
2. Gentelle 1978: 124—two plans published under the wrong number T95.
3. Gardin and Lyonnet 1978–9: pl. III—no. 97.
4. Lyonnet 1997: figs 13, 21–4—no. 97.
5. Gardin 1998: 42—no. 97.

DASHT-I RABĀT-I SARKŪFTA. See 2050 DASHT-I RABĀT-I SARKŪFTA in Supplement.

270. DASHT-I RŪD-I BĪYĀBĀN

Lat. 30° 18' N, long. 61° 24' E. approximately. Map 94.
Nīmrūz Province. In the desert south of the Rūd-i Bīyābān, 10 km east of Iran Border Post 20 and 8 km west of Gina.

Dates: Parthian/Indo Parthian, 2nd cent. BC–AD 2nd cent.; Sasanian, 3rd–7th cent. (ceramic).

Description: A low mound covered in silt and gravel.
Fieldwork: AMNH—sherds.
Source: Fairservis 1961: 63—mention (Site RB 21).

DASHT-I SANGAR. See 2051 DASHT-I SANGAR in Supplement.

DASHT-I TAMAKI. See 434 HUMAI QAL'A.

DAULATĀBĀD, Faryāb. See 1191 TIKAR and 430 HIRDAI TEPE.

DAULATĀBĀD, Minaret. See 2053 DAULATĀBĀD in Supplement.

271. DAULATĀBĀD TEPE

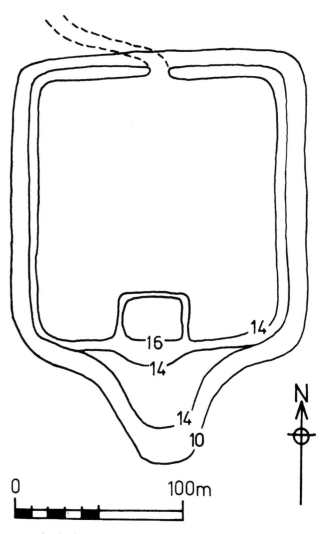

271 Daulatābād Tepe (M. Le Berre).

Original: Lat. 36° 58' N, long. 66° 50' E. Map 26.
Revised: 36.96973552 N, 66.83089101 E /
36° 58' 11.04787560 N, 66° 49' 51.20762484 E.
Balkh Province. 21 km north of this town, south-east of the village of Daulatābād.

Description: Very large quadrangular tepe (c.150 × 200 m), about 13 m high, with a protruding spur on the south, and surrounded by a ditch. A rampart encircles the tepe. On the south face, resting against the spur, a small platform (height 16–17 m) is dominant, about 50 m per side. South of the tepe, a cistern in fired bricks, circular in plan, topped by an ovoid dome, similar to that of one of the ruins at Qal'a-i Bust. Vast area of ruins surrounding the tepe.

Fieldwork: 1948 Le Berre, DAFA—survey.

Source: M. Le Berre: unpublished 1948 report, DAFA archives, tépé P. 55.

DAULAT KHĀN. See **2052 DAULAT KHĀN in Supplement.**

272. DAULAT KHĀN SULAR

Lat. 32° 35' N, long. 67° 25' E. Map 79.
Ghazni Province. On the northern shore of the Āb-i Istāda, c.40 km south-east of Muqqur and 15 km north-east of Gazkai.

Date: Hunnic-Late Sasanian, 5th–7th cent. (ceramic).

Description: None available.

Fieldwork: 1974 Dupree, AUFS—survey.

Source: L. Dupree.

273. DAULATYĀR

Lat. 34° 33' N, long. 65° 47' E. Map 55.
Ghūr Province. On the central road, c.60 km east of Chakhcharān.

Date: Ghurid, 12th–13th cent. (ceramic).

Description: A small isolated mound near the village.

Fieldwork: 1963 Thompson, Oxford University—survey.

Source: Thompson 1964: 10—mention.

DEH AS. See **2054 DEH AS in Supplement.**

DEH GAKI. See **2019 BURJ-I YAK in Supplement.**

DEH GHUNDI. See **404 HADDA.**

274. DEH-I ĀDĀM KHĀN
Or KUHNA GIRISHK or ZARANKA. See also 378 GIRDAI GHUNDAI.

Original: Lat. 31° 50' N, long. 64° 35' E. Maps 86, 87.
Revised: 31.84977969 N, 64.61939562 E /
31° 50' 59.20690056 N, 64° 37' 09.82424028 E.
Helmand Province. On a stony terrace above and to the west of the track from Girishk to Deh-i Adām Khān, on the west bank of the Helmand 2 km north-east of Girishk.

Dates: Early Islamic, 8th–13th cent.; Mongol-Timurid, 13th–16th cent. (ceramic).

Description: Traces of a fort and settlement area. The pottery included glazed, painted, and moulded wares, one sherd with 'cut out' decoration, a fragment of a large stone vessel and some glass.

Fieldwork:
1. 1885 Sahibdad Khan, ABC—topographical survey.
2. 1949 De Cardi—survey.
3. 1956 Ramachandran and Sharma, ASI—reconnaissance.

Sources:
1. Site information by B. De Cardi.
2. Ferrier 1857: 311—mentions remains.
3. Sahibdad Khan 1891b: 254—mention.
4. Holdich 1910: 492—mentions remains.
5. Ramachandran and Sharma 1956: I. 14—mention.
6. Fischer 1967a: 155—mention.
7. Fischer et al. 1974–6: 30—mention.

275. DEH-I ĀHANGARĀN
See also 330 FŪLĀDĪ.

Lat. 34° 48' N, long. 67° 46' E. Map 58.
Bāmiyān Province. In a side valley opening off the Fūlādī Valley, 4 km from Bāmiyān.

Date: Late Sasanian, 6th–7th cent. (stylistic).

Description: Many elaborate caves cut into the cliff face. Many have traces of decoration, and some have 'lantern' ceilings.

Source: Scerrato 1960—describes in detail the nearer caves (nos. I-VI). Photos, but no plans.

276. DEH-I JAUZ

Lat. 35° 39' N, long. 65° 22' E. Map 46.
Faryāb Province. In the Darra-i Jauz south-east of Bīlchirāgh. The site is 400 m south of the village of Deh-i Jauz.

Description: Remains of a stone wall with towers and loopholes barring the gorge at its narrowest point. The walls extend for some way up the hills.

Fieldwork: 1886 Griesbach, ABC—topographical survey.

Source: Griesbach 1888b: 198—brief description.

277. DEH-I KALĀN

Lat. 34° 19' N, long. 69° 10' E. Map 60.
On the west bank of the Lōgar River, in a gorge just south of where it opens out on to the Mūsa-i Lōgar plain.

Date: Early Sasanian, 3rd–4th cent. (architectural, ceramic).

Description: Three mounds, the largest surmounted by a recent mud-brick tower. On the northern and eastern sides of the mound, soil robbing has revealed good diaper masonry foundation walls with a *pakhsa* superstructure. On the northern side are two semi-circular towers and a square salient. The pottery is identical to that from Guldarra.

Fieldwork: 1963–4 Fussman and Le Berre, DAFA—survey.

Source: Fussman and Le Berre 1976: 101—brief description.

DEH-I KAMRĀN. See **2058 DEH-I KAMRĀN** in Supplement.

278. DEH-I MINĀR

Original: Lat. 34° 16–26' N, long. 62° 00' E. Map 52.
Revised: 34.26872392 N, 61.99447238 E /
34° 16' 07.40612244 N, 61° 59' 40.10055756 E.
Herat Province. 22 km due south-west of Herat, on the road from Zīyāratgāh to Ghūriyān.

Date: Timurid, 15th cent. (stylistic)

Description: The Khāniqāh-i Sard al-Dīn Armani. The remains of a square, two-storeyed brick building, originally covered by a dome. The exterior has brick and tile decoration, with some tile mosaic on the *iwān*s. In the vicinity are many marble gravestones.

Fieldwork:
1. 1967–9 Pugachenkova, Af/Sov. Mission—architectural survey.
2. 1978–9 Samizay, Kābul University/UNESCO—survey.

Sources:
1. Pugachenkova 1970: 41–5—full description and architectural analysis.
2. Pugachenkova 1976a: 78—brief description.
3. *Kabul Times* 1979a—brief report on repair work carried out.
4. Samizay 1981: 59—description and background, with plans and photos, of the monument, with a note on the conservation needs.
5. Golombek and Wilber 1988: 298—description.
6. Aalund 1990—photos and plan of the building.

DEH-I MIR. See **2059 DEH-I MIR** in Supplement.

DEH KHUSHK. See **2055 DEH KHUSHK** in Supplement.

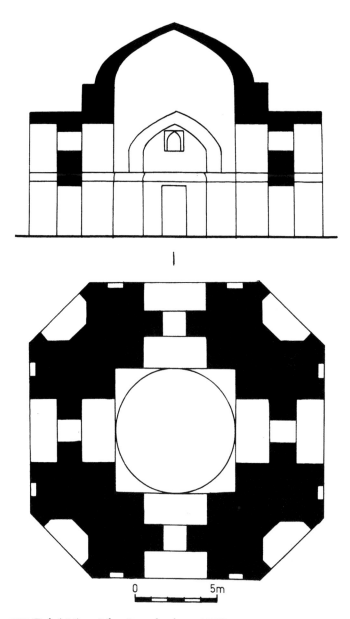

278 Deh-i Minār (after Pugachenkova 1970).

279. DEH MIRĀN

Lat. 35° 44' N, long. 65° 18' E. Map 46.
Faryāb Province. In the Yakh Darra *c*.16 km south of Bīlchirāgh.

Description: 120–30 chambers cut into the cliff faces of two ravines on the east side of the valley. Many are interconnecting, and are very well made with niches, bins, fireplaces, chimneys, etc. Landslips have obscured many of the openings. The chambers are in several tiers, often divided by harder conglomerate layers.

The location of these caves is still in doubt and their location as yet not ascertained, However, they could be associated with the site known as Kāfir Qal'a which is is an artificial mound with what appears to be some caves in the vicinity.

Fieldwork:
1. 1886 Griesbach, ABC—topographical survey.
2. 1996 Lee—reconnaisance.

Sources:
1. Additional information by Jonathan L. Lee.
2. Griesbach 1888b: 197—brief description.
3. Yate 1888: 239—mention.
4. Gazetteer 1979: IV. 416—summary description.

DEH-I NAU. See **2060 in Supplement.**

280. DEH-I QADIR

Original: Lat. 31° 31' N, long. 65° 32' E. Map 89.
Revised: 31.50772931 N, 65.52829152 E /
31° 30' 27.82552716 N, 65° 31' 41.84948856 E.
Kandahār Province. In the Panjwāyī area 27 km south-west of Kandahār. 1 km north of Lal Khān, 3.5 km from the right bank of the Tarnak and 12 km from Karīz-i Shamshir.

Description: On a ridge behind the village are the remains of an old fort partially excavated from the rock, with a commanding view of the surrounding countryside. Two bastions are still standing.

Source: Gazetteer 1980: V. 131—brief description.

281. DEH-I QĀZI

Original: Lat. 35° 03' N, long. 69° 37' E. Map 65.
Revised: 35.04246057 N, 69.62560927 E /
35° 02' 32.85805200 N, 69° 37' 32.19338424 E.
Kāpīsā Province. At the junction of five valleys in the centre of the Nijrau plain, 10 km north of Nijrau Bāzār.

Date: Kushan, 1st–3rd cent. (ceramic).

Description: A large mound.

Fieldwork: 1976 Kohl—survey.

Source: Kohl 1978: 72—brief description.

282. DEH-I QILA
Or SHĀHBAL.

Lat. 35° 07' N, long. 71° 21' E. Map 68.
Kunār Province. On the west bank of the Kunār River, *c.*45 km north of Chigha Sarāī.

Description: Ruins of a fortress.

Source: Fischer 1969: 358–359—mention after a description by Le Berre.

283. DEH-I RAHMĀN
Or AMARA KHĒL or UMAR KHĒL.

Original: Lat. 34° 28' N, long. 70° 22' E. Map 66.
Revised: 34.46596096 N, 70.35697247 E /
34° 27' 57.45944124 N, 70° 21' 25.10087616 E.
Laghmān Province. On the Darūnta plain, 1.5 km north of Bīmārān and 12 km west of Jalālābād.

Date: Indo-Parthian/Kushan, 1st cent. (stylistic).

Description: The remains of three stupas. One was in very fine condition in 1834, but is now completely destroyed, and consists almost entirely of rubble. It was 100 m in circumference, had flights of stairs on all four sides, and was in a square enclosure wall, *c.*50 m square and 1.20 m thick. Nothing was found in any of the stupas.

Fieldwork:
1. 1833 Honigberger—excavation in Stupa 2.
2. 1834 Masson—excavations.
3. 1965 Mizuno, Kyoto University—survey.

Sources:
1. Trebeck 1834—detailed description of the stupas and of coins found there.
2. Masson 1841: 79–80—brief descriptions.
3. Simpson 1881: 202—corrects Masson's measurements of Stupa 2.
4. Mizuno 1971: 116–17—description and photos of the present condition of the remains (Stupas 5–6).
5. Jongeward et al. 2012—catalogue and discussion of the reliquaries.
6. Errington 2017a: 121–4 and 2017b: 35, 42, 45—the Masson collection and archive relating to the site.

284. DEH-I SAMŪCH

Lat. 33° 59' N, long. 68° 02' E. Map 78.
Ghazni Province. 2 km north of Būkān, 4 km south of the junction of the Būkān and Khawā Rivers on the route from Sar-i Khawāt to Ghazni.

Description: A series of cave dwellings.

Fieldwork: 1887 Akbar Khan and Ata Muhammad, ABC—topographical survey.

Source: Akbar Khan and Ata Muhammad 1891: 445—mention.

DEH KUNDI. See **223 DAI KUNDI.**

285. DEHLA

Lat. 31° 51' N, long. 65° 53' E. Map 89.
Kandahār Province. C.26 km north-east of Kandahār on the Arghandāb River, just below the Arghandāb dam wall.

Description: Some huge boulders with many petroglyphs depicting ibex and hunting scenes.

Fieldwork: 1956 Ramachandran and Sharma, ASI—reconnaissance.

Source: Ramachandran and Sharma 1956: 111—brief description.

286. DEHMĀN
Or DEH IMĀN or SAMŪCHHĀ.

Original: Lat. 35° 12' N. long. 67° 37' E. Map 48.
Revised: 35.1931205 N, 67.62381182 E / 35° 11' 35,23378236 N, 67° 37' 25.72256460 E.
Bāmiyān Province. At the southern foot of the Dandān Shikān Pass, 3.5 km west of Saighān.

Date: Turk and/or pre-Mongol Islamic period, 7th–13th cent. (architectural).

Description: Two fortresses on the north (left) bank of the Saighān river. The main fortress contains a series of rooms and well-preserved bastions, the minor fort is a single-chambered, square structure. A group of artificial caves was also reported in the 19th century.

Fieldwork:
1. 1885 Maitland, ABC—topographical survey.
2. 2002 Lee, Society for South Asian Studies—reconnaissance

Sources:
1. Maitland 1888b: 11—mention.
2. Lee 2006: 248–9—mention.
3. Le Berre 1987: 62–3, pl. 75—detailed description of the main fortress.

DEH MĪR. See 723 MĪR BACHA KŪT.

287. DEH MORASI GHUNDAI

Original: Lat. 31° 32' N, long. 65° 30' E. Map 89.
Revised: 31.52040262 N, 65.49456017 E /
31° 31' 13.44942300 N, 65° 29' 40.41659508 E.
Kandahār Province. In the Panjwāyī area c.26 km southwest of Kandahār. 6.5 km east-south-east of Panjwāyī and 16 km south-west of Sa'id Qal'a Tepe.

Dates: Bronze Age, 3250–2000 BC; Sasanian, 3rd–7th cent.; early Islamic, 8th–13th cent. (C-14, ceramic).

Description: A mound, 140 × 80 m in area, almost entirely consisting of Bronze Age deposits. Excavations were too small to delineate structures, though mud-brick remains were found, with intrusive Sasanian burials and some early Islamic disturbance. Pottery bore close similarities to Mundigak IV. Other finds include some stone tools, bone artefacts, some copper fragments, figurines, domesticated sheep and goat remains, and both domesticated and wild wheats.

Fieldwork: 1951 Dupree, AMNH—excavations.

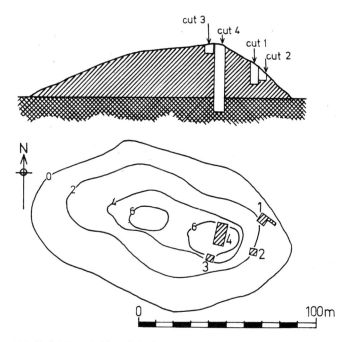

287 Deh Morasi Ghundai (after Dupree 1963).

Sources:
1. Dupree 1951—preliminary report on the excavations, with a list of the finds.
2. Fairservis 1952: 23—brief note on the excavations.
3. Fairservis 1953: 142–3—brief discussion of the general results.
4. Ramachandran and Sharma 1956: I. 10—brief description.
5. Chowdhury 1963—results of analyses of grain samples, with a discussion of its archaeological and botanical significance.
6. Dupree 1963—full report on the excavations, with detailed descriptions of the sequence and finds.
7. Matson 1963—note on the results of micro-analyses of pottery fabrics.
8. Thornton 1963—descriptive catalogue of selected geological samples.
9. Gouin 1969—includes one of the IIa figurines in a general catalogue and discussion.
10. Masson and Sarianidi 1969—discuss the site in its broad chronological and Near Eastern context.
11. Dales 1971—discusses the evidence from Deh Morasi for early contacts between the Gulf and the Indus.
12. Fairservis 1971: 122–3—brief summary of the excavations.
13. Dales 1973a: 125–6—very brief summary.
14. Dales 1973b—gives the range of corrected C-14 dates.
15. Dupree 1973: 266–9—summary of the results and comparison of the artefacts with those from Mundigak.
16. Meadow 1973—discussion of the chronology in the context of Indo-Iranian borderland sites.
17. Dales 1974—discussion of the figurines and of comparative material in Turkmenistan and Pakistan.
18. Shaffer 1974—discusses the evidence from the excavations in terms of analytical models.
19. Shaffer 1978b: 162–5—summary of the material.

288. DEH NAHR-I JADĪD
See also 933 QŪNSAI.

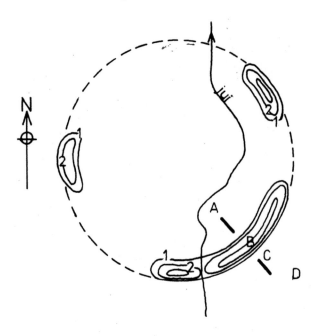

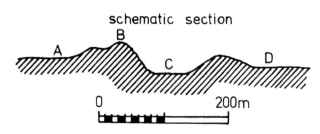

schematic section

0   200m

288 Deh Nahr-i Jadīd (J.-C. Gardin).

Original: Lat. 36° 59' N, long. 69° 11' E. Map 31, 32.
Revised:
36.98102321 N, 69.18278063 E / 36° 58' 51.68356644 N,
69° 10' 58.01025936 E (A).
36.98601777 N, 69.18565654 E / 36° 59' 09.66397848 N,
69° 11' 08.36355768 E (B).
Qundūz Province. 15 km south-west of Archi, by the new road (1977, not indicated on the 1:100,000 map) which links this town to the place called Deh Nahr-i Jadīd ('hamlet of the new canal'); site A, indicated on the 1:100,000 map (as a 'ruin'), is 1500 m north-west of this road.

Dates: Middle Bronze, c.2500–1500 BC; Achaemenid, 6th–4th cent. BC; Hellenistic, 3rd–1st cent. BC; Kushan and Hunnic-Turk, 1st–9th cent. (ceramic).

Description: (A) Circular enclosure (diam. c.350 m), of which only three segments remain, only 1 to 2 m high; the wall, visible in a cut, is about 4 m thick (mud-bricks of 40 cm, thickness 11–12 cm), with a large interior talus; on the exterior, redans spaced by about 10 m can be reconstituted, and at the foot of the wall a ditch. Local farmers remember the levelling of the enclosure and of several *extra muros* mounds (cf. B below); but there were no mounds within the walls,

according to them, when the development of irrigated agriculture in the region began to cause this levelling some 30 years before. The ground level within the enclosure is however higher by 1 m in relation to the level of the plain, on the exterior (fig. 16.3). (B) 200 m north-east of A, an artificial platform 2 to 3 m high, strongly damaged by cultivation (100 × 60 m). In a natural cut, fragments of a limestone column base worked by serrated chisel; the mouldings are broken.

Collection: National Museum/AIA—sherds.

Fieldwork:
1. 1955–65 Fischer, DAAD—survey.
2. 1977 Gardin et al., CNRS—survey.

Sources:
1. Site information by J.-C. Gardin.
2. Fischer 1969: 252 and 29–30—aerial and ground photos, with a brief summary as Dasht-i Ārchī II.
3. Gardin and Lyonnet 1978–9: pl. IV—nos. 45–6.
4. Gardin 1995: 89–90—description and plan.
5. Lyonnet 1997: figs 13, 25, 35, 39, 49, 68, 69—nos. 45, 46.
6. Gardin 1998: 57—nos. 45–6.

289. DEH NAU

Original: Lat. 36° 46'–37° 48' N, long. 67° 35'–67° 36' E. Map 29.
Revised:
36.78397233 N, 67.59464751 E / 36° 47' 02.30037432 N,
67° 35' 40.73102772 E (A).
36.80213427 N, 67.58557333 E / 36° 48' 07.68338892 N,
67° 35' 08.06397396 E (B).
36.76601745 N, 67.60623525 E / 36° 45' 57.66281820 N,
67° 36' 22.44690540 E (C).
Samangān Province. Near Deh Nau, a village situated 13 km north-west of Tāshqurghān.

Dates: Bronze, around the middle of the 2nd mill. BC (B, few sherds); beg. Iron, end 2nd–beg. 1st mill. BC (B); Achaemenid, 6th–4th cent. BC (C, few sherds); Kushan, 2nd–3rd cent. (C); pre-Mongol Islamic, 10th–13th cent. (C); Timurid, 15th–16th cent. (A, C) (ceramic).

Description: (A) extensive ruins of the Timurid period, indicated on the 1:100,000 map, 0.8 km north-west of Deh Nau; (B) 2 km north of these ruins, at the place called Safi on the map, mound 3 m high, surmounted by a geodesic marker; (C) 1.5 km south-east of Deh Nau, on the west coast of the Tāshqurghān track, a large rectangular enclosure (measurements not taken).

Collection: National Museum/AIA—sherds.

Fieldwork: 1969 Gouin, DAFA—survey.

Source: Gouin 1974, and unpublished report—site nos. 42 (B), 43 (A), 44 (C).

DEH QĀDĪ. See **974 SAKHĀR.**

DEH RĀN. See **2056 DEH RĀN** in Supplement.

DEH SABZ. See **2057 DEH SABZ** in Supplement.

290. DEH WARDA
Or ZAKAR TEPE.

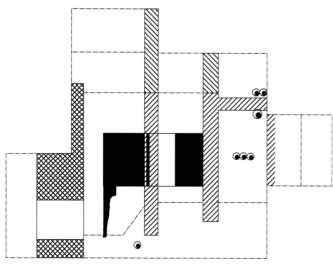

290 Deh Warda (after Carl 1959b).

Original: Lat. 36° 48' N, long. 67° 41' E. Map 92.
Revised: 36.79414899 N, 67.68981294 E /
36° 47' 38.93636256 N, 67° 41' 23.32658904 E.
Samangān Province. 11 km north of Tāshqurghān, north of
the hamlet of Deh Warda.

Dates: Sasanian, 3rd–4th cent. (numismatic); Hunnic-
Turk, 4th–9th cent.; Timurid, 15th–16th cent. (ceramic).

Description: Group of small tepes 3 to 6 m high. The tepe
situated the furthest to the east (height 6 m) is gullied; the
open gap in the tepe provides access to the interior of a
room covered by a dome.

Collection: National Museum/AIA – sherds.

Fieldwork:
1. 1948 Carl, DAFA – excavations.
2. 1969 Gouin, DAFA – survey.

Sources:
1. Carl 1959b – summary of excavation results.
2. Gouin 1974, and unpublished report – site no. 3.

291. DEH ZŪR
Or KĀFIR QAL'A.

Original: Lat. 32° 18' N, long. 64° 45' E. Map 87.
Revised: 32.30820648 N, 64.75052415 E /
32° 18' 29.54333988 N, 64° 45' 01.88694864 E.
Helmand Province. In Zamindāwar district, 3 km south of
Mūsa Qal'a.

Date: ?Turki Shahi, 7th cent. (documentary).

Description: A ruined fortress on top of a small hill. Possibly the location of the ancient temple of Zūr.

Sources:
1. Le Strange 1905: 345–6 – summary of the historical
references.
2. Caspani and Cagnacci 1951: 256 – mention.
3. Habibi 1972: 77 – mention.
4. Vercellin 1972: 372 – mentions Kāfir Qal'a.
5. Scarcia and Taddei 1973: 93 – mention ruins.

DESHU. See 2242 DAISHU.

**DIK-I DALĪL or DAM-I DALĪL. See 2061 DIK-I
DALĪL in Supplement.**

292. DILA

Original: Lat. 32° 36' N, long. 68° 02' E. Map 81.
Revised: 32.51986026 N, 68.08745634 E /
32° 31' 11.49694392 N, 68° 05' 14.84280960 E.
Ghazni Province. On the north-eastern shore of the Āb-i
Istāda, south-east of Muqqur.

Description: A series of small mounds, regularly spaced
along the original shoreline of the lake.

Fieldwork: 1976 Taddei, IsMEO – survey.

Sources:
1. Taddei 1976: 601 – brief description.
2. Verardi and Paparatti 2004: 93 – mention and sketch
plan.

293. DILĀRĀM

Original: Lat. 32° 10' N, long. 63° 26' E. Map 73.
Revised:
32.16013914 N, 63.43485579 E / 32° 09' 36.50091264 N,
63° 26' 05.48084724 E and
32.1608359 N, 63.43513155 E / 32° 09' 39.00923496 N,
63° 26' 06.47359008 E.
Farāh Province. On the west bank of the Khāsh Rūd on the
main Kandahār-Herat road, 133 km from Herat.

Description: A ruined fort *c.*60 m square, traditionally said
to be Hindu. Opposite is a low mound covered in occupation debris and Islamic pottery.

Fieldwork:
1. 1956 Ramachandran and Sharma ASI – reconnaissance.
2. 1960–70 Fischer, Bonn University – survey.

Sources:
1. Amir Khan and Shahzada Taimus 1888a: 129 – mention.
2. Ramachandran and Sharma 1956: I. 14–15 – mention.
3. Gazetteer 1973: I. 66 – mention.
4. Fischer et al. 1974–6: 30 – mention.

294. DILBAJĪN BĀLĀ

Original: Lat. 36° 51' N, long. 66° 40' E. Map 26.
Revised: 36.84508798 N, 66.67222725 E /
36° 50' 42.31672116 N, 66° 40' 20.01808812 E.
Balkh Province. 24.5 km north-west of Balkh, 1 km to the
south-west of the old route to Kilift via Khwāja Rushnai.

Description: Many small mounds, up to 6 m high.
Fieldwork: 1886 Maitland, ABC—topographical survey.
Source: Maitland 1888b: 193—mention.

295. DILBARJĪN
Or DALBARJIN.

295 Dilbarjīn (after Kruglikova 1979).

Original: Lat. 37° 01' N, long. 66° 40–53' E. Map 25.
Revised: 37.02053454 N, 66.52829205 E /
37° 01' 13.92433356 N, 66° 31' 41.85139368 E.
Jauzjān Province. 40 km north-west of Balkh and 20 km north-east of Āqcha.

Dates: Achaemenid, 6th–4th cent. BC; Hellenistic, 3rd–1st cent.; Kushan, 1st–3rd cent.; Kushano-Sasanian, 1st half of 5th cent. (architectural, ceramic, numismatic, stylistic).

Description: A large urban site surrounded by city walls reinforced with rectangular salients. It is dominated by a fortified enclosure and citadel in the centre, and has a vast unfortified urban area to the east and south of the city walls. Mounds to the south-east and south-west mark two probably monumental buildings. There is also a temple, of two main periods of construction, that contained many paintings of the Bāmiyān style, a Shiva-Parvati painting with inscription, a marble Bactrian inscription, a wall painting of the Dioscuri, many sculptural fragments, and many coins. Local pottery production is evident from a kiln producing many wasters.

Collection: National Museum.

Fieldwork: 1969–77 Kruglikova, Af/Sov. Mission — excavations.

Sources:
1. Kruglikova and Sarianidi 1971b: 27–42 — report on the 1970 season and detailed description of the paintings and sculptures.
2. Kruglikova 1973b: 25–91 — detailed excavation report on the 1973 season.
3. Dolgorukov 1974 — detailed report on the 1974 excavations at the inner part of the citadel.
4. Kruglikova 1974 — report on the 1970–2 excavations: area survey, the temple, the fortifications, and the western area.
5. Leriche 1974b: 265–6 — general discussion of Central Asian Hellenistic fortifications.
6. Pugachenkova 1974a — refers to Dilbarjin in a wider discussion of Bactrian art and architecture.
7. Pugachenkova 1974c — detailed report on the 1974 excavations at the city gates.
8. Pulatov 1974 — detailed report on the 1974 excavations in the outer part of the citadel.
9. Zaryab 1974b — brief report on the work.
10. Buri 1976 — technological analyses of the paintings.
11. Francfort 1976: 146–7 — brief description of the fortifications.
12. Kruglikova 1976 — detailed report and discussion on the paintings.
13. Kruglikova and Sarianidi 1976 — summary of the 1969–73 excavations.
14. Livshits 1976 — brief linguistic analysis of some fragmentary Bactrian inscriptions.
15. Pugachenkova 1976b — discussion of the architectural and constructional techniques.
16. Vainberg and Kruglikova 1976 — inventory of the coins.
17. Vorobieva-Desyatovskaya 1976 — brief note on a 5th-century Brahmi inscription.
18. Davary 1977 — list and bibliography of the inscriptions.
19. N. Dupree 1977: 363 — brief description of the site.
20. Kruglikova 1977a — report on the 1973 season: the large house, the cistern, the Buddhist sanctuary, and the artisan's house.
21. Kruglikova 1977b — brief note on the excavations.
22. Kruglikova 1977d — summary of the excavations to date.
23. Kruglikova 1978 — description and art-historical analysis of the temple paintings.
24. Mac Dowall and Taddei 1978b — brief summary of the art.
25. Bernard and Francfort 1979: 122–39 — summary and discussion of the latest discoveries.
26. Buri 1979 — detailed analysis of the techniques and styles of the paintings.
27. Francfort 1979a: 18–19 and 31–6 — lists the site and discusses the general characteristics of Achaemenid and Kushan fortifications.
28. Kruglikova 1979 — description and discussion of the latest paintings discovered.
29. Livshits 1979 — linguistic analysis of two Bactrian ostraca.
30. Livshits and Kruglikova 1979 — detailed linguistic analysis of the monumental Bactrian inscription.
31. Pugachenkova 1979a — discusses all aspects of the development of the architecture.
32. Sokolovsky 1979 — discusses two stucco heads.
33. Srivastava 1979c — review of the excavations.
34. Zhelninskaya et al. 1979 — results of scientific analyses of pigments used in the paintings.
35. Grenet 1982: 155–7 — discusses a 3rd–2nd BC Serapis intaglio found probably at Dilbarjin.
36. Lo Muzio 1999 — detailed discussion of the Dioscuri depicted at Dilbarjin, favouring a 2nd century AD date.
37. Tissot 2006: 73–93 — National Museum catalogue details and photos.
38. Ball 2008: 187–8 — summary.
39. Shenkar 2011: 124–6 — discusses the Temple of the Dioscuri.

296. DINAR TEPE

Lat. 37° 26' N, long. 65° 58' E. Map 24, 26.
Balkh Province. 19 km south-east of Khāmiyāb, 8 km from Qarqīn to the left of the road to Jar Quduq.

Description: A large artificial mound in a small open space, probably marking an ancient fort surrounded by a ditch. There are ruins of a later fort on top.

Fieldwork: 1886 Maitland, ABC—topographical survey.

Sources:
1. Maitland 1888b: 208—mention.
2. Gazetteer 1979: IV. 199—mention.

DINGHAL TEPE. See **2062 DINGHAL TEPE in Supplement.**

297. DĪNMUHAMMAD QAL'A

Original: Lat. 31° 14' N, long. 64° 14' E. approximately. Map 97.
Revised: 31.23106322 N, 64.23435649 E /
31° 13' 51.82759236 N, 64° 14' 03.68335860 E.
Helmand Province. On the east bank of the Helmand, opposite the village of Dīnmuhammad Qal'a between Bust and Hazārjuft.

Dates: Ghaznavid, 11th–12th cent.; Timurid, 15th–16th cent. (ceramic).

Description: Ruins of a small fort.

Fieldwork: 1966 Hammond, Cambridge University—survey.

Source: Hammond 1970: 449—lists site (No. 11) and describes the pottery and general survey results.

298. DIV QAL'A

Original: Lat. 37° 30' N, long. 65° 44' E. Map 24.
Revised: 37.50517091 N, 65.74116919 E / 37° 30' 18.61525800 N, 65° 44' 28.20906888 E.
Jauzjān Province. 3 km south of Khāmiyāb, on the left bank of the Āmū Daryā just before it turns northwards into Turkmenistan territory.

Description: Ruins of a fort on top of a detached, flat-topped limestone rock, some 45 m above the sand. There is evidence that the river once flowed at the foot of the rock. The first consists of a series of outer defences at the northern approach, and some towers still extant at the corners of the walls on top. Construction of very carefully fitted masonry blocks with very high-quality lime mortar. On the summit are two perfectly circular shafts, 2 m diameter and 7 m diameter respectively, with a masonry water channel connecting the two. They appear to extend to a considerable depth, though are now partially filled with debris. There may have been a well and associated cistern. Brief excavations produced no dating evidence.

Sources:
1. Durand 1885: II, pl. 25—distant sketch from Khamiyāb.
2. Holdich 1887: 34—mentions excavations.
3. Peacocke 1887a: 100—detailed description.
4. Yate 1888: 238—brief description.
5. Gazetteer 1979: IV. 198—detailed description.

DIV ZINDĀN. See **2063 DIV ZINDĀN in Supplement.**

DĪWĀLAK, Ghūr. See **2064 DĪWĀLAK in Supplement.**

299. DĪWĀLAK, HELMAND

Lat. 30° 33' N, long. 53° 57' E. Map 98.
Helmand Province. On the north bank of the Helmand, *c*.10 km south-west of Khwāja Sultān and 22 km east of Qal'a-i Nau.

Description: Extensive ruins

Source: Bellew 1874: 190—mention.

DĪWĀL-I GHUNDA. See **143 BURJ-I GHUNDA.**

300. DĪWĀL-I KHUDAIDĀD

Original: Lat. 31° 15'–31° 16' N, long. 62° 06'–62° 12' E. Map 84.
Revised: 31.24589025 N, 62.12449014 E /
31° 14' 45.20488920 N, 62° 07' 28.16449752 E.
Nīmrūz Province. 10 km north-east of Chakhānsūr and 7 km east of Pūst-i Gau, on the border of the irrigated land and the desert.

Dates: Ghaznavid-Ghurid, 11th–13th cent.; Mongol-Timurid, 13th–15th cent. (ceramic).

Description: An extensive area of remains, consisting of many ruins, mounds, *iwān* houses, and an ancient canal system. No fortifications apart from some one- and two-storeyed vaulted watch towers.

Fieldwork: 1970 Fischer et al., Bonn University—survey.

Sources:
1. Fischer 1971a: 47–8—photos.
2. Fischer 1973a—describes the work carried out.
3. Fischer 1973b—photogrammetrical elevations and description of the work carried out.
4. Fischer 1973c: 140—brief general discussion of the architecture.
5. Fischer et al. 1974–6—fully illustrated detailed description and discussion.
6. Fischer et al. 1976—describe the photogrammetrical work.
7. Fischer 1978c: 59—briefly summarises a typical *iwān* house.
8. Fischer 1983b—discussion in context of eastern Iranian architecture.
9. Klinkott 1982: 142–209—description of the *iwān* houses.
10. Ball 2008: 256—summary.

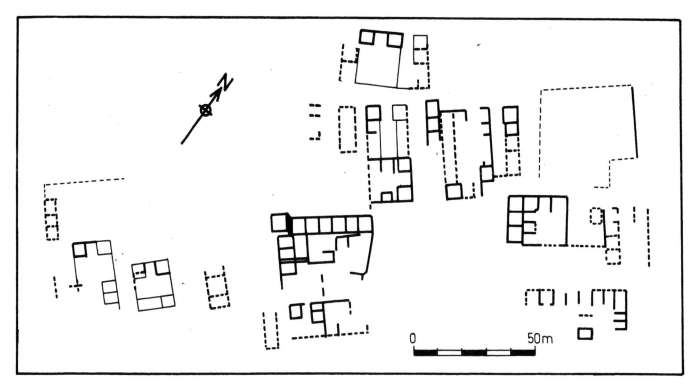

300 Dīwāl-i Khudaidād (after Fischer *et al.* 1974–6).

301. DĪWĀL-I LAWŪR

Original: Lat. 30° 56' N, long. 62° 02' E. Map 92.
Revised:
30.9393142 N, 62.02634617 E / 30° 56' 21.53113512 N,
62° 01' 34.84619652 E and
30.92371805 N, 62.01921751 E / 30° 55' 25.38496884 N,
62° 01' 09.18305364 E.
Nīmrūz Province. Between Dam and Surburt, 12.5 km
south-west of Zīyārat-i Amīrān Sāhib.

Date: Sasanian, 3rd–7th cent. (architectural, ceramic).

Description: Ruins of a town, consisting of extensive low
mounds, vaulted structures, and the remains of a fortress
containing vaulted halls (Fischer's Site 4). 2 km to the
north-east are some more small mud remains.

Fieldwork: 1965–70 Fischer, Bonn University — survey.

Sources:
1. Fischer 1970b: pls 41, 49–51, and 55 — photos.
2. Fischer 1971b: 43 — photo and brief summary.
3. Fischer 1972 — compares the vaults with Parthian
   architecture.
4. Fischer 1973c: 145 — mention.
5. Fischer et al. 1974–6: 38 — mention.

**DĪWĀL-I MAHMATA. See 2065 DĪWĀL-I MAHMATA
in Supplement.**

DIWANA GUR. See 909 QARA BAI.

DĪWĀR-I KĀFĪR. See 1007 SAR RUSTĀQ.

DĪWĀR-I TANG. See 1007 SAR RUSTĀQ.

DO GHĀR JŪI KHWĀJA. See 477 JŪI KHWĀJA.

DOLENA. See 306 DULĀNA.

DORĀHI. See 583 KHUSTI QISHLĀQ.

DOSHĀKH. See 350 GHANDAK.

DŪĀB, Faryāb. See 2066 DŪĀB in Supplement.

302. DŪĀB-I MĪKHZARĪN
See also 233 DARBAND.

Original: Lat. 35° 15'–35° 16' N, long. 67° 58'–68° 01' E.
Map 48.
Revised: 35.260834 N, 67.99019406 E / 35° 15' 39.00239460 N,
67° 59' 24.69862320 E.

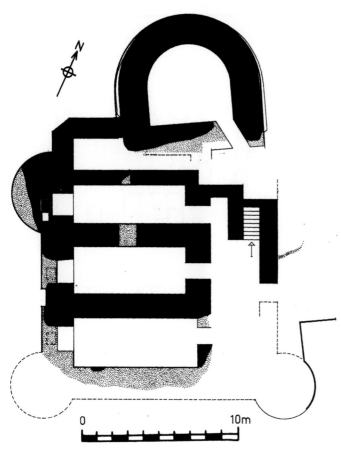

302 Dūāb-i Mīkhzarīn (after Le Berre 1987).

Bāmiyān Province. On either side of the Surkhāb, on the road from Bāmiyān to Dūshi, opposite the entrance to the Kahmard Valley.

Date: Late Sasanian, 6th–7th cent. (architectural, ceramic).

Description: (A) Ruins of a large fortress on a natural hill on the right bank of the Surkhāb commanding the entrance to the Kahmard Valley. Construction is of large mud-bricks and cut limestone. (Fischer's Duab I, Le Berre's A1 ruin 14.) (B) Ruins of a fortress on the right bank of the Surkhāb. Construction is of large mud-bricks. The interior has a two-storeyed elliptical vault and 'Sasanian' style semi-circular squinches. (Fischer's Duab II, Le Berre's A1 ruin 16.) (C) Ruins of several more forts on either side of the river. (Le Berre's A1 ruins 15 and 17, A2 ruins 1 and 2.)

Fieldwork:
1. 1955–60 Fischer, DAAD—survey.
2. 1974–5 Le Berre, DAFA—survey.

Sources:
1. Fischer 1966: 25—photo and discussion of the vaulting in terms of Indo-Iranian architectural connections.
2. Fischer 1969: 344–5—brief description and aerial photo.

3. Le Berre 1987: 33–7, pls 29–35—itineraries Al, ruins 14–17 and A2 Duab-i Mikhzarin, ruins 1 and 2; detailed descriptions and illustrations.

303. DUBAKH SAR
Or TABAK SAR or TAKHT-I SULTAN.

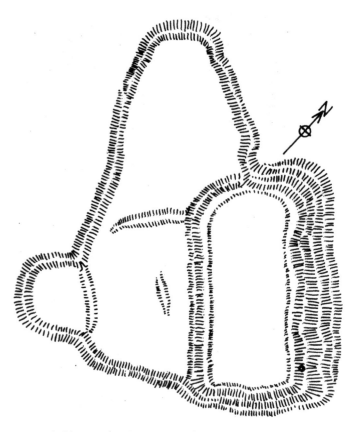

303 Dubakh Sar (after Scerrato 1967).

Original: Lat. 33° 46′ N, long. 68° 21′ E. Map 80.
Revised: 33.76744869 N, 68.3535946 E / 33° 46′ 02.81527932 N, 68° 21′ 12.94054308 E.
Ghazni Province. At the end of the Aftalā Valley, near Jaghatū, 4 km north-west of Band-i Sultan and *c*.20 km north-west of Ghazni.

Date: Turki Shahi, 7th–9th cent. (ceramic).

Description: A high mound, probably the remains of a fortification and adjacent town, commanding the ancient caravan route. On top are traces of mud-brick walls forming a vague square. Sherds are scarce, but some fragments of large storage jars containing Bactrian 'Hephthalite' inscriptions were later found in the Ghazni bazaar and described as coming from this site.

Fieldwork: 1966 Scerrato, IsMEO—survey.

Sources:
1. Scerrato 1967: 13–15—brief description and sketch plan.
2. Taddei 1975: 546—mentions the inscriptions.
3. Thomas 2015: 517—additional information from satellite imagery.

304. DUBANDI

Lat. 33° 57' N, long. 69° 18' E. Maps 65, 82.
Lōgar Province. In the mountains bordering the eastern end of the Lōgar Valley, on the Dubandi River *c.*30 km east of Hisārak.

Description: Remains of a large fortress, locally attributed to the /cGurgania Sultans.

Source: Raverty 1878: 70—mention.

DŪDĀN. SEE 862 QAL'A-I MADAR

305. DUKHTAR-I NŪSHĪRWĀN

Lat. 35° 35' N, long. 67° 50' E. Map 48.
Samangān Province. 3 km north of Dūāb-i Shāh, in a gorge on the route to Rūi.

Date: Turk, 7th–8th cent. (stylistic).

Description: A series of three artificial caves cut into the cliff face, containing paintings in the late Sasanian style. The main, central part of the painting represents an enthroned monarch with a tiger headdress, flanked by horsemen and attendants.

Fieldwork: 1924 Godard and Hackin, DAFA—survey.

Sources:
1. Buhot 1927: 145—brief description.
2. Godard and Hackin 1928: 65–74—description of the caves and paintings.
3. Grousset 1930—discusses the paintings.
4. Hackin 1933—description of the paintings.
5. Morgenstern 1935: 140–1—brief discussion of the Iranian style.
6. Foucher 1942–7: I. 123—mention.
7. Rowland 1946—discusses the fresco and its artistic connections to coin portraiture.
8. Bussagli 1953b—discusses some classical influence in the paintings.
9. Hallade 1962a—discusses the paintings in the context of Bactrian art.
10. Talbot Rice 1965: 165–6—briefly discusses the paintings.
11. Klimburg-Salter 1989: 74–5, 183–6—full discussion of the paintings.
12. Klimburg-Salter 1993—discussion against the background of the Muslim invasions.
13. Ball 2008: 188—summary.

DUKHTAR-I PĀDSHĀH. See 46 ĀQ KUPRUK.

306. DULĀNA
Or DOLENA.

Lat. 33° 05' N, long. 67° 28' E. Map 79.
Ghazni Province. In a gulley to the south-east of the Arghandāb River, 7 km south-east of Sang-i Māsha.

Description: Several petroglyphs and inscriptions inside a large cave, which is part of a complex of galleries and chambers up to 10 m high.

Source: Markham 1876: 245–6—brief description after an account by General Lynch, who visited there in 1841.

307. DŪN QISHLĀQ, TURĀNI
Including MAJAR, TEPE AFGHĀNI, and WATA-GAN TEPE.

Original: Lat. 37° 08–10' N, long. 68° 51–59' E. Map 31.
Revised:
37.16960351 N, 68.85714593 E / 37° 10' 10.57264248 N, 68° 51' 25.72535448 E (A).
37.16771718 N, 68.87863817 E / 37° 10' 03.78183072 N, 68° 52' 43.09740912 E (B).
37.16927838 N, 68.8812718 E / 37° 10' 09.40217196 N, 68° 52' 52.57847388 E (B).
37.15142432 N, 68.8966924 E / 37° 09' 05.12756604 N, 68° 53' 48.09264036 E (C).
Qundūz Province. Up to 7 km from Imām Sāhib in the south-west sector, by the Qundūz and Majar roads. (A) 5 km from the roundabout of Imām Sāhib by the Qundūz road, and 600 m south of this road, Watagan Tepe; (B) nearer the town, by the Majar road, Tepe Dūn Qishlāq, 500 m west of the road, at the level of the village which carries this name (access to the site by a road which follows a small canal, in the direction of a mill); (C) further south by the same road for 1.5 km, then by a road towards the south-east, in the direction of Turāni, to the tepe indicated on the 1:100,000 map as a mound of 7 m, west of the village of this name (Tepe Afghani). (D) Another mound indicated on the map in this sector, more to the south-west, is that of Majar, west of the village of this name; it is today completely razed.

Dates: Hunnic-Turk, 5th–9th cent.; pre-Mongol Islamic, 10th–13th cent. (ceramic).

Description: (A) Watagan Tepe: high rectangular east-west mound (100 × 75 m), damaged by irrigated fields (cotton), mainly on the south side, where a deep gap opens in a basin all the length of the tepe. At the top, sloping towards this depression, there are little hillocks with angles, and a slight protrusion in the middle of the sides, suggesting a fortified structure; the highest point is the south-west hillock (10 m). In the cuts visible at this place, traces of a thick wall in mud bricks (4.5 cm thick) and in *pakhsa*, against which lie layers indicative of fire. (B) Dūn Qishlāq: rectangular east–west platform (60 × 40 m), eaten into by irrigated fields: the site certainly extends towards the north (many sherds), and towards the north-east (up to a mound 200 m in this direction, in the process of being levelled: diam. 40 m, height 2.5 m). Flat top, with high part in the north (4.5 m). In the cuts visible in the north and the east, traces of a wall in mud-bricks (4.5 cm thick). (C) Tepe Afghāni: Turāni, high mound (10 m), steep, cut square at the base (60 × 60 m); the remains of a formerly much more extensive site, levelled in living memory by agriculture, as seen in the abundant sherds which were collected in the nearby fields. Column base of Kushan type and jar in place visible in a natural cut, to the east. (D) Majar: at the location of the mound of 4 m indicated on the 1:100,000 map, area of sherds in the irrigated fields, where not long ago stood a tepe 'razed five years ago', according to a villager (1978).

Collection: National Museum/AIA—sherds.

Fieldwork:
1. 1960 Fischer, DAAD—survey.
2. 1977 Gardin et al., CNRS—survey.

Sources:
1. Site information by J.-C. Gardin.
2. Fischer 1969: 351—cites Watagan Tepe under the name of Imam Sayyid I (sic).
3. Gardin and Lyonnet 1978–9: pl. V—nos. 110–13, 118.
4. Lyonnet 1997: fig. 69—nos. 110–13, 118.
5. Gardin 1998: 62—nos. 110–13, 118.

308. DŪRMAN, IMĀM SĀHIB

Original: Lat. 37° 10' N, long. 68° 49' E. Map 31.
Revised: 37.17244669 N, 68.81274934 E /
37° 10' 20.80806924 N, 68° 48' 45.89761968 E.
Qundūz Province. 9 km west of Imām Sāhib by the Qizil Qal'a road, and 200 m south of this road.

Dates: Kushan and Hunnic-Turk, 1st–9th cent.; some Islamic sherds (ceramic).

Description: Two mounds separated by a road: the highest (7 m), to the south-east, is square (50 × 50 m), rounded angles, steep on the east face; the lowest (2 m), crescent-shaped (100 × 50 m), is oriented north-east/south-west, steep on the north and west faces. These two mounds lie on the same low platform (0.50 m) of uncertain contours (150 × 100 m), eaten into by irrigated fields; the first carries traces of illegal digging at the top, the second, particularly rich in sherds, presents jars in place in a cut on the west face.

Collection: National Museum/AIA—sherds.

Fieldwork: 1977 Gardin et al., CNRS—survey.

Sources:
1. Site information by J.-C. Gardin.
2. Gardin and Lyonnet 1978–9: pl. V—no. 119.

3. Lyonnet 1997: figs 49, 68, 69—no. 119.
4. Gardin 1998: 62—no. 119.

309. DŪRMAN TEPE

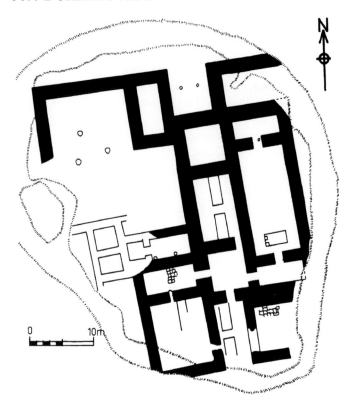

309 Dūrman Tepe (after Mizuno and Odani 1968).

Original: Lat. 36° 40' N, long. 68° 48' E. Map 32.
Revised: 36.67591022 N, 68.81403321 E /
36° 40' 33.27679992 N, 68° 48' 50.51957400 E.
Qundūz Province. Just north of Chahārdeh, 12 km south-west of Qundūz, 1.5 km to the south of the road to Tashqurghān.

Dates: Kushan and Kushano-Sasanian, 1st–5th cent. (ceramic, numismatic, stylistic).

Description: A low mound *c*.3 m high. Structures consisted of mud-brick and *pakhsa* remains of a single building divided into four periods. Finds include coins, terracottas, stuccos, sculptures, and limestone pillar bases.

Collection: National Museum.

Fieldwork: 1963–5 Mizuno and Odani, Kyoto University—excavations.

Sources:
1. Mizuno and Odani 1968: 1–57 (Japanese text) and 93–108 (English text)—richly illustrated report on the excavations, pottery, and other finds.
2. Kuwayama 1969—examination of the pillar bases and amphorae, and their relation to others in the Hellenistic East.

3. Fujita 1971 — detailed discussion of the material.
4. Higuchi 1972 — very brief summary of the excavations and finds.
5. Higuchi 1974b: 178 — very brief report.
6. H. Motamedi 1975c: 250–2 — summary of the excavations.

310. DŪST-I KHĒL
See also 1116 SULTĀNPŪR.

Lat. 34° 24' N, long. 70° 20' E. Map 66.
NangahārProvince. Between Sultānpūr stupa and Allahnazār caves, *c.*12 km west of Jalālābad to the south of the road to Nimla. The site is *c.*1 km south of the village of Dūst-i Khēl.

Description: A group of mounds and caves, possibly associated with the stupa of Sultanpur.

Fieldwork: 1834 Masson — survey.

Source: Masson 1841: 89 — mention.

DUST MUHAMMAD, Khwāja Ali. See **2067 DUST MUHAMMAD** in Supplement.

311. DŪST MUHAMMAD, DARWĪSHĀN

Original: Lat. 31° 02' N, long. 64° 11' E. Map 97.
Revised: 31.03718396 N, 64.19167997 E /
31° 02' 13.86227220 N, 64° 11' 30.04790316 E.
Helmand Province. On the left bank of the Helmand opposite Basābād, 10 km south of Darwīshān.

Dates: Indo-Parthian, 1st–3rd cent.; Sasanian, 3rd–7th cent.; Ghurid, 12th–13th cent. (ceramic).

Description: A mound and some ruins.

Collection: National Museum — sherds.

Fieldwork: 1966 Hammond, Cambridge University — survey.

Source: Hammond 1970: 449 — lists site (No. 16) and describes the pottery and general survey results.

312. DUZDULĀGH

Lat. 32° 23' N, long. 62° 18' E. Map 84.
Nīmrūz Province. 2 km north of Kadah near the west bank of the Khāsh Rūd.

Date: Timurid, 15th–16th cent. (ceramic).

Description: A small series of artificial caves cut into the cliff face. It is on three levels, with one of the lower caves containing a well. The scree below the caves is littered with Islamic glazed sherds. No ritual function is apparent; they were probably used as a temporary refuge for the inhabitants of Kadah.

Fieldwork: 1968 Fischer, Bonn University — survey.

Sources:
1. Fischer 1969–70: figs 14–15 — photos.
2. Fischer 1971b: 42 — photo and short description and discussion (Site 40).

313. EFENDI TEPE
Or MOMOKHIL. See also 173 CHĀR DARRA.

Original: Lat. 36° 45' N, long. 68° 45' E. Map 32.
Revised: 36.7542388 N, 68.7706339 E / 36° 45' 15.25968252 N, 68° 46' 14.28205800 E.
Qundūz Province. 11 km west of Qundūz, near the south bank of the Qundūz River.

Date: Kushan-Sasanian, 1st–7th cent. (ceramic).

Description: Mound *c.*15 m high with a second smaller one nearby. A simple column base — round drum on square base — was found on the larger mound. There are some large, complete jars in situ, where some alleged Kushan coin hoards may have been found.

Fieldwork: 1955–65 Fischer, DAAD — survey.

Sources:
1. Fischer 1969: 351 — brief summary.
2. Levi 1972: 159–60 — brief description.

314. EMSHI TEPE
Or IMSAK QAL'A.

314 Emshi Tepe (after Kruglikova and Sarianidi 1976).

Original: Lat. 36° 42' N, long. 65° 47' E. Map 24.
Revised: 36.70673779 N, 65.78703664 E /
36° 42' 24.25602600 N, 65° 47' 13.33191300 E.
Jauzjan Province. 4 km north-east of Shībarghān, to the left of the road to Āqcha.

Dates: Hellenistic, 4th–1st cent. BC; Kushan, 1st cent. BC–AD 3rd cent.; Sasanian/Kushano-Sasanian, 3rd–5th cent. (numismatic, stylistic).

Description: A large urban site covering *c*.18 hectares. It is enclosed by huge circular ramparts 1.5 km in circumference and up to 12 m in height. There are no towers. Inside, many small rooms were excavated, of mud-brick and *pakhsa* construction. The site was repaired then finally destroyed in the Sasanian period.

Finds included many coins, figurines, a Greek ostracon, bronze arrowheads, and a large amount of statuary.

Fieldwork:
1. 1886 Maitland, ABC—topographical survey.
2. 1938 Barger, ASI—survey.
3. 1969–70 Kruglikova and Musatamandi, Af/Sov. Mission—excavations.

Sources:
1. Peacocke 1887a: 106—mention.
2. Maitland 1888b: 169—mention.
3. Barger and Wright 1941: 45—very brief description (Site MD).
4. Kruglikova and Mustamandi 1970: 90–7—preliminary report on the excavations and finds, with photos of the statuary.
5. Kruglikova and Sarianidi 1971a: 20–1—brief description of the 1969 season. No illustrations.
6. Kruglikova 1973a—brief preliminary report on the excavations, with plans and sections.
7. Francfort 1976: 100–3—brief description of the ramparts.
8. Kruglikova and Sarianidi 1976—very brief summary of the work.
9. Francfort 1979a: 23–6—lists the site and discusses the general characteristics of Hellenistic fortifications.
10. Rougemont 2012a: 186—the Greek graffiti.

ERAGHLI. See 1244 YURUGHLI.

ESTOWAY. See 457 ISTAWAI.

EZĀBĀD. See 962 SABZ QAL'A.

315. FAIZĀBĀD
Or SANG-I MUR. See also 650 KURI and 2100 JOUZGUN in Supplement.

Original: Lat. 37° 06' N, long. 70° 34' E. Map 38.

Badakhshān Province. On a bluff on the south bank of the Kokcha River, immediately to the west of the town.

Date: Early Islamic, 10th–13th cent. (ceramic); Uzbek, 18th cent. (numismatic).

Description: Remains of a large enclosed citadel, commanding the entrance to the valley.

A hoard of 100 coins, including a number of Safavid *sahib qirans* of Muhammad Shah (1118–66/1706–52) was discovered in the vicinity of Faizābād, and a small selection shown by a local dealer in Mazār-i Sharīf, 1996.

Fieldwork:
1. 1960 Fischer, DAAD—survey.
2. 1975 Kohl—survey.

Sources:
1. Information on the coin hoard by Jonathan L. Lee.
2. Wood 1872: 162–3—brief description.
3. Fischer 1969: 350—brief summary.
4. Gazetteer 1972: 99—mention.
5. Kohl 1978: 64–5—mention.

316. FAIZĀBĀD TEPE
Or ISMA'IL QARA TEPE.

Original: Lat. 36° 53' N, long. 66° 27' E. Map 25.
Revised: 36.88549323 N, 66.43803595 E /
36° 53' 07.77562512 N, 66° 26' 16.92943692 E.
Jauzjān Province. 24 km south-east of Āqcha, about 2 km north of the Balkh road and 1.5 km north-east of Hustukh Tepe.

Dates: Hellenistic, 3rd–2nd cent. BC; pre-Mongol Islamic, 7th–13th cent. (ceramic).

Description: Rounded mound (diameter c.150 m), surrounded by a ditch. The heavy erosion has cut deeply into it and almost cut it in two.

Fieldwork:
1. 1886 Maitland, ABC—topographic exploration.
2. 1948 Le Berre, DAFA—survey.
3. 1960 Hayashi and Sahara, University of Kyoto—survey.

Sources:
1. Site information by M. Le Berre.
2. Maitland 1888b: 173—mention.
3. Hayashi and Sahara 1962: 65–6—photo and description in Japanese.

FAKHRĀBĀD. See 875 QAL'A-I QAISĀR.

317. FAKHRI

Original: Lat. 33° 34' N, long. 67° 57' E. Map 78.
Revised: 33.55499347 N, 67.96256822 E /
33° 33' 17.97650676 N, 67° 57' 45.24558660 E.

Ghazni Province. 46 km west of Ghazni on the road to Dasht-i Nāwar.

Date: ?Timurid, 15th cent. (stylistic).

Description: An octagonal domed tomb. The dome is mud-brick, the superstructure is *pakhsa* and the base is stone.

Sources:
1. Fussman 1974c: fig. 30—photo and brief description.
2. Thomas 2015: 517—additional information from satellite imagery.

Farad Jagani. See **2068 FARAD JAGANI in Supplement**.

318. FARĀH BĀLĀ HISĀR

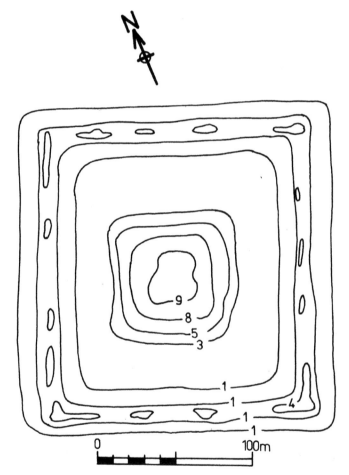

318 Farāh Bālā Hisār (M. Le Berre).

Original: Lat. 32° 23' N, long. 62° 07' E. Map 71.
Revised: 32.38210126 N, 62.11171096 E /
32° 22' 55.56453744 N, 62° 06' 42.15946536 E.
Farāh Province. 158 km south of Herat.

Dates: Achaemenid, 6th–4th cent. BC; Hellenistic, 3rd–1st cent. BC; Timurid and post-Timurid, 15th–17th cent. (ceramic).

Description: A vast fortified enclosure of mud with remains of a castle dating from the Timurid period in the north-west.

Fieldwork:
1. 1884 Peacocke, ABC—topographical survey.
2. 1952 Le Berre and Gardin, DAFA—survey.
3. 1960–70—Fischer, Bonn University—survey.

Sources:
1. Gardin and Lyonnet, 1980 chronological study of unpublished pottery from DAFA surveys.
2. Ferrier 1857: 393–4—brief description.
3. Peacocke 1885a: 25—brief description.
4. Yate 1900: 12—brief description.
5. Le Strange 1905: 341—summary of the historical references.
6. Caspani and Cagnacci 1951: 256–7—brief description.
7. Fischer 1967a: 129, 153, 188, 195, and 198—description and photo.
8. Gazetteer 1973: II. 76–9—good detailed description.
9. Fischer et al. 1974–6: 35 and pls 131–2—photos and very brief summary.
10. Klinkott 1982: 209–77—description of the fortifications.

319. FARĀHGIRD
   Or FŪLOJIRD.

Lat. 35° 00' N, long. 68° 47' E. Maps 49, 60.
Parwān Province. In the Ghūrband Valley, in a mountain on the right bank of the river, 6 km west of Siāhgird.

Description: The site of two ancient coal mines. The first consists of a tunnel descending for 15 m, the second is larger, but also 15 m long.

Fieldwork: 1957 Lindberg—speleological survey.

Sources:
1. Masson 1842: III. 169—mention.
2. Lindberg 1961: 9—brief description.

320. FARĀMĀZ
   See also 1221 ŪRUZGĀN.

Lat. 32° 58' N, long. 66° 40' E. Map 76.
Ūruzgān Province. 380 km north-east of Kandahār, on the route to Sang-i Māsha. The site is 8 km north of Ūruzgān, 3 km north-east of the Ūruzgān inscription.

Date: Turki Shahi, 7th–8th cent. (epigraphic).

Description: A boulder with a cursive Bactrian inscription in the same technique as Bād-i Asyā.

Sources: See the sources for Ūruzgān, Site 1221.

321. FARKHĀR, AND SURROUNDINGS TO THE SOUTH
Including DASHT-I BĀLĀ. See also 1093 SHURI.

Original: Lat. 36° 31'–36° 34' N, long 69° 52' E. Maps 37, 38.
Revised:
36.54257956 N, 69.87134464 E / 36° 32' 33.28641132 N, 69° 52' 16.84068816 E (A).
36.5689106 N, 69.86348582 E / 36° 34' 08.07816216 N, 69° 51' 48.54894948 E (B).
Takhār Province. Leaving Farkhār towards the south by the road, one passes beneath the peak of Chagarak, which overlooks the town, to arrive immediately in a narrow plain, squeezed between the Farkhār river to the west and the hills to the east. The first two projections of the hills, south of Chagarak, carry traces of ancient occupation (A). In the plain itself, the tepes are rare and small in size (B).

Dates: Hellenistic, 3rd–1st cent. BC (A); Kushan and Hunnic-Turk, 1st–9th cent.; pre-Mongol Islamic, 10th–14th cent. (ceramic).

Description: (A) On the first projection of the hills, south of the peak of Chagarak, an area of sherds (100 × 100 m)—some of the Hellenistic period—at the end and at the foot of the spur, about 1 km east of the Farkhār road. On the second projection, which reaches the road 300 m further to the south, a similar area of sherds at the base of the slopes, up to the road (100 × 50 m). (B) In the plain called Dasht-i Bālā, towards the south, a first tepe on the east side of the road, 500 m from the preceding tepe, place-name Mazār-i Shaikh: circular mound (diam. 50 m) cut into by cultivation (the sherds extend up to 80 m from the tepe), flat top (3 m). Second tepe 3 km further south, 200 m to the west of the road: hemispherical mound, diam. 25 m, height 3 m.

Collection: National Museum/AIA—sherds.

Fieldwork: 1977 Gardin et al., CNRS—survey.

Sources:
1. Site information by J.-C. Gardin.
2. Gardin and Lyonnet 1978–9: pl. X—nos. 328–32.
3. Lyonnet 1997: figs 39, 49, 68, 69—nos. 328–32.
4. Gardin 1998: 95—nos. 328–32.

FARMIS 'ALAQADARI. See 2069. FARMIS 'ALAQADARI in Supplement.

FĀRSĪ. See 2070 FĀRSĪ in Supplement.

322. FARUD BEG

Lat. 35° 34' N, long. 64° 34' E. Map 45.
Bādghīs Province. On the right bank of the Gaujan or Almar stream, 27 km south of Pa'in Guzar.

Description: Eight to ten artificial rock chambers, cut out of the conglomerate sandstone of the cliff face. Most are partly fallen away. There are several more caves high up on the hillside 1.5–2 km above the village.

Fieldwork: 1886 Griesbach, ABC—topographical survey.

Sources:
1. Griesbach 1888b: 191—brief description.
2. Yate 1888: 239—mention.
3. Gazetteer 1979: IV. 222–3—brief description.

323. FARUKHĀBĀD

Original: Lat. 37° 06' N, long. 66° 43' E. Map 26.
Revised: 37.07848163 N, 66.68383533 E / 37° 04' 42.53385684 N, 66° 41' 01.80719232 E.
Balkh Province. The area 1.5 km north and north-west of the village of Farukhābād, c.48 km north-west of Balkh, c.8 km to the east of the road to Kilift.

Date: Late Bronze Age, 2nd mill. BC. (ceramic).

Description: A series of ten small villages sites, stretching for some 9 km and totalling 26.2 hectares. The main settlement is Farukhābād 1, 110 × 80 m in area; Farukhābād 2 is smaller, 100 × 70 m in area. Both have remains of early cemeteries. The remaining settlements average 1.8 hectares each.

Fieldwork: 1973 Sarianidi, Af/Sov. Mission—survey.

Sources:
1. Kruglikova 1973b: 2–8—detailed report.
2. Zaryab 1974b—brief report on the Soviet work.
3. Biscione 1977: 125—brief description.
4. Sarianidi 1977c: 22–6—brief report on the survey results.
5. Srivastava 1979b: 57—summary of the Soviet work.
6. Kohl 1984: 161–2—brief summary.

324. FARUK QAL'A
See also 256 DASHLI.

Lat. 37° 02' N, long. 66° 25' E. Map 25.
Jauzjān Province. The southern end of the Dashli Oasis, 6–9 km south of Dashli 1 and 5 km east of the village of Faruk Qal'a. 30 km north-east of Āqcha.

Date: Achaemenid, 6th–4th cent. BC (ceramic).

Description: A very extensive surface scatter of Achaemenid sherds, stretching for some 3 km along the edge of the takir. No mounds.

Fieldwork: 1973 Sarianidi, Af/Sov. Mission—survey.

Source: Sarianidi 1977c: 29—mentions the scatter and discusses in general the Dashli material.

325. FAZILĀBĀD TEPE

Original: Lat. 36° 52' N, long. 66° 23' E. Map 25.
Revised: 36.86045599 N, 66.40118603 E /
36° 51' 37.64156400 N, 66° 24' 04.26972312 E.
Jauzjān Province. 21 km south-east of Āqcha, 200 m south
of the Balkh road.

Dates: Sasanian-Turk, 3rd–9th cent.; pre-Mongol Islamic,
10th–13th cent. (ceramic).

Description: Tepe on two levels, surrounded by a ditch.
Dimensions at the base, 180×170 m; in the upper part,
95×80 m, maximal height 12 m. The upper part possibly
corresponds to an Islamic reconstruction on an ancient
tepe. Many little mounds and area of ruins all around.

Fieldwork:
1. 1886 Maitland, ABC—topographic exploration.
2. 1938 Barger, ASI—survey.
3. 1946 Wheeler, ASI—reconnaissance.
4. 1948 Le Berre, DAFA—survey.
5. 1960 Hayashi and Sahara, University of Kyoto—survey.

Sources:
1. M. Le Berre: unpublished 1948 report, DAFA archives,
   tépé P. 20.
2. Maitland 1888b: 173—mention.
3. Barger and Wright 1941: 54–5—brief description of the
   site and the pottery (No. MK/K).
4. Shakur 1947: 69—mention.

FĪL KHĀNA. See **2174 PĪL KHĀNA in Supplement.**

326. FĪLKHĀNA
Or GUDARRA.

Original: Lat. 34° 27–45' N, long. 70° 23–38' E. Figs 21.1,
21.2, 21.3, Map 66.
Revised: 34.46269405 N, 70.38150971 E /
34° 27' 45.69858540 N, 70° 22' 53.43494628 E.
Nangahār Province. 5 km north-west of Jalālābād on the
north bank of the Kābul River, near the confluence with the
Surkhāb.

Date: Kushan, 1st–3rd cent. (architectural, stylistic).

Description: An artificial cave complex of 32 caves. One
of the chambers is a large circumambulatory pillar cave
surrounded by cells, in the tradition of Indian cave architecture. At the entrance to the main cave, two pieces of
sculpture were found in the 19th century.

On the summit of the hill above the caves are the remains
of two stupas, the northern one of which is better preserved. Inside was a gold-leafed reliquary compartment,
containing a gold and silver reliquary with a few beads.

Fieldwork:
1. 1834 Masson—excavation of stupa.
2. 1879 Tanner, Indian Army—excavation in main cave.
3. 1962 Mizuno and Nishakawa, Kyoto University—survey.

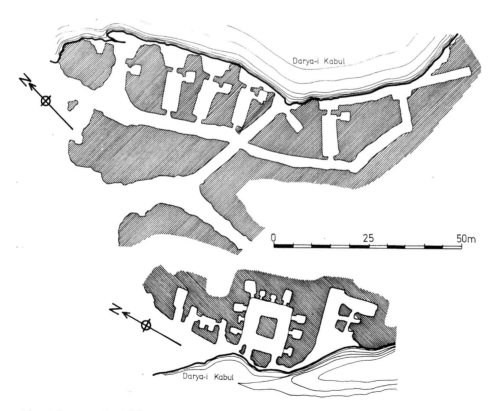

326 Fīlkhāna—caves (after Mizuno and Nishikawa 1967).

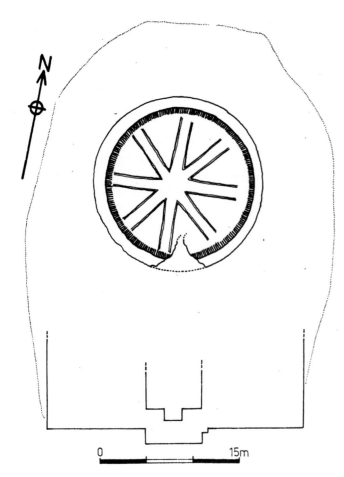

326 Fīlkhāna—stupa (after Mizuno and Nishikawa 1967).

Sources:
1. Masson 1833a: 9—description and sketch of the exterior of the caves.
2. Masson 1841: 87–8 and 98—brief description of the stupa and contents. Mentions the caves.
3. Simpson 1879a: 229—mentions Tanner's excavation.
4. Simpson 1879–80: 44 and 57–8—discusses the architecture of the caves and stupa with its Hellenistic connections.
5. Simpson 1881: 192–3 and 203–4—brief description of the caves and stupa.
6. Simpson 1882: 324–8—full description and plan of the caves and stupa.
7. Mizuno and Nishikawa 1967—fully illustrated summary description of the site.
8. Mizuno 1971: 122—brief description and photo of the stupa.
9. H. Motamedi 1975c: 269–70—summary of the Japanese survey.
10. Kuwayama 1997—discusses the possible influence of Roman funerary architecture on 'spoked' stupas from South Asia, including Filkhana.

11. Jongeward et al. 2012—catalogue and discussion of the reliquaries.
12. Errington 2017a: 133–7 and 2017b: 19–20, 32–3, 42, 45, 50, 59, 112—the Masson collection and archive relating to the site.

327. FIRINJAL

Lat. 34° 59' N, long. 68° 42' E. Maps 49, 60.
Parwān Provnce. In the Ghūrband Valley, c.15 km west of Siāhgird.

Description: An ancient lead mine, consisting of many chambers and galleries descending to a depth of up to 400 m, with ore being reached after 30 m.

Fieldwork:
1. 1837 Lord and Leech, Kābul Mission—geological survey.
2. 1957 Lindberg—speleological survey.

Sources:
1. Masson 1936a: 7—mention.
2. Lord 1838: 533–5—full description with geological observations.
3. Masson 1842: III. 169—mention.
4. Yate 1888: 330–1—brief description.
5. Lindberg 1949: 41–2—brief description.
6. Lindberg 1961: 9—brief description.

328. FIRITU

Original: Lat. 32° 27' N, long. 62° 06' E. Map 71.
Revised: 32.44579195 N, 62.11139407 E /
32° 26' 44.85102864 N, 62° 06' 41.01866784 E.
Farāh Province. 9 km north of Farāh, west of the Shindand road, south of the village of Firitu.

Dates: Beg. Iron, end 2nd–beg. 1st mill. BC; Hellenistic, 3rd–1st cent. BC; Indo-Parthian and Sasanian-Islamic, 1st–9th cent.; a few Islamic sherds (ceramic).

Description: Tepe of circular form (diam. c.120 m), height 8 m, with a protuberance in the north-west; it appears to be surrounded by a ditch which separates it, on the west, by a small long mound. The north part of the tepe is occupied by a cemetery with tombs in the form of beds of pebbles, oval in plan. The pebbles, set upright, are assembled in concentric rows (tombs of the same type on the cliffs of Lashkari Bāzār).

Collection: National Museum/AIA—sherds.

Fieldwork: 1952 Le Berre and Gardin, DAFA—survey.

Source: M. Le Berre: unpublished 1952 report, DAFA archives, tépé Shindand-Farah 5.

329. FIRŪZ NAKHSHIR

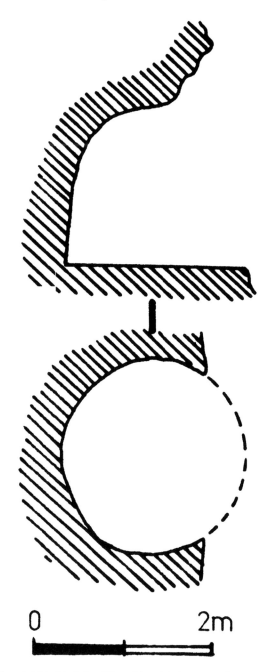

329 Firūz Nakhshir (after Hayashi and Sahara 1962).

Lat. 36° 33' N, long. 67° 41' E. approximately. Map 30.
Samangān Province. *C.*60 km north-west of Haibak, in the mountains near Pir Nakhshir, *c.*12 km to the west of the road to Tāshqurghān.

Description: A small artificial cave of uncertain date and function.

Fieldwork: 1960 Hayashi and Sahara, Kyoto University—survey.

Source: Hayashi and Sahara 1962: 44–5—photo and brief summary in Japanese.

330. FŪLĀDĪ
See also 100 BĀMIYĀN and 275 DEH-I ĀHANGARĀN.

Lat. 34° 48' N, long. 67° 48' E. Map 58.
Bāmiyān Province. A side valley branching off the main Bāmiyān Valley, 2 km to the west of the town.

Dates: Hunnic-Sasanian, 5th⁻7th (stylistic); Turk and/or pre-Mongol Islamic, 7th–13th cent. (architectural).

Description: A complex of some 30 artificial caves. Many have tunnel-like passageways connecting them to watch towers on the hills above. Some have decorations of 'lantern' ceilings and paintings.

There is also a line of later fortifications along the valley as far as Manāra, guarding the approach to the Bāmiyān Valley from the south.

Fieldwork:
1. 1962 Dagens, DAFA—survey of the caves.
2. 1974–75 Le Berre, DAFA—survey of the fortifications.
3. 1976 Higuchi and Miyaji, Kyoto University—survey of the caves.

Sources:
1. Dagens 1964b—descriptions and photos of the more elaborate caves.
2. H. Motamedi 1976—brief summary of the Japanese survey.
3. Tarzi 1977a—fully illustrated discussion of the art and architecture of the caves.
4. Le Berre 1987: 83–4, pl. 109—Itinerary B2, Darya-i Fuladi, ruins 106; description of the fortifications.
5. Suzuki and Aoki 2004: 34–5—brief description of the survey.

331. FULAKĀR
Or GAUHAR.

Lat. 35° 10' N, long. 65° 07' E. Map 46.
Ghūr Province. In the Chārsadda district in the headwaters of the Murghāb River, on the route from Chakhcharān to Bīlchirāgh, 6 km south of Gauhar.

Date: ?Ghurid, 12th–13th cent. (architectural, geographical).

Description: On two mounds on a long spur are some extensive brick remains of a palace complex, visible from a distance of 50 km away.

Fieldwork: 1886 Hira Singh, ABC—topographical survey.

Sources:
1. Holdich 1886: 6—mention.
2. Holdich 1887: 18—brief description.
3. Maitland 1888c: 20—mention.
4. Hira Singh 1891: 156—mention.

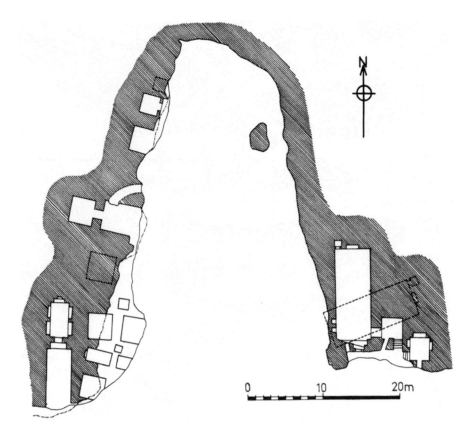

330 Fūlādi—caves (after Tarzi 1977a).

5. Gazetteer 1975: III. 66—mention.
6. Gazetteer 1979: IV. 221—mention.

FULLOL. See **582 KHUSH TEPE.**

FULOJIRD. See **319 FARĀHGIRD.**

332. FUNDUQISTĀN

Lat. 34° 58' N, long. 68° 53' E. Maps 49, 60.
Parwān Province. On a hill in the Ghūrband Valley 5 km
south of Siāhgird.

Date: Turki Shahi, late 7th cent. (numismatic, stylistic).

Description: A Buddhist monastery complex consisting of
a courtyard surrounded by niches decorated with elaborate
painted clay sculptures and paintings. Of particular importance is Niche E., which contained large numbers of sculptures and a hoard of Arabo-Sasanian coins. Construction is
of mud-brick and *pakhsa*.

Collections: National Museum and Musée Guimet.

Fieldwork:
1. 1936 Hackin, DAFA—survey.
2. 1937 Carl, DAFA—excavations.

Sources:
 1. Masson 1836a: 6—mentions coin finds from the site.
 2. Hackin 1936b—brief description of the discovery and
    catalogue of the six statuettes found.
 3. Auboyer 1938: 220–1—brief summary of the paintings.
 4. Hackin 1938a: 7–9—summary of the excavations and
    finds.
 5. Hackin 1938c: 9–11—summary of the work carried out
    in 1936–7.
 6. Vogel 1939: 32–3—brief summary of the site and
    finds.
 7. Monod-Bruhl 1939: 120—description of the objects on
    display in the Musée Guimet.
 8. Hackin 1940d—description and photos of the site and
    finds.
 9. Yoshikawa 1944—brief summary.
10. Ghirshman 1948: 28–31 discusses some possible
    Hephthalite coins from the site.
11. Deydier 1950: 190–1—summary of the site.
12. Hackin 1950b—account of the discovery and summary
    of the sculptures and paintings.
13. Henkl 1952—photos and artistic evaluation of the
    sculptures.
14. Bussagli 1953b—discusses some of the Hellenistic
    influence seen in the art.
15. Kohzad 1955c: 21–2—summary of the site and finds.

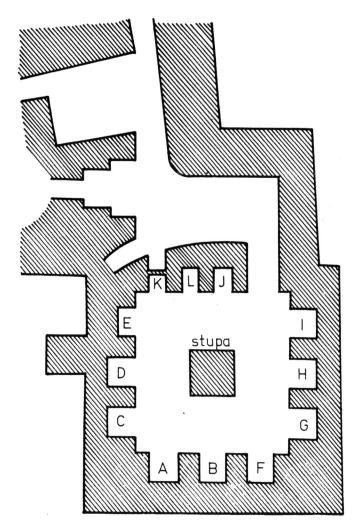

332 Funduqistān—monastery (after Hackin 1959).

16. Ramachandran and Sharma 1956: II. 7–8—discussion of the Buddha, Bodhisattva, and Naga figures.
17. Frumkin 1957—brief discussion of Graeco-Buddhist art.
18. Hackin 1959d—brief report on Carl's excavations in 1937 and photos and discussion of the sculptures.
19. Gullini 1961: pls 149–53—photos of the objects on display from the Kabūl Museum.
20. Rowland 1961—discusses the iconographical concept of the bejewelled Buddha depicted in one of the sculptures.
21. Hallade 1962b: 14–15—discussion of the evidence of Fundiqistān for Gupta and Sasanian relations.
22. Pugachenkova 1963: 80–3—general summary.
23. Mizuno 1964—illustrations and description of the objects exhibited in the Tokyo Museum.
24. Talbot Rice 1965: 172—briefly discusses the art as part of a Central Asian style.

25. Monod 1966: 329–33—description of the objects on display in the Musée Guimet.
26. Rowland 1966a: 114–23—photos and brief introduction to the art.
27. Göbl 1967: 313–14—discusses the documentation provided by the coins from Fundiqistān.
28. Auboyer 1968: pls 78–83—illustrates and discusses some of the sculptures and one of the paintings.
29. Hallade 1968:—discusses Funduqistān and the evolution of Gandharan art.
30. Hallade and Hinz 1968: pls XVI, XVII, 53, 126, 175, and 177—discuss the development of Gandharan art.
31. Hackin and Rowland 1971—brief notes on some of the sculptures and paintings.
32. H. Motamedi 1971b—art-historical analysis of some of the sculptures and paintings.
33. Rowland and Rice 1971: 43–8 and pls 147–64—summary and photos of the sculptures on display in the Kabūl Museum.
34. Taddei 1972b—discusses some of the art-historical problems.
35. N. Dupree et al. 1974: 99–103—summary of the sculpture and guide to the collection on display in the Kabūl Museum.
36. Rowland 1974: 107–19—discusses the styles represented in the sculptures and their Indian connections.
37. Tarzi 1975—good general summary of the excavations, the finds, and artistic parallels.
38. Gaulier et al. 1976—discussion of the religious iconography of the art.
39. Kuwayama 1976: 399–400—discusses the treatment of ribbons on some of the paintings.
40. Mac Dowall and Tadei 1978b: 239—brief discussion of the sculptures.
41. Rahman 1979: 286–7—discusses a possible later date for the sculptures.
42. Grenet 1984: 199–200—discusses the two urns found in the excavations.
43. Geoffroy-Schneiter 2001—photos of objects from the Musée Guimet.
44. Tissot and Darbois 2002—photos of objects from the Kabul Museum.
45. Tissot 2006: 120–33—National Museum catalogue details and photos.
46. Ball 2008: 87, 188–9—summary.

FŪSHANJ. See **1259 ZINDAJĀN.**

333. GALA QUDUQ
Or QAL'A-I QUDUQ.

Original: Lat. 36° 05' N, long. 66° 46' E. Map 47.

Revised: 36.09103657 N, 66.775178 E / 36° 05' 27.73163652 N, 66° 46' 30.64079604 E.

Balkh Province. On the south side of a small side valley opening off the Balkhāb, 6 km west of Āq Kupruk.

Description: No details provided.

Source: Information by L. Dupree.

334. GANDACHASHMA

Original: Lat. 34° 24' N, long. 79° 25' E. Map 66.
Revised: 34.40762718 N, 70.4145867 E / 34° 24' 27.45785448 N, 70° 24' 52.51210272 E.

Nangahār Province. On a hill 1.5 km west of the village of Gandachashma, 5 km south-west of Jalālābād between Chahārbāgh and Hadda.

Description: Some ruins, possibly of a stupa.

Fieldwork: 1834 Masson—survey.

Source: Masson 1841: 100—mention as an isolated tumulus associated with Ahin Push.

335. GARDAN RĪG

Lat. 30° 07' N, long. 61° 19' E. Map 94.
Nīmrūz Province. In the region between the Rūd-i Bīyābān and the Gaud-i Zarra, c. 15 km east of the Iranian border.

Dates: Bronze Age, late 3rd mill. BC; Islamic (ceramic).

Description: Remains of copper smelting and pottery manufacturing spread over some 200 square km. On the north side of the depression are some prehistoric burials containing grave goods. There is also a wide scatter of beads, seals, and much Islamic material.

Fieldwork:
1. 1951 Fairservis, AMNH—survey.
2. 1969 and 1871–3 Dales, University Museum Penn.—survey.

Sources:
1. McMahon 1906: 226–7—briefly describes the pottery scatter.
2. Fairservis 1952: 27–30—very brief summary of the survey.
3. Fairservis 1961: 68–76—detailed description of the pottery and summary of each site (nos. 104–14).
4. Dales and Flam 1969: 18–19—mention the work carried out.
5. Dales 1971—description of the site and discussion of the contacts with the Gulf and the Indus.
6. Dales 1972: 9–22—general description with photos of the finds.
7. Ball 2008: 48, 189—summary.
8. Thomalsky et al. 2013—discussion of metalworking at the site.

336. GARDAU
Or GARWAYI.

Lat. 34° 16' N, long. 70° 59' E. Map 68.
Nangahār Province. On the north bank of the Kābul River 6 km west of Lalpūra.

Description: Some ancient mounds and caves.

Source: Raverty 1878: 45—mention.

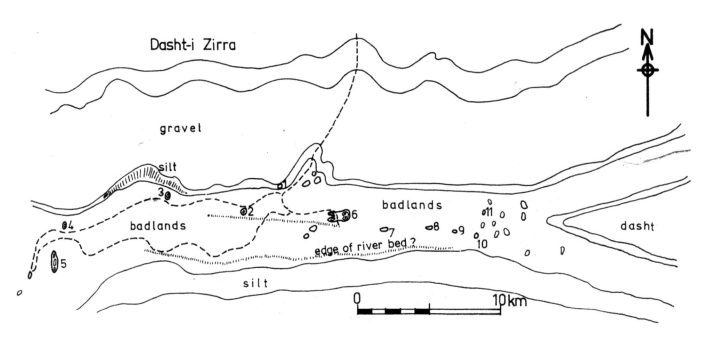

335 Gardan (after Fairservis 1961).

337. GARDĒZ

Original: Lat. 33° 36' N, long. 69° 14' E. Map 82.
Revised: 33.59729744 N, 69.23223289 E /
33° 35' 50.27076780 N, 69° 13' 56.03838780 E.
Paktiyā Province. 120 km south of Kābul.

Dates: Indo-Greek, 2nd cent. BC (numismatic); Kushan, 1st–3rd cent. (ceramic); Hunnic, 5th–6th cent. (ceramic, numismatic); Turki Shahi, 6th–9th. (ceramic, numismatic, stylistic); early Islamic, 10th–13th cent. (ceramic).

Description: Remains of a fort standing on an ancient mound surrounded by a ditch, near the present municipality. There have been various accidental finds from in and around Gardēz: some Hephthalite coins in 1962; a hoard of silver Turki Shahi coins in 1957; various Indo-Greek coins; a marble statue of Ganesha containing two lines of Brahmi inscription; two statues of Mahishāsura-mardinī; and a marble head of Shiva.

Fieldwork: 1960 Fischer, DAAD—survey.

Sources:

1. Gardin and Lyonnet, 1980 chronologcal study of pottery from unpublished DAFA surveys.
2. Raverty 1878: 685—mentions remains.
3. Caspani and Cagnacci 1951: 227—mention the Bālā Hisār mound.
4. Schlumberger 1955b—discusses the Shiva head.
5. Ramachandran and Sharma 1956: II. 1–4 and 6—description of the Ganesha statue and discussion of the date. Text and translation of the inscription.
6. Goetz 1957—discusses the Shiva head and its connections.
7. Tucci 1958: 328 n. 29—brief description of the Ganesha statue and transliteration of the inscription.
8. Fischer 1961c: 73—briefly discusses the Shiva head and Ganesha statue.
9. Sircar 1963—linguistic analysis and translation of the Ganesha inscription.
10. Petech 1964—discusses the historical implications of the Ganesha statue.
11. Bivar 1965: 97–8—mentions the Bālā Hisār mound and the Indo-Greek coin finds from the bazaar. Postulates a possible Indo-Greek capital at Gardēz.
12. Fischer 1967a: 166—mentions the site and finds.
13. Göbl 1967: 36–8—discusses the evidence of the Hephthalite coins for Hephthalite history.
14. Scerrato 1967: 23 n. 18—mentions the Turki Shahi coin hoard.
15. Agrawala 1968—discussion of the Ganesha statue.
16. Auboyer 1968: pl. 99—photo of the Mahishāsura statue with a brief note on this and other Hindu finds from Gardēz.
17. Fischer 1969: 340—brief summary of the site and finds.
18. Kuwayama 1972a—art-historical discussion of the Hindu statues.
19. Levi 1972: 122—mentions mound and large numbers of Graeco-Bactrian, Kushan, and Hephthalite coins in bazaar.
20. N. Dupree et al. 1974: 96–7—description of the Durga Mahishāsura in the National Museum.
21. Kuwayama 1976: 377–8—full description and discussion of both Mahishāsura-mardinī statues, with a review of the previous work.
22. Davary 1977—lists the Ganesha inscription and gives a bibliography.
23. Rahman 1979: 222–5 and 338—detailed analysis of the Ganesha inscription.
24. Stadtner 2000—discussion of the Ganesa statue in relation to two unprovenanced Bodhisattvas in a private collection.
25. Ball 2008: 189—summary.

338. GARGI RABĀT

Original: Lat. 36° 47' N, long. 67° 20' E. Map 30.
Revised: 36.78010382 N, 67.33185115 E /
36° 46' 48.37376100 N, 67° 19' 54.66414144 E.
Balkh Province. Just to the north of the main road to Tāshqurghān, 20 km east of Mazar-i Sharīf.

Description: Some mounds and ruins.

Source: Thompson 1964: 8—mention.

339. GARMĀB

Lat. 32° 21' N, long. 62° 29' E. Maps 72, 85.
Farāh Province. In the hills 9 km north of Khurmālaq, which is 39 km south-east of Farāh on the road to Dilārām.

Description: Ruins of a large building.

Source: Ferrier 1857: 271—mention.

GARMAU. See 2071 GARMAU in Supplement.

GAR NAO. See 404 HADDA.

GARSHASP. See 527 KARBĀSAK.

GARWAYI. See 336 GARDAU.

340. GASKIN

Original: Lat. 32° 28' N, long. 62° 08' E. Map 71.
Revised: 32.47093809 N, 62.15722277 E /
32° 28' 15.37712724 N, 62° 09' 26.00197956 E.
Farāh Province. 11 km north of Farāh between the route to Shindand and the Farāh Rūd.

Dates: Achaemenid, 6th–4th cent. BC; Hellenistic, 3rd–1st cent. BC; Indo-Parthian, 1st–4th cent; pre-Mongol Islamic, 10th–13th cent. (ceramic).

Description: A small circular mound, low elevation, with no visible structures.

Fieldwork: 1952 Le Berre and Gardin, DAFA—survey

Source: M. Le Berre: unpublished 1948 report, DAFA archives, tépé Shindand-Farah 4.

341. GAUBASTAK

Original: Lat. 31° 16' N, long. 62° 17' E. Map 84.
Revised: 31.25602913 N, 62.26826906 E /
31° 15' 21.70488240 N, 62° 16' 05.76861132 E.
Nīmrūz Province. C.35 km north-east of Chakhānsur, 2 km south of the Khāsh Rūd and 500 m north of the road to Dilārām.

Date: Mongol-Timurid, 13th–16th cent. (ceramic).

Description: A group of large mounds and mud ruins, including the remains of a gateway.

Fieldwork: 1969–70 Fischer, Bonn University—survey.

Source: Fischer et al. 1974–6: 33—mention and photos (Tappa 11).

GAUHAR, Bādghīs. See 331 FULAKĀR.

342. GAUHAR, KOKCHA

Lat. 36° 25' N, long. 70° 46' E. Map 38.
Badakhshān Province. On the east bank of the Kokcha River, *c.*7 km south of Hazrat Sa'id.

Date: Kushan, 1st–3rd cent. (ceramic).

Description: A settlement with a citadel to the south, occupying a rocky ledge in a naturally defensible position.

Fieldwork: 1975 Kohl—survey.

Source: Kohl 1978: 65—mention.

GAUKUSH. See 2072 GAUKUSH in Supplement.

GAURAGAI. See 2073 GAURAGAI in Supplement.

343. GAWARGĪN

Lat. 33° 14' N, long. 67° 45' E. Maps 78, 79.
Ghazni Province. In the Dehbadai Plain, 5 km east of Bārik and 5 km north-west of Humai Qal'a.

Description: A complex of artificial caves in three groups cut into the cliff face. They are on different levels connected by stairs. Condition is poor.

Fieldwork: 1976 Taddei and Verardi, IsMEO—survey.

Sources:
1. Verardi 1977a: 149—brief description.
2. Verardi and Paparatti 2004: 49–52—detailed description with drawings and photos.

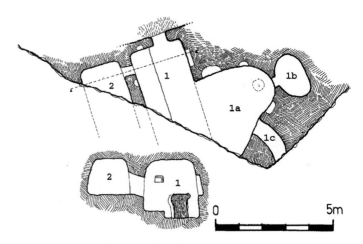

343 Gawargīn (after Verardi and Paparatti 2004).

344. GĀZA

Lat. 34° 49' N, long. 69° 00' E. Map 63.
Kābul Province. At the foot of the hills at the southern extremity of the Kūh-i Dāman Plain, 9 km north-west of the Khair Khāna Pass.

Description: Some mounds and tumuli.

Fieldwork: 1834 Masson—survey.

Source: Masson 1842: III. 112—mention.

GAZA BABRA KAMĀL. See 902 QANĀ-I BĀBĀ KAMĀL.

345. GAZKAI
   Or QAL'A-I MANSŪR.

Original: Lat. 32° 30' N, long. 67° 50' E. Map 79.
Revised: 32.52931021 N, 67.86668849 E /
32° 31' 45.51675240 N, 67° 52' 00.07857336 E.
Ghazni Province. On the western shore of the Āb-i Istāda, 38 km south of Muqqur.

Date: Harappan, 2nd mill. BC; Kushan, 2nd cent. (ceramic).

Description: A series of mounds near the village, some of them identified as three large stupa-monastery complexes.

Fieldwork:
1. 1960 Fischer, DAAD—survey.
2. 1974 Dupree, AUFS—survey.
3. 1976 Taddei, IsMEO—survey.

Sources:
1. Fischer 1967a: 164–5—mention.
2. Fischer 1969: 340—mention (Site A4).
3. Taddei 1976: 600—mention.
4. N. Dupree 1977: 34—mention.
5. Dupree 1981: 108, pls 15–20—describes 'Indus Valley' (Harappan) pottery from his Abib-i Istada survey.

346. GĀZURGĀH
See also **428 HERAT.**

Original: Lat. 34° 22–36' N, long. 62° 14–23' E. Map 52.
Revised: 34.37450357 N, 62.23894268 E /
34° 22' 28.21283796 N, 62° 14' 20.19365448 E.
Herat Province. At the edge of the Herat Plain, 4 km northeast of Herat.

Date: Timurid, 15th cent. (stylistic).

Description: The shrine complex of Khwāja 'Abdullah Ansārī. The shrine itself is a large courtyard building with a very high *iwān*. Much of it is covered in tile decoration. Other buildings in the complex are: the Namakdān, a 15th-century pavilion; the Hauz-i Zamzam, a cistern; and the Zarnīgar. In 1992–6 the whole courtyard in front of the shrine was repaved with marble slabs. There are also numerous elaborately carved marble gravestones.

Fieldwork:
1. 1937 Wilber, American Institute of Iranian Art—survey.
2. 1966 Golombek, ROM—survey.
3. 1978–9 Samizay, Kābul University/UNESCO—survey.
4. 2005–12 AKTC—conservation and renovation work on main buildings.

Sources:
1. Conolly 1834: II. 21–4—description of the shrine and garden in 1830.
2. Lal 1834: 12–14—description of the shrine, with texts and translations of some of the gravestones.
3. Ferrier 1857: 284–5—brief description.
4. Vambery 1864: 284–5—brief description.
5. Griesbach 1885: 5—detailed description.
6. Yate 1887: 85–93—description of the shrine and texts of many of the gravestones.
7. Maitland 1888c: 409—brief description.
8. Maitland 1888a: 409—description.

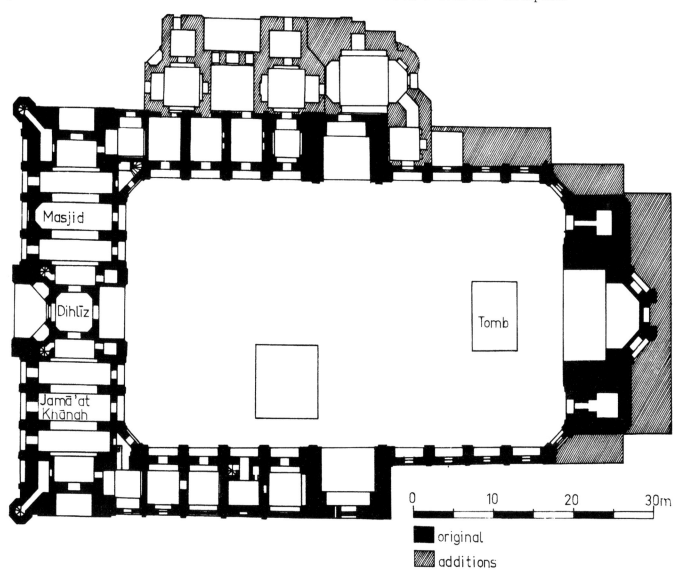

346 Gāzurgāh—Shrine of Abdullah Ansari (after Golombek 1969a).

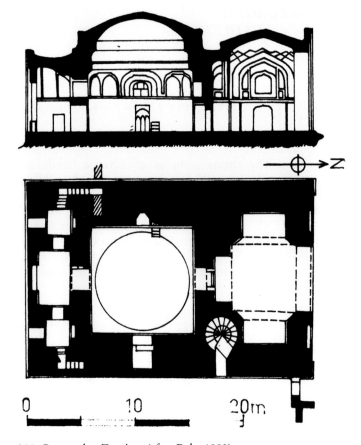

346 Gāzurgāh—Zarnigar (after Reha 1980).

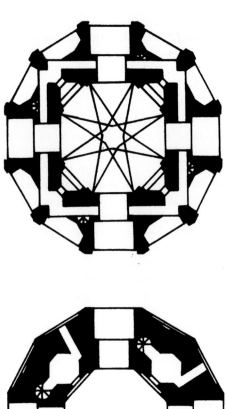

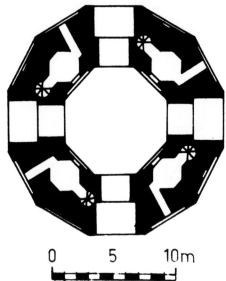

346 Gāzurgāh—Namakdān (after Golombek 1969a).

9. Yate 1888: 33–7—describes the shrine and many of the gravestones, giving their dates.
10. Niedemeyer and Diez 1924: pls. 167–74—photos.
11. Byron 1935b: 35—brief introduction to the monument.
12. Byron 1937: 105–6—brief description.
13. Wilber 1937: 121–6—photos and summary of the work carried out by the American Institute.
14. Byron 1938: 1126—brief description.
15. Frye 1948: 211–13—description and photos.
16. Seljuki 1962/63—study of the monument and inscriptions.
17. Pugachenkova 1963: 152–8—general summary.
18. Wolfe 1966: 48–57—good, illustrated guide to the complex.
19. Hill and Grabar 1967: pls 137–42—photos of architectural details.
20. Seljuki 1967a—texts of many of the gravestone inscriptions.

21. Ghawwās 1969: 12–13 and 18–20—description of the complex.
22. Golombek 1969a—very detailed analysis of the history, documentation, and architecture of the shrine. Full photographic coverage, though inadequate for drawings.
23. Anand 1970: 42–4—summary and photos.
24. Chaghatai 1970—discuss the influence of the dome-chamber on Mughul architecture.
25. Habibi 1971—photo of the Shamlu inscription and photo of the calligraphy.
26. Sourdel-Thomine and Spluler 1973: 355 and pl. 348—photo of the Namakdān.
27. Attar 1976—photos and texts of many of the inscriptions.
28. *Kabul Times* 1976a—brief mention of the repair work.
29. *Kabul Times* 1979a—brief report on the repair work.
30. Reha 1980—description and full architectural plans of the Khāna Zarnīgar, and parts of the shrine.
31. Samizay 1981: 64–8—good general summary and background, with photos, plans, and a note on the conservation needs.
32. O'Kane 1987: 149–152, 299–300, and 311–12—description of the shrine and associated monuments.
33. Michaud and Barry 1996: pls 74–5, 79—colour photos of the tilework.
34. Ball 2008: 210–12—summary.
35. Jodidio et al. 2017: 228–41—reports on the Aga Khan Trust for Culture conservation work.

347. GHAJAR

Lat. 31° 11' N, long. 62° 05' E. Map 84.
Nīmrūz Province. 3 km north-east of Chakhānsūr.

Date: Late Sasanian-early Islamic, 5th–10th cent. (ceramic).

Description: A site marked by a surface scatter of sherds around the modern village.

Fieldwork: 1960–70 Fischer, Bonn University—survey.

Source: Fischer et al. 1974: 40–1—brief description.

GHALBELA. See 2074 GHALBELA in Supplement.

348. GHĀL-I NAMAK

Lat. 35° 37' N, long. 65° 24' E. approximately. Map 46.
Faryāb Province. In the headwaters of the Darra-i Jauz, *c.*50 km south-east of Bīlchirāgh.

Description: Local reports of a complex of artificial caves.

Source: Lee 1980—mention.

349. GHALWAR
Or HAUZ-I KARBUZ. See also 428 HERAT.

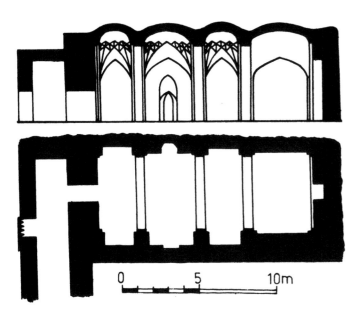

349 Ghalwar—Masjid-i Hauz-i Karbuz (after Pugachenkova 1970).

Original: Lat. 34° 21–35' N, long. 62° 09–15' E. Map 52.
Revised: 34.3501011 N, 62.15541845 E / 34° 21' 00.36395244 N, 62° 09' 19.50641064 E Herat Province. 4 km west of Herat, just to the north of the road to Zindajān.

Date: Timurid, 1441/2 (epigraphic, stylistic).

Description: A Timurid mosque with extensive later modifications. It contains a very fine mihrab, with calligraphic decoration in white and blue tile work. Opposite the mihrab is another inscription, giving the date of the building. The rest of the interior is covered in plain white plaster.

Fieldwork:
1. 1967–9 Pugachenkova, Af/Sov. Mission—architectural survey.
2. 1978–9 Samizay, Kābul University/UNESCO—survey.

Sources:
1. Herawi 1970—photo, brief description, and background.
2. Pugachenkova 1970: 28–31—full description and architectural discussion.
3. Habibi 1971: 219—photo of the mihrab and discussion of the calligraphy.
4. Pugachenkova 1976a—description and discussion.
5. Samizay 1981: 60–1—good description with a plan and photos.
6. O'Kane 1987: 207–9—description.
7. Wannell 2002: 245–6—description and translation of an insciption dated 1441 of an extract from Saadi's *Gulistān*.

350. GHANDAK
Including AUPAR and DOSHĀKH. See also 1199 TUGHAI.

Original: Lat. 34° 58'–35° 00' N, long. 67° 52'–68° 01' E. Map 58.
Revised:
34.95299157 N, 67.85588731 E / 34° 57' 10.76966352 N, 67° 51' 21.19431420 E,
34.98928046 N, 68.01417442 E / 34° 59' 21.40967364 N, 68° 00' 51.02791920 E, and
35.0043252 N, 68.0248068 E / 35° 00' 15.57070452 N, 68° 01' 29.30447640 E.
Bāmiyān Province. On the road from Bāmiyān to Dūshi, on the left bank of the Surkhāb and up the lateral Darra-i Ghandak, at Aupar and Doshākh.

Date: Turk and/or Islamic pre-Mongol, 7th–13th cent. (architectural).

Description: Remains of a mud fortress on the Surkhāb. The exterior is decorated with impressed diamonds in the form of lozenges and triangles. Inside the rooms have stepped, 'Sasanian' type squinches.
   There are remains of more ruined forts and towers up the Ghandak Valley.

Fieldwork:
1. 1955–68 Fischer, DAAD—survey.
2. 1974–5 Le Berre, DAFA—survey.

Sources:
1. Fischer 1966: 25—photos and discussion of the squinch in the context of Indo-Iranian contacts.
2. Auboyer 1968: pl. 100—photo and note.

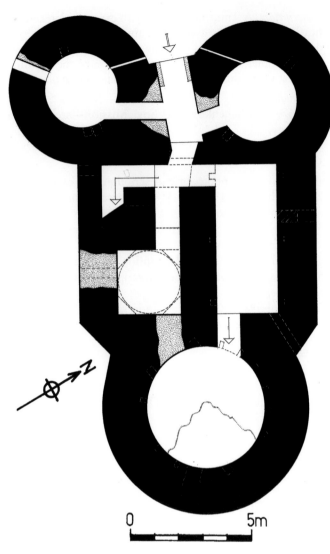

350 Ghandak (after Le Berre 1987).

3. Fischer 1969: 344 — brief summary.
4. Le Berre 1981: 27–32, 50–1, pls 4, 23–7, 49–51 — itineraries A1, ruins 8 and 9; A2, Dara-i Ghandak, ruins 1–3;
detailed description and photos.

GHĀRGHĀR. See 2075 GHĀR in Supplement.

GHARAMA. See 371 GHURAIDARAMA.

GHĀR-I ASB. See 46 ĀQ KUPRUK.

351. GHĀR-I DARWĪSHĀN
See also 2270 TEPE SAYYID MUKHTAR.

Lat. 34° 23' N, long. 62° 10' E. Map 52.

Herat Province. On a hill north of Bāgh-i Dasht, 5 km
north of Herat just to the north of the road to Islām Qal'a.

Date: Timurid, 15th cent. (epigraphic).

Description: A large, baked brick *iwān* with traces of a
mosaic tilework inscription.

Fieldwork: 1975 O'Kane, BIPS — survey.

Sources:
1. Seljuki 1967a: 61–2, pl. III — mention.
2. Ghawwās 1969: 39 — brief description.

GHĀR-I KARŪKH. See 2076 GHĀR-I KARŪKH in
Supplement.

GHĀR-I MĀR. See 46 ĀQ KUPRUK.

352. GHĀR-I MORDA GUSFAND

Lat. 35° 45' N., long. 65° 54' E. Map 46.
Faryāb Province. 10 km south of Bīlchirāgh and 9 km north
of Gurziwan at the head of a narrow valley formed by the
Rūd-i Chashma Khwāb.

Dates: Middle Palaeolithic, 50–30,000 BC (lithic); Late
Neolithic/Bronze Age, 5th-3rd mill. BC (ceramic, lithic).

Description: A very large rock shelter c. 300 m across by
100 m deep and 50 m high. Inside all the occupation was
stratified in loess deposits. No architecture was discernable.
Finds included both historic and proto-historic pottery,
stone scrapers, blades, flakes, cores, hand-axes, cleavers
and one worked bone. The site presented many geological
problems.

Fieldwork: 1969–70 Dupree, AMNH — excavations.

Sources:
1. Davis 1969–70: 78–80 — very summary report on the
1969 season.
2. Dupree, Lattman, and Davis 1970 — brief summary of
the excavations and material.
3. N. Dupree 1977: 353–4 — brief description.
4. Davis 1978: 43–4 — mention.
5. Zāhir 1980 — brief summary in Persian.

353. GHĀR-I SHĀH

Lat. 33° 17' N, long. 67° 35' E. Maps 77, 78, 79.
Ghazni Province. In the Ulyātū Valley on the route from
Jāghūri to Dasht-i Nāwar.

Date: Hunnic-Sasanian, 4th–6th cent. (architectural).

Description: A small, but well-preserved complex of artificial caves. Some are very high up in the cliff face, interconnected by stairs.

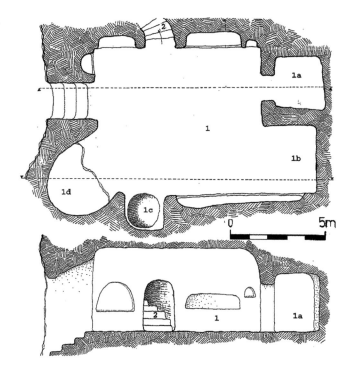

353 Ghar-i Shah 1 (after Verardi and Paparatti 2004).

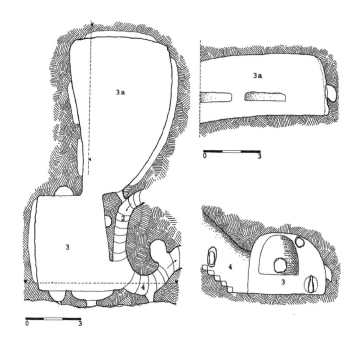

353 Ghar-i Shah 3 (after Verardi and Paparatti 2004).

Fieldwork: 1976 Taddei and Verardi, IsMEO—survey.

Sources:

1. Verardi 1977a: 149–50—brief description.
2. Verardi and Paparatti 2004: 56–60—detailed description with drawings and photos.

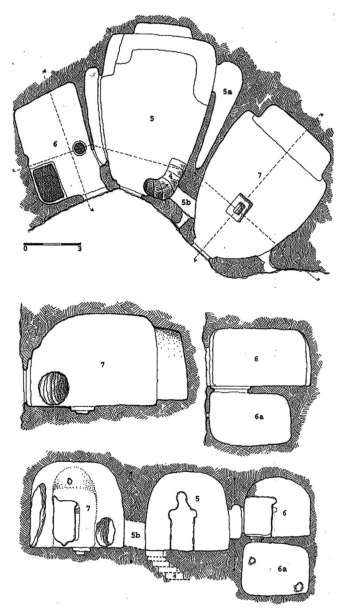

353 Ghar-i Shah 5–7 (after Verardi and Paparatti 2004).

354. GHĀR-I SUNI

Lat. 34° 21′ N, long. 63° 37′ E. Map 54.

Herat Province. 15 km to the west of Chisht, on the right bank of of the Harī Rūd.

Date: Middle Islamic, 11th–15th cent. (ceramic, Site K167).

Description: A small ruin (fort?) on the cliff constructed of stone, with a rubble facing. In the cliff face are some 200 inaccessible artificial caves (Soviet Site K165).

400 m from the caves is a small artificial mound measuring 3 × 40 m (Soviet Site K167).

Fieldwork:
1. 1952 Le Berre and Gardin, DAFA—survey.
2. 1968–78 Kruglikova, Af/Sov. Mission—survey.

Sources:
1. M. Le Berre: unpublished 1952 report, DAFA archives, tépé Chisht-Obeh 2.
2. Gaibov et al. 2010: 116—mention as living quarters for Muslim mystics (Site K165) and small mound (K167).

355. GHARLULI

Lat. 35° 45' N, long. 64° 54' E. Maps 45, 46.
Faryāb Province. 23 km south of Maimana near Takht-i Zaghan, a quarter of the way up a narrow valley formed by the Maimana River.

Dates: Iron Age, 2nd or 1st mill. BC (ceramic, lithic); Kushan and Sasanian, 1st–7th cent.; early Islamic, 8th–13th cent. (ceramic).

Description: A natural cave 13 × 23 m in area and 18 m in height. The material excavated ranges from 1st or 2nd millennium BC through to recent nomadic squatter occupation. The pottery includes a distinctive, regional hand-made ware.

Fieldwork: 1969 Dupree, AMNH—sondage.

Source: Davis 1969–70: 76–8—summary of the excavations.

GHAR TEPE. See 374 GHUZ TEPE.

GHARWAL. See 2077 GHARWAL in Supplement.

356. GHAT
Or GHET.

Original: Lat. 33° 18' N, long. 68° 17' E. Maps 78, 80.
Revised: 33.29301425 N, 68.27072047 E /
33° 17' 34.85131116 N, 68° 16' 14.59370136 E.
Ghazni Province. *C.*30 km south of Ghazni on the main road to Qarabāgh.

Description: Some mud-brick remains on a mound to the south of the village.

Fieldwork: 1960 Fischer, DAAD—survey.

Sources:
1. Fischer 1967a: 157—mention.
2. Fischer 1969: 339—mention.
3. Thomas 2015: 517—additional information from satellite imagery.

357. GHAZANA GHUNDAI

Lat. 34° 14' N, long. 69° 08' E. approximately. Map 60.
Lōgar Province. In the Surkhāb Valley below Shāhtūt Darra, well to the south of Mūsa-i Lōgar.

Description: A small square fort on a small rocky outcrop overlooking the valley. It has rounded angles and the remains of a semi-circular tower. Construction is of diaper masonry.

Fieldwork: 1963–4 Fussman and Le Berre, DAFA—survey.

Source: Fussman and Le Berre 1976: 102—mention.

358. GHAZNI
Including RAUZA. See also 1180 TEPE SARDAR.

Original: Lat. 33° 34–56' N, long. 68° 27–45' E. Map 80.
Revised:
Between 33.5683321 N, 68.43941332 E /
33° 34' 05.99554740 N, 68° 26' 21.88796496 E,
33.55626632 N, 68.42371745 E / 33° 33' 22.55873940 N, 068° 25' 25.38281136 E,
33.5641971 N, 68.4325741 E / 33° 33' 51.10957764 N, 068° 25' 57.26675892 E, and
33.58047969 N, 68.45255337 E / 33° 34' 49.72689336 N, 068° 27' 09.19213344 E.
Ghazni Province. 136 km south of Kābul. The remains of the old city stretch eastwards between the new city and the village of Rauza.

Dates: Ghaznavid and Ghurid, 11th–13th cent. (ceramic, documentary, stylistic, etc.); Timurid, 15th–16th cent. (stylistic).

Description: A large urban site consisting of a vast area of mounds and ruins littered with sherds and building debris. The most conspicuous remains are two elaborately decorated brick minarets or towers, both of which have only the first storey still standing, capped with modern tin roofs. Other remains are: the tomb of Sebuktegin on the hillside to the north of the minarets; the mausoleum of Shah Shahid or Muhammad Sharif Khan, a plain brick octagonal tomb, on a spur near the western minaret; the tomb of Mahmud, a modern building housing an extremely beautiful carved marble grave cover, in the village of Rauza; and the mausoleum of Abd al-Razzaq, a plain brick building now used as the Museum of Islamic Art, also in Rauza. In addition, there are many elaborately carved gravestones on and near the site. Excavations have revealed two more buildings: a private house and a palace. The palace is a complex of buildings surrounding a central, marble paved courtyard. The most significant find was a long, decorated marble frieze with an inscription in Persian, 250 m long. Other finds include objects of glass, ceramic, and bronze, decorative stuccos, paintings, marbles, and tilework.

During the 1980s the dome of the mausoleum of Abd al-Razzaq was damaged by rocket and artillery fire and the arch has collapsed at its apex. Extensive repairs were carried out to restore the roof, improve drainage from the dome, and to repair the collapsed arch. Internally, a large area of plaster was replaced and wooden window and door frames added.

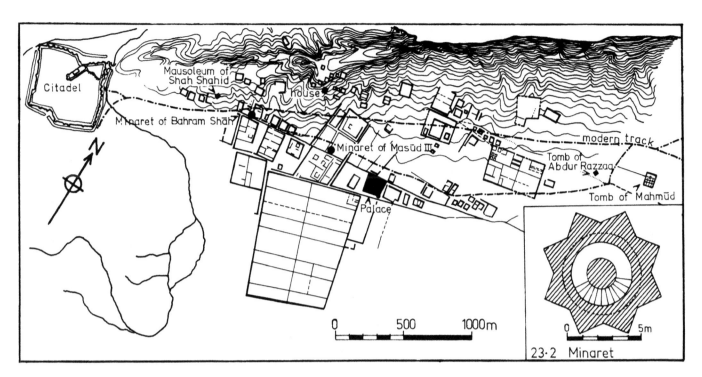

358 Ghazni—general plan (after Scerrato 1959 and St. G. Gore 1891: IX. 'Sketch Map of Ghazni and Surrounding Country', in Gazetteer of Afghanistan, IV. *Plans and Maps*. Simla).

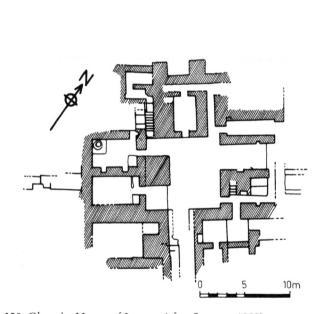

358 Ghazni—House of Lustres (after Scerrato 1959).

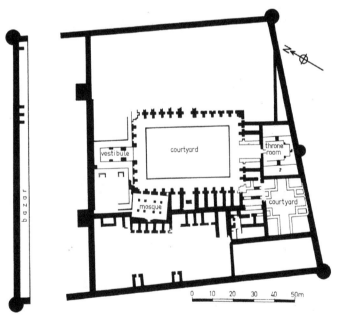

358 Ghazni—Palace of Masūd III (after Bombaci 1966).

Fieldwork:

1. 1923 Godard and Flury, DAFA—architectural and epigraphical survey.
2. 1956–64 Scerrato and Bombaci, IsMEO—excavations.
3. 1961–6 d'Amico and Bruno, IsMEO—restoration of the Mausoleum of Abdur Razzaq.
4. 1974 Orazi, IsMEO—architectural survey and conservation of the Mausoleum of Sharif Khan.
5. 1977–8 AIA—repair work on the minarets.
6. 2000 SPACH-UNESCO—repairs and consolidation to mausoleum of Abd-al Razzaq.
7. 2002–4 Taddei, IsIAO—survey and conservation work.

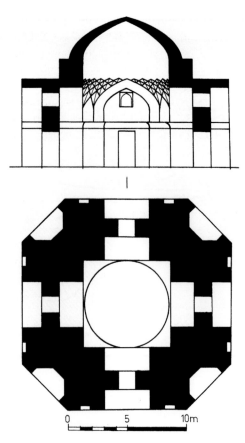

358 Ghazni—Mausoleum of Shāh Shāhid (after Pugachenkova 1970).

Sources:

1. Additional note on the Abd al-Razzaq mausoleum by Jonathan L. Lee.
2. Masson 1833c: 35—sketch depicting both minarets still with their second storeys.
3. Vigne 1837: 775—very brief description.
4. Kennedy 1840: II. 31 and 59–64—places both minarets at *c.*100 feet high, and gives a description of the garden and Tomb of Mahmud, including the grave cover and doors.
5. Vigne 1840: 128–33—estimates the height of the minarets as 140 feet, and describes the Tomb of Mahmud.
6. Atkinson 1842a: 217–22—detailed description of the minarets, estimated at 180 and 170 feet high each. Describes the Tomb of Mahmud and its surroundings, including the doors and some Hindu sculptures.
7. Atkinson 1842b: pl. 15—fairly detailed sketch of the minarets in 1839.
8. Jackson 1842: 11–12—brief description and sketch of the minarets.
9. Masson 1842: I. 219–22—description of the remains, mainly of the Tomb of Mahmud.

10. J. A. Rawlinson 1843—report on the removal to India of the wooden doors of the Tomb of Mahmud. Gives text and translations of the inscriptions.
11. Bellew 1862: 184–5—description of the minarets and tomb, condemning the British 'desecration'.
12. Fergusson 1876: II. 191–5—description of the minarets, the tomb, and the wooden doors.
13. Le Strange 1905: 348—summary of the historical references.
14. Flury 1918—analysis and discussion of the inscription in the Tomb of Mahmud.
15. Diez 1923: 159–64 and pls 70–2—describes the minarets and the Tomb of Mahmud.
16. Niedemeyer and Diez 1924: pl. 130—photos of the Tomb of Abdur Razzaq.
17. A. Godard 1925a: 26–9—historical background and brief report on all remains.
18. A. Godard 1925b—brief introduction to the most important remains.
19. Flury 1925—detailed epigraphical studies of the two minarets, the Tomb of Mahmud, and various other gravestones and fragmentary inscriptions from the site.
20. Byron 1935b: 34–5—brief introduction to the minarets and Tomb of Mahmud.
21. Hackin 1935b: 288–9—discusses briefly the provenance of coins of Gondophares and Napki found in Ghazni bazaar.
22. Diez 1936—discusses the development of the minaret form.
23. Y. Godard 1936—text and translation of the inscriptions on the minaret of Masud III.
24. Byron 1937: 322–6—good general description of the remains, with a photo and some background.
25. Pope 1938: 1280–1 and 1352–6—description of the brick ornament on the Bahram Shah minaret, and descriptions and drawings of other examples of carved stonework from the site.
26. Schroeder 1938: 983–5 and 1037—discusses the minaret of Mas'ūd and the general principles of Ghaznavid brick architecture.
27. Kohzad 1948a—discusses some of the Ghaznavid bronzes on display in the National Museum.
28. Diez 1950—discusses the minarets as possible victory towers.
29. Na'imi 1951—historical background of the site down to modern times. Description of many of the tombs and graves.
30. Sourdel-Thomine 1953: 110–21—art–historical study of the minaret of Bahram Shah and its inscriptions.
31. Bombaci 1957—historical-geographical background to Ghazni, Arachosia, and Zabulistan.
32. Bombaci 1959—historical background to the site and report on the excavations, mostly the finds.

33. Kessel 1959: pls 54–60—photos of many marble panels from Ghazni.
34. Scerrato 1959—report on the excavations: the architecture and finds.
35. Adamesteanu 1960: 21–7—brief summary of the excavations and the principal monuments.
36. Gullini 1960—plates and notes on an exhibition of photos and objects from Ghazni.
37. Bombaci 1961—short description of Ghaznavid art in terms of a broader Turk art style.
38. J. C. Courtois 1961: 27–8—summary of the excavations.
39. Fischer 1961c—discusses the Brahma statue discovered at the palace.
40. Gullini 1961: pls 154–78—photos of objects on display from the National Museum.
41. Scerrato 1961—discusses the art of Ghazni.
42. Bombaci 1962—outline of the main features of Ghaznavid architecture.
43. Bruno 1962: 100–4—summary description and many illustrations of the restoration of the Tomb of Abdur Razzaq.
44. Scerrato 1962a—discussion, artistic analysis, and photos of the Ghurid glazed tiles from the palace.
45. Klimburg 1963: 32–4—summary of the ornamentation of the monuments.
46. Pugachenkova 1963: 104–7, 121–5, and 162–5—general summary of all the remains.
47. Aziz 1964—good, light-hearted guide to the main monuments.
48. Mizuno 1964—illustrations and description of the Ghazni exhibition at the Tokyo Museum.
49. Otto-Dorn 1964: chapter 7—description of the Minaret of Mas'ūd III and the Tomb of Mahmūd.
50. Bombaci 1966—full linguistic analysis and translation of the Persian inscription. Discussion of its background and significance.
51. Rowland 1966a: 128–40—photos and description of some of the bronzes on display in the National Museum.
52. Hill and Grabar 1967: pls 145–50—photos of the minarets.
53. Riza 1967—texts of many inscriptions from Ghazni, including those on the minarets.
54. Taddei 1967: 345—mentions some massive stone foundations and marble pavement uncovered around the Tomb of Mahmūd.
55. Auboyer 1968: pls 108–16—illustrations and summary of some of the architecture and objects.
56. Hoag 1968—discusses the influence of the Mausoleum of Abdur Razzaq on Moghul architecture.
57. D. and J. Sourdel 1968: 359–62—brief discussion of the palace.
58. Anand 1970: 19–20—brief summary and photos of the remains.
59. Pugachenkova 1970: 37–41—full architectural study and discussion of the Shah Shahid Mausoleum.
60. Habibi 1971: 179–86—photos of some of the funerary and other inscriptions, and discussion of the calligraphy.
61. Rowland and Rice 1971: 51–2—description and photos of the objects on display from the National Museum.
62. Scerrato 1971a—discusses some bronze amulets from Ghazni.
63. Scerrato 1971b—describes and discusses some bronze harness pieces from Ghazni.
64. Hoag 1972—describes the Tomb of Abdur Razzaq and its later Indian connections.
65. Jalali 1972—extensive background to the site and the Ghaznavid dynasty.
66. H. Motamedi 1972—describes some of the objects in the Ghazni Museum.
67. Zander 1972: 563–4 and 570–6—describes in detail the IsMEO restoration project.
68. Rogers 1973: 239–44—discussion of the decoration on the wooden doors from the Tomb of Mahmūd and of other examples of Ghaznavid and Ghurid decoration. Suggests a date after the death of Mahmūd for the doors.
69. Sourdel-Thomine and Spuler 1973: 277–79—description and plan of the palace.
70. N. Dupree et al. 1974: 75–80—guide to the collection in the National Museum.
71. Kuwayama 1976: 384—description and discussion of a Brahma and a Jain statue found in the palace.
72. N. Dupree 1977: 179–90—good guide and historical background to the monuments and excavations.
73. Hutt 1977—links the minarets directly to the 8th- and 9th-century watch towers in eastern Tibet.
74. *Kābul Times* 1977a—very brief report on the repair work on the minarets.
75. Orazi 1977—detailed, fully illustrated architectural and engineering analysis of the Mausoleum of Sharif Khan.
76. Riza and Humayun 1977—catalogue and photos of many funerary inscriptions from in and around Ghazni.
77. Fischer 1978a: 311–13—brief description of the palace.
78. Galdieri 1978—details of the problems and plans for the conservation of the minarets, the Tomb of Mahmud, and other tombs.
79. H. Motamedi 1978a—historical account of Ghazni, with a summary of the excavations and remains and description of the collections in the Ghazni and National Museums.
80. Pinder-Wilson 2001—discusses in detail the decorations, inscriptions, and function of the minarets.
81. Hillenbrand 1984: 413–14—discussion in the context of Islamic palace architecture.
82. Golombek and Wilber 1988: 299–300—descriptions of the Abd ar-Razzaq and Shah-i Shahid monuments.

83. Blair 1992: 108–10—discusses the inscriptions of Masʿud I 1035–40.

84. Boardman in Errington and Cribb 1992: 105—describes a bronze Dionysus (?) figure of the 1st–2nd century found near Ghazni.

85. Hillenbrand 2000—discussion in the broader context of Ghaznavid and Ghurid architecture.

86. Flood 2002b—discussed the possible Indian inspiration both of the victory tower and the stellate plan.

87. Tissot 2006: 477–92—National Museum catalogue details and photos.

88. Flood 2007—discusses the motives behind the British removal of the so-called 'Gates of Somnath' and other spolia from Ghazni, and subsequent perceptions of Ghaznavid and Ghurid art.

89. Ball 2008: 92–3, 118, 190–3—summary.

90. Artusi 2009—analysis of brick and stucco decoration from the palace.

91. Giunta 2009—general account of the excavations and recent conservation work.

92. Rugiadi 2009—documentation of the marble decoration from the palace that has been taken and scattered in modern religious sites in the region.

93. Flood 2009b—discusses Indian influences on some of the carved stone work from Ghazni.

94. Giunta 2010—evidence for the reuse of the palace by Muizz al-Din under the Ghurids.

95. Rugiadi 2010—discusses the role of marble in the palace.

96. Rugiadi 2012—doctoral thesis: comprehensive discussion and catalogue of the marble decoration from the palace.

97. Allegranzi 2014—correlation of the extant remains with contemporary descriptions in Bayhaqi.

98. Allegranzi 2015—the early use of Persian royal epigraphy at the Ghaznavid court.

99. Filigenzi and Giunta 2015—brief summary of Italian work, including work after 2002.

100. Thomas 2015—summary of the excavations with information on sites in the region based upon sattelite imagery.

GHET. See 356 GHAT.

359. GHULĀM ʿALIKHĀN QALʾA

Original: Lat. 31° 13' N, long. 64° 11' E. approximately. Map 97.
Revised: 31.2212879 N, 64.19129901 E / 31° 13' 16.63642740 N, 64° 11' 28.67644284 E.
   Helmand Province. On the west bank of the Helmand *c.*12 km north of Hazārjuft, 2 km north of Shamala.

Dates: Sasanian, 3rd–7th cent.; Samanid, 10th cent.; Ghaznavid, 11th–12th cent. Timurid, 15th–16th cent. (ceramic).

Description: A group of ruins and mounds producing a large amount of sherds.

Fieldwork: 1966 Hammond, Cambridge University—survey.

Source: Hammond 1970: 449–50—lists sites (nos. 24 and 40) and describes the pottery and general survey results.

360. GHULĀMĀN

Lat. 31° 28' N, long. 65° 43' E. Map 89.
Kandahār Province. 21 km south of Kandahar between the Tarnak and Arghastān Rivers.

Dates: Sasanian, 3rd–7th cent.; Turki Shahi and early Islamic, 8th–13th cent. (ceramic).

Description: None available.

Fieldwork: 1950–1 Fairservis, AMNH—survey.

Source: Fairservis 1971: 394—mention.

361. GHULĀMĀN QALʾA

Original: Lat. 30° 33' N, long. 63° 46' E. Map 98.
Revised: 30.5617807 N, 63.75752504 E / 30° 33' 42.41051568 N, 63° 45' 27.09013608 E.
Helmand Province. On the north bank of the Helmand, 4 km east of Qalʾa-i Nau.

Description: Ruins of a large fort.

Source: Bellew 1874: 194—mention.

362. GHŪLBIYĀN

Lat. 35° 41' N, long. 65° 30' E. Map 46.
Faryāb Province, Gurziwan district. 35 km south-east of Bīlchirāgh. The site is in the mountains 15 km upstream south-east of the village of Ghūlbiyān in the Koh-i Larghajan area on the north side of a narrow limestone gorge.

Date: Early Sasanian AD 4th–early 5th cent. (stylistic).

Description: A mountain sanctuary located in a natural cave, possibly associated with a hunting reserve. Inside is a painting on the upper wall of the cave painted on a plastered surface. It consists of at least 16 figures, possibly more, as the painting has suffered from both weathering and deliberate vandalism, particularly on the extreme right. At the extreme top left is the figure of an an archer shooting an arrow at a springing ibex. The right side of the painting is occupied by at least three enthroned deities, the central one (and probable dedicatee) of which is identified with Tishtrya (Tir), the Iranian god of the star Sirius, provider of mountain game. A number of undersized female donors are depicted at the bottom right of the painting. To the left of the seated central deity are five standing male donors. Above and to the right of the central deity is a flying female deity or victory figure, possibly Fravasi. Under the feet of Tishtryais a representation of the Sea of Vurukasha (with fish swimming in it) the source from which this god collects the rains.

Nearby are some unidentified mud-brick and baked brick structures and a series of unidentified and undated incisions in the rock ledge to the left of the painting.

Fieldwork:
1. 1978 Lee, BIAS—survey.
2. 1996, Lee, SSAS—survey.

Sources:
1. Site description by F. Grenet and J. L. Lee.
2. Grenet and Lee 1980—summary description of the discovery of the painting (Lee). Detailed description and art-historical analysis with discussion of its historical background (Grenet).
3. Lee 1982: 107—briefly describes painting and discusses its implications on Ferrier's Sar-i Pul rock relief further east.
4. Grenet 1984: 134–5—discusses the funerary implications of the cave and painting.
5. Grenet and Lee, 1998—detailed description of the painting following a second field visit to the site, including detailed photographs, schematic drawing of the painting, detailed analysis, and revised dating and interpretation.
6. Ball 2008: 193—summary.
7. Ball 2017: 156–7—summary in the light of new discoveries in the Sasanian East.

363. GHULGHULA
See also 648 KŪRDŪ and 1044 SHAHR-I KALĀN.

Lat. 30° 44' N, long. 62° 02' E. Map 92.
Nīmrūz Province. In the dunes *c.*15 km south of Kūrdū and 18 km north of Sar-o Tar.

Description: A high ruined tower and a well-constructed baked brick building with a collapsed dome inside. There are many traces of ancient gardens and irrigation around.

Source: Tate 1910: 239—brief description.

364. GHUNDA CHASHMA
Or INDU KHĒL TUP.

Original: Lat. 34° 25' N, long. 70° 26' E. Map 66.
Revised: 34.40909934 N, 70.4274173 E / 34° 24' 32.75760636 N, 70° 25' 38.70227748 E.
Nangahār Province. 1.5 km west of Āhin Push stupa, 4 km south-west of Jalālābād.

Date: Kushan, 1st–3rd cent. (stylistic).

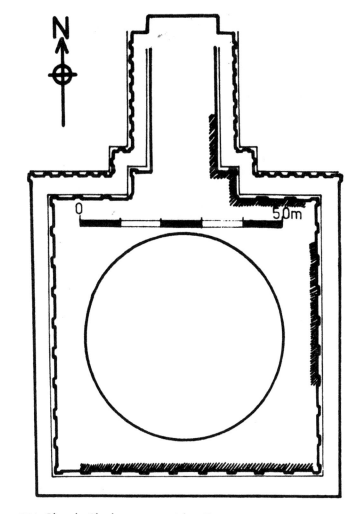

364 Ghunda Chashma—stupa (after Simpson 1879–80).

Description: Remains of a stupa. It stands on two platforms, the first 1.07 m high and *c.*25 m square, the second *c.*22 m square with 10 pilasters on each side. It has a stairway on the north side. The stupa contained nothing. To the south are the remains of a *vihara*.

Fieldwork:
1. 1834 Masson—survey.
2. 1879 Simpson, Indian Army—excavation.

Sources:
1. Masson 1841: 100—mention.
2. Simpson 1879a: 228–9—brief description of the stupa and its excavation.
3. Simpson 1879–80: 51—mentions the excavations and gives a plan.
4. Simpson 1881: 200–1—mention.
5. Errington 2017a: 156—the Masson collection and archive relating to the site.

365. GHUNDAI

Lat. 34° 39' N, long. 70° 11' E. Map 65.
Laghmān Province. In the foothills to the west of the
'Alishang River, 4 km west of Tigarhi on the road to Zīyā-
rat-i Mehtarlām.

Description: Ancient remains on top of the hills. There are
many fragments of white marble sculpture scattered
around, and reports of many finds of coins and other
antiquities.

Fieldwork: 1834 Masson—survey.

Sources:
1. Court 1837: 384—mention.
2. Masson 1842: III. 289 and 292—brief description.

366. GHUNDI BALUCH

Original: Lat. 34° 33' N, long. 68° 57' E. Map 63.
Revised: 34.54960041 N, 68.95568291 E /
34° 32' 58.56149292 N, 68° 57' 20.45847204 E.
Kābul Province. Near Sehgunbad, *c*.6 km south of Paghmān between Baiktūt and Arghandai.

Date: Kushan, 1st–4th cent. (ceramic).

Description: An artificial mound and the remains of a possible citadel.

Source: Caspani 1947b: 49—mention.

GHUNDI FATO. See 1025 SHĀH KHWĀJA.

367. GHUNDI GURGĀN

Original: Lat. 31° 29' N, long. 65° 35' E. Map 89.
Revised: 31.48144947 N, 65.57989139 E /
31° 28' 53.21809812 N, 65° 34' 47.60899788 E.
Kandahār Province. Near the left bank of the Tarnak, 19 km
south-west of Kandahār near Lal Khān, 13 km south-east of
Panjwāyī. The site is 1 km north of the village of Gurgān.

Description: A large, conspicuous artificial mound.

Source: Gazetteer 1980: V. 170—mention.

368. GHUNDI MANSŪR

Original: Lat. 31° 25' N, Long. 65° 38' E. Map 89.
Revised: 31.43633332 N, 65.6418875 E / 31° 26' 10.79995020 N,
65° 38' 30.79499316 E.
Kandahār Province. C.3 km from the right bank of the Dori
River and 3.5 km south-east of Karīz-i Shamshīr, *c*.22 km
south of Kandahār.

Dates: Sasanian, 3rd–7th cent.; Turki Shahi and early
Islamic, 8th–13th cent. (ceramic).

Description: A conspicuous, square artificial mound,
formed by the ruins of a large ancient fort. The remains of
four corner towers could still be seen in the late 19th
century.

Fieldwork:
1. 1950–1 Fairservis, AMNH—survey.
2. 1966 Fischer, DAAD—survey.

Sources:
1. Fischer 1967a: 151 and 183—mention and aerial photo.
2. Fischer 1969: 339—mention.
3. Fairservis 1971: 394—mention.
4. Gazetteer 1980: V. 170–1—brief description.

GHUNDI PAISA. See 2078 GHUNDI PAISA in Supplement.

369. GHUNDI RŪD-I BĪYĀBĀN

Lat. 30° 19' N, long. 61° 20' E. approximately. Map 94.
Nīmrūz Province. In the Rūd-i Bīyābān 2 km south-east of
Iran border post 10, 2 km south-west of the Rūd-i Bīyābān
sites.

Dates: Parthian/Indo-Parthian, 2nd cent. BC–AD 3rd cent.;
Sasanian, 3rd–7th cent. (ceramic).

Description: Ruins of a high buiding on a silt mound.
  A black chalcedony arrowhead was amongst the finds
from here.

Fieldwork: 1951 Fairservis, AMNH—survey.

Source: Fairservis 1961: 60—brief description (Site RB 12).

370. GHUNDI SHĀH NASR
Or TEPE ASHRAK.

Original: Lat. 34° 26' N, long. 70° 22' E. Map 66.
Revised: 34.43543396 N, 70.3787619 E / 34° 26' 07.56226140 N,
70° 22' 43.54284288 E.
Nangahār Province. Just to the north-west of Chahār Bāgh,
c.8 km west of Jalālābād on the road to Gandamak.

Description: A large mound with many other remains in
the vicinity. It is surmounted by a recent square building
known as Burj-i Jamadar. The mound is possibly the site of
ancient Nagara-hara.

Fieldwork:
1. 1834 Masson—survey.
2. 1965 Mizuno, Kyoto University—survey.

Sources:
1. Masson 1841: 99—brief description.
2. Mizuno 1971: 113—brief description and speculation.
3. Errington 2017a: 153–4 and 2017b: 33—the Masson collection and archive relating to the site.

GHŪRĀB. See 2080 GHŪRĀB in Supplement.

371. GHURAIDARAMA
Or GHARAMA.

Lat.36° 31' N, long. 70° 48' E. Map 38.
Badakhshān Province. On the east bank of the Kokcha,
*c.*10 km north of Hazrat Sa'id.

Date: Kushan, 1st–3rd cent. (ceramic).

Description: Remains of a fortified settlement on a natural
rocky ledge. Inside are two mounds 5 m high, containing
mud-bricks measuring 38 × 38 × 8 cm. The outer defensive
walls are of stone, and it has square towers. To the south is a
citadel measuring *c.*150 × 560 m. There was a surface find of
an unworked piece of lapis.

Fieldwork: 1875 Kohl—survey.

Sources: Kohl 1978: 65–7—brief description and photo.

372. GHŪRISANG

Lat. 35° 46' N, long. 69° 25' E. Map 50.
Baghlān Province. 3 km north of the village of Ghūrisang,
10 km north of Sayyad in the Andarāb Valley.

Description: Traces of ancient copper mining, consisting of
shallow excavations in the face of the vein.

Fieldwork: 1977 CNRS—geological survey.

Source: Berthoud et al. 1977: 17–18—brief description of
the geology and workings.

373. GHŪRIYĀN

Lat. 34° 21' N, long. 61° 30' E. Map 51.
Herat Province. 80 km west of Herat, on the south bank of
the Har-i Rūd.

Dates: Ghurid, 1198 (epigraphic); Timurid, *c.*1495 (stylistic).

Description: A Friday Mosque, similar to but smaller than
Zīyāratgāh. It is in very poor condition. There are also
remains of city walls and an old fort, overlooking the new
one. A three-part, Hebrew funerary inscription was found
in the region.

Fieldwork:
1. 1885 Griesbach, ABC—topographical survey.
2. 1975 O'Kane, BIPS—survey.
3. 1978–9 Samizay, Kābul University/UNESCO—survey.

Sources:
1. Lal 1846: 127—mentions many ruined buildings and
'ruined palaces' in the vicinity.
2. Anderson 1849: 582—mentions the remains as Fushanj.
3. MacGregor 1879: I. 232–4—description of the fort.
4. Griesbach 1885b: 1–2—description of fort.

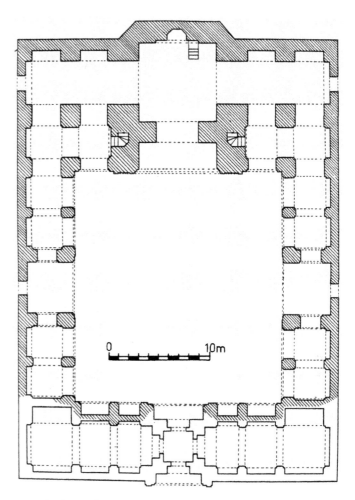

373 Ghūriyān (after O'Kane 1987).

5. Griesbach 1888a: 79—mentions the old fort.
6. Dupont-Sommer 1946—text, translation, and brief discussion of the Hebrew inscription, giving it a 5th-century date.
7. Fischel 1949—discusses the date of the inscription and concludes it is 1198.
8. Stern 1949—brief linguistic note and discussion of the date of the Hebrew inscription. New reading of Dupont-Sommer's version.
9. Rapp 1965—further analysis and commentary on the Hebrew inscription. Compares all four readings and confirms the 1198 date.
10. Seljuki 1967a: 146—describes the mosque.
11. Ghawwās 1969: 43–4—brief description of the remains.
12. *Kabul Times* 1979a—very brief report on the repair work on the mosque and fort.
13. Samizay 1981: 20–6—good description of all monuments, with photos, plans, and a note on the conservation needs.
14. O'Kane 1987: 351–2—description of the mosque.
15. Golombek and Wilber 1988: 300–1—description of the mosque.

GHŪRIYĀN TEPE See **794 PALGIRD.**

GHŪR-I ZARMAST. See **2079 GHŪR-I ZARMAST** in Supplement.

GHUR TEPE. See **400 GŪR TEPE.**

374. GHUZ TEPE
Or GHAR TEPE.

Original: Lat. 37° 18' N, long. 69° 29' E. Map 34.
Revised: 37.20611041 N, 69.4759502 E / 37° 12' 21.99746808 N, 69° 28' 33.42073116 E.
Tāluqān Province. In the modern village of Ghuz Tepe (or Ghur, Ghar Tepe, according to the maps), on the western edge of the modern canal which crosses the village towards the north, on an older course.
Dates: Achaemenid, 6th–4th cent. BC; Hellenistic, 3rd–1st cent. BC (A); Kushan and Hunnic-Turk, 1st–9th cent., pre-Mongol Islamic, 10th–13th cent. (ceramic).
Description: (A) High square mound (*c.*120 × 120 m, height 12 m), oriented north–south, sides very steep, damaged by irrigated fields (cotton): the original surface area of the site would have been considerably larger. A modern cemetery, to the north-west, extends up to the top of the mound, which is flattened, but very disturbed: wide funnel-shaped depressions at each of the four angles, themselves covered with tombs. (B) 100 m to the south-east, lower (by 3 m) and smaller but similar platform (c.50 × 50 m), cut on the east by a north–south road which follows the modern canal.
Collection: National Museum/AIA—sherds.
Fieldwork: 1974 Gardin et al., CNRS—survey.
Sources:
1. Site information by J.-C. Gardin.
2. Gardin and Lyonnet 1978–9: pl. III—nos. 57–8.
3. Lyonnet 1997: figs 25, 35, 39, 49, 68, 69—nos. 57, 58.
4. Gardin 1998: 42—nos. 57–8.

GHŪR-I ZARMAST. See **2079** in Supplement.

375. GIL-I SAFĪDKA

Original: Lat. 31° 21' N, long. 62° 04' E. Map 84.
Revised: 31.35235063 N, 62.07090303 E / 31° 21' 08.46228348 N, 62° 04' 15.25089576 E.
Nīmrūz Province. C.6 km north-west of Gul-i Safīd and 10 km east of Khwāja Siāh Push.
Dates: Late Sasanian–early Islamic, 5th–13th cent.; Mongol-Timurid, 13th–15th cent. (ceramic).

Description: Remains of a sizeable town stretching for *c.*1 km. It consists of a series of mud mounds with remains of walls and mud-brick towers (Fischer's Site 41).
Fieldwork: 1960–70 Fischer, Bonn University—survey.
Sources:
1. Fischer 1971b: 45—photos and brief description.
2. Fischer et al. 1974–6: 51—summary.
3. Ball 2008: 256—summary.

376. GĪNA KUHNA

Original: Lat. 30° 16' N, long. 61° 30' E. Map 94.
Revised: 30.2660886 N, 61.51217026 E / 30° 15' 57.91895172 N, 61° 30' 43.81292448 E.
Nīmrūz Province. In the Rūd-i Bībāyān 18 km east of Iran border post 20 and 5 km west of Tarākūn.
Date: ?Timurid, 15th cent. (traditional).
Description: Remains of a mud fort with square corner towers, surrounded by the ruins of domed tombs.
Fieldwork:
1. 1885 Merk, ABC—topographical survey.
2. 1903–5 Tate, SAC—survey.
Sources:
1. Merk 1888: 27—brief description.
2. Tate 1910: 163—brief description.

377. GĪRANAI

Lat. 32° 37' N, long. 62° 26' E. Map 72.
Farāh Province. On the left bank of the Farāh Rūd, just to the west of Shāhiwān, 41 km north-east of Farāh.
Description: Remains of a large, ancient baked brick fortress on a bluff above the river.
Sources:
1. Ferrier 1857: 269—brief description.
2. Gazetteer 1973: II. 91—mention.

GIRDĀB. See **1139 TĀLĀ.**

378. GIRDAI GHUNDAI
See also 274 DEH-I ADĀM KHĀN.

Lat. 31° 49' N, long. 64° 37' E. Map 86.
Helmand Province. On the east bank of the Helmand, 1 km north of the Girishk-Kandahār road, 5 km east of Girishk.
Date: Parthian, 2nd cent. BC (numismatic, stylistic).
Description: Some mud remains in the form of a large circle. Some pieces of terracotta frieze with egg-and-dart decoration in a classical style were found in 1977. Coins of

Pakores and Orthagnes were probably found from this site in the late 1920s.

Source:
1. Ferrier 1857: 311—mentions extensive remains.
2. Holdich 1910: 492—mentions remains.
3. Hackin 1935b: 288—mentions the coin finds.
4. Roberto Pagliero and Dirk Eenhooge 1977—personal communication on the remains and terracottas.

GIRDAI TEPE See **430 HIRDAI TEPE.**

379. GIRDI, JĀGHŪRĪ

Original: Lat. 33° 05' N, long. 67° 27' E. Map 79.
Revised: 33.07656527 N, 67.43506595 E /
33° 04' 35.63497272 N, 67° 26' 06.23740308 E.
Ghazni Province. On the east bank of the Arghandāb, 5.5 km south of Sang-i Māsha.

Description: A number of pyramid-shaped mounds, many of them containing caves. On the rocks are many inscriptions and graffiti, and in the vicinity are some old silver and lead mines.

Source: Markham 1876: 245—brief description, from a visit by Lynch in 1841.

380. GIRDI, NANGAHĀR

Original: Lat. 34° 14' N, long. 70° 58' E. Map 68.
Revised: 34.22524929 N, 70.97006925 E /
34° 13' 30.89742780 N, 70° 58' 12.24928884 E.
Nangahār Province. 50 km east of Jalālābād on the road to Tūrkhām.

Description: On top of a hill in the Girdi Valley are many ruins in diaper masonry. One building is still standing.

Fieldwork: 1879 Swinnerton, Indian Army—survey.

Sources:
1. Masson 1840: 32—mention.
2. Masson 1842: I. 168 and III. 245—mention.
3. Swinnerton 1879: 198—brief description.

381. GIRDI KAS

Original: Lat. 34° 23' N, long. 70° 40' E. Map 67.
Revised: 34.38761664 N, 70.68713296 E /
34° 23' 15.41990940 N, 70° 41' 13.67864160 E.
Nangahār Province. An island in the Kābul River, *c.*23 km east of Jalālābād.

Description: Remains of an ancient aqueduct of diaper masonry, and a tunnel through a spur of the hill. There are also remains of a stupa.

Sources:
1. Simpson 1879–80: 44—mention.
2. Simpson 1881: 194 and 206—mention.
3. Errington 2017a: 161—identified as Kameh in the Masson archives.

GIRISHK. See **274 DEH-I ĀDĀM KHĀN** and **378 GIRDAI GHUNDI.**

GOBAKLI TEPE See **941 QUSH TEPE, Imām Sahīb.**

GONDO. See **2081 GONDO in Supplement.**

GOOLJIN. See **656 KUSHK, Khwābgāh.**

GŪCHMACH. See **541 KAURMACH.**

382. GUCH TEPE

Original: Lat. 36° 49' N, long. 60° 48' E. Map 26.

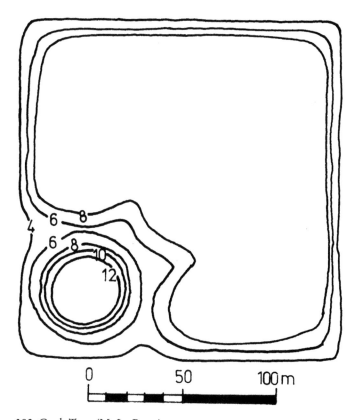

382 Guch Tepe (M. Le Berre).

Revised: 36.83198074 N, 66.80186082 E /
36° 49' 55.13067480 N, 66° 48' 06.69896748 E.
Balkh Province. 10 km north-west of this town. About
1.5 km north of the tepes described under no. 1227, east
of the same marshy depression. Access is by the road to
Kilift (about 1.5 km south of this road).

Description: Large square platform (about 170 × 170 m)
with a citadel in the south-west angle (height 12 m). The
whole is highly eroded, without any apparent trace of
constructions, surrounded by a ditch, and dominated by a
vast field of ruins.

Fieldwork: 1948 Le Berre, DAFA — survey.

Source: M. Le Berre: unpublished 1948 report, DAFA
archives, tépé P. 7.

GUDARA. See 326 FĪLKHĀNA.

383. GUDAR-I SHĀH
Or GUMBAZ-I SHĀH or SHĀH-I MARDĀN. See
also 229 DAM.

Original: Lat. 29° 55' N, long. 61° 20' E. Map 94.
Revised: 29.91127176 N, 61.34670524 E /
29° 54' 40.57832448 N, 61° 20' 48.13887336 E.
Nīmrūz Province. On the north bank of the Shaila Rūd,
north-west of the Gaud-i Zirra.

Date: Bronze Age, 3rd mill. (ceramic); ?Iron Age, c. 1800 BC
(stylistic); Timurid, 15th cent. (stylistic).

Description: A *zīyārat* and ruined mud-brick fort with one
arched doorway preserved, on a high, probably natural,
mound.

Scattered around are many alabaster objects, including
columns, discs, and weights, similar to objects found at
Tepe Hisār in Iran. In the vicinity are remains of many
ancient water-courses.

Shāh-i Mardān, or Zīyārat-i Shāh-i Mardān, is the more
correct name. Ruins of a small *gunbad* on a steep mound,
probably formed partly by earlier structures and also by the
deflation of the surrounding land. The visible structure is
no older than the 15th century (and possibly later), although
earlier tomb structures may underlie. The much reported
'Iron Age' stone objects have no relevance to the site. They
are deposited there by passing nomads and smugglers who
regard the site as a holy shrine. The stone objects probably
come from cemeteries associated with Khaimah Barang
(Site 229 Dam) and other similar, though smaller, sites in
the Shela Rūd. They in no way provide a date for Shāh-i
Mardān. The 'ancient water courses' are associated with a
typical 15th-century Timurid residence (presumably Site 393
Gumbad-i Sar-i Shaila) which is only a few hundred feet to
the east of 383. There are no Ghurid remains, or Ghurid
ceramic, in the area. There was no Islamic occupation in the
area until the 15th century. This is an isolated building. One

can see from it, more than a mile to the north-east, another
two similar buildings. Directly across the Shela Rūd (south)
from Shāh-i Mardān is a small tepe of 3rd mill. BC date with
plentiful evidence of copper smelting activity.

Fieldwork:
1. 1903–5 Tate, SAC — survey.
2. 1969 and 1971 Dales, University Museum Penn. — survey.
3. 1971–4 Trousdale, Smithsonian — survey.

Sources:
1. Additional information on revised date and nature of
   the site by W. Trousdale.
2. MacGregor 1882: 185 — brief description.
3. McMahon 1897: 407 and 412–13 — photo and brief
   description.
4. Yate 1900: 99–100 — mentions the *zīyārat* and stone
   objects.
5. Tate 1909: 40–1 — brief description.
6. Tate 1910: 161 — mention.
7. Dales and Flam 1969: 22–3 — brief description of the
   stone objects.
8. Dales 1972: 30–1 — description of the site with drawings
   and photos of the objects.
9. Dales 1977c — describes the survey and compares the
   objects with Hissar IIIc.
10. Deshayes 1977 — discusses the evidence of the stone
    objects for widespread trading connections in the
    Bronze Age of the Near East.

384. GUDĒLU
See also 2077 GHARWAL in Supplement.

Original: Lat. 33° 26' N, long. 69° 00' E. Map 82.
Revised: 33.43154291 N, 69.00537586 E /
33° 25' 53.55447384 N, 69° 00' 19.35309096 E.
Paktiyā Province. On the road between Ghazni and Gardēz, 11 km east of Kulālgu.

Description: A series of mounds.

Fieldwork: 1966 Fischer, DAAD — survey.

Sources:
1. Fischer 1967a: 166 — mention.
2. Fischer 1969: 340 — mention (Site A6).

GUDRI. See 479 JŪI NAU.

385. GUDUL-I ĀHANGARĀN

Lat. 33° 33' N, long. 68° 25' E. Map 80.
Ghazn-i Province. An area 2 km to the south-west of
Ghazn-i citadel.

Date: Turki Shahi, 7th cent. (stylistic).

Description: A chance find by construction workers of a very large number of objects. There was no recognizable stratigraphy or architecture in the find spot. The objects consist of miniature clay stupas, clay tablets with post-Gupta Sanskrit inscriptions, and clay bullae with seal impressions.

Fieldwork: 1962 Tadei, IsMEO—survey.

Sources:
1. Taddei 1968: 444—mentions the find.
2. Taddei 1970b—catalogues and makes a type series of the objects. Detailed descriptions, drawings, and photos.
3. Thomas 2015: 518—additional information from satellite imagery.

386. GŪGARI

Including KUHNA QAL'A and QARŪLŪ TEPE. See also 960 RUSTĀQ.

Original: Lat. 37° 08'–37° 09' N, long. 69° 49' E. Map 35.
Revised:
37.13669017 N, 69.81714366 E / 37° 08' 12.08461956 N, 69° 49' 01.71718140 E (A).
37.14411264 N, 69.80590996 E / 37° 08' 38.80551840 N, 69° 48' 21.27587040 E (C).
37.14315813 N, 69.80913361 E / 37° 08' 35.36928276 N, 69° 48' 32.88097836 E (C).
37.14220236 N, 69.8130086 E / 37° 08' 31.92851292 N, 69° 48' 46.83095424 E (C).
37.14454958 N, 69.80374853 E / 37° 08' 40.37848476 N, 69° 48' 13.49471628 E (C).
37.13966551 N, 69.81540821 E / 37° 08' 22.79584104 N, 69° 48' 55.46956536 E (B).
Takhār Province. At the exit from Rustāq on the road to Chayāb, on a terrace edge parallel to the Rustāq River (north-west orientation), 500 m west of the river. (A) The first tepe encountered (Qarūl Tepe) is at the fork in the road leading to the new bazaar of Rustāq, towards the south-west (in the course of construction, 1978); it rises in the middle of a cemetery which lies on both sides of this road. (B) The second, 400 m north of the first, is a small mound topped by a *ziyārat*. (C) Then there is a zone of regular hillocks covering 700 m on either side of the Chayāb road, some on the west side, on the edge of the road, the others on the east side, up to 300 m from the road. (D) The last tepe surveyed in this sector is located on the right bank of the Rustāq river (fordable in all seasons), at the end of a projection of the hills to the west which can be easily observed north of the preceding zone, overlooking the river by about 4 m.

Dates: Middle Bronze Age, *c.*2500–1500 BC (C); Achaemenid, 6th–4th cent. BC (B, D); Hellenistic, 4th–1st cent. BC (A, D); Kushan, 1st–4th cent. (B, C); Hunnic-Turk, 5th–9th cent. (A); Timurid, 15th–16th cent. (ceramic).

Description: (A) Qarūl Tepe: high pyramidal mound (sides 80 m at the base), in the middle of a large cemetery, on the edge of the terrace mentioned above; the narrow top rises to 6 m above the upper terrace (south-west side), but the north-east slopes of the tepe descend to the level of the lower terrace, 5 or 6 m further down. In the cuts on the north and east sections of the mound, 4 m below the top, burnt layers (alternating earth and charcoal), with complete jars in place. (B) Small rounded hillock (diam. 20 m), low (2 m), 100 m from the road (east side); many sherds between the road and this hillock, rare on the latter. (C) Area of hillocks located between the road and the terrace edge parallel to it, *c.*200 m to the east: many small mounds of various shapes (height generally less than 2 m), of which some are probably natural, but scattered with sherds of the same periods (Kushan and Islamic) over all the area (700 × 200 m). One of the highest is a mound called Kuhna Qal'a, located *c.*700 m from A (Qarūl Tepe), on the east side of the road (100 m): square platform (70 × 70 m), height 3 m, with a hillock of 5 m in the north-east angle; another mound of 5 m (rounded, diam. 50 m) 300 m south of the latter, on the west side of the road, near an active brick kiln. (D) Rounded rectangular platform aligned north-west/south-east (50 × 30 m), damaged by cultivation; flat top (3–4 m), ploughed (*lalmī*).

Collection: National Museum/AIA—sherds.

Fieldwork: 1978 Gardin et al., CNRS—survey.

Sources:
1. Site information by J.-C. Gardin.
2. Gardin and Lyonnet 1978–9: pl. II—nos. 507 to 513, 522.
3. Lyonnet 1997: figs 13, 25, 35, 39, 46, 49, 68, 69—nos. 507 to 513, 522.
4. Gardin 1998: 91—nos. 507 to 513, 522.

387. GULAZIRI KUL TEPE

Original: Lat. 36° 10' N, long. 65° 59' E. Map 24.
Revised: 36.17745728 N, 65.98946026 E / 36° 10' 38.84619108 N, 65° 59' 22.05693492 E.
Jauzjān Province. 9 km to the south-east of Sar-i Pul on the route to Sangchārak.

Dates: Hunnic-Turk, 5th–9th cent.; pre-Mongol Islamic, 10th–13th cent. (ceramic).

Description: None available.

Collection: National Museum/AIA—sherds.

Source: Gardin and Lyonnet, 1980 chronological study of unpublished pottery from DAFA surveys.

GULBĀGH. See **2082 GULBĀGH** in Supplement.

388. GULBAHĀR

Lat. 35° 08' N, long. 69° 18' E. Map 64.
Parwān Province. On the east bank of the Panjshīr River, 7 km east of Jabal as-Saraj, 84 km north of Kābul.

Date: ?Kushan, 1st–3rd cent. (stylistic).

Description: Many objects from the Buddhist period were found in *c.*1955 when building a factory. The finds included a fragmentary schist relief of Maitreya, the base of a statue with a Kharoshthi inscription, a small figure of Dipamkara Buddha, some column bases, various other miscellaneous Buddhist sculptures, and many coins.

Fieldwork: 1956 Ramachandran and Sharma, ASI—reconnaissance.

Sources:
1. Ramachandran and Sharma 1956: I. 30—brief description of the finds.
2. Mizuno 1971: 126—mention.
3. Fussman, Murad, and Ollivier 2008: 175—mention.

389. GULDARRA
Or MŪSA-I LOGAR.

Original: Lat. 34° 23–38' N, long. 69° 16–26' E. Map 62.
Revised: 34.39286658 N, 69.27853211 E /
34° 23' 34.31967864 N, 69° 16' 42.71558304 E.
Kābul Province. In the Mūsa-i Lōgar Valley, 22 km south-east of Kābul.

Date: Early Sasanian, 3rd–4th cent. (architectural, numismatic, stylistic).

Description: A large stupa-monastery complex, probably the best preserved in Afghanistan. The main stupa consists of a dome and two drums resting on a high, square platform with a staircase to the south-west, in turn resting on a lower square platform. Construction is of diaper masonry throughout. The high platform and both of the drums are decorated in friezes of blind arches and 'Indo-Corinthian' pilasters. Behind the stupa is a fortified monastery. It is of mud-brick construction on a stone foundation, and consists of a central courtyard surrounded by cells. To the south of

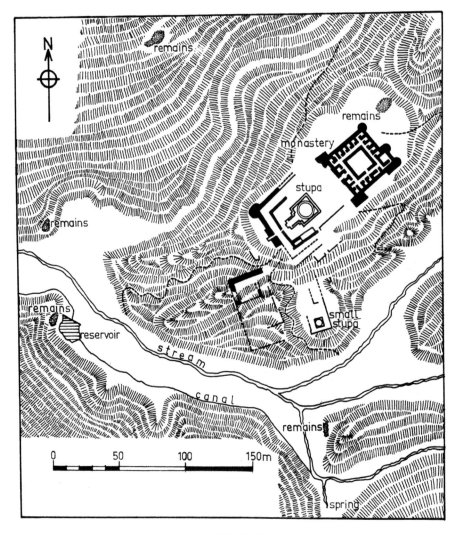

389 Guldarra (after Lézine 1964, Fussman and Le Berre 1976, and W. Ball).

the complex is a small stupa, almost a replica of the larger one, apart from the staircase.

In the 19th century, several gold ornaments, including a gold medallion of Mokadphises, were found in the stupa by Masson. In the DAFA excavations in the monastery many Kharoshthi ostraca were found, as well as some sculptures, including several stucco Garuda images.

The stupa dome was badly damaged in the 1980s as a result of a bomb being dropped on or in the vicinity of the site.

Fieldwork:
1. 1833 Honigberger—excavation.
2. 1834 Masson—excavation.
3. 1962–4 Lezine, Unesco—restoration of stupa.
4. 1963–4 Fussman and Le Barre—excavations in monastery.
5. 1965 Mizuno, Kyoto University—survey.
6. 1976–9 Rao, BIAS—preservation of stupa and monastery.

Sources:
1. Jacquet 1836b: 276—mentions the gold ornaments.
2. Masson 1841: 115—very brief description.
3. Carl 1959a: figs 38–40—photos of the monument before restoration.
4. Lézine 1962: 30–40—description of the site.
5. Lézine 1964—full examination of the architecture and decoration of the stupa, with notes on the restoration carried out. Many illustrations.
6. N. Dupree 1971a: 146–8—good general description.
7. Mizuno 1971: 125–6—brief description and photos.
8. Le Berre 1973:—brief report on the restoration with a list of equipment and costs.
9. Fussman and Le Berre 1976—detailed description of the excavations and of all architectural details. Analysis of the construction, catalogue of finds, and chronological discussion.

10. Davary 1977—mentions the inscriptions and gives a bibliography.
11. Franz 1977–8—discusses the development of the stupa.
12. Mac Dowall and Taddei 1978b: 241 and 267—summary of the ostraca and ceramics.
13. Rau 1979—brief preliminary report on the preservation work on the stupa and monastery.
14. Rao et al. 1985—full report on the preservation work.
15. Wightman 2007: 731—discusses the evolution of the stupa.
16. Ball 2008: 107, 194–8—summary.
17. Fussman, Murad, and Ollivier 2008: 71–8—argues for a 5th–6th-century date.
18. Jongeward et al. 2012—catalogue and discussion of the reliquaries.
19. Ball 2017: 162–3—summary in the light of new discoveries in the Sasanian East.
20. Errington 2017a: 77–81 and 2017b: 54, 56–7, 59, 113—the Masson collection and archive relating to the site.

GUL HAMID. See 19 AINAK.

390. GUL-I SAFĪD
  Or GUL-I SAFĪDKA.

Original: Lat. 31° 118' N, long. 62° 07–11' E. Map 84.
Revised: 31.3094853 N, 62.11370677 E / 31° 18' 34.14706668 N, 62° 06' 49.34436372 E.
Nīmrūz Province. 16 km north of Chakhānsūr and 9 km north-east of Pūst-i Gau.

Date: Early Islamic, 8th–13th cent. (architectural, ceramic).

Description: A very large unfortified area of remains. They include: some 90 houses, usually of the courtyard-*iwān*

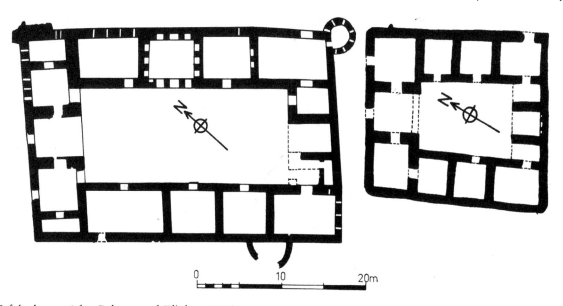

390 Gul-i Safīd—houses (after Behrens and Klinkott 1973).

type, with horseshoe arch decoration; a line of multi-storeyed watch towers in the north-west of the town; a central hill with a citadel, some cisterns, several tombs, a mosque, and a *zīyārat*; some high artificial mounds; and a canal system. Just to the north are some more ruins, standing on artificial mounds (Fischer's sites 32–4).

Fieldwork: 1971–2 Fischer, Bonn University — survey.

Sources:
1. Fischer 1970a — photos.
2. Fischer 1970b: pls 1–4 — photos.
3. Fischer 1971b: 42–3 and 45 — brief description with ground and aerial photos.
4. Fischer 1972 — discusses the pendentives.
5. Behrens and Klinkott 1973 — typology and architectural analysis of the *iwān* houses. Includes drawings.
6. Fischer 1973b — gives photogrammetrical drawings and describes the work carried out.
7. Fischer 1973c: 140 — brief description.
8. Reuther 1973 — discussion of the mud-brick architecture.
9. Fischer et al. 1974–6: 50 — summary and photos.
10. Fischer et al. 1976 — description of the photogrammetrical recording.
11. Fischer 1978b: 368–9 — brief description.
12. Fischer 1978c: 62 — brief summary and discussion in the context of medieval city types.
13. Fischer 1983b — discussion in context of eastern Iranian architecture.
14. Klinkott 1982: 142–209 — description of the *iwān* houses.
15. Ball 2008: 255–6 — summary.

GUL-I SHUTUR. See **2083 GUL-I SHUTUR** in Supplement.

391. GULRĀN

Original: Lat. 35° 06' N, long. 61° 41' E. Map 42.
Revised: 35.10436784 N, 61.68495538 E /
35° 06' 15.72421644 N, 61° 41' 05.83936188 E.
Herat Province. *c.*110 km north-west of Herat. The remains are to the east and south-east of the village.

Date: Bronze Age, 3rd mill. BC (ceramic); indeterminate Islamic.

Description: Remains of a large town. It consists of many ruined buildings and an extensive scatter of bricks and sherds, surrounded by remains of irrigation channels and gardens. In the centre are the remains of a citadel, consisting of a central keep *c.*10 m high on a mound surrounded by a ditch *c.*150 m square. There is also a ruined mosque and caravanserai.

Fieldwork:
1. 1885 Yate, ABC — topographical survey.
2. 2004–6 Franke and Urban, DAI — survey.

Sources:
1. *Pioneer*, 3 Apr. 1885 — brief description.
2. Maitland 1888a: 156–7, 254 — brief description, mentioning possible connections with the *Shāhnāma*.
3. Peacocke 1887b: 451 — mentions caravanserai.
4. A. C. Yate 1887: 284–5 — description of all remains.
5. C. E. Yate 1888: 68 — brief description of the fort.
6. Franke 2008: 31 and pl. 128 — notes pillaging at the site and illustrates a Bronze Age chlorite bowl from the site.
7. Franke 2016: 24 — mentions the Bronze Age date.

392. GUL TEPE
Or MIHR-I NIGĀ.

Lat. 35° 53' N, long. 64° 48' E. Map 24.
Faryāb Province. 5 km south-east of Maimana, just to the south of the village of Imām Sāhib.

Description: A series of small hills, one of which contains a complex of low, artificial caves. Most have fallen in, but some are at least 20 m deep. The surfaces show signs of having been plastered, and there is a scatter of coarse, hand-made sherds. The site was probably an interlinking dwelling place and had no ritual function.

Fieldwork: 1978 Lee, BIAS — survey.

Source: Jonathan L. Lee.

GUMBAD. See **786 PAI MŪRIMŪRI.**

393. GUMBAD-I SAR-I SHAILA
Or SHAILA RŪD.

Lat. 29° 50' N, long. 61° 23' E. Map 94.
Nīmrūz Province. At the western end of the Gaud-i Zirra depression, 10 km south-east of Gudar-i Shāh.

Date: Ghurid-Timurid, 12th–15th cent. (architectural, ceramic).

Description: Some ruined buildings and a scatter of sherds on both sides of the river. Construction is of mud-brick. The buildings have a decorated façade of blind arches and crosses.

Fieldwork: 1969 and 1971–2 Dales, AMNH — survey.

Sources:
1. Yate 1900: 96–7 — brief description.
2. Dales 1972: 24 — mention and photo.

394. GUMBAD-I YAK DAST

Lat. 30° 31' N, long. 61° 52' E. Map 93.
Nīmrūz Province. On the edge of the plateau 10 km south of Qal'a-i Fath, *c.*400 m to the east of the road to Chahār Burjak.

Description: Ruins of a square, baked brick tomb, roofed with a dome.

Fieldwork: 1903–5 Tate, SAC—survey.

Sources:
1. Smith 1876: 293—mention.
2. Peacocke 1885a: 5—mention.
3. Maitland 1888a: 67—mention.
4. A. C. Yate 1887: 80–1—brief description and associated legend.
5. Tate 1910: 247 and 249—brief description and photo.

GUMBAZ-I SHAH. See 383 GUDAR-I SHĀHSHĀH.

GUMBAZ AINADAH. See 820 PUL-I ZUHAK.

395. GUNĀBĀD

Lat. 34° 19' N, long. 63° 07' E. Map 53.
Herat Province. 9 km south-west of Obeh, in the direction of Herat: on the right bank of the Harī Rūd.

Description: Circular ruin sourrounded by a ditch, situated on a conical hill. At the base of this hill, another small tepe of rectangular shape.

Fieldwork: 1952 Le Berre and Gardin, DAFA—survey.

Source: M. Le Berre: unpublished 1952 report, DAFA archives.

GUNBAD-I SHUHADA. See 2084 GUNBAD-I SHU-HADA in Supplement.

GUNDA CHASHMA. See 364 GHUNDA CHASHMA.

GURĀZĀN. See 2086 GURĀZĀN in Supplement.

GŪR DARRA or GŪR TEPA. See 2085 GŪR DARRA or GŪR TEPA in Supplement.

396. GURGAK

Lat. 30° 53' N, long. 64° 20' E. approximately. Map 97.
Helmand Province. In the desert *c.*20 km from the left bank of the Helmand, east of Abbasābād.

Dates: Achaemenid, 6th–4th cent. BC; Sasanian, 3rd–7th cent. (ceramic).

Description: A mound and some scattered mud-brick ruins over a wide area.

Fieldwork: 1966 Hammond, Cambridge University—survey.

Source: Hammond 1970: 449—lists site (No. 9) and describes the pottery and general survey results.

397. GURG TEPE

Original: Lat. 36° 50' N, long. 66° 48' E. Map 26.
Revised: 36.83529531 N, 66.79810851 E /
36° 50' 07.06313220 N, 66° 47' 53.19062916 E.
Balkh Province. 12 km north-west of this town. About 500 m north of Guch Tepe, on the edge of the same marshy depression.

Description: Quadrangular platform (*c.*70 × 60 m), flattened top (height c.6 m).

Fieldwork: 1948 Le Berre, DAFA—survey.

Source: M. Le Berre: unpublished 1948 report, DAFA archives, tépe P. 8.

398. GURGURAWA
Or QAL'A-I HANĪFA. Including QAL'A-I SAR-I SANG and QURGHAN.

Lat. 35° 07'–35° 11' N, long. 67° 42' E. Map 48.
Bāmiyān Province. The Darra-i Gurgurawa south of the Saighān River, on the route leading from the Saighān to Bāmiyān.

Date: Turk/pre-Mongol Islamic, 7th–13th cent. (architectural).

Description: An imposing fort, said locally to be very ancient, containing a famous *zīyārat* dedicated to Muhammad Hanīfa. There are several more forts to the north and south along the valley.

Fieldwork:
1. 1885 Maitland, ABC—topographical survey.
2. 1974–75 Le Berre, DAFA—survey.
3. 2002 Lee, Society for South Asian Studies—reconnaissance.

Sources:
1. Maitland 1888b: 9—mention.
2. Gazetteer 1979: 477—mention.
3. Le Berre 1981—itineraries A2, Darya-i Saighān, ruin 4; F, ruins 1 and 2.
4. Lee 2006: 249–50—brief description, photo, and reproduction of Masson's sketch.

399. GUR-I MOGHUL

Original: Lat. 31° 40' N, long. 61° 29' E. Map 83.
Revised: 31.65226621 N, 61.49535894 E /
31° 39' 08.15835276 N, 61° 29' 43.29219192 E.
Nīmrūz Province. 16 km west of Lāsh Juwain and 7 km north of Jā-i Darg.

Date: Mongol-Timurid, 13th–15th cent. (ceramic).
Description: A series of mud-brick ruins.
Fieldwork: 1960–70 Fischer, Bonn University—survey.
Source: Fischer et al. 1974–6: 36—mention.

400. GŪR TEPE, QUNDŪZ
Or Ghur tepe.

Original: Lat. 36° 49' N, long. 68° 41' E. Map 32.
Revised: 36.8160307 N, 68.68723069 E / 36° 48' 57.71051568 N, 68° 41' 14.03046600 E.
Qundūz Province. Some 20 km north-west of Qundūz, by the Asqālan road and the road which forks at Larkhabi towards the village of Ghūr Tepe: the site is located on the road itself, a little before it meets the canal of Chim Tepe (no. 210) 300 m to the west; it was constructed on a high terrace of the Qundūz River, which slopes southward towards the river.
Dates: Achaemenid, 6th–4th cent. BC; Kushan, 1st–4th cent. (ceramic); Ghaznavid, 11th–12th cent. (stylistic).
Description: Square platform (50 × 50 m), oriented approximately north–south, height 4 m, dominated by a central hillock, also square (15 × 15 m), height 6 m, sloping gradually towards the terreplein. The base of the platform has been cut into by the roads (north, east, south sides) and by cultivation (west side), such that the mound should be reconstituted as wider, sloping less steeply towards the terrace.
  Surface finds: glass fragments, bronze Chinese mirror; other finds are reported but not confirmed: bronze objects and small bags [sachets: *sic*].
Collections: National Museum/AIA—sherds, Chinese mirror.
Fieldwork:
1. 1955 and 1960 Fischer, DAAD—survey.
2. 1975 Kohl—survey.
3. 1978 Gardin et al., CNRS—survey.
Sources:
1. Site information by J.-C. Gardin.
2. Fischer 1961a: 20-1—mention.
3. Trousdale 1964—stylistic commentary on mirror.
4. Fischer 1969: 349—mention.
5. Kohl 1978: 68—mention.
6. Gardin and Lyonnet 1978–9: pl. VII—no. 494.
7. Lyonnet 1997: figs 25, 35, 49—no. 494.
8. Gardin 1998: 80—no. 494.

401. GŪRZĪWĀN

Lat. 35° 42' N, long. 65° 14' E. Map 46.
Faryāb Province. 19 km south of Bīlchirāgh near Ghār-i Morda Gusfand.
Dates: Neolithic, *c.*6000 BC (ceramic, lithic); late Sasanian, 5th–7th cent.; Turk and early Islamic, 7th–13th cent. (ceramic).

Description: Some open-air sites on the river terraces, with a surface scatter of flint and pottery.
Fieldwork: 1970 Dupree, AUFS—survey.
Sources:
1. Information by L. Dupree.
2. N. Dupree 1977: 354—mentions Neolithic material.

402. GŪSHTA

Lat. 34° 21' N, long. 70° 47' E. Map 68.
Nangahār Province. On the north bank of the Kābul River, *c.*14 km south-east of Girdi Kach and *c.*40 km east of Jalālābād.
Date: Kushan-Hunnic, 1st–6th cent. (architectural).
Description: Remains of a stupa on a mound.
Sources:
1. Masson 1840: 33—mention.
2. Masson 1842: I. 169—mention.

GUZARA. See **2087 GUZARA** in Supplement.

403. GUZARPĀM

Original: Lat. 34° 07' N, long. 64° 38' E. Map 55.
Revised: 34.12818713 N, 64.66758323 E /
34° 07' 41.47366512 N, 64° 40' 03.29961108 E.
Ghūr Province. 8 km east of Hauz-i Bangi on the road from Shahrak to Chakhcharān.
Date: Ghurid, 12th cent. (architectural).
Description: A ruined fortress.
Sources:
1. Klimburg 1960: 47—mention.
2. Fischer 1969: 343—mention (Ruins P3).
3. Fischer 1978a: 335—mention.

404. HADDA
Including BĀGH GAI, DEH GHUNDI, GAR NAU, TEPE KĀFIRIHĀ, TEPE KALĀN, TEPE SHUTUR and TEPE ZARGARĀN. See also 165 CHAKHIL-I GHUNDI, 673 LALMA, and 815 PRATES.

Original: Lat. 34° 22–36' N, 70° 28–46' E. Map 67.
Revised: 34.35587127 N, 70.46291737 E /
34° 21' 21.13658136 N, 70° 27' 46.50253848 E.
Nangahār Province. 9 km by road south-east of Jalālābād.
Dates: Kushan-Sasanian, 1st–7th cent. (numismatic, stylistic).
Description: An extensive area of stupas, monasteries, and artificial caves covering approximately 15 km². All of the

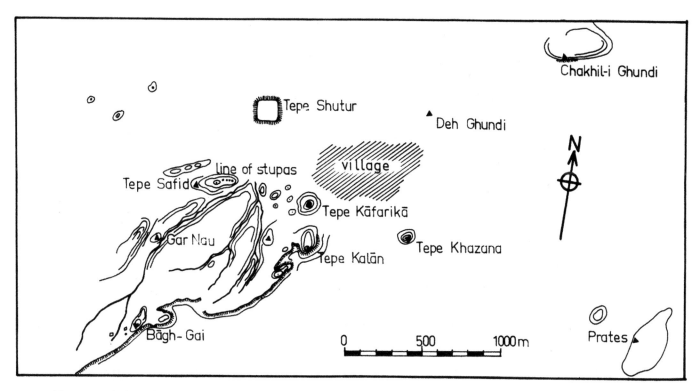

404 Hadda—general plan (after Masson 1841 and Barthoux 1933).

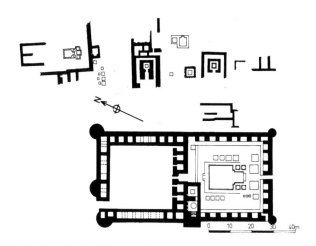

404 Hadda—Bāgh Gai (after Barthoux 1933).

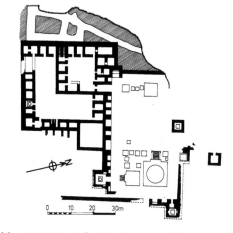

404 Hadda—Gar Nau (after Barthoux 1933).

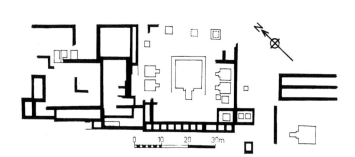

404 Hadda—Deh Ghundi (after Barthoux 1933).

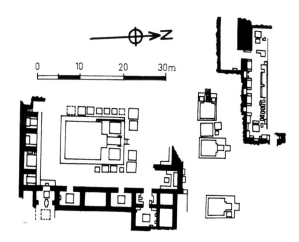

404 Hadda—Tepe Kāfarihā (after Barthoux 1933).

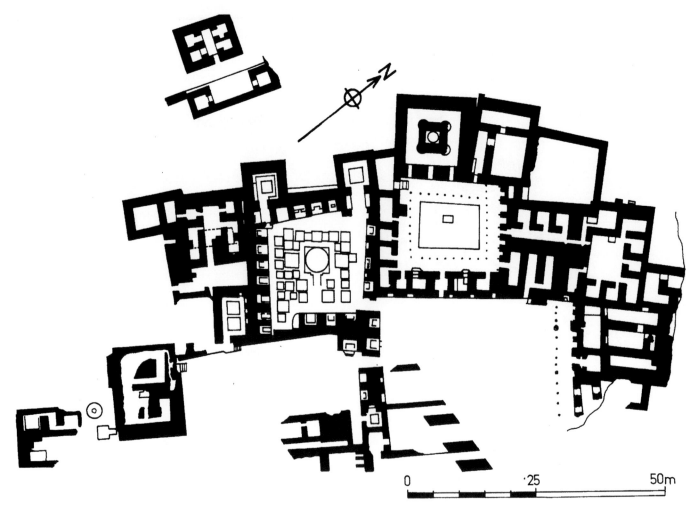

404 Hadda—Tepe Shutur (after Tarzi 1976a).

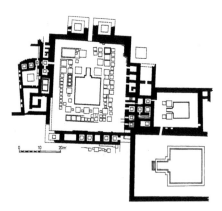

404 Hadda—Tepe Kalān (after Barthoux 1933).

sites are stupa-monastery complexes, often with more than one main stupa and always with many votive stupas. Hadda produced an immense artistic wealth of mud and stucco sculpture, many gold, silver, and steatite reliquaries, large numbers of coins—many of them Roman—several Kharoshthi inscriptions, and many other articles of gold, silver, and precious stone. The most spectacular finds came from Tepe Kalān, which produced a gold reliquary studded with emeralds and sapphires, and from Tepe Shutur, where reliefs include the well-known 'fish porch' and the statue of Heracles.

Some of the caves are decorated. Near Tepe Zargarān there is a series of domed caves, some of which have stucco decoration and paintings, and containing many sculptural fragments.

The Tepe Shutur reliefs and museum were completely destroyed in the fighting in 1980.

Collection: National Museum and Musée Guimet—objects from DAFA excavations.

Fieldwork:
1. 1834 Masson—survey.
2. 1879 Simpson, Indian Army—excavations in Tepe Zargarān caves.
3. 1923 Foucher and Godard, DAFA—sondages at Tepe Kalān.
4. 1926–8 Barthoux, DAFA—excavations at all sites except Tepe Shutur and Tepe Zargarān.
5. 1965–74 Mustamandi, AIA—excavations at Tepe Shutur.
6. 1974–9 Tarzi, AIA—excavations at Tepe Shutur.

Sources:

1. Masson 1833a: 4—description and sketches of some of the Hadda caves.
2. Jacquet 1839—general remarks on the work of Honigberger and Masson.
3. Masson 1841: 105–13—description of the remains and finds. List of the contents of Tepe Kalān.
4. Masson 1842: III. 254—mentions the work.
5. Dowson 1863: 230–4—discusses a Kharoshthi jar inscription excavated by Masson.
6. Thomas 1863: 235 n. 24—lists the Kharoshthi jar inscription in a discussion of the 'Bactrian' alphabet.
7. Fergusson 1876: 89–90—discusses Masson's excavations at Tepe Kalān and dates the stupa to the 7th century.
8. Simpson 1879a: 229—brief description of the Tepe Zargarān caves.
9. Swinnerton 1879: 198–200—description of the remains and the Tepe Zargarān caves.
10. Simpson 1879–80: 43–5 and 56–7—describes his own excavations in the caves and discusses the architecture of Hadda.
11. Leach 1880: 46—mentions Simpson's excavations.
12. Simpson 1881: 196–9—description of the site with reference to the travels of Huien Tsang.
13. Simpson 1882: 328–31—full description of the caves and paintings of Tepe Zargarān.
14. Simpson 1893: 99 and 107–10—briefly discusses the classical influence seen in some of the architectural decoration.
15. Cunningham 1894: 263–4 and 274–5—discusses some of the Hephthalite coins found by Masson.
16. Thomas 1915—linguistic analysis with text and translation of a Kharoshthi inscription on a jar found by Masson.
17. A. Godard 1925a: 16–17 brief report on the preliminary DAFA sondages.
18. Pandit 1927—photos and summary of the first DAFA excavations.
19. Barthoux 1928—preliminary report on the excavation results.
20. Foucher 1928: 23–4—brief summary of the first sondages by Godard.
21. Hackin 1928b—general preliminary report on the excavations 1923–8.
22. Bachhofer 1929: 159–61—photos and brief description of the DAFA excavations and some of the sculptures.
23. Barthoux 1929—photos and brief preliminary report on the art finds.
24. Du Colombier 1929—describes the stucco sculpture newly acquired by the Musée Guimet.
25. Foucher 1929—description and stylistic analysis of a bust in the Musée Guimet from Hadda.
26. Grousset 1929—discusses the importance of the sculptures in the Musée Guimet and describes 'Gothic-Buddhist'.
27. Hamada 1929—a study of two stucco heads from Hadda presented to the Kyoto Museum by DAFA.

28. Konow 1929: 157–8—text, translation, and linguistic analysis of the Kharoshthi jar inscription from Masson's excavations.
29. Migeon 1929a—brief review of the finds of the DAFA excavations.
30. Migeon 1929b—briefly summarises the excavations and the Musée Guimet sculptures.
31. Pandit 1929: 677–82—well illustrated description of the architecture, sculpture, and other results of the DAFA excavations.
32. Barthoux 1930a—photos of all the sculptures.
33. Barthoux 1930b—describes the excavations at Tepe Kalān and discusses the architecture of the stupa in general.
34. Barthoux 1930c—photos and description of the excavations.
35. Grousset 1930—discusses the excavations and the art.
36. Strzygowski 1930–2—discusses the revival of Hellenistic art in the later periods of Hadda.
37. Bachhofer 1931a—discusses some of the stucco sculptures found at Tepe Kāfirhā, Tepe Kalān, and Deh Ghundi.
38. Bachhofer 1931b—discusses some of the stucco sculptures.
39. Bachhofer 1932—discusses some of the stucco sculptures from Tepe Kāfirhā.
40. Barthoux 1933a—general analysis of the form, function, and decoration of the stupa. Descriptions of the various sites excavated from the point of view of their art.
41. Hackin 1933—summary of the results and the most important finds and their connections.
42. Combaz 1935: 96–7 and 101–3—discusses the construction and decoration of the remains and their part in the development of the stupa.
43. Okamoto 1935—dates Haddo to BC and discusses its 'Gothic' style.
44. Gray 1935—a note on 20 sculptures presented to the British Museum from the DAFA excavations.
45. Rowland 1936: 400—discusses Masson's finds as late examples of Gandharan art.
46. Monod-Bruhl 1939: 96–103 and 115–17—describes the Hadda objects on display in the Musée Guimet.
47. Yoshikawa 1941: 3–19—summarises the work at Hadda and describes the art.
48. Foucher 1942–7: 153 and 378–83—summary of the preliminary sondages at Tepe Kalān. Description of the sculptures and decorations and catalogue of the finds.
49. Yoshikawa 1944—summary of the DAFA excavations.
50. Ghosh 1945—describes some stucco sculptures from the DAFA excavations exhibited in the Calcutta Museum.
51. Schlumberger 1947a: 14–15—discusses the results of the excavations.
52. Shakur 1947: 9012—strong criticism of the state of the site left by its excavators.
53. Schlumberger 1949b: 11–12—brief summary of Barthoux's results.
54. Van Lohuizen-de Leeuw 1949: 140–3—discusses the sculptures.

55. Wheeler 1949—discusses the evidence of the sculptures and the problems of Romano-Buddhist art.
56. Deydier 1950: 155–70—summary of the site and its chronology, with a bibliography of the French work.
57. Bussagli 1953a—discusses the art of Hadda and its relation to Indian aesthetics.
58. Bussagli 1953b—discusses some classical influences on some of the paintings and sculptures from Hadda.
59. Curiel 1953: 124—discusses the Sasanian coins.
60. Kohzad 1953b: 3–4—brief summary.
61. Rowland 1953: 102–4—discusses the art.
62. Kohzad 1955c: 16–17—summary of the site and finds.
63. Bussagli 1956–7: 167–98 and 215–19—discusses the survivals of Hellenistic art at Hadda and the influence of Roman art.
64. Frumkin 1957—brief discussion of Graeco-Buddhist art.
65. Courtois 1961: 18–19—summary of the French work.
66. Gullini 1961: 66–138—photos of objects on display from the National Museum.
67. Gullini 1961—discusses the art.
68. Bussagli 1962a: 45—brief outline of the art.
69. Bussagli 1962b—outline of the main features of Gandharan art.
70. Mizuno 1962—introduction to the Japanese work in the Hadda area.
71. Courtois 1962–3—mineralogical analysis of a fragment of stone sculpture.
72. Pugachenkova 1963: 42–67—general summary.
73. Dagens 1964a: 11–34—descriptive catalogue of schist reliefs found in Barthoux's excavations.
74. Rowland 1964b—illustrates and discusses some of the objects exhibited at the Tokyo Museum.
75. Hallade 1964–5—stylistic discussion of the ornamental scarf depicted in some of the Hadda sculptures.
76. Fujita 1966a—general background to the site and stylistic summary of the sculptures.
77. Fujita 1966b—description of the site and stylistic discussion of the sculptures.
78. Monod 1966: 352–64—description of the objects on display in the Musée Guimet.
79. Rowland 1966a: 72–91—photos and description of the objects on display from the Kābul Museum.
80. Rowland 1966b—discussion and comparisons of a schist Tyche image.
81. Rosenfield 1967: 233–43—discussion of the reliefs in their wider context of Gandharan art.
82. Barret and Pinder-Wilson 1967–8: 21–3—description of some of the sculptures on exhibition.
83. S. and M. Mustamandi 1967/68a—report on the architecture, sculpture, and paintings of Tepe Shutur.
84. Auboyer 1968: pls 52–67—photos and notes on many objects from Hadda.
85. Hallade 1968—discusses the evolution of Gandharan art.
86. Hallade and Hinz 1968: pls 95, 105, 107–19—photos and discussion of the objects in the context of the development of Gandaran art.
87. Mustamandi 1968a—preliminary report on the third season at Tepe Shutur. Background to the site and summary of the finds.
88. Mustamandi 1968b—long description and stylistic analysis of the Fish Porch.
89. Fussmann 1969—study of a Kharoshthi inscription on a fragment of a jar.
90. Mustamandi 1969b—summary of the sculptures found at Tepe Shutur in the 1966/67 seasons.
91. S. and M. Mustamandi 1969—summary of the architecture, sculpture, paintings, and chronology of Tepe Shutur.
92. Azizi 1969/70a—discusses the art at Tepe Shutur.
93. Mustamandi 1969–70—long historical background and account of previous work at Hadda.
94. Habibi 1971: 28–9—discusses the Kharoshthi vase inscriptions.
95. Mustamandi 1971—brief report on the excavations at Tepe Shutur and 'East Tapa'.
96. Rowland and Rice 1971: 27–33, pls 109–10, 113–31 and 133–4—description and photos of the objects on display from the Kābul Museum.
97. Sadakata 1971—discusses the Greek and Roman influences on both the art and religion of Hadda.
98. Taddei 1972b—discusses some of the art-historical problems.
99. Kuwayama 1973—discusses the excavations and chronology of Tepe Shutur and questions the examination of the finds.
100. Mustamandi 1973—description of the excavations and finds at Tepe Shutur.
101. Shahrani 1963: 17–18—discusses the Graeco-Buddhist art of Hadda.
102. N. Dupree et al. 1974: 82–90—summary of the sculptures and styles and guide to the National Museum collection.
103. Iourkevitch 1974—summary of all the work carried out at Hadda.
104. Lévêque 1974—discusses the unity of Greek and Indian styles in the art.
105. Mustamandi 1974a—brief note on the discovery of the Herakles statue.
106. Mustamandi 1974b—summary of the excavations and sculptures from the 1966–7 seasons.
107. Zaryab 1974a—photos and description of the eighth season at Tepe Shutur.
108. Deshpande 1975a—traces the links between the sculpture of Hadda and Indian sculpture.
109. H. Motamedi 1975a: 71–5—discusses the sword depicted in some of the sculptures.
110. Trousdale 1975—discusses the sword depicted in some of the sculptures.
111. Gaulier et al. 1976—discuss the religious iconography of the art.
112. Tarzi 1976a—stylistic analysis of the sculptures and paintings from Tepe Shutur.

113. Tarzi 1976b—photos and description of the meditation cave at Tepe Shutur.
114. Tissot 1976—colour photos of the objects on display in the Musée Guimet and description of the art.
115. Tarzi 1976/77—description and photos of three niches on the north side of the Tepe Shutur monastery.
116. Davary 1977—lists the Kharoshthi vase inscription and gives its bibliography.
117. N. Dupree 1977: 214–25—some background on the development of the stupa and a good guide to Tepe Shutur.
118. Franz 1977–8—discusses the art and development of the stupa.
119. A. A. Motamedi 1978—discussion of a stucco trident sculpture found in Barthoux's excavations.
120. H. Motamedi 1978b—good general background and well illustrated summary of the excavations.
121. Sultan 1978—discusses Hellenistic influences in the art.
122. *Kabul Times* 1979b—brief report on the completion of the 1979 season.
123. Srivastava 1979c—review of the excavations.
124. Taddei 1979b—a study of two stucco heads.
125. Stwodah 1980: 7—describes the discovery and significance of an ancient bark book at Tepe Shutur.
126. Azizi 1981—brief history of Hadda and the results of the Tepe Shutur excavations.
127. Mustamandi 1997—discusses the impact of Hadda on Gandharan art generally.
128. Narain 1991—discusses possible Mauryan origins of Hadda Buddhism.
129. Salomon 1999—birch-bark scroll fragments from Hadda.
130. Geoffroy-Schneiter 2001—photos of objects from the Musée Guimet,
131. Tissot and Darbois 2002—photos of objects from the Kābul Museum.
132. Tissot et al. 2003—exhibition catalogue of some of the Buddha sculptures.
133. Allon 2001—publication of some birch-bark scroll fragments of the early 1st century AD.
134. Tissot 2006: 359–467—National Museum catalogue details and photos.
135. Ball 2008: 109, 114, 198–200—summary.
136. Jongeward et al. 2012—catalogue and discussion of the reliquaries.
137. Quagliotti 2012—discussion of the image of the starving Buddha from Tepe Shutur.
138. Errington 2017a: 162–99 and 2017b: 11–14, 20, 34–46—the Masson collection and archive relating to the site.

405. HADIRA
See also 2127 KHWĀJA ĀLI SEHYAKA in Supplement.

Lat. 31°21' N, long. 63°10' E. Map 98.
Helmand Province. An open plain on the right bank of the Helmand 25 km south-west of Malākhan.

Description: A large surface scatter of red pottery and glazed tiles. No trace of any buildings. This might have been pottery from nearby Khwāja Āli Sehyaka scattered in a graveyard.
Sources:
1. Additional note on possible source of pottery by W. Trousdale.
2. Bellew 1874: 198—mention.

406. HAFT CHAH

Original: Lat. 34° 10' N, long. 71° 05' E. Map 68.
Revised: 34.16768267 N, 71.07392697 E /
34° 10' 03.65762064 N, 71° 04' 26.13708228 E.
Nangahār Province. 8 km north-west of Tūrkhām on the Pakistan border, on the way to Dakka.
Date: ?Chaghatai, 14th cent. (traditional).
Description: Ruins of a very large fort on a mound, with a series of walls nearby.
Sources:
1. Masson 1840: 30—mention.
2. Masson 1842: II. 160–1—mention.
3. Raverty 1878: 43—mention.

HAFTŪ or **HAFTAU**. See **2088 HAFTŪ in Supplement**.

407. HAIBAK BĀLĀ HISĀR
Or AIBAK.

Original: Lat. 36° 14' N, long. 68° 03' E. Map 30.
Revised: 36.23859743 N, 68.0498152 E / 36° 14' 18.95073252 N, 68° 02' 59.33470884 E.
Samangān Province. 5 km south-east of the modern town of Haibak, 2 km south-east of Takht-i Rustam.
Date: Mongol-Timurid, 13th–15th cent. (ceramic).
Description: Remains of a citadel and other fortifications, consisting of a large, ruined outer enclosure with an inner keep at the northern end, built on a small hill. Probably the remains of ancient Samangān.
Fieldwork:
1. 1885–6 Maitland, ABC—topographical survey.
2. 1960 Hayashi and Sahara, Kyoto University—survey.
Sources:
1. Maitland 1888b: 42 and 310—brief description.
2. Hayashi and Sahara 1962: 41—photo and brief description in Japanese.

408. HAIRATĀN
Or AIRATĀN.

Lat. 37° 13' N, long. 67° 25' E. Map 30.
Samangān Province. On the Āmū Daryā north of Mazār-i Sharīf.

Dates: Middle and Upper Palaeolithic, *c.*30,000–10,000 BC (lithic); ?Seljuk, 11th–12th cent. (stylistic).

Description: An extensive area of remains and mounds. The only ruin standing (in 1886) is a baked brick gateway to a mosque, 3–4 m high. It is covered in brick patterns and has one fragmentary Kufic inscription, also in brick.

In dunes to the south of Hairatān is a wide surface scatter of Mousterian and Mesolithic stone tools.

Fieldwork:
1. 1886 Maitland, ABC—topographical survey.
2. 1975 Vinogradov, Af/Sov. Mission—survey.

Sources:
1. Holdich 1886: 9—mentions the ruins.
2. Holdich 1887: 36—mentions the ruins.
3. Maitland 1888b: 244–5—brief description of the ruins.
4. Vinogradov 1979—general discussion of the lithic assemblages from the survey with comparisons in Soviet Central Asia.

409. HĀJIGAK
See also 785 PAI KŌTAL.

Lat. 34° 40' N, long. 68° 06' E. Map 58.
Wardak Province. 1 km before the southern foot of the Hājigak Pass, near a school, on the road to Bāmiyān.

Description: A boulder beside the road with several petroglyphs, some at least probably ancient.

Source: N. Dupree 1977: 148—mention.

410. HĀJI PIYĀDA
Or NO GUMBAD.

Original: Lat. 36° 43' N, long. 66° 53' E. Maps 26, 27.
Revised: 36.7296953 N, 66.88514618 E / 36° 43' 46.90307388 N, 66° 53' 06.52626132 E.
Balkh Province. 3 km south of Balkh, 1.5 km to the west of the road to Pul-i Imāmbukri.

Date: Abbasid, late 8th cent. (stylistic).

Description: A small mosque measuring only some 10 m square. The outside walls are of mud-brick construction. The interior is divided into nine bays, each originally covered by a dome. The columns and the arches that divide the bays are exquisitely decorated in deeply carved stucco, depicting a wide variety of designs, stylistically comparable to Abbasid decoration in Mesopotamia.

The mosque itself is known as the Masjid-i Noh Gunbad; Haji Piyada is a modern shrine to the north.

Fieldwork:
1. 1966 Golombek and Salter—survey.
2. 1974–5 AIA—erection of protective roof.
3. 2006–8 AKTC and DAFA—preservation work.

Sources:
1. Peacocke 1887a: 357—description.

2. Pugachenkova 1968a: 18–27—detailed description and discussion.
3. Golombek 1969b—description and stylistic analysis of the stucco decoration.
4. Melikian-Chirvani 1969a—photos and discussion of the stucco work and its stylistic connections.
5. Anand 1970: 24–5—photos and brief summary.
6. Mandersloot and Powell 1972—brief description with very good photos of the mosque.
7. Zhwandun 1974—text of an interview with Melikian-Chirvani on the decoration.
8. *Kabul Times* 1975:—brief report on the preservation work.
9. *Kabul Times* 1976b—brief report on the preservation work.
10. N. Dupree 1977: 400–2—good summary description.
11. Fischer 1978a: 305–7—summary.
12. Mukhtarov 1980: 54–8—description.
13. O'Kane 2006—discussion in the broader context of nine-dome mosque plans.
14. Adle 2011—dates to end 8th century.
15. Adle 2015a—discussion of the mosque which he dates to 178/794–5 and relates to the building activity of Fazl the Barmakid.
16. Adle 2015b—summary of the recent investigations of the mosque.

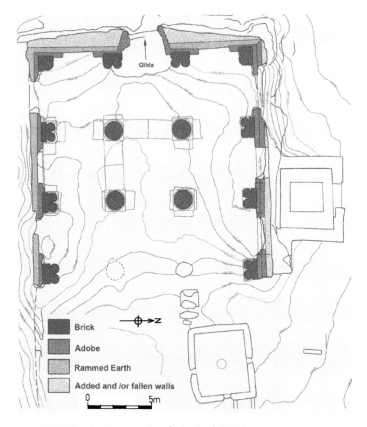

410 Hāji Piyāda (Boostani and Tonietti 2017).

17. Golombek et al. 2016—series of papers on the study and conservation.
18. Jodidio et al. 2017: 260–5—reports on the Aga Khan Trust for Culture conservation work.

411. HĀJIRANGĪN QAL'A

Lat. 31° 15' N, long. 64° 14' E. approximately. Map 97. Helmand Province. On the west bank of the Helmand 1 km south-west of Baikhān Qal'a, 3 km north-east of Nazār Muhammad Qal'a.

Date: Sasanian, 3rd–7th cent. (ceramic).

Description: An artificial mound.

Fieldwork: 1966 Hammond, Cambridge University—survey.

Source: Hammond 1970: 449—lists the site (no. 39) and describes the pottery and general survey results.

412. HĀJI YŪNUS

Original: Lat. 36° 41'–36° 42' N, long. 69° 33'–69° 34' E. Map 36.
Revised:
36.69355595 N, 69.55803244 E / 36° 41' 36.80140308 N, 69° 33' 28.91679264 E (A).
36.69409252 N, 69.55421686 E / 36° 41' 38.73308676 N, 69° 33' 15.18069600 E (A).
36.70517205 N, 69.56256182 E / 36° 42' 18.61939332 N, 69° 33' 45.22254516 E (B).
Takhār Province. On the left bank of the Tāluqān river, 5 km south-east of the bridge that crosses it near the town. The highest of the two tepes, A, corresponds to the mound of 4 m indicated on the 1:100,000 map, south of the village of Hāji Yūnus; tepe B is located 1.8 km north-north-east of this mound, on the edge of the canal which crosses the village of Muqim Qishlāq, coming from the Tāluqān River.

Date: Chalcolithic–Early Bronze Age, *c*.3500–2500 BC; Timurid, 15th–16th cent. (ceramic).

Description: (A) (Tepe Hāji Yunūs) Rectangular east–west platform (50 × 30 m), still hardly touched by cultivation; the shape and dimensions appear to be original. Flat top (5 m), high on the south side, with low hillocks at the south-west and south-east angles. 500 m to the west, lower platform (3 m), square in shape (40 × 40 m), north-north-east/south-south-west orientation. Very few sherds on these tepes, or in the surrounding fields. (B) Rounded mound (diam. 50 m, height 2 m), covered by a cemetery.

Collection: National Museum/AIA—sherds.

Fieldwork: 1978 Gardin et al., CNRS—survey.

Sources:
1. Site information by J.-C. Gardin.
2. Gardin and Lyonnet 1978–9: pl. VIII—nos. 401–3.

3. Lyonnet 1997: fig. 7—nos. 401–3.
4. Gardin 1998: 74—nos. 401–3.

413. HAJJAR TEPE

Original: Lat. 36° 50' N, long. 66° 26' E. Map 25.
Revised: 36.83995625 N, 66.42977192 E /
36° 50' 23.84248704 N, 66° 25' 47.17891020 E.
Jauzjān Province. 26 km south-east of Āqcha. About 600 m south of the road and the caravanserai of Nasratābād, west of the village of Fazilābād.

Description: Large circular mound (diam. *c*.250 m), height 13 m, without apparent relief. Small tepe to the east, separated from the main mound by a large depression. The existence of a ditch around the tepe is not certain.

Fieldwork: 1948 Le Berre, DAFA—survey.

Source: M. Le Berre: unpublished 1948 report, DAFA archives, tépé P. 25.

HAKAN. See 21 AKAM.

HALOBAD TEPE. See 550 KHALĀBĀD TEPE.

414. HAMĀM CHASHMA, BĪLCHIRĀGH

Lat. 35° 46' N, long. 65° 14' E. Map 46.
Faryāb Province. 9 km south of Bīlcharāgh on the west bank of the Chashma Khwāb River gorge, just before it opens out into the Gurziwan Valley.

Description: An artificial rock chamber very similar to Hamām Chashma at Nishar. It has an indecipherable inscription over the doorway, locally attributed to Jamshid.

Fieldwork: 1885–6 Amir Khan, Shahzada Taimus, Griesbach, ABC—topographical surveys.

Sources:
1. Amir Khan and Shahzada Taimus 1888b: 231—mention.
2. Griesbach 1888b: 196—mention.

415. HAMĀM CHASHMA, NĪSHAR
See also 777 NĪSHAR.

Lat. 35° 54' N, long. 65° 10' E. Maps 24, 46.
Faryāb Province. In the Shīrīn Tagau 38.5 km east of Maimana and *c*.12 km north-west of Bīlchirāgh. The site is 1 km upstream and on the opposite bank to Nīshar.

Date: ?Safavid, 16th cent. (traditional).

Description: A rock chamber cut into the cliff face on the right bank above a warm water spring. It is very neatly cut and measures *c*.2.5 m square. Said locally to date from the time of Shah Abbas.

Fieldwork: 1886 Griesbach, ABC—topographical survey.

Sources:
1. Griesbach 1888b: 196—brief description.
2. Maitland 1888b: 101—mention.
3. Gazetteer 1979: IV. 430—brief description.

HAROTE TEPE. See 564 KHARŪTI TEPE.

416. HASANĀBĀD

Original: Lat. 34° 11' N, long. 62° 02' E. Map 52.
Revised: 34.17850427 N, 62.01820852 E /
34° 10' 42.61536264 N, 62° 01' 05.55068100 E.
Herat Province. In the area south-west of Herat on the road from Zīyāratgāh to Zindajān. The site is *c.*2 km to the west of the village of Hasanābād.

Date: Timurid, 15th–16th cent. (ceramic).

Description: A small mound *c.*50 m diameter at the base and 3 m high. It is covered with a large number of green Islamic impressed and incised glazed sherds. Probably the remains of a farmhouse in the middle of the *dasht*. The *dasht* is periodically cultivated.

Fieldwork: 1974 Swiny, BIAS—survey.

Source: Site information by S. Swiny in unpublished BIAS archive.

417. HASANKHĀN
See also 824 PŪST-I GAU.

Original: Lat. 31° 15' N, long. 62° 00' E. Map 84.
Revised: 31.26074452 N, 62.01140834 E /
31° 15' 38.68028532 N, 62° 00' 41.07000780 E.
Nīmrūz Province. 4 km to the west of the Pūst-i Gau ruins, 11 km north-west of Chakhānsūr.

Description: An area of remains consisting of ruined buildings, low mounds, ramparts, and a ruined dwelling tower. Probably an extension of the Pust-i Gau remains.

Fieldwork: 1960–70 Fischer, Bonn University—survey.

Sources:
1. Fischer 1970b: pls 20–1—photos.
2. Fischer 1973c: 138—map reference.
3. Ball 2008: 254–5—summary.

418. HASHMATKHĀN
Including KHOL SHAMS and ZIRĀYAT-I PANJA-SHĀH. See also 483 KĀBUL.

Original: Lat. 34° 29' N, long. 69° 12' E. Map 61.
Revised: 34.49106589 N, 69.19427187 E /
34° 29' 27.83719104 N, 69° 11' 39.37873200 E.

Kābul Province. Between the Qul-i Hashmatkhān and the Kūh-i Takht-i Shāh, 3 km south-west of the Kābul Bālā Hisār.

Dates: Kushano-Sasanian, 3rd–5th cent.; Turki-Hindu Shahi, 7th–10th cent.; Timurid, 15th cent. (stylistic).

Description: A large area of mostly modern cemeteries where many antiquities have been found. The modern Zīyā-rat-i Panjashāh is built over a Buddhist stupa-monastery complex. In the 1830s this complex consisted of some caves, a cistern, and many cells, one of which was domed. Construction was of mud-brick. Finds included an arched niche supported by pillars, several tuz-leaf manuscripts, paintings, and much Buddhist and Hindu sculpture.

There is also a ruined tomb with a collapsed dome, the Zīyārat-i Sher Surkh, built in the Timurid style.

Fieldwork:
1. 1833 Masson—excavations.
2. 1833 Gérard, East India Company—excavations.

Sources:
1. Additional note on the rebuilding of the *zīyārat* by Jonathan L. Lee.
2. Masson 1833a: 5–6—brief summary of the results of his excavations.
3. Vigne 1840: 207—refers to some Hindu sculptures found.
4. Masson 1842: II. 235 and III. 92–8—detailed account of the excavations and finds.
5. Lal 1846: 214—description of a Buddha statue excavated by Gérard.
6. N. Dupree 1971a: 110–11 and 113—brief description of the remains.
7. Errington 2017a: 66–9 and 2017b: 15, 61—Masson documentation of the site (under the name Khol Shams, provisionally identified with Tepe Narenj).

HAUZ. See 792 PALANGI.

HAUZ-I 'ALĪĀBĀD. See 2089 HAUZ-I 'ALĪĀBĀD in Supplement.

HAUZ-I ANBAR SHĀH. See 2090 HAUZ-I ANBAR SHĀH in Supplement.

419. HAUZ-I BANGI

Original: Lat. 34° 06' N. long. 64° 33' E. Map 55.
Revised: 34.10522089 N, 64.56435884 E /
34° 06' 18.79519608 N, 64° 33' 51.69180636 E.
Ghūr Province. 8 km west of Guzarpam on the Chakhcharān-Shahrak road.

Date: Ghurid, 12th cent. (architectural).

Description: Remains of several forts.

Fieldwork: 1885 Maitland and Talbot, ABC.

Sources:
1. Maitland 1888a: 372 — mention. Two other forts lower down.
2. N. Dupree 1977: 77 — mention.

HAUZ-I KARBUZ. See 349 GHALWAR.

HAUZ-I JINDA KHĀN. See 2091 HAUZ-I JINDA KHĀN in Supplement.

HAUZ-I PALANGI. See 2092 HAUZ-I PALANGI in Supplement.

HAWAR SAI. See 959 RŪD-I SHĀHRAWĀN.

HAZĀRA QAL'A. See 2093 HAZĀRA QAL'A in Supplement.

420. HAZĀRA SAMŪCH

Lat. 37° 11' N, long. 69° 54' E. Maps 35, 38.
Takhār Province. 10 km north-east of Rustāq.

Date: Hunnic-Turk, 5th–9th cent. (architecture).

Description: The cliffs which overlook the river are riddled with artificial caves (semi-circular or triangular openings, height c.1 m; depth of the shelter: 2 to 3 m), reminiscent of those of Bāmiyān.

Fieldwork: 1978 Gardin et al., CNRS — survey.

Sources:
1. Site information by J.-C. Gardin.
2. Gardin and Lyonnet 1978–9: pl. II, no. 519.
3. Lyonnet 1997: fig. 69 — no. 519A.
4. Gardin 1998: 92 — no. 519A.

421. HAZĀR BĀGH

Lat. 37° 00'–37° 03' N, long. 69° 17'–69° 23' E. Maps 31, 35.
Takhār Province. North-west of Zagcha Guzar, a modern canal irrigates the little plain of Hazar Bagh, on a course parallel to that of an old canal along which several sites are located, small mounds which are hardly visible, surrounded by extensive areas of sherds.

Dates: Hellenistic, 3rd–1st cent. BC; pre-Mongol Islamic, 10th–13th cent. (ceramic).

Description: A series of low mounds and sherd scatters over a wide area.

Collection: National Museum/AIA — sherds.

Fieldwork: 1977 Gardin et al., CNRS — survey.

Sources:
1. Site information by J.-C. Gardin.
2. Gardin 1980 — describes the survey in the area in general terms.
3. Gardin and Lyonnet 1978–9: 52 — nos. 275–6, 278, 280, 286–8.
4. Lyonnet 1997: fig. 49 — nos. 74, 275–6, 278, 280, 286–8.
5. Gardin 1998: 50–2 — nos. 74, 275–6, 278, 280, 286–8.

422. HAZĀR GUSFAND

Lat. 36° 47' N, long. 70° 00' E. Map 38.
Badakhshān Province. 6 km north-east of Kalafgān, just to the south of the village of Chinār-i Gunjus Khān. Near Darra-i Kūr.

Dates: Late Iron Age, c.600 BC; early Islamic, 8th–13th cent. (ceramic, lithic).

Description: A cave site, the occupation was in layers of brown humus and loess, overlayed by much collapse. Finds included glazed sherds and slag, iron fragments, domesticated sheep and goat remains, and a fragment of a human skull.

Fieldwork:
1. 1959 Dupree, AUFS — survey.
2. 1966 Kolb and Khan, AMNH — sondage.

Sources:
1. Dupree and Howe 1963: 2 — mention.
2. Dupree 1967: 12 — mention.
3. Brill 1972b: 80 — table summarizing all the material and stratigraphy.
4. Caley 1972b: brief note on an iron object.
5. Dupree and Kolb 1972: 39–42 — ceramics discussed generally with the Āq Kupruk and Darra-i Kūr material and stratigraphy.

HAZĀRJUFT. See 709 MARKAZ-I HOKŪMATI, 898 QAL'AT-I CHAUKAKAT, 901 QAL'AT-I MAHMŪD and 1260 ZINDĀN.

423. HAZĀR NAU

Original: Lat. 34° 14' N, long. 70° 55' E. Map 68.
Revised: 34.23509301 N, 70.92987584 E /
34° 14' 06.33482556 N, 70° 55' 47.55302832 E.
Nangahār Province. 1 km to the south of the Jalālābād-Tūrkhām road, 4 km east of Bāsawal.

Description: A hill covered in ruined walls and building debris.

Source: Simpson 1879–80: 41 — mention.

424. HAZĀR SUM, HABASH

At. 35° 43' N, long. 67° 49' E. Map 30.
Samangān Province. In the Hazār Sum Valley, c.10 km south-west of Rūi Habash, in the mountainous area south of Haibak.

Description: Reports of a series of artificial caves in a white cliff.

Source: Maitland 1888b: 30—mention from hearsay.

425. HAZĀR SUM, HAIBAK

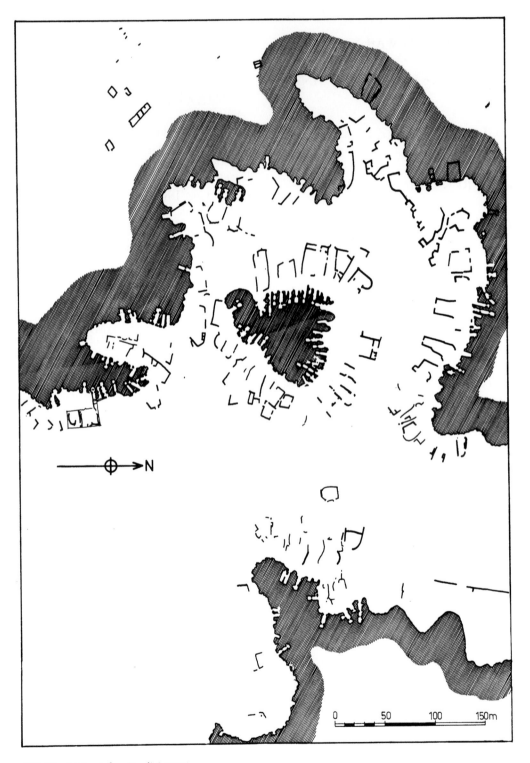

425 Hazā Sūm (after Puglisi 1963).

Lat. 36° 21' N, long. 67° 54' E. Maps 30, 84.
Samangān Province. 16 km north-west of Haibak, in a bend in the river through a valley.

Dates: Epi-Palaeolithic, *c.*10,000 BC (lithic); Neolithic, 8th–6th mill. BC. (Lithic); late Sasanian, 6th–7th cent. (stylistic); pre-Mongol Islamic, 10th–13th cent. (ceramic); Timurid, 15th–16th cent. (ceramic).

Description: A valley floor surrounded by low cliffs and wadis. On the valley floor is a site *c.*350,000 m² in area, consisting of an extensive scatter of prehistoric stone tools, a series of vertical stone slabs possibly representing primitive dwellings, and over 40 early Islamic mounds and burials. In the cliff faces are over 200 artificial caves, usually consisting of a front room, a central room with a fireplace, and a back room with a bench. Many are plastered, and some are decorated, though with no Buddhist paintings or images. In the wadi terraces are enormous amounts of chipped flint debris.

Fieldwork:
1. 1885 Talbot, ABC—survey.
2. 1960 Hayashi and Sahara, Kyoto University—survey.
3. 1962 Puglisi, IsMEO—excavations.

Sources:
1. Gardin and Lyonnet, 1980 chronological study of unpublished pottery from DAFA surveys.
2. Moorcroft and Trebeck 1841: II. 409–10—describe the caves and the remains of paintings inside.
3. Talbot et al. 1886: 345–7—description and sketches of some of the caves.
4. Holdich 1887: 39—brief description of the caves.
5. Maitland 1888b: 305—brief description.
6. Hayashi and Sahara 1962: 43–4—photos and description in Japanese.
7. Mizuno 1962—introduction to the Japanese survey of the site.
8. Puglisi 1962—summary of the site.
9. Castaldi 1963—detailed stylistic analysis of the graffiti and petroglyphs in the caves.
10. Puglisi 1963—very detailed map and description of the site and lithic industry.
11. N. Dupree 1967a: 30–2—describes the site and chronology.
12. Mizuno and Higuchi 1967—fully illustrated summary description of the caves in their various groups.
13. Davis 1978: 44—refutes Puglisi's conclusions on the prehistoric chronology and postulates later dates.
14. Gupta 1979: I. 137–41—discusses the lithic industry and its links in Central Asia.
15. Bassetti 2009—geological note on the stone tools.
16. Micheli 2009 2009—new data from a previously unpublished corpus of stone material that came to light in a storeroom in Rome, confirming a Levallois presence.
17. Michaeli 2013—further discussion of new date, and a perspective on the Palaeolithic of Afghanistan as a whole.

426. HAZRATĀN

Original: Lat. 34° 24' N, long. 70° 23' E. Map 66.
Revised: 34.40701538 N, 70.38660299 E /
34° 24' 25.25536188 N, 70° 23' 11.77077444 E.
Nangahār Province. *C.*2 km south of the village of Hazratan, in the foothills between Siāhsang and Qala'a-i Hāji stupas, *c.*9 km west of Jalālābād.

Dates: Kushan-Hunnic, 1st–6th cent. (architectural).

Description: Some badly eroded remains of a stupa, 5 m high and 13 m across. To the south are the remains of a monastery, and further south are more ruins.

Fieldwork:
1. Masson 1834—survey.
2. 1965 Mizuno, Kyoto University—survey.

Sources:
1. Masson 1841: 104—mention as a tumulus.
2. Mizuno 1971: 121—brief description (Stupa 45).

427. HAZRĀT-I BĀBĀ
See also 2120. KHALĪFA RAHMAT JAMSHĪDĪ in Supplement.

Lat. 34° 43' N, long. 62° 20' E. Maps 43, 52.
Herat Province. To the north of the Bābā Kotal north of Herat, in the northern foothills of the Kūh-i Hazrāt-i Bābā.

Description: A large grave surrounded by a wall of baked brick, with a tall stone monolith at the end of the grave. Adjacent are the remains of a small baked brick building, possibly a mosque, with three domes still surviving in 1886.

Fieldwork: 1884 Maitland, ABC—topographical survey.

Sources:
1. Maitland 1887c: 484—very brief description.
2. Maitland 1888a: 177—brief description.
3. Gazetteer 1975: III. 152—brief description.

HAZRĀT SAYYID. See 2094 HAZRĀT SAYYID in Supplement.

428. HERAT
Including KUHANDAZH. See also 66 ĀZADĀN, 84 BĀGH-I NAZĀRGĀH, 346 GĀZURGĀH, 349 GHALWAR, 819 PUL-I MALAN, and 1263 ZĪYĀRATGĀH.

Original: Lat. 34° 20–33' N, long. 62° 11–18' E. Map 52.
Revised: 34.34111392 N, 62.19080805 E /
34° 20' 28.01010228 N, 62° 11' 26.90897136 E.
Herat Province. 1,053 km by road west of Kābul.

Dates: ?Bronze Age, early 2nd mill. (epigraphic); Iron Age, 7th/6th–5th cent. (ceramic, C-14); Achaemenid, 6th–4th cent.

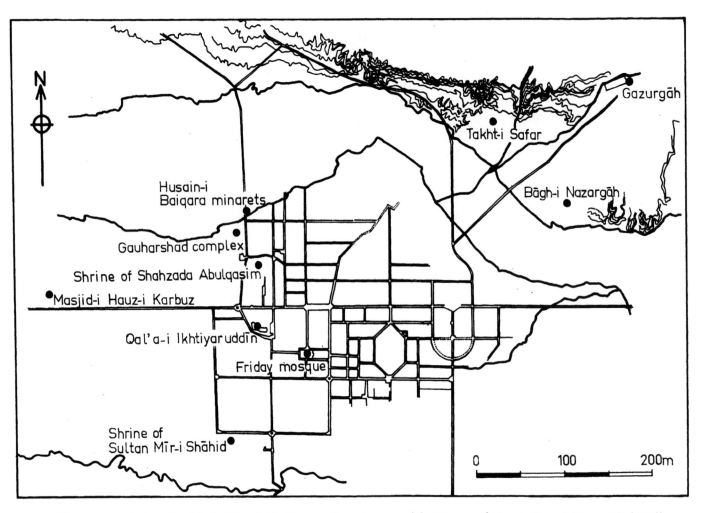

428 Herat—general plan (after Mas'ūd Rajāyi, 'A Glance at Some Aspects of the History of Herat', *Herat-i Bāstān*, 2/1 (1980)).

Gazurgāh

Takht-i Safar

Bāgh-i Nazargāh

Husain-i
Baiqara minarets

Gauharshad complex

Shrine of Shahzada Abulqasim

Masjid-i Hauz-i Karbuz

Qal'a-i Ikhtiyaruddīn

Friday mosque

Shrine of
Sultan Mīr-i Shāhid

0   100   200m

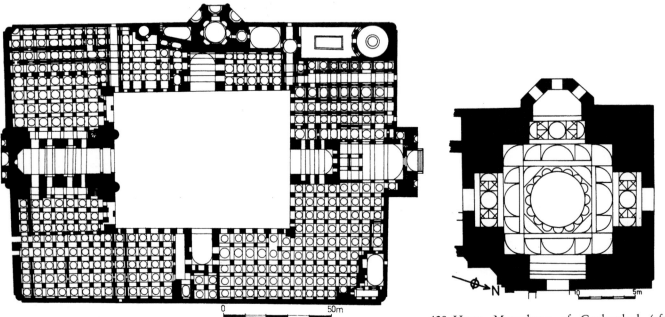

428 Herat—Friday Mosque (after Sālik 1979).

428 Herat—Mausoleum of Gauharshad (after Byron 1938).

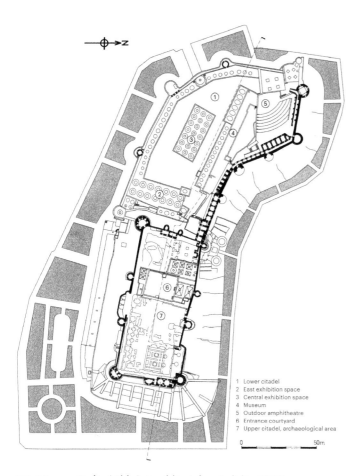

428 Herat—Qal'a-i Ikhtiyāruddīn (after Jodidio 2017).

1 Lower citadel
2 East exhibition space
3 Central exhibition space
4 Museum
5 Outdoor amphitheatre
6 Entrance courtyard
7 Upper citadel, archaeological area

0   50m

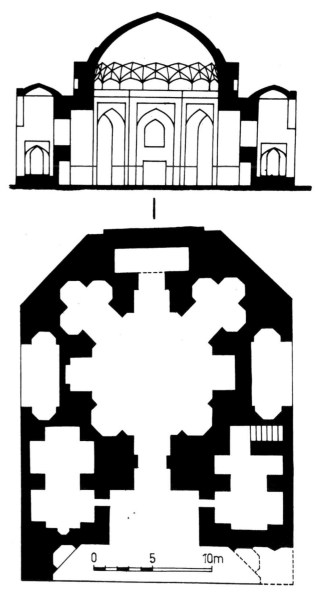

428 Herat—Shrine of Shāhzāda Abulqasim (after Pugachenkova 1970).

(ceramic, epigraphic); ?Sasanian, 3rd–7th cent. (numismatic, stylistic); Seljuk, Ghurid, Kart, and Timurid, 11th–16th cent. (architectural, documentary, stylistic, etc.).

Description: A large urban area, the old part of which is still partly surrounded by the remains of massive mud walls. Standing monuments within these walls include the immense fortress-palace of Qal'a-i Ikhtiyaruddīn, a mainly 15th-century citadel of baked brick standing on a mound and protected by a glacis, and the elaborate Friday Mosque, which, though largely modern, contains good examples of Islamic decoration from 12th-century Ghurid brickwork to 15th- and 16th-century Timurid tilework. The mosque included the Ghurid Mausoleum of Ghiyath al-Dīn, which was demolished in the 1950s. Excavations in the

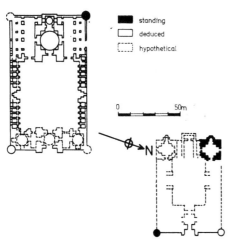

■ standing
□ deduced
⬚ hypothetical

0   50m

428 Herat—reconstruction of the Gauharshad Madrasa and Musalla (after Byron 1938).

citadel mound have found material going back to the Iron Age.

Most of the city's important monuments however lie outside the walls. Immediately to the north of the walls is a large artificial mound known as Kuhandazh, which represents the remains of the pre-13th-century city. On top is a monumental 15th-century Timurid shrine, the mausoleum of Shāhzāda 'Abulqāsim. A little further to the north is the mausoleum of Gauharshad and six minarets, all covered in fragments of extremely fine faience tilework from the 14th and 15th centuries. These remains are all that is left standing of a complex of three buildings: the Musalla of Gauharshad, the Mausoleum and Madrasa of Gauharshad, and the Madrasa of Husain-i Baiqara. 200 m to the south-west of the city walls is a large domed building dated 1485/6, the Shrine of Mir-i Shahid or Abdullah al-Walid.

In the early 19th century a cylindar seal and some Sasanian seals and gems were found by chance in or near Herat. The cylindar seal is Old Babylonian in style and includes and inscription in cuneiform. The empty space to the right of the inscription suggests that the seal was prefabricated and waiting for a customer to add a few motifs of his own choice. The signs are proper cuneiform signs but do not make obvious sense:

gìr en zi.ga
šu x me bi el
ki ti gar ir na

Possibly it is a magical. The seal has since been lost.

During the fighting of the 1980s there was extensive damage to the monuments in and around the Khiyābān and in the old city. Damage included shell holes in at least two of the minarets of the Gauhar Shah musalla and the Madrasa of Sultan Husain Baiqara. A number of other minor buildings were also damaged. In 2000 a 2.1 m wall was constructed all around the Musalla complex, it appears this wall was at least partially built on the former wall which once enclosed the area. In 2004 local contractors began to construct a modern monument to 'Ali Sher Nawai over his tomb. The brick structure around the tomb was demolished and deep excavations commenced around the tomb preparatory to the pouring of reinforced concrete foundations. These excavations were put on hold after representations were made by cultural heritage organisations.

Fieldwork:
1. 1936–7 Schroeder and Wilber, American Institute of Iranian art—survey of principal monuments.
2. 1942–3 Stuckert—architectural survey of Friday Mosque.
3. 1962–3 Lézine, UNESCO—survey.
4. 1964 Hansen, National Museum/UNESCO—restoration of the Ghurid portal.
5. 1967–9 Pugachenkova, Af/Sov. Mission—architectural surveys of principal monuments.
6. 1975–9 Bruno, Pagliero, and Van Eenhooge, Ministry of Information/UNESCO—excavations in the citadel and restoration and preservation of the citadel and minarets.

7. 1978–9 Samizay, Kābul University/UNESCO—architectural survey of all major and minor monuments.
8. 1996(?) DACAAR—repairs to roof of Gauhar Shad mausoleum.
9. 2005–9 Besenval, Marquis, and Franke, DAFA and DAI—excavations and architectural studies at Kuhandizh and on citadel mound.
10. 2007–11 Stevens, UNESCO/Norway Funds-in-Trust—conservation work on Gawharshad.
11. 2014–16 ACHCO—conservation of Shahzada Abdullah and Abul Qasim mausolea.

Sources:
1. Additional information on the seal by John Macginnis.
2. Additional notes on recent work by Jonathan L. Lee.
3. Conolly 1834: II. 2–3 and 19–20—general description of the city and musalla complex in 1830.
4. Lal 1834—brief description of the Musalla complex and the Friday Mosque, with the text and translation of an inscription of Husain-i Baiqara in the Tomb of Ghiyasuddīn.
5. Torrens 1842—very detailed description and drawings of the cuneiform inscription and of the 24 seals and gems found by Pottinger.
6. Ferrier 1857: 169–71 and 178–82—description of the citadel, which he dates as Timurid, and description of the Musalla complex and surrounding ruins in 1845.
7. Khanikoff 1860—brief discussion of the historical topography of the city and environs.
8. Durand 1885: pls 10, 13, 14, 16, 18, 19, and 30—views of main historic buildings. (Additional bibliographical information by Jonathan L. Lee.)
9. Holdich 1885b—detailed description of the defences and of the Mosalla.
10. Maitland 1885: 6–7—description of the Husain-i Baiqara complex, recommending 'they ought to be destroyed' and detailed description of Mir Shahid mound and tomb. (Additional bibliographical information by Jonathan L. Lee.)
11. Peacocke 1885b: 38–40—description of the town and defences from a military standpoint, as viewed from the Pahra hills.
12. Yate 1885: 3—describes remains of a massive masonry tomb under the Mosalla, reported to have originally been full of bones.
13. Peacocke 1887a: frontispiece, 51–4 and 150–60—sketches of many of the monuments and general description and military assessment of Herat. (Additional bibliographical information by Jonathan L. Lee.)
14. Yate 1887—brief notes on the architecture and epigraphy of the Zīyārat-i Wali, Zīyārat-i Mir-i Shahid, Musalla complex, and other inscriptions.
15. Maitland 1888a: 406–11—descriptions and sketches of many of the monuments. (Additional bibliographical information by Jonathan L. Lee.)

16. Yate 1888: 25–40—describes the layout, the walls, the citadel, the Friday Mosque, many ziyarats, and describes in detail the Musalla complex.

17. Saunders 1880s—detailed survey of Herat.

18. Wier 1893—18 plates of monumental tiles collected by the Afghan Boundary Commission 1884–6.

19. Le Strange 1905: 408–9—summary of the historical references.

20. Hamilton 1906: L 157–62—describes the walls and citadel as they existed in the late 19th century.

21. Niedemeyer and Diez 1924: pls 124–63—photos of the city and many of the monuments.

22. Yate 1926—description of the Gauhar Shad Musalla with texts and translations of many of its inscriptions.

23. Trinkler 1928—description of the main monuments in 1923.

24. Afghān 1930: 27–91—guide to the major monuments.

25. Royal Academy 1931—photo of a marble panel from the Musalla.

26. Byron 1935b: 35–7—brief introduction to the principal monuments.

27. Schroeder 1936: 135—mentions making a plan of the Friday Mosque.

28. Sālnāma 1936/7: opp. 300, 301, and 364–97—photos of some grave covers and of many of the monuments.

29. Byron 1937: 97–111—description of and background to the main monuments.

30. Wilber 1937: 120–6—summary of the American Institute work at the Friday Mosque and Musalla complex.

31. Byron 1938: 1125–35—full description and reconstruction of the Madrasa and Musalla of Gauhar Shad.

32. Hariri 1939: 2522—text of the dated inscription on the bronze basin in the Friday Mosque.

33. Sālnāma 1939/40: 240–1—photos of many of the monuments.

34. Belenistski 1945—describes the historical topography of Herat.

35. Erffa 1946—description and stylistic analysis of a grave cover originating at Herat.

36. Frye 1946b: 66–8—brief summary of the monuments and photo of the Gauhar Shad Mausoleum before its restoration.

37. Itemadi 1946—description and background of the Gauhar Shad Mausoleum and its inscriptions.

38. Sauvaget 1946: 27–9—texts and translations of inscriptions in the Tomb of Ghiyasaddīn, on the bronze basin in the Friday Mosque, and from the Musalla.

39. Frye 1948: 206–11—description, plan, and photos of the Ghurid parts of the Friday Mosque.

40. Zestovsky 1949—description and sketches of the main monuments.

41. Caspani and Cagnacci 1951: 260–2—good general description.

42. Itemadi 1953—a reconstruction of the history of the Friday Mosque from the Persian and Arabic sources.

43. Combe et al. 1954: 156–7—text and translation of the inscription on the bronze basin.

44. Kohzad 1955c: 45–53—recounts the legends surrounding the foundation of the city.

45. Butcher 1956: 73–5—colour photos and description of the restoration of the Friday Mosque.

46. Ramachandran and Sharma 1956: III. 12–13—summary of the coins in the Herat Museum.

47. Bussagli 1962a: 46–7—brief outline of the architecture of Herat.

48. Klimburg 1963: 34–5—summary of the Timurid architecture.

49. Pugachenkova 1963: 94–5 and 135–51—general summary.

50. Lézine 1963–4—description of the citadel and detailed report on the Ghurid portal. Many illustrations.

51. Wolfe 1966—good general guide and background to all principal monuments.

52. Hill and Grabar 1967: pls 126–9, 134–6, and 151–3—details of the main monuments.

53. Seljuki 1967a—descriptions of many of the decorated gravestones from in and around Herat.

54. Seljuki 1967b—complete text of the inscription on the Ghurid portal.

55. Ghawwās 1969—brief descriptions and guide to all the monuments.

56. Melikian-Chirvani 1969b—epigraphical analysis of the bronze basin inscription in the Friday Mosque and discussion of its mystical symbolism.

57. Habibi 1969–70a—discusses the Timurid calligraphy on some of the monuments and manuscripts of Herat.

58. Pugachenkova 1969–70—discusses the general forms of Timurid architecture.

59. Anand 1970: 27–45—good summary and photos of the major monuments.

60. Melikian-Chirvani 1970—discussion and translations of the Ghurid inscriptions in the Friday Mosque.

61. Pugachenkova 1970—full architectural analysis of the Shāhzāda Abul Qāsim Mausoleum.

62. Habibi 1971: 203—photo of the bronze basin inscription and discussion of the calligraphy.

63. Hansen 1971—preliminary results on a UNESCO study on the problems of restoration of the Herat monuments.

64. Caroe 1973—discusses the events surrounding the demolition of the Musalla and exonerates the British.

65. English 1973—describes the development and function of the old city.

66. Seljuki 1973—discusses the epigraphy of some of the gravestones found in the vicinity of the Gauhar Shad Mausoleum.

67. Grube 1974: 246–9—discusses some of the metalwork from Herat, including the bronze basin.

68. Hutt 1974: 169–70—description and discussion of the Ghurid portal.

69. Samizay 1974: 20–2—outlines the growth and character of the old city.

70. Attar 1976—photos and texts of many of the inscriptions from the buildings and gravestones of Herat.

71. Bruno 1976—proposals for conservation of the monuments of Herat. Very fine drawings and reproductions of many old photos.

72. *Kabul Times* 1976a—mentions the conservation work on the Friday Mosque.

73. Pugachenkova 1976a—discusses the layout of the main monuments.

74. Brandenberg 1977—some history and a general account of the architecture. Some photos and reprints of various plans.

75. Gaube 1977—detailed historical-geographical study of the evolution of the city.

76. Aalund 1978—very general background in terms of conservation need.

77. Fischer 1978b: 379–88—closely follows Wolfe's guide to most of the monuments.

78. Nāhiz 1978—brief description of the restoration work on the citadel.

79. Jawād 1979—photos and interim report on the restoration work at the citadel.

80. *Kabul Times* 1979a—report on the preservation work on the monuments.

81. Mac Dowall and Ibrahim 1979—catalogue and discussion of Hellenistic, Saka, Parthian, Kushan, Roman, and Sasanian coins in the Herat Museum.

82. Pugachenkova 1979c—discusses the Timurid architecture.

83. Sālik 1979—good plan and a summary of the history and architecture of the Friday Mosque.

84. Glatzer 1980—stylistic analysis of the Ghurid parts of the Friday Mosque. Annotated review of the previous literature.

85. Jawād 1980—photos and interim report on the restoration work at the citadel.

86. Rahīq 1980b—brief review of the *madrasa*s at Herat.

87. Stuckert 1980—brief description of the Friday Mosque and Mausoleum of Ghiyasaddīn before the modern alterations, with a plan and photos of the Ghurid parts now demolished.

88. Wāla 1980—brief discussion of the bronze bowl and inscriptions.

89. Ball 1981—description of the remains of a monumental terraced Timurid garden to the NW and discussion of its possible identification with Bāgh-i Jahān Ārā.

90. Samizay 1981: 15–255—good summary with photos and plans of all major and minor monuments, with an analysis of the old city and suggestions on its preservation.

91. Golombek 1983—discusses the history of the Friday Mosque.

92. Shokoohy 1983—plans, elevations, photos, description, and list of the Shāhzāda Alu'l Gāsim and Shāhzāda 'Abdullāh.

93. O'Kane 1984b—discussion of the Timurid stucco on the Friday Mosque.

94. O'Kane 1987: 115–18, 167–77, 203–5, 277–80, 330–43, 353–57 and 363–65—catalogue descriptions of all Timurid monuments.

95. Golombek and Wilber 1988: 301–21—descriptions of the Timurid monuments.

96. Aalund 1990: 20—axonometric reconstruction drawing of the citadel.

97. Boardman in Errington and Cribb 1992: 108–9—describes an AD 1st-century bronze statuette of a goddess found in the Herat region.

98. Michaud and Barry 1996: 14–41, pls 46–7, 66–7, 70–3, 81–2—general account of the main monuments, focusing on the tilework, with colour photos.

99. Hillenbrand 2000—discussion of the Ghurid sections in the Friday Mosque in the broader context of Ghaznavid and Ghurid architecture.

100. SPACH, 2001, *Newsletter*, 7: 13–15, report on restoration and cleaning work in musalla region with proposed plans to prevent imminent collapse of one of the surviving musalla minarets.

101. Hillenbrand 2002—detailed discussion of the demolished Ghurid tomb in the Friday Mosque and its decoration.

102. Gignoux 2003—discussion and illustration of a 7th-century bronze Christian cross from Herat.

103. Aga Khan Trust for Culture 2006—report on discoveries and restoration work in Herat.

104. Ball 2008: 95, 98, 200–10—summary.

105. Franke et al. 2008—general introduction to the city and its monuments arising from the DAI work on the citadel and museum and its collections, with specific essays on Herat metalwork, ceramics, glass, and the art of the book.

106. O'Kane 2009—discussion of the Persian inscriptions on the citadel.

107. O'Kane 2011—discussion of the tilework on the citadel.

108. Franke 2015a—discusses the evidence from the new excavations at the citadel and Kuhandizh for the pre-Islamic settlement.

109. Franke 2015b—summary of the DAI work in Herat.

110. Hansen et al. 2015—full detailed report on the 1964 restoration work on the Ghurid portal.

111. Stevens 2015—report on the conservation work on the Gawharshad Mausoleum.

112. Abassi 2016—history of the monuments at Kuhandizh and detailed report on their conservation.

113. Franke and Martina Müller-Wiener 2016—history of the Herat Museum and its restoration, with detailed catalogue of the collection.

114. Jodidio et al. 2017: 154–241—reports on the Aga Khan Trust for Culture conservation work.

429. HINDU HASAN GHAR

Lat. 31° 03' N, long. 64° 10' E. approximately. Map 97.
Revised: 31.05190153 N, 64.1747085 E / 31° 03' 06.84550944 N,
64° 10' 28.95058524 E.
Helmand Province. On the left bank of the Helmand
between Darwīshān and Basābād, 2 km west of Kamtudi
Wakīl Khān.

Dates: Parthian, 2nd–1st cent. BC; Into-Parthian, 1st–3rd
cent.; Sasanian, 3rd–7th cent.; Timurid, 15th cent. (ceramic).

Description: A mound.

Fieldwork: 1966 Hammond, Cambridge University—
survey.

Source: Hammond 1970: 450—lists site (no. 23) and discusses the pottery and general survey results.

430. HIRDAI TEPE
Or GIRDAI TEPE or TIKAR 4. See also 1191 TIKAR.

Lat. 36° 26' N, long. 64° 53' E. approximately. Map 24.
Faryāb Province. To the west of Daulatābād.

Date: Bronze Age, early 2nd mill. BC (C-14, ceramic).

Description: Remains of a square farming settlement measuring 100 × 95 m. It is surrounded by a defensive wall with
square towers.

Fieldwork: 1973 Sarianidi, Af/Sov. Mission—excavation.

Sources:
1. Biscione 1977: 125—mention.
2. Sarianidi 1977c: 22–6—brief description and discussion.
3. Srivastava 1979b: 57—summary of Sarianidi's work.
4. Kohl 1984: 161—summary of Soviet excavation.

431. HISĀR, JĀGHŪRĪ
Or SĀR.

Lat. 33° 12' N, long. 67° 35' E. Maps 78, 79.
Ghazni Province. In the Kūh-i Khūd Valley, c.16 km north
of Jāghūrī and 2 km west of Sarau.

Date: Early Sasanian, 4th–5th cent. (architectural).

Description: An isolated, impressive artificial cave complex.
It is heavily eroded and much has collapsed. There is a
tunnel-stairway connecting the north and south sides.

Fieldwork: 1974 Taddei and Verardi, IsMEO—survey.

Sources:
1. Taddei 1975: 547—mention.
2. Verardi 1977a: 141–2—brief description.

432. HISĀR, WĀKHĀN

Lat. 37° 00' N, long. 72° 43' E. Map 39.

Badakhshān Province. Near the junction of the Wākhān
and Panja Rivers, near the village of Āb Gāj. 12 km east of
Qal'a-i Panja.

Description: Reports of a large ruined fortress, locally
attributed to the Siāhpush Kāfirs.

Source: Gazetteer 1972: I. 83—mention.

HISĀRAK. See 817 PUL-I ALĀM.

433. HISĀR DARRA

Lat. 33° 04' N, long. 63° 53' E. Map 73.
Farāh Province. A small valley opening of the Larwand
Valley at the Masjid-i Sangi, c.10 km from Deh Tūrkān.

Description: 3 km from the mouth of the valley are remains
of a stone structure, locally known as a 'throne'. There are
more remains in the vicinity. At the end of the valley are
two caves in the side of the mountain, 500 m above the
valley floor. Coins were reported to have been found inside.
On top of the mountain above the caves some baked bricks
and sherds were found.

Fieldwork: 1946 Kohzad, HSA—survey.

Sources:
1. Kohzad 1951–4, 9/1: 42–3—brief description.
2. Ball 2002: 26—mention.

434. HUMAI QAL'A
Or DASHT-I TAMAKI.

Lat. 33° 13–21' N, long. 67° 47' E. Maps 78, 79.
Ghazni Province. At the eastern limits of the Dasht-i Tamaki, 15 km east of Nai Qal'a, 45 km north of Qarabāgh
near the road to Lūmān.

Date: Early Sasanian, 4th–5th cent. (stylistic).

Description: A complex of some 36 Buddhist caves. They
are irregularly situated in a cliff face, on several levels. Many
are quite large, some are just cells, interconnected by corridors and stairs. Most have elliptical vaults. There is no
decoration.

Fieldwork: 1974–5 Taddei and Verardi, IsMEO—survey.

Sources:
1. Taddei 1974b: 478—brief description and photo.
2. Taddei 1975: 545—mention.
3. Verardi 1977a: 143–7—description of the caves and discussion of the architectural parallels.
4. Verardi 1977c—full description and discussion of the
complex and its parallels.
5. Taddei 1978: 587–589—mention and photos.
6. Verardi and Parapatti 2004: 43—detailed description
with detailed drawings and photos.

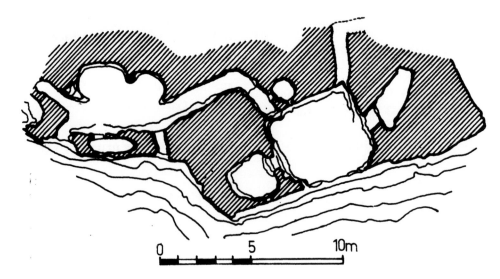

434 Humai Qal'a (after Verardi 1977a).

435. HUPIĀN

Original: Lat. 35° 02' N, long. 69° 09' E. Map 64.
Revised: 35.03699475 N, 69.15856052 E /
35° 02' 13.18111404 N, 69° 09' 30.81788676 E.
Parwān Province. 3 km north-west of Chārikār at the foot of the mountains bordering the west of the Kūh-i Dāman.

Description: Some large mounds built up from ancient deposits, built over by a modern village. Many antiquities are reported to have been found here.

Fieldwork:
1. 1834 Masson — survey.
2. 1923 Foucher, DAFA — survey.

Sources:
1. Masson 1842: III. 126 and 161 — discusses its history.
2. Cunningham 1846: 180-1 — briefly discusses the site in a reconstruction of ancient geography.
3. Foucher 1942-7: 143 — mention.
4. Caspani and Cagnacci 1951: 229 — brief description.
5. Fussman, Murad, and Ollivier 2008: 133-4 — brief discussion.

436. HUSAINĀBĀD

Lat. 30° 16' N, long. 62° 07' E. Map 95.
Nīmrūz Province. On the left (south) bank of the Helmand, 9 km above Chahār Burjak and 3 km below Ashkīnak.

Description: Remains of a fort on a slight rise, close to the river bank. Considerable areas of the walls still standing.

Fieldwork: 1884 Peacocke, Maitland, ABC — topographical survey.

Sources:
1. Peacocke 1885a: 4 — mention.
2. Maitland 1888a: 64 — mention.
3. Peacocke 1887a: 18 — mention.
4. Gazetteer 1973: II. 128 — mention.

437. HUSTUKH TEPE
Or NASRATĀBĀD or NASRAT TEPE.

Original: Lat. 36° 52' N, long. 66° 25' E. Map 25.
Revised: 36.8619128 N, 66.42629667 E / 36° 51' 42.88606380 N, 66° 25' 34.66799508 E.
Jauzjān Province. 24 km east of Āqcha, *c.*250 m south of the road to Balkh, to the east of the Zīyārat-i Sāhib Isma'īl Aghā.

Dates: Graeco-Bactrian, 3rd–2nd cent. BC; early Islamic, 10th–13th cent. (ceramic).

Description: A regular, rectangular mound *c.*40 × 50 m in area and 15 m in height, surrounded for a considerable area by smaller mounds, debris, and pottery of all types.

Fieldwork:
1. 1938 Barger, ASI — survey.
2. 1946 Wheeler, ASI — reconnaissance.
3. 1948 Le Berre, DAFA — survey.
4. 1956 Ramachandran and Sharma, ASI — reconnaissance.
5. 1960 Hayashi and Sahara, Kyoto University — survey.

Sources:
1. Barger and Wright 1941: 55 — brief description (Site ML).
2. Shakur 1947: 69 — mention.
3. Ramachandran and Sharma 1956: I. 20 — mention.
4. Hayashi and Sahara 1962: 65 — photo and description in Japanese.

438. IBRĀHĪMĪ

Original: Lat. 33° 10' N, long. 61° 45' E. Map 69.
Revised: 33.16478325 N, 61.74308557 E /
33° 09' 53.21969964 N, 61° 44' 35.10803508 E.
Herat Province. 5 km from Chah-i Puza-i Ibrāhīmī in a
valley of the Shikasta Ghuldam mountains, several km west
of the Herat-Kandahār road.

Description: Remains of an ancient copper mine. The workings extend along the richest part of the vein for *c.*15 m.

Fieldwork: 1977 CNRS—geological survey.

Source: Berthoud et al. 1977: 6–7—description of the geology and the workings.

IHSĀN RABĀT. See **2095 in Supplement.**

439. IMĀM SAHĪB, JAUZJĀN

Original: Lat. 36° 40' N, long. 66° 29' E. Map 28.
Revised: 36.66911169 N, 66.51596782 E /
36° 40' 08.80209480 N, 66° 30' 57.48413616 E.
Jauzjān Province. 54 km west of Mazār-i Sharīf on the
southern road to Āqcha.

Date: Ghaznavid, 11th cent. (stylistic).

Description: Two Ghaznavid shrines located adjacent to
each other, the Zīyārat-i Imām Zain al-'Abadin and the Zīyārat-i Bābā Hātim. The Zīyārat-i Bābā Hātim consists of a
square brick mausoleum with a simple entrance surrounded
by inscriptions and decorative brick panels. The interior has a
dome resting on stalactite quinches, and is decorated in
stucco, much of it imitating the brick patterns.

Fieldwork:
1. 1886 Peacocke, ABC—topographical survey.
2. 1978–9 de Valence, DAFA—restoration.

Sources:
1. Peacocke 1887a: 297—mentions the large domed
   ziyarat of Imam Zain al-Abuddin as well as a smaller
   ziyarat.
2. Melikian-Chirvani 1968—stylistic discussion of the
   monument, drawing widespread comparisons.
3. Sourdel-Thomine 1971—full description and stylistic
   analysis of the building and its decoration, with drawings and photos. Translation of the inscriptions.
4. Melikian-Chirvani 1972—art-historical description of
   the decoration and inscriptions.
5. Bivar 1977—a note on the exterior inscriptions.
6. Firūzi 1979—brief report on the completion of the
   restoration.
7. Gazetteer 1979: IV. 267—mention.
8. De Valence 1979—very brief outline of the restoration.
9. Bihdād 1981—report on the DAFA restoration.

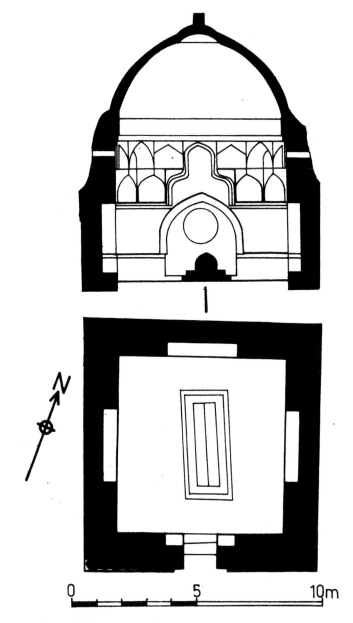

439 Imām-Sāhib, Jauzjān—Shrine of Bābā Hatim (after Bihdād 1981).

10. Hillenbrand 2000—discussion in the broader context
    of Ghaznavid and Ghurid architecture.
11. Ball 2008: 213—summary.

440. IMĀM SĀHIB, QUNDŪZ

Original: Lat. 37° 11' N, long. 68° 55' E. Map 31.
Revised: 37.1926996 N, 68.9022199 E / 37° 11' 33.71855064 N,
68° 54' 07.99165368 E.
Qundūz Province. In the town of Imām Sāhib, to the north-
west (Qarawul road).

Date: Timurid or post-Timurid, 15th–17th cent. (architectural).

Description: Octagonal citadel (*c*.200 × 200 m), surrounded by a terreplein of the same shape (width c.50 m, height 5 m), on the edge of which buildings were built whose ruined walls from a distance give the false impression of a second enclosure; but these thin walls, pierced with ogival windows, are not fortified. The rampart of the citadel is preserved to a considerable height (c.20 m); it is flanked by eight angle towers whose plan is still clearly apparent; its width on the curtain wall is 6 to 8 m. Many vestiges of mud-brick constructions inside the enclosure, mainly on the west side, where the entrance gate is located, flanked by two well-preserved towers. The access ramp to the terreplein, however, has not been located.

Collections: National Museum/AIA—sherds.

Fieldwork:
1. 1955–60 Fischer, DAAD—survey.
2. 1977 Gardin et al., CNRS—survey.

Sources:
1. Site information by J.-C. Gardin.
2. Fischer 1966: 27—mention and photo of the Timurid structures at the top.
3. Fischer 1969: 351—brief description and photo of the citadel called Imam Sayyid II (sic).
4. Gardin and Lyonnet 1978–9: pl. V—no. 105.
5. Gentelle 1989—full report on the ancient irrigation and hydrology of the area.
6. Gardin 1998: 62—no. 105.

IMĀM SHASH NŪR. See **2096 in Supplement.**

INDU KHĒL TUP. See **364 GHUNDA CHASHMA.**

IRAGHLI. See **1244 YURUGHLI.**

441. IRAQ AND JANDARGAL

Lat. 34° 47'–34° 50' N, long. 68° 02'–68° 05' E. Map 58.
Bāmiyān Province. Road from the Shībar Pass to Dūshi: in the side valleys south of Bulula (Darra-i 'Iraq and Darra-i Jandargal).

Date: Turk and/or pre-Mongol Islamic, 7th–13th cent. (architectural).

Description: Ruins of several towers and a castle, with brick decoration in the form of lozenges.

Fieldwork: 1974–5 Le Berre, DAFA—survey.

Source: Le Berre 1987: 46–50, pls 45–6—itinerary A2, Dara-i Eraq, ruins 1 to 6; Dara-i Jandargal, ruins 1 to 5.

442. ĪRGANAKH

Lat. 36° 39' N, long. 68° 39' E. Map 32.
Qundūz Province. A pass on the Qundūz-Tāshqurghān road, 22 km west of Qundūz.

Date: Graeco-Bactrian, 3rd–2nd cent. BC (stylistic).

Description: A small mound with traces of stone walls. A limestone column base in a pseudo-classical style was found on the surface.

Fieldwork: 1955 and 1960 Fischer, DAAD—survey.

Sources:
1. Fischer 1961a: 14–15—mention and photo of the column base.
2. Fischer 1969: 348—summary.

443. ĪRINDĀS

Original: Lat. 31° 14' N, long. 62° 12' E. Map 84.
Revised: 31.22389414 N, 62.19380556 E /
31° 13' 26.01889896 N, 62° 11' 37.70000412 E.
Nīmrūz Province. 14 km north-east of Chakhānsūr.

Description: A large artificial mound.

Source: Tate 1910: 211—mention.

444. ISHĀNĀN
Or DA MULLĀH TEPE.

Original: Lat. 36° 46' N, 68° 54' E. Map 85.
Revised:
36.77402315 N, 68.91196799 E / 36° 46' 26.48332776 N, 68° 54' 43.08475212 E (A).
36.77462918 N, 68.91936695 E / 36° 46' 28.66504044 N, 68° 55' 09.72101172 E (B).
Qundūz Province. 6 km north-east of Qundūz, in the village and outskirts of Ishānān. (A) The tepe of Ishānān itself is located 500 m north of the canal which crosses the village (direction north-west), on the west side of the road which leads to Gharau Shākh, to the north-north-east. (B) 700 m down the road, 200 m to the west is the tepe of Hazrat-i Sultān. (C) Finally, after A by the road that leads to Bakhshi, towards the east-north-east, at 600 m is a third tepe, on the north side of the road. The 1:100,000 map indicates a mound of 3 m at a point situated about 900 m to the west of A; this mound was not visited.

Dates: Achaemenid, 6th–4th cent. BC (A, C); Kushan and Hunnic-Turk, 1st–9th cent.; some Islamic sherds (A, C) (ceramic).

Description: (A) On a natural platform 2 m high (related to the geological past of the Khānābād river), two artifical mounds 200 m apart at the north-east and west ends of the platform (height 6 m). This site is today a cemetery, with a small mosque on the west mound. (B) Mound of irregular shape, cut straight by cultivation (25 × 25 m), flat top (3 m); in a cut on the south side, traces of a thick wall (1 m), and layers of ash at the present ground level. (C) Mound similarly reduced by cultivation, irregular shape (20 × 15 m), flat top (3–4 m); many sherds up to 30 m from the base, in the fields. In the cuts of the east face and the south angle, burnt layers at 1 m above the present ground level, 8 m long; under the layers, traces of a mud-brick structure which did not burn; above the burnt layers, walls with angles of which the coating indicates the interior of a building, after the fire. However, there is nothing to indicate that these three levels correspond to the three periods of occupation of the site indicated by the pottery.

Collections: National Museum/AIA — sherds.

Fieldwork:
1. 1960 Fischer, DAAD — survey.
2. 1978 Gardin et al., CNRS — survey.

Sources:
1. Site information by J.-C. Gardin.
2. Fischer 1961a: 17 — mention.
3. Gardin and Lyonnet 1978–9: pl. VII — nos. 464, 465, 469.
4. Lyonnet 1997: figs 25, 35, 49, 68, 60 — nos. 464, 465, 469.
5. Gardin 1998: 79 — nos. 464, 465, 469.

445. ĪSHĀN TŪP

Original: Lat. 35° 36'–36° 37' N, long. 69° 02'–69° 04' E. Map 32.
Revised:
36.63073016 N, 69.05315707 E / 36° 37' 50.62858896 N, 69° 03' 11.36545128 E (A).
36.61271968 N, 69.03988477 E / 36° 36' 45.79084944 N, 69° 02' 23.58518496 E (C).
Qundūz Province. On the plateau which dominates the plain of Qundūz-Khānābād, to the south: semi-desert zone, today without artificial irrigation, crossed by the road from Khānābād to 'Aliābād (Dasht-i Īshān Tūp). The tepes are situated between this road and the edge of the plateau, about 3 km farther north; a useful landmark is the fork of the Ishkamīsh road, which lies not far after the rise onto the plateau, coming from Khānābād, in the region of Chahār Tūt. (A) The most visible tepes are a group of mounds close together situated 4 km west of this point. (B) There is also 1 km south-west of the same point, on the edge of the road (west side), an area of extended fairly shallow gullying, of which the surface sherds confirm the artificial character. (C) Another zone of similar gullying lies 3.5 km south-west of the same point, on the same side of the road, between 300 and 1500 m distant from it.

Dates: Middle Bronze Age, *c.*2500–1500 BC; Beg. Iron, end 2nd–beg. 1st mill. BC (B, C); Kushan, 1st–4th cent. (C); Timurid, 15th–16th cent. (A, C) (ceramic).

Description: (A) Two round fairly high mounds (diam. 25 m, height 4 m), 100 m from each other, on an approximately

east–west line, flanked by two other smaller mounds (diam. 10 m, height 2 m), the same distance to the east and the north-east. These four mounds, probably kurgans, present all the traces of illegal excavations. 2 km to the north are other similar mounds visible on the edge of the plateau, in the region of Īshān Tūp (not surveyed). (B) Area of sherds in shallow gullies (max. height 2.5 m) extending over 400 × 400 m. (C) 300 m from the road indicated above, square mound (30 × 30 m), low (height 0.6 m), on the edge of long straight levees which probably indicate an ancient canal. 1000 m to the north, two low hillocks (height *c.*1 m), in a zone of gullying like B, where traces of canals may still be seen (on the ancient irrigation of the plateau of Īshān Tūp, see Gardin and Lyonnet 1978–9: 80, where this plateau is called Shākh Tepe). Achaemenid and Kushan sherds on the square mound, Islamic elsewhere (collection area: 200 × 200 m).

Collection: National Museum/AIA — sherds.

Fieldwork: 1978 Gardin et al., CNRS — survey.

Sources:
1. Site information by J.-C. Gardin.
2. Gardin and Lyonnet 1978–9: pl. VII — nos. 447–9, 499.
3. Lyonnet 1997: figs 13, 49 — nos. 447–9, 499.
4. Gardin 1998: 80 — nos. 447–9, 499.

446. ISHKAMĪSH, NORTH-EAST

Original: Lat. 36° 23' N, long. 69° 22' E. Map 37.
Revised:
36.385943 N, 69.35297201 E / 36° 23' 09.39479712 N, 69° 21' 10.69925004 E (A).
36.38653448 N, 69.34777177 E / 36° 23' 11.52414492 N, 69° 20' 51.97836696 E (B).
Takhār Province. Outskirts of Ishkamīsh in the north-east sector, up to 2 km from the town: the tepes are situated near springs or the streams which flow from them towards the north-west, in the direction of the Rūd-i Ishkamīsh. Access is by the Samandau-Chal road, which passes about 300 m east of of these springs. The largest tepe is directly above the spring situated 2.2 km from the roundabout of Ishkamīsh (A). Nearer the town, other less visible sites lie near a second spring, 1.3 km from the same point (B).

Dates: Hunnic-Turk, 5th–9th cent.; pre-Mongol Islamic, 10th–13th cent. (ceramic).

Description: (A) Rectangular site (100 × 80 m, north-west/south-east orientation in the length), constructed on terrain sloping to the north-west, between the road and the spring indicated above. A north-east/south-west depression, 10 m wide, divides the site into two unequal parts: the narrowest (40 × 80 m), south-east side, is 6 m above the level of the plain, the widest (50 × 90 m), north-west side, is 4 m above the level of the plain (measured at the foot of the tepe, west side). At the top, the terrain rises on the north-east and north-west sides; possible traces of a ditch (the south-west and south-east sides are edged re-pectively by a natural gully and by the road that passes at the foot of the tepe). None of these features, however, indicates that this is a fortified construction. (B) Near the spring and the stream situated halfway between the tepe above and the Bālā Hisār of Ishkamīsh (1.5 km away to the south-west), a zone of low mounds (1 to 2 m)—of which one is occupied by a cemetery—where the same type of pottery occurs as before: Hunnic and Islamic.

Collection: National Museum/AIA—sherds.

Fieldwork: 1978 Gardin et al., CNRS—survey.

Sources:
1. Site information by J.-C. Gardin.
2. Gardin and Lyonnet 1978–9: pl. XI—nos. 386–9.
3. Lyonnet 1997: figs 68, 69—nos. 386–9, 387, 388, 389.
4. Gardin 1998: 100—nos. 386–9.

447. ISHKAMĪSH BĀLĀ HISĀR
Or KALA TEPE.

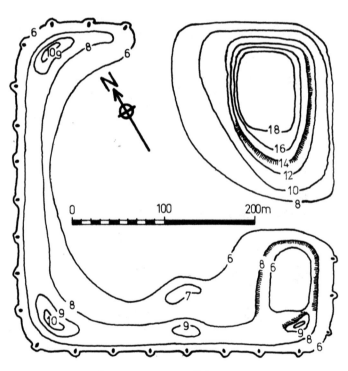

447 Ishkamish Bālā Hisar (J.-C. Gardin).

Original: Lat. 36° 23–38' N, long. 69° 22–36' E. Map 37. Revised: 36.3810802 N, 69.3366515 E / 36° 22' 51.88872828 N, 69° 20' 11.94540756 E. Takhār Province. In the town of Ishkamīsh, 500 m east-south-east of the central roundabout.

Dates: Hellenistic, 3rd–1st cent. BC; Kushan, 1st–4th cent.; pre-Mongol Islamic, 10th–13th cent.; and Timurid 15th–16th cent. (ceramic).

Description: Square fortification (340 × 340 m), oriented north-north-east/south-south-west, surrounded by a ditch where streams from nearby springs flow (south-east side); rectangular citadel (150 × 100 m)), same orientation, in the north-east angle. The wall, 8 m above the plain, has towers spaced every 40 m on the four sides, except in the north-east quadrant, where the talus of the citadel rises straight (height 18 m); a horizontal recess in the upper part of the talus suggests the occurrence of a curtain wall. Between the talus of the citadel and the first towers of the wall, towards the west and the south, the subsidence of the land possibly marks the location of a gate on the north side (where the expected fourth tower starting at the north-west angle is missing), or on the east side (under the 'curtain wall' of the citadel). On the interior, the terrain descends gently from the wall to the lower part of the site, in the west half; the east half is occupied—besides the north-east citadel—by a rectangular structure oriented like the latter, but much higher, in the south-east quadrant. In the lower part, the terrain is bumpy, but without clearly identifiable structures; on the walls, small hillocks rise at the three angles opposite the citadel, and in the middle of the south side. According to a local informant, all the surface area of the site is normally ploughed every year (*lalmī*)—it was not in 1978—and all sorts of materials were recovered (wood, stone, bricks, coins).

Collections: National Museum/AIA—sherds.

Fieldwork:
1. 1955–65 Fischer, DAAD—survey.
2. 1960 Hayashi and Sahara, University of Kyoto—survey.
3. 1978 Gardin et al., CNRS—survey.

Sources:
1. Site information by J.-C. Gardin.
2. Hayashi and Sahara 1962: 77—photos and description in Japanese.
3. Fischer 1969: 352–4 and pls. 27–8—photos and aerial views, description and commentary of the site.
4. Gardin and Lyonnet 1978–9: pl. XI—no. 398.
5. Lyonnet 1997: figs 39, 49—no. 398.
6. Gardin 1998: 100—no. 398.

448. ISHKĀSHIM

Original: Lat. 36° 42' N, long. 71° 34' E. Map 39. Revised: 36.70588848 N, 71.57144677 E / 36° 42' 21.19854384 N, 71° 34' 17.20836984 E. Badakhshān Province. At the entrance to the Wākhān corridor, just to the north of the town of Ishkāshim on the south side of the Panj River.

Description: A small ruined fort, locally attributed to the Siāhpush Kāfirs.

Fieldwork: 1898–9 Olufsen, Danish Army—survey.

Sources:
1. Olufsen 1904: 174—mention.
2. Gazetteer 1972: 85—mention.

449. ISHKĀZR

Lat. 36° 01' N, long. 70° 41' E. Map 38.
Badakhshān Province. C.10 km west of Munjān, up a tribu-
tary of the Kokcha River on the route from Munjān to
Anjumān.

Description: Remains of a stone fortress with a complex of
rooms inside. No sherds were found.

Fieldwork: 1963 Thompson, Oxford University—survey.

Sources:
1. Thompson 1964: 9—brief description.
2. Gardner 1971: 13—mention.

450. ISHKILI, IMĀM SĀHIB
    Including CHAKUR TEPE, PAS TEPE, and TĀSH
    WALTA TEPE.

Original: Lat. 37° 11'–37° 12' N, long. 69° 02' E. Map 31.
Revised:
37.19846409 N, 69.03986624 E / 37° 11' 54.47072580 N,
69° 02' 23.51847048 E (A).
37.20119532 N, 69.03054651 E / 37° 12' 04.30314552 N,
69° 01' 49.96742592 E (B).
37.19065015 N, 69.02659615 E / 37° 11' 26.34055368 N,
69° 01' 35.74612668 E (C).
Qundūz Province. 11 km east of Imām Sāhib, on the outskirts of the village of Ishkili; tepes A and B are the mounds
of 5 m and 7 m indicated on the 1:100,000 map, north and
north-west of Ishkili; tepe C is located in the village itself,
200 m west of the mosque.

Dates: Kushan and Hunnic-Turk, 1st–9th cent.; some
Islamic sherds. (ceramic).

Description: (A) Tāsh Walta Tepe: square mound (50 × 50 m),
tabular top (height 5 m) sloping gently towards the south;
80 m to the west, round hillock (diam. 10 m), lower (2.5 m).
(B) Chakur Tepe: similar mound (45 × 45 m), flat top (height
7 m), circular in shape (diam. 20 m); a few steps to the north, a
mound irregular in shape (50 × 25 m, height 2 m), damaged
by cultivation (Pas Tepe). (C) Oblong north–south mound
(20 × 10 m, height 3 m).

Collection: National Museum/AIA—sherds.

Fieldwork: 1977 Gardin et al., CNRS—survey.

Sources:
1. Site information by J.-C. Gardin.
2. Gardin and Lyonnet 1978–9: pl. V—nos. 143–5.
3. Lyonnet 1997: figs 49, 68, 69—nos. 143–5.
4. Gardin 1998: 64—nos. 143–5.

ISHKĪNAK. See 58 ASHKĪNAK.

451. ISKĀR

Original: Lat. 35° 34' N, long. 68° 31' E. Maps 33, 49.
Revised: 35.57978734 N, 68.52355881 E /
35° 34' 47.23443984 N, 68° 31' 24.81170376 E.
Baghlān Province. 2 km south of Dahan-i Kāyān up the
Qūl-i Iskār running into the right of the Surkhāb west of
Dūshi, on the Chahārdeh Pass from Dūshi to Siāgird.

Description: Some ruins.

Fieldwork: 1886 Drummond, ABC—topographical survey.

Source: Drummond 1888a: 335—mention.

452. ISLĀM PINJA

Lat. 37° 17' N, long. 66° 19' E. Maps 24, 28.
Jauzjān Province. On the south bank of the Āmū Daryā,
80 km north-west of Balkh on the road to Kilift.

Date: Upper Palaeolithic, c.10,000 BC (lithic).

Description: An alluvial plain with a surface scatter of
'Mesolithic' geometric microliths across a wide area.

Fieldwork: 1969 Vinogradov, Af/Sov. Mission—survey.

Source: Vinogradov 1979: 25–8—discussion of the lithics
together with others from the survey, with comparisons
with other material in Soviet Central Asia.

453. ISLĀMPŪR

Original: Lat. 34° 35' N, long. 70° 37' E. Map 67.
Revised: 34.58582354 N, 70.62521576 E /
34° 35' 08.96473320 N, 70° 37' 30.77675184 E.
Kunār Province. At the junction of the Darra-i Nūr with
the Darra-i Kunār, c.26 km north-east of Jalālābād on the
road to Nūristān.

Date: Hindu Shahi, 10th cent. (ceramic, stylistic); Timurid,
15th–16th cent. (ceramic).

Description: Some massive diaper masonry fortification
walls and ruins of houses. One building is very large and
has embellishments of schist slabs. There are also remains of
a possible stupa. Amongst the finds was some sculptured
stone work, possibly from a Hindu temple.

Fieldwork:
1. 1834 Masson—survey.
2. 1959 Fischer, DAAD—survey.

Sources:
1. Masson 1842: III. 280–1—mentions remains.
2. Simpson 1879–80: 97—mentions remains.
3. Caspani 1946a—discusses the possible classical origins
   of the site.
4. Fischer 1960: 9–10—brief description.
5. Fischer 1961c—mentions the Hindu remains.

6. Fischer 1969: 357 – brief summary.
7. Errington 2017a: 160 – the Masson collection and archive relating to the site.

454. ISLĀM QAL'A
Or KĀFIR QAL'A. See also 1165 TEPE GULAK.

Original: Lat. 34° 40' N, long. 61° 06' E. Map 51.
Revised:
34.67861037 N, 61.08049533 E / 34° 40' 42.99733668 N, 61° 04' 49.78319988 E to
34.67712879 N, 61.07949689 E / 34° 40' 37.66362816 N, 61° 04' 46.18880940 E.
Herat Province. The Afghan border post on the Herat-Mashhad main road, 116 km west of Herat.

Date: Sasanian, 5th cent. (ceramic); early Islamic, 8th–13th cent. (ceramic); 15th cent.(inscription).

Description: Square mound with a ruined fort on top and the remains of a caravanserai to the south. The fort was originally an irregular polygon, up to 112 m diameter. Only a few fragments of the towers were still standing in the late 19th cent. The caravanserai is a large, baked brick one with vaulted corridors and a cistern. The northern end is in bad condition. An inscription observed over the entrance in the 19th cent. recorded its building by Hasan Khan Shamlu in the late 15th cent. A separate inscription recorded the architects.

Fieldwork:
1. 1884 Maitland, Peacocke, ABC – topographical surveys.
2. 1949 Fischer, DAAD – survey.
3. 1955–68 Fischer, DAAD – survey.
4. 1956 Ramachandran and Sharma, ASI – reconnaissance.
5. 1968–78 Kruglikova, Af/Sov. Mission – survey.

Sources:
1. Ferrier 1857: 139 – mention.
2. MacGregor 1879: I. 243–4 – brief description.
3. Peacocke 1887a: 61–2 – brief description.
4. Maitland 1888a: 140–2 – descriptions of both buildings.
5. Durand 1, pl. 326 – sketch.
6. Yate 1888: 55 – mention.
7. Fox 1943: 138–9 – brief description and photo.
8. Ramachandran and Sharma 1956: I. 18 – mention.
9. Fischer 1969: 333–4 – brief summary and photo.
10. Gazetteer 1975: III. 214 – brief description.
11. Gaibov et al. 2010: 108 – brief description and corrections (Site K135).

ISMA'ĪL QARA TEPE. See 316 FAIZĀBĀD TEPE.

ISMA'ĪL QISHLĀQ. See 738 MULLĀH AFGHĀNI.

455. ISSIK TAL

Lat. 37° 00'–37° 03' N, long. 73° 19'–73° 21' E. Map 40. Badakhshān Province. In Wākhān *c.*14 km west of Sarhad on the route to Qal'a-i Panja.

Description: Large numbers of petroglyphs of ibex carved onto boulders around and to the north of the village.

Fieldwork: 1975 Gratzl et al. – survey.

Source: Gratzl et al. 1976: 329–33 and 337–40 – descriptions, photogrammetrical drawings, and colour photos of the petroglyphs.

456. ĪSTĀNHĀ

Lat. 35° 13' N, long. 67° 46' E. approximately. Map 48. Bāmiyān Province. At the western (upper) extremity of the Saighān Valley, between Saighān 'Alaqadari and Qal'a-i Bayani (q.v.).

Description: A series of caves cut into the side of a hill, on top of which is an ancient tower.

Sources:
1. Masson 1839: 90 – mention.
2. Masson 1842: II. 405 – mention.

ISTĀRĀB or ASTĀRĀB. See 2237 SANGCHĀRAK in Supplement.

457. ISTĀWAI
Or ESTOWAY.

Original: Lat. 32° 00' N, long. 63° 09' E. Map 73.
Revised: 32.00134884 N, 63.15291875 E /
32° 00' 04.85583156 N, 63° 09' 10.50750684 E.
Farāh Province. On the west bank of the Khāsh Rūd, 10 km north of Dehmazang.

Date: Early Islamic, 8th–13th cent. (ceramic).

Description: A mound.

Fieldwork: 1960–70 Fischer, Bonn University – survey.

Source: Fischer et al. 1974–6: 31 – mention.

JĀ-I DARK. See 652 KUSHĀBĀD.

458. JABAL AL-SARĀJ
Or PARWĀN or MIRWAN.

Lat. 35° 07' N, long. 69° 14' E. Map 64.
Parwān Province. At the southern foot of the Sālang Pass, just to the east of the main road. 77 km north of Kābul.

Description: In 1913 during construction work many remains of baked brick were uncovered. Finds included pottery, tilework, Islamic coins, arrowheads, a stone Buddhist relief, large storage jars, and an inscription. Many coins were also found here in the early 19th century.

Sources:
1. Masson 1842: III. 166—mentions coin finds.
2. Jewett 1948: 201–2—description of the objects found in 1913.
3. Fussman, Murad, and Ollivier 2008: 173–4—description and quote Jewett.

459. JABAR TEPE

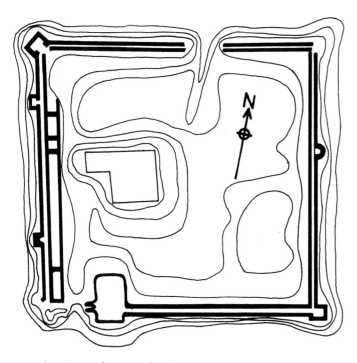

459 Jabar Tepe (after Pugachenkova 1976).

Original: Lat. 37° 03–05' N, long. 66° 50' E. Map 80.
Revised: 37.05484973 N, 66.83219603 E /
37° 03' 17.45902800 N, 66° 49' 55.90571088 E.
Balkh Province. 4 km north-east of Qarchikaq, just to the north of Mug Qal'a.

Date: Early Islamic, 10th–13th cent.

Description: An urban fortified site, with fortifications surrounding a central keep. Construction is of *pakhsa*.

Fieldwork: 1972–3 Pugachenkova, Af/Sov. Mission—survey.

Sources:
1. Pugachenkova 1976b– brief description and discussion of the architecture.
2. Francfort 1979a: 38—mentions the fortifications as continuing the traditions of Kushan military architecture.

460. JAGDALAK

Lat. 34° 25' N, long. 69° 45' E. Map 65.
Laghmān Province. Between Khurd Kābul and Gandamak, on the old route to Jalālābād.

Date: ?Chaghatai, 14th cent. (traditional).

Description: Remains of two forts and some mounds, marking the site of an ancient city. There are also some caves in the vicinity.

Sources:
1. Masson 1842: III. 179—mention.
2. Raverty 1878: 57—mention.

461. JAGHATŪ
See also 71 BĀD-I ĀSYĀ.

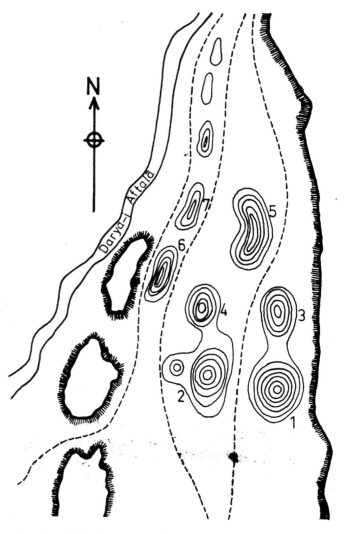

461 Jaghatu (after Scerrato 1967).

Lat. 33° 47' N, long. 68° 22' E. Map 80.
Ghazni Province. C.20 km north-west of Ghazni on the road to Wardak, at the foot of the Kūh-i Bād-i Āsyā.

Date: Turki Shahi, 7th–8th cent. (ceramic, numismatic, stylistic).

Description: A group of mounds containing mud-brick and *pakhsa* structures, one of which is vaulted. One mound has mud-brick fortifications on a stone foundation, with salients projecting from each wall. Finds include two late Bactrian inscriptions on boulders, stucco fragments, two coins, carnelian and lapis objects, but little pottery.

Fieldwork: 1958 Scerrato, IsMEO—sondages.

Sources:
1. Humbach, 1967: 25–6—discussion of the inscriptions.
2. Scerrato 1967—brief preliminary report on the remains and excavations.
3. Verardi 1977c: 119—brief summary of the discoveries.
4. Mac Dowall and Taddei 1978b: 263—summary of the remains.
5. Thomas 2015: 518—additional information from satellite imagery.

462. JALĀ'IR
Including TEPE CHIKAT.

Original: Lat. 36° 42' N, long. 69° 18' E. Map 32.
Revised:
36.68268797 N, 69.30758154 E / 36° 40' 57.67669200 N, 69° 18' 27.29353464 E. (A)
36.6839179 N, 69.30265038 E / 36° 41' 02.10445080 N, 69° 18' 09.54135252 E (B).
Takhār Province. In the plain of Jalā'ir, 5 km north-west of Bangui, tepes situated on the slopes which descend the road towards the Bangui River, to the height of of the last houses to the west of Jalā'ir-i Khurd: the first (A) is at the joining of the two roads indicated on the 1:100,000 map in this zone; the second (B) lies 500 more metres to the west by one of these roads.

Dates: Beg. Iron, end 2nd–beg. 1st mill. BC; Kushan and Hunnic-Turk, 1st–9th cent. (ceramic).

Description: (A) Rounded mound (diam. 20 m), cut into by irrigated fields (cotton), flattened top (2.5 m); in the cuts on the south-east, burnt layers, brick collapse, and mud-brick walls with coating reddened by the fire. 100 m to the northeast, another mound (Tepe Chikat) cut straight by ploughing (diam. 8 m, height 2 m), still with traces of walls or mud-bricks whose thickness (1 m) does not fit with the present dimensions of the tepe. (B) On a terrace edge followed by a small canal, oblong north-west/south-east mound also damaged on all sides by irrigation; present surface area 80 × 50 m, flattened top (threshing floor), dominating the plain by 3–4 m, north side, and 5–6 m south side (low terrace).

Collection: National Museum/AIA—sherds.

Fieldwork: 1978 Gardin et al., CNRS—survey.

Sources:
1. Site information by J.-C. Gardin.
2. Gardin and Lyonnet 1978–9: pl. XI—nos. 350–2.
3. Lyonnet 1997: figs 25, 35, 49, 68, 69—nos. 350–2.
4. Gardin 1998: 97—nos. 350–2.

463. JALĀLA

Lat. 35° 08' N, long. 71° 22' E. Map 68.
Kunār Province. On the west bank of the Kunār River, c.43 km north of Chaghān Sarāī.

Date: Kushan-Hunnic, 1st–6th cent. (architectural).

Description: Remains of a stupa.

Source: Fischer 1969: 359—mention, from Le Berre.

464. JALĀLĀBĀD

Lat. 34° 26' N, long. 70° 27' E. Map 66.
Nangahār Province. 150 km by road east of Kābul.

Dates: Achaemenid, 4th cent. BC (numismatic); Indo-Parthian, AD 25 (epigraphic); Hindu Shahi, 10th cent. (epigraphic, numismatic).

Description: A slight artificial mound, possibly from the Buddhist period, in the south-western corner of the town. There have been various accidental finds from in and around Jalālābād: a hoard of 100 bent bar Achaemenid coins, all of the same type; two Kharoshthi inscriptions dated AD 25; a defaced Hindu rock inscription and a hoard of 199 Hindu Shahi copper coins.

Sources:
1. Simpson 1881: 185—mentions the remains.
2. Vogel 1911: 259—mentions the Hindu Shahi inscription.
3. Konow 1938—photo with a translation and linguistic analysis of one of the Kharoshthi inscriptions.
4. Foucher 1942–7: 386—mentions the Kharoshthi inscription of the year 83.
5. Humbach 1968b—linguistic analysis of the Kharoshthi inscription in the National Museum.
6. Fussman 1970: 43–51—linguistic analysis of the Kharoshthi inscription in the National Museum.
7. Davary 1977—lists the Kharoshthi inscription and gives a bibliography.
8. Mac Dowall and Taddei 1978a and b: 200, 203, and 255—mention all the chance finds.

465. JALĀYUR

Lat. 36° 18' N, long. 64° 45' E. Map 24.
Faryāb Province. On the left bank of the Maimana River, 20 km south-south-west of Daulatābād.

Description: An old ruined fort.

Fieldwork: 1886 Maitland, ABC—topographical survey.

Sources:
1. Peacock 1887a: 247 and 288—mention.
2. Maitland 1888b: 157—mention.
3. Gazetteer 1979: IV. 270—mention.

466. JALMISH
Including QAL'A-I KHĀK-I SABŪR.

Lat. 35° 00' N, long. 68° 03'–68° 94' E. Map 58.
Baghlān Province. In the Darra-i Jalmish east of the Surkhāb, on the road from Bāmiyān to Dūshi, 5 km from Jalrīsh.

Date: Turki Shahi and/or Islamic pre-Mongol, 7th–13th cent. (architectural).

Description: Several ruined castles of brick and stone construction, on either side of the valley *c.*300 m apart. There are also many caves in the vicinity.

Fieldwork:
1. 1886 Peacocke, ABC—topographical survey.
2. 1974–5 Le Berre, DAFA—survey.

Sources:
1. Peacocke 1887: 398—mention.
2. Gazetteer 1910: IV. 213—mention.
3. Le Berre 1987—itinerary A2, Dara-i Jalmesh, runs 1–4.

467. JAL TEPE
Or JEL TEPE.

Original: Lat. 36° 33' N, long. 68° 54' E. Map 32.
Revised: 36.51595157 N, 68.90224944 E /
36° 30' 57.42563472 N, 68° 54' 08.09799120 E.
Qundūz Province. North of 'Aliābād, on the Baghlān-Qundūz road.

Date: Timurid, 15th–16th cent. (ceramic).

Description: A low-lying mound.

Fieldwork:
1. 1960 Fischer, DAAD—survey.
2. 1960 Hayashi and Sahara, Kyoto University—survey.

Sources:
1. Hayashi and Sahara 1962: 70, fig. 77—photo and description in Japanese.
2. Fischer 1969: 350—mention (Tepe B3).

468. JAM
Including KUSHKAK.

Original: Lat. 34° 23–38' N, long. 64° 31–51' E. Maps 54, 55.
Revised: 34.39729313 N, 64.51622607 E /
34° 23' 50.25526224 N, 64° 30' 58.41386136 E.

Ghūr Province. On the Harī Rūd between Kaminj and Āhangarān, where it is joined from the south by the Jam Rūd.

Date: Ghurid, 12th cent. (ceramic, epigraphic, stylistic).

Description: A minaret or victory tower, probably marking the site of the Ghurid capital of Fīrūzkuh. It stands 65 m high and has a diameter of 9 m at its base. It is made up of four tapering cylindrical shafts on an octagonal base, with a double spiral staircase inside. The outside is completely covered in decorative brickwork, except for one band of blue tile inscription near the top. The date inscription has been read as 570/1174–5 or 590/1193–4. Immediately to the east of the minaret the remains of a large courtyard was uncovered during excavations, and remains of a town recoded on either side of the valley, identified with the Ghurid capital of Fīrūzkuh.

On the hill of Kushkak between Jam village and the minaret are some Hebrew inscriptions dated 1153–1203. To the south of the river are mud-brick watch towers forming a fortification line. Another fortress with a stone reservoir lies on the north side of the river. There are several more mud remains in the immediate vicinity, including a possible bazaar and mosque, both to the east and west of the minaret.

Fieldwork:
1. 1956 Maricq and Le Berre, DAFA—survey.
2. 1959 J. Fischer et al., Cambridge University—topographical survey.
3. 1961–2 Bruno, IsMEO—architectural survey.
4. 1971 Scarcia, Venice University—survey.
5. 1973 Herberg, Berlin University—architectural survey.
6. 2000 Bruno and Akbari, Dept. of Historic Monuments—architectural and hydrological survey and construction of gabion walls to protect the base of the minaret.
7. 2003 and 2005 IsAIO/UNESCO Thomas, Pastori, Cucco—impact assessment for new road; excavations of robber holes on the upper slopes behind the minaret and ecavations to the east of the Minaret.
8. 2012 ACHCO—assessment work.

Sources:
1. Holdich 1886: 3—describes from local reports the minaret, the tunnel, and associated remains.
2. Holdich 1887: 24—mention.
3. Afghān 1930: 118–19—very brief description of the minaret, probably from hearsay. Describes it as being near Kāsh and that it was built by Husain-i Baiqara.
4. Kohzad 1951–4, 9/2: 6—brief description of the minaret from hearsay. Likens it to the Herat minarets.
5. Kohzad 1957—describes the discovery and identification of the minaret, with some historical-geographical background.
6. J. Fischer et al.1959—good topographical description of all the remains in the vicinity.

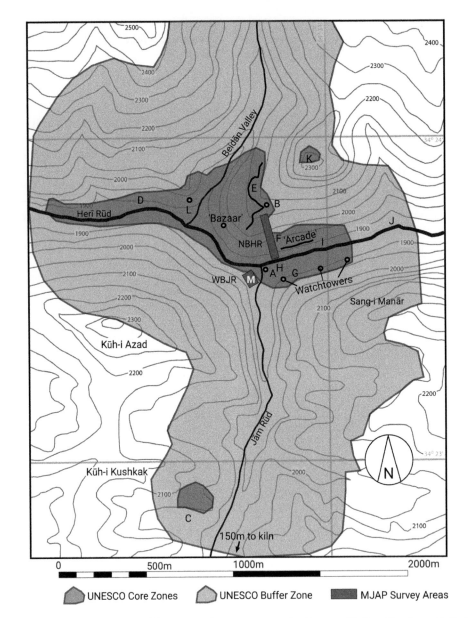

468 Jam—general plan. A: Minaret; B: Qaṣr Zarafshān; C: Hebrew cemetery; D: Zīyārat; E: Fortifications; F: Robber holes; G: Robber holes; H: 'Friday Mosque'; I: Ghūrid room in robber hole RH201; J: Eastern defences of the site; K: Kūh-i Khāra; L: Tāll Baydān; M: Robber holes (after Thomas 2007 and Herberg and Davary 1976).

7. Maricq 1959—brief description and preliminary account of the discovery.
8. Mariq and Wiet 1959—full account of the discovery, description of the minaret and decoration, and detailed historical background.
9. Kieffer 1960b—some historical-geographical background with a description of its discovery and identification.
10. Klimburg 1960: 49—photo and brief description.
11. Sourdel-Thomine 1960—general discussion of Ghurid art and its parallels.

12. Bruno 1962: 109–10—discusses the conservation problems of the minaret.
13. Gnoli 1962—brief note on the discovery of the Hebrew inscriptions.
14. Bruno 1963—architectural drawings of the minaret and description of the discovery of the Hebrew inscriptions.
15. Gnoli 1963b—brief note on the implications of the Hebrew inscriptions.
16. Klimburg 1963: 34—brief description.
17. Pugachenkova 1963: 108–12—general summary.

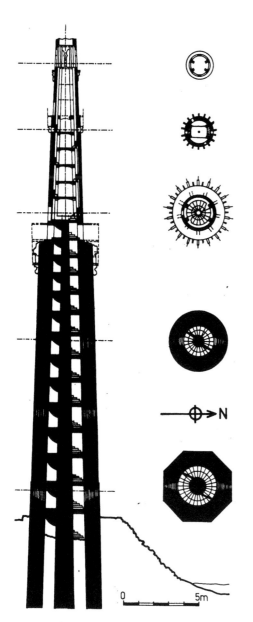

468 Jam—section of minaret (after Herberg and Davary 1976).

18. Gnoli 1964—texts, translations, and very full linguistic study of the Hebrew inscriptions and their implications.
19. Herrman 1965—brief general article on the discovery of the minaret and its implications.
20. Trousdale 1965a—description of the minaret and construction. Photos of the interior.
21. Hill 1966—diary of a visit to Jam. Brief description.
22. Leshnik 1968—discussion of the historical-geography of Ghūr, disputing the identification of Jam as Firuzkuh.
23. D. and J. Sourdel 1968: pl. III—photo and brief discussion of the minaret and its date.
24. Anand 1970: 23–4—brief summary and photos.

25. Stark 1970—popular tourist's account of a journey to Jam in 1968.
26. Janata 1971: 57–8—discusses the identification of Firuzkuh and other places in Ghūr.
27. Rapp 1971—detailed catalogue, with dates and texts, of all the Hebrew inscriptions.
28. Donini 1972—discusses the problem of identifying Firuzkuh with Jam.
29. Zander 1972: 565–8—describes the Italian project for conservation at Jam.
30. Herberg 1973—itinerary of a field trip into Central Afghanistan.
31. Rapp 1973—list of the new Hebrew inscriptions from Kushkak.
32. Hutt 1974: 166–9—description of the minaret in a study of the development of the minaret form.
33. Rapp 1974/75—texts of the new Hebrew inscriptions from Kushkak.
34. Desai 1975: 11–12—describes the architectural links with the Qutb Minar in Delhi.
35. Moline 1975—full discussion of the minaret: the date, decoration, history, and identification, concluding that it is the site of Firuzkuh.
36. Ettinghausen and Michaud 1976—photos and discussion of the ornament.
37. Herberg and Davary1976—very complete topographical and architectural study of all the remains and the surrounding area. Architectural drawings of the minaret.
38. Vercellin 1976a—discusses the identification of Firuzkuh.
39. Vercellin 1976b—points out some topographical features at Jam that support its identification as Firuzkuh.
40. Vercellin 1976—discusses Firuzkuh and its associations with the origins of the Firuzkuh.
41. N. Dupree 1977: 466–71—desctiption of the minaret and its discovery.
42. Davary 1978—discusses the remains and the historical geography, and refutes its identification with Firuzkuh.
43. Fischer 1978a: 331–2—very brief description of the minaret and the surrounding remains.
44. Herberg 1978: 216–19—description of the minaret and background on Firuzkuh.
45. Bruno 1979—describes the programme for conservation and excavation at the minaret.
46. Habibi 1980—reviews and reiterates Vercelin's new evidence.
47. UNESCO 1980—brief report on the conservation measures.
48. Pinder-Wilson 2001—discusses in detail the date and function of the minaret, and confirms its identification with Firuzkuh.
49. Samizay 1981: 12–13—summary and note on the need for preservation.
50. Michaud and Barry 1996: pls 52–4—colour photos.

51. Gilles 2000—discusses and illustrates current threats.
52. Hillenbrand 2000—discussion in the broader context of Ghaznavid and Ghurid architecture.
53. Ball 2002—discusses the fortification systems defending Firuzkuh.
54. Flood 2002b—discusses the possible Indian inspiration behind the idea of the victory tower.
55. Stewart 2004: 163–8—describes at some length the illicit excavations and both structures and objects that were turning up.
56. Thomas 2004—report on looting and preliminary investigations.
57. Flood 2005—discussion in the context of the Karramiyya sect.
58. Sourdel-Thomine 2004—comprehensive study of the minaret, its decoration, and inscription.
59. Flood 2005—discusses as a Karramiyya monument; supports Sourdel-Thomine's earlier dating.
60. Thomas et al. 2005—results of preliminary soundings around the minaret.
61. Thomas et al. 2006—results of environmental studies: geomorphological, archaeo-zoological, archaeo-botanical.
62. Thomas and Gascoigne 2006—report on the looting and subsequent damage to the site.
63. Thomas 2007—detailed description of the site and its history in the light of the latest investigations.
64. Ball 2008: 94, 118, 213–17—summary.
65. Flood 2009a—discusses the disputed dates, and the meaning behind the Sura of Maryam on the minaret and the possible Karramiyya associations.
66. Hunter 2009a—discusses a Jewish inscription discovered in 2005.
67. Hunter 2009b—further notes on the new Jewish inscription.
68. Gascoigne 2010—catalogue and discussion of the ceramics recovered from the 2005 investigations.
69. Shaked 2010—a note on the Jewish tombstones.
70. Filizenzi and Giunta 2015: 82—mention the Italian contribution to the Jam project.
71. Lintz 2015—discusses the evidence of the Judaeo-Persian inscriptions for a Jewish merchant colony.
72. Shaked 2016—discusses the Judaeo-Persian inscriptions in the context of newly discovered Jewish documents from Afghanistan.

JAMĀL KHĒL. See 481 JUMĀL KHĒL.

469. JAMĀL KĀLA
Or KUTPŪR 3. See also 667 KUTPŪR and 121 BĀZITKHĒL.

Original: Lat. 34° 26' N, long. 70° 19' E. Map 66.

Revised: 34.43992238 N, 70.32913922 E / 34° 26' 23.72057628 N, 70° 19' 44.90119956 E. Laghmān Province. C.7 km south-west of Darūnta between the Surkhāb and the road to Gandamak. 1 km south-west of Bāzitkhēl and 2 km south-west of Kutpūr.

Date: Kushan, 1st–3rd cent. (architectural).

Description: Remains of a stupa of inferior construction, 33 m in circumference. There is no decoration, and most of the plaster surface has disappeared. Inside was only ash and bone.

Fieldwork:
1. 1834 Masson—excavation.
2. 1965 Mizuno, Kyoto University—survey.

Sources:
1. Masson 1841: 66–7—brief description.
2. Mizuno 1971: 119—description and photo of the present condition (Stupa 25).

JAM QAL'A. See 875 QAL'A-I QAISĀR, 879 QAL'A-I SANGI.

JANDARGAL. See 441 'IRAQ.

470. JANGALAK-I QARABĀGH

Lat. 33° 17' N, long. 68° 04' E. Maps 78, 80. Ghazni Province. 11 km north of Qarabāgh, north-west of the Kābul-Kandahār road, c.45 km south-west of Ghazni.

Date: Early Sasanian, 4th–5th cent. (stylistic).

Description: A chance find of a small sandstone pilaster, c.30 cm high. It has a high base on which is carved a low relief of a female figure between two pilasters. The workmanship is rough, in the Gandharan style.

Sources:
1. Taddei 1969b: 546—mentions the discovery.
2. Verardi 1975—description and stylistic analysis of the sculpture.
3. Thomas 2015: 518—additional information from satellite imagery.

471. JĀNI TŪP
Or BĪMĀRĀN 5.

Original: Lat. 34° 27' N, long. 70° 21' E. Maps 66. Revised: 34.45532596 N, 70.34715268 E / 34° 27' 19.17347184 N, 70° 20' 49.74963900 E. Laghmān Province. C.1 km south of Bīmārān, across a gorge. C.4 km south of Darūnta.

Date: Indo-Parthian, 1st cent. (Numismatic).

Description: Remains of a stupa standing in a cultivated field. It is 46.70 m in circumference and is very solidly constructed, though without any decoration. It stands on a platform. Inside were gold ornaments, jewellery, 124 copper coins, and a steatite reliquary. Nearby are two mounds, possibly votive stupas.

Fieldwork:
1. 1833 Honigberger—excavation.
2. 1834 Masson—excavation.
3. 1965 Mizuno, Kyoto University—survey.

Sources:
1. Masson 1841: 75–9 and 97—description of the stupa and tumuli, and discussion of the coins.
2. Wilson 1841: pls V and IX—illustrations of the coins.
3. Mizuno 1971: 117—summary of Masson's work and description of the present condition (Siah Kūh Stupa 7).
4. Errington 2017a: 116–21 and 2017b: 30, 42, 45, 47—the Masson collection and archive relating to the site.

JAR-I SHĀKH BĀBA or **DARRA-I SHĀKH BĀBA. See 2097 in Supplement.**

472. JAR GUZAR

Original: Lat. 36° 40' N, long. 68° 58' E. Map 32.
Revised: 36.66326514 N, 68.97431609 E /
36° 39' 47.75451876 N, 68° 58' 27.53793840 E.
Qundūz Province. 12 km south-east of Qundūz, on the road to Khānābād: the tepe is located 800 m from the road, south side, near the village of Jar Guzar, which is situated on similar mounds, a few hundred metres to the south.

Dates: Achaemenid, 6th–4th cent. BC; Kushan and Hunnic-Turk, 1st–9th cent. (ceramic).

Description: Quadrangular north–south mound (60 × 40 m), surrounded by little canals and cut into at the base by irrigated fields; steep sides up to the flat top (height 15 m), on which there is a rectangular north–south structure, which occupies the east half of the surface. No traces of a way of access to the top, except perhaps for a depression on the north side. Sherds appear in the cuts almost to the present ground level, confirming the artificial character of this mound; those covered by the houses of Jar Guzar, to the south, also perhaps contain archaeological layers.

Collection: National Museum/AIA—sherds.

Fieldwork: 1978 Gardin et al., CNRS—survey.

Sources:
1. Site information by J.-C. Gardin.
2. Gardin and Lyonnet 1978–9: pl. VII—no. 419.
3. Lyonnet 1997: figs 25, 35, 49, 68, 69—no. 419.
4. Gardin 1998: 77—no. 419.

JAR QAL'A. See 2098 in Supplement.

473. JAR QUDUQ

Lat. 37° 17' N, long. 65° 46' E. Map 24.
Jauzjān Province. 27 km south of Khāmiyāb on the route to Āqcha.

Date: Neolithic, 7th–6th mill. BC (lithic).

Description: A well and a surface site. In the 1990s there were local reports of metal (bronze?) artefacts of high quality as well as much pottery recovered from the site.

Fieldwork: 1969 Vinogradov, Af/Sov. Mission—survey.

Sources:
1. Additional note on 1990s discoveries by Jonathan L. Lee.
2. Vinogradov 1979: 23—drawings of the material (Site 56).

474. JARWĪSH

Lat. 35° 26' N, long. 69° 44' E. Map 50.
Parwān Province. 1 km north of Khenj in the Panjshīr Valley, north-east of Umarz.

Description: An ancient site built over by a modern village.

Source: Kohl 1978: 72—mention from hearsay.

JAURU. See 2099 in Supplement.

JA'USHAN BEG. See 1019 SHĀH 'ALI.

JOUZGUN. See 2100 in Supplement.

JEL TEPE. See 467 JAL TEPE.

475. JIGA TEPE

Original: Lat. 37° 02–03' N, long. 66° 35' E. Map 26.
Revised: 37.02860435 N, 66.59068027 E /
37° 01' 42.97565748 N, 66° 35' 26.44898820 E.
Balkh Province. 5.5 km east of Dilbarjīn, 41 km north-west of Balkh, and 2 km to the west of the road to Kilift.

Dates: Hellenistic, 3rd–mid-2nd cent. BC; Kushan, 1st cent. BC–AD 3rd cent.; early Sasanian, 3rd–4th cent. (architectural, ceramic, numismatic).

Description: A hill up to 60 m high, with a site to the north and west. The first period consists of a circular fortification wall enclosing a possible temple. The wall is 150 m diam. With arrow slits on two levels, and is strengthened by semi-circular towers. There is a second wall 2.15 m inside, with a gallery and chambers in between. Construction is of mud and *pakhsa*. Finds include coins, a Greek ostracon, and bronze arrowheads. After the building's destruction and a long period of abandonment it was reoccupied during the Kushan period by a mud-brick building of uncertain

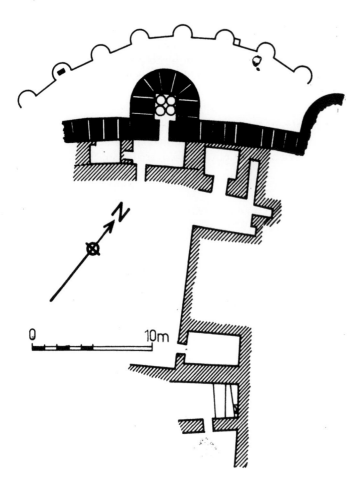

475 Jiga Tepe (after Pugachenkova 1979b).

function. The final period is represented by a large wealthy house of *pakhsa* and mud-brick construction. Finds from this period included large stamped pottery.

Fieldwork: 1974–6 Pugachenkova, Af/Sov. Mission—excavations.

Sources:
1. Kruglikova 1977d: 425—briefly discusses the Greek ostracon.
2. Pugachenkova 1979b– preliminary report on the excavations and brief discussion on the function of the site.
3. Nikitin 1995—discussion of a seal bearing a portrait of a Sasanian official.
4. Rougemont 2012a: 189–91—text and discussion of the Greek ostracon.

476. JIJA

Original: Lat. 32° 47' N, long. 61° 59' E. Map 69.
Revised: 32° 52' 36.977" N, 61° 59' 52.319" E.

Farāh Province. On the Adraskān River to the north of Farāh. 6.6 km to the north of a pass of the same name through the hills 33 km east of Anār Darra.

Description: Remains of an ancient stone wall defending the pass across a gap 80–100 m in width.

Source: Gazetteer 1973: II. 131—mention.

477. JŪI KHWĀJA
Or DO GHAR JŪI KHWĀJA.
See also 98 BĀLĀ MURGHĀB and 2199 QAL'A-I KHWĀJA in Supplement.

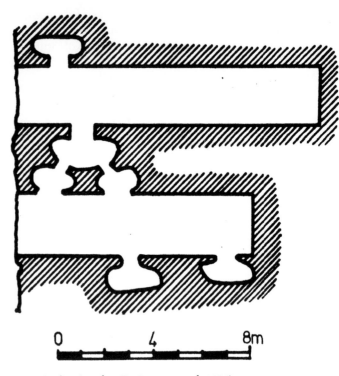

477 Jūi Khwāja (after De Laessoe et al. 1886).

Lat. 35° 33' N, long 63° 20' E. Map 44.
Bāghdīs Province. 3 km south of Bālā Murghāb on the west bank of the Murghāb River.

Description: An artificial cave complex consisting of two openings and seven small, partly obscured chambers. There is another small cave complex a few kilometres away.

Fieldwork:
1. 1885 De Laessöe, ABC—survey.
2. 1957 Lindberg—speleological survey.

Sources:
1. *Civ. and Milit. Gazette*, 24 July 1885—brief description and sketch.
2. De Laessöe 1886: 96—description and plan of the caves, ascribing them to the Buddhist period.
3. Lindberg 1961: 14–15—brief description.

478. JŪI KUHNA

Original: Lat. 31° 02' N, long. 62° 06' E. Map 92.
Revised: 31.02195261 N, 62.0965076 E / 31°01'19.02939492 N, 62° 05' 47.42736612 E.
Nīmrūz Province. At a point where the Chakhānsūr-Zaranj road intersects with Jūi Kuhna, *c*.22 km south of Chakhānsūr.

Dates: Sasanian, 3rd–7th cent. (B); Mongol-Timurid, 13th–15th cent. (A) (ceramic).

Description: (A) Remains of a silted up canal excavated. (B) A small mud ruin 1 km to the east.

Fieldwork: 1960–70 Fischer, Bonn University – survey and sondage (A).

Source: Fischer et al. 1974–6: 33 – brief summary.

479. JŪI NAU
 Or GUDRI or DAMB-I RUSTAM. Incl. BAD SHĀO. See also 2043 in Supplement.

Original: Lat. 30° 38' N, long. 61° 50' E. Map 93.
Revised:
Between 30.62061935 N, 61.85435093 E / 30° 37' 14.22967368 N, 61° 51' 15.66333108 E and 30.62207454 N, 61.8527823 E / 30° 37' 19.46835588 N, 61° 51' 10.01627532 E.
Nīmrūz Province. To the east of the Helmand 10 km north of Qal'a-i Fath. The site is actually closer to Gudri than Jūi Nau (although it has mainly been referred to under the latter name).

Dates: Early 1st mill. BC; Parthian–early Sasanian, 1st–3rd cent. (ceramic); Ghaznavid, 11th–12th cent. (stylistic); Timurid, 15th–16th cent. (ceramic).

Description: A conflation of sites here, hence the multiple names. Some mud-brick ruins surrounded by circular mud walls. The remains include a mosque with a richly decorated façade. Inside is a dome-chamber with a zone of transition formed by a series of horseshoe arches. There are also remains of many irrigation channels in the vicinity.

The small mosque is 16th century. Directly south of it is a larger, much eroded and deflated, oval qala called Bad Shāo (probably corruption from Bad-i Shād), probably early 1st mill. BC, based on comparison with other sites known to be of this date. Very sparse sherd cover. Many late Timurid structures around, with recent and older cemeteries with remains of mausolea.

Fieldwork:
1. 1960 Fischer, DAAD – survey.
2. 1971–4 Trousdale, Smithsonian – survey.

Sources:
1. Site information by W. Trousdale.
2. Fischer 1966: 27 – mention and photo.

3. Fsicher 1969: 335 – brief summary.
4. Fischer 1970a – photos of the remains.
5. Fischer 1971c: 50 – mention and photos.
6. Fischer et al. 1974–6: pls 180–1 – photos.

JUI YAL. See 2101 in Supplement.

480. JŪLAI

Lat. 34° 51'–34° 52' N, long. 68° 06' E. Map 58.
Bāmiyān Province. Road from the Shībar Pass to Dūshi: in the side valley south of Bulula (Darra-i Jūlai).

Date: Turk, 7th–9th cent. (ceramic).

Description: Badly eroded ruins of two towers and a small fort.

Collection: National Museum/AIA – sherds.

Fieldwork: 1974–6 Le Berre, DAFA – survey.

Source: Le Berre 1987: 45–6, pls 43c, 45 – itinerary A2, Dara-i Jolay, ruins 1 to 3; description and photos.

481. JUMĀL KHĒL
 Or JAMĀL KHĒL.

Lat. 32° 27' N, long. 67° 48' E. Map 79.
Ghazni Province. On the western side of the Āb-i Istāda, 6 km south-west of Gazkai.

Dates: Hunnic-Turki Shahi, 5th–9th cent. (ceramic).

Description: None available.

Fieldwork: 1974 Dupree, AUFS – survey.

Source: Information by L. Dupree.

482. JUWAIN
 See also **684 LĀSH**.

Original: Lat. 31° 42' N, long. 61° 38' E. Map 83.
Revised: 31.7136228 N, 61.62401328 E / 31°42' 49.04208612 N, 61° 37' 26.44780692 E.
Nīmrūz Province. Just to the south of the town of Lāsh Juwain.

Date: Timurid, 15th–16th cent. (ceramic).

Description: An artificial mound, 305 m high, with ruins of a large rectangular mud-brick fort on top, 150 × 200 m. Circular towers at angles and intervals along certain walls. Walls 17–20 m above plain, 60 cm thick at top, 1.60 m at bottom. Surrounded by ditch 2–5 m wide and 2–3 m deep. Ditch in turn surrounded by 3 m high wall. Main entrance on west side between two solid projecting towers. Many ruins to west towards Paydeh.

Collection: National Museum—sherds.

Fieldwork:

1. 1884 Peacocke, Maitland ABC—survey.
2. 1960–70 Fischer, Bonn University—survey.

Sources:

1. Smith 1876: 319–20—brief description.
2. Peacocke 1885a: 18–19—description.
3. Peacocke 1887a: 33—detailed description, sketch, and plan of fort.
4. A. C. Yate 1887: 99–100—brief description.
5. Maitland 1888a: 91–2—brief description.
6. Maitland et al. 1889: 40—mentions ruins to west.
7. Le Strange 1905: 341—summary of the historical references.
8. Fischer et al. 1974–6: 36—brief summary.
9. Klinkott 1982: 209–77—description of the fortifications.

483. KĀBUL

Including CHĀMAN-I HAUZURI. See also 418 HASHMATKHĀN, 555 KHĀNA SANGI, 1168 TEPE KHĀZANA, 1173 TEPE MARINJĀN, 2138 KHWĀJA SAFĀ in Supplement, and 2268 TEPE NARENJ in Supplement.

Original: Lat. 34° 32–53' N, long. 69° 11–18' E. Map 61.
Revised: 34.50778703 N, 69.191676 E / 34° 30' 28.03331124 N, 69° 11' 30.03360396 E.
Kābul Province. The area of the old city.

Dates: Achaemenid, 6th–4th cent. BC; Graeco-Bactrian and Indo-Greek, 3rd–2nd cent. BC; Hunnic-Turk, 5th–9th cent. (numismatic); Hindu Shahi 10th cent. (documentary, stylistic).

Description: A large urban site of uncertain character and extent due to modern overbuilding, between the three hills of Sher Darwāza, Asma'i, and Marinjān. The only extant remains are the Bālā Hisār and city walls most of which are 18th–19th century. The interior of the lower Bālā Hisār was destroyed in 1879 following the explosion of underground magazines and then a levelling of the old bazaars by Royal Engineers to make way for a new parade ground, barracks, and military hospital.

On the Sher Darwāza hill there is a Timurid shrine, known as the Zīyārat-i Takht-i Shah located at the extreme south apex of the Sher Darwāza, said to consist of an arched entrance way and a domed chamber with wall niches.

On Sher Darwāza hill, a series of stone and mud fortifications of possible Hunnic origins with extensive later rebuildings run from the upper Bālā Hisār along the Sher Darwāza hills to the base of the gorge leading to the modern, western, part of Kābul. The walls originally extended across Asma'i hill and over the plain around Deh Afghānān as well, and had six gateways.

There have been several significant accidental finds in and near Kābul, including many Buddhist artefacts found at Zīyārat-i Khwāja Safā on Shir Darwāza in 1905, and approximately 1000 Greek and Achaemenid coins from Chāman-i Hauzuri by construction workers in 1933.

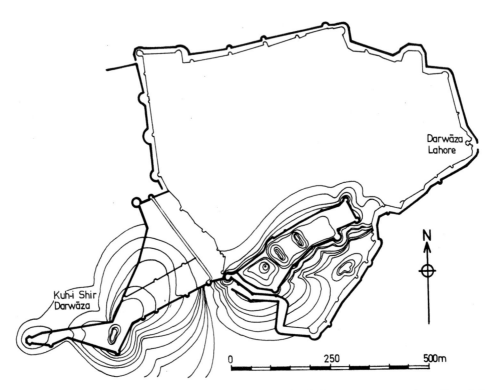

483 Kābul (after J. D. L. Sturt, *Plan and Survey of the Bala Hissar or Fort of Cabul*. Surveyor General's Office, Calcutta, 1878).

A hoard of 447 Hun coins was discovered in 1979 in a pot 10 km north of Kābul.

Fieldwork: 2007 Marquis, DAFA—archaeological studies of the Bālā Hisār.

Sources:
1. Additional notes by Jonathan L. Lee.
2. Masson 1842: II. 250–4—detailed descrption of the Bālā Hisār and defences.
3. Raverty 1878: 61–4—summary of early accounts of Kābul.
4. Le Strange 1905: 349–50—summary of the historical references.
5. Whitehead 1923—notes on some Indo-Greek tetra-drachms found in the Kābul area in 1917.
6. Niedemeyer and Diez 1924: pls 1–3 and 9–10—photos of the fortifications.
7. Sālnāma 1934/35: opp. 150—photo of a Buddha statue found at Kābul.
8. Foucher 1942–7: 146—mentions the Buddhist artefacts found at Khwājā Safā.
9. Caspani 1946b—description of the city walls, including the parts now demolished.
10. Caspani 1946c—guide to the principal historical monuments of Kābul.
11. Wheeler 1947: 58—describes briefly the discovery of the Chaman hoard.
12. Ghirshman 1948: 40—describes a Hephthalite coin from Deh Mazang.
13. Ghose 1952—description of a Hindu Shahi gold coin of Bhīma Deva.
14. Schlumberger 1953c—full report on the Chaman hoard: catalogue and discussion of comparisons with the Āmū Daryā Treasure and other material from the Achaemenid period.
15. Bivar 1954c—description and catalogue of the Chaman hoard.
16. Hulin 1954– discusses an Achaemenid silver piece with an Elamite cuneiform inscription from the Chaman hoard.
17. Kohzad 1955/56–56/57– a study of the history of the Bālā Hisār and walls of Kābul.
18. Pugachenkova 1963: 97—general summary of the Bālā Hisār.
19. Mac Dowall 1968b—discusses some collections of Shahi coins from Kābul.
20. N. Dupree 1971a—comprehensive guide and back-ground to all places of interest in and around Kābul.
21. N. Dupree et al. 1974: 106–8—summary of the Cha-man hoard displayed in the National Museum.
22. Samizay 1974: 31–2—outlines the growth and develop-ment of the old city.
23. Mac Dowall and Taddei 1978a: 202–3—brief descrip-tion of the Chāman hoard.
24. Bernard and Grenet 1981—publication of a Surya statue discovered in the Kābul region.
25. Alram 2000—catalogue of the hoard of Hun coins found north of Kābul.
26. Ball 2008: 218–27—summary.
27. Fussman, Murad, and Ollivier 2008: 105–12 and 303–4—general summary of Buddhism in and around Kābul.
28. Woodburn 2009—detailed historical study of the Bālā Hisār, documenting mainly its Mughal to 19th-century structures.

484. KĀBULI QISHLĀO

Original: Lat. 36° 43' N, long. 69° 05' E. Map 32.
Revised: 36.72476313 N, 69.08835169 E /
36° 43' 29.14727448 N, 69° 05' 18.06608040 E.
Qundūz Province. In the village of Kābuli Qishlāq, on the right bank of the Tāluqān-Khānābād river, about 5 km north-west of Khānābād as the crow flies. The tepe is today a cemetery, at the location of the mound indicated on the 1:100,000 map in the middle of the village.

Dates: Timurid, 15th–16th cent. (ceramic).

Description: Square enclosure (80 × 80 m), oriented approximately north-west/south-east, with a small square tower in the west angle (15 × 15 m) and possible traces of towers on the three other highest points. The wall is pre-served to an average height of 6 m; the talus of the tower rises to 10 m, flat top, with small hillock in the south angle (12 m). On the interior, the courtyard is 4 m higher than the level of the plain; no ancient structures visible, between the tombs that cover all the surface.

Collection: National Museum/AIA—sherds.

Fieldwork: 1978 Gardin et al., CNRS—survey.

Sources:
1. Site information by J.-C. Gardin.
2. Gardin and Lyonnet 1978–9: pl. VII—no. 444.
3. Gardin 1998: 83—no. 444.

485. KACHI GIRD

Original: Lat. 33° 27' N, long. 64° 32' E. Maps 55, 74.
Revised: 33.45245343 N, 64.53234812 E /
33° 27' 08.83236024 N, 64° 31' 56.45323524 E.
Ghūr Province. At the junction of four valleys 12 km east of Taiwāra on the route to Yamān.

Date: ?Ghurid, 12th cent. (architectural, geographical).

Description: An ancient fortress and many other ruins and towers extending for some distance.

Fieldwork: 1946 Kohzad, HSA—survey.

Source: Kohzad 1951–4, 9/1: 27 and 30—brief description.

486. KADAH

See also 601 KHWĀJA NAKHI.

Original: Lat. 31° 22' N, long. 62° 18' E. Map 84.
Revised: 31.35468526 N, 62.29541854 E /
31° 21' 16.86693564 N, 62° 17' 43.50673572 E.
Nīmrūz Province. On the Khāsh Rūd *c.*20 km north of
Chakhānsūr. The site is just to the west of the village of
Kadah.

Date: Timurid, 15th–16th cent.

Description: Many ruins, dominated by a post-Timurid
fortress (Fischer's Site 39), as well as mounds and a multi-
domed mosque. In the early 20th century a seal, depicting a
head surrounded by leaves and an inscription, was found in
the remains.

Fieldwork: 1969 Fischer, Bonn University—survey.

Sources:

1. Rawlinson 1873—historical-geography of this and other
   Seistan sites.
2. Peacocke 1885a: 15—mention from hearsay.
3. Peacocke 1887a: 29—mention from hearsay.
4. Tate 1904: 667—brief description of finds from the area.
5. Fischer 1969–70– photos of the remains.
6. Fischer 1971b: 45–6—photos and brief description of
   the remains.
7. Fischer et al. 1974–6: 235, 244, 253, and pls 255–7—
   description and photos.

KADU KHUR. See **135 BĪSH KAPA.**

KĀFARI or KĀFIRI. See **233 DARBAND.** See also **1021
SHAHĪDĀN.**

KĀFIRI. See **1021 SHAHĪDĀN.** See also **233 DARBAND.**

KAFIRIAT TEPE. See **19 AINAK.**

KĀFIR KOT. See **728 MIR ZAKAH.**

487. KĀFIR QAL'A, ARCHĪ

Original: Lat. 37° 03–05' N, long. 69° 09–15' E. Map 31.
Revised:
48737.05378835 N, 69.17303219 E / 37° 03' 13.63805676 N,
69° 10' 22.91586708 E (C).
48737.05300921 N, 69.17497986 E / 37° 03' 10.83313872 N,
69° 10' 29.92750140 E (A).
48737.05478743 N, 69.17382018 E / 37° 03' 17.23474656 N,
69° 10' 25.75264872 E (B).
48737.04924528 N, 69.17167627 E / 37° 02' 57.28299180 N,
69° 10' 18.03458316 E (D).
Qundūz Province. 6 km north-west of Archī, by the road
that links this town to Shāhrawān (road from Imām Sāhib

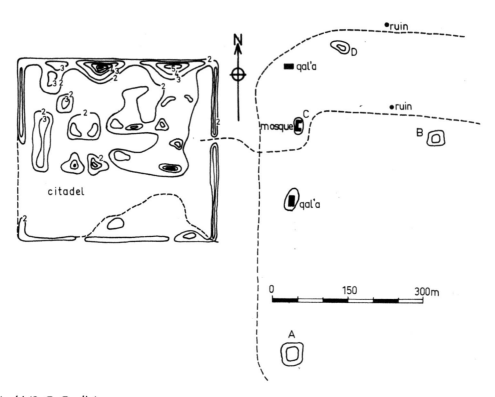

487 Kāfir Qal'a, Archi (J.-C. Gardin).

to Khwāja Ghar), then by a track crossing the middle of irrigated fields in the plain of Archī.

Dates: Achaemenid, 6th–4th cent. BC (some sherds on the rampart, east side); Hellenistic, 3rd–1st cent. BC; Kushan, 1st–4th cent.; pre-Mongol Islamic, 10th–13th cent. (ceramic).

Description: Extended habitation area (*c*.1 km square), around a large rectangular citadel (*c*.450 × 375 m) whose ramparts are preserved to an average height of 3 m. The cultivated fields (cotton) are erasing little by little the traces of constructions still visible inside the walls, mainly in the northern part (see figure); the same on the exterior, where the farmers report that many tepes have been razed during the last decades, to the east and south of the citadel. The four tepes *extra muros* visited in this direction (A, B, C, D in figure) are vestiges of this town, which developed beginning in the Kushan period near the older fortress (E). The largest of these tepes (A) is a large irregular platform (*c*.200 × 200 m), 1 to 2 m high, on which lie the remains of a taller (4 to 5 m at the highest points) square structure (70 × 70 m), with a central depression (body of buildings surrounding a large courtyard?). The others are smaller mounds, greatly damaged by cultivation; one of these (C) is occupied by a little modern mosque, in which a column base of Graeco-Bactrian type found in the citadel has been placed. Several jars of Graeco-Bactrian and Kushan type were reused in present-day (Islamic 10th–13th cent.?) houses; in one of them (?), a coin of Soter Megas.

Collection: National Museum/AIA — sherds.

Fieldwork: 1977 Gardin et al., CNRS — survey.

Sources:
1. Site information by J.-C. Gardin.
2. Gardin and Lyonnet 1978–9: pl. IV — nos. 36–40.
3. Gardin 1995: 87–8 — revised plan; suggests citadel might be later.
4. Lyonnet 1997: figs 25, 35, 39, 46, 49 — nos. 36–40.
5. Gardin 1998: 56 — nos. 36–40.

KĀFIR QAL'A, Buina Qara. See 138 BUINA QARA.

KĀFIR QAL'A, Darra-i Shakh. See 1129 TĀGH-I DARĀZ.

488. KĀFIR QAL'A, DARŪNTA

Original: Lat. 34° 29' N, long. 70° 22' E. Map 66.
Revised: 34.48515083 N, 70.36832099 E /
34° 29' 06.54297972 N, 70° 22' 05.95554852 E.
Laghmān Province. On the north bank of the Kābul River, opposite Pul-i Darūnta, *c*.15 km north-west of Jalālābād.

Description: Remains of ancient walls and terraces, probably a fort, on top of the hill.

Fieldwork: 1834 Masson — survey.

Sources:
1. Masson 1842: III. 285 — mention.
2. Leach 1880: 46 — mention.

KĀFIR QAL'A-I DEH GUL. See 2103 KĀFIR QAL'A-I DEH GUL in Supplement.

489. KĀFIR QAL'A, DEH IMĀN

Original: Lat. 35° 11' N, long. 67° 34' E. Map 48.
Revised: 35.18694176 N, 67.65442203 E /
35° 11' 12.99035220 N, 67° 39' 15.91929432 E.
Bāmiyān Province. On the south side of the Saighān Valley, 2 km west of Saighān 'Alaqadari on the route to Deh Imān and the Dandānshikān Pass.

Dates: Turk/pre-Mongol Islamic, 9th–13th cent. (architectural).

Description: Remains of two large fortresses on two spurs on the side of the valley, consisting of ruins of high mud walls and towers. Heavily looted following the discovery of a figurine after 2000.

Fieldwork:
1. 1885 Maitland, ABC — topographical survey.
2. 1974–5 Le Berre, DAFA — survey.
3. 2002 Lee, Society for South Asian Studies — reconnaissance.

Sources:
1. Maitland 1888b: 10 — mention.
2. Le Berre 1987 — itinerary A2, Darya-i Saighān, ruin 4.
3. Lee 2006: 247–8 — mention.

KĀFIR QAL'A, Deh Mirān. See 279 DEH MIRĀN.

KĀFIR QAL'A, Fārah. See 507 KĀKĀ-I KUHZĀDĀ.

KĀFIR QAL'A, Faryāb. See 2287 ZĪYĀRAT-I KHWĀJA GHAIB in Supplement.

490. KĀFIR QAL'A, GHŪLBIYĀN

Lat. 35° 44' N, long. 65° 22' E. Map 46.
Faryāb Province. Opposite the spring at the source of the Ghūlbiyān River, *c*.2 km upstream from the village of Ghūlbiyān, in the mountainous area south-east of Bīlchirāgh.

Description: An artificial cave complex, consisting of two low chambers, with low mud-brick walls across the front. Probably a fortification guarding the entrance to the valley.

Fieldwork: 1978 Lee, BIAS — survey.

Source: Site information by Jonathan L. Lee.

KĀFIR QAL'A, 'Iraq. See 739 MULLĀH MUHĪB.

KĀFIR QAL'A KHAIRĀBĀD. See 2102 in Supplement.

491. KĀFIR QAL'A, KŪH-I DĀMAN

Original: Lat. 34° 56' N, long. 69° 25' E. Map 64.
Revised: 34.93856845 N, 69.39698662 E /
34° 56' 18.84642648 N, 69° 23' 49.15182624 E.
Kāpīsā Province. 12 km south-east of Begram on the Kūh-i
Dāman stream where it joins the Panjshīr River.

Date: Kushan-Hunnic, 1st–7th cent. (architectural).

Description: Some remains forming a large rectangle, similar to Burj-i 'Abdullah, measuring 280 × 170 m. It is surrounded by walls 2.20 m thick. The whole site is heavily
eroded by water. 200 m to the north are the remains of a
stupa-monastery complex. The stupa now is only a mound
c.30 m diam., and the courtyard of the monastery is *c*.25 m
across.

The site is tentatively identified as ancient Rahula.

Fieldwork: 1923 Foucher, DAFA—survey.

Source: Foucher 1942–7: 141—description.

KĀFIR QAL'A, Kuhsān. See 454 ISLĀM QAL'A.

492. KĀFIR QAL'A, LANGAR

Original: Lat. 35° 59' N, long. 68° 02' E. Map 30.
Revised: 35.98359104 N, 68.0447198 E / 35°59' 00.92776200 N,
68° 02' 40.99129440 E.
Samangān Province. In the Khurram Valley south of Hai-
bak, between Ghazimard and Langar, 9 km north-east of
Khurram.

Description: Remains of fortifications on a bluff, with
another ruined tower on an isolated rocky outcrop in the
valley.

Fieldwork: 1885 Maitland, ABC—topographical survey.

Source: Maitland 1888b: 36—mention.

493. KĀFIR QAL'A, MADAR

Original: Lat. 35° 21' N, long. 67° 48' E. Map 48.
Revised: 35.34663354 N, 67.80238124 E /
35° 20' 47.88075300 N, 67° 48' 08.57245104 E.
Bāmiyān Valley. On the western side of a gorge leading
northwards to Madar from the Kahmard Valley.

Description: Two ranges of caves cut into the cliff face
15–20 m above the stream. They are protected by loopholed
defences, and there are some ruins at the foot. They were

not entered, but it is reported locally that they contain no
decorations.

On the east side of the gorge are the remains of a baked
brick fort.

Fieldwork:
1. 1885–86 Maitland, Griesbach, ABC—topographical
   surveys.
2. 1924 Godard and Hackin, DAFA—survey.

Sources:
1. Yavorski 1885: 118–19—brief description.
2. Griesbach 1888b: 211—mentions the caves.
3. Maitland 1888b: 211—mentions the caves.
4. Foucher 1942–7: 136—brief description and photo of
   the caves.

494. KĀFIR QAL'A, PUL-I KHUMRI

Lat. 35° 55' N, long. 68° 43' E. Fig 36.1, Map 33.
Baghlān Province. 1 km south of Pul-i Khumri, to the west
of the road to Dūshi.

Description: Remains of a fort on a mound. There are
glazed sherds on the top, but earlier material can be seen
on the western side where a stream has cut a section.

Fieldwork: 1946 Wheeler, ASI—reconnaissance.

Source: Shakur 1947: 42–3—brief description.

495. KĀFIR QAL'A, RUSTĀQ

Original: Lat. 37° 09' N, long. 69° 47' E. Map 35.
Revised: 37.14738528 N, 69.77759338 E /
37° 08' 50.58700224 N, 69° 46' 39.33616728 E.
Takhār Province. 3 km north-west of the last houses at
Rustāq, on the edge of a gully cut by the water flow from
the spring of Bulula (Chashma-i Bulula) to the south-east.
Ruin indicated on the 1:100,000 map.

Dates: Middle Bronze Age, *c*.2500–1500 BC; beg. Iron, end
2nd–beg. 1st mill. BC; Achaemenid, 6th–4th cent. BC; Hellenistic, 3rd–1st cent. BC; Kushan and Hunnic-Turk, 1st–9th
cent.; pre-Mongol Islamic, 10th–13th cent.; Timurid, 15th–
16th cent. (ceramic).

Description: Fortified site built on an islet of the terrace cut
out by water flow, at the foot of the hills which close the
plain of Rustāq to the west: gullying surrounds it on all
sides, forming natural ditches around the islet. The islet is
ovoid in shape (oriented north-north-west/south-south-
east, 300 × 200 m) and enclosed by a rampart, cut on the
north-west and south-east by the passage of the road which
leads from Rustāq to Khwāja Ghar across the hills; access to
the fortress was probably by one or the other of these two
gaps, no trace of a gate being visible anywhere else on the
rampart. The north-west part of the site is occupied by a

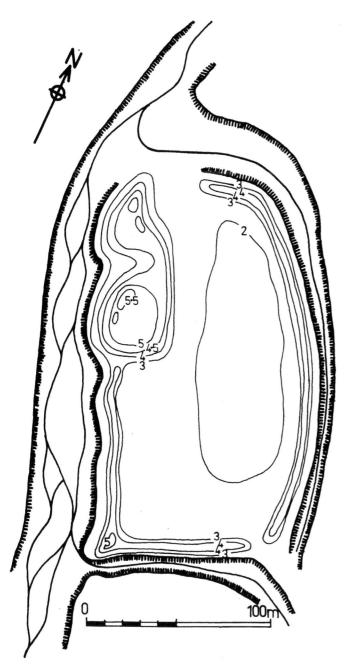

495 Kāfir Qal'a, Rustāq (J.-C. Gardin).

higher natural mound, lying along the edge of the stream (100 × 40 m), which it overlooks by some 30 m; this mound is not fortified, even on the exterior side, the rampart lying against it on the south and the north. It should thus be considered to be a high quarter of the fortification rather than a citadel. There are no visible redans or towers on the wall, except perhaps a projecting angle tower in the south-west. The average height of the talus is 4 m above the level of the plain (observed at the northern extremity of the site: the plain slopes toward the north-west); that of the

terreplein, *intra muros*, is 2 m, the highest part being the eastern half; finally, the 'high quarter' dominates the plain by about 5 m.

Collection: National Museum/AIA—sherds.

Fieldwork: 1978 Gardin et al., CNRS—survey.

Sources:
1. Site information by J.-C. Gardin.
2. Gardin and Lyonnet 1978–9: pl. II—no. 506.
3. Gardin 1995: 95–6—brief description and plan.
4. Lyonnet 1997: figs 13, 25, 35, 39, 68, 69—no. 506.
5. Gardin 1998: 91—no. 506.

KĀFIR QAL'A, Saighān. See 118 BAYANI.

496. KAFIR QAL'A, SHĀH ANJĪR

Original: Lat. 36° 23' N, long. 67° 12' E. Map 30.
Revised: 36.39385697 N, 67.21006339 E /
36° 23' 37.88509236 N, 67° 12' 36.22822056 E.
Balkh Province. At the top of a pass of the same name, 6 km north of Shāh Anjīr on the route leading to Shadiyān.

Description: Remains of an ancient fortress inaccessibly situated on the summit of the cliffs. The top is surrounded by walls over 1 m thick and over 1 km in circumference, and there is a double entrenchment surrounding the foot of the slope.

Fieldwork:
1. 1886 Maitland, ABC—topographical survey.
2. 1924 Foucher, DAFA—survey.

Sources:
1. Maitland 1888b: 279–80—brief description.
2. Foucher 1942–7: 116—brief description.
3. Gazetteer 1979: IV. 285—mention.

497. KĀFIR QAL'A, SHĪBAR
See also 1075 SHĪBAR, west.

Original: Lat. 34° 54' N, long. 68° 13' E. Map 48, 59.
Revised: 34.90098637 N, 68.21532149 E /
34° 54' 03.55093920 N, 68° 12' 55.15736904 E.
Bāmiyān Province. On the Shībar Pass between the Ghūr-band and Bāmiyān Valleys.

Date: Sasanian, 3rd–7th cent. (architectural, ceramic).

Description: Ruins of a fortress commanding the pass. Construction is mud-brick on a stone foundation. The rooms have Sasanian-style barrel vaults and domes.

Fieldwork:
1. 1955–68 Fischer, DAAD—survey.
2. 1974–5 Le Berre, DAFA– survey.

Source: Fischer 1969: 117—mention.

498. KĀFIR QAL'A, TIRĪN

Original: Lat. 32° 41' N, long. 66° 02' E. Map 76.
Revised: 32.67798535 N, 66.03365913 E /
32° 40' 40.74724560 N, 66° 02' 01.17285288 E.
Ūruzgān Province. 16 km north-east of the town of Tirīn, on the Kandahār-Ūruzgān road.
Description: A small, well-preserved stone fort to the left of the road.
Source: Bivar 1954a: 117 — mention.

KĀFIR QAL'A, Zādiyān. See 8 ABU HURAIRA.

KĀFIR QAL'A, Zamindāwar. See 291 DEH ZŪR.

KĀFIR SHAHR. See 565 KHARWAR.

KĀFIR TEPE. See 1022 SHĀHI KHAILA.

KAFSH KHĒL. See 2104 in Supplement.

499. KAFTARGHAR

Lat. 32° 51' N, long. 66° 07' E. approximately. Map 76.
Ūruzgān Province. In the Chūra district, on the upper Helmand not far from Ūruzgān.
Description: A cave, known from local reports as containing signs of prehistoric occupation.
Source: Bivar 1954a: 118 — mention from hearsay.

500. KAFTARKHĀN

Original: Lat. 34° 16' N, long. 61° 56' E. Map 52.
Revised: 34.26657716 N, 61.98451468 E /
34° 15' 59.67777312 N, 61° 59' 04.25285880 E.
Herat Province. 2 km to the east of the Kūh-i Kaftarkhān Pass, on the track from Zīyāratgāh to Zindajān.
Date: ?Timurid, 15th–16th cent. (ceramic).
Description: A mound *c.*50 m diam. and 3 m high, similar in all respects to Hasanābād (No. 416). It is covered in large amounts of green glazed pottery. Probably the remains of a farmhouse.
Fieldwork: 1974 Swiny, BIAS — survey.

Source: Site information by S. Swiny in unpublished BIAS archive.

501. KAFTARKHĀNA
Or TŪP-I ĀHANGARĀN

Lat. 33° 22' N, long. 67° 39' E. Maps 77, 78, 79.
Ghazni Province. Near Qūl-i Mīr, north of Ulyatu on the Jāghūri-Dasht-i Nāwar road.
Description: Reports of an artificial cave complex.
Source: Verardi 1977a: 150 — mention from hearsay.

502. KAIKĀBĀD
See also 863 QAL'A-I MĀDAR-I PĀDSHĀH.

Original: Lat. 30° 12' N, long. 62° 13' E. Map 95.
Revised: 30.2056393 N, 62.19240222 E / 30° 12' 20.30147208 N, 62° 11' 32.64799776 E.
Nīmrūz Province. On the Helmand 38.5 km below Rūdbār and 22.5 km above Chahār Burjak. 6 km west of Qal'a-i Mādar-i Pādshāh.
Description: Remains of several towers, probably part of a large city. 700m east are more ruins, with a minar to the south. The towers were once connected by a singular open-work ornamental wall, perhaps intended as a windbreak. While only two towers remain, there are ruins of four others at 300m intervals towards the east.
   On the opposite bank are ruins of a small town surrounding a ruined fort on a low, artificial mound.
Sources:
1. Additional notes by W. Trousdale.
2. Bellew 1874: 207 — brief description.

KAJAK. See 1074 SHĪBAR, east.

503. KAJARI

Lat. 34° 25' N, long. 70° 15' E. Map 65.
Laghmān Province. A gully leading north-westwards into the Siāhkuh from Tatang, *c.*20 km west of Jalālābād.
Description: Many caves cut into the rock face. There are also extensive masonry remains, including a round tower, many walls, a sherd scatter, burials, and funeral jars. There are also some simple petroglyphs depicting hunting scenes with elephants, stags, lion, hare, etc.
Fieldwork: 1833–4 Masson — survey.
Source: Masson 1842: III. 190–3 — description of the remains.

504. KAJITUTU

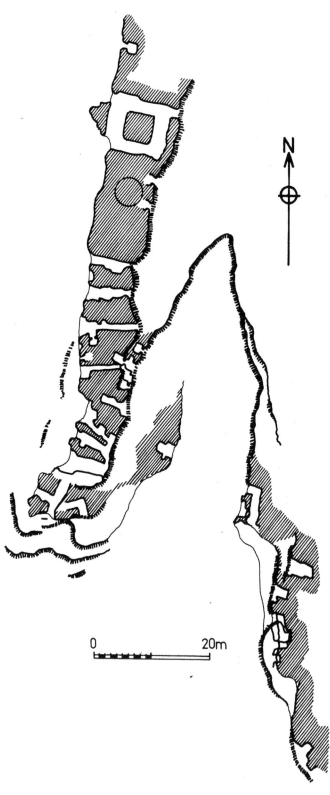

504 Kajituti (after Mizuno 1971).

Lat. 34° 27–45' N, long. 70° 24–40' E. Map 66.
Nangahār Province. On the north bank of the Kābul River, 203 km east of Fīlkhāna and 1–2 km west of Bārābād.

Date: Kushan-Hunnic, 1st–6th cent. (architectural).

Description: A series of caves cut into the river bank, with the much-ruined remains of a stupa and several walls on top. Most of the caves are single cells, except for one circumambulatory cave which appears ritual.

Fieldwork: 1962 Mizuno, Kyoto University − survey.

Sources:
1. Mizuno 1971: 80 and 123 − brief description and photos.
2. Errington 2017a: 136 − mention.

505. KĀKA BULAQ

Original: Lat. 36° 20' N, long. 69° 16' E. Map 37.
Revised:
36.33080421 N, 69.26607173 E / 36° 19' 50.89514304 N, 69° 15' 57.85824132 E and
36.33171438 N, 69.26378453 E / 36° 19' 54.17176152 N, 69° 15' 49.62430872 E.
Takhār Province. 9 km south-west of Ishkamīsh, by the Narīn road: zone of many quite high tepes (3 to 6 m), visible from several hundred metres on either side of the road. This zone is irrigated by many springs. Sherds were collected on only one of these sites, 6.5 km from the fork in the Narīn road to the west of Ishkamīsh, and 300 m to the east of this road.

Dates: Kushan and Hunnic-Turk, 1st–9th cent.; some Islamic sherds (A) (ceramic).

Description: (A) Oblong north–south platform (75 × 30 m), dominated by two hillocks, one in the centre (height 2 m), the other at the southern end, with a house in ruins (height 4–5 m). (B) 150 m west of A, a small rounded mound (diam. 20 m, height 2 m).

Collection: National Museum/AIA − sherds.

Fieldwork: 1978 Gardin et al., CNRS − survey.

Sources:
1. Site information by J.-C. Gardin.
2. Gardin and Lyonnet 1978–9: pl. XI − nos. 371–2.
3. Lyonnet 1978: figs 49, 68, 69 − nos. 371, 372.
4. Gardin 1979: 99 − nos. 371–2.

506. KĀKARĀN

Lat. 31° 32' N, long. 65° 30' E. Map 89.
Kandahār Province. 1 km north of Deh Morasi Ghundai, 6 km east of Panjwāyī.

Dates: Sasanian, 3rd–7th cent.; Mongol-Timurid, 13th–15th cent. (ceramic).

Description: None available.

Fieldwork: 1950–1 Fairservis, AMNH − survey.

Source: Fairservis 1971: 393 − mention (Site Khr–4).

507. KĀKĀ-I KUHZĀDĀ
Or KĀFIR QAL'A.

Original: Lat. 32° 17' N, long. 62° 15' E. Map 85.
Revised: 32.30591145 N, 62.25058062 E /
32° 18' 21.28120200 N, 62° 15' 02.09023776 E.
Farāh Province. 15 km south-east of Farāh, to the south of
the road to Dilārām.

Date: Ghaznavid and Ghurid, 11th–13th cent. (ceramic).

Description: Stone-built fortifications with bastions
defending a hill-fort. Some sections of baked brick masonry
(50×40×6 cm) noted near the summit. Evening light
showed the outline of a rectangular enclosure with towers
midway along each side in the plain below the hill-fort.
Pottery from below the fort included sgraffiato,
embossed/moulded, and glazed wares, glass, and a fragmentary stone (?) mortar.

Fieldwork:
1. 1949 De Cardi — survey.
2. 1952 Le Berre and Gardin, DAFA — survey.
3. 1956 Ramachandran and Sharma, ASI — reconnaissance.
4. 1960–70 Fischer, Bonn University — survey.

Sources:
1. Gardin and Lyonnet, 1980 chronological study of
   unpublished pottery from DAFA surveys.
2. Site description by B. De Cardi.
3. Ramachandran and Sharna 1956: I. 16 — brief
   description.
4. Fischer et al. 1974–7: 30 and pls 80–1 — mention and
   photos.
5. N. Dupree 1977: 271 — brief description and an account
   of the associated legend.

508. KAKRAK
See also 100 BĀMIYĀN.

Original: Lat. 34° 48' N, long. 67° 51' E. Map 58.
Revised: 34.83139532 N, 67.82648856 E /
34° 49' 53.02314192 N, 67° 49' 35.35882536 E.
Bāmiyān Province. A southern branch of the main Bāmiyān
Valley, 3 km south-east of Bāmiyān.

Dates: Late Sasanian, 6th–7th cent. (stylistic); Turk and/or
pre-Mongol Islamic, 9th–13th cent. (architectural).

Description: A large niche cut into the cliff face containing a
7 m statue of standing Buddha. It is surrounded by approximately 100 caves, including a sanctuary that contained
Sasanian style paintings in near perfect condition.

    There are also a number of later mud fortifications at and
around the caves defending the valley.

Collections:
1. National Museum — paintings.
2. Musée Guimet — paintings.

Fieldwork:
1. 1923 Godard, DAFA — survey.
2. 1930 Hackin, DAFA — survey.
3. 1974–5 Le Berre, DAFA — survey of fortifications.
4. 1876 Higuchi, Kyoto University — survey.

Sources:
1. Maitland 1888a: 319 — brief description.
2. Hackin 1932a — account of the 1930 expedition, with
   some historical and artistic background on the caves.
3. Hackin 1932b — summary of the work in 1930.

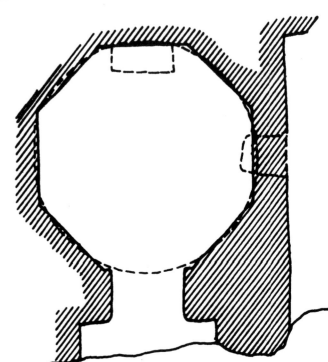

508 Kakrak — sanctuary (after Carl and Hackin 1933).

4. Hackin 1933—description of the caves.

5. Hackin and Carl 1933: 39–46—description of the Buddha, the caves, and the frescos.

6. Hackin 1934– briefly summarises the work of 1930.

7. J. and R. Hackin 1934: 51–2—brief description and guide.

8. Rowland 1938: 70–1—illustrates and discusses the frescos from the cupola.

9. Monod-Brühl 1939: 110–12—describes the fresco on display in the Musée Guimet.

10. Zestovski 1948: 51–3—summary description and sketches.

11. Bussagli 1953b—traces some classical influences in the frescos.

12. Talbot Rice 1965: 166–8—briefly discusses the Sasanian element in the frescos.

13. Monod 1966: 369–70—describes the fresco on display in the Musée Guimet.

14. N. Dupree 1967b: 50–2—description and guide.

15. Rowland and Rice 1971: 41–2 and pls 140 and 145–6—description and photos of the frescos on display from the National Museum.

16. Rowland 1972—discusses the evidence of the frescos in their wider Central Asian context.

17. N. Dupree et al. 1974: 93–5—guide to the frescos on display in the National Museum.

18. H. Motamedi 1975b– discusses four of the Sasanian-style paintings from the sanctuary.

19. H. Motamedi 1976—brief summary of the Japanese work.

20. Tarzi 1977a: 78 and 107—description of the Buddha and frescos.

21. Le Berre 1987: 81–2, pls 106–7– itinerary B2, Darya-i Kakrak, ruins 1–3; description and photos of towers.

22. Geoffroy-Schneiter 2001—photos of objects from the Musée Guimet.

23. Tissot and Darbois 2002—photos of paintings from the National Museum.

24. Tissot 2006: 116–19—National Museum catalogue details and photos.

25. Mateo 2008—discusses the 'hunter-king' painting and its possible identification with a planetary divinity.

26. Tarzi 2012: 92–7—report on the restoration of the Buddha.

509. KAKUL
Or ARAB KAKUL.

Original: Lat. 37° 15' N, long. 69° 28' E. Map 34.
Revised: 37.24798301 N, 69.46238446 E /
37° 14' 52.73882772 N, 69° 27' 44.58405924 E.
Takhār Province. About 10 km north of Dasht-i Qal'a, on the edge of the Āmū Daryā, near the modern village of Arab Kakul.

Dates: Hellenistic, 3rd–1st cent. BC; Kushan, 1st–4th cent.; some Islamic sherds (ceramic).

Description: On the edge of the cliff overlooking by some 20 m a branch of the Āmū Daryā, rectangular fortification oriented north–south (*c*.200 × 120 m); the remains of the wall rise little (1.50–2 m) above the level of the plain, no certain traces of towers or bastions. On the interior, vestiges of orthogonal north–south structures, height 1–1.5 m. About 150 m to the south-east, two small, low (height 2 m) quadrangular mounds (*c*.40 × 40 and 80 × 40 m) probably mark the location of houses, dated by the pottery like the fortification itself (Graeco-Bactrian and Kushan periods).

Collection: National Museum/AIA—sherds.

Fieldwork: 1975 Gardin et al., CNRS—survey.

Sources:
1. Site information by J.-C. Gardin.
2. Gardin and Lyonnet 1978–9: pl. 111—nos. 158–60.
3. Lyonnet 1997: figs 39, 49—nos. 158–60.
4. Gardin 1998: 43—nos. 158–60.

510. KALAFGĀN, NORTH

Original: Lat. 36° 47' N, long. 69° 57' E. Map 38.
Revised:
36.77686654 N, 69.94923438 E / 36° 46' 36.71954832 N, 69° 56' 57.24376800 E (A).
36.77529324 N, 69.95143671 E / 36° 46' 31.05566544 N, 69° 57' 05.17217112 E (C).
Takhār Province. Bālā Hisār of Kalafgān on the edge of the road which leads to Kishm.

Dates: Beg. Iron, end 2nd–beg. 1st mill. BC (A, B); Kushan, 1st–4th cent. (C); Hunnic-Turk, 5th–9th cent.; pre-Mongol Islamic, 10th–13th cent. (ceramic).

Description: (A) On a terrace sloping to the north, a tepe of trapezoid shape with rounded angles, oriented north-west/south-east, covering a surface area of 75 × 75 m. The top is flat, with the same shape (40 × 40 m), with a modern tomb in the middle; height about 10 m, steep slopes on the four sides. The terrace itself is strewn with sherds up to 100 m from the tepe; on the slopes, fired bricks (26 × 26 × 6 cm). On the same terrace: (B) 200 m to the west, small oblong mound (15 × 20 m), height 1–2 m; (C) 200 m to the south-east, round mound (diam. 30 m, height 2–3 m), damaged by ploughing, like the preceding mound (sherds up to 50 m around the mound). Probable remains of a habitation covering all the terrace in the Islamic period, on an older site.

Collection: National Museum/AIA—sherds.

Fieldwork: 1977 Gardin et al., CNRS—survey.

Sources:
1. Site information by J.-C. Gardin.
2. Gardin and Lyonnet 1978–9: pl. X—nos. 302–4.
3. Gardin 1995: 96–7—brief description and plan

4. Lyonnet 1997: figs 25, 35, 49, 68, 69 − nos. 302–4.
5. Gardin 1998: 93 − nos. 302–4.

511. KALAFGĀN, EAST

Original: Lat. 36° 46' N, long. 69° 58' E. Map 38.
Revised:
36.77126927 N, 69.96411808 E / 36° 46' 16.56936660 N,
69° 57' 50.82508764 E (A).
36.77167878 N, 69.96051315 E / 36° 46' 18.04360980 N,
69° 57' 37.84733172 E (B).
36.77396303 N, 69.96005231 E / 36° 46' 26.26691952 N,
69° 57' 36.18832248 E (C).
36.77201236 N, 69.96184033 E / 36° 46' 19.24450752 N,
69° 57' 42.62517792 E (D).
Takhār Province. 1.8 km east-south-east of the Bālā Hisār
of Kalafgān, near the source of the stream which passes to
the north of the village in the direction of the Kokcha. The
highest mound (A) probably corresponds to the tepe of 6 m
indicated on the 1:100,000 map, to the east of Kalafgān; but
the position of the mound is in this case erroneous and
should be placed 450 m to the east.

Dates: Beg. Iron, end 2nd–beg. 1st mill. BC (A); Achaemenid,
6th–4th cent. BC; Hellenistic, 3rd–1st cent. BC (B); Kushan
and Hunnic-Turk, 1st–9th cent. (B, C); some Islamic sherds
(ceramic).

Description: (A) The largest tepe of the group: oblong
north–south mound (75 × 40 m), height 4–5 m; the sherds
extend up to 100 m around the tepe, mainly to the east and
the north-east. (B) 300 m west of A, round mound (diam.
30), low (1.5 m); (C) 400 m north of B, identical mound,
higher (3m); (D) 100 m south-west of B, two similar
mounds (diam. 30 m), 25 m apart, height 2 and 3 m. The
surrounding plain, sloping towards the north-west, is
cultivated.

Collection: National Museum/AIA − sherds

Fieldwork: 1977 Gardin et al., CNRS − survey.

Sources:
1. Site information by J.-C. Gardin.
2. Gardin and Lyonnet 1978–9: pl. X − nos. 305–8.
3. Lyonnet 1997: pl. X − no. 305–8: figs 25, 35, 39, 49, 68,
   69 − nos. 305–8.
4. Gardin 1998: 94 − nos. 305–8.

512. KALAFGĀN, SOUTH

Original: Lat. 36° 46' N, long. 69° 57' E. Map 38.
Revised:
36.76532122 N, 69.94770233 E / 36° 45' 55.15639776 N,
69° 56' 51.72840312 E (A).
36.76830388 N, 69.9477344 E / 36° 46' 05.89395396 N,
69° 56' 51.84383388 E (B).

36.76657194 N, 69.94726958 E / 36° 45' 59.65897500 N,
069° 56' 50.17049160 E (B).
36.76329287 N, 69.95086526 E / 36° 45' 47.85433236 N,
069° 57' 03.11495328 E (C).
36.7635182 N, 69.95207098 E / 36° 45' 48.66553440 N,
069° 57' 07.45551540 E (C).
36.76393986 N, 69.94917558 E / 36° 45' 50.18348268 N,
069° 56' 57.03209448 E (C).
36.7607438 N, 69.94827554 E / 36° 45' 38.67767388 N,
069° 56' 53.79194940 E (D).
36.76207439 N, 69.94784465 E / 36° 45' 43.46779068 N,
069° 56' 52.24073100 E (D).
Takhār Province. About 1 km south-east of Kalafgān, by a
road which leaves the Tāluqān-Kishm road at 'Alaqadari,
towards the village of Zardalū Darra. Mounds A and D (the
latter cited below) correspond to the tepes of 5 m and 4 m
indicated respectively on the 1:100,000 map. A stream descending from the slopes to the south-east cross this zone
towards the Kokcha.

Dates: Kushan and Hunnic-Turk, 1st–9th cent.; some
Islamic sherds (ceramic).

Description: (A) 800 m from the main road and immediately to the left of the smaller road, rectangular mound
oriented east–west (100 × 50 m); flat top at two levels: 5 m
in the eastern half, rising gradually up to 8 m in the western
part. From the top of this tepe, there is a convenient view of
the lower mounds which surround it, all round in shape
(diam. 20 to 30 m), the height between 2 and 5 m, as follows:
(B) north sector, a mound 100 m distant (height 3 m),
another 300 m distant (height 5 m); (C) to the east-south-
east, a mound 250 m distant (height 1–2 m), another 500 m
distant (height 3 m), a third 700 m distant (height 4 m); (D)
in the south, a mound 400 distant (height 3 m), another 500 m
distant (height 4 m). Crops surround all these tepes and
damage them little by little; even the tops are flattened and
ploughed (*lalmī* crops).

Collections: DAFA and National Museum − sherds.

Fieldwork:
1. 1960 Fischer, DAAD − survey.
2. 1977 Gardin et al., CNRS − survey.

Sources:
1. Site information by J.-C. Gardin.
2. Fischer 1969: 350 − mention.
3. Gardin and Lyonnet 1978–9: pl. X − nos. 310–17.
4. Lyonnet 1997: figs 49, 68, 69 − nos. 310–17.
5. Gardin 1998: 94 − nos. 310–17.

513. KALAFGĀN, WEST

Original: Lat. 36° 46' N, long. 69° 54'–69° 56' E. Maps 35,
37, 38.
Revised:
36.76810112 N, 69.93103256 E / 36° 46' 05.16402768 N,
69° 55' 51.71722716 E (A).

36.77422472 N, 69.93521072 E / 36° 46' 27.20900424 N, 69° 56' 06.75859380 E (A).
36.767746 N, 69.9211201 E / 36° 46' 03.88561080 N, 69° 55' 16.03236720 E (B).
Takhār Province. 1 km south-west of Kalafgān, the Tāluqān road crosses a zone of little tepes very near to each other, the largest being close to the road, on the south side (A). The other remarkable site is located 1 km further in the same direction, 400 m north of the road, on the edge of the cliff which overlooks a branch of the stream of Kalafgān, a tributary of the Kokcha.

Dates: Beg. Iron, end 2nd–beg. 1st mill. BC (B); Achaemenid, 6th–4th cent. BC (B); Kushan, 1st–3rd cent.; Timurid, 15th–16th cent. (A) (ceramic).

Description: (A) Rectangular mound (80 × 40 m), parallel to the Kalafgān-Tāluqān road (north-east/south-west), 20 m to the south; height 3 m, with higher levees on the perimeter, indicating two bodies of buildings, each enclosing a courtyard (?). 100–200 m to the west, to the north-west and the north, on the north side of the road, small rounded mounds (diam. 20 m), low (1–2 m), like the preceding mound producing Islamic sherds, exclusively. (B) Between two gullies of the cliff indicated above, a rounded mound (diam. 50 m), rising from 2 to 3 m above the fields which extend to the south, where ancient sherds are also numerous; flat top, slightly depressed in the centre (threshing floor).

Collection: National Museum/AIA—sherds.

Fieldwork: 1977 Gardin et al., CNRS—survey.

Sources:
1. Site information by J.-C. Gardin.
2. Gardin and Lyonnet 1978–9: pl. X—nos. 322–6.
3. Lyonnet 1997: figs 25, 35, 46—nos. 322–6.
4. Gardin 1998: 94—nos. 322–6.

514. KALĀN GUZAR

Lat. 35° 33' N, long. 68° 24' E. Maps 33, 49.
Baghlān Province. Road from Chārikār to Dūshi by the Shībar Pass, in the valley of the Surkhāb (north of Dūāb-i Mīkhzarīn): on the left bank of the river (place-name Kalān Guzar).

Date: Turk and/or pre-Mongol Islamic, 7th–13th cent. (architectural).

Description: Ruin of a small castle.

Fieldwork: 1974–75 Le Berre, DAFA—survey.

Source: Le Berre 1987: 44—itinerary A1, ruin 30; brief description.

KALASHKAU. See 2105 KALASHKAU in Supplement.

515. KALDĪSH, NORTH-EAST

Lat. 37° 30' N, long. 69° 40' E. Map 34.
Takhār Province. Immediately north of the village of Kaldīsh, on the edge of the terrace where the village itself is situated, above the Āmū Daryā: the site is separated by a gully of the cliff where the road passes that descends to Darqad, in the river bed.

Dates: Middle Bronze Age, c.2500–1500 BC (B, D); Achaemenid, 6th–4th cent. BC; Hellenistic, 3rd–1st cent. BC; Timurid, 15th–16th cent. (ceramic).

Description: The site is not indicated visually by the presence of a tepe, but only by a slight rise on the edge of the cliff (c.1 m higher than the level of the terrace), and by the sherds of late periods which are found nearby (collection area up to 100 m from the cliff). A small fort in ruins, of late construction, occupies the high part of the site, towards the river.

Collection: National Museum/AIA—sherds.

Fieldwork: 1978 Gardin et al., CNRS—survey.

Sources:
1. Site information by J.-C. Gardin.
2. Gardin and Lyonnet 1978–9: pl. II—nos. 548–9.
3. Lyonnet 1997: figs 13, 25, 35, 49—nos. 305–8.
4. Gardin 1998: pl. II—nos. 305–8.

516. KALDĪSH, SOUTH

Original: Lat. 37° 29' N, long. 69° 39' E. Map 36.
Revised:
37.49321637 N, 69.65109811 E / 37° 29' 35.57893920 N, 69° 39' 03.95320464 E (A).
37.49195018 N, 69.65188339 E / 37° 29' 31.02065016 N, 69° 39' 06.78020580 E (A).
37.49300592 N, 69.65515714 E / 37° 29' 34.82131884 N, 69° 39' 18.56569752 E (B).
Takhār Province. About 1 km south-west of the village of Kaldīsh. (A) A first tepe rises at the edge of the cliff of the Āmū Daryā, immediately west of the cemetery situated between the villages of Kaldīsh and Khwāja Hāfiz (indicated on the 1:100,000 map); the archaeological site also occupies the west part of the cemetery. (B) The second tepe is the isolated mound of 6 m also indicated on the map, 400 m north-north-east of the same cemetery.

Dates: Beg. Iron, end 2nd–beg. 1st mill. BC; Achaemenid, 6th–4th cent. BC; some sherds of the Kushan and Islamic periods (ceramic).

Description: (A) Isolated mound on the edge of the terrace of the Āmū Daryā, of which the cliff overlooks the river from some 20 m; height 2 m in relation to the level of the terrace. Cut on the east by the road of Yangi Qal'a (which today joins Kaldīsh to Kwāja Hāfiz in a straight line, rather than the curved line indicated on the map), eroded on the west by the modern canal of Yangi Qal'a, at the foot of the cliff, and on the south by an arm of the Rūd-i Jilga-i Yangi Qal'a, this mound is reduced to a triangle of 80 m per side; the site continues however to the east, under the modern cemetery, on either side of the road. In the cuts of the cliff, in the south-west, there is, about 3 m beneath the summit, the traces of a hearth in place between two walls of the same room, and above, large jars also in place. (B) Rectangular north–south platform (20 × 15 m), visible from afar when approached on the plateau of Kaldīsh from the south (Rustāq, Chayāb) or the west (Darqad, Yangi Qal'a); tabular shape, flat top (4 m) in the northern part of the tepe. Cultivation of the surrounding fields, and on the mound itself (*lalmī* crops) have probably reduced the original dimensions of the site, but not apparently its shape, to judge from the regularity of the slopes on the four sides.

Collections: National Museum/AIA—sherds.

Fieldwork: 1978 Gardin et al., CNRS—survey.

Sources:
1. Site information by J.-C. Gardin.
2. Gardin and Lyonnet 1978–9: pl. II—nos. 543–5.
3. Lyonnet 1997: figs 25, 35, 49—nos. 543, 545.
4. Gardin 1998: 37—nos. 543–5.

517. KĀLŪ
Including QAL'A-I NAU and QAL'A-I SANGAK.

Original: Lat. 34° 39'–40' N, long. 68° 00'–68° 03' E. Map 58.
Revised: 34.66699974 N, 68.02653522 E /
34° 40' 01.19907912 N, 68° 01' 35.52677832 E.
Bāmiyān Province. At the foot of the Kotal-i Haft Pailān on the route from Hājigak to Bāmiyān via Kālū and Tupchi. Qal'a-i Nau is 3 km north-west of Kālū, Qal'a-i Sangak is just south of Kālū.

Date: Turk and/or pre-Mongol Islamic, 7th–13th cent. (architectural).

Description: Some baked brick ruins on a hill (Qal'a-i Nau) and the remains of a fort to the south-east (Qal'a-i Sangak).

Fieldwork: 1974–5 Le Berre, DAFA—survey.

Sources:
1. Masson 1842: II. 378—mentions Qal'a-i Nau.
2. Le Berre 1987: 79, pl. 101d–e—itinerary B2, ruin 8.

518. KAMA DAKKA
See also 226 DAKKA and 675 LALPŪRA.

Lat. 34° 13' N, long. 71° 07' E. Map 68.
Nangahār Province. C. 8 km north-west of the Khyber Pass, between the Jalālābād-Tūrkhām road and the Kābul River.

Date: Late Sasanian, 6th–7th cent. (stylistic).

Description: Accidental discovery of a fragmentary schist relief depicting the right footprint of Buddha, decorated with swastikas. Subsequent excavations revealed the remains of a Buddhist monastery and a stucco Buddha head.

Fieldwork: 1948 Le Berre, DAFA—sondage.

Sources:
1. Schlumberger 1949b: 16—very brief description.
2. Schlumberger 1957b: 12—mention.
3. Mizuno 1964—illustration and description of the objects displayed in the Tokyo Museum.
4. Rowland and Rice 1971: pl. 112—description and photo of the relief.
5. N. Dupree et al. 1974: 97—description of the objects on display in the National Museum.
6. H. Motamedi 1977—discusses this and other reliefs. Gives the religious connotations and traces the art-historical connections.
7. Tissot and Darbois 2002—photos of objects from the National Museum.
8. Tissot 2006: 468–9—National Museum catalogue details and photos.

KAMAL KHĀN QAL'A. See 2106 in Supplement.

KAMĀN-I BIHĪSHTĪ. See 2107 in Supplement.

519. KAMARĪ
Or KHĀNZĀDA.

Original: Lat. 34° 27' N, long. 69° 18' E. Map 62.
Revised: 34.44674835 N, 69.29650463 E /
34° 26' 48.29406468 N, 69° 17' 47.41666728 E.
Kābul Province. 14 km south-east of Kābul, 6 km to the east of Shīwakī stupa. The site is 3 km south-east of the village of Shīwakī.

Dates: Kushan, 1st–3rd cent. (architectural, numismatic); Hunnic-Turki Shahi, 5th–9th cent. (ceramic).

Description: Remains of two stupas, one of them fairly large *c.* 17 m high. Inside was a gold medal of Kadphises and several lamps filled with bones.

Fieldwork:
1. 1833 Gérard, East India Company—excavations.
2. 1834 Masson—survey.
3. 1922 Foucher, DAFA—survey.
4. 1972 Fussman, CNRS—survey.

Sources:
1. Gardin and Lyonnet, 1980 chronological study of unpublished pottery from DAFA surveys.
2. Jacquet 1839: 393–5—describes briefly Gerard's work.
3. Masson 1841: 114—mention.

4. Lal 1846: 213–14 — brief description of Gérard's work.
5. Holdich 1881b: 23 — brief description.
6. Foucher 1942–7: 147 — mention.
7. Fussman et al. 2008: 47–53, 206–14, and 300 — detailed description with photos and drawings.
8. Jongeward et al. 2012 — catalogue and discussion of the reliquaries.
9. Errington 2017a: 75–6 and 2017b: 26, 103 — the Masson collection and archive relating to the site.

KAM-I GAZAK. See 2108 in Supplement.

520. KAM PIRAK

See also 8 ABU HURAIRA, 814 PIT QAL'A TEPE, 1188 TEPE ZĀDIYĀN, 1245 ZĀDIYĀN, 2053 DAULATĀBĀD in Supplement and 2281 ZĀDI-YĀN KAFIR QAL'A in Supplement.

Original: Lat. 36° 55'–37° 04' N, long. 66° 18'–66° 57' E. Map 27.
Revised: 37.0636059 N, 66.94573387 E / 37° 03' 48.98125476 N, 66° 56' 44.64193128 E.
Balkh Province. From c.10 km west of Āqcha to several km to north-east of Zādiyān.

Date: Kushan–Kushano-Sasanian, 2nd–mid-4th cent. (C-14).

Description: A c.60 km long *pakhsa* wall stretching across the northern edge of the Balkh oasis from near Āqcha to just beyond Zādiyān. Its best preserved part is at Kam Pirak, where it is up to 3 m high for 4 km.

Fieldwork: 1970–2 Kruglikova, Af/Sov. Mission — survey.

Sources:
1. Lal 1846: 66 — mention.
2. Krugikova 1974: 105 — brief description.
3. Pugachenkova 1976b — brief architectural discussion.
4. De la Vaissière, Marquis, and Bendezu-Sarmiento 2015 — discussion in the context of the Zādiyān Kafir Qal'a complex, with C-14 date.
5. Ball 2008: 187 — summary.

521. KAMTUDI WAKĪL KHĀN

Original: Lat. 31° 03' N, long. 64° 11' E. Map 97.
Revised: 31.05835571 N, 64.19303535 E / 31° 03' 30.08054196 N, 64° 11' 34.92724740 E.
Helmand Province. On the left bank of the Helmand between Darwīshān and Basābād.

Dates: Indo-Parthian, 1st–3rd cent.; Sasanian, 3rd–7th cent.; Ghaznavid-Ghurid, 11th–13th cent. (ceramic).

Description: A mound.

Fieldwork: 1966 Hammond, Cambridge University — survey.

Source: Hammond 1970: 450 — lists site (no. 42) and discusses the pottery and general survey results.

KAMUS. See 2109 in Supplement.

KANGRAULI. See 2110 in Supplement.

522. KANDAHĀR

Or SHAHR-i KHUNA or TAQINĀBĀD or ZŪR SHAHR. See also 726 MIRWAIS BĀBĀ.

Original: Lat. 31° 37' N, long. 65° 39' E. Map 89.
Revised: 31.60119461 N, 65.66008776 E / 31° 36' 04.30061364 N, 65° 39' 36.31592232 E.
Kandahār Province. The old city of Kandahār is some 3 km to the west of the modern city, at the foot of the Qaitul Ridge.

Dates: Bronze Age, 2nd mill. BC; Iron Age, end 2nd–beginning 1st mill. BC; Iron Age/Achaemenid, 7th–4th cent. BC; Seleucid-Mauryan, 3rd–2nd cent. BC; Parthian-Saka. 2nd–1st cent. BC; Indo-Parthian, 1st–3rd cent.; Sasanian-Turki Shahi, 3rd–9th cent.; Timurid, 15th–16th cent.

Description: A large urban site at the foot of a precipitous ridge. It is surrounded by massive outer fortification walls and a moat, while interior secondary walls divide the site into nine quarters. Occupation is up to 8 m deep, but the site is heavily eroded and robbed in most places. The site is dominated by a massive citadel mound, c.30 m high.

A stupa-monastery complex on the ridge overlooks the site from the south, where there is also a series of stone cisterns dating from the latest period. In addition, there is an immense extramural necropolis, several times larger than the city itself, stretching southwards along the foot of the ridge.

Excavations concentrated on dating the fortifications and answering stratigraphic, chronological, and ceramic problems. Finds have included a large number of coins, mostly from the stupa, some fragmentary frescos, also from the stupa, a short Greek inscription (the 'Aristonax inscription') from the north-east area where most of the excavations have been concentrated, and two fragmentary cuneiform inscriptions from the foot of the citadel.

In addition, numerous important accidental finds have been made at Kandahār: a large stone bowl with a lotus leaf decoration and late 16th-century inscription; two bronze coffins discovered at the western edge of the Shahr-i Nau district (close to the site) in 1934, containing a glazed funerary urn with human bones inside and a silver urn and cover decorated with gold leaves; a number of possible Graeco-Bactrian seals found in 1840; a bilingual Greek and Aramaic Ashokan edict on bedrock at Sarpūza, just to the north of the site; another Ashokan edict in Greek from the site itself; a fragmentary Aramaic and Prakit inscription found in the

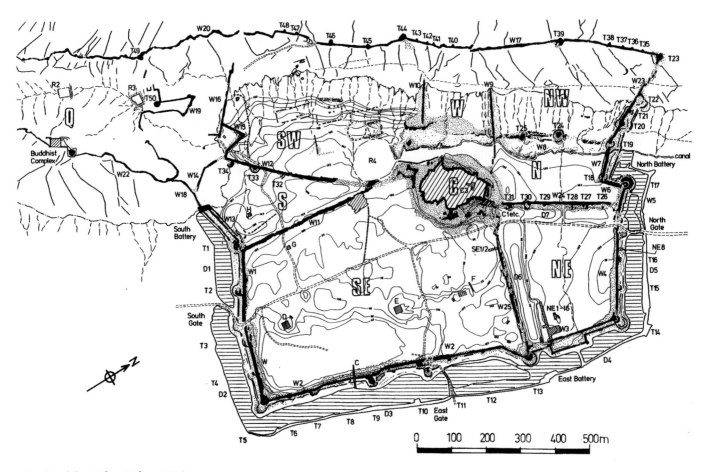

522 Kandahār (after Helms 1978).

bazaar; and another Greek inscription (the 'Sophytos inscription') purportedly from the site and now in a private collection.

Collections:
1. National Museum—stone bowl, Greek inscription, sherds.
2. Kandahār Museum—bronze coffins, coins.

Fieldwork:
1. 1946 Wheeler, ASI—reconnaissance.
2. 1951 Casal, DAFA—survey.
3. 1955 and 1960 Fischer, DAAD—survey.
4. 1964 Fussman and Le Berre, DAFA—survey.
5. 1974 Whitehouse, BIAS—excavations.
6. 1975 McNicoll, BIAS—excavations.
7. 1976–8 Helms, BIAS—excavations.

Sources:
1. Court 1836: 389—identifies the remains with Alexandria Arachosia.
2. Conolly 1840—illustrations, description, and discussion of a number of gems and seals discovered at Kandahār.
3. Kennedy 1840: I. 281–3—description of the remains and a proposal for the removal of the stone bowl to the British Museum.

4. Masson 1842: I. 279—mentions.
5. Cunningham 1846: 186—mentions finding coins of Maues and Azes at Kandahār.
6. Lal 1846: 187–8—briefly describes the remains and recounts legends about treasures down wells.
7. Ferrier 1857: 317–18—good description of the remains and its associated legends in 1845.
8. Bellew 1862: 232–3—describes the fortifications, the cisterns, and the stupa.
9. Bellew 1874: 142–4—description of the stone bowl.
10. Le Mesurier 1880: 245–7—describes the site and the cisterns.
11. Cunningham 1890: 122—refers to the many Saka coins of Gondophares found in 1840–1 by Stacy and Hutton.
12. Le Strange 1905: 347—summary of the historical references.
13. Horowitz 1913—analysis of the inscriptions on the stone bowl.
14. Sālnāma 1934/35: opp. 128—photo of the two funerary urns from the coffins.
15. Shakur 1947: 92–4—brief description.
16. Wheeler 1947: 64—brief assessment.
17. Caspani and Cagnacci 1951: 252–3—brief description of the site.

18. Ramachandran and Sharma 1956: III. 11–12—summary of the coins in the National Museum.
19. Altheim and Stiehl 1958—brief preliminary report on the discovery of the bilingual edict.
20. Fischer 1958b—description of the remains and discussion of its identification with Alexandria.
21. Scerrato 1958a—report on the discovery of the bilingual edict.
22. Scerrato 1958b—brief note on the discovery of the bilingual edict.
23. Scerrato et al. 1958—introduction to the discovery and full text, translation, and linguistic analysis of the bilingual edict.
24. Schlumberger et al. 1958—report on the discovery and full text, translation, and discussion of the bilingual edict.
25. Altheim and Stiehl 1959a—linguistic analysis of the Aramaic version of the bilingual edict.
26. Altheim and Stiehl 1959b—discuss the bilingual edict in the light of subsequent work and studies carried out by others.
27. Altheim and Stiehl 1959c: 21–32—linguistic discussion of the Aramaic version of the bilingual edict.
28. Gallavotti 1959a—translation and linguistic analysis of the Greek version of the bilingual edict.
29. Gallavotti 1959b—linguistic discussion of the bilingual edict and its importance for Mauryan history in Afghanistan.
30. Kosambi 1959—discusses the implications for Indian religion from the evidence of the bilingual edict.
31. Zucker 1959—note on the discovery of the bilingual edict.
32. Altheim 1959–61: 397–408—detailed linguistic analysis of the bilingual edict.
33. Alsdorf 1960—general discussion of Ashokan edicts from Kandahār and elsewhere.
34. Eggermont and Hoftijzer 1962: 42–5—text and translation of both versions of the bilingual edict.
35. Benveniste 1964—text, translation, and long linguistic analysis of the new Greek Ashokan edict, in the context of other Greek Ashokan edicts.
36. Scerrato et al. 1964—full report, linguistic analysis, and translation of the bilingual edict.
37. Schlumberger 1964b—text and translation of the new Greek Ashokan edict.
38. Benveniste and Dupont-Sommer 1966—full linguistic analysis of the new Aramaic-Prakit inscription.
39. Caillat 1966—linguistic discussion of the word *shyty* and its occurrence in the Aramaic version of the bilingual edict.
40. Dupont-Sommer 1966—text and long linguistic discussion on the fragmentary Aramaic-Prakit inscription.
41. Fussman 1966—extensive description and topographical analysis of the site. Divides the city into two sectors according to tentative periods.
42. Daffinà 1967: 22–43—discussion of the Achaemenid geography of Harahuvatish and the identification of Kandahār as the satrapal capital.
43. Fischer 1967a: 144–8—description of the site and its background.
44. Schlumberger 1967—discusses Hellenism in Afghanistan in the light of the discovery of the Greek inscriptions.
45. Schlumberger and Benveniste 1967—summary linguistic discussion with text and translation of the Greek edict.
46. Habibi 1968: 12—infers Achaemenid precedents in the Ashokan edicts.
47. Wheeler 1968: 65–70—discusses the Greek inscriptions and the identification as Alexandria.
48. Fischer 1969: 338—brief summary of the site and some of its pottery.
49. Shaked 1969—comments on the reading and interpretation of the new Greek edict.
50. Habibi 1971: 126—discusses the bilingual edict and the development of Afghan epigraphy.
51. Humbach 1971—discusses the significance of the inscriptions for western Mauryan history.
52. Norman 1972—linguistic notes on the Greek version of the bilingual edict.
53. Dupree 1973: 286–8—describes and assesses the importance of the inscriptions.
54. Rapp 1973: 66—discusses a Hebrew inscription from Kandahār.
55. Bernard 1974c—discusses the classical sources for Kandahār.
56. N. Dupree et al. 1974: 8–9 and 11–12—describe the two Ashokan edicts (one a copy) and the stone bowl on display in the National Museum.
57. Fischer et al. 1974–6: pls 1–3, 69, 70, and 76—photos and description of the site.
58. Deshpande 1975a—traces ceramic and epigraphic links with India.
59. Whitehouse 1976—detailed report on the excavation of two 12th-century burial mounds to the south of the city.
60. Davary 1977—lists the inscriptions and gives a bibliography.
61. N. Dupree 1977: 287–93—describes the bronze coffins and other finds, as well as the site and the excavations.
62. Itō 1977—text, new translation, and commentary on the Aramaic version of the bilingual edict.
63. Tarzi 1977d—discusses the background and the first results of the British excavations.
64. Fleming 1978—detailed description of the vertical photographic recording technique used in the excavations.
65. Mac Dowall 1978—brief note on coins from the Seleucid to Sasanian periods found during the 1975 season.

66. Mac Dowall and Ibrahim 1978−discussion and catalogue of coins in the Kandahār Museum, some at least of which were probably found at the site.
67. Mac Dowall and Taddei 1978a and b: 192−8, 230−2, and 262−3−discuss the inscriptions, the Achaemenid defences, the ceramics, and the brick sizes.
68. McNicoll 1978−interim report on the 1975 season, with tentative chronological and dynastic conclusions.
69. Whitehouse 1978−full report on the 1974 trench through the city walls: the pottery, sequence, and chronology.
70. Fraser 1979− text, translation, and linguistic analysis of the new Greek inscription found in the excavations.
71. Helms 1979− interim report on the 1976 season: the stupa, the citadel, and the city walls.
72. Taddei 1979a−discusses the burial mound excavated in 1974 and its Indian parallels.
73. Scerrato 1980−discussion of the funerary objects found outside Herat Gate.
74. Sikandarpūr 1980−summary of the excavations and main finds, including the cuneiform tablet.
75. Hansman 1981: 6−8−discusses the location of Arachosia at Kandahār.
76. Helms 1982−toponymic speculations on the name and identity of Kandahār, and the evidence from the excavation relating to the identification.
77. Helms 1983−summary of origins of name; earliest mentions; brief résumé of Islamic history from sources.
78. Allchin 1995: 127−30−brief description and discussion in the context of urbanism in South Asia.
79. McNicoll and Ball 1996−full report on 1975 and 1976 seasons.
80. Ball 1997−discussed Kandahār as a possible base for the Saka invasion of the Lower Indus.
81. Helms 1997−full report of the stratigraphy, pottery, and small finds from the 1976−8 seasons.
82. Bernard and Rougemont 2003−first announcement and translation of the Sophytos inscription.
83. Bernard et al. 2004−full discussion and translation of the Sophytos inscription.
84. MacDowall 2005−summary of the Indo-Greek coinage.
85. Tissot 2006: 504−National Museum catalogue details and photo of the stone bowl.
86. Ball 2008: 51−2, 228−3−summary.
87. Mairs 2008−discusses the evidence from the site for Greek ethnic identity in Arachosia.
88. Mairs 2011a−discusses the results of the excavations for cultural identity at Kandahār.
89. Rougemont 2012a: 165−82−full texts, translations, and discussion of the Greek inscriptions.
90. Rougemont 2012b−discusses the importance of the Greek inscriptions.
91. Mairs 2014a: 103−17−discussion of the Sophytos inscription and its implications for Indo-Greek identity at Kandahār.

92. Coningham and Young 2015: 331−2, 367−70−discuss Iron Age and Achaemenid period.
93. Fisher and Stolper 2015−detailed analysis of the fragmentery Elamite tablets with comparative material from Persepolis, confirming the identity of Kandahār as the Achaemenid regional capital.
94. Ball 2017: 161−2−evidence from the excavations for the Sasanian East.

KANDAKAU. See 1080 SHINGĀN.

523. KANGKRAK-I PĀ'ĪN
Or QAL'A-I MĀLIK.

Lat. 34° 22' N, long. 70° 09' E. Map 65.
Nangahār Province. On the south bank of the Surkhāb, 10 km west of Bālābāgh.

Description: A large number of caves, high up in the cliff face. They consist of some 30 square and triangular openings, with some semi-circular, possibly to take statues. There are no stupas or other ruins associated with the caves.

Fieldwork:
1. 1834 Masson−survey.
2. 1957 Lindberg−speleological survey.

Sources:
1. Masson 1833a: 10−brief description and sketch of the exterior.
2. Masson 1840: 38−mention.
3. Masson 1842: I. 3 and II. 186−mention.
4. Raverty 1878: 56−mention.
5. Lindberg 1961: 23−mention.

KANGRAULI. See 2110 in Supplement.

524. KANSĪR
Or SIRIGH CHAUPĀN.

Lat. 36° 58' N, long. 73° 26' E. Map 40
Badakhshān Province. On the crest of a spur opposite Pīrkhar, overlooking the west bank of the Barāghil stream, 4 km south of Sarhad in Wākhān.

Date: Tang Chinese, 8th cent. (architectural, documentary).

Description: Remains of an old fort guarding the approach to Karkat on the Āmū Daryā. It consists of a wall stretching for some 130 m, with three bastions facing westwards. There are no structures inside. Construction is of mud-brick, stone, and brushwood, similar to Chinese military outposts in the Tarim Basin.

Fieldwork:
1. 1901 Stein, ASI—survey.
2. 2013 DAFA—sondage.

Sources:
1. Stein 1904: 68–70—description and plan.
2. Gazetteer 1972: I. 135—mention under Pīrkhar.
3. Marquis 2013: 94—mentions new work at the site.
4. Mock 2011—photo of the fort and discussion of the historical background.
5. Mock 2016—mentions Stein's work at the site and discusses many other petroglyphs in the Wākhān.

525. KANUM

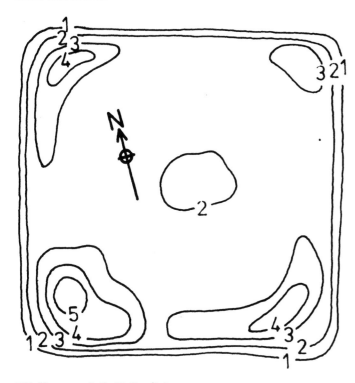

525 Kanum—A (J.-C. Gardin).

Original: Lat. 36° 48' N, long. 68° 57' E. Map 32.
Revised:
36.79079323 N, 68.95098214 E / 36° 47' 26.85562548 N, 68° 57' 03.53571876 E (A).
36.79844639 N, 68.94683181 E / 36° 47' 54.40700688 N, 68° 56' 48.59451708 E (B).
36.79894814 N, 68.94102829 E / 36° 47' 56.21331300 N, 68° 56' 27.70185876 E (C).

Qundūz Province. Some 10 km north-east of Qundūz as the crow flies, on the western outskirts of the village of Kanum, on the left bank of the Khānābād river. (A) A first tepe is located at the western edge of the village, recognizable by the area it occupies (1 hectare). (B) The second is situated about 500 m north-north-west of the last houses of

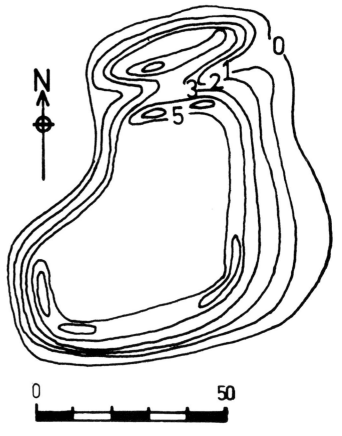

525 Kanum—C (J.-C. Gardin).

Kanum, on an advance of the terrace occupied by a cemetery, above the Khānābād River. To the west of this spur rises, below the terrace, two high natural mounds, vestiges of the geological history of this river (both indicated on the 1:100,000 map). The largest, to the west, is fortified (C); the smallest, to the east, presents no trace of structures, but produces sherds on the surface (D).

Dates: Beg. Iron, end 2nd–beg. 1st mill. BC (B, C, D); Achaemenid, 6th–4th cent. BC (B, C, D); Hellenistic, 3rd–1st cent. BC (A, B); Hunnic-Turk, 5th–9th cent. (B, D); pre-Mongol Islamic, 10th–13th cent. (A, D) (ceramic).

Description: (A) Square enclosure (100 × 100 m), oriented approximately north–south, probably with four angle towers: the wall, preserved to an average height of 2 m, is marked at the four angles of the square by little mounds (3–4 m), and runs more or less the length of the sides. No structures are identifiable on the interior, except for a slight rise in the central part. A gap used by an ancient canal, in the middle of the west side, possibly marks the position of the gate. (B) Advance of the north–south terrace overlooking the Khānābād river by some 15 m; on the western edge of the cliff, a rectangular structure (30 × 20 m, height 2 m) whose south-west side was carried away by a gully. No other recognizable vestiges, except for two narrow low mounds along the northern edge; but the surface of the site, which has become a cemetery (100 × 100), produces sherds of late periods in abundance. (C) Natural fortified mound, c.20 m above the low terrace where the Khānābād River today cuts its course: lying north-west/south-east (100 m), rectangular in the southern half (width 60 m), narrowing by the west in the northern half, whose extremity carries a distinct fortified construction (citadel?), separated from the rest of the site by a transverse north-east/south-west gully. The 'fortified' character lies in the traces of the walls which follow almost all the perimeter of the mound and the 'citadel', 1–2 m higher than the mound surface. (D) Lower natural mound (10 m above the low terrace), without visible structures, but not without sherds.

Collection: National Museum/AIA—sherds.

Fieldwork: 1978 Gardin et al., CNRS—survey.

Sources:
1. Site information by J.-C. Gardin.
2. Gardin and Lyonnet 1978–9: pl. VII—nos. 466–8.
3. Gardin 1995: 94–5—brief description and plan.
4. Lyonnet 1997: figs 25, 35, 49, 49, 68, 69—nos. 466–8.
5. Gardin 1998: 79—nos. 466–8.

KĀPĪSĀ. See **122 BEGRAM.**

KARABĀGH. See **907 QARABĀGH, Ghazni,** and **908 QARABĀGH, Gulrān.**

KARABASHAN TEPE. See **1217 URAZ BACHA.**

KARACHA. See **2111 KARACHA** in Supplement.

526. KARA KAMAR

Lat. 36° 26' N, long. 67° 54' E. Map 30.
Samangan Province. 23 km north of Haibak on the road to Tāshqurghān, above and behind the village of Hazrāt Sultān. Adjoins the Hazār Sūm Valley.

Dates: Middle Palaeolithic, 32,000–28,000 BC; Epi-Palaeolithic, 9300–9000 BC (C-14, lithic).

Description: A small rock shelter c.135 m above the valley floor, probably a transitory hunting station. Four cultural levels were differentiated typologically, but not stratigraphically, Period III being the most important. A total of 82 flint implements were found, most of them microliths. The materials bore no similarities to other material from Afghanistan, Soviet Central Asia, India, or Pakistan. The nearest parallel is the Baradostian culture in the Iranian Zagros.

Fieldwork:
1. 1954 Coon, University Museum, Penn.—excavations.
2. 1960 Hayashi and Sahara, Kyoto Museum—survey.
3. 1971 McBurney, Cambridge University—sondages.

Sources:
1. Coon and Coulter 1955—summary of the excavations and results.
2. Coon and Ralph 1955—brief note and table of the C-14 dates.
3. Ramachandran and Sharma 1956: I. 23–4—brief description and assessment.
4. Allchin 1957: 132—brief summary.
5. Coon 1957: 105–237—light account of the search for the site and its subsequent excavation.
6. Hayashi and Sahara 1962: 44—photo and brief description in Japanese.
7. Dupree 1967—summary, with a discussion on the chronology and comparative material.
8. N. Dupree 1967a: 34–5—brief description.
9. Masson and Sarianidi 1969—discuss the site in its wider chronological and Near Eastern context.
10. McBurney 1972: 23–4—brief discussion of Coon's work with a summary and plan of his own work.
11. Davis 1974: 60–1 and 177–208—full description of the excavations, stratigraphy, and lithics.
12. N. Dupree et al. 1974: 53–7—summary of the site and description of the objects on display in the National Museum.
13. Davis 1978: 45 and 50–5—good description of the material. Summary of the chronological controversy and refutation of the Middle Palaeolithic date.
14. Zahir 1980—summary of the results in Persian.

KARANGO. See **2112 in Supplement.**

KARA TEPE. See **1206 TŪRGHUNDI.**

KARĀWAL KHĀNA. See **2215 QARĀWAL KHĀNA** in Supplement.

527. KARBĀSAK
Or GARSHASP or QAL'A-I KUHNA.

Original: Lat. 30° 10' N, long. 62° 37' E. Map 96.
Revised: 30.16035749 N, 62.62455613 E /
30° 09' 37.28697660 N, 62° 37' 28.40207340 E.
Nīmrūz Province. On the south bank of the Helmand east of Rūdbār, towards Lat Qal'a.

Date: Partho-Sasanian, 1st–7th cent.; Ghaznavid, 10th–11th cent. (ceramic).

Description: An area of low mounds, and the ruins of an old fort.

Fieldwork:
1. 1884 Maitland, Peacocke, ABC—topographical survey.
2. 1966 Hammond, Cambridge University—survey.
3. 1967, 1971–4 Trousdale, Smithsonian—survey.

Sources:
1. Additional information on dates and location by W. Trousdale.
2. Bellew 1874: 202—mention.
3. Peacocke 1885a: 2—mention.
4. Maitland 1888a: 57—mention.
5. Peacocke 1887a: 16—mention.
6. Hammond 1970: 449—lists the sites (nos. 30 and 44) and describes the pottery and general survey results.
7. Gazetteer 1973: II. 148—mention.

KAR GUL. See 175 CHĀR GUL.

528. KARINJ

Lat. 34° 45' N, long. 70° 11' E. approximately. Map 65.
Laghmān Province. In the foothills of the Kūh-i Karinj, *c.*12 km due north of the junction of the ʿAlishang and ʿAlingār Rivers.

Description: Consistent but unconfirmed local reports of an inscription.

Source: Masson 1842: III. 293—mention.

KARI YAZI. See 2113 in Supplement.

529. KĀRĪZAK-I BĀLĀ

Original: Lat. 34° 38' N, long. 69° 02' E. Map 63.
Revised: 34.61959985 N, 69.03941609 E /
34° 37' 10.55946648 N, 69° 02' 21.89793444 E.
Kābul Province. At the foot of the hills at the southern extremity of the Kūh-i Dāman Plain, 5 km north-west of the Khair Khāna Pass.

Description: Some mounds and tumuli.

Fieldwork: 1834 Masson—survey.

Source: Masson 1842: III. 112—mention.

530. KĀRĪZAK-I PĀʾĪN

Lat. 34° 38' N, long. 69° 03' E. Map 63.
Kābul Province. At the southern extremity of the Kūh-i Dāman Plain, 5 km north-west of the Khair Khāna Pass.

Description: Some mounds and tumuli.

Fieldwork: 1834 Masson—survey.

Source: Masson 1842: III. 112—mention.

KĀRĪZ-I AMRUTAK. See 2114 in Supplement.

KĀRĪZ-I ZAMĀN. See 2115 in Supplement.

531. KARKACHA

Lat. 34° 22' N, long. 69° 38' E. Map 65.
Kāpīsā Province. At the top of a pass from the Surkhāb to Būtkhāk and Khurd Kābul.

Date: ?Chaghatai, 14th cent. (traditional).

Description: Ruins of two forts at the top of the pass. Below them are some ruined buildings, many mounds, and a scatter of bricks and pottery marking the remains of a town. There are also some caves nearby.

Sources:
1. Masson 1842: III. 178—mention.
2. Wood 1872: 107—brief description.

KARRACHA. See 1088 SHOTORAK.

KARSHIYAK. See 918 QARSHIYAK.

532. KARŪKH
Including TEPE AZĀDEH. See also 2076 GHĀR-I KARŪKH in Supplement.

Lat. 34° 29' N, long. 62° 35' E. Map 53.
Herat Province. 38 km north-east of Herat on the road to Maimana.

Date: Seljuk, 1128; Kart, 13th–14th cent. (epigraphic).

Description: A mosque containing inscriptions in *suls* characters, one of which dates it to 525 AH. Other inscriptions give a restoration in the time of Muhammad Kart, and again in the time of Sultān Abū Said Kuragān.

In addition to this mosque, the rear of the Friday Mosque is built of stone and may be earlier than the rest of the otherwise early 19th-century structure.

A number of 'blocks of great size' and a 'large round stone' were unearthed at Tepe Azādeh, a mound in the vicinity of Karūkh. The stones and blocks appear to have been some sort of foundations and were said to be composed of 'a mixture of asphalt and gypsum'.

Fieldwork:
1. 1978–9 Samizay, Kābul University/UNESCO—survey.
2. 2004–6 Franke and Urban, DAI—survey.

Sources:
1. Le Strange 1905: 410—summary of the historical references.
2. Samizay 1981: 50–5—summary, with drawings and photos of the remains.
3. Golombek and Wilber 1988: 327—description of the mosque.

4. Ball 2008: 233—summary.
5. Franke 2008: pl. 118—photo of Tepe Azādeh with illegal excavations.

533. KĀRWĀNBALASI

Lat. 37° 04' N, long. 73° 53' E. Map 40.
Badakhshān Province. 12 km north-east of Langar, just past the Mirza Murād Pass on the route to Bāzā-i Gumbad.
Description: A well-preserved small domed structure. Construction is of stones set in mortar. It has a corbelled dome. Possibly a converted *vihara*, like similar structures in Hunza.
Fieldwork: 1901 Stein ASI—survey.
Source: Stein 1904: 70–72—description and photo.

534. KASHINDA PĀ'ĪN

Lat. 36° 09' N, long. 66° 55' E. Map 47.
Balkh Province. On the Kushk Darra, *c.*7 km south-east of where it joins the Balkhāb, below Āq Kupruk. The site is just to the south of the village.
Description: A number of artificial caves cut into the white cretaceous limestone. Several are very large and show very careful skill.
Fieldwork: 1886 Griesbach, ABC—topographical survey.
Source: Griesbach 1888b: 203—mention.

535. KĀSHKOT

Lat. 34° 34' N, long. 70° 41' E. Map 67.
Kunār Province. Halfway between the Kundai Pass and Nūrgul on the south side of the Kunār River, 6 km east of Islāmpūr.
Description: Two ruined stone forts.
Source: Raverty 1878: 110—mention.

536. KATA BALANDI
Or PĀ-I MINĀR.

Lat. 35° 36' N, long. 69° 12' E. Map 61.
Kābul Province. On the Pā-i Minār hill to the north of the airport.
Dates: Hunnic-Turk, 5th–9th cent. (ceramic).
Description: Badly eroded remains of a stupa. There are no visible remains of an associated monastery, so it is presumed to have been a marker at the top of the pass.
Collection: National Museum/AIA—sherds.

Sources:
1. Gardin and Lyonnet, 1980 ceramic study of unpublished DAFA surveys.
2. Ball 1984: 119—discusses the possible location of a pre-Islamic 'minar' here.
3. Fussman, Murad, and Ollivier 2008: 138—mention.

537. KATA CHASHMA

Lat. 34° 07' N, long. 64° 09' E approximately. Map 54.
Ghūr Province. 6 km north-west of Shahrak.
Description: Several eroded artificial mounds.
Fieldwork: 1946 Kohzad, HAS—survey.
Source: Kohzad 1951–4, 9/2: 16—mention.

538. KATA QAL'A

Lat. 35° 55' N, long. 65° 02' E. Maps 24, 46.
Faryāb Province. In the Shīrīn Tagau *c.*26 km north-west of Bīlchirāgh and 26 km east of Maimana.
Description: None available.
Fieldwork: 1970 Dupree, AUFS—survey.
Source: Information by L. Dupree.

KATA SŪ. See 2116 in Supplement.

KATA TEPE. See 2117 in Supplement.

539. KATIKUTAR

Lat. 31° 03' N, long. 64° 13' E approximately. Map 97.
Helmand Province. On the left bank of the Helmand south of Darwīshān. 4 km north-east of Dūstmuhammad.
Date: Sasanian, 3rd–7th cent. (ceramic).
Description: A mound.
Fieldwork: 1966 Hammond, Cambridge University—survey.
Source: Hammond 1970: 23—drawing of material (Site 57).

KAUD-I GAZ. See 2118 in Supplement.

540. KAUK

Lat. 37° 25 N, long. 65° 42' E. Map 24.
Jauzjān Province. On the route from Khāmiyāb to Andkhui and Shībarghān via Jar Quduq, 15 km south of Khāmiyāb.
Date: Neolithic, 7th–6th mill. BC (lithic).
Description: A surface site surrounding a well.

Fieldwork: 1969 Vinogradov, Af/Sov. Mission—survey.

Source: Vinogradov 1979: 23—drawing of material (Site 57).

541. KAURMACH
Or GŪCHMACH. See also 890 QAL'A-I WALI.

Original: Lat. 35° 44' N, long. 63° 47' E. Map 44.
Revised: 35.74259015 N, 63.7781601 E / 35° 44' 33.32454648 N, 63° 46' 41.37636828 E.
Bādghīs Province. 19 km west of Chahārshamba on the left bank of the Qal'a-i Wali stream.

Description: Stone remains of an important town on an extensive plateau. It is dominated by the ruins of a mud fortress *c.*300 m square. Inside is an inner keep *c.*40 m square and a circular two-storey brick tower.

Fieldwork: 1886 Maitland, Yate, ABC—topographical surveys.

Sources:
1. Peacocke 1887a: 238—mention.
2. Holdich 1887: 17—mention.
3. Maitland and Drummond 1888: 97—mention.
4. Maitland 1888b: 143—mention.
5. Yate 1888: 188—brief description of the fort.
6. Gazetteer 1975: III. 247—mention.

KERĀNO-MUNJĀN. See 1230 WARZU.

542. KHAIRĀBĀD, FARYĀB
Or QAL'A-I JUBIN or QAL'A-I KAZAL or TŪP-KHĀNA QAL'A. See also 2102 KĀFIR QAL'A KHAIRĀBĀD in Supplement.

Original: Lat. 36° 22' N, long. 64° 53' E. Map 24.
Revised: 36.38828225 N, 64.89385344 E / 36° 23' 17.81609676 N, 64° 53' 37.87237320 E.
Faryāb Province. In the Shīrīn Tagau 7 km south of Daulatābād and 60 km north of Maimana.

Description: Remains of a medium-sized citadel on a mound, known as Qal'a-i Jubin. It is 8–10 m high with some towers still standing, and is completely surrounded by a ditch. Stretching irregularly to the east for several hundred metres are the remains of a city, consisting of very low mounds and Islamic glazed sherds, surrounded by a possible mud defensive wall. Outside are several more low mounds.

The site resembles early Islamic city patterns, and is probably the site of ancient Faryāb.

Fieldwork: 1885–6 Maitland, Peacocke, Yate, ABC—topographical survey.

Sources:
1. Peacocke 1887a: 108—mention.
2. Maitland 1888b: 158—mention.

3. Yate 1888: 233–4—mentions the remains and recounts the legends surrounding them.

543. KHAIRĀBĀD, HERAT

Lat. 34° 34' N, long. 61° 18' E. Map 51.
Herat Province. On the south bank of the Harī Rūd 5 km south-east of Tirpul.

Description: Ruins of some old buildings—possibly a caravanserai—and a domed cistern.

Fieldwork: 1885 Griesbach, ABC—topographical survey.

Source: Griesbach 1888a: 78—mention.

544. KHAIRĀBĀD, NĪMRŪZ
See also 810 PESHWĀRĀN.

Original: Lat. 31° 34' N, long. 61° 31' E. Map 83.
Revised: 31.56631051 N, 61.52014067 E / 31° 33' 58.71784284 N, 61° 31' 12.50640228 E.
Nīmrūz Province. At the northern end of the Peshwaran Plain, *c.*20 km south-west of Lāsh Juwain.

Description: Extensive remains dotted around the plain, mostly of detached *iwān* houses. There is also a wide surface scatter or iron slag.

Source: Bellew 1874: 273–5—description, mainly of the *iwān* houses.

545. KHAIRĀBĀD GHUNDAI

Original: Lat. 34° 25' N, long. 69° 11' E. Map 62.
Revised: 34.42247323 N, 69.1875259 E / 34° 25' 20.90362908 N, 69° 11' 15.09322848 E.
Kābul Province. A rocky outcrop between the west bank of the Lōgar River and the Gardēz Road, 2 km south of the turn-off to Guldarra and 13 km south of Kābul.

Date: Hunnic-Turki Shahi, 5th–9th cent. (ceramic).

Description: Remains of a small fortress.

Fieldwork: 1963–4 Fussman and Le Berre, DAFA—survey.

Sources:
1. Fussman and Le Berre 1976: 102—mention.
2. Gardin and Lyonnet, 1980 chronological study of unpublished DAFA surveys.

546. KHAIR KHĀNA

Lat. 34° 34' N, long. 60° 06' E. Map 61.
Kābul Province. 12 km north-west of Kābul, just to the north of the Khair Khāna Pass.

546 Khair Khāna (after Hackin 1936).

Dates: Kushano-Sasanian, 4th–5th cent. (ceramic); Turki and Hindu Shahi, 7th–10th cent. (stylistic).

Description: A large Hindu temple complex of two distinct periods. The first period consisted of a mud-brick temple with possible human sacrifice remains dedicating it. This was then superseded by three distinct sanctuaries built of schist slabs, surrounded by subsidiary buildings of diaper masonry construction and an open-air altar in a semi-circular enclosure. The most important finds were two marble statues of Surya, the first found during the excavations, the second found by accident in 1980.

Collections: National Museum and Musée Guimet.

Fieldwork: 1934 Carl, DAFA—excavations.

Sources:

1. Salnāma 1933/34: opp. 21—photos of some of the sculpture.
2. Hackin 1935c—brief discussion on the Sasanian artistic influences seen at Khair Khāna.
3. Hackin 1936a—summary of the excavations and description of the sculptures.
4. Hackin and Carl 1936—brief report on the excavations and full description of the sculptures and decorative elements.
5. Dollot 1937: 284–8—summary of the excavations.
6. Yoshikawa 1944—summary of the site.
7. Kohzad 1946/47—description of the Surya and the results of the excavations.
8. Schlumberger 1947a—brief discussion of the results.
9. Deydier 1950: 93–4—briefly discusses the Surya.
10. Ramachandran and Sharma 1956: II. 7—discuss the Hindu sculpture.
11. Barrett 1957—discusses the Hindu sculptures and their dates.
12. Goetz 1957—discusses the Surya and its stylistic connections.
13. Mizuno 1964—illustrations and descriptions of some of the objects displayed in the Tokyo Museum.

14. Rowland and Rice 1971: 19–50 and pls 165 and 167—description and photos of the Hindu sculptures on display from the National Museum.
15. Kuwayama 1972a—discusses and compares the Surya statue.
16. Dupree 1973: 309—summary of the site and mention of the human remains in the temple.
17. N. Dupree et al. 1974: 96—guide to the collection in the National Museum.
18. Deshpande 1975a—compares the Surya with other examples in India.
19. Trousdale 1975: 71–85—discusses the sword depicted on one of the marble reliefs.
20. Kuwayama 1976: 375–7—describes the Surya and other Hindu sculpture found.
21. Sharqi 1980—brief report on the discovery of the new Surya.
22. Kuwayama 1991: 92–4—discussion of the evidence from Begram III for the chronology.
23. Stadtner 2000—discussion of the two Surya statues from Khairkhana in relation to two unprovenanced Bodhisattvas in a private collection.
24. Tissot 2006: 355—National Museum catalogue details and photos.
25. Ball 2008: 233—summary.

KHAISTA TOPE See 761 NANDARRA.

547. KHĀK BATĀK

Lat. 35° 44' N, long. 66° 40' E. Map 47.
Balkh Province. 8 km south of Baiza in the headwaters of the Amrakh River.

Description: Remains of an old fort built of rough stone, only a portion of one tower of which is still standing.

Fieldwork: 1885 Sahibdad Khan, ABC—topographical survey.

Source: Sahibdad Khan 1888: 151—mention.

KHĀK-I BĀBĀ. See 1075 SHĪBAR, west.

548. KHĀK-I GHULĀM ‘ALI

Lat 34.58’ N, long. 68° 34’ E. Maps 49, 60.
Parwān Province. In the Ghūrband Valley *c.*31 km west of Siāhgird.

Description: Boulders with petroglyphs depicting ibex and hunting scenes.

Fieldwork: 1956 Ramachandran and Sharma, ASI— reconnaissance.

Sources:
1. Foucher 1942–7: 390—brief description and photo.
2. Ramachandran and Sharma 1956: I. 29–30

KHĀK-I HĀJI. See 2119 in Supplement.

549. KHĀK-I JABĀR
Or QABR-I JABĀR.

Lat. 34° 24’ N, long. 69° 30’ E. Map 65.
Kābul Province, Khak-i Jabbar district. 12 km east of Khurd Kābul, on the old route to Jalālābād.

Date: Gandharan, 1st–5th cent. (stylistic).

Description: Traces of drystone walls, possibly the remains of either a fort or Buddhist stupa, located on the hill directly behind the district offices of Khāk-i Jabar. In 2000, the approach up the hill was too risky due to mines. There is also a small series of caves to the south of the village.

Fieldwork: Lee 2000—reconnaissance and photographs.

Sources:
1. Site information by Jonathan L. Lee.
2. Masson 1840: 41—mentions the fort.
3. Masson 1842: 188—mentions the fort.
4. Raverty 1878: 59—mentions the caves.

550. KHALĀBĀD TEPE
Or HALOBAD TEPE or CHURUK TEPE.

Original: Lat. 36° 53’ N, 66° 17’ E. Maps 24, 25.
Revised: 36.89546787 N, 66.28454276 E /
36° 53’ 43.68433272 N, 66° 17’ 04.35394392 E.
Jauzjān Province. 11 km east of Āqcha. About 1 km north of the road to Balkh, between the Nar Mullāh Jum’a and the route to Murdiyān.

Dates: Graeco-Bactrian, 3rd–2nd cent. BC; Mongol-Timurid period 13th–15th cent. (ceramic).

Description: Rectangular platform (120 × 100 m), height 7 m, which dominates by 3 m a citadel situated in the south-east angle.

Collection: National Museum/AIA—sherds.

Fieldwork:
1. 1886 Maitland, ABC—topographical exploration.
2. 1948 Le Berre, DAFA—survey.
3. 1960 Hayashi and Sahara, University of Kyoto—survey.

Sources:
1. Maitland 1888b—mention.
2. DAFA archives: report M. Le Berre 1948, unpublished, tepe P. 11.
3. Hayashi and Sahara 1962: 61, fig. 65—photo and description in Japanese.
4. 1980 Gardin and Lyonnet, study of pottery from the DAFA surveys, unpublished.

551. KHĀL-I MUHAMMAD HĀSHIM KHĀN

Original: Lat. 30° 24’ N, long. 61° 51’ E. Map 93.
Revised: 30.40419714 N, 61.84240182 E /
30° 24’ 15.10970796 N, 61° 50’ 32.64655164 E.
Nīmrūz Province. On the east bank of the Helmand *c.*20 km south of Qal’a-i Fath, 150 m to the east of the road to Chahār Burjak.

Dates: Parthian and Indo-Parthian, 2nd cent. BC–AD 3rd cent.; Sasanian, 3rd–7th cent. (ceramic).

Description: A mound *c.*8 m in height and 80 × 50 m in area. There are the remains of a tower in the south-east corner.

Fieldwork: 1951 Fairservis, AMNH—survey.

Source: Fairservis 1961: 54—brief description and a summary of the pottery (Site, 34, KF–2).

KHALIFA RAHMAT JAMSHĪDĪ. See 2120 in Supplement.

KHAIMAH BARANG. See 229 DAM, Shaila Rūd.

KHAMCHĀN. See 650 KURI.

KHAM-I ĀB. See 2121 in Supplement.

KHAM-I ZARGAR. See 622 KŪH-I MŪRIMŪRI.

552. KHĀNĀBĀD, BALKH
Or TAKHT-I KHĀN, Including KUSHK-I SHĀH SANAM.

Original: Lat. 37° 04' N, long. 66° 37' E. Map 26.
Revised: 37.05878665 N, 66.62749952 E /
37° 03' 31.63194324 N, 66° 37' 38.99828388 E.
Balkh Province. 45 km south-east of Kilift and 20 km north-west of Daulatābād, north of Nikcha, to the north of the Balkh-Kilift road.

Description: A ruined town covering 203 square miles. Construction is mainly of mud and mud-brick, though there are many baked brick remains as well, the largest of which is known as the Kushk-i Shāh Sanam, said to have been an Idgāh. Also reports of a very large brick caravanserai called Takht-i Khān with a high mound in centre, four gates, and a cistern at each corner.

Fieldwork: 1886 Peacocke, ABC—topographical survey.

Sources:
1. Holdich 1886: 9—mention.
2. Holdich 1887: 36—mention.
3. Peacocke 1887a: 318–29—brief description.
4. Gazetteer 1979: 325—summary description.

553. KHĀNĀBĀD, QUNDŪZ

Original: Lat. 36° 41' N, long. 69° 06' E. Map 85.
Revised:
36.67713559 N, 69.10289322 E / 36° 40' 37.68813120 N, 69° 06' 10.41557724 E (A).
36.67707002 N, 69.10682408 E / 36° 40' 37.45206120 N, 69° 06' 24.56669520 E (B).
Qundūz Province. Less than a kilometre from the central crossroads of Khānābād on the road to Aliābād, 500 m east of this road: tepe A corresponds to the mound of 10 m indicated on the 1:100,000 map in the south-west quarter of Khānābād.

Date: Timurid, 15th–16th cent. (ceramic).

Description: (A) Rectangular platform (50 × 30 m) oriented north-east/south-west, height 6 m, dominated by a square mound (c.15 × 25 m) in the south-west half (height 10 m). (B) 400 m to the north-east of A, overlooking a large cemetery (called Naibullah Khān), rounded mound (diam. 30 m), 6 m high (with tombs and *zīyārat*).

Collections: National Museum/AIA—sherds.

Fieldwork:
1. 1955 and 60 Fischer, DAAD—survey.
2. 1978 Gardin et al., CNRS—survey.

Sources:
1. Site information by J.-C. Gardin.
2. Fischer 1961a: 15—mention and photo; photos of coins and seals.
3. Fischer 1969: 349–51—brief summary.

4. Gardin and Lyonnet 1978–9: pl. VII—nos. 435–6.
5. Gardin 1980—describes the survey of the Khanabad area in general terms.
6. Gentelle 1989—full report on the ancient irrigation and hydrology of the area.
7. Gardin 1998: 78—nos. 435–6.

554. KHĀNA GAUHAR

Lat. 31° 27' N, long. 64° 23' E. Map 97.
Helmand Province. On the east bank of the Helmand 17 km south-south-east of the bridge across the Helmand at Lashkar Gah, 8 km south of Khwāja Kanur.

Date: Sasanian, 3rd–7th cent. (architectural).

Description: Some Buddhist monastic remains consisting of a pillar of stone 100 m high separated from the cliff and crowned by a stupa. The stupa, 11 m diam., is of mud-brick and is surrounded by an ambulatory with a staircase to the east. The pillar has five single and multi-chambered caves cut into it on two levels.

Fieldwork: 1971–4 Trousdale, Smithsonian Institution—survey.

Source: Trousdale 1976a: 58–9—brief description.

KHĀNA LŪMĀN. See 1184 TEPE SINAUBAR.

KHĀNĀNĪ. See 2123 KHĀNĀNĪ in Supplement.

KHĀNIQĀH. See 960 RUSTĀQ.

555. KHĀNA SANGĪ
Or KHWĀJA SAFĀ.

Lat. 34° 30' N, long. 69° 10' E. Map 61.
Kābul Province. On the western side of the Kidar Pass over Shir Darwāza hill in Kābul, between Jangalak and the Bālā Hisār.

Dates: Kushan and Kushano-Sasanian, 2nd–4th cent. (numismatic, stylistic).

Description: Two artificial rock chambers with masonry doorways. There is a small terrace in front with several large blocks of masonry by the entrances.
Also remains of a stupa and associated monastery that contained Budhist sculptures in clay, still with traces of painting. A coin of Vima Kadphises was also found. This was also presumably the find spot in the 1930s of a seated Buddha in schist, deposited in the National Museum.

Collection: National Museum—schist Buddha.

Fieldwork: 2004–5 Paiman, AIA—excavation.

Sources:
1. Masson 1833a: 13—description and sketch.
2. Masson 1842: II. 235—brief description.
3. Paiman 2005—brief description of the excavations and finds.
4. Tissot 2006: 353—catalogue entry of the schist Buddha.
5. Errington 2017a: 66 and 2017b: 23–4—Masson documentation of the site.

556. KHĀNA YAHŪDA

Lat. 34° 54' N, long. 66° 39' E. Map 47.
Bāmiyān Province. 3 km south-east of Chehelburj, on the east bank of the Band-i Amīr River.

Dates: ?Ghurid, 12th–13th cent. (architectural, geographical).

Description: Remains of some fortifications.

Fieldwork:
1. 1885 Maitland and Talbot, ABC—topographical survey.
2. 1970 Brett et al., Bristol University—survey.

Sources:
1. Maitland 1888a: 485 and 498—brief description from hearsay.
2. Holdich 1910: 257—mention.
3. Brett et al. 1970—map reference.

557. KHANDŪD
See also 72. BĀD-I ĀSYĀ and 1204 TŪPKHĀNA.

Lat. 36° 57' N, long. 72° 19' E. Map 39.
Badakhshān Province. In Wākhān on the left bank of the Panja River, 29 km south-west of Qal'a-i Panja.

Date: Late Sasanian, 7th cent. (stylistic).

Description: In a recent mosque in the village are six reused stone columns. They are round or square in section, and three of them rest on sculpted lotus leaf bases in the Buddhist style. There are many other religious buildings in and around Khandūd, some of which have architectural features in the Buddhist tradition.

The site is probably associated with a Buddhist centre mentioned by Huien Tsang in the 7th century.

Sources:
1. Stein 1904: 64—assesses the strategical importance of Khandūd's position.
2. Mouchet and Blanc 1972: 60–5—brief description and sketch plans.
3. Ball 2008: 233–4—summary.
4. Mock 2011—discusses the Buddhist tradition and some of the carved stone remains.

KHĀN RAGĀB TEPE. See 2122 KHĀN RAGĀB TEPE in Supplement.

KHĀNZADA. See 519 KAMARI.

558. KHARĀBA-I IDUKHĀN
Or CHAPU. See also 824 PŪST-I GAU.

Original: Lat. 31° 17' N, long. 62° 02' E. Map 84.
Revised: 31.29370973 N, 62.03256418 E /
31° 17' 37.35501720 N, 62° 01' 57.23104980 E.
Nīmrūz Province. 3 km north-west of Pūst-i Gau, 13 km north of Chakhānsūr.

Date: Sasanian, 3rd–7th cent. (architectural).

Description: A series of ruins and mounds, probably an extension of the Pūst-i Gau remains. Dominated by the remains of a citadel, irregular in plan. In the centre of the citadel is a keep or palace, on a mound c.17 m high. Construction is mostly of large mud-bricks, but with some baked bricks being used. It has Sasanian-type vaults.

To the south of the citadel are the remains of another enclosure, c.40 m square, containing ruins of two buildings, the lower parts of which are of baked brick construction. To the west of the citadel are two more buildings with decorated façades.

There are more ruins and mounds stretching northwards towards Gul-i Safīdka.

Fieldwork:
1. 1903–5 Tate, SAC—survey.
2. 1950 Fairservis, AMNH—survey.
3. 1965–70 Fischer, Bonn University—survey.

Sources:
1. Tate 1910: 187 and 212—brief description and tentative identification as medieval Qarnein.
2. Fairservis 1961: 44—mention (Site 24).
3. Fischer 1970b: 12–13 and 17–19—photos.
4. Fischer 1971b: 42 and 46—photos and brief description (Sites 28–31).
5. Fischer 1973c: 138—map reference.
6. Ball 2008: 255—summary.

559. KHARĀBA-I SIĀH KHANA

Lat. 30° 23' N, long. 61° 52' E. Map 93.
Nīmrūz Province. On the east bank of the Helmand c.23 km south of Qal'a-i Fath, 100 m to the east of the road to Chahār Burjak.

Dates: Parthian and Indo-Parthian, 2nd cent. BC–AD 3rd cent.; Sasanian, 3rd–7th cent. (ceramic). ?Islamic (architectural).

Description: A tall, well-preserved building, perhaps a mosque, surrounded by sherds.

Fieldwork: 1951 Fairservis, AMNH—survey.

Source: Fairservis 1961: 54–5—brief description and summary of the pottery (Site 35, KF-3).

560. KHARĀBA-I SULTĀN SĀHIB

Lat. 30° 38' N, long. 64° 03' E. approximately. Map 97.
Helmand Province. On the east bank of the Helmand between Safar and Gauharkhān.

Dates: Achaemenid, 6th–4th cent. BC; Indo-Parthian, 1st–3rd cent.; Sasanian, 3rd–7th cent.; Samanid-Ghurid, 10th–13th cent.; Timurid, 15th–16th cent. (ceramic).

Description: An extensive sherd scatter.

Fieldwork: 1966 Hammond, Cambridge University—survey.

Source: Hammond 1970: 450—lists the site (no. 37) and discusses the pottery and general survey results.

KHARĀBA-I YĀR MUHAMMAD KHĀN. See 2124 in Supplement.

561. KHĀRĀN
See also 714 MASJIDAK.

Original: Lat. 31° 23' N, long. 61° 37' E. Map 83.
Revised: 31.39058196 N, 61.61679024 E /
31° 23' 26.09504592 N, 61° 37' 00.44486328 E.
Nīmrūz Province. 17 km south-east of Peshwaran, on the edge of the hāmūn.

Description: Some mounds, probably the remains of forts.

Fieldwork: 1903–5 Tate, SAC—survey.

Source: Tate 1910: 216—mention.

562. KHARGAI

Lat. 34° 33' N, long. 70° 13' E. approximately. Map 65.
Laghmān Province. On a hill north-east of Mandrawar bridge, c.33 km north-west of Jalālābād.

Description: Some scattered sherds and some petroglyphs on the rock face depicting animals.

Source: Fischer 1969: 357 and pl. 34—mention and photo.

563. KHĀRI
See also 983 SANGAR.

Original: Lat. 30° 55' N, long. 62° 05' E. Map 92.
Revised: 30.91829455 N, 62.09883096 E /
30° 55' 05.86037280 N, 62° 05' 55.79147184 E.
Nīmrūz Province. 2 km to the north of Sangar, 8 km south-west of Zīyārat-i Amīrān Sāhib.

Description: Some ruin fields, possibly a part of the Sangar remains.

Fieldwork: Fischer, Bonn University—survey.

Source: Fischer 1973c: 146—map reference.

564. KHARŪTI TEPE
Or HAROTE TEPE.

Original: Lat. 36° 41' N, long. 68° 49' E. Map 32.
Revised: 36.68155276 N, 68.81442268 E /
36° 40' 53.58992700 N, 68° 48' 51.92165556 E.
Qundūz Province. C.1 km north-east of Durman Tepe, 7 km south-west of Qundūz, to the south of the road to Tāshqurghān.

Description: A small artificial mound, c.3 m high.

Fieldwork: 1963 Mizuno and Odani, Kyoto University—survey.

Source: Mizuno and Odani 1968: 96—mention.

565. KHARWAR
Or KHURWAR or KĀFIR SHAHR or KĀFIR KŌT.

Original: Lat. 34° 43' N, long. 68° 52' E. Map 82.
Revised: 33.67236929 N, 68.92372916 E /
33° 40' 20.52945840 N, 68° 55' 25.42495800 E.
Ghazni Province. An extensive plain c.40 km north-east of Ghazni on the route to Charkh-i Lōgar in the upper Lōgar Valley.

Dates: Kushan, 1st–3rd cent; Sasanian-Turk, 5th–7th cent. (stylistic).

Description: Ruins of a large town and extensive area of Buddhist remains covering some 30 km², where many coins were found in the 19th century. Following extensive looting in recent years, investigations revealed the remains of numerous stupa-monastery complexes that contained many stucco Buddhist sculptures and other important art objects. Reports state that a number of the structures are several storeys high. It is reported to be one of the largest, most extensive and most important Buddhist sites in Afghanistan. Discoveries include wooden fragments dated to AD 2nd–3rd century, seven 'clay' heads from AD 5th–7th century (now in the National Museum), and parts of the feet of an enormous (standing) statue, possibly of Buddha. The area has been extensively looted.

An area of interest was the 'Buddhist Temple' consisting of a cylindrical tower type building about halfway up a mountain. Half of it was caved in, and locals in a nearby village told us the Taliban have tried to destroy it. Another area of interest was a sort of plateau feature located about 100 m on the northern side of the main river that runs through the valley. The plateau had many indented features in it that looked like collapsed cave openings. To me these caves looked intentionally destroyed and had been for some time.

Collections: National Museum—clay heads.

Fieldwork: 2003 Verardi and Paparatti, IsIAO/National Geographic—survey.

Sources:
1. Additional information by Mike Mantia.

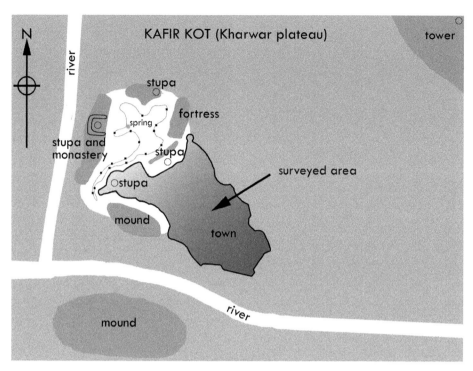

565 Kharwar (after Paparatti and Tilia in Verardi 2007).

2. Burnes 1843: 267 — report from hearsay.
3. Caspani and Cagnacci 1951: 227 — mention.
4. Verardi 2007: 239–48 — results of a brief survey, with a plans and photos.
5. Ball 2008: 234 — summary.
6. Filigenzi and Giunta 2015: 82–3 — mention of the Italian survey and photo showing the illicit excavations.

566. KHATIF

Original: Lat. 33° 27' N, long. 64° 37' E. Maps 55, 74.
Revised: 33.44315196 N, 64.62402887 E /
33° 26' 35.34705384 N, 64° 37' 26.50393164 E.
Ghūr Province. 33 km east of Taiwāra on the route to Yamān.

Description: Large numbers of artificial mounds — said to number thousands — with many ruins on top. There are reports of many more in the vicinity.

Fieldwork: 1946 Kohzad, HSA — survey.

Source: Kohzad 1951–4, 9/1: 28 — mention.

567. KHAWĀL

Lat. 36° 12' N, long. 68° 04' E. Map 30.
Samangān Province. On the west bank of the Khulm River, *c.*15 km south of Haibak.

Description: An artificial cave of uncertain date or function. It is high up in the cliff face and has a mud-brick wall across the opening.

Fieldwork: 1960 Hayashi and Sahara, Kyoto University — survey.

Source: Hayashi and Sahara 1962: 42 — photo and description in Japanese.

KHAWAR. See 2125 KHAWAR in Supplement.

KHAWĀT. See 1229 WARDAK.

KHAZANI. See 591 KHWĀJA GHALTĀN.

568. KHAZ TEPE

Original: Lat. 36° 48' N, long. 66° 44' E. Map 26.
Revised: 36.80354396 N, 66.74201589 E /
36° 48' 12.75826032 N, 66° 44' 31.25721300 E.
Balkh Province. 15 km north-west of this town, about 1 km north of the road to Āqcha, south of the village of Farari.

Description: Rectangular platform (130 × 140 m), slightly sunken in the centre, low (6 m).

Fieldwork:
1. 1886 Maitland, ABC — topographical exploration.
2. 1948 Le Berre, DAFA — survey.

Sources:
1. Le Berre: 1948 unpublished report, DAFA archives, tépé P. 48.
2. Maitland 1888b: 193 – mention.

KHIARZĀR. See 2126 KHIARZĀR in Supplement.

KHILGIAN. See 2141 KILLIGĀN in Supplement.

KHISĀR. See 875 QAL'A-I QAISĀR.

569. KHISHT TEPE
Or KHUSH TEPE (the 'TREASURE OF QUN-DUZ' or 'QUNDUZ HOARD'). See also 930 QUNDŪZ.

Original: Lat. 36° 57' N, long. 68° 05' E. Map 30.
Revised: 36.94462879 N, 68.08702928 E /
36° 56' 40.66364760 N, 68° 05' 13.30540980 E.
Qundūz Province. On the left bank of the Āmū Daryā, about 18 km downstream from its confluence with the Qundūz River. The site is found on an advance of the embankment, between the villages of Bāgicha and Khisht Tepe; it is occupied by a small modern fort, visible from afar (Tahana-i Khush Tepe).

Dates: Lithic? (a fragment of worked stone); Graeco-Bactrian, 3rd–2nd cent. BC (numismatic); Kushan and Hunnic-Turk, 1st cent. BC–9th cent.; pre-Mongol Islamic, 10th–13th cent.; Timurid, 15th–16th cent. (ceramic).

Description: Platform rising 3 m above the level of the plain, dominated in the north by a raised hillock of 5 m which overlooks the Āmū Daryā, directly 15 m below (the height of the natural terrace above the river is about 8 m). The platform follows in the north the contours of the curved advance of the terrace (east–west width *c.*100 m); it widens towards the south, up to 100 m from the river, thus covering a trapezoidal area of about 1.5 hectare, gently sloping towards the plain. The cuts in the cliff of the Āmū Daryā, to the north, reveal the calcareous base from which the site rises. Similar calcareous formations are visible on the opposite bank of the river, in Soviet territory, also used, it appears, for habitation sites; the nearest of these sites is found at about 100 m upriver, on the right bank. Piles for an ancient bridge were noted, visible on the right bank when the waters are low; but perhaps these are natural formations, as above, the river being very wide at this point. The surface of the platform is flat, without any apparent structures, but strewn with stones and fired bricks, as well as sherds; the steep mound which dominates in the north (oriented east–west, 30 × 20 m; geodesic marker on the top), where the heaps of stones are particularly dense: probable remains of an ancient fort reported in the 19th cent. by Maitland.

A treasure of 628 pieces of silver (the 'Qundūz treasure') was found on the site in 1946; it consists mainly of Graeco-Bactrian tetradrachmas.

Collections: National Museum – coin treasure; sherds.

Fieldwork:
1. 1886 Maitland, ABC – topographical exploration.
2. 1962 Le Berre, DAFA – trial excavation.
3. 1978 Gardin et al., CNRS – survey.

Sources:
1. Site information by J.-C. Gardin.
2. Holdich 1886: 5 – mentions remains.
3. Holdich 1887: 36 – mentions the remains of a bridge.
4. Maitland 1888b: 253–4 – brief description.
5. Bivar 1954d – brief note on the discovery of the hoard, including descriptions and illustrations of some of the coins and a complete inventory.
6. Bivar 1955a – description and discussion of the hoard, with detailed descriptions and photos of 54 of the coins.
7. Ramachandran and Sharma 1956: III. 1–3 – lists and illustrates the kings depicted on the coins.
8. Curiel and Fussman 1965 – inventory, catalogue of the monograms, photos, and discussion of the hoard.
9. Le Berre 1965 – summary description of the site, the citadel, and the pottery. No drawings.
10. N. Dupree 1967a: 104 – mentions the hoard.
11. Jenkins 1968: 25–7 – briefly discusses the mintage of the hoard.
12. Rowland and Rice 1971: 5–6 and pls 13–16 – description and photos of some of the coins.
13. Bivar 1972 – refers to the hoard in a discussion of Menander's coinage.
14. N. Dupree et al. 1974: 109 – summary of the hoard.
15. Bernard 1978a: 55 – tentatively identifies the site with Islamic Milla.
16. Gardin and Lyonnet 1978–9: 139 and pl. VI, no. 105 – mention.
17. Gazetteer 1979: IV. 330–1 – summary description of the mound.
18. Guillaume 1991: 8–24 – discusses the Graeco-Bactrian and Indian coins from the Qundūz Hoard.
19. Lyonnet 1997: figs 39, 46, 49. 68, 69 – no. 105.
20. Gardin 1997: 87 – no. 105.
21. Ball 2008: 234–5 – summary.
22. Holt 2012a: 174 and 182 – discusses the reworking of the dies on some of the coins from the hoard.

KHOL SHAMS. See 418 HASHMATKHĀN.

570. KHUDA BAKHSH
Or KHWĀJA CHEHELTĀN.

Lat. 34° 52' N, long. 68° 03' E. Map 58.

Bāmiyān Province. 4 km southwards up the 'Iraq River from its junction with the Shībar River.

Description: A series of caves both sides of the valley.

Fieldwork: 1885–6 Akbar Khan, Amir Khan, ABC—topographical surveys.

Sources:
1. Amir Khan 1888: 184—mention.
2. Akbar Khan 1891: 426—mention.

KHUGIYĀNI. See 782 PĀRCHIWAGĀM.

571. KHŪJAHĀ

Original: Lat. 34° 32' N, long. 69° 00' E. Map 63.
Revised: 34.53507379 N, 69.00682503 E /
34° 32' 06.26565984 N, 69° 00' 24.57009864 E.
Kābul Province. 12 km west of Kot-i Sangi on the outskirts of Kābul, on the road to Paghmān.

Date: Kushan—Hunnic, 1st–6th cent. (architectural).

Description: Remains of many stupa-monastery complexes on the spine of the hill above Khūjahā.

Source: Caspani 1947b: 49—mention.

KHŪJA HASAN. See 595 KHWĀJA HASAN.

572. KHUMDĀN

Lat. 36° 50' N, long. 67° 57' E. Map 29.
Samangān Province. 3.3 km north-east of Chit Rabāt Kuhna at the foot of the ascent towards Khisht Tepe, *c*.28 km north-east of Tāshqurghān.

Description: A small mound.

Fieldwork: 1886 Maitland, ABC—topographical survey.

Source: Maitland 1888b: 261—mention.

573. KHUNDUR

Original: Lat. 34° 13' N, long. 62° 31' E. Map 53.
Revised: 34.21884864 N, 62.45485324 E /
34° 13' 07.85508636 N, 62° 27' 17.47164816 E.
Herat Province. On the southern side of the Harī Rūd Valley, *c*.25 km east of the main Herat-Kandahar road. The turn-off is 12 km south of Herat.

Description: A large mound, well away from any settlement and visible for several miles. There is a spring at its base on the south-west side, and it has traces of clandestine digging. Length is *c*.100 m, height is *c*.10 m. There were no early-looking sherds.

Fieldwork:
1. 1952 Le Berre and Gardin, DAFA—survey.
2. 1974 Swiny, BIAS—survey.

Source: Site information by S. Swiny in unpublished BIAS archive.

574. KHURD KĀBUL

Lat. 34° 23' N, long. 69° 23' E. Map 63.
Kābul Province. 36 km south-east of Kābul and 17 km south of Būtkhāk, on the old route to Jalālābād.

Date: Kushan, 1st cent. (numismatic).

Description: Four or five stupa remains. One, though small, was fairly well preserved and contained two 'Indo-Saka' coins.

Fieldwork: 1834 Masson—excavation.

Sources:
1. Masson 1841: 115—mention.
2. Errington 2017a: 81 and 2017b: 66, 68—the Masson collection and archive relating to the site.

575. KHURD KHAIBAR

Original: Lat. 34° 14' N, long. 71° 01' E. Map 68.
Revised: 34.22285042 N, 71.03267782 E /
34° 13' 22.26152280 N, 71° 01' 57.64016208 E.
Nangahār Province. 18 km north-west of Tūrkhām and 4 km west of Lōya Dakka, on the road to Jalālābād.

Description: Many ancient mounds and caves.

Source: Masson 1842: III. 245—mention.

576. KHURMALIK

Original: Lat. 32° 17' N, long. 62° 28' E. Map 85.
Revised: 32.27604805 N, 62.46792681 E /
32° 16' 33.77299764 N, 62° 28' 04.53653220 E.
Farāh Province. 38 km from this town, on the road to Girishk, near the village of Khurmalik.

Description: Small tepe of conical form, west of the road.

Fieldwork: 1952, Le Berre and Gardin, DAFA—survey.

Source: M. Le Berre: unpublished 1952 report, DAFA archives, tépé Farah-Girishk 2.

577. KHURRAM

Lat. 35° 55' N, long. 68° 00' E. Map 30.
Samangān Province. C.50 km south of Haibak on the Darya-i Khurram, on the route to Rūi Habash.

Description: Local reports of some caves containing bone tools and other objects.

Source: Site information by Jonathan L. Lee.

KHURWAR. See 565 KHARWAR.

578. KHUSHĀB

Lat. 31° 30' N, long. 65° 49' E. Map 89.
Kandahār Province. 19 km south-east of this city.

Dates: Indo-Parthian and Sasanian, 1st–4th cent.; pre-Mongol Islamic, 10th–13th cent. (ceramic).

Description: Rectangular fortress (*c.*45 × 60 m), with bastions in the south and west.

Fieldwork: 1951 J.-M. Casal, DAFA—survey.

Source: J.-M. Casal: unpublished 1951 report, DAFA archives.

579. KHUSH BAI

Original: Lat. 36° 46' N, long. 69° 29' E. Maps 35, 36.
Revised:
36.76687969 N, 69.47385728 E / 36° 46' 00.76688004 N, 69° 28' 25.88622564 E (A).
36.76523744 N, 69.4842745 E / 36° 45' 54.85477320 N, 69° 29' 03.38819100 E (B).
Takhār Province. 7 km north-west of Tāluqān, accessible by the road which runs along the foothills of the plain of the same name, on the left bank of the Rūd-i Shāhrawān; the tepes are near this road, on the north side (A at 250 m, B at 500 m). The closest group of houses appears on the 1:100,000 map as part of the village of Kunchi; but the inhabitants of the place consider them to belong to the village of Sasmaq.

Dates: Late Chalcolithic–Early Bronze Age, *c.*3500–2500 BC (A); Middle Bronze Age, *c.*2500–1500 BC (A, B); Achaemenid, 6th–4th cent. BC; Hellenistic, 3rd–1st cent. BC (B); Kushan, 1st–4th cent. (B); Hunnic-Turk, 5th–9th cent. (A); some Islamic sherds (ceramic).

Description: (A) Group of mounds aligned west-north-west/east-south-east over 500 m, at the foot of the slopes which edge the route from Tāluqān to Cha'ila: (a) the furthest west is an oblong north-east/south-west mound (60 × 25 m), 5–6 m high with top at the north-east extremity (10 m); *zīyārat* to the south-west. 20 m towards the west, smaller parallel mound (30 × 20 m), flat (height 4–5 m), separated from the preceding one by a field; the two mounds most probably constituted one in the past. (b) Some 50 m to the east-south-east, rectangular platform north-west/south-east (60 × 40 m), average height 5 m with highest part (8 m) in the west, occupied by a modern cemetery (*zīyārat*). (c) 50 m further, to the east-south-east, similar mound north-west/south-east (200 × 80 m), average height 2–3 m, with high part (8 m) to the west; modern cemetery. On the north face, in section, pockets of ashes with sherds, bones, and broken, burnt pebbles. This line of mounds close together continues towards the east-south-east, up to the edges of the next tepe. (B) Rectangular mound north-west/south-east (80 × 30 m), flat top (height 3 m), steep flanks cut into by cultivation (cotton), where sherds are found in abundance, especially towards the north-east; burnt layers visible on the east face.

Collection: National Museum/AIA—sherds.

Fieldwork: 1977 Gardin et al., CNRS—survey.

Sources:
1. Site information by J.-C. Gardin.
2. Gardin and Lyonnet 1978–9: pl. IX—nos. 225, 233.
3. Lyonnet 1981—brief description of site, description, discussion, and illustration of the chalcolithic (mid-4th–mid-3rd mill.) pottery, and discussion of the geographical and historical implications.
4. Lyonnet 1997: figs 7, 13, 21–5, 35–37—nos. 225, 233.
5. Gardin 1998: 69—nos. 225, 233.

580. KHUSH GILDI

Includes ARAB TEPE.
Original: Lat. 37° 05'–37° 06' N, long. 68° 55'–68° 56' E. Map 34.
Revised: 37.10451051 N, 69.42879702 E / 37° 06' 16.23783672 N, 69° 25' 43.66926444 E.
Takhār Province. North of Khwāja Ghar on the road to Imām Sāhib, up to the bridge on the Rūd-i Shāhrawān, in the village of Khush Gildi, then by the roads leaving this bridge (right bank) towards the two following tepes: (A) one is 700 m east of the bridge, by a road edging the first canal coming from the Rūd-i Shāhrawān, right bank, from Khwāja Ghar; (B) the other lies 3 km north-east of the bridge, by a road which borders the right bank of this water course, then that of a second canal, towards Jau Gadi. These two tepes are in the process of being levelled by the irrigated crops, already the cause of the disappearance of many other tepes in the plain of Khwāja Ghar, the villagers confirm; their importance lies in the provision of information on the periods when the plain was populated, which will soon be lost.

Dates: Hephtalo-Turk, 5th–9th cent. (A); Islamic, not defined (B) (ceramic).

Description: (A) Rectangular east–west mound (30 × 20 m), only 0.5 m high, the remains of a tepe 'taller than a man' razed about five years ago, according to the villagers (1978). (B) Place-name Arab Tepe: square north-west platform (80 × 80 m), also hardly visible under the poplars and under the houses which today cover most of it.

Collection: National Museum/AIA—sherds.

Fieldwork: 1977 Gardin et al., CNRS—survey.

Sources:

1. Site information by J.-C. Gardin.
2. Gardin and Lyonnet 1978–9: pl. IV—nos. 1, 284.
3. Gardin 1980—describes in general terms the survey in the Khwāja Ghar area.
4. Lyonnet 1997: figs 68, 69—nos. 1, 284.
5. Gardin 1998: 49, pl. IV—nos. 1, 284.

581. KHUSHKĀBA

Original: Lat. 31° 40' N, long. 64° 39' E. Map 86.
Revised: 31.67017852 N, 64.65595007 E /
31° 40' 12.64266084 N, 64° 39' 21.42026460 E.
Helmand Province. C.5 km north of the Arghandāb River, 20 km south-east of Girishk, and 8 km west of Bālā Khāna.

Description: A mound.

Source: Bellew 1874: 169—mention.

582. KHUSH TEPE
Or FULLOL.

Lat. 36° 11' N, long. 69° 19' E. Map 37.
Baghlān Province. South-east of the village of Fullol on the road to Khost Farang, near the village of Sai Hazāra, at the junction of the Khost and Sai Valleys.

Date: Bronze Age, 2600–1700 BC (stylistic).

Description: A high mound, 14 × 18 m in area and 20 m in height. In 1966 there was an accidental discovery of a treasure consisting of gold and silver vessels. They are both plain and decorated with motifs such as the bearded bull, the serpent, and the vulture, reminiscent of contacts in Mesopotamia and Baluchistan. Subsequent excavations revealed a flexed burial, prehistoric in nature, but without any pottery.

Collection: National Museum—treasure.

Fieldwork:

1. 1966 Wardak, National Museum—excavations.
2. 1975 Kohl—survey.

Sources:

1. Dupree, Gouin, and Omer 1971—describe the discovery of the treasure, with photos and drawings of the objects.
2. Tosi and Wardak 1972—discuss the treasure and its implications in terms of trade contacts, with photos and drawings of the objects.
3. Dales 1973a: 126–7—very brief summary.
4. N. Dupree et al. 1974: summary of the discovery and description of the objects on display in the National Museum.

5. Deshayes 1977: 103–6—discusses the evidence of the treasure for widespread trade connections throughout western Asia in the Bronze Age.
6. Kohl 1978: 63–4—brief summary.
7. Dupree 1981: 108–9 and pls. 21–2—discusses implications of treasure for trade. Photos of objects found in the Kābul bazaar, probably originating from Khush Tepe.
8. Maxwell-Hyslop 1982—discusses the date and art-historical connections of each of the gold and silver pieces, then discusses the evidence of the hoard for identifying Afghanistan with Meluhha. Concludes with a date of c.2110–2003 BC for the hoard.
9. Tissot 2006: 12–14—National Museum catalogue detail and photoss.
10. Cambon and Jarrige 2006, 2007—discussion of the treasure in the context of the wider Bronze Age and catalogue of the objects in a touring exhibition.
11. Vidale 2017: 11–17—discusses a previously unpublished silver cup in relation to the Fullol treasure.

KHUSH TEPE, Imām Sāhib. See 1179 TEPE SALA.

KHUSH TEPE, Qundūz. See 569 KHISHT TEPE.

KHUSH TEPE, Qūzi. See 943 QŪZI.

583. KHUSTI QISHLĀQ
Or DORĀHI or PASHA KHĀNA. Includes QUL TEPE and RUSTAM TEPE.

Original: Lat. 36° 46' N, long. 69° 23' E. Maps 35, 36.
Revised:
36.77584414 N, 69.39330687 E / 36° 46' 33.03889536 N, 69° 23' 35.90473236 E (A).
36.77621843 N, 69.3890407 E / 36° 46' 34.38635484 N, 69° 23' 20.54653728 E (B).
Takhār Province. About 13 km west of Tāluqān, by the road that links this town to Khwāja Ghar, and which formerly forked at this place towards Khānābād (old road), after having forded a water course (called Shoratu) coming from the Rūd-i Shāhrawān. The two tepes are situated on the edges of this deeply cut water course, one on the left bank (A), the other on the right bank (B).

Dates: Middle Bronze Age, c.2500–1500 BC; beg. Iron, end 2nd mill.–beg. 1st mill. BC (A); Achaemenid, 6th–4th cent. BC (A); Kushan and Hunnic-Turk, 1st–9th cent. (B); pre-Mongol Islamic, 10th–13th cent. and Timurid, 15th–16th cent. (ceramic).

Description: (A) On a cliff eroded by a bend in the water course of the Shoratu, a crescent-shaped mound, oriented east–west (100 × 20 m), cut back in the south by cotton fields where sherds are abundant; a flat top (height 4 m), covered by a *zīyārat* and a cemetery which prevent for the moment the complete disappearance of the site. On the cuts of the south face, thick ashy layers with bones and and fragments of burnt jars, 1 m below the surface; on the north face, directly above the cliff, the thickness of the archaeological layer does not seem to be more than 2.5 m; traces of walls in place, in mud-brick. (B) Qul Tepe: On the edge of the cliff which overlooks the water course of Shoratu by about 8 m (right bank), rectangular platform (*c*.150 × 80 m), mainly oriented east–west; flat top, about 8 m above the level of the plain, with a depression in the east part, occupied by a modern cemetery. In the natural cuts of the cliff, archaeological layers visible in a thickness of about 4 m; ashes, charcoal, walls in *pakhsa* and mud-brick, bone debris, jars in place.

Collection: National Museum/AIA—sherds.

Fieldwork:
1. 1955 and 1960 Fischer, DAAD—survey.
2. 1975 Kohl—survey.
3. 1977 Gardin et al., CNRS—survey.

Sources:
1. Site information by J.-C. Gardin.
2. Fischer 1969: 350—brief description.
3. Gardin and Lyonnet 1978–9: pl. IX—nos. 240–1.
4. Kohl 1978: 64—brief description of Rustam Tepe.
5. Lyonnet 1997: figs 13, 21–4, 49, 68, 69—nos. 240, 241.
6. Gardin 1998: 71—nos. 240–1.

584. KHŪZYĀNI

Lat. 32° 08' N, long. 61° 55' E. Map 83.
Farāh Province. On the west bank of the Farāh Rūd, *c*.30 km south-west of Farāh on the road to Lāsh Juwain. The site of 3 km south of the village of Khūzyāni.

Description: A ruined Islamic building measuring *c*.75 × 50 m.

Fieldwork: 1949 Fairservis, AMNH—survey.

Source: Fairservis 1961: 40—mention.

585. KHWĀJA 'ABDUL HAQ WALI

Original: Lat. 34° 19' N, long. 61° 51' E. Map 52.
Revised: 34.30632881 N, 61.84186571 E /
34° 18' 22.78370196 N, 61° 50' 30.71655420 E.
Herat Province. 9 km to the south-east of Zindajān on the road to Zīyāratgāh.

Description: An area of ruins, one of which is a complex of indeterminate date known as Khwāja 'Abdul Haq Wali. The ruins consist of a mosque, a cistern, a tomb, many mounds, some miscellaneous ruins, and many graves. The mosque is 7.50 m square and consists of a dome-chamber fronted by an iwān. The dome and *iwān* is of baked brick construction; the remainder is mud-brick, except for baked brick quoining. The interior is plastered and painted.

The cistern is of baked brick and stone construction, and is entered by an *iwān* flanked by double-storey cells.

Fieldwork: 1978–9 Samizay, Kābul University/UNESCO—survey.

Source: Samizay 1981: 34–5—good description with a plan and photos of the remains.

586. KHWĀJA 'ALI

Lat. 30° 22' N, long. 63° 11' E. Map 98.
Helmand Province. On the south bank of the Helmand, *c*.25 km south-west of Daishu.

Description: A mound and a ruined tower surrounded by a surface scatter of pottery. There are no other buildings.

Source: Bellew 1874: 197–8—mention.

KHWĀJA ĀLI SEHYAKA. See 2127 in Supplement.

587. KHWĀJA BANDI KUSHA

Original: Lat. 36° 19' N, long. 69° 18' E. Map 37.
Revised: 36.33260721 N, 69.30700437 E /
36° 19' 57.38595024 N, 69° 18' 25.21572804 E.
Takhār Province. 6 km south–south-west of Ishkamīsh, by a track which leads to the place called Khwāja Bandi Kusha, famous for its springs. These flow in abundance at the foot of the mountainous spur where the track stops; they produce streams which flow towards the north, across a marshy zone, to form with the water from other sources the Rūd-i Ishkamīsh. The tepe of Khwāja Bandi Kusha lies 500 m north of the most eastern spring.

Date: Pre-Mongol Islamic, 10th–13th cent. (ceramic).

Description: Square platform (50 × 50 m), oriented northwest/south-east, rounded angles, height 3 m, with a raised mound in the centre (6 m), and another lower one at the northern angle (4 m).

Collection: National Museum/AIA—sherds.

Fieldwork:
1. 1960–8 Fischer, University of Bonn—survey.
2. 1978 Gardin et al., CNRS—survey.

Sources:
1. Site information by J.-C. Gardin.
2. Fischer 1969: 352—cited as Tepe B9.
3. Gardin and Lyonnet 1978–9: pl. XI—no. 390.
4. Gardin 1998: 100—no. 390.

KHWĀJA BRAHNE. See 2128 KHWĀJA BRAHNE in Supplement.

588. KHWĀJA BUGHRA

Original: Lat. 34° 35' N, long. 69° 10' E. Map 63.
Revised: 34.57571125 N, 69.16558909 E /
34° 34' 32.56050144 N, 69° 09' 56.12072976 E.
Kābul Province. Between the Wazīrābād marsh and the
hills behind the airport, 2–3 km west of the southern foot
of the Pā-i Minār Pass.

Description: A large mound.

Source: Masson 1842: III. 147—mention.

KHWĀJA CHEHELTĀN. See 570 KHUDA BAKHSH.

589. KHWĀJA DO KUH

Lat. 36° 49' N, long. 65° 37' E. Map 24.
Faryāb Province. 20 km north-west of Shībarghān, to the
east of the road to Andkhūī.

Date: Neolithic, 7th–6th mill. BC (lithic).

Description: A surface scatter of lithics. A heap of baked
bricks also marks the site of a caravanserai.

Fieldwork:
1. 1886 Peacocke, ABC—topographical survey.
2. 1969 Vinogradov, Af/Sov. Mission—survey.

Sources:
1. Peacocke 1887a: 291—mentions the brick scatter.
2. Vinogrdov 1979: 22—mentions the lithics (Site 51).

590. KHWĀJA DO KUH NAU

Lat. 36° 50' N, long. 65° 34' E. Map 24.
Faryāb Province. 25 km north-west of Shībarghān, to the
south of the road to Andkhūī, 5 km further on from Khwāja
do kuh.

Date: Neolithic, 7th–6th mill. BC.

Description: A surface site.

Fieldwork: 1969 Vinogradov, Af/Sov. Mission—survey.

Source: Vinogradov 1979: 22—mention (Site 52).

KHWĀJA GACHAI. See 2130 in Supplement.

591. KHWĀJA GHALTĀN
Includes KHAZANI.

Original: Lat. 36° 43' N, long. 68° 56' E. Map 85.
Revised:
59136.71858127 N, 68.92856639 E / 36° 43' 06.89256300 N,
68° 55' 42.83900256 E (A).

59136.72337709 N, 68.92895736 E / 36° 43' 24.15752004 N,
68° 55' 44.24648880 E (B).
59136.72376598 N, 68.92735042 E / 36° 43' 25.55751216 N,
68° 55' 38.46150264 E (B).
59136.72400544 N, 68.92997896 E / 36° 43' 26.41958832 N,
68° 55' 47.92426788 E (B).
59136.72865112 N, 68.92626685 E / 36° 43' 43.14402264 N,
68° 55' 34.56064812 E (C).
Qundūz Province. At about 5 km to the east of Qundūz, on
the western outskirts of the village of Khwāja Ghaltān: group
of tepes in the process of disappearing, in the rice fields that
tend to cover all the plain of Qundūz (1978). (A) The tepe
furthest to the south corresponds to the mound of 6 m indicated on the 1:100,000 map. (B) Three others, 600–700 m
further north, form a compact group also indicated on the
map (mounds of 7 m). (C) The fifth is 500 m to the north-west
of this group, in the eastern outskirts of the hamlet of Khazani.

Dates: Kushan and Hunnic-Turk, 1st–9th cent. (B, C); pre-
Mongol Islamic, 10th–13th cent. and Timurid, 15th–16th
cent. (ceramic).

Description: (A) Shapeless mound cut back by the crops
(cotton on the low parts, rice in the plain below), present
surface about 30 × 30 m; flat top (threshing floor), height
2 m. (B) Three mounds close together (80 to 100 m), in a
triangle, also eaten into by the rice fields: present surface of
each c.20 × 20 m, flat tops, height 2.5–3 m. In a cut of one of
these (the furthest south), east face, burnt layers containing
bone remains. (C) T-shaped mound, cut into by crops
(rice), present surface 50 m (east–west) × 40 m (north–
south); flat top (1–2 m), with higher hillocks to the north
(4 m) and the south-east (3 m).

Collection: National Museum/AIA—sherds.

Fieldwork:
1. Hayashi and Sahara, University of Kyoto—survey.
2. 1978 Gardin et al., CNRS—survey.

Sources:
1. Site information by J.-C. Gardin.
2. Hayashi and Sahara 1962: 74–5—summary in Japanese:
   description of the site and the pottery.
3. Gardin and Lyonnet 1978–9: pl. VII—nos. 453–7.
4. Lyonnet 1997: figs 49, 68, 69—nos. 453–7.
5. Gardin 1998: 78—nos. 453–7.

592. KHWĀJAGHĀR

Original: Lat. 34° 50'–34° 51' N. 67° 50' E. Map 58.
Revised: 34° 49' 59.988" N, 67° 49' 59.988" E.
Bāmiyān Province. Valley of the Bāmiyān river (Darya-i
Pahlawānsang): in the lateral valley of the Darya-i Khwāja-
ghār, to the north.

Date: Turk or pre-Mongol Islamic, 7th–9th cent.
(architecture).

Description: Ruins of three badly eroded small forts.

Fieldwork: 1974–5 Le Berre, DAFA—survey.

Source: Le Berre 1987: 82–3, pl. 108– itinerary B2, Darya-i Khwājaghār, ruins 1 to 3; brief description and photos.

KHWĀJA GIRUKI ZIRAYAT. See 2131 KHWĀJA GIRUKI ZIRAYAT in Supplement.

593. KHWĀJA GUL BARDAR
Or DALWARJĪN.

Original: Lat. 36° 50N, long. 66° 39' E. Map 26.
Revised: 36.82672074 N, 66.65641898 E /
36° 49' 36.19465716 N, 66° 39' 23.10833808 E.
Balkh Province. 14 km east of Nimlik, and north of the road to Balkh, 200 m south of the village of Dalwarjīn.

Description: Large circular enclosure, diam. *c.*140 m; terre-plein on two levels, height 15 m, surrounded by a deep ditch.

Fieldwork: 1948 Le Berre, DAFA—survey.

Source: M. Le Berre: unpublished 1948 report, DAFA archives, tépé P. 41.

594. KHWĀJA HĀFIZ

Original: Lat. 37° 29' N, long. 69° 39' E. Map 34.
Revised: 37.48203666 N, 69.65424352 E /
37° 28' 55.33198968 N, 69° 39' 15.27666012 E.
Takhār Province. 1 km east of the village of Khwāja Hāfiz, on a promontory of the high terrace of the Āmū Daryā formed by its confluence with the Rūd-i Jilga-i Yangi Qal'a.

Dates: Achaemenid, 6th–4th cent. BC; Hellenistic, 3rd–1st cent. BC. (B); Kushan and Hunnic-Turk, 1st–9th cent. (A); Timurid, 15th–16th cent. (ceramic).

Description: The orientation of the promontory is determined by that of the two water courses: north-north-west/south-south-east, Āmū Daryā side: north-north-east/south-south-west Jilga side. Study of the terrain shows that recently—'in human memory', according to the villagers—the Jilga cut a more direct passage towards the Āmū Daryā, by a gully which cuts the promontory in an east-north-east/south-south-west direction, the old course only being used as a secondary arm for feeding certain canals. It is on this triangular 'islet' thus formed that traces of ancient occupation were found. (A) The main vestiges, at the southern end, consist of a large fortified site, fed by water from a canal whose traces can be followed to the north-east up to the right bank of the Jilga (this canal was cut by the recently formed gully mentioned above; it is visible in section at the top of the cliffs of this gully, on the two banks). The site is in the shape of an irregular north–south lozenge, determined by the relief: the south

top is the extremity of the promontory described above, the south-west and south-east sides are the cliffs turned towards the Āmū Daryā and towards the old course of the Jilga, respectively, while the north-west and north-east sides are formed by an enclosure which closes the only access possible, by the north. The dimensions of the lozenge are about 400 m for the north–south axis, and 250 m for the largest east–west width. Along all the length of the south-east side (about 300 m), a natural mound about 80 m wide constitutes the 'high town', dominating the terrace by some 10 m; the top is flat, no structures are clearly visible, but there is no lack of sherds, of all periods (Achaemenid, Kushan, Islamic). The lower town, on the contrary, is undulating, with several little hillocks in the western part; it is crossed from north to south by the canal mentioned above. Of the enclosure, finally, there remains only a talus

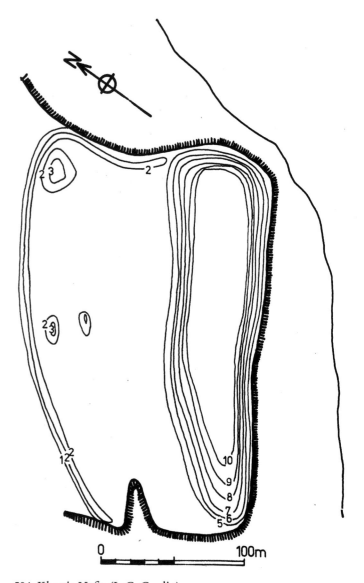

594 Khwāja Hāfiz (J.-C. Gardin).

2 m high, 6–8 m wide at the base, narrow at the top; a gap situated around the middle of the north-west segment suggests the possible location of a gate. (B) 500 m to the north-west of this 'gate', the western end is occupied by a less spectacular but older site, like those found more to the north on the same terrace edge (cf. nos. 515 and 516). It consists of a low hillock (diam. 6 m, height 0.5 m), around which many sherds lie scattered up to 50 m.

Collection: National Museum/AIA—sherds.

Fieldwork: 1978 Gardin et al., CNRS—survey.

Sources:
1. Site information by J.-C. Gardin.
2. Gardin and Lyonnet 1978–9: pl. II—nos. 546–7.
3. Gardin 1980—describes in general terms the survey in the Yangi Qal'a area.
4. Gardin 1995: 85–6—brief description and plan.
5. Lyonnet 1997: figs 25, 35, 49, 49, 68, 69—nos. 546, 547.
6. Gardin 1998: 37—nos. 546–7.

595. KHWĀJA HASAN
Or KHŪJA HASAN.

Lat. 31° 12' N, long. 64° 12' E. Map 97.
Helmand Province. On the east bank of the Helmand, near Khair Kūh, 6 km north of Darwīshān.

Dates: Bronze Age, 3rd mill. BC; Indo-Parthian, 1st–3rd cent.; Sasanian, 3rd–7th cent.; Timurid, 15th–16th cent. (ceramic).

Description: A mound and an Islamic cemetery on a bluff overlooking the river. A Buddhist stupa nearly destroyed by a substantial later *zīyārat* constructed over it. Dating is problematic here, as much of the material is stone and ceramic transported from elsewhere to decorate the graves. There is a large Islamic cemetery to the east of this *zīyārat* at the edge of the bluff, and one can find wares from the 3rd mill. BC onward on the graves.

Fieldwork:
1. 1966 Hammond, Cambridge University—survey.
2. 1966, 1971–4 Trousdale, Smithsonian—survey.

Sources:
1. Site information by W. Trousdale.
2. Hammond 1970: 449—lists site (no. 14) and discusses the pottery and general survey results.

596. KHWĀJA ISKANDAR

Original: Lat. 36° 22' N, long. 66° 53' E. Map 28.
Revised: 36.36942767 N, 66.91750289 E /
36° 22' 09.93961704 N, 66° 55' 03.01041948 E.
Balkh Province. On the west bank of the Balkhāb 23 km south of Chashma-i Shafā on the road to Āq Kupruk.

Description: A mound with a small building on top.
Fieldwork: 1885 Maitland, ABC—topographical survey.
Source: Maitland 1888b: 69—mention.

KHWĀJA JĪR. See **2132 KHWĀJA JĪR** in Supplement.

597. KHWĀJA KANUR
Or SULTAN BĀBĀ ZĪYĀRAT.
See also 736 MUKHTĀR.

Lat. 31 29 N, long. 64° 23 E. Map 86.
Helmand Province. On the south bank of the Arghandāb, just above the confluence with the Helmand. (Note erroneous location in previous edition.)

Dates: Hellenistic-Parthian, 3rd–1st cent. BC (stylistic); early Islamic, 8th–13th cent. (ceramic).

Description: The very eroded foundations of a sanctuary. The area is covered in limestone fluted columns and balustrade fragments, thousands of terracotta figurines, and architectural fragments of a large terracotta frieze of Hellenized busts and acanthus leaves.

It should also be noted here that Sultan Bābā Zīyārat is not a site: it is a small modern *zīyārat* 1 km to the south of Khwāja Kanur. The few pieces of glazed Islamic ceramic are simply grave decoration at Khwāja Kanur, as are all the other remains. All the finds from this high ridge come from another site—Mokhatar—and are simply transported to Khwāja Kanur by nomads to decorate graves.

Fieldwork:
1. 1960–70 Fischer, Bonn University—survey.
2. 1971–4 Trousdale, Smithsonian Institution—survey.

Sources:
1. Site information provided by W. Trousdale.
2. Fischer et al. 1974–6: 30–1—brief description (as Sultan Bābā Zīyārat), with drawings and photos of the column fragments.
3. Trousdale 1976a: 58—brief description.
4. Ball 2008: 235—summary.

KHWĀJA KAURĀTI. See **2133 KHWĀJA KAURĀTI** in Supplement.

KHWĀJA KINTI. See **2134 KHWĀJA KINTI** in Supplement.

KHWĀJA KUNDU. See **2135 KHWĀJA KUNDU** in Supplement.

598. KHWĀJA LAKAN

Original: Lat. 34° 33' N, long. 68° 57' E. Map 63.
Revised: 34.56007016 N, 68.96578471 E /
34° 33' 36.25258932 N, 68° 57' 56.82494124 E.
Kābul Province. 5 km south of Paghmān, between Baiktūt and Khūjahā.

Description: A number of artificial mounds.

Source: Caspani 1947b: 48 — mention.

KHWĀJA LANGĀR. See 2136 KHWĀJA LANGĀR in Supplement.

599. KHWĀJA MUHAMMAD SHURĀB

Original: Lat. 33° 42' N, long. 62° 43' E. Map 70.
Revised: 33.71459612 N, 62.67787994 E /
33° 42' 52.54603560 N, 62° 40' 40.36778688 E.
Herat Province. C.80 km south-east of Herat, 5 km west of Karaucha.

Description: A shrine and some ruins.

Source: Gazetteer 1975: III. 270 — mention.

600. KHWĀJA MUSAFFAR

Original: Lat. 34° 33' N, long. 69° 00' E. Map 63.
Revised: 34.54841752 N, 68.99848252 E /
34° 32' 54.30308892 N, 68° 59' 54.53705940 E.
Kābul Province. 14 km west of Kot-i Sangi on the outskirts of Kābul, just to the north of the southern road to Paghmān.

Date: Kushan, 1st–4th cent. (ceramic).

Description: A number of artificial mounds and an extensive later cemetery.

Source: Caspani 1947b: 48–9 — mention.

601. KHWĀJA NAKHI
  See also 486 KADAH.

Original: Lat. 31° 21' N, long. 62° 17' E. Map 84.
Revised: 31.34792357 N, 62.27941751 E /
31° 20' 52.52484984 N, 62° 16' 45.90304680 E.
Nīmrūz Province. 2 km south-west of Kadah and 31 km north-east of Chakhānsūr, to the west of the Khāshrūd.

Date: Safarid, 9th cent. (architectural).

Description: Many very ruined walls and buildings covering a vast area. It is dominated by huge mud-brick fortifications, surrounded by earthworks and a shallow moat. Inside is a palace area, the main building preserving a decorated façade. Possibly the site of ancient Qarnein.

Fieldwork: 1969 Fischer, Bonn University — survey.

Sources:
1. Le Strange 1905: 343 — summary of the historical references for Qarnein.
2. Fischer 1969–70 — photo.
3. Fischer 1970a — photos.
4. Fischer 1971b: 45 — photo and brief description (Site 36).
5. Fischer 1971c: 47–8 — brief description and photo.
6. Fischer et al. 1974–6: 257 — mention.
7. Ball 2008: 235 — summary.

KHWĀJA QĀSIM. See 2137 KHWĀJA QĀSIM in Supplement.

KHWĀJA PAHLAWĀN. See 89 BAHĀRAK and ŪCH ĀRIQĀRIQ.

602. KHWĀJA RAWĀSH

Lat. 34° 33' N, Long. 69° 13' E. Map 61.
Kābul Province. Immediately to the east of the Kābul Airport terminal.

Description: An artificial mound with the remains of a tower on top.

Source: Gazetteer 1910: IV. 302 — mention.

603. KHWĀJA RIA BĀBĀ

Lat. 33° 29' N, long. 62° 16' E. Map 70.
Farāh Province. About 100 km south of Herat, in the place called Zīyārat-i Khwāja Ria Bābā, on either side of the Shindand road.

Description: West of the road, ruins of a qal'a? To the east, another small ruin. Nearby, on a rocky outcrop, a *zīyārat*. Bridge and water point.

Fieldwork: 1952 Le Berre and Gardin, DAFA — survey.

Source: M. Le Berre: unpublished 1952 report, DAFA Archives, tépé Herat-Shindand 8.

KHWĀJA RUSHNĀI, Balkh. See 69 BĀBĀ RUSHNAI.

604. KHWĀJA RUSHNAI, BALKH-KILIFT

Original: Lat. 36° 55' N, long. 66° 36' E. Map 26.
Revised: 36.91622735 N, 66.60460599 E /
36° 54' 58.41845568 N, 66° 36' 16.58156004 E.
Balkh Province. 35 km north-west of Balkh on the old route to Kilift, south-west of the present road.

Description: Many mounds and ruins.

Fieldwork: 1886 Maitland, ABC—topographical survey.

Source: Maitland 1888b: 195—mention.

KHWĀJA SAFĀ. See **2138 KHWĀJA SAFĀ in Supplement.**

605. KHWĀJA SĀHIB KAUCH GIRĀN

Original: Lat. 36° 55' N, long. 66° 11' E. Maps 24, 25.
Revised: 36.92194259 N, 66.1957698 E / 36° 55' 18.99331824 N, 66° 11' 44.77128288 E.
Jauzjān Province. 1 km east of the town of Āqcha, on either side of the road to Balkh but particularly south of it.

Description: Vast area of low ruins. The western zone is partly cultivated; the eastern zone is a large cemetery dominated by a few hillocks. On one of them, about 150 m south of the road, lies the *zīyārat* of Khwāja Sāhib Kauch Girān.

Fieldwork: 1948 Le Berre, DAFA—survey.

Source: M. Le Berre: unpublished 1952 report, DAFA Archives, tépé P. 10.

KHWĀJA SĀLEH ZĪYĀRAT. See **2139 KHWĀJA SĀLEH ZĪYĀRAT in Supplement.**

606. KHWĀJA SEH YARĀN

Lat. 34° 59' N, long. 69° 10' E. Map 64.
Parwān Province. 3 km south-west of Chārikar towards Tope Darra.

Date: Kushan, 1st–3rd cent. (architectural).

Description: Remains of a stupa-monastery complex, and some associated indistinct ruins.

Fieldwork: 1923 Foucher, DAFA—survey.

Sources:
1. Foucher 1942–7: 142–3—brief description.
2. Fussman, Murad, and Ollivier 2008: 133—favour a later date.

607. KHWĀJA SIĀH PUSH

Original: Lat. 31° 26–43' N, long. 62° 02–03' E. Map 84.
Revised: 31.4251845 N, 62.03613587 E / 31° 25' 30.66418956 N, 62° 02' 10.08912300 E.

Nīmrūz Province. 28 km north of Chakhānsūr, to the north of Pūst-i Gau.

Date: Ghaznavid, 11th–12th cent. (stylistic).

Description: A vast area of unfortified, very ruined mud and mud-brick houses covering *c.* 1 km². The main feature is a baked brick minaret with eight alternating rounded and rectangular buttresses. It is decorated in a simple pattern formed by a series of alternately laid horizontal and vertical bricks.

Fieldwork:
1. 1903–5 Tate, SAC—survey.
2. 1969–72 Fischer, Bonn University—survey.

Sources:
1. Peacocke 1885a: 16—mention.
2. Peacocke 1887a: 31—mention.
3. Tate 1910: 187—mention.
4. Fischer 1969–70: 95 and fig. 205—brief description, plan, and photos.
5. Fischer 1970a—photos and comparisons with the minarets of Damghan, Ghazni, and the Qutb Minar.
6. Fischer 1971b: 45 and 47—photos and brief description of the site and minaret (Sites 42 and 43).
7. Fischer 1973c: 135–7—brief description and discussion of the minaret.
8. Fischer 1973d—report on the work carried out.
9. Fischer 1973e: 151—brief description of the site and minaret.
10. Fischer 1974b—drawing of the minaret.
11. Fischer et al. 1974–6: pls 252–4—photos.
12. Fischer 1976: 50—discusses the minaret in its Indian Islamic context.
13. Fischer et al. 1976—description of photogrammetrical recording.
14. Fischer 1978b: 366–7—brief description with a plan and photo.

607 Khwāja Siāh Push (after Fischer 1974b, 1978a, and 1978c).

15. Pinder-Wilson 2001 — discusses the date, the form, and the architectural parallels of the minaret.
16. Hillenbrand 2000 — discussion in the broader context of Ghaznavid and Ghurid architecture.
17. Ball 2008: 236 — summary.

608. KHWĀJA SULTĀN
Or QAL'A-I SULTĀN.

Original: Lat. 30° 39' N, long. 64° 03' E. Map 97.
Revised: 30.65657938 N, 64.05413334 E /
30° 39' 23.68575576 N, 64° 03' 14.88002652 E.
Helmand Province. On the left bank of the Helmand, c.16 km south of Safar.

Dates: Bronze Age, 3rd–2nd mill. BC; Seleucid, 4th–3rd cent. BC; Parthian and Indo-Parthian, 2nd cent. BC–AD 3rd cent.; Sasanian, 3rd–7th cent.; Ghurid, 10th–13th cent.; Timurid, 15th–16th cent. (ceramic).

Description: Extensive remains and mounds, dominated by a huge fortress mound in a walled enclosure. On the opposite side of the river is a baked brick tower.

Fieldwork: 1966 Hammond, Cambridge University — survey.

Sources:
1. Bellew 1874: 188 — brief description.
2. Hammond 1970: 449 — lists the sites (nos. 3, 5, 15, 20, and 21) and discusses the pottery and general survey results.
3. Besenval and Francfort 1994: 11 — reinterprets Hammond's Type 10 'cord marked' ware as Harappan.

KHWĀJA URYA. See **2140 KHWĀJA URYA** in Supplement.

KIAZĀR. See **2126 KHIARZĀR** in Supplement.

KILLIGĀN. See **2141 KILLIGĀN** in Supplement.

609. KILIFT

Lat. 37° 21' N, long. 66° 15' E. Maps 24, 28.
Balkh Province. On the Āmū Daryā 91 km north-west of Balkh. The site is to the east and west of Kilift. Kilift (or Kelif) is a former crossing point of the Āmū Daryā.

Dates: Upper Palaeolithic, 15,000–10,000 BC; Epi-Palaeolithic, 10,000 BC; Neolithic, 7th–6th mill. BC (lithic); Turk, 7th–8th century (epigraphic).

Description: An extremely rich area of surface sites in the dunes to the south of the river. Many flint tools, mainly a microlithic industry.

There are also remains of fortifications on the northern end of the hills overlooking the river, and some low mounds with a surface scatter of baked bricks.

Some Bactrian documents that came to light in 1999–2000 mention *Gōzgān*, i.e. Juzjān, but possibly originated from Kilift.

Fieldwork:
1. 1886 Maitland, ABC — topographical surveys.
2. 1969 Vinogradov, Af/Sov. Mission — survey.

Sources:
1. Peacocke 1887a: 339 — mentions caravanserai.
2. Maitland 1888b: 197 — brief description of the remains.
3. Kruglikova and Mustamandi 1970: 85 — mention the Neolithic sites.
4. N. Dupree 1977: 21 — mentions the Stone Age sites.
5. Srivastava 1979b: 55 — assesses the results of the Soviet survey.
6. Vinogradov 1979 — discusses the complete assemblage from the survey with comparative material in Soviet Central Asia.
7. Sims-Williams 2005 — discusses the Bactrian legal documents.
8. Sims-Williams 2007 — further discussion of a Bactrian legal document, dated AD 662/3.

610. KĪLRĪKHTA

Lat. 35° 15' N, long. 63° 28' E. Map 44.
Bādghīs Province. On the Murghāb River c.47 km south of Bālā Murghāb and 16 km south of Darband-i Jaukar.

Description: Remains of a high-arched bridge. Construction is of baked brick on a stone footing. On the right bank is a ruined fort on some cliffs overlooking the bridge.

Fieldwork:
1. 1884–5 Maitland and Shamsuddin Khan, ABC — topographical survey.
2. 1952 Le Berre and Gardin, DAFA — survey.

Sources:
1. Vambery 1864: 262–3 — mention.
2. A. C. Yate 1887: 233 — mentions the bridge and recounts its associated legend.
3. Maitland 1888a: 203 — brief description.
4. Maitland and Drummond 1888: 84 — brief description.
5. Griesbach 1885a: 13 — brief description.
6. Shamsuddin Khan 1888: 123 — mention.
7. Gazetteer 1975: III. 272 — mention.

8. N. Dupree 1977: 339—brief description and associated legend.
9. Le Berre 1952, unpublished report, DAFA Archives.

611. KIRGHIZ TEPE
Or TEPE GURGURI or TEPE KHĀTŪN QAL'A.

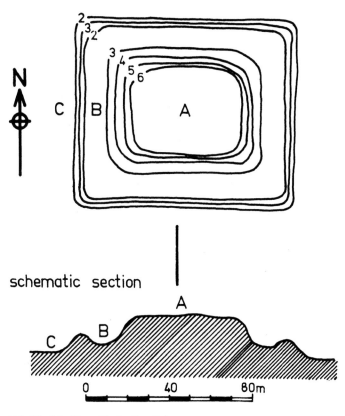

schematic section

611 Kirghiz Tepe (J.-C. Gardin).

Original: Lat. 37° 10' N, long. 69° 06' E. Map 31.
Revised: 37.16789103 N, 69.10901999 E /
37° 10' 04.40770440 N, 69° 06' 32.47197156 E.
Qundūz Province. On the edge of the terrace of the Āmū Daryā, 2 km north-east of the village of Khātūn Qal'a, situated some 15 km east of Imām Sāhib.

Dates: Iron Age 1700–800 BC; Achaemenid, 6th–4th cent. BC; Kushan, 1st–4th cent.; some Islamic sherds (ceramic).

Description: Rectangular fortified site, oriented east–west, including a citadel (80 × 65 m) surrounded by a rampart (110 × 90 m). These two structures are eroded, but their sides, still straight, rise to 9 m and 6 m respectively above the plain of Imām Sāhib; they are separated by a narrow terreplein (25 × 30 m) where traces of constructions are hardly visible.

Collection: National Museum/AIA—sherds.

Fieldwork: 1977 Gardin et al., CNRS—survey.

Sources:
1. Site information by J.-C. Gardin.
2. Gardin and Lyonnet 1978–9: pl. V—no. 146.
3. Gardin 1995: 92—brief description and plan.
4. Lyonnet 1997: figs 25, 35, 49—no. 146.
5. Gardin 1998: 64—no. 146.

612. KIRMĀNĀ, PANJAU

Lat. 34° 28' N, long. 66° 28' E. Map 56.
Ghūr/Bāmiyān Province. 13 km east of Lal, 79 km west of Panjau on the central road.

Description: A series of remains.

Fieldwork: 1946 Kohzad, HSA—survey.

Source: Kohzad 1951–4, 6/2: 13—mention.

KIRMĀN. See 2142 KIRMĀN in Supplement.

613. KISHM

Lat. 36° 43' N, long. 70° 06' E. Map 38.
Badakhshān Province. 106 km south-west of Faizābād and 52 km east of Farkhar.

Date: Middle Palaeolithic, 50,000–30,000 BC (lithic).

Description: A rock shelter at the top of a hill. Very little material was found; it was probably therefore a transitory hunting station rather than a settlement.

Fieldwork: 1971 McBurney, Cambridge University—sondage.

Source: McBurney 1972: 27–31—very brief report with a plan and section, but no analysis of the material.

614. KIZGHUNDI, CHEHEL DUKHTARĀN
Or SURKH TEPE.

Original: Lat. 35° 09' N, long. 62° 19' E. Map 43.
Revised: 35.11983127 N, 62.3117938 E / 35° 07' 11.39255760 N, 62° 18' 42.45767496 E.
Herat Province. On the left bank of the Kushk Rūd, 2 km north of Chehel Dukhtarān.

Description: Two large artificial mounds. The eastern one is surmounted by a *zīyārat*, and the western one is larger and higher and was probably an ancient fort.

Source: Gazetteer 1975: III. 274—mention.

KIZGHUNDI, Sar-i Chashma. See 2132 KHWĀJA JĪR in Supplement.

KLOLA TEPE. See 166 CHĀL.

KONDI. See **2144 KONDI** in Supplement.

KOT. See **KUT.**

615. KOTAL-I JAGDALAK

Original: Lat. 34° 24' N, long. 69° 46' E. Map 65.
Revised: 34.39719582 N, 69.77567288 E /
34° 23' 49.90495380 N, 69° 46' 32.42236188 E.
Laghmān Province. The top of a pass between Jagdalak and
Hisārak, on the old route from Kābul to Jalālābād.
Date: ?Chaghatai, 14th cent. (traditional).
Description: Remains of a castle.
Source: Masson 1842: 180 – mention.

616. KŌTAL-I KHĀWĀK

Lat. 35° 40' N, long. 69° 47' E. Map 50.
Baghlān Province. At the western foot of the Khāwāk Pass
11 km east of Dūāb-i Til.
Description: Remains of stone and baked brick buildings
on a hill.
Fieldwork: 1886 Shahzada Taimus, ABC – topographical
survey.
Source: Shahzada Taimus 1888: 318 – mention.

KUBA'I. See **927 QUCHI.**

617. KŪCHIKHĒL

Original: Lat. 33° 36' N, long. 69° 16' E. Map 82.
Revised: 33.58905553 N, 69.25511811 E /
33° 35' 20.59991592 N, 69° 15' 18.42520896 E.
Gardēz Province. In the hills 3 km east of Gardēz.
Description: Remains of fortifications.
Source: Fischer 1969: 340 – mention with Gardēz.

618. KUCH MUHAMMAD 'ALI

Lat. 34° 35' N, long. 70° 13' E. approximately. Map 65.
Laghmān. On the banks of the Laghmān River opposite
Kuch Muhammad 'Ali, *c*.5 km north of Mandrawar.
Description: Some artificial caves bordering the river.
Source: Holdich 1881a: 20 – mention.

KUHANDAZH. See **428 HERAT.**

619. KUHGĀH

Original: Lat. 31° 30' N, long. 61° 28' E. Map 83.
Revised: 31.5065125 N, 61.47097801 E / 31° 30' 23.44498812 N,
61° 28' 15.52084140 E.
Nīmrūz Province. On the west bank of the Farāh Rūd, 7 km
west of Peshwaran, on the eastern edge of the Hāmūn-i Sābiri.
Description: Remains of many *iwān* houses.
Source: Bellew 1874: 273–5 – brief description.

620. KŪH-I BACHA. SEE 1088 SHOTORAK.

KŪH-I CHATRĀBĀD. See **213 CHIT RABĀT
KUHNA.**

KŪH-I DIKSHA. See **1254 ZARGARĀN.**

KŪH-I EL. See **125 BĪDSAI.**

621. KŪH-I MANSŪR

Original: Lat. 34° 03–05' N, long. 68° 03–05' E. Map 59.
Revised: 34.06116656 N, 68.04173959 E /
34° 03' 40.19962392 N, 68° 02' 30.26253336 E.
Ghazni Province. On a bluff overlooking the confluence of
the Wardak and Jilga Rivers, *c*.20 km north of Dasht-i
Nāwar.
Date: Hunnic and Turki Shahi, 5th–9th cent. (ceramic);
Ghaznavid, 10th–11th cent. (architectural).
Description: A very high, almost inaccessible rocky bluff.
On top is a large castle *c*.300 m long, consisting of a curtain
wall strengthened with round towers, surrounding an inner
keep. Construction is of baked brick on a stone foundation.
Fieldwork: 1964–72 Fussman, CNRS – survey.
Sources:
1. Gardin and Lyonnet, 1980 chronological study of
   unpublished pottery from DAFA surveys.
2. Fussman 1974b: 92–3 – detailed description, with a plan
   and photos.
3. Fussman 1974c: 51–2 – brief description.

622. KŪH-I MŪRI
Or KHAM-I ZARGAR or NŪR.

Original: Lat. 35° 07' N, long. 69° 22' E. Map 64.
Revised: 35.1108689 N, 69.35081359 E / 35° 06' 39.12804396 N,
69° 21' 02.92891212 E.
Kāpīsā Province. 9 km south-east of Gulbahār at the foot of
the Kūh-i Kham-i Zargar.

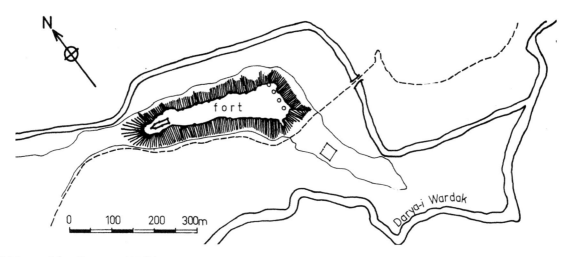

621 Kuh-i Mansūr (after Fussman 1974b).

Date: Kushano-Sasanian, 4th cent. (stylistic, ceramic).

Description: Remains of a stupa on a hill 20–5 m high. It is surrounded by several votive stupas and has an associated monastery down below, of three possible building periods. Construction is of diaper masonry. Finds include the arms of a throne in the form of lions, four unfinished lion statues, a schist relief, a statue of Buddha, a gold medallion, coins, and miscellaneous sculpture.

A second stupa-monastery complex is also recorded 2 km to the south-east.

Collections: National Museum and AIA—all excavated material.

Fieldwork:
1. 1965 Mizuno, Kyoto University—survey.
2. 1966 Mustamandi, AIA—excavations.

Sources:
1. Gardin and Lyonnet, 1980 chronological study of unpublished pottery from DAFA surveys.
2. S. and M. Mustamandi 1967/68b—brief preliminary report on the excavation.
3. Mizuno 1971: 126—mention and photos.
4. N. Dupree et al. 1974: 14—brief description of the Buddha on display in the National Museum.
5. *Kabul Times* 1978—photo of a vase from the excavations.
6. Miyaji 1978: 18—discusses some iconographical aspects of the relief.
7. Gardin 1982: 107—mentions African AIA work.
8. Tsushiya 2000—iconographical study of the Buddhist art.
9. Tissot 2006: 339–41—National Museum catalogue details and photos.
10. Ball 2008: 236—summary.
11. Fussman, Murad, and Ollivier 2008: 175–8, 216–17, and 308: detailed description.

623. KŪH-I NŪZŪL

Lat. 33° 12' N, long. 67° 37' E. Maps 78, 79.
Ghazni Province. In the Kūh-i Khūd Valley north-east of Jāghūrī, a few km east of Hisār.

Description: A few artificial caves cut into the cliff face.

Fieldwork: 1975 Taddei and Verardi, IsMEO—survey.

Source: Verardi 1977a: 142—mention and photo.

KŪH-I PAHLAWĀN. See 1088 SHOTORAK and 928 QUL-I NĀDIR.

KŪH-I PAZAK. See 2145 KŪH-I PAZAK in Supplement.

624. KŪH-I RAGHTU

Lat. 35° 40' N, long. 65° 26' E. Map 46.
Faryāb Province. On the route between Ghūlbiyān village and the Ghūlbiyān fresco, *c.*15 km upstream from the village, near an *ailāq* of Ghūlbiyān.

Description: A natural cave above a very steep glacis *c.*200 m above the valley floor, commanding the junction of two valleys. It has been built into a defensive system by a series of mud-brick walls on either side of the entrance, connected by a rock ledge cut into the side of the cave.

Fieldwork: 1978 Lee, BIAS—survey.

Sources:
1. Additional description by Jonathan L. Lee.
2. Lee 1980—mention.

625. KŪH-I SARHĀN

Lat. 35° 16' N, long. 64° 45' E. Map 45.
Bādghīs Province. At the confluence of the Khuranj with the upper Murghāb River, in the area south-east of Laulash.

Description: Local reports of ruins that include two minarets with tile decoration.

Source: Site information by Jonathan L. Lee.

626. KUHISTĀNIHĀ

Original: Lat. 36° 21–36° 23' N, long. 69° 20' E. Map 37.
Revised:
62636.36256796 N, 69.32791356 E / 36° 21' 45.24464016 N, 69° 19' 40.48880412 E (A).
62636.36553778 N, 69.33125515 E / 36° 21' 55.93599720 N, 69° 19' 52.51852596 E (B).
62636.36911104 N, 69.33411517 E / 36° 22' 08.79974004 N, 69° 20' 02.81460300 E (C).
62636.37629331 N, 69.33842311 E / 36° 22' 34.65591528 N, 69° 20' 18.32319888 E (D).
Takhār Province. Tepes located along the track from Ishkamīsh to Khwāja Bandi Kusha, west side, from the Bālā Hisār of Ishkamīsh to the village of Kuhistānihā. These tepes are each situated by one of the springs located along this line (four in number, indicated on the 1:100,000 map). Their respective positions are given hereafter by two numbers: the distance in km from the beginning of the track, to the south-east angle of the Bālā Hisār, and the distance in metres west of the track. (A) 2 km – 300 m; (B) 1.5 km – 400 m; (C) 1 km – 100 m; (D) 0.2 km – 100 m.

Dates: Hellenistic, 3rd–1st cent. BC (A, C); pre-Mongol Islamic, 10th–13th cent. and Timurid, 15th–16th cent. (ceramic).

Description: (A) Square north–south mound (30 × 30 m), flat top (4–5 m), on a natural terreplein surrounded by gullies in which flow streams from the nearby spring, to the north-east. (B) Rounded mound (diam. 30 m), flat top (1.5 m); another similar mound 200 m further south (not surveyed), near a second spring. (C) Square north–south mound (40 × 40 m), flat top (3 m), slightly rising in the north-west and south-east angles (4 m), 100 m east of a third spring. (D) Rounded mound (diam. 30 m) flat top (4 m); three similar mounds visible a few hundred metres distant in the south-west sector, not visited (height 2 to 3 m).

Collection: National Museum/AIA – sherds.

Fieldwork: 1978 Gardin et al., CNRS – survey.

Source:
1. Site information by J.-C. Gardin.
2. Gardin and Lyonnet 1978–9: pl. XI – nos. 394–7.
3. Lyonnet 1997: fig. 39 – nos. 394–7.
4. Gardin 1998: 100 – nos. 394–7.

627. KUHNA DEH, KUNAR

Original: Lat. 34° 34' N, long. 70° 34' E. Map 67.
Revised: 34.58225507 N, 70.56794273 E / 34° 34' 56.11826208 N, 70° 34' 04.59382620 E.
Nangahār Province. In the Kunar Valley near Kalatak, c. 24 km north-east of Jalālābād and 5 km south-west of Islāmpūr.

Date: Kushan, 1st–3rd cent. (stylistic).

Description: An extensive series of remains, dominated by a small but very perfect stupa in the same style as Nandarra. Both the square platform and the dome of the stupa are still intact. Beside it is a monastery, the walls of which are still standing, and the remains of aqueducts. A number of artificial caves are cut into the hill behind, and the nearby village is built of ancient masonry from the site.

Fieldwork: 1834 Masson – survey.

Sources:
1. Masson 1842: III. 276–8 – brief description.
2. Simpson 1879–80: 97 – mention.
3. Simpson 1881: 207 – brief description.
4. Ball 2008: 236 – summary.
5. Errington 2017a: 160 – the Masson collection and archive relating to the site.

KUHNA DEH, Sumara. See **2146 KUHNA DEH, Sumara in Supplement.**

628. KUHNA KHULM
Including SHUR TEPE.

Original: Lat. 36° 45' N, long. 67° 42' E. Map 29.
Revised: 36.76131322 N, 67.70604669 E / 36° 45' 40.72760460 N, 67° 42' 21.76809120 E.
Samangān Province. 7 km north of Tāshqurghān.

Dates: Sasanian, Hunnic, Turk, and pre-Mongol Islamic, 4th–13th cent.; Timurid, 15th–16th cent. (ceramic).

Description: A large mound c. 600 × 350 m in area and 10 m in height, covered in pottery. On the western side are the remains of a detached fort, and all round are many smaller mounds marking the remains of the surrounding town.

Fieldwork:
1. 1886 Maitland, ABC – topographical survey.
2. 1956 Ramachandran and Sharma, ASI – reconnaissance.
3. 1960 Hayashi and Sahara, Kyoto University – survey.
4. 1969 Gouin, DAFA – survey.

Sources:
1. Moorcroft and Trebeck 1841: 453 – brief description.
2. Yavorski 1885: 81 – mention.
3. Holdich 1887: 36 – mention.
4. Maitland 1888b: 262 – mention.
5. Yate 1888: 317 – brief description.
6. Le Strange 1905: 427 – summary of the historical references.
7. Caspani and Cagnacci 1951: 237 – mention.

8. Ramachandran and Sharma 1956: I. 23—mention.
9. Carl 1959b: 59—mention.
10. Hayashi and Sahara 1962: 45—photos and brief description in Japanese.
11. Muroga 1972: 140—discusses some pottery 'hand grenades' found at Shur Tepe.
12. Gouin 1974 and unpublished report (1970)—site no. 48.

629. KUHNA KHUSH RABĀT

Original: Lat. 36° 44' N, long. 67° 36' E. Map 29.
Revised: 36.73630673 N, 67.59698197 E /
36° 44' 10.70424348 N, 67° 35' 49.13510496 E.
Samangān Province. 11 km north-west of Tāshqurghān, to the north of the road to Mazār-i Sharīf.

Description: Some ruins.

Fieldwork: 1886 Maitland, ABC—topographical survey.

Source: Maitland 1888b: 263—mention.

630. KUHNA MASJID
See also 1123 SURKH KOTAL.

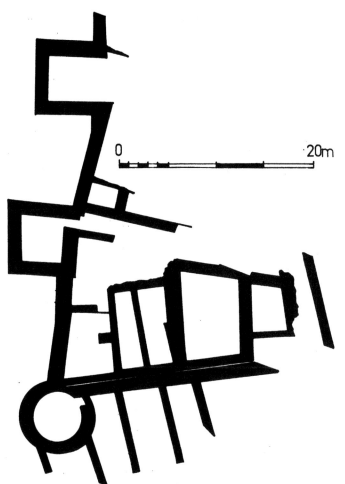

0   20m

630 Kuhna Masjid (after Bernard 1964).

Original: Lat. 36° 01' N, long. 68° 35' E. Map 33.
Revised: 36.03912023 N, 68.58459571 E /
36° 02' 20.83284384 N, 68° 35' 04.54454304 E.
Baghlān Province. 1 km south-east of Surkh Kotal.

Date: Sasanian, 3rd–7th cent. (architectural, ceramic).

Description: Some massive mud-brick fortifications on top of a hill. Finds include some large storage jars, an imported ceramic rhyton of unusual style, and a Kharoshthi ostracon.

Fieldwork: 1963 Bernard and Kieffer, DAFA—excavations.

Sources:
1. Bernard 1964—summary report on the stratigraphy, architecture, and finds.
2. Schlumberger 1971—brief summary of the excavations and discussion of the rhyton.
3. N. Dupree et al. 1974: 97—description of the rhyton.
4. Fussman 1974c: 53—brief note on the ostracon.
5. Kuwayama 1974b—discusses the architecture as dating evidence for Begram III.
6. Veuve 1974—detailed typology and ceramic analysis of the pottery.
7. Davary 1977—mentions the ostracon.
8. Francfort 1979a: 38—mentions the fortifications as a continuation of Kushan military traditions.
9. Tissot 2006: 70—National Museum catalogue details and photos.
10. Ball 2008: 267—summary.
11. Kuwayama 2010: 287–8—discusses the chronology.

KUHNA RABĀT. See **2147 KUHNA RABĀT in Supplement.**

631. KUHNA QAL'A, DASHT-I QAL'A

Original: Lat. 37° 11' N, long. 69° 25' E. Map 34.
Revised: 37.18855716 N, 69.42331968 E /
37° 11' 18.80578356 N, 69° 25' 23.95086456 E.
Takhār Province. 2 km north of the village of Dasht-i Qal'a, on the edge of the Āmū Daryā, left bank.

Dates: Beg. Iron, end 2nd–beg. 1st mill. BC; Achaemenid, 6th–4th cent. BC; Hellenistic, 3rd–1st cent. BC; Kushan, 1st–4th cent. (ceramic).

Description: On a cliff bend dominating the Āmū Daryā to the west, and north of a dead arm of the same river, a fortified place with a double circular enclosure wall, with a high citadel in the north-west part, at the location of the bend. The citadel is conical in shape, flat on top (height *c*.10 m above the level of the interior esplanade, 25 m above the Āmū Daryā), steep slopes. The double enclosure lies in a half circle around the citadel, towards the south and the east, diam. *c*.800 m for the exterior wall, 600 m for the interior wall; the taluses are preserved in height from 2 to 4 m, and are about 20 m wide at the base. Traces of

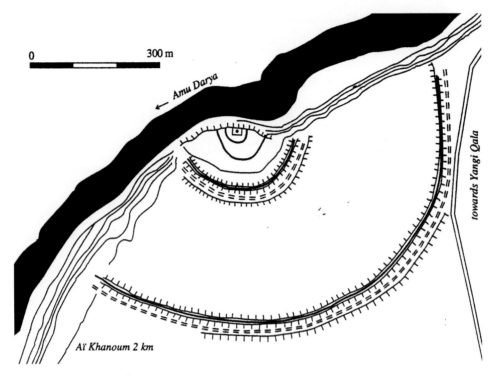

631 Kuhna Qal'a, Dasht-i Qal'a (J.-C. Gardin).

habitation between the two enclosure walls and at the foot of the citadel, in the south-east part principally.

Collection: National Museum/AIA—sherds.

Fieldwork: 1974 Gardin et al., CNRS—survey.

Sources:
1. Site information by J.-C. Gardin.
2. Gardin and Lyonnet 1978–9: pl. III—nos. 46–9.
3. Gardin 1995: 86–7—brief description and plan.
4. Fussman 1996—highlights the importance of the site as the possible Achaemenid precursor to Aï Khanoum.
5. Lyonnet 1997—nos. 46–9.
6. Gardin 1998: 41—nos. 46–9.

KUHNA QAL'A, Helmand. See **224 DAISHU.**

632. KUHNA QAL'A, KHĀNĀBĀD
Includes SAHAG.

Original: Lat. 36° 42' N, long. 69° 07'–69° 09' E. Map 32.
Revised:
36.69955224 N, 69.12548524 E / 36° 41' 58.38807336 N, 69° 07' 31.74688020 E (A).
36.69846639 N, 69.15264528 E / 36° 41' 54.47902056 N, 69° 09' 09.52301016 E (B).
Qundūz Province. Two sites on the edge of the Tāluqān river, right bank, 3.5 km and 1.2 km west-south-west of the village of Kuhna Kala. (A) The first is located on the edge of a cliff directly above the river (10 m), where the canal called Kaghiz-i Payān joins it (*c*.2 km north-north-east of Khānābād, as the crow flies). A new canal, being dug on the slopes which descend to the cliff (1978), crosses the site from east to west. (B) The second is 2.3 km to the east, also on a cliff on the edge of the Tāluqān River, near a house surrounded by barbed wire (depot for dynamite for the construction of a regulating dam).

Dates: Kushan, 1st–4th cent. (B); pre-Mongol Islamic, 10th–13th cent. and Timurid, 15th–16th cent. (A) (ceramic).

Description: (A) Polygonal fortress, with round towers at the angles. The enclosure wall is preserved in the northern part, above the new canal, on three sides (total length 100 m, height 5 m); in the southern part, on the edge of the river (cliff of 10 m above the present canal), a piece of north-west/south-east wall still standing with a vaulted opening (mud-bricks, width 28 cm, thickness 4–5 cm), filled in, and above, two racket-shaped windows, through which the town of Khānābād can be seen on the other side of the river. (B) Place called Sahag: rounded mound of irregular shape (30×30 m), height 2 m.

Collection: National Museum/AIA—sherds.

Fieldwork: 1978 Gardin et al., CNRS—survey.

Sources:
1. Site information by J.-C. Gardin.
2. Gardin and Lyonnet 1978–9: pl. VII—nos. 442–3.
3. Lyonnet 1997: fig. 49—nos. 442–3.
4. Gardin 1998: 83—nos. 442–3.

633. KUHNA QAL'A, TĀLUQĀN

Original: Lat. 36° 44' N, long. 69° 30' E. Map 36.
Revised: 36.73217437 N, 69.49794696 E /
36° 43' 55.82771976 N, 69° 29' 52.60906428 E.
Takhār Province. On the right bank of the Tāluqān River
(250 m from its closest arm), 1.4 km from the bridge of
Tāluqān by the embankment road. This tepe is located
opposite another Bronze Age site, on the left bank of the
river: Qurghān Tepe, cf. no. 937; the river is fordable
between these two points, except during the rise in water
level in spring.

Dates: Late Chalcolithic–Early Bronze Age, *c.*3500–2500
BC; Middle Bronze, *c.*2500–1500 BC; Timurid, 15th–16th
cent. (ceramic).

Description: Square mound (60×60 m) oriented north-
north-east/south-south-west, very steep slopes, cut at the
base to make place for crops and nearby houses. The top
(10–12 m) is flat, with a large central depression. In the cuts,
south face, traces of walls may be seen (alternating beds of
pakhsa and pebbles), as well as layers in place containing
Bronze Age sherds; at the base of the tepe, similar layers on
the east face, up to a height near the top. This tepe thus
appears to mainly contain vestiges of the 2nd mill. BC,
covered by a smaller Islamic settlement.

Collection: National Museum/AIA—sherds.

Fieldwork: 1977 Gardin et al., CNRS—survey.

Sources:
1. Site information by J.-C. Gardin.
2. Gardin and Lyonnet 1978–9: pl. IX—no. 299.
3. Lyonnet 1981—brief description, discussion, and illustration of the Chaleolithic (mid-4th–mid-3rd mill. BC)
   pottery, and discussion of the geographical and historical implications.
4. Gardin 1982: 105—mentions the identification of a Chaleolithic settlement.
5. Gardin 1995: 93—mention.
6. Lyonnet 1997: figs 7, 13, 21–24—no. 299.
7. Gardin 1998: 70—no. 299.

KUHNA QAL'A, Gūgari. See **386. GŪGARI.**

634. KUHSĀN

Original: Lat. 34° 39' N, long. 61° 12' E. Map 51.
Revised:
34.65628796 N, 61.19973472 E / 34° 39' 22.63666860 N,
61° 11' 59.04499776 E and
34.65186523 N, 61.19602625 E / 34° 39' 06.71483700 N,
61° 11' 45.69450396 E.
Herat Province. C.111 km west of Herat, near the Iranian
border north of Islām Qal'a.

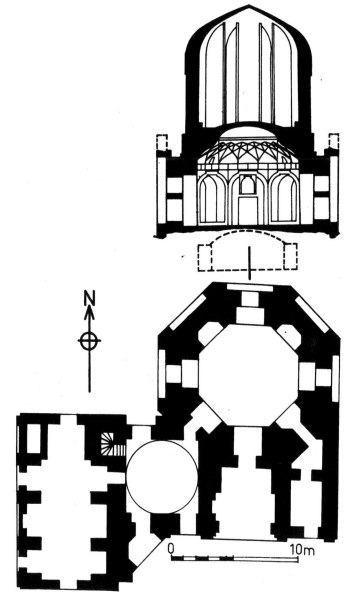

634 Kuhsān (after Pugachenkova 1968).

Date: Timurid, 15th cent. (stylistic).

Description: An octagonal mausoleum known locally as the
Tomb of Gauharshad. The exterior has mosaic tile decoration, mostly on the drum and dome, and the interior has
painted and plastered decoration. It is connected to an
undecorated mosque, now disused. This mausoleum is
now reported completely destroyed.

Just outside the village are the much eroded remains of a
mud fort. It is divided into two; the upper with barely
anything remaining, just a square mound, the lower part a
square enclosure, still with much of its mud walls standing.
The upper part is covered in Timurid and later pottery. No
baked brick scatter.

300 m to the south-west of the village is a low mound measuring 20 × 35 m with 15th-cent. pottery on the surface (Soviet Site K138).

Fieldwork:
1. 1967 Pugachenkova, Af/Sov. Mission—architectural survey.
2. 1978–9 Samizay, Kābul University/UNESCO—survey.
3. 1968–78 Kruglikova, Af/Sov.Mission—survey.

Sources:
1. Ferrier 1857: 140–1—brief description of the fort.
2. Peacocke 1885a: 46—brief description of fort.
3. A. C. Yate 1887: 150 and 162–3—brief description of the fort and '*madrasa*', dated correctly to the Timurid period.
4. C. E. Yate 1887: 98—mentions the mausoleum.
5. Maitland 1888a: 138–9—mentions the fort and '*madrasa*'.
6. C. E. Yate 1888: 53—brief description of a caravanserai and the fort.
7. Niedemeyer and Diez 1924: pl. 164—photo of the mausoleum before restoration.
8. Hill 1966: 391—mention.
9. Mustamandi 1967—brief preliminary description.
10. Pugachenkova 1968a: 27–41—description.
11. Pugachenkova 1968b– architectural study and discussion.
12. Ghawwās 1969: 1979: 44–5—brief description.
13. Pugachenkova 1970: 25–7—extensive architectural description and discussion.
14. N. Dupree 1977: 257–8—brief description.
15. *Kabul Times* 1979a—mentions the preservation work carried out.
16. Samizay 1981: 27–31—good description, with photos and drawings, of the remains, with a note on the conservation needs.
17. O'Kane 1987: 197–201—description.
18. Golombek and Wilber 1988: 325–7—description.
19. Aalund 1990—photos, plan, and assessment.
20. Ball 2008: 237–8—summary.
21. Gaibov et al. 2010: 108—brief description of Site K138.

KUHWĀT. See 1229 WARDAK.

KUHYĀN. See 2148 KUHYĀN in Supplement.

635. KUK JAR

Lat. 36° 21' N, long. 67° 55' E. Map 30.
Samangān Province. 14 km north-west of Haibak on the road to Tāshqurghān, *c.*3 km east of Darra-i Kalān and 8 km from Kara Kamar.

Date: Upper Palaeolithic, 15,000–10,000 BC (lithic).

Description: A surface site, possibly a hunting observation post, on top of a 30 m high mesa. Of the hundreds of stone artefacts collected, most were flakes and precisely struck micro-blades.

Fieldwork: 1969 Davis, Dupree, and Lattman, AMNH—survey.

Sources:
1. Davis 1969–70: 81–2—summary description of the site and material.
2. Davis 1974: 213–16—description of the lithic industry.
3. Davis 1978: 63–4—very brief description of the site.
4. Zāhir 1980—summary in Persian.

636. KULĀLGU

Original: Lat. 33° 27' N, long. 68° 53' E. Map 82.
Revised: 33.42917823 N, 68.89227196 E /
33° 25' 45.04161972 N, 68° 53' 32.17907220 E.
Paktiyā Province. 50 km east of Ghazni on the road to Gardēz.

Description: A series of mounds.

Fieldwork: 1966 Fischer, DAAD—survey.

Sources:
1. Fischer 1967a: 166—mention.
2. Fischer 1969: 340—mention (Site A5).
3. Thomas 2015: 518—additional information from satellite imagery.

637. KULĀNI

Lat. 35° 24' N, long. 64° 45' E. Map 45.
Faryāb Province. In the Laulash region *c.*60 km south of Maimana, to the south of the Band-i Turkistān. The site is just to the north of Qal'a-i Laulash.

Description: Local reports of an artificial mound, where objects have been found.

Source: Site information by Jonathan L. Lee.

638. KŪL MĀRŪT
See also 810 PESHWĀRĀN.

Original: Lat. 31° 30' N, long. 61° 30' E. Map 83.
Revised: 31.49412251 N, 61.50151399 E /
31° 29' 38.84102988 N, 61° 30' 05.45035860 E.
Nīmrūz Province. On the Farāh Rūd 5 km west of Pēshwārān.

Date: Ghaznavid, 11th cent. (stylistic).

Description: Part of the Pēshwārān area of remains. The main building is a large mosque and adjoining *madrasa*. The entrance *iwān* still preserves part of a floriated Kufic script in moulded plaster. Inside some painted plaster decoration is still preserved and there is the design of a moulded Masonic star over the mihrab. There are also remains of a solidly constructed bridge.

Fieldwork:
1. 1903–5 Tate, SAC—survey.
2. 1936 Hackin and Meunié, DAFA—survey.

Sources:
1. Bellew 1874: 272–3—brief description of the ruins and the mosque.
2. Smith 1876: 315–16—brief description.
3. Tate 1910: 198 and 217—photo of the mosque and mention of the bridge.
4. Hackin 1959c: figs 117–20—photos of the mosque.
5. Hill and Grabar 1967: pl. 608—photo of the *iwān* inscription.
6. Hillenbrand 2000—discussion in the broader context of Ghaznavid and Ghurid architecture.

639. KULŪKHI

Original: Lat. 31° 15' N, long. 62° 10' E. Map 84.
Revised: 31.2447083 N, 62.15883902 E / 31° 14' 40.94989044 N, 62° 09' 31.82048352 E.
Nīmrūz Province. 14 km north-east of Chakhānsūr. The site is *c.*1 km north-west of the village of Kulūkhi.

Dates: Late Sasanian-Early Islamic, 5th–13th cent.; Mongol-Timurid, 13th–16th cent. (ceramic).

Description: Remains of an Islamic mud tower and a pre-Islamic mound.

Fieldwork: 1960–70 Fischer, Bonn University—survey.

Source: Fischer et al. 1974–6: 42—mention (Tapa 43).

640. KULŪKH TEPE

Original: Lat. 36° 59' N, long. 68° 14' E. Map 30.
Revised: 36.98557969 N, 68.25754723 E /
36° 59' 08.08687536 N, 68° 15' 27.17002980 E.
Qundūz Province. 4.5 km west of the guard post of Kulūkh (Tahana-i Kulūkh), by the track leading from Qal'a-i Zāl to Khisht Tepe, on the Āmū Daryā; the site is located on the north side of the track, at the fork of a road leading to the village of Kulūkh Tepe, to the west-north-west.

Dates: Hunnic-Turk, 5th–9th cent.; pre-Mongol Islamic, 10th–13th cent. (ceramic).

Description: High conical mound (diam. 20 m, height 6 m), flanked by two lower hillocks (2–3 m); one 10 m to the west, irregular in shape (40 × 10 m), occupied by tombs and a *zīyārat*; the other 70 m south-east, of oblong shape, east–west, (60 × 15 m), parallel to the track. Seen in the main mound, in section, are large amounts of *pakhsa* (height 0.70 to 1 m), with the inclusion of calcareous boulders. These three eroded hillocks are the only vestiges of a site which was previously more extensive: similar sherds (Hunnic and Islamic periods) are scattered over the the ground, which rises in a gentle slope south of the track, in the direction of the dunes which dominate the plain of Kulūkh Tepe. The area of collection extends to the old canal whose traces may be seen on the slopes, 400 m south of the three hillocks—a canal coming from the Qundūz River, like the one which replaces it today to irrigate the same plain, on a curve of a slightly lower level.

Collection: National Museum/AIA—sherds.

Fieldwork:
1. 1886 Ata Muhammad, ABC—topographical exploration.
2. 1978 Gardin et al., CNRS—survey.

Sources:
1. Site information by J.-C. Gardin.
2. Maitland 1888b: 272—mention.
3. Gazetteer 1979: IV. 15—mention.
4. Gardin and Lyonnet 1978–9: pl. VI—no. 504. (The position of the site on this map is erroneous: it is located 1.8 km north-east of the point indicated.)
5. Lyonnet 1997: figs 68, 69—no. 504.
6. Gardin 1998: 87—no. 504.

641. KUMLI
Or NIKCHACH.

Original: Lat. 37° 06' N, long. 66° 34' E. Map 26.
Revised: 37.09369528 N, 66.5751545 E / 37° 05' 37.30302312 N, 66° 34' 30.55621152 E.
Balkh Province. 50 km north-west of Balkh, 2 km to the east of the road to Kilift. The main site is 9 km north of Nikcha.

Date: Bronze Age, 2nd mill. BC; Iron Age, 7th–6th cent. BC (ceramic).

Description: A line of eight heavily deflated Bronze and Iron Age settlements stretching northwards from Nikcha for 9 km. The northernmost site is a large brick platform functioning as a citadel, but with no traces of superstructures on top.

Fieldwork: 1973 Sarianidi, Af/Sov. Mission—excavations.

Sources:
1. Kruglikova 1973b: 8–13—detailed excavation report.
2. Sarianidi 1977c: 116—brief summary.
3. Francfort 1979a: 17—mention.
4. Kohl 1984: 161–2—brief summary.

642. KUMSAR

642 Kumsar (after Pugachenkova 1976).

Original: Lat. 37° 04' N, long. 66° 48' E. Map 26.
Revised: 37.06188834 N, 66.80429153 E /
37° 03' 42.79801500 N, 66° 48' 15.44949576 E.
Balkh Province, C.35 km north of Balkh, 2 km north-east of Qarchigak.

Date: Kushan, 1st cent. BC–AD 3rd cent. (ceramic).

Description: A large, L-shaped urban site measuring *c.*400 × 350 m. It is enclosed by 12 m high walls with rectangular corner towers and an internal gallery. In the middle of the enclosure is a mound.

Fieldwork:
1. 1886 Ata Muhammad, ABC—topographical survey.
2. 1972–3 Pugachenkova, Af/Sov. Mission—survey.

Sources:
1. Maitland 1888b: 274—mention.
2. Pugachenkova 1976b– brief description and illustrations.
3. Francfort 1979a: 32–6—lists the site and discusses the general principles of Kushan military architecture.

KŪNCHAK. See 738 MULLĀH AFGHĀNI.

643. KUNCHI QISHLĀQ

Original: Lat. 36° 46' N, long. 69° 28' E. Maps 35, 36.
Revised:
36.76346743 N, 69.46209574 E / 36° 45' 48.48273432 N, 69° 27' 43.54467372 E (A).
36.77007968 N, 69.46278874 E / 36° 46' 12.28686276 N, 69° 27' 46.03946148 E (B).
Takhār Province. 8 km north-west of Tāluqān, accessible by the road that edges the Rūd-i Shārawān; the two tepes are 300 m from this road, one to the south (A), the other to the north (B).

Dates: Hunnic-Turk, 5th–9th cent.; pre-Mongol Islamic, 10th–13th cent. (ceramic).

Description: (A) Mound of irregular shape (80 × 50 m), eaten into by cultivation; flat top (1.50 m), occupied by a modern cemetery. (B) Group of three mounds aligned east–west over about 200 m, at the foot of the slopes which edge the road from Tāluqān to Cha'ila; each is oblong in shape, north–south (c.70 × 20 m), the top is more or less flat (height 4 to 8 m depending on the slope of the land), occupied by a modern cemetery which at the present time protects the site from being razed by the cultivation of cotton. 100 m to the north-west of this zone, a small intact rectangular mound, 3 m high, whose form and dimensions (35 × 25 m) are those of a farm of the Kushan period.

Collection: National Museum/AIA—sherds.

Fieldwork: 1977 Gardin et al., CNRS—survey.

Sources:
1. Site information by J.-C. Gardin.
2. Gardin and Lyonnet 1978–9: pl. IX—nos. 228–9.
3. Lyonnet 1997: figs 68, 69—nos. 228–9.
4. Gardin 1998: 69—nos. 228–9.

644. KUNDI

Lat. 34° 35' N, long. 70° 39' E. Map 67.
Kunār Province. On the north bank of the Kunār River, 5 km east of Islāmpūr.

Source: Masson 1842: III. 281—mention from hearsay.

KUNDŪZ. See 930 QUNDŪZ.

KUNJAKAI. See 122. URYĀKHĒL.

645. KURAH DEH

Lat. 35° 43' N, long. 65° 19' E. Map 46.
Jauzjān Province. C.3 km south of Deh Mirān in Gurziwan, 20 km south-east of Bīlchirāgh.

Description: Some six or seven chambers cut out of the rock in a high cliff above the village, similar to those at Deh Mirān.

Fieldwork: 1886 Griesbach, ABC—topographical survey.

Sources:
1. Griesbach 1888b: 197—mention.
2. Gazetteer 1979: IV. 370—mention.

646. KURAGAZI

Original: Lat. 32° 07' N, long. 61° 53' E. Map 83.
Revised: 32.10940193 N, 61.89185169 E /
32° 06' 33.84696132 N, 61° 53' 30.66607932 E.

Farāh Province. On the south-east bank of the Farāh Rūd, 9 km north-east of Tujg on the Farāh-Lāsh Juwain road.

Date: Mongol-Timurid, 13th–16th cent. (ceramic).

Description: Remains of some walls.

Fieldwork: 1960–70 Fischer, Bonn University—survey.

Source: Fischer et al. 1974–6: 35—mention.

647. KŪRATĀS

Original: Lat. 35° 02' N, long. 69° 23' E. Map 64.
Revised: 35.04205338 N, 69.37887976 E /
35° 02' 31.39215972 N, 69° 22' 43.96714320 E.
Kāpisā Province. Near the foot of the Rīg-i Rawān, 3 km north-east of Sadiqābād.

Description: Some masonry remains known as Kāfir Qal'a in the hills, possibly a stupa. The site is covered in large amounts of sherds, and many coins had been found there.

Fieldwork: 1834 Masson—survey.

Sources:
1. Masson 1842: III. 166–7—mention.
2. Fussman, Murad, and Ollivier 2008: 178—mention.

648. KŪRDŪ
See also 363 GHULGHULA and 861 QAL'A-I KŪRDŪ.

Original: Lat. 30° 51' N, long. 62° 01' E. Map 92.
Revised:
Between 30.85643612 N, 62.01160936 E /
30° 51' 23.17001940 N, 62° 00' 41.79368880 E and
30.8544327 N, 62.0091546 E /
30° 51' 15.95772324 N, 62° 00' 32.95656648 E.
Nīmrūz Province. In the dunes 19 km south-west of Zīyā-rat-i Amirān Sāhib.

Dates: Sasanian, 3rd–7th cent.; early Islamic, 8th–13th cent.; Mongol-Timurid, 13th–16th cent. (ceramic).

Description: A vast area of remains stretching for a distance of several kilometres. To the north there are the remains of kilns, to the east is a square mud-brick tower with intact elliptical vaulting (Fischer's Tower 33), with another (Tower 34) just to the south. It is three-storey, and the ground floor is roofed with a dome on a simple octagonal zone of transition. To the west are extensive mud remains of walls and ruined towers (Ruinfield 35) and to the south are the remains of a mud-brick hall (Hall 36). In the surrounding area are traces of an extensive ancient irrigation system.

Fieldwork:
1. 1936 Meunié and Hackin, DAFA—survey.
2. 1970 Fischer, Bonn University—survey.

Sources:
1. Fischer 1971a—photos.
2. Fischer 1973c: 151—brief description.

3. Fischer et al. 1974–6: 38–9—description and photos (Sites 33–7).
4. Ball 2008: 238–9—summary.

649. KURGAL

Original: Lat. 34° 51' N, long. 69° 40' E. Map 65.
Revised: 34.85346858 N, 69.66233996 E /
34° 51' 12.48688908 N, 69° 39' 44.42387256 E.
Kāpīsā Province. 1 km east of Tagau, *c*.45 km north of Sarōbī on the road to Gulbahār.

Date: Hindu Shahi, 10th cent. (ceramic).

Description: A mound, *c*.20 m diam. and 5 m high, covered in marble fragments. Remains of some walls are visible.

Fieldwork: 1960 Fischer, DAAD—survey.

Sources:
1. Fischer 1964: 36—mention and photo.
2. Fischer 1969: 356—mention.

KURGHĀN. See 1029 SHĀH QURGHĀN.

650. KURI
Or KHAMCHĀN. See also 315 FAIZĀBĀD.

Original: Lat. 37° 06' N, long. 70° 31' E. Map 38.
Revised: 37.11906024 N, 70.52239686 E /
37° 07' 08.61687984 N, 70° 31' 20.62870860 E.
Badakhshān Province. On the Kokcha River, adjacent to Faizābād airport, 5 km west of the town.

Dates: Kushano-Sasanian, 4th–5th cent. (stylistic); early Islamic, 10th–13th cent. (ceramic); Timurid, 15th–16th cent. (ceramic).

Description: The probable remains of ancient Faizābād, consisting of an extensive low-lying site with traces of mud and baked brick structures covering an area of 1.5 square km. This site was the probable find spot of two Sasanian silver plates found by Lord in Faizābād.

Fieldwork:
1. 1960 Fischer, DAAD—survey.
2. 1975 Kohl—survey.

Sources:
1. Prinsep 1838—illustration and brief description of one of the Sasanian silver plates.
2. Cunningham 1841—illustration and brief description of the second silver Sasanian plate.
3. Wood 1872: 162–3—brief description of the remains.
4. Fischer 1969: 350—brief summary.
5. Gazetteer 1972: I. 99—mention.
6. Kohl 1978: 64–5—brief description.

651. KŪRRINDAR
Or BURJ KĀFIR.

Lat. 34° 44' N, long. 69° 08' E. Map 64.
Kābul Province. In the Kūh-i Dāman area, 33 km north of Kābul. The site is just north-east of Tepe Skandar, 2.5 km east of Sarāī Khūja.

Date: Kushano-Sasanian, 4th–5th cent. (stylistic).

Description: A stupa-monastery complex. The stupa is one of the largest in the region, 16 m high, with a well-preserved façade. It has a frieze of alternating blind arches and pilasters. Nothing was found inside.

Fieldwork:
1. 1833 Honigberger—excavation.
2. 1934 Masson—survey.
3. 1970 Ushikawa, Kyoto University—photogrammetrical survey.
4. 1972 Fussman, CNRS—survey.

Sources:
1. Masson 1936a: 5—mentions the stupa and large mound nearby.
2. Masson 1841: 116—mention.
3. Masson 1842: 145—mention.
4. Foucher 1942–7: 143—mention.
5. Caspani and Cagnacci 1951: 227—mention.
6. Ushikawa 1972—very brief description and an unfinished photogrammetrical drawing.
7. Fussman et al. 2008: 138–40, 217–19, and 306—description with photos and drawings.
8. Errington 2017a: 82–3—the Masson collection and archive relating to the site.

652. KUSHĀBĀD
Or JĀ-I DARG.

Original: Lat. 31° 36' N, long. 61° 29' E. Map 83.
Revised: 31.59232415 N, 61.48776315 E /
31° 35' 32.36693604 N, 61° 29' 15.94732560 E.
Nīmrūz Province. On the west bank of the Farāh Rūd 16 km south-west of Lāsh Juwain. The site is *c*.3 km south of the village of Kushābād.

Description: A mound, *c*.10 m high. Nearby are the remains of a manor house and windmills, together with a small fort and ruined mosque.

Source: Gazetteer 1973: II. 63 and 176—mention.

653. KUSHAK TIMŪRI
Or SHAHR-I TIMŪR.

Original: Lat. 34° 06' N, long. 65° 36' E. Map 55.
Revised: 34.10185785 N, 65.60255583 E /
34° 06' 06.68827584 N, 65° 36' 09.20097108 E.

Ūruzgān Province. In the Tagau Qurghān south of Chakh-charān. 3 km south-east of Gharghara in the Siāh Chub area on the Ūruzgān/Ghūr border.

Description: Reports of some ruins and walls.

Source: Kohzad 1951–4, 9/2: 13—mention from hearsay.

654. KUSH ĀSYĀ
Or QAL'A-I DAMBEG.

Original: Lat. 34° 58' N, long. 62° 21' E. Map 43.
Revised: 34.9644157 N, 62.35151712 E / 34° 57' 51.89653548 N, 62° 21' 05.46163632 E.
Bādghīs Province. On the Kush Rūd, 18.5 km below Kushk.

Description: A ruined fort and mosque.

Fieldwork: 1885 Peacocke, ABC—topographical survey.

Sources:
1. Peacocke 1887a: 180—mention.
2. Maitland 1888a: 171—mention.
3. Gazetteer 1975: III. 283—mention.

KUSH-I NAU and KUSH-I KUHNA. See 2149 KUSH-I NAU and KUSH-I KUHNA in Supplement.

KUSHK, Ibrāhīmābād. See 2150 KUSHK, Ibrāhīmābād in Supplement.

655. KUSHK, HERAT

Lat. 34° 19' N, long. 62° 01' E. Map 52.
Herat Province. 19 km west of Herat, just to the west of the Kārbar stream on the old route to Zindajān.

Description: Remains of a monumental building.

Source: Lal 1846: 130—mention.

KUSHK. See 2254 SURKHI in Supplement.

656. KUSHK, NĪMRŪZ
Or KHUSHAK or KHUSHK.
See also 2172 PASHTAU in Supplement.

Lat. 30° 45' N, long. 61° 47' E. Map 92.
Nīmrūz Province. On the Helmand *c*.4 km south of Khwābgāh, *c*.35 km south of Nād-i 'Alī. 8–9 km from Padah-i Sultān.

Description: Remains of a tower, probably an old 'summer house', on a mound, associated with stories of an ancient dam further upstream.

Fieldwork:
1. 1884 Peacocke, Maitland, ABC—topographical survey.
2. 1903–5 Tate, SAC—survey.

Sources:
1. Ferrier 1857: 411—mention.
2. Peacocke 1885a: 9—mention.
3. Maitland 1888a: 75—mention.
4. Tate 1910: 153—mention.

657. KUSHKAK
Or BABA KUSHKAK.

Original: Lat. 36° 48' N, long. 66° 34' E. Map 26.
Revised: 36.78980306 N, 66.57888639 E /
36° 47' 23.29100160 N, 66° 34' 43.99100976 E.
Balkh Province. 40 km west of Balkh, to the south of the road to Āqcha.

Description: A conspicuous mound with a *zīyārat* on top, at the south-eastern corner of the village. There are three more mounds on the east side of the village.

Fieldwork: 1886 Peacocke, Maitland, ABC—topographical survey.

Sources:
1. Peacocke 1887a: 298—mention.
2. Maitland 1888b: 175—mention.
3. Gazetteer 1979: IV. 372—mention.

658. KUSHK-I ĀGĀ BAHĀR

Lat. 35° 13' N, long. 66° 13' E. Map 47.
Jauzjān Province. On the left bank of the Band-i Amīr (Balkh) River near Dahān-i Kāshān, near the junction with the Ismaidān or Isfi Maidān River.

Date: Turk and/or Ghurid, 7th–13th cent. (architectural).

Description: Ruins of two mud-brick forts on stone footings. Inside are remains of vaulted rooms, and outside are arrow slits surmounted by three impressed triangles, as at Chahel Burj.

Source: Maricq and Wiet 1959: 84 and pl. XIV—mention and photo.

KUSHK-I BAHĀR. See **2151 KUSHK-I BAHĀR** in Supplement.

KUSHK-I FĪRŪZ. See **2152 KUSHK-I FĪRŪZ** in Supplement.

KUSHK-I KUHNA. See **2153 KUSHK-I KUHNA** in Supplement.

659. KUSHK-I NAKHŪD
Or PĪRZĀDA. See also 962 SABZ QAL'A.

Original: Lat. 31° 38' N, long. 65° 03' E. Map 88.
Revised: 31.62072073 N, 65.05868055 E /
31° 37' 14.59461756 N, 65° 03' 31.24998180 E.
Kandahār Province. 66 km west of Kandahār on the main road to Herat.

Date: Sasanian, 3rd–7th cent. (ceramic).

Description: Many mounds and remains in the vicinity of the bazaar.

Fieldwork: 1955–67 Fischer, DAAD—survey.

Sources:
1. Ferrier 1857: 316—mention.
2. Fischer 1967a: 146—mention.
3. Fischer 1969: 338—brief summary.
4. Fischer et al. 1974–6: 29—mention.

KUSHK-I SHĀH SANAM. See **552 KHĀNĀBĀD**, Balkh.

660. KUSHK KHAWĀL

Lat. 35° 09' N, long. 67° 07' E. Map 47.
Bāmiyān Province. 2 km south of Siāh Khawāl at the point where the gorge opens out, on the route from Darra-i Sūf to Bāmiyān.

Description: A group of cave dwellings.

Fieldwork: 1886 Amir Khan, ABC—topographical survey.

Source: Amir Khan 1888: 168—mention.

661. KUSH RABĀT
Or GUSHA RABĀT.

Original: Lat. 34° 39' N, long. 62° 06' E. Maps 92, 101.
Revised: 34.65581641 N, 62.10652179 E /
34° 39' 20.93907960 N, 062° 06' 23.47843356 E.
Herat Province. At the southern entrance to the Ardawān Pass, 36 km north–north-west of Herat.

Date: Timurid, late 15th cent. (architectural).

Description: A caravanserai on the old route from Herat to Merv. It has a monumental gateway and a mosque facing the entrance, with vaulted rooms around all sides of the courtyard. Construction is of baked brick, though in a poor state of preservation. Also ruins of a 'considerable tower' and of an eight-arched bridge over the Ardawān stream.

Fieldwork:
1. 1884 Maitland, ABC—topographical survey.
2. 1967–9 Pugachenkova, Af/Sov. Mission—survey.
3. 1978–9 Samizay, Kābul University/UNESCO—survey.

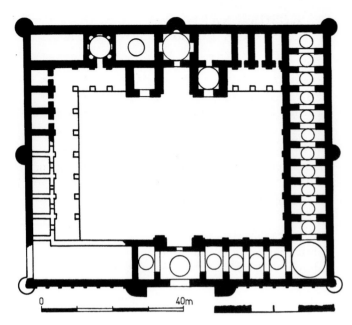

661 Kush Rabāt (after Pugachenkova 1970).

Sources:
1. Ferrier 1857: 190 — mention.
2. *Pioneer*, 17 June 1885 — mentions town and bridge.
3. Maitland 1887c: 479 — brief description of caravanserai.
4. Maitland 1888a: 164 — detailed description.
5. Pugachenkova 1970: 45–9 — full architectural analysis and drawings.
6. *Kabul Times* 1979a — mentions repair work carried out.
7. Samizay 1981: 56–8 — summary description with plans and photos of the monument, with a note on the need for conservation.
8. O'Kane 1987: 359–61 — full description.
9. Golombek and Wilber 1988: 341–2 — description of the caravanserai.
10. Ball 2008: 239 — summary.

662. KUSRUTĀBĀD

Or BULAN. See also 685 LASHKARI BĀZĀR and 1163 TEPE BULAND.

Original: Lat. 31° 34' N, long. 64° 20' E. approximately. Map 86.
Revised: 31° 35' 35.239" N, 64° 19' 44.383" E.
Helmand Province. On the right bank of the Helmand opposite Lashkari Bāzār.

Date: Ghaznavid, 11th–12th cent. (ceramic).

Description: Ruins of a town or palace, presumably a part of the Lashkari Bāzār remains. Only two sherds collected by the Cambridge survey.
Proper name is probably Bulan, hence it may well be the same as Site 1163, Tepe Buland. Consists of badly eroded enclosure wall surrounding an open space. Ceramic is

singularly absent: no sherds at all were found by the Smithsonian survey, except for a few pieces of recent ware dropped there because of its proximity to Lashkar Gah and numerous small villages. The qala walls are very eroded and there are no structural remains. It cannot be dated, though its eroded and deflated condition suggests considerable age. One side has been cut away during the construction of a modern canal.

Aerial photographs show a large semi-circular walled area on the west and north-west; the eastern half is obscured by modern cultivation. At the northern end is a circular citadel mound. The entire area is very heavily pitted by robber pits.

Fieldwork:
1. 1966 Hammond, Cambridge University — survey.
2. 1966, 1971–4 Trousdale, Smithsonian — survey.

Sources:
1. Additional site information by W. Trousdale.
2. Additional information from satellite image by D. Thomas.
3. Hammond 1970: 449 — lists the site (no. 17) and discusses the general survey results.

663. KUT-I ASHRU

See also 696 MAIDĀN.

Lat. 34° 27' N, long. 68° 48' E. Map 60.
Wardak Province. 45 km south of Kābul on the road to Hājigak.

Date: Early Sasanian, 1st half of 4th cent. (numismatic).

Description: Site of a chance discovery of ten gold Sasanian coins, mostly of Hormuzd II.

Source: Ramachandran and Sharma 1956: III. 11 — brief description of the hoard.

664. KUTI KHĒL

Lat. 34° 27' N, long. 70° 21' E. Map 66.
Laghmān Province. On the north bank of the Surkhāb, *c.*1 km south of Jāni Tūp.

Description: A large artificial mound, possibly containing ancient burials. There is an Islamic cemetery on top.

Fieldwork: 1834 Masson — survey.

Sources:
1. Masson 1841: 97 — mention.
2. Errington 2017a: 121 — the Masson collection and archive relating to the site.

665. KUT-I SITĀRA

Original: Lat. 34° 33' N, long. 68° 56' E. Map 63.
Revised: 34.55708271 N, 68.93275843 E /
34° 33' 25.49776500 N, 68° 55' 57.93033252 E.

Kābul Province. 1 km south-west of Baiktūt, 5 km south of Paghmān.

Date: Kushan, 1st–4th cent. (ceramic).

Description: Some remains, possibly of a stupa-monastery complex, on the heights enclosing the valley.

Source: Caspani 1947b: 49—mention.

666. KUTLUG TEPE

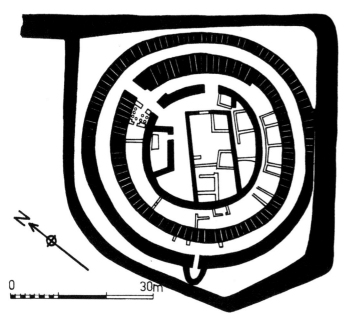

666 Kutlug Tepe (after Sarianidi 1977b).

Original: Lat. 37° 05' N, long. 66° 43' E. Map 26.
Revised: 37.08647884 N, 66.69536454 E /
37° 05' 11.32382400 N, 66° 41' 43.31232780 E.
Balkh Province. 3 km north-west of Farūkābād, 50 km north-west of Balkh, 10 km to the east of the road to Kilift.

Date: Achaemenid, 6th–4th cent. BC (ceramic).

Description: Remains of a round building, possibly a temple, fortified by massive mud walls pierced with embrasures.

Fieldwork:
1. 1886 Ata Muhammad, ABC—topographical survey.
2. 1973 Sarianidi and Tarzi, Af/Sov. Mission—excavations.

Sources:
1. Maitland 1888b: 274—mention.
2. Kruglikova and Sarianidi 1976—mention.
3. Sarianidi 1977b: 99—summary of the architecture.
4. Sarianidi 1977c: 116–21—description and discussion of the monumental architecture.
5. Francfort 1979a: 18–19—lists the site and discusses the general characteristics of Achaemenid military architecture.

667. KUTPŪR
See also 469 JAMĀL KĀLA and 121 BĀZITKHĒL.

Lat. 34° 27' N, long. 70° 20' E. Map 66.
Laghmān Province. At the foot of the Siāh Kūh, *c*.6 km south-west of Darūnta, just to the north of the road.

Date: Kushan, 1st cent. (stylistic).

Description: A large stupa *c*.53 m in circumference. It is covered in plaster and has a decorative frieze of alternating blind arches and pilasters. The condition is fairly good. At the centre was an empty baked brick chamber and underneath were some steatite fragments and a silver reliquary.

Fieldwork:
1. 1833 Honigberger—excavation.
2. 1834 Masson—excavation.
3. 1965 Mizuno, Kyoto University—survey.

Sources:
1. Masson 1841: 64–5—brief description of the stupa and contents (Tope 1).
2. Mizuno 1971: 119—summary of Masson's work and description and photos of the present condition (Stupa 23).
3. Ball 2008: 239—summary.
4. Jongeward et al. 2012—catalogue and discussion of the reliquaries.
5. Errington 2017a: 86–91 and 2017b: 18, 27–9—the Masson collection and archive relating to the site.

LAFTĀN. See 2154 LAFTĀN in Supplement.

668. LAGHMĀN

Lat. 35° 59' N, long. 66° 06' E. Maps 24, 47.
Faryāb Province. In the Astarāb Valley between Sar-i Pul and Bidistān, 6 km south of Sukhta Qal'a.

Description: Several caves of the 'Buddhist' period. Amongst them is a huge natural cave, reported to be very deep. It has stone fortification walls with loopholes defending the entrance.

There is also a nearby site with lots of surface finds of Ghaznavid metalwork, stucco, and ceramics (Jonathan L. Lee).

Fieldwork: 1886 Griesbach, ABC—topographical survey.

Sources:
1. Griesbach 1888b: 200—brief description of the caves.
2. Bivar 1966: 58—mentions the caves.

LAGHMĀN inscriptions. See 250 DARŪNTA and 1067 SHALATAK.

669. LAIRU

Lat. 32° 09' N, long. 66° 55' E. Maps 76, 91.
Zābul Province. 10 km north-east of Qal'at-i Ghilzai, just off the road to Kābul on the west bank of the Tarnak River.

The site is on top of the cliff which marks the boundary between the river channel and the surrounding plain.

Date: Neolithic/Chalcolithic, 10th–5th mill. BC (lithic).

Description: The site comprises a series of irregular mounds broken by water channels stretching along the cliff top for some 50 m, rising 0.50–1 m above the plain. No indication of occupation apparent in the cliff section or the water channels, but a thorough survey was not possible. It is therefore not certain that the mounds represent occupation and only one find was recorded, a blade or flake dark grey in colour, most probably of chert, or perhaps of obsidian. One edge is worn, but not retouched.

Source: Site information by P. Baker.

670. LAKSH

Lat. 36° 43’ N, long. 71° 56’ E. Map 39.
Badakhshān Province. In the Shkhaur Valley south of the Panja River, between Ishakāshim and Qal’a-i Panja.

Description: A group of petroglyphs depicting ibex and hunting scenes.

Source: Agresti 1970: 4–5—brief description.

LĀL SAR-I JANGAL. See 2155 LĀL SAR-I JANGĀL in Supplement.

671. LĀLĀKĒL

Lat. 33° 13’ N, long. 67° 36’ E. Map 78.
Ghazni Province. At the northern end of the Kūh-i Khūd Valley, *c.*18 km north of Sang-i Māsha.

Description: A complex of a few artificial caves at the foot of a large sandstone bluff.

Fieldwork: 1974 Taddei and Verardi, IsMEO—survey.

Sources:
1. Taddei 1975: 546—mention.
2. Verardi 1977a: 142—brief description.

672. LALKHĀN QAL’A

Lat. 31° 30’ N, long. 65° 31’ E. Map 89.
Kandahār Province. 9 km east of Panjwāyī, 2 km to the south of the road.

Dates: Sasanian, 3rd–7th cent.; Turki Shahi-early Islamic, 7th–13th cent.

Description: No details supplied.

Fieldwork: 1950–1 Fairservis, AMNH—survey.

Source: Fairservis 1971: 394—mention (Site Khr-6).

673. LALMA
See also 404 HADDA.

Original: Lat. 34° 20–33’ N, long. 70° 28–46’ E. Map 67.
Revised: 34.34523851 N, 70.46120193 E /
34° 20’ 42.85863024 N, 70° 27’ 40.32695916 E.
Nangahār Province. 3 km south-west of the main Hadda complex, 11 km south of Jalālābād.

Dates: Early Sasanian-Kushano Sasanian, 3rd–5th cent. (stylistic).

Description: A stupa-monastery complex consisting of three stupas and a group of 44 caves used as cells. The main stupa excavated, of two building periods, produced many stucco architectural fragments, statuary, and some traces of frescos.

Fieldwork: 1965–6 Mizuno and Fukita, Kyoto University— excavations.

Sources:
1. Fujita 1966b– brief discussion on the dating evidence.
2. Mizuno and Fujita 1968: 109–12—fully illustrated summary excavation report, without discussion.
3. H. Motamedi 1975c: 270–2—summary of the excavations.
4. Franz 1977–8– discusses the development and the art of the stupa.

674. LALMĪ BUZ
Or ARAP. Includes BĀGH-I MĪRI and CHINZAI.

Original: Lat. 36° 44’–36° 45’ N, long. 69° 18’–69° 20’ E. Maps 35, 36.
Revised:
36.74941268 N, 69.32548737 E / 36° 44’ 57.88566096 N, 69° 19’ 31.75453344 E (A).
36.73795241 N, 69.31947741 E / 36° 44’ 16.62867672 N, 69° 19’ 10.11866736 E (B).
36.73544817 N, 69.30710523 E / 36° 44’ 07.61341164 N, 69° 18’ 25.57881324 E (C).
Takhār Province. Some 20 km west of Tāluqān, by the road which links this town with Khānābād; the tepes are situated near to the mountainous spur of the Bāgh-i Mīri, on the edge of the terrace overlooking the village of Lalmī Buz and the plain to the south of the Tāluqān River (left bank).

Dates: Beg. Iron, end 2nd–beg. 1st mill. BC; Achaemenid, 6th–4th cent. BC; Hellenistic, 3rd–1st cent. BC; Timurid, 15th–16th cent. (ceramic).

Description: Place-name Arap: three mounds A, B, C, aligned east to west on the edge of the terrace, spaced by 200 m (A–B) and 400 m (B–C). (A) The first is a square platform (30 × 30 m), oriented east–west, with the high part in the east (2.5 m); (B) The second is oblong, same orientation (40 × 20 m), height 1 m with a small square edifice in the centre; (C) The third is rounded (diam. 30 m) and low (1.5 m). The importance of this site, besides its age, lies in its proximity to a Hellenistic zone of habitation to the south-west (plateau of Chinzai),

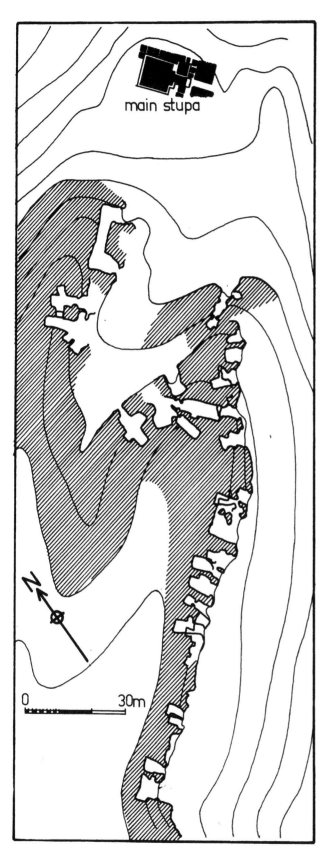

673 Lalma (after Mizuno and Fujita 1968).

main stupa

0   30m

indicated more by areas strewn with sherds rather than by mounds, and by traces of the canal which irrigated it, in the foothills south-west of Bagh-i Mīri.

Collection: National Museum/AIA—sherds.

Fieldwork: 1978 Gardin et al., CNRS—survey.

Sources:
1. Site information by J.-C. Gardin.
2. Gardin and Lyonnet 1978–9: pl. VIII—nos. 408–12.
3. Lyonnet 1997: figs 25, 35, 39—nos. 408–12.
4. Gardin 1998: 75—nos. 408–12.

LANDI BARECHI. See 2156 LANDI BARECHI in Supplement.

675. LALPŪRA
See also 226 DAKKA and 518 KAMA DAKKA.

Lat. 34° 14' N, long. 71° 02' E. Map 68.
Nangahār Province. On the north bank of the Kābul River, just west of the Khyber Pass.

Date: Kushano-Sasanian, 4th–5th cent. (epigraphic, stylistic).

Description: Find spot of a small stone relief, measuring 39×26 cm, depicting two wrestlers and containing a brief Kharoshthi inscription.

Sources:
1. Shakur 1946: 28–9—description of the relief and brief epigraphical analysis.
2. Davary 1977– mention.
3. Mac Dowall and Taddei 1978b: 241—mention.

LAL QAL'A. See 155 CHAHĀR BĀGH.

676. LĀMĀN
Including GUNBAD-I MIRĀN.

Lat. 34° 45' N, long. 63° 06' E. Map 53.
Bādghīs Province. *C.*37 km south of Qal'a-i Nau at the northern side of the Sabzak Pass on the road to Herat.

Date: Ghaznavid(?) stylistic; Timurid, 15th–16th cent. (stylistic).

Description: A high mound of two levels, the upper, to the east, probably a fortress. Ghaznavid bronzes (domestic) and pottery have been recovered from the site.

To the west of the village, on the south side of the road, is a large cemetery which includes two domed mausolea. The graveyard contains a number of red sandstone blocks now reused for headstones which appear to have come from a more ancient building. One of the headstones has what appears to be the carving of lion or fabulous beast, a second is inscribed with a series of angular characters in an indeterminate script. It is inscribed in red sandstone and appears to have been a lintel or similar architectural feature reused from a structure elsewhere in the area. There are two inscriptions: the first is deeply incised, and angular; the second appears on another face (below) and is faint but may be Arabic.

Fieldwork: 1992 Lee—reconnaissance.

Sources:
1. Site information by Jonathan L. Lee.
2. Gazetteer 1975: III. 287—mentions the fort and tomb.

LANDI BARECHI. See 2156 in Supplement.

LANGĀR. See 2157 LANGĀR in Supplement.

677. LANGAR KHĒL

Lat. 33° 35' N, long. 67° 20' E. Map 77.
Ūruzgān Province. In the Ajristān district, north or Ūruzgān. The site is 18 km north-east of Ajristān Woliswali, in a side valley to the east of the Ajristān River.

Description: Local reports of a site where a number of bronzes were found in the early 1950s.

Source: Bivar 1954a: 118—mention.

678. LANGARKISH

Lat. 37° 02' N, long. 73° 47' E. Map 40.
Badakhshān Province. Near the end of the Langarkish Valley where a small stream flows into the Panja River.

Date: ?Epi-Palaeolithic, 10,000 BC (stylistic).

Description: Three granite boulders with petroglyphs of ibex, hands, and figures. There are also traces of ancient cultivation in the vicinity.

Fieldwork:
1. 1898–9 Olufsen, Danish Army—survey.
2. 1901 Stein, ASI—survey.

Sources:
1. Olufsen 1904: 195—mentions the petroglyphs.
2. Stein 1904: 70—mentions the cultivation.
3. Gratzl et al. 1976: 315—mention the petroglyphs.

LARĀSĪ. See 2158 LARĀSĪ in Supplement.

679. LĀRGHA

Original: Lat. 33° 35' N, long. 64° 10' E. Map 54.
Revised: 33.57784162 N, 64.15493604 E /

33° 34' 40.22983452 N, 64° 09' 17.76976200 E.
Ghūr Province. 9 km west of Sab Talkh on the route from Taiwāra to Deh Tītān. The site is *c*.2 km north-east of the village of Lārgha.

Description: Many ruined towers.

Fieldwork: 1885 Sahibdad Khan, ABC—topographical survey.

Source: Sahibdad Khan 1891a: 242—mention.

680. LAR-I BĀLĀ

Original: Lat. 32° 08' N, long. 64° 18' E. approximately.
Maps 73, 87.
Revised: 32.13318451 N, 64.30206604 E /
32° 07' 59.46422556 N, 64° 18' 07.43775264 E.
Helmand Province. 19 km north-west of Qal'a-i Sa'ādat, just to the west of kārīz.

Description: A mound.

Source: Maitland 1879—mention.

LARĀSĪ. See 2158 in Supplement.

681. LARKHĀBI

Original: Lat. 35° 56' N, long. 68° 37' E. Map 33.
Revised: 35.95885147 N, 68.62050115 E /
35° 57' 31.86528336 N, 68° 37' 13.80414792 E.
Baghlān Province. On the Ghūri Plain west of Pul-i Khumri, 4 km south-east of Qal'a-i Ghūri.

Description: A line of small artificial mounds.

Fieldwork: 1886 Maitland, ABC—topographical survey.

Source: Maitland 1888b: 330—mention.

682. LARMUSH

Lat. 35° 20' N, long. 67° 44' E. Map 48.
Bamiyan province, Kahmard District. On the route from Chārikār to Dūshi by the Shībar Pass and Surkhāb Valley: in the lateral Kahmard Valley.

Date: Turk and/or pre-Mongol Islamic, 7th–13th cent. (architectural).

Description: A very badly ruined tower. There is also an artificial cave complex in the middle Kahmard valley below Payīn Bāgh.

Fieldwork: 1974–5 Le Berre, DAFA—survey.

Source: Le Berre 1987: 65–6—Itinerary A2, Darya-i Kahmard, ruin 6; brief description.

683. LARWAND

Or MALIKĀN.

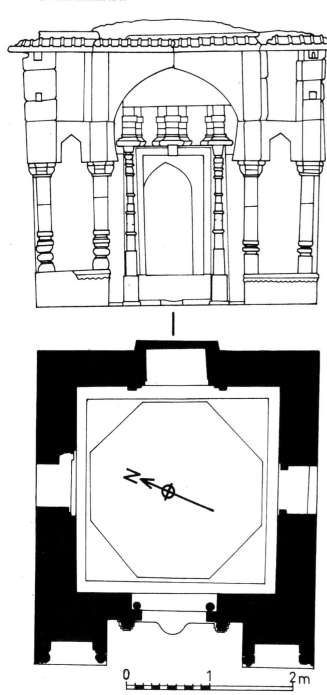

683 Larwand (W. Ball).

Lat. 33° 04' N, long. 63° 51' E. Map 73.
At the northern end of the Larwand Valley on the route to Parjuman from Mushkān. Near the village of Malikān.

Date: Ghurid, 12th–13th cent. (stylistic).

Description: The Masjid-i Sangi. A small building *c.*2.50 m square and 3 m high, of very carefully fitted masonry blocks. It has a very elaborately decorated façade and the remains of a dome inside. The architecture is entirely in the style of north-western India.

Nearby is the outline of a huge rectangular enclosure.

Fieldwork:
1. 1946 Kohzad, HAS—survey.
2. 1969 Scarcia, University of Venice—survey.
3. 1977 Ball—survey.

Sources:
1. Naïmi 1949– the article does not contain any mention of the monument but there is a good sketch of the façade of the monument on the front cover of the journal.
2. Kohzad 1951–4, 9/1: 42–3—summary description.
3. Klimburg 1958: 18—brief description.
4. Klimburg 1960: 49—photo and brief description.
5. Klimburg 1963 34—brief description.
6. Fischer 1969: 343—very brief summary.
7. Janata 1971: 58—brief discussion of its possible identification with the Ghurid capital of Zamindāwar.
8. Scarcia and Taddei 1973—detailed historical background and stylistic analysis.
9. Fischer 1974a: figs 173 and 174—photos and discussion of the Indian origins of the dome form.
10. Fischer 1978a: 339–43—summary.
11. Herberg 1978: 219—brief description.
12. Rafat 1980: 4—mentions a decorated manuscript found in the mosque, and the remains of a palace nearby.
13. Ball 1990—full description of the area and archaeological context.
14. Hillenbrand 2000—discussion in the broader context of Ghaznavid and Ghurid architecture.
15. Ball 2002: 26—brief description in the context of Ghurid fortifications.
16. Wannell 2002: 236—disscusses its possible construction by Indian prisoners.
17. Ball 2008: 240—summary.
18. Flood 2009b: 151–6—discusses the Indian elements in the stone carving.

684. LĀSH

See also 482 JUWAIN and 2250 SĪR HANGĀN in Supplement.

Original: Lat. 31° 43' N, long. 61° 35' E. Map 83.
Revised: 31.70872431 N, 61.58587086 E /
31° 42' 31.40751924 N, 61° 35' 09.13508052 E.
Nimrūz Province. On the Farāh Rūd, 95 km south-west of Farāh on the road to Zaranj.

Date: Timurid, 14th–16th cent. (ceramic, documentary).

Description: A series of fortifications overlooking the river, forming three successions of defensive works, consisting of two upper citadels on the plateau and a lower, badly ruined citadel on the river.

Fieldwork:
1. 1884 Peacocke, ABC—topographical survey.

2. 1950 Fairservis, AMNH—survey.

3. 1960–70 Fischer, Bonn University—survey.

Sources:

1. Ferrier 1857: 422—brief description.
2. Bellew 1874: 280—mention.
3. Smith 1876: 324–5—brief description.
4. Peacocke 1885a: 20–1—detailed description.
5. Peacocke 1887a: 34–5—detailed description and sketch.
6. A. C. Yate 1887: 99 and 102–4—description.
7. Tate 1910: 215–16—mention.
8. Fairservis 1961: 40—mention (Site 16).
9. Fischer et al. 1974–6: 36—mention.

685. LASHKARĪ BĀZĀR
See also 149 BUST and 662 KUSRUTĀBĀD.

Original: Lat. 31°33–55' N, long. 64°22–36' E. Map 86.

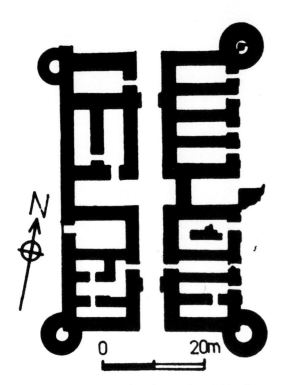

685 Lashkari Bāzār—Central Palace (after Schlumberger and Sourdel-Thomine 1978).

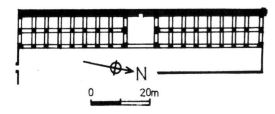

685 Lashkari Bāzār—Mosque (after Schlumberger and Sourdel-Thomine 1978).

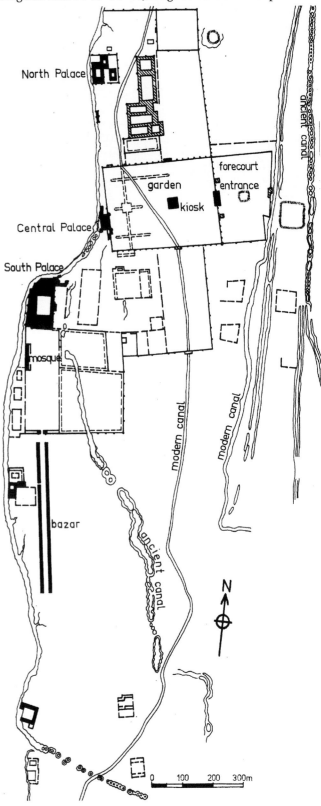

685 Lashkari Bāzār—general plan (after Schlumberger and Sourdel-Thomine 1978).

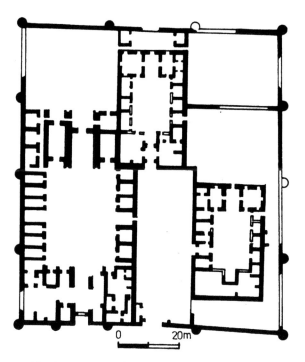

685 Lashkari Bāzār—North Palace (after Schlumberger and Sourdel-Thomine 1978).

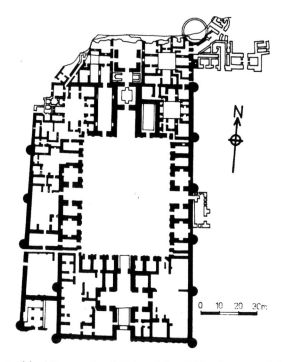

685 Lashkari Bāzār—South Palace (after Schlumberger and Sourdel-Thomine 1978).

Revised: 31.54234246 N, 64.35341676 E /
31° 32' 32.43283836 N, 64° 21' 12.30035328 E.
Helmand Province. On the left bank of the Helmand,
44 km to the south of the Kandahār-Herat road.

Dates: Ghaznavid and Ghurid, 11th–13th cent. (architectural, ceramic, documentary, stylistic, etc.)

Description: A vast concentration of palatial residences and public buildings stretching along the banks of the Helmand between Bust and the modern town of Lashkargāh for 6.5 km. The remains include three palaces on a bluff overlooking the river, a Friday Mosque, a bazaar, kilns with extensive local production, and many other buildings. The most important finds were decorative elements from the main palace—wall paintings, stuccos, inscriptions, etc.

Collections: National Museum—excavated material, including a reconstructed stucco mosque.

Fieldwork: 1949–52 Schlumberger, DAFA—excavations.

Sources:

1. A. H. Kohzad 1949a—discusses the history of the site and its relation to the existing monuments.
2. M. N. Kohzad 1949—describes an archaeological visit to the remains.
3. Schlumberger 1949a—historical background and summary of the results of the first season.
4. Schlumberger 1949e—brief report on a preliminary survey of the remains.
5. Schlumberger 1950—describes the excavation of the audience hall, the palace mosque, the garden pavilion, and the bazaar.
6. A. H. Kohzad 1951—discusses the evidence of the frescos for Ghaznavid uniforms.
7. Schlumberger 1952a—description and photos of the escavation of the Friday Mosque.
8. Schlumberger 1952d—summary of the architecture and frescos and discussion of Ghurid art.
9. M. N. Kohzad 1953—reviews A.A. Kohzad's book on Lashkari Bazar.
10. Sourdel-Thomine 1959—brief note on the stucco decorations.
11. Sourdel-Thomine 1960—discussion of Ghurid decorative art.
12. Bombaci 1961—brief description of the remains in the context of a broader Turk art style.
13. Bombaci 1962—outline of the main features of Ghaznavid architecture.
14. Boissier 1963—chemical analyses of some of the ceramic pastes and glazes.
15. Gardin 1963—typology and ceramic analysis of the pottery, and a catalogue of the coins.
16. Pugachenkova 1963: 116–21—general summary.
17. Otto-Dorn 1964: chapter 2—brief description of the south palace.
18. Bivar 1968– discusses some of the coins of the 'Sijistan barbarous' series found recently in and around the site.
19. D. and J. Sourdel 1968: 359–62—briefly discuss the south palace.

20. Rowland and Rice 1971: 52–3 and pls 191–3—description and photos of the frescos on display from the National Museum.
21. Sourdel-Thomine and Spuler 1973: 279–80—pl. XL—photo and description of the frescos.
22. N. Dupree et al. 1974: 75–8—guide to the exhibits in the National Museum.
23. Desai 1975: 11—discusses architectural parallels in India.
24. N. Dupree 1977: 312–15—guide to all the remains.
25. G. Casal 1978—catalogue and description of the frescos.
26. Fischer 1978a: 311—follows N. Dupree's guide to the site.
27. Le Berre 1978—brief note on the removal and lifting of the decorative panels.
28. Schlumberger 1978—full architectural record and analysis of all monuments, with many plans and photos.
29. Schlumberger and Gardin 1978—chronological table.
30. Sourdel-Thomine 1978—stylistic and epigraphic analyses of the decorations.
31. Hillenbrand 1984: 413—discussion in the context of Islamic palace architecture.
32. Allen 1988–90—architectural notes on many of the standing remains, supplementing the French records of the site.
33. Hillenbrand 2000—discussion in the broader context of Ghaznavid and Ghurid architecture.
34. Amirsoleimani 2005—discussed the clothes depicted on the paintings.
35. Tissot 2006: 494–503—National Museum catalogue details and photos.
36. Ball 2008: 94, 120, 240–6—summary.

686. LASHKARĪ BĀZĀR, PANJSHĪR

Lat. 35° 22' N, long. 69° 38' E. Map 50.
Parwān Province. On the east bank of the Panjshīr River, 2 km north of Umarz.

Date: Timurid,   15th–16th   cent.   (documentary, numismatic).

Description: Site of an extensive ancient settlement consisting of foundation walls and eroded copper coins and sherds. Probably associated with the ancient mines of Nuqri Khāna nearby.

Fieldwork: 1976 Kohl—survey.

Sources:
1. Kohl 1978: 71–2—brief description.
2. Thomalsky et al. 2013: 218–24—discussion of the Panjshīr silver mines.
3. Merkel et al. 2013—analysis of the slag from the silver mines.

687. LAT QAL'A
Or KONA QALA.

Original: Lat. 30° 10' N, long. 62° 42' E. Map 96.
Revised: 30.1710431 N, 62.68818771 E / 30° 10' 15.75517728 N, 62° 41' 17.47577256 E.
Nīmrūz Province. On the south bank of the Helmand east of Rūdbār, 10 km past Landi Barechi. The names 'Lat' and 'Lop' describe sectors along this stretch of the river and are not names of sites. The qal'a is called Kona (?Kuhna) Qal'a. Lat refers to the territorial region, of which Khel-i Bibarg Khān is the principal village. The next territory downstream is called Lop.

Dates: 2nd mill. BC; early 1st mill. BC; Achaemenid-Hellenistic, 6th–1st cent. BC; Parthian-Sasanian, 1st–7th cent.; Ghaznavid, 11th–12th cent.; Timurid, 15th–16th cent. (ceramic).

Description: The Qal'a is a steep-sided conical mound. The top has been flattened and a small, 19th-century ruinous fort with rifle ports occupies a small part of the top, covered with sherds—many of them glazed—and broken bricks. This is the only clearly multi-period site found by the Smithsonian survey in the Helmand Valley. The upper strata are Timurid. Below, there is relatively continuous occupation through Ghaznavid, Sasanian, Parthian, Hellenistic, Achaemenid, and Iron Age. It was not possible to continue the excavation, but numerous sherds in spoil suggest the site extends back to at least the 2nd millennium BC, and likely earlier. Owing to aggradation of the valley, the Parthian sherds were found more than 2 m below the present ground surface. The visible tepe is, therefore, but a small portion of the mound. The earliest strata are certainly below the present water table which is normally 4 m below the surface.

Fieldwork:
1. 1884 Maitland, ABC—topographical survey.
2. 1966 Hammond, Cambridge University—survey.
3. 1975 Trousdale, Helmand-Sistan Project—excavation.

Sources:
1. Site information by W. Trousdale.
2. Bellew 1874: 202—mention.
3. Maitland 1888a: 57—mention.
4. Hammond 1970: 449—lists sites (nos. 27 and 36) and describes the pottery types and general survey results.

688. LAWAR

Lat. 30° 57' N, long. 61° 58' E. Map 92.
Nīmrūz Province. 13 km due east of Zaranj, to the south of the road to Chakhānsūr.

Dates: Mongol-Timurid, 13th–16th cent. (ceramic).

Description: A surface site consisting of a scatter of sherds and baked bricks.

Fieldwork: 1960–70 Fischer, Bonn University—survey.

Sources:
1. Fischer 1969: 335—mention (Ruin D5).
2. Fischer et al. 1974–6: 34—mention.

689. LĪLĪ TEPE
See also 86 BAGHLĀN SHAHR-I KUHNA.

Original: Lat. 36° 11' N, long. 68° 45' E. Map 33.
Revised: 36.18283198 N, 68.75087781 E /
36° 10' 58.19512512 N, 68° 45' 03.16010376 E.
Baghlān Province. Next to the road about halfway between
Baghlān Shahr-i Jadīd and Baghlān Shahr-i Kuhna.

Date: Early Sasanian, 3rd–4th cent. (stylistic).

Description: A small, steep-sided mound with a modern
building on top. Surface finds of Buddhist stone sculpture,
bronzes, and beads.

Fieldwork: 1960 Hayashi and Sahara, Kyoto University –
survey.

Sources:
1. Dagens 1964a: 36–7 – brief description of the two reliefs
   found.
2. Hayashi and Sahara 1962: 68–70 – illustrations of the
   surface finds and summary of the site in Japanese.
3. Tissot 2006: 94 – National Museum catalogue details
   and photos.

LŪMĀN. See 1184 TEPE SINAUBAR.

690. MABIR TEPE

Original: Lat. 36° 52' N, long. 66° 48' E. Map 26.
Revised: 36.86180128 N, 66.80524534 E /
36° 51' 42.48461088 N, 66° 48' 18.88323696 E.
Balkh Province. 14 km north-west of this town on the road
to Kilift, north side, about 150 m.

Description: Square mound (*c.*120 × 120 m), height *c.*12 m,
slightly bumpy at the top, surrounded by a circular ditch
occupied in part by a pond (south-east zone of the tepe).

Fieldwork: 1948 Le Berre, DAFA – survey.

Source: M. Le Berre: unpublished 1948 report, DAFA
archives, tépé P. 2.

MADANIYAT TEPE. See 909 QARA BAI.

MADAR-I PĀDSHĀH. See 862 QAL'A-I MADAR-I
PĀDSHĀH.

MADDA KHĒL. See 693 MAHDI KHĒL.

MADRASA. See 136 BĪSH TAN TĒG.

691. MAGAS

Lat. 33° 27' N, long. 70° 00' E. Map 82.
Paktiyā Province. Near the village of Yakubi in Khūst
district, 11 km north of Matūn.

Description: Ruins of an old fort overlooking the village,
where ancient coins have been found.

Source: Gazetteer 1910: IV. 366 – mention.

692. MAHAJIRĪN

Original: Lat. 36° 47' N, long. 66° 42' E. Map 26.
Revised: 36.78717017 N, 66.69535974 E /
36° 47' 13.81259976 N, 66° 41' 43.29506580 E.
Balkh Province. 18 km south-east of Nimlik, about 500 m
south of the Balkh road, south-east of the village of Chahār
Bulaq.

Description: Rectangular platform (70 × 45 m), height
6.50 m; no particular relief. Two little tepes to the east and
north, the latter used as a cemetery.

Fieldwork: 1948 Le Berre, DAFA – survey.

Source: M. Le Berre: unpublished 1948 report, DAFA
archives, tépé P. 44.

MAHALLA-I MULLĀHĀ. See 702. MĀLĀN.

693. MAHDI KHĒL
Or MADDA KHĒL.

Original: Lat. 33° 22' N, long. 70° 01' E. Map 82.
Revised: 33.37180866 N, 70.0191901 E / 33° 22' 18.51117636 N,
70° 01' 09.08436288 E.
Paktiyā Province. On the Pakistani border 140 km east of
Gardēz, on a northern affluent of the Kurram River 10 km
east of Matūn.

Date: Ghurid, 12th–13th cent. (numismatic).

Description: A very ruined old fort. In 1969 a hoard of gold
coins was found here, most of them Khwarazmshahi.

Source: Bivar 1975 – description of the discovery and the
hoard.

694. MAHMUD KHĀN
Or MUHAMMAD KHĀN.

Original: Lat. 31° 32' N, long. 66° 37' E. Map 90.
Revised: 31.53723702 N, 66.62607727 E /
31° 32' 14.05327020 N, 66° 37' 33.87818604 E.
Kandahār Province. On the left side of the Lora River
Valley near Qal'a-i Nur Muhammad and Chighazai.

Description: A high artificial mound and a ruined octagonal
brick tower, said locally to be pre-Islamic.

Sources:
1. Clifford 1879: 4 – brief description of the tower and its
   associated legend.
2. Gazetteer 1980: V. 313 – mention.

695. MAIDACHAPA

Original: Lat. 36° 11' N, long. 69° 07' E approximately. Map 33.
Revised: 36.18909998 N, 69.11128317 E /
36° 11' 20.75991864 N, 69° 06' 40.61942568 E.
Takhār Province. To the west of the Narīn-Ishkamīsh road, near Tepe Qarya-i Afghān.

Date: Kushan-Sasanian, 1st–7th cent. (ceramic).

Description: A mound.

Fieldwork: 1960–8 Fischer, DAAD—survey.

Source: Fischer 1969: 352—mention (Tepe B 8).

696. MAIDĀN
See also 663 KUT-I ASHRU.

Original: Lat. 34° 28' N, long. 68° 46' E. Map 60.
Revised: 34.47704353 N, 68.77474046 E /
34° 28' 37.35672456 N, 68° 46' 29.06564412 E.
Maidān Province. On the western side of a lateral valley opening off the Maidān Valley, near the village of Molakhēl.

Description: Ancient mine workings, in part obscured by modern workings. To the south, a vein 20 m long has been excavated up to a depth of 2 m, and to the north, a small cave has been excavated. To the west is a series of four pits, 3 m in diameter. There are also traces of ancient structures.

Fieldwork: 1977 CNRS—geological survey.

Source: Berthoud et al. 1977: 11–12—description and sketch plan of the remains and the geology.

697. MAIMANA

Lat. 35° 55' N, long. 64° 46' E. Map 24.
Faryāb Province. 341 km south-west of Mazār-i Sharīf.

Dates: Early Iron Age, late 2nd–early 1st mill. BC. (ceramic), 10th–11th cent. (documentary, stylistic).

Description: A large artificial mound *c.*20 m high. A citadel originally stood on top, but has now been demolished. A medieval lacquered bronze ewer and 31 other metal objects were found by chance in 1953.

The shrine of Saif al-Muluk on the citadel mound, now destroyed, may suggest elements of Timurid glazed tiles in the dome. The minarets appear to be mid to late 19th-century additions. Traces of medieval walls around the city were still visible in 1978 in the south-west quarter of the city, around the prison.

Fieldwork:
1. 1885 Maitland, Peacocke, ABC—topographical survey.
2. 1952 Le Berre and Gardin, DAFA—survey.

Sources:
1. Gardin and Lyonnet, 1980 chronological study of pottery from unpublished DAFA surveys.

2. Additional notes on the shrine by Jonathan L. Lee.
3. Grodekoff 1880: 110—brief description of the citadel and mound.
4. Peacocke 1887a: 111—brief description of Bala Hisar.
5. Maitland 1888b: 107—brief description of the citadel.
6. Le Strange 1905: 424–5—summary of the historical references.
7. Niedermeyer and Diez 1924—photographs of Maimana citadel showing main entrance, walls, and bastions, and detail of shrine of Saif al-Muluk and the south-eastern aspects of the citadel.
8. Ramachandran and Sharma 1956: I. 19 and III. 14—describe several objects recovered from the citadel mound.
9. Rowland and Rice 1971: pl. 174—photo and note on the bronze ewer.
10. Melikian-Chirvani 1975b—discusses some of the bronzes.
11. Gazetteer 1979: IV. 398–9—brief description of the citadel.
12. Grötzbach 1979a—plan of citadel and town from 1949 prior to redevelopment.
13. Lee 1996: 6–7, 12–13—summary of pre-Islamic and early Islamic historical geography.
14. Tissot 2006: 493—National Museum catalogue details and photos.

698. MAIWAND

Original: Lat. 31° 45' N, long. 65° 08' E. Map 88.
Revised: 31.75260553 N, 65.13038443 E /
31° 45' 09.37989216 N, 65° 07' 49.38394548 E.
Kandahār Provnce. 60 km north-west of Kandahār, 2 km from the right bank of the Kushk-i Nakhud River.

Dates: Achaemenid, 6th–4th cent. BC; early Islamic, 10th–13th cent. (ceramic).

Description: A very high mound *c.*11 m high, surrounded by a ditch. Some Mundigak VI–VII sherds recovered.

Fieldwork: 1956 Ramachandran and Sharma, ASI—reconnaissance.

Sources:
1. Additional note on the ceramics by G. Willcox.
2. Ramachandran and Sharma 1956: I. 12–13—brief description.
3. Gazetteer 1980: V. 319—mention.

MAJAR. See 307. DŪN QISHLĀQ.

MAJNUN BEG. See 2159 MAJNUN BEG in Supplement.

699. MAKANDAK

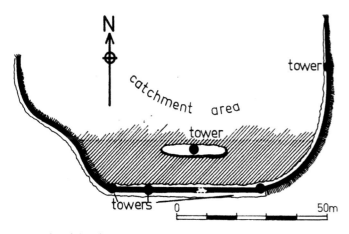

699 Makandak (after Balsan 1972a).

Lat. 30° 39' N, long. 66° 13' E. Map 99.
Kandahār Province. In Rīgīstān between Spīn Baldak and Shorawak, 9 km west of the Pakistan border.

Date: Timurid, 15th cent. (ceramic).

Description: Remains of a large earthen dam, 270 m long and 1.75 m high. There are four mud-brick towers along the dam wall at regular intervals, with a fifth and sixth on an 'island' in the catchment.

Sources:
1. Balsan 1972a: 30–4 — description and photos.
2. Balsan 1972b: 153 — mention.

Mala alau. See 732 MUNA 'ALĀ.

700. MALĀKHĀN
See also 881 QAL'A-I SIRAK.

Original: Lat. 30° 30' N, long. 62° 23' E. Map 98.
Revised:
Between 30.47471224 N, 63.34396976 E /
30° 28' 28.96404672 N, 63° 20' 38.29115220 E and
30.50684622 N, 63.39563673 E /
30° 30' 24.64638444 N, 63° 23' 44.29222440 E.
Helmand Province. A village and a geographical region on the right bank of the Helmand, an area of land about 10 miles in length, on the right bank flood plain, extending eastward from Daishu up to Khan Nashin area across the river.

Dates: Parthian to Ghaznavid, c.2nd –11th cent. (ceramic).

Description: Qal'a-i Sirak is a large site on this flood plain and near modern Malākhān village, located close to the Helmand River. Further north are a string of 17 sites running east–west on the Malākhān plain along an ancient canal. Malākhān Plain I (also called Bābā Qal'a) is likely a recent tower at the east end of the series; Malākhān Plain XVII also

exhibits remains likely from the Ghaznavid period. The remainder of the sites are badly eroded with few architectural remains visible. Sherd coverage on and between them is almost exclusively from the Parthian and Sasanian periods.

Fieldwork:
1. 1903–5 Tate, SAC — survey.
2. 1966, 1971–4 Trousdale, Smithsonian — survey.

Sources:
1. Site information by W. Trousdale.
2. 1857 Ferrier: 407 — brief notice.
3. Tate 1909: 64 — brief description.

701. MALĀKHĀNA

Lat. 31° 17' N, long. 64° 03' E. Map 97.
Helmand Province. In a wadi bed in the desert, 19 km west of the Helmand.

Dates: Achaemenid, 6th–4th cent. BC; Sasanian, 3rd–7th cent. (ceramic).

Description: An artificial mound.

Fieldwork: 1966 Hammond, Cambridge University — survey.

Source: Hammond 1970: 449 — lists site (no. 38) and describes the pottery types and general survey results.

702. MĀLĀN
Or MAHALLA-I MULLĀHĀ. See also 810 PESHWĀRĀN.

Original: Lat. 31° 32' N, long. 61° 32' E. Map 83.
Revised: 31.52814251 N, 61.53777495 E /
31° 31' 41.31304932 N, 61° 32' 15.98980380 E.
Nīmrūz Province. Near the Iranian border 2 km north of Peshwārān.

Description: A group of ruins.

Source: Bellew 1874: 246 — mention.

MALIKĀN. See 683. LARWAND.

703. MĀLISTĀN

Lat. 33° 18' N, long. 67° 10' E. Maps 77, 79.
Ghazni Province. In the headwaters of the Arghandāb River, c.35 km north-west of Sang-i Māsha.

Description: Ruins of a city.

Source: Markham 1876: 244 — mention.

MALMINJ. See 2160 MALMINJ in Supplement.

MAMALIK. See 776 NIMLIK.

704. MANĀRA

Original: Lat. 34° 06′ N, long. 64° 30′ E. Map, 54, 55.
Revised: 34.10505372 N, 64.49831101 E /
34° 06′ 18.19340352 N, 64° 29′ 53.91962808 E.
Ghūr Province. 5 km west of Chehel Gazari, on the
Chakhcharān-Taiwāra road.

Date: Ghurid, 12th–13th cent. (architectural).

Description: Remains of a castle.

Fieldwork: 1946 Kohzad, HSA—survey.

Source:
1. Maitland 1888a: 372—mention in general terms. Notes
   strategic siting.
2. Kohzad 1951–4, 8/4: 62—mention.

MANDI HISĀR. See 744 MUNDI HISĀR.

705. MANDRĀWAR

Original: Lat. 34° 33′ N, long. 70° 12′ E. Map 65.
Revised: 34.54646838 N, 70.20915234 E /
34° 32′ 47.28618528 N, 70° 12′ 32.94841104 E.
Laghmān Province. On the Laghmān River, 22 km north-
west of Pul-i Darūnta.

Description: Many mounds in and around the village. On a
hill to the north are some petroglyphs of ibex.

Fieldwork:
1. 1922 Foucher, DAFA—survey.
2. 1960 Fischer, DAAD—survey.

Sources:
1. Foucher 1939b—discusses the sites tentative identification with classical Nicaea.
2. Foucher 1942–7: 150 and 204–5—discussion of the location of Nicaea.
3. Caspani 1946a: 24—mention.
4. Fischer 1969: 357—brief description.

706. MANGIR SAR
   See also 154 CHĀGHAN SARĀI.

Original: Lat. 34° 54′ N, long. 71° 10′ E. Map 68.
Revised: 34.91037888 N, 71.16818221 E /
34° 54′ 37.36395216 N, 71° 10′ 05.45595024 E.
Kunār Province. The summit of a high mountain ridge 3 km
north of Chāghan Sarāi.

Dates: ?Kushan, 1st–3rd cent.; Hindu Shahi, 10th cent.
(ceramic).

Description: Some diaper masonry walls and ruins of more
stone structures to the south and east similar to the site of
Udegram in Swat.

Fieldwork: 1959 Fischer, DAAD—survey.

Sources:
1. Fischer 1960: opp. 7—photo.
2. Fischer 1969: 357–9—brief summary and aerial photos.

707. MANG QAL'A

Original: Lat. 36° 30′ N, long. 67° 51′ E. Map 30.
Revised: 36.47254524 N, 67.90139429 E /
36° 28′ 21.16285068 N, 67° 54′ 05.01943716 E.
Samangān Province. 33 km south-east of Tāshqurghān, just
to the east of the road to Haibak.

Date: Seljuk/Ghurid, 12th cent. (ceramic).

Description: A large mound c.10 m high, probably the
remains of a fort and associated settlement. There are Islamic
sherds on top but 'prehistoric' sherds at lower levels. A 12th-
cent. green glazed bowl was found by chance.

Fieldwork:
1. 1885 Maitland, ABC—topographical survey.
2. 1946 Wheeler, ASI—reconnaissance.

Sources:
1. Maitland 1888b: 46—mention.
2. Shakur 1947: 75—brief description.
3. Wheeler 1947: 63—mention.
4. Hayashi and Sahara 1962: 54 and fig. 95—mention the
   glazed bowl.

708. MARGIN TEPE

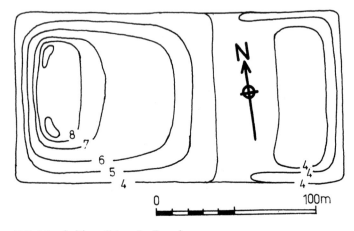

708 Margin Tepe (Marc Le Berre).

Original: Lat. 35° 45′ N, long. 66° 48′ E. Map 26.
Revised: 36.74518917 N, 66.79730143 E /
36° 44′ 42.68099832 N, 66° 47′ 50.28513576 E.
Balkh Province. 9 km south-west of this town, near the
village of Qal'a Ghundi, at the southern end of a marshy
depression along which other tepes are located (nos. 60,
382, 397, 1227). About 3.50 km south of the road to Āqcha.

Description: Rectangular mound about 200 × 100 m, oriented east–west, occupied by a modern cemetery. It appears to be composed of a courtyard in the east (low zone) with two openings in the north and the south, and buildings in the west (highest point 8.50 m) constructed in large mud bricks (outcropping at the north-west and south-west angles).

Fieldwork:
1. 1886 Maitland, ABC—topographical exploration.
2. 1948 Le Berre, DAFA—survey.

Sources:
1. Maitland 1888b: 176—mention.
2. M. Le Berre: unpublished 1948 report, DAFA archives, tépé P. 6.

709. MARKAZ-I HUKŪMATI

Original: Lat. 31° 08' N, long. 64° 11' E. Map 97.
Revised: 31.13444921 N, 64.20587339 E /
31° 08' 04.01715528 N, 64° 12' 21.14421732 E.
Helmand Province. On the east bank of the Helmand in the Hazārjuft district, *c.*2 km north-west of Darwīshān.

Dates: Achaemenid, 6th–4th cent. BC; Parthian, 2nd–1st cent. BC; Sasanian, 3rd–7th cent.; Timurid, 15th–16th cent. (ceramic).

Description: An artificial mound.

Fieldwork: 1966 Hammond, Cambridge University—survey.

Sources:
1. Bellew 1874: 183—mention.
2. Hammond 1970: 450—lists site (no. 45) and describes the pottery types and general survey results.
3. Gazetteer 1973: II. 107—mention.

MARKHANA. See **2161 MARKHANA** in Supplement.

710. MĀRKUH

Lat. 34° 16' N, long. 70° 48' E. Map 68.
Nangahār Province. On the northern skirts of the hills overlooking the Chahārdeh plain, *c.*43 km east of Jalālābād between the main road and the Kābul River.

Date: Kushan-Hunnic, 1st–6th cent. (architectural).

Description: Remains of a stupa on the hill.

Source: Masson 1842: III. 251—mention.

711. MARUCHĀQ

711 Maruchaq (after T. H. Holdich, *Plan of Maruchak*. Survey of India, Dehra Dun, 1887).

Original: Lat. 35° 49' N, long. 63° 08' E. Map 44.
Revised: 35.81575892 N, 63.1277823 E / 35° 48' 56.73212280 N, 63° 07' 40.01627640 E.
Bādghīs Province. On the Murghāb River just before the Soviet border, 35.5 km north-west of Bāla Murghāb. The site is a further 2 km north-west of the town of Maruchāq, 2 miles east of Maruchāq ford.

Date: ?Early Islamic, 10th–13th cent. (documentary).

Description: A circular artificial mound, *c.*13 m high and 250 m diam., inside a later fort. The walls of the fort are *c.*5 m high, and has a main entrance to the west.

1 km to the west are the remains of an ancient brick bridge, with three arches.

Old fort and town to south completely ruined inside. Outer walls and ditch enclose an irregular quadrilateral *c.*1 km square. Main gate to the west. Very high citadel in south-west corner, repaired in 19th cent. 1 km to west is an old bridge. The bridge is very ruined and appears very old and elaborate; baked brick; all arches gone, but piers still standing. Around Maruchāq are extensive ruins and remains of former *qal'as*.

Fieldwork:
1. 1884–5 Holdich, ABC—survey.
2. 1885–6 Maitland, Peacocke ABC.

Sources:
1. Additional notes by Jonathan L. Lee.
2. Durand 1884: 'Fort Maruchak', watercolour, British Library, Prints and Drawings, BL, OIC, Prints and Drawings WD408.
3. Durand 1885: illustrations of the bridge and fort.
4. Lumsden 1885: 565—mentions the bridge.
5. Rawlinson 1885: 578–80—discusses the site of Maruchāq and its tentative identification with ancient Marv ar-Rūd.
6. Maitland 1888a: 214–15—brief description.
7. Peacocke 1887a: 82–4 and 278–83—detailed description of all remains with plan, elevation, and sections of bridge.
8. A. C. Yate 1887: 191 and 276—mentions the bridge and describes the fortifications.
9. C. E. Yate 1888: 120–1—brief description of the fort.
10. Le Strange 1905: 405—summary of the historical references for Marv ar-Rūd.
11. Hamilton 1906: 141–2—brief description.
12. Hussein 1954: 13—brief description of the mound.

MARWA. See **2162 MARWA** in Supplement.

MARZ. See **1214 UMARZ.**

712. MĀSAMŪD

Lat. 34° 58' N, long. 70° 03' E. Map 65.
Laghmān Province. High valley of the Alishang.

Date: Hunnic-Turk, 5th–9th cent. (ceramic).

Description: None.

Collection: DAFA—sherds.

Source: Gardin and Lyonnet 1980, study of pottery from unpublished DAFA surveys.

713. MASALWANI

Lat. 34° 42' N, long. 70° 37' E. Map 67.
Kunār Province. In the Darra-i Nūr, *c.*5 km north of Qal'a-i Shāhi.

Date: Hindu Shahi, 10th cent. (ceramic).

Description: Remains of many schist buildings on the plain and the hill slopes around the village.

Fieldwork: 1959 Fischer, DAAD—survey.

Source: Fischer 1969: 358—very brief description (Ruins G 6).

MASHGAHI. See **2163 MASHGAHI** in Supplement.

714. MASJIDAK
Or TEPE SHAGĀLAK. See also **561 KHĀRAN.**

Original: Lat. 31° 25' N, long. 61° 32' E. Map 83.
Revised: 31.45116294 N, 61.50426813 E / 31° 27' 04.18657104 N, 61° 30' 15.36527304 E.
Nīmrūz Province. On the edge of the hāmūn, 10 km south of Pēshwārān.

Description: Five mounds of considerable size, with remains of canals and smaller mounds in the vicinity. Possibly the site of medieval Kuring.

Fieldwork: 1903–5 Tate, SAC—survey.

Source: Tate 1910: 216–17—brief description and historical note.

715. MASJID-I SHAHR-I KĀLĀN

Lat. 30° 48' N, long. 62° 05' E. Map 92.
Nīmrūz Province. In the dunes, *c.*3 km north-west of Shahr-i Kālān, 8 km south-east of Kūrdū.

Date: Timurid, 1428/9 (inscription).

Description: A large group of Timurid ruins: houses, windmills, granaries, mausolea, and possibly a mosque faced with brick (mentioned by Tate), probably also a mausoleum and a *madrasa*. Nearby is a cemetery with a dated inscription (a grave tile found by Tate possibly from elsewhere in the Sar-o-Tar region). Part of Helmand-Sistan Project site area h. 338.

Fieldwork:
1. 1903–5 Tate, SAC—survey.
2. 1971–4 Trousdale, Smithsonian—survey.

Sources:
1. Site information by W. Trousdale.
2. Tate 1910: 160 and 239—brief description of the mosque and the inscription.

716. MAZĀR-I SHARĪF

Original: Lat. 36° 42' N, long. 67° 07' E. Map 27.
Revised: 36.70902401 N, 67.11090234 E /
36° 42' 32.48645256 N, 67° 06' 39.24842832 E.
Balkh Province.

Dates: Ghaznavid, 1st half of 12th cent. (epigraphic, stylistic); Timurid, 15th–16th cent. (stylistic).

Description: The Shrine of 'Ali b Abi Tālib son-in-law and cousin of Prophet Muhammad, built during the reign of Sultān Husain-i Baiqara. The Timurid mausoleum remains as the central pivot of the shrine along with a second chamber which contains the tomb of Sultān Husain's architect but is now covered in more recent additions and decorations dating from the 16th to late 19th century. Additions include the tombs of the Afghan Amir Sher Ali Khān and his brothers, sons of Dost Muhammad Khān. In the east side is a large Friday mosque constructed by Sardar Muhammad Afzal Khān in the 1850s. There is also a large hall and *iwān* to the south-east of the shrine that is probably Timurid. In a small chamber to the left of the main entrance to the shrine is a decorated marble gravestone, probably from the Ghaznavid period.

A number of Timurid tombstones are also located in and around the shrine complex.

Sources:
1. Site information by Jonathan L. Lee.
2. Lal 1846: 65—describes a visit inside the dome-chamber and an adjacent room of decorated woodwork.
3. Yate 1888: 279–81—describes the complex, giving the dates on some of the mausoleums (now vanished) and summarizing some of the inscriptions.
4. Le Strange 1905: 422–3—summary of the historical references.
5. Miedemeyer and Diez 1924: pl. 192—photo of a Timurid mausoleum, now vanished.
6. Sālnāma 1936/37: 396–7—photo of a Timurid mausoleum, now vanished.
7. Byron 1938: 1136—brief description of the demolished mausoleum.
8. Frye 1946b: 69—brief summary of the shrine and photo of a ruined Timurid minaret base (now vanished).

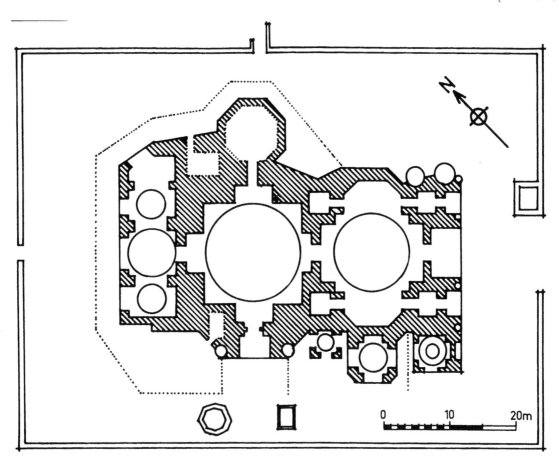

716 Mazār-i Sharīf (after O'Kane 1987 and Niedemeyer and Diez 1924).

9. Shakur 1947: 50—mentions the rich collection of Arabic and Persian manuscripts; coins of Greek, Saka, Kushan, and Muslim periods; Greek seals; and Sasanian heads and figurines in the museum.
10. Pugachenkova 1963: 168–71—general summary.
11. N. Dupree 1967a: 49–54—description and background of the shrine.
12. Golombek 1977—description and commentary of the Ghaznavid gravestone.
13. O'Kane 1987: 255–7—description of the shrine.
14. Golombek and Wilber 1988: 336–7—descriptions of the Timurid monuments.
15. McChesney 1991b—history of the shrine, its foundation and the *waqf* (religious endowment) documents.
16. Stuckert 1994: 36–8, 92, 190—sketches of shrine, bastions, etc. from various elevations, p. 38 drawing of now destroyed Timurid(?) covered bazaar in old Mazār.
17. Michaud and Barry 1996: 7–14—general account of the history of the shrine, focusing on the tilework, with photos.
18. Lee 1998: chapters 1–2—discusses the issue of the authenticity of the shrine and the Saljuq and Timurid foundation.
19. O'Kane 2000—argues that the Khwāja Akkasha shrine is not Timurid but Uzbek.
20. Ball 2008: 246–8—summary.

MIHR-I NIGĀ. See 392 GUL TEPE.

717. MINĀRA

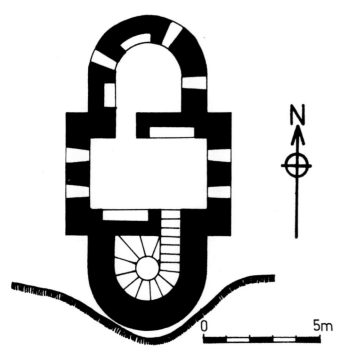

0   5m

717 Mināra (after Kästner 1968).

Lat. 34° 10' N, long. 63° 58' E. Map 54.
Ghūr Province. In the Tagau Ishlān, 3 km east of Nalbandan.

Date: Ghurid, 12th–13th cent. (architectural).

Description: Remains of many mud-brick towers to the east and west of the village, including one with a spiral staircase.

Source: Kästner 1968—brief description, plan, and photos.

718. MINĀR-I CHAKRI

Original: Lat. 34° 25' N, long. 69° 17' E. Map 62.
Revised: 34.41967222 N, 69.29274324 E /
34° 25' 10.81999488 N, 69° 17' 33.87568092 E.
Kābul Province. Overlooking the Kābul Valley 15 km south-east of Kābul, on top of a high pass from Shīwakī to Mūsa-i Lōgar.

Dates: Kushan, Sasanian and Turki Shahi, 1st–9th cent. (ceramic).

Description: A cylindrical diaper masonry pillar on a square base, surmounted by a lotus motif. Nearby are the remains of a monastery.

   This tower was originally one of three such monuments in the Shīwakī area, all of which have now collapsed. During the fighting in the 1980s, the tower received extensive shell damage on its northern face. By 1992 the tower was badly damaged and in danger of collapse. In 1998 the tower collapsed completely. Today only around 3 m of the structure remain.

Fieldwork: 1975–76 Rao, BIAS—preservation.

Sources:
1. Gardin and Lyonnet, 1980 chronological study of pottery from unpublished DAFA surveys.
2. Additional notes on the current state by by Jonathan L. Lee.
3. Masson 1833c: 32–7—sketches.
4. Masson 1841: 114—mention.
5. Burnes 1843: 263–4—brief description.
6. Eyre 1843: 317—brief, inaccurate description of the 'Grecian Pillar'.
7. Holdich 1881b—brief description and sketch.
8. Hayden 1910: 341–2—brief description.
9. Pandit 1927: 134 and 139—photo and brief description.
10. Foucher 1942–7: 147—brief description.
11. Caspani 1946c: 38–9—description and some tentative explanations.
12. Frye 1946a—photo and brief description and discussion.
13. Pugachenkova 1963: 34—general summary.
14. Dorneich 1968—very detailed study of the monument, though with no architectural plans.
15. Mizuno 1971: 125—brief description.
16. *Kābul Times* 1975—mentions the preservation work.

17. Franz 1978—discusses the monument and Buddhist pillar cults.
18. Rau 1979—brief preliminary report on the preservation work.
19. Ball 1984—discusses the function and a possible later date for the Minar.
20. Fischer 1987—discusses the Buddhist cult associations.
21. Dorneich 1999—discussion of the origins and significance of the tower with some comparative analysis. Argues for late 1st/early 2nd-century date.
22. Lewis 2000—photos of the destruction.
23. Ball 2008: 248–9—summary.
24. Fussman et al. 2008: 63–9 and 220–1—description with discussion of the function and name derivation.
25. Errington 2017a: 73–4 and 2017b: 25—the Masson collection and archive relating to the site.

719. MINĀR-I CHIGĪNĪ
Or KAUD-I GAZ or SĪKHSAR.

Original: Lat. 31° 02' N, long. 62° 04' E. Map 92.
Revised: 31.02797537 N, 62.05938868 E /
31° 01' 40.71133488 N, 62° 03' 33.79926384 E.
Nīmrūz Province. 3 km north-east of Chigīnī 11, between the *hāmūn* and the Chakhānsūr-Chahār Burjak road.

Description: An isolated square tower or minaret, resembling a multi-storeyed building. Construction is of mud-brick with baked brick quoining. Inside is a spiral staircase.
Fieldwork:
1. 1884 Maitland, ABC—topographical survey.
2. 1970 Fischer, Bonn University—survey.
Sources:
1. Maitland 1888a: 85—mention as Kaud-i Gaz.
2. Fischer 1971b: 46—description and photo (Site 17).

720. MINĀR-I SANG

Lat. 35° 58' N, long. 65° 25' E. Maps 24, 46.
Faryāb Province. 3 km east of Darzāb, between Maimana and Sar-i Pul.

Description: An ancient stone building, 10–15 m high, like a minaret, with a domed roof. It overlooks a stream, the banks of which have some artificial caves.
Fieldwork: 1886 Amir Khan and Shahzada Tamus, ABC—topographical survey.
Source: Amir Khan and Shahzada Tamus 1888c: 248—mention.

MĪN BASHI. See 160 CHAHĀR TŪT.

MĪN CHUKUR. See 917 QARLUQ.

MINGAJIK. See 2164 MINGLIK in Supplement.

MINGLIK. See 2164 MINGLIK in Supplement.

721. MĪRĀBĀD

Lat. 30° 26' N, long. 61° 50' E. Map 93.
Nīmrūz Province. 17 km south of Qal'a-i Fath, on the right bank of the Helmand to the east of the Chahār Burjak.

Dates: Early Islamic, 8th–13th cent.; Mongol-Timurid, 13th–16th cent. (architectural).

Description: A group of three small ruined mud-brick buildings standing *c.*75 m apart in a cemetery.
Fieldwork:
1. 1903–5 Tate, SAC—survey.
2. 1951 Fairservis, AMNH—survey.
Sources:
1. Bellew 1874: 214—mention.
2. Tate 1909: 96–7—mentions the remains of a dakhma.
3. Fairservis 1961: 53–4—brief description (Site 33).

722. MIR 'ALI

Original: Lat. 30° 57' N, long. 62° 02' E. Map 92.
Revised: 30.95116854 N, 62.03319291 E /
30° 57' 04.20674256 N, 62° 01' 59.49447276 E.
Nīmrūz Province. 10 km south-west of Zīyārat-i Amīrān Sāhib.

Description: An area of remains, including a two-storey mud-brick hall, some low mud ramparts, a baked brick gateway, and an ancient canal system.
Fieldwork: 1965–70 Fischer, Bonn University—survey.

MIR 'ALI KHAL. See 160 CHAHĀR TŪT.

723. MĪR BACHA KŪT
Or DAMĪR or DEH MĪR or SARĀĪ KHŪJA.

Lat. 34° 45' N, long. 69° 07' E. Map 64.
Kābul Province. In the Kūh-i Dāman plain 2 km west of the Sarāī Khūja, 33 km north of Kābul.

Dates: Early Sasanian, 3rd–4th cent. (ceramic, numismatic, stylistic); Turki Shahi, 7th–8th cent. (stylistic).

Description: A large mound, where two large schist statues of standing Buddha were accidentally found. Subsequent excavations revealed architectural remains and recovered pottery and coins. A statue of Shiva, now in a private collection, was also found at this site.

Fieldwork: 1967 Mustamandi, AIA—excavations.

Sources:
1. N. Dupree et al. 1974: 14 — brief description of one of the Buddhas in the National Museum.
2. Kuwayama 1976: 383 — mentions the Shiva statue.
3. N. Dupree 1977: 109 — mention.
4. Tissot 2006: 354 — National Museum catalogue details and photos.
5. Fussman, Murad, and Ollivier 2008: 140 — mention.

724. MĪR DAŪD
Or CHAHĀR BĀGH.

Original: Lat. 34° 05' N, long. 62° 13' E. Map 52.
Revised: 34.08208163 N, 62.2170422 E / 34° 04' 55.49387556 N, 62° 13' 01.35190956 E.
Herat Province. 30.5 km south of this city, along the route to Shindand, five sites spread out on either side of the road.

Date: Islamic period (A) (ceramic).

Description: (A) Near the the rocky ridge of the Band-i Badak, in the place called Hauz-i Mīr Daūd, to the west of the road, a small tumulus strewn with fragments of fired bricks and glazed Islamic pottery. Visible to the west, on the other side of a small stream, the ruins of a qal'a. (B) West of the road, a caravanserai constructed in bricks, partially ruined; on the other side of the road, ruins of a qal'a water point. (C) East of the road, ruins of a *qal'a* of the same type as the preceding ones. (D) East of the road, half-collapsed caravanserai, next to ruins of three qal'a and a little shapeless tumulus. (E) East of the road, tepe occupied by a cemetery (near an abandoned brick kiln). (F) There would be ancient copper and lead mines in the region.

Collection: National Museum/AIA — sherds.

Fieldwork:
1. 1885 Peacocke, ABC — reconnaissance.
2. 1952 Gardin and Le Berre, DAFA — survey.

Sources:
1. Le Berre, unpublished 1952 report, DAFA archives, tépés Herat-Shindand 1 to 5.
2. Lal 1846: 169 — mention.
3. Peacocke 1887a: 212–13, 216 — mentions brick ruins and traces of former fields and irrigation.
4. Gazetteer 1975: III. 298 — brief description.
5. N. Dupree 1977: 270 — mention and brief history.

725. MIR-I RUZADAR

Original: Lat. 36° 45' N, long. 66° 56' E. Map 27.
Revised: 36.74667438 N, 66.93348817 E / 36° 44' 48.02776008 N, 66° 56' 00.55739940 E.
Balkh Province. 3 km east of the outer walls of Balkh, near a small cemetery just off the Mazār-i Sharīf road.

Date: Timurid, 15th cent. (stylistic)

Description: A baked brick mausoleum on a baked brick platform *c.*50 cm high. The entrance is flanked by stairs to the roof. Inside there are four blocked windows in the upper level of the dome-chamber. The only decoration is some simple moulded plaster in the semi-domes, a stalactite niche head above the *mihrab* on the north side, and some remains of painted plaster on the walls. The dome of the ceiling is ornately decorated with floral patterns and blue glaze tiles.

Immediately to the south-west of the main shrine are the foundations of at least three minor, single-domed, shrines containing traces of fine blue glazed tiles in the Timurid style.

Fieldwork: 1972–4 Pugachenkova, Af/Sov. Mission — survey.

Sources:
1. Additional notes by Jonathan L. Lee.
2. Pugachenkova 1978: 33–5 — description of the building and discussion of its date.
3. Mukhtarov 1980: 72–94 — description and photo.
4. O'Kane 1987: 281–2 — description.
5. Golombek and Wilber 1988: 294–5 — description.

726. MIRWAIS BĀBĀ
Or PIR-I SABZ.

Original: Lat. 31° 37' N, long. 65° 37' E. Map 89.
Revised: 31.61817016 N, 65.60335703 E / 31° 37' 05.41257744 N, 65° 36' 12.08531340 E.
Kandahār Province. On the Herat road 8 km west of Kandahār.

Date: ?Hellenistic, 4th–1st cent. BC (stylistic).

Description: Remains of a tomb with terracotta pythons. Inside was a cylindrical marble funerary urn, a large silver vase, and an amphora containing gold ornaments.

Collection: Kandahar Museum — funerary objects.

Sources:
1. Scerrato 1958b: 6 n. 10 — mention.
2. Scerrato 1980 — discusses the funerary objects found (*c.*1 km from Shahr-i Kuhna on Herat road; old Islamic cemetery).

MIRWAN. See 458 JABAL AS-SARĀJ.

727. MIRZA JAHĀNGĪR
See also 155 CHAHĀR BĀGH.

Original: Lat. 34° 25' N, long. 70° 22' E. Map 66.
Revised: 34.41570429 N, 70.36493559 E / 34° 24' 56.53545912 N, 70° 21' 53.76811464 E.
Nangahār Province. *C.*2 km south of the village of Chahār Bāgh, between the Chahār Bāgh and Qal'ai Hāji stupas, 9 km west of Jalālābād.

Date: Kushan-Hunnic, 1st–6th cent. (architectural).

Description: Very badly ruined remains of a stupa, diam. 15 m, height 6 m. To the west are two small votive stupas, and to the south are the remains of a monastery, *c*.50 m square.

Fieldwork:
1. 1834 Masson—survey.
2. 1965 Mizuno, Kyoto University—survey.

Sources:
1. Masson 1841: 104—mention.
2. Mizuno 1971: 121—brief description (Stupa 47).
3. Errington 2017a: 151—the Masson collection and archive relating to the site.

728. MIR ZAKAH
Including KĀFIR KOT.

Original: Lat. 33° 46' N, long. 69° 29' E. Map 82.
Revised: 33.76714177 N, 69.47823627 E /
33° 46' 01.71035904 N, 69° 28' 41.65056804 E.
Paktiyā Province. 53 km north-east of Gardēz on the old route from Ghazni to Gandhara.

Dates: Achaemenid, Mauryan, Indo-Greek, Saka, Indo-Parthian, and Kushan, 6th cent. BC–AD 3rd cent. (numismatic); Kushan, Sasanian, Hunnic, Turki Shahi, and pre-Mongol Islamic, 1st–13th cent. (ceramic); Timurid, 15th–16th cent. (ceramic).

Description: A mound where over 11,000 coins were accidentally found in 1947. Subsequent excavations revealed architectural remains, more coins, and some gold and silver objects. In the 1990s another even larger treasure was discovered at Mir Zakah. This included a wide variety of objects covering some 400 years, including many Achaemenid and Hellenistic vessels, gold strips, and some 2 tons of coins—the largest coin hoard ever discovered anywhere in the world—that included nearly every variety from bent bars to Kushan coins. The treasure has been assembled from various localities, but mainly Bactria. It was not associated with a city or temple, so is presumed to have been plunder deposited in a temporary hiding place.

In the 1990s another even larger treasure reached the bazaar in Peshawar, later released onto the international trade in illicit antiquities. The hoard included a wide variety of objects covering some 400 years, including many Achaemenid and Hellenistic vessels, statuettes, jewellery, gold strips, and some 550,000 coins—approximately 2 tons—of gold, silver, and bronze, the largest coin hoard ever discovered anywhere in the world.

Collection: National Museum—first hoard.

Fieldwork: 1948 Le Berre, DAFA—excavations.

Sources:
1. Gardin and Lyonnet, 1980 chronological study of pottery from unpublished DAFA surveys.
2. Kohzad 1947/48—describes the discovery.
3. Schlumberger 1949b: 15—very brief description of the find and Le Berre's subsequent excavations.
4. Curiel and Schlumberger 1953—full inventory of the coins and catalogue of the excavated finds.
5. Ramachandran and Sharma 1956: III. 3–10—photos and brief study of the coins on display in the museum.
6. Narain 1957: 128–32—discusses and evaluates the hoard.
7. Jenkins 1959—discusses the Apollodotus coins from the hoard.

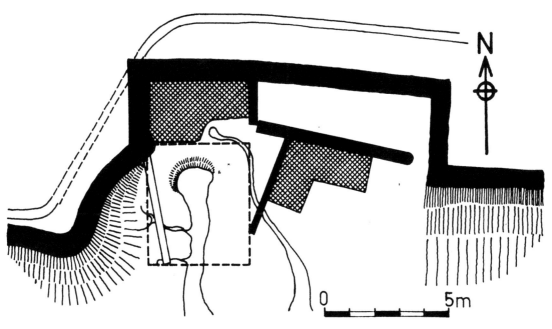

728 Mir Zakah (after Curiel and Schlumberger 1953).

8. Mac Dowall and Wilson 1960 — discuss the evidence of the Apollodotus coins.
9. Bivar 1965: 95–8 — discusses the hoard as evidence for a possible Indo-Greek mint at Gardéz.
10. Mac Dowall 1965 — discusses the hoard and the later Indo-Parthians.
11. Bivar 1972 — refers to the hoard in a discussion of the sequence of Menander's coinage.
12. N. Dupree et al. 1974: 110–11 — summary of the hoard and the display in the National Museum.
13. Mac Dowall 1974: 249 — discusses the evidence of the Hermaeus coins.
14. Mac Dowall and Taddei 1978a: 201–5 — brief summary.
15. Bivar 1982 — discusses the bar coinage from the hoard.
16. Guillaume 1991: 6–7 — discussion of the Graeco-Bactrian and Indian coins from the first discovery.
17. Pichikyan and Judelson 1998 — suggest that the second treasure discovered might be a part of the Āmū Daryā Treasure.
18. Bopearachchi 1999a — first report of the discovery.
19. Bopearachchi 2000a — two gold coins from the hoard, now in a private collection in London.
20. Bopearachchi 2002 — describes the discovery of the second hoard.
21. Bopearachchi 2003 — discusses some of the Graeco-Bactrian coins from Mir Zakah and elsewhere in an exhibition catalogue.
22. Ball 2008: 249 — summary.
23. Holt 2012a: 141–2 — brief description of the second treasure.

729. MISGARAN

Original: Lat. 33° 49' N. long. 62° 06' E. Map 70.
Revised: 33.82931746 N, 62.0993908 E / 33° 49' 45.54287040 N, 62° 05' 57.80687928 E.
Herat Province. 16 km west of a turn-off, 63 km south of Herat on the road to Kandahār.

Description: Some abandoned and eroded ancient copper inner workings. The workings extend along the face of the rock for several hundred metres, with one cave 4 m deep. Scattered around are rough stone pounding tools.

3 km to the north-west are some further signs of ancient mining.

Fieldwork: 1977 CNRS — geological survey.

Source: Berthoud et al. 1977: 4–5 — description of the workings and the geology.

MISHGHAN. See 751 MUSHKAN.

MOKHATAR. See 736 MUKHTĀR.

730. MUBARAK AND CHEHELDUKHTARĀN

Lat. 37° 03' N, long. 70° 40' E. Map 38.
Badakhshān Province. On the Kokcha River *c.* 16 km southeast of Faizābād.

Description: Some ruins, connected with legends 'too gross to notice'.

Source: Wood 1872: 164 — mention.

MUDELAKTAH SHADEH. See 2165 MUDELAKTAH SHADEH in Supplement.

731. MUGHULĀN-I KUHNA

Original: Lat. 33° 22' N, long. 62° 15' E. Map 70.
Revised: 33.41924232 N, 62.24997489 E / 33° 25' 09.27234192 N, 62° 14' 59.90959068 E.
Herat Province. Near the Shindand air base, *c.* 15 km northeast of Shindand.

Description: A large and interesting mound, containing a number of painted sherds.

Fieldwork: 1974 Swiny, BIAS — survey.

Source: Site information by S. Swiny in unpublished BIAS archive.

732. MUG QAL'A

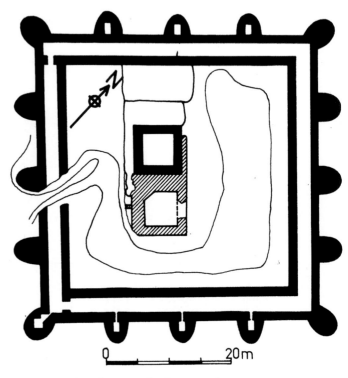

732 Mug Qal'a (after Pugachenkova 1976).

Original: Lat. 37° 03' N, long. 66° 50' E. Map 26.
Revised: 37.04893069 N, 66.82921496 E /
37° 02' 56.15049984 N, 66° 49' 45.17383908 E.
Balkh Province. 4 k m north-east of Qarchigak.

Date: Early Islamic, 10th–13th cent. (architectural).

Description: Remains of *pakhsa* fortifications.

Fieldwork: 1972–3 Pugachenkova, Af/Sov. Mission—survey.

Sources:
1. Pugachenkova 1976b—discussion of the building techniques.
2. Francfort 1979a: 38—mentions the survival of northern Kushan elements in the fortifications.

733. MUHAMMAD HASAN BŪZI

Original: Lat. 31° 14' N, long. 62° 02' E. Map 84.
Revised: 31.2260165 N, 62.05648088 E / 31° 13' 33.65938704 N, 62° 03' 23.33116728 E.
Nīmrūz Province. 6.5 km north-west of Chakhānsūr, on the main road.

Dates: Sasanian, 3rd–7th cent.; Timurid, 15th–16th cent. (ceramic).

Description: Some low mud walls just to the west of the village. A small mound covered in fragments of baked brick was noted here or near here in the 19th century.

Fieldwork:
1. 1884 Maitland, ABC—topographical survey.
2. 1965–70 Fischer, Bonn University—survey.

Sources:
1. Maitland 1888a: 82—mention (un-named).
2. Fischer 1969: 335—mention (Ruin D 1).
3. Fischer 1973c: 138—map reference.

734. MUHAMMAD HUSAIN

Lat. 30° 58' N, long. 61° 55' E. Map 92.
Nīmrūz Province. C.13 km north-east of Zaranj, 500 m north of the road to Chakhānsūr.

Date: Mongol-Timurid, 13th–16th cent. (ceramic).

Description: A surface site with a large area of scattered baked bricks, sherds, and stone vessels.

Fieldwork: 1960–70 Fischer, Bonn University—survey.

Sources:
1. Fischer 1969: 335—mention (Site D 4).
2. Fischer et al. 1974–6: 34—mention and photo (Position 18).

MUHAMMAD KHĀN. See 694 MAHMUD KHĀN.

735. MUHMAND DARRA
See also 116 BATI KŪT.

Lat. 34° 15' N, long. 70° 50' E. Map 68.
Nangahār Province. 5 km west of Bāsawal on the road from Tūrkhām to Jalālābād.

Description: An extensive surface scatter of sherds spreading without a break as far as Bati Kūt.

Sources:
1. Masson 1840: 32—mention.
2. Masson 1842: I. 168—mention.

736. MUKHTĀR
Or MOKHATAR.

Original: Lat. 31° 35' N, long. 64° 26' E. Map 86.
Revised: 31.59220937 N, 64.44103097 E /
31° 35' 31.95373272 N, 64° 26' 27.71149236 E.
Helmand Province. C.20 km north of Bust and 13 km north-east of Lashkargāh, halfway between the road and the Arghandāb.

Date: Hellenistic, 3rd–1st cent BC (ceramic).

Description: A large Hellenistic temple constructed on a high, stepped, artificial platform. The artefacts reported from Khwāja Kanur (597) and Sultan Bābā Zīyārat (1114) come from Mokhatar. Astonishingly, this site which looms so prominently along the Lashkar Gāh road has apparently not been investigated.

Sources:
1. Site information by W. Trousdale.
2. Bellew 1874: 170—mention.
3. Gazetteer 1973: II. 204—mention.

737. MULK 'ALI

Lat. 37° 17' N, long. 74° 13' E. Map 40.
Badakhshān Province. In the Little Pamirs c.6 km north-east of the Qūl-i Chaqmaqtīn, where the track from Langar crosses a small tributary on the north side of the Aqsū.

Description: A boulder with petroglyphs of ibex.

Source: Dor 1976: 124—mention.

738. MULLĀH AFGHĀNI
Includes ĀLCHĪN, CHAHĀR QISHLĀQ, ISMĀ'ĪL QISHLĀQ, KAL TEPE, KŪNCHAK, SHUR TEPE, and TĀSH TEPE.

Original: Lat. 37° 06'–37° 11' N, long. 68° 59'–69° 06' E. Map 31.

Revised:
37.18167164 N, 68.97877358 E / 37° 10' 54.01788636 N, 68° 58' 43.58489088 E (A).
37.16801399 N, 69.00646811 E / 37° 10' 04.85037480 N, 69° 00' 23.28519960 E (B).
37.15170351 N, 69.00211769 E / 37° 09' 06.13265184 N, 69° 00' 07.62367104 E (C).
37.17170756 N, 69.04343859 E / 37° 10' 18.14720412 N, 69° 02' 36.37891572 E (D).
37.13580006 N, 69.04617346 E / 37° 08' 08.88020196 N, 69° 02' 46.22445384 E (E).

Qundūz Province. Numerous tepes dispersed in the eastern part of the plain of Imām Sāhib in the region of Mullāh Afghāni between the two main branches of the canal that irrigates the whole region, the Nahr-i Shāhrawān. For unknown reasons, none of these tepes is indicated on the 1:100,000 map, while others, sometimes smaller, are so in other sectors; the following list is intended to correct this cartographic image of the distribution of the ancient sites in the plain of Imām Sāhib, and to widen the chronological base in reference to the linked development of human settlement and irrigation in this region. I. By the old road from Imām Sāhib to Shāhrawān, first of all, lies the access to the tepes situated in the following villages (distance in km measured from the central roundabout of Imām Sāhib): (A) 5.8 km, Ismā'īl Qishlāq, 400 m north of the road; (B) 9.5 km, place-name Mullāh Afghāni, 300 m north of the road, by a road leading from the well of this hamlet; (C) from the same well, towards the south (2 km over fields), Shur Tepe, to the south-west of the village of Kal Tepe; (D) 12 km, by the road from Diwana Qishlāq and Yaka Tūt, about halfway between these two villages, 700 m north-west of the road: Tash Tepe, occupied by a modern cemetery; (E) at the same distance, but by a road leading south from the hamlet of Kal Tepe to the village of Alchin, where the cemetery also indicates the location of an ancient site. II. Other tepes are accessible by the new road from Imām Sāhib to Shāhrawān, near the villages of Kunchak and Chahār Qishlāq, at the foot of the hills that border the plain in the south; still others can be reached only by tracks across fields, in the region of Gaurau especially. All these tepes present the same range of shapes and dimensions as the preceding ones; and the sherds found represent the same chronological range. The brief description that follows thus refers only to group I, considered to be representative for the sector under consideration.

Dates: Kushan and Hunnic-Turk, 1st–9th cent.; pre-Mongol Islamic, 10th–13th cent. (ceramic).

Description: (A) Low platform (0.50 m), damaged and soon to be razed by cultivation (cotton), whose original dimensions were 150 × 150 m, according to an informant from a neighbouring village (Ismā'īl Qishlāq); in the south-west angle, rectangular north-west/south-east mound (70 × 30 m), steep, high part in the south-east (5 m). (B) Square platform also damaged by irrigated crops (present dimensions 80 × 80 m), high part in the south (4 m). The site formerly extended much further to the north; according to the local farmers, many bricks and bone debris were found during ploughing. (C) Rounded mound eaten into on all sides by irrigated crops (cotton), diam. 60 m, height 3.5 m. (D) High rectangular east–west mound (80 × 50 m), high part in the west (8 m); many pebbles at the base, south and west sides (thus the name Tash Tepe given to this site?). (E) Rectangular east–west platform (100 × 80 m), surrounded by cotton fields; depressed top, with high slopes at the north-east (2.5 m) and south-west (3 m) angles.

Collection: National Museum/AIA—sherds.

Fieldwork: 1977 Gardin et al., CNRS—survey.

Sources:
1. Site information by J.-C. Gardin.
2. Gardin and Lyonnet 1978–9: pl. V—nos. 100–3, 106–9, 114–17.
3. Lyonnet 1997: figs 49, 68, 69—nos. 100–3, 106–9, 114–17.
4. Gardin 1998: 62—nos. 100–3, 106–9, 114–17.

MULLĀH 'ALĀ. See 732 MUNA 'ALĀ.

739. MULLĀH MUHĪB
Or KĀFIR QAL'A.

Lat. 34° 50' N, long. 68° 03' E. Map 58.
Bāmiyān Province. 2 km north of Qal'a-i 'Iraq in the 'Iraq gorge, at the point where a track goes westwards to Jola.

Description: The remains of a fort and a series of artificial caves.

Fieldwork: 1886 Amir Khan, ABC—topographical survey.

Sources:
1. Masson 1839: 110—mentions the caves.
2. Masson 1842: II. 443—mentions the caves.
3. Yavorski 1885: 155—mentions the fort.
4. Amir Khan 1888: 184—mentions the caves.

740. MULLĀH MŪSA

Original: Lat. 31° 07' N, long. 62° 05' E. Map 84.
Revised: 31.13029392 N, 62.08565972 E / 31° 07' 49.05809796 N, 62° 05' 08.37499272 E.
Nīmrūz Province. 4 km north-west of Qal'a-i Chigīnī on the edge of the hāmūn.

Dates: Sasanian-Early Islamic, 3rd–13th cent.; Mongol-Timurid, 13th–16th cent. (ceramic).

Description: Remains of fortification walls, with a high mound to the south-west in the hāmūn.

Fieldwork:
1. Peacocke 1884, ABC—topographical survey.
2. 1965–70—Fischer, Bonn University—survey.

Sources:
1. Peacocke 1885a: 13—mention ruins under the name of Aliābād.

2. Peacocke 1887a: 27 — mention.
3. Fischer 1970b: pl. 25 — photo.
4. Fischer 1973c: 144 — map reference.
5. Fischer et al. 1974–6: 37 — mention.

741. MULLĀH QŪLI

Original: Lat. 37° 05' N, long. 69° 09'–69° 10' E. Map 31.
Revised:
37.09155766 N, 69.15867112 E / 37° 05' 29.60758608 N,
69° 09' 31.21602300 E (A).
37.0895282 N, 69.14762923 E / 37° 05' 22.30150776 N,
69° 08' 51.46522872 E (B).
Qundūz Province. 6 and 7 km west of Shāhrawān, by the
road to Imām Sāhib, on the north (A) and south (B) sides of
the road, respectively: two tepes situated at the edge of the
zone irrigable by the northern branches of the canal of
Ārchī (region of Mullāh Qūli).

Dates: Achaemenid, 6th–4th cent. BC (B); Hellenistic, 3rd–
1st cent. BC (A, B); some Islamic sherds (A) (ceramic).

Description: (A) 150 m north of the road to Imām Sāhib,
rectangular north–south platform (100 × 50 m), flat top
(height 3–4 m), with a depression on the north side; today
occupied by a cemetery. (B) 300 m south of the same road,
rectangular north–south mound (40 × 30 m), eaten into by
irrigated fields, height 1.5 m.

Collection: National Museum/AIA — sherds.

Fieldwork: 1977 Gardin et al., CNRS — survey.

Sources:
1. Site information by J.-C. Gardin.
2. Gardin and Lyonnet 1978–9: pl. V — nos. 33–4.

3. Lyonnet 1997: figs 25, 35, 49 — nos 33–4.
4. Gardin 1998: 56 — nos. 33–4.

742. MUNA 'ALĀ
Or MULLĀH 'ALĀ or MALA ALAU.

Original: Lat. 33° 29' N, long. 64° 20' E. Maps 54, 74.
Revised: 33.50344845 N, 64.34666666 E /
33° 30' 12.41440380 N, 64° 20' 47.99997168 E.
Ghūr Province. 9 km to the south-west of Taiwāra on the
road to Parjuman.

Date: Ghurid, 12th–13th cent. (architectural, geographical).

Description: A group of ruined forts and towers, some
standing to a height of 10 m. Construction is of mud on a
stone foundation. The outside walls are decorated in simple
geometric patterns.

Fieldwork:
1. 1885 Sahibdad Khan, ABC — topographical survey.
2. 1946 Kohzad, HAS — survey.
3. 1977 Ball — survey.

Sources:
1. Sahibdad Khan 1891a: 243 — mention.
2. Kohzad 1951–4, 9/2: 13 — mention.
3. Klimburg 1960: 49 — mention.
4. Fischer 1978a: 335 — mention and photos.
5. Ball 2002: 33–5 — description and photos.
6. Wannell 2002.

743. MUNDIGAK

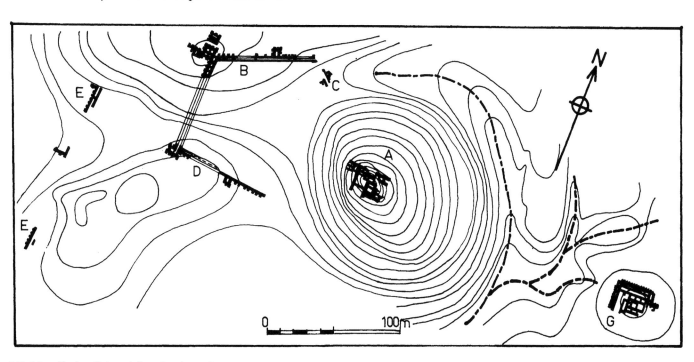

743 Mundigak — Palace (after Casal 1961).

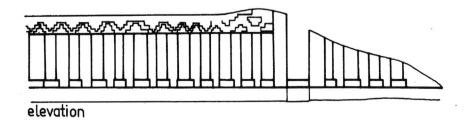

elevation

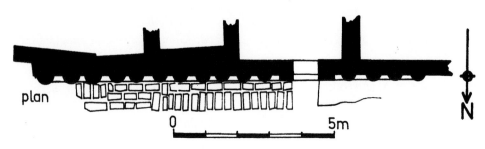

plan

0   5m

N

743 Mundigak—general plan (after Casal 1961).

Original: Lat. 31° 55' N, long. 65° 30' E. Map 89.
Revised:
Between 31.91221687 N, 65.50797162 E / 31° 54' 43.98073596 N,
65° 30' 28.69784208 E and 31.90655171 N, 65.49794379 E /
31° 54' 23.58614772 N, 65° 29' 52.59765372 E.
Kandahār Province. C.55 km north-west of Kandahār near
Shāh Maqsūd, on the upper drainage of the Kushk-i Na-
khud River.

Dates: Bronze Age, 4th–2nd mill. BC; Iron Age/Achae-
menid, 1st mill. BC. (C-14, ceramic).

Description: An extensive series of mounds marking the
site of a town. The chronology is still uncertain, but it has
tentatively been divided into seven main periods with many
subdivisions. The main period seems to be Period IV, which
saw a massive rebuilding after an earlier destruction. Both
the 'palace' and the 'temple' and possibly the city walls as
well date from this period. Another destruction layer and a
marked ceramic change indicate a period of abandonment
between IV and V, followed by a period of further rebuilding and construction of new monuments, including the
'massive monument'. Periods VI and VII saw only periodic
occupation on a small scale.

Collections: National Museum and Musée Guimet.

Fieldwork: 1851–8 Casal, DAFA—excavations.

Sources:
1. Casal 1952:—background and preliminary report on the
   1951 season.
2. Libby 1953: 7—results of C-14 analysis on a charcoal
   fragment—2937–2206 BC.
3. Casal 1954a—summary report on the excavations to
   date and description of the sequence and finds.

4. Casal 1954b—brief description of the first two seasons
   and the discovery of the 'massive monument'.
5. Falkner 1954–6—summary of the excavations.
6. Casal 1955a—preliminary account of the first two
   seasons.
7. Casal 1955b—brief outline of the excavations.
8. Casal 1956—brief description of the first five seasons
   and discussion of the site's role as a crossroads.
9. Casal 1957—summary of the excavations and of its
   archaeological links with Pakistan.
10. Bosch 1958: lxxxvii–lxxxix—summary of the excavations.
11. Auboyer 1960—127–33—summary of the excavations.
12. Casal 1961—full report on the excavations and cata-
    logue of the finds. Fully illustrated, though lacking in
    sections.
13. Gullini 1961—pl. 1–4—photos of the objects on dis-
    play from the National Museum.
14. Matheson 1961—very light account of the 1956 season
    by one of the members of the team.
15. Casal 1964a—describes the Period IV monumental
    buildings.
16. Casal 1964b—illustrates and discusses some of the
    objects exhibited in the Tokyo Museum.
17. Dales 1965—discusses the Bronze Age at Mundigak
    and its chronological connections.
18. Mendez 1966—anthropological analysis of the human
    remains.
19. Monod 1966: 370—description of some pottery on
    display in the Musée Guimet.
20. Poulain 1966—detailed catalogue and brief discussion
    of the fauna remains.

21. Rowland 1966a: 16–21—photos and brief introduction.
22. Sarianidi 1968—discusses connections with Badakhshan through the lapis trade.
23. Casal 1969: 57–82—describes and discusses the excavations and its significance for the study of Harappan civilisation.
24. Gouin 1969—catalogue and discussion of some Period IV remains.
25. Masson and Sarianidi 1969—detailed discussion of the site and material in its broader Near Eastern context.
26. Dales 1971—discusses the evidence of Mundigak for early contacts between the Gulf and the Indus.
27. Fairservis 1971: 123–34 and 396—good summary of the excavations, the finds, and the sequence, with a list of some of the C-14 dates.
28. Rowland and Rice 1971—1–2 and pls 7–9 and 11—very brief summary of the site and photos of some of the objects.
29. Dales 1973b—gives some corrected C-14 dates.
30. Dupree 1973: 266–9—summary of the results and comparisons of the artefacts with Deh Morasi.
31. Leriche 1973—discusses the archaeology of Central Asia.
32. Meadow 1973—discusses the chronology in the context of Indo-Iranian borderland sites.
33. Dales 1974—discussion (in German) of the ceramics and figurines and their links in Turkmenistan and Pakistan.
34. N. Dupree et al. 1974: 57–60—summary of the site and guide to the collection in the Kābul Museum.
35. Shaffer 1974—discusses the evidence of the excavations in terms of analytical models.
36. Deshpande 1975a—traces religious and ceramic links between Period IV and sites in India.
37. A. A. Motamedi 1975: 85–9—general summary of the excavations.
38. Cattenat and Gardin 1976—discuss the ceramic links for the Achaemenid period.
39. Dales 1977b—discusses the evidence from Mundigak for trade patterns between Central Asia, India, and Iran.
40. Deshayes 1977—compares the 'massive monument' with structures at Tureng Tepe.
41. N. Dupree 1977: 304–6—brief guide and description.
42. Pollack 1977b—discusses some of the Period IV pottery styles and their connections with the Quetta Valley and Susa.
43. Tosi 1977—discusses the evidence from Mundigak for the growth of Central Asian urbanization.
44. Schwartzenberg 1978: 157—good summary of the site and the development of South Asian Chalcolithic cultures.
45. Shaffer 1978b—91–149—detailed description and discussion of the stratigraphy, architecture, and finds.
46. Snead 1978—report on the geography of the Mundigak area.
47. Gupta 1979: II. 111–17 and 271–2—describes the main periods and their links with Central Asia and the Indian subcontinent in the Chalcolithic period.
48. Noorzai 1979—brief account of trade connections between Mundigak and the Indus Valley.
49. Tosi 1979—discusses Mundigak and early relations between India and Iran.
50. Sankalia 1980—general article in Pashto.
51. B. and R. Allchin 1982: 131–9—discuss the evidence of Mundigak in terms of the Indus civilization.
52. Dales 1985—discusses some unprovenanced stone sculptures from Sistan in relation to the Mundigak sculptures.
53. Tissot 2006: 15–19—National Museum catalogue details and photos.
54. Ball 2008: 45–6, 49–50, 249–51—summary.
55. Franke 2008—discusses the site within its broader Indo-Iranian borderlands context.
56. Thomalsky et al. 2013—discussion of metalworking at the site.

744. MUNDI HISĀR
Or MANDI HISĀR or MUNDI SAH or SHAHR-I KUHNA.

Lat. 31° 33' N, long. 65° 51' E. Map 89.
Kandahār Province. 16 km south-east of this city, on the edge of the Spīn Baldak road (west side) and the Tarnak River.

Dates: Bronze, 2nd mill. BC; Indo-Parthian, 1st–3rd cent.; Sasano-Turk, 5th–9th cent., pre-Mongol Islamic, 10th–13th cent. (ceramic).

Description: Square mound of about 50 m per side and 6 to 8 m high, occupied by a late cemetery in the north and west. East of the main tepe are two small mounds which are also covered by late tombs.

Collection: National Museum/AIA—sherds.

Fieldwork:
1. 1946 Wheeler, ASI—reconnaissance.
2. 1951 Casal, DAFA—survey.
3. 1966 Fischer, DAAD—survey.

Sources:
1. Unpublished 1951 report by J.-M. Casal in DAFA archives.
2. Shakur 1947: 104–5—mention.
3. Wheeler 1947: 61 and 64—mention.
4. Fisher 1967a: 151—survey.

MUNDI SAH. See **744. MUNDI HISĀR.**

745. MUNDIK TEPE

Original: Lat. 36° 47' N, long. 67° 27' E. Map 29.
Revised: 36.78658588 N, 67.4507179 E / 36° 47' 11.70917556 N, 67° 27' 02.58444576 E.
Samangān Province. About 25 km north-west of Tāshqur-ghān, by the road that links this town to Mazār-i Sharif (marker km 393): the tepe is cut in two by the road.

Dates: Some sherds of the Achaemenid and Hellenistic period, 6th–1st cent. BC; Kushan, 1st–3rd cent. (numismatic); Sasano-Hunnic period, 3rd–6th cent.; pre-Mongol Islamic, 10th–13th cent.; Timurid, 15th–16th cent. (ceramic).

Description: Tepe of irregular shape, covering a surface of about 2 hectares, cut in the middle by the road; height 5 m. The surface is covered by sherds, slag, terracotta debris (walls of kilns, firing waste).

Collection: National Museum/AIA—sherds.

Fieldwork:
1. 1956 Ramachandran and Sharma, ASI—reconnaissance.
2. 1969 Gouin, DAFA—survey.

Sources:
1. Ramachandran and Sharma 1956: I. 22–3—mention of the Kushan coin.
2. Gouin 1974 and unpublished report—site no. 16.

746. MUQQUR

Original: Lat. 32° 48' N, long. 67° 46' E. Map 79.
Revised: 32.83029317 N, 67.7906277 E / 32° 49' 49.05540768 N, 67° 47' 26.25970956 E.
Ghazni Province. On the main Kandahār-Kābul road, 103 km south-west of Ghazni.

Date: Sasanian, 3rd–7th cent.; Shahi 7th–8th cent. (ceramic, stylistic).

Description: Several low mounds. Several miniature clay stupas found on the site.

Fieldwork: 1966 Fischer, DAAD—survey.

Sources:
1. Fischer 1967a: 157—mention.
2. Fischer 1969: 338—mention.
3. Verardi and Paparatti 2004: 92—mention the stupas.

747. MUREHZAR

Lat. 34° 50' N, long. 63° 25' E. Map 53.
Bādghīs Province. Near Qadis, *c*.37 km south-east of Qal'a-i Nau.

Description: An artificial cave complex, cut into the side of the hill. It consists of a passage 203 m long opening into a small chamber; there is a blocked passage to the left and another passage to the right, 3–4 m long. There is a large chamber opening from the side of this passage, and a second large chamber is adjacent to the main complex.

Fieldwork: 1957 Lindberg—speleological survey.

Sources:
1. Lindberg 1961: 16—brief description.
2. Rafat 1980: 5—mention.

748. MURKI KHĒL

Original: Lat. 34° 12' N, long. 70° 02' E. Map 65.
Revised: 34.22559208 N, 70.04395965 E / 34° 13' 32.13148728 N, 70° 02' 38.25473208 E.
Nangahār Province. In the foothills of the Spīnghār, *c*.10 km south of Gandamak.

Date: Kushano-Sasanian, 4th–5th cent. (numismatic, stylistic).

Description: Remains of a stupa, stylistically similar to those at Hadda, surrounded by a very extensive surface scatter of large numbers of human bones. Many coins depicting fire altars were found on the surface.

Fieldwork: 1934 Masson—survey.

Sources:
1. Masson 1842: I and III. 225 and 299–301—brief description.
2. Errington 2017a: 161—the Masson archive relating to the site.

MURTAZAH. See **224 DAISHU.**

749. MŪSA-I LŌGAR

Original: Lat. 34° 24' N, long. 69° 13' E. Map 62.
Revised: 34.37519889 N, 69.21325575 E / 34° 22' 30.71598996 N, 69° 12' 47.72071404 E.
Kābul Province. On the left bank of the Lōgar River opposite where it is joined by the Guldarra stream, in the Mūsa-i Lōgar Valley *c*.20 km south of Kābul. Between the river and the mountainside.

Dates: Kushan, Sasanian, and Hunnic, 1st–6th cent.; pre-Mongol Islamic, 10th–13th cent. (ceramic).

Description: Three small mounds, the largest surmounted by a modern tower. Soil robbing on the northern and eastern sides has revealed ancient remains, consisting of a *pakhsa* superstructure on diaper masonry foundations. No plan was recognisable. The settlement possibly belonged to the Guldarra monastery.

Fieldwork: 1963–4 Fussman and Le Berre, DAFA—survey.

Sources:
1. Gardin and Lyonnet, 1980 chronological study of pottery from unpublished DAFA surveys.
2. Fussman and Le Berre 1976: 101—brief description.

750. MŪSA ZĀRI

Original: Lat. 36° 35' N, long. 69° 02' E. Map 32.
Revised:
36.58962233 N, 69.03122633 E / 36° 35' 22.64039196 N, 69° 01' 52.41478476 E (A).
36.59728455 N, 69.02449627 E / 36° 35' 50.22437964 N, 69° 01' 28.18658676 E (B).
36.59751551 N, 69.02825135 E / 36° 35' 51.05584176 N, 69° 01' 41.70486576 E (C).
Qundūz Province. On the plateau which dominates the plain of Qundūz-Khānābād, to the south: semi-desert zone, today without artificial irrigation, crossed by the Aliābād to Khānābād road (Dasht-i Ishān Tūp). 14 km from Aliābād, the road crosses a track which leads to the north-west towards Qundūz, passing through the nearby village of Shākh Tepe (at 1.5 km). From this point, visible a few km to the north-west, is the impressive necropolis called Shākh Tepe explored by J.-M. Casal (see site no. 1065). The tepes grouped under the present number are less spectacular: three little mounds situated in the east angle of the crossroads of the Khānābād road and the Qundūz track. (A) The first, at 1.5 km to the south-east of the crossroads, corresponds to the mound of 4 m indicated on the 1:100,000 map. (B) The second is on the south side of the road, 0.7 km from the crossroads. (C) The third is a little further from the road (200 m), on the same side, 1.1 km from the crossroads.

Dates: Kushan, 1st–4th cent. (A, C); Hunnic-Turk, 5th–9th cent. (A, C); some Islamic sherds (ceramic).

Description: (A) Square north–south mound (20 × 20 m), cut into by the surrounding crops (*lalmī*): abundant sherds up to 100 m to the north and to the south; height 5 m. 100 m and 300 m to the west, two small hillocks (diam. 10 m, height 1.5 m). (B) Square mound (15 × 15 m), flat top (1 m) depression in the centre. (C) Low platform (0.5 m) more or less square, north–south, with a bulge on the north side (total surface *c*.30 × 30 m), and some higher points on the top; hillock at the north-west angle (2 m), and T-shaped 'walls' on the south and east sides (1 m).

Collection: National Museum/AIA – sherds.

Fieldwork: 1978 Gardin et al., CNRS – survey.

Sources:
1. Site information by J.-C. Gardin.
2. Gardin and Lyonnet 1978–9: pl. VII – nos. 450–2.
3. Lyonnet 1997: figs 49, 68, 69 – nos. 450–2.
4. Gardin 1998: 80 – nos. 450–2.

751. MUSHKĀN
Or MISHGHĀN or SAR-I GHŪR MUSHKĀN.

Lat. 32° 59' N, long. 63° 52' E. Map 73.
Farāh Province. South-west of Zarnī, on the road from Dilārām to Taiwāra.

Date: ?Ghurid, 12th–13th cent. (stylistic).

Description: The modern mosque of Abu Bakr contains a reused ancient *mihrab* and two wooden pillars. The *mihrab*, though much damaged by modern reworking, has a horseshoe arch niche head and a Kufic inscription. The two pillars are completely covered with carved geometric patterns.

Sources:
1. Klimburg 1958: 19 – brief description.
2. Ball 2002: 26 – mention.

752. NĀD-I ʿALĪ
Or BINA-I KAI or SHAHR-I SISTĀN or ZARANJ. Including SAFĪD DAGH and SURKH DAGH.

Original: Lat. 30° 59' N, long. 61° 52' E. Map 92.
Revised: 30.99788057 N, 61.84942498 E / 30° 59' 52.37004804 N, 61° 50' 57.92993196 E.
Nīmrūz Province. *C*.24 km south-west of Chākhansūr and 6 km north of Zaranj. The site is *c*.1 km east of the village of Nād-i ʿAlī.

Dates: Bronze Age, 3rd–2nd mill. BC; Iron Age, early 1st mill. BC; Achaemenid, 6th–4th cent. BC; Seleucid and Parthian, 4th–1st cent. BC, early Islamic, 8th–13th cent. (ceramic).

Description: A large urban site consisting of massive fortification walls enclosing an irregular area of remains. The area is covered in alluvial deposit except for where mounds and ruins survive. These include a citadel surrounded by a ditch, a *madrasa* of part baked brick construction, a Friday Mosque, a bazaar, four gateways, the mound of Safīd Dagh, and the mound of Surkh Dagh, where excavations have revealed the remains of a Bronze or Iron Age 'massive monument' of uncertain function. In the early 20th century there were also remains of a brick minaret, 8–20 m high, that has since collapsed. In addition, there is a thick surface scatter of sherds and building debris with Iron Age bronze and gold objects coming from the excavations.

Fieldwork:
1. 1884 Peacocke, Maitland, ABC – topographical survey.
2. 1903–5 Tate, SAC – survey.
3. 1936 Ghirshman, DAFA – excavations at Surkh Dagh.
4. 1950 Fairservis, AMNH – survey.
5. 1968 Dales, University Museum, Penn. – excavations at Surkh Dagh.

Sources:
1. Conolly 1840 – description, illustrations, and discussion of some agate seals – some of them inscribed – found at the site.
2. Smith 1876: 298–9 – brief description.
3. Peacocke 1885a: 11–12 – brief description.
4. Maitland 1888a: 77–8 – brief description and sketch of ruins.

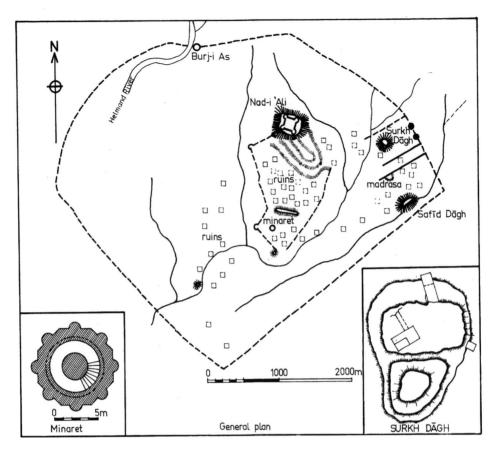

752 Nād-i ʿAli—general plan (after Tate 1910), (W. Ball—after a photo and description in Tate 1910), and Surkh Dāgh (after Dales 1977a).

5. Peacocke 1887a: 25–6—brief description.
6. Holdich 1885a: 163—brief description.
7. Holdich 1887: 9—mention.
8. A. C. Yate 1887: 94–6—brief description of the site and the associated legends.
9. McMahon 1906: 211—mention and photo of the citadel.
10. Tate 1909: 118–22—fairly detailed description of the site with a photo of Surkh Dagh.
11. Tate 1910: 198–204—detailed description of all remains and discussion of its historical sources. Photos of the minaret and Safīd Dagh and general plan of the site.
12. Stein 1928: 940–1—describes some bronze objects and pottery brought to him from the site.
13. Schroeder 1938: 1026—briefly discusses the minaret and its possible Sasanian form.
14. Ghirshman 1939—preliminary report on the excavations. Description of the architecture, pottery, and finds, with a note on the architectural links.
15. Kohzad 1950b—brief summary of Ghirshman's work.
16. Fairservis 1953: 144—briefly discusses the general results of Ghirshman's excavations.
17. Gardin 1959—summary of the Islamic pottery.
18. Hackin 1959c: 23–5—brief preliminary report on Ghirshman's excavations.
19. Fairservis 1961: 45–52—brief description of the site and summary of the material collected from Surkh Dagh (pottery, alabaster, glass, iron, slag).
20. Gnoli 1967: 106—brief discussion of the evidence of Ghirshman's work for pre-Achaemenid origins of the site.
21. Dales 1968: 41–5—brief account of his own excavations.
22. Fischer et al. 1974–6: 34—brief summary.
23. Cattenat and Gardin 1976—discusses the ceramics and its links in the Achaemenid period.
24. Dales 1977a—summary of Ghirshman's work and a brief report on the pottery and stratigraphy from his own excavations. Few drawings.
25. Fischer 1978b: 361—brief description.
26. Pinder-Wilson 2001—discusses the form and the architectural parallels of the minaret.
27. Vogelsang 1992: 263–7—discussion of the Achaemenid remains and pottery.
28. O'Kane 1984a—some new data on the minaret.
29. Besenval and Francfort 1994—redate the massive platform to the Bronze Age.
30. Ball 2008: 49, 251–2—summary.

753. NĀDIR TEPE, BALKH

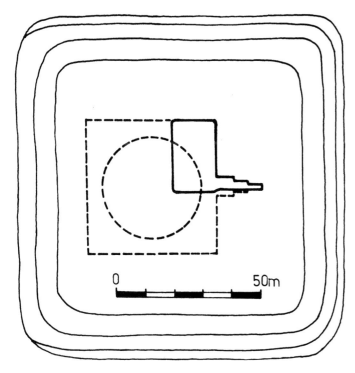

753 Nadir Tepe (after Foucher 1942–47).

Original: Lat. 36° 47' N, long. 66° 51' E. Map 26.
Revised: 36.78937546 N, 66.86349618 E /
36° 47' 21.75166932 N, 66° 51' 48.58623396 E.
Balkh Province. 3.5 km north-west of Balkh on the road to Kilift.

Date: Kushan and/or Sasanian, 1st–7th cent. (architectural).

Description: A large mound *c.*120 m square. On top are the remains of a possible stupa base with a stairway to the east, surrounded by a square wall marking a possible monastery.

Fieldwork:
1. 1886 Peacocke.
2. 1886 Maitland, ABC — topographical survey.
3. 1924 Foucher, DAFA — survey.
4. 1960 Hayashi and Sahara, Kyoto University — survey.

Sources:
1. Peacocke 1887a: 321 — brief description.
2. Maitland 1888b: 176 — mention.
3. Foucher 1942–7: 68 — brief description, with a plan and photo.
4. Hayashi and Sahara 1962: 57–8 — summary of the survey results.

754. NĀDIR TEPE, KANDAHĀR

Original: Lat. 31° 32' N, long. 65° 37' E. Map 89.
Revised: 31.53627575 N, 65.6398254 E / 31° 32' 10.59270432 N, 65° 38' 23.37143964 E.

Kandahār Province. 8 km south-west of Shar-i Kuhna of Kandahār and 4 km north-east of Zala Khān.

Dates: Indo-Parthian, 1st–3rd cent.; Sasano-Turk, 5th–9th cent. Timurid, 15th–16th cent. (ceramic).

Description: Small tepe.

Collection: National Museum/AIA — sherds.

Fieldwork: 1951 Casal, DAFA — survey.

Source: J.-M. Casal: unpublished 1951 report, DAFA archives.

755. NAGĀLA

Lat. 35° 55' N, long. 65° 53' E. Maps 24, 46.
Jauzjān Province. 7 km west of Jarghān, in the region of Sar-i Pul.

Dates: Hunnic-Turk, 5th–9th cent. (ceramic).

Description: None.

Collection: National Museum/AIA — sherds.

Source: Gardin and Lyonnet: 1980 study of pottery from unpublished DAFA surveys.

756. NAGARA GHUNDI

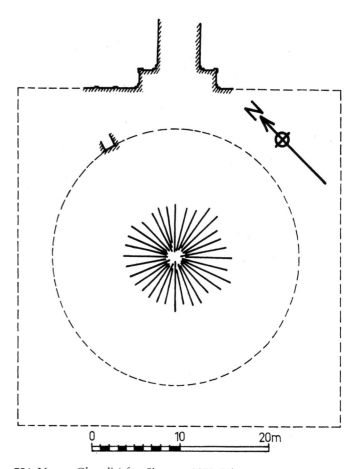

756 Nagara Ghundi (after Simpson 1879–80).

Original: Lat. 34° 26–43' N, long. 70° 23–38' E. Map 66.
Revised: 34.44657354 N, 70.39758843 E /
34° 26' 47.66473212 N, 70° 23' 51.31833180 E.
Nangahār Province. C.4 km west of Jalālābād near Tepe
Khwāja Lahōri, south of the junction of the Surkhāb and
Kābul Rivers.

Date: Kushan-Hunnic, 1st–6th cent. (architectural).

Description: A very large stupa, *c.*100 m in circumference.
Excavations revealed an unusual radial construction of the
dome, and a decorated, plastered exterior. Possibly identifiable with the Nagarahara stupa described by Huien Tsang.

Fieldwork:
1. 1934 Masson—survey.
2. 1879 Jenkins, Indian Army—excavation.

Sources:
1. Masson 1841: Sketch map—refers to the mound as a
   'tumulus of loose stones'.
2. Simpson 1879a: 229—mention.
3. Simpson 1879–80: 53–4—brief description.
4. Simpson 1881: 191–2—brief description.
5. Errington 2017a: 154–5—the Masson collection and archive relating to the site.

757. NAGARA KHĀNA

Lat. 35° 44' N, long. 63° 51' E. Maps 44, 45.
Faryāb Province. In the Hirak Valley, 9.5 km east of Qal'a-i
Wali in the Qaisār area.

Description: Several *zīyārats* surrounded by ruins.

Fieldwork: 1885 Peacocke, ABC—topographical survey.

Sources:
1. Peacocke 1887a: 115 and 239—mention.
2. Gazetteer 1979: IV. 266 and 425—mention.

NAHANGĀBĀD. See 820 PUL-I ZUHAK.

758. NAI QAL'A

Lat. 33° 14' N, long. 67° 52' E. Maps 78, 79.
Ghazni Province. 12 km north-east of the western end of
the Zardalu Pass (Qarabāgh-Lūmān road), 15 km west of
Humai Qal'a.

Date: Early Sasanian, 4th–5th cent. (stylistic).

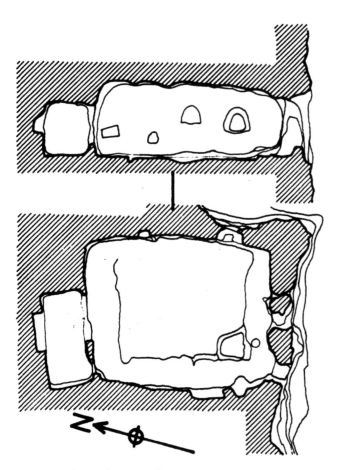

758 Nai Qal'a 1 (after Verardi 1977a).

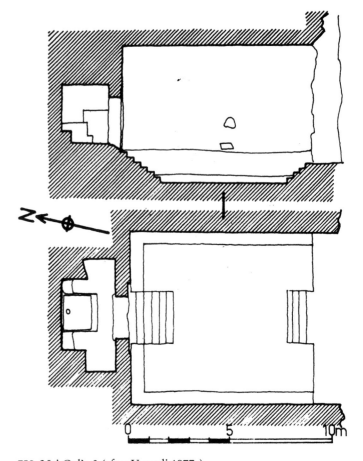

758 Nai Qal'a 2 (after Verardi 1977a).

Description: An extensive artificial cave complex of some 35 chambers, the largest in the Qarabāgh-Jāghūrī region, with quite large and relatively well-preserved chambers. It includes a large room (Cave 9) leading to a smaller inner room that contains a 'throne', presumably for a now lost image. There are traces of frescos on plastered surfaces.

Fieldwork: 1974 and 1975 Taddei and Verardi, IsMEO—survey.

Sources:
1. Taddei 1975: 545—mention and photo.
2. Verardi 1977a: 143–7—description with a discussion of the architectural parallels.
3. Verardi and Paparatti 2004: 27–37—detailed description with detailed drawings and photos.
4. Inaba in Verardi and Paparatti 2004: 105–8—discussion of the historical sources.

NAI SHAHR. See *777 NĪSHARĪ*.

759. NALBANDĀN

Lat. 34° 10' N, long. 63° 56' E. Map 54.
Ghūr Province. In the Tagau Ishlān, 3 km west of Mināra.

Date: Ghurid, 12th–13th cent. (architectural).

Description: Ruins of two mud-brick towers on either side of a gulley.

Source: Kästner 1968—brief description.

760. NAMŪSA

Original: Lat. 36° 03' N, long. 64° 39' E. Map 24.
Revised: 36.04074811 N, 64.65953171 E /
36° 02' 26.69318232 N, 64° 39' 34.31415600 E.
Faryāb Province. On the west bank of the Maimana River, c.20 km north of Maimana.

Description: A mound with remains of a fort on top.

Fieldwork: 1886 Maitland, ABC—topographical survey.

Source: Maitland 1888b: 155—mention.

761. NANDARRA
Or DARŪNTA or KHAISTA TOPE.

Original: Lat. 34° 28' N, long. 70° 21' E. Map 66.
Revised: 34.47067805 N, 70.35383704 E /
34° 28' 14.44099764 N, 70° 21' 13.81336056 E.
Laghmān Province. 12 km west of Jalālābād, between Darūnta and Bīmārān.

Date: Indo-Parthian, 1st cent. (numismatic).

Description: A large stupa on the side of the hill. It has an elaborate frieze of alternating blind arches and pilasters, and stands on a square platform. Inside was a bark box and some bullae. There are also remains of several smaller stupas, three of which were excavated by Pigou: 'Tope-i Kutchera' contained a jar with two coins of Hermaeus III and one of Azes; 'Tope-i fasl' contained a gold reliquary with pearls and bone; 'Tope-i Hosenamanat' contained a casket with three coins of Azes.

Other remains include a cave complex in an escarpment, some burials at the foot of the hill, and a large cistern c.100 m square between Nandarra and Deh Rahman.

Collections: BM—stupa deposits.

Fieldwork:
1. 1833 Honigberger—excavation.
2. 1834 Masson—excavation.
3. 1841 Pigou, Indian Army—excavations.
4. 1923 Foucher and Godard, DAFA—architectural study.
5. 1965 Mizuno, Kyoto University—survey.

Sources:
1. Gerard 1834—general remarks on Honigberger's findings.
2. Masson 1834b: 330—mentions own excavation.
3. Masson 1841: 81–6—descriptions of the stupas and discussion of their function.
4. Moorcroft and Trebeck 1841: 362–7—description of these and other stupas in the Darunta plain in 1820.
5. Pigou 1841—detailed description of the finds, and drawings of the coins.
6. Swinnerton 1879: 200—full description of the main stupas.
7. Simpson 1879–80: 44—brief description.
8. Holdich 1881a: 20—mention.
9. Simpson 1881: 202–3—brief description of the main stupa and associated remains.
10. Godard 1925a: 13–16—brief report on the survey carried out on the main stupa.
11. Pandit 1927: 135–7—photos and brief description.
12. Foucher 1942–7: 153—briefly mentions the survey of the stupa.
13. Caspani and Cagnacci 1951: 215 and fig. 181—mention and photo.
14. Mizuno 1971: 116—brief description and photos of the present condition (Stupa 104).
15. Franz 1977–8—stylistic discussion of the main stupa.
16. Ball 2008: 252—summary.
17. Jongeward et al. 2012—catalogue and discussion of the reliquaries.
18. Errington 2017a: 126–30 and 2017b: 31, 42–3, 45—the Masson collection and archive relating to the site.

762. NANGA

Lat. 32° 29' N, long. 67° 49' E. Map 79.
Ghazni Province. On the western side of the Āb-i Istāda, south-east of Muqqur.

Dates: Hunnic-Turki Shahi, 5th–9th cent. (ceramic).

Description: None available.

Fieldwork: 1974 Dupree, AUFS—survey.

Source: Information by L. Dupree.

NAQSHARA TEPE. See 909 QARA BAI.

NARAIMAN. See 764 NARIMAN.

763. NARANG

Lat. 34° 46' N, long. 71° 04' E. Map 68.
Kunār Province. On the right bank of the Kunār River, about halfway between Islāmpūr and Chaghan Sarāī.

Date: Hindu Shahi, 10th cent. (ceramic).

Description: Some mud-brick ruins and an Islamic cemetery on a natural hill.

Source: Fischer 1969: 357—brief description.

764. NARĪMĀN
Or NĀRĀTŪ or NĀRAIMĀN.

Original: Lat. 34° 42' N, long. 62° 57' E. Map 53.
Revised: 34° 44' 13.319" N, 63° 0' 33.509" E.
Bādghis Province. About 10 km west of Laman and 35 km south of Qal'a-i Nau on the road to Herat. 3 km north-east of Dehistān.

Dates: Achaemenid, 6th–4th cent. BC; pre-Mongol Islamic, 10th–13th cent.; Timurid, 15th–16th cent. (ceramic).

Description: Fortress of about 900 × 220 m. It occupies the whole of a rocky plateau oriented east–west, separated from a mountainous range by a narrow pass. The north and south faces are mostly sheer and thus impregnable. Access is by a winding ramp located in the south-east angle, immediately after the pass, leading to a gate which still exists. It is formed by a pointed arch made of narrow sandstone voussoirs, surmounted by a second ground arch, pointed and slightly protruding, constructed of bricks embedded in a masonry of stone blocks joined with lime plaster mortar. The interior left foot of the gate is preserved in a few courses of cut and dressed rubble stones. The few sections of walls which remain are built on the rock itself directly above the cliff, and are located mainly on the west and south faces. This rampart consisted of an exterior facing and a continuous interior archway, which probably carried a covered way. The construction of these archways is of the same type as the gate, although better adjusted. In the best preserved part of the rampart (south face) there is a little square room with a flat vault, 2.70 m per side, lit by two narrow windows which are flared and arched. The defensive system of the north face and the north-west angle is composed of very eroded towers constructed in the same way as the rest of the rampart. The north-west angle, not naturally well-defended, is doubled by an exterior enclosure of which a tower remains. Inside the fortress, at the highest point, are the remains of two monuments near one another. Of the first, only one room remains in the square plan, flanked by an *iwān* on the north and another on the south, and it is pierced by a door on both the east and west sides. The construction is of the same type as that of the rampart, with in addition some brick elements. Of the second monument, there remains only the central part, octagonal in plan. Each face contains a niche, with a pointed surbased arch faced with bricks. The whole is constructed in bricks on a foundation of masonry in stones with a facing of rough rubble stones. In the north and the west, within the fortress, are two wells. Finally, at about the centre, on the north side, is a *zīyārat*.

Collection: National Museum/AIA—sherds.

Fieldwork:
1. 1885 Maitland, Yate, ABC—topographic exploration.
2. 1952 Le Berre and Gardin, DAFA—survey.

Sources:
1. M. Le Berre: unpublished 1952 report, DAFA archives.
2. Durand 1885: I, pl. 27—sketch of fortifications.
3. Griesbach 1885a: 10–11—description.
4. *Pioneer*, 22 July 1885—description.
5. Maitland 1888a: 191–2—brief description; 322–44—detailed description and distant sketch, with mention by hearsay of gravestone with inscription 125 AH.
6. Yate 1888: 6–8—description of all the remains.
7. Le Strange 1905: 414–15—summary of the historical sources for Dehistān.
8. Niedemeyer and Diez 1924: pls 238–41—photos of many of the ruins.
9. Caspani and Cagnacci 1951: 247—mention.
10. Gazetteer 1975: III. 317—description.

765. NARĪN
Or ZARD TEPE.

Lat. 36° 03' N, long. 69° 08' E. Map 33.
Baghlān Province. C.48 km east of Baghlān.

Date: Early Islamic, 10th–13th cent. (documentary).

Description: A huge mound now occupied by modern military buildings.

Fieldwork:
1. 1886 Shahzada Taimus, ABC—topographical survey.
2. 1975 Kohl—survey.

Sources:
1. Shahzada Taimus 1888: 311—mention.
2. Caspani and Cagnacci 1951: 264—mention.
3. Fischer 1969: 352—mention.
4. Kohl 1978: 63—mention.

766. NASRATĀBĀD
See also 437 HUSTUKH TEPE.

Original: Lat. 36° 53' N, long. 66° 25' E. Map 25.
Revised: 36.87787036 N, 66.41439503 E /
36° 52' 40.33330968 N, 66° 24' 51.82209864 E.
Jauzjān Province. 24 km south-east of Āqcha, north of the Balkh road and north-east of the village of Nasratābād.

Description: Small quadrangular mound (80 × 80 m), height 9 m, surrounded by a ditch. Zone of ruins to the east and south, with scattered small hillocks.

Fieldwork: 1948 Le Berre, DAFA—survey.

Source: M. Le Berre: unpublished 1948 report, DAFA archives, tépé P. 24.

NAUĀR. See 769. NĀWA.

NAU NAGAK. See 2166. NAU NAGAK in Supplement.

767. NAURAK

Original: Lat. 33° 45' N, long. 64° 47' E. Maps 55, 74.
Revised: 33.75187827 N, 64.78635357 E /
33° 45' 06.76176948 N, 64° 47' 10.87285308 E.
Ghūr Province. A small plain, the Dasht-i Naurak, between Taiwāra and Shaharak.

Date: Ghurid, 12th–13th cent. (architectural, geographical).

Description: A ruined fort on a bluff and some scattered towers guarding the road.

Fieldwork:
1. 1946 Kohzad, HAS—survey.
2. 1977 Ball—survey.

Sources:
1. Kohzad 1951–4, 8/4: 62—mention.
2. Ball 2002: 33—description and photo.

768. NAURŪZ TEPE

Original: Lat. 35° 56' N, long. 64° 44' E. Map 24.
Revised: 35.93625246 N, 64.74318106 E /

35° 56' 10.50883980 N, 64° 44' 35.45182320 E.
Faryāb Province. Near Maimana airport, 5 km west of the town.

Description: A mound, where much glazed pottery has been found. On top are the remains of a fort.

Fieldwork:
1. 1885 Maitland, ABC—topographical survey.
2. 1978 Lee, BIAS—reconnaissance.

Sources:
1. Site information by Jonathan L. Lee.
2. Maitland 1888b: 108—mention.

769. NĀWA
Or NAUĀR.

Original: Lat. 32° 20' N, long. 67° 53' E. Map 79.
Revised: 32.33880663 N, 67.88227172 E /
32° 20' 19.70385252 N, 67° 52' 56.17817580 E.
Zābul Province. 14 km south of Āb-i Istāda.

Dates: Kushan-Sasanian, 1st–7th cent.; Turki Shahi-early Islamic, 8th–13th cent.; Timurid, 15th–16th cent. (ceramic).

Description: Extensive group of mounds and ruined walls.

Fieldwork:
1. 1966 Fischer, DAAD—survey.
2. 1976 Taddei and Verardi, IsMEO—survey.

Sources:
1. Fischer 1967a: 164—mention and ground aerial photos.
2. Fischer 1969: 340—mention.
3. Taddei 1976: 600—brief description.

NAWĀBĀD. See 48 ĀQ TEPE.

NAWĀBĀD, Rustāq. See 1235 YAKA TŪT.

770. NAWARID

Original: Lat. 36° 49' N, long. 66° 38' E. Map 26.
Revised: 36.81394258 N, 66.63089452 E /
36° 48' 50.19330204 N, 66° 37' 51.22028964 E.
Balkh Province. 11 km south-east of Nimlik, about 1.5 km north of the road to Balkh.

Description: Circular mound (diam. c.110 m), surrounded by a ditch; several hillocks around the tepe.

Fieldwork: 1948 Le Berre, DAFA—survey.

Sources: M. Le Berre: unpublished 1948 report, DAFA archives, tépé P. 40.

771. NAWARID LABAK

Original: Lat. 36° 48' N, long. 66° 37' E. Map 26.
Revised: 36.80362259 N, 66.61355453 E /
36° 48' 13.04131248 N, 66° 36' 48.79632276 E.
Balkh Province. 10 km south-east of Nimlik, 300 m south
of the Balkh road.

Description: Small circular tepe (diam. *c*.60 m), low (5 m),
surrounded by a ditch. One part of the top (east side) has
been subjected to digging (illegal excavation?). Several similar hillocks are visible to the east and the south-east; one of
these, north of the village of Nawarid, serves as a cemetery.

Fieldwork: 1948 Le Berre, DAFA—survey.

Source: M. Le Berre: unpublished 1948 report, DAFA
archives, tépé P. 39.

NĀYIBĀBĀD. See SHĀHTEPE

772. NAYIB DUM

Original: Lat. 37° 04–06' N, long. 69° 17–28' E. Maps 31, 35.

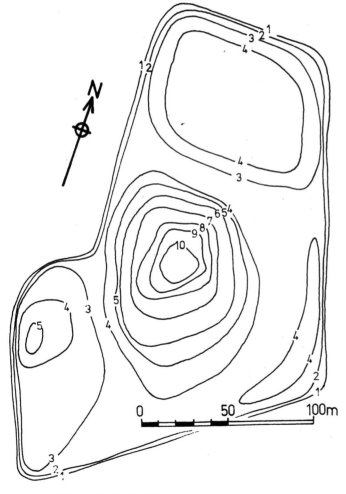

772 Nayib Dum (J.-C. Gardin).

Revised: 37.06405512 N, 69.27610977 E /
37° 03' 50.59843128 N, 69° 16' 33.99515508 E.
Qundūz Province. 5 km north-east of Archi, by the track
that links this town to Khwāja Ghar along the modern canal
of Ārchī (Nahr-i Ārchī), and about 1 km west of this canal,
in the irrigated fields (indicated on the 1:100,000 map).

Dates: Kushan and Hunnic-Turk, 1st–9th cent.; some
Islamic sherds (ceramic).

Description: Large hillock of irregular quadrilateral shape,
covering a surface of about 200×100 m at the base; the
platform rises to 3–4 m above the irrigated fields. A higher
mound dominates it in the south-west (5 m), another in the
centre (8–9 m).

Collection: National Museum/AIA—sherds.

Fieldwork: 1977 Gardin et al., CNRS—survey.

Sources:
1. Site information by J.-C. Gardin.
2. Gardin and Lyonnet 1978–9: pl. IV—no. 22.
3. Lyonnet 1997: figs 49, 68, 69—no. 22.
4. Gardin 1998: 55—no. 22.

773. NIJRAU
Or ASĀBĀD.
See also 928 QUL-I NĀDIR.

Lat 34° 57' N, long. 69° 36' E. approximately. Map 65.
Kāpīsā Province. 3 km south-west of Nijrau on the
Gulbahār-Sarōbi road.

Date: Kushan-Hunnic, 1st–6th cent. (stylistic).

Description: A large stupa-monastery complex. It has a
badly eroded dome on a high square platform, with a
stairway on one side. Construction is of diaper masonry.

Collections: National Museum—excavated objects.

Fieldwork:
1. 1933 Carl, DAFA—excavations.
2. 1976 Kohl—survey.

Sources:
1. Masson 1841: 117—mention.
2. Masson 1842: III. 168—mention.
3. Foucher 1942–7: 149—mention and photo before
   excavation.
4. Sālnāma 1933/34: opp. 31—photos of the stupa and
   some of the excavated objects.
5. Carl 1959a: figs 43–7—photos of the excavations.
6. Tarzi 2000—discussion of the schist sculptures.
7. Tissot 2006: 336—National Museum catalogue details
   and photos.
8. Jongeward et al. 2012—catalogue and discussion of the
   reliquaries.

NIKCHA. See 641 KUMLI.

774. NILĀB

Lat. 35° 00' N, long. 68° 52' E. approximately. Maps 49, 60. Parwān Province. On the Ghūrband River near Siāhgird.

Description: Remains of an immense fortress.

Sources:
1. Masson 1936a: 6—mention and historical discussion.
2. Masson 1842: III. 169—mention.
3. Cunningham 1846: 192—identifies the site with ancient Nilaubis.

775. NĪLĪ

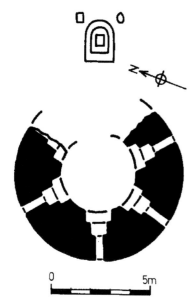

0   5m

775 Nili (W. Ball).

Original: Lat. 33° 14' N, long. 64° 22' E. Map 74.
Revised: 33.23103567 N, 64.3792902 E / 33° 13' 51.72840192 N, 64° 22' 45.44473368 E.
Ghur Province. On the route leading from Zarnī to Yamān, in the area south-east of Taiwāra.

Date: Ghurid, 12th–13th cent. (architectural, geographical).

Description: Very extensive remains of fortifications and towers defending the road.

Fieldwork: 1977 Ball—survey.

Sources:
1. Klimburg 1960: 49—mention.
2. Ball 2002: 29–32—detailed description and photos in the context of Ghurid fortifications.
3. Wannell 2002: 238—mention.

776. NIMLIK
Or MAMALIK.

Original: Lat. 36° 50' N, long. 66° 31' E. Maps 25, 26.
Revised: 36.83805995 N, 66.51059153 E / 36° 50' 17.01583008 N, 66° 30' 38.12949684 E.
Jauzjān Province. 36 km west of Balkh and 34 km east of Āqcha, immediately to the south of the road.

Dates: Graeco-Bactrian, 3rd–2nd cent. BC (epigraphic); early Islamic, 10th–13th cent. (ceramic).

Description: An extensive area of remains, stretching for several kilometres. It consists of houses, walls, and an arch, and is dominated by a very steep-sided mound, *c.* 17 m in height and 300 m in diameter, with more ruins on top. The mound was probably a citadel, and is surrounded by a ditch and defensive walls. A Greek ostracon was discovered here in 1946.

Fieldwork:
1. 1886 Maitland, ABC—topographical survey.
2. 1886 Peacocke, ABC—topographical survey.
3. 1938 Barger, ASI—survey.
4. 1946 Wheeler, ASI, and Schlumberger, DAFA—reconnaissance.
5. 1948 Le Berre, DAFA—survey.
6. 1956 Ramachandran and Sharma, ASI—reconnaissance.
7. 1960 Hayashi and Sahara, Kyoto University—survey.

Sources:
1. Ferrier 1857: 205—describes the site as probably Graeco-Bactrian.
2. Peacocke 1887a: 357—mention.
3. Maitland 1888b: 174—mention.
4. Yate 1888: 255—mention.
5. Barger and Wright 1941: 55—brief description.
6. Perkins and Braidwood 1947—brief note on the discovery of the ostracon.
7. Schlumberger 1947b—brief note on the ostracon.
8. Shakur 1947: 69–70—brief description.
9. Wheeler 1947: 63—brief description.
10. Ramachandran and Sharma 1956: I. 20—mention.
11. Hayashi and Sahara 1962: 66—photo and description in Japanese.
12. Davary 1977—mentions the ostracon.
13. Gazetteer 1979: IV. 430—mentions the remains.
14. Ball 2008: 252—summary.
15. Rougemont 2012a: 188–9—text and discussion of the ostracon.

NIOH. See 2167 NIOH in Supplement.

777. NĪSHAR

Or NAI SHAHR. See also 415. HAMAM CHASHMA.

Lat. 35° 54' N, long. 65° 09' E. Maps 24, 46.
Faryāb Province. On the south bank of the Shīrīn Tagau, 38.5 km east of Maimana and c.12 km north-west of Bīlchirāgh.

Description: Some 10–12 artificial rock chambers, most of them ruined. Probably associated with the cave of Hamam Chashma, further upstream.

Fieldwork:
1. 1886 Griesbach, ABC—topographical survey.
2. 1970 Dupree, AUFS—survey.

Sources:
1. Griesbach 1888b: 196—mention.
2. Gazetteer 1979: IV. 430—mention.
3. Lee (Sterling) 1991: 290—mentions the caves and a fort.

778. NISHK

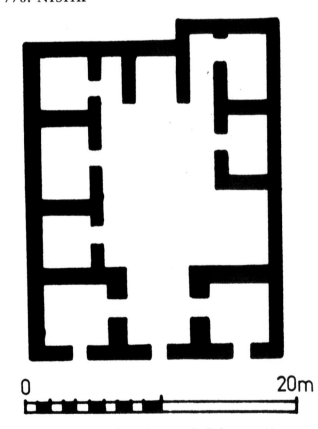

778 Nishk—house (after Behrens and Klinkott 1973).

Original: Lat. 31° 19–31' N, long. 62° 09–15' E. Map 84.
Revised: 31.2830706 N, 62.15855735 E /

31° 16' 59.05416216 N, 62° 09' 30.80644524 E.
Nīmrūz Province. 8 km north-east of Dīwāl-i Khudaidād on the Khāsh Rūd towards Kadah.

Dates: Sasanian, 3rd–7th cent.; early Islamic, 11th–13th cent. (architectural); Mongol-Timurid, 13th–16th cent. (ceramic).

Description: Remains of a large city. It is surrounded by fortification walls with a well-preserved monumental gateway. Inside are many *iwān* courtyard houses, and the centre is dominated by a citadel. It is multi-storey with round corner towers, and is decorated with a series of 'key-hole' shaped arches.

To the south is a large area of ruined houses, towers, and mounds.

Fieldwork: 1960–70 Fischer, Bonn University—survey.

Sources:
1. Fischer 1970b: pls 5–7—photos.
2. Fischer 1971b: 44—aerial and ground photos, and a summary of the ruin types (Site 35).
3. Behrens and Klinkott 1973—typology and architectural analysis of the *iwān* houses.
4. Fischer 1974b—photos.
5. Fischer et al. 1974–6: 49–51—brief description.
6. Fischer 1978b: 369—brief description of the gateway.
7. Fischer 1978c: 59–62—brief summary and discussion of medieval city types.
8. Ball 2008: 258—summary.

NOKEN KALAT. See 871. QAL'A-I NAU.

779. NŪKARKHĒL

Original: Lat. 34° 16' N, long. 70° 04' E. Map 65.
Revised: 34.26085064 N, 70.04090181 E /
34° 15' 39.06229140 N, 70° 02' 27.24652968 E.
Nangahār Province. In the northern foothills of the Spīn-ghār, c.8 km north of Murki Khēl and 7 km south-east of Gandamak.

Description: Remains of a large tumulus, possibly a stupa. There are also finds of many ancient burials consisting of skeletons with simple jewellery tied round their ankles.

Collections: BM—stupa deposits.

Fieldwork: 1834 Masson—survey.

Sources:
1. Masson 1842: III. 301 and 303—brief description.
2. Errington 2017a: 161—the Masson archive relating to the site.

780. NUQRI KHĀNA
Or BĀZĀRAK or DARRA-I SHARWA.

Lat. 35° 21' N, long. 69° 31' E. Map 50.
Parwān Province. In the Panjshīr Valley 5 km north of Bāzārak.

Description: An ancient abandoned silver and copper mine, consisting of a series of tunnels and caves excavated into a schist vein. In the vicinity are traces of old copper slag. There are also petroglyphs of simple figures and ibex.

Fieldwork: 1977 CNRS—geological survey.

Sources:
1. Dupree 1958a: 141—mention.
2. Berthoud et al. 1977: 16–17—description of the geology and the workings.
3. Kohl 1978: 71–2—mention.

NŪR. See 622 KŪH-I MŪRI.

NUR 'ALI. See 2168 NUR 'ALI in Supplement.

781. OBEH
See also 185 CHASHMA-I OBEH.

Lat. 34° 22' N, long. 63° 10' E. Map 53.
Herat Province. 107 km east of Herat, on the north bank of the Harī Rūd on the road to Chisht.

Date: Middle Islamic, 12th–15th cent. (ceramic); Timurid, 15th–16th cent. (ceramic, epigraphic, stylistic).

Description: In the town are the remains of a Bālā Hisār consisting of some fragmentary walls surrounded by a ditch. There is also a Friday Mosque containing a 15th-cent. inscription, although the mosque itself is probably later.
To the north-east of the town are the remains of a badly ruined qal'a of 12th–15th cent. (Soviet Site K164).

Fieldwork:
1. 1885 Maitland, ABC—reconnaissance.
2. 1952 Le Berre and Gardin, DAFA—survey.
3. 1960–1 Fischer and Dupree—survey.
4. 1975 O'Kane, BIPS—survey.
5. 1968–78 Kruglikova, Af/Sov. Mission—survey.

Sources:
1. M. Le Berre: unpublished 1952 report in DAFA Archives.
2. Maitland 1888a: 342—brief description of Bālā Hisar; 343—mentions gravestones north of the Bālā Hisar.
3. Fischer 1961d—mentions own survey.
4. O'Kane 1987: 156–7—description of the mosque.
5. Golombek and Wilber 1988: 340—description of the mosque.
6. Gaibov et al. 2010: mention (Sites K163 and K164).

OBLAU TEPE. See ĀBRAU.Ā

ORTA GUMBAZ. See 1243 YARTI GUMBAZ.

PADAH-I SULTĀN. See 792 PALANGI.

PADAH-I SULTĀN. See 2169 PADAH-I SULTĀN in Supplement.

PANJĀL. See 2171. PANJĀL in Supplement.

782. PĀCHIRWAGĀM
Or KHUGIYĀNI.

Lat. 34° 12' N, long. 70° 17' E. Map 65.
Ningrāhar Province. On the Chapryar River in Khugiyāni district, c.25 km south-west of Hadda.

Dates: Achaemenid, 4th cent. BC (numismatic); Kushano-Sasanian, 4th–5th cent. (stylistic).

Description: Some 50 bent bar silver Achaemenid coins were found here in 1962. Subsequent excavations revealed the remains of a fortress measuring c.200 × 100 m in area and finds of coins and fragmentary Buddhist sculpture.

Fieldwork: 1973 Mustamandi, AIA—excavations.

Sources:
1. Zafar, ed. 1973—mentions the excavations.
2. Mac Dowall and Taddei 1978a: 203—mention the coin hoard.

783. PAI HISĀR

Lat. 33° 49' N, long. 64° 16' E. Maps 54, 74.
Ghūr Province. North-west of Taiwāra and north-east of Sakhir.

Description: Some Ghurid remains reported by Muhammad Said Mashhal.

Source: Rafat 1980: 5—mention.

784. PAIKAR

Original: Lat. 34° 40' N, long. 68° 07' E. Map 58.
Revised: 34.671615 N, 68.12030421 E / 34° 40' 17.81398776 N, 68° 07' 13.09516356 E.
Bāmiyān Province. Road from Kābul to Bāmiyān, south slope of the Hājigak Pass: at the place called Kāfir Qal'a, in the valley of Darra-i Paikar.

Date: Turk and/or pre-Mongol Islamic period, 7th–13th cent. (architecture).

Description: The very eroded ruins of a castle defending the pass.

Fieldwork: 1974–5 Le Berre, DAFA—survey.

Sources:

1. Le Berre 1987: 87–8 and pl. 114—itinerary C, ruin 1.
2. Sims-Williams 2015—discussion of a Bactrian legal document that might have originated from this site or one nearby.

785. PAI KŌTAL

See also 409 HĀJIGAK.

Lat. 34° 40' N, long. 68° 05' E. Map 58.
Bāmiyān Province. At the northern foot of the Hāhigak Pass, just in the Kālu Valley, 7 km from the Hājigak petroglyphs.

Description: Several boulders on the left of the road with petroglyphs, of uncertain date.

Source: N. Dupree 1977: 148—mention.

PĀ-I MINĀR. See 536 KATA BALANDI.

786. PAI MŪRI

Including GUMBAD and SAUZAU.

Original: Lat. 34° 42'–34° 48' N, long. 68° 00' E. Map 58.
Revised:
Between 34.75927762 N, 68.00663296 E /
34° 45' 33.39942660 N, 68° 00' 23.87866608 E and
34.81234191 N, 67.99436568 E /
34° 48' 44.43088860 N, 67° 59' 39.71643180 E.
Bāmiyān Province. Along the Pāī Mūri gorge south of Shahr-i Zuhak, on the road from Bāmiyān to Kābul via the Hājigak Pass.

Date: Turk and/or pre-Mongol Islamic, 7th–13th cent. (ceramic, architectural).

Description: Remains of a watch tower guarding the entrance to the gorge and the approach to the Bāmiyān Valley. Construction is of baked brick. There is a line of five more forts guarding the road southwards to Gumbad. Only those at Pāī Mūri itself and Gumbad are dated by ceramics.

Fieldwork: 1974–5 Le Berre, DAFA—survey.

Sources:

1. Masson 1839: 108—mention.
2. Masson 1842: II. 438—mention.
3. Zestovsky 1948: opp. Sketch of Pai Mūri.
4. N. Dupree 1977: opp. 46—sketch of Pai Mūri.
5. N. Dupree 1977: 149—mention.
6. Le Berre 1987: 76–8 and pl. 98—brief description; itinerary B2, ruins 1–5.

787. PA'ĪN MAZĀR

Including QAL'A-I CHAHĀR BARADAR and QAL'A-I ZUHAK.

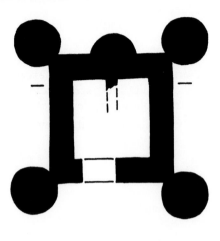

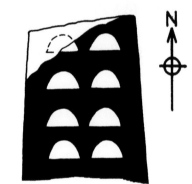

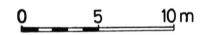

787 Pa'īn Mazār—Chahar Baradar 1 (W. Ball).

787 Pa'īn Mazār—Chahar Baradar 3 (W. Ball).

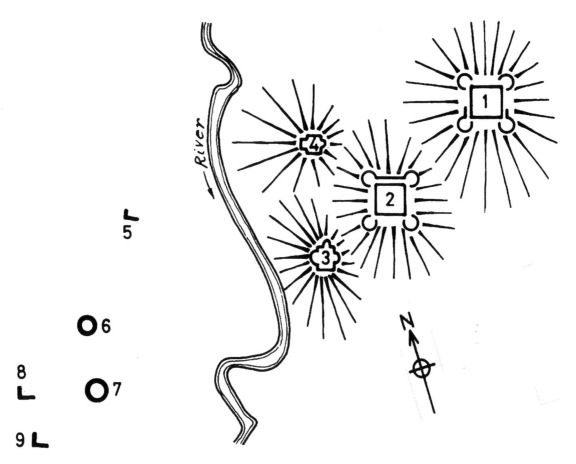

787 Pā'īn Mazār (W. Ball).

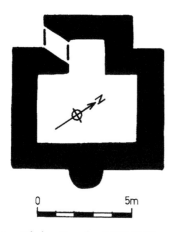

787 Pā'īn Mazār—Chahar Baradar 4 (W. Ball).

Original: Lat. 33° 22' N, long. 64° 19' E. Map 74.
Revised: 33.35273264 N, 64.31619011 E /
33° 21' 09.83749608 N, 064° 18' 58.28439492 E.
Ghūr Province. 35 km south of Taiwāra on the road to Zarnī.

Date: Ghurid, 12th–13th cent. (architectural, geographic).

Description: Two large complexes of ruined forts and towers known respectively as Qal'a-i Chahar Baradar and Qal'a-i Zuhak. Towers are mostly square and are mud-brick and *pakhsa* construction on a stone foundation. Many of the exterior walls have decorative panels of elaborate floriated patterns in mud plaster.

Fieldwork: 1977 Ball—survey.

Source: Ball 2002: 34–9—detailed description and photos.

788. PAISAI

Original: Lat. 30° 36' N, long. 61° 55' E. Map 93.
Revised: 30.58240425 N, 61.90163041 E /
30° 34' 56.65531080 N, 61° 54' 05.86947240 E.
Nīmrūz Province. C.7 km east of Zīyārat-i Shaikh Husain and 8 km north-east of Qal'a-i Fath.

Description: Some ruins.

Fieldwork:
1. 1903–5 Tate, SAC—survey.
2. 1936 Meunié and Hackin, DAFA—survey.

Source: Tate 1910: 139, 146, and 249—mention.

789. PĀ-I SHAHR

Lat. 37° 03' N, long. 70° 47' E. Map 38.
Badakhshān Province. On the road from Faizābād to Jurm, on the banks of the Kokcha *c.*14 km north-west of Bahārak.

Description: Remains of roughly finished masonry scattered over the valley for *c.*3 km, with some walls being recognizable. Possibly the site of the ancient capital of Badakhshān.

Fieldwork: 1938 Barger, ASI—survey.

Sources:
1. Barger 1939a: 389—brief description.
2. Emanuel 1939: 208–9—brief description.
3. Barger and Wright 1941: 49—brief description.

PAITAKHT-I CHANGIZ. See 1040 SHAHR-I CHANGIZ.

790. PAITĀVA

Lat. 34° 53' N, long. 69° 12' E. Map 64.
Parwān Province. 15 km south-west of Begram, 4 km to the east of the Kābul-Chārikār road, 50 km north of Kābul.

Date: Kushan, 1st–3rd cent. (stylistic).

Description: Remains of a stupa-monastery complex. Amongst the finds was a schist relief of Maitreya and other sculpture.

Collections: National Museum and Musée Guimet—objects from DAFA excavations.

Fieldwork: 1924–5 Hackin and Barthoux, DAFA—excavations.

Sources:
1. Hackin 1926—brief description and photo of the Maitreya relief.
2. Hackin 1933—summary of the results and the most important finds, with a note on the stylistic connections.
3. Deydier 1950: 93—briefly discusses the Buddha Sakyamuni statue.
4. Bussagli 1956–7: 198–205—discusses the survivals of Hellenistic art in the sculpture.
5. Plaeschke 1961—discussion of Gandharan art.
6. L. Courtois 1962–3—mineralogical analysis of the Maitreya relief.
7. Dagens 1964a: 35—description of a relief and statue base.
8. Mizuno 1964: illustrations and descriptions of objects displayed in the Tokyo Museum.
9. Rowland 1966a: 65–71—photos and brief introduction to the objects on display from the National Museum.
10. Hallade and Hinz 1968: pl 73—discussion of Paitava and the development of Gandharan art.
11. H. Motamedi 1971a—discussion of the Maitreya.

12. Rowland and Rice 1971: pls 106–8 and 111—description and photos of objects on display from the National Museum.
13. Gaulier et al. 1976—discussion of the religious iconography in the art.
14. Cambon 1996—discussion of the 'Buddha of the Great Miracle' and cognate sculptures.
15. Tsuchiya 2000—iconographical study of the Buddhist art.
16. Tissot and Darbois 2002—photos of objects from the Kābul Museum.
17. Tissot 2006: 330–3—National Museum catalogue details and photos.
18. Ball 2008: 253—summary.
19. Fussman, Murad, and Ollivier 2008: 142–54, 202, and 306—detailed description of the excavations based on Barthoux's notes, with discussion of the Paitāva sculptural style.

PAIWAN TEPE. See 172. CHAQALAQ TEPE.

791. PAKHRAK AND QANDAHĀRIHĀ
Or CHASMA QAINAR or TEPE QAINAR.

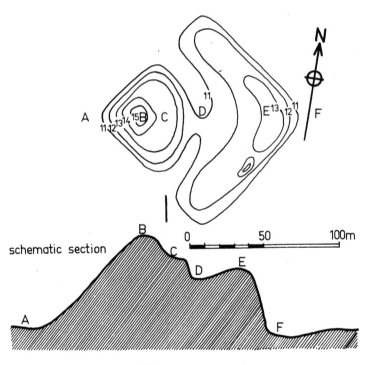

791 Pakhrak (J.-C. Gardin).

Original: Lat. 36° 25–41' N, long. 69° 25–41' E. Map 37.
Revised:
36.42898786 N, 69.40017114 E / 36° 25' 44.35631040 N, 69° 24' 00.61609932 E (A).

36.42409038 N, 69.397276 E / 36° 25' 26.72537664 N, 69° 23' 50.19360864 E (B).

Takhār Province. 8 km north-east of Ishkamīsh, by the Samandau-Chal road. Tepe A is located 300 m west of the road, near the spring of Qainar (indicated on the 1:100,000 map); ā\tepe B is located 800 m south-west of tepe A, beside the road, also on the west side. The present villages are a few hundred metres further west: Pakhrak for A, Qandahārihā for B.

Dates: Kushan and Hunnic-Turk; 1st–9th cent.; pre-Mongol Islamic, 10th–13th cent.; Timurid, 15th–16th cent. (ceramic).

Description: (A) Tepe Qainar (from the name of the spring above): at the western end of a natural east–west rise, a square site (100 × 100 m), north-east/south-west, surrounded by streams from the spring on three sides and by a gully (or ditch?) on the south-east side. The natural slope of the terrain, towards the north-west, causes the altitudes to be higher in the west than in the east, about 7 m, measured in relation to the plain to the west; they are 11 m for the eastern part of the site, which is more or less flat, and 13 m for the western part, rising as far as 15 m in the angle (small fort?). These two parts are separated by a crescent-shaped depression, oriented according to the north–south diagonal of the square. (B) Tepe Qandahārihā: quadrangular mound north-east/south-west (50 × 50 m), flat top inclined from the north-east to the south-west, punctuated by small hillocks on the north-east side and in the southern angle (2–3 m).

Collection: National Museum/AIA—sherds.

Fieldwork:
1. 1960 Hayashi and Sahara, University of Kyoto—survey.
2. 1978 Gardin et al., CNRS—survey.

Sources:
1. Site information by J.-C. Gardin.
2. Hayashi and Sahara 1962: 76—photo and description of the site, in Japanese.
3. Gardin and Lyonnet 1978–9: pl. XI—nos. 374–5.
4. Lyonnet 1997: figs 49, 68, 69—nos. 374, 375.
5. Gardin 1998: 99—nos. 374–5.

PAL PĪRĪ. See 2170 PAL PĪRĪ in Supplement.

792. PALANGI
See also 2254 SURKHI in Supplement.

Original: Lat. 30° 43' N, long. 61° 52' E. Map 93.
Revised:
Between 30.59957809 N, 61.89526699 E /
30° 35' 58.48112004 N, 61° 53' 42.96116616 E and
30.59657742 N, 61.88881106 E /
30° 35' 47.67869904 N, 61° 53' 19.71982644 E.
Nīmrūz Province. North of Qal'a-i Fath on the road from Chahār Burjak to Zaranj.

Dates: ?Parthian, 2nd–1st cent. BC (documentary); Timurid, 16th cent. (architectural, ceramic).

Description: A plain covered in ruins for several km. Palangi itself is a single building, about a kilometre east-north-east of Hauz. It was a prosperous 16th-century windmill, with adjoining house. The house is 70 m square and stands on a mud platform 2 m high, with walls a further 8 m high. The outer walls are mud-brick but decorated with baked brick patterns; the inside wall surfaces are plaster decorated. The residence part of the building has still later restorations. The name 'Palangi' derives from the stylised animals once depicted in tile, but now only identifiable by the holes where the tiles had been set.

The site is possibly to be identified with the Parthian town of Palakenti, mentioned by Isidor of Charax, although according to Trousdale the name 'Palangi' is recent and has no relationship to Palakenti.

Fieldwork:
1. Additional note on the name by by W. Trousdale.
2. 1884 Maitland, Peacocke ABC—reconnaissance.
3. 1903–5 Tate, ABC—survey.
4. 1936 Meunié and Hackin, DAFA—survey.
5. 1965–70 Fischer, Bonn University—survey.
6. 1966, 1971–4 Trousdale, Smithsonian—survey.

Sources:
1. Ferrier 1857: 410–11—brief description.
2. Peacocke 1885a: 9–10—description as Surkhi.
3. Maitland 1888a: 71—mention as Padah-i Sultan.
4. Tate 1909: 104—photo of the remains.
5. Tate 1910: 250–2—detailed description.
6. Gardin 1959—summary of the Islamic pottery.
7. Hackin 1959c: 28—brief description and photos.
8. Fischer 1969: 335—brief summary.
9. Fischer 1971c: 50—mention and photo.
10. Ball 2008: 253—summary.

793. PALANGKHĀNA

Lat. 34° 09' N, long. 63° 57' E. Map 54.
Ghūr Province. In the Tagau Ishlān, between Nalbandān and Mināra.

Date: Ghurid, 12th–13th cent. (architectural).

Description: Ruins of two towers on opposite sides of the valley.

Source: Kästner 1968—brief description.

794. PALGIRD AND GHŪRIYĀN TEPE

Original: Lat. 34° 20' N, long. 61° 25' E. Map 51.
Revised:
34.31431283 N, 61.39655505 E / 34° 18' 51.52617936 N, 61° 23' 47.59818504 E (A).

34.3216129 N, 61.41365408 E / 34° 19' 17.80642380 N, 61° 24' 49.15467936 E (B).
Herat Province. 65 km west of this city, on the left bank of the Harī Rūd, 7 km west of the oasis of Ghūriyān, south of the hamlet of Shahrābād.

Dates: Partho-Sasanian, 1st–4th cent.; pre-Mongol Islamic, 10th–13th cent. (A) (ceramic).

Description: A large urban site of ruins and mounds *c*.1.5 km in diameter. (A) A vast zone of hillocks, bordered on the east by a tepe. Remains include city walls, a citadel, residential and industrial areas covering a vast area. (B) Small mound to the east of this zone, low and very eroded.

Collection: National Museum/AIA – sherds.

Fieldwork:
1. 1952 Le Berre and Gardin, DAFA – survey.
2. Ramachandran and Sharma, ASI – reconnaissance.
3. 2004–6 DAI – survey.

Sources:
1. M. Le Berre: unpublished 1952 report, DAFA archives.
2. Ramachandran and Sharma 1956: I. 13 – mention.
3. Franke and Urban 2006: 18 – mention heavy looting.
4. Franke 2008: 74 and pls 122–4 – photo of robber pits on site and 11th-century glazed sherds.
5. Franke 2015: 73–4 – discussion of the remains.

795. PALWĀRI

Original: Lat. 34° 32' N, long. 70° 34' E. Map 67.
Revised: 34.53692948 N, 70.56776924 E / 34° 32' 12.94611576 N, 70° 34' 03.96926004 E.
Nangahār Province. On the west bank of the Kunār River, just to the south-east of the village of Palwāri *c*.22 km north-east of Jalālābād on the road to Islāmpūr.

Description: Extensive remains of walls and mounds on and around a hill by the river. Unconfirmed reports of an inscription here.

Fieldwork: 1834 Masson – survey.

Source: Masson 1842: III. 275–6 – brief description.

796. PANJDEH

Lat. 31° 45' N, long. 61° 35' E. Map 83.
Nīmrūz Province. On the west bank of the Farāh Rūd, 5 km north-west of Lāsh Juwain.

Description: A series of artificial caves cut into the banks of the river. Inside they open out into numerous chambers and passages. There is also a small ruined mud fort.

Fieldwork: 1884 Peacocke, Maitland, ABC – topographical survey.

Sources:
1. Bellew 1874: 280–1 – brief description.
2. Smith 1876: 325 – mention.
3. Peacocke 1885a: 20 – mentions ruined fort.
4. Maitland 1888a: 97 – mentions ruins.
5. Peacocke 1887a: 34 and 37 – mentions fort.

797. PANJIRI

Original: Lat. 36° 21'–36° 22' N, long. 69° 22' E. Map 37.
Revised:
36.3412369 N, 69.32405327 E / 36° 20' 28.45282812 N, 69° 19' 26.59175904 E (A).
36.34901055 N, 69.32613241 E / 36° 20' 56.43796776 N, 69° 19' 34.07667960 E (B).
36.35805077 N, 69.32764389 E / 36° 21' 28.98275796 N, 69° 19' 39.51800148 E (C).
Takhār Province. Tepes along the track from Ishkamīsh to Khwāja Bandi Kusha, west side, south of the village of Kuhistānihā (place-name Panjiri); their respective positions are given here by two numbers: the distance in km from the beginning of the track, at the south-east angle of the Bālā Hisār of Ishkamīsh, and the distance in metres west of this track. (A) 4.5 km – 80 m; (B) 3.5 km – 200 m; (C) 2.5 km – 400 m.

Dates: Hellenistic; 3rd–1st cent. BC (A); Kushan and Hunnic-Turk, 1st–9th cent. (A, B); pre-Mongol Islamic, 10th–13th cent. (B, C) (ceramic).

Description: (A) Two mounds 70 m apart (north-east/ south-west orientation), rounded (diam. 50 m), low (1–1.5 m). (B) low mound (1.5 m) in the shape of a long north-east/south-west barrier (80 m), between two zones of *lalmī* cultivation which have razed the rest of the tepe; many sherds in the fields up to 50 m to either side of the mound. (C) Rounded mound (diam. 50 m), 4 m high, on a terreplein occupied by houses and cultivation which have erased even the original edges of the site.

Collection: DAFA – sherds.

Fieldwork: 1978 Gardin et al., CNRS – survey.

Sources:
1. Site information by J.-C. Gardin.
2. Gardin and Lyonnet 1978–9: pl. XI – nos. 391–3.
3. Lyonnet 1997: figs 39, 49, 68, 69 – nos. 391–3.
4. Gardin 1998: 100 – nos. 391–3.

798. PANJWĀYĪ

Original: Lat. 31° 32' N, long. 65° 27' E. Map 89.
Revised: 31.52936508 N, 65.46398787 E / 31° 31' 45.71427072 N, 65° 27' 50.35632948 E.
Kandahār Province. 27 km south-west of Kandahār. The site is just south of the town of Panjwāyī.

Dates: Sasanian, 3rd–7th cent. (ceramic); Early Islamic, 10th–13th cent. (documentary); Mongol-Timurid, 13th–16th cent. (ceramic, documentary).

Description: A citadel mound some 10–12 m high, surrounded by a ditch. On top are remains of public buildings, and remains of more buildings are often found by farmers when digging in the surrounding fields.

Fieldwork:
1. 1950–1 Fairservis, AMNH—survey.
2. 1951 Casal, DAFA—survey.
3. 1960 Fischer, DAAD—survey.

Sources:
1. Masson 1836a: 9—mentions the site and tentatively identifies it as Alexandria Arachosia.
2. Le Strange 1905: 346–7—summary of the historical references.
3. Benava 1953—examines the sources and reconstructs the history and topography of the site. Relates some folklore and some of the learned men associated with the city.
4. Husain Shah 1962—historical geography of the area and description of the site.
5. Fischer 1967a: 149—mention.
6. Fairservis 1971: 393—mention (Site Khr-3).
7. Shah 1982—discussion of the sources.

799. PARCHAU
Or QARA PARCHAU.

Original: Lat. 36° 47' N, long. 69° 27' E. Maps 35, 36.
Revised:
36.77469869 N, 69.44810162 E / 36° 46' 28.91529300 N, 69° 26' 53.16584712 E (A).
36.7755821 N, 69.44574614 E / 36° 46' 32.09556000 N, 69° 26' 44.68610868 E (A).
36.77437066 N, 69.45066933 E / 36° 46' 27.73436196 N, 69° 27' 02.40957288 E (A).
36.78093172 N, 69.43842785 E / 36° 46' 51.35419056 N, 69° 26' 18.34026936 E (B).
Takhār Province. 10 km north-west of Tāluqān, accessible by the road that lies along the Rūd-i Shāhrawān; the two sites are located some hundred metres south of this road, below the slopes that descend from the Rūd-i Shāhrawān towards the plain of Tāluqān.

Dates: Late Chalcolithic–Early Bronze Age, *c.*3500–2500 BC; Middle Bronze Age, *c.*2500–1500 BC; beg. Iron, end 2nd–beg. 1st mill. BC; Achaemenid, 6th–4th cent. BC; Hellenistic, 3rd–1st cent. BC; some Islamic sherds (ceramic).

Description: (A) Long east–west mound (100 × 50 m), irregular in shape, attacked by the cotton cultivation which occupies terraces on the surrounding slopes; flat top (height 2 to 7 m measured from north to south in the direction of the slope), with a higher part in the west

(5 to 10 m). 100 m to the east, a smaller mound, sherds of the Achaemenid period. (B) 750 m to the west, two oblong mounds north-north-east/south-south-west, separated by a road. The largest is to the north (100 × 20 m, height 5 m), the highest to the south (60 × 20 × 8 m); flat top occupied in both cases by a modern cemetery; steep slopes, eaten into by crops.

Collection: National Museum/AIA—sherds.

Fieldwork: 1977 Gardin et al., CNRS—survey.

Sources:
1. Site information by J.-C. Gardin.
2. Gardin and Lyonnet 1978–9: pl. IX—nos. 230–1.
3. Lyonnet 1981—brief description of site, description, discussion, and illustration of the Chalcolithic (mid-4th–mid-3rd mill.) pattern and discuss of the geographical and historical implications.
4. Lyonnet 1997: figs 7, 13, 21–5, 35–7, 39—nos. 230, 231.
5. Gardin 1998: 69–70—nos. 230–1.

800. PARISHĀN TEPE
Or PRESHĀN TEPE.

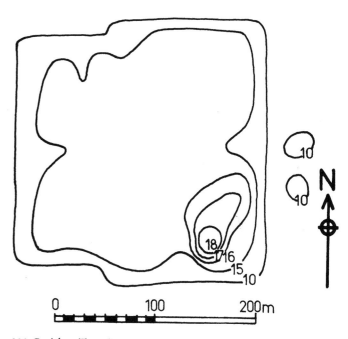

800 Parishān Tepe (M. Le Berre).

Original: Lat. 36° 54' N, long. 66° 18' E. Maps 25.
Revised: 36.89580023 N, 66.31181353 E / 36° 53' 44.88084456 N, 66° 18' 42.52870872 E.
Jauzjān Province. 11 km east of Āqcha on the road to Balkh, 2 km to the north of the road.

Dates: Graeco-Bactrian, 3rd–2nd cent. BC; Kushan, 1st cent. BC–AD 3rd (ceramic).

Description: A rectangular, 'lion-shaped' mound, some 15–20 m high. Signs of considerable robbing. There are several smaller mounds within *c.* 100 m, and the beginnings of an extensive ancient irrigation system. Five large jars were found in situ in 1946.

Fieldwork:
1. 1886 Maitland, ABC—topographical survey.
2. 1938 Barger, ASI—survey.
3. 1946 Wheeler, ASI—reconnaissance.
4. 1948 Le Berre, DAFA—survey.
5. 1956 Ramachandran and Sharma, ASI—reconnaissance.
6. 1960 Hayashi and Sahara, Kyoto University—survey.

Sources:
1. Maitland 1888b: 173—mention.
2. Barger and Wright 1941: 54—brief description (Site MG).
3. Shakur 1947: 69–71—description of the site and pottery.
4. Wheeler 1947: 63—mention.
5. Ramachandran and Sharma 1956: I. 20—mention.
6. Hayashi and Sahara 1962: 61–5—photo with a description of the site and pottery, in Japanese.
7. M. Le Berre: unpublished 1948 report, DAFA archives, Tépé P. 14.

801. PARJUMAN

Lat. 33° 09' N, long. 63° 52' E. Map 73.
Farāh Province. In the mountainous area south-west of Taiwāra.

Description: A large mud-brick mosque, probably quite old, near the village. It has two 'unusual towers' and is domed.

Sources:
1. Fox 1943: 164—very brief description.
2. Ball 1982: 26—mention from hearsay.

PARWAN. See 458 JABAL AL-SARĀJ.

802. PARWĀNA

Original: Lat. 34° 29' N, long. 62° 12' E. Map 52.
Revised: 34.47428143 N, 62.1868349 E /
34° 28' 27.41315232 N, 62° 11' 12.60563172 E.
Herat Province. 13 km north of this city, on either side of the road to Khushk Post, south-west of the village of Parwāna.

Description: Ruined zone covered by fired bricks; still recognizable is the plan of a quadrangular basin.

Fieldwork:
1. 1884 Maitland, Peacocke, ABC—topographic exploration.
2. 1952 Le Berre and Gardin, DAFA—survey.

Sources:
1. M. Le Berre: unpublished 1952 report, DAFA archives.
2. Gazetteer 1975: III. 329—brief description.

803. PASĀBAND
Or PASĀNGAN.

Original: Lat. 33° 42' N, long. 64° 51' E. Maps 55, 74.
Revised:
Between 33.69086823 N, 64.85122076 E /
33° 41' 27.12563556 N, 64° 51' 04.39474104 E and
33.69441039 N, 64.84831001 E /
33° 41' 39.87741120 N, 64° 50' 53.91604284 E.
Ghūr Province. To the east of the road from Chakhcharān to Taiwāra.

Description: Remains of a citadel. Also the Tomb of Khwāja Wajduddin, which is believed to be early.

Sources:
1. Kohzad 1951–4, 8/4: 62—mentions the citadel.
2. Rafat 1980: 4—mentions the tomb.

804. PASANG
Includes AMRŪD.

Lat. 35° 13'–35° 14' N, long. 67° 55–67° 58' E. Map 48.
Bāmiyān Province; Valley of the Darya-i Saighān, south of Dūāb-u Mīkhzarīn (road from Charikar to Dūshi by the Shībar Pass): between Dūāb and the place called Amrūd.

Dates: Turk and/or pre-Mongol Islamic period, 7th–13th cent. (architecture).

Description: Ruins of small forts.

Fieldwork: 1974–5 Le Berre, DAFA—survey.

Source: Le Berre 1987: 33 and 58—mention; itineraries A1, ruin 13; A2, Darya-i Saighān, ruin 2.

PASĀNGAN. See 803 PASĀBAND.

805. PASHAK

Original: Lat. 33° 30' N, long. 68° 33' E. Map 80.
Revised: 33.49494382 N, 68.54820592 E /
33° 29' 41.79774624 N, 68° 32' 53.54132640 E.
Ghazni Province. 13 km east of Ghazni on the road to Gardēz.

Date: Samanid, 10th cent. (ceramic).

Description: A large square ruined building with four corner towers. Construction of mud-brick, of two sizes.

Fieldwork: 1966 Fischer, DAAD—survey.

Sources:
1. Fischer 1967a: 166—mention.
2. Fischer 1969: 340—brief summary.

3. Thomas 2015: 519—additional information from satellite imagery.

PASHA KHĀNA. See 583 KHUSTI QISHLĀQ.

806. PASSANI
Including SIĀH KUH C. See also 855 QAL'A-I KACHALA.

Original: Lat. 34° 27' N, long. 70° 20' E. Map 66.
Revised: 34.45102994 N, 70.33774017 E /
34° 27' 03.70777968 N, 70° 20' 15.86462100 E.
Laghmān Province. At the foot of the Siāh Kūh, *c.*5 km south-west of Darūnta, immediately to the south-east of the road.

Date: Indo-Parthian, 1st cent. (stylistic).

Description: Remains of a stupa 33 m in circumference. Condition is poor, with no apparent decoration. Nothing was found inside. To the south and west are many mounds, and there is an Islamic cemetery and more mounds to the north. There are also many tumuli, presumably more stupas.

Fieldwork:
1. 1834 Masson—excavation.
2. 1965 Mizuno, Kyoto University—survey.

Sources:
1. Masson 1841: 68—brief description (Tope 1 of Passani).
2. Simpson 1881: 200–1—brief description.
3. Mizuno 1971: 118—summary of Masson's work and description and photos of the present condition (Stupas 12–22).
4. Jongeward et al. 2012—catalogue and discussion of the reliquaries.
5. Errington 2017a: 91–101 and 2017b: 52–3, 45, 47–8, 50, 52, 56–60, 108–19—the Masson collection and archive relating to the site.

PASHTAU. See 2172 PASHTAU in Supplement.

PASHTŪN ZARGHŪN. See 2173 PASHTŪN ZAR-GHŪN in Supplement.

PAS TEPE. See 450 ISHKILI.

807. PATANAK

Original: Lat. 34° 02' N, long. 68° 45' E. Map 60.
Revised: 34.03672895 N, 68.74247173 E /
34° 02' 12.22422324 N, 68° 44' 32.89823880 E.

Lōgar Province. On the main Kabūl-Ghazni road, just south of the Lōgar River. The site is *c.*1 km south-east of the village.

Dates: Kushan, Sasanian, Turki Shahi, 1st–9th cent. (ceramic).

Description: A large artificial mound with traces of mud-brick vaults.

Fieldwork: 1966 Fischer, DAAD—survey.

Sources:
1. Gardin and Lyonnet, 1980 chronological study of pottery from unpublished DAFA surveys.
2. Fischer 1967a: 158—mention.
3. Fischer 1969: 339—mention (Site A2).

808. PATANDAK

Original: Lat. 30° 54' N, long. 62° 02' E. Map 92.
Revised:
30.90355635 N, 62.03448703 E / 30° 54' 12.80284380 N, 62° 02' 04.15331268 E and
30.89247815 N, 62.05140856 E / 30° 53' 32.92134684 N, 62° 03' 05.07082608 E.
Nīmrūz Province. Between Dam and Kūrdū, 12 km south-west of Ziyārat-i Amīrān Sāhib.

Date: Iron Age, early 1st mill. BC; Partho-Sasanian, 1st–7th cent. (ceramic).

Description: Remains of a town. Ruins include a citadel and a baked brick house, where several complete vessels were found.

1 km to the south-east are the remains of a mud-brick fort (Fischer Ruin 28) and 2 km to the south is a ruined tower with a surface scatter of baked bricks and some buried pitoi (Fischer Ruin 30).

The central ruined qal'a is the largest early 1st mill. BC qal'a in the southern part of Afghan Sistan. In Partho-Sasanian times a new qal'a was constructed along its north-west side, but the earlier qal'a, except for the bala hisar, was not reoccupied. The name Patandak is attached only to the northernmost site.

Fieldwork:
1. 1970 Fischer, DAAD—survey.
2. 1971–4 Trousdale, Smithsonian—survey.

Sources:
1. Additional site information by W. Trousdale.
2. Fischer 1971a—brief description and photos.
3. Fischer et al. 1974–6: 38—mention and photo.

809. PATANNAH

Original: Lat. 33° 11' N, long. 68° 48' E. Map 82.
Revised: 33.18252437 N, 68.79585323 E /
33° 10' 57.08773524 N, 68° 47' 45.07163340 E.

Ghazni/Paktiyā Province. C.63 km south-east of Ghazni.

Date: Kushan-Sasanian, 1st–7th cent. (ceramic).

Description: A mound south of the village.

Fieldwork: 1966 Fischer, DAAD—survey.

Sources:
1. Fischer 1967a: 166—mention.
2. Fischer 1969: 340—mention.

810. PĒSHWĀRĀN
See also 544. KHAIRĀBĀD, 638. KŪL MĀRŪT, 702. MĀLĀN, and 979. SĀLIYĀN.

Original: Lat. 31° 31' N, long. 61° 32' E. Map 83.
Revised: 31.51211087 N, 61.53883455 E /
31° 30' 43.59913416 N, 61° 32' 19.80439008 E.
Nīmrūz Province. 25 km south of Lāsh Juwain, 5 km from the left bank of the Farāh Rūd.

Date: Early Islamic, 9th–13th cent. (architectural, documentary, numismatic).

Description: A vast area of extensive remains, known from the sources as Basher. It covers an area of *c.*9.3 × 13 km, but different parts appear under different catalogue entries (nos. 544, 638, 702, 979). The main feature of the central Pēshwārān complex is a huge circular citadel, some 200–300 m in diameter. The walls, of baked brick construction, are 17 m in height with a 2 m wide gallery around the top. There are two massive round entrance towers. Inside is a mound with the remains of a palace, and the surface is thickly covered with sherds, tiles, bricks, etc.

Many other ruins are scattered over the plain. Alternate layers of baked and mud-bricks seems to be a feature of these ruins.

Fieldwork:
1. 1903–5 Tate, SAC—survey.
2. 1936 Hackin and Meunié, DAFA—survey.
3. 1949 De Cardi—survey.
4. 1950 Fairservis, AMNH—survey.

Sources:
1. Ferrier 1857: 420—mention.
2. Bellew 1874: 245–7—brief description.
3. Smith 1876: 314–15—brief description.
4. Fairservis 1950—mention.
5. Hackin 1959c: figs 110–15—photos of the remains.
6. Fairservis 1961: 42–3—brief description with a summary of the pottery and finds (Site 21).
7. Ball 2008: 253–4—summary.

PĪL KHĀNA. See **2174 PĪL KHĀNA in Supplement.**

811. PIRA QAL'A

Original: Lat. 30° 55' N, long. 62° 03' E. Map 92.
Revised: 30.91986585 N, 62.05657967 E /
30° 55' 11.51706504 N, 62° 03' 23.68681560 E.
Nīmrūz Province. Between Burj-i Samad and Patandak, 10 km south-west of Zīyārat-i Amīran Sāhib.

Dates: Sasanian and early Islamic, 3rd–13th cent.; Mongol-Timurid, 13th–16th cent. (ceramic).

Description: Ruins of a courtyard *iwān* house. Construction is of mud-brick with baked brick quoining. The façade is decorated with blind arches.

Fieldwork: 1960–70 Fischer, Bonn University—survey.

Source: Fischer et al. 1974–6: 38—mention and photos.

812. PĪR GHUNDI ZĪYĀRAT

Lat. 34° 22' N, long. 70° 35' E. Map 67.
NangahārProvince. On the south bank of the Kābul River, near 'Ali Bughān *c.*19 km east of Jalālābād.

Description: Remains of a shrine, with some artificial caves—possibly Buddhist—behind.

Source: Simpson 1881: 206—mention.

PĪR KAMAL AL-DĪN. See **2175 PĪR-I KAMAL AL-DĪN in Supplement.**

813. PIR-I SURKH

Lat. 34° 04' N, long. 62° 25' E. Map 53.
Herat Province. 36 km south-east of Herat, on the road to Pushtu Zarghun.

Dates: Partho-Sasanian and/or Sasano-Islamic, 1st–9th cent.; Timurid, 15th–16th cent. (ceramic).

Description: None.

Collection: National Museum/AIA—sherds.

Fieldwork: 1952 Le Berre and Gardin, DAFA—survey.

Source: M. Le Berre: unpublished 1952 report, DAFA archives.

PĪR KAMAL BĀBĀ ZĪYĀRAT. See **158 CHAHĀRDEH.**

PĪRZĀDA. See **659 KUSHK-I NAKHUD.**

814. PIT QAL'A TEPE
See also 8 ABU HURAIRA, 520 KAM PIRAK, 1188 TEPE ZĀDIYĀN, 1245 ZĀDIYĀN, 2053 DAULA-TĀBĀD in Supplement, and 2281 ZĀDIYĀN KĀFIR QAL'A in Supplement.

Original: Lat. 37° 03' N, long. 66° 55' E. Map 27.
Revised: 37.04274565 N, 66.92078779 E /
37° 02' 33.88435224 N, 66° 55' 14.83605516 E.
Balkh Province. 49 km north of this town, north-west of the village of Zādiyān.

Description: Large rectangular tepe (about 140 × 80 m), height *c*.8 m, surrounded by a ditch, flanked on the east by a secondary ruin. The platform is surrounded by an enclosure wall in large mud-bricks, of which certain parts remain. Very strong erosion in the north.

Fieldwork:
1. 1948 Le Berre, DAFA—survey.
2. 2013 Besenval and Marquis, DAFA—survey.

Sources:
1. M. Le Berre: unpublished 1948 report, DAFA archives, tépé P. 50.
2. De la Vaissière, Marquis, and Bendezu-Sarmiento 2015—interprets as the western gateway to the Zādiyān Kāfir Qal'a complex.

815. PRATES
See also 404 HADDA.

Original: Lat. 34° 21' N, long. 70° 29' E. Map 67.
Revised: 34.35323683 N, 70.49182427 E /
34° 21' 11.65259124 N, 70° 29' 30.56737740 E.
Nangahār Province. *C*.2 km to the south-east of the main Hadda complex.

Date: Kushano-Sasanian, 4th–5th cent. (stylistic).

Description: A group of some 60 stupas covering an area of 19 × 40 m, dominated by four large stupas. Many reliefs of figures, religious scenes, etc. on the sides of the stupas.

Collections: National Museum and Musée Guimet—objects from the excavations.

Fieldwork: 1926 Barthoux, DAFA—excavations.

Source: Barthoux 1933a: 186–95—description of the stupas and sculptures.

PRESHĀN TEPE. See 800 PARISHĀN TEPE.

816. PTŪKH-TAL

Lat. 37° 01' N, long. 73° 22' E. Map 40.
Badakhshān Province. In Wākhān 9 km west of Sarhad.

Description: A large number of petroglyphs on the rock faces to the north of the village, depicting ibex and hunting scenes.

Fieldwork: 1975 'Exploration Pamir'—survey.

Source: Gratzl et al. 1978: 325–9—descriptions of each petroglyph and photos in colour.

817. PUL-I ALĀM
Or HISĀRAK.

Original: Lat. 33° 59' N, long. 69° 02' E. Maps 60, 82.
Revised: 33.98421187 N, 69.03324663 E /
33° 59' 03.16273668 N, 69° 01' 59.68787556 E.
Lōgar Province. On the left bank of the Lōgar River, on the Kābul-Gardēz road.

Dates: Hunnic-Turki Shahi, 5th–9th cent.; pre-Mongol Islamic, 10th–13th cent. (ceramic).

Description: Ruins of a fortress on a low hill. It is small, but is in a strong position commanding the Lōgar Valley and a fork in the roads. Also a stupa on a hill with massive stone walls 10–15 m high and 8–10 m diameter.

Fieldwork: 1966 Fischer, DAAD—survey.

Sources:
1. Gardin and Lyonnet, 1980 chronological study of pottery from unpublished DAFA surveys.
2. Holdich 1881a: 22—brief description.
3. Fischer 1967a: 166—mention.
4. Fischer 1969: 341—brief summary.
5. Levi 1972: 122—brief description.

PUL-I ALCHIN. See 218 CHUL-I ĀBDĀN.

818. PUL-I IMĀM BUKRI

Original: Lat. 36° 38' N, long. 66° 55' E. Map 28.
Revised: 36.63420611 N, 66.9244203 E /
36° 38' 03.14199384 N, 66° 55' 27.91309512 E.
Balkh Province. On the Balkhāb, 14 km south of Balkh.

Date: Timurid, 15th–16th cent. (ceramic).

Description: Many mounds and baked brick remains—although nothing standing—stretching westwards along the river banks for several kilometres. A bridge consisting originally of three arches of baked brick straddling the Balkh River just below the off take of the Balkh canal on the main road to Chashma-i Shafa to the east and Chimtal to the west. The footings of the bridge have been heavily eroded and undermined by the fast-flowing Balkh River which it straddles to the extent that at least two of the three arches are now at high risk of collapse. Severe damage has been caused to the upper part of the structure by its use by heavy military and other vehicles. In the mid-1990s a second bridge for heavy vehicles was constructed to the west and access across the medieval bridge was restricted to pedestrians and pack animals. However, in *c*.2005 a a slab of heavy concrete was laid on the medieval bridge and it was reopened for the use by heavy vehicles. Unable to bear the weight and vibration, the apex of the arches shows signs of severe stress with vertical cracks in the pointing.

Fieldwork:
1. 1955 and 1960 Fischer, DAAD—survey.
2. 1996–2006 Lee—various visits.

Sources:
1. Additional information on the bridge by Jonathan L. Lee.
2. Grodekoff 1880: 80—brief description of the site, identifying it with ancient Bactra.
3. Fischer 1961d—map reference.
4. Fischer 1969: 348—mention.
5. Stuckert 1994: 95—pen and ink sketch with brief description.

PUL-I KHAJIRA. See 2176 PUL-I KHAJIRA in Supplement.

819. PUL-I MALĀN

Original: Lat. 34° 17' N, long. 62° 11' E. Map 52.
Revised: 34.28618805 N, 62.19132361 E /
34° 17' 10.27698504 N, 62° 11' 28.76499528 E.
Herat Province. Across the Harī Rūd 6 km due south of Herat on the old road to Kandahār.

Date: ?Seljuk, 11th–12th cent. (documentary).

Description: A stone and brick bridge of 27 spans across the river. Although much of it is 20th-century rebuilding, the core of the structure is certainly earlier.

The road going south from Pul-i Malān towards Rabat-i Sāhibzāda is worn very deeply, up to *c.*1.50 m, indicating much use and age.

Fieldwork: 1995 DACAAR—repairs to the bridge.

Sources:
1. Lal 1834: 17—brief description.
2. Ferrier 1857: 261—brief description.
3. Peacocke 1887a: 154–5—brief description and sketch; 211–12—brief description.
4. Maitland 1888a: 414 and 418—brief description.
5. Yate 1888: 26–7—description of the present condition.
6. Le Strange 1905: 407—summary of the historical references.
7. Niedemeyer and Diez 1924: pls 175–6—photos.
8. Afghān 1930: 188–9—brief description.
9. Wolfe 1966: 58—brief description.
10. *Kabul Times* 1979a—mentions preservation work.

PUL-I NAU. See 2177 PUL-I NAU in Supplement.

PUL-I SANDAL. See 2178 PUL-I SANDAL in Supplement.

820. PUL-I ZUHAK
Or DAHAN-I PALIZAK or GUMBAZ AINA-DAH or NAHANGĀBĀD.

Original: Lat. 34° 06' N, long. 64° 17' E. Map 54.
Revised: 34.10639854 N, 64.26853137 E /
34° 06' 23.03475444 N, 64° 16' 06.71292372 E.
Ghūr Province. 2 km south-west of Shahrak.

Dates: Late Sasanian, 6th–7th cent.; early Islamic, 8th–13th cent. (ceramic).

Description: Remains of old fort consisting of just the bases of some mud-brick towers on a mound. There is also a large group of mounds to the south-west of the village.

Fieldwork:
1. 1885 Maitland and Talbot, ABC—reconnaissance.
2. 1960 Dupree and Fischer, AMNH—sondages.

Sources:
1. Maitland 1888a: 441—brief description.
2. Dupree and Fischer 1961—brief description of site and results.
3. A. A. Motamedi 1967: 33—mentions the excavations.
4. Fischer 1969: 343—mention.
5. Gazetteer 1975: III. 315—mentions ruins.
6. N. Dupree 1977: 477–8—mention.

821. PURI QAL'A

Original: Lat. 34° 37' N, long. 70° 37' E. approximately. Map 67.
Revised: 34.60977364 N, 70.62781171 E /
34° 36' 35.18511696 N, 70° 37' 40.12217292 E.
Kunār Province. In the hills 3 km north-east of Islāmpūr.

Date: Hindu Shahi, 10th cent. (ceramic).

Description: A huge fortification system consisting of schist walls and towers guarding the pass.

Fieldwork: 1960–8—Fischer, DAAD—survey.

Sources:
1. Fischer 1960: 10—mention.
2. Fischer 1969: 357—mention (Ruins G 5).

822. PUSHTA-I HASAN

Lat. 31° 40' N, long. 62° 57' E. Map 85.
Nīmrūz Province. Between the Khāsh Rūd and the Dilārām-Chakhānsūr road, 8 km north-east of Lokhi.

Date: Early Islamic, 8th–13th cent. (ceramic).

Description: Remains of a square mud-brick tower, probably a medieval staging post.

Fieldwork: 1960–70 Fischer, DAAD—survey.

Source: Fischer et al. 1974–6: 31—mention (Ruin 2).

823. PUSHT-I DASHT

Lat. 30° 20' N, long. 61° 54' E. Maps 93, 95.
Nīmrūz Province. On the east bank of the Helmand, c.8 km north-west of Qal'a-i Amīr, between Qal'a-i Fath and Chahār Burjak.

Dates: Sasanian, 3rd–7th cent.; early Islamic, 8th–13th cent. (ceramic).

Description: A semi-circular mound, c.8 m high.

Fieldwork: 1951 Fairservis, AMNH – survey.

Source: Fairservis 1961: 56 – brief description and summary of the pottery (Site 37, KF05).

PUSHT-I GAU See **77 BĀGHAK**.

824. PŪST-I GAU

See also 417 HASANKHĀN, 558 KHARĀBA-I IDU-KHĀN, and 836 QAL'A-I BĀYĀN.

Original: Lat. 31° 16' N, long. 62° 03' E. Map 84.
Revised: 31.26960125 N, 62.0514003 E /
31° 16' 10.56449496 N, 62° 03' 05.04107928 E.
Nīmrūz Province. 10 km north of Chakhānsūr. On the left (south) bank of Helmand, 2 miles west of Rūdhār.

Date: Indo-Parthian and Sasanian, 1st–7th cent. (architectural, ceramic).

Description: An extensive area of ruins and mounds. The main feature is a large, mud-brick rectangular enclosure on a mound, c.500 m. long, with 48 semi-circular or semi-polygonal towers and a large monumental gate. Possibly pre-Islamic (Fischer's Site 25).

Opposite the north angle of this enclosure is a late fort built on a solid *pakhsa* platform forming a mound c.17 m high (Site 27) with another, smaller mound (Site 26) adjacent. Both of these mounds are covered in pre-Islamic pottery and are surrounded by a wide scatter of baked bricks.

Fieldwork:
1. 1884 Maitland, Peacocke, ABC – topographical survey.
2. 1903–5 Tate, SAC – survey.
3. 1950 Fairservis, AMNH – survey.
4. 1968 Fischer, Bonn University – survey.

Sources:
1. Peacocke 1885a: 3 and 13 – mention.
2. Peacocke 1887a: 17 and 27 – mention.
3. Maitland 1888a: 59 – brief description.
4. Tate 1910: 187 and 212 – brief description of Site 27 and tentative identification of Site 27 with medieval Qarnein.
5. Stein 1928: 941 – describes some pottery brought to him from the site.
6. Fairservis 1961: 43 – brief summary (Site 22).

7. Gnoli 1967: 80 – discusses the possible historical identification of the site.
8. Fischer 1969–70 – photos.
9. Fischer 1970b: pls 8–10 and 14–18 – photos.
10. Fischer 1971b: 43–4 – brief descriptions of each site with ground and aerial photos.
11. Fischer 1971c: 48–9 – brief description and historical background.
12. Fischer 1973c: 139 – brief description.
13. Fischer 1973d – brief report on the survey.
14. Fischer et al. 1974–6: 49 – summary and photos.
15. Fischer 1978c: 59 – brief description.
16. Ball 2008: 254–6 summary.

PŪZA-I SHĀN. See **148 BŪS-I SHĀN**.

QABRI-I JABĀR. See **549 KHĀK-I JABĀR**.

QABRISTĀN-I GUDAMDAR. See **94 BĀJAURI TEPE GUDAMDAR**.

825. QADER

See 2179 QADER in Supplement.

826. QADIS

Lat. 34° 49' N, long. 63° 25' E. Map 53.
Bādghīs Province. C.37 km south-east of Qal'a-i Nau on the road to Jawānd.

Date: ?Sasanian, 3rd–7th; Ghaznavid, 11th cent. (stylistic).

Description: Some mud ruins. Some Sasanian silver bowls and coins were reported to have been illicitly excavated from a site here.

There is a large rectangular forecourt structure which may have been a mosque constructed on a pre-Islamic site (crude Qur'anic inscriptions incised in what appear to be 'Kushan-style' column bases).

Sources:
1. Information on the possible mosque and columns bases by Jonathan L. Lee.
2. Information on the silver bowls and coins by Z. Tarzi.
3. Maitland and Drummond 1888: 119 – mention ruined fort.

827. QĀDZYĀN

See also 154 CHĀGHAN SARĀI.

Lat. 34° 54' N, long. 71° 09' E. Map 68.

Kunār Province. 4 km north-west of Chāghan Sarāī, on the left side of the Pech Valley.

Date: ?Hindu Shahi, 10th cent. (ceramic).

Description: Stone foundations of several buildings on the mountain slopes.

Fieldwork: 1959 Fischer, DAAD—survey.

Sources:
1. Fischer 1960: opp. 6—photo of the walls.
2. Fischer 1969: 358—brief summary and aerial photo.

828. QAFLĀTŪN

Lat. 36° 03' N, long. 65° 50' E. Map 24.
Jauzjān Province. C.24 km south of Sar-i Pul on the road to Mirza Walang.

Description: Local reports of ruins.

Source: Reported by Jonathan L. Lee.

QAL'A GUSH. See 2180 QAL'A GUSH in Supplement.

QAL'A-I ĀB-I SAFĪD. See 2181 QAL'A-I ĀB-I SAFĪD in Supplement.

QAL'A-I ACHAKZAI. See 122. ŪRUZGĀN.

829. QAL'A-I AFZAL

Lat. 30° 16' N, long. 61° 46' E. Maps 94, 95.
Nīmrūz Province. On the south side of the Rūd-i Bīyābān, 13 km west of the Helmand.

Description: Ruins of a mud fort.

Fieldwork: 1885 Merk, ABC—topographical survey.

Source: Merk 1888: 26—mention.

830. QAL'A-I AKHURAQ

Original: Lat. 30° 14' N, long. 61° 36' E. Map 94.
Revised: 30.2380265 N, 61.6121856 E /
30° 14' 16.89541440 N, 61° 36' 43.86815460 E.
Nīmrūz Province. On a spur of the desert jutting south-wards into the Rūd-i Bīyābān depression, c.21 km west of Chahā Burjak.

Description: An area of remains. Between this site and Tarākūn there are also many more ruins of isolated tombs, houses, and settlements on either side of the river bed.

Fieldwork: 1885 Merk, ABC—topographical survey.

Source: Merk 1888: 26—mention.

831. QAL'A-I AMĪR

Original: Lat. 30° 18' N, long. 61° 57' E. Map 95.
Revised: 30.30364177 N, 61.92133902 E /
30° 18' 13.11037416 N, 61° 55' 16.82047560 E.
Nīmrūz Province. On the north bank of the Helmand, 10 km west of Chahār Burjak.

Date: Timurid, 15th–16th cent. (ceramic).

Description: A high, ruined fortress-like building.

Fieldwork: 1951 Fairservis, AMNH—survey.

Source: Fairservis 1961: 56—mention (Site 38).

QAL'A-I AMĪRĀN SĀHIB. See 2182 QAL'A-I AMĪRĀN SĀHIB in Supplement.

832. QAL'A-I AMĪR MUHAMMAD
Or TAGAU, Parvan.

Lat. 34° 53' N, long. 69° 41' E. Map 65.
Kāpīsā Province. In Tagau district near Shāhkōt, north of Sarōbī on the road to Gulbahār.

Date: Turki Shahi, 7th–8th cent. (ceramic, stylistic).

Description: A very small mound c.20 m diam. and 102 m high. It is covered with stone and baked brick, and the outline of a square building is just discernible. A small marble head of Durga was found here in 1960.

Fieldwork: 1960 Fischer, DAAD—survey.

Sources:
1. Fischer 1964—relates the discovery of the Durga and describes the site, with a discussion of the style.
2. Fischer 1969: 356—brief summary.
3. Kuwayama 1972a—discusses the Durga.
4. N. Dupree et al. 1974: 96—description of the Durga.
5. Kuwayama 1976—description and general discussion of Hindu sculpture in Afghanistan.
6. Tissot 2006: 342—National Museum catalogue details and photos.

QAL'A-I BAGHNĪ. See 2183 QAL'A-I BAGHNĪ in Supplement.

833. QAL'A-I BAJGĀH

Lat. 35° 21' N, long. 67° 48' E. Map 48.
Bāmiyān Province. Opposite the southern end of the Madar gorge in the south side of the Kahmard Valley c.5 km west of the village of Bajgāh.

Description: Ruins of a fort guarding the entrance to the gorge.

Fieldwork: 1885–6 Maitland, Griesbach, ABC— topographical surveys.

Sources:
1. Yavorski 1885: 119—mention.
2. Griesbach 1888b: 211—mention.
3. Maitland 1888b: 21—mention.

834. QAL'A-I BAKHTAGĀN

Lat. 35° 49' N, long. 66° 39' E. Map 47.
Balkh Province. On the west side of the Amrakh Valley 9.5 km north of Baiza on the road to Zari.

Date: ?Sasanian, 3rd–7th cent. (traditional).

Description: Remains of an ancient fort on top of a hill. Only one tower is still standing, a massive round tower *c*.20 m diam., built of baked bricks measuring *c*.30 × 15 × 15 cm. The remainder of the fort is completely ruined. It is locally said to have been built by Bakhtāq, a wazir of Nūshīrwan.

Fieldwork: 1885 Sahibdad Khan, ABC—topographical survey.

Sources:
1. Sahibdad Khan 1888: 150—brief description.
2. Gazetteer 1979: IV. 603—mention.

835. QAL'A-I BĀLĀ

Original: Lat. 36° 01' N, long. 68° 04' E. Map 30.
Revised: 36.01413673 N, 68.06322998 E /
36° 00' 50.89223700 N, 68° 03' 47.62794240 E.
Samingān Province. On the east side of the Khurram Valley south of Haibak, *c*.3 km north of Langar and 6 km south of Sarbāgh.

Description: A ruined fort on a high, isolated rocky outcrop.

Fieldwork: 1885 Maitland, ABC—topographical survey.

Source: Maitland 1888b: 37—mention.

836. QAL'A-I BĀYĀN
See also 824 PŪST-I GAU.

Original: Lat. 31° 17' N, long. 62° 04' E. Map 84.
Revised: 31.29149699 N, 62.0706086 E /
31° 17' 29.38914924 N, 62° 04' 14.19096612 E.
Nīmrūz Province. *C*.3 km to the north-west of Pūst-i Gau, 12 km north of Chakhānsūr.

Description: An area of remains. Construction seems entirely of mud; there are no baked bricks. Probably an extension of the Pūst-i Gau remains.

Fieldwork:
1. 1903–5 Tate, SAC—survey.
2. 1950 Fairservis, AMNH—survey.

Sources:
1. Tate 1910: 187—mention.
2. Fairservis 1961: 44—mention (Site 23).
3. Ball 2008: 255—mention.

QAL'A-I BĪN. See **187. CHĀYĀB.**

837. QAL'A-I BŪĪN QARA
Or KĀFIR QAL'A.

Original: Lat. 36° 12' N, long. 64° 52' E. Map 24.
Revised: 36.22590222 N, 64.8639177 E /
36° 13' 33.24800820 N, 64° 51' 50.10372144 E.
Faryāb Province. In the Shīrīn Tagau 16 km south of Khairābād.

Description: A large natural mound enlarged by artificial means to make a fort. *Pakhsa* block construction, with some traces of brick walls.

Fieldwork: 1885 Peacocke, ABC—topographical survey.

Sources:
1. Site information by F. Grenet.
2. Peacocke 1887a: 119—mention.
3. Gazetteer 1979: IV. 286—mention.

838. QAL'A-I BULAND

Original: Lat. 34° 59' N, long. 69° 17' E. Map 64.
Revised: 34.98798153 N, 69.27511953 E /
34° 59' 16.73350296 N, 69° 16' 30.43029576 E.
Parwān Province. At the north-western angle of the Begram Plain, *c*.4 km south-west of the Burj-i 'Abdullah bridge.

Description: Many mounds, including a very large one that may be a stupa. Also much ancient carved stone-work.

Fieldwork: 1834 Masson—survey.

Sources:
1. Masson 1836a: 3—brief description.
2. Masson 1842: III. 155—mention.

QAL'A-I BULDI. See **2184 QAL'A-I BULDI** in **Supplement.**

QAL'A-I BUST. See **149 BUST.**

QAL'A-I CHAHĀR BARADAR. See **787 PĀ'ĪN MAZĀR.**

QAL'A-I CHAKALA. See **855 QAL'A-I KACHALA.**

839. QAL'A-I CHIGĪNĪ
See also 201 CHIGĪNĪ 2.

Original: Lat. 31° 04' N, long. 62° 07' E. Maps 84, 92.
Revised: 31.07309821 N, 62.11563672 E /
31° 04' 23.15357364 N, 62° 06' 56.29220892 E.
Nīmrūz Province. 14 km by road south-east of Chakhānsūr,
c.10 km north of Chigīnī II.

Dates: Sasanian, 3rd–7th cent. (ceramic); Ghaznavid, 11th–
12th cent. (architectural).

Description: Extensive ruins of a town and irrigation
system. The town is walled and includes the remains of a
bazaar, a mosque, and houses. The most prominent features
are a large fortress-palace and adjacent dwelling tower. The
fortress-palace is enclosed in a low wall and has a decorated
façade of blind keyhole shaped arches. The dwelling tower is
square and entered high above ground level. Inside are two
barrel-vaulted rooms. Though Islamic architecturally it contains 'Kushano-Sasanian' pottery. Nearby are a series of low
mud ramparts.

Fieldwork:
1. 1936 Hackin and Meunié, DAFA—survey.
2. 1974 Fischer, Bonn University—survey and sondage in
   the irrigation area.

Sources:
1. Hackin 1959c: fig. 116—photo of a house.
2. Fischer 1970a—photos.
3. Fischer 1970b: pls 26–31—photos.
4. Fischer 1971b: 43–7—brief descriptions under their ruin
   types, with ground and aerial photos (Sites 18–21).
5. Fischer 1973c: 144—map reference.
6. Fischer et al. 1974–6: 369—mention and photo.
7. Fischer 1983a—discussion of the architecture.
8. Ball 2008: 256–7—summary.

QAL'A-I CHARA. See **2185 QAL'A-I CHARA in
Supplement.**

QAL'A-I CHASHMA KHŪNI. See **2186 QAL'A-I
CHASHMA KHŪNI in Supplement.**

QAL'A-I CHINGIZ. See **2123 KHĀNĀNĪ.**

QAL'A-I CHULAKAI. See **2187 QAL'A-I CHULAKAI
in Supplement.**

QAL'A-I DAHĀN-I NAU JŪI. See **2188 QAL'A-I
DAHĀN-I NAU JŪI in Supplement.**

840. QAL'A-I DASHT

Original: Lat. 34° 37' N, long. 69° 04' E. Map 63.
Revised: 34.62627598 N, 69.06956054 E /
34° 37' 34.59352008 N, 69° 04' 10.41793392 E.
Kābul Province. Along the northern approach of the Khair
Khāna Pass, c.15 km north-west of Kābul.

Description: A series of some half dozen mounds or tumuli
on either side of the road, spaced out at regular intervals.
Possibly the remains of towers or stupas.

Fieldwork: 1834 Masson—survey.

Sources:
1. Masson 1842: III. 111—mention.
2. Foucher 1942–7: 143—mention.

QAL'A-I DŪ ĀU. See **2189 QAL'A-I DŪ ĀU in
Supplement.**

841. QAL'A-I DUKHTAR
See also 874 QAL'A-I PESAR.

Original: Lat. 33° 17' N, long. 62° 11' E. Map 70.
Revised: 33.27995685 N, 62.19793751 E /
33° 16' 47.84466216 N, 62° 11' 52.57503852 E.
Farāh Province. On a ridge south-east of Shindand.

Date: Timurid, 15th–16th cent. (ceramic).

Description: A ruined fortress on a rocky spur. It consists
of a wall enclosing a very large area, c.350 × 150 m running
right down to the river. Construction is of brick and stone.

Fieldwork:
1. 1952 Le Berre and Gardin, DAFA—survey.
2. 1956 Ramachandran and Sharma, ASI—reconnaissance.
3. 1968–78 Kruglikova, Af/Sov. Mission—survey.

Sources:
1. Gardin and Lyonnet, 1980 chronological study of pottery from unpublished DAFA surveys.
2. Conolly 1841: 321—brief description.
3. Lal 1846: 172–3—mentions the fortress and recounts the
   legend surrounding its foundation.
4. Ferrier 1857: 443—brief description.
5. Yate 1900: 15–16—brief description.
6. Ramachandran and Sharma 1956: I. 16—brief
   description.
7. Gazetteer 1973: I. 278—mention.
8. Gaibov et al. 2010: 112—mentions the fortress destroyed
   by 1970.

QAL'A-I DUKHTAR, Bāmiyān. See **1042 SHAHR-I
GHULGHULA.**

842. QAL'A-I FATH

Original: Lat. 30° 33' N, long. 61° 51' E. Map. 93.
Revised: 30.54489823 N, 61.84999528 E /
30° 32' 41.63363376 N, 61° 50' 59.98302240 E.
Nīmrūz Province. On the east bank of the Helmand, 37 km
north of Chahār Burjak.

Dates: ?Bactrian, 3rd–1st cent. BC; ?Sasanian, 3rd–7th C.
(numismatic); Timurid, 15th–16th cent. (architectural).

Description: A very large area of ruins and mounds,
amongst the most extensive in Seistan. It is a square, walled
city with 94 round towers up to 10 m high (in 1905), though
with much of it washed away by floods. Construction is
mostly mud-brick. In the north-east is a citadel quarter on a
mound *c*.10 m high surrounded by a double line of walls,
strengthened by more round towers. The top of the mound
is divided into two huge buildings, with walls a further 22 m
high, with crenellations and loopholes. There are also
remains of many brick kilns or ice houses up to 13 m
diam., and a baked brick caravanserai or *madrasa*, known
as the Gumbaz-i Surkh, outside the walls to the south. In
the vicinity are extensive remains of gardens and canals.

Fieldwork:
1. 1884 Maitland and Peacocke, ABC — topographical survey.
2. 1903–5 Tate, SAC — survey.
3. 1936 Hackin and Meunié, DAFA — survey.
4. 1950 Fairservis, AMNH — survey.
5. 1960 Fischer, DAAD — survey.

Sources:
1. Ferrier 1857: 410 — mention.
2. Bellew 1874: 215–16 — brief description.
3. Smith 1876: 293–4 — brief description.
4. *Civ. and Milit. Gazette*, 18 Nov. 1884 — description,
   mentioning finds of 'Bactrian' and 'Sasanian' coins by
   the ABC.
5. Holdich 1885a: 162 — brief description.
6. Peacocke 1885a: 5–7 — fairly detailed description.
7. Holdich 1887: 6 — brief description.
8. Peacocke 1887a: 20–1 — brief description and sketches
   of citadel and the caravanserai.
9. A. C. Yate 1887: 80 and 83–5 — brief description of the
   site and associated legends.
10. Maitland 1888a: 69–70 — brief description.
11. McMahon 1906: 219 — mention.
12. Tate 1909: 105–6 and opp. 103 — brief description and a
    photo.
13. Tate 1910: 72, 78, and 245–9 — detailed description and
    photos of the remains.
14. Hackin 1959c: figs 121–3 — photos.
15. Fairservis 1961: 53 — mention (Site 32).
16. Fischer 1961: 34 — mention.
17. Fischer 1969: 335 — brief summary.
18. Fischer 1970a — photos.
19. Gazetteer 1973: II. 137–8 — detailed description.
20. Ball 2008: 257 — summary.

QAL'A-I FIRUZ HUSAIN. See 984 SANG BUR.

843. QAL'A-I GAURI

Original: Lat. 32° 19' N, long. 61° 31' E approximately.
Maps 69, 83.
Revised: 32.30471932 N, 61.49422767 E /
32° 18' 16.98954120 N, 61° 29' 39.21962568 E.
Farāh Province. Near the village of Dastgul, 20 km north of
Qal'a-i Kah.

Description: Remains of an ancient fort, said to be pre-
Islamic.

Fieldwork: 1884 Maitland, ABC.

Sources:
1. Maitland 1888a: 103 — mention.
2. Gazetteer 1975: III. 91 — mention.

844. QAL'A-I GAWAK

Original: Lat. 30° 42' N, long. 61° 50' E. Map 92.
Revised: 30.71374907 N, 61.84358995 E /
30° 42' 49.49664120 N, 61° 50' 36.92380560 E.
Nīmrūz Province. On the east bank of the Helmand
c.20 km north of Qal'a-i Fath.

Date: Ghaznavid, 11th–12th cent. (ceramic, stylistic).

Description: Remains of a mud-brick mansion with decorative features resembling those at Lashkari Bāzār.

Fieldwork:
1. 1884 Peacocke, ABC — topographical survey.
2. 1903–5 Tate, SAC — survey.
3. 1965–70 Fischer, Bonn University — survey.

Sources:
1. Peacocke 1885a: 8 — mention.
2. Peacocke 1887a: 22 — mentions fort.
3. Maitland 1888a: 71 — mentions remains of three forts,
   some distance apart, on a north–south line.
4. Tate 1910: 254 — brief description.
5. Fischer 1966: 27 — mention and photo.
6. Fischer 1969: 335 — mention.
7. Fischer 1970a — photos.
8. Fischer 1971c: 50 — mention.

845. QAL'A-I GĀWARGĪN

Original: Lat. 34° 45' N, long. 67° 06' E. Maps 47, 57.
Revised: 34.74156845 N, 67.09319295 E /
34° 44' 29.64642900 N, 67° 05' 35.49462000 E.
Bāmiyān Province. In the lower end of the Sarikol gulley,
c.12 km above Shahr-i Barbar.

Date: Ghurid (stylistic)

Description: Remains of an ancient mud-brick fort, built in a very inaccessible position with a ravine on two sides, and two subsidiary forts. It has several towers decorated with impressed ornamentation. Inside is a rock-cut staircase descending below ground level. Just below the fort is a mound resembling a stupa.

Fieldwork:
1. 1885 Talbot and Maitland, ABC — topographical survey.
2. 2002 Lee, Society for South Asian Studies — reconnaissance.

Sources:
1. Talbot et al. 1886: 331–2 — brief description.
2. Maitland 1888a: 503 — mention.
3. Kluyver 2000: 5 — detailed description.
4. Lee 2006: 229–32 — brief description and photos.

QAL'A-I GHAMBAR. See 2122 KHĀN RAGĀB TEPE in Supplement.

846. QAL'A-I GHŪRI

Original: Lat. 35° 58' N, long. 68° 36' E. Map 33.
Revised: 35.97338595 N, 68.62216877 E /
35° 58' 24.18942180 N, 68° 37' 19.80756624 E.
Baghlān Province. In the centre of the Ghūri Valley, some 27 km by road west of Pul-i Khumri.

Description: Remains of a citadel enclosed by a ditch, surrounded by ruins and mounds marking an ancient town.

Fieldwork: 1886 Maitland and Peacocke, ABC — topographical survey.

Sources:
1. Holdich 1887: 39 — brief description.
2. Peacocke 1887a: 370 — mention.
3. Maitland 1888b: 234 — mention.
4. Gazetteer 1972: I. 73 — mention.
5. Grenet 2002a: 215 — suggests the site as a location of the Hephthalite capital.

QAL'A-I GIUBI. See 29 'ALIĀBĀD.

847. QAL'A-I HĀJI
Or CHAHĀRBĀGH 5 and 6.

Original: Lat. 34° 25' N, long. 70° 24' E. Map 66.
Revised: 34.41767603 N, 70.39754264 E /
34° 25' 03.63371268 N, 70° 23' 51.15348636 E.
Nangahār Province. 1 km south of the village of Qal'a-i Hāji, at the eastern end of the Chahārbāgh group of stupas, 8 km west of Jalālābād.

Date: Kushan, 1st–3rd cent. (numismatic).

Description: Remains of two stupas, each with its associated monastery enclosure to the east. Both are 33 m circumference. The first contained a small steatite vase, bones, and one copper coin of Mokadphises. The second contained a gold reliquary and ashes inside a steatite vase. There are also 11 large mounds, possibly more stupas, and several smaller ones.

Fieldwork:
1. 1833 Gerard, East India Co. — excavation.
2. 1934 Masson — excavation.
3. 1965 Mizuno, Kyoto University — survey.

Sources:
1. Jacquet 1839 — general remarks on both Gerard's and Masson's work.
2. Masson 1841: 103–4 — brief description of the remains and the contents of the stupas.
3. Lal 1846: 213 — brief description of Gerard's excavation.
4. Mizuno 1971: 121–2 — summary of previous work and description and photos of the present condition (Stupas 49–53).

848. QAL'A-I HAUZ

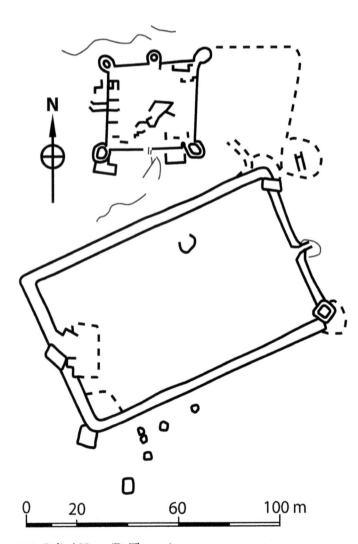

0   20   60   100 m

848 Qal'a-i Hauz (D. Thomas).

Original: Lat. 31° 00' N, long. 64° 52' E. Map 97.
Revised: 31.00752953 N, 64.87390988 E /
31° 00' 27.10629288 N, 64° 52' 26.07557412 E.
Kandahār Province. In the heart of the Rīgistān Desert, on the caravan route from Darwīshān on the Helmand to Kandahār.

Date: Ghaznavid, 11th–12th cent. (architectural).

Description: Ruins of a large mud-brick fortress. It is trapezoidal in plan, with a bastion to the north-west and a large tower to the north-east projecting from a square salient. There is some mud-brick decoration on the façade. Also remains of a reservoir and cultivation.

Sources:
1. Balsan 1972a: 169–73—account of a visit and a description of the remains.
2. Balsan 1972b: 156—mention.
3. Thomas et al. 2008—detailed satellite image of the remains.
4. Thomas and Kidd 2017—discuss the site in the context of a further 831 sites newly identified from satellite imagery in a sample 60 km study strip across the Rēgistān Desert.

QAL'A-I HAZHDA NAHR. See **2164 MINGLIK** in Supplement.

849. QAL'A-I HINDU
See also 77 BĀGHAK.

Original: Lat. 30° 08' N, long. 62° 26' E. Map 96.
Revised: 30.14625773 N, 62.4339362 E / 30° 08' 46.52781468 N, 62° 26' 02.17032576 E.
Nīmrūz Province. On the left bank of the Helmand, between 12 and 16 km west of Rūdbār; Qal'a-i Hindu itself is 16 km west.

Dates: Bronze Age, 3rd–2nd mill. BC; Seleucid, 4th–3rd cent. BC (numismatic); Indo-Parthian, 1st–3rd cent.; Sasanian, 3rd–7th cent. (ceramic).

Description: Extensive ruins and mounds, with a wide surface scatter of sherds. These comprise: at 12 km, ruins of a high walled fort, 25 m to the north of the road; at 14 km, an artificial mound to the north of the road; at 15 km, a few mounds and insignificant ruins; at 16 km, Qal'a-i Hindu to the south of the road, surrounded by extensive ruins and mounds. The toponym itself is uncertain: so far as we could ascertain there is no such place, although the toponym has, from time to time over the past 150 years, appeared on maps. The only one of the sources here that mention it is Maitland; the others do not give it this name.

Fieldwork:
1. 1884 Maitland, ABC—topographical survey.
2. 1966 Hammond, Cambridge University—survey.
3. 1971–4 Trousdale, Smithsonian—survey.

Sources:
1. Site information by W. Trousdale.
2. Ferrier 1857: 410—mentions the ruins and his own find of a Seleucid coin.
3. Maitland 1888a: 60—description of individual areas.
4. Tate 1909: 80—brief description.
5. Hammond 1970: 449—lists site (no. 8) and describes the pottery types and general survey results.
6. Gazetteer 1973: II. 140—mention.

QAL'A-I ISFANDIAR. See **199 CHICHAKTU.**

QAL'A-I ĪSHTAR. See **2190 QAL'A-I ĪSHTAR** in Supplement.

QAL'A-I ISKĪCH. See **2191 QAL'A-I ISKĪCH** in Supplement.

QAL'A-I ISMĀ'ĪLI. See **2192 QAL'A-I ISMĀ'ĪLI** in Supplement.

850. QAL'A-I ISMĀ'ĪL
Or RABĀT-I ISMĀ'ĪL.

Original: Lat. 35° 57' N, long. 63° 19' E. Map 44.
Revised: 35.6142115 N, 63.31033809 E / 35° 36' 51.16139100 N, 63° 18' 37.21711752 E.
Bādghīs Province. On the west bank of the Murghāb River, 6.5 km north of Bālā Murghāb.

Description: A mound c.200 m square and 7 m high, with another mound, probably the remains of a fort, a further 15 m higher in the north-western corner. In the vicinity are extensive remains of ancient vine cultivation, and 1 km downstream are the remains of an old baked brick bridge. There is also a report of caves.

Fieldwork: 1886 Yate, ABC—topographical survey.

Sources:
1. Maitland 1888a: 212—mentions caves.
2. Yate 1888: 223–24—brief description of remains.
3. Hamilton 1906: 142—mentions remains.
4. Gazetteer 1975: III. 218—mentions remains.

851. QAL'A-I JAFAR SULTĀN

Lat. 33° 08' N, long. 67° 29' E. Map 79.
Ghazni Province. 5 km east of Sang-I Māsha, at the point where the Lūmān stream meets the Arghandāb River.

Description: Several inscriptions on the rocks in the valley, in a script that Rawlinson was unable to identify.

Source: Markham 1876: 244—mention, after a journey by Lynch in 1841.

852. QAL'A-I JAMAL

Original: Lat. 33° 06' N, long. 62° 06' E. Map 70.
Revised: 33.06814129 N, 62.11419198 E /
33° 04' 05.30863752 N, 62° 06' 51.09111756 E.
Farāh Province. Along the road from Shindand to Farāh, south of Darauji, 150 m west of the road.

Dates: Beg. Iron, end 2nd-beg. 1st mill. BC; Indo-Parthian, 1st–4th cent.; Sasano-Islamic, 3rd–9th cent. (ceramic).

Description: Small mound 6 m high, irregular shape. Large mud-bricks are visible; the surroundings are strewn with sherds.

Collection: National Museum/AIA—sherds.

Fieldwork: 1952 Le Berre and Gardin, DAFA—survey.

Source: M. Le Berre: unpublished 1952 report, DAFA archives, tépé Shindand-Farah 2.

853. QAL'A-I JAMSHID

Lat. 36° 35' N, long. 69° 24' E. Map 37.
Takhār Province. In the valley of the Darya-i Chal which continues towards the south of the Bangui valley, 10 km upriver from its confluence with the Rūd-i Ishkamīsh. The site is located on an outcrop which overlooks the Darya-i Chal by about 150 m, right bank, at its juncture with a stream called Nahr-i Jamshid; the access road, from Bangui, follows the left bank of the river, which is forded at the foot of the outcrop (northern outskirts of the village of Chār Chinār).

Dates: Achaemenid, 6th–4th cent. BC.; some Islamic sherds (ceramic).

Description: No artificial mound visible near the top, periodically farmed for *lalmī* crops; but the surface produces very old sherds, and a recent find from this same place has been reported, an inscribed stone, which has since disappeared (1978).

Collection: National Museum/AIA—sherds.

Fieldwork: 1978 Gardin et al., CNRS—survey.

Sources:
1. Site information by J.-C. Gardin.
2. Gardin and Lyonnet 1978–9: pl. XI—no. 353.
3. Lyonnet 1997: figs 25, 35—no. 353.
4. Gardin 1998: 97—no. 353.

QAL'A-I JAN BEG. See **2193 QAL'A-I JAN BEG in Supplement.**

QAL'A-I JUBĪN. See **2194 QAL'A-I JUBĪN in Supplement.**

854. QAL'A-I JUGHIR KHĒL

Lat. 34° 50' N, long. 67° 51' E. Map 58.
Bāmiyān Province. 3 km east of Bāmiyān, on the north side of the valley opposite Shahr-i Ghulghula.

Description: A series of artificial caves.

Source: Amir Khan 1888: 176—mention.

QAL'A-I KACHAK. See **2195 QAL'A-I KACHAK in Supplement.**

855. QAL'A-I KACHALA
Or QAL'A-I CHAKALA.
See also 806 PASSANI.

Original: Lat. 34° 27' N, long. 70° 20' E. Map 67.
Revised: 34.45311975 N, 70.33392912 E /
34° 27' 11.23110792 N, 70° 20' 02.14483236 E.
Laghmān Province. A gully in the Kūh-i Siāh on the north bank of the Surkhāb. The gully is north-west of Zīyārat-i Sa'id Ilias Aliah, 1 km north-west of Passani, just behind the village of Qal'a-i Kachala.

Date: Indo-Parthian, 1st cent. (numismatic).

Description: Either side of the gully is honeycombed with artificial caves, with more in the foothills. One is a circumambulatory chamber. On the tops of the hills are remains of many walls, mounds, and stupas. One of the stupas contained small gold and silver reliquaries inside a steatite vase, together with jewellery, a Kharoshthi tuz-leaf manuscript, and six copper coins of Azes. Another excavated stupa contained nothing. The whole area is scattered with bones, ashes, and sherds.

Collections: British Museum—stupa contents.

Fieldwork:
1. 1833 Honigberger—excavation.
2. 1834 Masson—excavations.
3. 1965 Mizuno, Kyoto University—survey.

Sources:
1. Masson 1841: 68–9 and 94–5—brief description of the caves, the stupa (Tope 2 of Passani) and the tumuli.
2. Wilson 1841: pl. 1—drawing of the steatite vase.
3. Caspani 1945—brief description of the caves and tentative identification as the 'Cave of the Shadow of the Buddha' mentioned by Huien Tsang.
4. Mizuno 1971: 124—description of the caves.
5. Jongeward et al. 2012—catalogue and discussion of the reliquaries with the Passani material.
6. Errington 2017a: 91–101 and 2017b: 52–3, 45, 47–8, 50, 52, 56–60, 108–19—the Masson collection and archive relating to the site with the Passani material.

QAL'A-I KALĀR. See **2196 QAL'A-I KALĀR in Supplement.**

QAL'A-I KADAH. See **486 KADAH.**

856. QAL'A-I KAMAR

Original: Lat. 34° 26' N, long. 62° 12' E. Map 52.
Revised: 34.45870464 N, 62.1978917 E / 34° 27' 31.33671192 N, 62° 11' 52.41013116 E.
Herat Province. 11 km north of this city, west of the road to Khushk Post, about 1 km south of the pass of Qal'a-i Kamar, near a modern mill.
Date: Timurid, 15th–16th cent. (ceramic).
Description: Ruins of a small building and a courtyard, built in stone.
Collection: National Museum/AIA — sherds.
Fieldwork: 1952 Le Berre and Gardin, DAFA — survey.
Source: M. Le Berre: unpublished 1952 report, DAFA archives.

857. QAL'A-I KANG
See also 2202 QAL'A-I KUHNA in Supplement.

Original: Lat. 31° 06' N, long. 61° 53' E. Map 83.
Revised: 31.1034459 N, 61.8857609 E / 31° 06' 12.40525188 N, 61° 53' 08.73925008 E.
Nīmrūz Province. C.15 km north of Zaranj and 6 km east of the Iranian border.
Description: A relatively modern fort, c.300 m diam., built on a large, ancient mound.
Fieldwork: 1903–5 Tate, SAC — survey.
Source: Tate 1909: 130–1 — mention.

QAL'A-I KAZAL. See **542 KHAIRĀBĀD.**

QAL'A-I KHĀK-I SABŪR. See **466 JALMISH.**

QAL'A-I KHALIFA. See **1197 TOPDARRA.**

QAL'A-I KHALIL JĀN. See **2197 QAL'A-I KHALIL JĀN in Supplement.**

QAL'A-I KHALSANG. See **2198 QAL'A-I KHALSANG in Supplement.**

858. QAL'A-I KHĀRĀN
Or QAL'A-I KHĀZĀN.

Original: Lat. 30° 18' N, long. 61° 50' E. Maps 94, 95.

Revised: 30.30418312 N, 61.83213785 E / 30° 18' 15.05924676 N, 61° 49' 55.69627440 E.
Nīmrūz Province. 6 km west of Bandar-i Kamāl Khān on the Helmand on the route to Burri, on a cliff above the old bed of the Rūd-i Bīyābān.
Description: Some large mud ruins, probably a fort, on a low bluff.
Fieldwork:
1. 1885 Merk, ABC — topographical survey.
2. 1903–5 Tate, SAC — survey.
Sources:
1. Merk 1888: 26 — mention.
2. Tate 1910: 241 — mention.

QAL'A-I KHĀZĀN. See **858 QAL'A-I KHĀRĀN.**

QAL'A-I KHWĀJA. See **2199 QAL'A-I KHWĀJA in Supplement.**

859. QAL'A-I KIRTA

Original: Lat. 32° 13' N, long. 62° 59' E. Map 85.
Revised: 32.17351333 N, 62.98132835 E / 32° 10' 24.64797900 N, 62° 58' 52.78207008 E.
Farāh Province. About 115 km from this city, in the village of Qal'a-i Kirta, on either side of the road to Girishk, 5 km south-east of Sultān Bakwa.
Description: Several tumuli on either side of the road; largest tepe to the south.
Fieldwork: 1952 Le Berre and Gardin, DAFA — survey.
Source: M. Le Berre: unpublished 1952 report, DAFA archives, tepe Farah-Girishk 6.

QAL'A-I KOMAGHAI. See **2200 QAL'A-I KOMAGHAI in Supplement.**

860. QAL'A-I KUHNA, JURM

Lat. 35° 55' N, long. 70° 52' E, Map 38.
Badakhshān Province. On the east bank of the Kokcha at the northern entrance to the Jurm plain, 7 km north of Jurm.
Description: Remains of stone walls, probably originally a part of larger fortifications. Some interior walls of baked brick. One mud-brick wall decorated with inlaid river pebbles. Two distinct building phases discernible.
Fieldwork: 1975 Kohl — survey.
Sources:
1. Levi 1972: 172–3 — brief description.
2. Kohl 1978: 65 — mention.

QAL'A-I KUHNA, Kang. See 2202 QAL'A-I KUHNA, Kang in Supplement.

QAL'A-I KUHNA KULAGH PARDAI. See 2201 QAL'A-I KUHNA KULAGH PARDAI in Supplement.

QAL'A-I KUHNA, Nīmrūz. See 527 KARBĀSAK.

861. QAL'A-I KŪRDŪ
See also 648 KŪRDŪ.

Original: Lat. 30° 54' N, long. 61° 57' E. Map 92.
Revised: 30.86277681 N, 61.97827317 E /
30° 51' 45.99650484 N, 61° 58' 41.78341596 E.
Nīmrūz Province. C.5 km west of the Kūrdū ruins, in the dunes 14 km south-east of Zaranj.

Date: Timurid, 15th–16th cent. (documentary).

Description: Some very prominent ruins of a large mud-brick fort built on an artificial platform c.5 m high. The walls are a further 13 m high, and c.70 m square. There is an entrance in the south wall.

Fieldwork:
1. 1903–5 Tate, SAC—survey.
2. 1936 Hackin and Meunié, DAFA—survey.

Sources:
1. Tate 1910: 240—brief description.
2. Klinkott 1982: 209–77—description of the fortifications.

862. QAL'A-I MĀDAR
Or Dūdān.

Lat. 35° 22' N, long. 67° 48' E. Map 48.
Bāmiyān Province. C.3 km east of Madar at the northern end of the Madar gorge leading to Kahmard. On the east side of the valley.

Description: Ruins of an ancient mud fort on a low hill, the base of which has many artificial caves. There are also many more caves, often in several tiers, along the eastern side of the valley. Most are collapsed and filled in.

Fieldwork: 1885–6 Maitland, Griesbach, ABC—topographical surveys.

Sources:
1. Yavorski 1885: 117—brief description of the caves.
2. Griesbach 1888b: 211—mentions the fort and caves.
3. Maitland 1888b: 22—mentions the fort.
4. Lee 2006: 250—mention as 'Dūdān'.

863. QAL'Ā-I MĀDAR-I PĀDSHĀH
See also 502 KAIKĀBĀD.

Original: Lat. 30° 11' N, long. 61° 16' E. Map 95.

Revised: 30.18769621 N, 62.2689412 E / 30° 11' 15.70636608 N, 62° 16' 08.18832756 E.
Nīmrūz Province. On the south bank of the Helmand 23 km west of Rūdbār.

Date: Early Islamic, 8th–13th (architectural).

Description: A large ruined fort or palace surrounded by many more remains and mounds stretching to the east and west for some distance. The fort measures c.160 × 120 m with walls up to 8 m high surrounding a central courtyard, dominated by two ruined towers at each end, 300 m apart. Construction is of mud-brick on a baked brick foundation. The inside is divided into courtyards and includes remains of domed rooms and a mosque. The mosque has a courtyard and a prayer hall two bays deep.

Fieldwork:
1. 1884 Maitland and Peacocke, ABC—topographical survey.
2. 1966 Hammond, Cambridge University—survey.

Sources:
1. Bellew 1874: 206–7—brief description.
2. *Civil and Milit. Gazette*, 18 Nov. 1884—detailed description.
3. Durand 1885: I, pl 57—sketch.
4. Holdich 1885a: 161—brief description.
5. Peacocke 1885a: 3—brief description.
6. Holdich 1887: 6—brief description.
7. Peacocke 1887a: 17—brief description.
8. A. C. Yate 1887: 82–3—mention.
9. Maitland 1888a: 60–1—fairly detailed description.
10. Hammond 1970: 440 n. 20—very brief description and photo.
11. Gazetteer 1973: II. 143–4—detailed description.
12. Ball 2008: 257–8—summary.

QAL'A-I MĀLIK. See 523 KANGKRAK-I PĀ'ĪN.

864. QAL'A-I MĀLIK ANTAR
See also 1234 WURSHAK.

Original: Lat. 33° 22' N, long. 64° 34' E. Maps 55, 74.
Revised: 33.37089002 N, 64.57473656 E /
33° 22' 15.20407632 N, 64° 34' 29.05160808 E.
Ghūr Province. Just to the south of Wurshak, 13 km south-west of Yamān.

Date: Ghurid, 12th–13th cent. (architectural, geographical).

Description: A 10 m high square stone fort with snakelike decoration on the east and south walls. There are remains of several more stone and mud-brick forts on either side of the valley.

Fieldwork: 1946 Kohzad, HSA—survey.

Source: Kohzad 1951–4, 9/1: 31—brief description.

QAL'A-I MAMBAR BASHI. See 2203 QAL'A-I MAMBAR BASHI in Supplement.

QAL'A-I MANSŪR. See **345 GAZKAI.**

865. QAL'A-I MĪR 'ALĀM
Or RABĀT-I MĪR 'ALĀM.

Original: Lat. 33° 47' N, long. 62° 15' E. Map 70.
Revised:
33.78897107 N, 62.24847385 E / 33° 47' 20.29586460 N,
62° 14' 54.50585568 E and 33.79010122 N, 62.24805242 E /
33° 47' 24.36439308 N, 62° 14' 52.98869868 E.
Herat Province. At the southern end of the Mīr 'Alām Pass,
on the east side of the main road to Kandahār, c.60 km
south of Herat.

Date: Partho-Sasanian, 1st–7th cent. (ceramic).

Description: A small mound c.15 m long at the top and 8 m
high. To the south of the mound are the remains of a small
square fort. One sherd of red spiral-burnished ware was
recovered from the mound.

Fieldwork:
1. 1885 Peacocke.
2. 1974 Swiny, BIAS—survey.

Sources:
1. Site information by S. Swiny in unpublished BIAS archive.
2. Peacocke 1887a: 213—mentions ruined caravanserai.
3. Maitland et al. 1889: 80—mention ruined caravanserai.

QAL'A-I MĪR. See **2204 QAL'A-I MĪR in Supplement.**

QAL'A-I MUFTI. See **1087 SHĪWAKĪ.**

866. QAL'A-I MUHAMMAD

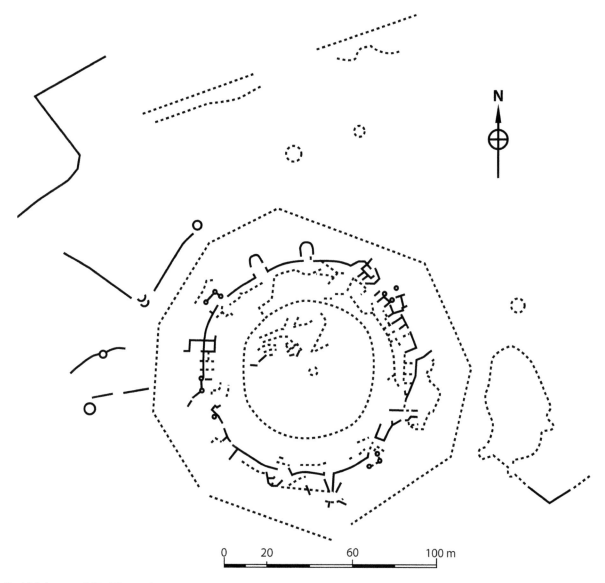

866 Qal'a-i Muhammad (D. Thomas).

Original: Lat. 30° 58' N, long. 61° 52' E. Map 92.
Revised: 30.97018511 N, 61.88401476 E /
30° 58' 12.66638304 N, 61° 53' 02.45314464 E.
Nīmrūz Province. 4 km north-east of Zaranj on the road to Chakhānsūr.

Date: Mongol-Timurid, 13th–16th cent. (ceramic).

Description: Some mud-brick remains of a large polygonal fortress. Some vaults are still preserved.

Fieldwork:
1. 1884 Maitland, Peacocke ABC—topographical survey.
2. 1970 Fischer, Bonn University.

Sources:
1. Maitland 1888a: 77—mention.
2. Peacocke 1887a: 25—mention.
3. Fischer 1971a—photos.
4. Fischer et al. 1974–6: 34—brief description.
5. Klinkott 1982: 209–77—description of the fortifications.

867. QAL'A-I MUHAMMAD AZIM

Lat. 34° 50' N, long. 67° 47' E. Map 58.
Bāmiyān Province. 3 km west of Bāmiyān on the north side of the valley. The village of Qal'a-i Muhammad Azim is on the south side.

Description: A series of artificial caves, presumably an extension of the Bāmiyān ones.

Fieldwork: 1885 Maitland and Talbot—topographical survey.

Sources:
1. Yavorski 1885: 129—mention.
2. Amir Khan 1888: 174—mention.
3. Maitland 1888a: 514—mention.

868. QAL'A-I MUHAMMAD KHĀN TEPE
Or ĀBDĀN.

Original: Lat. 36° 44' N, long. 67° 13' E. Map 27.
Revised: 36.74085161 N, 67.20835087 E /
36° 44' 27.06578808 N, 67° 12' 30.06313056 E.
Balkh Province. 10 km east of Mazār-i Sharīf on the road to Tāshqurghān.

Date: Mongol-Timurid, 13th–16th cent. (ceramic).

Description: Large numbers of mounds and ruins.

Fieldwork: 1960 Hayashi and Sahara, Kyoto University—survey.

Sources:
1. Ferrier 1875: 210—mention.
2. Hayashi and Sahara 1962: 53—photo and description in Japanese.

869. QAL'A-I NAQSHI

Lat. 34° 11' N, long. 65° 06' E. Map 55.
Ghūr Province. In the mountains south of the Band-i Bāyān, south of Chakhcharān.

Date: Ghurid, 12th–13th cent. (architectural).

Description: Remains of an ancient baked brick fortress with baked brick patterns on the walls.

Fieldwork: 1885 Maitland, ABC—topographical survey.

Sources:
1. Maitland 1888a: 447—brief description from hearsay.
2. Gazetteer 1975: III. 219—mention.

QAL'A-I NASHAN. See 2206 QAL'A-I NASHAN in Supplement.

870. QAL'A-I NAU, BĀDGHĪS

Lat. 34° 58' N, long. 63° 06' E. Map 53.
Bādghīs Province. On the Herat road 2 km south of the town of Qal'a-i Nau.

Description: Some artificial caves cut into the hillside. There are no traces of carvings or frescos.

Sources:
1. A. C. Yate 1887: 200—mention.
2. Byron 1937: 120—mention.

QAL'A-I NAU, Juwain. See 2207 QAL'A-I NAU, Juwain in Supplement.

QAL'A-I NAU, Kalu. See 517 KALU.

871. QAL'A-I NAU, SEISTAN
Or BAGHLAR or NOKEN KALAT or CHA-KHĀN-SŪRAK.

Original: Lat. 30° 56' N, long. 62° 08' E. Map 92.
Revised: 30.93036067 N, 62.13708568 E /
30° 55' 49.29841092 N, 62° 08' 13.50846132 E.
Nīmrūz Province. 5 km due south of Zīyārat-i Amīrān Sāhib.

Dates: Indo-Parthian-Sasanian, 1st–7th cent. (ceramic); early Islamic, 8th–13th cent. (architectural, ceramic).

Description: A large, well-preserved Islamic fortress (Tate's Noken Kalat, Hackin's Chakhānsūrak, Fischer's Site 6) connected to a probably pre-Islamic high tower (Fischer's Site 5). Inside the fort are several ruins, including the remains of a mosque. The tower, of possible pre-Islamic origins and later Islamic reuse, contained human remains.

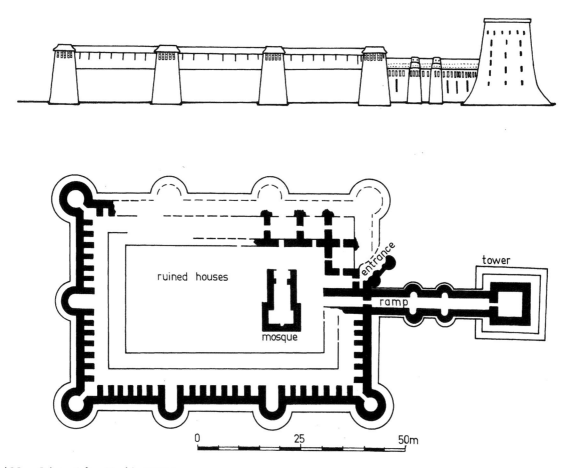

871 Qal'a-i Nau, Seistan (after Hackin 1959c).

There is also a series of square pillars with baked brick bases to the south.

The tower is certainly pre-Islamic in plan and elevation, as is the qal'a itself; both were heavily rebuilt in Islamic times. There is no possibility that the tower is connected with Zoroastrianism. It conforms to standard fortress and/ or dwelling towers of a type known widely throughout West Turkistan and Afghanistan. Burials, in some cases quite fresh, were encountered, unmarked, in several ruins and qal'a towers. Suspicion attends some of them, but not the possibility that they have anything to do with latent Zorastrianism. The square pillars with baked brick bases are piers of ruined Timurid mausolea and have nothing to do with Qala-i Nau.

Fieldwork:
1. 1884 Maitland, ABC—topographical survey.
2. 1903–5 Tate, SAC—survey.
3. 1936 Hackin and Meunié, DAFA—survey.
4. 1968 Fischer, Bonn University—survey.
5. 1971–4 Trousdale, Smithsonian—survey.

Sources:
1. Additional site information by W. Trousdale.
2. Maitland 1888a: 194—mention.

3. Tate 1910: 121 and 239—mentions the tower and the human remains. Brief description of the fortress.
4. Hackin 1959c: 27—mention, with a plan and photos.
5. Fischer 1969–70—photos.
6. Fischer 1970b: pl. 48—photo.
7. Fischer 1971b: 44 and 46–7—photos and brief description of the fortress and brief discussion of the tower.
8. Klinkott 1982: 209–77—description of the fortifications.
9. Ball 2008: 258—summary.

872. QAL'A-I PĀDSHĀH

Original: Lat. 35° 17' N, long. 67° 36' E. Map 48.
Revised: 35.30196921 N, 67.62258577 E /
35° 18' 07.08917148 N, 67° 37' 21.30875472 E.
Bāmiyān Province. In the Kahmard Valley near Laghaki, near the mouth of the Haftadārān Valley.

Description: An isolated mass of rock with some ruins on top.

Fieldwork: 1885 Maitland, ABC—topographical survey.

Source: Maitland 1888b: 17—mention.

873. QAL'A-I PANJA
See also 236 DARGAH-I QAL'A-I PANJA.

Original: Lat. 37° 00' N, long. 72° 34' E. Map 39.
Revised: 37.00382716 N, 72.57989275 E /
37° 00' 13.77776340 N, 72° 34' 47.61391404 E.
Badakhshān Province. On the south bank of the Panja River in Wākhān.

Description: Remains of two 'Siāhpush Kāfir' fortresses on adjacent hills, with more ruins and cemeteries in the vicinity. The main fortress has high walls and towers constructed of slate bonded with clay.

Fieldwork: 1989–99—Olufsen, Danish Army—survey.

Sources:
1. Olufsen 1904: 94—brief description.
2. Gazetteer 1972: I. 91—mention.
3. Mock 2011—discusses shrines at the fort and in the vicinity.

874. QAL'A-I PESAR
Or QAL'A-I BACHA.
See also 841 QAL'A-I DUKHTAR.

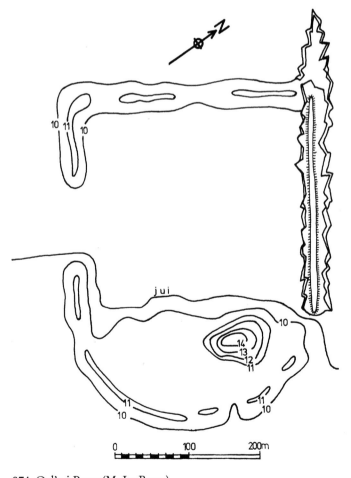

874 Qal'a-i Pesar (M. Le Berre).

Original: Lat. 33° 17–28' N, long. 62° 10–16' E. Map 70.
Revised: 33.28459172 N, 62.21502116 E /
33° 17' 04.53020352 N, 62° 12' 54.07616484 E.
Farāh Province. On the north bank of the Shindand River, 3 km south-east of Shindand on the road to Farāh.

Dates: Indo-Parthian, 1st–4th cent.; some Islamic sherds (ceramic).

Description: Vast enclosure (c.450 × 350 m) oriented north-west/south-east, of square plan in the north-west part and closed by a half-oval in the south-east, surrounded by a ditch. The north-east wall is built on a rocky ridge; only a few fragments (large mud bricks) remain of the other walls, mostly ruined. The south-east interior part of the enclosure is constructed on a rocky protrusion and partly occupied by a cemetery. There also the highest point in the enclosure (c.14 m) is located, formed by a tumulus whose southern base presents a vault fitted with very large mud-bricks. The north-west interior part is entirely under cultivation. A *jūi* crosses the enclosure. The exterior walls are also occupied by tombs.

Collection: National Museum/AIA—sherds.

Fieldwork:
1. 1952 Le Berre and Gardin, DAFA—survey.
2. 1956 Ramachandran and Sharma, ASI—reconnaissance.
3. 1974 Swiny, BIAS—survey.
4. 1968–78 Kruglikova, Af/Sov. Mission—survey.

Sources:
1. M. Le Berre: unpublished 1952 report, DAFA archives.
2. Yate 1900: 15–16—brief description.
3. Ramachandran and Sharma 1956: I. 16–17—brief description.
4. Gaibov et al. 2010: 112—fortress no longer standing by 1970.

875. QAL'A-I QAISĀR
Or QAL'A-I KAISĀR or KHISĀR or JAM QAL'A. Including BŪTGĀH and FAKHRĀBĀD.

Original: Lat. 33° 07' N, long. 64° 08' E. Map 73.
Revised: 33.1208357 N, 64.13529931 E / 33° 07' 15.00850956 N, 64° 08' 07.07752392 E.
Ghūr Province. 33 km north-east of Parjuman and 50 km south-west of Taiwāra.

Date: Ghurid, 12th–13th cent. (architectural).

Description: A large, well-preserved stone fortress in a high position guarding the route. It consists of an inner and outer enclosure surrounded by walls 4 m thick and round and hexagonal towers up to 8 m high. There is a main entrance defended by two towers to the north. Inside, the walls have decorative bands of impressed triangles in yellow plaster, c.20 cm wide. In the western enclosure are the remains of a mosque. The fortress is said by local tradition to have been begun by Alā ud-Dīn and completed by Ghiyās ud-Dīn.

'Two hours march' to the south are many more ruins and fortifications known as Fakhrābād, where some gold and silver coins were reported to have been found in the early 19th century. Nearby is a very small lake with some ruins known as Būtgāh on an island in the middle.

Fieldwork:
1. 1885 Imam Sharif, ABC—topographical survey.
2. 1946 Kohzad, HSA—survey.

Sources:
1. Ferrier 1857: 250–1—brief description.
2. Holdich 1887: 30—mention.
3. Imam Sharif 1891b: 217—mention.
4. Naïmi 1949: 15–17—brief description.
5. Kohzad 1951–4, 9/2: 5–9—very detailed description of the fortress and assessment of its strategic importance.
6. M. N. Kohzad 1959: 7—mention.
7. Klimburg 1960: 49—photo and brief description.
8. *Kabul Times* 1970: 197—mention.
9. Gazetteer 1975: III. 183–4—brief description.
10. Fischer 1978a: 335—mention and photos.
11. Ball 1982: 26—brief description in the context of Ghurid fortifications.
12. Wannell 2002: 236–8—brief description.
13. Ball 2008: 258–9.

QAL'A-I QAZI. See 2208 QAL'A-I QAZI in Supplement.

QAL'A-I QUDUQ. See 333 GALA QUDUQ.

QAL'A-I RAJPUT. See 1185 TEPE SKANDAR.

876. QAL'A-I RĀMRŪD

Lat. 30° 17' N, long. 61° 18' E approximately. Map 94.
Nīmrūz Province. 6 km south of the Rūd-i Bīyābān sites, 3 km east of the Iranian border and 17 km west of Gina.

Date: Sasanian, 3rd–7th cent. (ceramic).

Description: A mound 75 × 60 m in area and 7 m in height. On top are the remains of a square building. To the south are many more mounds and ruined towers that were unvisited.

Fieldwork: 1951 Fairservis, AMNH—survey.

Source: Fairservis 1961: 67—brief description (Site RB 34).

877. QAL'A-I RUSTAM
See also 265 DASHT-I NĀWAR.

Original: Lat. 33° 29' N, long. 67° 44' E. Maps 78, 79.
Revised: 33.48239587 N, 67.73667284 E /
33° 28' 56.62514100 N, 67° 44' 12.02221716 E.
Ghazni Province. 89 km west of Ghazni at the southwestern edge of the Dasht-i Nāwar.

Description: An isolated hill entirely surrounded by an immense fortification wall. On the south slope of the hill are the remains of stone fortifications in a vague triangle, measuring *c.*300 m each side. To the north, on the crest of the hill, is a second large stone fort.

Source: Fussman 1974c: 5–6—brief description.

878. QAL'A-I SA'ĀDAT

Original: Lat. 32° 03' N, long. 64° 27' E. Map 87.
Revised: 32.04967285 N, 64.44584059 E /
32° 02' 58.82227692 N, 64° 26' 45.02611932 E.
Helmand Province. 29 km north-west of Girishk and 32 km south-west of Nauzad.

Description: An old ruined fort surrounded by a ditch and secondary wall. The walls are *c.*8 m high and 3–3.50 m thick at the base, and have polygonal salients and corner towers.

Source: Gazetteer 1973: I. 144–5—description.

QAL'A-I SAM. See 1046 SHAHR-I KUHNA, Farāh.

QAL'A-I SANGAK. See 517 KALU.

879. QAL'A-I SANGĪ
Or JAM QAL'A.

Lat. 33° 10' N, long. 64° 03' E. Map 73.
Ghūr Province. 8 km north-west of Qal'a-i Qaisār, between Taiwāra and Parjuman.

Date: Ghurid, 12th–13th cent.

Description: Remains of a fortress on top of a hill. It is built of large, roughly cut stones without mortar. There was once an aqueduct leading into an immense central cistern.

Sources:
1. Ferrier 1857: 251—brief description.
2. *Kabul Times* 1970: 197—mentions the date.
3. Ball 1982: 26—mention.

QAL'A-I SAR-I SANG. See 398 GURGURAWA.

SARKARI. See 2209 QAL'A-I SARKARI in Supplement.

880. QAL'A-I SHĀHI

Original: Lat. 34° 38' N, long. 70° 35' E. Map 67.
Revised: 34.64955543 N, 70.58248021 E /
34° 38' 58.39956060 N, 70° 34' 56.92875204 E.
Kunār Province. In the Darra-i Nūr, c.10 km upstream from its junction with the Darra-i Kunār.

Dates: Kushan, 1st–3rd cent. (numismatic, stylistic); Hindu Shahi, 10th cent. (numismatic).

Description: Remains of a stupa and monastery. A stucco Buddha head was found here, as well as Kushan, Hindu Shahi, and Islamic coins, and some stone axes.

Fieldwork: 1959 Fischer, DAAD—survey.

Sources:
1. Fischer 1960: 9—mention.
2. Fischer 1969: 358—brief summary.

SIĀH BŪMAK. See **2210 QAL'A-I SIĀH BŪMAK** in Supplement.

881. QAL'A-I SIRAK
See also 700 MALĀKHĀN.

Original: Lat. 30° 27' N, long. 63° 22' E. Map 98.
Revised: 30.45853036 N, 63.36239907 E /
30° 27' 30.70930032 N, 63° 21' 44.63664012 E.
Helmand Province. In the Kūh-i Khān Nashin region, on a bend on the north bank of the Helmand, 4 km south-west of the modern village of Malākhān.

Date: Sasanian, 3rd–7th cent. (ceramic); Timurid, 15th–16th cent. (architectural).

Description: A large complex pre-Islamic site, heavily disturbed. Amongst the surface finds was an inscription in an unidentified script.

Across the river, on the south side, is cemetery containing several plain mausolea of probable 15th-century date. Ferrier hid in one of these mausolea trying to escape Baluch marauders. There is also a large ruined fort.

Fieldwork:
1. 1903–5 Tate, SAC—survey.
2. 1971–4 Trousdale, Smithsonian Institution—survey.

Sources:
1. Additional note on remains across river by W. Trousdale.
2. Ferrier 1857: 407–8—mention.
3. Tate 1909: 64—brief description (as Malākhān).
4. Trousdale 1976a: 59—mention.

882. QAL'A-I SULTĀN, GHŪR

Lat. 33° 42' N, long. 63° 53' E. Map 54.
Ghūr Province. 3 km east of Deh Titān on the slopes of the Kūh-i Sultān, near Tūlak on the Shahrak-Adraskan road.

Date: Ghurid, 12th–13th cent. (architectural).

Description: Remains of a fort associated with Qal'a-i Zārmurgh.

Source: M. N. Kohzad 1959: 7—mention.

QAL'A-I SULTĀN, Helmand. See **608 KHWĀJA SULTĀN.**

883. QAL'A-I SURKH, NĪMRŪZ
Or SOHREN KALAT.

Original: Lat. 30° 56' N, long. 62° 12' E. Map 92.
Revised: 30.93627561 N, 62.19821196 E /
30° 56' 10.59220644 N, 62° 11' 53.56305528 E.
Nīmrūz Province. 6 km east of Qal'a-i Nau, 8 km southeast of Zīyārat-i Amīrān Sāhib.

Date: Pre-Islamic (indeterminate); early Islamic, 8th–13th cent; Timurid 15th–16th cent. (architectural).

Description: A large area of pre-Islamic fortification walls—now only long mounds—and an Islamic fortress. The fortress is c.35 m square and has four corner towers and four salients, with an entrance on the east side. The interior consists of a courtyard surrounded by two storeys of rooms. The silt level now reaches the second storey of the building.

The fortress is 15th century, Timurid, but within a broad sector of earlier date, as described. The qal'a itself is actually in a quite isolated position, and probably commanded one of the main routes from the Sistan Basin up to the Dasht-i Margo.

Fieldwork:
1. 1903–5 Tate, SAC—survey.
2. 1936 Hackin and Meunié, DAFA—survey.
3. 1965–70 Fischer, Bonn University—survey.
4. 1974 Trousdale, Smithsonian Institution—survey.

Sources:
1. Additional information supplied by W. Trousdale.
2. Tate 1910: 239—brief description and photo of the fort.
3. Fischer 1971b: 43–4—photo and brief description (Sites 7 and 8).
4. Fischer 1973c: 148—mention.

884. QAL'A-I SURKH, PARWĀN

Lat. 35° 03' N, long. 60° 10' E. Map 64.
Parwān Province. To the north of Chārikār, to the east of the main road.

Date: Kushan-Hunnic, 1st–6th cent. (architectural).

Description: A small abandoned fort built on the remains of an ancient monastery. A circular mound in front is probably the remains of a stupa.

Fieldwork: 1923 Foucher, DAFA—survey.

Sources:
1. Foucher 1942–7: 143 — brief description.
2. Fussman, Murad, and Ollivier 2008: 134–5 — brief discussion.

885. QAL'A-I SURKH, SAMANGĀN

Lat. 35° 32' N, long. 67° 58' E. Map 48.
Samangān Province. Near Dūāb-i Shāh, *c.*6 km east of Pā-īn Tangi on the road from Dūāb-i Shāh to Dūāb-i Mīkhzarin.

Description: Several almost inaccessible caves cut into the cliff face. Some have walls built across the openings, and contained human and animal remains.

Fieldwork: 1924 Godard and Hackin, DAFA — survey.

Source: Foucher 1942–7: 122–3 — brief description and photo.

886. QAL'A-I SURKHAT

Original: Lat. 32° 07' N, long. 64° 20' E. Map 87.
Revised: 32.10722944 N, 64.36988357 E /
32° 06' 26.02599624 N, 64° 22' 11.58084804 E.
Helmand Province. 4 km west of Qal'a-i Sa'ādat, in the area north-west of Girishk towards Pusht-i Rūd.

Description: A mound with the remains of a small fort on top.

Source: Maitland 1879 — mention.

887. QAL'A-I SUSAN

Lat. 34° 55' N, long. 68° 18' E. Maps 48, 49, 59.
Parwān Province. At the eastern foot of the Shībar Pass in the Ghūrband Valley, 5 km east of Tang-i Taidukal.

Description: A series of roughly cut artificial caves.

Fieldwork: 1956 Ramachandran and Sharma, ASI — reconnaissance.

Source: Ramachandran and Sharma 1956: I. 29 — mention.

QAL'A-I SUSANAK. See 894 QAL'A-I ZARIN.

888. QAL'A-I TAPAQI

Original: Lat. 30° 16' N, long. 61° 36' E. Map 94.
Revised: 30.26243524 N, 61.60798745 E /
30° 15' 44.76686616 N, 61° 36' 28.75483512 E.
Nīmrūz Province. On the north side of the Rūd-I Bīyābān 26 km west of Chahar Burjak on the route to Tarākūn.

Description: Some ruins.

Fieldwork: 1885 Merk, ABC — topographical survey.

Source: Merk 1888: 26 — mention.

QAL'A-I TUNISH BEG. See 2211 QAL'A-I TUNISH BEG in Supplement.

QAL'A-I UNDI. See 962 SABZ QAL'A.

889. QAL'A-I WĀBU

Original: Lat. 31° 24' N, long. 62° 37' E. Map 85.
Revised: 31.40695578 N, 62.60984539 E /
31° 24' 25.04081448 N, 62° 36' 35.44339716 E.
Farāh Province. 21 km south-west of the town of Khāsh Rūd, just south of the Pul-i Ghurghuri across the Khāsh Rūd.

Dates: Sasanian, 3rd–7th cent. (architectural, ceramic); early Islamic, 8th–13th cent. (ceramic).

Description: An area of ancient remains dominated by a large citadel. The citadel has massive mud-brick walls and three-quarter bastions, with decorative façades of arrow-shaped slits and pointed and geometric blind arches. The interior contains several two-storey halls roofed by elliptical vaults. The citadel is probably pre-Islamic with later Islamic reuse.

To the south is a long line of square watch towers, many containing pre-Islamic pottery. One tower has a domed roof and stepped 'Sasanian' squinches.

Fieldwork: 1968 and 1969 Fischer, Bonn University — survey.

Sources:
1. Fischer 1969–70: 95 — mention and photos.
2. Fischer 1970a — photos.
3. Fischer 1971b: 43–4 and 47 — photos and summary description.
4. Fischer 1972 — compares the stepped squinches to others in Iran.
5. Fischer 1973d — brief report on the survey.
6. Fischer et al. 1974–6: 32 — mention.

890. QAL'A-I WALI
See also 541 KAURMACH.

Original: Lat. 35° 46' N, long. 63° 46' E. Map 44.
Revised: 35.78641477 N, 63.72404105 E /
35° 47' 11.09316588 N, 63° 43' 26.54776272 E.
Bādghīs Province. 43.5 km east of Bālā Murghāb, at the junction of the Shur Aghiz and Qarawāl Khāna Valleys.

Description: A ruined fort surrounded by mounds with baked brick remains. The fort consists of outer mud walls *c.*100 × 80 m enclosing an inner fort, *c.*35 m square, and a baked brick two-storey circular tower. The site can possibly be identified with ancient Qaisar.

Fieldwork: 1885–6 Maitland, Peacocke, ABC — topographical surveys.

Sources:
1. Grodekoff 1880: 146—mention.
2. *Pioneer*, 3 July 1886—brief description.
3. Holdich 1887: 17—mention.
4. Peacocke 1887a: 237—mention.
5. Maitland and Drummond 1888: 97—mention.
6. Maitland 1888b: 143—brief description.
7. Yate 1888: 125–6—brief description.
8. Gazetteer 1975: III. 244—brief description.

891. QAL'A-I ZAFAR
Or ALTAN JALAB.

Lat. 37° 04' N, long. 70° 09' E. Map 38.
Badakhshān Province. In the Teshkān Valley *c.*40 km north of Kishm, on the road midway between Faizābād and Rustāq.

Description: Reports of extensive ruins of an ancient town and citadel, said to be the ancient capital of Badakhshān.

Source: Gazetteer 1972: I. 18 and 179—mention.

892. QAL'A-I ZĀL

Original: Lat. 36° 59' N, long. 68° 22' E. Map 30.
Revised: 36.98885979 N, 68.37031215 E /
36° 59' 19.89525300 N, 68° 22' 13.12375656 E.

Qundūz Province. On the left bank of the Qundūz river, west of the last houses of the Qal'a-i Zāl district: the site is on the edge of a north–south segment of the river, before its change of course towards the west in the direction of the Āmū Dāryā, only some 10 km away.

Dates: Kushan and Hunnic-Turk, 1st–9th cent.; Timurid, 15th–16th cent. (ceramic).

Description: Large fortified town, surrounded by a rampart 1800 m long (east–west, almost to the degree) and 900 m wide (north–south), flanked by towers spaced by 40 m: 44 towers on the long sides, 22 on the short sides. The south rampart is interrupted by a gate, between the 17th and the 18th tower from the south-east angle. On the interior, in the north-west angle of the enclosure, a square platform (360 × 360 m) rises 2 m above the level of the plain, marking the location of a high town, also fortified: 12 towers on each side, spaced by 30 m. Finally, in the same north-west angle, a rectangular citadel (200 m north–south × 100 m east–west) dominates the high town by 6 m; its north and west sides rise directly on the edge of the terrace which overlooks the Qundūz River, *c.*20 m below. (A) The low town lies on this terrace, without any general rise in elevation of the land; but it is occupied by scattered mounds (several reaching 3 m in height) and gullies, mainly in the western part, not yet affected by the extension of irrigated fields from Qal'a-i Zāl; five of these mounds have been surveyed, but systematic study of the relief remains to be done. The rampart appears to be constructed entirely of mud-bricks (length

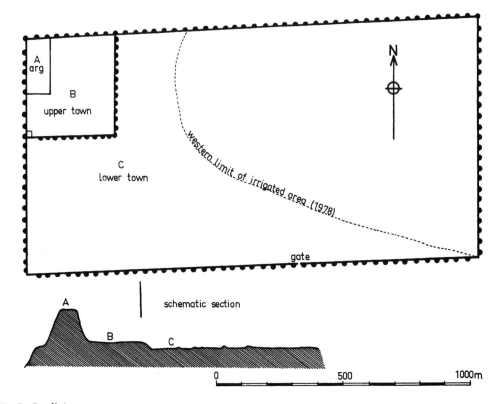

892 Qal'a-i Zāl (J.-C. Gardin).

41–2 cm), the walls as well as the towers; the latter are 12 to 15 m wide. (B) The rampart of the high town is constructed in the same way; thanks to the layers of bricks visible on the surface on the east and north walls, it is possible to measure approximately the width of these layers (c.4 m) and the projection of the towers (about 10 m). In the south-west angle, at the point where the south wall of the high town meets the west rampart, along the river, rises a bastion projecting on the north side, higher by one or two metres than the towers; a depression between the bastion and the citadel possibly marks an ancient way of access to the river, while a gate is apparent at the foot of the bastion in the wall of the high town, where the latter communicates with the low town. The surface of the bastion is strewn with burnt bricks, charcoal, and other debris; that of the high town is gullied (study to be done), but uniformly covered with sherds. (C) The surface of the citadel is quite flat, hardly undulating, and also covered with sherds, again mixed with debris (iron, clay, ashes, and charcoal). In the side gullies, it is possible to measure the large volumes of masonry in mud bricks which surround the construction, resting on the natural layers in place (pebbles and grey sand, covered by an artificial bed of red clay); in a cut of the south face, traces of a sloping area of worked (reworked?) calcareous stones. The tops of these structures, preserved in some 15 courses, sometimes exceed the level of the ground, the only vestiges of the walls which would have surrounded the citadel; dimensions of the bricks: thickness 13–14 cm, length either 36–7 cm or 39–40 cm.

Collection: National Museum/AIA—sherds.

Fieldwork: 1978 Gardin et al., CNRS—survey.

Sources:
1. Site information by J.-C. Gardin.
2. Maitland 1888b: 272—mention.
3. Barger and Wright 1941: 44—mention.
4. Le Berre 1965: 87–8—brief description.
5. Francfort 1976a: 151—brief description of the fortifications.
6. Gardin and Lyonnet 1978–9: pl. VI—no. 503.
7. Bernard and Francfort 1978a: 55—brief description.
8. Francfort 1979a: 31–6—examination of the general characteristics of Kushan military architecture.
9. Gardin 1982: 107—mention.
10. Lyonnet 1997: figs 46, 49, 68, 69—no. 503.
11. Gardin 1998: 86—no. 503.

893. QAL'A-I ZANGI
Or DARRA-I ZANG.

Lat. 35° 37' N, long. 65° 17' E approximately. Map 46. Faryāb Province. In the upper Darra-i Zang, c.6 km south of Qarya-i Darra-i Zang.

Description: A complex of artificial caves on the eastern side of the valley reported. It consists of a stone doorway opening into a tunnel lined with niches, associated with a brick, plaster lined cistern. Nearby are the remains of stone buildings. The site is locally said to be the capital of King Zangbar.

Sources:
1. Additional information by Jonathan L. Lee.
2. *Kabul Times* 1970: 189—mention.
3. Lee 1980—mention.

894. QAL'A-I ZARIN
Or QAL'A-I SUSANAK.

Original: Lat. 31° 06' N, long. 62° 05' E. Map 84.
Revised: 31.10047022 N, 62.08364082 E /
31° 06' 01.69280676 N, 62° 05' 01.10696784 E.
Nīmrūz Province. Just to the north-west of Qal'a-i Chigīnī.

Date: Late Sasanian-early Islamic, 5th–13th cent. (ceramic).

Description: A mound with mud-brick remains and a low rampart.

Fieldwork: 1965–70 Fischer, Bonn University—survey.

Sources:
1. Peacocke 1885a: 13—mention.
2. Peacocke 1887a: 27—mention.
3. Fischer 1970b: pls 23–4—photos.
4. Fischer 1973c: 144—map reference.
5. Fischer et al. 1974–6: 37—mention.

QAL'A-I ZĀRMURGH. See 974. SAKHĀR.

895. QAL'A-I ZINDAJĀN

Original: Lat. 34° 20' N, long. 61° 41'–61° 42' E. Map 51.
Revised: 34.34121147 N, 61.69426098 E /
34° 20' 28.36129704 N, 61° 41' 39.33952764 E.
Herat Province. 44 km west of this city and 23 km east of Ghūriyān.

Date: Early Islamic (ceramic).

Description: (A) Vast enclosure about 800 m per side of which only the south face and the southern ends of the east and west faces remain. The road from Ghūriyān to Zindajān crosses it. No trace of construction is visible on the interior, and there are no sherds. (B) Small undulating area situated between (A) and the village of Zindajān, 200 m south of the road. Most of it is occupied by a modern cemetery.

Fieldwork:
1. 1952 Le Berre and Gardin, DAFA—survey.
2. 1968–78 Kruglikova, Af/Sov. Mission—survey.

Sources:
1. M. Le Berre: unpublished 1952 report, DAFA archives.
2. Gaibov et al. 2010: 110—mention (Site K145—although it is not certain this is the same as Qal'a-i Zindajān).

896. QAL'A-I ZIRAU

Lat. 31° 45' N, long. 61° 20' E approximately. Map 83.
Nīmrūz Province. North of Chung-i Marghun in the area west of Lāsh Juwain.

Description: An old ruin.

Source: Tate 1910: 238—mention.

QAL'A-I ZUHAK. See 787 PĀ'ĪN MAZĀR.

897. QAL'A-I ZULKHAMAR

Lat. 35° 39' N, long. 66° 08' E. Map 47.
Juazjān Province. 5 km south-east of Qal'a-i Tak at the junction of two rivers, on the route from Sar-i Pul to Yakaulang.

Description: Some ruins on a hill overlooking the two rivers.

Fieldwork: 1886 Amir Khan and Shahzada Taimus, ABC—topographical survey.

Source: Amir Khan and Shahzada Taimus 1888c: 255—mention.

898. QAL'AT-I CHAUKAKAT

Original: Lat. 31° 09' N, long. 64° 12' E. Map 97.
Revised: 31.14709212 N, 64.19491162 E /
31° 08' 49.53162624 N, 64° 11' 41.68183272 E.
Helmand Province. On the left bank of the Helmand 2.5 km north of Darwīshān.

Date: Sasanian, 3rd–7th cent. (ceramic).

Description: A ruin.

Fieldwork: 1966 Hammond, Cambridge University—survey.

Sources:
1. Bellew 1874: 183—mention.
2. Hammond 1970: 450—lists the site (no. 35) and describes the pottery types and general survey results.
3. Gazetteer 1973: II. 107—mention.

899. QAL'AT-I GHILZAI

Original: Lat. 32° 07' N, long. 66° 54' E. Map 91.
Revised: 32.11160978 N, 66.90815985 E /
32° 06' 41.79521052 N, 66° 54' 29.37547008 E.
Zābul Province. On the main Kandahār-Kābul road, 138 km north of Kandahār.

Description: A mud and stone fort on a natural hill c.70 m above the plain. It has round towers and walls 2.5–3 m thick pierced with a double line of loopholes. At the southern end of the fort is a large artificial mound, c.30 m high.

Sources:
1. Griffith 1879—good description of the fort.
2. Fischer 1967a: 157—mention.
3. Fischer 1969: 338—mention.

900. QAL'AT-I GIRDI

Original: Lat. 30° 16' N, long. 61° 19' E. Map 94.
Revised: 30.2652565 N, 61.30858822 E / 30° 15' 54.92339244 N, 61° 18' 30.91759272 E.
Nīmrūz Province. On the Dasht-i Tuba, 6 km south of the Rūd-i Bīyabān and 5 km east of the Iranian border.

Dates: Parthian and Indo-Parthian, 2nd cent. BC–AD 3rd cent.; Sasanian, 3rd–7th cent. (ceramic).

Description: A mound c.20 m diam. With the ruins of a 20 m high rectangular building c.100 m to the west. There is another small mound, 300 m south of the building.

Fieldwork: 1951 Fairservis, AMNH—survey.

Source: Fairservis 1961: 67—brief description (Site 103).

901. QAL'AT-I MAHMŪD

Original: Lat. 31° 08' N, long. 64° 12' E. Map 97.
Revised: 31.14339356 N, 64.18734724 E /
31° 08' 36.21679908 N, 64° 11' 14.45006760 E.
Helmand Province. On the left bank of the Helmand in the Hazārjuft area north of Darwīshān.

Dates: Late Sasanian, 5th–7th cent. AD; Ghaznavid, 11th–12th cent. (ceramic).

Description: The remains of a large *rabāt*.

Fieldwork: 1966 Hammond, Cambridge University—survey.

Sources:
1. Bellew 1874: 183—mention.
2. Hammond 1970: 449—lists the site (no. 13) and describes the pottery types and general survey results.
3. Gazetteer 1973: I. 107—mention.

902. QANĀ-I BĀBĀ KAMĀL
Or GAZA BARBRA KAMĀL or QARYĀ-YI BĀBĀ KAMĀL.

Lat. 33° 18' N, long. 67° 37' E. Maps 77, 78, 79.
Ghazni Province. In the Ulaitu Valley several km north of Tepe Zaitūn on the Jāghūrī-Dasht-i Nawār road.

Dates: Early Sasanian, 5th–6th cent.; Ghaznavid, 11th–12th cent. (stylistic).

Description: A group of artificial caves. The main cave is a *vihara* with carved lotus and lozenge decoration, with a later Islamic mihrab inserted framed by a polylobate arch.

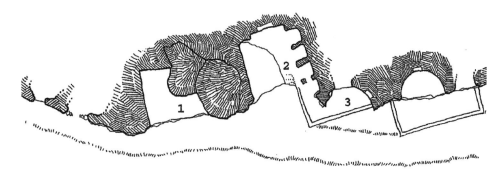

902 Qanā-i Bābā Kamāl (after Verardi and Paparatti 2004).

Fieldwork: 1976 Taddei and Verardi, IsMEO—survey.

Sources:
1. Taddei 1976: 601—brief description.
2. Verardi 1977a: 150—brief description.
3. Verardi and Paparatti 2004: 70–3—detailed description with drawings and photos.

QANDAHĀR. See **522 KANDAHĀR.**

QANDAHĀRIHĀ. See **791 PAKHRAK.**

903. QAND-I PĪR

Original: Lat. 34° 57' N, long. 69° 35' E approximately. Map 65.
Revised: 34.95726305 N, 69.58810069 E / 34° 57' 26.14699152 N, 69° 35' 17.16247176 E.
Kāpīsā Province. On the southern edge of the Nijrau plain, west of Asābād.

Date: Kushan, 1st–3rd cent. (ceramic).

Description: A fairly large tepe (*c.*10 m high) with considerable horizontal expanse. The site was covered in plain red Kushan pottery; there was no evidence of earlier occupation.

Fieldwork: 1976 Kohl—survey.

Source: Site information by P. L. Kohl.

904. QANJUGHA, QARĀWAL
Includes TEPE BURHAN BAI.

Original: Lat. 37° 12'–37° 13' N, long. 68° 47'–68° 51' E. Map 31.
Revised:
37.1997224 N, 68.86534142 E / 37° 11' 59.00063244 N, 68° 51' 55.22909976 E (A).
37.20217737 N, 68.84803461 E / 37° 12' 07.83853344 N, 68° 50' 52.92459384 E (B).
37.21708976 N, 68.79970393 E / 37° 13' 01.52314860 N, 68° 47' 58.93415052 E (C).
37.22048892 N, 68.78701651 E / 37° 13' 13.76012064 N, 68° 47' 13.25943744 E (D).
Qundūz Province. West-north-west of Imām Sāhib, by the road that ends on the edge of an old meander of the Āmū Dāryā, in the region of Qarāwal. (A) 3 km from the last houses of Imām Sāhib to the north-west, the first tepe rises on the southern edge of the road, not far from a small road which leads to the village of Qanjugha-i Uzbekiya, to the south. (B) The second is located 1 km further west, 400 m from the road, near the last houses of the same village towards the north-west. (C) By the road from Qarāwal, the next tepe is located 4.5 km further on the north side of the road, recognizable by the tombs which cover it; (D) the last tepe is located on the same side of the Qarāwal road, 300 m west-north-west of the previous one, on the edge of the 'jangāl' which extends along the left bank of the Āmū Dāryā.

Dates: Kushan and Hunnic-Turk, 1st–9th cent.; pre-Mongol Islamic, 10th–13th cent. (ceramic).

Description: (A) Oblong north–south mound (30 × 15 m), surrounded by crops which reduce it from year to year; flat top (4 m). (B) Tepe Burhan Bai: a square hillock (30 × 30 m), oriented north-west/south-east, flat top (6 m); 20 m to the south-east, small round mound (diam. 10 m) still 4 m high. The crops are also eating into the last vestiges of a site whose contours are indicated by a low platform emerging from the irrigated crops: irregular shape, 80 × 50 m. (C) Round hillock, diam. 10 m, height 1 m. (D) Mound in the shape of an isosceles triangle oriented north–south (base 30 m, height 50 m); highest point at the south-east angle (10 m), gentle slope towards the north-west. Around the site, *lalmī* crops on very saline land.

Collection: National Museum/AIA—sherds.

Fieldwork: 1977 Gardin et al., CNRS—survey.

Sources:
1. Site information by J.-C. Gardin.
2. Gardin and Lyonnet 1978–9: pl. V—nos. 133–6.
3. Lyonnet 1997: figs 49, 68, 69—nos. 133–6.
4. Gardin 1998: 63—nos. 133–6.

905. QAQ

Lat. 37° 11' N, long. 65° 30' E. Map 24.
Faryāb Province. 7 km south of the Soviet border, on the route from Andkhūī to Khāmiyāb via Qara Tepe, 15 km south-west of Qara Tepe.

Date: Neolithic, 7th–6th mill. BC (lithic).

Description: A surface site surrounding a well.

Fieldwork: 1969 Vinogradov, Af/Sov. Mission—survey.

Source: Vinogradov 1979: 23—drawing of the material (Site 54).

906. QAQ-I NAZAR AGHA

Lat. 37° 05' N, long. 65° 28' E. Map 24.
Faryāb Province. 17–18 km north-east of Chār Bāgh on the route from Andkhūī to Khāmiyāb via Jar Quduq.

Date: Neolithic, 7th–6th mill. BC (lithic).

Description: An extensive surface site stretching for c.1 km around a well.

Fieldwork: 1969 Vinogradov, Af/Sov. Mission—survey.

Source: Vinogradov 1979: 22–5—description with drawings of the site and material (Site 53).

907. QARABĀGH, GHAZNI
See also 470 JANGALAK-I QARABĀGH.

Original: Lat. 33° 12' N, long. 68° 07' E. Maps 78, 80.
Revised: 33.24762483 N, 68.11499749 E /
33° 14' 51.44939304 N, 68° 06' 53.99097336 E.
Ghazni Province. 55 km south-west of Ghazni on the road to Kandahār.

Date: Kushan-Sasanian, 1st–7th cent. (ceramic).

Description: A large mound and several smaller mounds to the north-east of the bazaar. A reworked stone doorpost in Gandharan style was found on the mound.

Fieldwork: 1966 Fischer, DAAD—survey.

Sources:
1. Masson 1842: II. 218—mention.
2. Fischer 1967a: 157—mention.
3. Fischer 1969: 339—mention.
4. Verardi 1977a: 147—mention.
5. Verardi and Paparatti 2004: 92—mention the doorpost.
6. Thomas 2015: 519—additional information from satellite imagery.

908. QARABĀGH, GULRĀN

Original: Lat. 34° 56' N, long. 61° 47' E. Map 42.
Revised: 34.93232308 N, 61.78118142 E /
34° 55' 56.36309916 N, 61° 46' 52.25310768 E.
Herat Province. 26 km south-east of Gulrān.

Date: Sasanian, 5th–7th cent.; Timurid, 14th–15th cent. (ceramic).

Description: Remains of a fort with a double line of ramparts standing on a high mound. The mound is c.17 m high and is surrounded by a ditch. An Arabic inscription was found on top of the mound.

Fieldwork:
1. 1884 Maitland, ABC—topographical survey.
2. 1968–78 Kruglikova, Af/Sov. Mission—survey.

Sources:
1. *Pioneer*, 7 Jan. 1885: 3—brief description.
2. A. C. Yate 1887: 178—brief description.
3. Maitland 1888a: 159—brief description.
4. Gazetteer 1975: III. 247—mention.
5. Gaibov et al. 2010: 114—mention ceramic dates (Site K155).

909. QARA BAI

Includes DIWĀNA GUR and NAQSHARA TEPE or MADANIYAT TEPE.
Original: Lat. 36° 45' N, long. 69° 32'–69° 33' E. Map 36.
Revised:
36.74657343 N, 69.54882571 E / 36° 44' 47.66434260 N, 69° 32' 55.77254268 E (A).
36.74475039 N, 69.54017624 E / 36° 44' 41.10141336 N, 69° 32' 24.63446112 E (B).
36.7520991 N, 69.54062671 E / 36° 45' 07.55676576 N, 09° 32' 26.25616284 E (B).
36.74354228 N, 69.53624283 E / 36° 44' 36.75219036 N, 69° 32' 10.47417972 E (C).
36.74259989 N, 69.53776869 E / 36° 44' 33.35960940 N, 69° 32' 15.96728724 E (D).
Takhār Province. In the west part of the village of Qara Bai which extends along the Rūd-i Shārawān, 1.5 km north of the central crossroads of Tāluqān; tepes A and B are on the right bank of the Rūd-i Shārawān, tepes C and D on the left bank, just next to the water.

Dates: Hellenistic, 3rd–1st cent. BC (B); Kushan and Hunnic-Turk, 1st–9th cent.; pre-Mongol Islamic, 10th–13th cent. (ceramic).

Description: (A) Naqshara Tepe (old name) or Madaniyat Tepe: high oblong east–west mound (100 × 50 m), with steep flanks, cut into by the surrounding crops; flat top (5 m), dominated by two hillocks, to the east (6 m) and to the west (10 m). In the cuts visible at the base of the tepe, alternating layers of ashes and earth in a height of 2 m, with bone debris and jars. (B) 700 m west of A, a small oblong mound (20 × 15 m), low (3.5 m), eaten into by the crops, with the same burnt layers as A; another similar mound (30 × 15 × 2.5 m) 750 m further north. (C) Diwāna Ghur: high mound rounded at the base (50 × 50 m), steep slopes up to the flat top (10 m); the north face, almost vertical, is eroded by a canal coming from the nearby Rūd-i Shārawān; thick burnt layers at the base of the tepe, like A and B, with jars in place. (D) Some 100 m to the south-east, low platform (2 m), east–west and rectangular (70 × 50 m), occupied by a modern cemetery; the little canals which surround it are filled with sherds.

Collection: National Museum/AIA—sherds.

Fieldwork: 1977 Gardin et al., CNRS—survey.

Sources:
1. Site information by J.-C. Gardin.
2. Gardin and Lyonnet 1978–9: pl. IX—nos. 212, 218–21.
3. Lyonnet 1997: figs 39, 49, 68, 69—nos. 212, 218–21.
4. Gardin 1998: 69—nos. 212, 218–21.

QARA-I GHŪRI. See **2212 QARA-I GHŪRI** in Supplement.

910. QARA KUL

Lat. 37° 07' N, long. 66° 05' E. Map 24.
Jauzjān Province. On the southern edge of the dunes north of Āqcha, 5 km north-west of Sararwal and 8 km north-east of Sayyidābād, 6 km north of the village of Qara Kul.

Date: Neolithic, 7th–6th mill. BC (lithic).

Description: A surface scatter with stone tools scattered across a wide area.

Fieldwork: 1976 Vinogradov, Af/Sov. Mission—survey.

Source: Vinogradov 1979: 41–2—description of the site and drawings of the material (Site 424).

911. QARA KŪTARMA, QIZIL QAL'A

Original: Lat. 37° 09'–37° 10' N, long. 68° 37'–68° 42' E. Map 31.
Revised:
37.1601798 N, 68.65435632 E / 37° 09' 36.64729692 N, 68° 39' 15.68276748 E (C).
37.16576109 N, 68.66098207 E / 37° 09' 56.73992904 N, 68° 39' 39.53543868 E (C).
37.16835127 N, 68.63993882 E / 37° 10' 06.06457272 N, 68° 38' 23.77976568 E (B).
Qundūz Province. On the outskirts of Qizil Qal'a, between the fork in the road from Qundūz towards Imām Sāhib (at Qara Kūtarma) and the turn to Qizil Qal'a, about 3 km further. Several tepes are located along this road, mainly on the south side, near the modern canal which, coming from Shāhrawān across the plain of Imām Sāhib, ends in this region. The old canal more or less follows the same course: its last mounds are visible west of the end of the modern canal, in the direction of Qazaq on the Āmū Dāryā. The importance of the tepes in this region lies in establishing, in

relation to the vestiges of irrigation, the western edges of settlement in the plain of Imām Sāhib during the main periods of its development. (A) In this perspective, the most important tepe is the westernmost, also the largest: 2.5 km south-east of Qizil Qal'a on the north side of the road that turns in this place towards the east, in the direction of the Imām Sāhib-Qundūz fork. (B) A similar tepe 2.5 km further east dominates the southern edge of the road; (C) the other mounds are smaller and lie in an arc between the road and the village of Qara Kūtarma, to the north and east of the latter.

Dates: Kushan, 1st–4th cent.; Timurid, 15th–16th cent. (ceramic).

Description: (A) Oblong east–west (100 × 30 m) mound, on the edge of a cliff overlooking an old meander of the Āmū Dāryā; the highest part is in the western part of the mound (2 m). Visible from there, in the arid steppe that extends towards the west, the mounds of two old canals which continue in the same direction, 800 m and 300 m from the site; the higher of the two (at 800 m, height reaching 2 m) was recently re-excavated (1977) in the continuation of the modern canal. Found on the surface, between the two canals, are sherds similar to those of the above tepe. (B) Rectangular east–west (100 × 40 m) platform, flat top (1 m), slightly raised in the north-west and south-east angles (1.5 m); many fragments of fired bricks and sometimes whole bricks (30 × 30 cm), reused in the nearby houses. (C) The other nearby mounds of Qara Kūtarma have the same oblong or rectangular form, all oriented east–west, variable in size (between 60 × 30 and 15 × 10 m), height between 0.5 and 1.5 m.

Collection: National Museum/AIA—sherds.

Fieldwork: 1977 Gardin et al., CNRS—survey.

Sources:
1. Site information by J.-C. Gardin.
2. Gardin and Lyonnet 1978–9: pl. V –nos. 121–8.
3. Lyonnet 1997: fig. 49—nos. 121–8.
4. Gardin 1998: 63 –nos. 121–8.

QARA PARCHAU. See **799 PARCHAU**.

QARA RABĀT, Ardawān. See **2214 QARA RABĀT, Ardawān** in Supplement.

QARA RABĀT, Hazrat-i Bābā. See **2213 QARA RABĀT, Hazrāt-i Bābā** in Supplement.

912. QARA TEPE, JAUZJĀN

Lat. 37° 15' N, long. 65° 38' E. Map 24.
Jauzjān Province. 13 km south-west of Jar Quduq on the route to Andkhūī, c.30 km south of Khāmiyāb.

Date: Neolithic, 7th–6th mill BC (lithic).

Description: A rocky mound *c.*60 m high, rising steeply above the plain, with a surface scatter of stone tools on top.

Fieldwork: 1969 Vinogradov, Af/Sov. Mission—survey.

Source: Vinogradov 1979: 25—description (Site 55).

QARA TEPE, Khulm. See 141 BURAT TEPE.

913. QARA TEPE, KŪCHI

Original: Lat. 36° 23' N, long. 69° 17' E. Map 37.
Revised: 36.38295962 N, 69.27888415 E /
36° 22' 58.65463164 N, 69° 16' 43.98292668 E.
Takhār Province; 4 km west of Ishkamīsh, at the north-east outskirts of the village of Kūchi: the tepe corresponds to the mound of 5 m indicated on the 1:100,000 map near Kūchi.

Date: Islamic. (ceramic).

Description: Conical mound, diam. 60 m, height 10 m; flat circular top (diam. 20 m), with a funnel-shaped central depression which continues on the west face of the tepe down to the base. This is surrounded by a shallow gully. 100 m to the west, a modern cemetery.

Collection: National Museum/AIA—sherds.

Fieldwork: 1978 Gardin et al., CNRS—survey.

Sources:
1. Site information by J.-C. Gardin.
2. Gardin and Lyonnet 1978–9: pl. XI—no. 369.
3. Gardin 1998: 99—no. 369.

QARĀWAL. See 904 QANJUGHA.

914. QARĀWAL KHĀNA

Original: Lat. 35° 42' N, long. 63° 15' E approx. Map 44.
Revised: 35.68583775 N, 63.25015084 E /
35° 41' 09.01591080 N, 63° 15' 00.54300960 E.
Bādghīs Province. On the right bank of the Murghāb River at its confluence with the Qal'a-i Wali stream, about 30 km north-west of Bālā Murghāb and 22 km south-east of Māruchāq.

Description: Very extensive brick ruins, in the midst of which is the Zīyārat-i Shaikh Auliah.

Fieldwork: 1884–5 Maitland and Peacocke, ABC—topographical survey.

Sources:
1. Peacocke 1887a: 84—mention.
2. Maitland 1888a: 213—brief description.
3. Maitland and Drummond 1888: 86—mention.
4. Yate 1888: 122—mention.

QARĀWAL TEPE, QUNDŪZ. See 194 CHEHEL DUKHTARĀN, QUNDŪZ.

915. QARĀWAL TEPE, TĀSHQURGHĀN

Original: Lat. 36° 45' N, long. 67° 45' E. Map 29.
Revised: 36.75682233 N, 67.75667772 E /
36° 45' 24.56039700 N, 67° 45' 24.03980496 E.
Samangān Province. 9 km north-east of Tāshqurghān.

Dates: Kushano-Sasanian Hunnic, 4th–6th cent.; Samanid, 9th–10th cent.; Timurid, 15th–16th cent. (ceramic).

Description: A large mound *c.*500 × 250 m in area and 4 m in height, with remains of walls and towers on top and surrounded by smaller mounds.

Fieldwork:
1. 1886 Maitland, ABC—topographical survey.
2. 1969 Gouin, DAFA—survey.

Sources:
1. Gardin and Lyonnet, 1980 chronological study of pottery from DAFA unpublished surveys.
2. Maitland 1888b: 262—brief description.

916. QARĀYĪ

Lat. 36° 45' N, long. 64° 32' E approximately. Map 45.
Faryāb Province. To the south of Almar, west of Maimana, through a gorge called Dahān-i Darra.

Description: Local reports of a long, tunnel-like cave in the mountainside, *c.*100 m above the valley floor, where much archaeological material has been found. The tunnel opens out at the end into individual chambers, possibly containing paintings.

Source: Site information by Jonathan L. Lee.

917. QARLUQ
Including CHĪCHKA and MIN CHUKUR.

Original: Lat. 37° 04'–37° 07' N, long. 69° 19'–69° 22' E. Map 34.
Revised: 37.1326168 N, 69.36888696 E / 37° 07' 57.42047424 N, 69° 22' 07.99305492 E.
Qundūz Province. North-east of Archi, by the track which edges the southern branch of the Ārchī canal, at the base of the foothills of the Ambar Kūh, in the direction of Khwāja Ghar: traces of ancient occupation on the narrow bands of land squeezed between the canal to the west (edge of terrace) and the hills to the east, near the villages of Chīchka, Qarluq, and Min Chukur (4, 7, and 9 km from Archi, respectively).

Dates: Hellenistic, 3rd–1st cent. BC; pre-Mongol Islamic, 10th–13th cent. (ceramic).

Description: The sites are reduced here to undulating areas (less than 1 m in height), where only the sherds confirm that these are not, or not exclusively, natural. Neither the exact situation, nor a detailed description of each site is appropriate here; to be retained is the overall fact of the development of this zone of foothills in the Hellenistic period and the first centuries of Islam, thanks to the particularly skilful construction of irrigation canals.

Collection: National Museum/AIA—sherds.

Fieldwork: 1977 Gardin et al., CNRS—survey.

Sources:
1. Site information by J.-C. Gardin.
2. Gardin and Lyonnet 1978–9: pl. IV—nos. 4–6, 14–20.
3. Lyonnet 1997: fig. 39—nos. 4–6, 14–20.
4. Gardin 1998: 55—nos. 4–6, 14–20.

QARQĪN. See **2216 QARQĪN in Supplement.**

918. QARSHĪYAK

Original: Lat. 37° 02' N, long. 66° 48' E. Map 26.
Revised: 37.04658236 N, 66.81185326 E /
37° 02' 47.69650896 N, 66° 48' 42.67171800 E.
Balkh Province. 38 km north-west of Balkh, to the east of the road to Kilift.

Description: Several square miles of ruins, including gateways, towers, and a square building with several intact domes.

Fieldwork: 1886 Ata Muhammad, ABC—topographical survey.

Sources:
1. Yavorski 1885: 63–4—brief description.
2. Maitland 1888b: 274—mention.
3. Gazetteer 1979: IV. 315—mention.

QĀSH QAL'A. See **239 DARRA-I 'ALI.**

QARŪL TEPE. See **386 GŪGARI.**

QARYĀ-YI BĀBĀ KAMĀL. See **902 QANĀ-I BĀBĀ KAMĀL.**

QASR-I GUL ANDAM. See **9. BAIZA.**

QASR-I TULAK. See **2217 QASR-I TULAK in Supplement.**

919. QAURACHI

Original: Lat. 36° 48' N, long. 66° 41' E. Map 26.
Revised: 36.79965151 N, 66.69448586 E /
36° 47' 58.74545040 N, 66° 41' 40.14909960 E.

Balkh Province. 18 km south-east of Nimlik; about 300 m north of the road from Balkh, east of the village of Chahār Bulaq.

Description: Slightly convex platform, square in plan (130 × 130 m), height 12 m, surrounded by a ditch.

Fieldwork:
1. 1946 Wheeler, ASI—reconnaissance.
2. 1948 Le Berre, DAFA—survey.

Sources:
1. M. Le Berre: unpublished 1948 report, DAFA archives, tepe P. 43.
2. Shakur 1947: 68—mention.

920. QIPCHAQ TEPE

Original: Lat. 36° 49' N, long. 66° 31' E. Maps 25, 26.
Revised: 36.80744027 N, 66.52889134 E /
36° 48' 26.78495472 N, 66° 31' 44.00883660 E.
Jauzjān Province. 3 km south-east of Nimlik, south of the Balkh road, south-west of the village of Qipchak.

Description: Circular platform (diam. 140 m), height 12 m, dominated on the south by a small rounded mound (height 14.50 m). Three small tepes surround it on the south (remains of an enclosure?). In the north and the south-west, zones of late ruins.

Fieldwork: 1948 Le Berre, DAFA—survey.

Source: M. Le Berre: unpublished 1948 report, DAFA archives, tepe P. 29.

921. QISHLĀQ

Original: Lat. 34° 22' N, long. 69° 15' E. Map 62.
Revised: 34.36688168 N, 69.24198617 E /
34° 22' 00.77405772 N, 69° 14' 31.15022928 E.
Kābul Province. In the valley immediately to the south-west of Guldarra, above the villages of Gumbaza and Kūtgai.

Description: Remains of a diaper masonry wall climbing almost vertically up the side of a mountain.

Fieldwork: 1963–4 Fussman and Le Berre, DAFA—survey.

Source: Fussman and Le Berre 1976: 102—mention.

922. QISHLĀQ-I SUFLA

Original: Lat. 34° 25' N, long. 69° 13' E. Map 62.
Revised: 34.40384548 N, 69.21905448 E /
34° 24' 13.84371108 N, 69° 13' 08.59611612 E.
Kābul Province. On a spur of the mountain overlooking the right bank of the Lōgar River gorge, 4 km south of Saka, at the point where the river enters the gorge from the Mūsa-i Lōgar plain.

Date: ?Kushan, 1st–3rd cent. (architectural).

Description: Remains of a small much ruined fort, almost identical to Saka.

Fieldwork: 1963–4 Le Berre and Fussman, DAFA—survey.

Sources:
1. Carl 1959a: 13—mention.
2. Fussman and Le Berre 1976: 102—mention.

QIZIL KUCHA. See **959 RŪD-I SHĀHRAWĀN.**

QIZIL SAI. See **959 RŪD-I SHĀHRAWĀN.**

QIZIL QAL'A, Imām Sāhib. See **911 QARA KŪTARMA.**

QIZIL QAL'A, Rustāq. See **1235 YAKA TŪT.**

923. QIZIL QAL'A, SIĀH KHAWĀL

Original: Lat. 35° 07' N, long. 67° 08' E. Map 47.
Revised: 35.11354815 N, 67.12721598 E /
35° 06' 48.77333280 N, 67° 07' 37.97753916 E.
Bāmiyān Province. In the Darra-i Siāh Khawāl, just north of a lateral gorge from the south-east, on the route from Darra-i Sūf to Bāmiyān.

Description: Remains of a fort.

Fieldwork: 1886 Amir Khan, ABC—topographical survey.

Source: Amir Khan 1888: 168—mention.

924. QIZIL QAL'A TEPE

Original: Lat. 36° 49' N, long. 66° 42' E. Map 26.
Revised: 36.82395566 N, 66.70791549 E /
36° 49' 26.24038140 N, 66° 42' 28.49574708 E.
Balkh Province. 18 km east of Nimlik, 3 km north of the Balkh road, south of the village of Qizil Qal'a.

Description: Quadrangular mound (200 × 200 m), slightly sunken in the centre (height 12 m), dominated by a slightly higher mound in the south-west angle (height 14 m), surrounded by a ditch. Immediately to the south-east, a large enclosure of the same size, surrounded by walls, low (height 3 m).

Fieldwork: 1948 Le Berre, DAFA—survey.

Source: M. Le Berre: unpublished 1948 report, DAFA archives, tepe P. 45.

925. QIZIL SAI
Or TEPE NAU KALIN.

Original: Lat. 36° 26' N, long. 68° 54' E. Map 32.
Revised: 36.44476464 N, 68.89207432 E /
36° 26' 41.15268960 N, 68° 53' 31.46754084 E.
Qundūz Province. 7 km south of 'Aliābād on the road to Baghlān.

Date: Kushan, 1st–3rd cent. (ceramic).

Description: A small, steep-sided mound.

Fieldwork:
1. 1956 Ramachandran and Sharma, ASI—reconnaissance.
2. 1960 Hayashi and Sahara, Kyoto University—survey.

Sources:
1. Ramachandran and Sharma 1956: I. 24–5—mention.
2. Hayashi and Sahara 1962: 70—photo and description in Japanese.

QIZLA TEPE. See **54. ARCHI.**

926. QIZ QAL'A

Lat. 36° 00' N, long. 65° 37' E. Maps 24, 46.
Jauzjān Province. 35 km east of Darzāb, 2 km north of the route to Sar-i Pul.

Description: Remains of an old fort.

Source: Amir Khan and Shahzada Taimus 1888c: 249—mention.

927. QUCHI
Includes BUTA KASHAN and KUBA'I.

Original: Lat. 36° 43'–36° 45' N, long. 68° 57'–68° 59' E. Map 32.
Revised:
36.75850367 N, 68.92351025 E / 36° 45' 30.61322712 N, 68° 55' 24.63688812 E (A).
36.75240434 N, 68.93482934 E / 36° 45' 08.65563192 N, 68° 56' 05.38563408 E (B).
36.74469922 N, 68.95311496 E / 36° 44' 40.91720676 N, 68° 57' 11.21384412 E (C).
36.74767601 N, 68.94976462 E / 36° 44' 51.63361872 N, 68° 56' 59.15263632 E (C).
36.75209136 N, 68.94729347 E / 36° 45' 07.52887836 N, 68° 56' 50.25650964 E (C).
36.72659566 N, 68.97489889 E / 36° 43' 35.74436484 N, 68° 58' 29.63599536 E (D).
Qundūz Province. 6 km east-north-east of Qundūz, in the village of Quchi (B, C), and in the neighbouring villages of Buta Kāshān (A) and Kuba'i (D), respectively north-west and south-east of Quchi. (A) The tepe of Buta Kāshān is

situated on the right bank of the canal which crosses the village, in a north-west direction, 300 m north of a pronounced turn in the road from Qundūz. (B) Along this road to the east, in the direction of Quchi, with the first houses of this village, lies a group of four tepes spaced regularly on the north side of the road, and a fifth on the south side; (C) then, at the exit of the village, lies a group of three tepes, two on the south side, on the edge of the road, and one on the north side, at a distance of 200 m; south of the same road, an isolated tepe, used as a cemetery.

Dates: Achaemenid, 6th–4th cent. BC (B); Hunnic-Turk, 5th–9th cent.; pre-Mongol Islamic, 10th–13th cent., and Timurid, 15th–16th cent. (ceramic).

Description: (A) Rectangular north-west/south-east platform (30×20 m), damaged on the south-west, height 3 m, 4 m in the south-east half. (B) Five mounds spaced from 50 to 100 m along the road, mostly damaged by the rice fields. The most damaged are those to the west, which are steep (diam. at the base 20 m, at the top 15 m, height 3 m) and that on the east, used as a source of clay for a brick kiln located on the site (10×10 at the base, height 6 m). The best preserved are the next-to-last ones to the west (oblong east–west, 50×50 m, height 4 m), and to the east (round, diam. 30 m, height 5 m), both occupied by a cemetery. On the first cited, to the west, visible in a cut (north side) at mid-height, are burnt layers about 1 m thick, 4 m long, above which blocks of *pakhsa* had fallen. (C) Three mounds spaced by 400 m, one to the north of the road (25×15 m, height 4 m), the two others on the south side; that on the west is almost entirely razed (15×10, height 2 m), that on the east is still only damaged (40×40 m, height 5 m). (D) Round mound (diam. 30 m, height 3 m), covered with scrub, with tombs, and a *zīyārat*.

Collection: National Museum/AIA—sherds.

Fieldwork: 1978 Gardin et al., CNRS—survey.
Sources:
1. Site information by J.-C. Gardin.
2. Gardin and Lyonnet 1978–9: pl. VII –nos. 458–63.
3. Lyonnet 1997: figs 25, 35, 68, 69—nos. 458–63.
4. Gardin 1998: 78–9—nos. 458–63.

928. QUL-I NĀDIR
Or KŪH-I PAHLAWĀN. Including NIJRAU.

Lat. 35° 00' N, long. 69° 22' E. Map 64.
Parwana Province. 5 km east of Begram, at the foot of the Kūh-i Pahlawān.

Date: Kushan, 2nd–4th cent. (stylistic).

Description: A stupa-monastery complex. In the centre of the stupa was a blue painted reliquary chamber containing gold and silver reliquaries wrapped in silk, inside a stone casket. Very little sculpture except for one schist relief fragment.

Several more stupa complexes east and west of Qul-i Nādir have also been recorded.

Collections: National Museum and Musée Guimet—objects from DAFA excavations.

Fieldwork: 1939 Meunié, DAFA—excavations.
Sources:
1. Meunié 1943–5—discusses the evidence for identifying the site as a Chinese convent.
2. Meunié 1959c—detailed description of the architecture and finds.
3. N. Dupree et al. 1974: 97–8—brief summary and guide to the collection in the National Museum.
4. Tissot 2006: 337—National Museum catalogue details and photos.

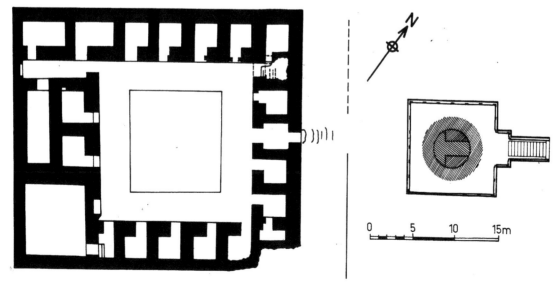

928 Qul-i Nādir (after Meunié 1959).

5. Fussman, Murad, and Ollivier 2008: 167–72 and 307–8—description of the excavations, as well as the unpublished excavations in the vicinity of Qul-i Nādir.

6. Jongeward et al. 2012—catalogue and discussion of the reliquaries.

QUL-I MAQSŪD. See 1121 SURKHDAR.

QUL-I TŪT. See 2268 TEPE NĀRENJ in Supplement.

QUL TEPE. See 583 KHUST-I QISHLĀQ.

929. QUNDUG

Lat. 35° 12' N, long. 54° 51' E. Map 45.
Bādghīs Province. In the upper Murghāb region, *c.*18 km east of its junction with the Khuranj River.

Description: Local reports of ruins.

Source: Site information by Jonathan L. Lee.

930. QUNDŪZ
Or KUNDŪZ.
See also 194 CHEHEL DUKHTARĀN, 569 KHISHT TEPE (the 'Qundūz Hoard'), 931 QUNDŪZ BĀLĀ HISĀR, and 1160 TEPE ĀHINGRĀN.

Lat. 36° 43' N, long. 68° 51' E. Map 32.
Qundūz Province. In the western part of the new town.

Date: Kushan, 2nd–3rd cent. (ceramic, stylistic).

Description: Many remains in and around Qundūz, which in addition to the ones cross-referenced above, include some ruined square structures on the plain immediately to the west, a group of seven mounds with large mud-brick structures, and a site in the west part of the town where some stone column bases and baked brick remains were discovered by accident in 1938. There have also been many chance finds from in and around Qundūz, including a Kharoshthi inscription on a vase, now in a private collection.

Fieldwork:
1. 1938 Barger, ASI—survey.
2. 1955 and 1960 Fischer, DAAD—survey.

Sources:
1. Barger 1939a: 374–85—mentions the discovery of the column base.
2. Barger 1939b—description and photos of the column bases.
3. Emanuel 1939: 207–8—account of the discovery of the column bases.

4. Barger and Wright 1941: 43–4—brief description of the column bases and their discovery.
5. Wheeler 1947: 61–2—mentions the site and finds.
6. Fischer 1961a—gives the literary background and mentions some of the remains.
7. Bussagli 1962a: 42—mentions the significance of the discovery of the column bases.
8. Talbot Rice 1965: 132—briefly discusses the evidence of the column bases for a possible Hellenistic site.
9. Fischer 1969: 349—summary and bibliography of the site and finds.
10. Fussman 1974c: 58–61—linguistic analysis of the Kharoshthi vase inscription.
11. Ball 2008: 259–60—summary.

931. QUNDŪZ BĀLĀ HISĀR

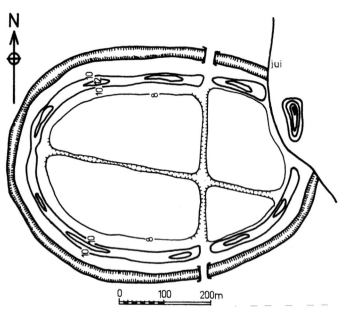

931 Qundūz Bālā Hisar (J.-C. Gardin).

Original: Lat. 36° 45' N, long. 68° 52' E. Map 32.
Revised: 36.74286928 N, 68.87170604 E /
36° 44' 34.32940620 N, 68° 52' 18.14172888 E.
Qundūz Province. 1.5 km north of the central crossroads of Qundūz, by the road to Qizil Qal'a, on the east side of the road.

Dates: Achaemenid, 6th–4th cent. BC; Hellenistic, 3rd–1st cent. BC; Kushan and Hunnic-Turk, 1st–9th cent.; pre-Mongol Islamic, 10th–13th cent.; Timurid, 15th–16th cent. (ceramic).

Description: Fortification ovoid in shape, oriented approximately east–west (600 × 400 m), with a high citadel at the east end, separated from the enclosure by a canal which flows below, towards the north. The wall dominates the plain of Qundūz by some 10 m; the tabular mound of the citadel (east–west, 70 × 40 m) by about 15 m. A ditch some 20 m wide and 4 m deep surrounds the site, except in the east under the citadel. No trace of redans or towers on the wall or on the citadel, whose top is completely flat. Within the enclosure, the ground is rugged in relief; a systematic study remains to be carried out. A north–south gully crosses the site at its widest point, in the eastern half, cutting through the north and south ramparts through two gaps: this is today a frequented route, with a wooden bridge over the ditch on the north and the south, possibly indicative of an old route.

Fired bricks at the base of the walls. Finds: many limestone fragments and a head of Buddha.

Collections: National Museum/AIA—sherds; finds from excavations.

Fieldwork:
1. 1937 Hackin, DAFA—trial trench.
2. 1938 Barger, ASI—survey.
3. 1946 Wheeler, ASI—reconnaissance.
4. 1955 and 1960 Fisher, DAAD—survey.
5. 1960 Hayashi and Sahara, University of Kyoto—survey.
6. 1963 Mizumo, University of Kyoto—trial trench.
7. 1977 Gardin et al., CNRS—survey.

Sources:
1. Wood 1872: 138—briefly describes the citadel and mound as it appeared in 1837.
2. Barger 1938: 114–15—brief note on the site and Hackin's discoveries.
3. Barger 1939a: 384–5—brief description.
4. Barger 1939b—brief description.
5. Barger and Wright 1941: 43–4—speculations on the possible Sasanian origins of the mound.
6. Shakur 1947: 46–9—description of the mound and discussion of Wood's observations.
7. Wheeler 1947: 61—brief description.
8. Allchin 1957: 135–6—discusses Graeco-Bactrian sherds found at the site.
9. Fischer 1961a—mentions the remains and gives the literary background for Qunduz.
10. Hayashi and Sahara 1962—summary in Japanese of survey results.
11. Mizuno 1962—introduction to the Japanese survey.
12. Mizuno and Odani 1968: 95—mentions the trial soundings.
13. Fischer 1969: 349—summary and bibliography of the site.
14. Higushi 1969—discusses the Buddha head and its relationship to a supposed Āmū Daryā school of Gandharan art.
15. Gardin and Lyonnet 1978–9: 135–6 and pl. VII—mention the pre-Hellenistic date (Site 490).
16. Gentelle 1989—full report on the ancient irrigation and hydrology of the area.
17. Gardin 1982: 106–7—mentions the post-Greek settlement.
18. Gardin 1980—describes the survey in the Qunduz area in general terms.
19. Gardin 1995: 93–4—brief description and plan.
20. Lyonnet 1997: figs 25, 35, 39, 49, 68, 69—no. 490.
21. Gardin 1998: 79—no. 490.

932. QUNDŪZ TEPE

Original: Lat. 36° 04' N, long. 68° 37' E approximately. Map 33.
Revised: 36.07073145 N, 68.62102188 E /
36° 04' 14.63323476 N, 68° 37' 15.67878348 E.
Baghlān Province. On the eastern side of the Chashma-Shir Plain, near the Qundūz River.

Description: A line of mounds.

Source: Maitland 1888b: 323—mention.

933. QŪNSAI
See also 288 DEH NAHR-I JADĪD and 260 DASHT-I ARCHI.

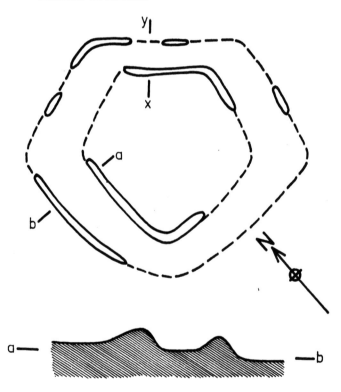

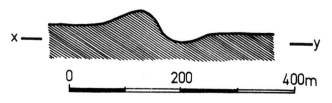

schematic sections

933 Qūnsai (J.-C. Gardin).

Original: Lat. 36° 59' N, long. 69° 10' E. Maps 31, 32.
Revised: 36.98552136 N, 69.17271258 E /
36° 59' 07.87688952 N, 69° 10' 21.76530600 E.
Qundūz Province. 700 m west of Deh Nahr-i Jadid
(no. 288), by a small road across fields.

Dates: Bronze, 2nd mill. BC; beg. Iron, end 2nd–beg. 1st
mill. BC; Achaemenid, 6th–4th cent. BC; Hellenistic, 3rd–1st
cent. BC; Kushan, 1st–4th cent. (ceramic).

Description: Fortified city with a double pentagonal
enclosure, covering a surface of about 500 × 500 m; the
two ramparts, of which the space between varies between
50 and 200 m (see figure), are slightly curved on the sides of
the pentagon, straight at the base; only a few segments with
eroded profiles remain, 3 m high, about 30 m wide at
ground level. The exterior rampart follows a line of inden-
tations (towers? face: 5 m spaced by about 10 m; mud bricks
38 to 41 cm, thickness 10 to 12 cm). The ground is raised in
comparison to the level of the plain, 2 m inside the small
enclosure, 1 m between the two ramparts. Stone column
base seen on the SE exterior rampart, with plinth 60 cm per
side, polished base (diam. 38 cm).

Collection: National Museum/AIA—sherds.

Fieldwork:
1. 1955–65 Fischer, DAAD—survey.
2. 1977 Gardin et al., CNRS—survey.

Sources:
1. Site information by J.-C. Gardin.
2. Fischer 1969: 252 and 29–30—aerial and ground photos,
   with a brief summary as Dasht-i Ārchī II.
3. Gardin and Lyonnet 1978–9: pl. IV—no. 47.
4. Gardin 1995: 89–90—description and plan.
5. Lyonnet 1997: figs 13, 25, 35, 39, 49—no. 47.
6. Gardin 1998: 57—no. 47.

934. QURAISH TEPE

Original: Lat. 36° 54' N, long. 66° 36' E. Map 26.
Revised: 36.90497054 N, 66.58354644 E /
36° 54' 17.89393896 N, 66° 35' 00.76717608 E.
Balkh Province. 2 km south-west of Khwāja Rushnai and
1 km north of the village of Quraish Tepe, 35 km north-
west of Balkh.

Description: A large mound *c.*8 m high, covered in ruins,
with more ruins at the foot stretching for *c.*400 m to the
north and west. There are many more mounds of various
sizes scattered over the plain.

Fieldwork: 1886 Maitland, ABC—topographical survey.

Source: Maitland 1888b: 195—mention.

935. QURBAQA

Original: Lat. 36° 53' N, long. 66° 20' E. Map 25.
Revised: 36.88282987 N, 66.32934944 E /
36° 52' 58.18752192 N, 66° 19' 45.65798436 E.

Jauzjān Province. 15 km south-east of Āqcha, 300 m north
of the road to Balkh.

Description: Small very eroded tepe of irregular form
(*c.*50 × 70 m), height *c.*6 m. All around are scattered low
ruins which are probably the continuation of tepe no. 978.

Fieldwork: 1948 Le Berre, DAFA—survey.

Source: M. Le Berre: unpublished 1948 report, DAFA
archives, tepe P. 16.

QURGHĀN. See 398 GURGURAWA

936. QURGHĀN TEPE, IMĀM SĀHIB

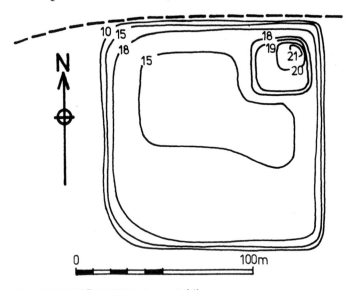

936 QURGHĀN TEPE, Imām Sāhib

Original: Lat. 37° 13' N, long. 68° 55' E. Map 31.
Revised:
Between 37.21713614 N, 68.92917674 E /
37° 13' 01.69011984 N, 68° 55' 45.03626040 E,
37.21813674 N, 68.92684024 E / 37° 13' 05.29227732 N,
68° 55' 36.62487228 E,
37.21693676 N, 68.9267234 E / 37° 13' 00.97231980 N,
68° 55' 36.20424108 E,
37.217828 N, 68.92594957 E / 37° 13' 04.18080648 N,
68° 55' 33.41846604 E and
37.21319606 N, 68.9253688 E / 37° 12' 47.50581276 N,
68° 55' 31.32769368 E.
Qundūz Province. 4.5 km north-east of Imām Sāhib, on the
edge of the *jangal* which extends up to the Āmū Dāryā,
6 km away.

Dates: Iron Age, 1700–800 BC; Achaemenid, 6th–4th cent.
BC; Kushan and Hunnic-Turk, 1st–9th cent.; pre-Mongol
Islamic, 10th–13th cent.; Timurid, 15th–16th cent. (ceramic).

Description: Square fortification built on the eroded edge of a terrace of the Āmū Dāryā, which forms with the *jangal* a slope of 2 to 3 m. The ramparts, well-preserved, dominate the plain of Imām Sāhib by about 15 m; no trace of towers, but at the north-east angle a square citadel rises to 20 m (marker). The interior of the enclosure has the form of a basin with a gentle slope, around a large depression whose bottom nevertheless lies above the level of the plain, on the outside; a modern cemetery occupies the slopes on three sides (west, north, and south). On the exterior, several little circular or oblong mounds, 1 to 2 m high, are spaced around the fortification at distances of between 100 and 400 m; they could be the remains of a large semi-circular enclosure lying against the edge of the terrace (diam. *c*.700–800 m) before the building of the square construction, which occupies the centre. In such a case, the circular enclosure would be attributed to the Achaemenid period, and the square fortification to the Kushan period.

Collection: National Museum/AIA — sherds.

Fieldwork: 1977 Gardin et al., CNRS — survey.

Sources:
1. Site information by J.-C. Gardin.
2. Gardin and Lyonnet 1978–9: pl. V — nos. 137–42.
3. Gardin 1995: 91–2 — description and plan.
4. Lyonnet 1997: figs 25, 35, 49, 68, 69 — nos. 137–42.
5. Gardin 1998: 63 — nos. 137–42.

937. QURGHĀN TEPE, TĀLUQĀN

Original: Lat. 36° 43' N, long. 69° 29' E. Map 36.
Revised:
36.72214348 N, 69.4927015 E / 36° 43' 19.71651936 N, 69° 29' 33.72540432 E and
36.72129467 N, 69.4901417 E / 36° 43' 16.66080660 N, 69° 29' 24.51012504 E.
Takhār Province. 2 km west of the modern bridge on the Tāluqān River by the road from Tāluqān to Khānābād: the tepe is located 200 m north of the road, on the left bank of the river, about 500 m to the north.

Dates: Chalcolithic-Early Bronze Age, *c*.3500–2500 BC; Bronze, 2nd mill. BC; beg. Iron, end 2nd–beg. 1st mill. BC; Achaemenid, 6th–4th cent. BC; Hellenistic, 3rd–1st cent. BC; some Islamic sherds (ceramic).

Description: Circular enclosure (diam. 200 m) marked by a line of trees (willows) in the middle of irrigated fields; both are missing in the northern part, levelled by the crops (but where, however, most of the sherds are found). All that remains of the enclosure is a large circular ridge 3 to 5 m wide at the base, and about 3 m high above the level of the plain; within the enclosure, the surface of the ground is raised 1.5 m in relation to the plain. In a cut at the north-west end of the preserved enclosure, burnt layers are lying against beds of *pakhsa*, covered by collapsed earth. According to an informant, systematic levelling of the

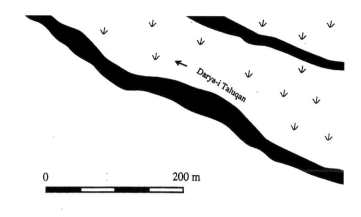

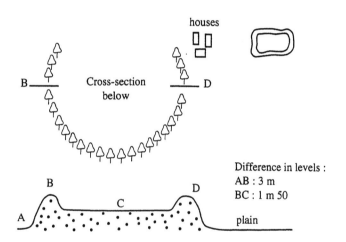

937 Qurghān Tepe, Tāluqān (after Gardin 1998)

site began fairly recently, just a few decades ago. 100 m north-east of the site, a rectangular east–west platform (40 × 30 m); flat top, inclined from west to east (2–1 m). This tepe is cut into by the crops; another tepe, reported to the north-west of the site, has completely disappeared.

Collection: National Museum/AIA — sherds.

Fieldwork: 1978 Gardin et al., CNRS — survey.

Sources:
1. Site information by J.-C. Gardin.
2. Gardin and Lyonnet 1978–9: 6 and pl. VIII — nos. 400, 405.
3. Gardin 1995: 92–3 — description and plan.
4. Lyonnet 1997: figs 7, 13, 25, 35, 39 — nos. 400, 405.
5. Gardin 1998: 6 and 75 — nos. 400, 405.

938. QŪRI

Original: Lat. 31° 22' N, long. 64° 10' E approximately. Map 97.
Revised: 31.3218961 N, 64.21741729 E / 31° 19' 18.82597728 N, 64° 13' 02.70223284 E.

Helmand Province. *C.*23 km south-west of Bust, in the desert between Nād-i ʿAlī and the Helmand.

Dates: Parthian-Saka, 2nd–1st cent. BC; Indo-Parthian, 1st–3rd cent.; Sasanian, 3rd–7th cent.; Ghurid, 12th–13th cent. (ceramic).

Description: A mound and an Islamic cemetery.

Fieldwork: 1966 Hammond, Cambridge University—survey.

Source: Hammond 1970: 449—lists the site (no. 28) and describes the pottery types and general survey results.

939. QUR QUDUQ

Lat. 37° 11–37° 12' N, long. 66° 03' E. Map 24.
Jauzjān Province. In the dunes between 11 and 13 km north of Sayyidābād on the route to Shur Tepe on the Āmū Daryā.

Date: Neolithic, 7th–6th mill. BC (lithic).

Description: Several surface sites covering several square km.

Fieldwork: 1976 Vinogradov, Af/Sov. Mission—survey.

Source: Vinogradov 1979: 44–51—description of the sites and drawings of the material (Sites 428–33).

940. QURŪGH

Original: Lat. 36° 21' N, long. 69° 20' E. Map 37.
Revised: 36.35876327 N, 69.30793844 E /
36° 21' 31.54777272 N, 69° 18' 28.57838148 E.
Takhār Province. 3 km south of Ishkamīsh on the northern edge of the lake.

Dates: Kushan-Sasanian, 1st–7th cent.; early Islamic, 10th–13th cent. (ceramic).

Description: Some mounds.

Fieldwork: 1960–8 Fischer, DAAD—survey.

Source: Fischer 1969: 352—mention (Ishkamīsh II).

941. QUSH TEPE, IMĀM SĀHIB
Or GOBAKLI TEPE.

Original: Lat. 36° 42' N, long. 66° 29' E. Map 25.
Revised: 36.7310214 N, 66.47917957 E / 36° 43' 51.67705368 N, 66° 28' 45.04643472 E.
Jauzjān Province, 5 km north-west of Imām Sāhib, 1 km to the east of the road to Āqcha.

Dates: Sasanian, 3rd–7th cent.; Turk and early Islamic, 8th–13th cent. (ceramic).

Description: A large circular mound, 30 m diam. and 10 m high, with a square of mud fortification walls 100 m to the east.

Fieldwork:
1. 1955–60 Fischer, DAAD—survey.
2. 1956 Ramachandran and Sharma, ASI—reconnaissance.
3. 1960 Hayashi and Sahara, Kyoto University—survey.

Sources:
1. Ramachandran and Sharma 1956: I. 20—mention.
2. Hayashi and Sahara 1962: 60—photo and description in Japanese.
3. Fischer 1969: 348—brief description with ground and aerial photos (Imām Sāhib).

942. QUSH TEPE, QUNDŪZ

Original: Lat. 36° 47' N, long. 68° 37' E. Map 32.
Revised: 36.77689359 N, 68.61664593 E /
36° 46' 36.81692112 N, 68° 36' 59.92533216 E.
Qundūz Province. On the south bank of the Qundūz River, *c.*16 km west of Qundūz.

Date: Kushan, 1st–3rd cent. (architectural, ceramic).

Description: A very large mound with a square structure characteristic of the Kushan period. On the surface were several pseudo-Hellenistic limestone fragments.

Fieldwork:
1. 1955 and 1960 Fischer, DAAD—survey.
2. 1975 Kohl—survey.

Sources:
1. Fischer 1961a: 17—mention.
2. Fischer 1969: 351—mention.
3. Kohl 1978: 68—mention.

QUTANK. See 2068 FARAD JAGANI in Supplement.

943. QŪZI
Includes KHUSH TEPE, TEPE AFGHĀNHĀ, and TEPE SAFDARI.

Original: Lat. 36° 42' N, long. 68° 59' E. Map 32.
Revised:
36.69541905 N, 68.99590609 E / 36° 41' 43.50856308 N, 68° 59' 45.26193804 E (A).
36.70433772 N, 68.98100757 E / 36° 42' 15.61577688 N, 68° 58' 51.62724480 E (B).
36.70489844 N, 68.9790749 E / 36° 42' 17.63438292 N, 68° 58' 44.66963064 E (B).
36.70793426 N, 68.98327492 E / 36° 42' 28.56332160 N, 68° 58' 59.78971560 E (C).
36.71055645 N, 68.99760377 E / 36° 42' 38.00321208 N, 68° 59' 51.37356732 E (D).
Qundūz Province. Group of tepes near the village of Qūzi, about 11 km west of Khānābād, accessible by a track from this village. (A) The first is located by the track, at the

eastern edge of the village; it corresponds to the square structure indicated at this place on the 1:100,000 map. (B) The next two are 1.7 km further, on the north side of the track (general west-north-west direction), just before the track crosses the road between Tarnau and Nawābād. The last two are accessible by this road: (C) one lies 600 m from the crossroads (corresponding to a mound indicated on the 1:100,000 map, without altitude measurement, immediately to the east of the road); (D) the other lies 1.2 km north-east of C, in the hamlet which carries its name, Tepe Safdari (indicated on the map by an unnamed group of houses between Qūzi and Nawābād).

Dates: Achaemenid, 6th–4th cent. BC (B, C); Hunnic-Turk, 5th–9th cent.; some Islamic sherds (ceramic).

Description: (A) Rectangular east–west platform (80 × 50 m), rounded at the angles, height 3 m, on which rises, to the north, an oblong east–west mound which is higher (7 m)— with a *ziyārat*—and to the south, three small hillocks also aligned east–west (4–5 m). (B) Place-name Khush Tepe: two mounds 100 m apart, aligned east–west. The highest, to the west, is square (25 × 25 m), with an appendage in the north, surmounted by a *ziyārat*; flat top, also square (10 × 10 m), height 7 m, regular slopes occupied by a cemetery which delays the levelling of the mound. The lowest has a similar shape (30 × 30 m), but eroded in the angles, height 6 m; the Achaemenid sherds of site B come from this mound. (C) Place-name Tepe Afghānhā: long east–west mound of irregular shape (200 × 100 m), damaged by the rice fields, average height 2–3 m, occupied by the hamlet which carries this name. (D) Place-name Tepe Safdari: oblong east–west mound (100 × 80 m), low (1–2 m), occupied by the hamlet of the same name.

Collection: National Museum/AIA—sherds.

Fieldwork: 1978 Gardin et al., CNRS—survey.

Sources:
1. Site information by J.-C. Gardin.
2. Gardin and Lyonnet 1978–9: pl. VII—nos. 437–41.
3. Lyonnet 1997: figs 25, 35, 68, 69—nos. 437–41.
4. Gardin 1998: 78—nos. 437–41.

944. RABĀTAK KĀFIR QAL'A

Original: Lat. 36° 09' N, long. 68° 24' E. Maps 30, 33.
Revised: 36.15458392 N, 68.40714495 E /
36° 09' 16.50212856 N, 68° 24' 25.72182684 E.
Baghlān Province. C.40 km east of Haibak on the road to Pul-i Khumri.

Dates: Kushan, Hunnic, and Turk, 1st–9th cent. (ceramic); Timurid, 15th–16th cent. (architectural, ceramic).

Description: Remains of an old brick caravanserai and various miscellaneous mud-brick structures. The caravanserai has a rectangular courtyard with four or five domed chambers opening into it on the north and south sides.

In the 1990s a sanctuary was uncovered consisting of a series of terraces similar to Surkh Kotal, but much was destroyed before it could be recorded. However, an inscription was saved and taken to Kābul, which records the genealogy of Kanishka, together with some sculptural fragments of pilasters, a stone lion, and lotus.

The Rabatak site is similar but smaller, to Surkh Kotal. What is different is that Rabatak has a perimeter wall with well-defined gateway on the north which leads directly onto a processional way(?) to the upper terrace(s). The ancient road to Balkh ran past this site to the west (not the east as the modern road does). In the area where the inscription was found (at the apex of the site) there were several Kushan-style column bases as well as other monumental fragments.

To the north are remains of mud-brick towers on the hillside.

Fieldwork:
1. 1886 Maitland, ABC—topographical survey.
2. 1955–65 Fischer, DAAD—survey.

Sources:
1. Information on the sanctuary site by Jonathan L. Lee.
2. Gardin and Lyonnet, 1980 chronological study of pottery from DAFA unpublished surveys.
3. Peacocke 1887a: 368—mention.
4. Maitland 1888b: 319—brief description.
5. J. C. Courtois 1961: 26—mention.
6. Fischer 1969: 351—mention (Ruins B6).
7. Gazetteer 1979: IV. 467—mention.
8. Sims-Williams and Cribb 1996—discuss the newly discovered inscription, together with other fragments discovered with it.
9. Fussman 1998—discussion of the inscription and its evidence for chronology.
10. Sims-Williams 1998b—revised reading of the inscription.
11. Mac Dowall 2002—discusses what the inscription reveals about the ancestry of Kanishka in reference to their coinage.
12. Ball 2008: 260—summary.
13. Bopearachchi 2008—discusses chronology of the early Kushan kings in the light of the inscription, questioning the identification of Vima Takto with Soter Megas. Pls 14 and 18 shows a Brahma statue and another relief in a private collection in Pakistan 'probably from Rabatak'.
14. Sims-Williams 2008—further revised reading of the inscription.
15. Falk 2009—discussion of the name Wema Takhtu.
16. Gnoli 2009—discussion of the religious significance of the inscription.
17. Sims-Williams 2012—discussion and translation of the inscription.
18. Sims-Williams and Falk 2014—summary of the evidence.

RABĀT-I ABDULLAH KHĀN. See **2218 RABĀT-I ABDULLAH KHĀN** in Supplement.

RABĀT-I AUDĀN. See **2219 RABĀT-I AUDĀN** in Supplement.

RABĀT-I BĀTUN. See **2220 RABĀT-I BĀTUN** in Supplement.

RABĀT-I CHAWNI. See **2221. RABĀT-I CHAWNI** in Supplement.

945. RABĀT-I CHUPUL TEPE

Lat. 37° 29' N, long. 65° 50' E. Map 24.
Jauzjān Province. On the bank of the Āmū Daryā 20 km north-west of Qarqīn, to the north of the road to Khāmiyāb.

Description: A ruined brick *rabāt*.

Fieldwork: 1886 Maitland, ABC—topographical survey.

Source: Maitland 1888b: 209—mention.

RABĀT-I GHANDAU. See **2222 RABĀT-I GHANDAU** in Supplement.

RABĀT-I KHISHT-I PUKHTA. See **2231 RŪZANAK** in Supplement.

946. RABĀT-I MIRZA

Original: Lat. 34° 43' N, long. 62° 08' E. Map 43.
Revised: 34.71710142 N, 62.12665259 E /
34° 43' 01.56511524 N, 62° 07' 35.94932436 E.
Herat Province. 47 km north of Herat, 2 km to the east of the road to Kushk.

Date: Timurid, 15th cent. (epigraphic).

Description: A baked brick caravanserai, once very fine but now probably completely ruined. An Arabic inscription was seen lying outside the entrance in 1884 with the name of Sultān Husain Mirza and the date 111 AH [*sic*].

Fieldwork: 1884 Maitland, ABC—topographical survey.

Sources:
1. Maitland 1887c: 478—brief description.
2. Maitland 1888a: 164—brief description of the Husain Mirza inscription with the (incorrect) date of 111 *hijri*.

RABĀT-I MULLAH MURDAN-I MURTAZAI. See **2220 RABĀT-I BĀTUN** in Supplement.

947. RABĀT-I PAI

Original: Lat. 34° 16' N, long. 61° 44' E. Map 52.
Revised: 34.27077589 N, 61.74177156 E /
34° 16' 14.79318744 N, 61° 44' 30.37762284 E.
Herat Province. In a narrow valley in the hills 8 km south of Zindajān.

Dates: Kart-Timurid, 13th–16th cent. (architectural, epigraphic).

Description: A stone mosque, 9 m square inside, built on an earlier brick structure, commemorating Tughril bin Shamsuddin, who died in 1355. It has a double brick dome and inside are remains of frescos, now plastered over, and pierced stone windows. Of possible pre-Islamic origins, it is known locally as a second Ka'ba. Nearby is an open shrine built in 1363.

Fieldwork:
1. 1884 Maitland, ABC—topographical survey.
2. 1885 Peacocke, ABC—topographical survey.
3. 1978–9 Samizay, Kābul University/Unesco—survey.

Sources:
1. Peacocke 1887a: 215—brief description.
2. Maitland 1888a: 129—brief description (from Griesbach).
3. Yate 1888: 23—mention.
4. Seljuki 1967a: 144—photo and description.
5. Ghawwās 1969: 22—brief description.
6. Gazetteer 1975: III. 326—mention.
7. Samizay 1981: 36–7—good description of the remains, with photos and plans.
8. Wannell 2002: 245—brief description and photo.

RABĀT-I RŪZANAK or **RĀBĀT-I KHISHT-I PUKHTA.** See **2231** in Supplement.

948. RABĀT-I SĀHIB ZĀDA

Original: Lat. 34° 13 N, long. 62° 12 E. Map 52.
Revised: 34.22544891 N, 62.20177436 E /
34° 13' 31.61607816 N, 62° 12' 06.38768916 E.
Herat Province. 12 km due south of Herat on the edge of the cultivation, between Zīyāratgāh and the main Kandahār road.

Date: Seljuk-Kart, 11th–14th cent. (stylistic).

Description: An immense circular earthworks on the *dasht* measuring *c.*733 m diam. but only *c.*80 cm high, with its only feature a very low mound *c.*50 cm high in the exact centre. No occupation debris was apparent, apart from some modern pottery. Much of the northern part is obscured by modern cultivation. High resolution satellite images show abandoned irrigation channels and fields cutting through the earthworks, i.e. post-dating it (I am grateful to Antony Lauricella of the Oriental Institute, Chicago, for the satellite images).

To the north is a mud-brick structure with a baked brick dome, the Khāniqāh Maulānā Jalāluddīn Mahmūd. The interior is completely plain, with no decoration. Outside are several carved white marble gravestones.

Fieldwork:
1. 1975 O'Kane, BIPS—survey.
2. 1977 Ball—survey.

Sources:
1. Site description by W. Ball.
2. Information on the date of the khāniqāh by B. O'Kane.
3. Seljuki 1967a: 111—photo and brief description of the khāniqāh.

949. RABĀT-I SANGARDĀN

Original: Lat. 34° 51' N, long. 61° 53' E. Map 42.
Revised: 34.85030289 N, 61.87315536 E /
34° 51' 01.09039896 N, 61° 52' 23.35930356 E.
Herat Province. Halfway between Sang Kōtal and Qarabāgh on the road to Gulrān from Herat.

Description: An old ruined caravanserai.

Sources:
1. Maitland and Drummond 1888: 40—mention.
2. C. E. Yate 1888: 68—mention.

950. RABĀT-I SANG-I BĀLĀ

Lat. 35° 46' N, long. 62° 06' E. Maps 43, 52.
Herat Province. C.50 km north of Herat on the road to Kushk, 3 km south of the village of Rabāt-i Sang.

Date: Timurid, 15th–16th cent. (ceramic).

Description: A small mound c.80 × 50 m in area and 10 m in height.

Fieldwork: 1974 Swiny, BIAS—survey.

Source: Site information by S. Swiny in unpublished BIAS archive.

951. RABĀT-I SANG-I PĀ'ĪN

Original: Lat. 34° 48' N, long. 62° 09' E approximately. Map 43.
Revised: 34.80220648 N, 62.15348403 E /
34° 48' 07.94334312 N, 62° 09' 12.54252348 E.
Herat Province. In the Dūāb Valley 4 km south of Dūāb, c.56 km north of Herat, 1.5 km east of the road to Kushk.

Description: A large and obviously important site, producing a varied and interesting assemblage of pottery. The most diagnostic pieces consist of bold linear motifs in dark paint (brown to purple) applied to the buff surface of the unburnished vessel.

There is also a ruined caravanserai of rough masonry arches and domes in baked brick just to the north on a hill to the west.

Fieldwork:
1. 1884 Maitland, ABC—topographical survey.
2. 1974 Swiny, BIAS—survey.

Sources:
1. Site information by S. Swiny in unpublished BIAS archive.
2. Maitland 1888a: 163—brief description of the caravanserai.
3. Maitland 1887c: 477—brief description of the caravanserai.
4. Maitland and Drummond 1888: 62—mentions the caravanserai.

RABĀT-I SAPCHA. See **2223 RABĀT-I SAPCHA** in Supplement.

RABĀT-I SHĀHBID. See **1020 SHĀHBID**.

RABĀT-I SHŪRĀU. See **2224 RABĀT-I SHŪRĀU** in Supplement.

RABĀT-I SURKH, Herat. See **2225 RABĀT-I SURKH, Herat** in Supplement.

RABĀT-I SURKH, Farāh. See **2226 RABĀT-I SURKH, Farāh** in Supplement.

952. RABĀT-I YAN CHASHMA
Or RABĀT-I GALLA CHASHMA.

Original: Lat. 35° 43' N, long. 63° 29' E. Map 44.
Revised: 35.70635033 N, 63.47319716 E /
35° 42' 22.86120312 N, 63° 28' 23.50976232 E.
Bādghīs Province. In the Qarāwal Khāna Valley c.28 km east of its junction with the Murghāb River.

Description: Ruins of an old baked brick *rabāt* and cistern, surrounded by many mounds and a wide scatter of building debris.

Fieldwork: 1886 Maitland, Peacocke, ABC—topographical surveys.

Sources:
1. *Pioneer*, 3 July 1886—brief description.
2. Peacocke 1887c: 115 and 326—mention.
3. Maitland and Drummond 1888: 97—mention.
4. Maitland 1888b: 142—brief description.
5. Gazetteer 1975: III. 129—mention.

RAG-I BĪBĪ. See **2227 RAG-I BĪBĪ** in Supplement.

953. RAHMAN GUL

Lat. 37° 19' N, long. 74° 34' E approximately. Map 40.
Badakhshān Province. In the Little Pamirs in a valley form-
ing an ancient tributary to the Āq Sū, parallel to the Tergen
Gorum-Jar Turuk track.

Date: ?Epi-Palaeolithic, *c*.10,000 BC (stylistic).

Description: Three granite boulders with petroglyphs of
hunting scenes of many ibex and human figures with dogs.

Source: Dor 1976: 124–8—description and photos.

954. RAHMATĀBĀD

Original: Lat. 36° 49' N, long. 66° 35'–66° 36' E. Map 26.
Revised:
36.81995314 N, 66.58627669 E / 36° 49' 11.83130040 N,
66° 35' 10.59609768 E (A).
36.81942798 N, 66.58784849 E / 36° 49' 09.94071576 N,
66° 35' 16.25457696 E (B).
Balkh Province. 7 km south-east of Nimlik, 300 m north of
the Balkh road, the same distance to the south from the
village of Rahmatābād: two tepes 100 m apart.

Description: (A) Quadrangular mound (120 × 130 m), with
a low part (2 m) in the south-west, topped by a higher
platform (6.50 m) in the north-east, suggesting the plan of
a building surrounded by a courtyard. (B) East of A, a small
quadrangular tepe (70 × 55 m), height 4–5 m.

Fieldwork: 1948 Le Berre, DAFA—survey.

Source: M. Le Berre: unpublished 1948 report, DAFA
archives, tepes P. 35 and 36.

RAUZA BĀGH. See **2228 RAUZA BĀGH in Supplement.**

955. RĪG GARDŪN

Lat. 33° 10' N, long. 67° 32' E. Maps 78, 79.
Ghazni Province. At the foot of the Kūh-i Khūd at the end
of the Lūmān Valley, in the Jāghūrī district.

Description: Some rocks with petroglyphs of Persian graffiti, ibex, and hunters.

Source: Bivar 1971: 84—brief description.

956. RĪG GHUNDAI

Lat. 31° 37' N, long. 65° 54' E approximately. Map 89.
Kandahār Province. To the east of Kandahār below Sāhibzāda Qal'acha.

Date: Islamic (ceramic).

Description: A low, probably natural mound, mostly
blown sand on bedrock, with no sign of artificial build-
up. There are however a few sherds on the eastern side.

Fieldwork: 1974 Whitehouse and Swiny, BIAS—survey.

Source: Site information by D. Whitehouse and S. Swiny in
unpublished BIAS archive.

ROBATAK. See **944 RABĀTAK.**

RUCH. See **2229 RUCH in Supplement.**

957. RŪD-I BĪYĀBĀN

Original: Lat. 30° 19' N, long. 61° 21' E. Map 94.
Revised: 30.31684076 N, 61.37612615 E /
30° 19' 00.62673348 N, 61° 22' 34.05415044 E.
Nīmrūz Province. In the Rūd-i Bīyābān 3 km east of Iran
Border Post 20.

Date: Sasanian, 3rd–7th cent. (ceramic).

Description: An area of *c*.2 km² of mud ruins and mounds
with widely scattered sherds and building debris. Among
the ruins are two small square buildings.

Fieldwork: 1951 Fairservis, AMNH—survey.

Source: Fairservis 1961: 60—description of the site and
outline of the pottery (Sites RB 3–11).

958. RŪDĪN

Original: Lat. 30° 17' N, long. 61° 58' E. Map 95.
Revised: 30.26958153 N, 61.96081626 E /
30° 16' 10.49350260 N, 61° 57' 38.93852412 E.
Nīmrūz Province. On the edge of a cliff overlooking the left
bank of the Helmand, 8 km west of Chahār Burjak.

Date: Kayani, 14th cent. (traditional).

Description: Ruins of a small fortification said to guard the
site of a dam across the Helmand, the Band-i Rustam,
destroyed by Tamurlane.

Fieldwork: 1903–05 Tate, SAC—survey.

Source: Tate 1909:90–91—mention.

959. RŪD-I SHĀHRAWĀN
  Includes HAWAR SAI, QIZIL KUCHA, QIZIL
  SAI, SHIR GUZAR, TURIGH, and ZAGHCHA
  GUZAR.

Original: Lat. 36° 52'–36° 59' N, long. 69° 22'–69° 23'
E. Maps 35, 36.
Revised:
36.87412639 N, 69.382324 E / 36° 52' 26.85501300 N,
69° 22' 56.36640504 E (A).

36.95670434 N, 69.38113604 E / 36° 57' 24.13561932 N, 69° 22' 52.08974220 E (D).

Takhār Province. Between the plain of Tāluqān and the plain of Khwāja Ghar, the road which links these two villages runs along the valley of the Rūd-i Shāhrawān, passing through villages situated on the cliffs which dominate this water course: (A) Turigh, (B) Hawar Sai, (C) Qizil Sai, (D) Qizil Kucha, (E) Zaghcha Guzar. For the exact locations of these sites, see Gardin and Lyonnet 1978–9.

Dates: Middle Bronze Age, *c*.2500–1500 BC; Beg. Iron, end 2nd–beg. 1st mill. BC (except E); Achaemenid, 6th–4th cent. B (except E); Hellenistic, 3rd–1st cent. BC (except B, C); pre-Mongol Islamic, 10th–13th cent. (ceramic).

Description: Ancient sites exist in each of these five zones, in the form of small mounds, or more often as simply areas of sherds on the flat parts of the terrace, between the Rūd-i Shāhrawān and the road.

Collection: National Museum/AIA—sherds.

Fieldwork: 1977 Gardin et al., CNRS—survey.

Sources:
1. Site information by J.-C. Gardin.
2. Gardin and Lyonnet 1978–9: pl. IX—nos. 260, 266, 269–74.
3. Gardin 1980—describes the area survey in general terms.
4. Lyonnet 1997: figs 12, 25, 35–57—nos. 259, 260, 266, 269–74.
5. Gardin 1998: 51–2, 70—nos. 259, 260, 266, 269–74.

RUSTAM TEPE. See **383 KHUSTI QISHLĀQ.**

960. RUSTĀQ

Includes KHĀNIQĀH. See also 131. BINI MA-LAKH, 386. GŪGARI.

Original: Lat. 37° 07' N, long. 69° 49' E. Maps 35, 38.
Revised:
37.12975079 N, 69.82612129 E / 37° 07' 47.10285768 N, 69° 49' 34.03665732 E (A).
37.11986662 N, 69.84388556 E / 37° 07' 11.51981796 N, 69° 50' 37.98800304 E (B).
37.11792149 N, 69.8663289 E / 37° 07' 04.51736148 N, 69° 51' 58.78404468 E (C).

Takhār Province. Along the road which crosses the village of Rustāq, towards the east-south-east, starting with Qarūl Tepe (no. 386, A), tepes are located at the following points: (A) at 1 km, south side of the road, in the middle of a wasteland where formerly the garrison buildings were situated; (B) at 3.5 km, hamlet of Khāniqāh, north side of the road, Zīyārat-i Khūja 'Ala'uddīn; (C) near the hamlet of Samarghyan, next to the road, north side.

The village of Rustāq contains several monuments of the Islamic period, which are ruins but still standing (principally the mausoleums of Chehel Dukhtarān and Hazrat-i Waqf).

Dates: Pre-Mongol Islamic, 10th–13th cent. (ceramic); Timurid, 15th–16th cent. (architecture).

Description: (A) Rectangular north-west/south-east mound (60 × 40 m), flat top (height 4 m). (B) rectangular east–west mound (40 × 20 m), height 3 m, continued on the east by a lower appendage. On this mound lies the square tomb of a holy man (Khūja 'Ala'uddīn), with moulded pillars in the angles, surrounded by more modest steles and tombs; this *zīyārat* is built on a platform 2 m high, in the northern part of the mound. (C) Round hillock (diam. 15 m), height 2 m.

Collection: National Museum/AIA—sherds.

Fieldwork:
1. 1955–65 Fischer, DAAD—survey.
2. 1978 Gardin et al., CNRS—survey.

Sources:
1. Site information by J.-C. Gardin.
2. Fischer 1969: 353—brief description of the monuments, and photo of a Timurid dome.
3. Gardin and Lyonnet 1978–9: pl. 11—nos. 514, 520–1.
4. Gardin 1998: 91—nos. 514, 520–1.

RŪI. See **2230. RŪI in Supplement.**

RŪZANAK. See **2231 RŪZANAK in Supplement.**

SĀBARI. See **1010 SĀWARI.**

961. SABARZ

Original: Lat. 34° 20' N, long. 63° 34' E. Map 54.
Revised: 34.34860455 N, 63.56972781 E / 34° 20' 54.97638396 N, 63° 34' 11.02010808 E.

Herat Province. 20 km west of Chisht, on the road to Obeh, right bank of the Harī Rūd, between the river and the village of Sabarz, on a promontory.

Dates: Parthian, 1st–3rd cent.; Timurid 15th cent. (ceramic; stylistic).

Description: Small enclosure of irregular trapezoidal shape (about 100 × 70 m), which presents some traces of digging. There is also an elaborate marble gravestone of a Timurid prince, Ghiyath al-Din Jamshid bin 'Izzuddin Muhammad.

Collection: National Museum/AIA—sherds.

Fieldwork:
1. 1885 Maitland ABC—topographical survey.
2. 1952 Le Berre and Gardin, DAFA—survey.

Sources:
1. M. Le Berre: unpublished 1952 report, DAFA archives, tepe Sabarz 4.

2. Maitland 1888a: 353 — mentions old ruined fort and ziyarat of Khwāja Nizamuddīn.
3. Wannell 2002: 243–4 — mentions the gravestone.

SABZAK, Bāmiyān. See 47 ĀQ RABĀT.

SABZAK. See 1021 SHAHĪDĀN.

SABZAWAR. See 1079 SHINDAND.

962. SABZ QAL'A

Or EZĀBĀD or QAL'A-I UNDI. See also 659 KUSHK-I NAKHUD.

Original: Lat. 31° 38' N, long. 65° 02' E. Map 88.
Revised: 31.63498379 N, 65.04646925 E /
31° 38' 05.94163932 N, 65° 02' 47.28930576 E.
Kandahār Province. 4 km north-west of the Kushk-i Nakhūd bazaar, north of the main road 69 km west of Kandahār.

Dates: Indo-Parthian, 1st–4th cent.; pre-Mongol Islamic, 10th–13th cent.; Timurid, 15th–16th cent. (ceramic).

Description: A large citadel mound, *c.*35 m square and 20–5 m high. Remains and walls extend for some distance around the citadel, with several more mounds continuing up to Maiwand.

Fieldwork:
1. 1949 De Cardi — survey.
2. 1951 Casal, DAFA — survey.
3. 1956 Ramachandran and Sharma, ASI — reconnaissance.
4. 1960–70 Fischer, Bonn University — survey.

Sources:
1. Gardin and Lyonnet, 1980 chronological survey of pottery from unpublished DAFA surveys.
2. Ferrier 1857: 316 — mention.
3. Ashe 1881: 37 and 47 — mention.
4. Holdich 1910: 492 — mention.
5. De Cardi 1950: 56 — mention.
6. Ramachandran and Sharma 1956: I. 13 — mention.
7. Fischer 1967a: 156 — mention and photo.
8. Fischer 1969: 338 — brief summary.
9. Fischer 1973b: 214 — mention.
10. Kalb 1973: discussion of the glazed pottery.
11. Fischer et al. 1974–6: 29 — mention.

963. SADIQĀBĀD

Lat. 35° 01' N, long. 69° 22' E. Map 64.
Kāpīsā Province. On the north bank of the Panjshīr River opposite Shotorak.

Date: Hunnic, 5th–6th cent. (numismatic).

Description: A small Hephthalite cemetery. One grave was excavated, containing burial objects of simple jewellery, pots, and coins.

Fieldwork: 1942 Ghirshman, DAFA — excavations.

Sources:
1. Ghirshman 1948: 1–8 — brief description of the grave and catalogue of the objects.
2. Kohzad 1953b: 6 — mention.

964. SAFAR

Lat. 30° 42' N, long. 64° 06' E. Map 97.
Helmand Province. On the left bank of the Helmand, *c.*8 km upstream from Banadir.

Date: Late Sasanian, 7th cent. (architectural).

Description: An artificial cave cut into the river bluff, consisting of an outer terrace measuring 5 × 2 m and an inner chamber. The walls of the cave are covered in graffiti of gazelle, hands, figures, miscellaneous lines, etc.

Fieldwork: 1966 Hammond, Cambridge University — survey.

Sources:
1. Additional note by W. Trousdale that there are no cliffs or caves near Safar.
2. Hammond 1970: 457–9 — description and brief discussion of the petroglyphs.

SAFAR KHĀN KŪSHTAK. See 2233 SAFAR KHĀN KŪSHTAK in Supplement.

965. SAFARWAL

Lat. 37° 07' N, long. 66° 07' E. Map 24.
Jauzjān Province. On the southern edge of the dunes *c.*23 km north of Āqcha 9 km east of Sayyidābād.

Date: Neolithic, 7th–6th mill. BC (lithic).

Fieldwork: 1976 Vinogradov, Af/Sov. Mission — survey.

Description: A surface site with a very large number of stone tools scattered across the surface for a large area.

Source: Vinogradov 1979: 39–41 — general discussion of the survey results with comparisons in Soviet Central Asia (Sites 418–23).

SAFĪD DAGH. See 752 NĀD-I 'ALĪ.

966. SAFĪDSANG

Original: Lat. 34° 18' N, long. 69° 08' E. approximately. Map 60.
Revised: 34.29489731 N, 69.139688 E / 34° 17' 41.63032140 N, 69° 08' 22.87678308 E.

Lōgar Province. 40 km north of Pul-i Alām, c.1 km to the east of the road to Gardēz from Kābul.

Dates: Kushan-Sasanian, 1st–7th cent.; Timurid, 15th–16th cent. (ceramic).

Description: Some ruins on both sides of the road, as well as unconfirmed reports of a stone inscription.

Fieldwork: 1966 Fischer, DAAD—survey.

Sources:
1. Fischer 1967a: 167—mention.
2. Fischer 1969: 341—mention (Site A7).

SĀFIYA. See 2234 SĀFIYA in Supplement.

SAHAG. See 632 KUHNA QAL'A, Khānābād.

967. SĀHIBZĀDA QAL'ACHA

Lat. 31° 36' N, long. 65° 54' E. approximately. Map 89. Kandahār Province. Overlooking Rīg Ghundai from the south, east of Kandahār.

Date: Sasanian, 3rd–7th cent. (ceramic).

Description: A narrow, low rocky spur c.8 m high, overlooking the plain. On the tip of the spur is a small mudbrick structure 10 m square and up to 4 m high. Some of the walls are built on a rubble and mud footing. The building has some traces of internal rooms.

Fieldwork: 1974 Whitehouse, BIAS—survey.

Source: Site information by D. Whitehouse in unpublished BIAS archive.

SAHRĀ YAMAK. See 2235 SAHRĀ YAMAK in Supplement.

968. SA'ID QAL'A TEPE
Or CHEHELGHAR GHUNDAI or CHILA GOR TEPE.

Original: Lat. 31° 33–55' N, long. 65° 35–58' E. Map 89. Revised: 31.5520486 N, 65.57967394 E / 31°33' 07.37497656 N, 65° 34' 46.82619228 E. Kandahār Province. 15 km south-west of Kandahār on the road to Panjwāyī.

Dates: Bronze Age, c.3500–2100 BC; early Sasanian, 3rd–5th cent. (C-14, ceramic).

Description: A mound c.200 m diam. and 8 m high. The early periods (I–III, corresponding to Mundigak III–IV) consist of a series of mud-brick structures divided by collapses and rebuildings, with only minor ceramic changes. Period IV consists of a late cemetery surrounding the mound. There are some traces of fortifications. The finds from the early period included some minor stone tools (but no flints), a few bone points, bronze fragments, miscellaneous stone vessels, simple jewellery, and figurines.

Fieldwork:
1. 1951 Casal, DAFA—survey.
2. 1951 Fairservis, AMNH—sondages.
3. 1970/71 Shaffer, AMNH—excavations.

Sources:
1. Fairservis 1952: 24—brief note on the sondages.
2. Fairservis 1953: 142–3—briefly discusses the general results of the sondages.
3. Masson and Sarianidi 1969—discuss the site in its wider chronological and Near Eastern context.
4. Fairservis 1971: 123—very brief summary of the first sondages.
5. Shaffer 1971—preliminary report on the early levels, with photos mainly of the finds.
6. Shaffer and Hoffman 1971—detailed description and analytical tables of the late cemetery, with physiological analyses and cultural and religious conclusions.
7. Dales 1973a: 125–6—very brief summary.
8. Shaffer et al. 1973—summary of the 1970/71 season, with a long discussion of the problems and methods.
9. Shaffer 1974—discusses the evidence from the excavations in terms of analytical models.
10. Shaffer 1976: 74–5—brief discussion of the architectural remains and finds.
11. Shaffer 1978a—full report on the excavations, with an environmental background and extensive comparisons.

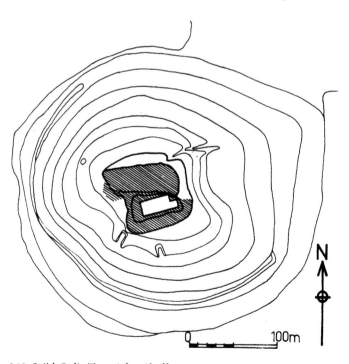

968 Sa'id Qal'a Tepe (after Shaffer 1978a).

12. Shaffer 1978b: 149–62—discussion and reinterpretation of the material.

969. SAIGHĀN ALĀQADĀRĪ
See also 398 GURGURAWA.

Original: Lat. 35° 11' N, long. 67° 41' E. Map 48.
Revised: 35.17822011 N, 67.67736417 E /
35° 10' 41.59237872 N, 67° 40' 38.51100228 E.
Bāmiyān Province. Valley of Darya-i Saighān, south-west of Dūāb-i Mīkhzarīn (road from Chārikār to Dūshi by the Shībar Pass).

Date: Turk, 7th–10th cent. (ceramic).

Description: Ruins of a small fort comprising several towers, one still with an intact dome.

Collection: National Museum/AIA—sherds.

Fieldwork: 1974–5 Le Berre, DAFA—survey.

Source: Le Berre 1987: 59–60, pl. 69c and d—description and photos; itinerary A-II, Darya-i Saighān, ruin 5.

970. SAIN

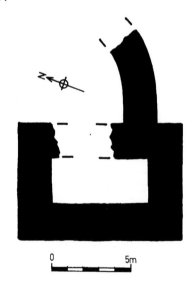

970 Sain 1 (W. Ball).

Original: Lat. 33° 21' N, long. 64° 18' E. Map 74.
Revised: 33.34058439 N, 64.31008305 E /
33° 20' 26.10379932 N, 64° 18' 36.29896740 E.
Ghūr Province. 35 km south-east of Taiwāra on the road to Zarnī.

Date: Ghurid, 12th–13th cent. (architectural, geographic).

Description: A very small group of towers defending the road. Construction is of mud on a stone foundation.

Fieldwork: 1977 Ball—survey.
Source: Ball 2002: 37—brief description.

971. SAJĀWAND
Or SAKAWAND or TAKHT-I JAMSHID.

Original: Lat. 33° 54' N, long. 68° 48' E. Map 82.
Revised: 33.90721711 N, 68.79397749 E /
33° 54' 25.98158160 N, 68° 47' 38.31895572 E.
Lōgar Province. In the mountains c.15 km south-west of Baraki, which is 70 km south of Kābul to the west of the road to Gardēz.

Date: Hindu Shahi, 10th cent. (architectural, ceramic, documentary).

Description: On a saddle of a hill is a huge platform and many walls of diaper masonry, with later mud-brick structures from the Islamic period on top. The remains are the site of a major Hindu Shahi temple.

Sources:
1. Raverty 1878: 72–4 and 679–80—mentions the remains and gives a detailed documentary summary.
2. Kohzad 1944/45c—background to the site and temple.
3. Caspani and Cagnacci 1951: 226—mention the remains.
4. Kohzad 1953a—extensive discussion on the historical, religious, and geographical background.
5. Fischer 1959a: 130—background to the temple.
6. Mac Dowall and Taddei 1978b: 263—mention the remains.

972. SAKA

Original: Lat. 34° 27–45' N, long. 69° 12–20' E. Map 62.
Revised: 34.44587087 N, 69.20549205 E /
34° 26' 45.13512588 N, 69° 12' 19.77138108 E.
Kābul Province. On a spur overlooking the east bank of the Lōgar River at the point where it enters the Kābul plain, 12 km south of Kābul.

Dates: Hellenistic, 3rd–1st cent. BC (ceramic), Kushano-Sasanian, 4th–5th cent. (numismatic); Hephthalite and Turki Shahi, 5th–8th cent. (ceramic).

Description: Two small mounds representing a small, elongated fort and a rectangular building with a gateway. Construction is of mud-brick on a diaper masonry foundation. Amongst the finds were some bronze coins and much incised and stamped pottery.

Two badly eroded mounds nearby mark the possible remains of two stupas.

Fieldwork:
1. 1935 Carl, DAFA—excavations.
2. 1972 Fussman, CNRS—survey.

972 Saka (after Carl 1959a).

Sources:
1. Gardin and Lyonnet, 1980 chronological study of pottery from unpublished DAFA surveys.
2. Dollot 1937: 289–90 — brief summary of the excavations.

3. Carl 1959a — brief summary of the excavations.
4. N. Dupree 1971: 208 — mention.
5. Fussman et al. 2008: 46 — mention the possible stupa remains.

SAKAR DARRA. See 1064 SHAKAR DARRA.

SAKAWAND. See 971 SAJAWAND.

973. SAKHA

Lat. 32° 49' N, long. 69° 07' E. Map 82.
Paktiyā Province. About 10 km south of Urgūn.
Dates: Turki Shahi — Hindu Shahi, 8th–10th cent. (ceramic).
Description: A small mound.
Collection: National Museum/AIA — sherds.
Source: Gardin and Lyonnet, 1980 study of the pottery from the unpublished DAFA surveys.

974. SAKHĀR
Or SAKHĪR or SAGHĀR or QAL'A-I ZĀR-MURGH. Correctly DEH QĀDĪ.

Lat. 33° 43' N, long. 63° 52' E. Map 54.
Ghūr Province. In the district of Saghār, C. 5 km north-west of Deh Titān below the Kūh-i Zārmurgh, south of the Shahrak-Adraskan road.
Date: Ghurid, 12th–13th cent. (architectural).
Description: In the 19th century reports of the remains of a Ghurid palace that included a baked brick minaret 30 m high reached members of the Afghan Boundary Commission. Investigations in 2013 confirmed the existence of a minaret, somewhat less than 30 m high, with a tapering shaft of mud-brick but the top decoration of interlaced lozenges and zig-zags in baked brick. Local reports confirm the one-time existence of a mosque, now gone. The reported 'palace' might the fort of Qal'a-i Sultān (Site 882) nearby.
Sources:
1. Maitland 1888a: 363 — report from hearsay of 'ancient city'.
2. Sahibdad Khan 1891a: 240 — mentions the minaret.
3. M. N. Kohzad 1959: 7 — brief description.
4. Rafat 1980: 4 — mention.
5. Zeymal Haidari — personal communication.
6. Thomas et al. 2014 — description, context, and photos of the minaret.

975. SĀLĀR TEPE

Original: Lat. 36° 46' N, long. 66° 26' E. Map 25.
Revised: 36.76820166 N, 66.43681515 E /
36° 46' 05.52597564 N, 66° 26' 12.53453244 E.
Balkh Province. On the left bank of the Balkhāb, 12 km
north-west of Imām Sāhib on the road to Āqcha.

Dates: Graeco-Bactrian, 3rd–2nd cent. BC; Mongol-
Timurid, 13th–16th cent. (ceramic).

Description: A mound, 150 m square and 15 m high, surrounded by remains of mud walls.

Fieldwork:
1. 1956 Ramachandran and Sharma, ASI—reconnaissance.
2. 1960 Hayashi and Sahara, Kyoto University—survey.

Sources:
1. Ramachandran and Sharma 1956: I. 20—mention.
2. Hayashi and Sahara 1962: 60—photo and description in
   Japanese.

976. SALAWĀT

Lat. 31° 32' N, long. 65° 33' E. Map 89.
Kandahār Province. 11 km east of Panjwāyī, 1 km south of the
road. The site is 1.5 km north-east of the village of Salawāt.

Dates: Sasanian, 3rd–7th cent.; Turki Shahi and early
Islamic, 8th–13th cent. (ceramic).

Description: None available.

Fieldwork: 1950–1 Fairservis, AMNH—survey.

Source: Fairservis 1971: 394—mention (Khr–8).

SĀLIHĀN. See 979 SĀLIYĀN.

977. SĀLIQ BAI

Lat. 37° 27' N, long. 65° 54' E. Map 24.
Jauzjān Province. 13 km west of Qarqīn between the road
to Khāmiyāb and the left bank of the Āmū Daryā.

Description: Ruins of a large fortified enclosure.

Fieldwork: 1886 Maitland, ABC—topographical survey.

Source: Maitland 1888b: 209—mention.

978. SALTUQ

Original: Lat. 36° 53' N, long. 66° 19' E. Map 25.
Revised: 36.87977147 N, 66.31240894 E /
36° 52' 47.17730280 N, 66° 18' 44.67218040 E.
Jauzjān Province. 15 km south-east of Āqcha, on the southern edge of the road to Balkh.

Description: Field of low ruins: traces of old irrigation
canals are visible.

Fieldwork: 1948 Le Berre, DAFA—survey.

Source: M. Le Berre: unpublished 1948 report, DAFA
archives, site P. 15.

979. SĀLIYĀN
Or SĀLIHĀN. See also 810. PESHWĀRĀN.

Original: Lat. 31° 29' N, long. 61° 34' E. Map 83.
Revised: 31.4939017 N, 61.56095929 E / 31° 29' 38.04612864 N,
61° 33' 39.45343320 E.
Nīmrūz Province. 5 km south-east of Peshwārān, 30 km
south of Lāsh Juwain.

Description: Part of the Peshwārān series of remains, consisting of many ruins and a scatter of sherds and bricks.

Fieldwork: 1950 Fairservis, AMNH—survey.

Sources:
1. Bellew 1874: 243—mention.
2. Stein 1928: 938 and 941—describes some pottery
   brought to him from the site.
3. Fairservis 1961: 44–5—mention (Site 16).
4. Gazetteer 1973: II. 252—mention.

980. SAMANDAU

Lat. 36° 27' N, long. 69° 28' E. Map 37.
Takhār Province. 14 km north-east of Ishkamīsh, by a road
that stops at the village of Samandau and continues towards
the north-east in the direction of Chal. The tepe is located
20 m to the west of the last houses of Samandau, on the southern
edge of the stream formed by the spring of the same name.

Dates: Hellenistic, 3rd–1st cent. BC; some Islamic sherds
(ceramic).

Description: Small round mound (diam. 15 m, height 2.5 m),
with rises of land and sherds over an area around the mound
up to some 60 m from it.

Collection: National Museum/AIA—sherds.

Fieldwork: 1978 Gardin et al., CNRS—survey.

Sources:
1. Site information by J.-C. Gardin.
2. Gardin and Lyonnet 1978–9: pl. XI—no. 373.
3. Lyonnet 1997: fig. 39—no. 373.
4. Gardin 1998: 99—no. 373.

981. SAMTI
Includes DAHĀNA-I QISHLĀQ and TAHANA-I
AIQULI.

Original: Lat. 37° 34'–37° 36' N, long. 69° 50'–69° 53'
E. Maps 35, 38.

Revised: 37.5696476 N, 69.82606426 E / 37° 34' 10.73136540 N, 69° 49' 33.83135220 E.

Takhār Province. The little plain of Samti, situated in a curve of the Āmū Daryā, contains no notable tepe; but there exist in the village of Samti some clear traces of ancient occupation. (A) The most eloquent are the areas of sherds of the Kushan and pre-Mongol period found at the location of a disused cemetery, between the two groups of houses that form the east and west parts of the village. This area scattered with pottery appears to continue up to the Āmū Daryā, 600 m to the north. (B) 4 km south-west of Samti, a small artificial mound rises 300 m east-north-east of a lookout post (Tahana-i Aiquli), on the north side of the track that leads to Khasar and Chayāb, along the edge or in the bed itself of the stream of Shāh-i Maslan. (C) 1 km south of Dahāna-i Qishlāq, this road leads away from the stream to climb an advance of the slopes towards the east; the heights that separate the road from the stream carry traces of ancient occupation.

Dates: Achaemenid, 6th–4th cent. BC (A); Kushan, 1st–4th cent. (A); pre-Mongol Islamic, 10th–13th cent.; Timurid, 15th–16th cent. (ceramic).

Description: (A) Hillocky area covering a surface of about 1.5 hectares (600 × 250 m) between the disused cemetery of Samti and the Āmū Daryā: many little bumps are no higher than 0.5 m and between them fragments of fired bricks and pottery are found in abundance, but the bumps do not present any particular plan. The sherds of the early periods only come from the zone of the cemetery, while those of the Islamic period cover the entire area. 300 m west of the cemetery, a tepe was razed several years ago in order to build a little mosque; sherds of the pre-Mongol period are found in its garden. (B) Small mound (diam. 10 m, height 2 m) on which is a tomb surrounded by a low wall: pre-Mongol sherds around it. (C) Line of a ridge overlooking the stream (to the east) by some 30 m, and the road (to the west) by about 10 m; the upper part of the slopes, on the road side, is flat, and carries traces of structures oriented north–south/east–west, probably small houses. Sherds cover almost all the slope, up to the road (50 m), over a distance of about 100 m along the ridge. The surface of the site is worked (*lalmī*).

Collection: National Museum/AIA — sherds.

Fieldwork: 1978 Gardin et al., CNRS — survey.

Sources:
1. Site information by J.-C. Gardin.
2. Gardin and Lyonnet 1978–9: pl. II — nos. 537–42.
3. Lyonnet 1997: figs 25, 35, 49 — nos. 537–42.
4. Gardin 1998: 36 — nos. 537–42.
5. Grenet 2002b — discusses Samti in connection with a place associated with Zoroaster.

SAMŪCHHĀ. See 286 DEHMĀN.

982. SANDUKTI

Lat. 37° 12'–37° 14' N, long. 66° 25'–66° 26' E. Maps 25, 28. Jauzjān Province. Just to the east of the Kilift-Balkh road, 12 km south-east of Islām Pinja.

Date: Epi-Palaeolithic, 10,000–8,000 BC (lithic).

Description: A group of four surface sites, with a fifth 3 km further south.

Fieldwork: 1969 Vinogradov, Af/Sov. Mission — survey.

Source: Vinogradov 1979: 28–30 — description and drawings of the material (Sites 67 and 68).

SANGANDĀB. See 1074 SHĪBAR, east.

SANGAR, Deh Khaju. See 1252 ZANGU.

983. SANGAR, ZĪYĀRAT-I AMĪRĀN SĀHIB
See also 563 KHĀRI.

Original: Lat. 31° 54' N, long. 62° 05' E. Map 92.
Revised: 30.89554663 N, 62.08625583 E /
30° 53' 43.96785108 N, 62° 05' 10.52098944 E.
Nīmrūz Province. On the northern edge of the dunes south of Zīyārat-i Amīrān Sāhib.

Description: Remains of a huge Islamic fortress.

Fieldwork:
1. 1936 Hackin and Meunié, DAFA — survey.
2. 1969–74 Fischer, Bonn University — survey.

Source:
1. Fischer 1969–70 — photos.
2. Fischer 1970a — photos.
3. Fischer 1970b: pls 56–7 — photos.
4. Fischer 1973c: 148 — mention.
5. Fischer et al. 1974–6: pl. 178 — photo.

984. SANG BUR
Or QAL'A-I FĪRŪZ HUSAIN.

Lat. 35° 01' N, long. 62° 18' E. Map 43.
Herat Province. On the east side of the Kushk Rūd, opposite the confluence with the Chahār Darracha, 87 km north of Herat.

Date: Middle Islamic (ceramic).

Description: A large mound *c.*15 m high and a smaller one adjacent. It was covered in an extensive scatter of broken baked bricks and glazed and unglazed ceramics.

Fieldwork:
1. 1885 Maitland, ABC, Peacocke — topographical survey.
2. 1974 Swiny, BIAS — survey.
3. 1968–78 Kruglikova, Af/Sov. Mission — survey.

Sources:
1. Site information by S. Swiny in unpublished BIAS archive.
2. Peacocke 1887a: 179 and 376 — mentions two large artificial mounds in centre of valley, one surmounted by a *ziyārat*, and an old fort.
3. Maitland 1888a: 294 — mentions old fort mound, with several more higher up. 4½ miles from Kush Asya to Tunish Beg.
4. Maitland and Drummond 1888: 63 — mention.
5. Gaibov et al. 2010: 112 — brief description (Site K152).

SANGCHĀRAK. See **2237 SANGCHĀRAK** in Supplement.

985. SANGDARRA

Lat. 33° 11' N, long 67° 33' E. Maps 78, 79.
Ghazni Province. In the Kūh-i Khūd Valley 3 km north of Jāghūrī, near the village of Wakilkhēl.

Date: Early Sasanian, 4th–5th cent. (architectural).

Description: An artificial cave complex. The main feature is the assembly hall (Cave 3), in bad condition, that is divided by two rows of three columns each into a central 'Nave' and two outer 'aisles', 1 m lower than the 'Nave'.

Fieldwork: 1974–5 Taddei and Verardie, IsMEO — survey.

Sources:
1. Taddei 1975: 546 — brief description.
2. Verardi 1977a: 139–41 — description and photos.
3. Taddei 1978: 587–9 — mention and photo.
4. Verardi and Paparatti 2004: 62–5 — detailed description with drawings and photos.

SANG HISĀR. See **988 SANG-I SAR.**

986. SANG-I FARHĀD

Original: Lat. 34° 23' N, long. 70° 23' E. Map 66.
Revised: 34.39293419 N, 70.37154082 E /
34° 23' 34.56307212 N, 70° 22' 17.54694336 E.
Nangahār Province. In the hills between Sultānpūr and Hadda, 6 km south-west of Sultānpūr and 9 km northwest of Hadda.

Date: Kushan-Hunnic, 1st–6th cent. (architectural).

Description: Ruins of stupas and other remains.

Fieldwork: 1965 Mizuno, Kyoto University — survey.

Source: Mizuno 1971: 121 — mention (Stupas 42–4).

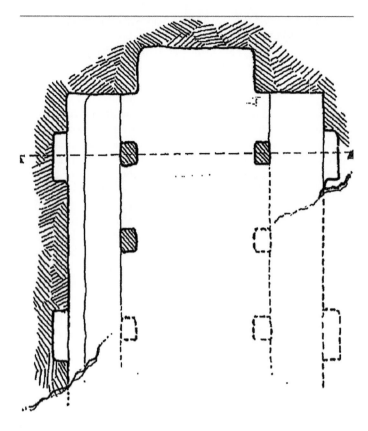

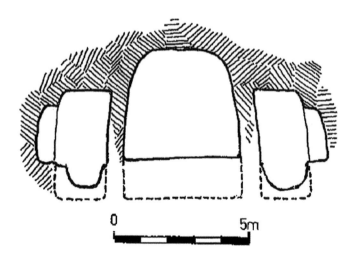

985 Sangdarra (after Verardi and Paparatti 2004).

987. SANG-I MAZĀR

Lat. 33° 08' N, long. 64° 17' E. Maps 73, 74.
Ghūr Province. Between 37 and 39 km north of Sar-i Mushkān on the road to Zarnī and Taiwāra, at the northern foot of the low pass between the Mushkān and Zarnī Valleys.

Date: ?Late Bronze, 2nd mill. (stylistic); Ghurid, 12th–13th cent. (architectural, geographical).

Description: A line of five watch towers guarding the road for almost 2 km. Most are round and are *pakhsa* construction on a stone foundation. A silver bracelet with paired birds in roundels and a cursive Arabic inscription, and a bronze tripod with three ibex heads comparable to Bactrian and Luristan bronzes, were found locally.

Fieldwork: 1977 Ball—survey.

Sources:
1. Ball 2002: 29—detailed description and photo in the context of Ghurid fortifications.
2. Wannell 2002: 238—describes the bracelet and bronze.

SANG-I MUR. See **315 FAIZĀBĀD.**

SANGINA TEPE. See **2238 SANGINA TEPE** in Supplement.

988. SANG-I SAR
Or SANG HISĀR.

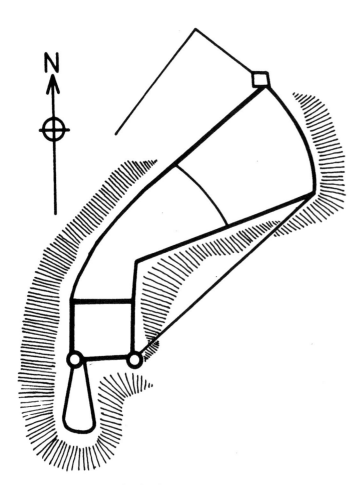

988 Sang-i Sar (David Whitehouse).

Original: Lat. 31° 32' N, long. 65° 20' E. Maps 88, 89.
Revised: 31.5255504 N, 65.28404416 E / 31°31' 31.98144864 N, 65° 17' 02.55898752 E.
Kandahār Province. A bluff overlooking the Arghandāb River 39 km west of Kandahār, some 3 km south of the road to Herat.

Dates: Indo-Parthian and Sasanian, 1st–7th cent.; Timurid, 15th–16th cent. (ceramic).

Description: A very large mud-brick fortress or fortified town in a commanding position on a natural hill. It consists of a citadel *c*.45 m square at the top, with two round towers and a lower outer work to the south. To the north is a lower enclosure containing very many building remains, and further to the north-east is a second lower enclosure on a steep slope. The foot of the hill to the south-east, north-east, and north-west has an outer curtain wall.

Fieldwork:
1. 1955–67 Ficher, DAAD—survey.
2. 1974 Whitehouse, BIAS—survey.

Sources:
1. Site information by D. Whitehouse in unpublished BIAS archive.
2. Ferrier 1857: 316—mention.
3. Ashe 1881: 37—mention.
4. Holdich 1910: 492—mention.
5. Fischer 1967a: 168—mention.
6. Fischer 1969: 338—brief summary.
7. Whitehouse 1978: 15—mentions the pottery.

989. SANG TAKHTA

Original: Lat. 34° 15' N, long. 66° 08' E. Map 56.
Revised: 34.25895316 N, 66.13187229 E /
34° 15' 32.23139328 N, 66° 07' 54.74023644 E.
Ūruzgān Province. In the Daikundi area, *c*.110 km west of Panjau.

Description: Some ruins.

Source: Kohzad 1951–4, 6/2: 13—mention.

990. SANGZAR

Lat. 31° 11' N, long. 62° 15' E. Map 84.
Nīmrūz Province. 18 km due east of Chakhānsūr, 500 m south of the road to Kilārām.

Date: Early Islamic, 8th–13th cent. (ceramic).

Description: A mound, probably marking the remains of an early Islamic staging post.

Fieldwork: 1960–70 Fischer, Bonn University—survey.

Source: Fischer et al. 1974–6: 33—mention (Tappa 12).

SANJITAK. See **2239 SANJITAK** in Supplement.

SANJIT DARRA. See 1087 SHĪWAKĪ.

SĀR. See 431 HISĀR.

SARĀI KHŪJA. See 723 MĪR BACHA KŌT.

991. SARĀI RŪD-I BĪYĀBĀN

Original: Lat. 30° 18' N, long. 61° 23' E. approximately.
Map 94.
Revised: 30.30116977 N, 61.40352193 E /
30° 18' 04.21117308 N, 61° 24' 12.67896240 E.
Nīmrūz Province. In the Rūd-i Bīyābān 3 km south-east of
the Iranian border and 11 km west of Gina Kuhna.
Dates: Parthian and Indo-Parthian, 2nd cent. BC−AD 3rd
cent.; Sasanian, 3rd–7th cent.; early Islamic, 8th–13th cent.
(ceramic).
Description: Remains of a rectangular building, probably a
caravanserai, measuring *c.*180 × 150 m with a tower at each
corner. There is a second, smaller building to the south-
west.
Fieldwork: 1951 Fairservis, AMNH—survey.
Source: Fairservis 1961: 60 and 63—brief description
(Site RB 14).

992. SARĀI SIĀH ĀB

Original: Lat. 32° 14' N, long. 62° 43' E. Map 85.
Revised:
32.22337257 N, 62.72057379 E / 32° 13' 24.14126640 N,
62° 43' 14.06563788 E (A).
32.2231212 N, 62.72990957 E / 32° 13' 23.23632252 N,
62° 43' 47.67445920 E (B).
32.22205084 N, 62.72165901 E / 32° 13' 19.38303732 N,
62° 43' 17.97245112 (C).
Farāh Province. About 70 km from this town, at the village
of Siāh Āb, near the caravanserai, on either side of the road
to Girishk.
Description: (A) West of the road, platform of square plan.
(B) East of the road, 300 m from the caravanserai, a tepe
established on a rocky outcrop: fragments of small bricks
are present. (C) Remains of a caravanserai (identified from
satellite image).
Fieldwork: 1952 Le Berre and Gardin, DAFA—survey.
Source: M. Le Berre: unpublished 1952 report, DAFA
archives, tepe Farah-Girishk 3 and 4.

**SARAK-I KHALIFA. See 2240 SARAK-I KHALIFA in
Supplement.**

993. SĀR BĀGH

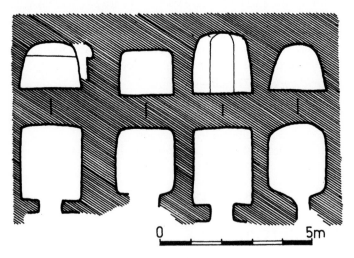

993 Sār Bāgh (after Hayashi and Sahara 1962).

Lat. 36° 03–05' N, long. 68° 04–06' E. Map 30.
Samangān Province. On the west side of a narrow gorge
formed by the Khurrum River, *c.*30 km south of Aibak.
Description: Four groups of artificial caves, each a series
of openings in the cliff face. Their date and function are
uncertain.
Fieldwork: 1960 Hayashi and Sahara, Kyoto University—
survey.
Source: Hayashi and Sahara 1962: 42–3—photos and
description in Japanese.

**SARDEH ULYA. See 2241 SARDEH ULYA in
Supplement.**

**SARGAH-I SISTAN. See 2043 DAM-I MALIK KHAN
in Supplement.**

SARHANGI. See 2250 SĪR HANGĀN in Supplement.

994. SAR-I BĪD

Lat. 35° 31' N, long. 68° 32' E. Maps 33, 49.
Baghlān Province. On the Chahārdeh Pass from Dūshi to
Siāhgird, in the Qūl-i Iskār 6.5 km south of Dahān-i Kāyān.
Description: A ruin.
Source: Drummond 1888: 335—mention.

**SAR-I CHASHMA, Baghlān. See 1123 SURKH
KOTAL.**

995. SAR-I CHASHMA, MUQQUR

Lat. 32° 51' N, long. 67° 47' E. Map 79.
Ghazni Province. At the foot of the hills 4 km north of Muqqur, at the supposed source of the Tarkal River.

Description: An artificial mound, marking the source of the river.

Source: Masson 1842: II. 216—mention.

996. SAR-I DARRA-I DARZĀB

Lat. 35° 58' N, long. 65° 27' E. Maps 24, 46.
Faryāb Province. *C.*20 km north-east of Bīlchirāgh, up the Darzāb Valley 8 km east of Darzāb.

Description: Local reports of a cave with many stone items found in its recesses.

Source: Site information by Jonathan L. Lee.

SAR-I GAU, Kandahār. See 1041 SHAHR-I GAI.

SAR-I GAU, Qundūz. See 1160 TEPE ĀHINGARĀN.

SAR-I GHŪR MUSHKĀN. See 751 MUSHKĀN.

997. SARIKOL

Lat. 34° 44' N, long. 67° 07' E. approximately. Maps 47, 57.
Bāmiyān Province. A small gulley at the head of the Balkh (Band-i Amīr) River, south of Qal'a-i Gawargīn.

Description: Many artificial caves cut into the cliff face. Several have ledges across their ends, 1 m wide and 30 cm high. The best preserved cave is a barrel-vaulted chamber 8–10 m long and 3 m high and wide.

Fieldwork: 1885 Talbot and Maitland, ABC—survey.

Source: Talbot et al. 1886: 331—brief description.

998. SAR-I MASJID

Lat. 35° 24' N, long. 64° 57' E. Map 46.
Faryāb Province. In the Darra-i Khuranj just north of where it meets the upper Murghāb River, in the area east of Laulash.

Date: Samanid, 961/2 (epigraphic).

Description: Local reports in Maimana of a building dated 350 AH.

Source: Information by Jonathan L. Lee.

999. SAR-I NAMAK

Lat. 36° 57' N, long. 67° 28' E. Map 29.
Samangān province. On the southern edge of the dunes 39 km north-west of Tāshqurghān.

Dates: Middle Palaeolithic, 30,000–10,000 BC; Upper Palaeolithic, *c.*10,000 BC (lithic).

Description: A surface site with a wide scatter of Mousterian and Mesolithic artefacts.

Fieldwork: 1975 Vinogradov, Af/Sov. Mission—survey.

Source: Vinogradov 1979—discusses the lithic assemblage generally with the rest of the survey results.

1000. SAR-I PUL

Original: Lat. 36° 13' N, long. 65° 56' E. Map 24.
Revised: 36.21188146 N, 65.92094376 E /
36° 12' 42.77325384 N, 65° 55' 15.39754644 E.
Faryāb Province. On the southern road from Shībarghān to Maimana via Sar-i Pul and Bīlchirāgh.

Dates: Early Sasanian, 3rd cent. (numismatic); Seljuk, 11th–12th cent. (stylistic).

Description: A number of medieval *zīyārat*s in and around the town, the most notable of which are the Zīyārat-i Imām-i Khurd and the Zīyārat-i Imām-i Kalān. Both are small, simple domed structures of mud-brick with elaborate stucco decoration inside. One contains an inscription identifying Sar-i Pul with medieval Anbir.

Some Bactrian documents that came to light in 1999–2000 mention *Gōzgān*, i.e. Juzjān, but possibly originated from Sar-i Pul.

A day's march to the south of Sar-i Pul, a Sasanian style rock relief was reported by Ferrier in 1845. Although the exact location of this relief is still not known, despite many attempts to locate it, its existence is in part confirmed by local reports of the relief in 1977. The finds of Roman coins, mainly of Gordion III, in the bazaar in the early 1930s, and the discovery of the Sasanian style painting of Ghulbiyān to the west in 1977, does in any case prove the existence of settlements and monuments of this date and nature in the area.

Sources:
1. Ferrier 1857: 229–30—detailed description of the rock relief.
2. Le Strange 1905: 426—summary of the historical references for Anbir.
3. Hackin 1935b: 292—mentions the coin finds.
4. Caspani 1948—discusses the rock relief and briefly describes the Italian search for it in 1946.
5. Maricq and Wiet 1959: 71–6—discuss the rock relief and Ferrier's route.
6. Bruno 1962: 107—mentions his own search for the rock relief.

7. Bivar 1966—describes his own search for the rock relief, and the two *zīyārats* and their decoration. Photos of the interiors only; no drawings.
8. Lee 1982—investigation of the whereabouts of the rock relief and revision of its location.
9. Blair 1992: 198–202—the monumental inscription dated 500/1106 of the Imamzada Yahya.
10. Hillenbrand 2000—discussion of the tombs in the broader context of Ghaznavid and Ghurid architecture.
11. Sims-Williams 2005—discusses the Bactrian documents.
12. Ball 2008: 261—summary.
13. Ball 2017: 155–6—summary of the evidence for the relief in the light of new discoveries in the Sasanian East.

1001. SAR-I SANG

Lat. 36° 13' N, long. 70° 48' E. Map 38.
Badakhshān Province. On a steep mountainside 330 m above the valley floor on the east side of the Kokcha River, *c.*56 km south of Jurm.

Description: A famous lapis lazuli mine, probably dating from proto-historic times. It consists of one old disused shaft and two new shafts.

Fieldwork: 1963 Thompson, Oxford University—survey.

Sources:
1. Wood 1872: 170–2—description of the mines and mining techniques.
2. Le Strange 1905: 436–7—summary of the historical references.
3. Barthoux 1933b—description of the mines and mineralogical analyis of the lapis.
4. Fox 1943: 61–3—description of the mines.
5. Kohzad 1948b—brief discussion of the lapis trade, mentioning the mines and listing some of the early sites where it has been found.
6. Nasiri 1962–3—detailed general background on lapis and the trade, with a description of all mines in the vicinity.
7. Thompson 1964: 1–8—geological report and account of the Oxford University expedition.
8. Herrman 1970: 22–7—detailed study of the mines, with drawings and photos, in an account of the early lapis trade with Mesopotamia.
9. Kulke 1976—detailed geological and mineralogical study of the mines, with many photos.
10. Bernard 1978a: 49–51—description of the mines and discussion of their historical importance.
11. Maxwell-Hyslop 1982—discusses the historical-geographical background of the mines and the lapis routes.
12. Ball 2008: 261—summary.

1002. SAR-I ZINDĀN

Lat. 35° 24' N, long. 65° 11' E. Map 46.
Bādghīs/Faryāb Province. On the Hashtumin River tributary of the upper Murghāb River.

Description: Local reports of a large ancient fortress, associated with a mythical king.

Source: Information by Jonathan L. Lee.

1003. SARKAR

Original: Lat. 33° 06' N, long. 61° 40' E. Map 69.
Revised: 33.08347992 N, 61.66850814 E /
33° 05' 00.52771992 N, 61° 40' 06.62929572 E.
Farāh Province. Along the valley to the south-east of the village of Sarkar west of the Kūh-i Shams and Kūh-i Bulghaja, to the west of the track from Aukal to Anārdarra.

Description: Traces of ancient mining along the valley.

Fieldwork: 1977 CNRS—geological survey.

Source: Berthoud et al. 1977: 7–8—geological description of the area.

1004. SARKHUSHAK

Original: Lat. 34° 57' N, long. 68° 00' E. Map 58.
Revised: 34.95343691 N, 68.01060555 E /
34° 57' 12.37288608 N, 68° 00' 38.17996560 E.
Overlooking the west bank of the Bāmiyān River, 31 km from Bāmiyān and 20 km from the entrance to the Shikari Valley, on the road to Dūāb-i Mīkhzarīn.

Dates: Ghaznavid and Ghurid, 10th–13th cent. (architectural, ceramic).

Description: An immense fortified complex on a bluff. It is divided into two parts by a ridge, the first part an administrative area with a palace, a mosque and a small domed tomb, the second part a citadel. The whole area is completely walled. Construction is mud-brick.

Fieldwork:
1. 1951 Allchin and Codrington—survey.
2. 1956 Ramachandran and Sharma, ASI—reconnaissance.
3. 1970 Brett et al., Bristol University—survey.
4. 1974–5 Le Berre, DAFA—survey.

Sources:
1. J. and R. Hackin 1934: 48—brief description.
2. Sidqi 1952: 34—mention.
3. Ramachandran and Sharma 1956: 127—brief description.
4. N. Dupree 1967b: 86–7—brief description.
5. Brett et al. 1970: 32–3—description and plan of the fortifications.
6. Le Berre 1987: 27–32—itinerary A-I, ruins 7 and 8.

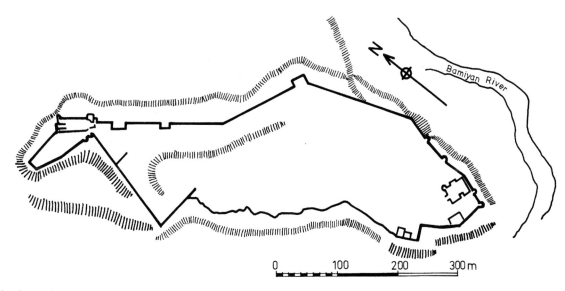

1004 Sarkhushak (after Brett et al. 1970).

7. Ball 2008: 261–2 — summary.
8. Allchin 2012: 147 — brief account of the Allchin survey.

1005. SAR KIAR

Lat. 36° 25' N, long. 67° 53' E. Map 30.
Samangān Province. Between Haibak and Tāshqurghān, c.12 km north of Kuk Jar.

Description: A possible prehistoric rock shelter.

Source: Coon 1957: 219 and 222 — mention.

1006. SAR-O-TAR
Or TAR-O SAR or SAR-O SAR. Including SHAHR-I GHULGHULA.

Original: Lat. 30° 44' N, long. 62° 07' E. Map 93.
Revised: Between 30.57893266 N, 62.09031513 E /
30° 34' 44.15758464 N, 62° 05' 25.13446188 E, 30.58688491 N, 62.10075399 E / 30° 35' 12.78569364 N,
62° 06' 02.71435788 E and 30.58984617 N, 62.08273353 E / 30° 35' 23.44622856 N, 62° 04' 57.84070152 E.
Nīmrūz Province. In the middle of the dunes 86 km southeast of Zaranj and 22 km east of Qal'a-i Fath.

Dates: Iron Age, early 1st mill. BC (architectural, ceramic); Parthian, 2nd–1st cent. BC (architectural, ceramic, numismatic); Indo-Parthian and Sasanian, 1st–7th cent. (architectural, ceramic, numismatic); Saffarid, 9th cent. (architectural, ceramic, numismatic); Ghaznavid, 11th–12th cent. (architectural, ceramic, numismatic); Ghurid, 12th–13th cent. (architectural, ceramic, numismatic); Timurid, 15th–16th cent. (architectural, ceramic, numismatic).

Description: A vast area of remains and ancient cultivation stretching for several hundred square km across the large field of sand dunes. The main part is the remains of Shahr-i Ghulghula itself, a large fortified urban site covering c.1 square km. It consists of a first, square enclosure and ditch (rounded in the southern part) 120 m wide, with remains of many houses and graves inside. There is then a second, circular enclosure and 90 m wide ditch with a third, innermost pentagonal enclosure and 45 m wide ditch marking a probable palatial complex. This stands on a mound 25 m high, and includes the remains of a mosque and over 100 rooms, many of them domed and containing stucco decoration. Most of the fortifications are mud, though there is extensive baked brick foundations and construction as well. A lower palace, bath house and numerous other structures from Saffarid/Ghaznavid times cover the lower portion inside the walls. Excavation of the main citadel shows the Islamic structures were built upon a foundation of Parthian and Sasanian remains. Finds from the area include many Parthian, Sasanian, and early Islamic coins, and a hoard of 406 copper coins dated 1167–1221 from the mosque.

Sar-o Tar is a term designating the sanded part of the southern Afghan Sistan basin, and is improperly applied sometimes to the ruins of the city of Shahr-i Gholhola. All the ruins such as the so-called 'Shahr-i Kalan' (1044) and its Masjid (715) and many other sites are in Sar-o Tar. The Smithsonian survey identified approximately 150 sites from the the Iron Age (late 2nd–early 1st mill. BC) through the Timurid period in this region. We could find no evidence of occupation prior to the Iron Age in this basin, implying that the basic engineering of the canal system upon which this region depended appears to have been done at this time. The area was densely settled with farms

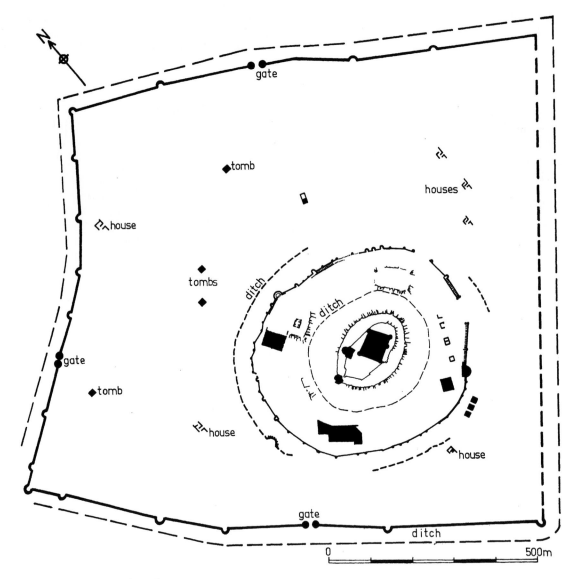

1006 Sar-o-Tar (after Tate 1910 and Hackin 1959).

in Parthian and Sasanian times and reinhabited in Saffarid/ Ghaznavid/Ghurid periods. The area was abandoned after Timurid times, leaving possibly the largest unmodified series of architectural remains from the 15th century in the world, many still standing three storeys high. Remains of extensive canals and field walls are still visible on the landscape.

Fieldwork:
1. 1903–5 Tate, SAC—survey.
2. 1936 Hackin and Meunié, DAFA—survey.
3. 1851 Fairservis, AMNH—survey.
4. 1968–71 Dales, University Museum Penn.—survey.
5. 1966, 1971–6 Trousdale, Smithsonian Institution—excavations and area survey.

Sources:
1. Additional information on the site by W. Trousdale.
2. *Civil and Mil. Gazette*, 25 Nov. 1884: 5—description of several 'Assyrian' objects found by the ABC.
3. A. C. Yate 1887: 85–6—mentions the site and some of the surface finds.
4. Codrington 1904—catalogue of the Islamic coins found at the site.
5. Rapson 1904—catalogue of the pre-Islamic coins found at the site.
6. Tate 1904: 668–70—mentions the Ghaznavid coins and a copper lamp found at the site.
7. Le Strange 1905: 343–4—summary of the historical references.

8. MacMahon 1906: 219–20—some photos and brief general references to the site and area.
9. Tate 1909: 106–8—photos and description.
10. Tate 1910: 107 and 224–34—photos and a historical geography and detailed description of the area, concentrating on the military architecture.
11. Stein 1928: 942—describes some bronze objects brought to him from the site.
12. Dollot 1937: 292–3—brief dummary of the DAFA survey.
13. Sālnāma 1937/38: between 228 and 229—photos.
14. Gardin 1959—summary of the Islamic pottery.
15. Hackin 1959c: 25–7—brief preliminary note on the survey, with photos and plans.
16. Fairservis 1961: 52–3—brief summary (Site 30).
17. Sistani 1967—good description and photos of the remains.
18. Amiri 1973—description of the site with some historical background. Photos and a plan.
19. Zaryāb 1974b—brief report on the American mission.
20. Trousdale 1976a: 59–60—desdription of the remains.
21. Trousdale 1976b—discusses the area in general terms.
22. Amiri 1979—photos and description in Persian.
23. Vincent 1979—photos and brief account of the Smithsonian mission.
24. Ball 2008: 49, 262–3.

1007. SAR RUSTĀQ
Includes DĪWĀR-I KĀFĪR and DĪWĀR-I TANG. See also 420 HAZĀRA SAMŪCH.

Original: Lat. 37° 03'–37° 08' N, long. 69° 54'–69° 58' E. Maps 35, 38.
Revised:
37.11257341 N, 69.91130156 E / 37° 06' 45.26426556 N, 69° 54' 40.68561132 E (A).
37.04054 N, 69.9687616 E / 37° 02' 25.94398416 N, 69° 58' 07.54175496 E (B).
37.1290331 N, 69.89676771 E / 37° 07' 44.51917008 N, 69° 53' 48.36376284 E (C).
37.13458383 N, 69.8930564 E / 37° 08' 04.50180348 N, 69° 53' 35.00302884 E (C).
Takhār Province. 6 km east-south-east of Rustāq, the village of Sar Rustāq is located in the centre of an archaeological region which can be divided into three sectors: (A) the village itself, with the vestiges of a kilometre-long wall (Dīwār-i Kāfir) which formerly closed access to the plain of Rustāq by the valleys and passes indicated below, in the south-east; (B) the natural road links the region of Rustāq to the valley of the Kokcha, to the south-east (Pul-i Begum), in the direction of Badakhshān, with here again a wall closing a narrow pass (Dīwār-i Tang), 8.5 km south-east of Sar Rustāq (this road uses a pass that is easily accessible by the valleys of the two streams which flow down them: the Wadi Tarāzu towards the north-west, towards the Rustāq River, and the Darya-i Dīwār-i Tang towards the south-east, in the direction of the Kokcha); (C) finally, the plateau of Sar Rustāq, north of the village, whose archaeological importance lies in a well-defined zone of kurghans, as well as in the natural road which links the plateau to a region of formerly inhabited caves, from which the nearby village of Hazāra Samūch takes its name, 6 km to the north (see no. 420).

Dates: Kushan, 1st–4th cent. (A, C); pre-Mongol Islamic, 10th–13th cent. (ceramic).

Description: (A) Dīwār-i Kāfir: strongly eroded traces of a rectilinear wall about 1 km long, oriented north–north-east/south-south-west, joining the two mountainous spurs between which flows the stream of Sar Rustāq (Wadi Tarāzu), towards the Rustāq River (to the west-north-west). The wall is rooted in the slopes of these two spurs, about 40 m above the bottom of the valley where the village lies, and then continues between the houses, which have erased it in some places. In the best-preserved segments, the height is hardly higher than 1 m and the length on the ground, 5–6 m; there is no cut to expose the structure. (B) Dīwār-i Tang: remains of a wall about 300 m long, closing the narrow passage of the stream that carries this name, between a mountainous spur to the north and a scree of large rocks to the south. The line of the wall, slightly curved in the direction of the slope of the stream (southeast), is oriented north-north-east at the northern end, south-west at the southern end. In the southern part of the line of the wall, a few irregularly spaced protrusions are observable, on the west side, of which at least one, halfway between the two ends, suggests a tower or a small fort (retaining a central passage?). The talus is made of earth and pebbles, but many remains of fired bricks (25×25 cm, 5.5 thick) are found nearby. (C) Group of closely spaced mounds, on the plateau of Sar Rustāq, about 2.5 km northwest of the village of this name; the location is indicated on the 1:100,000 map by a tepe of 5 m, which constitutes the highest of these mounds (diam. 60 m; flat top, height 5–6 m). The others, about ten in number, are grouped 200 m northeast of this mound, in a small area (150×100 m): small round (diam. 30 m) or long hillocks, height 2–2.5 m. The configuration of the site suggests a necropolis, in the Kushan tradition (kurghans); but the surface sherds are Islamic. 800 m north-west of this zone, on the left bank of the Rustāq river, an islet of terrace cut out by the latter (identifiable by a *zīyārat* at the south-west end) also produces Islamic sherds.

Collection: National Museum/AIA—sherds.

Fieldwork: 1978 Gardin et al., CNRS—survey.

Sources:
1. Site information by J.-C. Gardin.
2. Gardin and Lyonnet 1978–9: pl. II—nos. 515–17.
3. Lyonnet 1997: fig. 49—nos. 515–17.
4. Gardin 1998: 91—nos. 515–17.

1008. SASMĀQ

Original: Lat. 36° 47' N, long. 69° 28' E. Map 37.
Revised:
36.77809939 N, 69.4710628 E / 36° 46' 41.15781048 N, 69° 28' 15.82609692 E (A).
36.77497789 N, 69.46814294 E / 36° 46' 29.92038780 N, 69° 28' 05.31459156 E (B).
Takhār Province. 8 km north-west of Tāluqān, accessible by the road that runs along the Rūd-i Shārawān; tepe A is on the edge of this water course, right bank, tepe B lies 200 m away, on the left bank.

Dates: Late Chalcolithic–Early Bronze Age, *c.*3500–2500 BC (A); Achaemenid, 6th–4th cent. BC (B); Kushan, 1st–4th cent. (A); some Islamic sherds (ceramic).

Description: (A) In a bend of the Rūd-i Shārawān, on the edge of a terrace, a small, long east–west (20 × 10 m) mound, low (1.5–2 m). (B) 400 m to the south, in cotton fields, T-shaped north–south mound (40 × 40 m), flat top (2m). These two tepes, greatly damaged by cultivation, will probably soon disappear.

Collection: National Museum/AIA—sherds.

Fieldwork: 1977 Gardin et al., CNRS—survey.

Sources:
1. Site information by J.-C. Gardin.
2. Gardin and Lyonnet 1978–9: pl. IX—nos. 226–7.
3. Lyonnet 1997: figs 7, 25, 35, 49—nos. 226, 227.
4. Gardin 1998: 69—nos. 226–7.

SAUZAU. See 786 PAI MŪRIMŪRI.

1009. SAUZMA QAL'A

Lat. 36° 06' N, long. 66° 12' E. Maps 24, 47.
Balkh Province. 25 km north-west of Tukzar and *c.*58 km east of Sar-i Pul in the Sanghārak district south of Balkh.

Date: Sasanian, 3rd–7th cent. (stylistic).

Description: A chance find of a three-headed, four-armed composite figure in limestone, representing Shiva, Buddha, and Heracles. The figure may be a fake.

Collection: Mazār-i Sharīf Museum—figure.

Sources:
1. Ramachandran and Sharma 1956: I. 21 and III. 15—brief description.
2. Fischer 1957—description of the find and discussion of other Shiva-Heracles images.
3. Fischer 1959a: 131—mention.
4. Fischer 1961c—mention.
5. Bussagli 1962c: 86 n. 2—brief discussion.
6. Tucci 1968—brief discussion of its authenticity.

7. Fischer 1969: 348—mention.
8. Mustamandy 1997—discusses the Herakles figure in the context of Gandharan art generally.

SAWĀL. See 1073 SHAWĀL.

1010. SĀWARI
Or SĀBARI.

Lat. 31° 33' N, long. 61° 17' E. approximately. Map 83.
Nīmrūz Province. In the middle of the Hāmūn-i Sāwari, only visible when it is dry.

Description: Remains of a large town, much of it of baked brick. Many coins and seals were found there when the *hāmūn* ran dry in 1902.

Source: Tate 1910: 115—brief description.

SAYYAD. See 1207 TURT QUL TEPE.

1011. SAYYADĀN DARRA

Original: Lat. 35° 41' N, long. 69° 18' E. Map 50.
Revised: 35.68626971 N, 69.32564366 E /
35° 41' 10.57093944 N, 69° 19' 32.31717492 E.
Baghlān Province. In a branch of the Andarāb Valley, 10 km north-east of Banū.

Date: ?Ghurid, 12th–13th cent. (traditional).

Description: Reports of the remains of a fortress, locally attributed to Sultān Ghiyyas al-Dīn.

Sources:
1. Maitland 1888b: 435—mention.
2. Gazetteer 1972: I. 73—mention.

1012. SAYYIDĀBĀD

Lat. 37° 06' N, long. 66° 02' E. Map 24.
Juazjān Province. On the southern edge of the dunes *c.*26 km north-west of Āqcha and 2 km north of the village of Sayyidābād.

Date: Neolithic, 7th–6th mill. BC (lithic).

Description: A group of four surface sites with a very extensive scatter of stone tools.

Fieldwork: 1976 Vinogradov, Af/Sov. Mission—survey.

Source: Vinogradov 1979: 42–4—general discussion of the lithic assemblage from the survey with comparisons in Soviet Central Asia (Sites 426–7).

1013. SEH DARRA

Lat. 36° 42' N, long. 68° 52' E. Map 32.
Qundūz Province. 3 km south of Qundūz on the road to 'Aliābād.

Date: ?Kushan. 1st–3rd cent. (architectural).

Description: A mound containing a square structure, characteristic of the Kushan period.

Fieldwork: 1955 and 1960 Fischer, DAAD—survey.

Source: Fischer 1961a: 17—mention.

1014. SEH PISTA

Lat. 35° 32' N, long. 68° 22' E. Map 49.
Baghlān Province. On the left bank of the Surkhāb between Bāmiyān and Dūshi, *c.*30 km north-east of Tālā.

Dates: Kushan and early Sasanian, 2nd–6th cent.; Turk, 7th–10th cent. (ceramic).

Description: Ruins of a building in the style of a caravanserai. The rooms inside are barrel-vaulted or domed. Construction is of large mud-bricks.

Fieldwork:
1. 1955–68 Fischer, DAAD—survey.
2. 1974–5 Le Berre, DAFA—survey.

Sources:
1. Fischer 1969: 345—summary.
2. Le Berre 1987—itinerary A-I, ruin 29.
3. Gardin and Lyonnet, 1980 chronological study of pottery from unpublished DAFA surveys.

1015. SEHSHAMBA

Lat. 36° 11' N, long. 65° 57' E. Map 24.
Jauzjān Province. 5 km south-east of Sar-i Pul on the road to Sangchārak.

Description: Some ruins.

Source: Amir Khan and Shahzada Taimus 1888c: 250—mention.

1016. SEH TŪPĀN

Original: Lat. 34° 27' N, long. 69° 18' E. Map 62.
Revised: 34.44857168 N, 69.31148026 E /
34° 26' 54.85805808 N, 69° 18' 41.32895364 E.
Kābul Province. 7.5 km east of the village of Shīwakī and 1.5 km east of Kamari stupa.

Date: Kushan-Sasanian, 1st–7th cent. (architectural).

Description: A series of ruins that include the remains of probably six stupas. One is reasonably well preserved, still with much of its frieze of blind arches and pilasters.

Collections: BM—stupa deposits.

Fieldwork:
1. 1833 Honigberger—excavation.
2. 1934 Masson—survey.
3. 1923 Foucher, DAFA—survey.
4. 1971 Fussman, CNRS—survey.

Sources:
1. Jacquet 1836b: 246–7—mentions Honigberger's work and illustrates the stupas.
2. Masson 1841: 114—mention.
3. Pandit 1927: 132—photo of the main stupa.
4. Foucher 1942–7: 147—mention.
5. Fussman et al. 2008: 55–62, 224–33, and 300—detailed description, photos, and drawings.
6. Errington 2017a: 76–7 and 2017b: 103—the Masson collection and archive relating to the site.

SEIĀB. See 1229 WARDAK.

1017. SHĀBASH

Original: Lat. 34° 30' N, long. 61° 23' E. Map 51.
Revised:
34.48324654 N, 61.38509497 E / 34° 28' 59.68752816 N, 61° 23' 06.34188984 E (A).
34.49602965 N, 61.38475654 E / 34° 29' 45.70672272 N, 61° 23' 05.12355696 E (B).
34.5026692 N, 61.38410709 E / 34° 30' 09.60911892 N, 61° 23' 02.78552184 E (B).
Herat Province. (A) 101 km north-west of Herat, just to the south of the main road to Islām Qal'a. (B) 16 km from Ghuriyān on the route to Kuhsan, 6 km west of Shābash.

Date: Early Islamic, 8th–13th cent. (ceramic).

Description: (A) A site; surface sherds included incised and moulded wares (B. De Cardi). A few low mounds, covered in many broken baked bricks and building debris on either side of the road to the west of the village (presumably all that remains of the baked brick fort recorded in the 19th century, below). Stretches for a few hundred metres in either direction, near a modern mud-brick caravanserai. Very little pottery (W. Ball). (B) A small, irregular fort *c.*90 m diam. Mostly baked brick, with square towers at irregular intervals. Walls 10–13 m high. 3 m wide ditch to north and west. Nearby are ruins of a large (according to Peacocke) or small (according to Maitland) caravanserai.

Fieldwork:
1. 1884 Peacocke, Maitland, ABC—topographical survey.
2. 1949 De Cardi—survey.
3. 1977 Ball, BIAS—survey.

Sources:
1. Peacocke 1885a: 45 — detailed description.
2. Maitland 1888a: 137 — mentions caravanserai.
3. Maitland and Drummond 1888: 6 and 22 — mention ruins of 'small but handsome' baked brick caravanserai west of Shābash.

1018. SHADYĀN TANGI

Original: Lat. 36° 34' N, long. 67° 09' E. Map 28.
Revised: 36.5686523 N, 67.14223526 E / 36° 34' 07.14827316 N, 67° 08' 32.04693384 E.
Balkh Province. A ravine through the Kūh-i Alburz *c.*16 km south of Mazār-i Sharīf on the road to Marmul.

Description: At a point in the ravine that is only 8 m wide there is an ancient stone and mortar arch with remains of brick chambers on top.

Fieldwork:
1. 1886 Maitland and Peacocke, ABC — topographical survey.
2. 1924 Foucher, DAFA — survey.

Source:
1. Peacocke 1887a: 359 — brief description.
2. Maitland 1888b: 183–4 — brief description.
3. Yate 1888: 260 — brief description.
4. Foucher 1942–7: 174 and pl. IIc — description and photo.
5. Gazetteer 1979: IV. 524 — mention.

SHAHĀR KALĪL or CHAHĀR DARRA. See 2243 SHAHĀR KALĪL in Supplement.

1019. SHĀH 'ALI

Includes BAGHA-I ZAGHIRAH and JA'USHAN BEG.
Original: Lat. 36° 42'–36° 43' N, long. 69° 13'–69° 16' E. Map 36.
Revised:
36.7054632 N, 69.26911602 E / 36° 42' 19.66751280 N, 69° 16' 08.81767956 E (A).
36.70469101 N, 69.26902353 E / 36° 42' 16.88762952 N, 69° 16' 08.48470764 E (B).
Takhār Province. In the lower part of the Bangui River, followed upstream by the road from its confluence with the Tāluqān river: the first tepe (A) is 1.9 km from the fork in the road from Khānābād to Tāluqān, on the left bank of the river; the second (B) is on the right bank, on the edge of the river, near the village of Qul Braq (or Barak).

Dates: Achaemenid, 6th–4th cent. BC; Kushan and Hunnic-Turk, 1st–9th cent. (B); some Islamic sherds (ceramic).

Description: (A) On the edge of the Bangui road, south side, in the courtyard of a house: small round mound (diam. 10 m, height 1 m), with sherds of the Achaemenid period. (B) Hamlet of Bagha-i Zaghirah, 1 km south of the Bangui road (by a small road on the western edge of the village of Qul Braq): tepe Ja'ushan Beg, on the edge of the terrace that overlooks the Bangui River, right bank. This tepe, height 6 m (terrace side), has been strongly eaten into by crops, as well as by a canal dug below (river side): the surface area of the site, at the time about 80 × 80 m, would have been larger in the past (50 m to the north-east, a similar but lower mound, *c.*1 m, was part of it, producing the same sherds of the Achaemenid and Kushan periods). On the north face, in the cuts, traces of east–west wall in *pakhsa*, surmounted by layers of ashes, some burnt (charcoal, ashes), some not (waste, debris?).

Collection: National Museum/AIA — sherds.

Fieldwork: 1978 Gardin et al., CNRS — survey.

Sources:
1. Site information by J.-C. Gardin.
2. Gardin and Lyonnet 1978–9: pl. XI — nos. 347–9.
3. Lyonnet 1997: figs 25, 35, 49, 68, 69 — nos. 347–9.
4. Gardin 1998: 97 — nos. 347–9.

SHĀHBAL. See 282 DEH QILA.

1020. SHĀHBID
Or RABĀT-I SHĀHBID.

Lat. 33° 56' N, long. 62° 14' E. Map 70.
Revised: 33.94265442 N, 62.23736459 E / 33° 56' 33.55590804 N, 62° 14' 14.51251212 E.
Herat Province. 33 km south of Herat on the road to Adraskān, on the left bank of a stream.

Description: A ruined caravanserai dedicated to Shaikh Ismā'īl Khān Mustaufī. There are a few badly damaged inscriptions, one of them giving the dedication.

Fieldwork: 1885 Peacocke, ABC — topographical survey.

Sources:
1. Lal 1846: 169–70 — mention and translation of the inscription.
2. Peacocke 1887a: 213 — mention.

1021. SHAHĪDĀN
Including KĀFIRI andI SABZAK. See also 233 DARBAND.

Original: Lat. 34° 53'–34° 54' N, long. 67° 37'–67° 38' E. Map 48.

Revised: 34.88096706 N, 67.65235968 E /
34° 52' 51,48142212 N, 67° 39' 08.49486276 E.
Bāmiyān province. Along the valley of the Shahīdān/Gumbad River, beginning 1 km north of Deh Sauzak and continuing up to the village of Shahīdān, c.20 km north-west of Bāmiyān.

Date: Turk and/or pre-Mongol Islamic, 7th–13th cent. (architectural).

Description: Ruins of a line of fortifications along the sides of the valley. North of Deh Sauzak is an ancient well-preserved building like a 'Hindu temple' according to 19th-century reports, known as Kāfiri, high up above the valley. It has a low dome with a pointed arch, and is baked brick construction. This presumably refers to the conical tower with elaborate external decoration of impressed triangles and lozenges separated by a 'herringbone' brick course described by Le Berre.

Fieldwork:
1. 1885 Sahibdad Khan, ABC—topographical survey.
2. 1974–5 Le Berre, DAFA—survey.
3. 2002 Lee, Society for South Asian Studies—reconnaissance.

Sources:
1. Maitland 1888b: 4—quotes Sahibdad Khan's description of the 'Hindu temple'.
2. Le Berre 1987: 76 and pl. 98—description and photo; itinerary B-I, ruins 17–19.
3. Lee 2006: 245–7—mention and photo.
4. Baumer 2014: 202–3—photo of a huge fortress.

1022. SHĀHI KHAILA
Or KĀFIR TEPE.

Original: Lat. 36° 44' N, long. 67° 41' E. Map 29.
Revised: 36.73054915 N, 67.68744944 E /
36° 43' 49.97693784 N, 67° 41' 14.81799444 E.
Samangān Province. 4 km north of Tāshqurgān.

Dates: Beg. Iron, end 2nd–beg. 1st mill. BC; Sasanian-Hunnic, 4th–6th cent.; pre-Mongol Islamic, 10th–13th cent.; Timurid, 15th–16th cent. (ceramic).

Description: Tepe of 6 m (no other data).

Collection: National Museum/AIA—sherds.

Fieldwork: 1969 Gouin, DAFA—survey.

Source: Gouin 1974 and unpublished report in DAFA archives—site no. 47.

SHĀH-I MARDAN. See 383 GUDAR-I SHĀH

1023. SHĀH-I MASHHAD

Original: Lat. 35° 02–03' N, long. 63° 59' E. Map 45.
Revised: 35.03534828 N, 63.99258629 E /
35° 02' 07.25379864 N, 63° 59' 33.31064436 E.

Bāgdhīs Province. In the Jawand area on the left bank of the Murghāb River, c.2 km downstream from its confluence with the Kucha River.

Date: Ghurid, 1165–76 (epigraphic).

Description: Ruins of an elaborately decorated baked brick *madrasa* and mausoleum of Sultan Saif al-Dīn. Only parts of the northern and eastern sides are still standing, the best preserved of which is the east part of the façade. This includes an entrance *iwān* and two originally domed rooms. There are 15 bands of Kufic and *naskhī* inscription. On the surface are some scattered sgraffiato sherds.

Fieldwork:
1. 1886 Hira Singh, ABC—topographical survey.
2. 1970 Casimir and Glatzer, Heidelberg University—survey.
3. 1977 Aalund, DACAAR—survey.
4. 1993 Glatzer and Najimi, DACAAR—survey.

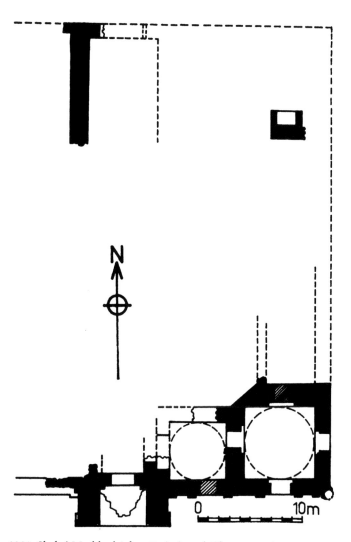

1023 Shāh-i Mashhad (after Casimir and Glatzer 1971).

Sources:

1. Hira Singh 1891: 146 — mentions baked brick remains.
2. Achak 1970 — description.
3. Casimir and Glatzer 1971a — brief preliminary report and historical background.
4. Casimir and Glatzer 1971b — full description and discussion of the architecture and decoration.
5. Glatzer 1973 — description of the architecture and inscriptions.
6. Gazetteer 1975: III. 360 — mentions ruins of an ancient city.
7. Habibi 1977 — analysis of the inscriptions.
8. Herberg 1978: 220 — brief description.
9. *Kabul Times* 1979a — mentions repair work carried out.
10. Samizay 1981: 15 — summary of the remains and note on the conservation needs.
11. Aalund 1990: 8–12 — plans and photographs.
12. Michaud and Barry 1996: pls 48–9 — colour photos of the brick work.
13. Hillenbrand 2000 — discussion in the broader context of Ghaznavid and Ghurid architecture.
14. Wannell 2002: 239–42 — brief description and historical discussion, with photos taken in 1989.
15. Flood 2005a: 280–1 — discusses possible Karramiyya associations of the monument.
16. Ball 2008: 263 — summary.
17. Flood 2009a: 103–5 — further discussion of possible Karramiyya associations.
18. Najimi 2015 — detailed analysis of the history, architecture, and epigraphy, including some hitherto unpublished inscriptions.

1024. SHĀH-I WALAYAT

Lat. 33° 07' N, long. 64° 30' E. Maps 55, 74.
Farāh Province. North of Gulistān in the mountainous area north of Dilārām.

Description: Some historical remains reported by Muhammad Said Mashhal.

Source: Rafat 1980: 5 — mention.

1025. SHĀH KHWĀJA
Or GHUNDI FATO.

Original: Lat. 33° 08' N, long. 67° 37' E. Maps 78, 79.
Revised: 33.12777538 N, 67.62038061 E /
33° 07' 39.99138132 N, 67° 37' 13.37018196 E.
Ghazni Province. In the Jāghūrī area 2 km west of Lūmān and 1 km east of tepe Sinaubar.

Dates: Early Sasanian, 3rd–4th cent. (architectural); Turki Shahi, 7th–8th cent. (ceramic).

Description: A group of three mounds. The largest has some mud-brick structures, one of them a *pakhsa* passage with a mud-brick vault, and a few partly filled-in caves. The main cave has a row of niches inside, probably representing the 'thousand Buddha' iconography.

Fieldwork: 1974 Taddei and Verardi, IsMEO — survey.

Sources:
1. Taddei 1974b: 546 — brief description and photo.
2. Verardi 1977a: 138 — description and photos.
3. Verardi and Paparatti 2004: 47 — detailed description with drawing and photos.

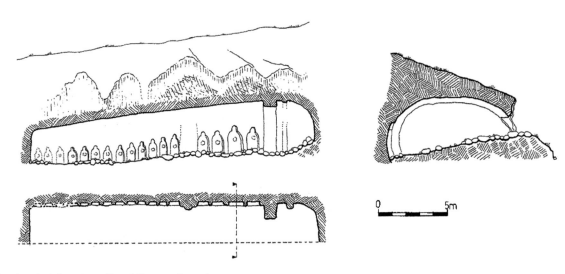

1025 Shah Khwāja (after Verardi and Paparatti 2004).

1026. SHĀHKŌT

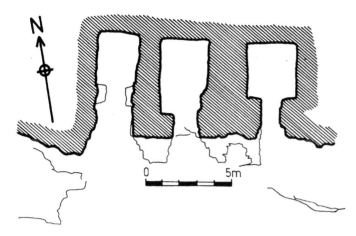

1026 Shāhkōt (after Mizuno 1971).

Lat. 34° 18' N, long. 79° 55' E. Map 68.
Nangahār Province. C.5 km north-east of the Chakanūr caves, between the villages of Guldāg and Khūzāzo Kalay.

Description: A small series of artificial caves.

Fieldwork: 1965 Mizuno, Kyoto University—survey.

Source: Mizuno 1971: 8—plan and photo.

1027. SHĀHMAQ

Lat. 34° 58' N, long. 69° 08' E. Map 64.
Parwān Province. At the foot of the hills on the western side of the Kūh-i Dāman Plain, 2 km south of Tūp Darra.

Description: Some mounds and some remains of stone terraces, with some caves in the hills.

Fieldwork: 1834 Masson—survey.

Source: Masson 1842: III. 139—mention.

1028. SHĀH MAQSŪD

Original: Lat. 31° 59' N, long. 65° 28' E. Map 89.
Revised: 31.98656567 N, 65.47358415 E /
31° 59' 11.63640372 N, 65° 28' 24.90295188 E.
Kandahār Province. In the Khākrīz Valley 56 km north of Kandahār. The site is to the west of the shrine.

Description: A cemetery, associated with a famous shrine, covered in many fragments of ancient worked marble.

Source: N. Dupree 1977: 307—mention.

SHĀH MĀR. See 2242 SHĀH MĀR in Supplement.

1029. SHĀH QURGHĀN

Lat. 33° 33' N, long. 67° 15' E. Map 77.
Ūruzgān Province. C.7 km north-east of Ajristān bazaar, in the mountains north of Ūruzgān.

Description: Reports of the remains of an ancient town, covering a considerable area, where large numbers of coins and other antiquities have been found.

Sources:
1. Masson 1842: II. 223–4—mentions the site and finds.
2. Gazetteer 1910: IV. 325—mention.
3. Bivar 1954a: 118—mention.

1030. SHAHRĀBĀD

Original: Lat. 34° 22' N, long. 61° 24' E. Map 51.
Revised: 34.34341461 N, 61.42284182 E /
34° 20' 36.29259924 N, 61° 25' 22.23054372 E.
Herat Province. 10 km west of Ghūriyān to the north-east of the field of ruins of Palgird, near Shahrābād.

Dates: Beg. Iron, end 2nd–beg. 1st mill. BC; Timurid, 15th–16th cent. (ceramic).

Description: Quadrangular platform (c.120 × 120 m), 8.5 m high, surrounded by enclosure walls.

Collection: National Museum/AIA—sherds.

Fieldwork: 1952 Le Berre and Gardin, DAFA—survey.

Source: M. Le Berre: unpublished 1952 report, DAFA archives.

1031. SHAHRAK

Original: Lat. 34° 07' N, long. 64° 18' E. Map 54.
Revised: 34.08702247 N, 64.32334863 E /
34° 05' 13.28088624 N, 64° 19' 24.05508456 E.
Ghūr Province. (A) On the central road between Chakhchārān and Adraskan. (B) 5 km east of Shahrak on road to Chakhchārān.

Dates: Sasanian, 3rd–7th cent.; early Islamic, 10th–12th cent. (ceramic).

Description: (A) Many mounds and remains in the vicinity of the town of Shahrak, producing pseudo-prehistoric painted pottery. (B) A ruined mud-brick tower, and another further up the valley.

Fieldwork:
1. 1885 Maitland and Talbot, ABC—topographical survey.
2. 1961 Dupree and Fischer—sondages.

Sources:
1. Maitland 1888a: 371—mentions the towers.
2. Dupree and Fischer 1961—brief description of the sondages.
3. Dupree 1964: 1—brief description.
4. Fischer 1969: 343—brief summary (Sites P1 and P2).

SHAHRAK KUHNA. See **2244 SHAHRAK KUHNA** in Supplement.

1032. SHĀHRAWĀN GUR TEPE

Original: Lat. 37° 05'−37° 06' N, long. 69° 15'−69° 17' E. Maps 31, 35.
Revised:
37.09520439 N, 69.27563045 E / 37° 05' 42.73580472 N, 69° 16' 32.26960704 E (A).
37.09142557 N, 69.24488836 E / 37° 05' 29.13205380 N, 69° 14' 41.59809096 E (B).
Qundūz Province. East of Shāhrawān, on the edge of the road from Imām Sāhib to Khwāja Ghar: (A) at 3 km, north side, Gur Tepe: (B) at 1 km, north and south sides, two little mounds in the process of disappearing.

Dates: Hellenistic, 3rd–1st cent. BC; Kushan and Hunnic-Turk, 1st–9th cent.; pre-Mongol Islamic, 10th–13th cent. (ceramic).

Description: (A) High rectangular mound (c.100 × 80 m, height 10 m) on the edge of a terrace of the Āmū Dāryā (like no. 209). The top is flat, without a trace of visible structures; the flanks are eaten into by the surrounding crops. (B) Oblong north–south mounds, greatly damaged by the crops: the largest, south side of the road (c.50 × 40 m, height 1 m), produces thick fired bricks (7 cm) and cut blocks of limestone; the smallest, 100 m east of the preceding one, on the north side of the road, will soon no longer exist (c.30 × 20 m, height 0.5 m).

Collection: National Museum/AIA — sherds.

Fieldwork: 1977 Gardin et al., CNRS — survey.

Sources:
1. Site information by J.-C. Gardin.
2. Gardin and Lyonnet 1978–9: pl. IV — nos. 11–13.
3. Lyonnet 1997: figs 39, 49, 68, 69 — nos. 11–13.
4. Gardin 1998: 55 — nos. 11–13.

1033. SHAHR-I ARMĀN

Original: Lat. 34° 38' N, long. 63° 52' E. Map 54.
Revised: 34.63633916 N, 63.86375462 E / 34° 38' 10.82096448 N, 63° 51' 49.51663956 E.
Bādghīs Province. South-east of Qal'a-i Nau in the northern foothills of the Band-i Bādghīsāt.

Date: Ghurid, 11th–13th cent. (ceramic).

Description: Remains of a small town, consisting of a ruined stone fort surrounded by mounds, ruins, and ancient gardens and irrigation, possibly the site of the Ghurid city of Shurmin. Many Seljuk ceramics found at the site, seen in local houses. The site has been extensively robbed.

Fieldwork: 1886 Hira Singh, ABC — topographical survey.

Sources:
1. Holdich 1886: 6 — mention.
2. Holdich 1887: 20 — brief description.
3. Maitland 1888a: 359 — mention from hearsay.
4. Hira Singh 1891: 145 — mention.
5. Sidqi 1952: 6 — mention.
6. Kohzad 1951–4, 9/2: 19 — mention from hearsay.
7. Wannell 2002: 242–3 — brief description and photos of some of the objects recovered.

1034. SHAR-I BANŪ, WEST

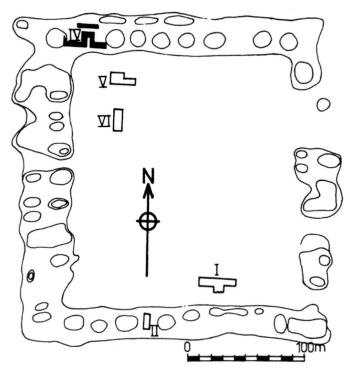

1034 Shahr-i Banu, west (after Carl 1959b).

Original: Lat. 36° 50' N, long. 67° 40' E. Map 29.
Revised: 36.82857563 N, 67.66114152 E / 36° 49' 42.87228204 N, 67° 39' 40.10947992 E.
Samangān Province. In the dasht 18 km north of Tāshqurghān.

Dates: Bronze and Iron Age, 2nd and early 1st mill. BC (A few sherds only); Hellenistic, 3rd–1st cent. BC; Kushan, 1st–3rd cent. (numismatic): Sasanian, Hunnic, and Turk, 3rd–9th cent.; pre-Mongol Islamic, 10th–13th cent.; Timurid, 15th–16th cent. (ceramic).

Description: Remains of several superimposed settlements surrounding a rectangular fortification wall, c.6 m high. The walls are massive mud construction with hollow square towers less than 20 m apart. Excavations consisted of several trenches in the settlement and walls, and fnds included several coins, terracotta reliefs, and various sculptures.

Fieldwork:
1. 1934 Hackin, DAFA—excavations.
2. 1938 Carl, DAFA—excavations.
3. 1960 Hayashi and Sahara, Kyoto University—survey.
4. 1969 Gouin, DAFA—survey.

Sources:
1. Gardin and Lyonnet, 1980 chronological study of pottery from unpublished DAFA surveys.
2. Hackin 1935b: 290—mentions Kushan coins found.
3. Carl 1959b—summary report on the excavations and catalogue of the finds.
4. Hayashi and Sahara 1962: 46–53—photos, drawings, and summary of the pottery.
5. Gouin 1974 and unpublished report—Site 6.
6. Pugachenkova 1974a—refers to Shahr-i Banu in a wider discussion of Bactrian art and architecture.
7. Francfort 1979: 32–6—lists the site and discusses the general principles of Kushan fortifications.

1035. SHAHR-I BANŪ, EAST

Original: Lat. 36° 50' N, long. 67° 40' E. Map 29.
Revised: 36.83263546 N, 67.6673354 E / 36° 49' 57.48765492 N, 67° 40' 02.40745332 E.
Samangān Province. 15 km north of Tāshqurgān and about 1 km east of the main ruins of Shahr-i Banū.

Dates: Kushan and Sasanian, 1st–5th cent.; Hunnic-Turk, 5th–9th cent.; pre-Mongol Islamic, 10th–13th cent.; Timurid, 15th–16th cent. (ceramic).

Description: (A) 0.7 km east-north-east of Shahr-i Banu, a quadrangular tepe of about 50 m per side, with traces of a rampart, 6 m; a gap on the north side. (B) 1.2 km east of Shahr-i Banu, area of sherds.

Collection: National Museum/AIA—sherds.

Fieldwork: 1969 Gouin, DAFA—survey.

Source: Gouin 1974 and unpublished report—sites no. 21 (A) and 19 (B).

1036. SHAHR-I BANŪ, SOUTH-EAST

Original: Lat. 36° 49' N, long. 67° 40'–67° 41' E. Map 29.
Revised:
36.81762004 N, 67.66698706 E /
36° 49' 03.43214220 N, 67° 40' 01.15339980 E (A).
36.8210242 N, 67.67705363 E /
36° 49' 15.68713620 N, 67° 40' 37.39305576 E (B).
36.81705706 N, 67.68601175 E /
36° 49' 01.40542284 N, 67° 41' 09.64230180 E (C).
Samangān Province. 15 km north of Tāshqurghān and about 2 km south-east of the main ruins of Shahr-i Banū.

Dates: Hellenistic, 3rd–1st cent. BC (A); Kushan, Sasano-Hunnic, and Turk, 1st–9th cent. (A, B, C); pre-Mongol Islamic, 10th–13th cent.; Timurid, 15th–16th (C). (ceramic).

Description: Group of three sites south-east of Shahr-i Banu: (A) at 1.3 km, square enclosure (c.100 × 100 m), very eroded, max. height 2 m; (B) at 1.8 km, rectangular enclosure (c.130 × 70 m), very eroded, max. height 1.5 m; (C) 1 km east of the preceding tepe, a tepe 4 m high, with a depression at the top; traces of walls in large square bricks (30 × 30 cm).

Collection: National Museum/AIA—sherds.

Fieldwork: 1969 Gouin, DAFA—survey.

Source: Gouin 1974 and unpublished report, DAFA archives—sites no. 5 and 18 respectively.

1037. SHAHR-I BARBAR, BADAKHSHĀN
   Or BAHĀRAK.

Original: Lat. 36° 59' N, long. 70° 53' E. Map 38.
Revised: 37.00277912 N, 70.90539235 E / 37° 00' 10.00482444 N, 70° 54' 19.41246288 E.
Badakhshān Province. In the foothills immediately to the east of Barak on the Kokcha River, guarding the approach to the Darya-i Zardū.

Date: Early Islamic, 10th–13th cent. (ceramic).

Description: A large settlement with remains of massive stone walls. There are also two large mounds of rough masonry known as Kafir Qal'a that may be ruined stupas.

Fieldwork:
1. 1938 Barger, ASI—survey.
2. 1975 Kohl—survey.

Sources:
1. Barger 1938: 116—mention.
2. Barger 1939a: 389–90—mention.
3. Barger 1939b: brief description and photo.
4. Barger and Wright 1941: 50—brief description.
5. Kohl 1978: 65—mention.

1038. SHAHR-I BARBAR, BALKH

Original: Lat. 37° 00' N, long. 66° 46' E. Map 26.
Revised: 36.99918667 N, 66.77090316 E / 36° 59' 57.07202424 N, 66° 46' 15.25139076 E.
Balkh Province. 3 km south of Aliyak just to the east of Hayatān on the road from Kilift to Balkh.

Description: An artificial mound surrounded by a ditch with fortifications on top. Said to be the remains of a town contemporary with Termez.

Fieldwork: 1886 Ata Muhammad, ABC—topographical survey.

Sources:
1. Yavorski 1885: 65—mention.
2. Maitland 1888a: 502–3—brief description.
3. Maitland 1888b: 274—mention.
4. Gazetteer 1979: IV. 315—mention.

1039. SHAHR-I BARBAR, BĀMIYĀN
See also 189 CHEHEL BURJ, Bāmiyān.

Original: Lat. 34° 45' N, long. 67° 00' E. Map 47.
Revised: 34.74892618 N, 67.01776926 E /
34° 44' 56.13425772 N, 67° 01' 03.96934716 E.
Bāmiyān Province. 40 km downstream from Band-i Amīr and *c.*53 km upstream from Chehel Burj, where the Sarikol stream joins the Band-i Amīr River.

Date: Turk and/or Ghurid, 7th–13th cent. (architectural).

Description: Not to be confused with Chehel Burj (Site 189) which is also known as Shahr-i Barbar. Remains of a fortified town on an escarpment *c.*400 m above the valley. It consists of a curtain wall, 2.5 m thick and up to 4 m high, in rough stone courses around the north side of the escarpment. Some domed chambers are built into the thickness of the walls. Inside are various remains of stone and baked brick, including four cisterns. The site is traditionally said to be the capital of the kingdom of Gurgin, pre-dating the Mongol conquest.

Fieldwork:
1. 1885 Talbot and Maitland, ABC—survey.
2. 2002 Lee, Society for South Asian Studies—reconnaissance.

Sources:
1. Talbot et al. 1886: 330–1—fairly detailed description.
2. Gazetteer 1910: IV. 466—mention.
3. Holdich 1910: 257—mention.
4. Kohzad 1951–4, 6/2: 3 and 8—mention from hearsay.
5. Lee 2006: 235–6—brief description and photo.
6. Ball 2008: 264—summary.

1040. SHAHR-I CHANGIZ
Or TĀH-I SHAHR. Including PAITAKHT-I CHANGIZ.

Lat. 35° 41' N, long. 67° 16' E. Maps 30, 47.
Samangān Province. In the Darra-i Sūf, 4 km south of Kamach.

Description: Remains of an ancient city, that include the ruins of a mosque and a 'darbar hall', still in good condition, of baked brick construction. On top of some cliffs to the south-east are some ruins of more baked brick buildings, known as Paitakht-i Changiz.

Fieldwork: 1886 Amir Khan, ABC—topographical survey.

Sources:
1. Amir Khan 1888: 163–4—brief description.
2. Gazetteer 1979: IV. 552—mention.

1041. SHAHR-I GAI
Or SAR-I GAU.

Lat. 31° 41' N, long. 65° 37' E. Map 89.
Kandahār Province. In the Arghandāb Valley on the north side of the village of Manāra, to the west of the road to Shāh Maqsūd.

Dates: Sasano-Hunnic, 3rd–5th cent.; Mongol-Timurid, 14th–15th cent. (ceramic).

Description: A small irregular mound, *c.*20 m across and 4 m high, with very little pottery.

Fieldwork:
1. 1950–1 Fairservis, AMNH—survey.
2. 1974 Whitehouse, BIAS—survey.

Source: Fairservis 1971: 393—mention (Site Khr 1).

SHAHR-I GHULGHULA, Kūh-i Bābā. See 2245
SHAHR-I GHULGHULA, Kūh-i Bābā in Supplement.

1042. SHAHR-I GHULGHULA, BĀMIYĀN
Including QAL'A-I DUKHTĀR. See also 100 BĀMIYĀN.

Original: Lat. 34° 49' N, 67° 51' E. Map 58.
Revised: 34.81817797 N, 67.83870579 E /
34° 49' 05.44068444 N, 67° 50' 19.34084112 E.
Bāmiyān Province. 3 km south-east of the Bāmiyān bazaar.

Dates: Late Sasanian and Turk, 6th–9th cent. (ceramic); Ghaznavid, 11th–12th cent. (stylistic); Ghurid, 12th–13th cent. (architectural, ceramic, and epigraphic).

Description: Remains of a fortified urban site, with the remains of a mud-brick fort, the Qal'a-i Dukhtar, 1 km to the east. Construction is mostly mud. The remains include two early Islamic mosques, and accidental finds have included an elaborately engraved Ghaznavid brass bowl and an early 13th-cent. carved wooden door. To the north-east are the remains of a stupa constructed of stone and bonded with mud. It measures 24 × 16 m and survives to a height of 2.5 m, within a 100 × 70 m enclosure.

Fieldwork:
1. 1951 Allchin and Codrington—sondage.
2. 1970 Brett et al., Bristol University—survey.

Sources:
1. Masson c. 1833c: 30 sketch of the remains.
2. Jacquet 1837: 420–1—general discussion of the remains.
3. Masson 1839: 100–1—brief description.
4. Moorcroft and Trebeck 1841: II. 387–93—brief description.
5. Masson 1842: II. 390–3—detailed description of the site, mentions finds of manuscripts and Islamic coins.
6. W. Griffith 1847: 403—summary description.
7. Yavorski 1885: 136 and 151–2—brief description and discussion.
8. Maitland 1888a: 519—brief description.
9. Le Strange 1905: 418–19—summary of the historical references for Bāmiyān.
10. Foucher 1942–7: 134–5—brief description.
11. Kohzad 1950a—brief background and guide.
12. Godard 1951: 4–5 and figs 1 and 4—describes two mosques and their place in the development of the iwān mosque.

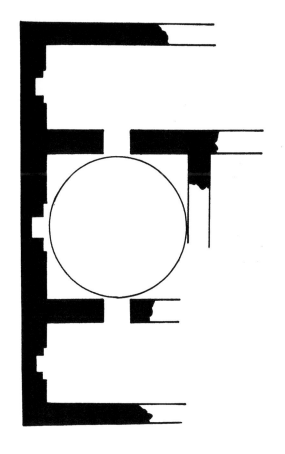

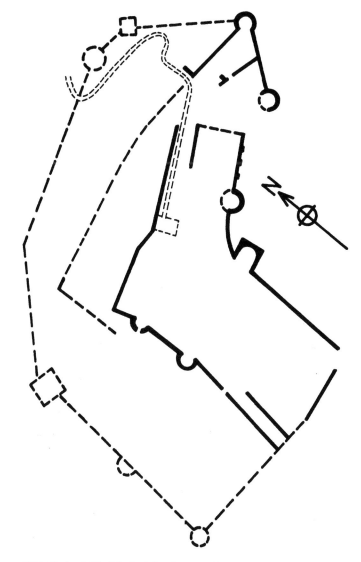

1042 Shahr-i Ghulghula (after Brett et al. 1970).

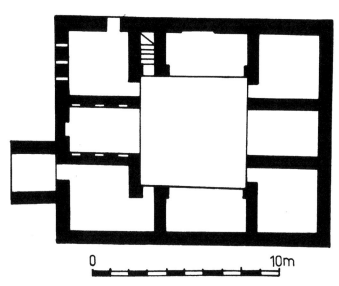

1042 Shahr-i Ghulghula, Bāmiyān—mosques (after Godard 1951).

13. Kohzad 1955/56—analysis of the decoration on the early Islamic pottery.
14. Pugachenkova 1963: 96—general summary.
15. N. Dupree 1967b—background and guide.
16. A. A. Motamedi 1967: 32—mentions Allchin and Codrington's sondage.

17. Brett et al. 1970: 33–4—description and plan of the fortifications.
18. Rowland and Rice 1971: pl. 173—photo and note on the Ghaznavid bowl.
19. N. Dupree et al. 1974: 76–9—description of the objects on display in the National Museum.
20. Hillenbrand 2000—discussion of the two mosques in the broader context of Ghaznavid and Ghurid architecture.
21. Suzuki and Aoki 2004: 33—describe the newly discoved stupa.
22. Allchin 2012: 137–44—account of the Allchin-Codrington survey.
23. Maeda 2015—report on a hoard of Chinese bronzes from the site.

SHAHR-I GHULGHULA, Seistan. See 1006 SAR-O TAR.

1043. SHAHR-I HINDŪAN
See also BALKH.

Original: Lat. 36° 45' N, long. 66° 55' E. Map 27.
Revised: 36.75769647 N, 66.91499023 E /
36° 45' 27.70730820 N, 66° 54' 53.96483124 E.
Balkh Province. Just to the east of the Balkh Bālā Hisār, on the old road to Mazār-i Sharīf.

Date: Early Islamic, 10th–13th cent. (traditional).

Description: Remains of an old city, possibly an urban extension of Balkh itself. It is enclosed by walls *c.*600 × 200 m in area and up to 10 m in height, with many mounds, bricks, and walls—many still standing in 1886—inside. The site is locally said to have been destroyed by Chingis Khān.

Fieldwork: 1886 Yate, ABC—topographical survey.

Sources:
1. Maitland 1888b: 179—mention.
2. Yate 1888: 257—brief description.

1044. SHAHR-I KALĀN
See also 363 GHULGHULA and 1006 SAR-O TAR.

Original: Lat. 30° 48' N, long. 62° 06' E. Map 92.
Revised: 30.79215858 N, 62.10428855 E /
30° 47' 31.77088908 N, 62° 06' 15.43879224 E.
Nīmrūz Province. In dunes *c.*11 km south-east of Kūrdū and 10 km north-east of Shahr-i Ghulghula.

Date: Timurid, 15th–16th cent. (documentary).

Description: Two high mounds surrounded by ruined houses, some tombs and ancient gardens, and irrigation canals. One of the mounds consists of a platform, *c.*13 m high, with the remains of a mud-brick fort a further 20 m high on top. Inside is a scatter of baked bricks.

The above ruins described (mainly by Tate) are too nebulous for identification, and are just a part of the general remains of the Sar-o Tar area. There are numerous clusters of Timurid houses in Sar-o Tar, this one might be the ones we designated as House 338, which contains numerous buildings and extends over several kilometres, but uncertain based on the description here.

Fieldwork:
1. Additional site information by W. Trousdale.
2. 1903–5 Tate, SAC—survey.
3. 1936 Hackin and Meunié, DAFA—survey.
4. 1950 Fairservis, AMNH—survey.
5. 1971–4 Trousdale, Smithsonian—survey.

Sources:
1. Tate 1910: 239 and 276—brief description of all the remains.
2. Fairservis 1961: 51–2—brief description.

1045. SHAHR-I KHAWAT

Lat. 34° 04' N, long. 67° 59' E. Map 59.
Ghazni Province. 16 km north of Dūābi, in the mountains to the north of the Dasht-i Nāwar.

Description: Some artificial caves in a cliff face. No paintings or sculptures.

Source: Fussman 1974c: 510–52—brief description.

1046. SHAHR-I KUHNA, FARĀH
Or KHUSHANA or QAL'A-I SAM.

Original: Lat. 32° 26–43' N, long. 62° 03–5' E. Map 71.
Revised: 32.43716839 N, 62.05914973 E /
32° 26' 13.80619464 N, 62° 03' 32.93904528 E.
Farāh Province. 10 km north-west of this town, south of the village called Shahr-i Kuhna.

Dates: Indo-Parthian, 1st–4th cent.; pre-Mongol Islamic, 10th–13th cent. Timurid, 15th–16th cent. (ceramic).

Description: Fortress with square plan (about 200 × 200 m), probably flanked by angle towers, surrounded by an interior ditch and a rampart (height *c.*4 m), of which remain some fragments of walls and towers. The whole is surrounded by a second ditch. The interior of the fortress is dominated by a citadel of about 50 × 50 m, height 9 m.

Collection: National Museum/AIA—sherds.

Fieldwork: 1952 Le Berre and Gardin, DAFA—survey.

Sources:
1. Ferrier 1857: 442—mention.
2. Yate 1900: 13—mention.
3. M. Le Berre: unpublished 1952 report, DAFA archives, Tepe Shindand-Farāh 7.

SHAHR-I KUHNA, Kandahār Province. See 744 MUNDI HISĀR.

1047. SHAHR-I KUHNA, ZĀMINDĀWAR

Original: Lat. 32° 21' N, long. 64° 59' E. Map 87.
Revised: 32.35530497 N, 64.98592179 E /
32° 21' 19.09789236 N, 64° 59' 09.31843068 E.
Helmand Province. 26 km east of Mūsa Qal'a on the road to Kajakī, south of the village of Sikandarābād.

Date: Early Islamic, 10th–13th cent. (ceramic).

Description: Remains of a walled town. The walls are of mud measuring *c.*1 km square and up to 10 m high, with traces of towers and salients on the outside. Inside are many mounds and artificial deposits probably several metres deep, with many sherds and baked bricks scattered on the surface. The centre is dominated by a roughly square mud citadel mound, *c.*20 m high and some 60 m square. Many cannon balls are said to have been found at the site. Local tradition associates the founding of the city with Darius; the site is probably to be identified with early Islamic Shahr-i Dāwar.

Fieldwork: 1885 Sahibdad Khan, ABC—topographical survey.

Sources:
1. Sahibdad Khan 1891a: 250—brief description.
2. Sahibdad Khan 1891b: 254—mentions the association with Darius.
3. Vercellin 1972: 372—mention.
4. Gazetteer 1973: II. 273—brief description.

1048. SHAHR-I SAFĀ

Original: Lat. 31° 48' N, long. 66° 20' E. Map 90.
Revised: 31.80439245 N, 66.32836109 E /
31° 48' 15.81280632 N, 66° 19' 42.09993372 E.
Zābul Province. 120 km north-east of Kandahār on the road to Kābul. The site is to the east of the road, *c.*200 m northeast of the toll barrier.

Dates: Bronze Age, 2nd mill. BC; Indo-Parthian, 1st–4th cent.; pre-Mongol Islamic, 10th–13th cent. (ceramic).

Description: A very high conical mound *c.*35 m high and 200 × 190 m in area, with an 11 m ledge a quarter of the distance from the top. There are two other low inconspicuous mounds to the south-west of the road.

North of the road is a large area of mounds, probably representing the remains of a considerable town, with the outline of buildings and streets just discernible from aerial photos.

Fieldwork:
1. 1951 Casal, DAFA—survey.
2. 1956 Ramachandran and Sharma, ASI—reconnaissance.
3. 1966 Fischer, DAAD—survey.
4. 1974 Swiny and Whitehouse, BIAS—survey.

Sources:
1. Site information by D. Whitehouse in unpublished BIAS archive.
2. Gardin and Lyonnet, 1980 chronological study of pottery from unpublished DAFA surveys.
3. Masson 1833c: 21—sketch.
4. Court 1836: 389—mention.
5. Kennedy 1840: II. 5—brief description.
6. Masson 1842: II. 195–6—brief description.
7. Bellew 1862: 26—mention.
8. Ramachandran and Sharma 1956: I. 18—brief description.

9. Fischer 1967a: 156—brief summary and photo.
10. Fischer 1969: 338—brief summary and aerial photos.
11. Whitehouse 1978: 15—mentions the pottery.

1049. SHAHR-I SAGĀN

Original: Lat. 35° 26' N, long. 68° 15' E. Maps 48, 49.
Revised: 35.42590655 N, 68.24677579 E /
35° 25' 33.26359692 N, 68° 14' 48.39285192 E.
Baghlān Province. On the left bank of the Surkhāb, 13.5 km south of Shuturjangāl, on the road from Bāmiyān to Dūshi.

Date: Ghaznavid and Ghurid, 11th–13th cent. (architectural, ceramic).

Description: Extensive mud and stone remains, with many cave dwellings in the hillside. The site is locally said to have been destroyed by the Mongols.

Fieldwork:
1. 1886 Peacocke, ABC—topographical survey.
2. 1974–5 Le Berre, DAFA—survey.

Source:
1. Peacocke 1887a: 381—brief description.
2. Gazetteer 1979: IV. 257—mention.
3. Le Berre 1987: 41–2 and pl. 40d–f—description and photos; itinerary A–I, ruins 27 and 28.

SHAHR-I SANG. See 180 CHĀR SANG TEPE.

1050. SHAHR-I SIKANDARI

Lat. 34° 17' N, long. 68° 52' E. Map 60.
Maidān Province. 1 km east of the Kandahār road, near Sarāī Khwāja, *c.*30 km south of Kābul.

Dates: Hellenistic, 3rd–1st cent. BC. Hunnic and Turki Shahi, 6th–9th cent.; pre-Mongol Islamic, 10th–13th (ceramic).

Description: None.

Collection: DAFA—sherds

Source: Gardin and Lyonnet 1980, study of the pottery from unpublished DAFA surveys.

SHAHR-I SISTĀN. See 752 NĀD-I 'ALĪ.

SHAHR-I TĪMŪR. See 653 KUSHAK TĪMŪRI.

1051. SHAHR-I WAIRĀN

Original: Lat. 35° 46' N, long. 65° 37' E. Map 46.
Revised: 35.76804839 N, 65.61707099 E /
35° 46' 04.97418888 N, 65° 37' 01.45556292 E.

Faryāb Province. On the border of Faryāb and Sar-i Pul provinces, on the plateau in the high mountains of the Gurziwān plateau, above the upper reaches of the Deh-i Jauz river, some 6 km due west of Khawāl.

Description: The ruins of 'what once must have been a considerable city' with surface covering of baked bricks, artificial mounds, and a large cemetery. The site is said to cover some 2.5 km. According to local sources, the site was 'the summer residence of a former king'. It is possible that this is the site of ancient Gurzivān, said to have been the residence of the pre-Islamic 'kings' of Guzgānān.

Fieldwork: 1886 Imam Sharif, ABC—topographical survey.

Sources:
1. Further site information by Jonathan L. Lee.
2. Ferrier 1857: 229—passing reference to the 'ruined city'.
3. Holdich 1886: 6—mention.
4. Holdich 1887: 70—brief description.

5. Imam Sharif 1888: 222—very brief description.
6. Caspani 1948: 24—mention.
7. Gazetteer 1979: IV. 159—brief description.
8. Lee 1982: 104—mention in relation to Ferrier's disputed itinerary.

1052. SHAHR-I ZUHAK

Original: Lat. 34° 50' N, long. 67° 59' E. Map 58.
Revised: 34.82653736 N, 67.98267378 E /
34° 49' 35.53448628 N, 67° 58' 57.62561088 E.
Bāmiyān Province. Guarding the eastern entrance to the Bāmiyān, Hājigak, and Shikāri Rivers, 17 km from Bāmiyān.

Dates: Hunnic-Turk, 5th–9th cent.; early Islamic, 10th–13th cent.; Timurid, 15th–16th cent. (ceramic).

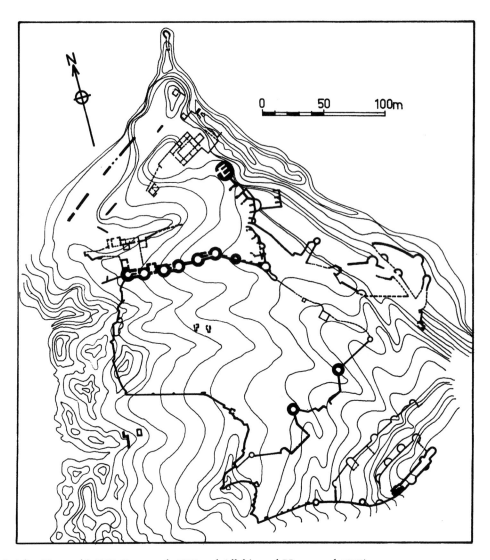

1052 Shahr-i Zuhak (after Zestovski 1948, Brett et al. 1970 and Allchin and Hammond 1978).

Description: A large fortified complex on a high bluff. It is in three parts: a residential area and an upper and lower citadel. There is a particularly complex entrance. Construction is mostly of mud, with only some baked brick, and decoration consists of simple impressed triangles on the outside walls. In the north part is a 20 m long rock-cut tunnel, descending at 45° to a well-head.

Fieldwork:
1. 1951 Allchin and Codrington—excavations.
2. 1966 Bernard, DAFA—excavations.
3. 1970 Brett et al., Bristol University—survey.
4. 1974–5 Le Berre, DAFA—survey.

Sources:
1. Masson 1836d: 708—mention.
2. Masson 1842: II. 389–90—brief description and discussion of the origins.
3. Lal 1846: 50–1—describes a visit to the site and some of the legends associated with it.
4. W. Griffith 1847: 405–6—good brief description.
5. Wood 1872: 131—brief description, giving it a late date.
6. Yavorski 1885: 137—brief description.
7. Maitland 1888a: 522–3—brief description.
8. J. and R. Hackin 1934: 49–50—brief description.
9. Foucher 1942–7: 135—brief description.
10. Codrington 1944: 88–9—photos and discussion of its importance.
11. Frye 1946a—photo and brief discussion.
12. Frye 1946c: 135—photos of the site and discussion of the general architectural principles.
13. Zestovski 1948: 44–51—description, sketches, and plans of the remains, and discussion whether it is a fort or city.
14. Allchin 1957: 139—discusses the Turk period at the site.
15. N. Dupree 1967b: 81–2—guide and background.
16. Pauly 1967—linguistic analysis and translation of some 7th-cent. Sanskrit texts on wood found at the site.
17. Auboyer 1968: pls 92 and 95—photos.
18. Fischer 1969: 344—very brief summary.
19. Brett et al. 1970: 30–2—detailed description of the remains and the construction techniques, with a plan.
20. Fischer 1974a: fig. 124—photo and discussion of the dome form in one of the buildings.
21. Mac Dowall and Taddei 1978b: 276–7—plan and photo.
22. Francfort 1979a: 38—mentions the survivals of Kushan military architecture in the fortifications.
23. Le Berre 1987: 66–72—itinerary B–I, Shahr-i Zahuk ruins 205.
24. Baker and Allchin 1991—thorough architectural and historical analysis of the buildings.

SHAHR-I ZUHAK, Zābul. See 1211 ULĀN RABĀT.

1053. SHAHRZA'IDA

Lat. 33° 12' N, long. 67° 41' E. Maps 78, 79.
Ghazni Province. In the Barik Valley, *c.* 8 km north-west of Tamaki and 10 km north-east of Lūmān.
Description: An artificial cave complex.
Fieldwork: 1976 Taddei and Verardi, IsMEO—survey.
Source: Verardi 1977a: 136 and 149—mention.

1054. SHĀH SALĪM BĀBĀ TEPE
Or WARQA-I GULSHĀH.

Original: Lat. 36° 49' N, long. 66° 34' E. Maps 25, 26.
Revised:
36.82200271 N, 66.57188739 E /
36° 49' 19.20974520 N, 66° 34' 18.79461336 E (A).
36.81877501 N, 66.56808034 E /
36° 49' 07.59002484 N, 66° 34' 05.08923012 E (B).
Balkh Province. 5 km south-east of Nimlik, two tepes situated on either side of the road to Balkh: (A) 150 m north of the road; (B) 150 m south of the road.
Description: (A) Circular mound on two levels, diam. *c.* 160 m, height 15 m. In the centre of the upper platform, recent tomb and ruins of a tower. A ditch surrounds the tepe, which is located in a zone of ruins which are probably not old. (B) Small circular platform, diam. *c.* 50 m, low.
Fieldwork: 1948 Le Berre, DAFA—survey.
Source: M. Le Berre: unpublished 1948 report, DAFA archives, tepes P. 33 and 34.

1055. SHĀH SALĪM PASHA TEPE

Original: Lat. 36° 50' N, long. 66° 33' E. Maps 25, 26.
Revised: 36.83289523 N, 66.54848587 E /
36° 49' 58.42282332 N, 66° 32' 54.54912696 E.
Balkh Province. About 1 km east of Nimlik, north of the road to Balkh, north-east of the hamlet of Shāh Salīm Pacha.
Dates: Hellenistic, 3rd–2nd cent. BC (ceramic).
Description: Small circular mound, diam. 50 m, height 3.5 m, without any particular relief.
Fieldwork:
1. 1946 Wheeler, ASI—reconnaissance.
2. 1948 Le Berre, DAFA—survey.
3. 1960 Hayashi and Sahara, University of Kyoto—survey.
Sources:
1. M. Le Berre: unpublished 1948 report, DAFA archives, tepe P. 32.
2. Shakur 1947: 68—mention.
3. Hayashi and Sahara 1962: 66–7—photo and brief description in Japanese.

SHĀH TEPE, Lōgar. See 19 AINAK.

1056. SHĀH TEPE
Or NĀYIBĀBĀD.

Original: Lat. 36° 47'–36° 48' N, long. 67° 27'–67° 30' E.
Map 29.
Revised:
36.79687005 N, 67.48158008 E / 36° 47' 48.73216848 N,
67° 28' 53.68827720 E (A).
36.78494682 N, 67.5004146 E / 36° 47' 05.80854264 N,
067° 30' 01.49254992 E (C).
Samangān Province. About 23 km north-west of Tāshqurghān, north of the road which links this town to Mazār-i
Sharīf (between markers 389 and 391, from Kābul): zone of
tepes called Shāh Tepe, from the name given to the largest of
them (A).

Dates: Epi-Palaeolithic, about the 7th mill. BC (lithic material); beg. Iron, end 2nd–beg. 1st mill. BC (ceramic); some
traces of Islamic occupation, pre-Mongol, 10th–13th cent.,
and Timurid, 15th–16th cent. (ceramic).

Description: (A) 1.5 km north of the road from Tāshqurghān
to Mazār-i Sharīf, at km marker 391 (from Kābul), large east-
west tepe (600 × 300 m), very eroded (height 3 m); (B) many
hillocky areas are visible up to 2 km from this tepe, in the
south-east and south-west sectors mainly: those visited are
located respectively 2.3 km in the east-north-east, at 0.8 km in
the south-south-east, at 1.2 km in the south, and at 1.5 km in
the west-south-west. (C) Two little low tepes, with remains
of potters' kilns, were found 1.2 km south-south-east and
1.5 km south-east of tepe A, not far north of the road from
Tāshqurghān to Mazār-i Sharīf, near the fork towards the
village of Nāyibābād; three hillocky areas covered with sherds
of the same period were visited to the east of these tepes (at 0.6,
0.9, and 1.2 km from the last cited), in the direction of the zone
of Burat Tepe (no. 141, D), which probably formed with Shāh
Tepe a single area of occupation, in the Iron Age. All this
region is covered with sherds, glass fragments, iron slag,
worked stone (as at Siāh Rīgān, cf. no. 1101).

Collections: National Museum/AIA– pottery.

Fieldwork:
1. 1946 Wheeler, ASI—reconnaissance.
2. 1969 Gouin, DAFA—survey.
3. 1975 Sarianidi and Vinogradov, AfSov. Mission—
survey.

Sources:
1. Shakur 1947: 52–3 and 73—brief description of the site
and the remains of iron workings.
2. Wheeler 1947: 62—brief description.
3. Gouin 1974: 111–51 and unpublished report in DAFA
Archives—brief description of the site and detailed typological analysis and discussion of the ceramics (Sites 49 (A),
50–3 (B), and 45–58 (C).

4. Sarianidi 1977c—general discussion of the lithics and
ceramics.
5. Vinogradov 1979—general discussion on the lithics from
the survey as a whole with comparisons in Soviet Central
Asia.

1057. SHĀH UZBEG

Original: Lat. 33° 28' N, long. 62° 14' E. Map 70.
Revised: 33.48956299 N, 62.26803518 E /
33° 29' 22.42677336 N, 62° 16' 04.92664800 E.
Farāh Province. About 110 km south of Herat, on either
side of the road to Shindand.

Description: (A) To the west of the road, on the edge, small
ruin: (B) To the east, caravanserai, with a platform nearby.

Fieldwork: 1952 Le Berre and Gardin, DAFA—survey.

Source: M. Le Berre: unpublished 1952 report, DAFA
archives, tepe Herat-Shindand 10.

1058. SHA'IDA

Original: Lat. 33° 51' N, long. 61° 51' E. Map 69.
Revised: 33.85850815 N, 61.84605266 E /
33° 51' 30.62933532 N, 61° 50' 45.78956772 E.
Herat Province. 6 km from the track from Herat to Farāh
via the Wadi Sha'ida.

Description: Remains of old copper mine workings,
extending over an area of c.200 × 40 m. There are several
excavations into the vein, now filled in. Little slag, though
two large slag heaps were found 15 km further south.

Fieldwork: 1977 CNRS—geological survey.

Source: Berthoud et al. 1977: 5–6—description of the geology and mine workings.

1059. SHAIKHĀBĀD

Original: Lat. 34° 41' N, long. 69° 41' E. Map 65.
Revised: 34.68536432 N, 69.68692634 E /
34° 41' 07.31156604 N, 69° 41' 12.93483912 E.
Laghmān Province. On the Mahipar River 14 km north of
Sarōbī on the road to Gulbahār.

Date: Hindu Shahi, 10th cent. (ceramic).

Description: Remains of walls on a mountain overlooking
the river. In one corner is a small mound, c.10 m diam. and
4 m high, covered in bricks, stone remains, and sherds.

Sources:
1. Fischer 1964: 36—brief description.
2. Fischer 1969: 356—mention.

1060. SHAIKH BAHLŪL

Original: Lat. 34° 53' N, long. 62° 01' E. Maps 42, 43.
Revised: 34.88688082 N, 62.0090615 E / 34° 53' 12.77096388 N, 62° 00' 32.62139712 E.
Herat Province. C.12 km north-west of Khwāja Gul Bed and 88 km east of Qarabāgh, in the Gulrān area.
Description: Remains of an ancient fort and extensive cemetery.
Fieldwork: 1968–78 Kruglikova, Af/Sov. Mission—survey.
Sources:
1. A. C. Yate 1887: 181—mention.
2. Gaibov et al. 2010: 112—mention (Site 154).

SHAIKH TASH TAIMUR. See **2246 SHAIKH TASH TAIMUR** in Supplement.

SHAILA RŪD. See **393 GUMBAD-I SAR-I SHAILA.**

1061. SHAIRĀBĀD, SOUTH

Original: Lat. 36° 50'–36° 51' N, long. 67° 38' E. Map 29.
Revised:
36.83985852 N, 67.6430471 E /
36° 50' 23.49067236 N, 67° 38' 34.96956396 E (A).
36.8500606 N, 67.653033 E /
36° 51' 00.21817296 N, 67° 39' 10.91879172 E (B).
36.84749464 N, 67.65084408 E /
36° 50' 50.98070076 N, 67° 39' 03.03869520 E (C).
Samangān Province. 16 km north of Tāshqurghān, principal ruins of the place called Shairābād (A), and neighbouring sites to the north-north-east (B, C).
Dates: Beg. Iron, end 2nd–beg. 1st mill. BC (A); Hellenistic, 3rd–1st cent. BC (B); Kushan, 3rd cent. (A, B, C); Sasanian-Hunnic, 4th–6th cent. (A, C) (ceramic).
Description: (A) Large quadrangular site (about 400 × 400 m), eroded, low; (B) 1.3 km north-north-east of the preceding site, small tepe surrounded by an extended area of sherds, square bricks (25 × 25 cm); (C) 500 m south-west of the preceding tepe, small rectangular tepe, cut by an east–west trench, many sherds around.
Collection: National Museum/AIA—sherds.
Fieldwork: 1969 Gouin, DAFA—survey.
Source: Gouin 1974 and unpublished report, DAFA archives—sites no. 7 (A), 25 (B), 24 (C).

1062. SHAIRĀBĀD, EAST

Original: Lat. 36° 50'–36° 51' N, long. 67° 39' E. Map 29.
Revised: 36.83335017 N, 67.66134587 E /
36° 50' 00.06060516 N, 67° 39' 40.84514352 E.
Samangān Province. 16 km north of Tāshqurghān and about 1.5 km east of the principal ruins of Shairābād.
Dates: Kushan, Sasanian, and Hunnic, 1st–6th cent. (A, B); Turk and pre-Mongol Islamic, 7th–13th cent. (A) (ceramic).
Description: (A) 1.7 km east-south-east of Shairābād, small tepe 3 m high, cut by a rectangular trench; (B) 1.2 km east-north-east of Shairābād, area of sherds, with many fragments of mortars for grinding.
Collection: National Museum/AIA—sherds.
Fieldwork: 1969 Gouin, DAFA—survey.
Source: Gouin 1974 and unpublished report—sites no. 22 (A), 23 (B).

1063. SHAIRĀBĀD, NORTH-WEST

Original: Lat. 36° 50'–36° 52' N, long. 67° 37'–67° 38' E. Map 29.
Revised:
36.86224808 N, 67.62655725 E /
36° 51' 44.09307756 N, 67° 37' 35.60609172 E (A).
36.85213 N, 67.61742169 E /
36° 51' 07.66801656 N, 67° 37' 02.71809156 E (B).
Samangān Province. About 18 km north of Tāshqurghān and at 2–3 km in the north-west sector of the principal ruins of Shairābād.
Dates: Bronze and beg. Iron, 2nd mill.–beg. 1st mill. BC (D); Hellenistic, 3rd–1st cent. BC (A, D); Kushan, 1st–4th cent. (A–D); Sasanian-Hunnic, 4th–6th cent. (B, C); some Islamic sherds (A) (ceramic).
Description: (A) 3 km north-west of Shairābād, ruins square in plan (70 × 70 m); (B) 2.5 km west-north-west of Shairābād, rectangular site (150 × 100 m); (C) 1 km east and 1.5 km south-east of the preceding site, extensive area of sherds (diam. c.100 m); (D) 1 km east-south-east of ruins A, very extensive area of sherds, some of these dating to the Bronze Age; small oblong mound 700 m to the south-east (Kushan sherds).
Collection: National Museum/AIA—sherds, bronze arrowhead with three barbs (A), fluted bead in lapis lazuli (C).
Fieldwork: 1969 Gouin, DAFA—survey.
Source: Gouin 1974 and unpublished report—sites no. 8 (A), 9 (B), 10–11 (C), 26 and 27 (D).

SHAIRKHAJ. See **2247 SHAIRKHAJ** in Supplement.

SHAKAR. See **974 SAKHĀR.**

1064. SHAKAR DARRA
Or SAKAR DARRA or SHANKAR DHAR.

Lat. 34° 41' N, long. 69° 00' E. Map 63.

Parwān Province. 8 km west of the main road to the north, the turn-off 22 km north of Kābul.

Date: Kushano-Sasanian, mid-4th cent.; late Sasanian, 6th–7th cent. (stylistic).

Description: The site of several chance finds of Hindu sculpture, including images of Ganesha, Surya, and Shiva. The Ganesha is a marble statue, possibly the earliest such image known, that may have originated in Afghanistan.

Sources:
1. Ramachandran and Sharma 1956: II. 4–6—discusses the sculpture and dates it to the 4th cent.
2. Agrawala 1968: 167—photo and brief description of the Ganesha.
3. Dhavalikar 1971—description of the Ganesha and discussion of the implications.
4. Yamada 1972: 21–2—dates the Ganesha to the 7th cent.
5. Kuwayama 1976—full description and discussion of all the Hindu sculpture, with a summary of previous work.

1065. SHĀKH TEPE

Original: Lat. 36° 36N, long. 69° 00' E. Map 32.
Revised: 36.62258077 N, 68.95577407 E /
36° 37' 21.29076084 N, 68° 57' 20.78664876 E.
Qundūz Province. 18 km south of Qundūz immediately to the east of the road to ʿAliābād.

Date: Hunnic, 5th–6th cent. (numismatic, stylistic).

Description: A flat plateau with some 100 tumulus burial mounds, each 3–4 m high, stretching in an east–west direction for c.2 km. Finds include a gold Byzantine coin of Anastasius (491–518), gold jewellery set with semi-precious stones, and joint human and animal burials.

Fieldwork:
1. 1952 Schlumberger, DAFA—reconnaissance.
2. 1953 Casal, DAFA—excavation of 11 tumuli.
3. 1955 and 1960 Fischer, DAAD—survey.
4. 1956 Ramachandran and Sharma, ASI—reconnaissance.
5. 1963 Le Berre, DAFA—excavation of 9 tumuli.

Sources:
1. Casal 1954c—brief summary report and photos of the excavations.
2. Ramachandran and Sharma 1956: I. 25—mention.
3. Fischer 1961a: 19—brief topographical description.
4. Schlumberger 1964c: 208–11—very brief summary of the 1963 excavations and the Byzantine coin.
5. Fischer 1969: 350—brief summary (Tepe B4).
6. N. Dupree 1977: 409—brief description.
7. Gardin and Lyonnet 1978–9: 140–1—brief discussion.
8. Gardin 1998: 140–1—brief discussion.

1066. SHĀKI NAUKA
Or BĀRIK.

Lat. 33° 14' N, long. 67° 42' E. Maps 78, 79.
Ghazni Province. In the Bārik plain, c.10 km north-west of Tamaki on the road from Qarabāgh to Lūmān.

Date: Hunnic-Sasanian, 5th–7th cent. (stylistic).

Description: An artificial cave complex, one (Cave 4) a square *vihara* with four pilasters.

Fieldwork: 1976 Taddei and Verardi, IsMeEO—survey.

Sources:
1. Taddei 1976: 601—mention and photo.
2. Verardi 1977a: 136 and 149—brief description.
3. Verardi and Paparatti 2004: 47–9—detailed description with drawings and photos.

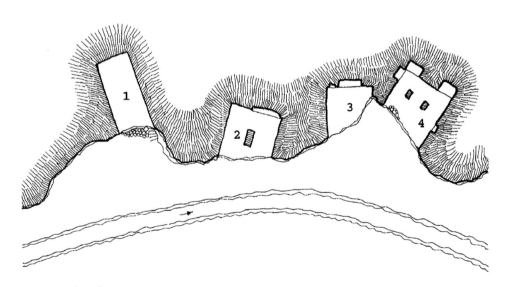

1066 Shāki Nauka (after Verardi and Paparatti 2004).

SHAKOTE. See 1026 SHĀHKŌT.

1067. SHALATAK
Or LAGHMĀN.

Lat. 34° 36' N, long. 70° 14' E. Map 65.
Laghmān Province. On the east bank of the Laghmān River, midway between the villages of Shalatak and Qargha.

Dates: Mauryan, *c.*250 BC (A—epigraphic); Kushan, 1st–4th cent. (B—ceramic).

Description: (A) An Ashokan edict on the rock face above the river was discovered in 1968. There are four texts, three in Sanskrit and one in Aramaic. A second Ashokan inscription, in Aramaic, was discovered in 1973. There are also many petroglyphs of animals.
   (B) In the village of Shalatak to the north is a Kushan site.

Fieldwork:
1. 1950 Dupree, AMNH—excavations.
2. 1957–8 Lindberg—speleological survey.

Sources:
1. Gardin and Lyonnet, 1980 chronological study of pottery from unpublished DAFA surveys.
2. Ahang 1969–70—report on the discovery.
3. Dupont-Sommer 1970—very detailed record and linguistic analysis and discussion.
4. Bourgeois 1971—describes the inscription and petroglyphs.
5. Habibi 1971: 128—photo of the inscription and discussion of the development of Afghan epigraphy.
6. Humbach 1971—discusses the significance of the inscription for western Mauryan history.
7. Bogolyubov 1973—linguistic discussion and review of Dupont-Sommer's work.
8. Humbach 1973—linguistic discussion of the inscription and review of Dupont-Sommer's work.
9. Davary and Humbach 1974—full linguistic analysis of the Aramaic text.
10. Davary 1977—mention and bibliography.
11. Mac Dowall and Taddei 1978a: 192—mention.
12. Itō 1979—discussion.
13. Dupont-Sommer 1980: 706–11—discusses the possible reference to Tadman in the inscription, and its implications for possible Buddhist influence on the Essenes.
14. Davary 1981—discusses the Aramaic text.

1068. SHAMALA

Original: Lat. 31° 12' N, long. 64° 11' E. approximately. Map 97.
Revised: 31.19822441 N, 64.17927263 E /
31° 11' 53.60787312 N, 64° 10' 45.38148240 E.

Helmand Province. On the right bank of the Helmand *c.*10 km north of Hazārjüft.

Dates: Late Sasanian, 5th–7th cent.; early Islamic, 9th–13th cent.; Timurid, 15th–16th cent. (ceramic).

Description: A large group of ruins and mounds with a large number of sherds.

Fieldwork: 1966 Hammond, Cambridge University—survey.

Source: Hammond 1970: 350—lists the sites (nos. 10 and 43) and discusses the pottery types and general survey results.

SHAM QAL'A. See 169 CHAM QAL'A.

1069. SHAMSHIR GHAR
Or BADWAN.

Lat. 31° 35' N, long. 65° 30' E. Map 89.
Kandahār Province. Overlooking the left bank of the Arghandāb River near Badwan, 5.5 km north-north-east of Panjwāyī and 24 km south-west of Kandahār.

Dates: Bronze Age, *c.*1300–600 BC; early Kushan; late Kushan, 1st–3rd cent.; Kushano-Sasanian, 3rd–7th cent.; Turki Shahi, 7th–9th cent.; early Islamic, 10th–13th cent. (ceramic).

Description: A large natural cave. Inside four periods were distinguished in the deposits. There was no architecture, and on the cave walls are simple fragmentary frescos. Finds included bronze and iron harness pieces and projectile points, some 8th–11th cent. coins, simple jewellery, and a series of Indo-Sasanian and Sasanian seals.

Fieldwork:
1. 1950 Dupree, AMNH—excavations.
2. 1957–8 Lindberg—speleological survey.

Sources:
1. Dupree 1951—very summary report on the stratigraphy and sequence.
2. Benava 1953: 24—describes some of the legends connected with the cave.
3. Dupree 1956—preliminary report on the excavations, with fairly detailed descriptions and photos of the pottery.
4. Dupree 1957—summary report on the excavations and results.
5. Dupree 1958a—full report and catalogue of the finds, prefaced by a detailed history of archaeological research in Afghanistan.
6. Dupree 1958b—description of the finds and sequence.
7. Matson 1958—notes on selected ceramic wares and conclusions on the manufacture.
8. Fischer 1961c—discusses a Shivaite trident painted on the cave wall.
9. Lindberg 1961: 21—brief speleological and meteorological observations.

10. N. Dupree et al. 1974: 58—describe some of the objects on display in the National Museum.
11. Dupree 1981: 1 n. 1—revised chronology.
12. Tissot 2006: 20—National Museum catalogue details and photos.

1070. SHAND-I MA'SŪMKHĀN

Lat. 31° 19' N, long. 61° 53' E. Map 83.
Nīmrūz Province. In the middle of the dasht, *c.*26 km south-east of Tepe Khākak, 23 km north of Kang and 7 km east of Deh Yak-i Bālā.

Dates: Sasanian, 3rd–7th cent.; early Islamic, 9th–13th cent. (ceramic).

Description: A flat area covered in pottery and glass.

Fieldwork: 1950 Fairservis, AMNH—survey.

Source: Fairservis 1961: 41—mention and summary of the pottery (Site 18, Tell 4).

SHANKAR DHAR. See 1064 SHAKAR DARRA.

1071. SHARABIYA

Lat. 32° 06' N, long. 64° 20' E. Map 87.
Helmand Province. 14.5 km by road north-west of Sa'adat Qal'a. 3 km to the south of the road to Washīr from Girishk.

Description: Some ruins marking an old site.

Source: Maitland 1897—mention.

1072. SHĀRĀN

Original: Lat. 35° 59' N, long. 70° 54' E. Map 38.
Revised: 35.9824012 N, 70.8980935 E / 35° 58' 56.64433080 N, 70° 53' 53.13661548 E.
Badakhshān Province. On the Munjān (Kokcha) River, *c.*18 km south-east of Munjān.

Description: Remains of a fortress on an isolated rocky bluff in the centre of the valley. Inside are many rooms, with walls still standing up to a height of 1 m. Construction is of stone. Opposite the fortress are the remains of a large wall, closing off the valley.

Fieldwork: 1963 Thompson, Oxford University—survey.

Sources:
1. Thompson 1964: 9—brief description.
2. Gardner 1971: 14–15—brief description.

SHASOLIM-POCHA TEPE. See 1055 SHĀH SĀLIM PASHA TEPE.

1073. SHAWĀL
Or SAWĀL or ASHKINAK.

Original: Lat. 31° 03' N, long. 62° 03' E. Map 92.
Revised: 31.05797855 N, 62.04606347 E /
31° 03' 28.72277892 N, 62° 02' 45.82849020 E.
Nīmrūz Province. On the edge of the hāmūn 13 km south of Chakhānsūr and 2 km north-west of Dīwāl-i Ghundi.

Dates: Sasanian, 3rd–7th cent. (architectural); early Islamic, 8th–13th cent.; Timurid, 15th–16th cent. (ceramic).

Description: Remains of a fortified city, half submerged in the lake. The remains include a rectangular citadel, several watch towers, and many standing pillars and other structures. Construction is both mud-brick and baked brick. Near a *zīyārat* to the south is a square two-storey watch-tower of mud-brick, preserving several Sasanian architectural features.

Fieldwork: 1955, 1960, 1968, and 1970 Fischer, Bonn University—survey.

Sources:
1. Fischer 1961b—brief description.
2. Fischer 1966: 27—mention and photos.
3. Fischer 1969: 335 and pls 3–6—brief summary with ground and aerial photos.
4. Fischer 1969–70: 93—mention and photos.
5. Fischer 1970a—photos.
6. Fischer 1970b: pls 32–4—photos.
7. Fischer 1973c: 142—mention.
8. Fischer et al. 1974–6: 37—mention.

SHAWRA CHELAKHĀNA. See 2248 SHAWRA CHE-LAKHĀNA in Supplement.

1074. SHĪBAR, EAST
Includes DAHĀNA KUTAK, KAJAK, and SANGANDĀB.

Lat. 34° 54'–34° 57' N, long. 68° 15'–68° 25' E.
Maps 48, 49, 59.
Bāmiyān Province. Road from Chārikar to Dūshi, on the east slopes of the Shībar Pass: from east to west, ruins of small forts or castles at the place called Sangandāb and in the side valleys of the Darra-i Kajak and Dahāna Kutak.

Date: Turk and/or pre-Mongol Islamic period, 7th–13th cent. (architectural).

Description: Very eroded remains of a fort guarding the pass. More very ruined forts in the side valley and on the descent to Ghurband Valley.

Fieldwork: 1974–5 Le Berre, DAFA—survey.

Source: Le Berre 1987: 86–7, pl. 113—brief descriptions and photos; itinerary D, ruins 1 to 3.

1075. SHĪBAR, WEST
Includes DAHĀNA KHUKKUSHTA, KHĀK-I BĀBĀ, and SUMBUL.
See also 497 KĀFIR QAL'A, Shībar.

Lat. 34° 52'–34° 54' N, long. 68° 09'–68° 11' E. Maps 48, 59. Bāmiyān Province. Road from Chārikār to Dūshi, on the west slopes of the Shībar Pass: from east to west, ruins of small forts or castles in the places called Dahāna Khukkushta, Khāk-i Bābā, and 'Alaqadari Shībar (at the confluence of the side valley of the Darra-i Sumbul).

Date: Turk and/or pre-Mongol Islamic, 7th–9th cent. (architectural).

Description: Very badly eroded mud remains, presumably fortifications, guarding the pass (A-I, 1–5), and a ruined tower at the confluence with 'Sasanian' style squinches (A-II, 1).

Fieldwork: 1974–5 Le Berre, DAFA—survey.

Source: Le Berre 1987: 25–6 and 44, pls 20, 21, 43—description and photos; itineraries A1, ruins 1 to 5; A2, Darra-i Sumbul, ruin 1.

1076. SHĪBARGHĀN

Original: Lat. 36° 40' N, long. 65° 45' E. Map 24.
Revised: 36.67266108 N, 65.74292504 E /
36° 40' 21.57989736 N, 65° 44' 34.53014004 E.
Juazjān Province. 132 km west of Mazār-i Sharif and 55 km north of Sar-i Pul.

Dates: Kushan-Sasanian, 1st–7th cent. (ceramic); early Islamic, 10th–13th cent. (documentary, stylistic).

Description: A high citadel mound on the east side of the town. In the 1930s, two elaborately decorated early Islamic stone panels were found here. Many mounds around, and especially above the town.

Fieldwork:
1. 1885 Maitland and Peacocke, ABC—topographical survey.
2. 1955–68, Fischer, DAAD—survey.

Sources:
1. Peacocke 1887a: 293—brief description.
2. Maitland 1888b: 167—mentions the mound.
3. Le Strange 1905: 426—summary of the historical references.
4. Sālmāna 1937/38: opp. 229—photo of the panels.
5. Fischer 1969: 348—mentions the site and gives a bibliography of the historical sources.
6. Gazetteer 1979: IV. 538—mentions the mound.

1077. SHIKĀRI

Original: Lat. 34° 53' N, long. 68° 02' E. Map 58.
Revised: 34.89641765 N, 68.03704531 E /
34° 53' 47.10354432 N, 68° 02' 13.36312860 E.

Bāmiyān Province. 41 km north-east of Bāmiyān, at the junction of the Dūshi and Shībar roads, 2 km south of the village of Shikāri.

Date: Early Islamic, 10th–13th cent. (architectural).

Description: Remains of a small fort of mud-brick on a stone base, guarding the roads.

Fieldwork:
1. 1886 Peacocke, ABC—topographical survey.
2. 1974–5 Le Berre, DAFA—survey.

Sources:
1. Peacocke 1887a: 403—mention.
2. N. Dupree 1977: 149—mention.
3. Le Berre 1987: 26–7, pl. 22—description and photos; itinerary A-I, ruins 6 and 7.

1078. SHIKARĪN HASAN KHĒL

Lat. 32° 28' N, long. 67° 48' E. Map 79.
Ghazni Province. On the western side of the Āb-i Istāda, 5 km south-west of Ghazkai.

Dates: Hunnic and Turki Shahi, 5th–9th cent. (ceramic).

Description: None available.

Fieldwork: 1974 Dupree, AUFS—survey.

Source: Information by L. Dupree.

1079. SHINDAND
Or SABZAWAR.

Original: Lat. 33° 18' N, long. 62° 08' E. Map 70.
Revised: 33.30636556 N, 62.14597202 E /
33° 18' 22.91602968 N, 62° 08' 45.49927956 E.
Farāh Province. 120 km south of Herat on the road to Nīmrūz.

Date: Middle Islamic, 11th–15th cent. (ceramic); ?Timurid, 15th–16th cent. (documentary).

Description: Ruins of a square fort in the centre of the town with inner and outer fortifications measuring 40 × 400 m, standing on an artificial mound 2 m high (Soviet K148). There are four circular towers on each side. In 1833 a large portal of a mosque was still standing.

On the northern outskirts of the town are the remains of a large medieval town with ruins of many buildings built of mud-brick and *pakhsa* (Soviet K160). Outlying suburbs 2 km further north-west consisting of pottery scatters (Soviet K149).

Fieldwork: 1968–78 Kruglikova, Af/Sov. Mission—survey.

Sources:
1. Lal 1846: 171—mentions the remains of a mosque.
2. Ferrier 1857: 265—mentions large ruins.
3. Yate 1900: 15—mentions the fort.
4. Le Strange 1905: 412—summary of the historical references.

5. Sidqi 1952: 7—mentions the ruins and discusses the historical background.
6. Ramachandran and Sharma 1956: III. 4—brief summary of a coin collection in the local government hotel.
7. Vercellin 1974—discusses the topography of Shindand.
8. Gaibov et al. 2010: 112—brief description of fort (Site K148), town (Site K160), and suburb (K149).

1080. SHINGĀN
Including KANDAKAU.

Original: Lat. 36° 37' N, long. 69° 48' E. Maps 37, 38.
Revised:
36.63002481 N, 69.79261149 E / 36° 37' 48.08932176 N, 69° 47' 33.40138020 E (B).
36.63022959 N, 69.79638399 E / 36° 37' 48.82652400 N, 69° 47' 46.98236220 E (D).
Takhār Province. On the left bank of the Farkhar River, west of the village of Shingan, in the little plain called Dasht-i Nawad Jarīb which lies between the river and the hills to the south. This plain is crossed by two large north–south lines of stones, which have descended from the reliefs (indicated on the 1:100,000 map); it is accessed by the road from Tāluqān to Farkhar, by a footbridge situated near the western line of stones. The position of the tepes described is given in relation to this bridge.

Dates: ?Chalcolithic-Early Bronze Age, *c.*3500–2500 BC (D); Beg. Iron, end 2nd–beg. 1st mill. BC (A); Kushan, 1st–4th cent.; pre-Mongol Islamic, 10th–13th cent. (C) (ceramic).

Description: (A) 700 m south-east of the bridge, between the two lines of stones, mound in the form of a crescent (50×50 m), height 1.5–2 m. (B) On the eastern edge of the eastern line of stones, 300 m from the river, rectangular east–west mound (50×40 m), height 2.5 m, with top in the eastern part (4 m); 200 m further north, along the same line of stones, area of sherds of the same period (Kushan), about 30×30 m (C) 1.3 km south-east of the bridge, on the edge of a terrace midway between the river and the hills, a group of three small tepes close together (less than 100 m), one rectangular north–south (70×40 m), height 1–3 m; the two others circular (diam. 30 to 50 m), height 1–2 m. These tepes, situated in an irrigated zone, are eaten into by cultivation. (D) on the edge of the river, 1 km upriver from the bridge, oblong north–south mound (80×30 m), height 2–3 m; according to an informant, the river has taken away part of the tepe, also damaged by ploughing.

Collection: National Museum/AIA—sherds.
Fieldwork: 1977 Gardin et al., CNRS—survey.
Sources:
1. Site information by J.-C. Gardin.
2. Gardin and Lyonnet 1978–9: pl. X—nos. 338–41, 343–5.
3. Lyonnet 1997: figs 7, 25, 35, 49—nos. 338–41, 343–5.
4. Gardin 1998: 96—nos. 338–41, 343–5.

1081. SHĪNIYĀ
Or SHINA. See also 27 ALAYĀR.

Original: Lat. 34° 32' N, long. 65° 40' E. Map 55.
Revised: 34.51930912 N, 65.65297664 E / 34° 31' 09.51282804 N, 65° 39' 10.71590832 E.
Ghūr Province. 13 km west of Daulatyār on the road to Panjau.
Date: Ghurid, 12th–13th cent. (architectural).

Description: Many circular and square towers on the hills to the east and west of Shīniyā. They are usually of stone with loopholes towards the top.
Fieldwork:
1. 1885 Maitland and Talbot, ABC—topographical survey.
2. 1946 Kohzad, HAS—survey.
Sources:
1. Maitland 1888c: 388—mention.
2. Kohzad 1951–4, 7/2: 50—mention.
3. N. Dupree 1977: 457—mention.

1082. SHIRĀBĀD

Original: Lat. 36° 41' N, 67° 01' E. Map 27.
Revised: 36.70483366 N, 67.04282226 E / 36° 42' 17.40118068 N, 67° 02' 34.16012844 E.
Balkh Province. 6 km west of Mazār-i Sharif on the road to Dehdādi.
Dates: Hunnic-Turk, 5th–9th cent.; pre-Mongol Islamic, 10th–13th cent. (ceramic).
Description: A high mound with a ruin on top.
Fieldwork: 1885 Maitland and Peacocke, ABC—topographical survey.
Sources:
1. Gardin and Lyonnet, 1980 chronological study of pottery from unpublished DAFA surveys.
2. Peacocke 1887a: 301—mention.
3. Maitland 1888b: 64—mention.

1083. SHĪRBAND

Original: Lat. 35° 02' N, long. 61° 39' E. Map 42.
Revised: 35.0446214 N, 61.64345393 E / 35° 02' 40.63703352 N, 61° 38' 36.43414116 E.
Herat Province. C.8 km south-west of Gulrān, at the southern extremity of the plain.
Description: Ruins of a small fort and other structures.
Sources:
1. *Pioneer,* 3 Apr. 1885—mention.
2. A. C. Yate 1887: 284—mention.

SHIR GUZAR. See 959 RŪD-I SHĀHRAWĀN.

1084. SHIR-I HAIDAR
Or ANGURI.

Original: Lat. 32° 58' N, long. 67° 32' E. Map 79.
Revised: 32.95311009 N, 67.55326627 E /
32° 57' 11.19633696 N, 67° 33' 11.75858244 E.
Ghazni Province. 25 km north-west of Muqqur, on the north-western side of the Kūh-i Bauri Dalkhush, c.1 km south of the village of Anguri.

Description: The workings of an ancient mine. The vein has been excavated at two points, the main part being an area 8 m long with galleries descending 6–7 m deep.

Fieldwork: 1977 CNRS—geological survey.

Source: Berthoud et al. 1977: 9–10—description of the workings and the geology.

SHISHAGI GHUNDAY. See 2127 KHWĀJA ĀLI SEHYAKA in Supplement.

1085. SHISHĀWA

Original: Lat. 31° 30' N, long. 62° 42' E. Map 85.
Revised: 31.49426274 N, 62.66007361 E /
31° 29' 39.34585536 N, 62° 39' 36.26500104 E.
Nīmrūz Province. 24 km south-west of Dilārām on the road to Chakhānsūr.

Date: Timurid, 15th–16th cent. (ceramic).

Description: Remains of a large mud fort.

Fieldwork: 1960–70 Fischer, Bonn University—survey.

Source: Fischer et al. 1974–6: 32—mention.

1086. SHISH TEPE

Original: Lat. 36° 46'–36° 47' N, long. 69° 25'–69° 26' E. Map 37.
Revised:
36.77979968 N, 69.43088922 E /
36° 46' 47.27885412 N, 69° 25' 51.20119344 E (A).
36.76877973 N, 69.42415477 E /
36° 46' 07.60703628 N, 69° 25' 26.95717308 E (B).
Takhār Province. 11 km west of Tāluqān, zone accessible by the road which runs along the Rūd-i Shārawān (A) or by the road along the Tāluqān River (B): the two sites are located between these two roads, respectively 700 m south of the first (A) and north of the second (B).

Dates: Achaemenid, 6th–4th cent. BC (B); Hellenistic, 3rd–1st cent. BC (A); Kushan and Hunnic-Turk, 1st–9th cent.; some Islamic sherds (ceramic).

Description: (A) High mound of conical aspect, quadrangular at the base (80 × 70 m), rising about 10 m above the plain, eaten into by irrigated crops. In the cuts thus created, archaeological layers are visible in a thickness of about 4 m: charcoal, detritus, mud-brick walls with burnt coating.
(B) Mound of irregular form (30 × 25 m) cut into by cultivation; surface inclined from north to south, with *zīyārat* at the highest point (4.5 m) and modern cemetery on the slopes.

Collection: National Museum/AIA—sherds.

Fieldwork: 1977 Gardin et al., CNRS—survey.

Sources:
1. Site information by J.-C. Gardin.
2. Gardin and Lyonnet 1978–9: pl. IX—nos. 232, 239.
3. Lyonnet 1997: figs 25, 35, 39, 49, 68, 69—nos. 232, 239.
4. Gardin 1998: 70—nos. 232, 239.

1087. SHĪWAKĪ
Or BURJ-I KEMRI or QAL'A-I MUFTI or SAN-JITAK or SANJIT DARRA.
See also 1237 YAKHDARRA.

Original: Lat. 34° 26' N, long. 69° 17' E. Map 62.
Revised: 34.44110048 N, 69.28111701 E /
34° 26' 27.96174312 N, 69° 16' 52.02122988 E.
Kābul Province. 11 km south of Kābul at the foot of the mountains near the village of Yakhdarra, 5 km south-east of the village of Shīwakī.

Dates: Kushan, 1st–3rd cent. (architectural, numismatic, stylistic); Hunnic and Turki Shahi, 5th–9th cent. (ceramic); Hindu Shahi, 10th cent. (numismatic).

Description: Remains of a stupa and at least one monastery enclosure, covering a wide area. The stupa has a well-preserved frieze of alternating pilasters and blind arches. Inside was a steatite vase with a Kharoshthi inscription, some gold Kushan coins, and a Roman coin of Trajan. In 1970 a silver Hindu Shahi coin hoard was found at Shīwakī.

Fieldwork:
1. 1833 Honigberger—excavation.
2. 1834 Masson—survey.
3. 1962–5 Mizuno, Kyoto University—survey.
4. 1972 Fussman, CNRS—survey.

Sources:
1. Gardin and Lyonnet, 1980 chronological study of pottery from unpublished DAFA sherd collections.
2. Jacquet 1836b: 262–74:—full description and illustrations of Honigberger's discoveries.
3. Niedemeyer and Diez 1924: pl. 52—photo of the stupa.
4. Jacquet 1839: 393–4—describes Honigberger's results.
5. Masson 1841: 114—mention.
6. Masson 1842: II. 237—mention.
7. Honigberger 1852: 60—mentions his own work.
8. Foucher 1942–7: 147—mention.
9. Caspani 1946c: 41—brief description.
10. Lézine 1962: 44–5—description of the stupa and comparisons with Guldarra.

11. Lézine 1964: 19–20—brief description and illustrations, using the profile of the dome for a reconstruction of the dome at Guldarra.
12. Mizuno 1971: 124–5—brief description and photos.
13. Franz 1977–8—discusses the development of the stupa and its art.
14. Mac Dowall and Taddei 1978b: 247 and 255—mention the various coin finds.
15. Ball 2008: 264–5—summary.
16. Fussman et al. 2008: 28–35, 234–41, and 299–300—detailed description, photos, and drawings ('Shevaki 1 and 2').
17. Jongeward et al. 2012—catalogue and discussion of the reliquaries.
18. Errington 2017a: 71–5 and 2017b: 25–6, 103—the Masson collection and archive relating to the site.

1088. SHOTORAK

Or KŪH-I PAHLAWĀN. Including KARRA-CHA and KŪH-I BACHA.

Original: Lat. 35° 00' N, long. 69° 20' E. Map 64.
Revised: 35.0079059 N, 69.33989678 E / 35° 00' 28.46125476 N, 69° 20' 23.62839612 E.
Kāpīsā Province. On the south bank of the Panjshīr River at the foot of the Kūh-i Pahlawān, 4 km north of Begram.

Date: Kushan, 3rd cent. (architectural, stylistic).

Description: A small monastery complex with some seven or eight stupas. The main stupa was surrounded by a cloistered courtyard, and decorated in figures in bas-relief. Finds included many clay stupa models and many schist sculptures. The site may have been the living quarters of Kanishka's Chinese hostages.

There are numerous other remains in the close vicinity which have been published under different names of uncertain locality. Agents of Masson excavated a small stupa called Kūh-i Bacha (Site 620 in original Gazetteer), which Fussman has identified with Shotorak.

There were also sherds in the DAFA collection from a site in the same locality known as 'Ghundi Paisa' which may be the same site.

Collections: National Museum and Musée Guimet—objects from DAFA excavations.

Fieldwork:
1. 1834 Masson—excavation of 'Kūh-i Bacha'.
2. 1936–7 Meunié, DAFA—excavations.

Sources:
1. Gardin and Lyonnet 1980 chronological study of pottery from DAFA surveys, unpublished, under the name 'Ghundi Paisa'.
2. Masson 1836a: 2—mention as 'Kūh-i Bacha'.
3. Masson 1841: 117—mention as 'Kūh-i Bacha'.

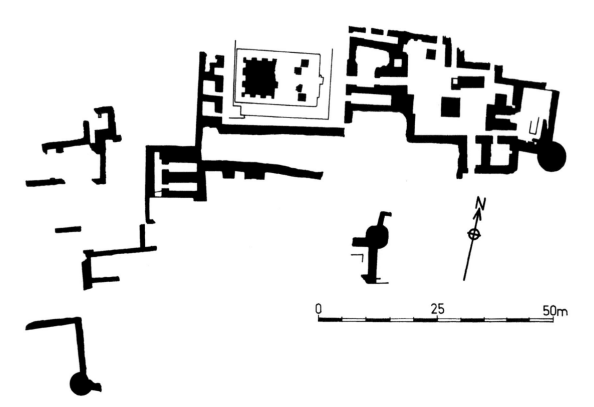

1088 Shotorak (after Meunié 1942).

4. Masson 1842: III. 141 and 165—mention as 'Kūh-i Bacha'.
5. Auboyer 1938: 221—brief summary of the finds.
6. Hackin 1938a: 6–7—brief summary of the excavations.
7. Hackin 1938c: 7–9—brief summary.
8. Monod-Bruhl 1939: 119—description of some reliefs in the Musée Guimet.
9. Meunié 1942—full description of the architecture of the stupas, and of the sculptures and decorative elements.
10. Meunié 1943–5—discusses the evidence for the site being a Chinese convent.
11. Yoshikawa 1944—summary of the excavations.
12. Van Lohuizen-de Leeuw 1949: 111–14—discusses a relief of a throned Buddha.
13. Yoshikawa 1949—account of the excavations and stylistic analysis of the sculpture.
14. Soper 1949–50: 77—discusses the light symbolism in the stele.
15. Kohzad 1953b: 5—mentions the excavations.
16. Bussagli 1956–7: 198–205—discusses the survival of Hellenistic art at Shotorak.
17. Carl 1959d—brief catalogue of the small finds.
18. Gullini 1961: pls 139–44—photos of objects on display from the National Museum.
19. Plaeschke 1961—discusses Shotorak's place in the Gandharan school.
20. L. Courtois 1962–3—mineralogical analyses of some of the stone sculptures.
21. Pugachenkova 1963: 38–9—general summary.
22. Mizuno 1964—illustrations and descriptions of the objects exhibited in the Tokyo Museum.
23. Hallade 1964–5—stylistic discussion of the occurrence of the ornamental scarf in some of the sculpture.
24. Monod 1966: 348–51—describes some of the reliefs on display in the Musée Guimet.
25. Rowland 1966a: 65–71—photos and brief introduction to the sculptures on display from the National Museum.
26. Rosenfield 1967—discusses the sculpture as a whole with other Gandharan art.
27. Auboyer 1968: pls 42–51—illustrates and discusses many of the objects.
28. Bussagli 1968: 49–50—evaluation of the architecture and sculptures as evidence for the date of Kanishka.
29. Hallade 1968—discusses the evolution of Gandharan art.
30. Hallade and Hinz 1968: pls 32, 71, 72, 96, 100—photos and discussion of the place of Shotorak in the development of Gandharan art.
31. Kuwayama 1969—examines the column bases from Shotorak and compares them to those north of the Hindu Kush.
32. H. Motamedi 1971a—discusses the Dipankara Buddha statue.
33. Rowland and Rice 1971: 135–6 and pl. 105—brief summary and photos of the art.
34. N. Dupree et al. 1974: 61–9—brief outline of the art and guide to the collection in the National Museum.
35. Taddei 1974c—discusses the iconography of the Buddhist sculpture from Shotorak.
36. Gaulier et al. 1976—discuss the religious iconography in the art.
37. Rhie 1976—compares some of the sculpture with Chinese art.
38. Trousdale 1975: 71–85—discusses the swords depicted on some of the reliefs.
39. Tarzi 1977c—good summary of the site and finds.
40. Miyaji 1978: 18—discusses some iconographyical aspects of the Parinirvana relief.
41. Tissot 1980—describes the evidence of the sculpture for daily life in Kushan times.
42. Kuwayama 1991: 103–9—discussion of the evidence from Begram III for the chronology.
43. Tsuchiya 2000—iconographical study of the Buddhist art.
44. Tissot and Darbois 2002—photos of objects from the National Museum.
45. Tissot 2006: 307–29, 334–335—National Museum catalogue details and photos.
46. Ball 2008: 175—summary.
47. Fussman 2008: 157–65 and 307—identifies Shotorak with Masson's 'Kūh-i Bacha'; description of the excavations.
48. Errington 2017a: 84—the Masson collection and archive relating to the site.

1089. SHŌRTŪGHAI

Original: Lat. 37° 18' N, long. 69° 30' E. Map 34.
Revised: 37.28076126 N, 69.49430783 E /
37° 16' 50.74051944 N, 69° 29' 39.50819628 E.
Takhār Province. About 17 km north-north-east of Dasht-i Qal'a, by the road from Khwāja Ghar and Yangi Qal'a, between this road and the Āmū Dāryā, south of the village of Shōrtūghai.

Dates: Bronze, end 3rd–beg. 2nd mill. BC; Hellenistic, 3rd–1st cent. BC (ceramic).

Description: Group of mounds close together (height 2 to 4 m) on the edge of an old meander of the Āmū Dāryā. The excavation brought to light: (A) a Bronze Age settlement, (B) partly covered by a farm of the Hellenistic period. (A) In the first, two main levels, distinguished especially by different styles of pottery. The oldest presents links with the Indus civilisation: the settlement is interpreted to be a commercial trading post founded by Harappan colonists. The finds provide evidence of metalworking (gold, copper) and precious stones (lapis lazuli in large quantity); Harappan seal. Other neighbouring sites, less than 2 km from this tepe, provide Harappan pottery on the surface. (B) Farm or manor of the Hellenistic period (8 × 16 m at least), with several rooms, north–south orientation; constrtuction in mud-bricks. The main room, containing a silo, is surrounded by smaller rooms, with hearths, querns, weighing instruments. Abundant pottery, many finds: figurines, lamps, schist vessel, iron objects, one bronze coin; storage jars in an adjoining building, east side.

Collections: National Museum/AIA—finds from the excavation.

Fieldwork:
1. 1975 Gardin, Gentelle, and Lyonnet, CNRS—survey.
2. 1976–9 Francfort, CNRS—excavations.

Sources:
1. Site information by H.-P. Francfort.
2. Lyonnet 1977—full report on the discovery, the pottery and the implications.
3. Francfort and Pottier 1978—preliminary report on the 1976 season: the stratigraphy, architecture, and finds. Discussion of the implications.
4. Gardin and Lyonnet 1975–9: 129–31 and pl. III, nos. 78, 166, 168–9, 20—discuss the importance of the excavations and the hydrological and geographical aspects of the site.
5. Francfort 1979b—brief summary of the excavations.
6. Gardin and Gentelle 1979—discuss the land usage and irrigation system in ancient times around Shōrtūghai.
7. A. A. Motamedi 1979—summary of the Bronze Age ceramics and review of the work of Francfort, Lyonnet, and Pottier.
8. A. A. Motamedi 1980—outline of the site from an interview with Pottier.
9. Qadriyan 1980—description in Persian of the excavations and results.
10. Dupree 1981—summary based on published accounts to Jan. 1980; personal speculations.
11. Francfort 1981a—general summary in English.
12. Francfort 1981b—discussion in the broader context of the Bactrian Bronze Age.
13. Francfort 1983—brief summary.
14. Francfort and Pottier 1981—full preliminary report.
15. Francfort 1989—full detailed report of the excavations.
16. Gentelle 1989—full report on the ancient irrigation and hydrology of the area.
17. Chakrabarti 1990: 1–3 and 85–93—discusses the evidence for the external trade of the Indus.
18. Ball 2008: 49, 100, 102, 265—summary.
19. Thomalsky et al. 2013—discussion of metalworking at the site.

1090. SHURĀBĀD

Original: Lat. 36° 42' N, long. 68° 55' E. Map 32.
Revised: 36.692111 N, 68.91837919 E / 36° 41' 31.59959100 N, 68° 55' 06.16507320 E.

Qundūz Province. About 6 km south-east of Qundūz, on the road to Khānābād: the tepe is located 1 km from the road, south side; it corresponds to the mound indicated on the 1:100,000 map south-east of the village of Shurābād, without altitude measurement.

Date: Hunnic-Turk, 5th–9th cent. (ceramic).

Description: Round mound (diam. 80 m), rising to an off-centre top (10 m) which overlooks to the south-west the canal called Nahr-i Naqi; in the cuts visible on this face of the tepe, layers of ashes and burnt earth, at various heights. A modern cemetery covers the slopes of the mound.

Collection: National Museum/AIA—sherds.

Fieldwork: 1978 Gardin et al., CNRS—survey.

Sources:
1. Site information by J.-C. Gardin.
2. Gardin and Lyonnet 1978–9: pl. VII—no. 421.
3. Lyonnet 1997: figs 68, 69—no. 421.
4. Gardin 1998: pl. VII—no. 421.

1091. SHŪRĀBI

Lat. 36° 33' N, long. 69° 03' E. Map 32.
Qundūz Province. At the edge of the Qundūz plain 26 km south-east of Qundūz.

Date: Kushan, 2nd cent. (ceramic, stylistic).

Description: A mound cut by a canal. The resulting section shows a mud-brick vaulted structure. A stone Atlante figure was found by chance here.

Fieldwork: 1955 and 1960 Fischer, DAAD—survey.

Sources:
1. Fischer 1958a: 250–3—description of the Atlante figure and long discussion on comparative material.
2. Fischer 1961a: 17—mention and photo of the site.
3. Fischer 1969: 349—brief summary.

1092. SHŪRATŪ
Includes TEPE MAHMŪD or SHĀH MAHMŪD.

Original: Lat. 36° 47' N, long. 69° 24' E. Map 36.
Revised:
36.78251276 N, 69.39554181 E /
36° 46' 57.04592736 N, 69° 23' 43.95052608 E (A).
36.78308432 N, 69.39519744 E /
36° 46' 59.10356820 N, 69° 23' 42.71076672 E (B).
36.78241999 N, 69.39356897 E /
36° 46' 56.71194672 N, 69° 23' 36.84828696 E (C).
36.78166268 N, 69.39335958 E /
36° 46' 53.98566312 N, 69° 23' 36.09449052 E (D).
36.78651215 N, 69.39597341 E /
36° 47' 11.44374324 N, 69° 23' 45.50427600 E (E).
Takhār Province. Some 15 km from Tāluqān on the road that links this town with Khwāja Ghar: group of tepes

*c.*500 m east of the rozd, in the village of Shūratū. The most visible is that indicated on the 1:100,000 map, on the edge of the Shūratū water course, right bank (A); it is surrounded by smaller mounds, one very close, 20 m to the north-north-west (B), two others *c.*100 m to the west (C) and the south-west (D), a fourth 200 m to the north (E.), corresponding to the 'ruin' indicated on the 1:100,000 map in this position. All these hillocks are damaged by the surrounding cultivated fields, which have probably already destroyed others.

Dates: Achaemenid, 6th–4th cent. BC (C, E); Kushan, 1st–4th cent. (except C); Hunnic-Turk, 5th–9th cent. (except C); some Islamic sherds (ceramic).

Description: (A) High mound of 12 m, oval, oriented north–south (60 × 30 m); steep slopes, strongly cut into at the base by crops, especially on the east and north. The top is flat, circular (diam. 15 m). (B) Rectangular east–west platform (30 × 15 and 20 m, east and west sides respectively, low (2.5 m), with remains of walls at the south-west angle, which appear recent. (C) Oblong north-west/south-east mound (30 × 15 m), sloping towards the south-east (2.5 to 1 m). (D) Square platform (20 × 20 m), low (2 m); on the cuts of the north face, 1.5 m below the top, burnt layers 50 cm thick (charcoal, ashes, earth with remains of white coating). (E) Tepe Mahmūd, or Shāh Mahmūd: quadrangular platform (60 × 50 m), 3 m high, with a rise on the west side (4 m) and a depression on the east side; wall visible on the west side, mud-bricks.

The interpretation of all these observations (descriptions and dates) could be this: vestiges of a town of the Kushan period of which A is the hub, built on the remains of an Achaemenid site; destruction before or during the Muslim conquest, then reoccupation at the beginning of the Islamic period.

Collection: National Museum/AIA—sherds.

Fieldwork: 1977 Gardin et al., CNRS—survey.

Sources:
1. Site information by J.-C. Gardin.
2. Gardin and Lyonnet 1978–9: pl. IX—nos. 242–6.
3. Lyonnet 1997: figs 25, 35, 49, 68, 69—nos. 242–6.
4. Gardin 1998: 71—nos. 242–6.

1093. SHURI
See also 321 FARKHAR.

Original: Lat. 36° 35' N, long. 69° 52' E. Map 37.
Revised:
36.59062982 N, 69.858924 E /
36° 35' 26.26734768 N, 69° 51' 32.12640612 E (A).
36.59219021 N, 69.8592071 E /
36° 35' 31.88477148 N, 69° 51' 33.14556648 E (B).
36.59138067 N, 69.85894362 E / 36° 35' 28.97039904 N, 069° 51' 32.19701400 E (B).
Takhār Province. 1 km north of Farkhar, on the edge of the road to Tāluqān, east side. The southernmost tepe of the

group (A) corresponds to the mound of 5 m indicated on the 1:100,000 map.

Dates: Achaemenid, 6th–4th cent. BC (B); Hunnic-Turk, 5th–9th cent. (ceramic).

Description: (A) Rectangular mound (40 × 30 m) along the road, which at the time cut across a part of the site, according to a local informant; flat top (3 m). (B) 100 m to the north, small round mound (diam. 25 m, height 3 m); between these two mounds, a modern cemetery, with a hillock 0.5 m high, on which sherds of the same period are found.

Collection: National Museum/AIA—sherds.

Fieldwork: 1977 Gardin et al., CNRS—survey.

Sources:
1. Site information by J.-C. Gardin.
2. Gardin and Lyonnet 1978–9: pl. X—nos. 335–7.
3. Lyonnet 1997: figs 25, 35, 68, 69—nos. 335–7.
4. Gardin 1998: 96—nos. 335–7.

1094. SHUR TEPE, CHUSHKA

Original: Lat. 37° 21' N, long. 66° 50' E. Map 28.
Revised: 37.3351527 N, 66.83361592 E / 37° 20' 06.54971712 N, 66° 50' 01.01730480 E.
Balkh Province. Just to the south of the Āmū Daryā at Chushka Guzar, *c.*37 km north of Qarchi Gak.

Description: A very large mound rising above the river flats.

Fieldwork: 1886 Maitland, ABC—topographical survey.

Sources:
1. Maitland 1888b: 234—mention.
2. Gazetteer 1979: IV. 172—mention.

1095. SHUR TEPE, DĀLĪ

Original: Lat. 37° 19' N, long. 66° 37' E. Map 28.
Revised: 37.31711848 N, 66.60292411 E /
37° 19' 01.62652116 N, 66° 36' 10.52677944 E.
Balkh Province. On the banks of the Āmū Daryā 20 km east of Islām Pinja, 2 km east of the village of Dālī.

Description: A mound *c.*8 m high, not to be confused with Shur Tepe further east along the Āmū Daryā.

Fieldwork: 1886 Maitland, ABC—topographical survey.

Source: Maitland 1888b: 232—mention.

SHUR TEPE, Imām Sāhib. See **738 MULLĀH AFGHĀNI.**

SHUR TEPE, Khulm. See **628 KUHNA KHULM.**

SHUTUR. See **2190 QAL'A-I ĪSHTAR in Supplement.**

1096. SHUTURGHAR

Lat. 33° 20' N, long. 67° 39' E. Maps 77, 78, 79.
Ghazni Province. Near Siabam *c.*10 km north of Ulyatu on the Jāghūrī-Dasht-i Nāwar road.

Description: A small complex of artificial caves.

Fieldwork: 1976 Taddei and Verarddi, IsMEO—survey.

Sources:
1. Verardi 1977a: 150—mention.
2. Verardi and Paparatti 2004: 89—description with drawing and photos.

1097. SHŪYIN

Lat. 31° 44' N, long. 65° 41' E. Map 89.
Kandahār Province. On the west bank of the Arghandāb River, 16 km north-east of the turn-off from the Kandahār-Herat road.

Dates: Sasanian, 3rd–5th cent.; Hunnic-early Islamic, 5th–13th cent. (ceramic).

Description: Three low mounds, each measuring *c.*15 × 20 m in area and 4 m in height, with many potsherds in the adjacent fields. Possibly burial mounds.

Fieldwork:
1. 1950–1 Fairservis, AMNH—survey.
2. 1974 Swiny, BIAS—survey.

Source: Site information by S. Swiny in unpublished BIAS archive.

1098. SIĀH ĀB

Lat. 32° 14' N, long. 62° 35' E. Map 85.
Fārah Province. In an isolated valley 13 km west of the village of Siāh Āb, on the Dilārām-Farāh road.

Date: Late Sasanian, 5th–7th cent. (stylistic).

Description: Rock carvings on many boulders edging a small stream bed for *c.*1 km, just south of the road and near a conical cairn to the east. They represent pastoral and hunting scenes, and individual horned animals. About 50 carvings could be traced upstream and further search might yield additional examples. The date is uncertain, but stylistically they belong to three different periods.

Fieldwork:
1. 1949 De Cardi—survey.
2. 1956 Ramachandran and Sharma, ASI—reconnaissance.

Sources:
1. Additional site information by B. De Cardi.
2. De Cardi 1950: 56—brief description.
3. Ramachandran and Sharma 1956: I. 15—brief description.

1099. SIĀHGIRD
Including ORTAKUL KUHNA. See also 1243 YARTI GUMBAZ.

Original: Lat. 36° 55' N, long. 67° 05' E. Map 27.
Revised: 36.92921856 N, 67.07137959 E /
36° 55' 45.18679980 N, 67° 04' 16.96653300 E.
Balkh Province. 24 km north of Mazār-i Sharīf on the road to Pata Kisar.

Description: Extensive remains of old buildings, forts, and canals covering an area of some 10 km². In 1886 many were still standing up to two and three storeys. In the centre is a large mound and many brick ruins.

Fieldwork: 1886 Peacocke, ABC—topographical survey.

Sources:
1. Grodekoff 1880: 14—mention.
2. Holdich 1886: 9—mention.
3. Holdich 1887: 36—mention.
4. Peacocke 1887a: 303–4—brief description.
5. Yate 1888: 247—quotes a brief description by Peacocke.
6. Caspani and Cagnacci 1951: 239—mention.
7. Gazetteer 1979: IV. 545–6—summary description.

1100. SIĀH KHAWĀL

Lat. 35° 10' N, long. 67° 07' E. Map 47.
Bāmiyān Province. 22 km south of Chashma Duzdān and 25 km north of Khākdau on the route from Darra-i Sūf to Bāmiyān, at the point where the route enters the Darra-i Siāhkhawāl.

Description: A series of artificial caves and the remains of an old fort above.

Fieldwork: 1886 Amir Khan, ABC—topographical suvey.

Source: Amir Khan 1888: 168—mention.

SIĀH KUH. See **127 BĪMĀRĀN** (A and B) and **806 PASSANI** (C).

SIĀH QANDŪQ. See **63 ĀSYĀ-I QUNĀK.**

1101. SIĀH RĪGĀN

Lat. 36° 51'–36° 53' N, long. 67° 39'–67° 40' E. Map 29.
Samangān Province. About 20 km north of Tāshqurgān, and at 3–4 km in the north-east sector of the main ruins of Shairābād (no. 1061, A): sites marked by little eroded hillocks, covered and surrounded by sherds. Some of them (D, E, F) are located immediately next to the dunes that separate the oasis of Tāshqurgān from the Amu Darya, the region called Siāh Rīgān (Black Sands).

Dates: Epi-Palaeolithic, 7th mill. BC (lithic material); Bronze, 2nd mill. BC (A?, D); beg. Iron, end 2nd–beg. 1st mill. BC (C, D, E); Hellenistic, 3rd–1st cent. BC (B); Kushan, 2nd–3rd cent. (A, B, F); Sasanian-Hunnic, 4th–6th cent. (F?); some Islamic sherds (E) (ceramic).

Description: (A) 2 km north-east of Shairābād (no. 1061, A) and 2.5 km north of Shahr-i Banu (no. 1034); (B) 1.2 km south of A; (C) two hillocky areas (diam. *c*.100 m) 1.2 km east-north-east and north-north-east of A, respectively (many flints on the first of these two areas); (D) 1.5 km north-east of A (many fragments of large jars, flints); (E) 1.3 km north of A (many flints); (F) 2.7 km north-north-east of A, a hillocky area covered by sherds over an extensive surface (diam. *c*.300 m), at the edge of the zone of dunes which is covering the site little by little.

The D–E region (Siāh Rīgān) is covered with sherds and knapped stone, probably dispersed by water; only for the lithic material, a collection of more than 3000 objects was collected, of which 400 tools: many micro-burins, retouched blades, points, end-scrapers.

Collections: National Museum/AIA– pottery; bronze objects: head of pin (E), lid (C), arrowhead with two barbs (D); lapis lazuli bead (E); flint (C, D, E).

Fieldwork:
1. 1969 Gouin, DAFA—survey.
2. 1976 Vinogradov, Af/Sov. Mission—survey.

Sources:
1. Gouin: unpublished report in DAFA Archives—sites nos. 28 (E), 36 (B), 37–8 (C), 39 (D), 40 (F), 41 (A).
2. Gouin 1973a: 78–86—preliminary report on the stone artefacts, with photos and drawings.
3. Sarianidi 1977c: 7–11—discusses the lithics from the Soviet survey.
4. Davis 1978: 67–8—brief summary and comparisons of the Palaeolithic site and material.
5. Srivastava 1979b: 55—assessment of Vinogradov's work.
6. Vinogradov 1979—discusses the general lithic assemblage from the survey, with comparisons in Soviet Central Asia.
7. Zahir 1980—summary in Persian of the results.

1102. SIĀHSANG
See also 155 CHAHĀR BĀGH.

Original: Lat. 34° 24' N, long. 70° 23' E. Map 66.
Revised: 34.40504138 N, 70.36847767 E /
34° 24' 18.14898528 N, 70° 22' 06.51961344 E.
Nangahār Province. In the foothills of the Siāhkuh, 3 km south-west of the village of Chahār BāghB.

Date: Kushan-Hunnic, 1st–6th cent. (architectural).

Description: Ruins of five stupas and other remains, containing nothing.

Fieldwork:
1. 1834 Masson—excavations.
2. 1965 Mizuno, Kyoto University—survey.

Sources:
1. Masson 1841: 104—mention (Chahār Bāgh tumuli).
2. Mizuno 1971: 121—brief description (Stupas 37–41).

1103. SIBAK

Original: Lat. 33° 29' N, long. 64° 40' E. Maps 55, 74.
Revised: 33.48580603 N, 64.66222168 E /
33° 29' 08.90171628 N, 64° 39' 43.99805088 E.
Ghūr Province. At the foot of the Kūh-i Pasangān near Khatif, east of Taiwāra, 5 km west of Yamān.

Date: Ghurid, 12th–13th cent. (architectural, geographical).

Description: Remains of towers and other structures.

Fieldwork: 1946 Kohzad, HAS—survey.

Source: Kohzad 1951–4, 9/1: 28—mention.

1104. SIBI CHUB

Lat. 33° 11' N, long. 67° 27' E. Map 79.
Ghazni Province. C.10 km north of Sang-i Māsha on the road to Malistān.

Description: Some inscriptions on a large block of dark-coloured granite.

Source: Markham 1876: 244—mention, from a journey by Lynch in 1841.

SĪMKUHĪ. See 2249 SĪMKUH in Supplement.

SĪR HANGĀN. See 2250 SĪR HANGĀN in Supplement.

SIRIGH CHAUPAN. See 524 KANSIR.

1105. SIRKAYI

Original: Lat. 31° 51' N, long. 68° 04' E. Map 81.
Revised: 31.83012648 N, 68.06922633 E /
31° 49' 48.45533088 N, 68° 04' 09.21479448 E.
Zābul Province. In the Katawāz district near Turkhel, *c*.7 km north-west of the Pakistan border.

Description: Remains of a tower and stone walls on top of a hill *c*.35 m high.

Source: Wazir Taniwal—personal communication.

1106. SIRWĀN

Lat. 34° 18' N, long. 63° 03' E. Map 53.
Herat Province. On the south bank of the Harī Rūd, *c*.15 km south-west of Obeh.

Date: Ghaznavid or Seljuk, 11th cent. (stylistic).

Description: A decorated brick minaret, similar to Ghazni and Herat, now collapsed. It had a fluted shaft 29 m high, and a two-line Kufic inscription.

Sources:
1. Khanikoff 1861: 370—brief description.
2. Maitland and Drummond 1888: 135—mention.
3. Diez 1923: 166-7—includes the site in an inventory of 11th- and 12th-century minarets.
4. Creswell 1927: 292—discusses the evolution of the minaret.
5. Combe et al. 1936: 141—text of the inscription.
6. Sourdel-Thomine 1953: 118 and 134—quotes Khanikoff's description and discusses the form of the minaret.
7. Mayer 1956: 55—brief note on the architect of the minaret.
8. Pinder-Wilson 1981—discusses the form and the architectural parallels of the minaret.

1107. SNA QAL'A
Or QAL'A-I SABZ or SHNA QAL'A.

Original: Lat. 30° 33' N, long. 63° 132' E. Map 98.
Revised: 30.55628608 N, 63.54418529 E /
30° 33' 22.62989880 N, 63° 32' 39.06703788 E.
Helmand Province. On the right bank of the Helmand across the river from Kūh-i Khān Nashīn, *c*.20 km west of Qal'a-i Nau.

Dates: ?Sasanian, 3rd–7th cent. (architectural); Ghaznavid, 11th–12th cent. (ceramic).

Description: The possible remains of a large fire temple. It consists of a sanctuary, preserved by later conversion into an Islamic tomb, resting on four broad terraces cut from the hilltop. One sherd was found containing a three-letter Aramaic inscription. A small Ghaznavid town occupied the lower terraces of the site.

Ferrier did not get a close look at it as it was dark and he was fleeing from Baluch marauders who already had murdered members of his party; but even under these circumstances, well calculated to produce anxiety, he was able to report the site. Access to the site is very difficult as it lies within many square miles of very broken terrain, and I do not believe any subsequent traveller along the Helmand saw it. It is, however, quite spectacular, owing to the green colour of the volcanic rock outcrop.

Fieldwork: 1971-4 Trousdale, Smithsonian Institution—survey.

Sources:
1. Additional site information by W. Trousdale.
2. Ferrier 1857: 407—mention.
3. Trousdale 1976: 59—brief description.

SOHREN KALAT. See **883 QAL'A-I SUKH, Nīmrūz.**

SORBOG. See **993 SĀR BĀGH.**

1108. SPĪN BALDAK
Or the 'CHĀMAN HOARD'.

Original: Lat. 31° 00' N, long. 66° 24' E. Map 99.
Revised: 31.01168996 N, 66.40227696 E /
31° 00' 42.08384988 N, 66° 24' 08.19705240 E.
Kandahār Province. The Afghan border post on the main Kandahār-Quetta road.

Date: Saka, 1st cent. BC (numismatic).

Description: A hoard of 75 silver Saka coins found at a site near here in about 1940.

Aerial photographs have also recorded the remains of a large caravanserai with a double set of rooms surrounding two courtyards.

Sources:
1. Additional information from aerial photographs by D. Thomas.
2. Jenkins 1955: 25-6—discusses the hoard and gives a brief catalogue.
3. Mac Dowall and Taddei 1978a: 212—mention.

1109. SPIRWAN

Original: Lat. 31° 30' N, 65° 25' E. Map 89.
Revised: 31.49738795 N, 65.41919092 E /
31° 29' 50.59660668 N, 065° 25' 09.08732388 E.
Kandahār Province. 5 km south-west of Panjwāyī, on the right bank of the Arghandāb.

Dates: Bronze, 3rd–2nd mill. BC; Indo-Parthian, 1st–4th cent.; Timurid, 15th–16th cent. and post-Timurid, 17th cent. (ceramic).

Description: Large enclosure of irregular shape (cf. fig. 51.2), rectangular on the east and south faces, semi-circular on the north-west faces, about 250 m long. In the rounded north-west part a citadel rises (height *c*.25 m) lying on a rectangular platform. The rest of the enclosure appears to be entirely constructed. The east face is pierced by two gates.

Collection: National Museum/AIA—sherds.

Fieldwork:
1. 1951 Casal, DAFA—survey.
2. 1956 Ramachandran and Sharma, ASI—reconnaissance.
3. 1966 Fischer, DAAD—survey.

Sources:
1. J.-M. Casal: unpublished 1951 report, DAFA archives.
2. Ramachandran and Sharma 1956: I. 11—mention.
3. Fischer 1967a: 149—mention.

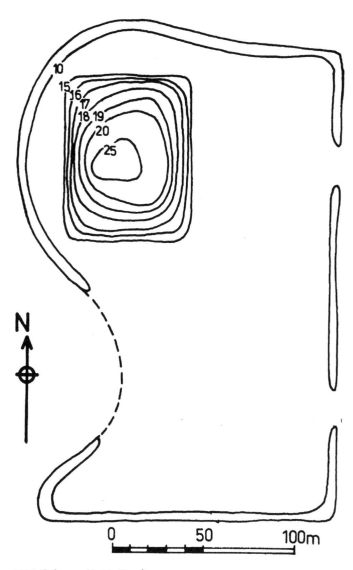

1109 Spirwan (J.-M. Casal).

1110. SRA GHUNDAI, GHAZNI

Original: Lat. 32° 20' N, long. 67° 53' E. Map 79.
Revised: 32.33194789 N, 67.88604183 E /
32° 19' 55.01241228 N, 67° 53' 09.75058404 E.
Ghazni Province. C.2 km north of Nāwa south of the Āb-i Istāda, to the east of the road to Muqqur.

Dates: Late Sasanian and Turki Shahi, 6th–9th cent.; early Islamic, 10th–12th cent. (ceramic).

Description: Remains of a city in the form of a vast rectangle, orientated north–south. It is surrounded by a double set of fortification walls, the outermost one having four corner towers and two gateways each on the north and south walls. The most elaborate gate is one of the northern ones. Inside, the remains include a large mound in the exact centre, a probable mosque to the east, a possible palace or caravanserai, and numerous ruins of baked brick, mud-

brick, and *pakhsa*. There are large numbers of sherds across the surface.

Fieldwork: 1976 Taddei, IsMEO – survey.

Sources:
1. Taddei 1976: 600–1 – brief description.
2. Verardi and Paparatti 2004: 92–3 – mention and sketch plan.

1111. SRA GHUNDAI, HELMAND

Lat. 31° 37' N, long. 64° 20' E. approximately. Map 86. Helmand Province. On the right bank of the Helmand opposite Lashkargāh.

Dates: Sasanian, 3rd–7th cent.; early Islamic, 8th–13th cent.; Timurid, 15th–16th cent. (ceramic).

Description: Ruins of a small fort.

Fieldwork: 1966 Hammond, Cambridge University – survey.

Source: Hammond 1970: 459 – lists the site (no. 34) and describes the pottery types and general survey results.

1112. SŪCH

Lat. 36° 46' N, long. 70° 50' E. Map 38. Badakhshān Province. At a bridge across the Kokcha River 11 km south of Jurm.

Description: Many petroglyphs of possible prehistoric date on a series of large boulders, stretching southwards along the valley for 4 km. Most are hunting scenes; one depicts a snake swallowing a goat.

Source: N. Dupree 1977: 427–8 – brief description and photo.

SUJĀWAND. See 971 SAJĀWAND.

SUKHTA CHINĀR. See 2251 SUKHTA CHINĀR in Supplement.

SUKHTA QAL'A. See 2252 SUKHTA QAL'A in Supplement.

1113. SULDUZ TEPE

Original: Lat. 36° 54' N, long. 65° 07' E. Map 24.
Revised: 36.89923094 N, 65.10372487 E /
36° 53' 57.23138940 N, 65° 06' 13.40954460 E.
Faryāb Province. 6 km south of Andkhūī, to the east of the road to Maimana.

Description: An extremely large, flat-topped mound, probably the remains of a fort or small town.

Fieldwork: 1886 Maitland, ABC—topographical survey.

Source: Maitland 1888b: 162—mention.

1114. SULTĀN BĀBĀ ZĪYĀRAT
See 597 KHWĀJA KANUR.

1115. SULTĀN BAKWĀ

Original: Lat. 32° 14' N, long. 62° 57' E. Map 85.
Revised: 32.23688624 N, 62.94615478 E /
32° 14' 12.79045068 N, 62° 56' 46.15720152 E.
Farāh Province. On the Dilārām-Farāh road, 186 km west of Girishk.

Description: A small mound and some mud remains, surrounded by an ancient canal system.

Fieldwork:
1. 1952 Le Berre and Gardin, DAFA—survey.
2. 1960–70 Fischer, Bonn University—survey.

Sources:
1. Yate 1900: 10—mentions ancient cultivation.
2. Gazetteer 1973: II. 285—mentions remains.
3. Fischer et al. 1974–6: 30—mention remains.

1116. SULTĀNPŪR
See also 310 DŪST-I KHĒL.

Original: Lat. 34° 25' N, long. 70° 20' E. Map 66.
Revised: 34.41517538 N, 70.32499621 E /
34° 24' 54.63137304 N, 70° 19' 29.98636248 E.
Nangahār Province. 3 km from Chahār Bāgh and 1 km south of the village of Sultānpūr-i Sufla, 13 km west of Jalālābād.

Date: Kushan, 1st–2nd cent. (architectural, stylistic).

Description: Remains of an undecorated stupa in very bad condition. It seems completely isolated, with no mounds or remains in the vicinity apart from a ruined Hindu shrine. Inside was a pyramid-shaped steatite reliquary.

Collections: BM—stupa deposits.

Fieldwork:
1. 1834 Masson—excavation.
2. 1965 Mizuno, Kyoto University—survey.

Sources:
1. Jacquet 1837: 424–5—discusses Masson's work.
2. Masson 1841: 89–90—brief description.
3. Wilson 1841: pl. III—drawing of the reliquary.
4. Fergusson 1876: 91—discusses the construction of the stupa.
5. Mizuno 1971: 122—brief description and photo.

6. Irwin 1979: 808–10—discussion of the cosmic significance of the reliquary.
7. Jongeward et al. 2012—catalogue and discussion of the reliquaries.
8. Errington 2017a: 139–40 and 2017b: 33, 42, 52, 59, 112, 117–18—the Masson collection and archive relating to the site.

1117. SUMAQULI
Includes SUMARA. See also 2146 KUHNA DEH, Sumara, in Supplement.

Lat. 34° 46'–34° 48' N, long. 67° 53'–67° 54' E. Map 58.
Bāmiyān Province. Valley of the river of Bāmiyān (Darya-i Pahlawānsang): region of Sumaquli and the side valley of Darya-i Sumara, to the south.

Date: Turk, 8th–10th cent. (ceramic, architecture).

Description: A castle, only lowest of a curtain of five or six mud-brick towers standing, which once blocked the valley. There is then a line of ten-sided polygonal towers on high positions. Mud-brick on stone foundations; arrow slits. Similar to Shahr-i Ghulghula towers. Little pottery (Le Berre B-I, 10–12).
　There are then two further ruined towers up the Sumara Valley (Le Berre B-II, 1 and 3).

Collection: National Museum/AIA—sherds.

Fieldwork: 1975–6 Le Berre, DAFA—survey.

Sources:
1. Levi 1972: 73–4—description.
2. Le Berre 1987: 74–5, 80–1, pls 94, 95, 105—itinerary B-I, ruins 10 to 12; B-II, Darya-i Somara, ruins 1 and 3.

SUMBUL. See 1075 SHĪBAR, west.

SUM-I SANGAR. See **2253 SUM-I SANGAR in Supplement.**

1118. SUNDURWAR

Original: Lat. 34° 52' N, long. 70° 22' E. Map 65.
Revised: 34.87463782 N, 70.36397246 E /
34° 52' 28.69614228 N, 70° 21' 50.30086860 E.
Laghmān Province. On the west bank of the 'Alingār River, 7 km north of 'Alingār Woleswali to the west of the road to 'Alaqadari Shāhi.

Date: Hindu Shahi, 10th cent. (ceramic).

Description: Some stone walls on a hill. There is also a cave by the river.

Fieldwork: 1955–68 Fischer, DAAD—survey.

Source: Fischer 1969: 357—brief summary (Ruins G2).

1119. SUR

Lat. 34° 23' N, long. 63° 28' E. Maps 53, 54.
Herat Province. A valley descending southwards to the
Harī Rūd, 29 km west of Chisht.

Description: Some ruins.

Sources:
1. Gazetteer 1975: III. 378 — mention.
2. Rafat 1980: 5 — mention.

1120. SŪRBURT
Or SURKH BARUT.

Original: Lat. 30° 51' N, long. 62° 05' E. Map 92.
Revised: 30.84900423 N, 62.07839547 E /
30° 50' 56.41524600 N, 62° 04' 42.22368156 E.
Nīmrūz Province. In the dunes 15 km south of Zīyārat-i
Amīrān Sāhib and 5.5 km south of Sangar.

Description: Remains of a huge fortress.

Fieldwork: 1965–70 Fischer, Bonn University — survey.

Sources:
1. Fischer 1970b: pl. 58 — photo.
2. Fischer 1971b: 44 — mention and photo (Site 1).
3. Fischer 1973c: 148 — mention.

SURKH BARUT. See **1120 SŪRBURT.**

SURKH DAGH. See **752 NĀD-I 'ALĪ.**

1121. SURKHDAR
Or QUL-I MAQSŪD.

Lat. 34° 51' N, long. 67° 46' E. Map 58.
Bāmiyān Province. 7 km west of Bāmiyān in the hills just to
the north of the road to Band-i Amīr.

Description: Some ancient ruins and a cave village.

Fieldwork: 1886 Amir Khan, ABC — topographical survey.

Sources:
1. Masson 1839: 84 — mentions ruins.
2. Masson 1842: II. 395 — mentions ruins.
3. Amir Khan 1888: 174 — mentions caves.

1122. SURKH DĀWAR

Lat. 34° 18' N, long. 70° 34' E. Map 67.
Nangahār Province. To the south-west of the main road from
Jalālābād to Tūrkhām, between Bati Kot and 'Ali Baghan.

Date: ?Chaghatai, 14th cent. (traditional).

Description: Ruins of a large castle.

Source: Masson 1842: III. 251–2 — mention.

SURKHI. See **2254 SURKHI in Supplement.** See also **792
PALANGI.**

1123. SURKH KOTAL
Or CHASHMA-I SHIR or SAR-I CHASHMA. See
also 630 KUHNA MASJID.

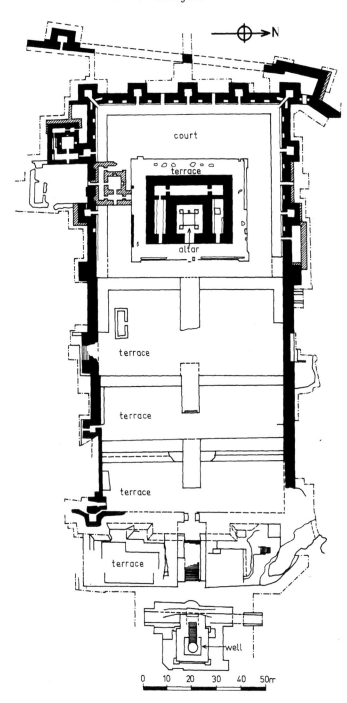

1123 Surkh Kotal (after Schlumberger 1964d).

Original: Lat. 36° 02–03' N, long. 68° 33–55' E. Map 33.
Revised: 36.03604605 N, 68.58952582 E /
36° 02' 09.76577280 N, 68° 35' 22.29293724 E.
Baghlān Province. On a hill to the west of the road to
Haibak, 18.5 km north of Pul-i Khumri.

Date: Kushan and Kushano-Sasanian, 2nd–4th cent. (ceramic, numismatic, stylistic).

Description: A major Kushan dynastic shrine complex on top of a hill overlooking the Baghlān plain. It is approached by a monumental brick and masonry staircase, flanked by four massive terraces, cut out of the hillside. The temple itself—possibly a fire temple—is in the centre of a paved courtyard, and consists of a masonry altar with four Hellenistic column bases at each corner, in a sanctuary with massive mud walls.

The most important finds have been inscriptions. The most notable one is the foundation inscription, a monumental inscription in the Bactrian language, made up of a series of stone blocks that originally lined the front of the third terrace. The other main inscription is the Nokonzoko inscription, an elaborate, very controversial inscription in three versions, that describes the construction and restoration of the complex, also in the Bactrian language. Other finds include a life-size headless statue of Kanishka, several more inscriptions, many coins, and various sculptural fragments in stone and stucco.

Collections: National Museum and Musée Guimet—objects from DAFA excavations.

Fieldwork: 1952–63 Schlumberger, DAFA—excavations.

Sources:
1. Schlumberger 1952b—brief note on the discovery of the site.
2. Schlumberger 1952c—report on the excavations of the temple with a description of the architecture and sculpture.
3. Kohzad 1952/53—describes the first season's excavations.
4. Kohzad 1953e—description of the discovery of the site and the first season's excavations.
5. Schlumberger 1953a—account of the discovery and brief report on the first season.
6. Schlumberger 1953b—brief description of the temple and discussion of the implications.
7. Curiel 1954—epigraphical analyses of seven blocks of the great inscription, the Palomedes inscription, and one other inscription.
8. Mandelshtam 1954—summary of the excavations.
9. Schlumberger 1954a—account of the discovery, summary of the first two seasons, and discussion of the date and implications.
10. Schlumberger 1954b—description and appraisal of the main results of the first season.
11. Schlumberger 1954c—brief note on the second season's excavations: the temple, the inscriptions, sculptures, and coins.
12. Schlumberger 1954d—interim report on the excavation of the sanctuary terrace and on the finds, with a discussion on the religious aspects.
13. Kohzad 1954/55—brief report on the results of the second season.
14. Schlumberger 1955a—brief report on the results of the second season.
15. Schlumberger 1955c—brief note on the third season's excavations: the stairway, the statue of Kanishka, and the platform.
16. Schlumberger 1955d—interim report on the excavation of the stairway, the terraces, and some of the sculpture.
17. Henning 1956—brief note on the ancient, medieval, and modern names of the site.
18. Picard 1956—brief note on the excavation of the temple.
19. Bussagli 1956–7: 156–67—discusses the survivals of Greek art at Surkh Kotal.
20. Altheim and Stiehl 1957: 127–8—brief linguistic discussion of the grat inscription.
21. Schlumberger 1957a—brief summary of the fourth, fifth, and sixth seasons: the stairway and the long inscription.
22. Bertrand 1958—a general account: the background, discovery, and excavations.
23. Bosch 1958: LXXXIX–LCI—brief introduction to the results of the 1952 and 1953 seasons.
24. Maricq 1958—text, translation, detailed commentary, and very full linguistic analysis and discussion.
25. Fischer 1959a: 130—brief summary of its relation to Indian culture.
26. Katsuno 1959—summary of the excavations and finds.
27. Schlumberger 1959—summary of the discovery, the temple, the architecture, and the sculpture.
28. Jettmar 1959–60—discusses the connections with Central Asian architecture.
29. Auboyer 1960: 122–7—summary of the excavations.
30. Henning 1960—summary and detailed linguistic analysis of the long inscription.
31. Humbach 1960—detailed linguistic and historical study of the long inscription; interpretation as Mithraic hymn.
32. Kieffer 1960a—very detailed linguistic analysis of the long inscription.
33. Schlumberger 1960a—detailed discussion of the historical, cultural, and linguistic implications of the site.
34. Schlumberger 1960b: 143–50—describes Surkh Kotal in the context of eastern Hellenistic art.
35. Benveniste 1961—new eedition and catalogue of all the inscriptions. Texts of all versions, with chronological and historical discussion. Rejection of Humbach's interpretation.
36. Brandenstein 1961—discusses the derivation and etymology of one of the Bactrian words.
37. J.C. Courtois 1961: 24–6—summary of the excavations.

38. Fischer 1961c—mentions the tridents carved on the staircase.
39. Humbach 1961a—new studies on the language and religion of the Kushans from the new evidence of the Surkh Kotal inscriptions.
40. Humbach 1961b—note on the religion of the Kushans.
41. Schlumberger 1961a—discusses the art of Surkh Kotal in relation to Parthian and Graeco-Roman art.
42. Kieffer 1961—discusses the characteristics of Kushan art from the site and the influences of Greek art.
43. Schlumberger 1961b—full summary of the site and finds, with speculations on the origins of Indo-Greek art.
44. Bussagli 1962a: 42—brief summary of the art.
45. Bussagli 1862b—outline of the main features of Gandharan art.
46. Hallade 1962a—discusses Surkh Kotal and Bactrian art.
47. Humbach 1962—brief note on the Kanishka inscription.
48. Kieffer 1962—compares the sculpture of Surkh Kotal and Mat, concluding that Surkh Kotal art is closer to its Hellenistic origins.
49. Mayrhofer 1962—discusses the great inscription.
50. Bivar 1963—discusses the evidence from Surkh Kotal for the date of Kanishka.
51. Gershevitch 1963—review and rejection of Humbach's interpretation of the inscription.
52. Humbach 1963—an answer to Gershevitch's arguments on the inscription.
53. Pugachenkova 1963: 19–21—general summary.
54. Habibi 1963/64a—very detailed linguistic analysis of the inscriptions, proposing Bactrian as the forerunner of modern Dari.
55. Habibi 1963/64b—brief version of Habibi 1963/64a.
56. Ali 1964: 24–5—discusses the importance of the discoveries for the origins of Gandharan art.
57. Göbl 1964—discusses the evidence from Surkh Kotal for a date of Kanishka.
58. Hansen 1964—a new interpretation of two passages of the long inscription, with a discussion of the phonetics.
59. Harmatta 1964—long linguistic analysis and interpretation of the great inscription.
60. Mukherjee 1964—brief note on the dating of the year 31 referred to in the inscription, fixing it at AD 108/9.
61. Schlumberger 1964a—illustrates and discusses some of the objects exhibited at the Tokyo Museum.
62. Schlumberger 1964d—summary of the previous seasons and preliminary report on the 1963–4 season: the full temple complex and discussion of the history of the monument.
63. Göbl 1965—new complete edition and linguistic analysis of the three versions of the inscription.

64. Harmatta 1965—full linguistic analyses and discussion of the Palomedes, unfinished, and wall inscriptions.
65. Henning 1965—discusses Kanishka and the Bactrian inscriptions at Surkh Kotal.
66. Talbot Rice 1965: 143–44—good summary of the site.
67. Gershevitch 1966—reviews the problems of the inscriptions and their different interpretations.
68. Göbl 1966—discusses the inscriptions in relation to Vasishka II.
69. Humbach 1966–7: I. 76–103—texts and linguistic discussion of all inscriptions.
70. N. Dupree 1967a: 13–19—good description of the temple complex.
71. Gershevitch 1967: 21–32—discusses the erection of the inscription and its implications.
72. Mukherjee 1967: 70–2—refers to the inscriptions in a discussion of Kushan genealogy.
73. Rosenfield 1967: 154–62—discusses the art and the inscriptions.
74. Schlumberger 1967—discusses the evidence from Surkh Kotal for Hellenism in Afghanistan.
75. Auboyer 1968: pls 38–41—photos of the site, the inscription, and the Kanishka statue.
76. Barnett 1968—general discussion on Surkh Kotal and the derivations of Bactrian art.
77. Bussagli 1968: 43–5 and 50—discusses the evidence of the sanctuary and inscriptions for a date of Kanishka.
78. Habibi 1968: 13–14—discusses the derivations of Bactrian art and the origins of Kushan art, and the consequent emergence of a national style.
79. Humbach 1968a—brief note on two points of historical interest in the inscription.
80. Kosambi 1968—supports Humbach's interpretation of the inscription as a hymn.
81. Mustamandi 1968c—discusses the survivals of Graeco-Bactrian art at Surkh Kotal.
82. Narain 1968: 230–1—discusses the archaeological evidence from Surkh Kotal for Kushan chronology.
83. Kuwayama 1969—examination of the pillar bases and comparison of them with those from south of the Hindu Kush.
84. Mustamandi 1969a—discusses the Kushan art of Surkh Kotal.
85. Dobbins 1970—refers to the evidence from the inscriptions in a discussion of Kushan chronology.
86. Schlumberger 1970: 60–6—photos and brief summary of the site and its decoration in the context of Iranian Hellenistic art.
87. Habibi 1971: 54 and 5 and 137—photos of the inscription and discussion of the development of Afghan epigraphy.

88. Schippmann 1971: 492–8 — discusses the temple in the context of Sasanian fire temples.
89. Mustamandi 1972 — discusses the origin of the eagle motif found in the temple.
90. Dupree 1973: 292–5 — brief discussion of the main problems.
91. Kumar 1973: 286–8 — brief discussion of the inscription.
92. Sims-Williams 1973 — brief discussion of some syntactical aspects of the inscription.
93. Staviski 1973 — discusses and compares the capitals from Surkh Kotal.
94. N. Dupree et al. 1974: 4–7 — brief outline of the site and guide to the exhibits in the Kābul Museum.
95. Habibi 1974 — summary of the linguistic evidence of the inscriptions.
96. Mekarska 1974 — reviews the problems of the inscriptions and attempts an etymological dictionary of each word.
97. Pugachenkova 1974a — discusses the broad aspects of Bactrian art and architecture.
98. Rowland 1974: 80–2 — briefly discusses the sculptures and possible Parthian prototypes.
99. Sidqi 1975 — discusses the religious and cultural aspects of the Kushans in the light of Surkh Kotal.
100. Trousdale 1975: 71–85 — discusses the sword depicted in some of the sculpture.
101. Azizi 1976 — discusses the archaeological evidence for Kushan history.
102. Francfort 1976a: 147–8 — brief description of the defences around the sanctuary.
103. Davary 1977 — lists the inscriptions and gives a bibliography.
104. Fussman 1977 — discusses the essentially Iranian aspects of the temple.
105. Mac Dowall and Taddei 1978a: 235–8 — brief introduction to the inscriptions.
106. Sultan 1978 — discusses the Hellenistic influences in the art.
107. Francfort 1979a: 32–6 — discusses the general characteristics of Kushan fortifications.
108. Gershevitch 1979 — a new translation and discussion of the inscription.
109. Pugachenkova 1979a — discusses the general principles of Kushan religious architecture.
110. Srivastava 1979c — summary of the excavations.
111. Gershevitch 1980 — discusses the inscription and associated well.
112. Fraser 1982 — brief note on the Palamedes inscription and origins of the name.
113. Lazard, Grenet, and Lamberterie 1984 — discussion of the inscriptions.
114. Fussman and Guillaume 1990 — final report on the coins and small finds.
115. Tissot and Darbois 2002 — photos of objects from the Kābul Museum
116. Tissot 2006: 51–69 — National Museum catalogue details and photos.
117. Cambon and Jarrige 2006, 2007 — mention the restoration of the Kanishka statue that had been smashed in 2001.
118. Wightman 2007: 688–694 — discusses in context of Central Asian fire and water cults.
119. Ball 2008: 266–8 — summary.
120. Rougemont 2012a: 194–5 — discussion of the Palamedes signature.
121. Sims-Williams 2012 — discussion and translation of the Bactrian inscriptions.
122. Canepa 2015 — discussion of Surkh Kotal in the context of Middle Iranian dynastic sanctuaries.
123. Green 2017 — discusses Surkh Kotal and the establishment of pre-Taliban Afghan national identity.

1124. SURKH MINĀR

Lat. 34° 26' N, Long. 69° 15' E. Map 62.
kābul province. 2 km south-east of the village of Shīwakī, 3 km west of the stupa.

Date: Kushan-Turki Shahi, 1st–9th cent. (architectural).

Description: The site of a diaper masonry column, now collapsed, similar to the Minār-i Chakri. There is also a small, badly damaged stupa with a frieze of blind arches and pilasters, and an associated monastery.

Fieldwork:
1. 1962 Mizuno, Kyoto University — survey.
2. 1972 Fussman, CNRS — survey.

Sources:
1. Jacquet 1837: 406–7 — brief description.
2. Masson 1841: 114 — brief description.
3. Burnes 1843: 263–4 — brief description.
4. Niedemeyer and Diez 1924: pl. 53 — photo.
5. Dorneich 1968 — discusses all aspects of the monument.
6. Mizuno 1971: 125 — mention, with a photo of the stupa.
7. Fischer 1987 — discussion.
8. Ball 1984 — discusses the function and the evidence for possible later date.
9. Fussman et al. 2008: 43–5, 253–6, and 299–300 — detailed description, photos, and drawings ('Shevaki 3, 4, and 5').

SURKH TEPE. See 614 KIZGHUNDI.

1125. SURKH TŪP

Original: Lat. 34° 28' N, long. 70° 21' E. Map 66.
Revised: 34.46807847 N, 70.35145913 E /
34° 28' 05.08247508 N, 70° 21' 05.25286584 E.

Laghmān Province. Between Bīmārān and Darunta, c. 700 m west of the large stupa at Deh Rahman.

Date: Indo-Parthian, 1st cent. (architectural, numismatic).

Description: A stupa complex consisting of a large stupa in very poor condition, surrounded by votive stupas, two of them quite large, and some caves cut into the hillside below. The central chamber of the stupa had a fresco of a human figure. A coin of Azes I was found on the surface.

Collections: BM—stupa deposits.

Fieldwork:
1. 1833 Honigberger—excavation of main stupa.
2. 1834 Masson—excavation of votive stupa.
3. 1965 Mizuno, Kyoto University—survey.

Sources:
1. Masson 1841: 81 and 96—brief description.
2. Wilson 1841: pls III and VIII fig. I—illustrations of coins found.
3. Mizuno 1971: 119—brief description and photo (Stupas 26–8).
4. Jongeward et al. 2012—catalogue and discussion of the reliquaries.
5. Errington 2017a: 124–6 and 2017b: 301—the Masson collection and archive relating to the site.

1126. SUST-I BĀLĀ

Lat. 36° 58' N, long. 72° 48' E. Map 39.
Badakhshān Province. On the south side of the Wākhān River 15 km east of Qal'a-i Panja.

Description: A number of petroglyphs on six boulders near the village, depicting ibex, hands, and hunters.

Fieldwork: 1975 'Exploration Pamir'—survey.

Source: Gratzl et al. 1978: 324–5—description and drawings.

TABAK SAR. See 303 DUBAKH SAR.

TAGAO YĀRĪ. See 2255 TAGAO YĀRĪ in Supplement.

TAGAU, Parvan. See 832 QAL'A-I AMĪR MUHAMMAD.

1127. TAGAU DEHTAI

Lat. 33° 34' N, long. 64° 21' E. Maps 54, 74.
Ghūr Province. 10 km east of Sab Talkh on the road from Deh Tītān to Taiwāra, 4 km west of the village of Dehtai.

Description: Remains of several ancient towers.

Fieldwork: 1885 Sahibdad Khan, ABC—topographical survey.

Source: Sahibdad Khan 1891a: 242—mention.

TAGAU-I MAGH. See 2257 TAGAU-I MAGH in Supplement.

TAGAU QAL'A. See 2258 TAGAU QAL'A in Supplement.

TAGAU RABĀT. See 2256 TAGAU RABĀT in Supplement.

1128. TAGHĀ'I

Original: Lat. 36° 42' N, long. 68° 56' E. Map 85.
Revised:
36.70097196 N, 68.94094283 E /
36° 42' 03.49905276 N, 68° 56' 27.39418008 E (A).
36.69904771 N, 68.94035412 E /
36° 41' 56.57176824 N, 68° 56' 25.27481616 E (B).
36.69511327 N, 68.94426145 E /
36° 41' 42.40776444 N, 68° 56' 39.34121712 E (C).
Qundūz Province. 7.5 km south-east of Qundūz, on the road to Khānābād, a group of three tepes 300 m apart, 600–800 m north of this road; indicated on the 1:100,000 map as mounds of 7 m (A), 6 m (B), 7 m (C), from north-west to south-west, east of the village of Taghā'i.

Dates: Achaemenid, 6th–4th cent. BC (A); Hunnic-Turk, 5th–9th cent.; pre-Mongol Islamic, 10th–13th cent.; Timurid, 15th–16th cent. (B) (ceramic).

Description: (A) Mound of irregular shape, covering a surface of 70 m (east–west) × 40 m (north–south), damaged by rice fields on the north and the east, but apparently intact on the two other sides, which form in the south-west a right angle. The western half, the highest (8 m), looks like a tetrahedron with a flat top (12 × 12 m), with a protuberance in the north-east; the eastern half is irregular, in elevation and plan, with two hillocks (2 m and 3 m) in the south-east and the north-east of the mound, respectively. (B) Very diminished vestiges of the mound of '6 m' indicated on the 1:100,000 map: low platform (1–2 m) with irregular contours (30 × 30 m). (C) Square platform (40 × 40 m), shaped by the terracing undertaken at the moment of the construction of the paved Qundūz-Khānābād road (about 1974), as well as by the surrounding rice fields; flat top (10 m), with a T-shaped rise higher in the north-west angle (12 m). In the cuts of the south face, 4–5 m above the present ground level, burnt layers (ashes and earth mixed), surmounted by the remains of construction in mud-bricks and *pakhsa*.

Collection: National Museum/AIA—sherds.

Fieldwork: 1978 Gardin et al., CNRS—survey.

Sources:
1. Site information by J.-C. Gardin.
2. Gardin and Lyonnet 1978–9: pl. VII—nos. 428–30.
3. Lyonnet 1997: Figs 25, 35, 28, 29—nos. 428–30.
4. Gardin 1998: 78—nos. 428–30.

1129. TĀGH-I DARĀZ
Or KĀFIR QAL'A.

Lat. 35° 36' N, long. 65° 14' E. Map 46.
Faryāb Province. cent. 4 km south-east of Darra-i Shākh, in the headwaters of the Shīrīn Tagau c.40 km south of Bīlchirāgh.

Description: A group of artificial caves, interconnected by a tunnel, with mud-brick walls across the entrances. The caves probably served as fortifications guarding the route.

Fieldwork: 1978 Lee, BIAS—survey.

Source: Lee 1980: 76–7—full description and plan.

TAHANA-I AIQULI. See 981 SAMTI.

TAHARI TEPE. See 29 'ALIĀBĀD.

TĀH-I SHAHR. See 1040 SHAHR-I CHANGIZ.

1130. TAIWĀRA

Original: Lat. 33° 31' N, long. 64° 25' E. Maps 54, 74.
Revised: 33.52224608 N, 64.41172514 E /
33° 31' 20.08587936 N, 64° 24' 42.21050508 E.
Ghūr Province. Capital of Ghūrāt sub-province, 185 km by road south-west of Chakhcharān on the road to Kilārām.

Description: Local reports of ancient remains on the hill now occupied by the modern administrative fort. There are also remains of many towers in the vicinity.

Fieldwork: 1946 Kohzad, HSA—survey.

Sources:
1. Kohzad 1951–4, 9/1: 21—mention
2. Ball 2002: 32–3—mention

1131. TĀJ-I BAI TEPE
Or YAKA TŪTU TEPE.

Original: Lat. 36° 40' N, long. 68° 49' E. Map 32.
Revised: 36.67667779 N, 68.82090172 E /
36° 40' 36.04004184 N, 68° 49' 15.24619416 E.
Qundūz Province. C.1 km east of Durman Tepe, 8 km south-west of Qundūz just to the left of the road to Tāshqurghān.

Description: A small mound.

Fieldwork: 1963 Mizuno, Kyoto University—survey.

Source: Mizuno and Odani 1968: 96—mention.

TAKHĀRĀ. See 2259 TAKHT-I ĀRĀ in Supplement.

1132. TAKHNĀBĀD

Original: Lat. 37° 22–23' N, long. 69° 49' E. Maps 35, 38.
Revised: 37.38802627 N, 69.78788007 E /
37° 23' 16.89457488 N, 69° 47' 16.36826568 E.
Takhār Province. About 3 km south-west of Chah Āb, near the village of Takhnābād, constructed on the slopes of the mountains which close the plateau of Chayāb to the south-west. (A) The most remarkable site is Qal'a-i Hisār, 600 m south-south-west of the last village houses; it is located at the end of an advance of the slopes (orientation south-east), which overlooks the narrow pass cut into the relief by the Rūd-i Khwāja Jurghailu, towards the south-west. The road that leads from Yangi Qal'a or from Rustāq to Chayāb runs through this narrow pass, then climbs the slopes of Qal'a Hisār which it skirts, leaving the end of the spur to the right (south-east). (B) After crossing the village of Takhnābād, the road turns toward the plateau of Chayāb, to the north-east, passing through the small valley of a stream flowing from a nearby spring, to the north (indicated on the 1:100,000 map). The edges of this valley are punctuated by small hillocks around which sherds are scattered, from the spring itself to the slopes which dominate the small valley, towards the east, on both sides of the road, as far as 500 m downstream.

Dates: Hellenistic, 3rd–1st cent. BC (A); Hunnic-Turk, 5th–9th cent.; pre-Mongol Islamic, 10th–13th cent. (ceramic).

Description: (A) Between the road and the end of the spur (distance about 200 m), three bumps more or less aligned with the spur (north-west/south-east): the area of sherds (100 × 50 m) is between the last and the next-to-last bump, towards the end of the spur. (B) The most visible mound (diam. 20 m, height 2.5 m), partly natural, is above the spring (Sar-i Chashma), continuing an east–west advance of the relief; it is occupied by a cemetery. 200 m to the south, on the eastern slopes of the small valley, an area of sherds (100 × 100 m) in the *lalmī* fields: place-name Paliz, without any topographical particularities; fragments of fired bricks on the surface (width 27–8 cm, thickness 5.5 cm). 300 m further south, high on the slopes that descend towards the Rūd-i Khwāja Jurghailu, a bumpy area in the *lalmī* fields, where the same type of pottery is to be found.

Collection: National Museum/AIA—sherds.

Fieldwork: 1978 Gardin et al., CNRS—survey.

Sources:
1. Site information by J.-C. Gardin.
2. Gardin and Lyonnet 1978–9: pl. II—nos. 532–5.
3. Lyonnet 1997: figs 39, 68, 69—nos. 532–5.
4. Gardin 1998: 90—nos. 532–5.

TAKHTA KUPRUK. See 1220 URTA BUZ.

TAKHT-I ĀRĀ. See 2259 TAKHT-I ĀRĀ in Supplement.

1133. TAKHT-I BĀLĀ

Original: Lat. 32° 07' N, long. 61° 55' E. Map 83.
Revised: 32.13514593 N, 61.93015492 E /
32° 08' 06.52534908 N, 61° 55' 48.55771344 E.
Farāh Province. 12 km north-east of Tujg on the Farāh-Lāsh Juwain road.

Date: Timurid, 15th–16th cent. (ceramic).

Description: Remains of a high mud fortress with a gateway on the south side. Many silted up irrigation canals in the vicinity.

Fieldwork: 1960–70 Fischer, Bonn University—survey.

Source: Fischer et al. 1974–6: 35—brief description and photos.

TAKHT-I JAMSHID. See 971 SAJĀWAND.

TAKHT-I KHĀN. See 552 KHĀNĀBĀD, Balkh.

1134. TAKHT-I KHĀTŪN

Original: Lat. 35° 37' N, long. 63° 48' E. Maps 44, 45.
Revised: 35.62422452 N, 63.81001356 E /
35° 37' 27.20825688 N, 63° 48' 36.04882536 E.
Faryāb Province. At the foot of the mountains near the junction of the Kara Jangal and Khwāja Langari streams, 14 km south of Kaurmach.

Date: Early Islamic, 10th–13th cent. (traditional).

Description: Remains of many old *kārīz* and mud remains, including a fort measuring *c.*600 × 200 m, locally said to have been destroyed by the Mongols.

Fieldwork:
1. 1885 Peacocke, ABC—topographical survey.
2. 1886 Yate, ABC—topographical survey.

Sources:
1. Grodekoff 1880: 145—mention.
2. Holdich 1887: 17—mention.

3. Peacocke 1887a: 238—mention.
4. Yate 1888: 195–6—brief description.
5. Caspani and Cagnacci 1951: 246—mention.

TAKHT-I PĀDSHĀH. See 2260 TAKHT-I PĀDSHĀH in Supplement.

TAKHT-I RUSTAM, Balkh. See 99 BALKH.

1135. TAKHT-I RUSTAM, HAIBAK

Original: Lat. 36° 15–25' N, long. 68° 02–03' E. Map 30.
Revised: 36.24572113 N, 68.02218099 E /
36° 14' 44.59606800 N, 68° 01' 19.85156004 E.
Samangān Province. 2 km south of the centre of Haibak.

Dates: Kushano-Sasanian, 4th–5th cent. (architectural); Ghaznavid and Seljuk, 11th–12th cent. (numismatic).

Description: A stupa-monastery complex, all completely carved from the bedrock. The monastery consists of five chambers, two of them sanctuaries. One of them has a domed ceiling with an elaborate lotus leaf decoration. On an adjacent hill is the stupa, surmounted by a *harmika*, with several more rough caves around the base.

A hoard of Ghaznavid coins was found by chance in one of the caves.

Fieldwork:
1. 1886 Talbot and Maitland, ABC—survey.
2. 1923 Foucher, DAFA—survey.
3. 1956 Ramachandran and Sharma, ASI—reconnaissance.
4. 1960 Muzuno and Nashikawa, Kyoto University—survey.
5. 2015–16 ACHCO—conservation assessment.

Sources:
1. Moorcroft and Trebeck 1841: II. 402–7—description of the stupa and caves.
2. Talbot et al. 1886: 344–5—description and sketch plan of the stupa.

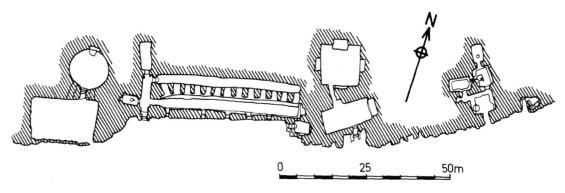

1135 Takht-i Rustam (after Mizuno and Nishikawa 1962).

3. Holdich 1887: 39—brief description.
4. Maitland 1888b: 308–9—detailed description.
5. Yate 1888: 321–2—brief description.
6. Foucher 1924—description and plans of the complex.
7. Foucher 1942–7: 123–9—description and photos.
8. Ramachandran and Sharma 1956: II. 10–13—discuss the architecture and some petrolyphs in the caves.
9. Bussagli 1962a: 42–3—brief summary.
10. Hallade 1962—discusses the caves as a part of Bactrian art.
11. Hayashi and Sahara 1962: 106—mention the coin hoard.
12. Mizuno 1962—introduction to the Japanese survey.
13. Mizuno and Nishikawa 1962—fully illustrated summary description of the complex.
14. N. Dupree 1967a: 22–7—description and guide.
15. Ball 2008: 269—summary.

1136. TAKHT-I RUSTAM, SEISTAN

Lat. 31° 35' N, long. 61° 47' E. Map 83.
Nīmrūz Province. On the northern edge of the Hāmūn-i Pūzak, *c*.20 km south-east of Lāsh Juwain.

Date: Sasanian, 3rd–7th cent. (ceramic).

Description: A long mound.

Fieldwork: 1950- Fairservis, AMNH—survey.

Sources:
1. Stein 1928: 938 and 942—describes some pottery brought to him from the site.
2. Fairservis 1961: 45—mention (Site 27).

1137. TAKHT-I SHĀH
See also 2268 TEPE NĀRENJ in Supplement.

Original: Lat. 34° 29' N, long. 69° 10' E. Map 61.
Revised: 34.48681566 N, 69.17666194 E /
34° 29' 12.53637564 N, 69° 10' 35.98298184 E.
Kābul Province. The top of a hill 3 km south-west of the Kābul Bālā Hisār, above the Qūl-i Hashmat Khān.

Date: ?Timurid, 15th–16th cent. (architectural, documentary).

Description: A large building, probably a tomb, measuring *c*.11 m long, 6 m wide, and 4 m high. On the western side is a small arched entrance opening into a dome-chamber *c*.3.50 m square, with four niches in each corner and four in each side. Construction is of uncut stones with a plaster surface. It is connected to masonry walls along the summit of the hill. From Babur's description the building is known to pre-date the Mughal period. Underneath the building on the western side of the hill is an artificial cave.

Sources:
1. Masson 1833a: 12—description and sketch.

2. Masson 1842: II. 234–5—detailed description and tentative date.
3. Holdich 1881b: 22—mentions the cave and building as the remains of a stupa.
4. N. Dupree 1971a: 112—mention.
5. Errington 2017a: 66 and 2017b: 22–3—the Masson collection and archive relating to the site.

1138. TAKHT-I SHIR KHĀN

Lat. 37° 06' N, long. 65° 21' E. Maps 24, 28.
Jauzjān Province. To the south of the road 7 km south-west of Bulut Kak and 11 km north-east of Chahārbān the road from Khāmiyāb to Andkhūī.

Description: A small but conspicuous mound.

Fieldwork: 1886 Maitland, ABC—topographical survey.

Source: Maitland 1888b: 214—mention.

1139. TĀLĀ
Or TĀLĀ-O BARFAQ or GIRDĀB or KĀFIR QAL'A BARFAQ. See also 263 DASHT-I LAJAM.

Original: Lat. 35° 22' N, long. 68° 13' E. Map 48.
Revised: 35.37190106 N, 68.20617149 E /
35° 22' 18.84383184 N, 68° 12' 22.21734708 E.
Baghlān Province. On the right bank of the Surkhāb, *c*.4 km south of the village of Tālā, on the road from Bāmiyān to Dūshi.

Date: Turk and/or pre-Mongol Islamic, 7th–13th cent. (architectural).

Description: Remains of a palatial residence that has both circular domed rooms and long barrel-vaulted rooms. Construction is of large mud-bricks for the walls and towers, on stone foundations. In the hillside are many caves.

Fieldwork:
1. 1886 Peacocke, ABC—topographical survey.
2. 1951 Allchin and Codrington—survey.
3. 1960 Hayashi and Sahara, Kyoto University—survey.
4. 1955–68 Fischer, DAAD—survey.
5. 1974–5 Le Berre, DAFA—survey.
6. Grenet 2002: 217—identifies the site with 'Kurz' in the sources for the Hephthalite wars.

Sources:
1. Peacocke 1887a: 382—mention.
2. Hayashi and Sahara 1962: 77–8—description of the site and discussion in Japanese of the pottery.
3. Fischer 1969: 345—brief summary and photos.
4. Gazetteer 1979: IV. 227—mention.
5. Le Berre 1987: 38–9, pls 36–8—itinerary A1, ruin 19 (Kāfir Qal'a).

1140. TĀLĀ BEGUM

1140 Tālā Begum (W. Ball—after a photo and description in Fussman 1974c).

Lat. 33° 36' N, long. 68° 03' E. Maps 78, 80.
Ghazni Province. 33 km west of Ghazni on the road to Dasht-i Nāwar.

Date: Ghurid or Timurid, 12th–13th or 15th–16th cent. (stylistic).

Description: A small polygonal tomb tower of baked brick. It has some simple decoration and a slightly pointed dome.

Sources:
1. Fussman 1974c: fig. 31—photo and brief description.
2. Verardi 1977a: 135—mentions a Ghurid date.
3. Thomas 2015: 519—additional information from satellite imagery.

1141. TALŪKHĀN

Original: Lat. 31° 27' N, long. 65° 20' E. Maps 88, 89.
Revised: 31.45931473 N, 65.31870865 E /
31° 27' 33.53302584 N, 65° 19' 07.35113676 E.
Kandahār Province. On the left bank of the Arghandāb River near its junction with the Tarnak, 39 km from Kandahār and *c.*13 km south-west of Panjwāyī.

Description: A low, artificial mound, built over by a modern village.

Source: Site information by G. Willcox.

1142. TĀLUQĀN
Including TEPE KLUB and TEPE SHAHR.

Original: Lat. 36° 44' N, long. 69° 32' E. Map 36.
Revised: 36.73304222 N, 69.53849844 E /
36° 43' 58.95198408 N, 69° 32' 18.59437428 E.
Takhār Province. In the town of Taluqān, some 100 m to the south-west (A) and the south-east (B) of the central crossroads.

Date: Hunnic, 492/3 AD (epigraphic); Islamic period, not specified (ceramic).

Description: (A) 'Tepe Shahr': near the *Madrasa* Abdul Masjid, a large oval mound (60 × 60 m), oriented north–south, flat top, highest point in the south (8 m), occupied by a modern cemetery. (B) 'Tepe Klub': square platform (30 × 30 m, height 4 m) on which the 'club' of Taluqān was built.

Some time in the early 21st century a copper scroll was found with an inscription in Brahmi by the 'lord of Tālagānika' and dedicating a stupa in the names of four Alkhan Hun kings.

Collections:
1. National Museum/AIA—sherds.
2. Schøyen Collection, Oslo—copper scroll.

Fieldwork: 1977 Gardin et al., CNRS—survey.

Sources:
1. Site information by J.-C. Gardin.
2. Gardin and Lyonnet 1978–9: pl. IX—nos. 211–13.
3. Gardin 1980—describes the survey in the Taluqan area in general terms.
4. Lyonnet 1981—discussion of the Chalcolithic sites.
5. Gentelle 1989—full report on the ancient irrigation and hydrology of the area.
6. Lyonnet 1997: figs 9–12—pottery and discussion of the Chalcolithic-Bronze Age.
7. Gardin 1998: 68—nos. 211–13.
8. Melzer 2006—full description, discussion, translation, and interpretation of the copper scroll.
9. De la Vaissière 2007—discussion of the scroll, locating its origin in Talagang in northern Pakistan.
10. Vondrovec 2008—discussed the evidence of the scroll in the context of Alkhon coinage.
11. Alram and Pfisterer 2010: 20–6—discusses the evidence of the scroll and coins for Hunnic history.

1143. TAM'ALI

Original: Lat. 37° 03'–37° 04' N, long. 68° 27'–68° 29' E. Map 34.
Revised:
37.05457938 N, 69.45336081 E /
37° 03' 16.48576728 N, 69° 27' 12.09889800 E (A).
37.05319448 N, 69.46678905 E /
37° 03' 11.50011396 N, 69° 28' 00.44058000 E (B).

37.05886777 N, 69.4703001 E /
37° 03' 31.92397920 N, 69° 28' 13.08036540 E (C).
37.06601048 N, 69.47228385 E /
37° 03' 57.63771288 N, 69° 28' 20.22184200 E (D).

Takhār Province. To the east of Khwāja Ghar, on the road to Dasht-i Qal'a: traces of ancient occupation at the foot of the slopes which dominate the plain of Khwāja Ghar to the south, between this village and the bridge on the Kokcha. On a naturally hilly terrain, four little artificial tepes were discovered, presenting the same configuration and the same assemblages of sherds; their importance lies in the information they can provide on settlement in this zone of foothills in the Hellenistic period and probably during the first centuries of Islam, thanks to a canal from the Rūd-i Shārawān, abandoned since the Mongol invasion (see Gardin and Lyonnet 1978–9: 137–8 and 151–4). The position of these sites is indicated hereafter by two numbers: the distance from the exit of Khwāja Ghar, in kilometres, and the distance to the south or to the north of the road, in metres. (A) 1.9 km/300 m south; (B) 2.7 km/500 m south; (C) 3.8 km/300 m south; (D) 3.2 km/200 m north. This last tepe is occupied by the cemetery indicated on the 1:100,000 map, at the southern end of the village of Qarya-i Lab-i Kokcha.

Dates: Middle Bronze Age, *c.*2400–1500 BC (B); Hellenistic, 3rd–1st cent. BC; some Islamic sherds (C, D) (ceramic).

Description: Sites A, C, D are little square mounds, 30 to 40 m per side, oriented north–south, with a flat top (C) including a high part in the east (D), and a central depression (A): these are probably isolated farms, opening onto courtyard-gardens surrounded by walls. Mound B is even smaller, and rounded (diam. 10 m). The height varies between 1.5 and 2.5 m.

Collection: National Museum/AIA—sherds.

Fieldwork: 1977 Gardin et al., CNRS—survey.

Sources:
1. Site information by J.-C. Gardin.
2. Gardin and Lyonnet 1978–9: pl. IV—nos. 200–3.
3. Lyonnet 1997: figs 13, 21–4—nos. 200–3..
4. Gardin 1998: 49—nos. 200–3.

TANDURAK. See 224 DAISHU.

1144. TANG-I AZAU

Lat. 34° 08' N, long. 64° 12' E. Map 54.
Ghūr Province. In the west wall of a gorge, 2 km upstream from its entrance. 19 km west of Shahrak.

Date: Ghurid, *c.*1300 (epigraphic).

Description: A roughly carved, badly eroded Hebrew inscription cut into a boulder. It consists of three lines on one side and five or six on the other. Medieval metalwork has also been found at the site.

Fieldwork:
1. 1885 Talbot and Maitland, ABC—topographical survey.
2. 1946 Kohzad, HSA—survey.
3. 1952 Ghirshman and Frye—survey.
4. 1956 Bell, Evans, Holland, Oxford University—survey.
5. 1959—Fischer, Lonsdale, Owen, Cambridge University—survey.

Sources:
1. Talbot et al. 1886: 239—mentions visiting and copying the inscriptions.
2. Maitland 1888a: 364 and 393—mentions the inscription, which he copies and calls Pali.
3. Kohzad 1951–4, 9/2: 17–18—brief description.
4. Frye 1954—account of an expedition to the site. Describes it as Parthian.
5. Ramachandran and Sharma 1956: I. 18–19—mentions it as an Aramaic inscription.
6. Henning 1957—linguistic analysis and translation.
7. J. Fischer et al. 1959—describe a visit to the inscription.
8. Rapp 1967—text, translation, and brief analysis.
9. Rapp 1973: 66—lists the three inscriptions.
10. Wannell 2002: 144—mentions the metalwork.
11. Lintz 2015: 163–6—brief overview of the inscriptions.

TANG-I SAFIDAK. See 2261 TANG-I SAFIDAK in Supplement.

1145. TANG-I TIZAU

Lat. 34° 08' N, long. 64° 20' E. Map 54.
Ghūr Province. 4 km north of the Herat-Chakhcharān road, 3 km east of Shahrak.

Description: Some simple petroglyphs of two stylised ibex cut into the side of the gorge. There are two more animal petroglyphs, probably ibex, on two boulders further upstream.

Source: Trousdale 1965b—detailed description and discussion.

TĀQ-I AMĪRĀN. See 2182 QAL'A-I ZĪYĀRAT-I AMĪRĀN SĀHIB in Supplement. See also 1264 ZĪYĀRAT-I AMĪRĀN SĀHIB.

1146. TARA KHĒL

Original: Lat. 34° 35' N, long. 69° 15' E. Map 61.
Revised: 34.57234627 N, 69.26462583 E /
34° 34' 20.44655904 N, 69° 15' 52.65298476 E.
Kābul Province. 6 km north-east of Kābul airport, 6 km south-east of Pai Minār.

Date: Kushan, 1st–4th cent. (ceramic).

Description: A large mound.

Fieldwork: 1923 Foucher, DAFA—survey.

Sources:

1. Gardin and Lyonnet, 1980 chronological study of pottery from unpublished DAFA surveys.
2. Foucher 1942–7: 143—mention.

1147. TARĀKŪN
Or TRĀKHŪN.

Original: Lat. 30° 16' N, long. 61° 30' E. Map 94.
Revised: 30.27071606 N, 61.4875519 E / 30° 16' 14.57782032 N, 61° 29' 15.18684288 E.
Nīmrūz Province. On a terrace of the Rūd-i Bīyābān between the Helmand and the Iranian border.

Date: Late Islamic, 16th–17th cent. (architectural, ceramic).

Description: Some huge mud ruins, dominated by the remains of a fortress on a mound *c.*50 m above the plain. The outer walls of the fortress have loopholes but no towers, and have a narrow vaulted gallery around the top. The lower part of the walls are built of baked bricks *c.*45 cm square; the upper parts are of mud-brick. There is a main gateway on the north-eastern side. Inside is a large baked brick bastion at the northern end with an elaborately decorated hall underneath. At the southern end are the remains of a palace, a mosque, and a hammam. There is also a deep, brick-lined well and a subterranean gallery descending some 35 m to a vaulted, brick-lined chamber *c.*5 m square. In the vicinity of the fortress are the remains of many houses, cemeteries, and tombs. Local tradition associates the remains with fire worship.

Trākhun, according to local use. There is absolutely nothing of early Islamic times here. There was evidence only of a dried-up canal in the Rūd-i Biyābān at that period. The site is one of the latest sites in Afghan Sistan.

Fieldwork:

1. 1885 Merk, ABC—topographical survey.
2. 1903–5 Tate, SAC—survey.
3. 1968–71 Dales, University Museum Penn.—survey.
4. 1971–4 Trousdale, Smithsonian Institution—survey.

Sources:

1. Additional information on the date by W. Trousdale.
2. Durand 1885: I, pl. 54—sketch.
3. Peacocke 1885a: 8—mentions the large area of coins and other finds laid bare after rain.
4. Merk 1888: 27—fairly detailed description.
5. Yate 1888: 145–6—quotes Merk's description.
6. Tate 1900: 104–6—brief description.
7. McMahon 1906: 218—mention and photo.
8. Tate 1909: 98–9—brief description.
9. Tate 1910: 242–4—fairly detailed description. Mentions the fire worship associations.

10. Fairservis 1961: 64—mention.
11. Dales and Flam 1969: 18—photos and brief description.
12. Dales 1972: 18—mention and photo.
13. Gazetteer 1973: II. 289–90—quotes Merk's description.
14. Ball 2008: 270—summary.

1148. TARIKĪ

Original: Lat. 34° 23' N, long. 69° 27' E. Map 65.
Revised: 34.38641906 N, 69.44315864 E / 34° 23' 11.10861348 N, 69° 26' 35.37110580 E.
Kābul Province. Between Khurd Kābul and Khāk-i Jabār, just to the east of the gorge.

Date: ?Chaghatai, 14th cent. (traditional).

Description: Remains of a 'Chaghatai fortress' built of white argillaceous stone.

Sources:

1. Masson 1840: 41—mention.
2. Masson 1842: I and III. 188 and 303–4—mention.

TAR-O SAR. See 1006 SAR-O TAR.

1149. TĀSH GUZAR, BALKH
Or GUZAR TEPE.

Original: Lat. 37° 15' N, long. 67° 12' E. Map 30.
Revised: 37.24652342 N, 67.20734511 E / 37° 14' 47.48430408 N, 67° 12' 26.44240392 E.
Balkh Province. On the banks of the Āmū Daryā opposite Termez, 64 km north of Mazār-i Sharīf.

Dates: Epi-Palaeolithic, 10,000–7000 BC (B, lithic); early Islamic, 10th–13th cent. (A, documentary); Timurid, 15th–16th cent. (A, ceramic).

Description: (A) Extensive remains of a town forming a rectangle *c.*200 × *c.*800 m. It consists of many mounds and a wide scatter of baked bricks enclosed on three sides by mud fortification walls, with baked brick towers at frequent intervals. When the river is low a baked brick pier can be seen, possibly the remains of a bridge across the Āmū Daryā. The site is probably the remains of medieval Aqsikh, mentioned by Ibn Hauqal.

(B) In the dunes to the south of Tāsh Guzar is a surface site consisting of a wide scatter of Late Mesolithic artefacts similar to those from Siāh Rīgān.

Fieldwork:

1. 1885–6 Maitland and Peacocke, ABC—topographical survey.
2. 1975 Vinogradov, Af/Sov. Mission—survey.

Sources:

1. Gardin and Lyonnet, 1980 chronological study of pottery from unpublished DAFA surveys.

2. Holdich 1886: 9—mentions the ruins.
3. Holdich 1887: 36—mentions the bridge.
4. Peacocke 1887a: 243 and 308—mentions bridge.
5. Maitland 1888b: 239—brief description of the remains.
6. Sarianidi 1977c: 7–11—discusses the lithics from the Soviet survey.
7. Gazetteer 1979: IV. 562–3—summary description of Maitland's survey.
8. Vinogradov 1979—discusses the general lithic assemblage from the survey, and compares them with material in Soviet Central Asia.

1150. TĀSH GUZUR, FARYĀB

Original: Lat. 35° 55' N, long. 64° 17' E. Map 45.
Revised: 35.92240563 N, 64.28881424 E /
35° 55' 20.66027412 N, 64° 17' 19.73127660 E.
Faryāb Province. At the junction of the Qaisār valley with the Galla valley, near Khwāja Gauhar north of Qaisār.

Description: Remains of an old baked brick *rabāt*.

Fieldwork: 1886 Peacocke, ABC—topographical survey.

Source: Gazetteer 1979: IV. 563—mention.

1151. TĀSHQURGHĀN

Lat. 36° 42' N, long. 67° 44' E. Map 29.
Samangān Province. 3 km to the east of the town.

Date: ?Epi-Palaeolithic, 10,000–8000 BC (lithic).

Description: A low mound covered in microlithic flints; no pottery.

Fieldwork: 1959 Dupree, AUFS—survey.

Source: Dupree and Howe 1963: 2—mention.

1152. TĀSHQURGHĀN BĀLĀ HISĀR

Original: Lat. 36° 41' N, long. 67° 41' E. Map 29.
Revised: .68751366 N, 67.69856295 E / 36° 41' 15.04917060 N, 67° 41' 54.82660524 E.
Samangān Province. On the southern edges of the town of Tāshqurghān, where the Samangān River flows out of the gorges.

Date: Timurid, 15th–16th cent. (ceramic).

Description: Fortification perched on a rocky point dominating the town.

Collection: National Museum/AIA—sherds.

Fieldwork: 1969 Gouin, DAFA—survey.

Sources:
1. Gouin 1974 and unpublished report—site no. 12.
2. Bernard 1999: 52–5—identifies the site with Aornos of the classical accounts of Alexander's campaign.

1153. TĀSH TEPE

Lat. 36° 15' N, long. 68° 02' E. Map 30.
Samangān Province. 2 km south-east of the modern town of Haibak, halfway to the Bālā Hisār.

Description: A mound.

Fieldwork: 1885 Maitland and Talbot, ABC—topographical survey.

Source: Maitland 1888b: 44—mention.

TĀSH TEPE, Imām Sāhib. See 738 MULLĀH AFGHĀNI.

TĀSH WALTA TEPE. See 450 ISHKILI.

1154. TĀTARANG ZĀR

Lat. 34° 49' N, long. 69° 13' E. Map 64.
Parwān Province. At the foot of the hills on the eastern side of the Kūh-i Damān plain, c. 8 km east of the Istālif turn-off, 50 km north of Kābul. Between the river and the hills.

Description: Extensive remains of a city, consisting of many mounds. Numerous coins and other antiquities found.

Fieldwork: 1834 Masson—survey.

Sources:
1. Masson 1836: 5—mention.
2. Masson 1842: III. 143–4—mention.

1155. TAWACHI

Original: Lat. 36° 56' N, long. 65° 10' E. approximately. Map 24.
Revised: 36.91936303 N, 65.14365917 E /
36° 55' 09.70692492 N, 65° 08' 37.17300156 E.
Faryāb Province. Just to the east of Andkhūī, to the south of the road to Shībarghān.

Description: An artificial mound.

Fieldwork: 1886 Maitland, ABC—topographical survey.

Source: Maitland 1888b: 163—mention.

1156. TAWISK

Original: Lat. 32° 12' N, long. 61° 00' E. Map 83.
Revised: 32.19200825 N, 61.98361932 E /
32° 11' 31.22969712 N, 61° 59' 01.02954228 E.
Farāh Province. 22 km south-west of Farāh on the road to Lāsh Juwain.

Dates: Sasanian, 3rd–7th cent.; early Islamic, 8th–13th cent. (ceramic).

Description: A mound *c.*100 × 60 m in area and 20 m in height. There is another low mound covered in ruins *c.*1 km to the north.

Fieldwork: 1949 Fairservis, AMNH—survey.

Source: Fairservis 1961: 40—brief description and summary of the pottery (Site 14, Tell 1).

1157. TĀZI

Lat. 32° 22' N, long. 67° 18' E. Maps 79, 91.
Zābul Province. 3 km east of the Kābul-Kandahār road, 20 km south-west of Shāhjūi.

Description: No details of the site available. The sherds include buffwares with incised meanders and cables, black-on-buff painted and a little black-on-red.

Fieldwork: 1959 De Cardi—survey.

Source: Site information by B. De Cardi.

TEMORSHO TEPE. See 166 CHĀL.

TEKIR. See 2262 TEKIR in Supplement.

1158. TEPE ĀB BAKHSH

Original: Lat. 30° 17' N, long. 61° 29' E. approximately. Map 94.
Revised: 30.27352697 N, 61.47688566 E / 30° 16' 24.69709884 N, 61° 28' 36.78838068 E.
Nīmrūz Province. In the Rūd-i Bīyābān, 1 km north of Gina.

Date: Sasanian, 3rd–7th cent. (ceramic).

Description: A mound, *c.*35 m square, on a natural bluff.

Fieldwork: 1951 Fairservis, AMNH—survey.

Source: Fairservis 1961: 63—mention (Site RB 24).

TEPE ABDAL. See 1220 URTA BUZ.

1159. TEPE 'ABDULLAH

Original: Lat. 35° 41' N, long. 63° 17' E. Map 44.
Revised: 35.6768457 N, 63.28971365 E / 35° 40' 36.64451424 N, 63° 17' 22.96914720 E.
Bādghīs Province. 13 km north-west of Bālā Murghāb, on the right bank of the Murghāb River.

Description: A small circular mound *c.*13 m high, with the remains of a fort on top.

Fieldwork: 1885 Maitland, ABC—topographical survey.

Sources:
1. Maitland 1888a: 213—mention.

2. Maitland and Drummond 1888: 86—mention.
3. Gazetteer 1975: III. 422—mention.

TEPE AFGHĀNHĀ. See 943 QŪZI.

TEPE AFGHĀNI. See 307 DŪN QISHLĀQ.

1160. TEPE ĀHINGARĀN
Or ĀKHUNDZĀDA TEPE or SAR-I GAU. See also 930 QUNDŪZ.

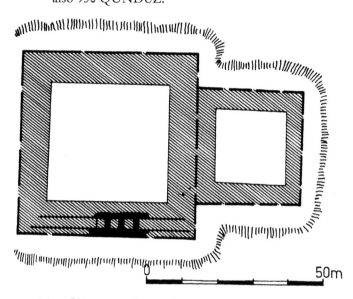

1160 Tepe Āhingarān (after Hackin 1950a).

Original: Lat. 36° 44' N, long. 68° 52' E. Map 32.
Revised: 36.74629235 N, 68.90494192 E / 36° 44' 46.65245244 N, 068° 54' 17.79089616 E.
Qundūz Province. 3 km north-east of Qundūz.

Dates: Kushan-Sasanian, 1st–7th cent. (architectural, ceramic, stylistic).

Description: A series of mounds, the main one measuring 80 × 70 m in area and 2.5 m in height. In 1936 a series of stucco relief panels, Buddha heads, and Corinthian capitals were discovered by chance in a ditch at the site, leading to subsequent excavations by Hackin. The excavations revealed a stupa-monastery complex consisting of two enclosures surrounded by walls. Architecture included mud-brick vaulting and several column bases. Further excavations by Cammann revealed a second monastery complex, where many sculptures and decorative elements were found. In addition there have been other chance finds at the site of a series of limestone friezes, and of a fragmentary relief in 1960.

Collections: National Museum—sculptures and friezes.

Fieldwork:
1. 1937 Hackin, DAFA—excavations.
2. 1938 Barger, ASI—survey.

3. 1946 Wheeler, ASI—reconnaissance.
4. 1953 Cammann, University Museum, Penn.—excavations.
5. 1955 and 1960 Fischer, DAAD—survey.
6. 1956 Ramachandran and Sharma, ASI—reconnaissance.
7. 1960 Hayashi and Sahara, Kyoto University—survey.

Sources:
1. Hackin 1937—photos and preliminary report on the stuccos and the excavations.
2. Barger 1939a: 385—mentions the discovery of the stuccos.
3. Barger 1944: 8–9—brief discussion of the stucco heads and photos of the Buddhist remains.
4. Shakur 1947: 49–51—brief description.
5. Wheeler 1947: 62—brief description.
6. Deydier 1950: 204—brief summary of Hackin's excavations.
7. Hackin 1950a—sketch plan of the excavations and discussion of the stucco heads.
8. Rainey 1953: 41—mentions Cammann's excavations.
9. Young 1954—mentions Cammann's excavations.
10. Ramachandran and Sharma 1956: I. 25 and II. 19–20—mention Cammann's excavations and describes the finds.
11. Allchin 1957: 139—discusses the remains in the context of the Turki Shahis.
12. Matson 1957—very brief summary of the American excavations.
13. Fischer 1958a—detailed description and discussion of the limestone frieze panels.
14. Fischer 1959b—brief discussion of the friezes.
15. Hackin 1959b—very brief summary of the excavations and the stucco heads.
16. Fischer 1961a: 16—mention of the finds and photo of the mounds.
17. Fischer 1961c—discusses a Garuda plaque found at the site.
18. Bussagli 1962a: 42—summary of the finds.
19. Hallade 1962a—discusses the sculptures as part of Bactrian art.
20. Hayashi and Sahara 1962: 71–3—photos and description (in Japanese) of the stucco reliefs and column bases in a private collection in Qundūz.
21. Ali 1964: 22–3—discusses the discoveries and the origins of Gandharan art.
22. Dagens 1964a: 39—brief description of a fragmentary relief found in 1960.
23. Motamedi 1967: 33—mentions Cammann's excavations.
24. Fischer 1969: 349—general summary.
25. Rowlands and Rice 1971: pl. 132—photo and summary of the stucco heads.
26. Fischer 1974a: fig. 123—photo and discussion of the vaulting system.
27. Tissot 2006: 97–101—National Museum catalogue details and photos.

TEPE ASHRAK. See **370 GHUNDI SHĀH NASR.**

TEPE AZAM QAL'A. See **73 BĀD-I SAH GHUNDĀI.**

TEPE AZĀDEH. See **53 KARŪKH.**

TEPE BĀGH-I SŪR Or BĀGHSŪR. See **2263 TEPE BĀGH-I SŪR in Supplement.**

1161. TEPE BALKHI

Lat. 34° 30' N, long. 69° 13' E. Map 61.
Kābul Province. C.1 km south of the Kābul Bālā Hisār, outside the Lahori Gate.
Description: A mound.
Source: Information by A. D. H. Bivar.

TEPE BANAUSHAK. See **2264 TEPE BANAUSHAK in Supplement.**

TEPE BARANGTŪT. See **108 BARANGTŪT.**

1162. TEPE BARZANGI

Original: Lat. 37° 10' N, long. 68° 44' E. Map 31.
Revised: 37.16306652 N, 68.72666253 E /
37° 09' 47.03948712 N, 68° 43' 35.98510584 E.
Qundūz Province. 16.5 km from Imām Sāhib, by the road to Qizil Qal'a, and 300 m south of this road: indicated as a tepe of 10 m on the 1:100,000 map.
Dates: Hunnic-Turk, 5th–9th cent.; pre-Mongol Islamic, 10th–13th cent. (ceramic).
Description: High very steep mound (14 m), greatly damaged by gullying (north-east side) which gives access to the top; this is tabular (70 × 70 m), with two small rises on the eastern edge of the tepe. The base of the mound, cut into by the crops which extend at its feet, occupies a surface of about 130 × 100 m. Two lower platforms emerge from the fields at around 100 m to the north-east (one of 200 × 100 m, the other 100 × 20 m); they are part of the same site, originally more extensive. There are traces of walls in *pakhsa* and in bricks in the cuts visible on the west face of the large tepe.
Collection: National Museum/AIA—sherds.
Fieldwork: 1977 Gardin et al., CNRS—survey.
Sources:
1. Site information by J.-C. Gardin.
2. Gardin and Lyonnet 1978–9: pl. V—no. 129.
3. Lyonnet 1997: figs 28, 29—no. 129.
4. Gardin 1998: 63—no. 129.

1163. TEPE BULAND
See also 662 KUSRUTĀBĀD.

Original: Lat. 31° 36' N, long. 64° 19' E. Map 86.
Revised: 31.59523545 N, 64.33116322 E /
31° 35' 42.84761388 N, 64° 19' 52.18758876 E.
Helmand Province. On the high river terrace opposite Lashkargāh.

Dates: Parthian and Saka, 2nd–1st cent. BC; Indo-Parthian, 1st–3rd cent.; Sasanian, 3rd–7th cent.; Ghurid, 12th–13th cent. (ceramic).

Description: A series of mounds, possibly the same as Site 662, Kusrutābād.

Fieldwork:
1. 1956 Ramachandran and Sharma, ASI—reconnaissance.
2. 1966 Hammond, Cambridge University—survey.

Sources:
1. Ramachandran and Sharma 1956: I. 14—mention.
2. Hammond 1970: 459—lists the site (no. 26) and describes the pottery types and general survey results.

TEPE BURHAN BAI. See 904 QANJUGHA.

1164. TEPE CHAHĀR BĀGH

Original: Lat. 36° 52' N, long. 66° 27' E. Map 25.
Revised: 36.87625573 N, 66.4491859 E / 36° 52' 34.52063412 N, 66° 26' 57.06923208 E.
Jauzjān Province. 30 km south-east of Āqcha, north of the road to Balkh, about 600 m north-east of Hustukh Tepe, near the village of Chāhar Bāgh.

Description: Small very eroded tepe, height 6.5 m, oval in form (110 × 80 m) with a small excrescence on the east face.

Fieldwork: 1948 Le Berre, DAFA—survey.

Source: M. Le Berre: unpublished 1948 report, DAFA archives, tepe P. 23.

TEPE CHAHĀR DARRA. See 2265 TEPE CHAHĀR DARRA in Supplement.

TEPE CHIKAT. See 462 JALĀ'IR.

TEPE DŪN QISHLĀQ. See 307 DŪN QISHLĀ.

TEPE FIRUZ HUSAIN. See 1206 TŪRGHUNDI.

TEPE GUDAMDAR. See 94 BĀJAURI TEPE GUDAMDAR.

1165. TEPE GULAK
See also 454 ISLĀM QAL'A.

Original: Lat. 34° 40' N, long. 61° 05' E. Map 51.
Revised: 34.69460191 N, 61.0863861 E / 34° 41' 40.56686160 N, 61° 05' 10.98995604 E.
Herat Province. On the Iranian border 2 km north-west of the Afghan border post of Islām Qal'a, 118 km west of Herat.

Dates: Early Islamic, 8th–13th cent.; Timurid, 15th–16th cent. (ceramic); Safavid, 1628 (epigraphic).

Description: An artificial mound, c.100 m diam. and 15 m high, and several smaller mounds. On top, the remains of a mud-brick fort, with an inscription dated 1037 AH (1628), were standing in the 1880s.

Fieldwork:
1. 1884 Maitland, ABC—topographical survey.
2. 1949 De Cardi—survey.
3. 1955–68—Fischer, DAAD—survey.
4. 1956 Ramachandran and Sharma, ASI—reconnaissance.
5. 1968–78 Kruglikova, Af/Sov. Mission—survey.

Sources:
1. Ferrier 1857: 139—mention.
2. MacGregor 1879: I. 243–4—brief description of the fort.
3. Maitland 1888a: 141—brief description.
4. Yate 1888: 55—brief description of the fort.
5. Ramachandran and Sharma 1956: I. 18—mention.
6. Fischer 1969: 333–4—brief summary of the mound.
7. Gazetteer 1975: III. 214—brief description.
8. Gaibov et al. 2010: 108—brief description.

TEPE GURGURI. See 611 KIRGHIZ TEPE.

TEPE HISĀR. See 96 BĀLĀ KHĀNA.

TEPE JAMSHID. See 853 QAL'A-I JAMSHID.

TEPE KĀFIRIHĀ. See 404 HADDA.

TEPE KALĀN. See 404 HADDA.

TEPE KALĀN. See 1088 SHOTORAK.

TEPE KASHKARI. See 5 ABRAU.

1166. TEPE KHĀRAK

Original: Lat. 31° 26' N, long. 61° 37' E. Map 83.
Revised: 31.43660297 N, 61.61012577 E /
31° 26' 11.77070244 N, 61° 36' 36.45276768 E.

Nīmrūz Province. *C.*8 km south-east of Salyān, just to the west of the Lāsh Juwain-Chakhānsūr road.

Dates: Sasanian, 3rd–7th cent.; early Islamic, 8th–13th cent. (ceramic).

Description: A low mound, *c.*80 m square and 6 m high. The sides are eroded or dug away.

Fieldwork: 1950 Fairservis, AMNH—survey.

Sources: Fairservis 1961: 41—brief description and summary of the pottery (Site 17, Tell 3).

1167. TEPE KHĀKRĪZ

Lat. 33° 12' N, long. 67° 35' E. Map 79.
Ghazni Province. *C.*17 km north of Jāghūri in the Kūh-i Khūd Valley near Hisār.

Date: Turki Shahi, 7th–8th cent. (ceramic).

Description: A small mound.

Fieldwork: 1975 Taddei and Verardi, IsMEO—survey.

Source: Verardi 1977a: 142—mention.

TEPE KHĀTŪN QAL'A. See 611 KIRGHIZ TEPE.

1168. TEPE KHĀZANA

Lat. 34° 31' N, long. 69° 10' E. Map 61.
Kābul Province. On a spur of the Shir Darwāza hill overlooking the Kābul River.

Date: Hunnic, 5th–7th cent. (stylistic).

Description: Remains of a Buddhist stupa and monastery, now destroyed. In 1930 a series of 50 stucco and terracotta heads and other sculptural fragments were found by chance. The heads reflect different artistic styles from Hellenistic to Gupta.

Collections: National Museum—sculptures.

Sources:
1. Sālnāma 1933/34: opp. 20—photo of the objects.
2. Rowland 1966a: 112—photo of one of the terracotta heads.
3. Barrett and Pinder-Wilson 1967–8: 26—photo of one of the heads and description of two more.
4. Rowland and Rice 1971: 139—photo and note of a terracotta relief and three birds.
5. N. Dupree et al. 1974: 103–5—description of the objects on display in the National Museum.
6. Tissot and Darbois 2002—photos of objects from the Kābul Museum.
7. Tissot 2006: 347–51—National Museum catalogue details and photos.

TEPE KHUSH. See 1179 TEPE SALA.

1169. TEPE KHWĀJA LAHŌRĪ

Original: Lat. 34° 27' N, long. 70° 24' E. Map 66.
Revised: 34.44838288 N, 70.39511089 E /
34° 26' 54.17836008 N, 70° 23' 42.39921876 E.
Nangahār Province. 6 km west of Jalālābād near the Kābul River, just north of the turn-off to Gandamak.

Description: A huge mound, *c.*600 m circumference at the base and 30 m high. It has stone remains on the top and is surrounded by many smaller mounds and extensive sherds and occupation debris. A series of long earthern ridges near the junction of the Surkhāb and Kābul Rivers, with more to the south and north-east, may mark the position of city walls. Many coins and other antiquities are frequently found. There are also some caves in the bank of the river. The site may have been ancient Nagarahara.

Collections: BM—coins.

Fieldwork:
1. 1834 Masson—survey.
2. 1965 Mizuno, Kyoto University—survey.

Sources:
1. Masson 1833a: 5–6 description and sketch of the mound, and discussion of its tentative identification with Nagarahara.
2. Masson 1841: 99—brief description.
3. Simpson 1881—brief description of this and other antiquities in the Jalālābād area.
4. Mizuno 1971: 113—mention and photo.
5. Errington 2017a: 154 and 2017b: 14, 33—the Masson collection and archive relating to the site.

TEPE KLUB. See 1142 TĀLUQĀN.

TEPE KUNDUR. See 2266 TEPE KUNDUR in Supplement.

1170. TEPE KURKURAK
Or TEPE SHĀHID BUSTĀN.

Original: Lat. 36° 52' N, long. 66° 16' E. Maps 24, 25.
Revised: 36.87186971 N, 66.26659698 E /
36° 52' 18.73094196 N, 66° 15' 59.74911972 E.
Jauzjān Province. 10 km south-east of Āqcha, 1 km south of the road to Balkh, west of Nahr Mullāh Jum'a.

Description: Two tepes 50 m apart. (A) Rounded mound (diam. *c.*80 m, height 7 m), occupied by a late cemetery, very deteriorated by erosion. (B) Shapeless mound partly razed by farmers, about 3 m high, to the south-east of A.

Fieldwork: 1948 Le Berre, DAFA—survey.

Source: M. Le Berre: unpublished 1948 report, DAFA archives, tepes P. 12.

1171. TEPE MAHI

Original: Lat. 33° 35' N, long. 68° 28' E. Map 80.
Revised: 33.59371866 N, 68.46976079 E /
33° 35' 37.38718860 N, 68° 28' 11.13885804 E.
Ghazni Province. 2 km north-east of Rauza, just to the west
of the main road to Kābul.

Date: Turki Shahi, 7th–9th cent. (ceramic, numismatic).

Description: Remains of a settlement where pottery similar
to Jaghatū and coins of Napti Malka have been found.

Sources:
1. Adamesteanu 1960: 29 – mention.
2. Thomas 2015: 519 – additional information from satellite imagery.

TEPE MAHMŪD. See 1092 SHŪRATŪ.

1172. TEPE MAHMŪDIYA

Original: Lat. 33° 35' N, long. 69° 15' E. Map 82.
Revised: 33.5835854 N, 69.25088852 E / 33° 35' 00.90744396 N,
69° 15' 03.19868856 E.
Paktiyā Province. In the hills 3 km east of Gardēz.

Description: Ruins of fortifications.

Source: Fischer 1969: 340 – mention.

1173. TEPE MARANJĀN

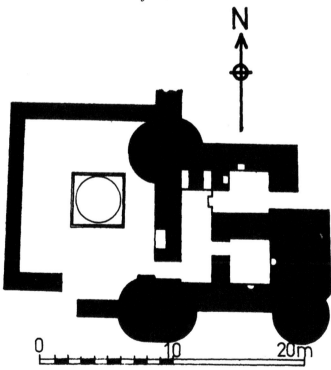

1173 Tepe Maranjān (after Carl and Hackin 1959).

Original: Lat. 34° 31–51' N, long. 69° 15–25' E. Map 61.
Revised: 34.51235526 N, 69.20729469 E /
34° 30' 44.47893672 N, 69° 12' 26.26086744 E.
Kābul Province. At the eastern end of the Maranjān hill,
4 km east of the Kābul Bālā Hisār, just to the north of the
road to Būtkhāk.

Dates: Kushano-Sasanian, 3rd–4th cent. (numismatic, stylistic); Hunnic-Turki Shahi, 5th–9th cent. (ceramic).

Description: A Buddhist monastery complex, of which
almost nothing remains today. Finds include sculpture,
frescos, and a hoard of 368 Sasanian silver drachmae, dating
from AD 383 to 388. In 1981, a second monastic complex
was discovered by chance and later excavated that includes a
diaper masonry stupa, and a thick ash layer that may mark
the Hephthalite invasion.

At the foot of the hill at the south side are 12 artificial
caves with low parallel openings. Immediately to the east of
these caves are many mounds.

Collections: National Museum.

Fieldwork:
1. 1933 Carl, DAFA – excavations.
2. 1981–7 Joyenda, AIA – excavations.
3. 2017–18 Noori, ACHCO and Oriental Institute
Chicago – restoration work.

Sources:
1. Gardin and Lyonnet, 1980 chronological study of pottery from unpublished DAFA surveys.
2. Masson 1833a: 11 – description and sketch of the exterior of the caves and the mounds.
3. Sālnāma 1933/34: opp. 24–5 – photos of the excavations and the sculpture.
4. Dollot 1937: 284–5 – brief summary of the excavations.
5. Caspani 1946c – guide to the site.
6. Kohzad 1949b – description of the coin hoard.
7. Curiel 1953 – reports the discovery of the coin hoard.
8. Carl and Hackin 1959 – very summary report on the
excavations and sculptures.
9. Pugachenkova 1963: 41 – general summary.
10. Talbot Rice 1965: 164 – brief discussion of the frescos.
11. Göbl 1967: 29–36 – discusses the evidence of the coins
for Hephthalite history.
12. N. Dupree 1971a: 118–19 – brief summary.
13. Rowland and Rice 1971: pl. 137–8 – photos and
descriptions of some of the objects.
14. N. Dupree et al. 1974: 81 and 108 – description of the
coin hoard and other objects on display in the National
Museum.
15. Fussman and Le Berre 1976: 95–9 – analysis of the
architecture and chronological conclusions.
16. Zeymal Haidari 1980 – personal communication on the
new discovery.
17. Kuwayama 1991: 100–3 – discussion of the evidence
from Begram III for the chronology.

18. Tissot and Darbois 2002—photos of objects from the National Museum
19. Tissot 2006: 343–6—National Museum catalogue details and photos
20. Cambon and Jarrige 2006, 2007—mention the restoration in the National Museum of the Boddhisattva that had been smashed in 2001.
21. Paiman 2008: 59—mentions the recent excavations.
22. Fussman, Murad, and Ollivier 2008: 95–103, 262–9, and 302–3—description and photos of both the earlier and more recent excavations.
23. Errington 2017a: 69–70 and 2017b: 21–2: Masson documentation of the site.

TEPE MUCHAK. See **2267 TEPE MUCHAK** in Supplement.

1174. TEPE NĀRANJ, GHAZNI

Original: Lat. 33° 01' N, long. 67° 56' E. approximately. Map 79.
Revised: 33.01309133 N, 67.93638136 E /
33° 00' 47.12879412 N, 67° 56' 10.97287872 E.
Ghazni Province. On the main Kābul-Kandahār road, c. 30 km south-west of Qarabāgh and 30 km north-east of Muqqur.

Date: Sasanian, 3rd–7th cent. (ceramic).

Description: Four or five mounds on either side of the road, dominated by a large one to the north.

Fieldwork: 1965 Fischer, DAAD—survey.

Sources:
1. Masson 1842: II. 217—brief description.
2. Fischer 1967a: 165—mention.
3. Fischer 1969: 339—mention (Site A1).

TEPE NĀRENJ, Kābul. See **2268 TEPE NĀRENJ, Kābul, in Supplement.**

TEPE NAU KALIN. See **925 QIZIL SAI TEPE.**

1175. TEPE QABR-I TURKMAN
Or CHISH TEPE.

Original: Lat. 36° 52' N, long. 66° 21' E. Map 25.
Revised: 36.87125106 N, 66.35748663 E /
36° 52' 16.50380484 N, 66° 21' 26.95188312 E.
Jauzjān Province. 17 km south-east of Āqcha, 300 m south of the road to Balkh, near the late cemetery of Qabr-i Turkman.

Dates: Hellenistic, 3rd–2nd cent. BC; Mongol-Timurid period, 13th–16th cent. (ceramic).

Description: Small quadrangular platform (c.30 × 30 m), quite high; possibly surrounded by a ditch. Several ruins nearby.

Fieldwork:
1. 1948 Le Berre, DAFA—survey.
2. 1960 Hayashi and Sahara, University of Kyoto—survey.

Sources:
1. M. Le Berre: unpublished 1948 report, DAFA archives, tepe P. 18.
2. Hayashi and Sahara 1962: 65—photo and brief description.

TEPE QAINAR. See **791 PAKHRAK.**

1176. TEPE QARYA-I AFGHĀN

Original: Lat. 36° 13' N, long. 69° 10' E. Map 33.
Revised: 36.22654851 N, 69.16096221 E /
36° 13' 35.57465076 N, 69° 09' 39.46395276 E.
Takhār Province. On the main Narīn-Ishkamīsh road, c.22 km north of Narīn.

Date: Kushan-Sasanian, 1st–7th cent. (ceramic).

Description: A very large, steep, pyramid-shaped mound.

Fieldwork: 1955–65 Fischer, DAAD—survey.

Source: Fischer 1969: 352—mention.

TEPE QURSI. See **1 ABAKA.**

1177. TEPE RĀMRŪD

Lat. 30° 18' N, long. 61° 19' E. approximately. Map 94.
Nīmrūz Province. C.2 km east of the Iranian border, 4 km south-west of the Rūd-i Biyābān sites and 17 km west of Gina.

Dates: Parthian and Indo-Parthian, 2nd cent. BC–AD 3rd cent.; Sasanian, 3rd–7th cent. (ceramic).

Description: Two small mounds, c.300 m apart. The first is 40 × 20 m in area and 5 m in height, the second is 6 m in height.

Fieldwork: 1951 Fairsevis, AMNH—survey.

Source: Fairservis 1961: 64 and 66—brief description (Sites RB 32 and 33).

1178. TEPE RŪD-I BIYĀBĀN

Original: Lat. 30° 18' N, long. 61° 24' E. approximately. Map 94.
Revised: 30.29973653 N, 61.41611873 E /
30° 17' 59.05149036 N, 61° 24' 58.02743124 E.

Nīmrūz Province. On a bluff overlooking the south side of the Rūd-i Bīyābān, 9 km east of Iran border post 20 and 8 km west of Gina.

Date: Sasanian, 3rd–7th cent. (ceramic).

Description: Two small mounds, *c.*100 m apart.

Fieldwork: 1951 Fairservis, AMNH—survey.

Source: Fairservis 1961: 63—brief description (Sites RB 15 and 16).

TEPE RUSTAM. See 99 BALKH.

TEPE SAFDARI. See 943 QŪZI.

1179. TEPE SALA
Or TEPE KHUSH.

Lat. 36° 40' N, long. 66° 29' E. Map 28.
Balkh Province. 3 km west of Imām Sāhib, 60 km from Mazār-i Sharīf.

Dates: Turk, 7th–9th cent.; Timurid, 15th–16th cent. (ceramic).

Description: A large, irregular mound, 30 m across and 10 m high.

Fieldwork: 1960 Hayashi and Sahara, Kyoto University—survey.

Sources:
1. Gardin and Lyonnet, 1980 chronological study of pottery from unpublished DAFA surveys.
2. Hayashi and Sahara 1962: 60—photo and description in Japanese.

TEPE SALĀM. See 2269 TEPE SALĀM in Supplement.

1180. TEPE SARDAR

Original: Lat. 33° 32' N, long. 68° 27' E. Map 80.
Revised: 33.5581385 N, 68.45648676 E / 33° 33' 29.29859028 N, 68° 27' 23.35235328 E.
Ghazni Province. 4 km south-east of Ghazni.

Dates: Sasanian, 3rd–7th cent.; Turki Shahi, 7th–9th cent. (architectural, ceramic, stylistic).

Description: A very large stupa-monastery complex, consisting of a main stupa (the largest in Afghanistan) surrounded by many votive stupas and chapels, richly decorated in high clay relief. The remains in the sanctuary include fragments of several colossal Buddha statues, including a monumental seated Buddha and a 15 m long reclining Buddha, all made from unbaked clay. There is also a Hindu shrine in the complex, where a statue of Durga Mahishasuramardini was found. Other finds include frescos, manuscripts, and many more sculptures.

By 1999 much of the Tepe Sardar complex had been pillaged or destroyed by acts of deliberate iconoclasm

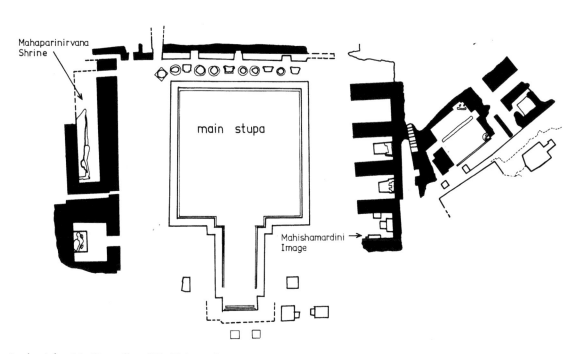

1180 Tepe Sardar (after MacDowall and Taddei 1978b).

during the 1980s. In addition, the roofs of many of the chapels had been badly damaged or completely removed, exposing the interiors to the weather.

Fieldwork:

1. 1959–60 Adamesteanu, IsMEO—excavations.
2. 1961 Puglisi, IsMEO—excavations.
3. 1967–77 Taddei, IsMEO—excavations.
4. 2003 Verardi, IsIAO—limited soundings.

Sources:

1. Adamesteanu 1960: 28–9—brief report on the excavations and finds.
2. Gullini 1960—photos and notes on an exhibition of the excavations.
3. Taddei 1967—brief interim report: clearing on the northern and western sides of the terrace.
4. Taddei 1968: 444—brief interim report: the area east of the Buddha.
5. Taddei 1969a—report on the excavations up to 1967: architecture and sculptures.
6. Taddei 1969b: 545–7—brief interim report on the excavations and finds.
7. Taddei 1970a—very brief summary of the 1970 season.
8. Taddei 1970c: 509–10—brief interim report on the excavations and finds.
9. N. Dupree 1971a: 213–16—good description.
10. Taddei 1971—brief interim report: trial trenches around the mound.
11. Kuwayama 1972a—discusses and compares the Hindu sculpture.
12. Taddei 1972a—brief interim report: upper terrace, Stupa 64, sculpture, restorations.
13. Taddei 1972b—discusses some of the art-historical problems.
14. Taddei 1973—detailed report on Chapel 23 and its associated Hindu sculpture.
15. Taddei 1974a—discusses the reclining Buddha and its architectural associations.
16. Taddei 1974b—mentions the restoration work at Chapel 17.
17. Deshpande 1975—brief interim report on the 1975 season.
18. Taddei 1975—brief interim report on the 1975 season.
19. Taddei 1976—brief interim report on the 1976 season.
20. N. Dupree 1977: 190–6—good guide and background to the excavations.
21. Mac Dowall and Taddei 1978b: 280–3 and 290–4—photos and plan.
22. Taddei 1978—summary of the excavations, architecture, and sculpture.
23. Taddei and Verardi 1978—fully illustrated preliminary report on the excavations and finds, with extensive stylistic discussion.
24. Antonini 1979a—discusses the main features of some of the pottery, though without drawings.
25. Antonini 1979b—discusses the motifs depicted in area 64.
26. Parlato 1979—text and brief inguistic discussion of a 2nd–3rd cent. Brahmi inscription found between stupa 64 and Monument 69.
27. Kuwayama 1991: 95–100—discussion of the evidence from Begram III for the chronology.
28. Taddei 1999—discussion of the chronology of the clay sculpture, arguing for a later date than hitherto thought.
29. Stadtner 2000—discussion of the Uma Maheswara statue in relation to two unprovenanced Bodhisattvas in a private collection.
30. Verardi and Paparatti 2004: 93–4—discussion of the chronology of the early phases.
31. Ball 2008: 270–1—summary.
32. Filigenzi 2009a—general summary of the excavations and main results.
33. Filigenzi 2009b—discussion of the sculptures and their relation to Buddhist art generally.
34. Verardi 2010—discussion of some of the problems of the excavation and chronology of the site, with circumstantial evidence for a Kanishka I foundation.
35. Filigenzi and Giunta 2015—brief summary of Italian work, including work after 2002.
36. Thomas 2015: 519—additional information from satellite imagery.

TEPE SAYYID MUKHTAR. See 2270 TEPE SAYYID MUKHTAR in Supplement.

TEPE SHAGĀLAK. See 714 MASJIDAK.

1181. TEPE SHAHIDĀN

Original: Lat. 36° 42' N, long. 67° 49' E. Map 29.
Revised: 36.70328114 N, 67.81485908 E /
36° 42' 11.81210436 N, 67° 48' 53.49268044 E.
Samangān Province. 10 km east of Tāshqurghān on the road to Qundūz.

Dates: Kushan, Sasanian, Hunnic, Turk, 1st–8th cent. (ceramic).

Description: Two tepes with fortifications on the western edges of the hamlet of Shahidān.

Collection: National Museum/AIA—sherds.

Fieldwork:

1. 1960–8 Fischer, DAAD—survey.
2. 1969 Gouin—survey.
3. 1970 White, AMNH—survey.

Sources:
1. Fischer 1969: 348—mention (Tepes B2).
2. Gouin 1974 and unpublished report—site no. 14.
3. Mac Dowall and Taddei 1978a: 299—mention.
4. Srivastava 1979c—description.

TEPE SHĀHID BUSTĀN. See 1170 TEPE KURKURAK.

TEPE SHĀH MAMŪD. See 1092 SHŪRATŪ.

TEPE SHAHR. See 1142 TĀLUQĀN.

1182. TEPE SHIRWANI

Lat. 35° 00' N, long. 69° 35' E. Map 65.
Kāpīsā Province. 5 km north-east of Nijrau bazaar, on the north side of the plain near Tepe Tughak.

Description: A small and not very interesting mound. It is reported locally that a tunnel existed from the site down into the present lower village.

Fieldwork: 1976 Kohl—survey.

Source: Site information by P. L. Kohl.

1183. TEPE SHUR SHURAK

Original: Lat. 36° 47' N, long. 66° 45' E. Map 26.
Revised: 36.77975874 N, 66.75602016 E /
36° 46' 47.13145212 N, 66° 45' 21.67259040 E.
Balkh Province. 12 km north-west of this town, south of the road to Āqcha, east of the village of Sabzikar.

Description: Rectangular platform (140 × 90 m), low (height 6 m), dominated by a citadel in the south-east angle (height 7.5 m) and surrounded by a ditch.

Fieldwork: 1948 Le Berre, DAFA—survey.

Source: M. Le Berre: unpublished 1948 report, DAFA archives, tepe P. 47.

TEPE SHUTUR. See 404 HADDA.

1184. TEPE SINAUBAR
   Or KHĀNA LŪMĀN.

Lat. 33° 08' N, long. 67° 36' E. Maps 78, 79.
Ghazni Province. Just west of Lūmān, *c.*52 km west of Qarabāgh on the road to Sang-i Māsha.

Date: Early Sasanian, 3rd–4th cent. (architectural).

Description: A large, dome-shaped rock *c.*8 m high, that has been cut from the end of a limestone ridge by a ditch to form a stupa. It has many artificial caves cut into it, one of which (Cave 2) has a blind arcade of three or four parabolic niches, similar to Bāmiyān and a carved garlanded *boukephalion* decoration.

Fieldwork:
1. 1962 Bivar, SOAS—survey.
2. 1974–5 Taddei and Verardi, IsMEO—survey.

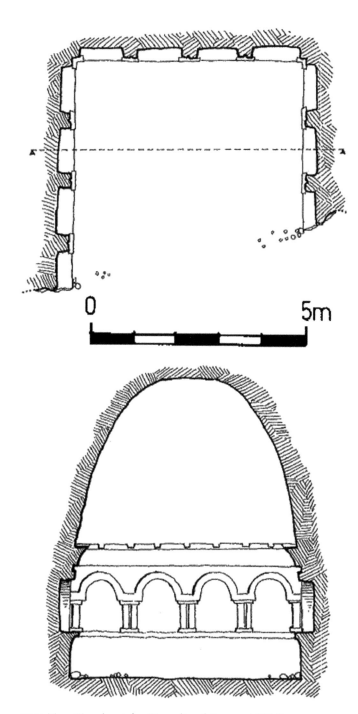

1184 Tepe Sinaubar (after Verardi and Paparatti 2004).

Sources:
1. Bivar 1971: 85–6—brief description.
2. Taddei 1975: 455–6—brief description.
3. Verardi 1977a: 136–8—description.
4. Verardi and Paparatti 2004: 43–6—detailed description with detailed drawings and photos.

1185. TEPE SKANDAR
Or QAL'A-I RAJPUT.

Original: Lat. 34° 43' N, long. 69° 07' E. Map 63.
Revised: 34.72117251 N, 69.12556975 E /
34° 43' 16.22101872 N, 69° 07' 32.05111368 E.
Kābul Province. 31 km north of Kābul, to the east of the road to Chārikār, 3 km south of Sarāī Khūja.

Dates: Late Sasanian-Turki Shahi, late 6th–early 9th cent. (numismatic, stylistic).

Description: A large mound measuring 440 × 280 m in area. It consists of two sanctuaries, a fort, and several small shrines, one of them containing a fire altar. One of the most important finds is a marble Hindu statue of Uma Maheshvara, which has a Sanskrit inscription on its base. Other finds include coins, sculpture, and miscellaneous artefacts.

Collections: National Museum—objects from the excavations.

Fieldwork:
1. 1834 Masson—survey.
2. 1923 Foucher, DAFA—survey.
3. 1946 Wheeler, ASI—reconnaissance.
4. 1970, 72, 74, 76, and 78 Higuchi, Kyoto University—excavations.

Sources:
1. Masson 1842: III. 145—mention.
2. Foucher 1942–7: 144–5—brief description.
3. Shakur 1947: 23–5—brief description.
4. Caspani and Cagnacci 1951: 277—mention.
5. Dagens 1964a: 35—brief description of a statue base found by chance.
6. Higuchi et al. 1971—interim report (in Japanese) on the excavations, the architecture, and sculpture.
7. Kuwayama 1972a—discusses and compares the Hindu sculpture found.
8. Kuwayama 1972b—preliminary report on the shrine, terrace, dwelling area, and Maheshvara statue.
9. Yamada 1972b—linguistic analysis and translation of the Sanskrit inscription.
10. Higuchi 1974a—preliminary report on the 1972 excavations at the fort, with photos and summary of the finds.
11. Kuwayama 1974a—preliminary report on the excavations at the fort.
12. Zaryab 1974b—brief report on the Japanese mission.

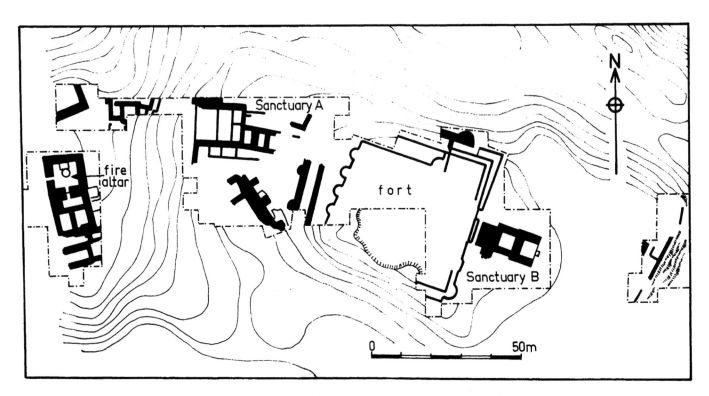

1185 Tepe Skandar (after Kuwayama 1974a, Kuwayama and Momono 1976, Kuwayama 1978 and 1980).

13. Kuwayama 1976—detailed description and discussion of the Maheshvara and other Hindu sculpture found at the site.
14. Kuwayama and Momono 1976—preliminary report on and tentative sequence for the fort, Sanctuary A, and minor buildings.
15. H. Motamedi 1976: 58–60—summary of the excavations.
16. Davary 1977—mentions the Sanskrit inscription.
17. Kuwayama 1978—interim report on the fourth season: the western building and the north-western corridor.
18. Kuwayama 1980—interim report on the fifth season, on the lower, western end of the site.
19. Kuwayama 1991: 86–92—discussion of the evidence from Begram III for the chronology.
20. Tissot 2006: 358—National Museum catalogue details and photos.
21. Ball 2008: 271—summary.
22. Kuwayama 2010: 288–9—the evidence from Tepe Skandar for a long gap between Begram II and III.

1186. TEPE TUGHAK

Original: Lat. 34° 59’ N, long. 69° 35’ E. Map 65.
Revised: 34.98412007 N, 69.58144791 E /
34° 59’ 02.83223868 N, 69° 34’ 53.21247564 E.
Kāpīsā Province. 3 km north of Nijrau bazaar, on the north side of the plain just to the north-east of the road to Gulbahar.

Description: Tepe Tughak was visible from the road and seems to have been built partly on a natural rock outcrop; it may have been a Kushan citadel.

Fieldwork: 1976 Kohl—survey.

Source: Site information by P. L Kohl.

1187. TEPE TŪP

Lat. 34° 58’ N, long. 69° 34’ E. approximately. Map 65.
Kāpisā Province. In the valley immediately to the south of Nijrau.

Date: Kushan, 1st–3rd cent. (ceramic).

Description: A Kushan building on a rock outcrop. A chamber had been partly exposed by villagers digging for soil and diaper masonry was visible. There was little pottery and most of the outcrop is natural.

Fieldwork: 1976 Kohl—survey.

Source: Site information by P. L Kohl.

TEPE WĀKIL DIRĀZ KHAN. See 94 BĀJAURI TEPE GUDAMDAR.

TEPE WALI BABA. See 19 AINAK.

1188. TEPE ZĀDIYĀN

See also 8 ABU HURAIRA, 520 KAM PIRAK, 814 PIT QAL'A TEPE, 1245 ZĀDIYĀN, 2053 DAU-LATĀBĀD in Supplement, and 2281 ZĀDIYĀN KĀFIR QAL'A in Supplement.

Original: Lat. 37° 01’ N, long. 66° 55’ E. Map 27.
Revised: 37.00375155 N, 66.90727211 E /
37° 00’ 13.50558072 N, 66° 54’ 26.17960572 E.
Balkh Province. About 40 km north of this town, west of the village of Zādiyān.

Description: Quadrangular mound (*c*.40 × 40 m), height about 3 m, probably surrounded by a wall.

Fieldwork: 1948 Le Berre, DAFA—survey.

Source: M. Le Berre: unpublished 1948 report, DAFA archives, tepe P. 54.

1189. TEPE ZAHIDĀN

Original: Lat. 36° 44’ N, long. 67° 11’ E. Map 27.
Revised: 36.73007308 N, 67.17667243 E /
36° 43’ 48.26307324 N, 67° 10’ 36.02075736 E.
Balkh Province. C.8 km east of Mazār-i Sharīf.

Dates: Kushan-Sasanian, 1st–7th cent.; early Islamic, 10th–13th cent. (ceramic).

Description: A series of low mounds on either side of the road, up to 4 m high. One is square, and contains remains of structures in small and large mud-bricks.

Fieldwork:
1. 1956 Ramachandran and Sharma, ASI—reconnaissance.
2. 1960 Hayashi and Sahara, Kyoto University—survey.
3. 1960–8 Fischer, Bonn University—survey.

Sources:
1. Ramachandran and Sharma 1956: I. 22—mention.
2. Hayashi and Sahara 1962—photo and brief description in Japanese.
3. Fischer 1969: 348—brief description (Tepes B1).

1190. TEPE ZAITUN

Lat. 33° 17’ N, long. 67° 36’ E. Maps 77, 78, 79.
Ghazni Province. Near Ulyatu on the Jāghūrī-Dasht-i Nāwar road.

Date: Early Sasanian, 4th–5th cent. (architectural).

Description: A very large complex of artificial caves, cut into a ridge. Most are very small chambers, except for one huge cave (Cave 23) that contains a row of large elliptical arch niches resembling Haibak, and another (Cave 24) in the form of a tetrapylon covered with a dome.

Fieldwork: 1976 Taddei and Verardi, IsMEO—survey.

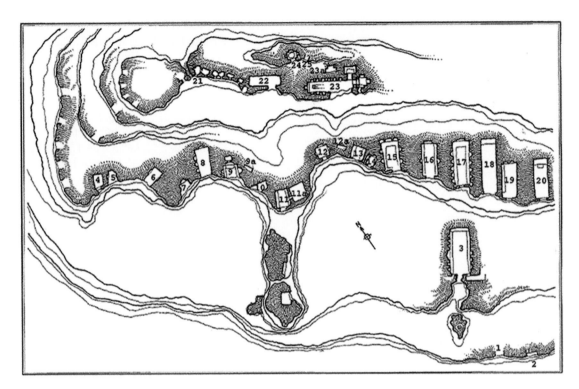

1190 Tepe Zaitun (after Verardi and Paparatti 2004).

Sources:
1. Taddei 1976: 601 — brief description.
2. Verardi 1977a: 150 — mention.
3. Verardi and Paparatti 2004: 73–88 — detailed description with many drawings and photos.

TEPE ZARGARĀN, Balkh. See **99 BALKH.**

TEPE ZARGARĀN, Hadda. See **404 HADDA.**

1191. TIKAR
See also **430 HIRDAI TEPE.**

Lat. 36° 25' N, long. 64° 53' E. approximately. Map 24.
Faryāb Province. West of Daulatābād.

Date: Bronze Age, early 2nd mill. BC (ceramic).

Description: Five artificial mounds, each 2.5–3.5 m high, totalling *c.*5 hectares in area. They are probably small unfortified farming settlements or manors, containing small mud-brick houses.

Fieldwork:
1. 1969 Kruglikova and Mutamandi, Af/Sov. Mission — survey.
2. 1973 Sarianidi, Af/Sov. Mission — survey.

Sources:
1. Kruglikova and Mustamandi 1970: 85 — mention.
2. Biscione 1977: 125 — very brief description.
3. Sarianidi 1977c: 22–6 — brief description and discussion.
4. Srivastava 1979b: 57 — summary of the Soviet work.
5. Kohl 1984: 161 — summary of the Soviet work.

1192. TILLYA TEPE
Or TILLA TEPE.

Original: Lat. 36° 43' N, long. 65° 44' E. Map 24.
Revised: 36.69460304 N, 65.78972843 E /
36° 41' 40.57095876 N, 65° 47' 23.02235772 E.
Jauzjān Province. 5 km north of Shībarghān, 2 km to the east of the road to Andkhūī.

Dates: Early Iron Age, *c.*1300–800 BC (C-14, ceramic); Kushan, 100 BC–AD 100 (stylistic).

Description: A mound *c.*80 m diam. and 4 m high, enclosed by mud-brick walls *c.*1.5 m high. Inside is a temple consisting of two halls with 15 columns and a cruciform altar. The site is possibly a very early Indo-Iranian settlement.

In the 1st century Tilla Tepe was reused as a necropolis for a wealthy elite, perhaps associated with nearby Effendi Tepe. In 1978 six burials were excavated, consisting of raised wooden coffins containing burial adornments of silk, gold, and silver. Some 20,000 gold objects were recovered, consisting of bracelets, bowls, clasps, buttons,

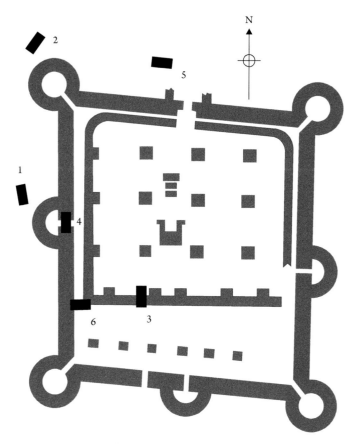

1192 Tillya Tepe (after Sarianidi).

weapons, statuary jewellery, etc., representing a mixture of Indian, Central Asian, Iranian, and Hellenistic styles.

In 1995 the site had been heavily dug by looters to the extent that only a few walls remained. Reports of a seventh burial containing extensive amounts of jewellery on a par with the other six graves were confirmed by local officials and villagers.

The collection was removed to the vaults of the Dikusha Palace in c.1981 where it was later recovered intact in April 2004.

Collections: National Museum—treasure.

Fieldwork: 1969–78 Sarianidi and Tarzi, Af/Sov. Mission—excavations.

Sources:

1. Kruglikova and Sarianidi 1971c: 87–90—brief description of the site and finds.
2. Sarianidi 1972a—preliminary report on the excavations to date: stratigraphy, chronology, and ceramic type series, with a discussion of the cultural origins and affinities.
3. Cattenat and Gardin 1976—discuss the ceramics and its links.
4. Sarianidi 1977c: 107–8—discussion of the ceramics and chronology.
5. Azimi 1979—report on the discovery of the treasure.
6. Kato 1979—general article on the discovery and significance of the treasure.
7. Sarianidi 1979a—report and photos, some in colour, of some of the gold objects.
8. Srivastava 1979c—good review of the excavations.
9. Time 1979—summary of the discovery and descriptions of some select objects.
10. Zafar 1979—brief report and photos on the discovery of the treasure.
11. Koshalenko and Sarianidi 1992—discuss the coins from the necropolis.
12. Sarianidi 1980—description of the treasure and discussion on the evidence it presents for the origins of the Kushans.
13. Sarianidi 1985—full colour illustrations of the most important items from the hoard with brief discussion of the history and origins of the artefacts.
14. Bernard 1987—discusses the treasure in the context of the nomadic conquest of Graeco-Bactria.
15. Zeymal 1999—argues for second quarter of the 1st century AD for the treasure.
16. Boardman 2003—discusses three gold objects from the hoard.
17. Brown 2003—discusses a gold token as a possible prototype Buddha figure.
18. Cambon and Schiltz in Cambon and Jarrige 2006, 2007, and 2008—brief description of the discovery of the treasure and catalogue of objects in a European touring exhibition.
19. Calligaro in Cambon and Jarrige 2007—analysis of the origins of the gold and stones from the treasure.
20. Ball 2008: 272—summary.
21. Baumer 2012: 291–6—summary of the excavations and discoveries.
22. Boardman 2012—discusses the links of the treasure with Greek art.
23. Francfort 2012—discusses the links of the treasure with the art and burials of the Eurasian steppe.
24. Leidy 2012—discusses the Chinese and Chinese influenced objects from the treasure.
25. Rougemont 2012a: 187–8—discusses the images of Athena from the treasure.

1193. TĪRĀNDĀZ

Original: Lat. 31° 52' N, long. 66° 28' E. Map 90.
Revised: 31.85269029 N, 66.46365455 E /
31° 51' 09.68503068 N, 66° 27' 49.15637136 E.
Zābul Province. 18 km north-east of Shahr-i Safā, just to the south of the Kandahār-Kābul road.

Date: Sasanian, 3rd–7th cent. (B, ceramic); 18th cent. (A, stylistic).

Description: (A) A baked brick pillar some 10–15 m high, with simple chevron pattern decoration. (B) A small mound near the village.

Fieldwork:
1. 1965 Fischer, DAAD—survey.
2. 1971–4 Trousdale, Smithsonian Institution—survey.

Sources:
1. Masson 1833c: 22—sketch of the pillar.
2. Masson 1842: I and II. 269–70 and 196—brief description of the pillar.
3. Bellew 1862: 216—mention.
4. Shakur 1947: 91—brief description of the pillar.
5. Ramachandran and Sharma 1956: I. 8—mention.
6. Fischer 1967a: 156 nn. 109–11—mention.
7. Fischer 1969: 338—mentions the mound.
8. Gazetteer 1980: V. 478—brief description of the tower.

1194. TIRKHĀNA

Lat. 34° 26' N, long. 68° 32' E. Map 60.
Wardak Province. On the north side of a gorge *c.*14 km west of Jalrēz, on the road from Kot-i Ashru to Hājigak.

Description: Remains of an ancient tower.

Sources:
1. Masson 1939: 54—mention.
2. Masson 1842: II. 327—mention.

1195. TĪRKŪH

Lat. 30° 28' N, long. 61° 48' E. Map 93.
Nīmrūz Province. On a 'peninsular' jutting into the Helmand opposite Dakdila, between Chahār Burjak and Qal'a-i Fath.

Description: A large natural mound, 200 × 300 m in area and *c.*15m in height, surrounded on three sides by the river. On top are a number of ruins.

Fieldwork: 1884 Peacocke, ABC—topographical survey.

Sources:
1. Smith 1876: 286—mention.
2. Peacocke 1885a: 7—very brief description.
3. Peacocke 1887a: 21—very brief description.
4. Gazetteer 1973: II. 291—mention.

1196. TIRPUL

Original: Lat. 34° 36' N, long. 61° 16' E. Map 51.
Revised: 34.59564268 N, 61.26161358 E /
34° 35' 44.31363576 N, 61° 15' 41.80890276 E.
Herat Province. On the Harī Rūd 95 km downstream from Herat, just to the east of where the modern Herat-Mashhad road crosses the river.

Date: ?Timurid, 15th–16th cent. (architectural).

Description: Remains of a caravanserai and a stone baked brick bridge, of six arches. It is 180 m long with a parapet 60 cm high above a flagstoned roadway.

Fieldwork:
1. 1884 Peacocke Maitland, ABC—topographical survey.
2. 1979 AIA—preservation.

Sources:
1. Holdich 1885a: 277–8—brief description.
2. Peacocke 1885a: 46—detailed description.
3. Peacocke 1887a: 59—description of bridge.
4. A. C. Yate 1887: 149–50—brief description.
5. Maitland 1888a: 137—brief description of bridge; 275—mentions rabat.
6. Gazetteer 1975: III. 425—brief description.
7. *Kabul Times* 1979a—mentions repair work.

TĪZNAI TAGAU. See **2271 TĪZNAI TAGAU** in Supplement.

TOLO BARFAQ. See **1139 TĀLĀ.**

1197. TOPDARRA
Including QAL'A-I KHALIFA.

Original: Lat. 34° 59' N, long. 69° 08' E. Map 64.
Revised: 34.98877317 N, 69.11910531 E /
34° 59' 19.58341524 N, 69° 07' 08.77911024 E.
Parwān Province. 58 km north of Kābul, 5 km south-west of Chārikār.

Dates: Kushan, 1st–3rd cent. (architectural); Hunnic-Hindu Shahi, 5th–10th cent. (ceramic).

Description: A very intact stupa over 20 m high and 30 m diam., with a decorative frieze of alternating Indo-Corinthian pilasters and blind arches. There is no sign of a platform. Its foundation is attributed to Kanishka. The remains of two more stupas were recorded further north. To the south, near the village of Qal'a-i Khalifa, two mounds probably mark the remains of two more stupas.

Towards Chārikār are the remains of two complete monasteries with courtyards and small stupas.

Collections: BM—stupa deposits.

Fieldwork:
1. 1834 Masson—survey.
2. 1923 Foucher, DAFA—survey.
3. 1965 Mizuno, Kyoto University—survey.
4. 1972 Fussman, CNRS—survey.
5. 2017–18 Noori, ACHCO and Oriental Institute Chicago—restoration work.

Sources:
1. Gardin and Lyonnet, 1980 chronological study of pottery from unpublished DAFA surveys.

2. Jacquet 1836b: 275–6 — brief description.
3. Masson 1841: 116 — mention.
4. Masson 1842: III. 135 — mention.
5. Foucher 1942–7: 142 — brief description of all the remains.
6. Lézine 1962: 45–6 — description of the main stupa.
7. Lézine 1964: description of the stupa.
8. Mizuno 1971: 126 — brief description and photos.
9. Ball 2008: 272 — summary.
10. Fussman et al. 2008: 126–33, 276–83, and 305 — description and photos of the remains.
11. Jongeward et al. 2012 — catalogue and discussion of the reliquaries.
12. Errington 2017a: 83–4 and 2017b: 54 — the Masson collection and archive relating to the site.

1198. TOPRAKKALE

Original: Lat. 37° 00' N, long. 67° 08' E. Map 27.
Revised: 37.03741217 N, 67.18107891 E /
37° 02' 14.68382640 N, 67° 10' 51.88409328 E.
Balkh Province. Near Mumīnābād, 34 km north of Mazār-i Sharīf, 2 km to the east of the road to the Āmū Daryā.

Date: Kushan, 1st cent. BC–AD 3rd cent (architectural).

Description: A large square urban site surrounded by monumental ramparts. The ramparts have square towers and internal galleries, with many arrow slits on the outside. Inside the town are the remains of a large stupa-monastery complex.

Fieldwork: 1972–3 Pugachenkova, Af/Sov. Mission — survey.

Sources:
1. Pugachenkova 1976b — brief description and drawing.
2. Francfort 1979a: 32–6 — lists the site in a general discussion of Kushan military architecture.

TRĀKŪN. See 1147 TARĀKŪN.

1199. TUGHAI
Or JALMISH TUGHAI. Including TURKAI MA-ZĀRA. See also 350 GHANDAK.

Lat. 35° 02' N.–35° 05' N, long. 68° 01' E. Map 58.
Baghlān Province. On the Surkhāb between Shikari and Dūāb-i Mikhzarīn, on the road to Dūshi.

Date: Turk and/or pre-Mongol Islamic, 7th–13th cent. (architectural).

Description: Remains of a small fort of carefully made mud-brick. The exterior is decorated. Inside is a dome-chamber with squinches very similar to Haibak, but with the distinctive feature of an engaged colonette between each squinch.

There are the remains of two more small forts further downstream on the Surkhāb.

Fieldwork:
1. 1951 Allchin and Codrington — survey.
2. 1974–5 Le Berre, DAFA — survey.

Source: Le Berre 1987: 32–3, pls 27e and 36 — itinerary A1, ruins 10–12.

1200. TUJG

Original: Lat. 32° 04' N, long. 61° 48' E. Map 83.
Revised: 32.04064603 N, 61.80009917 E /
32° 02' 26.32572312 N, 61° 48' 00.35700264 E.
Farāh Province. On the north-west bank of the Farāh Rūd, c.45 km south-west of Farāh.

Date: Mongol-Timurid, 15th–16th cent. (ceramic).

Description: Some mud-brick ruins.

Fieldwork: 1960–70 Fischer, Bonn University — survey.

Source: Fischer et al. 1974–6: 35 — mention.

1201. TUKHM TEPE

Original: Lat. 36° 02' N, long. 69° 07' E. Map 33.
Revised: 36.04083509 N, 69.10821377 E /
36° 02' 27.00632904 N, 69° 06' 29.56956624 E.
Baghlān Province. At the south-eastern end of the Narīn plain, c.3 km south of the bazaar.

Description: An extremely steep, cone-shaped mound covered in crude red pottery. It is 20 m high and is 15 × 10 m in area at the summit.

Fieldwork: 1975 Kohl — survey.

Source: Kohl 1978: 63 — brief description.

TUNUK. See 134 BISH KA'IK.

1202. TŪPCHI

Original: Lat. 34° 45'–34° 49' N, long. 67° 56'–67° 57' E. Map 58.
Revised: 34.81234753 N, 67.94073031 E /
34° 48' 44.45109216 N, 67° 56' 26.62913148 E.
Bāmiyān. A lateral valley leading to the Haft Pailān Pass opening southwards off the Bāmiyān Valley, 4 km west of Shahr-i Zuhak.

Date: Turk, 8th–10th cent. (ceramic).

Description: A series of ruins and towers guarding the approach to the Bāmiyān Valley.

Fieldwork: 1974–5 Le Berre, DAFA — survey.

Sources:
1. Gardin and Lyonnet, 1980 chronological study of pottery from unpublished DAFA surveys.
2. Masson 1839: 82—mention.
3. Masson 1842: II. 378–9—mention.
4. Le Berre 1987—itineraries B1, ruins 6–9; B2, Darya-i Panjpalan, ruins 104.

1203. TŪP-I ĀHANGARĀN
See 501 KAFTARKHĀNA

TŪPKHĀNA QAL'A. See 542 KHAIRĀBĀD.

1204. TŪPKHĀNA
See also 557 KHANDŪD.

Original: Lat. 36° 57' N, long. 72° 20' E. Map 39.
Revised: 36.95888476 N, 72.33181074 E /

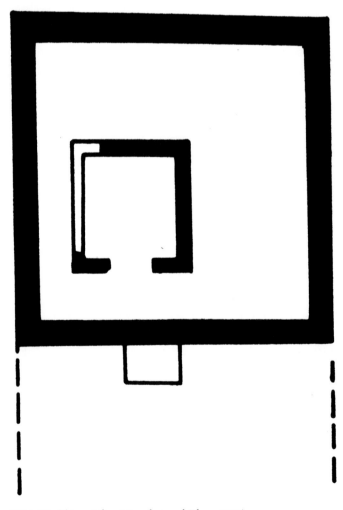

1204 Tūpkhāna (after Mouchet and Blanc 1972).

36° 57' 31.98514680 N, 72° 19' 54.51865356 E.
Badakhshān province. 2 km east of Khandūd in Wākhān.

Date: ?Late Sasanian, 7th cent. (architectural).

Description: A double stone platform on a hill, with a square mud-brick structure on top, possibly a Buddhist stupa. It is covered in painted geometric sherds.

Source: Mouchet and Blanc 1972: 65–6—brief description.

TURĀNI. See 307 DŪN QISHLĀQ.

1205. TURGHAI TEPE

Original: Lat. 37° 09' N, long. 69° 30' E. Map 34.
Revised: 37.15535616 N, 69.48755326 E /
37° 09' 19.28219004 N, 69° 29' 15.19175328 E.
Takhār Province. 5 km east of the village of Dasht-i Qal'a on the edge (south side) of the track that leads from this village to Nawābād.

Dates: Middle Bronze Age. C.2500–1500 BC; Hellenistic, 3rd–1st cent. BC; Kushan, 1st–3rd cent. (ceramic).

Description: High conical mound, round at the base (diam. *c*.60 m, height 10 m), without visible structures; traces of illegal digging on the flanks and at the top of the mound. This tepe is the highest in the surrounding plain, to which it has given its name (Dasht-i Turghai Tepe); it is flanked by a little low mound (height *c*.3 m), some 10 m to the north. Many smaller tepes are located in this plain, more or less eroded (height 2–4 m), on either side of an old canal whose trace is indicated by high slender mounds, about 1.5 km south and east of the tepe.

Collection: National Museum/AIA—sherds.

Fieldwork: 1974 Gardin et al., CNRS—survey.

Source:
1. Site information by J.-C. Gardin.
2. Gardin and Lyonnet 1978–9: pl. III—no. 4.
3. Gardin and Gentelle 1979: the history of the settlement of this region.
4. Lyonnet 1997: figs 13, 21–4, 39, 49—no. 4.
5. Gardin 1998: 42—no. 4.

1206. TŪRGHUNDI
Or KARA TEPE or TEPE FĪRŪZ HUSAIN.

Original: Lat. 35° 14' N, long. 62° 17' E. Map 43.
Revised: 35.23719359 N, 62.28572663 E /
35° 14' 13.89692220 N, 62° 17' 08.61586188 E.
Herat Province. The Afghan border post on the left bank of the Kushk River, 113 km north of Herat.

Description: A large artificial mound *c*.17 m high, surrounded by a ditch. On top are the remains of a baked brick and mud fort, c.100 m square, with a gateway to the south. In the vicinity are many ancient irrigation canals.

Fieldwork:
1. 1884–5 Maitland, Peacocke, Yate, ABC—topographical survey.
2. 1968–78 Kruglikova, Af/Sov. Mission—survey.

Sources:
1. Abbot 1884: I. 11–12—mention.
2. *Pioneer*, 5 Jan. 1886—description.
3. Peacocke 1887a: 178, 270, and 276—brief description; 376—mention as Tepe Fīrūz Husain.
4. Maitland 1888a: 169—brief description.
5. Maitland and Drummond 1888: 63—mention.
6. Yate 1888: 103—brief description.
7. Gaibov et al. 2010: 112—mention (Site K153).

TURIGH. See 959 RŪD-I SHĀHRAWĀN.

TŪRSHAIKH. See 2273 TŪRSHAIKH in Supplement.

1207. TURT GUL TEPE
Or SAYYAD.

Original: Lat. 36° 16' N, long. 64° 53' E. Map 24.
Revised: 36.2892752 N, 64.87672801 E / 36° 17' 21.39073116 N, 64° 52' 36.22082376 E.
Faryāb Province. On the east side of the Shīrīn Tagau 13 km south of Khairabād and c.50 km north of Maimana.

Description: A natural mound considerably enlarged by artificial means to form a very regularly delineated fortress. Length is c.100 m, height over 15 m. Construction is of *pakhsa* blocks. On top is a *zīyārat* and some traces of walls, but no signs of any defensive walls.

Fieldwork: 1886 Peacocke, ABC—topographical survey.

Sources:
1. Site information by F. Grenet.
2. Peacocke 1887a: 248—mention as ancient Faryab.
3. Gazetteer 1979: IV. 473—mention.

1208. TŪSHKĀN

Lat. 36° 53' N, long. 70° 17' E. Map 38.
Badakhshān. In the mountains c.20 km north-east of Kishm.

Date: Seljuk, 12th cent. (stylistic).

Description: Site of an accidental find of 14 white bronzes, with hammered decoration and *naskhī* inscriptions.

Source: Melikian-Chirvani 1975a: 141–2—brief description with photos of three of the bronzes.

TŪTACHĪ. See 2274 TŪTACHĪ in Supplement.

TUTAK-I ĀBLĀN. See 2173 PASHTŪN ZARGHŪN in Supplement.

TŪTA KHĀN. See 2275 TŪTA KHĀN in Supplement.

ŪCH ĀRIQ. See 89 BAHĀRAK.

1209. ŪCH TEPE

Original: Lat. 36° 54' N, long. 67° 13' E. Map 27.
Revised: 36.90213935 N, 67.225604 E / 36° 54' 07.70165352 N, 67° 13' 32.17438812 E.
Balkh Province. In the dasht 24 km north-east of Mazār-i Sharīf.

Date: Epi-Palaeolithic, c.7000 BC (lithic).

Description: A mound 4 m high, with a second, 3 m high, 900 m to the south. The site is covered in Late Mesolithic artefacts similar to Siāh Rīgān.

Fieldwork: 1975 Vinogradov, Af/Sov. Mission—survey.

Sources:
1. Sarianidi 1977c: 7–11—discusses the lithics.
2. Vinogradov 1979—general discussion of the lithics together with others from the survey, with comparisons in Soviet Central Asia.

1210. UD KHĒL TEPE

Lat. 34° 32' N, long. 69° 16' E. Map 61.
Kābul Province. 9 km east of Kābul, south of the road to Jalālābād.

Date: Hunnic-Turk, 5th–9th cent. (ceramic).

Description: None.

Collection: National Museum/AIA—sherds.

Source: Gardin and Lyonnet 1980, study of pottery from unpublished DAFA surveys.

1211. ŪLĀN RABĀT
Or SHAHR-I ZUHAK.

Original: Lat. 32° 37' N, long. 67° 25' E. Map 79.
Revised: 32.59870273 N, 67.40698317 E / 32° 35' 55.32984276 N, 67° 24' 25.13942964 E.
Zābul Province. Near Deh Zangi, 11 km north of Shāhjūi on the Kandahār-Kābul road.

Dates: Hellenistic, 4th–1st cent. BC; Indo-Parthian and Sasanian, 1st–7th cent. (ceramic).

Description: A mound and associated ruins, in a square enclosure wall. There is also a ruined mud-brick pillar. Possibly ancient Arachosia.

Fieldwork: 1966 Fischer, DAAD—survey.

Sources:
1. Rawlinson 1842—mentions the remains and summarizes the sources for Arachosia.
2. Fischer 1967a: 163–4—mention and aerial photo.
3. Fischer 1969: 339—brief summary.

1212. ŪLJATŪ, SOUTH

Original: Lat. 36° 43' N, long. 67° 38' E. Map 29.
Revised: 36.72717227 N, 67.64459119 E /
36° 43' 37.82018208 N, 67° 38' 40.52827608 E.
Samangān Province. 7 km north-west of Tāshqurghān, on the road to Mazār-i Sharīf, south side (marker 374 km, from Kābul).

Dates: Beg. Iron, end 2nd–beg. 1st mill. BC; Hellenistic, 3rd–1st cent. BC; Kushan 1st–3rd cent.; pre-Mongol Islamic, 10th–13th cent. (ceramic).

Description: Quadrangular enclosure (measurements not taken); traces of interior walls in mud-bricks.

Collection: National Museum/AIA—sherds, cornelian bead.

Fieldwork:
1. 1885 Maitland, ABC—topographical exploration.
2. 1969 Gouin, DAFA—survey.

Sources:
1. Maitland 1888b: 54 and 263—mention.
2. Gouin 1974 and unpublished report—site no. 45.
3. Gazetteer 1979: IV. 583—mention.

1213. ŪLJATŪ, NORTH
　　See also 289 DEH NAU.

Original: Lat. 36° 45' N, long. 67° 37' E. Map 29.
Revised:
36.74583069 N, 67.61978445 E /
36° 44' 44.99049732 N, 67° 37' 11.22400524 E (A).
36.75881009 N, 67.61823957 E /
36° 45' 31.71631356 N, 67° 37' 05.66246712 E (B).
Samangān Province. 9 km north-west of Tāshqurghān, on the edge of the track that links this town with Deh Nau.

Dates: Kushan, 1st–3rd cent. (A); Sasanian-Hunnic and Turk, 4th–9th cent.; Timurid, 15th–16th cent. (A and B) (ceramic).

Description: (A) On the south side of the track, 6 km from the point where it separates from the Tāshqurghān-Mazār-i Sharīf road: oblong east–west mound (length 75 m), flattened (height 4 m), with two adjoining hillocks to the west; mud-bricks visible in the cuts (40 × 40 cm); (B) on the north

side of the track, 1 km north of the preceding tepe, oblong east–west mound (70 m), surrounded by small hillocks.

Collection: National Museum/AIA—sherds and round cornelian bead.

Fieldwork: 1969 Gouin, DAFA—survey.

Source: Gouin 1974 and unpublished report—sites no. 1 (A), 2 (B).

1214. UMARZ

Lat. 35° 22' N, long. 69° 38' E. Map 50.
Parwān Province. In the upper Panjshīr Valley.

Description: An ancient settlement built over by a modern village.

Fieldwork: 1976 Kohl—survey.

Source: Kohl 1978: 72—mention.

1215. ŪNAI

Lat. 34° 27' N, long. 68° 25' E. Maps 59, 60.
Wardak Province. On the eastern ascent of the Ūnai Pass between Kot-i Ashru and Jājigak.

Description: Remains of many walls and terraces on the sides of the hills. They are probably fortifications, though they may be stupas.

Sources:
1. Masson 1839: 55—mention.
2. Masson 1842: II. 328—mention.

1216. ŪNPAIKĀL

Original: Lat. 36° 55' N, long. 66° 26' E. Map 25.
Revised: 36.92628044 N, 66.44192346 E /
36° 55' 34.60957968 N, 66° 26' 30.92444268 E.
Jauzjān Province. On the Kilift-Balkh road between Chilik and Chahār Bāgh, c.22 km east of Āqcha.

Description: A very extensive area of mud remains, mounds, and ancient vineyards. The remains include many walls of large houses with double rows of windows.

Fieldwork: 1886 Peacocke, Yate, ABC—topographical survey.

Sources:
1. Peacocke 1887a: 356—mention.
2. Yate 1888: 254—brief description.

1217. URAZ BACHA
　　Includinging KARABASHAN TEPE.

Original: Lat. 37° 05'–37° 06' N, long. 69° 24' E. Map 34.

Revised:
37.0877363 N, 69.40439768 E / 37° 05' 15.85069440 N,
69° 24' 15.83165484 E (A).
37.09839343 N, 69.3990122 E / 37° 05' 54.21636240 N,
69° 23' 56.44391964 E (B).
37.09732604 N, 69.40774559 E / 37° 05' 50.37373572 N,
69° 24' 27.88412076 E (C).

Takhār Province. About 3 km north-north-west of Khwāja Ghar, by the road to Imām Sāhib, near the villages of Khush Gildi and Uruz Bacha. Two small tepes are located on the slopes of the hills which dominate the Rūd-i Shārawān and the plain of Khwāja Ghar, to the west; they lie on the edge of an old canal whose traces can be followed all along the promontory formed by these hills towards the north, in the direction of the Āmū Dāryā. This canal skirts the promontory, to irrigate, on the western slopes, the little plateau of Qarluk and Chichka. (A) the first tepe is located on the left bank of the Rūd-i Shārawān, 20 m upstream from the bridge where the road to Khwāja Ghar crosses this river, at Khush Gildi; (B) the second is 1 km downstream, 300 m west of the road, at the location of the cemetery indicated on the 1:100,000 map west of the village of Uruz Bacha. (C) A third larger tepe, in the process of being razed, is situated 400 m east of the preceding one, at the location of the last houses north of Khush Gildi.

Dates: Hellenistic, 3rd–1st cent. BC (B); Hunnic-Turk, 5th–9th cent.; some Islamic sherds (ceramic).

Description: (A) Round mound eaten into on all sides by irrigated crops (diam. 50 m, height 6 m). (B) Oblong north–south mound (30 × 15 m), height 2 m. (C) Round mound (diam. 80 m), in the process of disappearing under irrigated crops (maize and cotton): height 0.5 m, with a little hillock of 1 m in the centre, carrying the ruins of a late house. Place-name Karabashan Tepe. The importance of these two tepes is to confirm the periods when the canal functioned, indicated by the sites on the plateau of Chichka (see no. 917).

Collection: National Museum/AIA—sherds.

Fieldwork: 1977 Gardin et al., CNRS—survey.

Sources:
1. Site information by J.-C. Gardin.
2. Gardin and Lyonnet 1978–9: pl. IV—nos. 2, 76, 285.
3. Lyonnet 1997: figs 39, 68, 69—nos. 2, 76, 285
4. Gardin 1998: 49–50—nos. 2, 76, 285.

1218. URLAMISH

Original: Lat. 36° 13' N, long. 67° 31' E. Map 30.
Revised: 36.23526032 N, 67.52586451 E /
36° 14' 06.93713508 N, 67° 31' 33.11224212 E.
Samangān Province. On the mountainous road from Haibak to Mazār-i Sharīf, *c.*50 km west of Haibak.

Date: Hunnic-Turk, 5th–9th cent. (stylistic).

Description: Some ruins and caves. A stucco Shiva figure was found by chance here.

Source: Hayashi and Sahara 1962: 106—mention.

1219. URLAND TEPE

Original: Lat. 36° 52' N, long. 66° 20' E. Map 25.
Revised: 36.87182555 N, 66.32756415 E /
36° 52' 18.57197712 N, 66° 19' 39.23092848 E.
Jauzjān Province. 18 km south-east of Āqcha, 1 km south of the road to Balkh, more or less in front of tepe no. 935.

Description: Rectangular platform (*c.*100 × 80 m), surrounded by a ditch (under cultivatation); maximum height in the south-east (6 m). Small mounds nearby; all are very eroded.

Fieldwork: 1948 Le Berre, DAFA—survey.

Source: M. Le Berre: unpublished 1948 report, DAFA archives, tepe P. 17.

1220. URTA BUZ
Including TAKHTA KUPRUK and TEPE ABDAL.

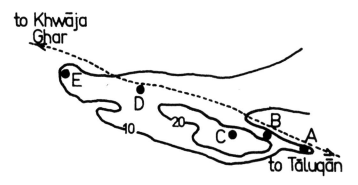

1220 Urta Buz (J.-C. Gardin).

Original: Lat. 36° 44'–36° 45' N, long. 69° 26'–69° 30' E.
Fig 54.3, Map 36.
Revised:
36.75038286 N, 69.4575223 E /
36° 45' 01.37829924 N, 69° 27' 27.08029368 E (D).
36.75622524 N, 69.43313927 E /
36° 45' 22.41085320 N, 69° 25' 59.30138352 E (E).
Takhār Province. Natural promontory parallel to the Tālu-qān River, (right bank), a few km west of the town of the same name; length 6 km, width 1 km, variable altitude (10–20 m), higher on the slope to the river, to the south, than on the side of the plain, to the north.

Dates: Late Chalcolithic–Early Bronze Age, *c.*3500–2500 BC; Bronze, 2nd mill. BC; beg. Iron, end 2nd–beg. 1st mill. BC; Hellenistic, 3rd–1st cent. BC (D); some sherds of the Kushan (except E) and Islamic (except A) periods (ceramic).

Description: (A) Area of sherds (100 × 20 m) at the eastern end of Urta Buz, on the top (height 8 m), on the edge of the road from Tāluqān to Khwaja Ghar. (B) Area of sherds (100 × 50 m) 1.2 km west of A, at the top of Urta Buz (10 m) on the edge of the same road. (C) Area of sherds 1 km west of B, near two little mausolea 100 m apart, located on the southern edge of Urta Buz, at about 500 m south of the road. (D) Tepe Abdal, in the village of the same name: two round mounds (diam. 30 m, height 3 and 5 m), situated on the northern edge of Urta Buz, above the same road; modern tombs on both mounds. (E) 600 m east of Takhta Kupruk, on the Tāluqān road (200 m south of the road), oval east–west mound (300 × 100 m), at the foot of the western end of Urta Buz; flat top, on two levels; 5 m at western end, 7 m in the eastern half, with a *zīyārat* on each bump and modern tombs over all the surface. This long mound, evidence of a geological period, provides sherds of the Bronze Age collected over quite extensive areas, either on flat ground (A, B), sometimes near relatively late ruins (C), or on tepes of the Hellenistic or Kushan period (D, E). The location of these five points is indicated in figure 54.3.

Collection: National Museum/AIA — sherds.

Fieldwork: 1977 Gardin et al., CNRS — survey.

Sources:
1. Site information by J.-C. Gardin.
2. Gardin and Lyonnet 1978–9: pl. IX — nos. 234–8.
3. Lyonnet 1981 — brief description of site, description, discussion, and illustration of the Chal. (mid-4th–mid-3rd mill.) pottery, and discussion of the geographical and historical implications.
4. Gardin 1995: 93 — mention.
5. Lyonnet 1997: figs 7, 25, 35–7 — nos. 234–8.
6. Gardin 1998: 70 — nos. 234–8.

1221. ŪRUZGĀN
Or QAL'A-I ACHAKZAI. See also 320 FARĀMĀZ.

Lat. 32° 58' N, long. 66° 39' E. Map 76.
Ūruzgān Province. 280 km north-east of Kandahār, in the Hazārajāt. The site is 5 km north of the town.

Dates: Turki Shahi, 7th–8th cent.; Ghaznavid, 11th–12th cent. (epigraphic).

Description: A boulder with a cursive Bactrian inscription, in the same style as Bād-i Asyā, and an Arabic inscription.

Sources:
1. Bivar 1954a — description and linguistic analysis.
2. Humbach 1966–7: I. 103–4 — brief linguistic analysis.
3. Habibi 1969/70b: 2–11 — photos and linguistic discussion of the Bactrian inscription.
4. Habibi 1971: 55–6 — discusses the inscription and the development of Afghan epigraphy.
5. Habibi 1974 — summary of the inscriptions, ascribing them to the Hephthalite period.

6. Davary 1977 — mention and bibliography.
7. Habibi 1977 — discusses the inscription.
8. Rahman 1979: 235–7 — linguistic analysis.

1222. URYĀKHĒL
Or KUNJAKAI.

Lat. 34° 33' N, long. 68° 58' E. Map 63.
Kābul Province. 5 km south of Paghmān, between Cheheltān and Baiktūt.

Date: Kushan-Kushano-Sasanian, 1st–4th cent AD (stylistic).

Description: Remains of a very large diaper masonry stupa on a square base decorated with Indo-Corinthian pilasters with a staircase on one side. Very similar in size and construction to Guldarra.

Fieldwork: 2005 Paiman, AIA — excavation.

Sources:
1. Caspani 1947b: 49 — mentions Buddhist remains.
2. Paiman 2005 — brief report on the discovery and excavations.
3. Fussman, Murad, and Ollivier 2008: 113–17, 201, and 304 — description and photo of the excavations.

ŪSHTAR. See **2190 QAL'A-I ĪSHTAR** in Supplement.

1223. USMĀN

Original: Lat. 34° 25' N, long. 69° 16' E. Map 62.
Revised: 34.42411147 N, 69.26204347 E /
34° 25' 26.80127616 N, 69° 15' 43.35649812 E.
Kābul Province. C. 1 km south-east of the Yakh-darra stupa between Surkh Minār and the Minār-i Chakri, 2.5 km south-east of the village of Usman.

Date: Kushan-Turki Shahi, 1st–9th cent. (architectural).

Description: The very badly eroded remains of several stupas and associated monastery enclosures, together with a well-preserved stupa, still with a frieze of blind arches and Indo-Corinthian pilasters.

Fieldwork: 1972 Fussman, CNRS — survey.

Sources:
1. Holdich 1881b: 23 — brief description of the stupa, mistaking it for the base of a minar.
2. Ball 1984 — discusses evidence for the function and a possible later date, on the mistaken interpretation by Holdich as a minar.
3. Fussman et al. 2008: 37–43, 245–52, and 299–300 — detailed description, photos, and drawings ('Shevaki 6–9').

USTKHĀN ZĀR. See **2276 USTKHĀN ZĀR** in Supplement.

1224. UTĀQ
Including BĀJAURI.

Original: Lat. 37° 00' N, long. 69° 10'–69° 11' E. Maps 31, 32.
Revised: 37.00446891 N, 69.17063025 E /
37° 00' 16.08808104 N, 69° 10' 14.26890216 E.
Qundūz Province. 12 km south-west of Archi, between two branches of the canal called Nahr-i Ārchī Kuhna; accessible by a dirt road which runs along the canal from Archi. Tepe A is located 100 m north of this road.

Dates: Hellenistic, 3rd–1st cent. BC (B); Kushan and Hunnic-Turk, 1st–9th cent. (A, B); some Islamic sherds (ceramic).

Description: (A) High quadrangular mound (c.100 × 100 m), cut into at the base by irrigated crops which surround it on all sides. The top is a square platform (c.50 × 50 m) whose highest point is at the north-west angle (about 12 m). (B) 900 m to the east, on the northern side of the same road, a low platform (0.60 m) of irregular form (c.70 × 30 m) is hardly distinguishable in the fields of cotton, detectable in three little mounds (2–3 m) which mark the angles.

Collection: National Museum/AIA—sherds.

Fieldwork: 1977 Gardin et al., CNRS—survey.

Sources:
1. Site information by J.-C. Gardin.
2. Gardin and Lyonnet 1978–9: pl. IV—nos. 43–4.
3. Lyonnet 1997: figs 39, 49, 68, 69—nos. 43, 44
4. Gardin 1998: 57—nos. 43–4.

1225. UVLIA TEPE
Or AULIA TEPE.

Original: Lat. 37° 06' N, long. 66° 42' E. Map 26.
Revised: 37.07777518 N, 66.71790917 E /
37° 04' 39.99065232 N, 66° 43' 04.47301020 E.
Balkh Province. 2 km north-west of Farukhābād 1, in the dunes north of Qarchigak, c.40 km north-west of Balkh.

Date: Achaemenid, 6th–4th cent. BC (ceramic).

Description: A large site c.1 km diam., partially buried in the sands. On the south side is a mound, c.60 m diam. and 4 m high, circular in plan, reminiscent of the round temple at Dashli 3. It has double circular walls forming an internal gallery, enclosing a series of transverse walls. Two periods of construction were recognised. Construction is of *pakhsa* block.

Fieldwork: 1973 Kruglikova, Af/Sov. Mission—excavations.

Source: Kruglikova 1973b: 13–24—detailed excavation report.

1226. WAHANA NAWARID

Original: Lat. 36° 45' N, long. 66° 46' E. Map 26.
Revised: 36.74629123 N, 66.76239661 E /
36° 44' 46.64843304 N, 66° 45' 44.62781184 E.
Balkh Province. 2 km due west of Balkh and 5 km east of Chār Būlāq, just to the east of the canal.

Description: A group of mounds.

Fieldwork: 1886 Maitland, ABC—topographical survey.

Source: Maitland 1888b: 175—mention.

WAISUR. See 2144 KONDI in Supplement.

WAKHSHI. See 2277 WAKHSHI in Supplement.

1227. WALAKAI

Original: Lat. 36° 47' N, long. 66° 49' E. Map 26.
Revised:
36.79542154 N, 66.80635178 E /
36° 47' 43.51753824 N, 66° 48' 22.86641844 E (A).
36.79133868 N, 66.81581024 E /
36° 47' 28.81925916 N, 66° 48' 56.91686652 E (B).
Balkh Province. 8 km north-west of this town; c.1.5 km north of the Āqcha road, on the eastern edge of a marshy depression extending from north to south over several kilometres (old river bed?), along which several tepes are located.

Description: Two mounds about 500 m apart. From north to south: (A) Small tepe of square plan (c.100 × 100 m), height 8 m, surrounded by a ditch; in the eastern part, traces of constructions; to the west, courtyard enclosed by walls, the whole suggesting a 'farm'. (B) Rectangular mound (c.150 × 110 m), height 12 m, very damaged by erosion, possibly surrounded by a ditch (stagnant water at the western base of the tepe).

Fieldwork:
1. 1946 Wheeler, ASI—reconnaissance.
2. 1948 Le Berre, DAFA—survey.

Sources:
1. M. Le Berre: unpublished 1948 report, DAFA archives, tepes P. 3 and P. 4.
2. Shakur 1947: 68—mention.

WAL'A-I KIZIL KUL. See 2274 TŪTACHĪ in Supplement.

1228. WALI KHĀN

Original: Lat. 30° 58' N, long. 64° 10' E. approximately. Map 97.
Revised: 31.00535988 N, 64.17868208 E /
31° 00' 19.29557304 N, 64° 10' 43.25550276 E.
Helmand Province. On the left bank of the Helmand just south of Basābād, between Kuchnai Darwīshān and Miānpushta.

Date: Samanid-Ghaznavid, 10th–12th cent. (ceramic).

Description: A mound.

Fieldwork: 1966 Hammond, Cambridge University—survey.

Source: Hammond 1970: 449—lists site (no. 22) and describes the pottery types and general survey results.

1229. WARDAK
Or BĪRĀNA or KHAWĀT or KUHWĀT or SEIĀB.

Original: Lat. 34° 08' N, long. 68° 38' E. Map 60.
Revised: 34.12477847 N, 68.50252463 E /
34° 07' 29.20248012 N, 68° 30' 09.08867160 E.
Wardak Province. Near Chak-i Wardak 14 km west of the Kābul-Ghazni road, on the road to Besūd.

Date: Kushan, 2nd–3rd cent. (architectural, ceramic).

Description: A large fortified urban site with a regular, grid street plan and inner and outer enclosures. The outer enclosure is strengthened at regular intervals by round towers, and is further defended on two sides by a ditch.

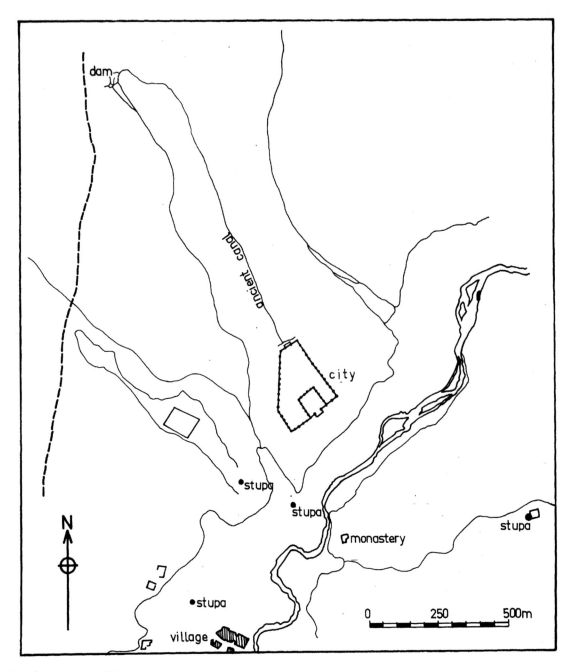

1229 Wardak (after Fussman 1974a).

There is only one entrance. Outside the walled city there are many more remains, including a dam and canal system, a fortified monastery complex, and some five or six stupas, one of which contained metal vases, a steatite vase with a Kharoshthi inscription, and several Kushan coins.

Collections: BM—stupa deposits and coins.

Fieldwork:
1. 1836 Masson (absentee), East India Co.—excavation.
2. 1964, 1967, 1969–72 Fussman, CNRS—survey.
3. 2005 Besenval, DAFA.

Sources:
1. Vigne 1840: 140—mentions the site and Masson's work.
2. Masson 1841: 117–18—vague description of the site and the contents of the stupa.
3. Masson 1842: II. 223—mentions the site and dates it to 4th–5th cent. AD.
4. Prinsep 1858: 161–5—transliteration and discussion of the inscription.
5. Bayley 1861—discusses Mitra's translation of the inscription.
6. Mitra 1861—very detailed linguistic analysis of the inscription, with transcription and translation of the text.
7. Dowson 1863: 229–34 and 255–66—detailed discussion and translation of the inscription.
8. Thomas 1863: 235 n. 24—lists the inscription in a general discussion of the Bactrian alphabet.
9. Senart 1890: 121—text and note on the inscription.
10. Senart 1894: 515—brief note on the translation of the inscription.
11. Lüders 1909: 661–2—discusses the inscription.
12. Pargiter 1912—brief linguistic analysis, text, translation, and conclusion that it is a monastery dedication.
13. Grierson 1913—linguistic discussion of the phonestics of the inscription and its modern linguistic connotations.
14. Partiger 1914—brief linguistic note on the phonetics of the inscription, and corrections of his earlier translation.
15. Senart 1914—detailed linguistic discussion and new reading of the inscription.
16. Hultzsch 1919—linguistic discussion of the inscription.
17. Konow 1929: 157–8—full linguistic analysis, translation, and discussion of the inscription, with photos. Review of previous work.
18. Caspani and Cagnacci 1951: 248—mention the site and inscription.
19. Habibi 1971: 132—photos of the vase and discussion of the development of Afghan epigraphy.
20. Fussman 1974—detailed description of the remains and description and catalogue of the surface pottery.
21. Kieffer 1975: 49—mention (as Bīrāna).
22. Davary 1977—mentions the inscription and gives a bibliography.
23. Kuwayama 1991: 84–6—discussion of the evidence from Begram III for the chronology.
24. Ball 2008: 272–3—summary.
25. Jongeward et al. 2012—catalogue and discussion of the reliquaries.
26. Errington 2017a: 200–11 and 2017b: 64, 113, 115—the Masson collection and archive relating to the site.

WARQA-I GULSHĀH. See 1054 SHĀH SALĪM BĀBĀ TEPE.

1230. WARZU
Or KERĀNO-MUNJĀN.

Original: Lat. 36° 01' N, long. 70° 43' E. Map 38.
Revised: 36.01729281 N, 70.72120512 E /
36° 01' 02.25412392 N, 70° 43' 16.33841472 E.
Badakhshān Province. On the Kokcha, near the junction of routes to Wākhān, Andarāb, and Nūristān, 4 km east of Iskazr.

Date: Ghaznavid, 1st half of 11th cent. (stylistic).

Description: The Madrasa-i Warzu, a building with a primitive form of squinch and the remains of paintings.

Sources: Gardner 1971: 121–3—brief description.

WATAGAN TEPE. See 307 DŪN QISHLĀQ.

1231. WAZĀN

Lat. 35° 53' N, long. 66° 40' E. Map 47.
Balkh Province. On the west bank of the Amrakh River about midway between Zari and Bakhtagān.

Description: A group of ruined forts and castles high up on the hill behind the village. They have many large towers still standing, similar to Chehel Burj.

Fieldwork: 1885 Sahibdad Khan, ABC—topographical survey.

Source: Sahibdad Khan 1888: 149—brief description.

1232. WAZĪRĀBĀD
Or DAHAN-I SHIR.

Original: Lat. 35° 59' N, long. 68° 40' E. Map 33.
Revised: 35.97822388 N, 68.6820752 E / 35° 58' 41.60595936 N, 68° 40' 55.47070236 E.

Baghlān Province. 6 km north-west of Pul-i Khumri on the east bank of the river.

Date: Kushan, 1st–3rd cent. (numismatic, stylistic).

Description: Remains of a large Buddhist monastery complex, much of it destroyed by road building. The main stupa had been opened illicitly; it stands in a rectangular enclosure. There are two more stupas to the north-west and north-east, and another stupa-monastery complex higher up on the hill. The finds include fragments of a near life-size statue of a horse and rider, decorations of unbaked clay, and coins.

Fieldwork:
1. 1946 Wheeler, ASI—reconnaissance.
2. 1956 Ramachandran and Sharma, ASI—reconnaissance.
3. 1968 Mustamandi, AIA—excavations.

Sources:
1. Shakur 1947: 43–4—brief description.
2. Caspani and Cagnacci 1951: 236—mention.
3. Ramachandran and Sharma 1956: I. 26—brief description.
4. N. Dupree 1977: 369—brief description.

1233. WAZĪR KHĀN

Original: Lat. 36° 58' N, long. 69° 09' E. Maps 31, 32.
Revised:
36.9608614 N, 69.15342439 E /
36° 57' 39.10102668 N, 69° 09' 12.32779968 E,
36.9616018 N, 69.15860851 E /
36° 57' 41.76649008 N, 69° 09' 30.99063564 E, and
36.96093583 N, 69.15471332 E /
36° 57' 39.36898944 N, 69° 09' 16.96795092 E.
Qundūz Province. About 1 km north of the village of Wazīr Khān, itself situated at about 7 km south-west of Archi, by the Qundūz road; access to the site is to the north by a road which leads from the mosque of Wazīr Khān, on the southern branch of the Ārchī canal (Nahr-i Jadīd).

Dates: Hellenistic, 3rd–1st cent. BC; Kushan, 1st- 3rd cent.; Islamic period, not specified (ceramic).

Description: Two tepes 500 m apart (on an east–west line): rectangular east–west platforms (100 × 80 m), height 3–4 m with the highest part at the western end (5–6 m). Smaller mounds 100 m to the north and the south.

Collection: National Museum/AIA—sherds.

Fieldwork: 1977 Gardin et al., CNRS—survey.

Sources:
1. Site information by J.-C. Gardin.
2. Gardin and Lyonnet 1978–9: pl. IV—nos. 62–5.
3. Lyonnet 1997: 39, 49—nos. 62–6.
4. Gardin 1998: 57—nos. 62–6.

1234. WURSHAK
See also 114 BASHURA and 864 QAL'A-I MĀLIK ANTAR.

Lat. 33° 23' N, long. 64° 34' E. Maps 55, 74.
Ghūr Province. 13 km south-west of Yamān, south-east of Taiwāra.

Date: Ghurid, 12th–13th cent. (architectural, geographic).

Description: Remains of a square fort on a hill overlooking the village. The foundations, up to 3 m high, are built of large stones, and the mud-brick walls on top of that are covered in a yellow clay plaster.

Fieldwork: 1946 Kohzad, HSA—survey.

Sources:
1. Kohzad 1951–4, 9/1: 31—brief description.
2. Ball 2002: 39—mention.

YAHAN. See 1236 YAKHAN-I PA'IN.

1235. YAKA TŪT
Includes NAWĀBĀD and QIZIL QAL'A.

Original: Lat. 37° 13'–37° 20' N, long. 69° 44' E. Map 35.
Revised:
37.21664031 N, 69.74196109 E /
37° 12' 59.90512896 N, 69° 44' 31.05991860 E (A).
37.2473072 N, 69.74432177 E / 37° 14' 50.30593188 N, 69° 44' 39.55837452 E (C).
37.33378012 N, 69.73492811 E / 37° 20' 01.60843164 N, 69° 44' 05.74117836 E (D).
Takhār Province. On the outskirts of the villages which edge the left bank of the Rustāq River north of Bish Kapa: Qizil Qal'a, Nawābād, Yaka Tūt. These villages are situated on a terrace edge which continues the alignment already observed for the sites of the region of Bish Kapa itself, due to the same topographical factor (see no. 135). (A) The tepe of Qizil Qal'a is 1 km north-north-west of the point where the stream descending from the foothills of Rustāq (see no. 960) flows into the Rustāq River; the village school is constructed on the tepe. (B) About 2 km to the north, in the village of Nawābād, the edge of the terrace is hillocky, but sherds are found only near certain mounds, near the place where the river narrows between Bai Nazar and Nawābād. (C) 1 km further north, a small tepe appears some 300 m south-east of the ruins (late) which extend to the south of Yaka Tūt (indicated on the 1:100,000 map); its importance lies in the age of the sherds found, from the Achaemenid period. (D) From there up to the fork to Chayāb, the only apparent tepes are two neighbouring mounds located on the edge of the plateau which overlooks by 20 m the Rustāq River on the right bank, about 1 km east-north-east of the village of Pushtak-i Bālā.

Dates: Beg. Iron, end 2nd–beg. 1st mill. BC (C); pre-Mongol Islamic, 10th–13th cent.; Timurid, 15th–16th cent. (ceramic).

Description: (A) Rectangular platform (70 × 30 m) recut to serve as a terreplein for the school of Nawābād, height 6 m. (B) Area of collection in the hillocky zone indicated above, *c*.100 × 100 m. (C) Low mound of irregular form (20 × 20 m), surrounded by crops (*lalmī*); *zīyārat* on the top (1m). (D) Two hillocks 20 m apart in a zone of cultivation (*lalmī*); diam. 15 m, height 2 m.

Collection: National Museum/AIA—sherds.

Fieldwork: 1978 Gardin et al., CNRS—survey.

Sources:
1. Site information by J.-C. Gardin.
2. Gardin and Lyonnet 1978–9: pl. II—nos. 528–31.
3. Lyonnet 1997: figs 25, 35—nos. 528–31.
4. Gardin 1998: 92—nos. 528–31.

YAKA TŪTU TEPE. See 1131 TĀJ-I BAI TEPE.

YAK DARAKHT. See **2278 YAK DARAKHT** in Supplement.

1236. YAKHAN-I PĀ'ĪN
Or YAHAN.

Original: Lat. 33° 27' N, long. 64° 17' E. Maps 54, 74.
Revised: 33.45987383 N, 64.29087031 E /
33° 27' 35.54577288 N, 64° 17' 27.13311204 E.
Ghūr Province. 5 km south-east of Waras, *c*.15 km south-west of Taiwāra on the road to Parjuman.

Date: Ghurid, 12th–13th cent. (architectural).

Description: Ruins of many mud-brick forts and towers, up to 12 m high, connecting with a line of watch towers. North of the ruins are the remains of some tombs.

Fieldwork: 1885 Imam Sharif, ABC—topographical survey.

Sources:
1. Holdich 1887: 26—mentions the ruins and tombs.
2. Imam Sharif 1891a: 207—brief description.
3. Sahibdad Khan 1891a: 244—mention.
4. Klimburg 1958: 18—mention.
5. Klimburg 1960: 49—mention.
6. Fischer 1978a: 335—mention and photos.
7. Rafat 1980: 5—mention.
8. Ball 2002: 33–6—description and photos.

1237. YAKHDARRA
See also 1087 SHĪWAKĪ.

Original: Lat. 34° 25' N, long. 69° 16' E. Map 62.
Revised: 34.43169977 N, 69.26937669 E /
34° 25' 54.11918928 N, 69° 16' 09.75610128 E.
Kābul Province. 2 km south-west of Shīwakī stupa, 1 km south of the village of Yakhdarra, at the foot of the hills to the south of Kābul.

Date: Kushan-Hunnic, 1st–6th cent. (architectural).

Description: The remains of two stupas and associated monastery enclosures.

Fieldwork:
1. 1833 Honigberger—excavation.
2. 1834 Masson—survey.
3. 1965 Mizuno, Kyoto University—survey.
4. 1972 Fussman, CNRS—survey.

Sources:
1. Jacquet 1836b: 254–62—full description and illustrations of Honigberger's discoveries.
2. Masson 1841: 114—mention.
3. Frye 1946a—photo and brief description and discussion.
4. Mizuno 1971: 124–5—brief description and photos.
5. Fussman et al. 2008: 35–7, 242–4, and 299–300—detailed description, photos, and drawings ('Shevaki 3, 4, and 5').

1238. YAKHKHĀNA

Lat. 30° 49' N, long. 62° 05' approximately. Map 92.
Nīmrūz Province. In the dunes north of Masjid-i Shahr-i Kalān, between Shahr-i Kalān and Kūrdū.

Description: Ruins of an old ice-house or cistern with a collapsed dome. This was probably a seasonal open pool of water, or large excavation to a high water table, in a small 15th–century bazaar. It is just one remain in the vast Sar-o-Tar region of 150 sites, and hardly merits separate mention.

Fieldwork:
1. 1903–5 Tate, SAC—survey.
2. 1971–4 Trousdale, Smithsonian Institution—survey.

Sources:
1. Additional information by W. Trousdale.
2. Tate 1910: 239–40—brief description.

1239. YAMĀN

Original: Lat. 33° 28' N, long. 64° 43' E. Maps 55, 74.
Revised: 33.47486652 N, 64.70837244 E /
33° 28' 29.51946552 N, 64° 42' 30.14079408 E.
Ghūr Province. 38 km east of Taiwāra.

Date: ?Ghurid, 12th–13th cent. (architectural, geographical).

Description: Ruins covering a very extensive area, consisting of isolated, unconnected towers and small forts. Each is separated by *c*.100 m, they do not appear to form any pattern. They are round or square, with plain arched entrances. Construction is generally of mud-brick, though stone and even wood are sometimes used. There are also many burials with 'brass' burial cups at their heads and feet.

Fieldwork:
1. 1885 Imam Sharif, ABC—topographical survey.
2. Peacocke 1887a: 211—report from hearsay.
3. 1946 Kohzad, HSA—survey.

Sources:
1. Holdich 1887: 30—mentions the remains and the burials.
2. Imam Sharif 1891b: 217—brief description.
3. Kohzad 1951–4, 9/1: 29—description.
4. Klimburg 1958: 18—mention.
5. Klimburg 1960: 49—brief description and photo.
6. Janata 1971: 57—mentions the ruins.
7. Ball 2002: 37–9—brief description.
8. Wannell 2002—brief description.
9. Ball 2008: 273—summary.

1240. YANGI ĀRIQ
Or KUHNA QAL'A.

Original: Lat. 36° 42' N, long. 67° 54' E. Map 29.
Revised: 36.70301768 N, 67.90399528 E /
36° 42' 10.86363072 N, 67° 54' 14.38301448 E.
Samangān Province. 12 km east of Tāshqurghān, on the Qundūz road.

Dates: Sasanian-Hunnic, Turk, pre-Mongol Islamic, 4th–13th cent.; Timurid, 15th–16th cent. (ceramic).

Description: Area of sherds around ruins of an abandoned village. The water for irrigation from the Samangān River does not come this far.

Collection: National Museum/AIA—sherds.

Fieldwork: 1969 Gouin, DAFA—survey.

Source: Gouin 1974 and unpublished report—site no. 13.

YANG QAL'A. See **2279 YANG QAL'A, Jauzjān, in Supplement.**

1241. YANG QAL'A, BALKH

Original: Lat. 36° 41' N, long. 66° 45' E. Map 28.
Revised: 36.68442807 N, 66.76084028 E /
36° 41' 03.94106316 N, 66° 45' 39.02500836 E.
Balkh Province. On the river c.16 km south-west of Balkh.

Description: A conspicuous mound in the centre of the village, with a domed *zīyārat* known as Bābā Kushkak on top.

Source: Gazetteer 1979: IV. 598—mention.

1242. YARIK SARDĀBA

Original: Lat. 37° 07' N, long. 66° 31' E. Maps 25, 26.
Revised: 37.1232275 N, 66.51994421 E / 37° 07' 23.61900612 N, 66° 31' 11.79914700 E.

Balkh Province. 53 km north-west of Balkh on the road to Kilift, north of the Dashli Oasis.

Description: A mound covered in baked bricks, marking the site of an old caravanserai and cistern.

Fieldwork: 1886 Peacocke, ABC—topographical survey.

Sources:
1. Peacocke 1887a: 318—mention.
2. Gazetteer 1979: IV. 598—mention.

1243. YARTI GUMBAZ
Or ORTA GUMBAZ. See also 1099 SIĀHGIRD.

Original: Lat. 36° 59' N, long. 67° 07' E. Map 27.
Revised: 36.98441042 N, 67.12740803 E /
36° 59' 03.87751596 N, 67° 07' 38.66891412 E.
Balkh Province. 8 km north of Siāhgird, 32 km north of Mazār-i Sharīf.

Date: Late Sasanian, 6th–7th cent. (architectural).

Description: Extensive mounds and ruins marking an urban site, surrounding a large mud-brick stupa on a larger mound. This consists of a large mud-brick dome on a slight rise, solid apart from two double-storeyed through passages at right angles to each other. Surrounded by entrance area of mound. One of the passages bears on Pata Hisar; a beacon at night therefore would be a guide over main caravan route to Balkh.

Fieldwork:
1. 1886 Peacocke, ABC—topographical survey.
2. 1972–3 Pugachenkova, Af/Sov. Mission—survey.

Sources:
1. Peacocke 1887a: 304—detailed description.
2. Hackin 1933: 63—mention.
3. Melikian-Chirvani 1974: 5—mention as a possible 'Buddho-Islamic' site.
4. Pugachenkova 1976b—mention.
5. Gazetteer 1979: IV. 546—mention.

1244. YURUGHLI

Original: Lat. 36° 45' N, long. 65° 53' E. Maps 24.
Revised: 36.75695858 N, 65.87562132 E /
36° 45' 25.05090168 N, 65° 52' 32.23674156 E.
Jauzjān Province. C.16 km north-east of Shībarghān, just to the south of the road to Āqcha.

Date: Early Islamic, 10th–13th cent. (ceramic).

Description: A complex of mounds and ruined walls surrounded by debris. It is dominated by a square, steep-sided fortress mound, 300 m square and 13 m high, surrounded by a ditch.

Fieldwork:
1. 1886 Maitland, ABC—topographical survey.
2. 1938 Barger, ASI—survey.

Sources:
1. Maitland 1888b: 169—mention.
2. Barger and Wright 1941: 54—brief description and photo.

YŪSUF DARRA. See 2280 YŪSUF DARRA in Supplement.

1245. ZĀDIYĀN

See also 8 ABU HURAIRA, 520 KAM PIRAK, 814 PIT QAL'A TEPE, 1188 TEPE ZĀDIYĀN, 2053 DAULATĀBĀD, Minaret, in Supplement, and 2281 ZĀDIYĀN KĀFIR QAL'A in Supplement.

Original: Lat. 37° 02' N, long. 66° 56' E. Map 27.
Revised:
37.04225323 N, 66.94542819 E /
37° 02' 32.11161360 N, 66° 56' 43.54150020 E (A).
37.03665555 N, 66.94535932 E /
37° 02' 11.95998900 N, 66° 56' 43.29355884 E (B).
Balkh Province. 34 km north of this town, north of and near the town of Zādiyān; 14 km north-east of the village of Daulatābād.

Dates: Kushan-Hunnic-Turk, 1st–9th cent. (ceramic).

Description: An extremely ruined, but recognizable, large stupa built in mud-bricks of the same type as those of the stupas of Balkh. At the centre of the monument a central bulb appears which could be a smaller more primitive stupa. South of the stupa is the minaret of Daulatābād (see separate entry).

Fieldwork: 1948 Le Berre, DAFA—survey.

Source:
1. Le Berre 1958: unpublished report, DAFA archives, tepes P. 52 and P. 53.
2. Ball 2008: 187—summary.

ZĀDIYĀN KAFIR QAL'A. See 2281 ZĀDIYĀN KĀFIR QAL'A in Supplement.

ZAGHCHA GUZAR. See 959 RŪD-I SHĀHRAWĀN.

1246. ZĀHIR KHĀN

Original: Lat. 32° 19' N, long. 63° 13' E. approximately. Map 73.
Revised: 32.36729074 N, 63.20820103 E /
32° 22' 02.24666904 N, 63° 12' 29.52369576 E.
Farāh Province. C.110 km south of Farāh Rūd on the west side of the road, on the Charāgh Rūd near the 775 km post (from Kābul).

Description: Remains of a rectangular fortress, c.35 × 20 m in area and 12 m in height, built of slabs of stone in mud mortar.

Fieldwork: 1974 Swiny, BIAS—survey.

Source: Site information by S. Swiny in unpublished BIAS archive.

1247. ZAKAN-O ZURKAN

Original: Lat. 31° 03' N, long. 62° 07' E. Map 92.
Revised: 31.04700154 N, 62.10211599 E /
31° 02' 49.20552816 N, 62° 06' 07.61757840 E.
Nīmrūz Province. C.15 km south of Chakhānsūr, between Qal'a-i Chigīnī and the site of Jūi Nau.

Dates: Sasanian, 3rd–7th cent.; early Islamic, 8th–13th cent. (ceramic).

Description: Remains of a polygonal mud-brick structure. 2 km to the east is another small ruin.

Fieldwork: 1965–8 Fischer, Bonn University—survey.

Sources:
1. Fischer 1969: 335—mention (Ruin D2).
2. Fischer et al. 1974–6: 37—mention (Ruins 14 and 26).

ZAKAR TEPE. See 290 DEH WARDA.

1248. ZAKIRD

Original: Lat. 31° 32' N, long. 65° 45' E. Map 89.
Revised: 31.54321299 N, 65.74596882 E /
31° 32' 35.56677264 N, 65° 44' 45.48776388 E.
Kandahār Province. 9 km south-east of this city.

Dates: Indo-Parthian, 1st–4th cent.; Sasano-Turki Shahi, 5th–9th cent.; pre-Mongol Islamic, 10th–13th cent.; Timurid, 15th–16th cent. (ceramic).

Description: Large shapeless tepe located near a village, serving as a source of fuel for it. According to some informants, excavations have already been carried out on this tepe.

Collection: National Museum/AIA—sherds.

Fieldwork:
1. 1951 Casal, DAFA—survey.
2. 1966 Fischer, DAAD—survey.

Sources:
1. Casal: unpublished 1951 report, DAFA archives.
2. Fischer 1967a: 151—mention.
3. Fischer 1969: 339—mention.

1249. ZALA KHĀN

Original: Lat. 31° 32' N, long. 65° 35' E. Map 89.
Revised: 31.53028059 N, 65.60335623 E /
31° 31' 49.01011644 N, 65° 36' 12.08244456 E.
Kandahār province. 15 km east of Panjwāyī and 1.5 km south-east of Chilkur.

Dates: Indo-Parthian, 1st–4th cent.; pre-Mongol Islamic, 10th–13th cent. (ceramic).

Description: Low square mound, flat top about 4 m high, cut by a 'jui' and surrounded by crops.

Collection: National Museum/AIA—sherds.

Fieldwork: 1951 Casal, DAFA—survey.

Source: Casal: unpublished 1951 report, DAFA archives.

1250. ZĀL QALʼA

Original: Lat. 36° 48' N, long. 66° 43' E. Map 26.
Revised: 36.80196692 N, 66.71217116 E /
36° 48' 07.08092820 N, 66° 42' 43.81616520 E.
Balkh Province. 19 km south-east of Nimlik, south of the village of Zāl Qalʼa, north of the road to Balkh.

Description: Shapeless mound, about 6 m high; the top carries traces of excavation.

Fieldwork: 1948 Le Berre, DAFA—survey.

Source: Le Berre 1958: unpublished report, DAFA archives tepe P. 46.

1251. ZĀMBUKĀN

Lat. 36° 42' N, long. 66° 56' E. Map 27.
Balkh Province. 7 km south-east of Balkh, between the Pul-i Imāmbukri and Dehdādi roads.

Date: Middle Palaeolithic, 50,000–30,000 BC (lithic).

Description: Accidental discovery from an irrigation canal near here of a Mousterian flake tool, similar to material from Teshik Tash.

Sources:
1. Allchin 1953—brief note and drawing of the tool.
2. Allchin 1957: 132—mention.

1252. ZANGU
Or SANGAR.

Original: Lat. 30° 10' N, long. 62° 18' E. Map 95.
Revised: 30.20464247 N, 62.22442475 E /
30° 12' 16.71289560 N, 62° 13' 27.92908272 E.
Nīmrūz Province. On the left bank of the Helmand, opposite and a little upstream from Deh Khaju. 2 km west of Qalʼa-i Madar-i Padshah, on left (south) bank.

Dates: Achaemenid, 6th–4th cent.; Seleucid and Parthian, 4th–1st cent. BC; Indo-Parthian and Sasanian, 1st–7th cent. (ceramic).

Description: Two parallel banks of earth with a high mound at one end. In the eroded surface of the mound some drystone walls are visible. Remains of a small fort surrounded by a ditch. Inside is a high rectangular

mound. There are more remains further west on the river bank.

Fieldwork:
1. 1884 Maitland, Peacocke, ABC—topographical survey.
2. 1966 Hammond, Cambridge University—survey.

Sources:
1. Peacocke 1885a: 3—mention (unnamed).
2. Maitland 1888a: 61–2—brief description.
3. Peacocke 1887a: 17—mention.
4. Hammond 1970: 450—lists site (no. 450) and describes the pottery types and general survey results.

ZARANJ. See 75. NĀD-I 'ALĪ.

ZARANKA. See 274 DEH-I ĀDĀM KHĀN.

1253. ZARD KAMAR

Original: Lat. 37° 26'–37° 28' N, long. 69° 37'–69° 39' E. Map 34.
Revised:
37.49954161 N, 69.65987314 E / 37° 29' 58.34980212 N, 69° 39' 35.54329212 E,
37.50023605 N, 69.66089112 E / 37° 30' 00.84976416 N, 69° 39' 39.20803848 E,
37.45095097 N, 69.63597887 E / 37° 27' 03.42350964 N, 69° 38' 09.52394244 E,
37.44630024 N, 69.62660762 E / 37° 26' 46.68088164 N, 69° 37' 35.78741508 E, and
37.42425585 N, 69.60577611 E / 37° 25' 27.32105316 N, 69° 36' 20.79398592 E.
Takhār Province. At the foot of the hills that edge the plain of Yangi Qalʼa, towards the east, several small sites which are difficult to find line the foothills for a distance of about 3 km, from the village of Zard Kamar to the hamlet of Kalafgani, to the north-east.

Dates: Beg. Iron, end 2nd–beg. 1st mill. BC; Achaemenid, 6th–4th cent. BC; Kushan, 1st–4th cent.; pre-Mongol Islamic, 10th–13th cent. (ceramic).

Description: Hillocky area covering a surface of about 2 hectares (200 m north-east/south-west × 100 m north-west/south-east), on the south-west edge of the road that links Zard Kamar to Yangi Qalʼa from this site. In the holes dug for the tombs which today occupy this area, whole jars are often visible, fallen or standing, as well as fragments of fired brick. According to the villagers, digging the ground, among the houses of Zard Kamar, produces similar pottery in quantity (verified by a collection of sherds from one of the last houses of the village, in a gully in the south-east); the same information and the same observation in the hamlet of Kalafgar, of recent construction, 3 km north-east of Zard Kamar on the same terrace. The importance of these sites is to bring into evidence the irrigation practised in this zone from the Achaemenid period onward, by means of a canal coming from the Jilga (see Gardin and Lyonnet 1978–9: 134). The easiest to locate is 500 m north-north-east of Zard Kamar, on an advance of the terrace edge which runs along the hills, towards the north-east, 3–4 m above the plain of Yangi Qal'a; a modern cemetery occupies the site. The other traces of ancient occupation are indicated only by little undulations observed from place to place near the edge of the terrace, and especially the areas scattered with sherds, all more or less within the same chronological range.

Collection: National Museum/AIA — sherds.

Fieldwork: 1978 Gardin et al., CNRS — survey.

Source:
1. Site information by J.-C. Gardin.
2. Gardin and Lyonnet 1978–9: pl. II — nos. 550–6.
3. Lyonnet 1997: figs 25, 35, 49 — nos. 550–7.
4. Gardin 1998: 38 — nos. 550–6.

ZARD TEPE. See 765 NARĪN.

1254. ZARGARĀN, KĀBUL
Or KŪH-I DIKSHA.

Lat. 34° 47' N, long. 69° 04' E. Map 64.
Kābul Province. At the foot of the hills on the west side of the Kūh-i Dāman Plain, on the south side of the Farza Valley *c.*6 km south of Istālif.

Description: The entrance to a cave at the top of a hill, with a flight of stairs descending to a large underground chamber surmounted by a dome.

Fieldwork: 1834 Masson — survey.

Sources:
1. Masson 1842: III. 117 — brief description.
2. Caspani and Cagnacci 1851: 228 — brief description.

ZARGĀRĀN, Bāmiyān. See 2282 ZARGĀRĀN, Bāmiyān, in Supplement.

1255. ZARKASHĀN

Lat. 32° 51' N, long. 67° 37' E. approximately. Map 79.
Ghazni Province. 13 km north-west of Muqqur on the south-eastern flanks of the Kūh-i Kachal.

Description: Remains of an ancient gold mine. Along the extent of the vein are several millstones, 80–120 cm diam., for crushing the ore, and the foundations of several buildings.

Fieldwork: 1977 CNRS — geological survey.

Source: Berthoud et al. 1977: 10–11 — description of the geology and workings.

1256. ZARKHARID

Lat. 34° 31' N, long. 68° 14' E. Map 59.
Bāmiyān Province. Road from Kābul to Bāmiyān, south slope of the Hājigak road: on the right bank of the Helmand in the place called Zarkharid.

Date: Turk and/or pre-Mongol Islamic period, 7th–10th cent. (architecture).

Description: Badly eroded ruin of a small fort.

Fieldwork: 1974–5 Le Berre, DAFA — survey.

Source: Le Berre 1987: 86, pl. 115 — brief description and photo; itinerary C, ruin 2.

ZARKHARID-I SULTAN. See 194 CHEHEL DUKHTARĀN, Qundūz.

1257. ZARNĪ

Lat. 33° 12' N, long. 64° 20' E. Map 74.
Ghūr Province. 190 km north of Dilārām, on the road to Taiwāra.

Description: A ruined tower just outside the village.

Fieldwork: 1885 Imam Sharif, ABC — topographical survey.

Sources:
1. Ferrier 1857: 248 — mentions ruins.
2. Holdich 1886: 5 — mention.
3. Imam Sharif 1891a: 207 — mention.
4. Klimburg 1960: 49 — mention.
5. Naïmi 1949: 14 — mention.
6. Ball 2002: 26 — mention.

1258. ZARSHOY

Lat. 35° 54' N, long. 65° 06' E. Map 24, 46.
Faryāb Province. In the Shīrīn Tagau *c.*8 km west of Nishar, *c.*20 km north-west of Bīlchirāgh on the road to Maimana.

Dates: Parthian-Hunnic, 1st–6th cent.; Timurid, 15th–16th cent. (ceramic).

Description: None available.

Fieldwork: 1970 Dupree, AUFS — survey.

Source: Site location and date by L. Dupree.

ZARU GHUNDAI. See 2283 ZARU GHUNDAI in Supplement.

1259. ZINDAJĀN
Or FŪSHANJ.

Original: Lat. 34° 21' N, long. 61° 45' E. Map 52.
Revised: 34.34971633 N, 61.73667797 E /
34° 20' 58.97880132 N, 61° 44' 12.04070172 E.
Herat Province. On the left bank of the Harī Rūd, 44 km downstream from Herat.

Dates: Late Sasanian, 5th–6th cent. (ceramic, stylistic); early Islamic, 8th–13th cent. (ceramic, documentary); Kart, 14th cent. (stylistic); Timurid, 15th–16th cent. (ceramic).

Description: Inside the town is the Mausoleum of Khwāja Muhammad Ghazi, a 14th-century cubical dome-chamber with a plain brick exterior. Inside is a fragmentary decorated stone inscription around the grave, commemorating Nasruddīn Alp Ghazi who died in 1202.

Just to the west of the town is a thin scatter of sherds and some unidentifiable mud remains. There are no mounds or building debris.

A small ivory statue of a Buddha was found by chance at Zindajān in the 1950s.

Collections: Herat Museum—cenotaph.

Fieldwork:
1. 1952 Le Berre and Gardin, DAFA—survey.
2. 1977 Ball—survey.
3. 1978–9 Samizay, Kābul University/UNESCO—architectural survey.
4. 1968–78 Kruglikova, Af/Sov. Mission—survey.

Sources:
1. Gardin and Lyonnet, 1980 chronological study of pottery from unpublished DAFA surveys.
2. Ferrier 1857: 142—identifies the site with Fūshanj.
3. Maitland 1888a: 128—mentions a few ruins to east.
4. Le Strange 1905: 411—summary of the historical references for Fūshanj (mistakenly identified with Ghūriyān).
5. Frye 1954: 116—mentions the Buddhist find.
6. Ghawwās 1969: 43—mentions the grave cover.
7. Ghūriyāni 1971—general background to the site.
8. Attar 1976—photo of the mud remains to the west of the town.
9. *Kabul Times* 1979a—mentions repair work carried out.
10. Samizay 1981: 32–3—description, with plans and photos of all remains, and a note on the conservation needs.
11. O'Kane 1985—detailed publication of the mausoleum.
12. Gaibov et al. 2010: 110—mention mounds to the west (Site K144).
13. Haase and Franke 2016—detailed description and discussion of the glazed cenotaph (now in the Herat Museum).

1260. ZINDĀN

Original: Lat. 31° 08' N, long. 64° 13' E. approximately. Map 97.
Revised: 31.14255634 N, 64.20570167 E /
31° 08' 33.20282976 N, 64° 12' 20.52601704 E.
Helmand Province. On the left bank of the Helmand, *c.*3 km north-east of Darwīshān.

Dates: Bronze Age, 3rd–2nd mill. BC; Achaemenid, 6th–4th cent. BC; Seleucid and Parthian, 4th–1st cent. BC;

Indo-Parthian and Sasanian, 1st–7th cent.; Timurid, 15th–16th cent. (ceramic).

Description: A mound with ruins on top. A wide range of sherds were collected.

Fieldwork: 1966 Hammond, Cambridge University—survey.

Sources:
1. Bellew 1974: 183—mention.
2. Hammond 1970: 449—lists site (no. 6) and describes the pottery types and general survey results.
3. Gazetteer 1973: II. 107—mention.
4. Besenval and Francfort 1994: 11—reinterpret Hammond's Type 10 'cord marked' ware as Harappan.

1261. ZINGI BAR

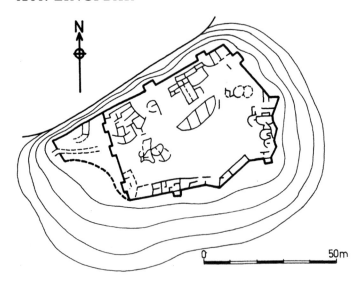

1261 Zingi Bar (after Olufsen 1904).

Original: Lat. 37° 00' N. long. 73° 35' E. Map 40.
Revised: 37.00490091 N, 73.600563 E /
37° 00' 17.64327960 N, 73° 36' 02.02680036 E.
Badakhshān Province. 13 km west of Langarkish in Wākhān.

Description: Remains of a 'Siāhpush Kāfir' fortress on a bluff, in a very well defended position. The walls are up to 7 m high and 1 m thick and are pierced by loopholes. The gateway to the south-east is approached by an artificial ramp, with the gateway itself built of large, roughly cut granite blocks. Construction elsewhere is of flat slates. On either side of the gateway are plaster surfaced guardrooms with arched ceilings. Inside, remains include several buildings, one quite large and possibly plastered, and three vaulted cisterns. There is an underground tunnel from the ramparts to a water channel to the north-east. All roofs throughout are either flat or vaulted.

Fieldwork: 1898–9 Olufsen, Danish Army—survey.
Sources:
1. Wood 1872: 218—mentions Zoroastrian affinities.
2. Olufsen 1904: 176–83—detailed description and photo, with some historical background.

1262. ZIRAK KĀRĪZ

Original: Lat. 32° 05' N, long. 64° 25' E. Map 87.
Revised: 32.07030444 N, 64.40340788 E /
32° 04' 13.09598544 N, 64° 24' 12.26837772 E.
Helmand Province. 6 km north-west of Qal'a-i Sa'ādat, just to the west of the village of Zirak Kārīz, north of Sharza.
Description: Some ruins.
Source: Maitland 1879—mention.

ZĪR-I SŪM. See **2284 ZĪR-I SŪM in Supplement.**

1263. ZIYĀRATGĀH

Original: Lat. 34° 12' N, long. 62° 08' E. Map 52.
Revised: 34.18844358 N, 62.1400536 E / 34° 11' 18.39687000 N, 62° 08' 24.19295640 E.
Herat Province. 21 km south of Herat.
Dates: ?Seljuk, 11th–12th cent.; Timurid, late 15th–early 16th cent. (architectural, epigraphic).

Description: Three monuments in and near the village. The Masjid-i Chehel Sitūn, a mosque of possible Seljuk foundation, is divided into winter and summer prayer halls, with an artificial cave underneath used as a *chilla-khāna*. It has a *mihrab* with a dated inscription from the time of Shah Rukh (1510). The Friday Mosque is a large mosque surrounding a central courtyard. It is undecorated except for an entrance inscription dating from the time of Husain-i Baiqara, and some traces of tilework outside. The Khāniqāh-i Mullāh Kalān is to the south of the village in a cemetery. It consists of three brick tombs, the largest of which at the western end is called Mullah Kalān. It is in ruins, and originally had a central dome-chamber. Over the entrance is an inscription from the time of Husain-i Baiqara.

C. 1 km to west of Ziyāratgāh is an old ruined fort surrounded by shallow ditch.

To the east of the town is a small artificial mound (12 × 15 m) with 14th–15th cent. pottery (Soviet Site K142).

Fieldwork:
1. 1967–9 Pugachenkova, Af/Sov. Mission—architectural survey.
2. 1978–9 Samizay, Kābul University/Unesco—architectural survey.
3. 1968–78 Kruglikova, Af/Sov. Mission—survey.

Sources:
1. Ferrier 1857: 262—mentions the Friday Mosque.
2. Peacocke 1887a: 216—mentions Friday Mosque.
3. Maitland 1888a: 400—mentions the Hāniqāh and the Friday Mosque.

1263 Zīyāratgāh—Friday Mosque (after Pugachenkova 1968).

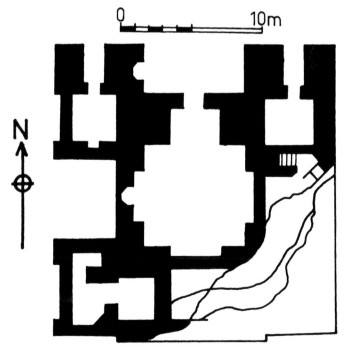

1263 Zīyāratgāh—Khāniqāh of Mullāh Kalān (after Pugachenkova 1968).

4. Maitland 1888c: 399–400 – description.
5. Niedemeyer and Diez 1924: pl. 165–6 – photos of the Friday Mosque before 20th-century restoration.
6. Wolfe 1966: 60 – brief description of all three monuments.
7. Ghawwās 1969: 41–2 – brief description of all three monuments.
8. Pugachenkova 1969 – descriptions and plans of all monuments.
9. Pugachenkova 1970 – brief description of the monuments.
10. Pugachenkova and Khakomov 1972 – brief study of the Khāniqāh.
11. Ghawwās 1974 – background and history of the ancient and modern monuments.
12. Pugachenkova 1976a: 32 – brief discussion.
13. Pugachenkova 1979c – discusses the Khāniqāh.
14. Samizay 1980: 42–9 – good summary description, with photos and plans, of all three monuments, with a note on the conservation needs.
15. O'Kane 1987: 259–63, 303–10, and 319–21 – full descriptions of the Timurid monuments.
16. Golombek and Wilber 1988: 350–3 – descriptions of the Timurid monuments.
17. Ball 2008: 274–6 – summary.
18. Gaibov et al. 2010: 110 – mentions mound to east of town (Site K142).

ZĪYĀRAT-I ABDUL HAKIM. See **2285 ZĪYĀRAT-I ABDUL HAKIM** in Supplement.

1264. ZĪYĀRAT-I AMĪRĀN SĀHIB
See also 2182 QAL'A-I AMĪRĀN SĀHIB in Supplement.

Original: Lat. 30° 59' N, long. 62° 08' E. Map 92.
Revised: 30.97812764 N, 62.13123234 E /
30° 58' 41.25948636 N, 62° 07' 52.43643300 E.
Nīmrūz Province. C.10 km east of Chigīnī, just to the north-east of the village of Amīrān Sāhib.

Dates: Saffarid/Ghaznavid, 10th–12th cent.; Timurid, 15th cent. (stylistic).

Description: The *zīyārat* is composed of a modern mosque converted to tomb chamber (and cemetery) and an adjoining 15th-century mosque (which probably once held the graves of the three martyrs). Isolated as it is, it is still an important shrine, and operates as a true sanctuary for those who need it, for whatever reason, as well as serving the normal functions of cure and retreat. The ruinous octagonal minaret had an interior staircase and is located at the north-east corner of the 15th-century mosque. Remains of earlier structures surround the complex. The earliest extant

architectural remains at the *zīyārat* appear to be Ghaznavid, but I would expect the site to be older.

Fieldwork:
1. 1903–5 Tate, SAC – survey.
2. 1936 Hackin and Meunié, DAFA – survey.
3. 1965–70 Fischer, Bonn University – survey.
4. 1971–4 Trousdale, Smithsonian – survey, excavation.

Sources:
1. Site information by W. Trousdale.
2. Tate 1910: 254–5 – brief description with a photo of the *zīyārat* and minaret.
3. Fischer 1970a – photo of the minaret.
4. Fischer 1970b: pls 38–9 – photos.
5. Fischer 1973c: 145 – mention.

ZĪYĀRAT-I ASĀB-I QĀF. See **35 ĀLTĪ KHWĀJA.**

1265. ZĪYĀRAT-I BĀBĀ FURQ

Lat. 34° 55' N, long. 61° 43' E. Map 42.
Herat Province. 6 km south-west of Qarabāgh, *c.*25 km south-east of Gulrān.

Description: A ruined mud-brick dome-chamber in a cemetery that contains many carved black and white marble gravestones.

Sources:
1. *Pioneer*, 7 Jan. 1885: 3 – brief description.
2. A. C. Yate 1887: 177–8 – brief description.

1266. ZĪYĀRAT-I DŪST MUHAMMAD

Original: Lat. 30° 22' N, long. 61° 52' E. Maps 93, 95.
Revised: 30.36338307 N, 61.86802533 E /
30° 21' 48.17906316 N, 61° 52' 04.89119556 E.
Nīmrūz Province. On the east bank of the Helmand *c.*24 km south of Qal'a-i Fath on the road to Chahār Burjak.

Dates: Parthian and Indo-Parthian, 2nd cent. BC–AD 3rd cent.; Sasanian, 3rd–7th cent. (ceramic).

Description: A series of 20–30 small buildings, all in various states of decay.

Fieldwork: 1951 Fairservis, AMNH – survey.

Source: Fairservis 1961: 55–6 – brief description and summary of the pottery (Site 36, KF–4).

ZĪYĀRAT-I HAZRĀT SULTAN MUHAMMAD DEOBAND. See **2286 ZĪYĀRAT-I HAZRAT SULTĀN MUHAMMAD DEOBAND** in Supplement.

1267. ZĪYĀRAT-I IMĀM

Original: Lat. 32° 22' N, long. 64° 59' E. Map 87.
Revised: 32.36227398 N, 64.98234312 E /
32° 21' 44.18634492 N, 64° 58' 56.43524892 E.
Helmand Province. 1 km north-west of Shahr-i Kuhna in Zamīndāwar, halfway between Kajaki and Mūsa Qal'a.

Date: Ghaznavid, 1092 (inscription).

Description: A *zīyārat* containing a dated inscription.

Fieldwork: 1885 Sahibdad Khan, ABC—topographical survey.

Source: Sahibdad Khan 1891b: 254—mention.

ZĪYĀRAT-I IMĀM ASKAR. See 764 NĀRĪMĀN.

ZĪYĀRAT-I KHALIFA RAHMAT JAMSHIDI. See 2120 KHALIFA RAHMAT JAMSHĪDĪ in Supplement.

ZĪRĀYAT-I KHWĀJA GHAIB or KAFIR WAL'A. See 2287 ZĪYĀRAT-I KHWĀJA GHAIB in Supplement.

ZĪYĀRAT-I KHWĀJA JINN. See 2288 ZĪYĀRAT-I KHWĀJA JINN in Supplement.

ZĪRĀYAT-I KHWĀJA QĀSIM. See 2289 ZĪYĀRAT-I KHWĀJA QĀSIM in Supplement.

ZĪYĀRAT-I MĪR HAIDAR. See 2290 ZĪYĀRAT-I MĪR HAIDAR in Supplement.

ZĪYĀRAT-I PANJESHĀH. See 418 HASHMAT KHĀN.

ZĪRĀYAT-I SAYYAD TAJDĀR AQĀ. See 2291 ZĪYĀRAT-I SAYYAD TAJDĀR AQĀ in Supplement.

1268. ZĪYĀRAT-I SAYYAD WAKĀS

Lat. 34° 10' N, long. 63° 06' E. Map 53.
Herat Province. In the Tang-i Azau *c*.7 km north-west of Taghān Kūh.

Description: Some artificial caves.

Fieldwork: 1885 Sahibdad Khan, ABC—topographical survey.

Sources:
1. Maitland et al. 1889: 111—mention.
2. Sahibdad Khan 1891a: 235—mention.

1269. ZĪYĀRAT-I SHAIKH HUSAIN

Lat. 30° 35' N, long. 61° 51' E. Map 93.
Nīmrūz Province. South of Sargah-i Sīstān near Qal'a-i Fath, 7 km west of Paisai.

Dates: Mongol, 1227; Timurid, 1517 (epigraphic).

Description: A domed mausoleum of baked brick construction, on a *pakhsa* platform. There are several other tombs in the vicinity and some fragmentary inscriptions dated 623 and 923 AH.

Immediately to the south is a splendid late Timurid cemetery with several tolerably preserved mausolea constructed of baked and mud-brick.

Fieldwork: 1903–5 Tate, SAC—survey.

Sources:
1. Additional information on the cemetery by W. Trousdale.
2. Tate 1910: 258–9—brief description.

ZŪR SHAHR. See 522 KANDAHĀR.

1270. ZUHAKA

Lat. 33° 37' N, long. 69° 30' E. approximately. Map 82.
Paktiyā Province. On the western side of the Kūh-i Siāh or Mihtar Sulaiman, near Gardēz.

Description: A large ruined city, about half the size of old Kandahār, surrounded by broad, high ramparts pieced by three gates of baked brick. Inside the remains include a cistern and several wells. The site could possibly be the ancient city of Zābul.

Sources:
1. Vigne 1840: 109—mention from hearsay.
2. Raverty 1878: 457 and 506–7—very brief description and discussion of the location.
3. Gazetteer 1908: V. 287—mention from hearsay, as being 'probably near Kandahar'.
4. Ball 2008: 275—summary.

1271. ZULM

Lat. 37° 10' N, long. 69° 30' E. Map 34.
Takhār Province. About 500 m north-east of the village of Nawābād, in the plain of Turghai Tepe (q.v.), on an advance of the hills which close this plain to the east. The site is located on the slopes of this spur, at the foot of which are traces of an old canal which drew water from the Kokcha, and irrigated the plain towards the north, up to the outskirts of the present village of Lala Guzar.

Dates: Beg. Iron, end 2nd–beg. 1st mill. BC (B, C); Achaemenid, 6th–4th cent. BC (B); Hellenistic, 3rd–1st cent. BC (C); pre-Mongol Islamic, 10th–13th cent. (A, C) (ceramic).

Description: (A) The main site is an area of undulations strewn with fired bricks and sherds that covers a surface of about 20 hectares, below the slopes that descend towards the village of Nawābād (previous name: Zulm). The surface area of the site and the abundance of the bricks suggest a small city, razed in the Mongol period; H.-P. Francfort (1978) proposes an identification as Andijarag of the Muslim geographers. (B) In the southern part of the area above, the ancient canal (oriented here south-east–north-west) skirts a natural mound which had probably been adapted, tabular in shape (*c.*150 × 100 m), where sherds of the Achaemenid period were collected. A trial trench dug by P. Bernard in this mound produced much pottery of this period, but no trace of architecture. (C) North of this site, on either side of the same canal, vestiges of hamlets or farms close together, of the Islamic period, of which some produce older pottery (Achaemenid, Graeco-Bactrian, and Kushan).

Collection: National Museum/AIA—sherds.

Fieldwork:
1. 1974 Gardin et al., CNRS—survey.
2. 1975 Bernard, DAFA—trial trench.

Sources:
1. Site information by J.-C. Gardin.
2. Francfort 1978—historical geography of the region, identification of Zulm as Andijaragh from medieval sources.
3. Gardin and Lyonnet 1978–9: 143 and pl. III, nos. 111–13—brief description.
4. Lyonnet 1997: figs 25, 35–7—nos. 111–13
5. Gardin 1998: 43, 143, and pl. III, nos. 111–13—brief description.

ZURĀBĀD. See 2292 ZURĀBĀD in Supplement.

Site Catalogue Supplement

2000. ABBĀSĀBĀD

Original: Lat. 30° 49′ N, long. 64° 03′ E. Map 97.
Revised: 30.89182426 N, 64.14857268 E /
30° 53′ 30.56733240 N, 64° 08′ 54.86163360 E approx.
Helmand Province. Approximately 2 km south of Mīān-pushta on route to Safār, on the east bank of the Helmand.

Description: Three artificial caves with arched entrances, in the cliff face 300–400 ft above the river.

Source: Maitland et al. 1889: 64—mention.

2001. ABDULĀBĀD

Original: Lat. 30° 28′ N, long. 63° 15′ E. Map 98.
Revised: 30.48024033 N, 63.2477723 E /
30° 28′ 48.86519412 N, 63° 14′ 51.98027604 E.
Helmand Province. On the left bank of the river *c*.10 km upstream from Khwāja ʿAli.

Description: A circular artificial mound, *c*.75 m diameter.

Source: Peacocke 1887a: 13—mention.

2002. ĀB-I RASŪL DĀD

Lat. 35° 36′ N, long. 65° 50′ E approx. Map 46.
Faryāb Province. Eastern Gurziwān district, in Kūh-i Larghajān area south-east of Ghulbiyān in a deep gorge.

Date: Seljuk? 12th–13th cent. (stylistic).

Description: A shrine approximately 6 × 8 m. located by a spring of water. It consists of four walls of square fired brick. No inscriptions or decoration.

Source: Site information by Jonathan L. Lee (recorded October 1996 and in photographic archive).

2003. AHMADĀBĀD

Lat. 34° 34′N, long. 61° 19′ E. Map 51.
Herat Province. On the north bank of the Harī Rūd just to the north of the road from Kuhsān to Herat, just to the south-west of Ahmadābād.

Date: Middle Islamic (ceramic).

Description: A low artificial mound, *c*.4 m high, 20 × 15 m in area. There is a scattering of building debris within a radius of *c*.30 m.

Fieldwork: 1968–78 Kruglikova, Af/Sov. Mission—survey.

Source: Gaibov et al. 2010: 108 and 110.

2004. ALLAH KĀRĪZ

Lat. 31° 31′ N, long. 65° 14′ E. Map 88.
Kandahār Province. In the right bank of the Arghandāb Valley about halfway between Kandahār and Kushk-i Nakhud, to the south of the main road.

Description: A site dominating the plain.

Source: Ashe 1881: 37—mention.

2005. ĀQĪNA

Original: Lat. 37° 08′ N, long. 65° 11′ E. Map 24.
Revised: 37.13203605 N, 65.1930878 E /
37° 07′ 55.32977676 N, 65° 11′ 35.11606380 E.
Faryāb Province. Some 20–5 km north of Andkhūī beside the new road to the Turkmenistan frontier.

Date: 18th cent. (stylistic).

Description: A caravanserai and a cistern. A large, baked brick sunken cistern approx. 10 m square, with a domed roof. Access to the water is by the descent of a brick staircase. Similar in style and size to the urban cisterns of the old city of Herat and surrounding area. The remains of a medieval canal lie to the south-east of the cistern, and the broken walls of a caravanserai and other buildings lie to the north and east of the cistern.

Fieldwork:
1. 1885 Peacocke, ABC.
2. 1995–8 Lee.

Sources:
1. Peacocke 1887a: 76—mention.
2. Site information by Jonathan L. Lee (recorded 1995–8 and in photographic archive).

2006. ATA KHĀN KHWĀJA

Lat. 36° 12′ N, long. 64° 41′ E. Map 24.
Revised: 36.22916125 N, 64.73544481 E /
36° 13′ 44.98051656 N, 64° 44′ 07.60133400 E.
Faryāb Province. Between Mīn Darakht and Jālayur.

Description: An old ruined fort.

Fieldwork: 1885 Peacocke, ABC—topographical survey.

Source: Peacocke 1887a: 247—mention.

2007. AUSAK

Original: Lat. 31° 08′ N, long. 61° 52′ E approx. Map 83.
Revised: 31.14673568 N, 61.88731197 E /
31° 08′ 48.24843576 N, 61° 53′ 14.32307472 E.
Nīmrūz Province. On edge of Naizār just out from Ibrāhīmābād on road to Makbarah-i Ābīl.

Description: Mounds and ruins.

Fieldwork: 1884 Maitland, ABC—topographical survey.

Source: Maitland 1888a: 85—mention.

2008. AZĪZĀBĀD

Original: Lat. 33° 43′ N, long. 68° 31′ E. Map 80.
Revised: 33.72932991 N, 68.54262656 E /
33° 43′ 45.58766088 N, 68° 32′ 33.45562212 E.
Ghazni Province. Approximately 20 km north-east of
Ghazni just to the east of the main road.

Date: Ghaznavid, 11th–12th cent. (stylistic).

Description: A caravanserai where a fragment of a Ghaznavid stucco has been found.

Source: Site information by A. D. H. Bivar.

2009. BĀBĀ KUZAM

Original: Lat. 36° 40′ N, long. 66° 40′ E approx. Map 28.
Revised: 36.68520877 N, 66.69387596 E /
36° 41′ 06.75157560 N, 66° 41′ 37.95345960 E approx.
Balkh Province. Between 14 and 24 km from Imām Sāhib
on road to Imām Bukri.

Description: Ruins.

Source: Peacocke 1887a: 298—mention.

2010. BĀGH-I SHŪR
Or BĀGHSŪR or BUKSHOR.

Lat. 36° 56′ N, long. 66° 50 E. Map 80.
Balkh Province. To the west of the Balkh-Daulātabād road
near Bāghsūr settlement, south of Daulātabād.

Description: A low mound. The site is elevated on the
western end and there are several other low mounds in the
area. It appears to have been part of a series of fortified
positions built around the main fortress of Shahr-i Barbar
(q.v.), or Kāfir Qal'a-i Daulātabād. Local villagers report
recovering glass beads. Pottery sherds scattered across site
include burnished red ware and unornamented plain
domestic ware.

Source: Site information by Jonathan L. Lee.

2011. BANĀQ

Original: Lat. 35° 22′ N, long. 67° 23′ E approx. Map 48.
Revised: 35.31370719 N, 67.59991859 E /
35° 18′ 49.34589804 N, 67° 35′ 59.70694092 E.
Bāmiyān Province. North part of Kahmard valley, at the
base of the Ājār Valley.

Description: Reports of ruins and ancient remains.

Source: Site information by Jonathan L. Lee, 2005.

2012. BAND-I DARRA-I BAND

Original: Lat. 36° 05′ N, long. 65° 47′ E approx. Map 24.
Revised: 36.09319827 N, 65.70926875 E /
36° 05′ 35.51378640 N, 65° 42′ 33.36748200 E approx.
Jauzjān Province. Sayyad district some 1.5 hours drive
south-west of Sayyid settlement south-west of Sar-i Pul.

Description: A high and impressive earth and stone dam
some 10–15 m in height constructed in a narrow gorge.
with interior walkways which dammed a branch of the
Sar-i Pul River. The dam used to divert the catchment
waters into a series of irrigation canals but is now defunct
and has been cut through at the base to make way for road
transport into the mountains. At the top of the dam are
remains of a sluice gate system and various chambers
constructed inside the dam. Locally the dam is said to
have been constructed during the reign of Sultān Husain
Baiqara.

Source: Site information by Jonathan L. Lee (and in photographic archive).

2013. BĀRKĀH

Original: Lat. 36° 41′ N, long. 66° 48′ E approx. Map 28.
Revised: 36.68778086 N, 66.41819328 E /
36° 41′ 16.01107908 N, 66° 25′ 05.49581196 E.
Balkh Province. A village in Chimtāl District south-east of
Balkh.

Dates: Achaemenid, 6th–4th cent., Hellenistic, 4th–1st
cent. (ceramic).

Description: A round Achaemenid structure associated with a round Hellenistic structure.

Source: Site information by P. Marquis.

2014. BĀZĀR GAI
(Formerly 1273.)

Original: Lat. 32° 58′ N, long. 67° 56′ E approx. Map 79.
Revised: 32.96296229 N, 67.9404741 E /
32° 57′ 46.66424040 N, 67° 56′ 25.70677080 E approx.
Ghazni Province. In the Āb-I Istāda area.

Date: Hunnic-Turki Shahi, 5th–9th cent. (ceramic).

Description: None available.

Fieldwork: 1974 Dupree, AUFS — survey.

Source: Site information by Louis Dupree.

2015. BUNYĀD KHĀN

Original: Lat. 35° 50′ N, long. 61° 06′ E approx. Map 51.
Revised: 34.81975331 N, 61.08581377 E /
34° 49′ 11.11191960 N, 61° 05′ 08.92958640 E approx.
Herat Province. Overlooking the right bank of Harī Rūd just on the Afghan side of the Iran–Afghan border, approximately 20 km north of Islām Qal'a.

Description: A ruined fort.

Fieldwork: 1884 Peacocke, ABC — topographical survey.

Source: Peacocke 1887a: 63–4 — mention.

2016. BURJ-I GHUS KARI

Original: Lat. 31° 14′ N, long. 61° 52′ E approx. Map 83.
Revised: 31.22479366 N, 61.89638049 E /
31° 13′ 29.25716412 N, 61° 53′ 46.96975176 E.
Nīmrūz Province. 11 km north of Ībrāhīmābād to right of the road to Makbarah Abīl.

Description: Some ruins on a mound.

Fieldwork: 1884 Peacocke, ABC — topographical survey.

Source: Peacocke 1887a: 30 — mention.

2017. BURJ-I SHAIKH SULAIMĀN

Lat. 34° 45′ N, long. 62° 55′ E. Map 53.
Bādghīs Province. 7 km north of Dehistān.

Description: Remains of an old tower.

Fieldwork: 1885 Maitland, ABC — topographical survey.

Source: Maitland 1888a: 320 — mention.

2018. BURJ-I TĀJARMĪN

Original: Lat. 34° 21′ N, long. 64° 02′ E. Map 54.
Revised: 34.31877704 N, 64.03640457 E /
34° 19′ 07.59735192 N, 64° 02′ 11.05646136 E.
Herat Province. On the north bank of the Harī Rūd, 7 km from Darra-i Takht on the route to Naspanj and Lāshwa up the Tagau Tajarmīn, on the Beshwa-Kaminj route.

Description: A large mud tower.

Fieldwork:
1. 1884–7 Maitland, ABC — topographical survey.
2. 2004–6 Franke and Urban, DAI — survey.

Sources:
1. Maitland and Drummond 1888: 158 — mention.
2. Franke and Urban 2006: 11 — mention; 13 — photo.

2019. BURJ-I YAK
Or DEH GAKI.

Original: Lat. 34° 07′ N, long. 64° 11′ E. Map 103.
Revised: 34.1097885 N, 64.32451195 E /
34° 06′ 35.23858920 N, 64° 19′ 28.24300920 E approx.
Ghūr Province. Shahrak plain, near river bank 13 km south of the Tang-i Azau-Shahrak road, opposite two gorges: Mahmūd Yamar and Shorawak. 5 km east of Nahangābād.

Description: Mounds and a ruined tower.

Fieldwork: 1885 Lal, ABC — topographic survey.

Source: Maitland 1888a: 366 and 442 — mention.

2020. BUTKĀK
See 75 BĀDQĀQ.

2021. CHAHĀR BURJAK

Original: Lat. 30° 17′ N, long. 62° 03′ E. Map 95.
Revised: 30.28478367 N, 62.04279614 E /
30° 17′ 05.22122748 N, 62° 02′ 34.06610040 E.
Nīmrūz Province. 1 km west of Chahār Burjak, to south of road to Qal'a-i Fath, beyond the canals. Chahār Burjak is on the north bank.

Description: Some ruins.

Fieldwork: 1884 Maitland, ABC — topographical survey.

Source: Maitland 1888c: 65 — mention.

2022. CHAHĀR DĪWĀL

Original: Lat. 34° 08′ N, long. 65° 04′ E. Maps 55, 74.
Revised: 33.83678095 N, 64.93366338 E /
33° 50′ 12.41141640 N, 64° 56′ 01.18816080 E approx.

Ghūr Province. 2 km from Sar-i Akhtam to left of road to Kata Chashma Tagau on the road from Guzarpām to Chakhcharān.

Description: Remains of mud tower on a mound.

Fieldwork: 1885 Maitland and Lal, ABC—topographical survey.

Source: Maitland 1888a: 446—mention.

2023. CHAHĀR SHANBEH TEPE

Original: Lat. 36° 18′ 21″ N, long. 68° 49′ 34″ E. Map 33.
Revised: 36.30716502 N, 68.82673328 E /
36° 18′ 25.79408568 N, 68° 49′ 36.23982492 E.
Baghlān Province. Some 20 km north-east of Baghlān to the right of the Baghlān-Qundūz highway to the south of the settlement of this name.

Dates: ?Graeco-Bactrian, 3rd–1st cent. BC; Kushan, 1st–3rd cent. AD (ceramic; stylistic).

Description: An impressive and extensive series of ruins surrounding a central, elevated mound consisting of a series of three level, artificial terraces rising from the north-west to the south-east. At the high (south-east) end the site has been heavily undercut and eroded by the waters—a fast-flowing, seasonal wash, the Jar-i Khushk. A series of lower mounds are located to the east and south of the main site, one of which may possibly be the remains of a stupa.

In 2004 the Historic Monument Department of Baghlān Province recovered two Kushan column bases and other fragments of monumental architecture from the bed of the river after the collapse of part of the southern end of the site into the wash. On the south wall traces of arches and mud-brick structures can be clearly seen from the river bed. There are also traces of plaster exposed by the erosion of the site by the waters of the wash.

The site abounds in surface pottery including incised and plain red burnished(?) domestic ware.

Collections:
1. ASA—sherds.
2. Dept. of Information and Culture, Pul-i Khumri—column bases.

Fieldwork: 2004 Lee—reconnaissance.

Source: Site information by Jonathan L. Lee (recorded 2004 and in photographic archives).

2024. CHAKHĀNSŪR

Original: Lat. 31° 10′ N, long, 62° 04′ E. Map 84.
Revised: 31.18082236 N, 62.0520004 E /
31° 10′ 50.96049096 N, 62° 03′ 07.20145728 E.
Nīmrūz Province. The main town in the province in the 19th century.

Description: A low mound, *c.*7 m high, probably artificial, surrounded by the remains of an old fort. On top is a large well-preserved fort, probably mainly modern. Walls in shape of irregular polygon, with small round towers at angles, up to 20 m above mound. Mud-brick. Entrance on south west side in centre of a watch tower *c.*27 m high.

Fieldwork: 1884 Peacocke, ABC—topographical survey.

Sources:
1. Peacocke 1885a: 13—description.
2. Peacocke 1887a: 27—description and sketch of fort.

2025. CHAMBAR QAL'A

Original: Lat. 34° 28′ N, long, 66° 30′ E approx. Map 56.
Revised: 34.46089821 N, 66.52123533 E /
34° 27′ 39.23353836 N, 66° 31′ 16.44717468 E.
Bāmiyān Province. 16 km east of Lal, opposite Dahān-i Tamburak (q.v.).

Description: A ruined fort.

Fieldwork: 1885 Maitland and Lal, ABC—topographical survey.

Source: Maitland 1888a: 466—mention.

2026. CHĀRBĀGH

Original: Lat. 34° 32N long, 70° 19′ E. Map 66.
Revised: 34.42487971 N, 70.38002173 E /
34° 25′ 29.56696680 N, 70° 22′ 48.07822440 E approx.
Nangahār Province. Surkhrūd district, 10 km north-west of Jalālābād.

Date: Ghaznavid, 11th cent. (stylistic).

Description: The grave of Shah Faizullah Agha, thought to be the first Hindu who converted to Islam in eastern Nangahār province. The grave has two domes, one of them completely damaged, and calligraphic works on the half-crumbled walls painted in black. The dome and other portions of the shrine are on the verge of collapse.

Source: Mahbob Shah Mahbob (<http://www.pajhwok.com/en/2013/03/03/ancient-dome-verge-destruction#.UTl9p6wv_DA.email> accessed Jan. 2016, brought to my attention by Jonathan L. Lee).

2027. CHILANG

Original: Lat. 30° 13′ N long, 62° 51′ E. Map 96.
Revised: 30.22563926 N, 62.89514153 E /
30° 13′ 32.30132880 N, 62° 53′ 42.50949360 E approx.
Helmand Province. On the left bank of Helmand, 21 km below Khwāja 'Ali on road to Landi Barechi, 2 km below Pulālak.

Description: Remains of 2 towers, probably the gateway to a fort.

Fieldwork: 1884 Maitland, Peacocke, ABC—topographical survey.

Sources:
1. Peacocke 1887a: 15—mention.
2. Maitland 1888a: 55—mention.

2028. CHILSITŪN
See also 99 BALKH.

Lat. 36° 45′ N, long 66° 56′ E. Map 27.
Balkh Province. South-east of Balkh near Bāgh-i Uraq.

Dates: Kushan, 1st–3rd cent; early Islamic, 9th–10th cent. (ceramic).

Description: An extensive, low mound, heavily dug and full of robber pits. On the east side of the site looters have dug down and uncovered a mud-brick stairway leading into a series of low chambers. There are also local reports of carved column bases and what may have been an inscription on a stone, possibly a foundation stone or dedicatory tablet, being uncovered. As well as Kushan remains, sherds of glazed Nispahur style pottery and baked bricks scattered the site. The remains of at least four lined wells have also been excavated on the west of the site.

Fieldwork: 1996 and 1998, Lee—reconnaissance.

Source: Site information by Jonathan L. Lee (recorded in photographic archive).

2029. CHIM QAL'A, JAUZJĀN

Lat. 36° 35′ N, long 65° 24′ E. Map 24.
Jauzjān Province. 27 km from Shibarghān to right of road to Rabāt Audān and Daulatābād.

Description: Ruins of an old fort.

Fieldwork: 1885 Peacocke, ABC—topographical survey.

Source: Peacocke 1887a: 107—mention.

2030. CHIM QAL'A, BAGHLĀN

Original: Lat. 36° 15′ N, long. 68° 50′ E. Map 33.
Revised: 36.29371437 N, 68.84983936 E /
36° 17′ 37.37173920 N, 68° 50′ 59.42169960 E approx.
Baghlān Province. Some 15 km north-east of Baghlān and east of the Baghlān-Qundūz highway. (Note: this is not the same as Site 169 Cham Qal'a.)

Description: A large, square fortress some 50 m in width contained within acutely angled mud walls some 15 m in height surrounded by the remains of a deep wet ditch. To the south-west the bed of a canal which brought water

for the ditch is clearly seen. There are remains of two entranceways in the south-east and north-west. A medieval guard house with tower in red baked brick (40 × 40 × 5 cm) was built as an extension to the gate on the north-west, which was presumably the main entrance. The medieval gate is built upon courses of more ancient, mud-bricks (16 × 7 × 8 cm). The latter brick courses also show traces of white plaster.

Outside the south-east walls are two low mounds which flank the entrance. Beyond this is an ancient caravan route from Pul-i Khumri to Qundūz. A number of other low mounds on the south-east and south-west of the citadel suggest minor fortications or barracks.

On the south-west wall an artificial, arched tunnel some 1.5 m high has been cut into the side of the walls and exits inside the fortification.

A modern concrete pavilion on the north wall has been erected for officials to watch buzkashi games.

Fieldwork: 2004 Lee—reconnaissance.

Source: Site information by Jonathan L. Lee (recorded in photographic archive).

2031. CHOR GUNBĀD

Lat. 29° 48′ N, long. 61° 22′ E. Map 94.
Nīmrūz Province. On the high ground among sand dunes to the south of the Shēla Rūd in the far south-west of the province.

Date: Timurid, 15th–16th cent. (ceramic).

Description: A large cemetery of Timurid date, with the ruins of several simple mausolea.

Source:
1. Site information by W. Trousdale.
2. MacGregor 1882: 184–5—brief description.

2032. CHURUK TEPE

Original: Lat. 37° 10′ N, long. 66° 12′ E. Maps 24, 25.
Revised: 37.17278054 N, 66.21993758 E /
37° 10′ 22.00993716 N, 66° 13′ 11.77528584 E.
Jauzjān Province. 18.5 km from Kilift to left of road to Chilik.

Description: A mound with a ruined fort on top.

Fieldwork: 1885–6 Peacocke, ABC—topographical survey.

Source: Peacocke 1887a: 104 and 332—mention.

2033. DAHĀN-I CHOQUR

Original: Lat. 34° 29′ N, long. 65° 00′ E. Map 55.
Revised: 34.57594831 N, 64.66731429 E /
34° 34′ 33.41390160 N, 64° 40′ 02.33142960 E approx.
Ghūr Province. West of Chashm Sakina between Jam and Chakhcharān.

Description: Illicit excavations in 2002 revealed a pre-Islamic burial beside a *pakhsa* pillar shaped like a serpent, as well as communal burials containing some eight to nine inhumations that contained grave goods consisting of wooden bowls depicting mounted warriors holding lances.

Source: Stewart 2004: 185—brief description.

2034. DAHĀN-I GHŪRĪ

Original: Lat. 35° 54′ N, long. 68° 30'E. Maps 30, 33.
Revised: 35.91195801 N, 68.48850456 E /
35° 54′ 43.04885040 N, 68° 29′ 18.61641960 E approx.
Baghlān Province. In the south-west of the province at the end of the Ghūrī Plain, west of Pul-i Khumri.

Description: Reports by officials in the Department of Historic Monuments of Baghlān Province of a site with traces of ancient ruins.

Source: Site information by Jonathan L. Lee 2004.

2035. DAHĀN-I SAHRĀK

Original: Lat. 35° 08′ N, long. 67° 41′ E approx. Map 48.
Revised: 35.11803796 N, 67.69147789 E /
35° 07′ 04.93666320 N, 67° 41′ 29.32038600 E approx.
Bāmiyān Province. On the Bāmiyān-Saighān road on the left (west) side of the valley of the same name, opposite the village of Sūkhta Chinār.

Description: A series of artificial caves.

Fieldwork: 2000, Lee—reconnaisance.

Source: Site information by Jonathan L. Lee.

2036. DAHĀN-I SIĀH BUMAK

Original: Lat. 34° 20′ N, long. 67° 02′ E. Map 56.
Revised: 34.41972787 N, 66.53135687 E /
34° 25′ 11.02033272 N, 66° 31′ 52.88472192 E.
Bāmiyān Province. 25 km from Dahan-i Kushnau or Nawa Agha in the Lāl Valley at the entrance to the side valley of Siāh Bumak; 4.5 km after Qal'a-i Qomaghai.

Description: Small ruined fort at entrance of valley, and another a little further up the valley.

Fieldwork: 1885 Maitland and Lal, ABC—topographical survey.

Source: Maitland 1888a: 467—mention.

2037. DAHĀN-I TAMBURAK

Original: Lat. 34° 26′ N, long. 66° 31′ E approx. Map 56.
Revised: 34.46939026 N, 66.49803103 E /
34° 28′ 09.80494212 N, 66° 29′ 52.91171952 E.

17 km from Dahan-i Kushnan or Nawa Agha in Lal Valley, on road to Siah Bumak.

Description: Two towers at the mouth of the ravine.

Fieldwork: 1885 Maitland and Lal, ABC—topographical survey.

Source: Maitland 1888a: 466—mention.

2038. DAHĀN-I ZŪLFIQĀR

Lat. 35° 35′ N, long. 61° 19′ E. Map 41.
Herat Province. C.1.2 km from the river just before reaching Zūlfiqār from Gulrān.

Description: A flat-topped clay mound *c*.5 m high, with an old watch tower on top.

Source: Maitland and Drummond 1888: 42—mention.

2039. DAK-I MARI

Original: Lat. 30° 55′ N, long. 61° 48′ E. Map 92.
Revised: 30.91603419 N, 61.80009192 E /
30° 54′ 57.72307284 N, 61° 48′ 00.33089652 E.
Nīmrūz Province. *c*.11 km south of Nād-i 'Ali, to west of road to Qal'a-i Fath.

Description: An artificial mound representing the site of an old village.

Fieldwork: 1884 Peacocke, ABC—topographical survey.

Sources:
1. Peacocke 1885a: 11—mention.
2. Peacocke 1887a: 25—mention.

2040. DALKHAK

Original: Lat. 32° 02′ N, long. 63° 55′ E. Map 73.
Revised: 32.03121688 N, 63.92204505 E /
32° 01′ 52.38077520 N, 63° 55′ 19.36218000 E approx.
Helmand Province. 77 km from Girishk on the old route to Dilārām.

Description: A ruined fort.

Source: Maitland et al. 1889: 84—mention.

2041. DAMB

Lat. 30° 34′ N, long. 61° 52′ E. Map 93.
Nīmrūz Province. 3 km north of Qal'a-i Fath and to east of road to Zaranj.

Description: Some ruins, probably an extension of Qal'a-i Fath. Some distance to east is a long line of ruins marking former gardens and villages.

Fieldwork: 1884 Maitland, Peacocke, ABC—topographical survey.

Sources:
1. Peacocke 1885a: 8—mention in general terms.
2. Maitland 1888a: 70—brief description.

2042. DAMB KURUDI
Or DAM-I KALAN.

Lat. 30° 36′ N, long. 61° 52′ E. Map 93.
Nīmrūz Province. 7 km north of Qal'a-i Fath to right of road to Zaranj.

Description: A large area of ruins.

Fieldwork: 1884 Maitland, Peacocke, ABC—topographical survey.

Sources:
1. Peacocke 1885a: 8—mention in general terms.
2. Peacocke 1887a: 22—mention.
3. Maitland 1888a: 70–1—mention.

2043. DAM-I MALIK KHĀN

Lat. 30° 34′ N, long. 61° 50. Map 93.
Nīmrūz Province. To the east of the Helmand 2 km north of Qal'a-i Fath.

Dates: Early 1st mill. BC; Parthian-early Sasanian, 1st–3rd cent. (ceramic).

Description: A very large, partly natural and partly constructed, segmented mound. Ceramics of the early 1st mill. BC, very heavy sherd cover for Parthian to early Sasanian times.

Fieldwork: 1971–4 Trousdale, Smithsonian—survey.

Source: Site information by W. Trousdale.

2044. DARAKHT-I TŪT

Lat. 35° 05′ N, long. 62° 18′ E. Map 43.
Revised: 35.08870663 N, 62.30573831 E /
35° 05′ 19.34387844 N, 62° 18′ 20.65790916 E.
Herat Province. 20 km south of Tūrghundi on left bank of Kushk Rūd.

Date: ?Timurid (stylistic).

Description: A shrine, with beautifully carved calligraphy on the marble headstone and footstone.

Fieldwork: 1884 Maitland, ABC—topographical survey.

Sources:
1. Peacocke 1887a: 275—mention.
2. Maitland 1888c: 170—mention.

2045. DARRA-I SABZ

Original: Lat. 34° 52′ N, long. 66° 42′ E. Map 47.
Revised: 34.81646161 N, 66.69239398 E /
34° 48′ 59.26180680 N, 66° 41′ 32.61833160 E approx.
Bāmiyān Province. At the base of a low pass between the Dargāh and Darra-i Sabz Valleys on the road between Yakaulang and Chehel Burj.

Description: A series of artificial caves.

Fieldwork: 2002 Lee—reconnaissance.

Source: Lee 2006: 236—mention.

2046. DARRA-I SABZAK

Original: Lat. 34° 51′ 31″ N, long. 66° 41′ 44″ E. Map 48.
Revised: 34.85994716 N, 67.70592925 E /
34° 51′ 35.80979040 N, 67° 42′ 21.34531440 E approx.
Bamiyān Province. 25 km north-west of Bamiyān on the road to Yakaulang.

Description: A square 'Ghurid' fortress located in the mouth of the valley of the same name, high up on the western ridge,

Fieldwork: 2002 Lee, Society for South Asian Studies—reconnaissance.

Source: Lee 2006: 236—mention.

2047. DARRA-I TAKHT
Including ASYĀB-I BĀDĪ.

Original: Lat. 34° 22′ N, long. 64° 03′ E. Map 54.
Revised: 34.36853487 N, 64.04442489 E /
34° 22′ 06.72554388 N, 64° 02′ 39.92960904 E.
Herat Province. On the right bank of the Harī Rūd approximately 30 km above Chisht-i Sharif.

Date: ?Ghurid (architectural).

Description: Remains of a watch tower amd other remains in the vicinity. On the western edge of the village are some very eroded mud remains whose name implies a windmill (Asyā-i Bādī), and there are several settlement remains in the valley between 1.3 and 1.5 hectares in area, both of which showed signs of looting.

Fieldwork: 2004–6 DAI—survey.

Source: Franke and Urban 2006: 11 and 15—brief description; figs 14, 18–19 and 21, photos.

2048. DASHT-I BIYĀBĀN-I RAY MUHAMMAD

Lat. 34° 38′ N, long. 61° 16′ E. Map 51.
Herat Province. 16 km south-east of Kuhsān.

Date: Late Islamic, 14th–15th cent. (ceramic).

Description: A small tepe.

Fieldwork: 1968–78 Kruglikova, Af/Sov. Mission— survey.

Source: Gaibov et al. 2010: 108—mention (Site K140).

2049. DASHT-I JALAUGĪRAK

Original: Lat. 33° 23 N, long. 62° 02′ E approx. Map 69.
Revised: 33.40195547 N, 61.98082681 E /
33° 24′ 07.03970676 N, 61° 58′ 50.97651132 E.
Farāh Province. Between 20 and 22 km north-west of Shindand.

Date: Early Islamic (ceramic).

Description: Two small artificial mounds measuring 3 × 20 m and 2–2.5 m in height.

Fieldwork: 1968–78 Kruglikova, Af/Sov. Mission— survey.

Source: Gaibov et al. 2010: 111–12—brief description (Sites K146 and K147).

2050. DASHT-I RABĀT-I SARKŪFTA

Original: Lat. 33° 20′ N′ long. 62° 02′ E approx. Map 70.
Revised: 33.37623352 N, 62.07745576 E /
33° 22′ 34.44068856 N, 62° 04′ 38.84074788 E.
Farāh Province. 13 km west of Shindand on the road to Katat-i Nazār Khān.

Date: Middle Islamic, 11th–15th cent. (ceramic).

Description: An artificial mound.

Fieldwork: 1968–78 Kruglikova, Af/Sov. Mission— survey.

Source: Gaibov et al. 2010: 112—mention (Site K161).

2051. DASHT-I SANGAR
      See also 77 BĀGHAK and 527 KARBĀSAK.

Original: Lat. 30° 05′ N, long. 62° 30′ E approx. Map 96.
Revised: 30.15032808 N, 62.58555889 E /
30° 09′ 01.18107468 N, 62° 35′ 08.01198888 E.
Nīmrūz Province. On the south bank of the Helmand between Rūdbār and Khājū. Along part of southern cliffs.

Description: A plain covered in the ruins of old forts and other buildings, mostly of mud-brick. Many have traces of painted arches and domes.

Fieldwork: 1884 Peacocke, ABC—topographical survey.

Sources:
1. Peacocke 1885a: 3—brief description.
2. Peacocke 1887a: 16—brief description.

2052. DAULAT KHĀN

Original: Lat. 33° 31′ N, long. 68° 48′ E. Map 82.
Revised: 33.51016546 N, 68.79757434 E /
33° 30′ 36.59565240 N, 68° 47′ 51.26762400 E approx.
Ghazni/Paktia Province border. On the road between Ghazni and Gardez.

Date: Ghaznavid (epigraphic).

Description: A marble gravestone containing a *naskhī* inscription.

Source: Bivar 1986: 133: mention and photographs.

2053. DAULATĀBĀD, MINARET
      (Previously under 1245 ZĀDIYĀN). See also 8 ABU HURAIRA, 520 KAM PIRAK, 814 PIT QAL'A, 1188 TEPE ZĀDIYĀN, 2281 ZĀDIYĀN KAFIR QAL'A.

Lat. 37° 01′ N, long. 66° 56′ E. Map 27.
Balkh Province. Actually located 14 km north-east of the village of Daulatābād, north of and near the town of Zādiyān.

Date: Seljuk, 1108/09 (epigraphic).

Description: A cylindrical minaret built in fired bricks joined with lime mortar. The upper part has disappeared, a stairway provided access. This is composed of a first flight, of which only 16 steps remain. It is lit by two narrow openings. The exterior is extensively decorated with baked brick and stucco decoration, including three inscriptions, one of which provides the date.

Fieldwork: 1935 Schroeder, American Institute of Iranian Art—survey.

Sources:
1. Schroeder 1936: 135—photo and mention of the minaret.
2. Sourdel-Thomine 1953: 122–30—stylistic and epigraphical analysis of the minaret.
3. Pugachenkova 1963: 102—general summary of the minaret.
4. Hill and Grabar 1967: pls 167–8—photos.
5. Anand 1970: 26—brief summary and photo of the minaret.
6. Pugachenkova 1975—description.
7. Hillenbrand 2000: 152—discussion in the broader context of Ghaznavid and Ghurid architecture.
8. Ball 2008: 186–7—summary.

2054. DEH AS

Original: Lat. 36° 52′ N, long. 66° 45′ E. Map 26.
Revised: 36.93727584 N, 66.67515418 E /
36° 56′ 14.19303372 N, 66° 40′ 30.55503504 E.

Balkh Province. 4 km from Adīna Masjid, 2 km to right of road to Balkh.

Description: A mound and some ruins.

Fieldwork: 1886 Peacocke, ABC—topographical survey.

Source: Peacocke 1887a: 321—mention.

2055. DEH KHUSHK

Original: Lat. 31° 39′ 26.99″ N, long. 65° 40′ 59.54″ E. Map 89.
Revised: 31° 39′ 23.922″ N, 65° 40′ 59.584″ E.
Kandahār Province. At the base of the mountain to the north of Kandahār.

Description: Remains of a possible fort in what appears to be diaper masonry, but it *might* have been a water catchment system that would then redirect the water to a *qanat* system; there was definitely an old tunnel system near the base of the mountain as well.

Source: Ken Zemach (information by D. Thomas).

2056. DEH RĀN

Original: Lat. 34° 15 N, long. 63° 59′ E. Map 54.
Revised: 34.24600509 N, 63.96898456 E /
34° 14′ 45.61831680 N, 63° 58′ 08.34441960 E approx.
Herat Province. Approximately 9 km up a valley south of the Harī Rūd, 25 km east of Chisht.

Date: ?Ghurid (architectural).

Description: A ruined mud fort now only comprising two very fragmentary ruined towers on a mound. Originally an oval-shaped building on a spur overlooking the village.

Fieldwork: 2004–6 Franke and Urban, DAI—survey.

Source: Franke and Urban 2006: 11—brief description; figs 15–16—photos.

2057. DEH SABZ

Or KŪH-I MOHRA or TEPE MOHRA. See also 13 ADRASKĀN RŪD.

Lat. 33.63940412 N, long. 62.26462473 E /
33° 38′ 21,85482264 N, 62° 15′ 52.64901036 E. Map 70.
Herat Province. Adraskān district, near the modern Herat-Kandahar road.

Date: Early Islamic, 10th–12th cent. (ceramic).

Description: A large, prominent artificial mound measuring 90 × 80 m and approximately 10 m high. On the surface were found quantities of 'pseudo-prehistoric' early Islamic painted pottery.

Fieldwork: 2004–6 Franke and Urban, DAI—survey.

Source: Franke and Urban 2006: 20—mention; figs 27 and 28—photos of the mound and surface sherds.

2058. DEH-I KAMRĀN

Lat. 30° 53′ N, long. 61° 47′ E approx. Map 92.
Nīmrūz Province. 11 km from Deh-i Kamrān on road to Deh-i Dādi. To left of road.

Description: A mound covered in baked bricks.

Fieldwork: 1884 Maitland, Peacocke, ABC—topographical survey.

Sources:
1. Peacocke 1885a: 11—mention in general terms.
2. Maitland 1888a: 25—mention.

2059. DEH-I MIR

Lat. 34.76084923 N, long. 69.12938838 E /
34° 45′ 39.05721000 N, 69° 07′ 45.79816800 E approx. Map 64.
Kābul Province. In the Kūh-i Dāman c. 35 km north of Kābul, just to the east of the main road.

Description: None available.

Fieldwork: Mustamandi, ASA.

Source: Gardin 1982: 107 and 108–9—mention.

2060. DEH-I NAU

Original: Lat. 36° 57′ N, long. 67° 09′ E. Map 27.
Revised: 36.94491095 N, 67.14412079 E /
36° 56′ 41.67943656 N, 67° 08′ 38.83482744 E.
Balkh Province. Between Mohminabad and Padah Khāna to the west of Siāhgird.

Description: Ruins.

Fieldwork: 1886 Peacocke, ABC—topographical survey.

Source: Peacocke 1887a: 304—mention.

2061. DIK-I DALĪL

Or DAM-I DALĪL. See also 788 PAISAI.

Original: Lat. 30° 37′ N, long. 61° 55′ E approx. Map 93.
Revised: 30.60741962 N, 61.99348419 E /
30° 36′ 26.71063200 N, 61° 59′ 36.54306960 E approx.
Nīmrūz Province. In the gravel plain north-east of Qal'a-i Fath.

Description: A prominent mound near the ruins of Paisai.

Sources:
1. Site information by W. Trousdale.
2. Tate 1910: 249–50—brief description.

2062. DINGHAL TEPE

Lat. 36° 32′ N, long. 65° 37′ E approx. Map 24.
Faryāb Province. 9.5 km from Yang Qal'a, to left of road to
Alti Khwāja (14.5 km, Shibarghān).
Description: Two mounds.
Fieldwork: 1886 Peacocke, ABC—topographical survey.
Source: Peacocke 1887a: 293—mention.

2063. DIV ZINDĀN

Original: Lat. 36° 17′ N, long. 67° 59′ E. Map 30.
Revised: 36.31066923 N, 67.9300919 E /
36° 18′ 38.40924060 N, 67° 55′ 48.33082344 E.
Samangān Province. 50 km from Urlamish, a little above
Dalkhākī, after Darra-i Kalan, on road to Haibak.
Description: A circular excavation in the rock *c*.50 m
diam. and 20–5 m deep, with sheer vertical sides. No trace
of spoil around it, and no debris at the bottom. Seems
unlikely to have been a cistern; said locally to have been a
prison.
Fieldwork: 1886 Peacocke, ABC—topographical survey.
Source: Peacocke 1887a: 366—mention.

2064. DĪWĀLAK

Lat. 34° 45′, long. 64° 30′ approx. Map 55.
Lat. 34.60922005 N, long. 64.6540816 E /
34° 36′ 33.19219440 N, 64° 39′ 14.69376360 E approx.
Ghūr Province. On the route between Jam and Jawand.
Description: A brick wall with windows and machicloula-
tion blocking a hollow in a cliff face. Probably a guard post.
Source: Wannell 2002: 239—mention.

2065. DĪWĀL-I MAHMATA
(Formerly 1283.)
Or DĪWĀL-I MAHWATA.

Original: Lat. 31° 17′ N, long. 62° 11′ E. Map 84.
Revised: 31.28813527 N, 62.18524386 E /
31° 17′ 17.28697272 N, 62° 11′ 06.87791400 E.
Nīmrūz Province. 15 km north-east of Chakhānsūr.
Date: Ghurid, 12th–13th cent. (ceramic).
Description: Mud-brick ruins of iwan courtyard houses in
the character of a village-like rustaq. Remains of true vault-
ings and well-preserved wall decoration. On the surface are
baked bricks from the wall decoration and pottery.
Fieldwork: 1974 Fischer, Bonn University—survey.
Source: Site information by K. Fischer.

2066. DŪĀB

Lat. 35.73333 N, long. 65.25 E /
35° 43′ 59.9880 N, 65° 15′ 00. E.
Faryāb Province. 10 km south of Bilchirāgh in Gurziwān
district in the valley near Deh Mirān.
Description: Remains of a medieval fortress,
Fieldwork: 1996 Lee—reconnaissance.
Source: Site information by Jonathan L. Lee.

2067. DUST MUHAMMAD, KHWĀJA 'ALI

Original: Lat. 30° 15′ N, long. 62° 58′ E. Map 96.
Revised: 30.24120538 N, 62.97106692 E /
30° 14′ 28.33937340 N, 62° 58′ 15.84092820 E.
Helmand. 8 miles from Khwāja Ali to right of road to Landi
Barechi.
Description: A ruined fort.
Fieldwork: 1884 Peacocke, ABC—topographical survey.
Source: Peacocke 1887a: 15—mention.

2068. FARAD JAGANI
Or QUTANK.

Lat. 36° 48′ N, Long. 70° 07′ E. Map 38.
Badakhshān Province. On the Kokcha River 1 km east-
south-east of Kishm near the village of Farad Jagani ('Far-
aghajaniha') at the foot of the Tepe Surkh hill. The site itself
is known as 'Qutank'.
Date: Islamic, pre-Mongol (?) (stylistic, from poor
photos).
Description: A graveyard said to contain some 20 burials.
According to villagers who robbed the tombs, one grave
alone yielded some 170 beads carved from semi-precious
stones, possibly the remains of a necklace, a pair of gold
earrings, wrist bangles, and a knife. 'Greek' coins were also
said to have been recovered as well as many earthenware
pots and 'an antique instrument'. This may be the site
marked as Sar-i Mashhad on the Russian topographic
maps located 1 km south-south-west of the village of
Farad Jagani.
Source: SPACH, *Newsletter*, 5, 1999: 30—brief notice of
discoveries, a photograph of some of the ornamental carving and pottery.

2069. FARMIS 'ALAQADARI
(Formerly 1274.)
Unlocated.

Ghūr Province. [No such 'Alaqadari of this name known in
Ghūr.]

Description: Reports by Said Muhammad Mashal of the remains of a city with '30 minarets'. Parts are still known as the 'drummers home', 'King's throne', etc. More likely to be towers, a familiar enough building in the Ghūr landscape, than minarets.

Source: *Kabul Times* 1970: 197—mention.

2070. FĀRSĪ

Lat. 33° 47′ N, long. 63° 15′ E. Map 53.
Ghūr/Farāh Province. On the Hārūt Rūd on the route from Shindand up into central Ghūr.

Description: A ruined, very high mud fort *c.*400 m square. No ditch. There are also said to be 'historical ruins' in the area.

Sources:
1. Maitland et al. 1889: 107—mentions the fort.
2. *Gazetteer* 1975: III. 105—mentions historical ruins.

2071. GARMAU

Original: Lat. 34° 28′ N, long. 65° 59′ E. Map 56.
Revised: 34° 27′ 25.858″ N, 65° 57′ 15.521″ E.
Ghūr Province. 20 km east of Daulatyār, on a spur above the village to the east.

Description: A 'neat large tower'.

Fieldwork: 1885 Maitland and Lal, ABC—topographical survey.

Source: Maitland 1888a: 459—mention.

2072. GAUKŪSH

Original: Lat. 34° 47′ N, long. 66° 45′ E approx. Map 58.
Revised: 34.80384609 N, 67.80449873 E /
34° 48′ 13.84593840 N, 67° 48′ 16.19542440 E approx.
Bāmiyān Province. Across the Tagau-i Shahār on the Dasht-i Sarkār.

Description: Ruins of buildings, some with pointed arches.

Fieldwork: 1885 Maitland, ABC—topographical survey.

Source: Maitland 1888a: 519—mention.

2073. GAURAGAI

Original: Lat. 32° 10′ N, long. 61° 32′ E approx. Map 83.
Revised: 32.16356101 N, 61.55348179 E /
32° 09′ 48.81961944 N, 61° 33′ 12.53446164 E.
Farah Province. 5 km from 'Ken' (Qal'a-i Kah?) on the way to Kang, 3 km to the west of the road; to north of Dezak. South of the Hārūt Rūd.

Description: Ruins. More ruins visible among the hills.
Fieldwork: 1884 Maitland, ABC—topographical survey.
Source: Maitland 1888a: 102—mention.

2074. GHALBELA

Original: Lat. 35° 59′ N, long. 64° 27′ E. Map 45.
Revised: 35.98610771 N, 64.44897898 E /
35° 59′ 09.98777220 N, 64° 26′ 56.32432692 E.
Faryāb Province. Maimana district. 22 km from Kaftarkhāna on the road to Kassaba Qal'a, in the Qaisār valley, 16 km below Tash Guzār.

Description: Ruins of an old fort and large village.

Fieldwork: 1885 Peacocke, ABC—topographical survey.

Sources:
1. Peacocke 1887a: 244—mention.
2. Gazetteer 1979: IV. 224—mention.

2075. GHĀR

Original: Lat. 34° 34′ N, long. 64° 59′ E. Map 55.
Revised: 34° 31′ 20.8″ N, 64° 36′ 13.789″ E approx.
Ghūr Province. Before Barra Khāna, between Jām and Chakhcharān.

Description: Illicit excavations in 2002 revealed decorated anthropomorphic polychrome beakers.

Sources:
1. *Gazetteer* 1975: III, Map III-10-B—marks ruins just before Barra Khāna.
2. Stewart 2004: 184–5—mentions the excavations.

2076. GHĀR-I KARŪKH
See also 532 KARŪKH.

Original: Lat. 34° 27′ N, long. 62° 31′ E. Map 53.
Revised: 34.44854369 N, 62.55345232 E /
34° 26′ 54.75728400 N, 62° 33′ 12.42835200 E approx.
Herat Province. 6 km south-west of the town of Karūkh on the left bank of the Karūkh River.

Date: Timurid, 15th cent. (epigraphic).

Description: A small mosque in a cave in the side of the hill near the spring. There are a series of inscriptions set in the cave wall, one 767/1365–6.
   (Note: catalogued in the first edition under **185 CHASHMA-I OBEH.**)

Sources:
1. Samizay 1981: 50—brief description.
2. O'Kane 1987: 251–3—full description and photos.

2077. GHARWAL
See also 384 GUDĒLU.

Lat. 33° 30′ N, long. 69° 00′ E approx. Map 82.
Paktiyā Province. C.50 km east of Ghazni.

Date: Hunnic-Turk, 5th–9th cent. (numismatic).

Description: A hoard of eight coins and four gold bracteates found in 2004.

Source: Vondrovec 2007 – publication of the hoard.

2078. GHUNDI PAISA

Original: Lat. 34° 56′ N, long. 69° 20′ E. Map 64.
Revised: 35.0079059 N, 69.33989678 E /
35° 00′ 28.46125476 N, 69° 20′ 23.62839612 E.
Kāpīsā Province. A small hill on the south side of the Begram plain.

Dates: Kushan, Sasanian, and Turki Shahi, 1st–9th cent.; a few Islamic sherds, Ghaznavid or Ghurid, 11th–13th cent. (ceramic).

Description: Formerly Masson's Kūh-i Bacha, now identified with Kūh-i Pahlawān, probably Shotorak.

Source: Gardin and Lyonnet, 1980 chronological study of unpublished pottery from DAFA surveys.

2079. GHŪR-I ZARMAST

Original: Lat. 35° 57′ N, long. 68° 35′ E approx. Map 33.
Revised: 35.71357691 N, 68.36990763 E /
35° 42′ 48.87688320 N, 68° 22′ 11.66746800 E approx.
Baghlān Province. Dahān-i Ghūri area.

Description: Local reports of an artificial cave or tunnel.

Source: Site information by Jonathan L. Lee (recorded 1996).

2080. GHŪRĀB

Original: Lat. 35° 02′ N, long. 67° 15′ E. Map 48.
Revised: 35.0164252 N, 67.71589529 E /
35° 00′ 59.13071280 N, 67° 42′ 57.22304400 E approx.
Bāmiyān Province. Saighān District. In the Kokadayi valley to the east of Sūkhtar Chinār valley on the north face of the pass between Saighān and Bāmiyān valleys.

Description: A small, square fortress. According to local reports there are also artificial caves in the area.

Fieldwork: 2005 Lee – reconnaissance.

Source: Site information by Jonathan L. Lee.

2081. GONDO

Lat. 30° 14′ N, long. 62° 06′ E. Map 95.
Nīmrūz Province. On left (south) bank of the Helmand, 14.5 km west of Khāyū and c.8 km east of Chahār Burjak.

Description: Ruins, and a surface sherd scatter.

Fieldwork:
1. 1884 Peacocke, ABC – topographical survey.
2. 1966 Hammond, Cambridge University – survey.

Sources:
1. Peacocke 1885a: 4 – mention.
2. Peacocke 1887a: 18 – mention.
3. Hammond 1970: 449 – lists the site (no. 12).

2082. GULBĀGH

Lat. 34.41892767 N, Long. 69.12661232 E /
34° 25′ 08.13961920 N, 69° 07′ 35.80433400 E approx.
Map 62.
Kābul Province. South of Kābul region.

Date: ?Kushan, 3rd–4th cent. (architectural).

Description: A small monastery with a vaulted chamber.

Source: Carl 1959a: 15 – mention.

2083. GUL-I SHUTUR

Original: Lat. 34° 26′ N, long. 61° 11′ E. Map 51.
Revised: 34.43530084 N, 61.18603035 E /
34° 26′ 07.08303120 N, 61° 11′ 09.70925640 E.
Herat Province. 27 km from Ghuriyān on the road to Khwāf (Iran), just before the ascent to Hauz-i Sang-i Dukhtar.

Description: An old caravanserai and cistern.

Source: Maitland and Drummond 1888: 3 – mention.

2084. GUNBAD-I SHUHADA

Original: Lat. 34° 21′ N, long. 63° 39′ E. Map 54.
Revised: 34.34624769 N, 63.57534205 E /
34° 20′ 46.49166672 N, 63° 34′ 31.23138432 E.
Herat Province. Overlooking the south side of the Harī Rūd between Chisht and Obeh, 15 km west of Chisht.

Date: Ghurid (stylistic).

Description: An octagonal mausoleum of baked brick surmounted by a dome 11 m high. It is surrounded by a cemetery that includes inscribed marble.

Fieldwork: 2005 Franke and Urban, DAI – survey.

Source: Franke and Urban 2006: 7–10 – brief description with photos and plan.

2085. GŪR DARRA OR GŪR TEPE

Lat. 35° 43' N, long. 64° 55' E. Maps 45, 46.
Faryāb Province. Near Qal'a-i Niyāz Beg in the upper Maimana River above Maimana.

Description: An artificial mound atop a hill where there have been reports of some gold and other metal items being recovered after rain.

Source: Site information by Jonathan L. Lee.

2086. GURĀZĀN

Original: Lat. 34° 17' N, long. 62° 13' E. Map 52.
Revised: 34.27994606 N, 62.22010944 E /
34° 16' 47.80581600 N, 62° 13' 12.39398760 E approx.
Herat Province. 12 km south of Herat 150 m to the east of the new road to Kandahār just before it crosses the Harī Rūd.

Date: Late Islamic, 16th–17th cent. (ceramic).

Description: A circular artificial mound 35 m in diameter and 1 m in height. 40 m further east is another square mound (40 × 40 m) less than 1 m high. 50 m further east is a third rectangular mound (6 × 60 m) 60–70 cm high. All three probably belonged to a single structure.

Fieldwork: 1968–78 Kruglikova, Af/Sov. Mission—survey.

Source: Gaibov et al. 2010: 110—brief description (Site K156).

2087. GUZARA

Original: Lat. 34° 12' N, long. 62° 14' E. Map 52.
Revised: 34.15729354 N, 62.21045182 E /
34° 09' 26.25674544 N, 62° 12' 37.62656784 E.
Herat Province. Approximately 16 km south of Herat.

Description: A rubble stone fortress on top of a hill.

Fieldwork: 2004–6: DAI—survey.

Source: Franke 2008: pl. 119—photo.

2088. HAFTŪ
     Or HAFTAU.

Original: Lat. 34° 54' N, long. 62° 08' E. Map 43.
Revised: 34.88811881 N, 62.16057244 E /
34° 53' 17.22770232 N, 62° 09' 38.06078004 E.
Herat Province. On the Herat-Batun Kotal-Kara Tepe road.

Description: A large artificial mound with traces of a fort on top.

Fieldwork: 1884 Maitland, ABC—topographical survey.

Source: Maitland 1888a: 162—mention.

2089. HAUZ-I 'ALIĀBĀD

Lat. 34° 20' N, long. 62° 31' E. Map 53.
Herat Province. Pushtūn Zarghūn district. To the north of the Herat-Marwa (Marābād) road above Tūnyān.

Description: Local reports of a covered cistern of baked brick.

Source: Site information by Jonathan L. Lee, 2005.

2090. HAUZ-I ANBAR SHĀH

Original: Lat. 34° 32' N, long. 62° 46' E. Map 53.
Revised: 34.53646635 N, 62.77875171 E /
34° 32' 11.27885388 N, 062° 46' 43.50616932 E.
Herat Province. 14 km from Chakār Shamba-Karukh on the road to Qal'a-i Nau.

Description: Old baked brick cistern and heaps of baked bricks marking the site of a caravanserai.

Fieldwork: 1885 Maitland, ABC—topographical survey.

Source: Maitland 1888a: 329—mention.

2091. HAUZ-I JINDA KHĀN

Lat. 34° 20' N, long. 62° 27' E. Map 53.
Herat Province. Pushtūn Zarghūn district, just to the north of the main Herat-Marwa road.

Description: A covered cistern of baked brick behind the Friday Mosque.

Fieldwork: 2004, 2005 Lee—reconnaissance.

Source: Site information by Jonathan L. Lee.

2092. HAUZ-I PALANGI

Original: Lat. 30° 40' N, long. 61° 52' E. Map 93.
Revised: 30.58119415 N, 61.88747288 E /
30° 34' 52.29893712 N, 61° 53' 14.90238276 E.
Nīmrūz Province. To south of Palangi.

Description: A modern village constructed amidst the ruins of a 15th–16th-century town. The name 'Hauz' refers to the remains of a cistern, originally roofed, and to the southwest are many more ruined mansions and other structures, including a baked brick kiln with glass and pottery wasters. There are also remains of ancient canal systems.

Source: Site information by W. Trousdale.

2093. HAZĀRA QAL'A

Lat. 34° 55' N, long. 62° 25' E approx. Maps 43, 53.
Herat Province. On the right (east) bank of the Kushk River, 16 km down (north) from Kushk towards Kush Āsyā.

Description: A mound, and a second mound further down.

Fieldwork: 1885 Maitland, ABC—topographical survey.

Source: Maitland 1888a: 292—mention.

2094. HAZRAT SAYYID

Original: Lat. 36° 47′ N, long. 70° 47′ E. Map 38.
Revised: 36.46286064 N, 70.77978006 E /
36° 27′ 46.29830400 N, 70° 46′ 47.20822680 E approx.
Badakhshān Province. An exposed rock outcrop overlooking the remote village of Hazrat Sayyid on the Yamgān valley off the Kokcha in southern Badakhshān.

Date: 11th–18th cent. (architectural).

Description: The *zīyārat* or shrine of Nasir Khusraw marks the site where the 11th-century poet-philosopher is believed to have been buried. Built soon after his death, sometime between 1072 and 1076, the shrine today is made up of four small, flat-roofed rooms clustered together, two of which have open verandas. Earlier modifications to the shrine are believed to been made in the 12th century and during the Chaghatai period in the 14th century. During the comprehensive renovation and expansion of the building in the late 17th century, the verandas, supported by carved wooden columns, were constructed and the main tomb chamber was reroofed with cedar wood beams on which verses from the Qur'an are delicately inscribed in *naskhī* script. Renovations carried out in the second half of the 18th century included the replastering of the inner walls of the shrine in a typical Mughal-era motif, which together with previous renovations, spans nine centuries of architectural development and ornamentation.

Fieldwork: 2007–12 AKTC—survey and preservation.

Sources: Jodidio et al. 2017: 312–19—reports on the AKTC conservation work.

2095. IHSĀN RABĀT

Original: Lat. 36° 36′ N, long. 65° 32′ E approx. Map 24.
Revised: 36.55416264 N, 65.59637633 E /
36° 33′ 14.98552128 N, 65° 35′ 46.95480168 E.
Jauzjān Province.18.5 km from Shibarghān on road to Rabāt Audān and Daulatābād.

Description: Ruins of old caravanserai.

Fieldwork: 1885 Peacocke, ABC—topographical survey.

Source: Peacocke 1887a: 107—mention.

2096. IMĀM SHASH NŪR

Original: Lat. 34° 15′ N; Long 62° 20′ E. Map 52.
Revised: 34.27566443 N, 62.32676976 E /
34° 16′ 32.39195268 N, 62° 19′ 36.37113744 E.

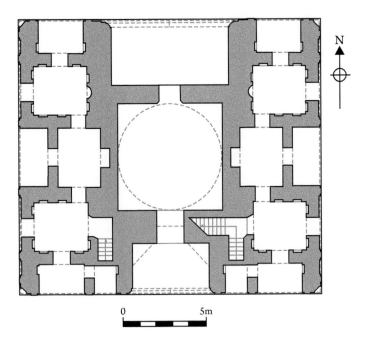

2096 Imām Shash Nūr (J. Leslie, AKTC).

Herat Province. Injīl district, 1 km north-north-east of the settlement of Khisht Pashān on the north side of the road to Sar-i Asyā at the junction of this road and the road to Katani.

Date: Timurid 16th cent. (stylistic).

Description: A fine, well-preserved two-storeyed, baked brick shrine with imposing iwan front and rear. The iwan and elements of the exterior walls are ornamented with blue tiles. The ribbed hood and squinches of the entrance under the iwan are painted. The shrine is situated in a large, medieval cemetery. Some 100 m to the south west, on the opposite side of the road, is a large covered cistern in baked brick.

Fieldwork:
1. 2004, Lee—reconnaissance.
2. 2006, AKTC—preliminary survey and assessment of repair work.

Sources:
1. AKTC, *Afghanistan Newsletter*, July 2006—report, with photographs of destruction of old city, modern development, and discovery of Timurid domestic housing.
2. AKTC, *Afghanistan Newsletter*, August 2006—photograph of hood of arch and painting and brief report on the shrine.
3. Site information by Jonathan L. Lee (recorded in photographic archive).

2097. JAR-I SHĀKH BĀBA
Or DARRA-I SHĀKH BĀBA.

Lat. 36° 47′ N, Long. 70° 08′ E. Map 38.
Badakhshān Province. Approximately 3 km south-east of Kishm.

Description: Remains of 'old castles'.

Source: SPACH, *Newsletter,* 5, 1999: 30—brief notice of discovery.

2098. JAR QAL'A
Or ZAR QAL'A.

Original: Lat. 36° 41′ N, long. 65° 10′ E. Map 9465.
Revised: 35.69422733 N, 65.16407044 E /
35° 41′ 39.21839160 N, 65° 09′ 50.65358040 E approx.
Faryāb Province. Gurziwān district, south-east of Maimana.

Description: Local reports of the remains of a fortress or fortifications on the hillside at rear of this village.

Source: Site information by Jonathan L. Lee (recorded 1996).

2099. JAURU
(Formerly 1284.)

Original: Lat. 31° 21′ N, long. 62° 07′ E. Map 84.
Revised: 31.34680718 N, 62.13196087 E /
31° 20′ 48.50585484 N, 62° 07′ 55.05913128 E.
Nīmrūz Province. 18 km north of Chakhānsur.

Dates: Ghaznavid and Ghurid, 11th–13th cent. (architectural, ceramic).

Description: Open settlement of rural iwan courtyard-houses adjacent to now abandoned canals and fields, a kind of *rustaq*. Ruins of mud-brick houses with remains of vaultings and wall decoration. Abundant pottery on the surfaces in the open courtyards, iwans, and chambers.

Fieldwork: 1969, 1970, 1974 Fischer, Bonn University—survey.

Source: Site information by K. Fischer.

2100. JAUZGUN
See also 315 FAIZĀBĀD.

Lat. 37° 06′ N, long. 70° 34′ E. Map 38.
Badakhshān Province. Location uncertain. The above coordinates refer to a place called 'Jaūzān' north-east of Faizābād in the *Gazetteer,* I (1973), where the 1:100,000 map shows ruins.

Description: Ruins of a 'palace' said to have been built by Zubaida Khatun during the reign of Caliph Abu Jafar Mansur (754–775). The ruins were visible in 1871.

Sources:
1. Faiz Bakhsh 1872, *Report on Badakhshan, Balkh and Bokhara.* British Library: OIC, L/PandS/5/270, fols 152–90.
2. Site information by Jonathan L. Lee.

2101. JUI YAL

Lat. 33° 49′ N, long. 63° 39′ E. Maps 53, 54.
Ghūr Province. 4.4 km from Deh Khuramshahr in the plain 1.6 km to the left of the route to Fārsī, at a point where the route crosses a large water course called Jin Yal 1.6 km after Khurramshahr Tagau.

Description: A ruined fort.

Source: Maitland et al. 1887: 107—mention.

2102. KĀFIR QAL'A KHAIRĀBĀD
See also 542 KHAIRĀBĀD.

Original: Lat. 36° 22′ N, long. 64° 52′ E. Map 24.
Revised: 36.37438459 N, 64.88459446 E /
36° 22′ 27.78453732 N, 64° 53′ 04.54004592 E.
Faryāb Province. South of Khairābād village, 10 km south of Daulatābād and 53 km north of Maimana.

Description: A large mound with traces of brick walls. (It might be the same as the extensive remains that other members of the ABC described under Khairābād.)

Fieldwork: 1885 Peacocke, ABC—topographical survey.

Source: Peacocke 1887a: 109—mention.

2103. KĀFIR QAL'A-I DEH GUL

Original: Lat. 34° 20′ N, long. 63° 21′ E. Map 53.
Revised: 34.33744487 N, 63.35517408 E /
34° 20′ 14.80153452 N, 63° 21′ 18.62668728 E.
Herat Province. In the Sirvān region of Obeh district, 17 km east of Obeh and 5 km north of the Harī Rūd.

Description: Remains of a drystone structure on top of a hill overlooking the village of Deh Gul.

Fieldwork: 2004–6 Franke and Urban, DAI—survey.

Source: Franke and Urban 2006: 15—mention; fig. 22—photo.

2104. KAFSH KHĒL

Lat. 35° 11′ 38″ N, long. 67° 44′ 17.16″ E. Map 48.
Bāmiyān Province. Saighān district, a side valley to the south-west of Saighān settlement.

Description: A series of artificial caves in the mountain side and a small fortress.

Fieldwork: 2005 Lee, reconnaissance.

Source: Site information by Jonathan L. Lee.

2105. KALASHKAU

Revised: 33.65198367 N, 62.30909422 E /
33° 39′ 07.14122820 N, 62° 18′ 32.73920640 E. Map 70.

Herat Province. Adraskān district, spproximately 5 km east of the main Herat-Kandahār road on the edge of a wide wadi.

Description: Two small mounds covered with much mainly undecorated pottery. Remains of mud walls and a stone lined well.

Fieldwork: 2004–6 Franke and Urban, DAI—survey.

Source: Franke and Urban 2006: 20—mention.

2106. KAMĀL KHĀN QAL'A

Original: Lat. 30° 13′ N, long. 62° 45′ E. Map 95.
Revised: 30.3073056 N, 61.87984272 E /
30° 18′ 26.30016360 N, 61° 52′ 47.43380352 E.
Nīmrūz Province. 1.6 km from Landi Barechi, to the right of the road to Rūdbār.

Description: Ruined fort.

Fieldwork: 1884 Peacocke, ABC—topographical survey.

Source: Peacocke 1887a: 16—mention.

2107. KAMĀN-I BIHĪSHT

Original: Lat. 35° 02′ N, long. 61° 07′ E. Map 41.
Revised: 35.04684548 N, 61.12923236 E /
35° 02′ 48.64371684 N, 61° 07′ 45.23648772 E.
Herat Province. At the 14th mile north of Toman Agha, about 84 km north of Kuhsān, on the right bank of the Harī Rūd.

Description: A ruined caravanserai.

Fieldwork: 1884 Peacocke, ABC—topographical survey.

Source: Peacocke 1887a: 63–4 and 451—mention.

2108. KAM-I GAZAK

Original: Lat. 34° 21′ N, long. 63° 39′ E. Map 54.
Revised: 34.34292195 N, 63.64723919 E /
34° 20′ 34.51901280 N, 63° 38′ 50.06107320 E approx.
Herat Province. 11 km below Chisht on the right bank of the Harī Rūd.

Description: A ruined fort. 2.4 km further downstream, where the Tagau Gazak enters from the north, is a pier in the middle of the river, marking the site of an old bridge.

Source: Maitland and Drummond 1888: 156—mention.

2109. KAMUS

Lat. 35° 24′ N, long. 71° 20′ E approx. Map 68.
Kunār Province. 'About a quarter or half an hour's walk from lower Kamdesh close beside the road below the hill and not towards the river' to police station at Bashgul confluence.

Description: Extensive foundations of a building of large, dressed masonry blocks, with some of marble. No decoration or architectural clues. Probably not a fort, as it is in a hollow overlooked by unfortified hills. May therefore have been a temple. No dating evidence.

Source: Levi 1972: 225—brief description.

2110. KANGRAULI

Original: Lat. 35° 25′ N, long. 61° 31′ E approx. Map 42.
Revised: 35.30423591 N, 61.47281821 E /
35° 18′ 15.24929184 N, 61° 28′ 22.14554304 E.
Herat Province. Between Gulrān and the Turkmenistan frontier.

Description: Ruins of an old caravanserai.

Fieldwork: 1885 Peacocke, ABC—topographical survey.

Source: Peacocke 1887a: 139—mention.

2111. KARACHA

Original: Lat. 34° 59′ N, long. 69° 19′ E. Map 64.
Revised: 35.00159859 N, 69.33076395 E /
35° 00′ 05.75490672 N, 69° 19′ 50.75023800 E.
Kābul Province. At the western end of Kūh-i Pahlawān, c.3 km north-east of Begram and to the west of Shotorak.

Dates: Kushan, 1st–3rd cent. (stylistic).

Description: Remains of a stupa on a square base, with a monastery higher up the slope. Several Buddhist sculptures in plaster and schist were recovered.

Collection: Musée Guimet—schist relief.

Fieldwork: 1925 Barthoux, DAFA—excavations.

Sources:
1. Cambon 1996—description of the excavation and discussion of the sculptures.
2. Fussman, Murad, and Ollivier 2008: 160–2 and 307—description of the excavations from Barthoux's unpublished notes.

2112. KARANGO

Lat. 35° 07′ N, long. 61° 17′ E. Map 41.
Herat Province. 12.4 km from Chashma Karango to the west of the route to Karīz Ilyas from Kuhsān.

Description: Ruins of an old village.

Source: Maitland and Drummond 1888: 31—mention.

2113. KARI YAZI

Original: Lat. 36° 37′ N, long. 65° 23′ E. Map 24.
Revised: 36.59629585 N, 65.40411198 E /
36° 35′ 46.66507224 N, 65° 24′ 14.80311324 E.

Faryāb Province. 31.4 km from Shibarghān on road to Rabāt Audān and Daulatābād.

Description: Ruins of a domed building.

Fieldwork: Peacocke, ABC—topographical survey.

Source: Peacocke 1987a: 107—mention.

2114. KARĪZ-I AMRUTAK

Original: Lat. 34° 53′ N, long. 61° 57′ E approx. Maps 42, 43, 52.
Revised: 34.84383758 N, 61.95260838 E /
34° 50′ 37.81528080 N, 61° 57′ 09.39016440 E approx.
Herat Province. Approximately 2 km south-west of Qashawri on road to Sang Kotal.

Description: Ruins of an old fort or caravanserai.

Fieldwork: 1885 Peacocke, ABC—topographical survey.

Sources:
1. Peacocke 1887a: 175—mention.
2. *Gazetteer* 1975: III. 355—mention under the name Sargardān, presumably the same as Karīz Amrutak.

2115. KARĪZ-I ZAMĀN

Lat. 34° 39′ N, long. 62° 16′ E approx. Maps 43, 52.
Herat Province. 6.4 km up the Bābā Pass to the north of the Herat Valley, to left of road. 14 km from Hazrat-i Bābā to right of route to Kushki.

Description: Ruins of a fort.

Sources:
1. Peacocke 1887a: 489—mention.
2. Maitland and Drummond 1888: 70—mention.

2116. KATA SŪ

Original: Lat. 35° 05′ N, long. 67° 06′ E. Map 48.
Revised: 34.99945039 N, 67.67643731 E /
34° 59′ 58.02138600 N, 67° 40′ 35.17432320 E approx.
Bāmiyān Province. Saighān district. On the north side of the Āq Rabāt Pass on the east bank of the Sūkhta Chinār River north of Bāmiyān on the road to Saighān.

Description: A series of artificial caves, heavily blackened by soot.

Fieldwork: 2002 Lee, Society for South Asian Studies—reconnaissance.

Source: Lee 2006: 245–7—mention.

2117. KATA TEPE

Lat. 36° 39′ N, long. 66° 53′ E. Maps 27, 28.
Balkh Province. 12 km from Yang Qal'a to left of road to Takhti.

Description: A large mound.

Fieldwork: 1886 Peacocke, ABC—topographical survey.

Source: Peacocke 1887a: 299—mention.

2118. KAUD-I GAZ
Or SĪKHSAR. See 719 MINAR-I CHIGĪNĪ.

2119. KHĀK-I HĀJI

Original: Lat. 34° 08′ N, long. 64° 45′ E approx. Map 55.
Revised: 34.14968273 N, 64.76223797 E /
34° 08′ 58.85784312 N, 64° 45′ 44.05670604 E.
Ghūr Province. 11 km east of Guzārpām on road to Chakhcharān (Sarah Khalifa).

Description: A *zīyārat* and cemetery, among mounds that appear to be ancient remains.

Fieldwork: 1885 Maitland and Talbot, ABC—topographical survey.

Source: Maitland 1888a: 373—mention.

2120. KHALĪFA RAHMAT JAMSHĪDĪ
See also 427 HAZRĀT-I BĀBĀ.

Lat. 34° 46′ 30.3″ N.; 62° 17′ 08″ E. Maps 43, 52.
Herat Province. Rabāt-i Sangīn district. At the site of the grave of a 19th-century Sufi *pir* located on a high dune (elevation 1318 m) near the village of the same name.

Date: ?Early Islamic (stylistic).

Description: A few metres outside the perimeter of the shaikh's tomb lies the ruins of a much earlier domed complex, part of which is now buried under collapsed walls and roof. Robber pits reveal a baked bricked, arched entrance way leading to a domed chamber. The walls of the chamber are in a herring-bone pattern using square, baked brick bonded with lime mortar.

To the south of the structure is the remains of a wall standing some 1.5 m above the surface with a centre niche. The hillside appears to have once been artificially terraced and there are indications of a more extensive area of buried walls in the immediate area.

Fieldwork: 2005, Lee—reconnaisance.

Source: Site information by Jonathan L. Lee (recorded in photographic archive).

2121. KHAM-I ĀB

Lat. 37° 32′ N, long. 65° 42′ E. Map 24.
Jauzjān Province. In the far north of the province on the left bank of the Āmū Dāryā just before it leaves Afghan territory.

Description: Ruins of a baked brick caravanserai.
Fieldwork: Peacocke, ABC—topographical survey.
Source: Peacocke 1887a: 339—mention.

2122. KHĀN RAGĀB TEPE
Or QAL'A-I GHAMBAR.

Original: Lat. 35° 46' N, long. 63° 10' E. Map 44.
Revised: 35.76181636 N, 63.1627647 E /
35° 45' 42.53890608 N, 63° 09' 45.95291568 E.
Bādghīs Province. On the right bank of the Murghāb River,
7 km above Maruchaq on the route to Qarāwal Khāna, in
the valley to the right and below a low terrace called Pūza
Takhta Hamwār.
Description: A low mound.
Fieldwork: 1884 Peacocke, ABC—topographical survey.
Source: Peacocke 1887a: 84—mention.

2123. KHĀNĀNĪ
Or QAL'A-I CHINGIZ.

34.27704857 N, 62.42487538 E /
34° 16' 37,37486568 N, 62° 25' 29.55136044 E. Map 53.
Herat Province. The very east of Injīl district.
Description: A large mud fortification known as Qal'a-i
Chingiz.
Fieldwork: 2004–6 Franke and Urban, DAI—survey.
Source: Franke and Urban 2006: 18—mention.

2124. KHARĀBA-I YĀR MUHAMMAD KHĀN
(Formerly 1285.)

Original: Lat. 31° 16' N, long. 62 ° 13' E. Map 84.
Revised: 31.2832075 N, 62.21796215 E /
31° 16' 59.54698956 N, 62° 13' 04.66375512 E.
Nīmrūz Province. 16 km north-east of Chakhānsūr.
Date: Ghurid, 12th–13th cent. (ceramic).
Description: Mud-brick ruins of *iwan* courtyard-houses in
the character of a village-like *rustaq*. Remains of true vault-
ings and well-preserved wall decoration. On the surface are
baked bricks from the wall decoration and pottery.
Fieldwork: 1974 Fischer, Bonn University—survey.
Source: Site information by K. Fischer.

2125. KHAWAR

Original: Lat. 34° 47' N, long. 67° 50' E. Map 58.
Revised: 34.78001157 N, 67.84579037 E /
34° 46' 48.04164120 N, 67° 50' 44.84533560 E approx.

Bāmiyān Province. At the southern end of the Kakrak Valley.
Description: The remains of two watch towers.
Source: Suzuki and Aoki 2004: 35—mention.

2126. KHIARZĀR
Or KIAZĀR.

Original: Lat. 32° 58' N, long. 61° 41' E. Map 69.
Revised: 32.95250772 N, 61.65667127 E /
32° 57' 09.02780748 N, 61° 39' 24.01655472 E.
Farah Province. 1.6 km to the west of the entrance to Jamāl
Ghazi Pass at 10 km on the route from Sangbūr northwards
to Karēz Dasht.
Description: Old ruined fort on a mound.
Fieldwork: 1884 Peacocke, ABC—topographical survey.
Sources:
1. Peacocke 1887a: 44—mention.
2. Maitland et al. 1889: 46—mention.

2127. KHWĀJA 'ALI SEHYAKA
Or SHISHAGI GHUNDAY. See also 405
HADIRA.

Original: Lat. 30° 15' N, long. 63° 11' E. Map 98.
Revised: 30.29095828 N, 63.17777022 E /
30° 17' 27.44982528 N, 63° 10' 39.97280172 E.
Helmand Province. On the left bank of the Helmand.
Dates: Hellenistic, late 3rd cent. BC; early Sasanian, late 3rd
cent. AD (ceramic, C-14).
Description: Khwāja 'Ali. (This is Khwāja 'Ali Sehyaka (the
village).) The site is locally known as Shishagi Ghunday.
On a low, broad, rounded, and natural rock outcrop, at the
edge of the flood plain, are the very scant remains of a large
Hellenistic sanctuary and contiguous structures. There is an
excellent ceramic sequence here, probably beginning in the
late 3rd century BC, and continuing until late 3rd century
AD. The sanctuary was destroyed at the beginning of the
Sasanian period and much rubble was recovered from the
well (inscriptions in Aramaic and in Greek alphabet, carved
stucco, gold leaf, probably from a wooden coffer, fragments
of various classical architectonic forms both in white limestone and carved brick.
Fieldwork: 1975, Trousdale, Smithsonian Helmand-Sistan
Project—excavation.
Source: Site information by W. Trousdale.

2128. KHWĀJA BRAHNE
Unlocated.

Herat Province. Chisht region.
Date: ?Ghurid (architectural).

Description: Heavily eroded square mud-brick tower on a stone footing, *c*.10.50 × 9.20 m. There is a glass smelting site 600 m to the south down the valley.

Fieldwork: 2004–6 Franke and Urban, DAI—survey.

Source: Franke and Urban 2006: 11—brief description; fig. 17—photo.

2129. KHWĀJA DŌ KŪH
See 589 KHWĀJA DO KUH.

2130. KHWĀJA GACHAI

Original: Lat. 36° 06′ N, long. 64° 30′ E. Map 45.
Revised: 36.09925338 N, 64.49757654 E /
36° 05′ 57.31217556 N, 64° 29′ 51.27552888 E.
Faryāb Province. On the *chūl* 11–13 km north of Qasaba Qal'a in Qaisār area. Zīyārat-i Khwāja Gachai is 2.5 km further north of the fort.

Description: Remains of a large settlement that includes a ruined fort and a zīyārat on a mound. Surrounded by traces of former cultivation.

Fieldwork: 1885 Peacocke, ABC—topographical survey.

Sources:
1. Peacocke 1887a: 244–5—brief description.
2. Gazetteer 1979: IV. 339—brief description.

2131. KHWĀJA GIRUKI ZĪYĀRAT

Lat. 31° 15′ N, long. 61° 52′ E. Map 83.
Nīmrūz Province. 11 km from Ibrāhīmābād close to the left of the road to Makburah Abīl.

Description: Ruins on a low mound.

Fieldwork: 1884 Peacocke, ABC—topographical survey.

Source: Peacocke 1885a: 16—mention.

2132. KHWĀJA JĪR
Or KIZGHUNDI.

Original: Lat. 35° 08′ N, long. 62° 17′ E. Map 43.
Revised: 35.15252442 N, 62.2948383 E /
35° 09′ 09.08792136 N, 62° 17′ 41.41788972 E.
Herat Province. 93 km north of Herat on the road to Tūrghundi. On the left bank of the Kushk Rūd, 1 km below Sar-i Chashma. Chapgul Tagau joins the left side of the river at the castle.

Date: Middle Islamic (ceramic).

Description: Two artificial mounds. The east is surmounted by a zīyārat, the west is higher and larger, probably an ancient fort. 1 km below the mounds are the remains of an old mud castle or tower, on edge of low cliff, 5 m high, overlooking the left bank of the river.

Fieldwork:
1. 1886 Peacocke, ABC—topographical survey.
2. 1968–78 Kruglikova, Af/Sov. Mission—survey.

Sources:
1. Peacocke 1887a: 376—description.
2. Maitland and Drummond 1888: 63—mention.
3. Gazetteer 1975: III. 274—mention.
4. Gaibov et al. 2010: 112—mention (Site K151).

2133. KHWĀJA KAURĀTI

Lat. 36° 38′ N, long. 66° 23′ E. Map 28.
Jauzjān Province. 10.5 km east of Imām Sāhib on the road to Shibarghān, between Khwāja Kaurati and the hills.

Description: Many old mounds and ruined villages.

Fieldwork: 1886 Peacocke, ABC—topographical survey.

Source: Peacocke 1887a: 296—mention.

2134. KHWĀJA KINTI

Original: Lat. 35° 35′ N, long. 64° 01′ E. Map 45.
Revised: 35.59604753 N, 64.02401603 E /
35° 35′ 45.77111520 N, 64° 01′ 26.45770800 E approx.
Faryāb Province. Qaisār district.

Description: Local reports of many artefacts found here, including coins, pottery, bronze(?) weapons and statuettes.

Source: Site information by Jonathan L. Lee (recorded 1978, 1996).

2135. KHWĀJA KUNDU

35.72492602 N, 64.08936611 E /
35° 43′ 29,73368640 N, 64° 05′ 21.71797872 E. Map 45.
Faryāb Province. On the main Chahār Shanba to Maimana road, at the point where the route to Khwaja Kundu to the south-west branches off.

Description: Some ruins.

Source: Maitland and Drummond 1888: 129—mention.

2136. KHWĀJA LANGĀR

Lat. 35° 56′ N, long. 68° 34′ E approx. Map 33.
Baghlān Province. Dahān-i Ghūri district, to the west of Pul-i Khumri.

Date: Kushan-Hunnic, 1st–6th cent. (stylistic).

Description: A shrine on an artificial mound from which dressed stone masonry fragments were recovered after a targeted looting.

Collection: Department of Information and Culture, Pul-i Khumri—stone objects.

Source: Site information by Jonathan L. Lee (2004).

2137. KHWĀJA QĀSIM

Lat. 34° 48′ N, long, 62° 05′ E. Maps 43, 52.
Herat Province. 24 km from Rabāt-i Sangardān in valley on route to Hazrat-i Bābā.

Description: An old ruined fort.

Source: Maitland and Drummond 1888: 103—mention.

2138. KHWĀJA SAFĀ
See also 483 KĀBUL.

Original: Lat. 34° 30′ N, long. 69° 10′ E. Map 61.
Revised: 34.50862695 N, 69.17660221 E /
34° 30′ 31.05701316 N, 69° 10′ 35.76793836 E.
Kābul Province. On Shir Darwāza Hill overlooking the old city of Kābul to the west of the Bālā Hisār.

Date: Kushan-Turki Shahi, 3rd–9th cent. (stylistic, ceramic, numismatic)

Description: An Islamic shrine built over a series of older terraces on the side of the hill. Several 3rd-century Buddhist sculptures were discovered here in 1905. Excavations in 2004 found traces of a Buddhist monastery complex, although much is obscured underneath the Muslim holy site. The excavations produced many more Buddhist sculptures, mainly 4th–5th century, and a coin of Vima Kadphises.

Collection: ASA—excavated material.

Fieldwork: 2004 Paiman, Afghan ASA—excavations.

Sources:
1. Foucher 1942–7: 146—mentions the Buddhist artefacts found at Khwāja Safā.
2. Paiman 2005: 24–42—description and photos of the excavations and finds.
3. Tissot 2006: 353—National Museum catalogue details and photos.
4. Fussman, Murad, and Ollivier 2008: 81–2 and 302—brief account of the excavations.

2139. KHWĀJA SĀLEH ZĪYĀRAT

Lat. 37° 22′ N, long. 66° 03′ E. Map 24.

Balkh Province. 'Half a farsakh' below Khwāja Sāleh Zīyārat, on the right bank of the Āmū Dāryā between Kilif and Khāmiyāb.

Description: Reports of many baked brick ruins that include a bazaar and kilns.

Source: Peacocke 1887a: 333—mention from hearsay.

2140. KHWĀJA URYA

Original: Lat. 33° 33′ N, long. 62° 16′ E. Map 70.
Revised: 33.51986562 N, 62.27332307 E /
33° 31′ 11.51623596 N, 62° 16′ 23.96304228 E.
Farāh Province. 87 km south of Herat to the east of the main road to Kandahār.

Date: Islamic, 11th–15th cent. (ceramic).

Description: An artificial mound 45 m square and 2 m high.

Fieldwork: 1968–78 Kruglikova, Af/Sov. Mission—survey.

Source: Gaibov et al. 2010: 112—brief description (Site K159).

2141. KILLIGĀN
Or KHILGIAN.

Original: Lat. 34° 52′ N, long. 66° 41′ E. Map 47.
Revised: 34.87085875 N, 66.68934214 E /
34° 52′ 15.09151620 N, 66° 41′ 21.63169932 E.
Bāmiyān Province. Some 15 km south-east of Chehel Burj to the south of the road to Darra-i Chāsht.

Date: Kushan-Hunnic, 2nd–7th cent. (stylistic).

Description: Remains of a very large stupa-monastery complex. The monastery courtyard is very large and surrounded by cells, some still with traces of stucco decoration. There are several larger rooms to the north and east, presumably for communal use.

Fieldwork: 2002 Lee, Society for South Asian Studies—reconnaissance

Source:
1. Lee 2006: 241–6—detailed description and photos, with schematic plan of the complex.
2. Baumer 2014: 75, pl. 55—photo of the remains.

2142. KIRMĀN

Original: Lat. 34° 27′ N, long. 66° 08′ E approx. Map 56.
Revised: 34.47038711 N, 66.3006505 E /
34° 28′ 13.39359240 N, 66° 18′ 02.34180000 E approx.
Ghūr/Bāmiyān Province. Kirmān Valley, north valley, Hazarajat, 24 km east of Sakāba.

Description: A high sandstone cliff with 'Buddhist' caves flanked by crudely carved pilasters.

Source: Dobbs 1904: 6-7—mention.

2143. KIZGHUNDI, SAR-I CHASHMA
See 2132 KHWĀJA JĪR.

2144. KONDI
Including WAISUR.

Original: Lat. 33° 22′ N, long, 69° 59′ E approx. Map 82.
Revised: 33.36746463 N, 69.99285244 E /
33° 22′ 02.87265720 N, 69° 59′ 34.26879480 E approx.
Paktiyā Province. In the north-east of Khūst district centre.

Date: Kushan-Kushano-Sasanian, 2nd–4th cent. (stylistic).

Description: As artificial mound known locally as Waisur. Illicit excavations have uncovered walls, and stones have been removed. There are also remains of a Buddhist stupa where 'treasures' have been illicitly excavated as well as Buddhist sculpture.

Collection: National Museum—sculpture.

Source: Pajhwok Afghan News website, Kābul, in Dari (information by Jonathan L. Lee).

2145. KŪH-I PAZAK

Lat. 35° 11′ N.; long. 67° 35′ E. Map 48.
Bāmiyān Province. On the south side of the upper Saighān valley above Deh Imām and opposite Samūchha on the right bank of the Saighān River.

Description: Local reports of a site where considerable pottery and other material have been found.

Source: Lee 2006: 249—mention.

2146. KUHNA DEH, SUMARA
See also 1117 SUMAQULI.

Lat. 34° 46′ N, long. 67° 54′ E. Map 107.
Bāmiyān Province. Approximately 5 km up the Sumara Valley, to the south of the main Bāmiyān Valley, on an alluvial bluff overlooking the left bank of the stream.

Date: Kushan-Sasanian, 3rd–7th cent. (stylistic).

Description: Very badly eroded remains of a stupa. The (assumed) square base has almost completely eroded apart from its rubble core, precariously supporting a still intact drum of 'diaper masonry' decorated in a double frieze of blind arches and pseudo-Corinthian pilasters separated by pseudo-classical entablatures. The dome has disappeared. Below some artificial caves are probably the remains of its associated monastery. (*Note*: previously included with 1117 SUMAQULI.).

Fieldwork: 1975–6 Le Berre, DAFA—survey.

Source: Le Berre 1987: 80 and pl. 105—brief description and photos; itinerary B-II ruin 2.

2147. KUHNA RABĀT

Lat. 34° 36′ N, long. 62° 13′ E approx. Maps 43, 52.
Herat Province. 8 km from top of Bābā Pass and 11 km from Hazrat-i Bābā. 7 km from Khwāja Jīr up in the Bedak Ravine on route to Hazrat-i Bābā.

Description: A low, barely noticeable heap of ruins.

Fieldwork: 1884 Maitland, ABC—topographical survey.

Sources:
1. Maitland 1888a: 177—mention.
2. Maitland and Drummond 1888: 68—mention.

2148. KUHYĀN

Original: Lat. 34° 23′ N, long. 63° 07′ E. Map 53.
Revised: 34.39540822 N, 63.09666551 E /
34° 23′ 43.46959452 N, 63° 05′ 47.99583924 E.
Herat Province. To the north of the Herat-Obeh road, approximately 8 km before Obeh.

Description: Remains of a settlement, 12.5 hectares in area.

Fieldwork: 2004–6 Franke and Urban, DAI—survey.

Source: Franke and Urban 2006: 15—brief description.

2149. KUSH-I NAU AND KUSH-I KUHNA

Original: Lat. 32° 26′ N, long. 61° 32′ E approx. Maps 69, 83.
Revised: 32.39018138 N, 61.52593512 E /
32° 23′ 24.65297232 N, 61° 31′ 33.36642840 E.
Farah Province. Between 8 and 9 km on the route from Kang to Zikin.

Description: Two mounds with remains of towers on each.

Fieldwork: 1884 Maitland, ABC—topographical survey.

Source: Maitland 1888a: 106—mention.

2150. KUSHK, IBRĀHĪMĀBĀD

Lat. 31° 10′ N, long. 61° 50′ E. Map 83.
Nīmrūz Province. 6.5 from Ibrāhīmābād, 1.6 km to the left of the road to Makbarah-i Abīl.

Description: Ruins.

Fieldwork: 1884 Peacocke, Maitland, ABC—topographical survey.

Sources:
1. Peacocke 1885a: 16—mention.
2. Maitland 1888a: 85—mention.

2151. KUSHK-I BAHĀR

Original: Lat. 34° 31′ N, long. 65° 38′ E. Map 55.
Revised: 34.52685953 N, 65.51314767 E /
34° 31′ 36.69431160 N, 65° 30′ 47.33159400 E approx.

Ghūr Province. 26 km west of Daulatyār, west of Shīniya.

Description: A small ruined fort.

Fieldwork: 1885 Maitland and Lal, ABC—topographical survey.

Source: Maitland 1888c: 388—mention.

2152. KUSHK-I FĪRŪZ

Original: Lat. 34° 32′ N, long. 65° 28′ E approx. Map 55.
Revised: 34.52329509 N, 65.47701223 E /
34° 31′ 23.86232148 N, 65° 28′ 37.24402728 E.
Ghūr Province. On the right (north) bank of the Harī Rūd at the mouth of a *tagau* running into the river, opposite the point at 3.6 km from Puzalich to Bādgah-Daulatyār road.

Description: A fort. On opposite (south) side of river is an old canal.

Fieldwork: 1885 Maitland and Talbot.

Source: Maitland 1888a: 385—mention.

2153. KUSHK-I KUHNA

Lat. 34° 52′ N, long. 62° 30′ E. Maps 43, 53.
Herat Province. 86 km north of Herat on the Kushk Rūd on the road to the Turkmenistan border.

Description: A large fort. All mud-brick, apart from one tower which is made of baked bricks, probably reused from an older building.

Opposite Kushk is a small domed *zīyārat* called Imam Sher Surkh, containing the brother of Imām Reza.

Fieldwork: 1884 Maitland, ABC—topographical survey.

Source: Maitland 1888a: 173–4—brief description.

2154. LAFTĀN

Original: Lat. 31° 41′ N, long. 61° 36′ E. Map 83.
Revised: 31.68980104 N, 61.60063815 E /
31° 41′ 23.28376092 N, 61° 36′ 02.29732524 E.
Nīmrūz. 3.5 km south of Juwain fort.

Description: Ruins.

Fieldwork: 1884 Peacocke, ABC—topographical survey.

Sources:
1. Peacocke 1885a: 18—mention.
2. Peacocke 1887a: 33—mention.

2155. LĀL SAR-I JANGĀL

Original: Lat. 34° 30′ N, long. 66° 18′ E. Map 47/56.
Revised: 34.57073436 N, 65.82117578 E /
34° 34′ 14.64369600 N, 65° 49′ 16.23281880 E approx.

Ghūr Province. Lāl wa Sar-i Jangāl district, Kirmān valley.

Date: Hunnic, 6th cent. AD (epigraphic).

Description: In 2003 there were reports of 'mummified' human remains recovered by looters from under, or adjacent to, a Shi'i shrine. Some archaeological material also appears to have been found. A series of small scrolls containing texts had been found by the local population in this area.

The manuscript is written in a widely spread ornate script, mainly known from manuscripts found in Pakistan and Afghanistan. I named it 'Gilgit/Bamiyan-Type I'. On palaeographical grounds this script can be dated at the earliest into the 6th century AD. Three fragments are overlapping. Two words may point towards a philosophical text, but this is a mere suggestion. They are *avidya* (frgm. 1) 'wrong knowledge' and *samskaranirodha* 'the destruction of individual disposition' (frgm. 3).

Sources:
1. Site information by Jonathan L. Lee.
2. Information on the texts by Lore Sander from photographs by Lee.

2156. LANDI BARECHI

Lat. 30° 15′ N, long. 62° 46′ E. Map 96.
Nīmrūz Province. About 1 hour north of Landi Barechi and 2 hours from the desert cliffs. On bluff on left.

Description: An old fort, a 'conspicuous ruin'.

Fieldwork: 1884 Maitland, Peacocke, ABC—topographical survey.

Sources:
1. Maitland 1888a: 55–6—mention.
2. Peacocke 1887a: 16—mention.

2157. LANGĀR
Including KHWĀJA CHARĀN.

Original: Lat. 34° 52′ N, long. 63° 27′ E. Map 53.
Revised: 34.87221872 N, 63.45525359 E /
34° 52′ 19.98739452 N, 63° 27′ 18.91293480 E.
Bādghis Province. Qadis District. Some 15 km north-north-east of Qadis.

Date: ?Timurid, 15th–16th cent. (stylistic).

Description: A series of Sufi *khanaqāh*s centred around the graves of at least four shaikhs. The main complex, which includes the main *khanaqāh*, lies 1 km south-south-west of the village. A second series of shrines is located to the east-south-east at Khwāja Charan.

The main grave is of Qutb al-Dīn, which is surrounded by a cemetery which contains a series of fine carved and inscribed headstones in *naskhī* script, each between 1.5 and 2 m in height. A number of the graves are carved with what appears to be a symbol of the deceased's trade. The earliest graves may date back to the Timurid period, although many appear to be somewhat later (17th–19th cent.).

To the south of the village there is a mound where coins, rings, and other artefacts have been recovered.

Fieldwork : 1994, Lee—reconnaisanance.

Source: Site information by Jonathan L. Lee (recorded in photographic archive).

2158. LARĀSĪ

Original: Lat. 34° 45′ N, long. 66° 50′ E. Map 47.
Revised: 34.73257923 N, 66.89737756 E /
34° 43′ 57.28523880 N, 66° 53′ 50.55921240 E approx.
Bāmiyān Province. On the Band-i Amīr River 10 km north-west of Yakaulang.

Description: A series of artificial caves on the right bank of the Band-i Amīr River.

Fieldwork: 2002 Lee, Society for South Asian Studies—reconnaissance.

Source: Lee 2006: 236—brief description.

2159. MAJNŪN BEG

Original: Lat. 34° 56′ N, long. 61° 35′ E. Map 42.
Revised: 34.9582879 N, 61.5792897 E /
34° 57′ 29.83645800 N, 61° 34′ 45.44293656 E.
Herat Province. 17 km from Chashma Sabz (which is 38 km from Kuhsān) to the right of the pass over to Asyā Dīn and thence to Gulrān.

Description: A ruined fort on a mound.

Source: Maitland and Drummond 1888: 113—mention.

2160. MALMINJ

Lat. 35.31873361 N, long. 64.98875864 E /
35° 19′ 07.44097800 N, 64° 59′ 19.53109680 E approx.
Map 46.
Bādghīs Province. On the Murghab River, three to four days' journey from Jam between Maimana and Chakhcharān.

Description: Unconfirmed reports of two rock reliefs, one on either side of the river, depicting men and lions.

Source: Levi 1972: 99—report from hearsay.

2161. MARKHANA

Original: Lat. 34° 24′ N, long. 67° 25′ E. Map 57.
Revised: 34.36321317 N, 67.47357224 E /
34° 21′ 47.56741812 N, 67° 28′ 24.86005068 E approx.

Wardak Province. Just to the west of the Nāwur Pass, west of the upper reaches of the Helmand, to the north of the road into the Hazārajat from Kābul.

Description: Some ruins. Marked on the 2001 *Reise Know-How* 1:1,000,000 map of Afghanistan with the same weighting as for Bāmiyān, Surkh Kotal, and similar major sites.

Source: Gazetteer 1985: VI. 555—mentions ruins.

2162. MĀRWA

Original: Lat. 34° 15′ N, long. 62° 55′ E. Map 53.
Revised: 34.25699059 N, 62.89798404 E /
34° 15′ 25.16612580 N, 062° 53′ 52.74255840 E.
Herat Province. On the north bank of the Harī Rūd on the road between Herat and Obeh.

Date: Ghurid, 11th cent.? (documentary).

Description: Remains of a *pakhsa rabāt* to the north of the village measuring 5 × 45 m. Walls survive only to a height of 1 m. Originally it had many baked bricks in its construction, but all had been robbed and reused in the modern village.

Fieldwork: 1968–78 Kruglikova, Af/Sov. Mission—survey.

Source: Gaibov et al. 2010: 116—brief description (Site K162).

2163. MASHGAHI
(Formerly 1286.)

Original: Lat. 31° 19′ N, long. 62° 16′ E. Map 84.
Revised: 31.31434247 N, 62.26213218 E /
31° 18′ 51.63287616 N, 62° 15′ 43.67584692 E.
Nīmrūz Province. 25 km north-east of Chakhānsur.

Dates: Ghurid, 12th–13th cent.; Timurid, 14th–15th cent. (architectural, ceramic).

Description: Scattered ruins of mud-brick *iwan* courtyard-houses and low mud walls for the protection of cattle. The area is strewn with fragmentary baked bricks and both coarse and fine-glazed pottery.

Fieldwork: 1974 Fischer, Bonn University—survey.

Source: Site information by K. Fischer.

2164. MINGLIK
Or MINGAJIK or QAL'A-I HAZHDA NAHR.

Original: Lat. 36° 54′ 39.11″ N, long. 66° 03′ 28.14″ E. Map 24.
Revised: 36.92268782 N, 66.1397689 E /
36° 55′ 21.67616928 N, 66° 08′ 23.16805044 E.
Jauzjān Province. South-west of Aqcha on the old caravan road to Andkhūī to the south of the settlement of the same name.

Description: A moated fortress situated on a circular, artificial mound some 20 m high. Traces of walls are visible at the apex of the mound. This fortress historically guarded the approaches to Āqcha and Balkh from the ford over the Āmū Dāryā at Qarqi and Kilift. During the wars between the Afghans and Uzbeks in the 18th–19th centuries the fortress was besieged and sacked several times.

Fieldwork: 1996 Lee—reconnaisance.

Sources:
1. Additional site information by Jonathan L. Lee.
2. Ferrier 1857: 202—mention.
3. Lee 1996: 319–20—description of seige and sack of 1868.

2165. MUDELAKTAH SHADEH

Original: Lat. 34° 21′ N, long. 61° 43′ E. Map 51.
Revised: 34.39983611 N, 61.6657422 E /
34° 23′ 59.40998520 N, 61° 39′ 56.67192360 E approx.
Herat Province. 3 km from Zindajān on road to Rozanak. Augha is at 5 km.

Description: Ruins of 'some antiquity'.

Fieldwork: 1884 Maitland, ABC—topographical survey.

Source: Maitland 1888a: 130—mention.

2166. NAU NAGAK
(Formerly 1277.)
Unlocated.

Parwān Province. Near Khishtkār, pool of the former prime minister ('piscine de l'ancien premier ministre').

Dates: Hunnic-Turk, 5th–9th cent.; pre-Mongol Islamic, 10th–13th cent. (ceramic).

Description: None available.

Source: Gardin and Lyonnet, 1980 ceramic study of unpublished DAFA surveys.

2167. NIOH
(Formerly 1278.)
Unlocated.

Kandahār Province.

Date: Indo-Parthian, 1st–4th cent. (ceramic).

Description: None available.

Source: Gardin and Lyonnet, 1980 ceramic study of unpublished DAFA surveys.

2168. NUR 'ALI

Lat. 35° 19′ 45″ N, long. 67° 39′ 16″ E. Map 48.
Bāmiyān Province. Kahmard district.

Description: A series of artificial caves located low down on the hillside above the settlement of the same name and on the left bank of the Kahmard River.

Fieldwork: 2005, Lee—reconnaissance.

Source: Site information by Jonathan L. Lee.

2169. PADAH-I SULTĀN

Lat. 30° 46′ N, long. 61° 46′ E. Map 92.
Nīmrūz Province. On the right bank of the Helmand 18.5 km below Qal'a-i Fath.

Description: Three lines of artificial mounds. Some more 'unimportant' ruins lie 3 km to the north.

Source: Site information by W. Trousdale.

2170. PAL PĪRĪ

Original: Lat. 34° 21′ N, long. 62° 23′ E. Map 53.
Revised: 34.35342409 N, 62.40169843 E /
34° 21′ 12.32673516 N, 62° 24′ 06.11434008 E.
Herat Province. Karūkh district, in the village of the same name located at the base of the Pashdan wash on the Herat-Marwa road some 25 km east of Herat.

Description: An imposing, two-storey, baked brick *hauz*. The cistern is one of several located along the highway from Herat to Mārwa but of all of them ('Aliābād, Jinda Khūn) this is the finest, best preserved, and largest, and is comparable to the cistern of Imām Shash Nūr (q.v.).

Fieldwork: 2005 Lee—reconnaissance.

Source: Site information by Jonathan L. Lee.

2171. PANJĀL

Lat. 36.98655868 N, long. 66.44082466 E /
36° 59′ 11.61125880 N, 66° 26′ 26.96877960 E approx. Map 25.
Balkh Province. Near Akbarābād, north of Balkh towards the Āmū Dāryā.

Description: Large silver coins reportedly found. Also a number of gold coins with the figure of a man.

Source: Moorcroft, 1841: II. 495—mention.

2172. PASHTAU
See also 656 KUSHK.

Lat. 30° 50′ N, long. 61° 49′ E. Map 92.
Nīmrūz Province. 8 km from Padah-i Sultān on road to Zaranj.

Description: A broken baked brick arch on a spur.

Fieldwork: 1884 Maitland, ABC—topographical survey.

Source: Maitland 1888a: 74—mention.

2173. PASHTŪN ZARGHŪN
Including TUTAK-I ĀBLĀN.

Original: Lat. 34° 18' N, long. 62° 38' E. Map 53.
Revised: 34.29779873 N, 62.63951618 E /
34° 17' 52.07542188 N, 62° 38' 22.25826096 E.
Herat Province. On the Herat-Obeh road about halfway between Herat and Mārwa.

Description: Two small tells, in both of which stone vaulting has been revealed by illicit excavation.

Fieldwork: 2004–6 Franke and Urban, DAI—survey.

Source: Franke and Urban 2006: 26—brief description.

2174. PĪL KHĀNA
Or FĪL KHĀNA (Persian).

Lat. 36° 39' N, long. 66° 51' E. Map 82.
Balkh Province. 6 miles from Yang Qal'a, close to right of road to Takhti following the course of the Jui Yang Qal'a.

Description: Ruins.

Fieldwork: 1886 Peacocke, ABC—topographical survey.

Source: Peacocke 1887a: 299—mention.

2175. PĪR-I KAMAL AL-DĪN

Original: Lat. 36° 45' 38" N, long. 66° 54' 28" E. Map 27.
Revised: 36.75790884 N, 66.91509863 E /
36° 45' 28.47182040 N, 66° 54' 54.35507520 E approx.
Balkh Province. North-north-east of the modern town of Balkh.

Description: A baked brick single-domed shrine containing a finely carved screen, or *katara*, around the tomb, a motif repeated in the wooden lattice work of the arched windows. The tomb appears to be undated but was doubtless originally part of what was once a large garden (*bāgh*), in which the Timurid shrine of Khwāja Agha Shāh Wali, which lies to the north, was the central focus.

Fieldwork: 2000, Lee—reconnaissance.

Source: Site information by Jonathan L. Lee (recorded, with photographs in archive).

2176. PUL-I KHAJIRA

Original: Lat. 35° 14' N, long. 51° 07' E approx. Map 41.
Revised: 35.23073856 N, 61.10088965 E /
35° 13' 50.65880484 N, 61° 06' 03.20275728 E.
Herat Province. 14 miles north of Kamān-i Bihisht, 1 mile before Tang-i Malu, on Harī Rūd.

Description: A few traces of masonry marking the site of a bridge, said to be very ancient, across the Harī Rūd.

Fieldwork: 1884 Peacocke, ABC—topographical survey.
Sources:
1. Peacocke 1887a: 64—mention.
2. Peacocke 1887b: 451—mention.

2177. PUL-I NAU

Lat. 34°22' N, long. 63° 31' E. Map 54.
Herat Province. 18 km from Obeh, before Sabarz on road to Chisht. 1.6 km past Deh Nau.

Description: Remains of an ancient bridge across the Harī Rūd consisting of two masonry footings.

Source: Maitland and Drummond 1888: 135—mention.

2178. PUL-I SANDAL

Original: Lat. 34° 19' N, long. 62° 07' E. Map 52.
Revised: 34.36025767 N, 62.07166249 E /
34° 21' 36.92762244 N, 62° 04' 17.98495032 E.
Herat Province. 9 km west of Herat, at the Karabar stream.

Description: An old bridge across the Karabar stream. Consisted originally of three arches, one now disappeared. Length approx. 30 m, width 3.5 m.

Source: Maitland and Drummond 1888: 21—brief description.

2179. QADER
Or BĀGH-I SŪFĪ.

Lat. 34.30904821 N, Long. 62.39999016 E /
34° 18' 32.57354160 N, 62° 23' 59.96458320 E approx.
Map 53.
Herat Province. The very east of Injīl district.

Description: Remains of a garden, where pottery and clay pipes were collected.

Fieldwork: 2004–6 Franke and Urban, DAI—survey.

Source: Franke and Urban 2006: 18—mention.

2180. QAL'A GUSH
(Formerly 1276.)
Unlocated.

Laghmān Province. In the Charada district on the 'Alishang River, adjacent to Darra-i Paryāna.

Date: Hindu Shahi, 9th–10th cent. (epigraphic).

Description: Some rock-cut Sanskrit inscriptions, probably marking the Islamic conquest of Laghmān.

Source: Foucher 1942–7: 386–7—description and photos; no linguistic analysis.

2181. QAL'A-I ĀB-I SAFĪD

Original: Lat. 34° 59′ N, long. 61° 37′ E. Map 42.
Revised: 34.99275151 N, 61.62046406 E /
34° 59′ 33.90544464 N, 61° 37′ 13.67063328 E.
Herat Province. 22 km from Chashma Sabz (from Rūzanak) on route to Gulrān.

Description: Ruins of an old fort.

Source: Maitland and Drummond 1888: 46 — mention.

2182. QAL'A-I AMĪRĀN SĀHIB

Or TAQ-I AMĪRĀN. See also 1264 ZĪYĀRAT-I AMĪRĀN SĀHIB.

Original: Lat. 30°59′ N, long. 62°08′ E. Map 92.
Revised: 30.99105979 N, 62.14352657 E /
30° 59′ 27.81522744 N, 62° 08′ 36.69564156 E.
Nīmrūz Province. C.10 km east of Chigīnī, to the north of the Zīyārat-i Amīrān Sāhib.

Date: Timurid, 15th cent. (architectural).

Description: An area of ruins known as Tāq-i Amīrān, including a large, well-preserved Timurid mansion or palatial building measuring 70 × 20 m, with walls 10 m high pierced by ventilation shafts. It has several courtyards and is typical of such large 15th-century houses. The house (House 4 of the Smithsonian project) is sometimes known as Qal'a-i Amīrān Sāhib/Bābā.

Fieldwork:
1. 1903–5 Tate, SAC — survey.
2. 1936 Hackin and Meunié, DAFA — survey.
3. 1965–70 Fischer, Bonn University — survey.
4. 1971–4 Trousdale, Smithsonian — survey.

Sources:
1. Site information by W. Trousdale.
2. Tate 1910: 254–55 — brief description.
3. Fischer 1970b: pls 38–9 — photos.
4. Fischer 1973c: 145 — mention.

2183. QAL'A-I BAGHNĪ

Lat. 34.35313497 N, Long. 62.40073268 E /
34° 21′ 11.28588120 N, 62° 24′ 02.63765520 E approx. Map 53.
Herat Province. The very east of Injīl district.

Description: A large mud fortification with walls standing several metres high.

Fieldwork: 2004–6 Franke and Urban, DAI — survey.

Source: Franke and Urban 2006: 18 — mention; fig. 26 — photo.

2184. QAL'A-I BULDI

Original: Lat. 34° 53′ N, long. 62° 28′ E. Maps 43, 53.
Revised: 34.8993009 N, 62.45514483 E /
34° 53′ 57.48325008 N, 62° 27′ 18.52139304 E.

Herat. 14 km from Kush Asyā to Kushk, at the junction of the Kushk River with the Darra-i Chahār Dabah.

Description: Ruins on top of a high rocky promontory.

Fieldwork: 1885 Peacocke, ABC — topographical survey.

Source: Peacocke 1887a: 181 — mention.

2185. QAL'A-I CHARA

Or KĀFIR QAL'A.

Lat. 32° 23′ N, long. 63° 28′ E approx. Map 73.
Farāh Province. 13 km from Ghanimurgh on the route to Jut-i Kasarmin (72 km from Wāshīr on the route to Sabzavār via Daulatābād). A short distance on is Karīz-i Jaqira.

Description: A ruined fort.

Source: Maitland et al. 1889: 86 — mention.

2186. QAL'A-I CHASHMA KHŪNI

Or KARIZ TAWARKAH or RABĀT-I SAR-HANG RAHMAT ALIKOZAI.

Original: Lat. 33° 57′ N, long. 62° 12′ E. Map 70.
Revised: 33.96124984 N, 62.18973688 E /
33° 57′ 40.49941644 N, 62° 11′ 23.05277448 E.
Herat Province. 10 km from Rabāt-i Mīr Dāūd on road to Chahār Gazab. To the west of the main Herat-Kandahār road.

Description: A ruined fort.

Fieldwork: 1885 Peacocke, ABC — topographical survey.

Source: Peacocke 1887a: 216 — mention.

2187. QAL'A-I CHULAKAI

Original: Lat. 35° 04′ N, long. 62° 05′ E approx. Maps 42, 43.
Revised: 34.8722182 N, 61.92929462 E /
34° 52′ 19.98552576 N, 61° 55′ 45.46062804 E.
Herat Province. 6 km from Kashawri on the route to Qizil Kul.

Description: A ruined fort.

Fieldwork: 1885 Peacocke, ABC — topographical survey.

Source: Peacocke 1887a: 175 — mention.

2188. QAL'A-I DAHĀN-I NAU JŪI

Unlocated.

Ghūr/Bāmiyān Province. 18.5 km from Dahān-i Kushnān or Nawa Agha in the Lāl Valley on the road to Siāh Bumak. 1.6 km after Dahān-i Tamburak.

Description: A large ruined fort.

Fieldwork: 1885 Maitland and Lal, ABC—topographical survey.

Source: Maitland 1888a: 466—mention.

2189. QAL'A-I DŪ ĀU

Original: Lat. 34° 48′ N, long. 62° 14′ E. Maps 43, 52.
Revised: 34.82480122 N, 62.23588743 E /
34° 49′ 29.28439920 N, 62° 14′ 09.19476240 E approx.
Herat Province. 11 km from Karaghaitu (which is 26 km from Kushk) on the route to Hafta thence Kuhsān, at the junction with the Rabāt-i Sangi stream.

Description: A ruined fort.

Source: Maitland and Drummond 1888: 101—mention.

2190. QAL'A-I ĪSHTAR
Or ŪSHTAR or SHUTUR.

Original: Lat. 34° 24′ N, long. 64° 36 E. Map 55.
Revised: 34.45964969 N, 65.01979735 E /
34° 27′ 34.73888760 N, 65° 01′ 11.27047080 E approx.
Ghūr Province. 30 km from Sarāī Khalīfa on the road to Āhangārān.

Description: A small mud fort and other ruins and some artificial mounds.

Fieldwork: 1885 Maitland and Talbot, ABC—topographical survey.

Sources: Maitland 1888a: 378—mention.

2191. QAL'A-I ISKĪCH

Original: Lat. 34° 08′ N, long. 64° 50′ E. Map 55.
Revised: 34.19212282 N, 64.86860175 E /
34° 11′ 31.64215920 N, 64° 52′ 06.96629352 E.
Ghūr Province. On the route from Guzarpām to Chakhcharān at the junction of the Brinji valley with the Tarbulāq valley.

Description: An old fort, with the remains of a tower on a spur to the east.

Source: Maitland 1888a: 44—mention.

2192. QAL'A-I ISMĀ'ĪL
See 850 QAL'A-I ISMĀ'ĪL

2193. QAL'A-I JAN BEG
See also 58 ASHKINAK.

Lat. 30° 13′ N, long. 62° 11′ E. Map 95.
Nīmrūz Province. 7 km west of Khaju to Chahār Burjak, on the left (south) bank of Helmand.

Description: An area of ruins dominated by a relatively modern fort.

Fieldwork: 1884 Maitland, ABC—topographical survey.

Source: Maitland 1888a: 63—mention.

2194. QAL'A-I JUBĪN

Lat. 36° 28′ N, long. 68° 51′ E approx. Map 32.
Qundūz Province. South-west of 'Aliābād.

Date: Kushan, late 4th–7th cent. (stylistic).

Description: Accidental find of a large, seated Buddha in limestone, 1.14 m high.

Source: Site information by K. Fischer.

2195. QAL'A-I KACHAK

Lat. 34° 03′ N, long. 61° 24′ E. Map 51.
Herat Province. 1.6 km from Nayak, on a rock to the right of the road to Fīrūzbahān south of Ghūriyān.

Description: Remains of a square tower on a rock.

Fieldwork: 1885 Maitland and Talbot.

Source: Maitland 1888a: 502—mention.

2196. QAL'A-I KALĀR

Original: Lat. 34° 28′ N, long. 62° 19′ E. Map 52.
Revised: 34.45230874 N, 62.28822892 E /
34° 27′ 08.31145752 N, 62° 17′ 17.62412784 E.
Herat Province. In the plain 11 km from Palikzār, 1.2 km to the right of the road to Āb-i Kalār (near the Gāzurgāh Pass). 8 km from Parwāna on the route to Khwāja Jīr.

Description: A ruined fort.

Fieldwork: 1885 Peacocke, ABC—topographical survey.

Sources:
1. Peacocke 1887a: 189—mention.
2. Maitland and Drummond 1888: 61 and 100—mention.

2197. QAL'A-I KHALIL JĀN
(Formerly 1279.)

Lat. 33.92094821 N, long. 68.09728333 E /
33° 55′ 15.41353800 N, 68° 05′ 50.21997000 E approx.
Map 78.
Ghazni Province. On the road to Ghazni from Dasht-i Nāwar.

Date: Hunnic-Turk, 5th–9th cent. (ceramic).

Description: None available.

Source: Gardin and Lyonnet, 1980 chronological study of unpublished pottery from DAFA surveys.

2198. QAL'A-I KHALSANG

Original: Lat. 34° 50 N, long. 61° 15' E approx. Map 51.
Revised: 34.80451983 N, 61.098047 E /
34° 48' 16.27139520 N, 61° 05' 52.96918200 E approx.
Herat Province. At the seventh mile north of Toman Agha on the right bank of the Harī Rūd.

Description: Ruined fort.

Fieldwork: 1884 Peacocke, ABC—topographical survey.

Source: Peacocke 1887a: 63–4—mention.

2199. QAL'A-I KHWĀJA
See also 477 JŪI KHWĀJA.

Original: Lat. 35° 33' N, long. 63° 20' E. Map 44.
Revised: 35.55375385 N, 63.33272114 E /
35° 33' 13.51387080 N, 63° 19' 57.79610400 E approx.
Bādghīs Province. 1.5 km south of Bālā Murghāb and 4 km north of Jauhār, to the west of the road.

Description: Ruins of a fort.

Fieldwork: 1884 Maitland, ABC.

Sources:
1. Maitland 1888a: 206—mention.
2. Maitland and Drummond 1888: 85—mention.

2200. QAL'A-I KOMAGHAI

Lat. 34.47654779 N, long. 66.52836004 E /
34° 28' 35.57203320 N, 66° 31' 42.09612600 E approx.
Map 56.
Ghūr/Bāmiyān Province. 20.5 km from Dahān-i Kushnān or Nawa Agha in Lāl Valley on road to Siāh Bumak. 3 km after Qal'a-i Dahān-i Nau junction.

Description: A ruined fort.

Fieldwork: 1885 Maitland and Talbot.

Source: Maitland 1888a: 467—mention.

2201. QAL'A-I KUHNA KULAGH PARDAI

Lat. 36.0819689 N, long. 64.85613688 E /
36° 04' 55.08802200 N, 64° 51' 22.09276080 E approx.
Map 24.
Faryāb Province. 26 km from Islam Qal'a on the route to Farzanak.

Description: Remains of a large town.

Source: Maitland and Drummond 1888: 117—mention.

2202. QAL'A-I KUHNA, KANG
See also 857 QAL'A-I KANG.

Lat. 31° 04' N, long. 61° 53' E Map 138.
Nīmrūz Province. Kang is *c.*30 km north of Zaranj; the Qal'a-i Kuhna of Kang is 'Not far south of Kang' and seems to be different from the modern fort described by Tate as Qal'a-i Kang.

Description: A ruined fort.

Fieldwork: 1884 Maitland, ABC—topographical survey.

Source: Maitland 1888a: 105—mention.

2203. QAL'A-I MAMBAR BASHI

Lat. 34° 33' N, long. 62° 03' E. Maps 43, 52.
Herat Province. 27 km from Mamizak on the right bank of the Sinjau stream on the route to Kush Rabāt.

Description: Ruins of a small fort.

Sources:
1. Maitland and Drummond 1888: 116—mention.
2. Gazetteer 1975: III. 219—mention.

2204. QAL'A-I MĪR

Original: Lat. 30° 13' N, long. 62° 00' E. Map 95.
Revised: 30.28064057 N, 61.95415128 E /
30° 16' 50.30606280 N, 61° 57' 14.94460440 E approx.
Nīmrūz Province. On the left (south) bank of the Helmand, 6 km to the west of Chahār Burjak and *c.*1 km to south of road to Qal'a-i Fath.

Description: Some ruins.

Fieldwork: 1884 Peacocke, ABC—topographical survey.

Sources:
1. Peacocke 1885a: 5—mention.
2. Peacocke 1887a: 19—mention.

2205. QAL'A-I MUHAMMAD
See 866 QAL'A-I MUHAMMAD.

2206. QAL'A-I NASHAN

Original: Lat. 37° 19' N, long. 66° 17' E. Map 28.
Revised: 37.31211925 N, 66.29840565 E /
37° 18' 43.62928200 N, 66° 17' 54.26035080 E approx.
Jauzjān Province. At the end of a low sandstone ridge close to the banks of the Āmū Dāryā on the road from Islām Pinja to Kilift.

Description: Remains of a large brick building, probably a caravanserai.

Fieldwork: 1886 Peacocke, ABC—topographical survey.

Source: Peacocke 1887a: 313—mention.

2207. QAL'A-I NAU, JUWAIN

Lat. 31° 42' N, long. 61° 41' E. Map 83.
Nīmrūz Province. 5 km south-east of Juwain fort.

Description: Ruins of a fort.

Fieldwork: 1884 Peacocke, ABC—topographical survey.

Sources:
1. Peacocke 1885a: 18—mention.
2. Peacocke 1887a: 33—mention.

2208. QAL'A-I QAZI
Or DARWĪSH ALI KUSA.

Lat. 34° 36' N, long. 62° 18' E. Maps 43, 52.
Herat Province. 39 km from Kush Asyā to Tunish Beg.

Description: A large ruined fort.

Fieldwork: 1885 Maitland, ABC.

Source: Maitland 1888a: 294—mention.

2209. QAL'A-I SARKARI

Original: Lat. 34° 21' N, long. 63° 42' E. Map 54.
Revised: 34.33925256 N, 63.7118909 E /
34° 20' 21.30920088 N, 63° 42' 42.80724936 E.
Herat Province. 2.5 km west of Chisht-i Sharif.

Description: Remains of a caravanserai.

Fieldwork: 2004–6 DAI—survey.

Source: Franke and Urban 2006: 11—mention; fig. 10—plan; fig. 11—photo.

2210. QAL'A-I SIĀH BŪMAK

Original: Lat. 34° 37' N, long. 66° 13' E. Map 56.
Revised: 34.4273044 N, 66.54692504 E /
34° 25' 38.29585260 N, 66° 32' 48.93013536 E.
Bāmiyān Province. On the road from Lal to Chehelburj.

Description: A small ruined fort.

Fieldwork: 1885 Maitland and Talbot.

Source: Maitland 1888a: 467—mention.

2211. QAL'A-I TUNISH BEG

Lat. 34° 48' N, long. 62° 06' E. Maps 43, 52.
Herat Province. 1.5 km from Karaghaita (which is 26 km from Kushk) on the route to Kafta thence to Kuhsān.

Description: Some artificial mounds.

Source: Maitland and Drummond 1888: 1010—mention.

2212. QARA-I GHŪRI

Original: Lat. 35° 35' N, long. 64° 10' E. Map 45.
Revised: 35.59741523 N, 64.14764782 E /
35° 35' 50.69481468 N, 64° 08' 51.53215380 E.
Faryāb Province. Qaisār district, about 20 km south-west of Qaisār. Exact location uncertain but in the vicinity of Qara-i Ghūri.

Description: Local reports of a fortified town(?) where walls and domestic dwellings have been uncovered, revealing considerable archaeological material. Local tradition associates the site with the Sultan Sanjar.

Source: Site information by Jonathan L. Lee (recorded October 1996).

2213. QARA RABĀT, HAZRĀT-I BĀBĀ

Lat. 34° 41' N, long. 62° 24' E. Maps 43, 53.
Herat Province. 9 km from Hazrāt-i Bābā on the route to Palikzār.

Description: An old, ruined baked brick caravanserai.

Fieldwork: 1885 Peacocke, ABC—topographical survey.

Sources:
1. Peacocke 1887a: 185—mention.
2. Maitland 1887c: 478—mentions it as a heap of ruins only.
3. Peacocke 1887c: 491—mentions ruins.

2214. QARA RABĀT, ARDAWĀN

Lat. 34° 40' N, long. 62° 07' E. Maps 43, 52.
Herat Province. 18.5 km from Dūāb on the south side of Ardawān Pass, 3 km from Kush Rabāt (Site 641) to the right of the route to Rabāt-i Sangi (Site 950).

Description: A heap of stones, the site of a former caravanserai.

Fieldwork: 1884 Maitland, ABC—topographical survey.

Sources:
1. Maitland 1888a: 1641—mention.
2. Maitland and Drummond 1888: 62—mention.

2215. QARĀWAL KHĀNA
See 914 QARĀWAL KHĀNA.

2216. QARQĪN

Lat. 37° 25' N, long. 66° 03' E. Map 24.
Jauzjān Province. 21 km below Kilif, near the Khwāja Saleh crossing of the Āmū Dāryā.

Description: Reports of an old brick caravanserai, next to the Zīyarāt-i Khwāja Sāleh. East of the *zīyarāt* is an artificial mound surmounted by a citadel.

Source: Peacocke 1887a: 339—mention.

2217. QASR-I TULAK

Original: Lat. 33° 58′ N, long. 63° 44′ E. Map 54.
Revised: 33.97157769 N, 63.70422913 E /
33° 58′ 17.67969588 N, 63° 42′ 15.22488564 E.
Ghūr Province. A valley in the upper reaches of the Farāh Rūd.

Description: Extensive remains.

Fieldwork: Wardak, ASA.

Source: Gardin 1982: 107 and 108–9—mention.

2218. RABĀT-I ABDULLAH KHĀN

Lat. 37° 24′ N, long. 65° 41′ E. Map 24.
Jauzjān Province. 13 km south of Khamiāb on the road to Dali.

Description: Ruins of a baked brick caravanserai with a large dome.

Fieldwork: 1885 Peacocke, ABC—topographical survey.

Source: Peacocke 1887a: 101—mention.

2219. RABĀT-I AUDĀN

Original: Lat. 36° 37′ N, long. 65° 25′ E. Map 24.
Revised: 36.56702821 N, 65.32417065 E /
36° 34′ 01.30155240 N, 65° 19′ 27.01432920 E approx.
Faryāb Province. 41 km from Shibarghān on the road to Daulatābād.

Description: A ruined caravanserai with a large domed cistern.

Fieldwork: 1885 Peacocke, ABC—topographical survey.

Source: Peacocke 1887a: 108—mention.

2220. RABĀT-I BĀTUN
Or RABĀT-I MULLAH MURDAN-I MURTAZAI.

Original: Lat. 34° 39′ N, long. 62° 02′ E. Maps 43, 52.
Revised: 34.66652604 N, 62.02990472 E /
34° 39′ 59.49375048 N, 62° 01′ 47.65699452 E.
Herat Province. 21 km up the Bātun Pass north of the Herat Valley. Just above the junction of the Bātun Valley with the Ahmad Kal Valley, on the route from Parwāna to Jutachi.

Description: A ruined caravanserai.

Fieldwork: Maitland, ABC—topographical survey.
Sources:
1. Maitland 1887b: 470, 474—mention.
2. Maitland and Drummond 1888: 50—mention.

2221. RABĀT-I CHAWNĪ

Lat. 34.30087624 N, long. 63.98049456 E /
34° 18′ 03,15445500 N, 63° 58′ 49.78041672 E. Map 54.
Herat Province. In the mountains south of the Harī Rūd near Qarya-i Khārzār, 25 km from the Qal'a-i Sarkārī caravanserai.

Description: A ruined caravanserai.

Fieldwork: 2004–6 Franke and Urban, DAI—survey.

Source: Franke and Urban 2006: 10—schematic plan; fig. 12—photo.

2222. RABĀT-I GHANDAU

Original: Lat. 34° 29′ N, long. 62° 10′ E. Map 52.
Revised: 34.50604605 N, 62.17014573 E /
34° 30′ 21.76576632 N, 62° 10′ 12.52462548 E.
Herat Province. 5.6 km from Parwāna in a hollow to the left of the road to Sinjau.

Description: Ruins of an old caravanserai.

Fieldwork: 1885 Peacocke, ABC—topographical survey.

Source: Peacocke 1887a: 191—mention.

2223. RABĀT-I SAPCHA

Original: Lat. 34° 07′ N, long. 62° 13′ E. Map 52.
Revised: 34.1570075 N, 62.22498038 E /
34° 09′ 25.22701476 N, 62° 13′ 29.92938564 E.
Herat Province. 20 km from Herat to the east of the main road to Kandahār.

Date: Ghaznavid-Mongol, 12th–14th cent. (ceramic).

Description: Remains of a square caravanserai measuring 12 × 120 m. Towers are visible in the corners and the centre.

Fieldwork: 1968–78 Kruglikova, Af/Sov. Mission—survey.

Source: Gaibov et al. 2010: 110—mention (Site K158).

2224. RABĀT-I SHŪRĀU

Lat. 35° 05′ N, long. 63° 15′ E. Map 53.
Herat Province. 14.5 km from Rabāt-i Mir Dāūd on road to Bichagai (east).

Description: A ruined caravanserai and *zīyārat*.

Fieldwork: 1885 Peacocke, ABC—topographical survey.

Source: Peacocke 1887a: 218—mention.

2225. RABĀT-I SURKH, HERAT

Original: Lat. 35° 04′ N, long. 61° 30′ E. Map 42.
Revised: 35.05016025 N, 61.63890213 E /
35° 03′ 00.57688560 N, 61° 38′ 20.04767160 E approx.
Herat Province. On the pass separating Ghuriyān and Bādghīs, south-west of Gulrān.

Description: A small fort or caravanserai.

Fieldwork: 1884-85 Peacocke and Maitland, ABC—topographical survey.

Sources:
1. Maitland 1888a: 151—mention.
2. Peacocke 1887a: 121—mention.
3. Maitland 1887a: 448—brief description.
4. Peacocke 1887b: 453—mention.

2226. RABĀT-I SURKH, FARĀH

Original: Lat. 32° 40′ N, long. 61° 56′ E. Maps 69, 71.
Revised: 32.62969241 N, 61.99434256 E /
32° 37′ 46.89266052 N, 61° 59′ 39.63320088 E.
Farāh Province. On the road to Sangbūr, north of the Kūh-i Ghulghish.

Description: An 'old ruined village' close to the road.

Fieldwork: 1884 Peacocke, ABC—topographical survey.

Source: Peacocke 1885a: 30—mention.

2227. RAG-I BĪBĪ

Original: Lat. 35° 53′ N, long. 68° 44′ E. Map 33.
Revised: 35.87959901 N, 68.74813129 E /
35° 52′ 46.55644680 N, 68° 44′ 53.27264040 E approx.
Baghlān Province. A kilometre south of the village of Shamarq on the west bank of the Pul-i Khumri River, just off the main road connecting Kabul with northern Afghanistan, and 11 km south of Pul-i Khumri.

Date: Sasanian, mid-3rd cent. (stylistic).

Description: A rock relief depicting a Sasanian emperor, probably Shapur I, hunting rhinoceros, and a captive Kushan king. It first became known to scholarship in 2002. It may have been erected here because it overlooked the ancient road to the Kushan dynastic centre of Surkh Kotal, some 25 km further north, hence commemorating Shapur's conquest of the Kushan Empire and advance to the Indus (where there were rhinoceroses).

Fieldwork: 2004 Grenet and Lee, DAFA and SPACH—survey.

Sources:
1. Barthélemy 2004—first announcement of the discovery.
2. Grenet 2005—preliminary report on the discovery.
3. Grenet, Lee et al. 2007—full account of the discovery and interpretation.

4. Ball 2008: 267—summary.
5. Ball 2017: 157–60—summary in the light of new discoveries in the Sasanian East.

2228. RAUZA BĀGH

Lat. 34° 15′ N, long. 62° 13′ E. Map 52.
Herat Province. 14 km south of Herat 100 m to the east of the main road to Kandahār.

Description: Three low artificial mounds with a scatter of pottery and fragments of square baked bricks representing the remains of buildings.

Fieldwork: 1968–78 Kruglikova, Af/Sov. Mission—survey.

Source: Gaibov et al. 2010: 110—brief description (Site K157).

2229. RUCH

Original: Lat. 34° 24′ N, long. 61° 33′ E. Map 51.
Revised: 34.41317939 N, 61.55970237 E /
34° 24′ 47.44581768 N, 61° 33′ 34.92853344 E.
Herat Province. On the right bank of the Harī Rūd, 10.5 km above Rūzanak and 11 km north-east of Ghuriyān, 5 km south of the main road, 69 km from Herat.

Description: The remains of a tomb, the Zīyārat-i Haft Baradārān, a few hundred metres to the west of the village. It consists of a polygonal mud wall, surrounding a brick foundation, with broken bricks, debris, and a few blue tiles scattered around. There is a square undercroft, plastered and in good preservation, under the foundation. Entered by what remains of stairs going down. Contains a plain unmarked grave cover. In 1884 a baked brick dome covered in blue tiles was still standing, but this had collapsed in 1977.

Fieldwork: 1977 Ball, BIAS—survey.

Sources:
1. Site information by W. Ball.
2. Gazetteer 1975: III. 341—mention.

2230. RUI

Original: Lat. 35° 47′ N, long. 67° 52′ E. Map 30.
Revised: 35.77540178 N, 67.86442031 E /
35° 46′ 31.44639360 N, 67° 51′ 51.91311600 E approx.
Samangān Province. On the left bank of the Tashkurghān River 45 km south of Aibak.

Description: 19th-century reports of a ruined fort of indeterminate age. It is possible that Rui—or its vicinity—might be the find spot (or at least the main find spot) of the Bactrian documents, 150 documents on leather, parchment, cloth, and wood that appeared on the international antiquities market in the 1990s and are now in private collections in London and Hiroshima. Their exact provenance is unknown, but it is known they came from northern Afghanistan. Many of the documents mention the locality 'Rob' which corresponds to modern Rui.

Collections:
1. Khalili Collection, London.
2. Hirayama Museum, Hiroshima.

Sources:
1. Sims-Williams 1998 — discusses a deed of manumission in the Hirayama collection.
2. Sims-Williams and de Blois 1998 — evidence of the documents for a Bactrian calendar.
3. Sims-Williams 1999 — initial results of the discovery.
4. Sims-Williams 2000 — discussion of four economic documents.
5. Sims-Williams 2000–12 — full translations of the documents in the Khalili collection in London.
6. Sims-Williams 2002 — brief report of the discovery and significance of the documents.
7. Tanabe 2008 — documents in the Hirayama collection in Hiroshima.
8. Lerner 2009 — discussed the headdresses depicted on the sealings.
9. Rezakhani 2010 — discussion of the evidence of the documents for everyday life in the region.

2231. RŪZANAK
Or RABĀT-I KHISHT-I PUKHTA.

Original: Lat. 34° 27′ N, long. 61° 30′ E. Map 51.
Revised: 34.44621912 N, 61.50910974 E /
34° 26′ 46.38882480 N, 61° 30′ 32.79506400 E.
Herat Province. About 3 km north of the Harī Rūd on the road to the Iranian border.

Description: A ruined baked brick caravanserai.

Fieldwork: 1884 Maitland, Peacocke, ABC — topographical survey.

Sources:
1. Peacocke 1887a: 56 — mention.
2. Maitland 1888a: 132 — mention.
3. Maitland and Drummond 1888: 22 — mention.

2232. SABZAK
See 1021 SHAHĪDĀN.

2233. SAFAR KHĀN KŪSHTAK

Lat. 30° 14 N, long. 62° 58′ E. Map 141.3.
Helmand Province. On left bank of Helmand, 8–10 km south of Khwāja ʿAli on the road to Landi Barechi.

Description: A ruined tower on a mound. The surrounding plain is covered in sherds.

Fieldwork: 1884 Maitland, Peacocke, ABC — topographical survey.

Sources:
1. Peacocke 1885a: 1 — mention.
2. Peacocke 1887a: 15 — mention.
3. Maitland 1888a: 55 — mention.

2234. SĀFIYA

Original: Lat. 30° 15′ N, long. 66° 12′ E approx. Map 99.
Revised: 30.17028701 N, 66.16443455 E /
30° 10′ 13.03325256 N, 66° 09′ 51.96436992 E.
Kandahār Province. On the route from Nushki (in Pakistan) to Khwāja ʿAli below Kandahār, 66 km before Arbu.

Description: Some wells with a low, square mound to the west, probably the remains of a fort.

Fieldwork: 1884 Maitland, ABC — topographical survey.

Source: Maitland 1888a: 14 — mention.

2235. SAHRĀ YAMAK

Original: Lat. 34° 22′ N, long. 63° 32′ E. Map 54.
Revised: 34.36502207 N, 63.53850155 E /
34° 21′ 54.07947000 N, 63° 32′ 18.60557064 E.
Herat Province. 8 km from Walang-i Rakwaja (which is 30 km from Obeh) on the south bank of the Harī Rūd on the route to Sabarz.

Description: A ruined fort.

Source: Maitland and Drummond 1888: 155 — mention.

2236. SAMŪCHHĀ
See 286 DEHMĀN.

2237. SANGCHĀRAK

Original: Lat. 35° 55′ N, long. 66° 27′ E. Map 47.
Revised: 35° 55′ 22.231″ N 66° 21′ 47.259″ E approx.
Jauzjān Province. Sangchārak is a village and district.

Description: Local reports of figures and other remains from the village of Istārāb in Sangchārak district. A 'Kushan' column base has also been recorded.

From a cave in Sangchārak district a Greek tax receipt in leather was recovered and is now in the Ashmolean Museum.

Sources:
1. Local reports by Jonathan L. Lee.
2. Rea, Senior, and Hollis 1994 — detailed translation, analysis, and account of the discovery of the Greek document.
3. Grenet 1996 — discussion of names mentioned in the document.
4. Rapin 1996 — discussion of the Greek document.
5. Rougemont 2012a: 191–2 — full text, translation, and discussion.

2238. SANGINA TEPE

Original: Lat. 33° 40′ N, long. 69° 15′ E approx. Map 82.
Revised: 33.5946381 N, 69.23341484 E /
33° 35′ 40.69715640 N, 69° 14′ 00.29340960 E approx.
Paktiyā Province. Near the town of Gardez.

Dates: Hunnic-Turk, 5th–9th cent. AD; early Islamic, 10th–13th cent. (ceramic).

Description: None available.

Source: Gardin and Lyonnet, 1980 chronological study of unpublished pottery from DAFA surveys.

2239. SANJITAK

Original: Lat. 34° 27′ N, long. 69° 18′ E. Map 62.
Revised: 34.44891811 N, 69.30177165 E /
34° 26′ 56.10521040 N, 69° 18′ 06.37792740 E.
Kābul Province. In the foothills between Saka and Butkhāk.

Description: A spring. Many mounds and caves, where funeral jars have been found. Also a deep rock-cut cistern.

Source: Masson 1842: II. 237 — brief description.

2240. SARAK-I KHALIFA

Lat. 34° 15′ N, long. 64° 54′ E. Map 55.
Ghūr Province. 28 km north-east of Guzarpām on the road to Chakhcharān. 10 km from Tarbulah to the left of the road to Au Chush.

Description: Two ruined towers.

Fieldwork: 1885 Maitland and Talbot, ABC — topographical survey.

Sources:
1. Maitland 1888a: 395–6 — mention.
2. Maitland and Drummond 1888: 162 — mention.
3. Gazetteer 1975: III. 354 — mentions a ruined fort.

2241. SARDEH ULYA

Original: Lat. 31° 43′ N, long. 65° 43′ E approx. Map 89.
Revised: 31.71015279 N, 65.69955813 E /
31° 42′ 36.55005120 N, 065° 41′ 58.40927808 E.
Kandahār Province. In the Arghandāb valley approximately halfway between Kandahār and the bridge across the Arghandāb River on the road to the Arghandāb Dam. 2 km north of a square tower on the west side of the road.

Date: ?Kushan, 1st–3rd cent. (ceramic).

Description: Three low mounds, two to the west of the road and one to the east, that look like burial mounds. Sherd scatters both on the mounds and the adjacent fields.

Fieldwork: 1974 Swiny, BIAS — survey.

Source: Site information by S. Swiny in unpublished BIAS archive.

2242. SHĀH MĀR

Original: Lat. 33° 50′ N, long. 68° 37′ E. Map 80.
Revised: 33.84398266 N, 68.61989814 E /
33° 50′ 38.33758500 N, 68° 37′ 11.63332056 E.
Ghazni Province. Near the village of Haft Asyā in the Chakar valley near Ghazni.

Description: A tepe known as Shāh Mār, 'king of snakes', tentatively identified with the abode of the god Zuna or Suna in Buddhist mythology.

Source: Verardi and Paparatti 2004: 91 — mention.

2243. SHAHĀR KALĪL
Or CHAHĀR DARRA.

Original: Lat. 34° 57′ N, long. 62° 15′ E. Map 43.
Revised: 35.03684109 N, 62.29406847 E /
35° 02′ 12.62792040 N, 62° 17′ 38.64649560 E approx.
Herat Province. On the left (west) bank of the Kushk river, 26 km south of Tūrghundi.

Description: Remains of an ancient fort.

Fieldwork: 1884–5 Maitland and Peacocke, ABC — topographical survey.

Sources:
1. Maitland 1888a: 171 — mention.
2. Peacocke 1887a: 180 — mention.

2244. SHAHRAK KUHNA

Original: Lat. 36° 52′ N, long. 67° 09′ E. Map 27.
Revised: 36.87437019 N, 67.14651609 E /
36° 52′ 27.73269408 N, 67° 08′ 47.45791932 E.
Balkh Province. East of the mound of Āq Tepe, 16 km north of Mazār to the east of the road to Siahgird.

Description: Ruins.

Fieldwork: 1886 Peacocke, ABC — topographical survey.

Source: Peacocke 1887a: 303 — mention.

2245. SHAHR-I GHULGHULA, KŪH-I BĀBĀ

Lat. 34° 48′ N, long. 67° 51′ E. Map 58.
Bāmiyān Province. About 1 hour's walk just to the south of Shahr-i Ghulghala, towards the Kūh-i Bābā.

Date: ?Hunnic.

Description: A line of four burial mounds, reminiscent of Hunnic qurghans. No pottery. They appear unexcavated, though one is partly washed away and another has been cut by a canal.

Source: Levi 1972: 69–70 and 72 — brief description.

2246. SHAIKH TASH TAIMUR

Original: Lat. 36° 51′ N, long. 66° 45′ E. Map 26.
Revised: 36.83598743 N, 66.75918634 E /
36° 50′ 09.55474044 N, 66° 45′ 33.07081716 E.
Balkh Province. 8 km from Adīna Masjid, 1.5 km to the right of the road to Balkh.

Description: A large mound.

Fieldwork: 1886 Peacocke, ABC – topographical survey.

Source: Peacocke 1887a: 321 – mention.

2247. SHAIRKHAJ

Original: Lat. 34° 21′ N, long. 63° 55′ E. Map 54.
Revised: 34.35988294 N, 63.90519284 E /
34° 21′ 35.57859480 N, 63° 54′ 18.69421680 E approx.
Herat Province. A ravine running southwards into the Harī Rūd between Chisht and Dahān-i Hamwār.

Description: Remains of a settlement, 1 hectare in area.

Fieldwork: 2004–6 Franke and Urban, DAI – survey.

Source: Franke and Urban 2006: 15 – mention.

2248. SHAWRA CHELAKHĀNA

Lat. 34° 26′ N, long. 63° 10′ E. Map 53.
Herat Province. 7 km north of Obeh.

Description: Remains of a settlement, 1.85 hectare in area. Illicit excavations have revealed traces of drystone walls. There is also a cemetery stretching for some 500 m, none of the graves in Islamic orientation and many of them looted, so presumed non-Islamic.

Fieldwork: 2004–6 Franke and Urban, DAI – survey.

Source: Franke and Urban 2006: 15 and 18 – mention; fig. 24 – photo.

2249. SĪMKŪH

Lat. 35° 13′ N, long. 61° 24′ E. Maps 41, 42.
Herat/Bādghīs Province. On the road from the head of the Chilgazi Rūd across two low passes to Chashma Sīmkūh, in a hollow on the south side of the saddle.

Description: Traces of ancient copper mining.

Fieldwork: 1885 Peacocke, ABC – topographical survey.

Source: Peacocke 1887a: 127 – mention.

2250. SĪR HANGĀN
Or SARHANGI. See also 684 LĀSH.

Lat. 31° 42′ N, long. 61° 33′ E. Map 83.
Nīmrūz Province. To the north-west of Juwain fort.

Description: Ruins of an 'old Turkman city' (mentioned by Peacocke quite separately from his descriptions of Lāsh, with which it might otherwise be confused).

Fieldwork: 1884 Peacocke, ABC – topographical survey.

Sources:
1. Peacocke 1885a: 18 – mention.
2. Peacocke 1887a: 33 – mention.

2251. SUKHTA CHINĀR

Original: Lat. 35° 07′ N, long. 67° 43′ E. Map 48.
Revised: 35.11803796 N, 67.69147789 E /
35° 07′ 04.93666320 N, 67° 41′ 29.32038600 E approx.
Bāmiyān Province. Saighān district. About 20 km south of Saighān on the road to Bāmiyān.

Description: A complex of some 15 artificial caves behind the village.

Fieldwork: 2002 Lee, Society for South Asian Studies – reconnaissance.

Source: Lee 2006: 245–7 – mention and photo.

2252. SUKHTA QAL'A

Original: Lat. 36° 03′ N, long. 66° 04′ E. Maps 24, 47.
Revised: 36.02115928 N, 66.11275286 E /
36° 01′ 16.17340440 N, 66° 06′ 45.91029276 E.
Faryāb Province. 8 km from Laghmān on the route to Sar-i Pul.

Description: A ruined fort.

Source: Maitland 1888c: 16 – mention.

2253. SUM-I SANGAR

Original: Lat. 36° 18′ N, long. 67° 52′ E approx. Map 30.
Revised: 35.72292565 N, 67.81347738 E /
35° 43′ 22.53235080 N, 67° 48′ 48.51857520 E approx.
Samangān Province. West or south-west of Hazār Sum.

Description: Another series of artificial caves, similar to Hazār Sum.

Sources:
1. Holdich 1887: 39 – mention.
2. Yate 1888: 322 – mention.

2254. SURKHI
Or KUSHK.

Lat. 30° 42′ N, long. 61° 51′ E. Map 92.
Nīmrūz Province. 16 km north of Qal'a Fath to left of road to Padah-i Sultān. Also at 3.6 km after Padah-i Sultān to Deh-i Kamrān.

Description: The entire plain around covered in ruins, stretching for 5.6 km.

Fieldwork: 1884 Peacocke, ABC—topographical survey.

Sources:
1. Peacocke 1885a: 8–9—mention.
2. Peacocke 1887a: 22—mention.

2255. TAGAU YĀRĪ

Original: Lat. 34° 27′ N, long. 63° 16′ E. Map 53.
Revised: 34.46366913 N, 63.27862078 E /
34° 27′ 49.20885720 N, 63° 16′ 43.03479000 E approx.
Herat Province. Obeh region.

Description: Remains of a settlement, 1.1 hectare in area.

Fieldwork: 2004–6 Franke and Urban, DAI—survey.

Source: Franke and Urban 2006: 15—mention.

2256. TAGAU RABĀT

Original: Lat. 34° 38′ N, long. 62°50′ E. Map 53.
Revised: 34.6366436 N, 62.83709854 E /
34° 38′ 11.91694704 N, 62° 50′ 13.55474580 E.
Herat Province. At the northern foot of Zarmast Pass, 9 km from Armalik.

Description: A ruined caravanserai.

Fieldwork: 1885 Peacocke, ABC—topographical survey.

Source: Peacocke 1887a: 224—mention.

2257. TAGAU-I MAGH

Original: Lat. 35° 23′ N, long. 65° 15′ E. Map 46.
Revised: 35.3945877 N, 65.26005247 E /
35° 23′ 40.51572000 N, 65° 15′ 36.18890280 E approx.
Faryāb Province. Laulāsh district, in the vicinity of Guzān and Hashtomīn.

Description: Local reports of the discovery of a manuscript in a wooden cover.

Source: Information reported by Jonathan L. Lee (1996).

2258. TAGAU QAL'A

Original: Lat. 35° 53′ N, long. 65° 24′ E. Maps 24, 46.
Revised: 35.88200791 N, 65.41187767 E /
35° 52′ 55.22847456 N, 65° 24′ 42.75959436 E.
Faryāb Province. Gurziwān district, near Kauliyān.

Description: Local reports of a fort or fortified position in the main Shirin Tagau valley. Baked brick and a number of metal items are reported to have been discovered here by local villagers.

Source: Information reported by Jonathan L. Lee (1996).

2259. TAKHT-I ĀRĀ
Or TAKHĀRĀ.

Original: Lat. 35° 43′ N, long. 65° 20′ E. Map 46.
Revised: 35.70525723 N, 65.33302466 E /
35° 42′ 18.92603520 N, 65° 19′ 58.88879040 E approx.
Faryāb Province. Gurziwān district, near Ghulbiyān.

Description: Local reports of antiquities.

Source: Information reported by Jonathan L. Lee (1996).

2260. TAKHT-I PĀDSHĀH

Lat. 35° 57′ N, long. 68° 35′ E approx. Map 33.
Baghlān Province. Location unknown, but said to be in the region of Dahān-i Ghūri, to the west of Pul-i Khumri.

Description: A series of artificial caves and passageways, possibly of Buddhist origin, reported by the Department of Information and Culture in Baghlān.

Source: Information reported by Jonathan L. Lee (1996).

2261. TANG-I SAFIDAK

Original: Lat. 34° 44′ N, long. 66° 46′ E. Map 47.
Revised: 34.74684371 N, 66.7720166 E /
34° 44′ 48.63733800 N, 66° 46′ 19.25975280 E approx.
Bāmiyān Province. A side gully to the south of the Band-i Amīr River approximately 25 km to the west of Yakaulang, between Shahr-i Barbar and Chehel Burj. The site is 1 km south of the village of Tang-i Safīdak.

Date: Turk, 8th cent. (epigraphic).

Description: The remains of a Buddhist stupa made of lime-stone, discovered in 1996. On the east side is a 13-line Bactrian dedicatory inscription. Inside the stupa a vase, some coins, and a manuscript were discovered. On the ridge adjacent are a number of artificial caves, mostly now collapsed, and the foundations of further remains are reported in the vicinity.

Sources:
1. Lee and Sims-Williams 2003—description of the remains and analysis and translation of the inscription, dated to the 8th century.
2. Ball 2008: 270—summary.
3. Sims-Williams 2010: 203–5—publication of a Bactrian document said to have come from Bamiyan, but more likely the manuscript found in the Tang-i Safīdak stupa.
4. Davary 2012—discussion of the inscription, favouring an earlier date of AD 624.

2262. TEKIR

Original: Lat. 34° 37′ N, long. 61° 16′ E. Map 51.
Revised: 34.62720826 N, 61.28241998 E /
34° 37′ 37.94971800 N, 61° 16′ 56.71191000 E approx.

Herat Province. To the north of the road from Kuhsān to Herat, approximately 3 km to the north of the bridge over the Harī Rūd at Tīrpul.

Date: Middle Islamic (ceramic).

Description: A small mound.

Fieldwork: 1968–78 Kruglikova, Af/Sov. Mission—survey.

Source: Gaibov et al. 2010: 108—mention (Site K140).

2263. TEPE BĀGH-I SŪR
Or BĀGHSŪR.

Original: Lat. 36° 56′ N, long. 66° 50′ E. Map 80.
Revised: 36.92827594 N, 66.83002108 E /
36° 55′ 41.79339552 N, 066° 49′ 48.07589016 E.
Balkh Province. South of Daulatābād on the west side of the main road to Balkh.

Date: Kushan(?), 1st–3rd cent. (ceramic).

Description: A low dual-level mound, higher on the north. A number of similar low mounds in the same area. Unglazed red ware shards scatter the site

Fieldwork: 2000 Lee—reconnaissance.

Source: Site information by Jonathan L. Lee.

2264. TEPE BANAUSHAK

Lat. 34° 18′ N, long. 63° 37′ E approx. Map 54.
Herat Province. 12.5 km south-west of Chisht, high up in the hills and isolated from any settlement.

Description: Remains of a pottery kiln, with a scatter of waster fragments. Traces of a square stone building 150 m to the north.

Fieldwork: 2004–6 Franke and Urban, DAI—survey.

Source: Franke and Urban 2006: 18—brief description; fig. 25—photo.

2265. TEPE CHAHĀR DARRA

Original: Lat. 35° 01′ N, long. 62° 18′ E. Map 43.
Revised: 35.02455422 N, 62.29555321 E /
35° 01′ 28.39519884 N, 62° 17′ 43.99154052 E.
Herat Province. 23 km from Tūrghundi on the road to Kush Asyā. 1.5 km after Shahar Khalīl.

Description: An old fort on a mound.

Fieldwork: 1885 Peacocke, ABC—topographical survey.

Source: Peacocke 1887a: 180—mention.

2266. TEPE KUNDUR

Lat. 34° 18′ N, long. 62° 38′ E approx. Map 52.
Herat Province. Pashtūn Zarghūn region.

Description: A large artificial mound measuring 120 × 90 m, approximately 10 m high.

Fieldwork: 2004–6 Franke and Urban, DAI—survey.

Source: Franke and Urban 2006: 15—brief description.

2267. TEPE MUCHAK
(Formerly 1281.)

Original: Lat. 36° 48′ N, long. 66° 00′ E approx. Map 24.
Revised: 36.80751934 N, 65.979326 E /
36° 48′ 27.06960672 N, 065° 58′ 45.57359820 E.
Jauzjān Province. Between Shibarghān and Āqcha.

Dates: Achaemenid, 6th–4th cent. BC; Kushan and Hunnic-Turk, 1st–9th cent.; Timurid, 15th–16th cent. (ceramic).

Description: None available.

Source: Gardin and Lyonnet, 1980 chronological study of unpublished pottery from DAFA surveys.

2268. TEPE NĀRENJ, KĀBUL
See also 1137 TAKHT-I SHĀH. Including QUL-I TŪT.

Original: Lat. 34° 29′ N, long. 69° 10′ E. Map 61.
Revised: 34.49205226 N, 69.18185904 E /
34° 29′ 31.38815040 N, 69° 10′ 54.69253320 E approx.
Kābul Province. On a northern spur of the Kūh-i Zamburak (formerly Kūh-i Takht-i Shāh) between the mountain and the Kul-i Hashmat Khān, south of the Bālā Hisār.

Dates: Hunnic-Hindu Shahi, 5th–9th cent. (numismatic, stylistic).

Description: A very large Buddhist monastic complex of five groups of buildings on a series of nine artificial terraces, possibly the main Buddhist centre for the Kābul region that remained active until the Muslim conquest. It comprises one large stupa and five small stupas. The associated chapels contained many votive stupas and large numbers of Buddhist sculptures of clay coated with stucco.

400 m to the north is a small monastery, Qul-i Tūt, excavated during the Tepe Nārenj excavations.

Possibly the same as Site 1137, Takht-i Shāh, excavated by Masson, but the identification is disputed so the two are treated separately.

Fieldwork: 2004–12 Paiman, ASA—excavations.

Sources:
1. Paiman 2005—brief description with photos of the excavations and main discoveries.
2. Fussman, Murad, and Ollivier 2008: 83–93 and 270–5—detailed description and photos of the excavations.
3. Paiman 2008—report on the 2007 excavations.
4. Paiman and Alram 2010—summary of the historical background, the excavations, and the coin finds.

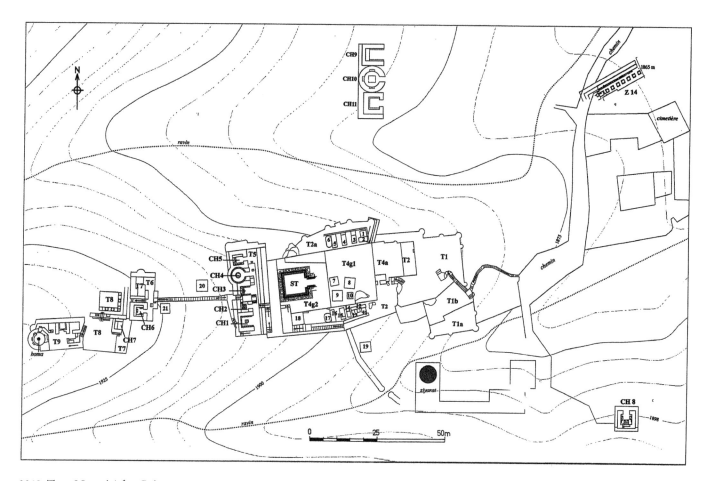

2268 Tepe Nārenj (after Paiman 2013).

5. Paiman and Alram 2013—full report on the excavations, the main finds, and the coins.
6. Baumer 2014: 75—brief mention.

2269. TEPE SALĀM

Lat. 34° 31′ N, long. 69° 08′ E. Map 61.
Kabul Province. Aliābād village, west of Kūh-i Asmāī.
Description: Buddhist remains.
Source: ?Masson.

2270. TEPE SAYYID MUKHTAR
See also 351 GHĀR-I DARWĪSHĀN.

Original: Lat. 34° 27′ N, long. 62° 06′ E approx. Map 52.
Revised: 34.38750485 N, 62.17860061 E /
34° 23′ 15.01746324 N, 62° 10′ 42.96218808 E.
Herat Province. Approximately 15 km to the north-west side of Herat on the side of a hill.
Date: Timurid, 16th cent. (stylistic).
Description: The grave of the painter Behzād. There are also several other old decorated and inscribed tombstones.

Satellite photographs reveal a further shrine/grave complex to the south-west of the building. There is also a small shrine of Sayed Mukhtar on the hill, 10 m from Behzād's tomb with attractive decorated brickwork.
Source: Zia Langari (information by Jonathan L. Lee).

2271. TĪZNAI TAGAU

Original: Lat. 32° 42′ N, long. 64° 41′ E. Map 87.
Revised: 32.71424287 N, 64.66476656 E /
32° 42′ 51.27431832 N, 64° 39′ 53.15961132 E.
Helmand Province. On the route from Girishk to Ghūr, sub-route Sarbesha to Pai Tīznai, at the junction of the Tīznau Tagau with the Rūd-i Mūsa Qal'a.
Description: An old ruined fort.
Source: Maitland et al. 1889: 92—mention.

2272. TŪPKHĀNA QAL'A
See also 542 KHAIRĀBĀD.

Original: Lat. 36° 22′ N, long. 64° 54′ E. Map 24.
Revised: 36.38598294 N, 64.91572163 E /

36° 23′ 09.53859120 N, 64° 54′ 56.59787484 E.
Faryāb Province. 30 km from Rabāt-i Audān on the road to
Daulatābād.

Description: A ruined fort.

Fieldwork: 1885 Peacocke, ABC—topographical survey.

Source: Peacocke 1887: 108—mention.

2273. TŪRSHAIKH

Original: Lat. 35° 24′ N, long. 62° 57′ E. Map 44.
Revised: 35.38614263 N, 62.97955034 E /
35° 23′ 10.11345468 N, 62° 58′ 46.38123876 E.
Herat Province. On the Āb-i Garm north-east of Kushk
just before the Turkmenistan border

Description: Ruins of a large, old baked brick caravanserai
with a domed cistern and ruined village.

Fieldwork: 1886 Peacocke, ABC—topographical survey.

Source: Peacocke 1887a: 268—mention.

2274. TŪTACHĪ
Or WAL'A-I KIZIL KUL.

Original: Lat. 35° 00′ N, long. 61° 55′ E. Maps 42, 43.
Revised: 35.00782276 N, 61.94244991 E /
35° 00′ 28.16192304 N, 61° 56′ 32.81968968 E.
Herat Province. A village south-east of Gulrān.

Description: Ruins of an old fort or caravanserai.

Fieldwork: 1885 Peacocke, ABC—topographical survey.

Sources:
1. Peacocke 1887a: 176—mention.
2. Peacocke 1887b: 451—mention.
3. Maitland and Drummond 1888: 52—mention.

2275. TŪTA KHĀN

Original: Lat. 34° 52′ N, long. 69° 14′ E. Map 64.
Revised: 34.87565584 N, 69.24296882 E /
34° 52′ 32.36103480 N, 69° 14′ 34.68773436 E.
34.87578969 N, 69.24289654 E /
34° 52′ 32.84289480 N, 69° 14′ 34.42755120 E approx.
Kābul Province. On the eastern edge of the Kūh-i Dāman
plain on a low ridge 3 km. south-east of Paitava.

Description: Two mounds on top of the ridge. Excavations
to test whether these represented a stupa-monastery complex revealed several parallel walls of *pakhsa*, possibly passageways or corridors, and possible retaining wall, but were
otherwise inconclusive.

Fieldwork: 1925 Barthoux, DAFA—excavations.

Source: Fussman, Murad, and Ollivier 2008: 140–2, 202, and
306—reproduces Barthoux's notes, with some comment.

2276. USTKHĀN ZĀR

Original: Lat. 36° 52′ N, long. 67° 51′ E approx. Map 29.
Revised: 36.69141512 N, 67.70998796 E /
36° 41′ 29.09441400 N, 67° 42′ 35.95664160 E approx.
Samangān Province. C.25 km north-east of Tāshqurghān.

Description: A site where painted pottery has been found.
Painted in black or dull grey.

Source: Hayashi and Sahara 1962: 106—brief description of
the pottery in the Mazār Museum.

2277. WAKHSHI

Original: Lat. 36° 50′ N, Long. 70° 09′ E. Map 8389.
Revised: 36.82459898 N, 70.18184747 E /
36° 49′ 28.55633160 N, 70° 10′ 54.65087400 E approx.
Badakhshān Province. 5 km east-north-east of Kishm in the
valley of the same name.

Description: Local reports of the discovery of jewels and
architectural features including dressed stone and baked
brick in the hillside.

Source: SPACH, *Newsletter*, 5, 1999: 30—brief mention of
site.

2278. YAK DARAKHT

Lat. 34° 52′ N, long. 62° 15′ E. Map 43.
Herat Province. 12 km from Kush Rabāt on the Kushk Rūd
on the route to Sar-i Chashma. At 16 km the Chahār Darra
stream joins the Kushk Rūd.

Description: An old fort on a mound.

Source: Maitland and Drummond 1888: 67—mention.

2279. YANG QAL'A, JAUZJĀN

Original: Lat. 36° 32′ N, long. 64° 54′ E. Map 24.
Revised: 36.52753327 N, 64.90583933 E /
36° 31′ 39.11975832 N, 64° 54′ 21.02160384 E.
Jauzjān Province. 7 km north of Daulatābād, half a km to
the left of the route to Chap Gudar.

Description: Ruins of an old fort.

Fieldwork: 1885–6 Peacocke, ABC—topographical survey.

Source: Peacocke 1887a: 92 and 289—mention.

2280. YŪSUF DARRA
Or DARRA-I YŪSUF.

Original: Lat. 35° 55′ N, long. 67° 17′ E approx. Maps
30, 47.
Revised: 35.90834876 N, 67.28449908 E /

35° 54′ 30.05553240 N, 67° 17′ 04.19669160 E approx. Balkh Province. A tributary to the Balkh River in the hills to the south of Balkh.

Description: Two Greek texts on skin supposedly discovered at an unspecified site in the Yūsuf Darra and now in a private collection.

Sources:
1. Clarysse and Thompson 2007—detailed translation, analysis, and discussion of the texts.
2. Rougemont 2012a: 193–4—full text, translation, and discussion.

2281. ZĀDIYĀN KĀFIR QAL'A
See also 8 ABU HURAIRA, 520 KAM PIRAK, 814 PIT QAL'A TEPE, 1188 TEPE ZĀDIYĀN, 2053 DAULATĀBĀD, and 1245 ZĀDIYĀN.

Lat. 37° 02–05′ N, long. 66° 56–95′ E. Figs 1.2, 1.4; Map 81. Balkh Province. 34 km north of this town, north of and near the town of Zādiyān; 14 km north-east of the village of Daulatābād.

Dates: (A) Kushan—Kushano-Sasanian, 1st cent. BC–4th cent. AD (C-14); (B) Kushan-Hephthalo-pre-Mongol Islamic, 6th–12th cent. (ceramic).

Description: A vast complex comprising a number of different elements.

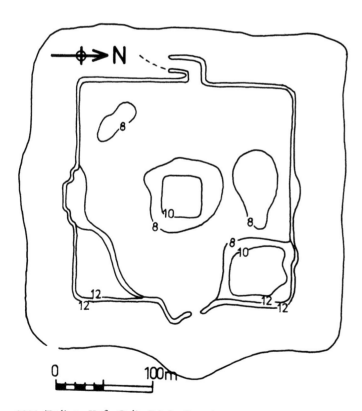

2281 Zādiyān Kāfir Qal'a (M. Le Berre).

(A) A 4 km long west–east *pakhsa* rampart, that turns south at its eastern end for a further 1.3 km, preserved up to 7 m high in places. Satellite images reveal that this is part of an immense walled enclosure forming an exact square, 4 km square. The northern rampart incorporates the long oasis wall of Kam Pirak (Site 520).

(B) In the exact centre of the west wall is a square mound, Pit Qal'a (Site 814), now interpreted as part of the Zādiyān complex, presumed to be a gateway.

(C) In the exact centre of the enclosure is the large square citadel mound of Zādiyān Kāfir Qal'a itself, measuring approximately 200 m square with walls standing up to 12 m high surrounded by a ditch. Construction is large-size mudbricks. There is an entrance ramp—a bent entrance—in the centre of the west side, i.e. exactly opposite the Pit Qal'a 'gateway'. The south and east sides have salients. The interior is heavily disturbed and is covered in baked brick fragments. On the walls is the mausoleum of Abu Huraira (Site 8).

A, B, and C appear to have been built as one single complex. Apart from the citadel mound, the enclosure is entirely empty of settlement remains; i.e. it was not urban, but is interpreted as a fortified military camp.

Fieldwork:
1. 1948 Le Berre, DAFA—survey.
2. 1973 Pugachenkova, Af/Sov. Mission—survey.
3. 2013 Besenval and Marquis, DAFA—survey.

Sources:
1. Le Berre 1958: unpublished report DAFA archives, tepe P.49.
2. La Vaissière, Marquis, and Bendezu-Sarmiento 2015—full description, date, and interpretation of the enclosure and citadel complex.
3. Omelchenko and Mirzaahemedov 2015: 400—brief description.

2282. ZARGĀRĀN, BĀMIYĀN

Lat. 34° 49N, long. 67° 50′ E. Map 58.
Bāmiyān Province. Just to the east of the main cliff containing the caves and giant Buddhas.

Description: A pot burial indication a possible Zoroastrian cemetery. Buddhist manuscripts have also supposedly been discovered here.

Source: Suzuki and Aoki 2004: 32–3—mention.

2283. ZARU GHUNDAI
(Formerly 1282.)

Lat. 34° 38′ N, long. 70° 14′ E approx. Map 65.
Laghmān Province. Alishang Valley.

Date: Hunnic-Turk, 5th–9th cent. (ceramic).

Description: None available.

Source: Gardin and Lyonnet, 1980 chronological study of unpublished pottery from DAFA surveys.

2284. ZĪR-I SŪM

Original: Lat. 35° 20′ N, long. 67° 15′ E. Map 48.
Revised: 35.36119815 N, 67.71677064 E /
35° 21′ 40.31333640 N, 67° 43′ 00.37430400 E approx.
Bāmiyān Province. Kahmard district, in the Qara Kotal area above Larmush.

Description: A series of artificial caves located in the gorge behind the village of the same name.

Fieldwork: 2005 Lee—reconnaissance.

Source: Site information by Jonathan L. Lee.

2285. ZĪYĀRAT-I ABDUL HĀKIM

Lat. 37° 10′ N, long. 67° 17′ E. Map 30.
Balkh Province. On the left bank of the Āmū Dāryā opposite Termez, in the Hairatān region.

Description: A large domed building containing Arabic and Persian Kufic inscriptions.

Source: Peacocke 1887a: 307.

2286. ZĪYĀRAT-I HAZRAT SULTĀN MUHAMMAD DEOBAND

Original: Lat. 36° 08′ N, long. 65° 50′ E. Map 78.
Revised: 36.14813165 N, 65.83193401 E /
36° 08′ 53.27392452 N, 65° 49′ 54.96243708 E.
36.14819271 N, 65.83208784 E /
36° 08′ 53.49376320 N, 65° 49′ 55.51621680 E approx.
Jauzjān Province. 1 km north of Sayyad, south-west of Sar-i Pul.

Date: Seljuk(?), 12th cent. (architectural).

Description: A single dome tomb, recently renovated, but which contained elements of medieval square, baked brick. Some 50 m to the south-west is a second, unadorned, tomb of square baked brick said to be used as a *chilla khāna* (meditation chamber for Sufis). Neither tomb contains any inscriptions or glazed tilework. Both tombs are located on an artificial mound from which villagers report recovering bronze coins and pottery

Fieldwork: 1995 Lee—reconnaissance.

Source: Site information by Jonathan L. Lee (recorded

2287. ZĪYĀRAT-I KHWĀJA GHAIB
Or KĀFIR QAL'A.

Original: Lat. 35° 44′ N, long. 64° 04′ E approx. Map 45.
Revised: 35.73926032 N, 64.01777705 E /
35° 44′ 21.33716388 N, 64° 01′ 03.99737460 E.
Faryāb Province. 23 km from Yangi Āriq (Qaisar) on the top of a hill to the left of the road to Chahā Shanba.

Description: Remains of an old earthwork on top of the hill.

Fieldwork: 1885 Peacocke, ABC—topographical survey.

Source: Peacocke 1887a: 114—mention.

2288. ZĪYĀRAT-I KHWĀJA JINN

Original: Lat. 34° 45′ 9.83″ N. Long. 63° 5′ 48.29″ E. Map 53.
Revised: 34.83031145 N, 63.11524452 E /
34° 49′ 49.12120920 N, 63° 06′ 54.88026480 E approx.
Bādghīs Province. In the mountains around the settlement of Laman.

Description: Local reports of an ancient shrine high in the mountains which can only be reached during the summer months. The community reports the shrine contains Arabic inscriptions and glazed tiles.

Source: Information reported by Jonathan L. Lee (1994).

2289. ZĪYĀRAT-I KHWĀJA QĀSIM

Lat. 34° 48′ N, long. 62° 05′ E. Maps 43, 52.
Herat Province. 14 km after Kashawri, 37 km to Sangi Rabāt.

Description: An old ruined fort 1 km below the *zīyārat*.

Fieldwork: 1885 Maitland, ABC—topographical survey.

Source: Maitland 1888a: 286—mention.

2290. ZĪYĀRAT-I MĪR HAIDAR

Lat. 35° 53′ 11.47″ N, long. 65° 23′50.06″ E. Map 24, 46.
Faryāb Province. Gurziwān district, 5 km from Kauliyān.

Description: A shrine of sun-dried bricks around which a number of figurines and other carved items, some covered in gilt, have been unearthed by local villagers. Items included a bronze figurine of a man holding a bow and arrow.

Source: Site information by Jonathan L. Lee (recorded 1996).

2291. ZĪYĀRAT-I SAYYAD TAJDĀR AQĀ

Original: Lat. 31° 51′ N, long. 64° 33′ E approx. Map 86.
Revised: 31.81848524 N, 64.56993723 E /
31° 49′ 06.54686040 N, 64° 34′ 11.77402080 E approx.
Helmand Province. Near Girishk.

Description: An ancient *zīyārat* reported.

Source: Sahibdad Khan 1891b: 254—mention.

2292. ZURĀBĀD

Original: Lat. 31° 10′ N, long. 62° 05′–62° 98′ E. Map 84.
Revised: 31.15774869 N, 62.07794002 E /
31° 09′ 27.89527680 N, 62° 04′ 40.58405400 E approx.
Nīmrūz. Around Chakhansūr.

Description: Ruins. (Maps mark many ruins to the east of Chakhansūr.)

Sources:
1. Peacocke 1885a: 13—mention.
2. Peacocke 1887a: 27—mention.

Map Concordance

For ease of reference, below are the original 1982 map numbers with the corresponding new map numbers.

Original	New	New	Original
77 bis	23	23	77 bis
78	24	24	78
79	25	25	79
80	26	26	80
81	27	27	81
82	28	28	82
83	29	29	83
84	30	30	84
85	31 & 32	31	85
86	33	32	85
87	34 & 35	33	86
88	36 & 37	34	87
89	38	35	87
90.1	39	36	88
90.2	40	37	88
91	42	38	89
92	43	39	90.1
93	44	40	90.2
94	45	41	new
95	46	42	91
96	47	43	92
97	48	44	93
98	49	45	94
99	50	46	95
100	51	47	96
101	52	48	97
102	53	49	98
103	54	50	99
104	55	51	100
105	56	52	101
106	57	53	102
107	58	54	103
108	59	55	104
109	60	56	105
110	61, 62, & 63	57	106
111	64	58	107

(continued)

Continued

Original	New	New	Original
112	65	59	108
113	66 & 67	60	109
114	68	61	110
115	69	62	110
116	70	63	110
117	71	64	111
118	72	65	112
119	73	66	113
120	74	67	113
121	75	68	114
122	76	69	115
123	77	70	116
124	78	71	117
125	79	72	118
126	80	73	119
127	81	74	120
128	82	75	121
129	83	76	122
130	84	77	123
131	85	78	124
132	86	79	125
133	87	80	126
134	88	81	127
135	89	82	128
136	90	83	129
137	91	84	130
138	92	85	131
139	93	86	132
140.1	94	87	133
140.2	95	88	134
140.3	96	89	135
141.1	97	90	136
141.2	98	91	137
142	99	92	138
		93	139
		94	140.1
		95	140.2
		96	140.3
		97	141.1
		98	141.2
		99	142

Period Maps

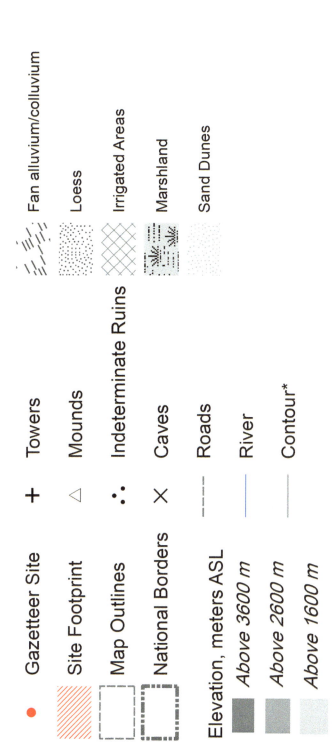

●	Gazetteer Site
▨ (orange hatched)	Site Footprint
⬚ (dashed outline)	Map Outlines
▢ (dashed dark)	National Borders

Elevation, meters ASL

▪ (dark)	Above 3600 m
▪ (medium)	Above 2600 m
▪ (light)	Above 1600 m

+	Towers
△	Mounds
∴	Indeterminate Ruins
✕	Caves
– – –	Roads
——	River
——	Contour*

(hatched lines)	Fan alluvium/colluvium
(dotted)	Loess
(cross-hatch)	Irrigated Areas
(marsh pattern)	Marshland
(fine dots)	Sand Dunes

*contour lines are drawn at 250m intervals on maps at or below 1:500,000 scale, and at 500m intervals on maps above 1:500,000 scale. A few maps at 1:100,000,000 scale have 1000m contours.

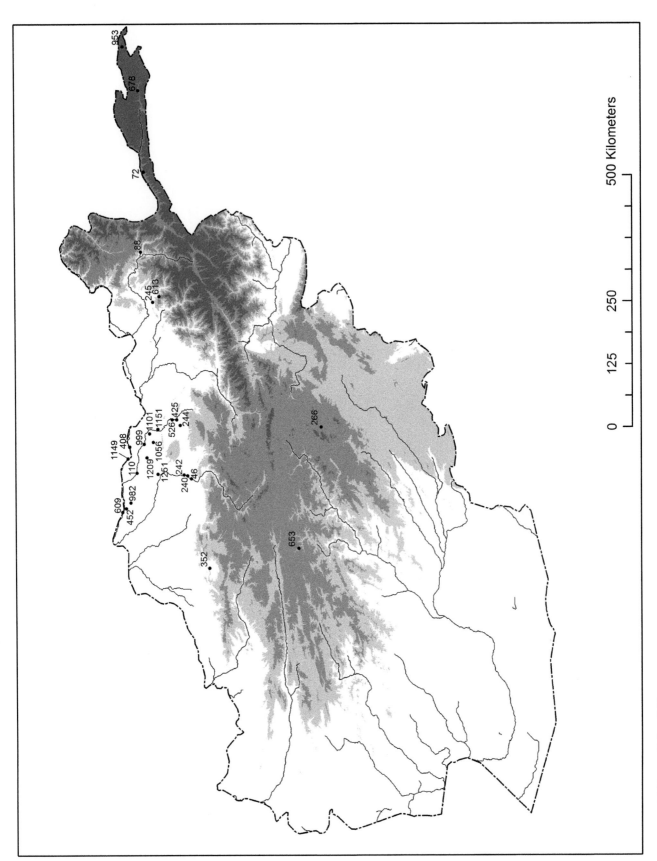

1 50,000–8,000 BC—Palaeolithic.

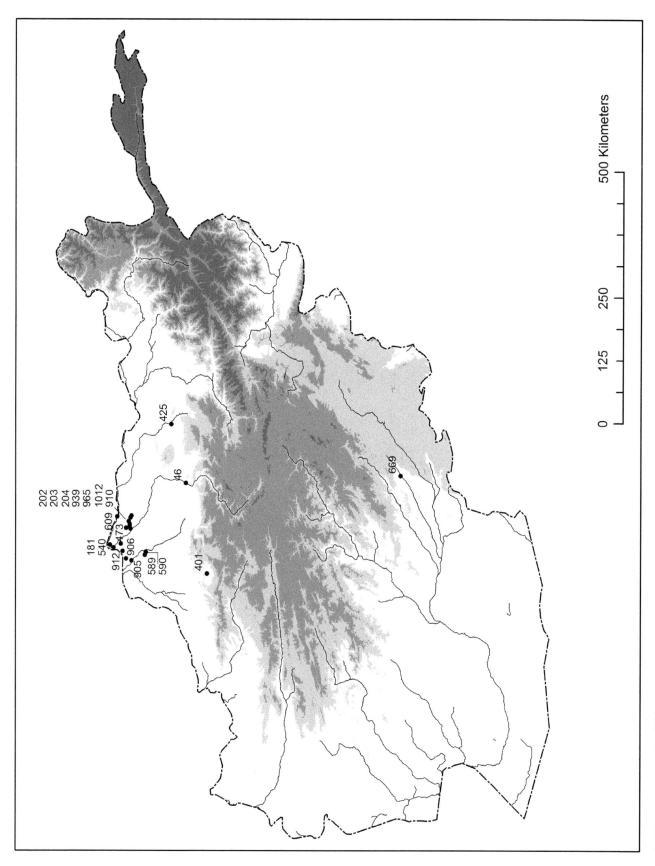

202
203
204
939
965
1012
910
609
473
181
540
906
912
905
589
590
401
425
46
669

2 8,000–4,000 BC—Neolithic.

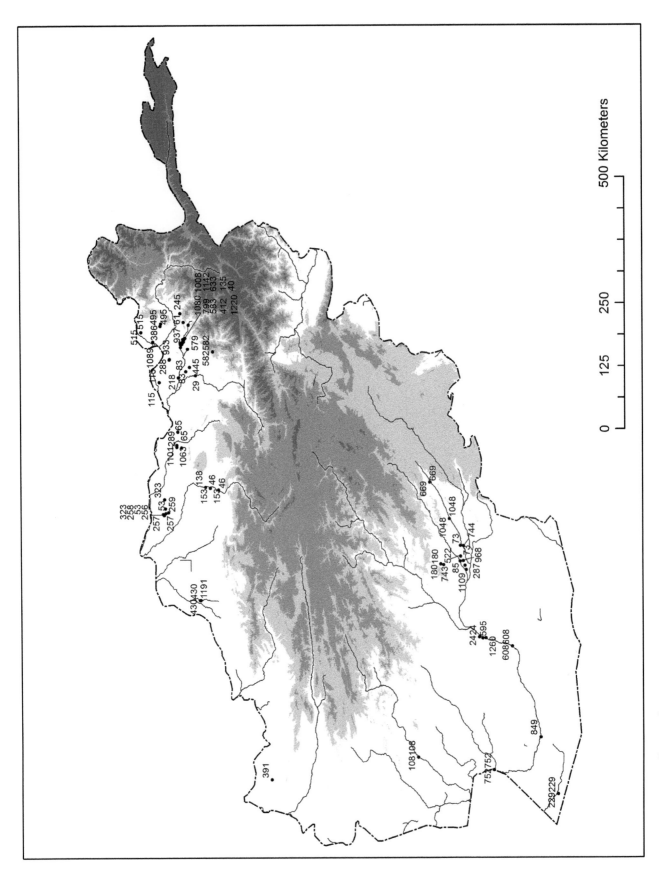

3 4,000–1,500 BC—Bronze Age.

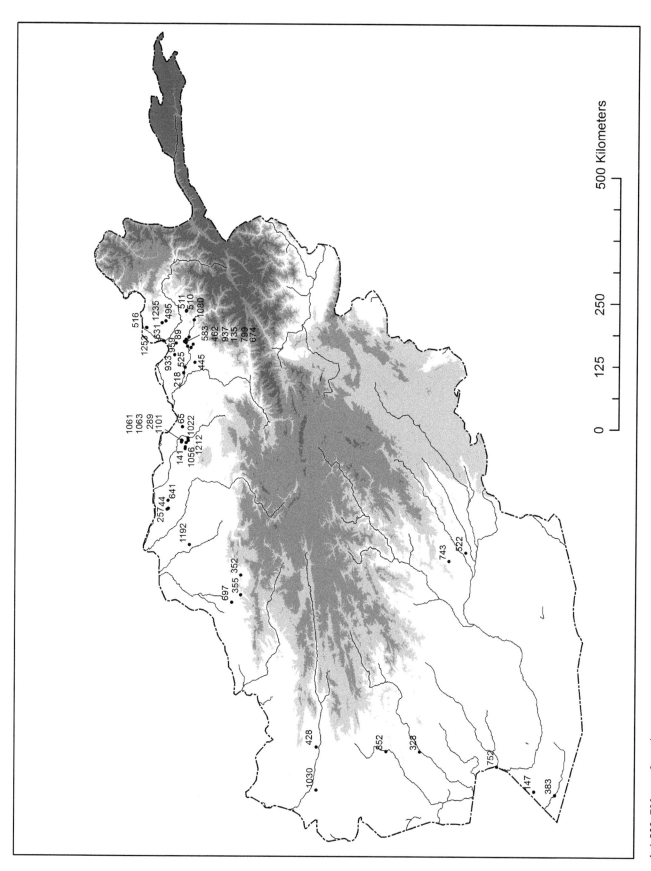

4 1,500–700 BC—Iron Age.

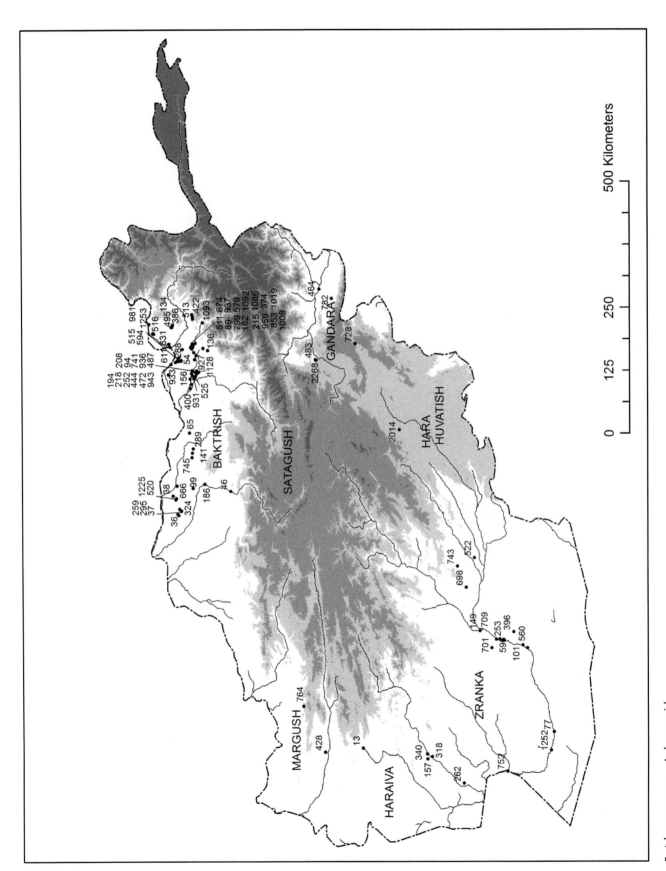

5 4th century BC—Achaemenid.

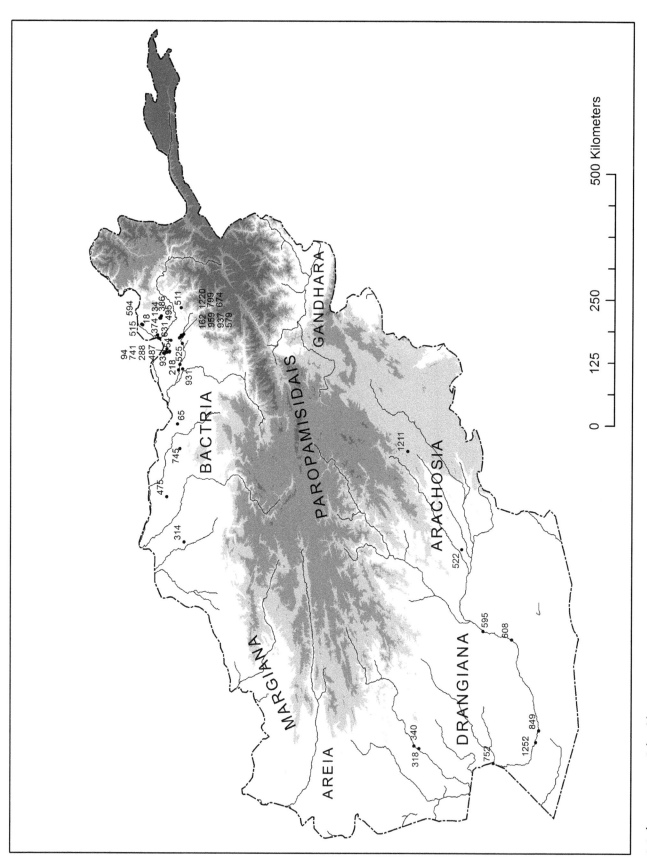

6 3rd century BC—Seleucid.

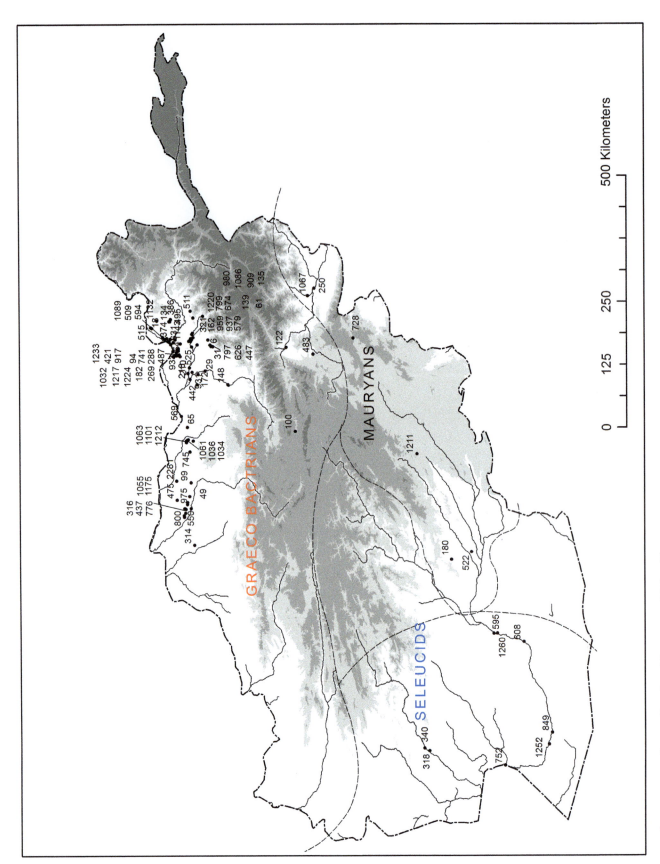

7 3rd century BC—Graeco-Bactrian, Mauryan, and Seleucid.

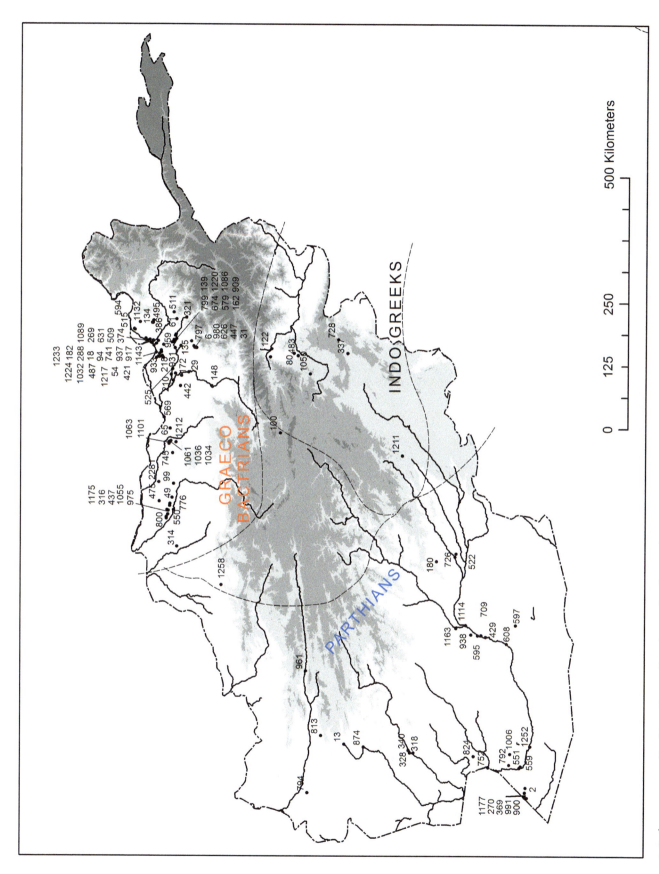

8 2nd century BC—Parthian, Graeco-Bactrian, and Indo-Greek.

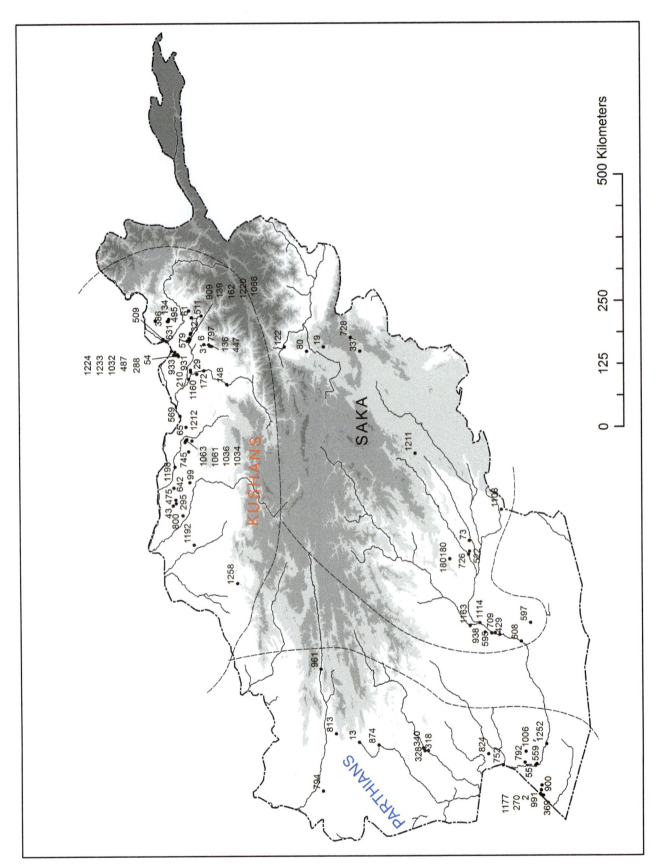

9 1st century BC — Parthian, Kushan, and Saka.

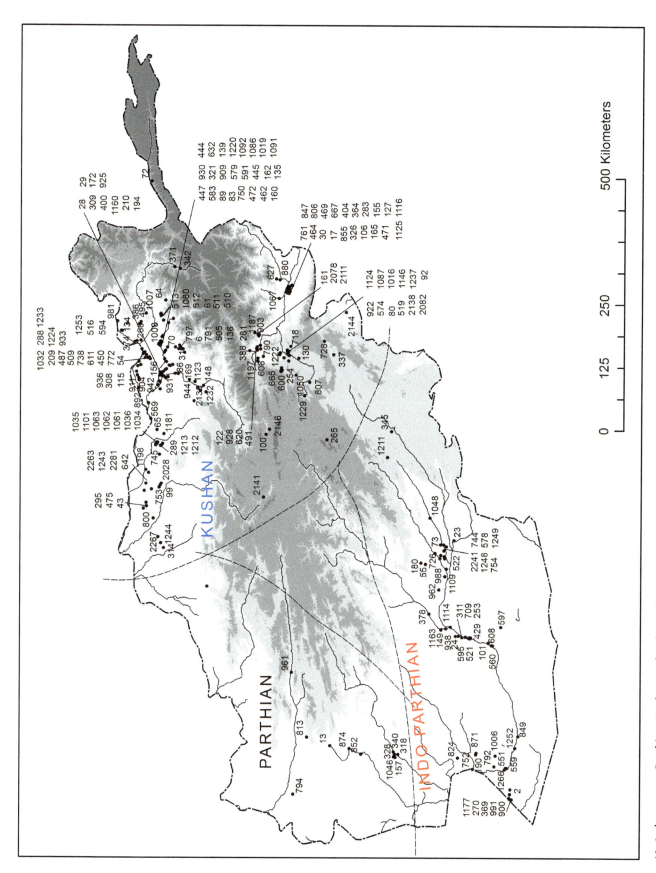

10 2nd century—Parthian, Kushan, and Indo-Parthian.

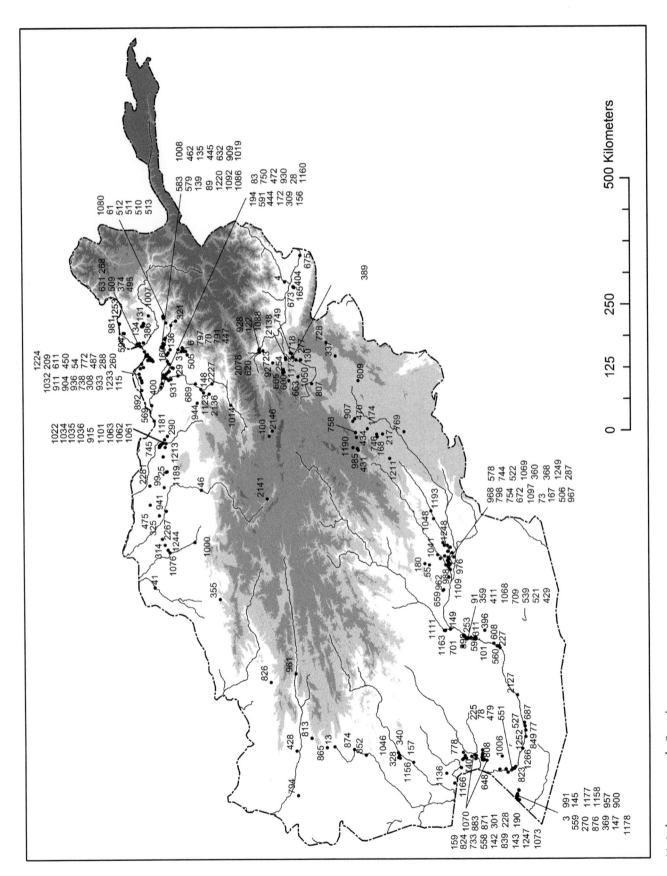

11 3rd century—early Sasanian.

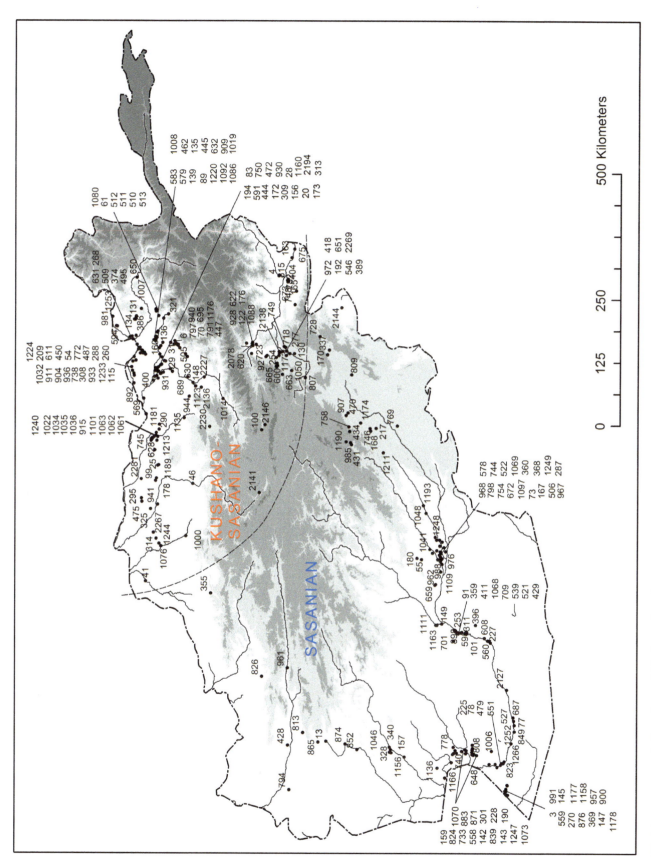

12 4th century – early Sasanian and Kushano-Sasanian.

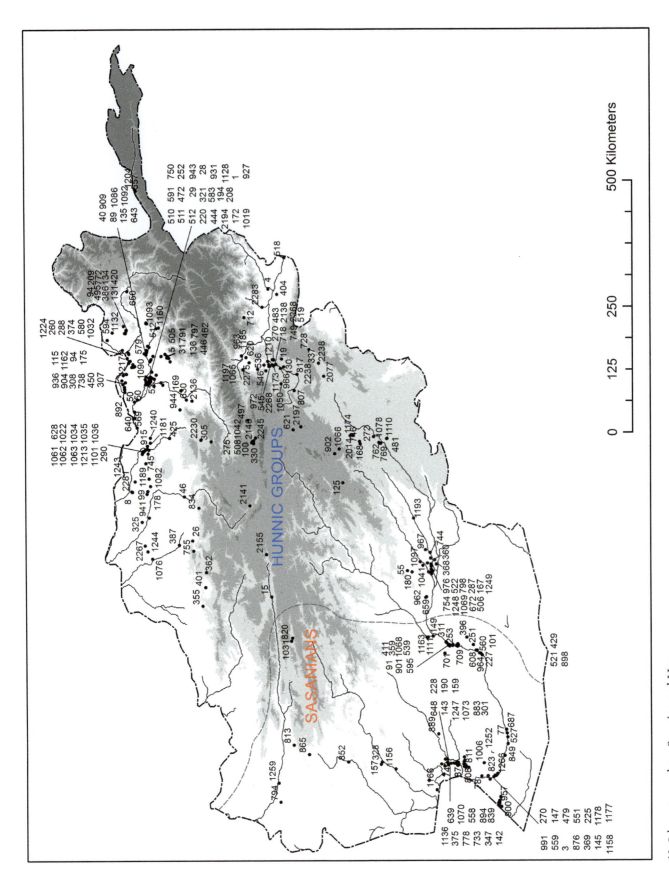

13 5th century—later Sasanian and Hun.

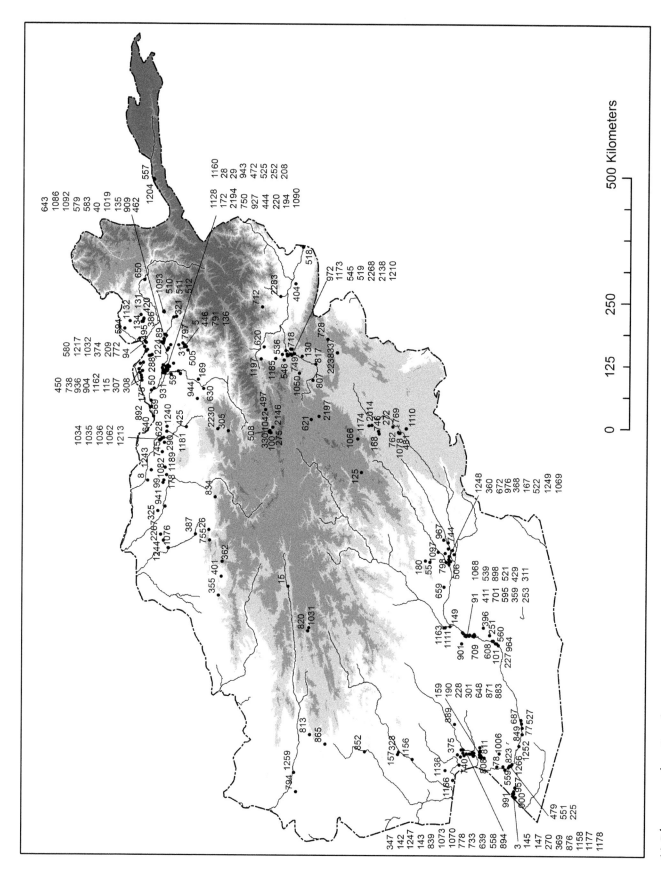

14 7th century—later Sasanian.

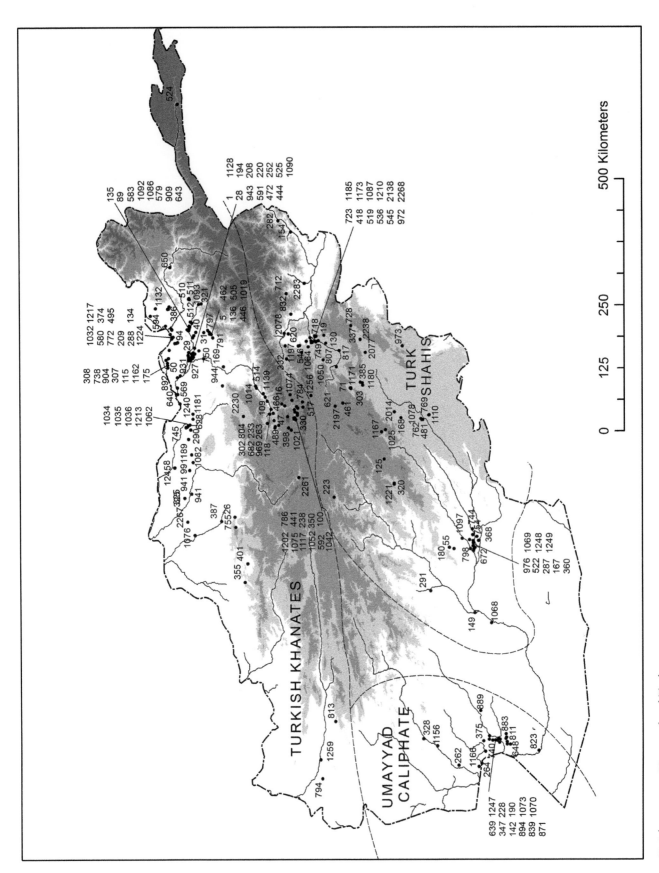

15 8th century—Umayyad and Turk.

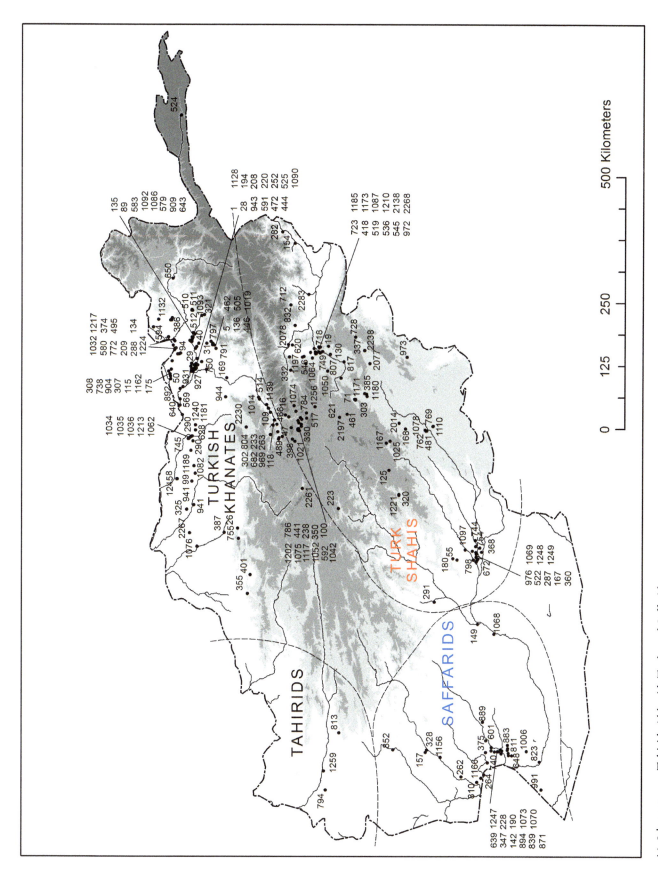

16 9th century—Tahirid, Abbasid, Turk, and Saffarid.

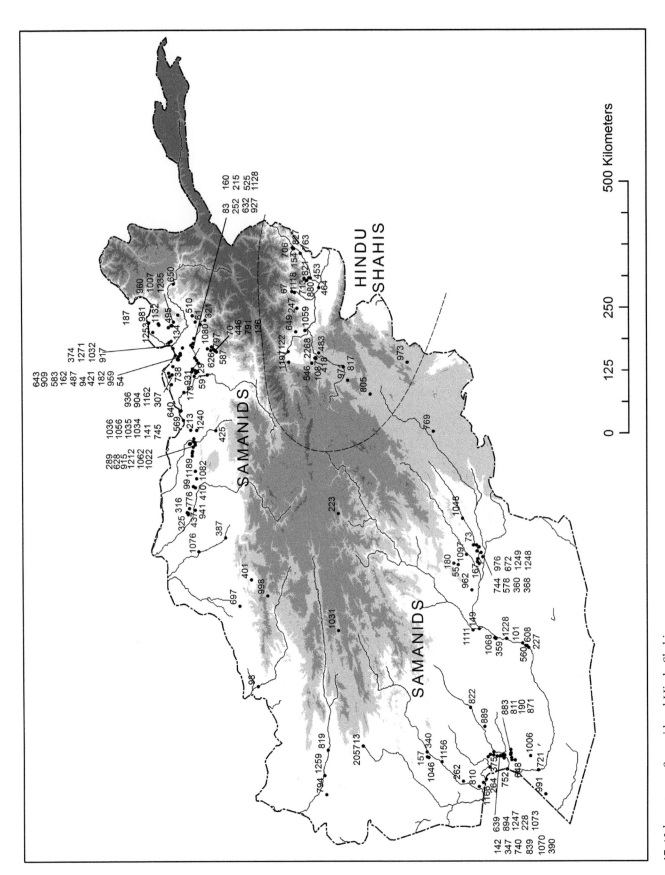

17 10th century—Samanid and Hindu Shahi.

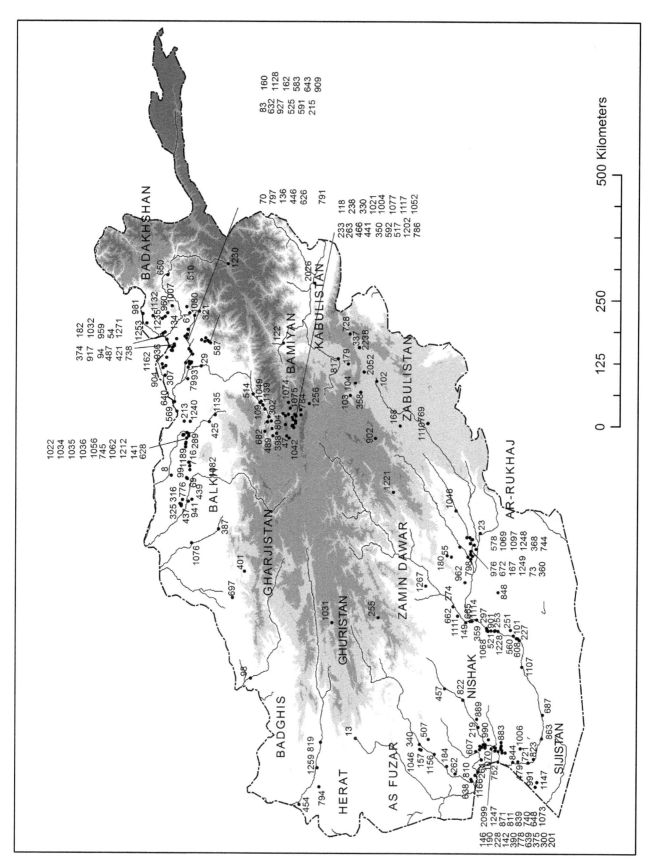

18 11th century—Ghaznavid.

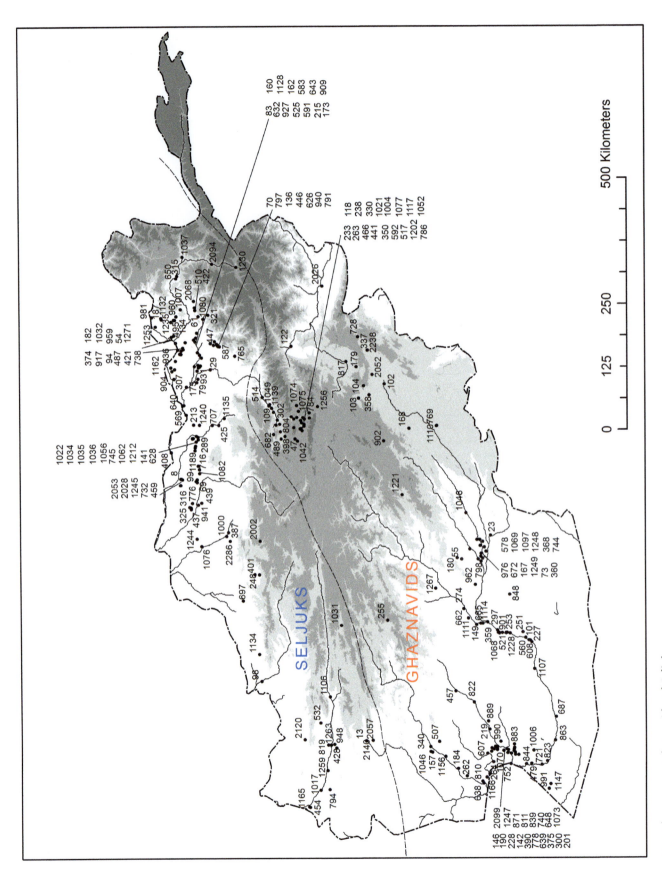

19 11th century — Ghaznavid and Seljuk.

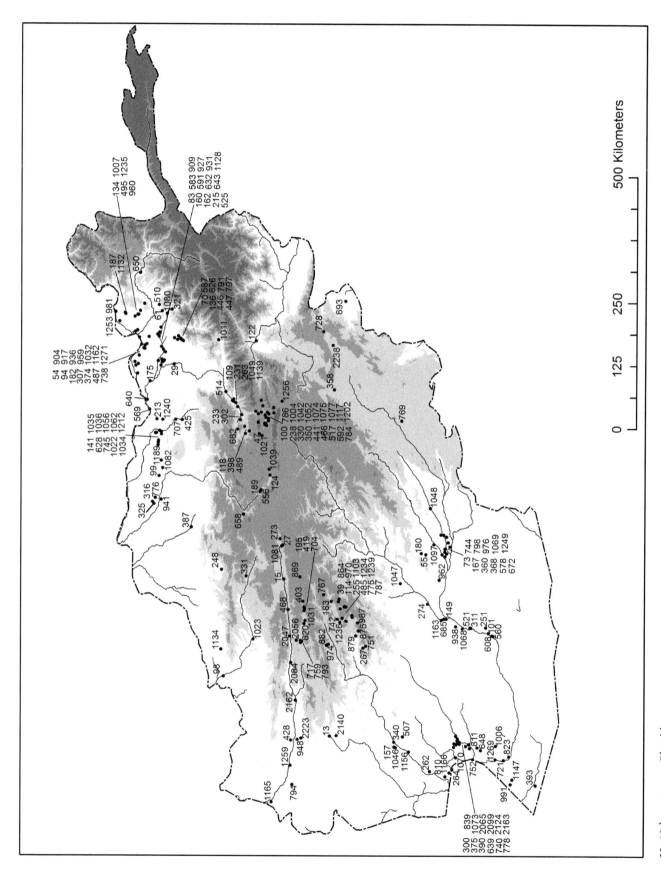

20 12th century—Ghurid.

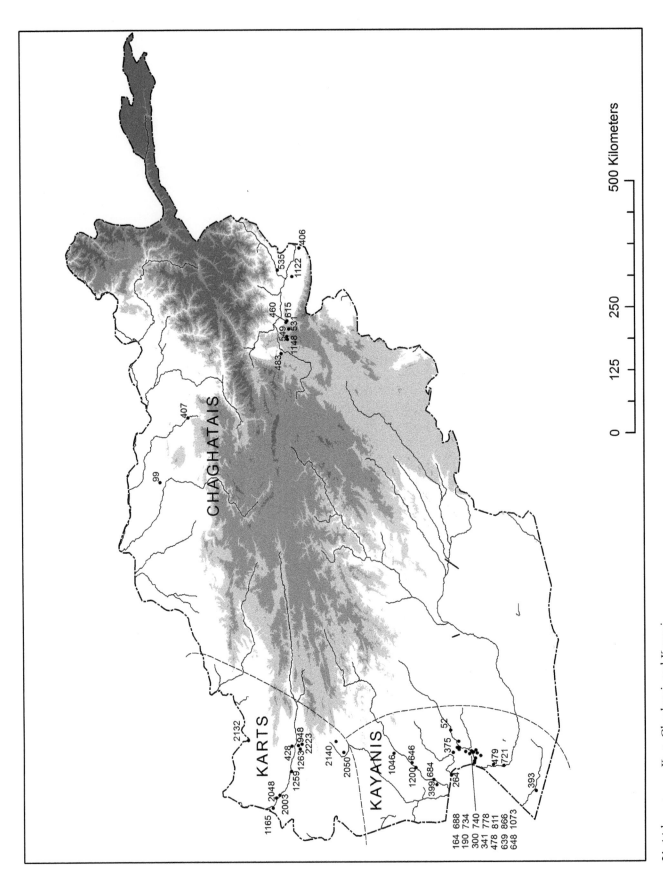

21 14th century — Kart, Chaghatai, and Kayani.

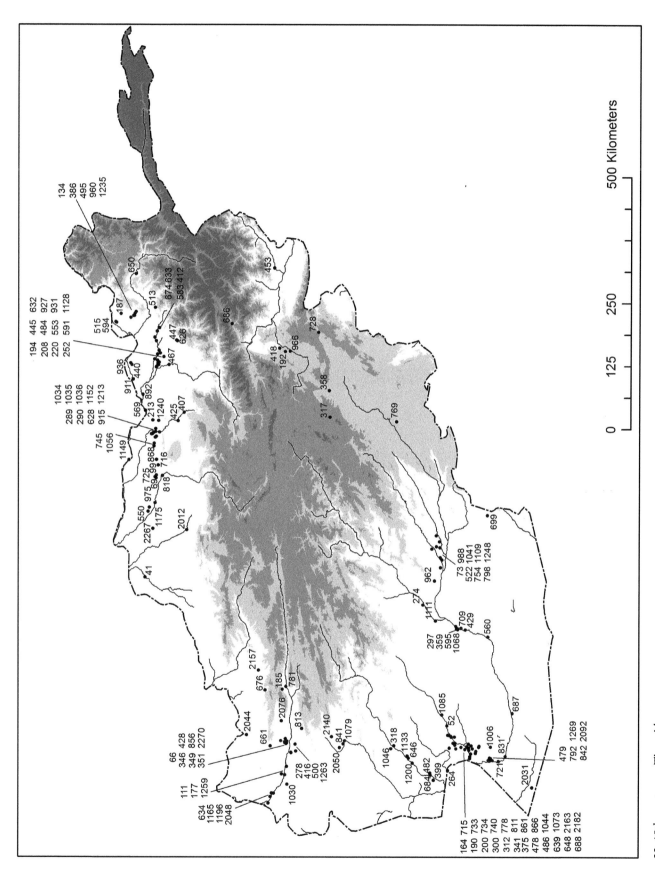

194 445 632
208 484 927
220 553 931
252 591 1128

134
386
495
960
1235

650

674 633
583 412
513

453

187

515
594

936
440

447
626

418
192

686

728

966

911 892
569 213
915 1240
1034
1035
1036
1152
1213

289
290
628

745
1056
1149

425
407

317

358

769

699

868
975 725
692 699 716
818
550
2267 1175
2012

73 988
522 1041
754 1109
798 1248

962

41

274
1111

2157

297
359
595
1068

709
429
560

676 185
781

1085

2076
813
2044

2140
841
1079

52

687

66 428
346 856
349 2270
351

661

1046 318
1133
646

1006
831

479
792 1269
842 2092

111
177
1259

278
416
500
1263

2050

1200
684 482
399
264

721
2031

1030

634
1165
1196
2048

164 715
190 733
200 734
300 740
312 778
341 811
375 861
478 866
486 1044
639 1073
648 2163
688 2182

0   125   250   500 Kilometers

22 15th century—Timurid.

Regional Maps

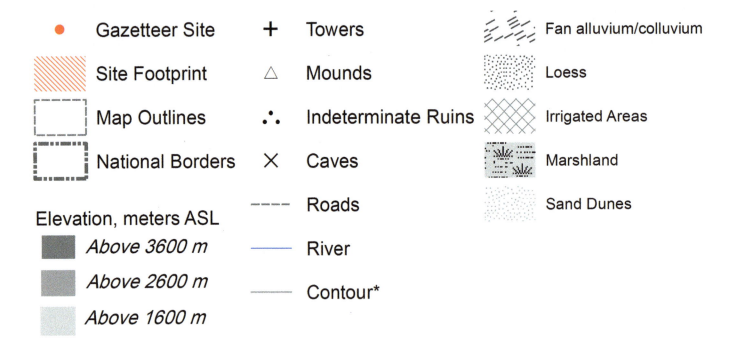

● Gazetteer Site	+ Towers	Fan alluvium/colluvium
Site Footprint	△ Mounds	Loess
Map Outlines	∴ Indeterminate Ruins	Irrigated Areas
National Borders	✕ Caves	Marshland
	----- Roads	Sand Dunes

Elevation, meters ASL

Above 3600 m

Above 2600 m

Above 1600 m

—— River

—— Contour*

*contour lines are drawn at 250m intervals on maps at or below 1:500,000 scale,
 and at 500m intervals on maps above 1:500,000 scale.
A few maps at 1:100,000,000 scale have 1000m contours.

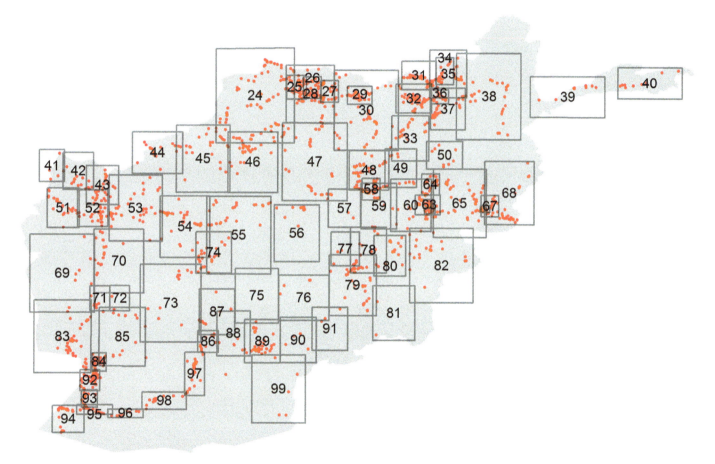

23 Map extents.

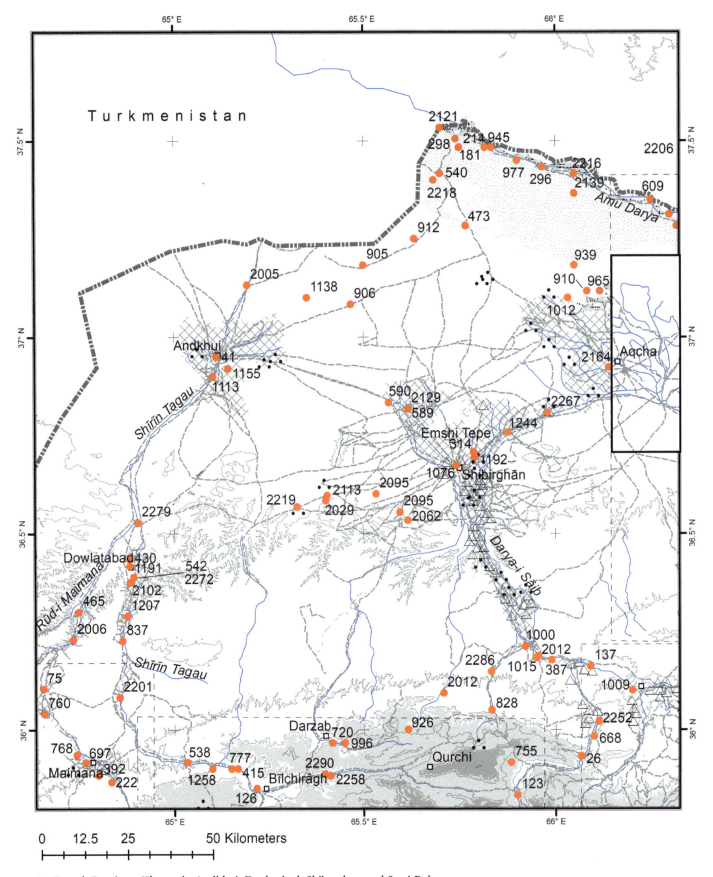

24 Faryāb/Jauzjān—Khāmyāb, Andkhui, Daulatābād, Shibarghān, and Sar-i Pul areas.

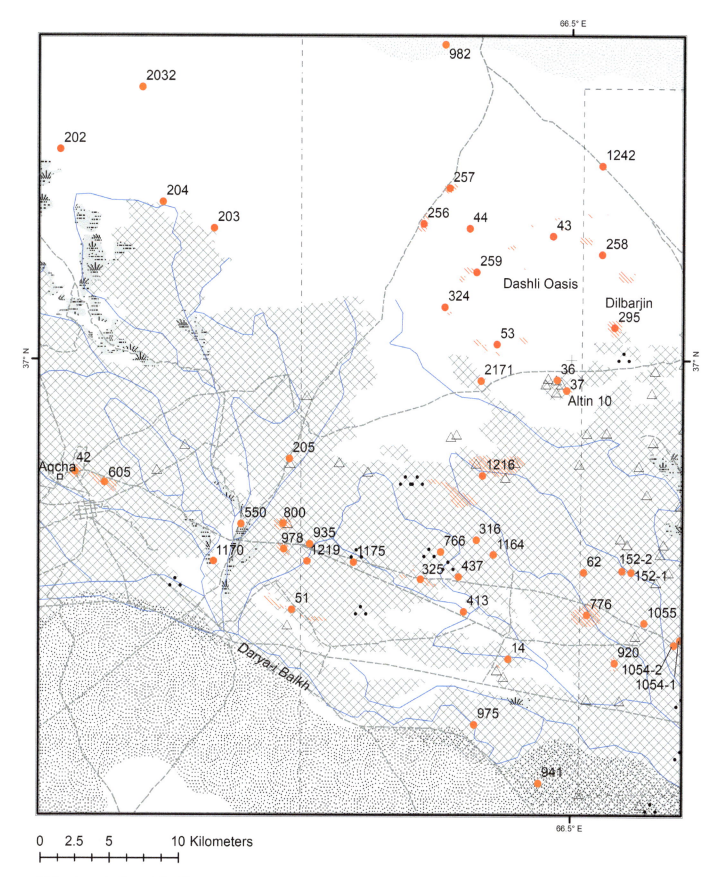

25 Jauzjān—Aqcha and Dashli areas.

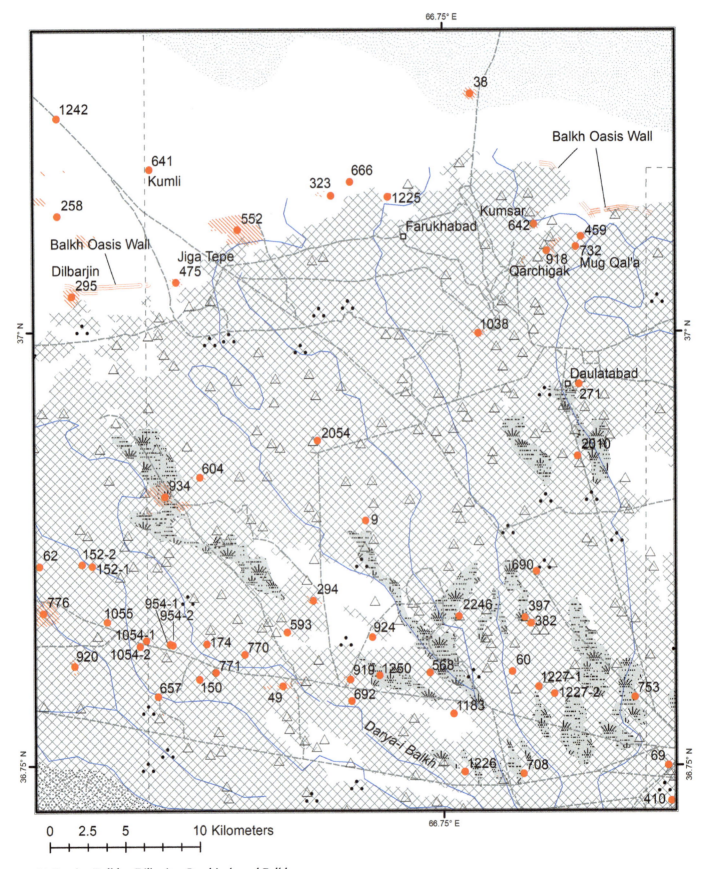

26 Jauzjān/Balkh—Dilbarjīn, Qarchigak, and Balkh areas.

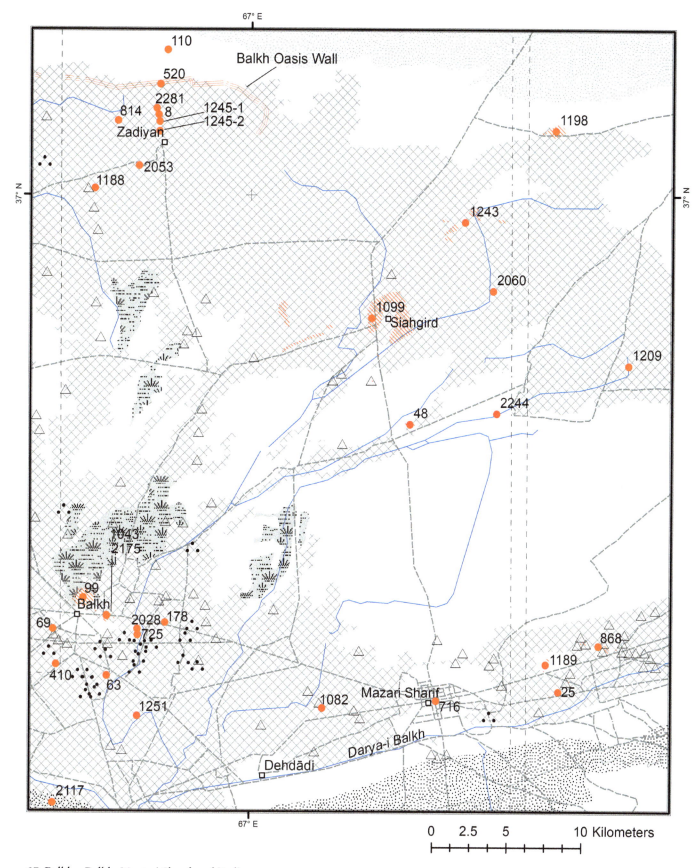

27 Balkh—Balkh, Mazār-i Sharīf, and Zādiyān areas.

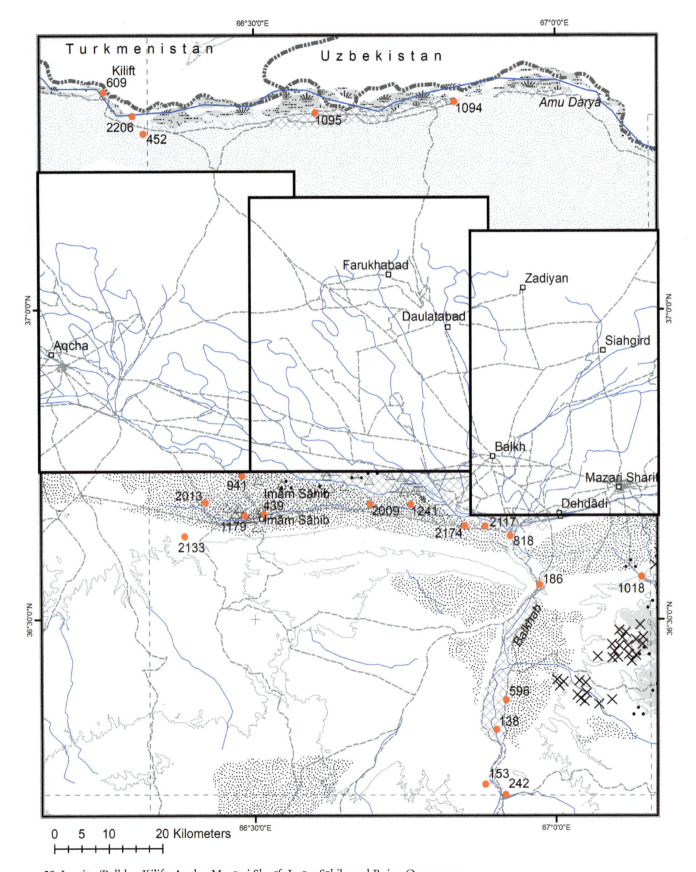

28 Jauzjān/Balkh—Kilift, Aqcha, Mazār-i Sharīf, Imām Sāhib, and Buina Qara areas.

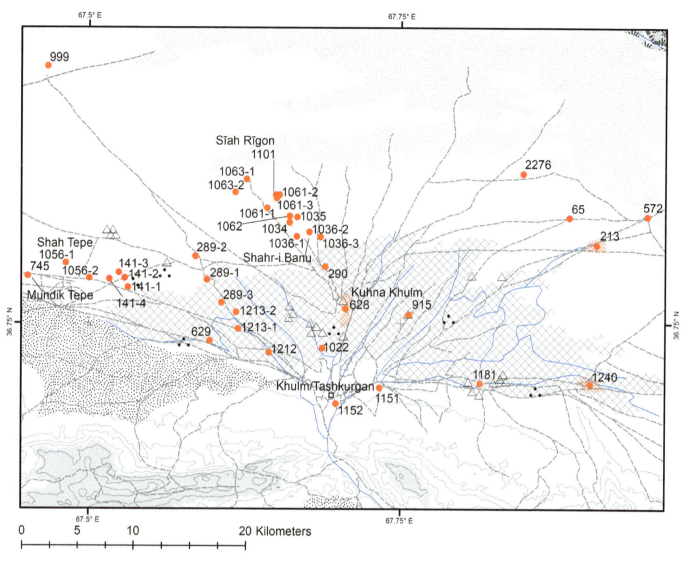

29 Samangān—Tāshqurghān area.

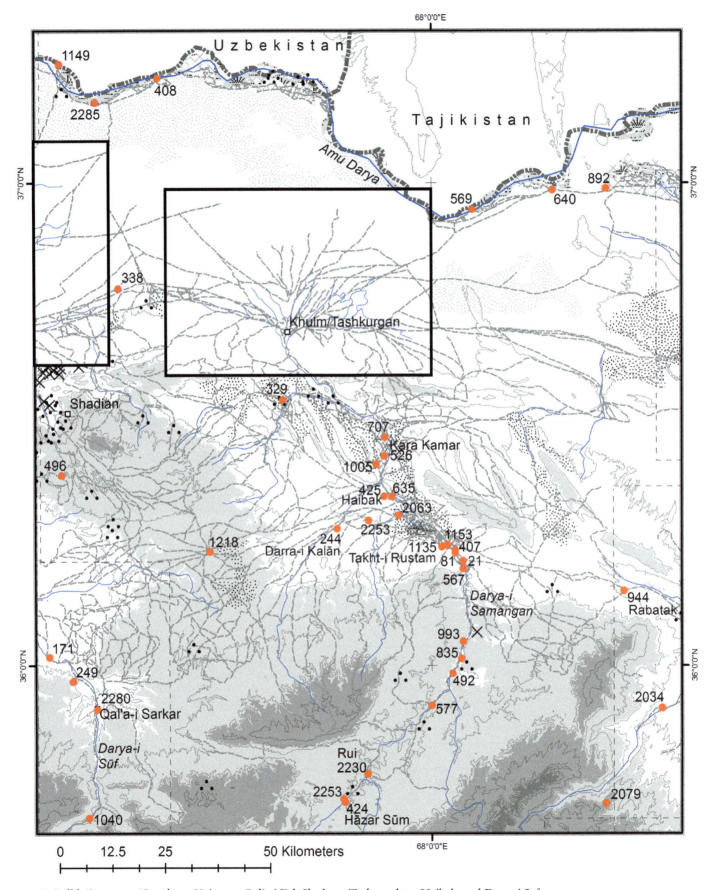

30 Balkh/Samangān/Qundūz—Hairatān, Qal'a-i Zāl, Shadyān, Tāshqurghān, Haibak, and Darra-i Sūf areas.

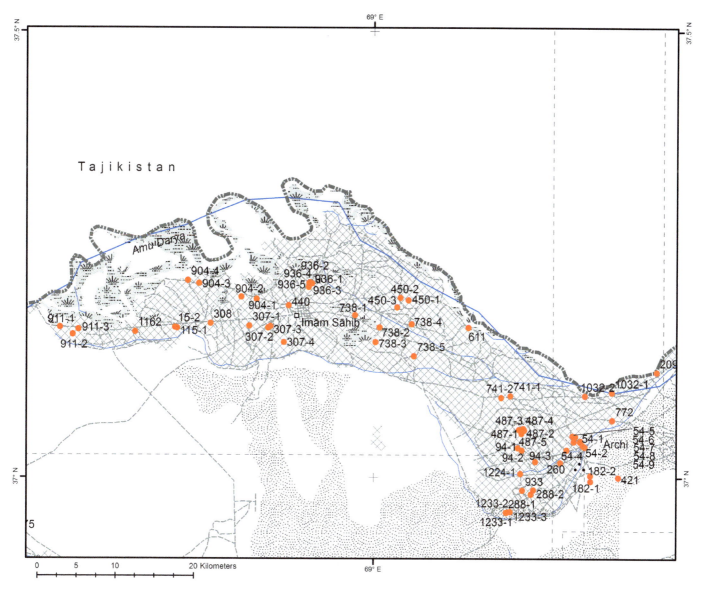

31 Qundūz — Imām Sāhib, Archi areas.

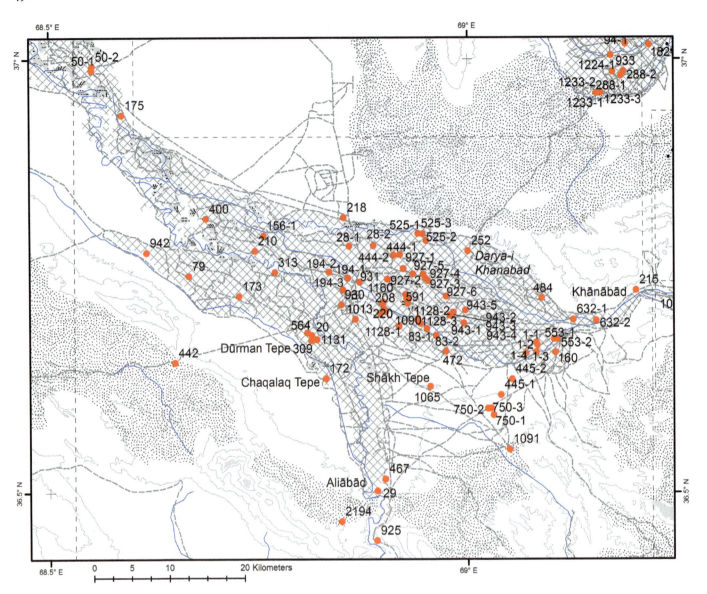

32 Qundūz—Qundūz and Khānābād areas.

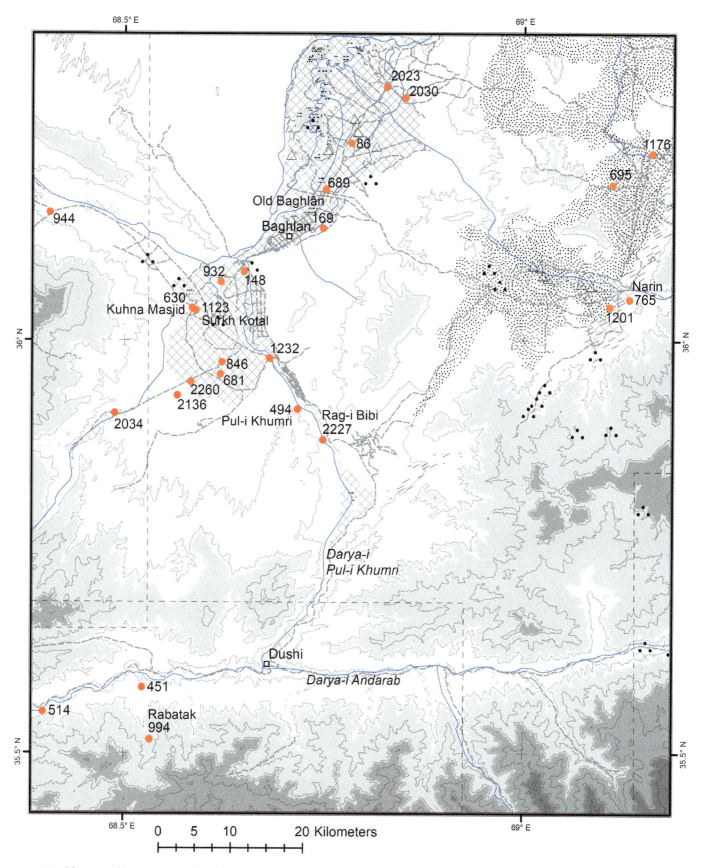

33 Baghlān—Baghlān, Narīn, Pul-i Khumri, and Dūshi areas.

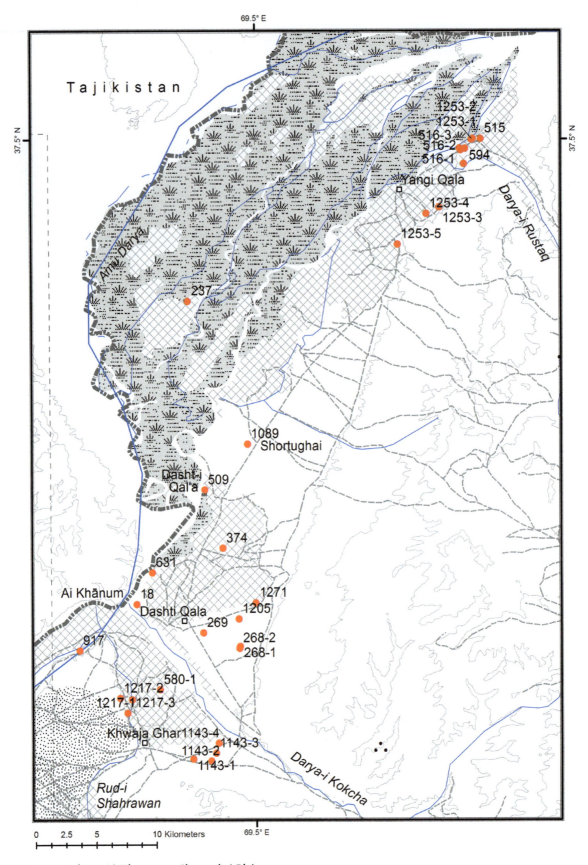

34 Qundūz—Ai Khanoum—Shortughai Plain.

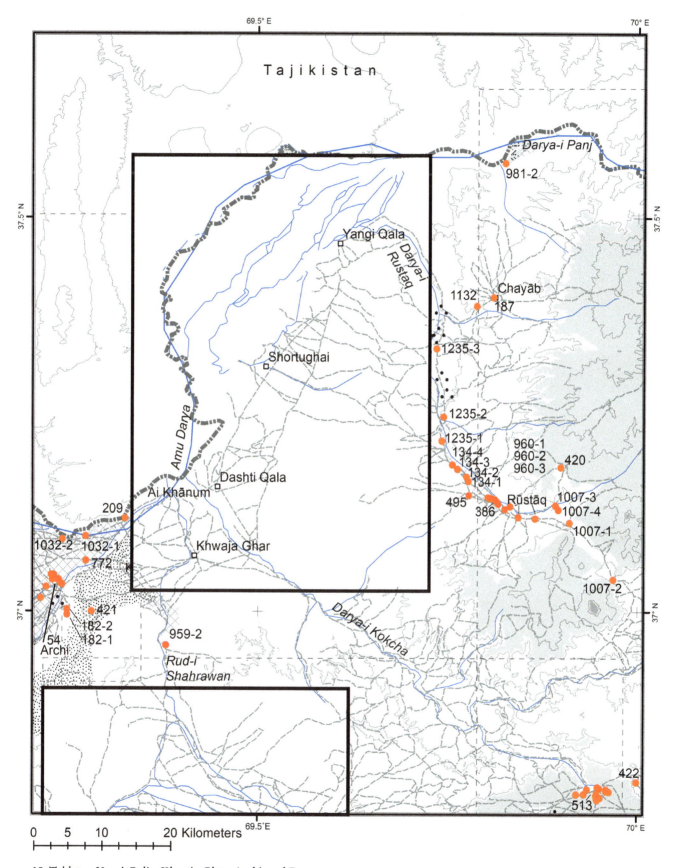

35 Takhār—Yangi Qal'a, Khwāja Ghār, Archi, and Rustāq areas.

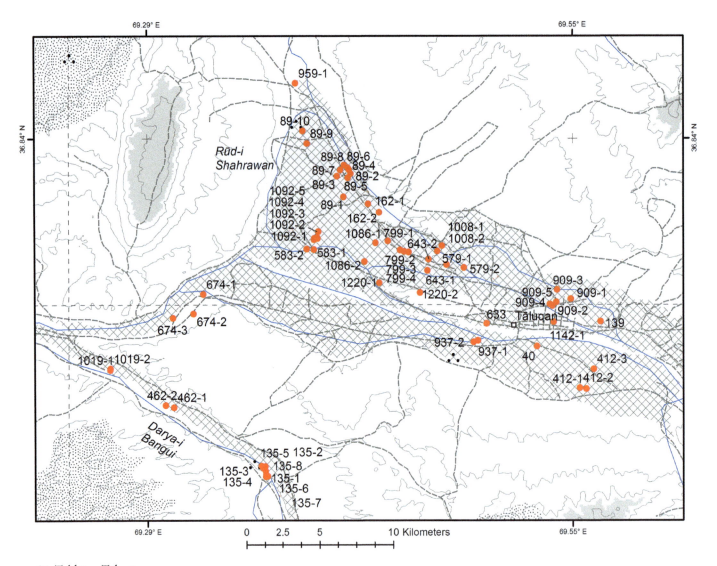

36 Takhār—Tāluqān area.

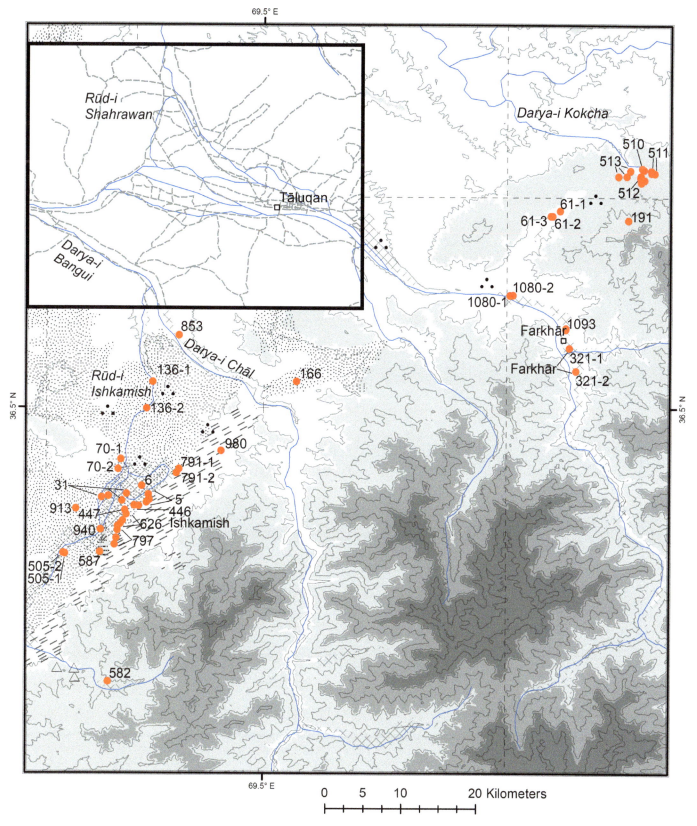

37 Takhār—Tāluqān, Farkhār, and Ishkamish areas.

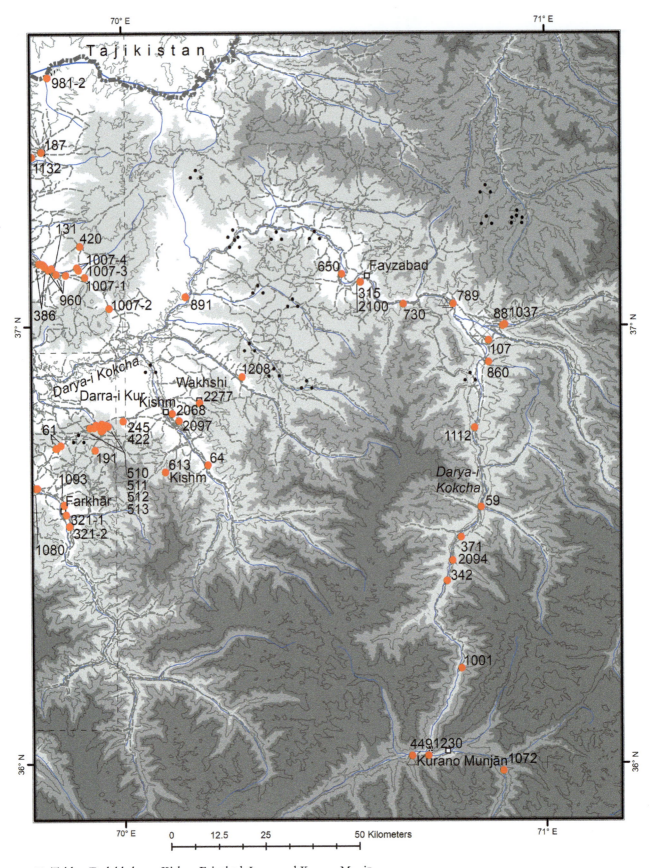

38 Takhār/Badakhshān—Kishm, Faizābād, Jurm, and Kerano-Munjān areas.

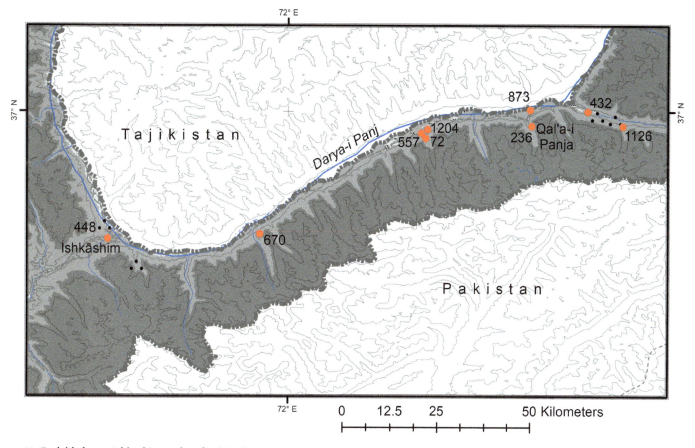

39 Badakhshān—Ishkāshim and Qal'a-i Panja areas.

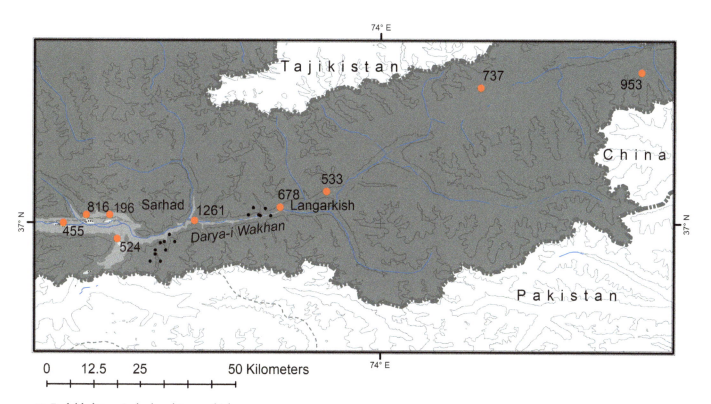

40 Badakhshān—Sarhad and Langarkish areas.

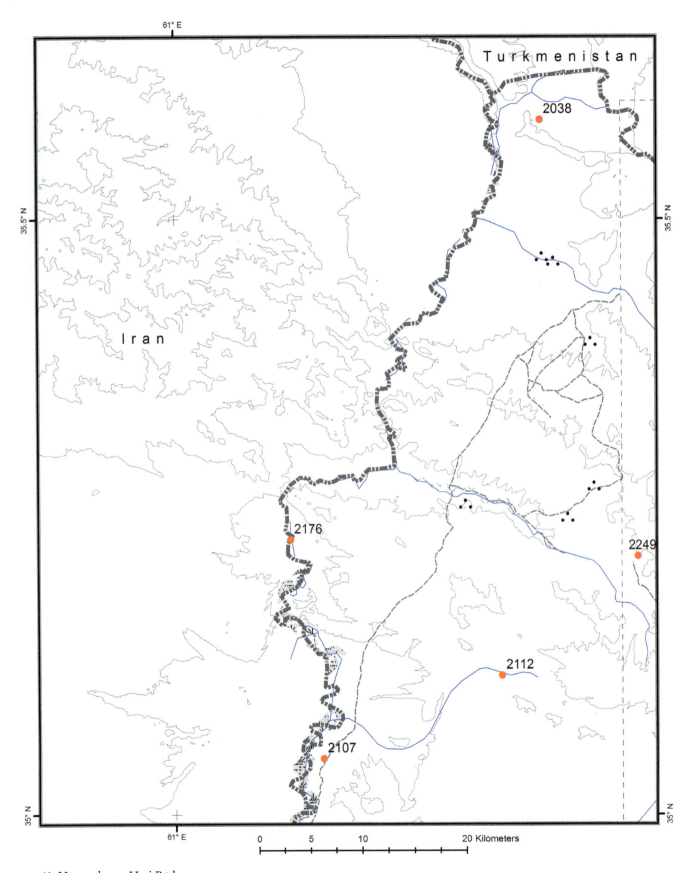

41 Herat—lower Hari Rūd area.

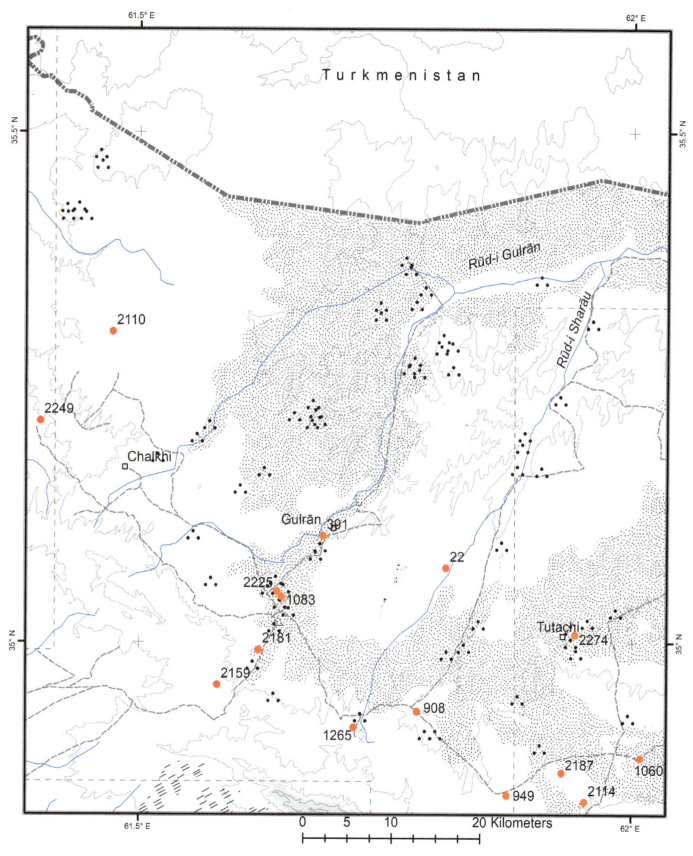

42 Herat—Gulrān area.

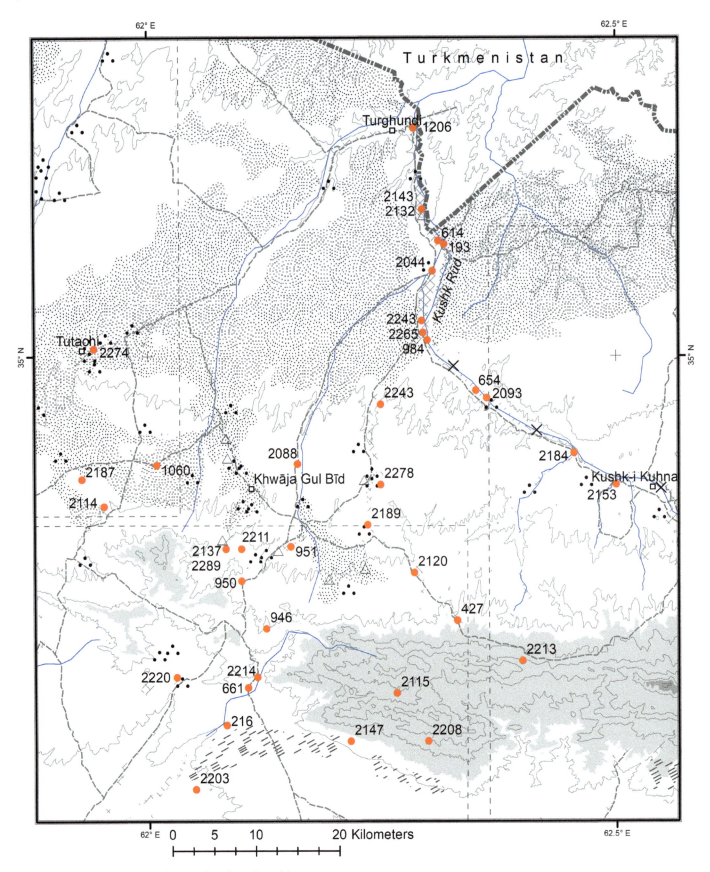

43 Herat/Bādghīs—Tutachi, Tūrghundi, and Kushk areas.

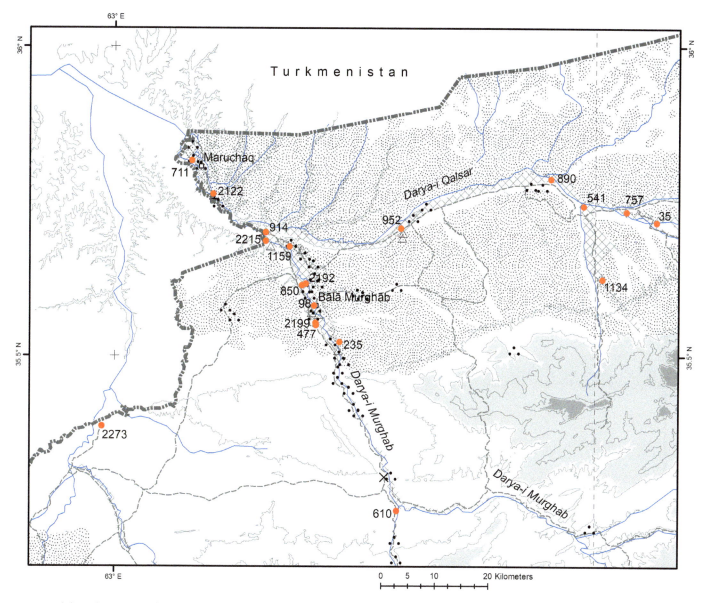

44 Bādghīs—lower Murghāb area.

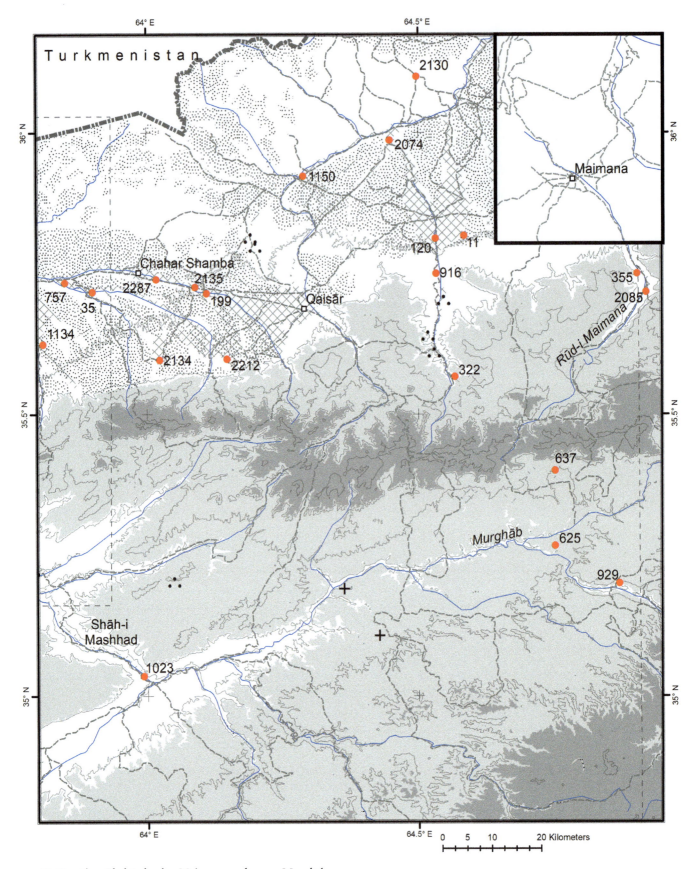

45 Faryāb—Chahārshanba, Maimana, and upper Murghāb areas.

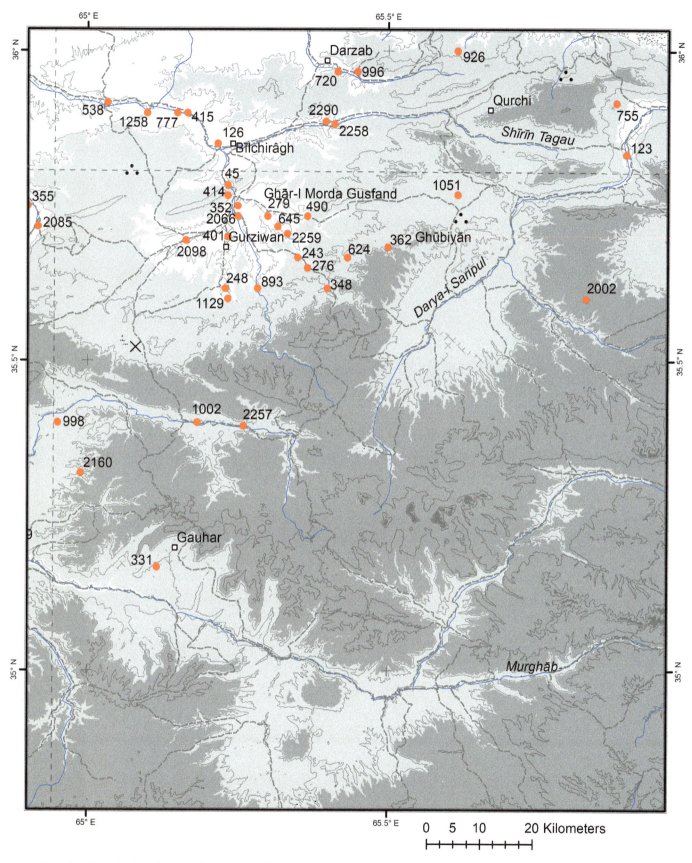

46 Faryāb—Darzāb, Gurziwan, and upper Murghāb areas.

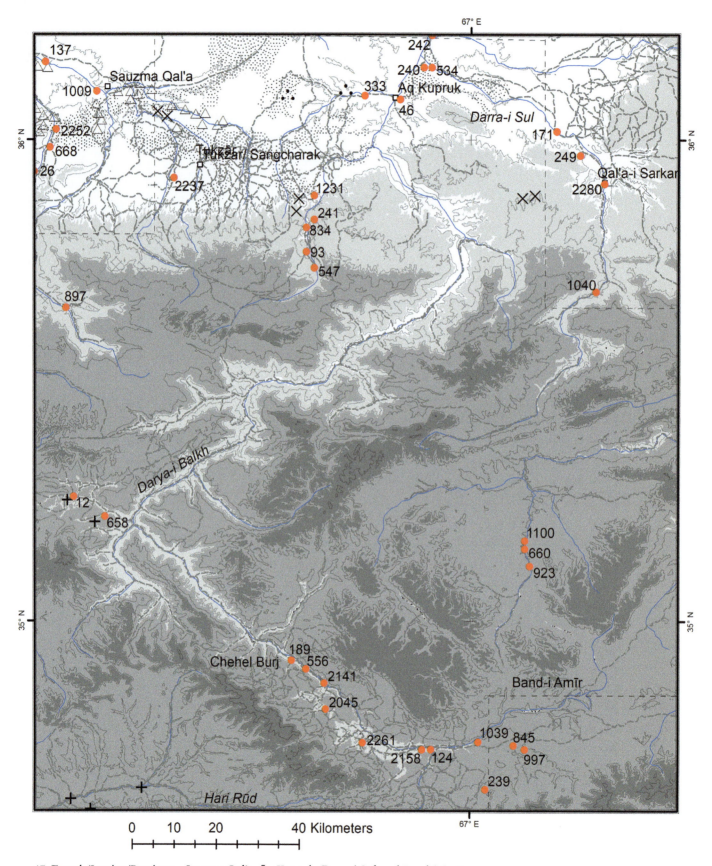

47 Faryāb/Jauzjān/Bāmiyān—Sauzma Qal'a, Āq Kupruk, Darra-i Sūf, and Band-i Amīr areas.

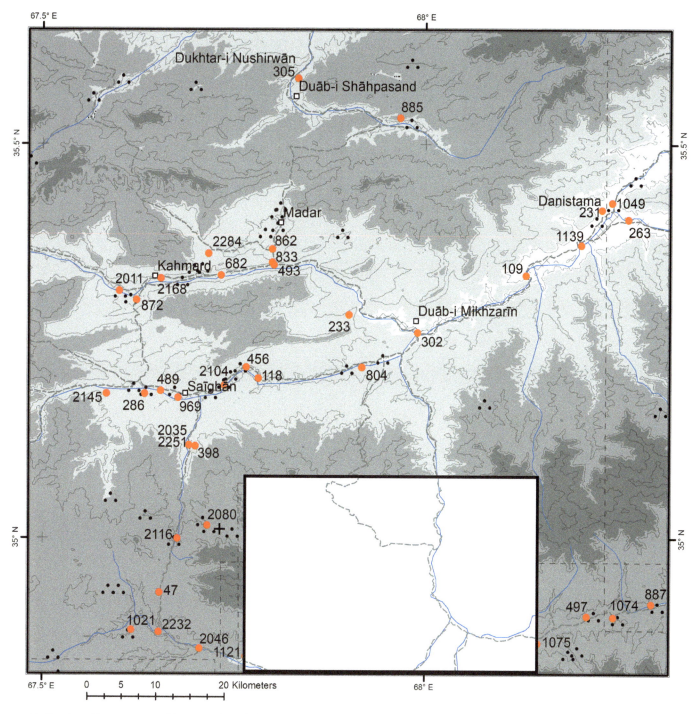

48 Bāmiyān/Samangān/Baghlān—Dūāb-I Shāhpasand, Tālā, Kahmard, Saighān, Bāmiyān, and Surkhāb areas.

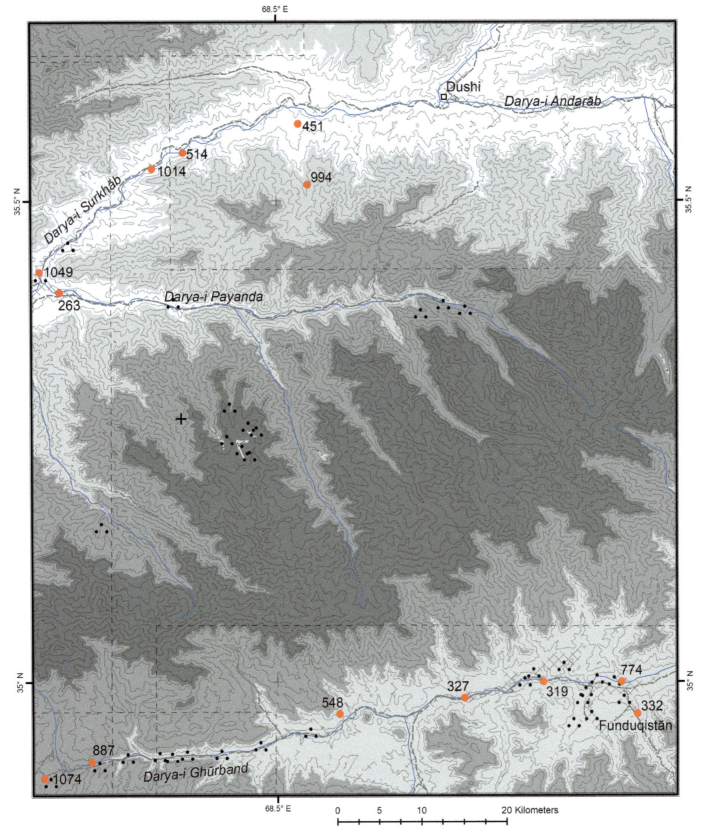

49 Baghlān/Parwān—Dūshi and Ghūrband areas.

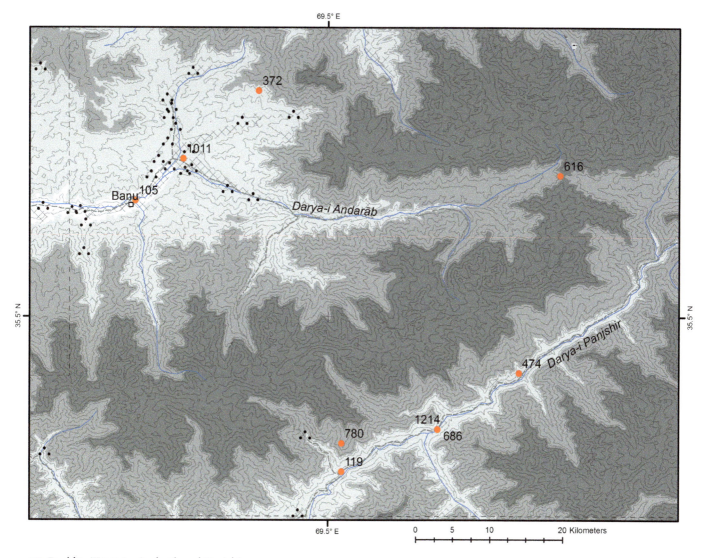

50 Baghlān/Kāpīsā—Andarāb and Panjshir areas.

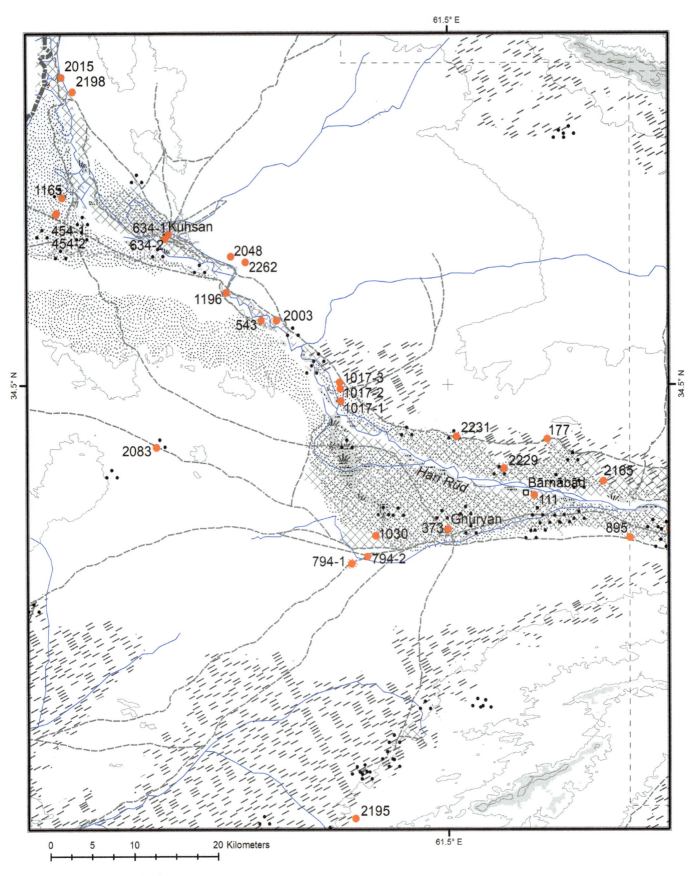

51 Herat—Kuhsān and Ghūriyān areas.

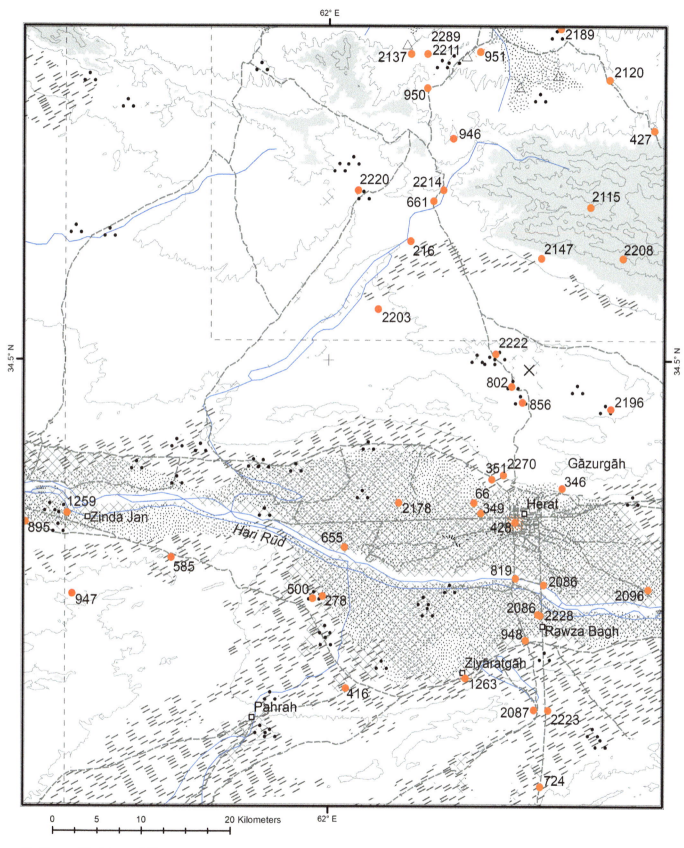

52 Herat—Zindajān and Herat areas.

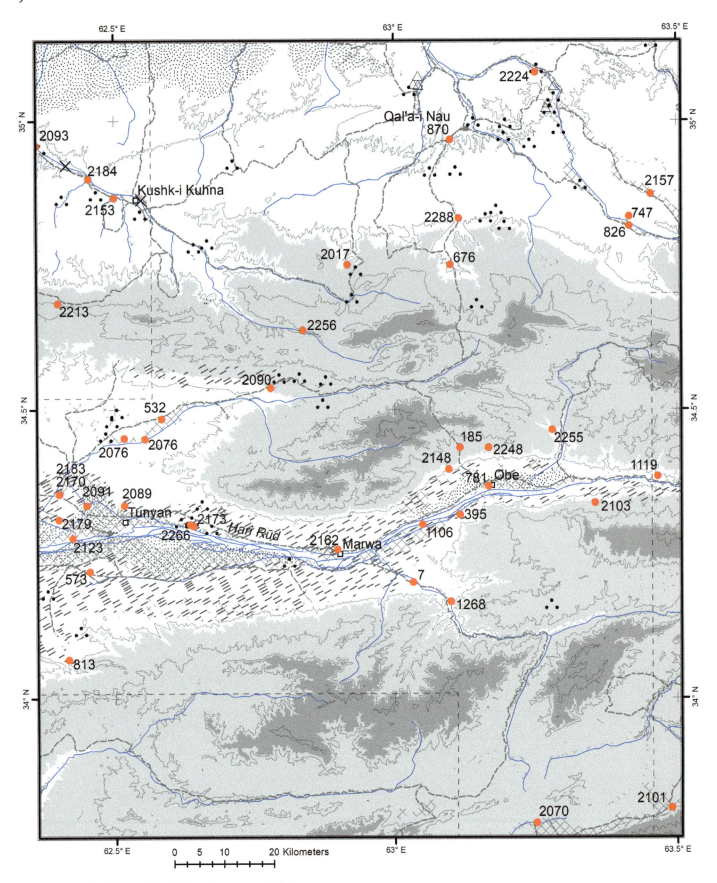

53 Herat/Bādghīs—Qal'a-i Nau, Tunyān, and Obeh areas.

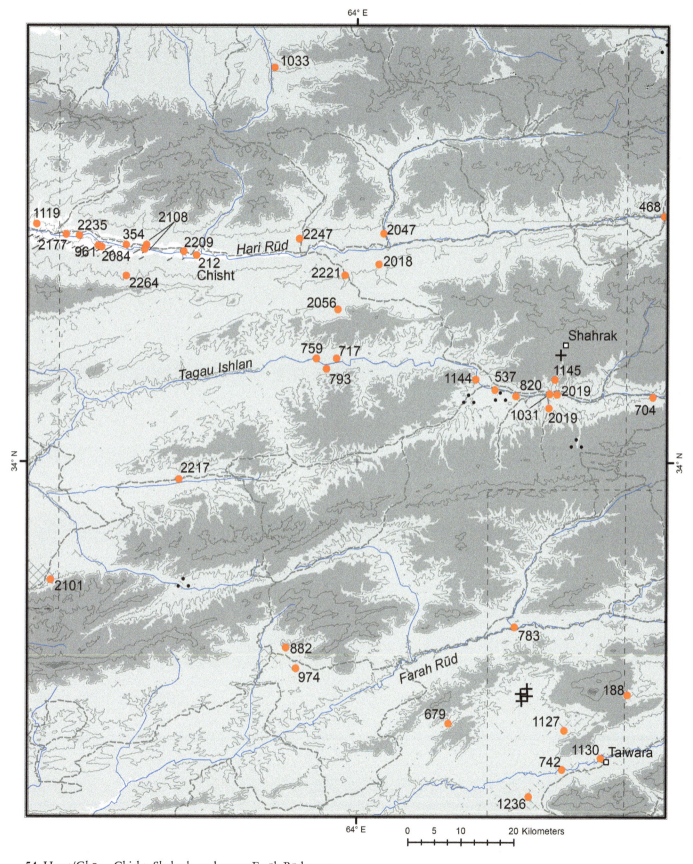

54 Herat/Ghūr—Chisht, Shahrak, and upper Farāh Rūd areas.

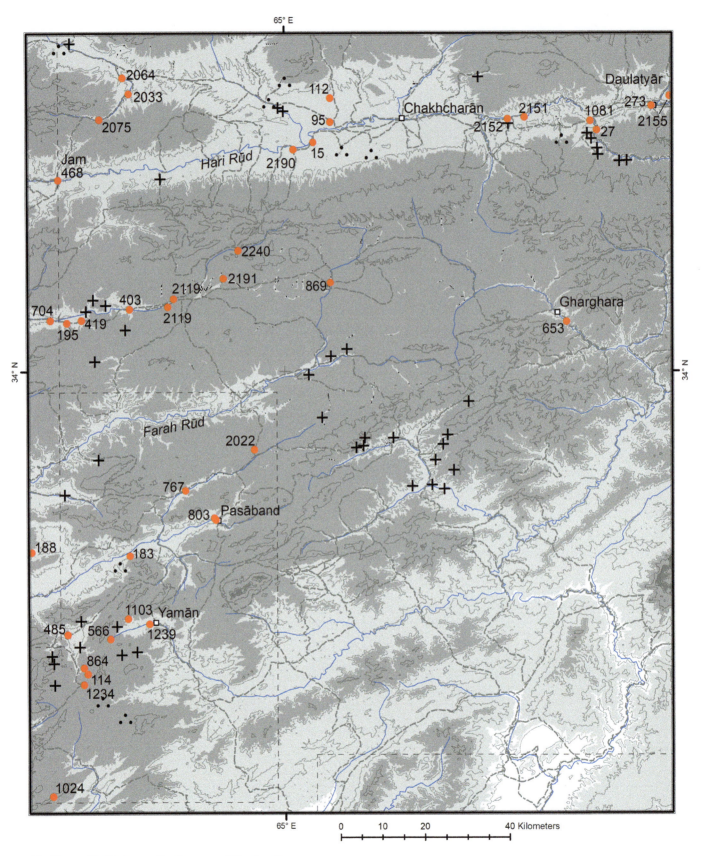

55 Ghūr—Chakhcharān, Daulatyār, and Pasāband areas.

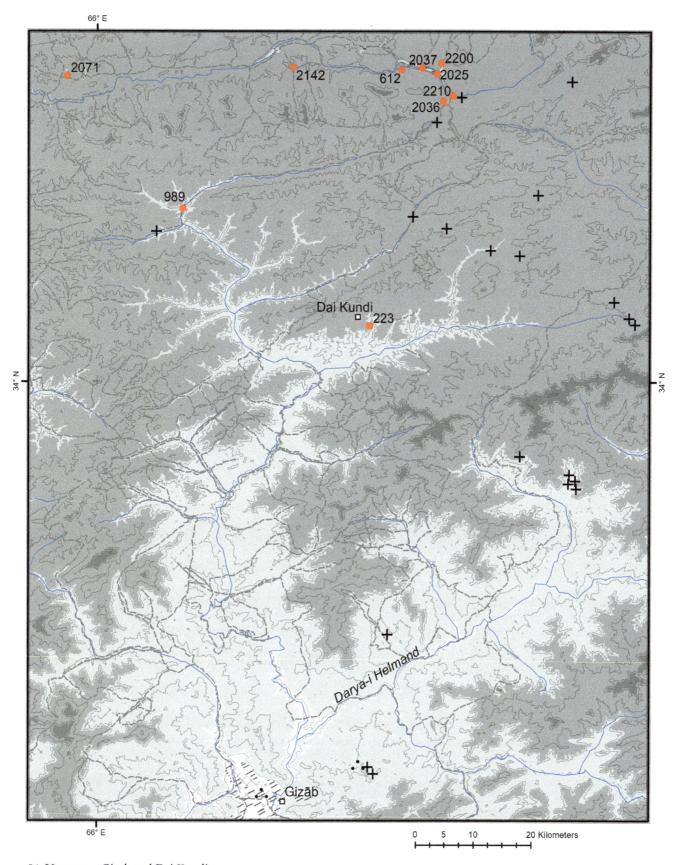

66° E

2071

2142

2037 2200
612 2025
2210
2036

989

Dai Kundi
223

34° N

34° N

Darya-i Helmand

Gizāb

66° E

0   5   10   20 Kilometers

56 Uruzgān—Gizāb and Dai Kundi areas.

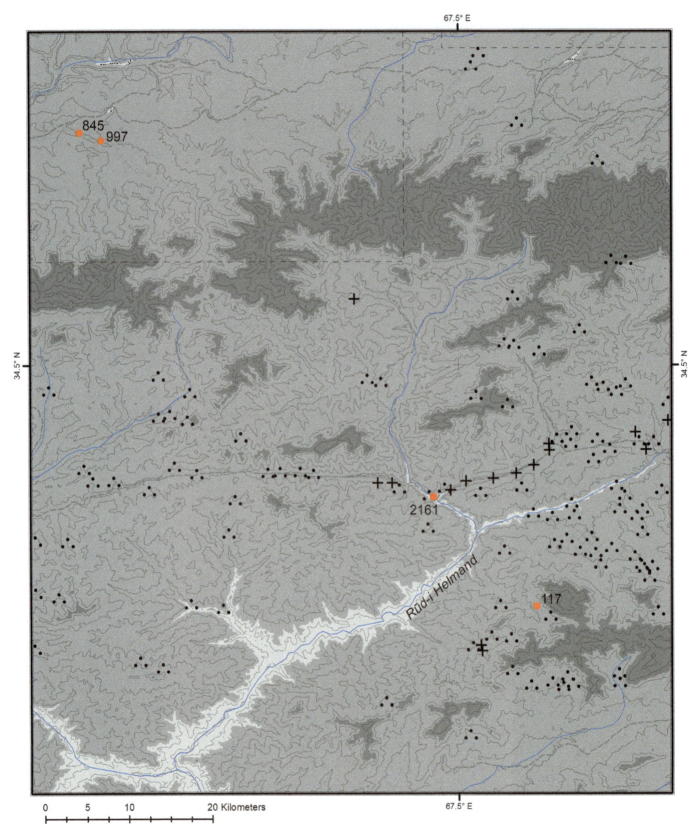

57 Bāmiyān/Maidān/Uruzgān/Ghazni—Yakaulang, Paniau, and Behsud areas.

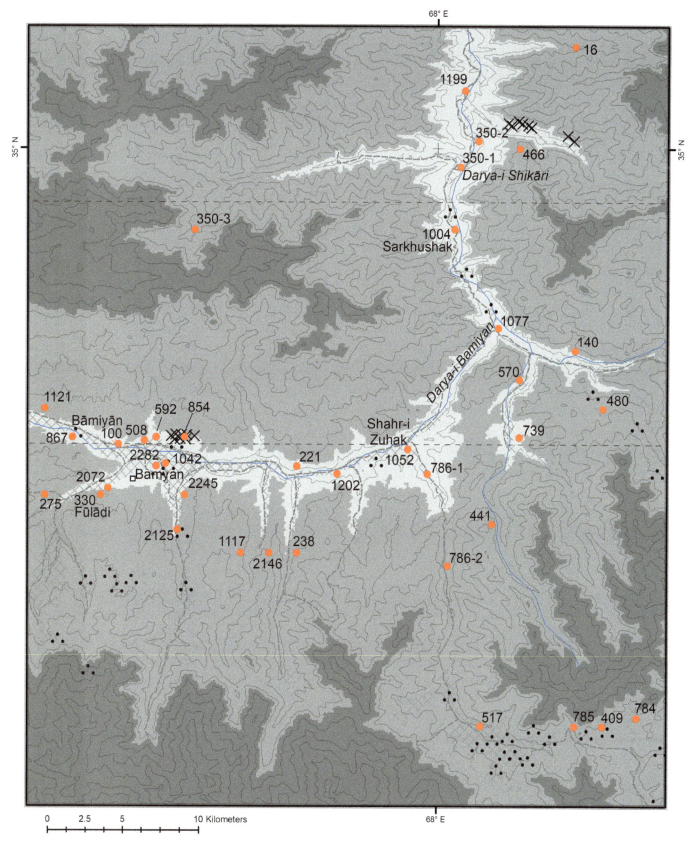

58 Bāmiyān—Bāmiyān and Shikarī areas.

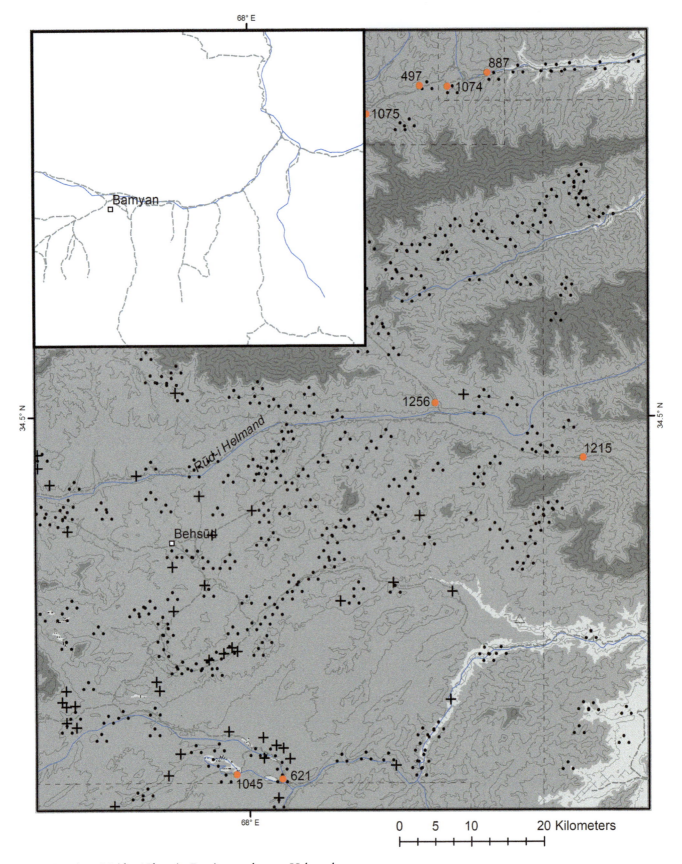

59 Bāmiyān/Maidān/Ghazni—Bāmiyān and upper Helmand areas.

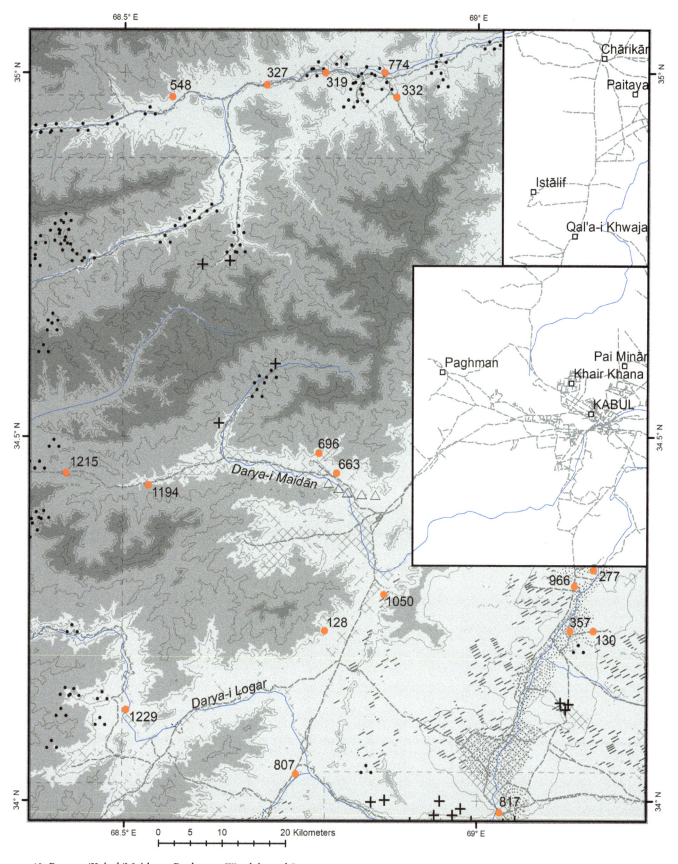

60 Parwān/Kābul/Maidān—Paghman, Wardak, and Logar areas.

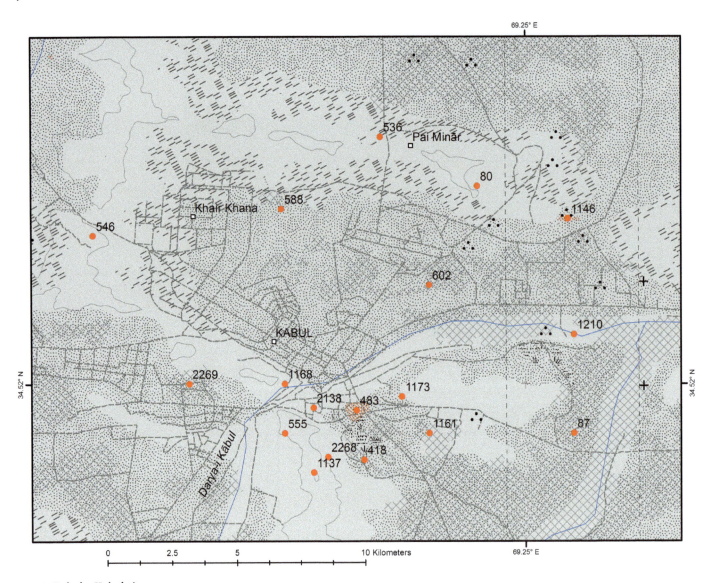

61 Kābul—Kābul city.

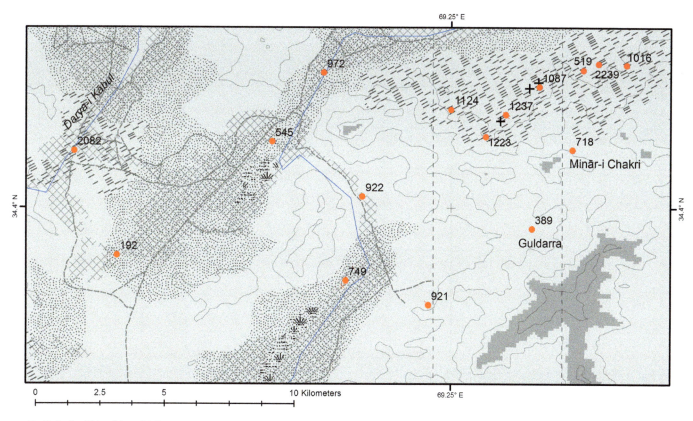

62 Kābul—Shiwaki and Minār area.

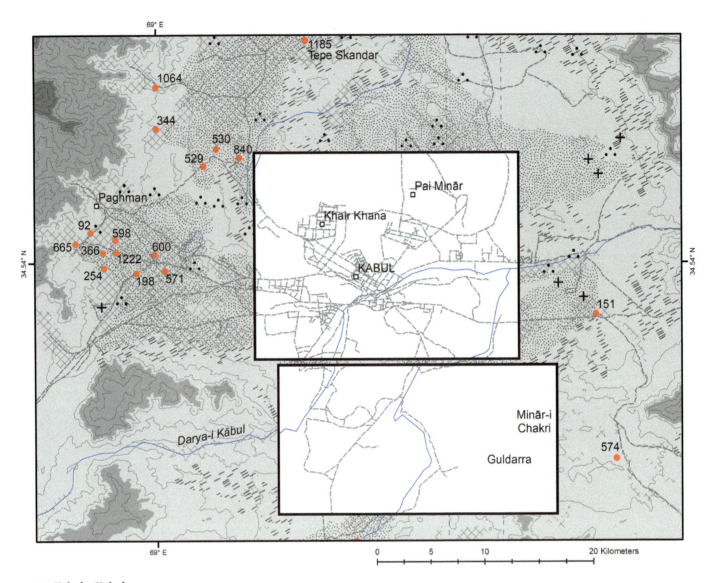

63 Kābul—Kābul area.

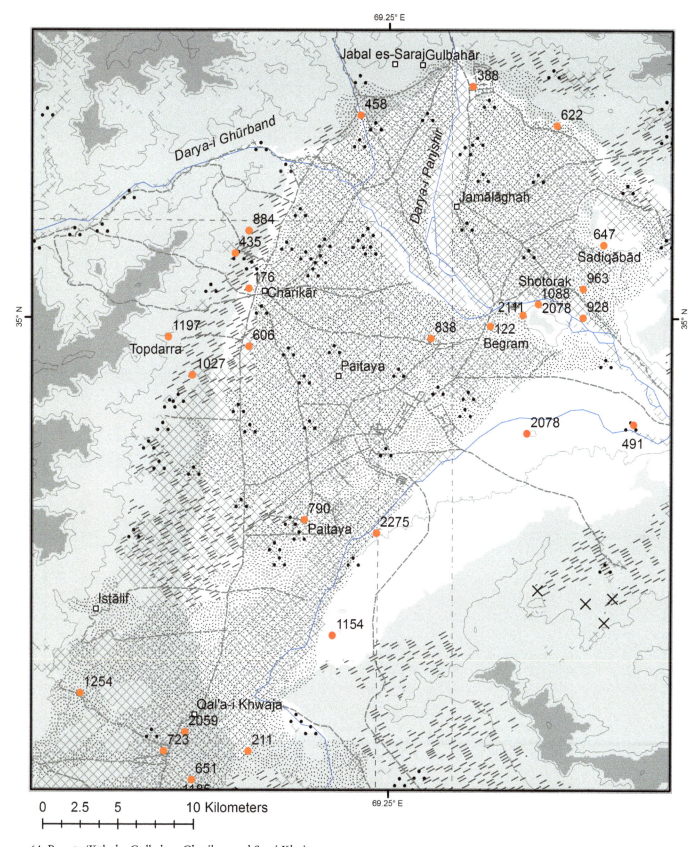

64 Parwān/Kābul—Gulbahār, Chārikār, and Sarai Khuja areas.

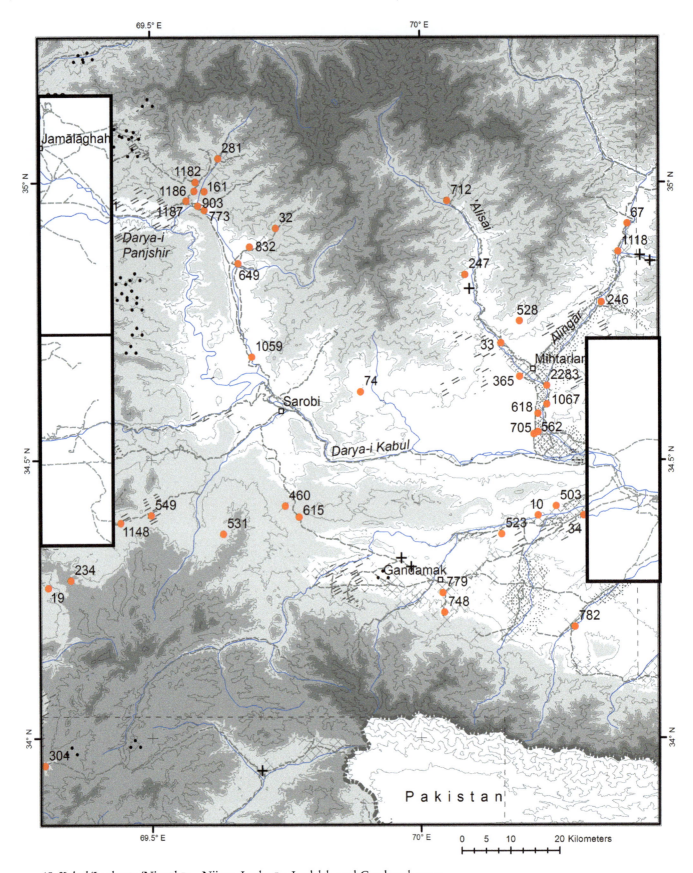

65 Kābul/Laghmān/Ningāhār—Nijrau, Laghmān, Jagdalak, and Gandamak areas.

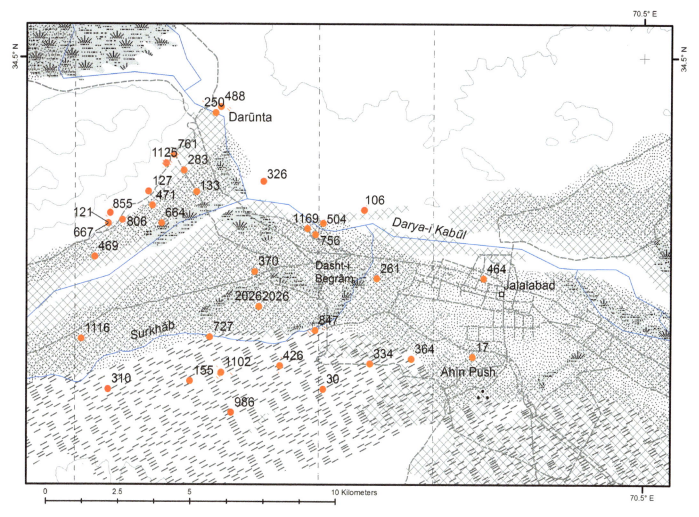

66 Ningāhār—Darūnta and Jalālābād area.

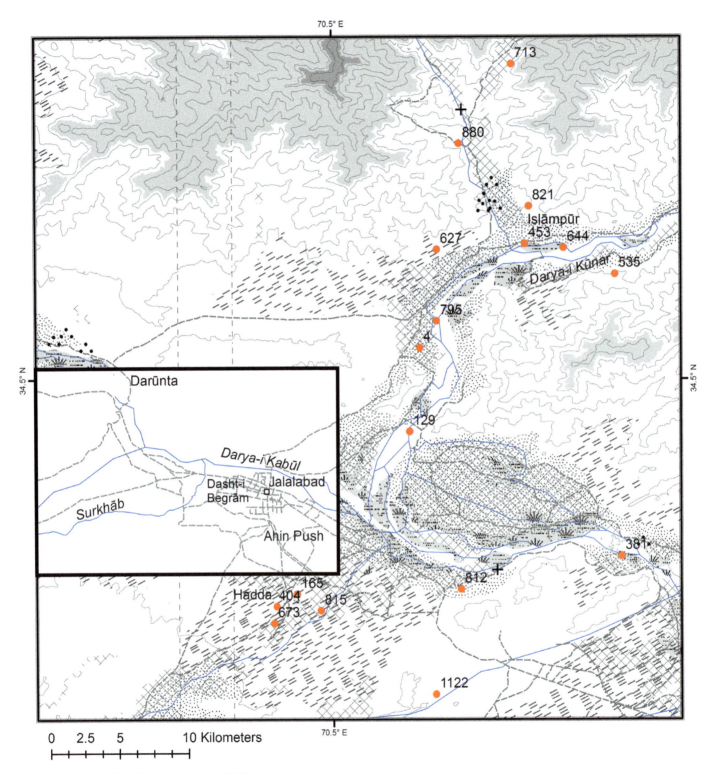

67 Laghmān/Ningāhār—Jalālābād and Islāmpūr areas.

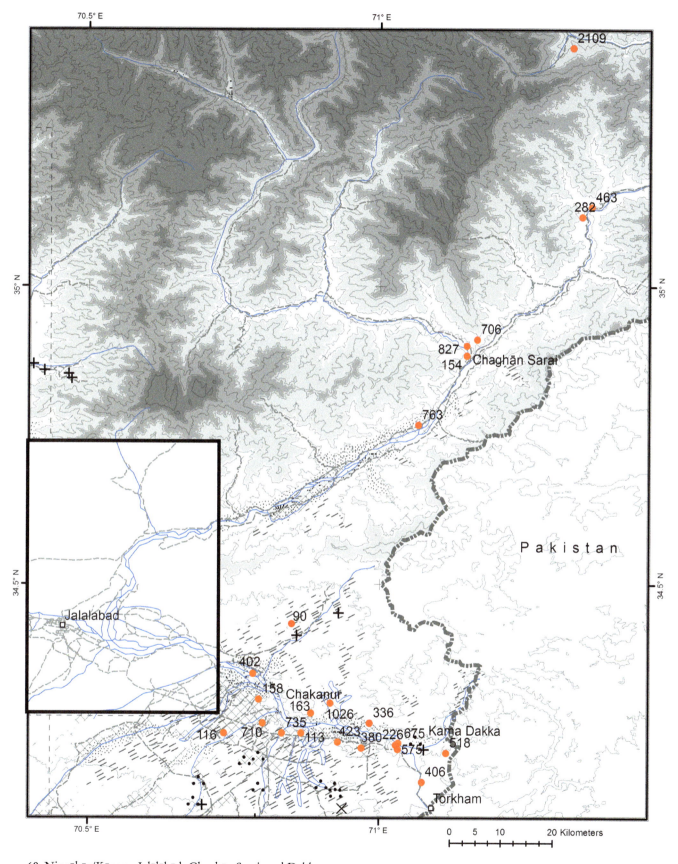

68 Ningāhār/Kūnar—Jalālābād, Chaghān Sarai, and Dakka areas.

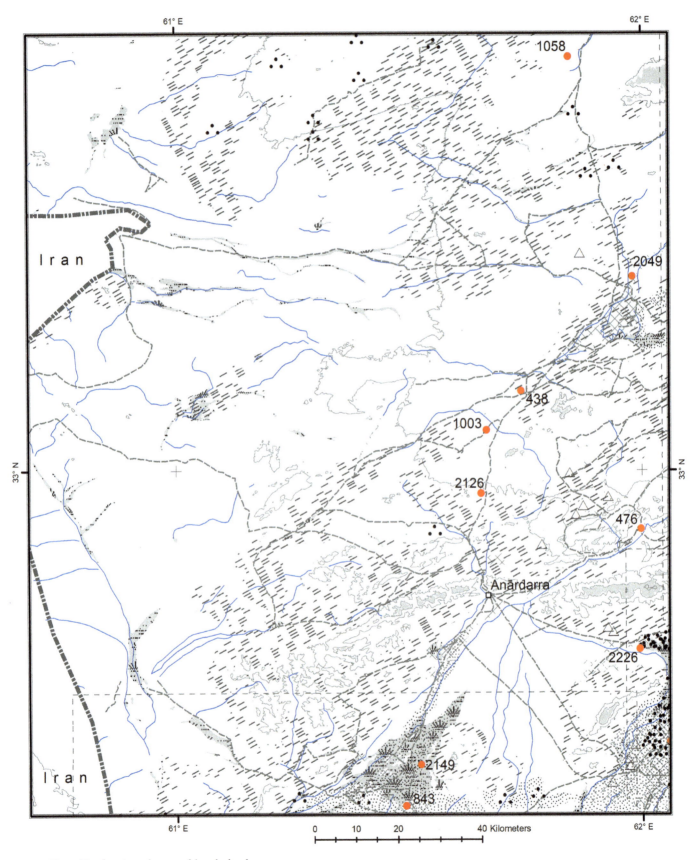

69 Herat/Farāh—Anārdarra and borderland area.

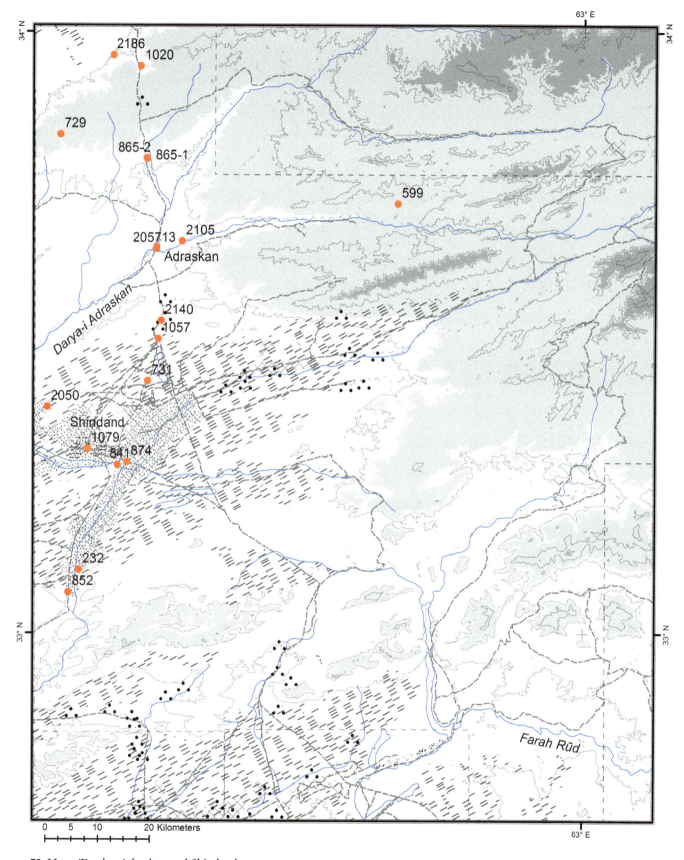

70 Herat/Farāh—Adraskān and Shindand areas.

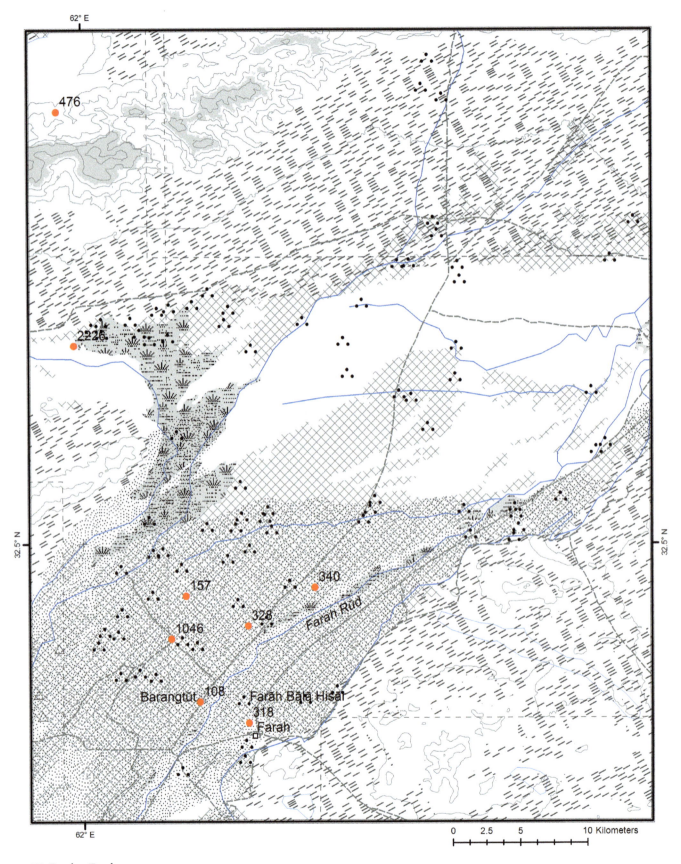

71 Farāh—Farāh area.

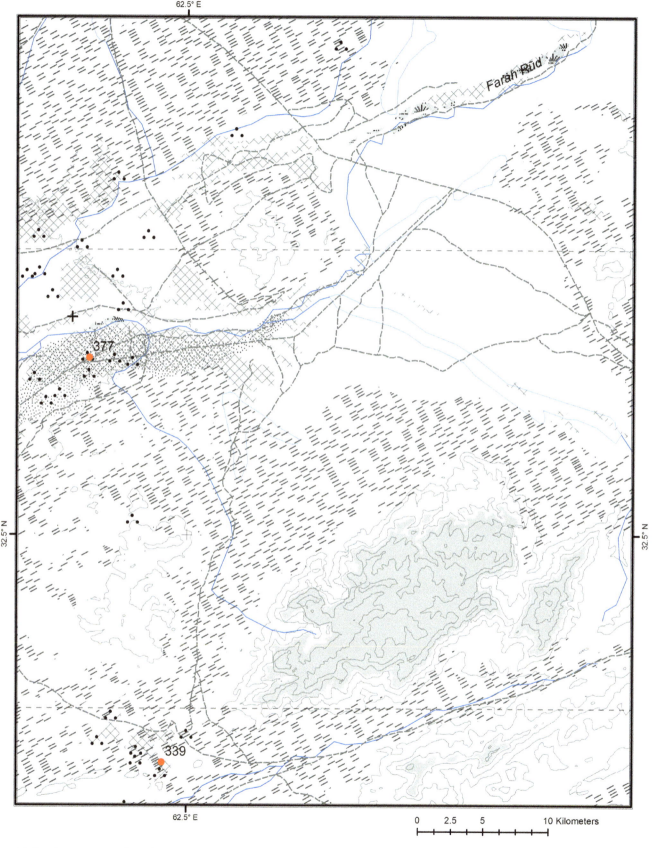

72 Farāh—area east of Farāh.

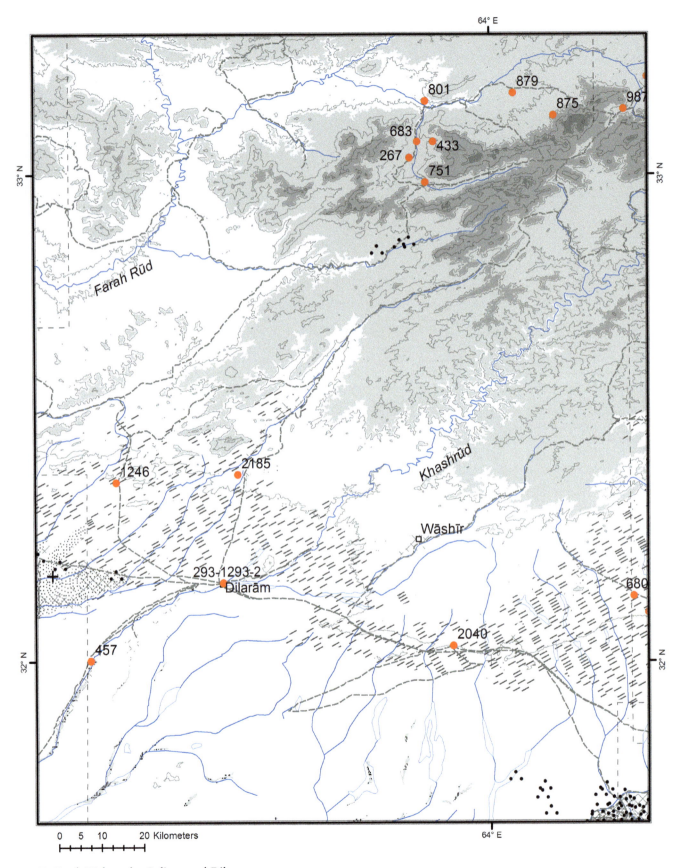

73 Farāh/Helmand—Gulistān and Dilārām areas.

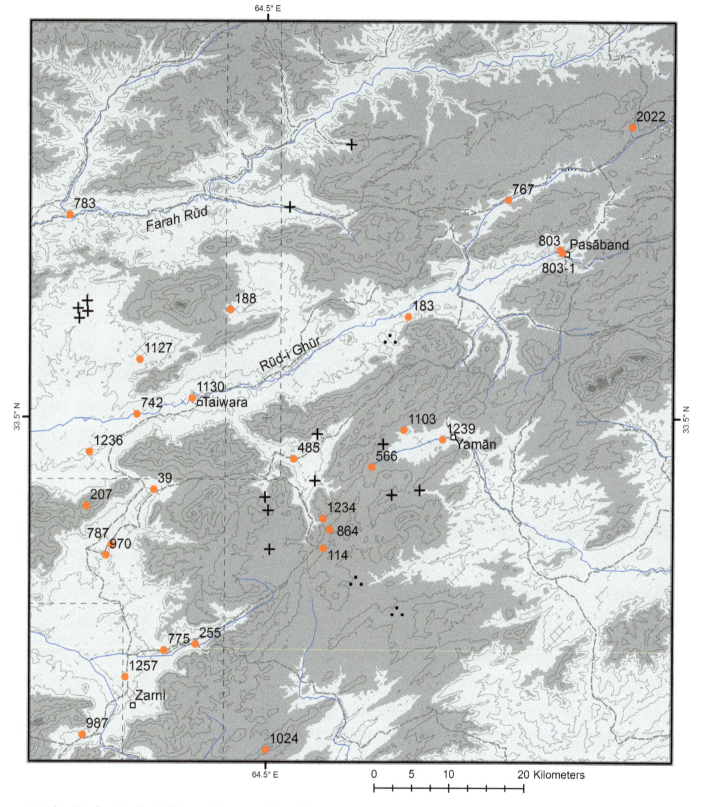

74 Ghūr/Farāh—Pasāband, Taiwara, Yamān, and Mushkan areas.

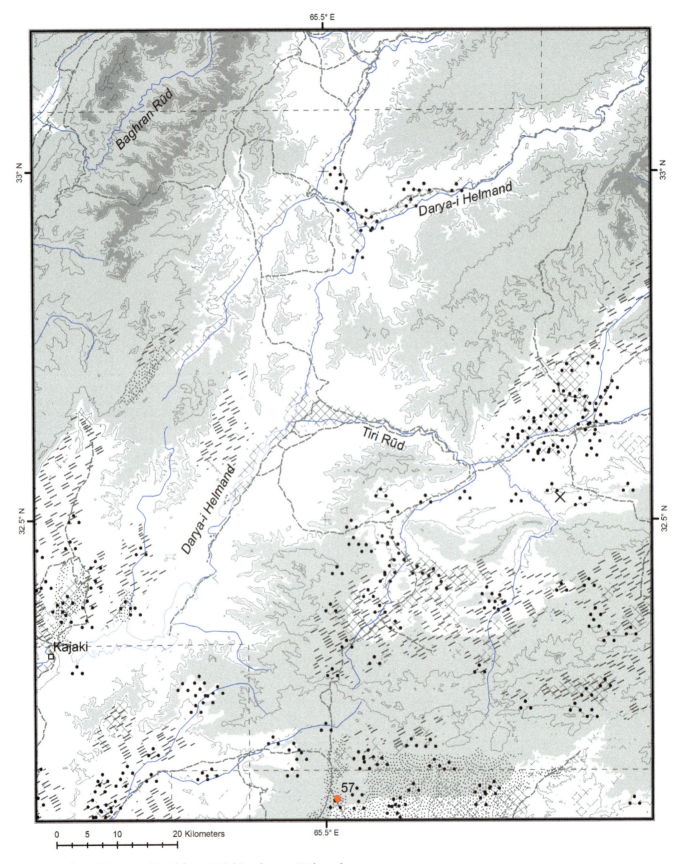

75 Helmand/Uruzgān/Kandahār—Kajaki and upper Helmand areas.

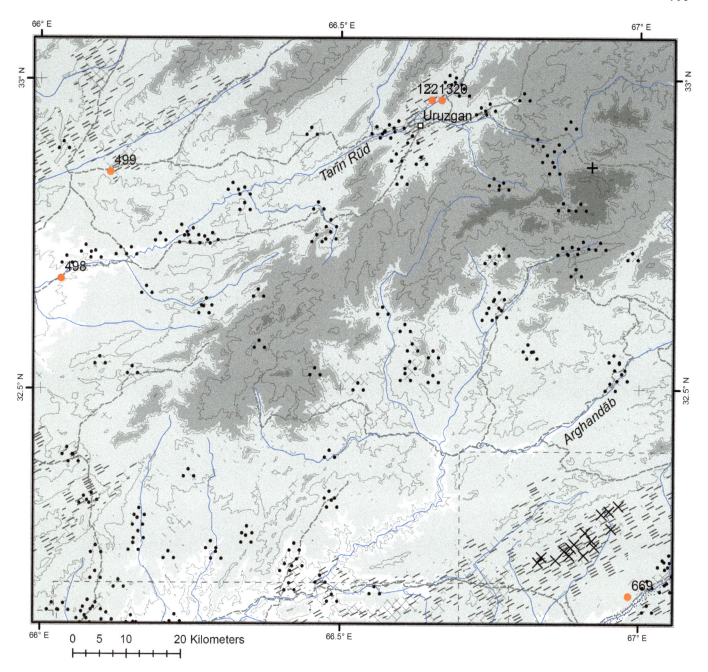

76 Uruzgān/Zābul — Uruzgan and Tarīn areas.

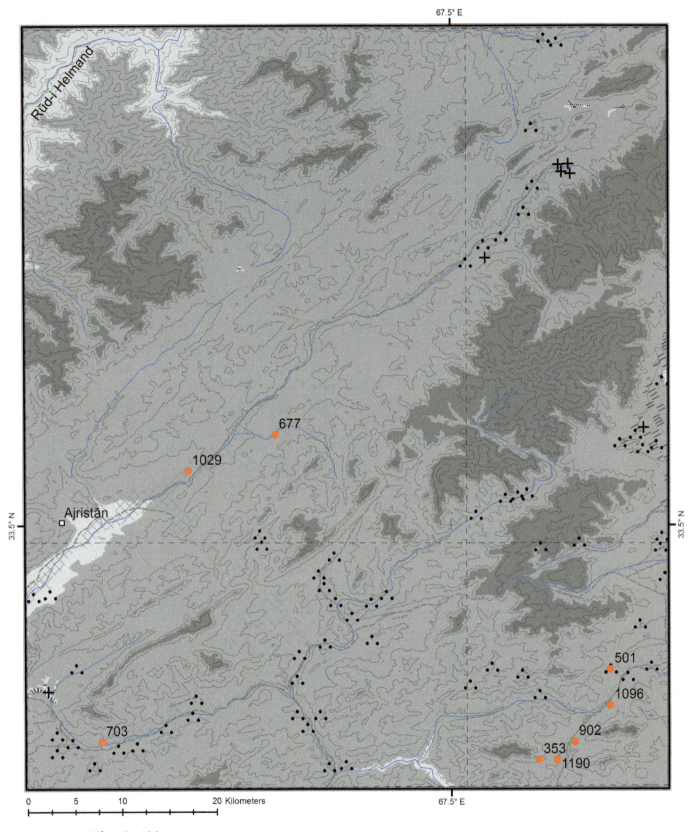

77 Uruzgān/Ghazni—Ajristān area.

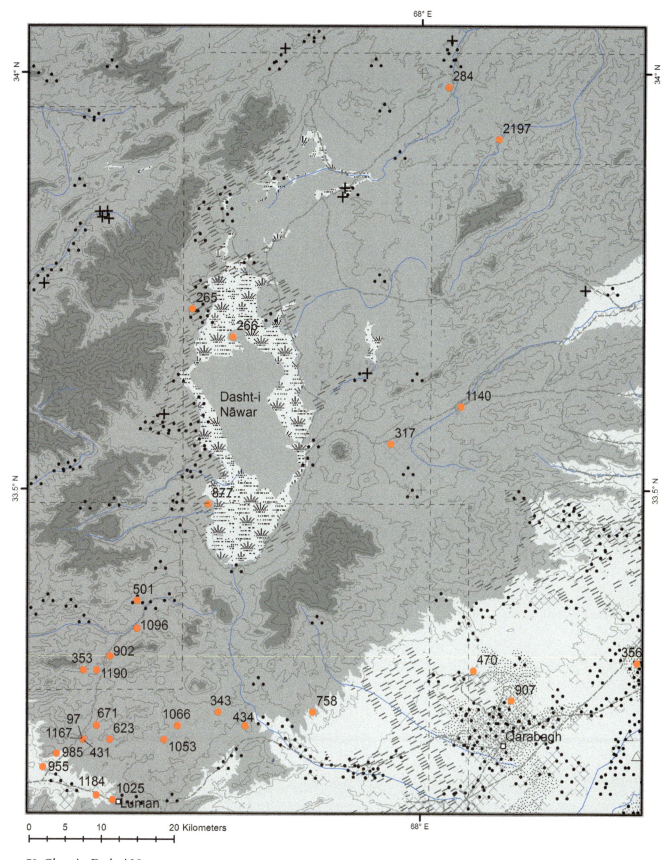

78 Ghazni—Dasht-i Nāwar area.

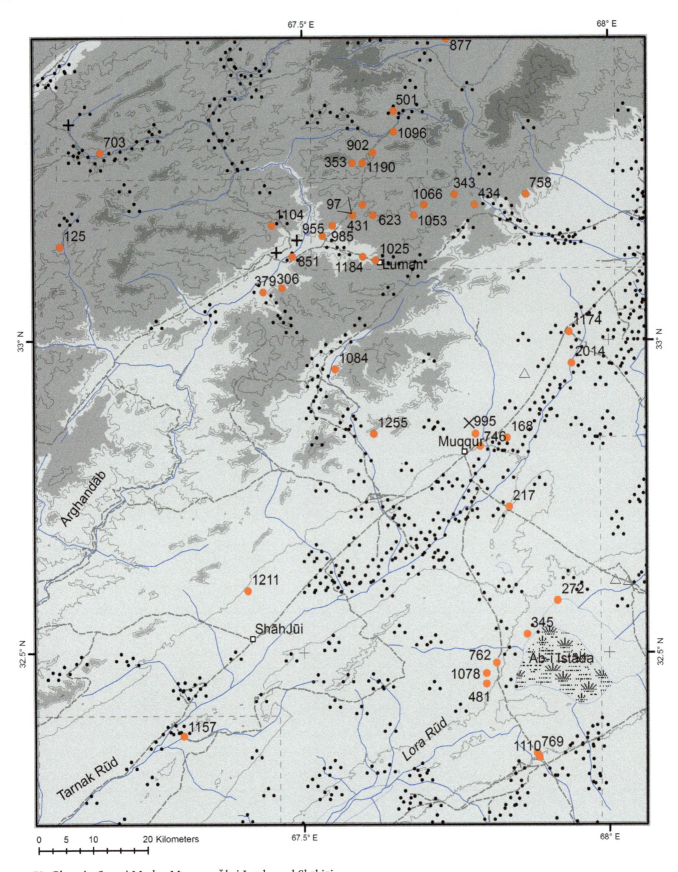

79 Ghazni—Sang-i Māsha, Muqqur, Āb-i Istāda, and Shāhjūi areas.

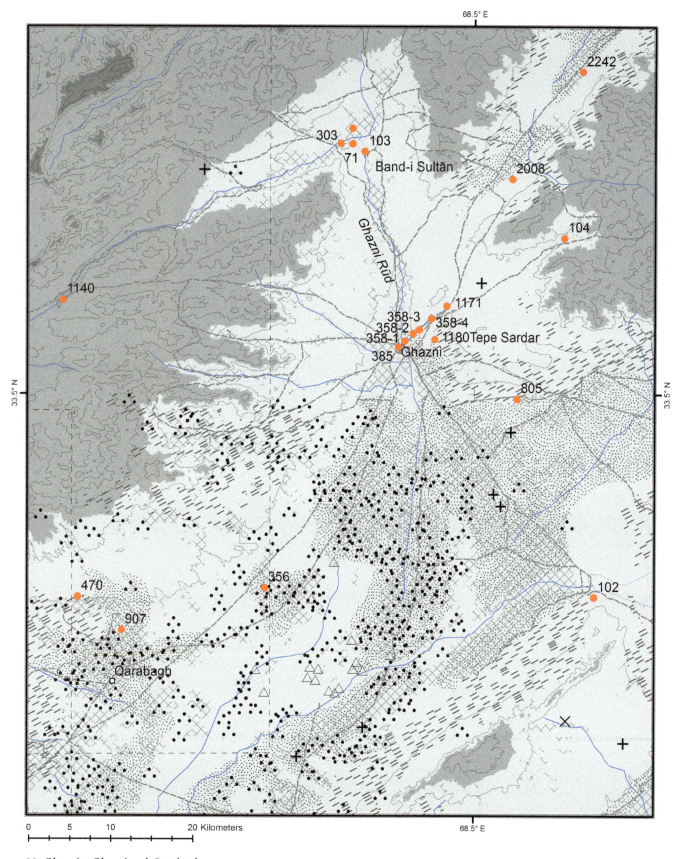

80 Ghazni—Ghazni and Qarabāgh areas.

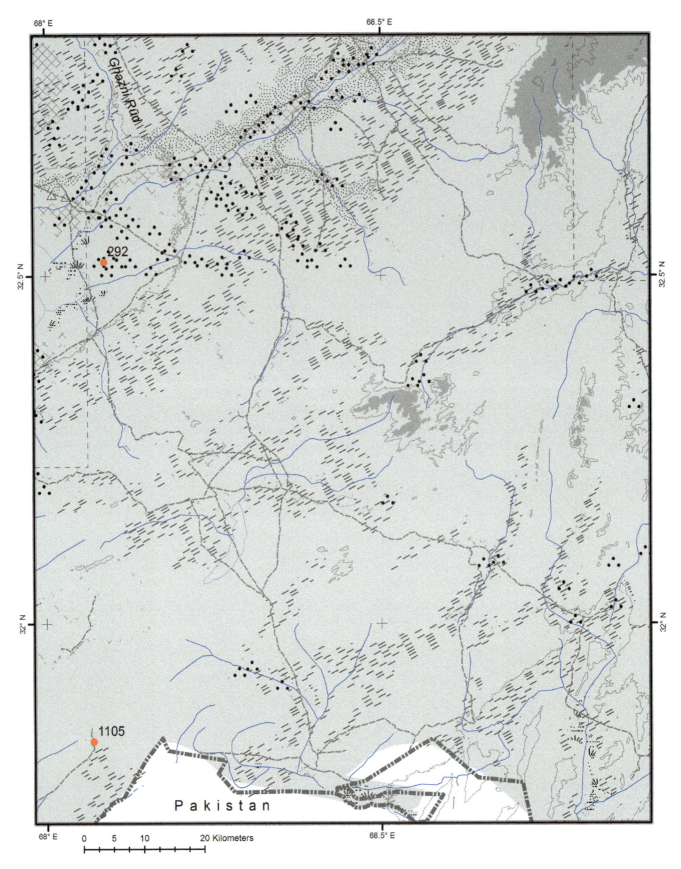

81 Ghazni/Paktiya—Katawaz area.

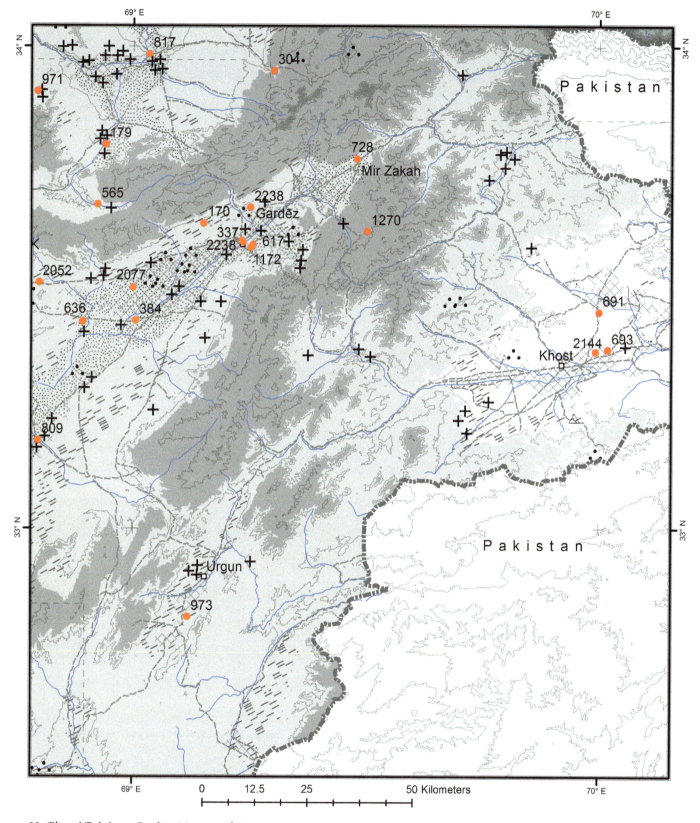

82 Ghazni/Paktiya—Gardēz, Matūn, and Urgūn areas.

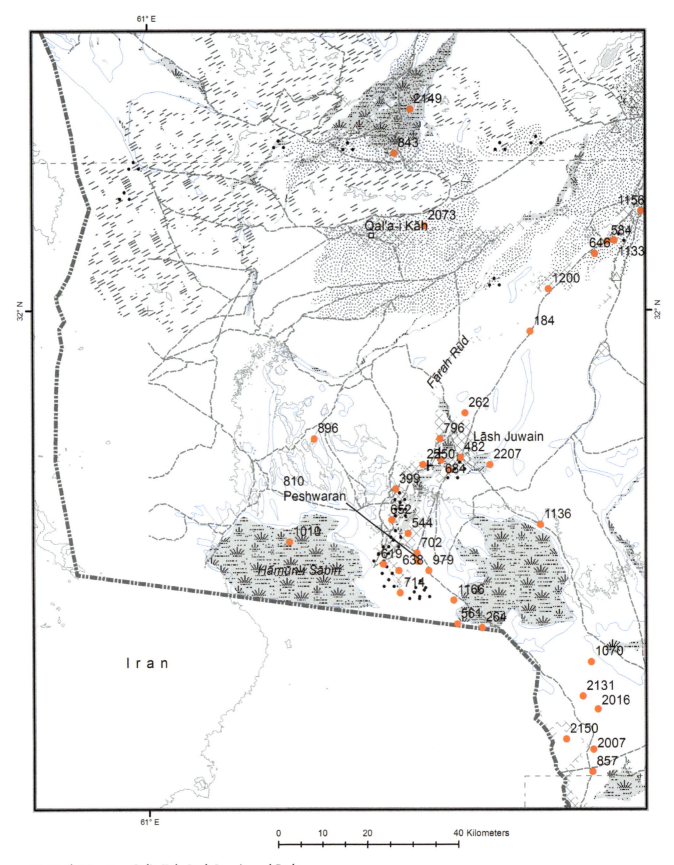

83 Fārāh/Nīmrūz — Qal'a Kāh, Lāsh Juwain, and Peshwaran areas.

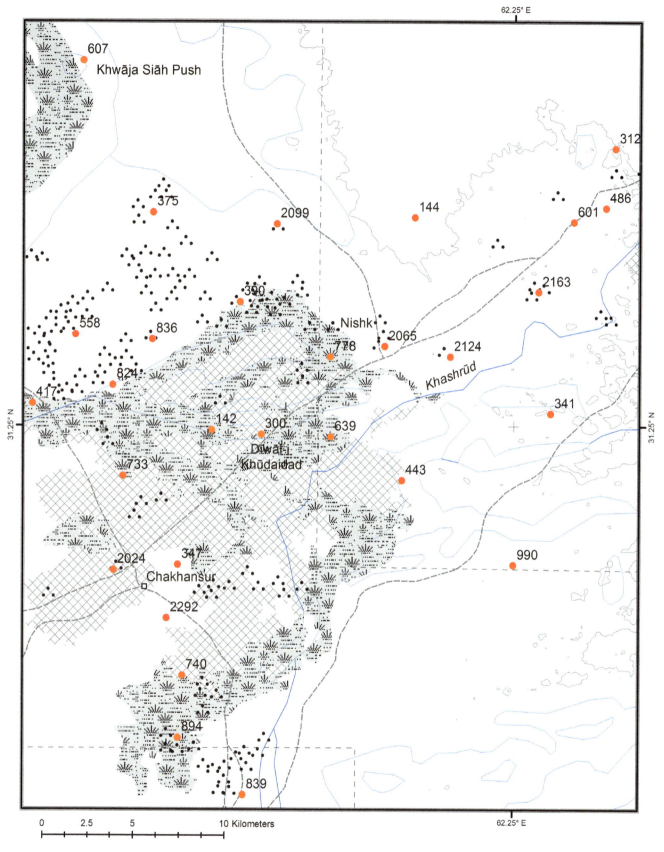

62.25° E

607
Khwāja Siāh Push

312

486

144
601

375

2099

2163

390

558
836
Nishk
2065
2124

824
Khashrūd

417
341

142   300
639
Dīwāl-i
Khudaidad
443

733

990

347

2024

Chakhānsūr

2292

740

894

839

31.25° N   31.25° N

62.25° E

0   2.5   5   10 Kilometers

84 Nīmrūz — Chakhānsūr and Nishk areas.

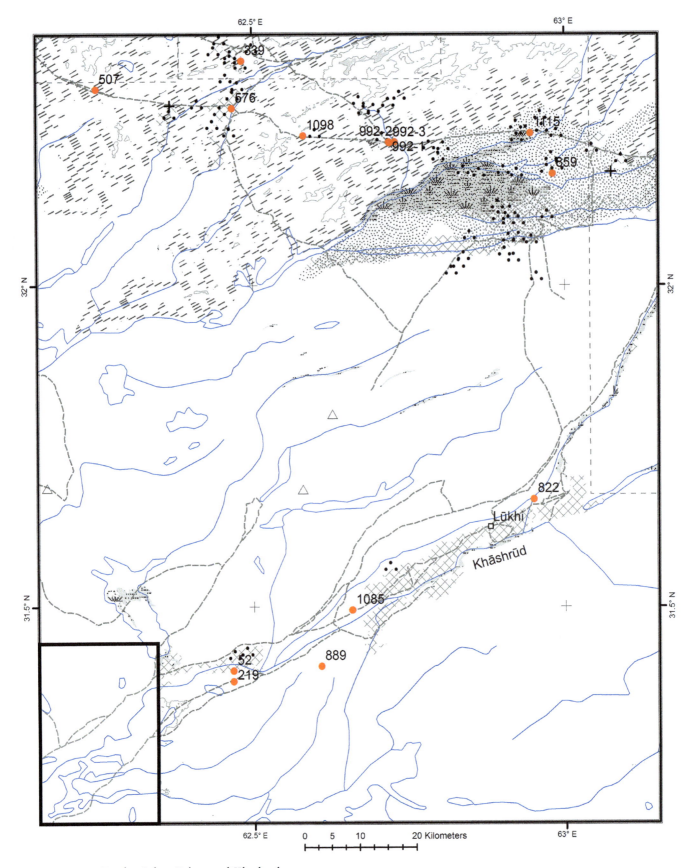

85 Nīmrūz/Farāh—Sultān Bakwa and Khāshrūd areas.

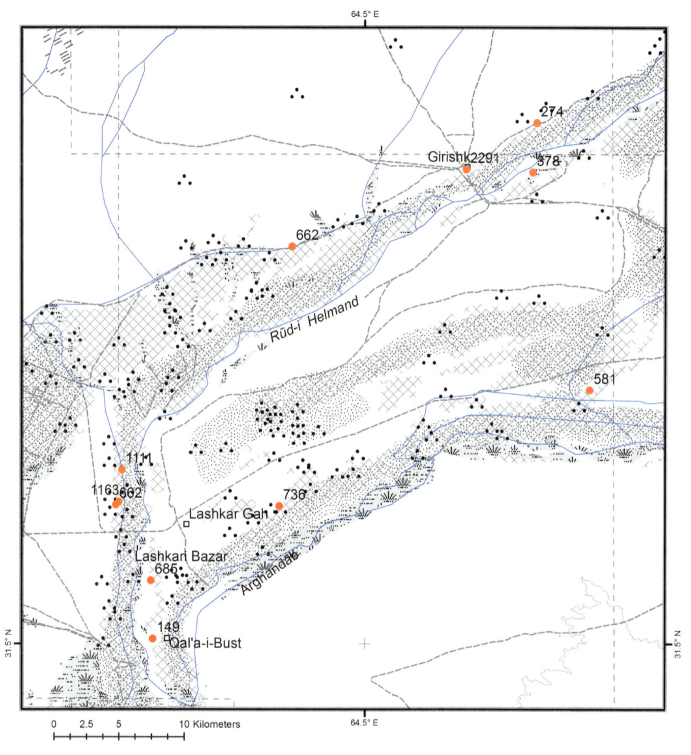

64.5° E

274

Girishk 2291   378

662

Rūd-i Helmand

581

1111

1163 662

736

Lashkar Gah

Lashkari Bazar
685

Arghandab

149
Qal'a-i-Bust

31.5° N

31.5° N

64.5° E

0   2.5   5   10 Kilometers

86 Helmand—Girishk and Lashkargāh areas.

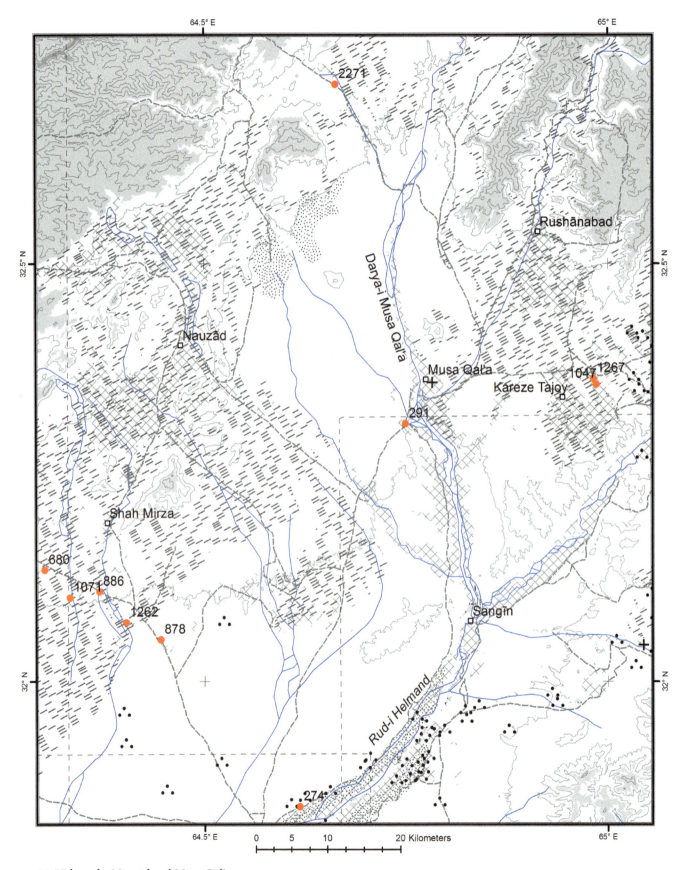

87 Helmand—Nauzād and Mūsa Qal'a areas.

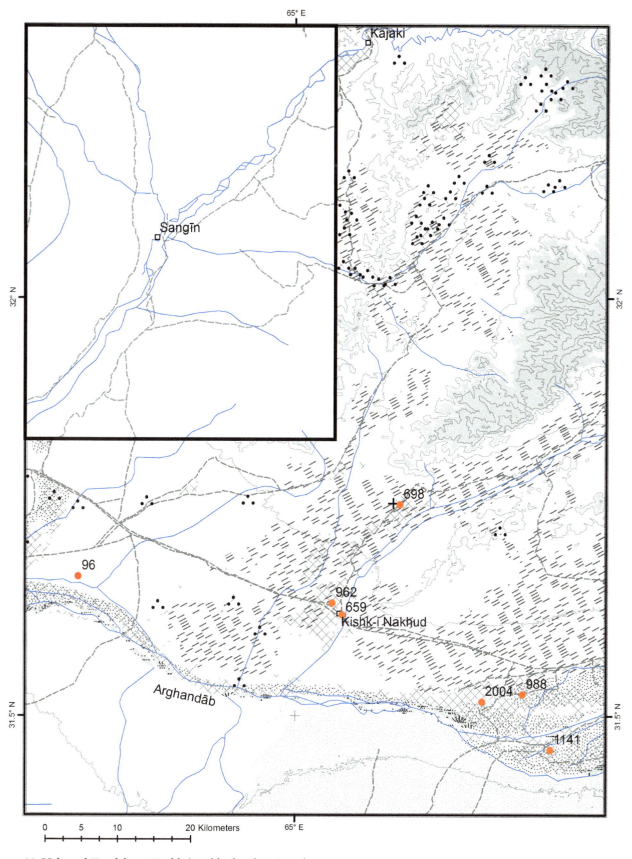

88 Helmand/Kandahār—Kushk-i Nakhūd and Maiwand areas.

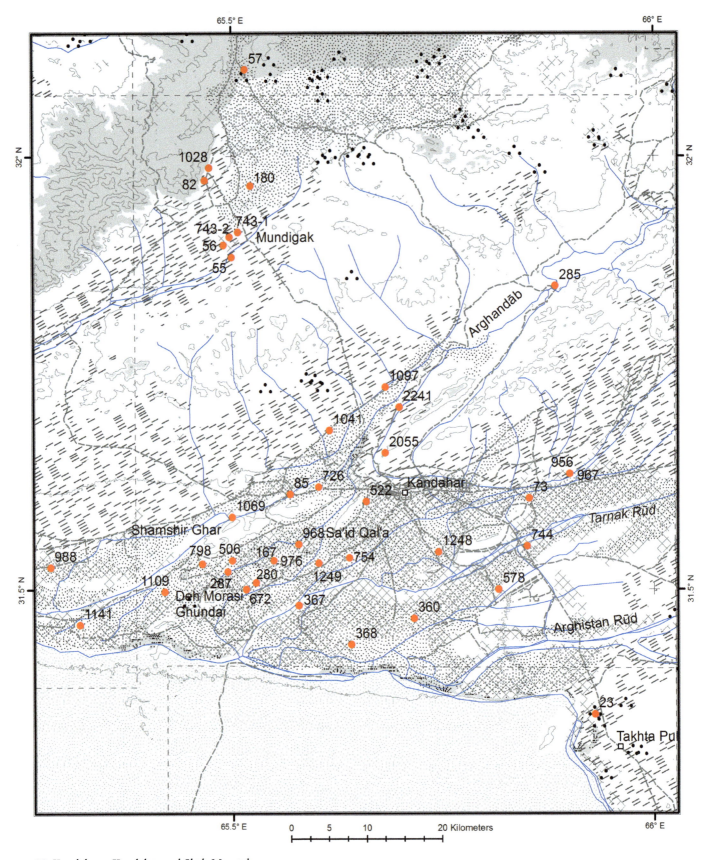

89 Kandahār—Kandahār and Shāh Maqsūd areas.

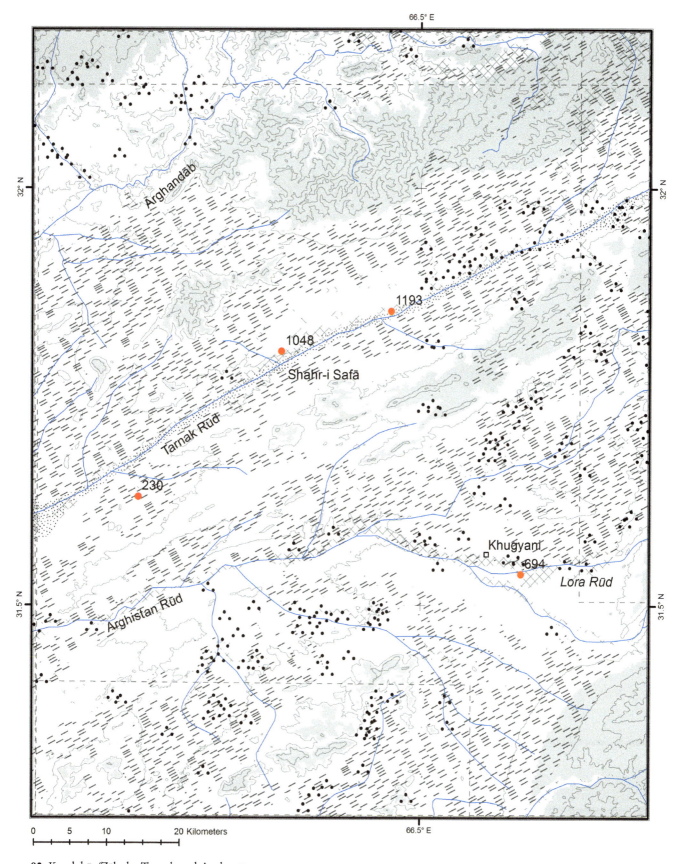

90 Kandahār/Zābul—Tarnak and Arghastān areas.

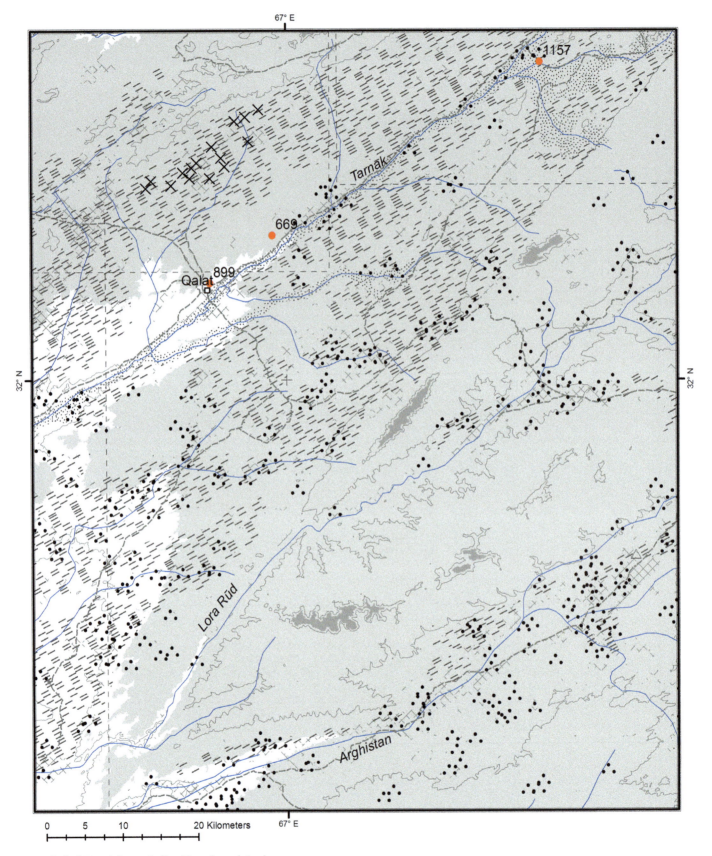

91 Zābul/Kandahār—Qal'at, Tarnak, and Arghastān areas.

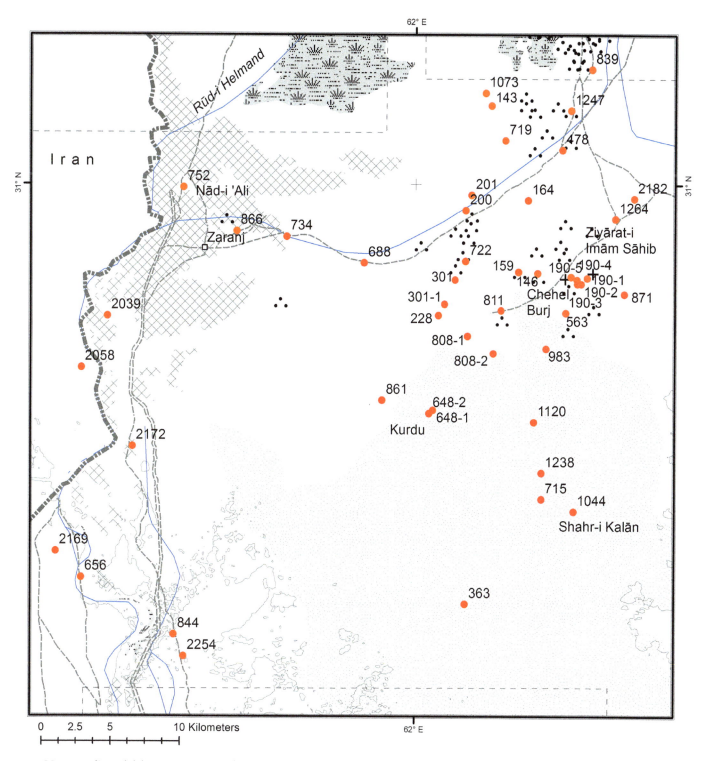

92 Nīmrūz—Zaranj, Ziyārat-i Amirān Sāhib, and Kurdu areas.

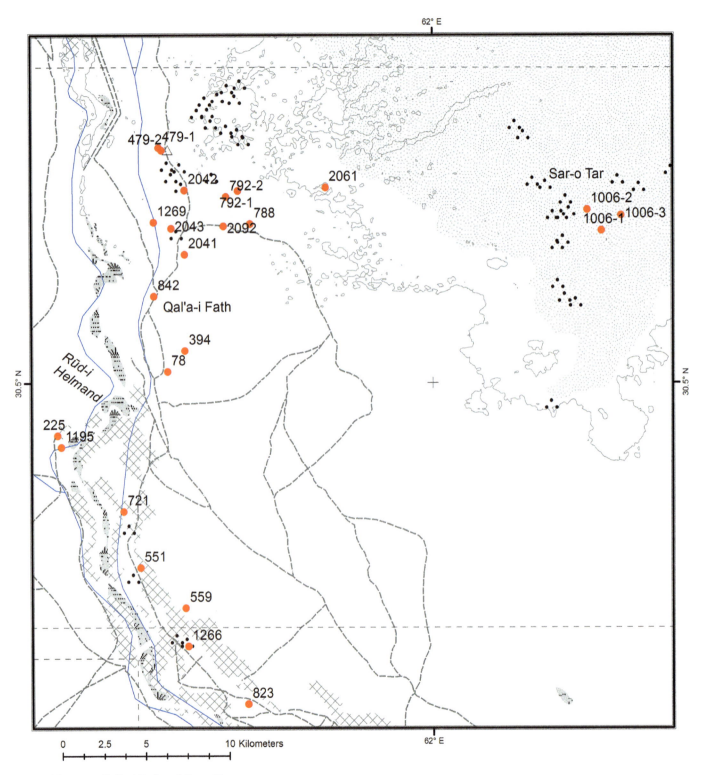

93 Nīmrūz—Qal'a-i Fath and Sar-o Tar areas.

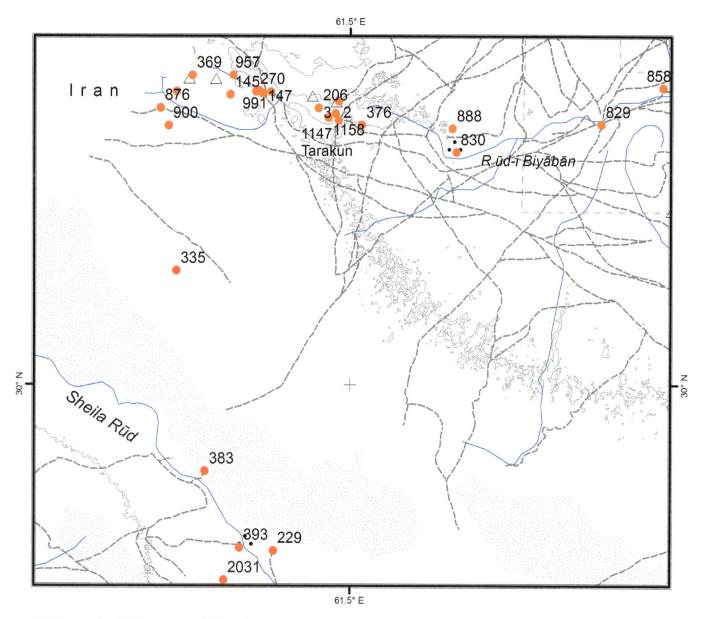

94 Nīmrūz—Rūd-i Biyābān and Shaila Rūd areas.

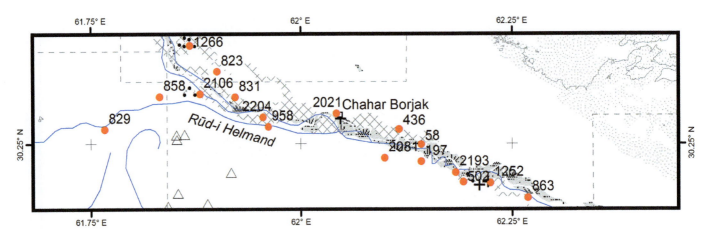

95 Nīmrūz—Chahārburjak area.

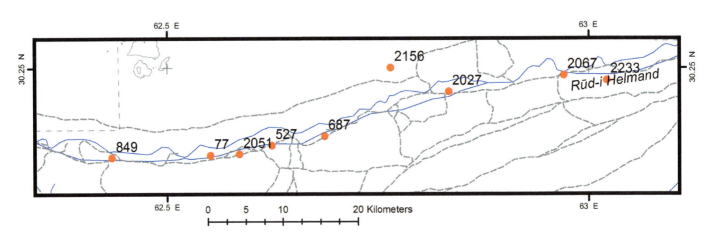

96 Nīmrūz—Rūdbār area.

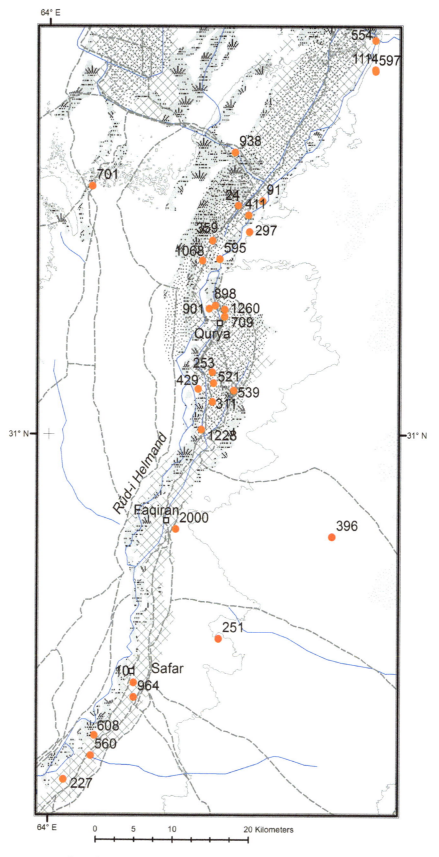

97 Helmand—Darwīshān and Safar areas.

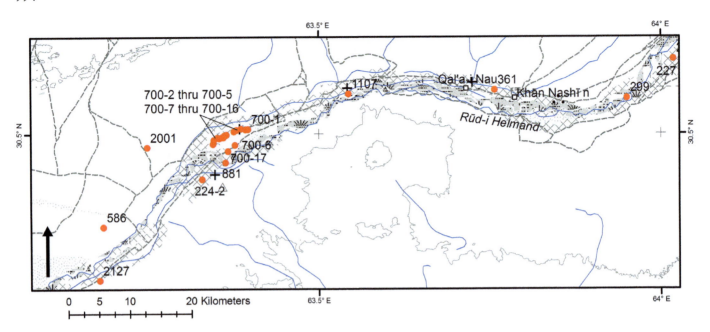

98 Helmand—Khān Nashīn and Daishu areas.

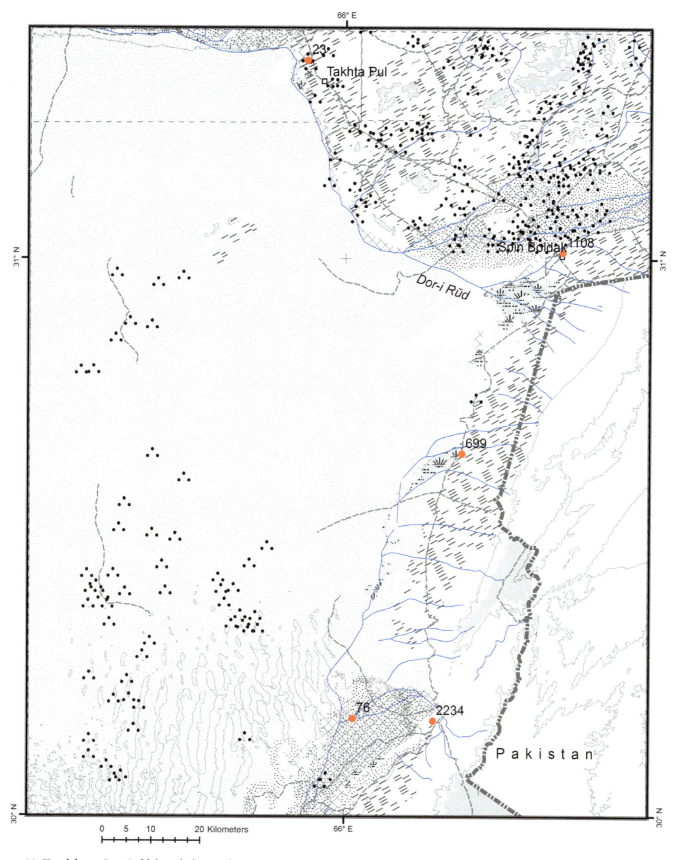

99 Kandahār—Spīn Baldak and Shorawak areas.

APPENDIX 1

Chronological Concordance

The first column gives the site name and the second one the site number.

Lower Palaeolithic (Map 56).

Dasht-i Nāwur	266

Middle Palaeolithic (Map 56): 50,000–30,000 BC

Darra-i Chakhmakh	240
Darra-i Dadil	242
Darra-i Kūr	245
Dasht-i Nāwur	266
Ghār-i Morda Gusfand	352
Hairatān	408
Kara Kamar	526
Kishm	613
Sar-i Namak	999
Zambukan	1251

Upper Palaeolithic (Map 56): 15,000–10,000 BC

Āq Kupruk	46
Darra-i Kalān	244
Hairatān	408
Islām Panja	452
Kilift	609
Kuk Jar	635
Sar-i Namak	999

Epi-Palaeolithic (Map 56): 10,000–8000 BC

Āq Kupruk	46
Bād-i Asyā?	72
Bahārak?	88
Barkhan-i Zādiyān	110
Darra-i Kalān	244
Hazār Sūm, Haibak	425
Kara Kamar	526
Kilift	609
Langārkish?	678
Rahman Gul?	953
Sandukti	982
Shāh Tepe	1056
Siāh Rigān	1101
Tāsh Guzar	1149
Tāshqurghān	1151
Ūch Tepe	1209

Neolithic (Map 57): 8000–4000 BC

Āq Kupruk	46
Chāsh Bābā	181
Chilik-i Qul	202
Chilik-i Yaldash	203
Chilik-i Yass Khān	204
Gurziwan	401
Hazār Sūm	425
Jar Quduq	473
Kauk	540
Khwāja Do Kuh	589
Khwāja Do Kuh Nau	590
Kilift	609
Lairu?	669
Qaq	905
Qaq-i Nazār Aghā	906
Qara Kul	910
Qara Tepe	912
Qur Quduq	939
Safarwal	965
Sayyidābād	1012

Bronze Age (Map 58): 4000–1500 BC

Akram Qal'a	24
Aliābād	29
Andarābi	40
Āq Kupruk	46
Aranji	53
Astāna Tepe	61
Ayatan Tepe	65
Bād-i Sah Ghundai	73
Bāgh-i Mīr	83
Bāgh-i Pul Ghundai	85
Barangtūt	108
Bāsiz	115
Bīsh Kapa	135
Buina Qara	138
Chadur Tepe?	153
Chār Sang Tepe	180
Chul-i Abdān	218

(continued)

Bronze Age (Map 58): 4000–1500 BC

Dam, Shaila Rūd	229
Darra-i Kūr	245
Dashli 1	256
Dashli 3	257
Dashli East	258
Dashli South	259
Deh Morasi Ghundai	287
Deh Nahr-i Jadīd	288
Deh Nau	289
Farukhābād	323
Gardan Rīg	335
Gudar-i Shāh	383
Gūgari	386
Gulrān	391
Hāji Yūnis	412
Herat?	428
Hirdai Tepe	430
Īshān Tūp	445
Kāfir Qal'a Rustāq	495
Kaldīsh	515
Kandahār	522
Khush Bai	579
Khush Tepe	582
Khusti Qishlāq	583
Khwāja Hasan	595
Khwāja Sultān	608
Kuhna Qal'a Tāluqān	633
Mundigak	743
Mundi Hisār	744
Nād-i 'Ali	752
Parchau	799
Qal'a-i Hindu	849
Qūnsai	933
Qurghān Tepe	937
Rūd-i Shahrawān	956
Sa'id Qal'a Tepe	968
Sang-i Mazār?	987
Sasmāq	1008
Shahr-i Safā	1048
Shairābād, north-west	1063
Shingān	1080
Shōrtūghai	1089
Siāh Rīgān	1101
Spirwan	1109
Tam 'Ali	1143
Tikar	1191
Urta Buz	1220
Zindān	1260

Iron Age (Map 59): 1500–700 BC

Aq Chapar 2	44
Ayatan Tepe	65
Bahārak	89

Bīsh Kapa	135
Burat Tepe	141
Burri	147
Bust	149
Chul-i Abdān	218
Dam-i Malik Khān	2043
Dashli 3	257
Deh Nau	289
Firitu	328
Ghārluli	355
Gudar-i Shāh	383
Herat	428
Ishān Tūp	445
Jalā'ir	462
Kāfir Qal'a Rustāq	495
Kalafgān	510
Kalafgān, east	511
Kaldīsh, south	516
Kandahār	522
Kanum	525
Khusti Qishlāq	583
Kirghiz Tepe	611
Kuhna Qal'a	631
Kumli	641
Lalmi Buz	674
Maimana	697
Mundigak	743
Nād-i 'Ali	752
Parchau	799
Qal'a-i Jamal	852
Qūnsai	933
Qurghān Tepe	937
Rūd-i Shāhrawān	959
Shāhi Khaila	1022
Shahrābād	1030
Shāh Tepe	1056
Shairābād	1061
Shairābād, north-west	1063
Shingān	1080
Siāh Rīgan	1101
Tilla Tepe	1192
Uljatu	1212
Urta Buz	1220
Yaka Tūt	1235
Zard Kamar	1253
Zulm	1271

Achaemenid (Map 60): c.530–330 BC

Adraskan Rud	13
Altin 1	36
Altin 10	37
Altin Dilyar Tepe	38
Āq Kupruk	46
Archi	54
Ayatan Tepe	65

Bahārak and Uch Ariq	89	Mir Zakah	728
Bājauri Tepe Gudamdar	94	Mullāh Qūli	741
Balkh	99	Mundigak	743
Banādir Jum'a Khān	101	Mundik Tepe	745
Barkah	2013	Nād-i 'Ali	752
Bīsh Ka'ik	134	Nariman	764
Bīsh Tan Tēg	136	Pachīrwagām	782
Burat Tepe	141	Parchau	799
Bust	149	Qal'a-i Jamshid	853
Chahār Darracha	156	Quchi	927
Chahārdeh	157	Qundūz Bālā Hisār	931
Cha'ila	162	Qūnsai	933
Chehel Dukhtarān	194	Qurghān Tepe, Imām Sāhib	936
Chilla Mazār	208	Qurghān Tepe, Tāluqān	937
Chugha-i Ulyā	215	Qūzi	943
Chul-i Abdān	218	Rūd-i Shahrāwān	959
Darwāza Kam	252	Samti	981
Darwīsh Anrar Khān Qal'a	253	Sasmāq	1008
Dashli, south	259	Shāh 'Ali	1019
Dasht-i Qal'a, north	268	Shish Tepe	1086
Deh Nahr-i Jadīd	288	Shūratū	1092
Deh Nau	289	Shūri	1093
Dilbarjīn	295	Taghā'i	1128
Farāh Bālā Hisār	318	Tepe Muchak	2267
Faruk Qal'a	324	Uvlia Tepe	1225
Gaskin	340	Zangu	1252
Ghuz Tepe	374	Zard Kamar	1253
Gūgari	386	Zindān	1260
Gurgak	396	Zulm	1271
Gūr Tepe, Qundūz	400		

Seleucid (Map 61): c.330–185 BC in Seistan, 330–250 BC in the remainder of the country

Hazār Gusfand	422		
Herat	428		
Ishānān	444	Ai Khānum	18
Jalālābād	464	Archi	54
Jar Guzar	472	Ayatan Tepe	65
Kābul	483	Bājauri Tepe Gudamdar	94
Kāfir Qal'a, Archi	487	Barkah	2013
Kāfir Qal'a, Rustāq	495	Bīsh Ka'ik	134
Kalafgān, east	511	Cha'ila	162
Kalafgān, west	513	Chul-i Abdān	218
Kaldīsh	515	Deh Nahr-i Jadīd	288
Kaldīsh, south	516	Emshi Tepe	314
Kandahār	522	Farāh Bālā Hisār	318
Kanum	525	Firitu	328
Kharāba-i Sultān Sāhib	560	Gaskin	340
Khush Bai	579	Ghuz Tepe	374
Khusti Qishlaq	583	Gūgari	386
Khwāja Hāfiz	594	Jiga Tepe	475
Kirghiz Tepe	611	Kāfir Qal'a, Archi	487
Kuhna Qal'a	631	Kāfir Qal'a, Rustāq	495
Kutlug Tepe	666	Kalafgān, east	511
Lalmi Buz	674	Kaldīsh	515
Maiwand	698	Kandahār	522
Malakhāna	701	Kanum	525
Markaz-i Hokūmati	709	Khush Bai	579

(continued)

Seleucid (Map 61): *c.*330–185 BC in Seistan, 330–250 BC in the remainder of the country

Khwāja 'Alī Sehyaka	2127
Khwāja Hāfiz	594
Khwāja Hasan	595
Khwāja Sultān	608
Kuhna Qal'a	631
Lalmi Buz	674
Mullāh Qūli	741
Mundik Tepe	745
Nād-i 'Ali	752
Parchau	799
Qal'a-i Hindu	849
Qundūz Bālā Hisār	931
Qūnsai	933
Qurghān Tepe	937
Rūd-i Shāhrawān	959
Ulān Rabāt	1211
Urta Buz	1220
Zangu	1252
Zindān	1260

Mauryan (Map 62): *c.* 275–185 BC in Jalālābād, Ghazni, Kandahār, and Bust areas only

Chār Sang Tepe	180
Darūnta	250
Kandahār	522
Mir Zakah	728
Shalatak	1067
Ulān Rabāt	1211

Graeco-Bactrian (Maps 62 and 63): *c.*250–110 BC in Balkh and Badakhshān areas, 250–160 BC in Herat, Bādghīs, and Kābul areas, 185–110 BC in the remainder of the country

Abrau, north-west	6
Ai Khānum	18
Aliābād	29
Ali Qutan	31
Aq Tepe Nawarid	49
Archi	54
Astāna Tepe	61
Ayatan Tepe	65
Bāgh-i Mīr	83
Bājauri Tepe Gudamdar	94
Balkh	99
Bāmiyān?	100
Barkah	2013
Begram	122
Bīsh Ka'ik	134
Bīsh Kapa	135
Būlaq Urta Buz	139
Būs-i Shān	148
Chaqalaq Tepe	172
Cha'ila	162

Chashma	182
Chim Tepe	210
Chul-i Abdān	218
Dasht-i Qal'a, south	269
Deh Nahr-i Jadīd	288
Dilbarjin	295
Emshi Tepe	314
Faizābād Tepe	316
Farkhar	321
Ghuz Tepe	374
Gūgari	386
Hazār Bāgh	421
Hustukh Tepe	437
Irganakh	442
Ishkamish Bālā Hisār	447
Jiga Tepe	475
Kābul	483
Kāfir Qal'a, Archi	487
Kāfir Qal'a, Rustāq	495
Kakul	509
Kalafgān, east	511
Kaldīsh	515
Kanum	525
Khalābād Tepe	550
Khisht Tepe	569
Khush Bai	579
Khwāja Hāfiz	594
Kuhistānihā	626
Kuhna Qal'a	631
Lalmi Buz	674
Mir Zakah	728
Mullāh Qūli	741
Mundik Tepe	745
Nimlik	776
Panjiri	797
Parchau	799
Parishān Tepe	800
Qara Bai	909
Qarluq	917
Qundūz Bālā Hisār	931
Qūnsai	933
Qurghān Tepe	937
Rūd-i Shāhrawān	959
Sālār Tepe	975
Samandau	980
Shāhrawān Gur Tepe	1032
Shahr-i Banu	1034
Shahr-i Banu, south-east	1036
Shāh Salim Pacha Tepe	1055
Shairābād	1061
Shairābād, north-west	1063
Shish Tepe	1086
Shōrtūghai	1089
Siāh Rīgān	1101
Takhnābād	1132
Tam 'Ali	1143

Tepe Qabr-i Turkman	1175
Uljatu	1212
Uraz Bacha	1217
Urta Buz	1220
Utāq	1224
Wazir Khān	1233
Yūsuf Darra	2280
Zulm	1271

Parthian (Maps 63, 64, and 65): *c.*160 BC–AD 225 in Herat and Bādghīs areas, 155 BC–AD 20 in Seistan, and 155–90 BC in Kandahar and Bust areas

Ab Bakhshi-i Bālā	2
Adraskan	13
Baghak	77
Chahārdeh	157
Chār Sang Tepe	180
Dam-i Malik Khān	2043
Dasht-i Rūd Bīyābān	270
Farāh Bālā Hisār	318
Firitu	328
Gaskin	340
Ghundi Rūd-i Bīyābān	369
Hindu Hasan Ghār	429
Kandahār	522
Khāl-i Muhammad Hāshim Khān	551
Kharāba-i Siāh Khāna	559
Khwāja Hasan	595
Khwāja Kanūr	597
Khāja Sultān	608
Markaz-i Hokūmati	709
Mirwais Bābā	726
Nād-i ʿAli	752
Palangi?	792
Palgird	794
Pir-i Surkh	813
Pūst-i Gau	824
Qalʾa-i Pesar	874
Qalʾat-i Girdi	900
Qūri	938
Sabarz	961
Sarai Rūd-i Bīyābān	991
Sar-o Tar	1006
Sultān Bābā Ziyārat	1114
Tepe Buland	1163
Tepe Rāmrūd	1177
Ulān Rabāt	1211
Zangu	1252
Zarshoy	1258
Zindān	1260
Zīyārat-i Dust Muhammad	1266

Indo-Greek (Map 63): *c.*155–90 BC in Kābul, Jalālābād, and Ghazni areas only

Bāgh-i Asyā	80
Begram	122
Chārikar	176

Gardēz	337
Kābul	483
Mir Zakah	728
Shahr-i Sikandari	1050

Saka (Map 64): *c.*90 BC–AD 2 in Kābul, Jalālābād, Ghazni, Kandahār, and Bust areas only.

Ainak	19
Bād-i Sah Ghundai	73
Bāgh-i Asyā	80
Begram	122
Chār Sang Tepe	180
Gardēz	337
Kandahār	522
Mir Zakah	728
Spīn Baldak	1108

Early Kushan (Map 64): *c.*110 BC–AD 75 in Balkh and Badakhshān areas only

Abrau, north-west	6
Aliābād	29
Ali Qutan	31
Aq Chapar 1	43
Archi	54
Astāna Tepe	61
Ayatan Tepe	65
Bāgh-i Mīr	83
Bajauri Tepe	94
Balkh	99
Bīsh Kaʾik	134
Bīsh Tan Tēg	136
Būlaq Urta Buz	139
Būs-i Shān	148
Chaʾila	162
Chaqalaq Tepe	172
Chim Tepe	210
Deh Nahr-i Jadīd	288
Dilbarjīn	295
Farkhar	321
Gūgari	386
Ishān Tūp	445
Ishkamish Bālā Hisār	447
Jiga Tepe	475
Kāfir Qalʾa, Archi	487
Kāfir Qalʾa, Rustāq	495
Kakul	509
Kalafgān, east	511
Khist Tepe	569
Khush Bai	579
Kuhna Qalʾa	631
Kumsar	642
Mundik Tepe	745
Panjiri	797
Parishān Tepe	800
Qara Bai	909
Qundūz Bālā Hisār	931

(*continued*)

Early Kushan (Map 64): *c.*110 BC–AD 75 in Balkh and Badakhshān areas only

Qūnsai	933
Sasmāq	1008
Shāhrawān Gur Tepe	1032
Shahr-i Banu	1034
Shahr-i Banu, south-east	1036
Shairābād	1061
Shairābād, north-west	1063
Shish Tepe	1086
Tepe Ahingarān	1160
Tilla Tepe	1192
Toprakkale	1198
Uljatu	1212
Urta Buz	1220
Utāq	1224
Wazir Khān	1233

Indo-Parthian (Map 65): *c.*AD 20–225 in Kandahār, Bust, and Seistan areas, AD 20–75 in Kābul, Jalālābād, and Ghazni areas

Ab Bakhsh-i Bālā	2
Akhundzāda	23
Akram Qal'a	24
Arūkh, south	55
Bād-i Sah Ghundai	73
Bāgh-i Asyā	80
Banadir Jum'a Khān	101
Bārābād	106
Bazitkhēl	121
Begram	122
Bīmārān	127
Bust	149
Chahārdeh	157
Chār Sang Tepe	180
Chehel Burj	190
Dam-i Malik Khān	2043
Darwīsh Anrar Khān Qal'a	253
Dasht-i Rūd-i Bīyābān	270
Dūst Muhammad	311
Firitu	328
Gardēz	337
Gaskin	340
Ghundi Rūd-i Bīyābān	369
Girdai Ghundai	378
Hindu Hasan Ghār	429
Jalālābād	464
Jāni Tūp	471
Kamtudi Wakīl Khān	521
Kandahār	522
Khāl-i Muhammad Hāshim Khān	551
Kharāba-i Siāh Khāna	559
Kharāba-i Sultān Sāhib	560
Khurd Kābul	574
Khushāb	578

Khwāja Hasan	595
Khwāja Sultān	608
Mir Zakah	728
Mundi Hisār	744
Nadir Tepe	754
Nandarra	761
Nioh	2167
Passani	806
Pūst-i Gau	824
Qal'a-i Hindu	849
Qal'a-i Jamāl	852
Qal'a-i Kachala	855
Qal'a-i Nau	871
Qal'at-i Girdi	900
Qūri	938
Sabz Qal'a	962
Sang-i Sar	988
Sarai Rūd-i Bīyābān	991
Sardeh Ulya	2241
Sar-o Tar	1006
Shahr-i Kuhna Farāh	1046
Shahr-i Safā	1048
Spirwan	1109
Surkh Tūp	1125
Tepe Buland	1163
Tepe Rāmrūd	1177
Ulān Rabāt	1211
Zakird	1248
Zala Khān	1249
Zangu	1252
Zindān	1260
Zirārat-i Dust Muhammad	1266

Great Kushan (Map 65): *c.*AD 75–225 in Balkh, Badakhshān, Kābul, Jalālābād, and Ghazni areas only

Abrau, north-west	6
Ahin Push Tepe	17
Alchīn	28
Aliābād	29
Aligul	30
Ali Qutan	31
Aq Chapar 1	43
Archi	54
Astāna Tepe	61
Awarzan	64
Ayatan Tepe	65
Bād Guzar	70
Bād-i Asyā	72
Bāgh-i Mir	83
Baghlān Shahr-i Kuhna	86
Bahārak	89
Baiktūt	92
Bajauri Tepe	94
Balkh	99
Bāmiyān	100
Bāsiz	115

Begram	122	Kāfir Qal'a, Rustāq	495
Bīmārān	127	Kaka Bulaq	505
Bin-i Gaugir	130	Kakul	509
Bīsh Ka'ik	134	Kalafgān	510
Bīsh Kapa	135	Kalafgān, east	511
Bīsh Tan Tēg	136	Kalafgān, south	512
Būlaq Urta Buz	139	Kalafgān, west	513
Būs-i Shān	148	Kaldīsh, south	516
Chahār Bāgh	155	Kamari	519
Chahār Darracha	156	Kam Pirak	520
Chahār Tūt	160	Karacha	2111
Chai Khanjar	161	Khisht Tepe	569
Cha'ila	162	Khurd Kābul	574
Chakhil-i Ghundi	165	Khush Bai	579
Cham Qal'a	169	Khusti Qishlāq	583
Chaqalaq Tepe	172	Khwāja Ghaltān	591
Chehel Dukhtarān	194	Khwāja Hāfiz	594
Chilsitūn	2028	Khwāja Langār	2136
Chim Qurghān	209	Khwāja Musaffar	600
Chim Tepe	210	Khwāja Safā	2138
Daryābād	254	Khwāja Seh Yārān	606
Dasht-i Nāwar	265	Killigān	2141
Dasht-i Qal'a, north	268	Kirghiz Tepe	611
Deh-i Qazi	281	Kondi	2144
Deh-i Rahman	283	Kuh-i Bacha	620
Deh Nahr-i Jadīd	288	Kuhna Deh	627
Deh Nau	289	Kuhna Qal'a Dasht-i Qal'a	631
Dilbarjīn	295	Kuhna Qal'a Khānābād	632
Dūrman	308	Kuhna Deh Sumara	2146
Dūrman Tepe	309	Kumsar	642
Emshi Tepe	314	Kut-i Sitāra	665
Farkhar	321	Kutpūr	667
Fil Khāna	326	Minār-i Chakri	718
Gardēz	337	Mir Zakah	728
Gauhar	342	Mullāh Afghāni	738
Gazkai	345	Mundik Tepe	745
Gharluli	355	Mūsa Zāri	750
Ghunda Chashma	364	Nādir Tepe	753
Ghundi Paisa	2078	Nayib Dum	772
Ghuraidarama	371	Paitāva	790
Ghuz Tepe	374	Pakhrak	791
Gūgari	386	Panjiri	797
Gulbāgh?	2082	Parisān Tepe	800
Gulbahār	388	Passani	806
Gur Tepe	400	Patanak	807
Hadda	404	Qal'a-i Hāji	847
Ishānān	444	Qal'a-i Kachala	855
Ishān Tūp	445	Qal'a-i Shāhi	880
Ishkamish Bālā Hisār	447	Qal'a-i Zāl	892
Ishkili	450	Qand-i Pir	903
Jala'ir	462	Qanjugha	904
Jamāl Qal'a	469	Qara Bai	909
Jar Guzar	472	Qara Kūtarma	911
Jiga Tepe	475	Qishlāq-i Suflā	922
Kāfir Qal'a, Archi	487	Qizil Sai	925
Kāfir Qal'a, Kuh-i Dāman	491		

(continued)

Great Kushan (Map 65): c.AD 75–225 in Balkh, Badakhshān, Kābul, Jalālābād, and Ghazni areas only

Qul-i Nādir	928
Qundūz	930
Qundūz Bālā Hisār	931
Qūnsai	933
Qurghān Tepe	936
Qush Tepe	942
Rabātak Kāfir Qal'a	944
Samti	981
Sar Rustāq	1007
Sasmāq	1008
Seh Tūpān	1016
Shāh 'Ali	1019
Shāhrawān Gur Tepe	1032
Shahr-i Banu	1034
Shahr-i Banu, east	1035
Shahr-i Banu, south-east	1036
Shahr-i Sikandari	1050
Shairābād	1061
Shairābād, east	1062
Shairābād, north-west	1063
Shalatak	1067
Shingān	1080
Shish Tepe	1086
Shiwaki	1087
Shūrābi	1091
Shūratū	1092
Siāh Rīgān	1101
Sultānpūr	1116
Surkh Kotal	1123
Surkh Minār?	1124
Tara Khēl	1146
Tepe Ahingarān	1160
Tepe Bāgh-i Sūr?	2263
Tepe Muchak	2267
Tepe Sala	1179
Tepe Shāhidān	1181
Tepe Tūp	1187
Top Darra	1197
Toprakkale	1198
Uljatu	1212
Uljatu-Deh Nau	1213
Urta Buz	1220
Uryākhēl	1222
Utāq	1224
Wardak	1229
Wazīrābād	1232
Wazīr Khān	1233
Yakhdarra	1237
Yarti Gumbaz	1243
Zādiyān	1244
Zādiyān Kāfir Qal'a	2281
Zard Kamar	1253

Early Sasanian (Map 66): c.275–345 in Balkh, Badakhshān, Kābul, and Jalālābād areas, 275–450 in all other areas

Ab Bakhsh-i Pa'in	3
Abdulkhēl?	4
Abrau, north-west	6
Adraskan	13
Ala Chapan	25
Alchīn	28
Aliābād	29
Ali Qutan	31
Andkhui	41
ĀqKupruk	46
Archi	54
Arūkh, south	55
Astāna Tepe	61
Bād Guzar	70
Bad-i Sah Ghundai	73
Bāghak	77
Bāghak-i Bālā	78
Bāgh-i Mir	83
Bahārak	89
Baikhān Qal'a	91
Baiktūt	92
Bajauri Tepe	94
Balkh	99
Bāmiyān	100
Banadir Jum'a Khān	101
Bāsiz	115
Begram	122
Bin-I Gaugir	130
Bini Malakh	131
Bīsh Ka'ik	134
Bīsh Kapa	135
Bīsh Tan Tēg	136
Būlaq Urta Buz	139
Burj-i Ghunda	143
Burj-i Rūd-i Bīyābān	145
Burkhankhān	142
Burri	147
Būs-i Shān	148
Bust	149
Chahār Shakhlak	159
Chahārdarracha	156
Chahārdeh	157
Chakhil-i Ghundi	165
Chalghūr	167
Chambāra	168
Chaqalaq Tepe	172
Chār Sang Tepe	180
Chār Tūt	160
Chehel Burj	190
Chehel Dukhtarān	194
Chiling	206

Chim Qurghān	209	Kakul	509
Chūla	217	Kalafgān	510
Da Loy Wyālā Qal'a	227	Kalafgān, east	511
Dakdila	225	Kalafgān, west	513
Dam	228	Kalafgān, south	512
Dam-i Malik Khān	2043	Kam Pirak	520
Darwīsh Anrar Khān Qal'a	253	Kamtudi Wakīl Khān	521
Daryābād	254	Kandahār	522
Dasht-i Archi	260	Karbāsak	527
Dasht-i Qal'a, north	268	Katikutar	539
Dasht-i Rūd-i Bīyābān	270	Khāli-i Muhammad Hāshim Khān	551
Deh Morasi Ghundai	287	Kharāba-i Idukhān	558
Deh Nahr-i Jadīd	288	Kharāba-i Siah Khāna	559
Deh Warda	290	Kharāba-i Sultān Sāhib	560
Deh-i Kalān	277	Khisht Tepe	569
Dīwāl-i Lawūr	301	Khush Bai	579
Dūrman	308	Khushāb	578
Dūrman Tepe	309	Khusti Qishlāq	583
Dūst Muhammad	311	Khwāja 'Ali Sehyaka	2127
Emshi Tepe	314	Khwāja Ghaltān	591
Farkhar	321	Khwāja Hāfiz	594
Fazilābād Tepe	325	Khwāja Hasan	595
Firitu	328	Khwāja Langār	2136
Gardēz	337	Khwāja Musaffar	600
Gaskin	340	Khwāja Safā	2138
Ghārluli	355	Khwāja Sultān	608
Ghulām 'Ali Khān Qal'a	359	Killigān	2141
Ghulāmān	360	Kirghiz Tepe	611
Ghundi Mansūr	368	Kondi	2141
Ghundi Paisa	2078	Kuh-i Bacha	620
Ghundi Rūd-i Bīyābān	369	Kuhna Deh Sumara	2146
Ghuz Tepe	374	Kuhna Qal'a Dasht-i Qal'a	631
Gūgari	386	Kuhna Qal'a Khānābād	632
Guldarra	389	Kurdu	648
Gurgak	396	Kushk-i Nakhud	659
Gur Tepe	400	Kut-i Ashru	663
Hadda	404	Kut-i Sitāra	665
Hājirangīn Qal'a	411	Lalkhān Qal'a	672
Herat	428	Lalma	673
Hindu Hasan Ghār	429	Lalpūra	675
Hisār	431	Lat Qal'a	687
Humai Qal'a	434	Līli Tepe	689
Ishānān	444	Malakhāna	701
Ishān Tūp	445	Markaz-i Hokūmati	709
Ishkamish Bālā Hisār	447	Minār-i Chakri	718
Ishkili	450	Mīr Bacha Kot	723
Jalā'ir	462	Mīr Zakah	728
Jangalak-i Qarabāgh	470	Muhammad Hasan Būzi	733
Jār Guzar	472	Mullāh Afghāni	738
Jiga Tepe	475	Mullāh Mūsa	740
Jui Nau	479	Mundi Hisār	744
Kāfir Qal'a, Archi	487	Mundik Tepe	745
Kāfir Qal'a, Rustāq	495	Muqqur	746
Kaka Būlaq	505	Mūsa Zāri	750
Kākarān	506	Mūsa-i Logar	749

(continued)

Early Sasanian (Map 66): *c.*275–345 in Balkh, Badakhshān, Kābul, and Jalālābād areas, 275–450 in all other areas

Nādir Tepe	754
Nai Qal'a	758
Nāwa	769
Nayib Dum	772
Nioh	2167
Nishk	778
Pakhrak	791
Palgird	794
Panjiri	797
Panjwāyi	798
Patanak	807
Patandak	808
Patannah	809
Pir-i Surkh	813
Pusht-i Dasht	823
Pūst-i Gau	824
Qadis?	826
Qal'a-i Chigini	839
Qal'a-i Hindu	849
Qal'a-i Jamāl	852
Qal'a-i Mir 'Alam	865
Qal'a-i Nau	871
Qal'a-i Pesar	874
Qal'a-i Rāmrūd	876
Qal'a-i Surkh	883
Qal'ai Zāl	892
Qal'at-i Chaukakat	898
Qal'at-i Girdi	900
Qanjugha	904
Qara Bai	909
Qara Kūtarma	911
Qarabāgh-i Ghazni	907
Qarawul Tepe	915
Qul-i Nādir	928
Qundūz	930
Qundūz Bālā Hisār	931
Qūnsai	933
Qurghān Tepe	936
Qush Tepe	941
Rabātak Kāfir Qal'a	944
Rag-i Bībī	2227
Rūd-i Bīyābān	957
Sa'id Qal'a Tepe	968
Sabarz	961
Sabz Qal'a	962
Sāhibzāda Qal'acha	967
Salawāt	976
Samti	981
Sangdarra	985
Sang-i Sar	988

Sar Rustāq	1007
Sarai Rūd-i Bīyābān	991
Sar-i Pul	1000
Sar-o Tar	1006
Sasmāq	1008
Sehpista	1014
Shāh 'Ali	1019
Shāhi Khaila	1022
Shāhrawān Gur Tepe	1032
Shahr-i Banu	1034
Shahr-i Banu, east	1035
Shahr-i Banu, south-east	1036
Shahr-i Gai	1041
Shahr-i Kuhna Farāh	1046
Shahr-i Safā	1048
Shahr-i Sikandari	1050
Shairābād	1061
Shairābād, east	1062
Shairābād, north-west	1063
Shamala	1068
Shamshir Ghār	1069
Shand-i Ma'sūm Khān	1070
Shawāl	1073
Shibarghān	1076
Shingān	1080
Shish Tepe	1086
Shotorak	1088
Shūratū	1092
Shūyin	1097
Siāh Rīgān	1101
Spirwan	1109
Sra Qal'a	1111
Surkh Kotal	1123
Takht-i Rustam	1136
Tawisk	1156
Tepe Ab Bakhsh	1158
Tepe Ahingarān	1160
Tepe Buland	1163
Tepe Khākak	1166
Tepe Maranjān	1173
Tepe Muchak	2267
Tepe Nāranj	1174
Tepe Rāmrūd	1177
Tepe Rūd-i Bāyābān	1178
Tepe Sala	1179
Tepe Shāhidān	1181
Tepe Sinaubar	1184
Tepe Zahidān	1189
Tepe Zaitun	1190
Tirandaz	1193
Ulān Rabāt	1211
Uljatu-Deh Nau	1213
Urta Buz	1220
Utāq	1224

Wazīr Khān	1233	Hadda	404
Zādiyān	1244	Hashmatkhān	418
Zādiyān Kāfir Qal'a	2281	Ishānān	444
Zakan-o Zurkan	1247	Ishkili	450
Zakird	1248	Jalā'ir	462
Zala Khān	1249	Jar Guzar	472
Zangu	1252	Jiga Tepe	475
Zard Kamar	1253	Kāfir Qal'a, Rustāq	495
Zarshoy	1258	Kaka Bulaq	505
Zindān	1260	Kalafgān	510
Zīyārat-i Dūst Muhammad	1266	Kalafgān, east	511

Kushano-Sasanian (Map 67): c.345-425 in Balkh and Badakhshān and 345-450 in Kābul and Jalālābād areas

		Kalafgān, south	512
Abdulkhēl	4	Kam Pirak	520
Ajamandan Tepe	20	Khair Khāna	546
Alchīn	28	Khisht Tepe	569
Ali Qutan	31	Khusti Qishlāq	583
Aliābād	29	Khwāja Ghaltān	591
Āq Kupruk	46	Khwāja Hāfiz	594
Bahārak	89	Khwāja Langār	2136
Bajauri Tepe	94	Khwāja Safā	2138
Balkh	99	Kih-i Mūri	622
Bāmiyān	100	Killigān	2141
Bāsiz	115	Kondi	2144
Begram	122	Kuh-i Bacha	620
Bin-i Gaugir	130	Kuhna Deh Sumara	2146
Bini Malakh	131	Kuhna Khulm	628
Bīsh Ka'ik	134	Kuhna Masjid	630
Bīsh Kapa	135	Kuri	650
Chakanūr	163	Kurrindar	651
Chakhil-i Ghundi	165	Lalma	673
Chanwar	170	Lalpura	675
Chaqalaq Tepe	172	Līli Tepe	689
Chārdarra	173	Maidachapa	695
Chārikār	176	Minār-i Chakri	718
Charkh-i Falak	178	Mullāh Afghāni	738
Chehel Dukhtarān, Kabul	192	Mundik Tepe	745
Chehel Dukhtarān, Qūnduz	194	Murki Khēl	748
Chim Qurghān	209	Mūsa-i Logar	750
Chūla	217	Nayib Dum	772
Dasht-i Archi	260	Pachīrwagām	782
Deh Nahr-i Jadīd	288	Pakhrak	791
Deh Warda	290	Panjiri	797
Deh-i Kalān	277	Prates	815
Dilbarjīn	295	Qal'a-i Jubīn	2194
Dūrman	308	Qal'a-i Zāl	892
Dūrman Tepe	309	Qanjugha	904
Efendi Tepe	313	Qara Bai	909
Farkhar	321	Qarawul Tepe	915
Fazilābād Tepe	325	Qul-i Nādir	928
Ghārluli	355	Qundūz Bālā Hisār	931
Ghundi Paisa	2078	Qurghān Tepe	936
Ghuz Tepe	374	Qurūgh	940
Guldarra	389	Qush Tepe	941
		Rabātak Kāfir Qal'a	944
		Rui	2230

(continued)

Kushano-Sasanian (Map 67): c.345–425 in Balkh and Badakhshān and 345–450 in Kābul and Jalālābād areas

Saka	972
Sehpista	1014
Shāh 'Ali	1019
Shāhi Khaila	1022
Shāhrawān Gur Tepe	1032
Shahr-i Banu	1034
Shahr-i Banu, east	1035
Shahr-i Banu, south-east	1036
Shairābād	1061
Shairābād, east	1062
Shairābād, north-west	1063
Shish Tepe	1086
Siāh Rīgān	1101
Surkh Kotal	1123
Takht-i Rustam	1135
Tepe Ahingarān	1160
Tepe Maranjān	1173
Tepe Muchak	2267
Tepe Qarya-i Afghān	1176
Tepe Salam	2269
Tepe Shāhidān	1181
Tepe Zahidān	1189
Uljatu-Deh Nau	1213
Utāq	1224
Yangi Ariq	1240
Zādiyān	1244
Zādiyān Kāfir Qal'a	2281

Hunnic (Map 68): c.475–565 in Balkh and Badakhshān, 450–535 in Kābul, Jalālābād, Ghazni, and Kandahār areas, and 485–565 in Bādghīs

Abaka	1
Abdulkhēl	4
Abrau	5
Ainak	19
Alafsafīd	26
Alchīn	28
Aliābād	29
Ali Qutan	31
Andarābi	40
Āq Kupruk	46
Aq Tepe	50
Arūkh, south	55
Bahārak	89
Bajauri Tepe Gudamdar	94
Balkh	99
Bāmiyān	100
Bāsiz	115
Bazār Gai	2014
Bīdsai	125
Bin-i Gaugir	130
Bini Malakh	131

Bīsh Ka'ik	134
Bīsh Kapa	135
Bīsh Tan Tēg	136
Chalghūr	167
Cham Qal'a	169
Chambāra	168
Chaqalaq Tepe	172
Chār Gul	175
Char Sang Tepe	180
Charkh-i Falak	178
Chehel Dukhtarān	194
Chilla Mazār	208
Chim Qurghān	209
Dāg-i Nāsir	220
Darwāza Kam	252
Dasht-i Archi	260
Daulat Khān Sular	272
Deh Morasi Ghundai	287
Deh Nahr-i Jadīd	288
Deh Warda	290
Dūn Qishlāq	307
Dūrman	308
Farkhar	321
Fazilābād Tepe	325
Fūlādi	330
Gardēz	337
Ghārluli	355
Gharwal	2077
Ghulāmān	360
Ghundi Mansūr	368
Ghuz Tepe	374
Gūgari	386
Gulaziri Kul Tepe	387
Gurziwan	401
Hadda	404
Hazāra Samūch	420
Ishānān	444
Ishkamish	446
Ishkili	450
Jalā'ir	462
Jar Guzar	472
Jumāl Khēl	481
Kābul	483
Kāfir Qal'a, Rustāq	495
Kaka Bulaq	505
Kākarān	506
Kalafgān	510
Kalafgān, east	511
Kalafgān, south	512
Kandahār	522
Kanum	525
Kata Balandi	536
Khair Khāna	546
Khairābād Ghundai	545

Later Sasanian (Map 69): *c.*450–650 in Herat, Bust, and Seistan, 565–650 in Bādghīs, Balkh, and Badakhshān, and 535–650 in the remainder of the country

Kamtudi Wakīl Khān	521	Palgird	794
Kandahār	522	Panjiri	797
Kanum	525	Panjwāyi	798
Karbāsak	527	Patanak	807
Kata Balandi	536	Patandak	808
Katikutar	539	Pira Qal'a	811
Khair Khāna	546	Pir-i Surkh	813
Khairābād Ghundai	545	Pul-i Zuhak	820
Khāl-i Muhammad Hāshim Khān	551	Pul-i'Alam	817
Khandūd	557	Pusht-i Dasht	823
Kharāba-i Idukhān	558	Qal'a-i Bakhtagān?	834
Kharāba-i Siah Khāna	559	Qal'a-i Chigini	839
Kharāba-i Sultān Sāhib	560	Qal'a-i Hindu	849
Khisht Tepe	569	Qal'a-i Jamāl	852
Khush Bai	579	Qal'a-i Jubīn	2194
Khush Gildi	580	Qal'a-i Khalīl Jān	2197
Khusti Qishlāq	583	Qal'a-i Mīr 'Alam	865
Khwāja Ghaltān	591	Qal'a-i Nau	871
Khwāja Hāfiz	594	Qal'a-i Rāmrūd	876
Khwāja Safā	2138	Qal'a-i Surkh	883
Khwja Hasan	595	Qal'a-i Wabu	889
Khwāja Sultān	608	Qal'a-i Zāl	892
Kuh-i Bacha	620	Qal'a-i Zarin	894
Kuh-i Mansūr	621	Qal'at-i Chaukakat	898
Kuhna Deh Sumara	2146	Qal'at-i Girdi	900
Kuhna Khulm	628	Qal'at-i Mahmud	901
Kuhna Masjid	630	Qanjugha	904
Kulūkh Tepe	640	Qara Bai	909
Kulūkhi	639	Quchi	927
Kunchi	643	Qundūz Bālā Hisār	931
Kurdu	648	Qurghān Tepe	936
Kuri	650	Qush Tepe	941
Kushk-i Nakhud	659	Qūzi	943
Lalkhān Qal'a	672	Rabātak Kāfir Qal'a	944
Lat Qal'a	687	Rūd-i Bīyābān	957
Malākhāna	701	Rui	2230
Markaz-i Hokūmati	709	Safar	964
Māsamūd	712	Sāhibzāda Qal'acha	967
Minār-i Chakri	718	Saka	972
Mir Zakah	728	Salawāt	976
Muhammad Hasan Būzi	733	Sangīna Tepe	2238
Mullāh Afghāni	738	Sarai Rūd-i Bīyābān	991
Mullāh Mūsa	740	Sar-o Tar	1006
Mundi Hisār	744	Shāh 'Ali	1019
Mundik Tepe	745	Shahrak	1031
Muqqur	746	Shāhrawān Gur Tepe	1032
Musā Zāri	750	Shahr-i Banu	1034
Musā-i Logar	749	Shahr-i Banu, east	1035
Nagāla	755	Shahr-i Banu, south-east	1036
Nanga	762	Shahr-i Ghulghula	1042
Nau Nagak	2166	Shahr-i Sikandari	1050
Nāwa	769	Shairābād, east	1062
Nayib Dum	772	Shāki Nauka	1066
Nishk	778	Shamala	1068
Pakhrak	791		

(continued)

Later Sasanian (Map 69): *c.*450–650 in Herat, Bust, and Seistan, 565–650 in Bādghīs, Balkh, and Badakhshān, and 535–650 in the remainder of the country

Shamshir Ghār	1069
Shand-i Ma'sūmkhān	1070
Shawāl	1073
Shibarghān	1076
Shikarīn Hasan Khēl	1078
Shirābād	1082
Shish Tepe	1086
Shurābād	1090
Shūratū	1092
Shūri	1093
Shūyin	1097
Siāh Ab	1098
Sra Ghundai	1110
Sra Qal'a	1111
Taghā'i	1128
Takhnābād	1132
Takhnāil Rustam	1136
Tawisk	1156
Tepe Ab Bakhsh	1158
Tepe Ahingarān	1160
Tepe Barzangi	1162
Tepe Buland	1163
Tepe Khākak	1166
Tepe Khazana	1168
Tepe Maranjān	1173
Tepe Muchak	2267
Tepe Nāranj	1174
Tepe Nārenj	2268
Tepe Rāmrūd	1177
Tepe Rūd-i Bīyābān	1178
Tepe Shāhidān	1181
Tepe Skandar	1185
Tepe Zahidān	1189
Topdarra	1197
Tūpkhāna?	1204
Ud Khēl Tepe	1210
Uljatu-Deh Nau	1213
Uraz Bacha	1217
Utāq	1224
Yangi Ariq	1240
Yarti Gumbaz	1243
Zādiyān	1244
Zakan-o Zurkan	1247
Zakird	1248
Zala Khān	1249
Zangu	1252
Zaru Ghundai	2283
Zindajān	1259
Zindān	1260
Zīyārat-i Dūst Muhammad	1266

Turk Khanate (Maps 70, 71): *c.*650–875 in Balkh, Badakhshān, and Bāmiyān areas, 650–820 in Bāghdīs

Abaka	1
Abrau	5
Abu Huraira	8
Ahangarān	16
Alafsafīd	26
Alchīn	28
'Aliābād	29
'Ali Qutan	31
Andarābi	40
Aq Rabāt	47
Aq Tepe	50
Bahārak	89
Bājauri Tepe Gudamdar	94
Balkh	99
Bāmiyān	100
Barfaq	109
Bāsiz	115
Bayani	118
Bazār Gai	2014
Bīsh Ka'ik	134
Bīsh Kapa	135
Bīsh Tan Tēg	136
Cham Qal'a	169
Chār Gul	175
Chehel Dukhtarān	194
Chilla Mazār	208
Chim Qurghān	209
Dāg-i Nāsir	220
Darband	233
Darra-i Ahangarān	238
Darwāza Kam	252
Dasht-i Lajam	263
Deh Nahr-i Jadīd	288
Deh Warda	290
Duāb-i Mīkhzarīn	302
Dun Qishlāq	307
Dūrman	308
Farkhar	321
Fazilābād Tepe	325
Fūlādi	330
Ghandak	350
Ghārluli	355
Gharwal	2077
Ghuz Tepe	374
Gūgari	386
Gulaziri Kul Tepe	387
Gurgurawa	398
Gurziwan	401
'Iraq	441
Ishānān	444
Ishkamish	446

Ishkili	472	Shahr-i Zuhak	1052
Jalā'ir	462	Shairābād	1062
Jalmish	466	Shibar, east	1074
Jar Guzar	472	Shibar, west	1075
Julai	480	Shibarghān	1076
Kābul	483	Shirābād	1082
Kāfir Qal'a, Deh Imām	489	Shish Tepe	1086
Kāfir Qal'a, Rustāq	495	Shurābād	1090
Kaka Bulaq	505	Shūratū	1092
Kalafgān	510	Shūri	1093
Kalafgān, east	511	Sumaquli	1117
Kalafgān, south	512	Taghā'i	1128
Kalān Guzar	514	Takhnābād	1132
Kalu	517	Tāla	1139
Kansir	524	Tang-i Safidak	2261
Kanum	525	Tepe Barzangi	1162
Khisht Tepe	569	Tepe Shāhidān	1181
Khush Bai	579	Tepe Zahidān	1189
Khush Gildi	580	Tughai	1199
Khusti Qishlāq	583	Tūpchi	1202
Khwāja Ghaltān	591	Uljatu-Deh Nau	1213
Khwājaghār	592	Uraz Bacha	1217
Khwāja Hāfiz	594	Utāq	1224
Kuhna Khulm	628	Yangi Ariq	1240
Kulūkh Tepe	640	Zādiyān	1245
Kunchi	643	Zarkharid	1256
Kuri	650	Tepe Muchak	2267
Larmush	682	Zaru Ghundai	2283
Mullāh Afghāni	738		
Mundik Tepe	745		
Mūsa Zāri	750		

Umayyad-Abbasid (Map 70): c.650–800 in Seistan and 650–820 in Herat

Nagāla	755		
Nayib Du,	772	Balkh	99
Paikar	784	Burkhankhān	142
Pai Muri	786	Chahārdeh	157
Pakhrak	791	Chehel Burj	190
Panjiri	797	Chiling	206
Pasang	804	Dam	228
Qal'a-i Zāl	892	Dasht-i Hauz	262
Qanjugha	904	Dasht-i Mīshkushi	264
Qara Bai	909	Firitu	328
Quchi	927	Ghajar	347
Qundūz Bālā Hisār	931	Gil-i Safīdka	375
Qush Tepe	941	Hazār Gusfand	422
Qūzi	943	Kulūkhi	639
Rabātak Kāfir Qal'a	944	Kurdu	648
Rui	2230	Mullāh Mūsa	740
Saighān 'Alaqadari	969	Palgird	794
Seh Pista	1014	Pira Qal'a	811
Shāh 'Ali	1019	Pir-i Surkh	813
Shāhidān	1021	Pusht-i Dasht	823
Shāhrawān Gur Tepe	1032	Qal'a-i Chigini	839
Shahr-i Banu	1034	Qal'a-i Jamāl	852
Shahr-i Banu, east	1035	Qal'a-i Nau	871
Shahr-i Banu, south-east	1036	Qal'a-i Surkh	883
Shahr-i Ghulghula	1042	Qal'a-i Wabu	889
		Qal'a-i Zarin	894

(continued)

Umayyad-Abbasid (Map 70): c.650–800 in Seistan and 650–820 in Herat

Sarai Rūdi-i Bīyābān	991
Sar-o Tar	1006
Shamala	1068
Shand-i Ma'sūmkhān	1070
Shawāl	1073
Tawisk	1156
Tepe Khākak	1166
Zakan-o Zurkan	1247
Zindajān	1259

Turki Shahis (Maps 70 and 71): c.650–850 in Kābul, Jalālābād, Ghazni, and Kandahār areas, 650–800 in Bust area

Ainak	19
Arūkh, south	55
Bād-i Asyā	71
Bāzār Gai	2014
Bīdsai	125
Bin-i Gaugir	130
Bust	149
Chaghan Sarai	154
Chalghūr	167
Chambara	168
Chār Sang Tepe	180
Dai Kundi	223
Deh Morasi Ghundai	287
Deh Zūr?	291
Deh-i Qila	282
Dubakh Sar	303
Farāmāz	320
Funduqistān	332
Gardēz	337
Ghulāmān	360
Ghundi Mansūr	368
Ghundi Paisa	2078
Gudul-i Ahangarān	385
Hashmatkhān	418
Jaghatu	461
Jumāl Khēl	481
Kamari	519
Kandahār	522
Kata Balandi	536
Khair Khāna	546
Khairābād Ghundai	545
Khwāja Safā	2138
Kuh-i Bacha	620
Kuh-i Mansūr	621
Lalkhān Qal'a	672
Māsamūd	712
Minār-i Chakri	718
Mir Bacha Kot	723
Mir Zakah	728
Mundi Hisār	744

Mūsa- Logar	749
Nādir Tepe	754
Nanga	762
Nau Nagak	2166
Nawa	769
Panjwāyi	798
Patanak	807
Pul-i 'Alam	817
Qal'a-i Amīr Muhammad	832
Qal'a-i Khalīl Jān	2197
Saka	972
Sakha	973
Salawāt	976
Sangīna Tepe	2238
Shāh Khwāja	1025
Shahr-i Sikandari	1050
Shakar Darra	1064
Shamshir Ghār	1069
Shikarīn Hasan Khēl	1078
Shiwaki	1087
Shūyin	1097
Sra Ghunda	1110
Tepe Khākrīz	1167
Tepe Māhi	1171
Tepe Marinjān	1173
Tepe Nārenj	2268
Tepe Sardar	1180
Tepe Skandar	1185
Top Darra	1197
Ud Khēl Tepe	1210
Uruzgan	1221
Zakird	1248
Zala Khān	1249
Zaru Ghundai	2283

Tahirid (Map 71): c.820–75 in Herat and Bādghīs areas only

Gulaziri Kul Tepe	387
Gurziwan	401
Palgird	794
Pir-i Surkh	813
Shibarghān	1076
Zindajān	1259

Saffarid (Map 71): c.860–920 in Bust and Seistan, 875–900 in Kandahār area

Burkankhān	142
Chahārdeh	157
Chehelburj	190
Chiling	206
Dam	228
Dasht-i Hauz	262
Dasht-i Mīshkushi	264
Firitu	328
Ghajar	347
Gil-i Safīdka	375

Khwāja Nakhi	601
Kulūkhi	639
Kurdu	648
Mullāh Mūsa	740
Peshwaran	810
Pira Qal'a	811
Pusht-i Dasht	823
Qal'a-i Chigini	839
Qal'a-i Jamāl	852
Qal'a-i Nau	871
Qal'a-i Surkh	883
Qal'a-i Wabu	889
Qal'a-i Zarin	894
Sarai Rūd-i Bīyābān	991
Sar-o Tar	1006
Shamala	1068
Shand-i Ma'sūmkhān	1070
Shawāl	1073
Tawisk	1156
Tepe Khākak	1166
Zakan-o Zurkan	1247

Samanid (Map 70): c.875–1000 in Herat, Bādghīs, Balkh, and Badakhshān areas, 900–80 in Kandahār area, and 910–1000 in Bust and Seistan areas

Adraskan	13
'Aliābād	29
Archi	54
Arūkh, south	55
Astāna Tepe	61
Bād Guzar	70
Bād-i Sah Ghundai	73
Bāgh-i Mir	83
Bājauri Tepe Gudamdar	94
Bvv Murghāb	98
Balkh	99
Bandadir Jum'a Khān	101
Bīsh Ka'ik	134
Bīsh Tan Tēg	136
Burat Tepe	141
Burhankhān	142
Bust	149
Chahārdeh	157
Chahār Tūt	160
Cha'ila	162
Chalghūr	167
Chār Gul	175
Chār Sang Tepe	180
Chashma	182
Chayāb	187
Chehel Burj	190
Chiling	206
Chit Rabāt Kuhna	213
Chugha-i Ulyā	215
Da Lōy Wyālā Qal'a	227

Dam	228
Darwīsh Anrar Khān Qal'a	252
Dasht-i Hauz	262
Dasht-i Mīshkushi	264
Deh Nau	289
Deh Sabz	2057
Dun Qishlāq	307
Faizābād Tepe	316
Farkhār	321
Fazilābād Tepe	325
Gaskin	340
Ghajar	347
Ghulām 'Alikhān Qal'a	359
Ghulāmān	360
Ghundi Mansūr	368
Ghuz Tepe	374
Gil-i Safīdka	375
Gulaziri Kul Tepe	387
Gul-i Safīd	390
Gurziwan	401
Hāji Piyada	410
Hazār Bāgh	421
Hazār Gusfand	422
Hazār Sūm	425
Hustukh Tepe	437
Ishkamish	446
Kāfir Qal'a, Archi	487
Kāfir Qal'a, Rustāq	495
Kalafgān	510
Kanum	525
Kharāba-i Sultān Sāhib	560
Khisht Tepe	569
Khushāb	578
Khusti Qishlāq	583
Khwāja Bandi Kusha	587
Khwāja Ghaltān	591
Kuhistānihā	626
Kuhna Khulm	628
Kuhna Qal'a Khānābād	632
Kulūkhi	639
Kulūkh Tepe	640
Kunchi	643
Kurdu	648
Kuri	650
Lalkhān Qal'a	672
Maimana	697
Maiwand	698
Mirābād	721
Mullāh Afghāni	738
Mullāh Mūsa	740
Mundi Hisār	744
Mundik Tepe	745
Nād-i 'Ali	752
Nariman	764
Nāwa	769

(continued)

Samanid (Map 70): *c.*875–1000 in Herat, Bādghīs, Balkh, and Badakhshān areas, 900–80 in Kandahār area, and 910–1000 in Bust and Seistan areas

Nimlik	776
Pakhrak	791
Palgird	794
Panjiri	797
Peshwaran	810
Pira Qal'a	811
Pul-i Malān?	819
Pushta-i Hasan	822
Qal'a-i Chigini	839
Qal'a-i Nau	871
Qal'a-i Surkh	883
Qal'a-i Wabu	889
Qal'a-i Zarin	894
Qanjugha	904
Qara Bai	909
Qarawul Tepe	915
Qarluq	917
Quchi	927
Qundūz Bālā Hisār	931
Qurghān Tepe	936
Qush Tepe	941
Rud-i Shāhrawān	959
Rustāq	960
Sabz Qal'a	962
Salawāt	976
Samti	981
Sarai Rūd-i Biyābān	991
Sar-i Masjid	998
Sar-o Tar	1006
Sar Rustāq	1007
Shāhi Khaila	1022
Shahrak	1031
Shāhrawān Gur Tepe	1032
Shahr-i Banu	1034
Shahr-i Banu, east	1035
Shahr-i Banu, south-east	1036
Shahr-i Kuhna Farāh	1046
Shahr-i Safā	1048
Shāh Tepe	1056
Shairābād	1062
Shamala	1068
Shand-i Ma'sūmkhān	1070
Shawāl	1073
Shibarghān	1076
Shingān	1080
Shirābād	1082
Shūyin	1097
Sra Qal'a	1111
Taghā'i	1128
Takhnābād	1132
Tāsh Guzar	1149

Tawisk	1156
Tepe Barzangi	1162
Tepe Khākak	1166
Tepe Sahidān	1189
Uljatu	1212
Wali Khān	1228
Yaka Tūt	1235
Yangi Ariq	1240
Zakan-o Zurkan	1247
Zakird	1248
Zala Khān	1249
Zard Kamar	1253
Zindajān	1259
Zulm	1271

Hindu Shahi (Map 72): *c.* 875–1000 in Jalālābād, 875–980 in Kābul, and 875–960 in Ghazni area

Bābā Kala	67
Begram	122
Chaghān Sarai	154
Dai Kundi	223
Darra-i Paryana	247
Hashmatkhān	418
Islāmpūr	453
Jalālābād	464
Kābul	483
Kala Gush	2180
Khair Khāna	546
Kurgal	649
Mangir Sar	706
Masalwani	713
Nārang	763
Pashak	805
Pul-i 'Alam	817
Puri Qal'a	821
Qadzyān?	827
Qal'a-i Gush	2180
Qal'a-i Shāhi	880
Sajawand	971
Sakha	973
Shaikhābād	1059
Shiwaki	1087
Sundurwar	1118
Tepe Nārenj	2268
Top Darra	1197

Ghaznavid (Maps 73 and 74): *c.*960–1150 in Ghazni, 980–1150 in Kābul and Kandahār areas, 1000–1150 in Jalālābād, Bust, and Seistan areas, and 1000–50 in Herat, Bādghīs, Balkh, and Badakhshān areas

Abu Huraira	8
Adraskan	13
Akhundzāda	23
'Aliābād	29

(continued)

Ghaznavid (Maps 73 and 74): *c.*960–1150 in Ghazni, 980–1150 in Kābul and Kandahār areas, 1000–1150 in Jalālābād, Bust, and Seistan areas, and 1000–50 in Herat, Bādghīs, Balkh, and Badakhshān areas

Kulūkhi	639
Kulūkh Tepe	640
Kunchi	643
Kurdu	648
Kuri	650
Kusrutābād	662
Lalkhān Qal'a	672
Larmush	682
Lashkari Bāzār	685
Lat Qal'a	687
Maimana	697
Maiwand	698
Mazār-i Sharīf	716
Mirābād	721
Mir Zakah	728
Mullāh Afghāni	738
Mullāh Mūsa	740
Mundi Hisār	744
Mundik Tepe	745
Nād-i 'Ali	752
Nariman	764
Nau Nagak	2166
Nāwa	769
Nimlik	776
Nishk	778
Paikar	784
Pai Muri	786
Pakhrak	791
Palgird	794
Panjiri	797
Panjwāyi	798
Pasang	804
Peshwaran	810
Pira Qal'a	811
Pul-i 'Alam	817
Pul-i Malān?	819
Pushta-i Hasan	822
Pusht-i Dasht	823
Al'a-i Chigini	839
Qal'a-i Gawak	844
Qal'a-i Hauz	848
Qal'a-i Madar-i Padshāh	863
Qal'a-i Nau	871
Qal'a-i Surkh	883
Qal'a-i Wabu	889
Qal'at-i Mahmud	901
Qana-i Bābā Kamāl	902
Qanjugha	904
Qara Bai	909
Qarluq	917

Quchi	927
Qundūz Bālā Hisār	931
Qurghān Tepe	936
Qush Tepe	941
Rūd-i Shāhrawān	959
Rustāq	960
Sabz Qal'a	962
Salawāt	976
Samti	981
Sangzar	990
Sarai Rūd-i Biyābān	991
Sarkhushak	1004
Sar-o Tar	1006
Sar Rustāq	1007
Shāhidān	1021
Shāhi Khaila	1022
Shahrak	1031
Shāhrawān Gur Tepe	1032
Shahr-i Banu	1034
Shahr-i Banu, east	1035
Shahr-i Banu, south-east	1036
Shahr-i Ghulghula	1042
Shahr-i Kuhna Farāh	1046
Shahr-i Safā	1048
Shahr-i Sagan	1049
Shahr-i Zuhak	1052
Shāh Tepe	1056
Shairābād	1062
Shamala	1068
Shamshir Ghār	1069
Shand-i Ma'Sūmkhān	1070
Shawāl	1073
Shibar, east	1074
Shibar, west	1075
Shibarghān	1076
Shikari	1077
Shingān	1080
Shirābād	1082
Shūyin	1097
Sangina Tepe	2238
Sna Qal'a	1107
Sra Ghundai	1110
Sra Qal'a	1111
Sultān Bābā Zīyārat	1114
Sumaquli	1117
Taghā-i	1128
Takhnābād	1132
Takht-i Rustam	1135
Tālā	1139
Tarakun	1147
Tawisk	1156
Tepe Barzangi	1162
Tepe Khākak	1166
Tepe Zahidān	1189
Tughai	1199

Tūpchi	1202	Gurziwan	401
Tushkan	1208	Hairatān	408
Uljatu	1212	Hazār Bāgh	421
Uruzgan	1221	Hazār Gusfand	422
Wali Khān	1228	Hazrat Sayyid	2094
Warzu	1230	Herat	428
Yaka Tūt	1235	Hustukh Tepe	437
Yangi Ariq	1240	Ishkamish	446
Zakan-o Zurkan	1247	Ishkamish Bālā Hisār	447
Zakird	1248	Islām Qal'a	454
Zala Khān	1249	Jabar Tepe	459
Zard Kamar	1253	Kāfir Qal'a, Archi	487
Zarkharid	1256	Kāfir Qal'a, Rustāq	495
Zindajān	1259	Kalafgān	510
Zīyārat-i Imām	1267	Kanum	525
Zulm	1271	Karūkh	532
		Khalīfa Rahmat Jamshīdī	2120

Seljuk (Map 74): c.1050–1150 in Herat, Bāghdīs, Balkh, and Badakhshān areas only

Āb-i Rasūl Dād	2002	Khisht Tepe	569
Adraskan	13	Khusti Qishlāq	583
'Aliābād	29	Khwāja Bandi Kusha	587
Archi	54	Khwāja Ghaltān	591
Astāna Tepe	61	Khwāja Urya	2140
Bād Guzar	70	Kuhistānihā	626
Bāgh Arāgh	79	Kuhna Khulm	628
Bāgh-i Mir	83	Kuhna Qal'a Khānābād	632
Bājauri Tepe Gudamdar	94	Kulūkh Tepe	640
Bālā Murghāb	98	Kunchi	643
Balkh	99	Kuri	650
Bīsh Ka'ik	134	Mang Qal'a	707
Bīsh Tan Tēg	136	Mug Qal'a	732
Burat Tepe	141	Mullāh Afghāni	738
Chahār Tūt	160	Mundik Tepe	745
Cha'ila	162	Nariman	764
Chārdarra	173	Narin	765
Chār Gul	175	Nimlik	776
Chashma	182	Pakhrak	791
Chayāb	187	Palgird	794
Chilsitūn	2028	Panjiri	797
Chit Rabāt Kuhna	213	Pul-i Malān	819
Chugha-i Ulyā	215	Qanjugha	904
Darra-i Shākh	248	Qara Bai	909
Daulatābād	2053	Qarluq	917
Deh Nau	289	Quchi	927
Deh Sabz	2057	Qundūz Bālā Hisār	931
Dun Qishlāq	307	Qurghān Tepe	936
Faizābād	315	Qurugh	940
Faizābād Tepe	316	Qush Tepe	941
Farad Jaghani?	2068	Rabāt-i Sāhib Zāda	948
Farkhar	321	Rūd-i Shāhrawān	959
Fazilābād Tepe	325	Rustāq	960
Ghuz Tepe	374	Samti	981
Gulaziri Kul Tepe	387	Sar-i Pul	1000
		Sar Rustāq	1007
		Shabash	1017

(continued)

Seljuk (Map 74): *c.*1050–1150 in Herat, Bāghdīs, Balkh, and Badakhshān areas only

Shāhi Khaila	1022
Shahrak	1031
Shāhrawān Gur Tepe	1032
Shahr-i Banu	1034
Shahr-i Banu, east	1035
Shahr-i Banu, south-east	1036
Shahr-i Barbar	1037
Shāh Tepe	1056
Shairābād	1062
Shingān	1080
Shirābād	1082
Sirwan	1106
Taghā'i	1128
Takhnābād	1132
Takht-i Khātūn	1134
Tāsh Guzar	1149
Tepe Barzangi	1162
Tepe Gulak	1165
Tepe Zahidān	1189
Uljatu	1212
Yaka Tūt	1235
Yangi Ariq	1240
Yurughli	1244
Zādiyān	1245
Zard Kamar	1253
Zindajān	1259
Zīyāratgāh	1263
Zīyārat-i Hazrat Sultān	2286
Zulm	1271

Ghurid (Map 75): *c.*1150–1220

Adraskan	13
Ahangarān	15
Alayar	27
'Aliābād	29
Ana	39
Aq Rabāt	47
Archi	54
Arūkh, south	55
Astāna Tepe	61
Bād Guzar	70
Bād-i Sah Ghundai	73
Bāgh-i Mir	83
Bājauri Tepe Gudamdar	94
Bālā Murghāb	98
Balkh	99
Bāmiyān	100
Banādir Jum'a Khān	101
Barfaq	109
Bashura	114
Bayani	118

Begram	122
Bidmushki	124
Bīsh Ka'ik	134
Bīsh Tan Tēg	136
Burat Tepe	141
Burj-i Lar	144
Bust	149
Chahārdeh	157
Chahār Tūt	160
Cha'ila	162
Chalghūr	167
Chārgul	175
Chār Sang Tepe	180
Chashma	182
Chashma-i Khuni	183
Chayāb	187
Chehel Burj	189
Chehel Gazari	195
Chiling	206
Chisht	212
Chit Rabāt Kuhna	213
Chugha-i Ulyā	215
Danistama	231
Darband	233
Darra-i Ahangarān	238
Darra-i Shākh	248
Darra-i Takht	2047
Darwāza	251
Darzāb	255
Dasht-i Hauz	262
Dasht-i Lajam	263
Dasht-i Mīshkushi	264
Dasht-i Qal'a	267
Daulatyār	273
Deh Adam Khān	274
Deh Rān?	2056
Dīwāl-i Khudaidād	300
Dīwāl-i Mahmata	2065
Duāb-i Mīkhzarīn	302
Dun Qishlāq	307
Dūst Muhammad	311
Faizābād Tepe	316
Farkhar	321
Fazilābād Tepe	325
Fūlādi	330
Fulakar?	331
Gaskin	340
Ghandak	350
Ghazni	358
Ghulāmān	360
Ghundi Mansūr	368
Ghūriyān	373
Ghuz Tepe	374
Gil-i Safīdka	375

Gulaziri Kul Tepe	387	Marwa	2162
Gul-i Safīd	390	Mashgahi	2163
Gumbad-i Sār-i Shaila	393	Mināra	717
Gunbad-i Shuhada	2084	Mīrābād	721
Gurgurawa	398	Mir Zakah	728
Guzar-i Pam	403	Mullāh Afghāni	738
Hauz-i Bangi	419	Mullāh Mūsa	740
Hazār Gusfand	422	Muna Ala	742
Hazār Sūm	425	Mundi Hisār	744
Herat	428	Mundik Tepe	745
ʻIraq	441	Mushkan	751
Ishkamish	446	Nād-i ʻAli	752
Ishkamish Bālā Hisār	447	Nalbandan	759
Jalmish	466	Nariman	764
Jam	468	Naul Nagak	2166
Jauru	2099	Naurak	767
Kachi Gird	485	Nawa	769
Kāfir Qalʼa, Archi	487	Nili	775
Kāfir Qalʼa, Deh Imām	489	Nimlik	776
Kāfir Qalʼa, Rustāq	495	Nishk	778
Kak-i Kuhzad	507	Paikar	784
Kalafgān	510	Pai Muri	786
Kalān Guzar	514	Paʼin Mazār	787
Kalu	517	Pakhrak	791
Kamtudi Wakīl Khān	521	Palangkhāna	793
Kanum	525	Palgird	794
Khāna Yahuda	556	Panjiri	797
Kharāba-i Sultān Sāhib	560	Panjwāyi	798
Kharāba-i Muhammad Khān	2124	Peshwaran	810
Khisht Tepe	569	Pira Qalʼa	811
Khushāb	578	Pul-i Zuhak	820
Khusti Qishlāq	583	Pusht-i Dasht	823
Khwāja Bandi Kusha	587	Qalʼa-i Chigini	839
Khwāja Brahne	2128	Qalʼa-i Malik Antar	864
Khwāja Ghaltān	591	Qalʼa-i Naqshi	869
Khwājaghār	592	Qalʼa-i Qaisār	875
Khwāja Sultān	608	Qalʼa-I Sangi	879
Khwāja Urya	2140	Qalʼa-I Sultān	882
Kuhistāniha	626	Qanjugha	904
Kuhna Khulm	628	Qara Bai	909
Kuhna Qalʼa Khānābād	632	Qarluq	917
Kulūkhi	639	Quchi	927
Kulūkh Tepe	640	Qundūz Bālā Hisār	931
Kunchi	643	Qurghān Tepe	936
Kurdu	648	Quri	938
Kuri	650	Qush Tepe	941
Kushk-i Aghā Bahār	658	Rabāt-i Sāhib Zāda	948
Lalkhān Qalʼa	672	Rabāt-i Sapcha	2223
Larmush	682	Rūd-i Shāhrawān	959
Larwand	683	Rustāq	960
Lashkari Bāzār	685	Sabz Qalʼa	962
Mahdi Khēl	693	Sain	970
Maiwand	698	Sākhir	974
Manāra	704	Salawāt	976
Mang Qalʼa	707	Samti	981

(continued)

Ghurid (Map 75): *c.*1150–1220

Sang-i Mazār	987
Sangina Tepe	2238
Sarai Rūd-i Bīyābān	991
Sarkhushak	1004
Sar-o Tar	1006
Sar Rustāq	1007
Sayyadān Darra	1011
Shāhidān	1021
Shāhi Khaila	1022
Shāh-i Mashhad	1023
Shahrak	1031
Shāhrawān Gur Tepe	1032
Shahr-i Banu	1034
Shahr-i Banu, east	1035
Shahr-i Banu, south-east	1036
Shahr-i Barbar	1039
Shahr-i Ghulghula	1042
Shahr-i Kuhna Farah	1046
Shahr-i Kuhna Zamīndāwar	1047
Shahr-i Safā	1048
Shahr-i Sagān	1049
Shahr-i Zuhak	1052
Shāh Tepe	1056
Shairābād	1062
Shamala	1068
Shamshir Ghār	1069
Shand-i Ma'Sūmkhān	1070
Shawāl	1073
Shibar, east	1074
Shibar, west	1075
Shikari	1077
Shingān	1080
Shiniya	1081
Shirābād	1082
Shūyin	1097
Sibak	1103
Sumaquli	1117
Taghā'I	1128
Takhnābād	1132
Takht-i Khātūn	1134
Tālā	1139
Tang-i Azau	1144
Tarakun	1147
Tawisk	1156
Tepe Barzangi	1162
Tepe Buland	1163
Tepe Gulak	1165
Tepe Khākak	1166
Tepe Zahidān	1189
Tughai	1199
Tūpchi	1202
Uljatu	1212

Wurshak	1234
Yaka Tūt	1235
Yakhan-i Pa'in	1236
Yaman	1239
Yangi Ariq	1240
Zala Khān	1249
Zard Kamar	1253
Zarkharid	1256
Zindajān	1259
Zīyārat-i Shaikh Husain	1269
Zulm	1271

Kart (Map 76): *c.*1245–1350 in Herat and Bādghīs only

Ahmadābād	2003
Ghūriyān	373
Herat	428
Khwāja Jīr	2132
Khwāja Urya	2140
Nariman	764
Rabāt-i Sāhib Zāda	948
Rabāt-i Sapcha	2223
Tepe Gulak	1165
Zindajān	1259
Zīyāratgāh	1263

Kayani (Map 76): *c.*1260–1380 in Bust and Seistan areas only

Arairi	52
Burj-i Lar	144
Chakhansurak	164
Chehel Burj	190
Dasht-i Mīshkushi	264
Dīwāl-i Khudaidād	300
Gaubastak	341
Gil-i Safīdka	375
Gunbad-i Sar-i Shaila	393
Gur-i Mughul	399
Jui Kuhna	478
Jui Nau	479
Kulūkhi	639
Kuragazi	646
Kurdu	648
Lash	684
Lawar	688
Mīrābād	721
Muhammad Husain	734
Mullāh Mūsa	740
Nishk	778
Pira Qal'a	811
Qal'a-i Muhammad	866
Shahr-i Kuhna Farāh	1046
Shawāl	1073
Tujg	1200

(continued)

Timurid (Map 77): c.1380–1500

Kulūkhi	639	Qarawul Tepe	915
Kuragazi	646	Quchi	927
Kurdu	648	Qundūz Bālā Hisār	931
Kuri	650	Qurghān Tepe	936
Kush Rabāt	661	Rustāq	960
Lalmi Buz	674	Sabz Qal'a	962
Laman	676	Safīdsang	966
Langār	2157	Salar Tepe	975
Lash	684	Sang-i Sar	988
Lashkari Bāzār Panjshir	686	Sar-o Tar	1006
Lat Qal'a	687	Shāhi Khaila	1022
Lawar	688	Shahrābād	1030
Makandak	699	Shahr-i Banu	1034
Markaz-i Hokūmati	709	Shahr-i Banu, east	1035
Masjid-i Shahr-i Kalān	715	Shahr-i Banu, south-east	1036
Mashgahi	2163	Shahr-i Gai	1041
Mazār-i Sharīf	716	Shahr-i Kalān	1044
Mītābād	721	Shahr-i Kuhna Farāh	1046
Mīr-i Ruzadar	725	Shāh Tepe	1056
Mīr Zakah	728	Shamala	1068
Muhammad Hasan Būzi	733	Shawāl	1073
Muhammad Husain	734	Shindand	1079
Mullāh Mūsa	740	Shishawa	1085
Mundik Tepe	745	Spirwan	1109
Nādir Tepe	754	Sra Qal'a	1111
Nariman	764	Taghā-i	1128
Nāwa	769	Takht-i Bālā	1133
Nishk	778	Tālā Bēgum	1140
Obeh	781	Tāsh Guzar	1149
Palangi	792	Tāshqurghān Bālā Hisār	1152
Panjwāyi	798	Tepe Gulak	1165
Pira Qal'a	811	Tepe Muchak	2267
Pir-i Surkh	813	Tepe Qabr-i Turkman	1175
Pul-i Imāmbukri	818	Tepe Sayyid Mukhtar	2270
Qal'a-i 'Amīr	831	Tirpul	1196
Qal'a-i 'Amirān Sāhib	2182	Tujg	1200
Qal'a-i Dukhtar	841	Uljatu-Deh Nau	1213
Qal'a-i Fath	842	Yaka Tūt	1235
Qal'a-i Kamar	856	Yangi Ariq	1240
Qal'a-i Kurdu	861	Zakird	1248
Qal'a-i Muhammad	866	Zarshoy	1258
Qal'a-i Muhammad Khān Tepe	868	Zindajān	1259
Qal'a-i Zāl	892	Zindān	1260
Qara Kūtarma	911	Zīyāratgāh	1263
		Zīārat-i Shaikh Husain	1269

APPENDIX 2

Concordance of Collections

Of the collections listed in the original edition, only those in the BIAS and the DAFA were checked personally. Those collections have since been handed to the Afghan authorities, and are now housed in the AIA and/or the National Museum; they are therefore listed under both.

The collections in the National Museum have undergone considerable changes, from looting and destruction to resurrection, since the original edition. At the time of writing the Museum is engaged a long-term project of cataloguing its collections, so those listed here will soon be superseded.

The sources of collections elsewhere are listed to the best of my knowledge based mainly upon publications of the sites from which they originated. It has not been possible to check these personally, either by visiting the collections or by examining online or printed catalogues. The lists therefore may long have been superseded, but are repeated here as possible guides to future research.

AIA, Kabul—collections from some of the missions, both Afghan and foreign. (Sites 1, 5, 6, 13, 16, 18, 19, 23, 26, 28, 29, 31, 37, 40, 46, 50, 54, 55, 56, 61, 65, 70, 73, 80, 83, 84, 85, 89, 94, 98, 99, 100, 115, 122, 130, 134, 135, 136, 139, 141, 148, 149, 156, 157, 160, 161, 162, 169, 175, 175, 180, 182, 187, 194, 208, 209, 210, 212, 213, 215, 218, 220, 231, 242, 244, 245, 248, 252, 266, 268, 269, 272, 274, 281, 287, 288, 289, 290, 295, 302, 307, 308, 318, 321, 328, 333, 337, 340, 346, 352, 355, 358, 371, 374, 378, 386, 387, 389, 400, 401, 404, 412, 421, 425, 428, 440, 444, 445, 446, 447, 450, 462, 468, 472, 480, 481, 484, 487, 495, 505, 507, 509, 510, 511, 512, 513, 515, 516, 519, 522, 535, 536, 538, 545, 553, 569, 578, 579, 580, 583, 587, 591, 594, 611, 620, 622, 626, 628, 630, 631, 632, 633, 640, 643, 674, 685, 686, 697, 712, 718, 728, 738, 741, 743, 744, 745, 749, 750, 752, 754, 755, 762, 764, 772, 777, 781, 786, 791, 794, 797, 798, 799, 807, 813, 817, 841, 852, 853, 856, 874, 892, 903, 904, 909, 911, 913, 915, 917, 927, 931, 933, 936, 937, 941, 943, 944, 948, 956, 959, 960, 961, 962, 968, 969, 971, 972, 973, 980, 988, 1007, 1008, 1022, 1030, 1032, 1034, 1035, 1036, 1037, 1041, 1042, 1047, 1048, 1049, 1050, 1052, 1056, 1061, 1062, 1063, 1067, 1078, 1080, 1082, 1086, 1087, 1089, 1090, 1092, 1093, 1097, 1101, 1109, 1117, 1128, 1132, 1142, 1143, 1146, 1149, 1152, 1162, 1173, 1179, 1181, 1185, 1185, 1186, 1197, 1202, 1205, 1210, 1211, 1213, 1217, 1220, 1224, 1229, 1233, 1235, 1240, 1246, 1248, 1249, 1253, 1258, 1259, 1273, 1277, 1278, 1279, 1280, 1281, 1282, 2138, 2268). See also the National Museum.

Agra Fort, Agra, the Diwan-i Khass—wooden doors from the Tomb of Mahmud, Ghazni. (Site 358).

Al-Sabah Museum in Kuwait—mainly precious metalwork and other precious objects. All unprovenanced, but most have been traced stylistically to Bactria or to Afghanistan broadly. Probably not from a single hoard (although some might be); it is possible that some might be from the second Mir Zakah discovery (Site 728).

AMNH, New York—sherds from Fairservis's surveys and Dupree's excavations. (Sites 2, 3,46, 145, 147, 167, 206, 245, 262, 264, 270, 287, 335, 360, 368, 369, 506, 551, 559, 672, 752, 798, 810,823, 876, 900, 957, 976, 991, 1041, 1070, 1136, 1156, 1166, 1177, 1178, 1266).

Ashmolean Museum, Oxford—sherds collected by Bivar; Greek document from Sangcharak. (Sites 723, 1161, 2237).

BIPS, Tehran—a few miscellaneous sherd collections amongst those from Iran. (Sites 99, 100, 428, 1042).

BM, London—coins and objects from Masson's collection, and some sculptures from early DAFA excavations. (Sites 17, 107, 121, 122, 127, 155, 283, 326, 332, 389, 404, 483, 620, 667, 761, 779, 806, 855, 1016, 1087, 1116, 1125, 1169, 1197, 1229).

Dargah Pir Rattan lath Temple, Kabul—statue of Ganesha, from Gardez. (Site 337).

Gardner Museum, Boston—carved marble grave cover, probably from Herat. (Site 428).

Herat Museum—various chance finds of coins and objects from the west, as well as from the DAI survey of 2005–6. (Sites 185, 212, 255, 391, 428, 697, 794, 1259, 2018, 2047, 2056, 2057, 2084, 2105, 2123, 2128, 2148, 2173, 2179, 2183, 2247, 2248, 2255, 2264, 2266).

Hirayama Museum, Hiroshima—Bactrian documents from northern Afghanistan. (Site 2230).

Kandahar Museum—various chance finds of coins and objects from the region. (Sites 358, 522, 726).

Khalili Collection, London—Aramaic documents from Balkh; Bactrian documents from northern Afghanistan. (Sites 99, 2230).

Kyoto Museum—sculptures from DAFA excavations at Hadda. (Site 404).

Lahore Museum—Kharoshthi inscription from Jalalabad. (Site 464).

Maimana Museum—various chance finds of objects from the region. (Site 697).

Mazar-i Sharif Museum—various chance finds of coins and objects from the north. (Sites 41, 99, 707, 1009, 1135, 1218).

Musée Guimet, Paris—objects from the earlier DAFA excavations. (Sites 100, 122, 165, 332, 404, 508, 546, 743, 790, 815, 1088, 1123).

National Museum, Kabul—naturally the biggest collection in the world of objects from Afghanistan. Major museum objects on display, as well as more objects and sherd collections in storage from most 20th-century fieldwork, particularly from fieldwork after c.1960. (Sites 1, 5, 6, 8, 13, 15, 16, 18, 19, 23, 24, 26, 28, 29, 31, 36, 37, 38, 40, 46, 50, 52, 54, 55, 56, 61, 65, 67, 70, 73, 77, 78, 79, 80, 83, 84, 85, 86, 89, 91, 94, 98, 99, 100, 101, 115, 122, 130, 134, 135, 136, 139, 141, 142, 143, 144, 146, 148, 149, 153, 154, 156, 157, 159, 160, 161, 162, 163, 164, 165, 168, 169, 170, 172, 173, 175, 180, 182, 184, 187, 190, 194, 200, 208, 209, 210, 212, 213, 215, 217, 218, 219, 220, 227, 228, 231, 242, 244, 245, 248, 251, 252, 253, 256, 257, 260,

266, 268, 269, 272, 274, 281, 287, 288, 289, 290, 295, 297, 300, 301, 302, 307, 308, 309, 311, 312, 313, 314, 315, 318, 321, 328, 332, 333, 337, 340, 341, 345, 346, 347, 352, 355, 358, 359, 368, 371, 373, 374, 375, 378, 386, 387, 389, 390, 396, 399, 400, 401, 404, 404, 411, 412, 421, 425, 428, 429, 440, 444, 445, 446, 447, 450, 453, 454, 457, 462, 464, 467, 468, 472, 475, 478, 479, 480, 481, 482, 483, 484, 487, 495, 497, 505, 507, 508, 509, 510, 511, 512, 513, 515, 516, 518, 519, 521, 522, 526, 527, 535, 536, 538, 539, 545, 546, 553, 553, 560, 569, 578, 579, 580, 582, 583, 583, 587, 591, 594, 595, 608, 611, 620, 622, 622, 626, 628, 630, 631, 632, 633, 639, 640, 643, 646, 648, 649, 650, 659, 663, 674, 684, 685, 686, 687, 688, 689, 693, 695, 697, 701, 706, 709, 712, 713, 718, 723, 728, 734, 738, 740, 741, 743, 744, 745, 746, 749, 750, 752, 754, 755, 762, 763, 764, 769, 772, 776, 777, 778, 781, 782, 786, 790, 791, 792, 794, 797, 798, 799, 805, 807, 808, 809, 811, 813, 817, 818, 820, 821, 822, 824, 827, 832, 839, 841, 844, 849, 852, 853, 856, 866, 871, 874, 880, 892, 894, 898, 901, 903, 904, 907, 909, 911, 913, 915, 917, 927, 928, 931, 933, 936, 937, 938, 940, 941, 942, 943, 944, 948, 956, 959, 960, 961, 962, 963, 968, 969, 971, 972, 973, 980, 988, 990, 1007, 1008, 1014, 1022, 1030, 1031, 1032, 1034, 1035, 1036, 1037, 1041, 1042, 1047, 1048, 1049, 1050, 1052, 1056, 1056, 1059, 1061, 1062, 1063, 1067, 1068, 1069, 1073, 1076, 1078, 1080, 1082, 1085, 1086, 1087, 1088, 1089, 1090, 1091, 1092, 1093, 1097, 1101, 1109, 1111, 1114, 1117, 1118, 1123, 1128, 1132, 1133, 1142, 1143, 1146, 1149, 1152, 1160, 1162, 1163, 1165, 1168, 1173, 1176, 1179, 1181, 1185, 1186, 1192, 1197, 1200, 1202, 1205, 1208, 1210, 1211, 1212, 1213, 1217, 1220, 1224, 1228, 1229, 1232, 1233, 1235, 1240, 1246, 1247, 1248, 1249, 1252, 1253, 1258, 1259, 1260, 1273, 1277, 1278, 1279, 1280, 1281, 1282, 2138, 2268). See also the collections in the Afghan Institute of Archaeology.

Peshawar Museum—stone relief from Lalpura. (Site 675).

Schøyen Collection, Norway—Buddhist manuscripts from Bamiyan (Site 100).

SOAS, London—sherds from Allchin and Codrington's survey of the Bamiyan-Surkhab region. (Sites 1004, 1042, 1052, 1139).

University Museum, University of Pennsylvania—finds from Kara Kamar. (Site 526).

University of Rome—lithics from Darra-i Kalan. (Site 244).

APPENDIX 3

Fieldwork Concordance

1833

- J. G. Gerard, East India Company—excavations at stupas in Kabul and Jalalabad areas. (Sites 418, 519, 847).
- Martin Honigberger—excavations of stupas in Kabul and JaIalabad areas. (Sites 106, 127, 283, 389, 469, 471, 651, 667, 761, 855, 1016, 1087, 1125, 1137).
- Charles Masson—excavations at Begram and Hashmatkhan, and survey in Kuh-i Daman area. (Sites 122, 211, 261, 344, 418, 435, 529, 530, 620, 647, 651, 840, 1027, 1087, 1154, 1185, 1197, 1254).

1834

- Charles Masson—excavations at Begram (Site 122) and surveys and excavation of stupas in Kabul and Jalalabad areas. (Sites 4, 10, 17, 30, 33, 106, 121, 122, 127, 129, 133, 155, 283, 310, 326, 334, 364, 365, 370, 389, 404, 426, 453, 469, 471, 488, 503, 523, 574, 627, 664, 667, 727, 748, 761, 779, 795, 806, 847, 855, 1102, 1116, 1125, 1169).

1835

- Charles Masson, East India Company—excavations at Begram (Site 122).

1836

- Charles Masson, East India Company—excavations at Wardak (Site 1229).

1841

- Pigou, Indian Army—excavations in Barabad caves and Nandarra stupa. (Sites 106, 761).

1879

- Amesbury, Indian Army—excavations at Ahin Push Tepe. (Site 17).
- Jenkins, Indian Army—excavations at Nagara Ghundi. (Site 756).
- Tanner, Indian Army—excavations in Fil Khana caves. (Site 326).
- William Simpson, Indian Army—Excavations at Ahin Push Tepe, Ghunda Chashma, and the Tepe Zargaran caves at Hadda. (Sites 17, 364, 404).
- C. Swinnerton, Indian Army—topographical survey of Buddhist monuments in the Jalalabad area. (Sites 163, 380).

1883

- P. J. Maitland, ABC—topographical survey in Seistan. (Sites 58, 77, 842, 863).
- W. Peacocke, ABC—topographical survey in Seistan. (Sites 48, 58, 77).

1884

- P. J. Maitland, ABC—topographical surveys in Herat area. (Sites 654, 666, 802, 908, 946, 947, 1165).
- A. C. Yate, ABC—topographical surveys in the north-west. (Site 711).

1885

- Akbar Khan, ABC—topographical survey in the centre. (Site 570).
- F. de Laessöe, ABC—survey of caves on the Murghab. (Site 447).
- C. L. Griesbach, ABC—topographical surveys in the north, west, and centre. (Sites 45, 373, 543).
- Imam Sharif, ABC—topographical surveys in the centre. (Sites 188, 207, 875, 1236, 1239, 1257).
- P. J. Maitland, ABC—topographical surveys in the centre and north. (Sites 47, 137, 153, 186, 189, 193, 199, 212, 239, 286, 398, 407, 492, 493, 596, 697, 707, 764, 768, 833, 835, 862, 869, 872, 890, 1082, 1153, 1212, 1263).
- C. S. Merk, ABC—topographical surveys in Seistan and Herat area. (Sites 7, 147, 206, 376, 489, 829, 830, 858, 888, 1147).
- W. Peacocke, ABC—topographic surveys in the north, north-west, and west. (Sites, 205, 697, 757, 837, 890, 1206).
- Sahibdad Khan, ABC—topographical surveys in the north-west and centre. (Sites 93, 241, 249, 274, 547, 679, 742, 834, 1021, 1047, 1127, 1231, 1267, 1268).
- Shamsuddin Khan, ABC—topographical survey in the north-west. (Site 610).
- M. G. Talbot and P. J. Maitland, ABC—surveys around Bamiyan and at Hazar Sum. (Sites 100, 425, 845, 997, 1039, 1144).
- A. C. Yate, ABC—topographical surveys in the west. (Sites 391, 711, 764, 914, 1206).

1886

- Amir Khan, ABC—topographical survey in the centre. (Sites 570, 739, 923, 1040, 1100, 1121).
- Amir Khan and Shahzada Taimus, ABC—topographical surveys in the north-west. (Sites 45, 171, 414, 720, 897).
- Ata Muhammad, ABC—topographical survey in the Balkh-Qunduz area. (Sites 38, 640, 642, 666, 918, 1038).
- F. H. R. Drummond, ABC—topographical surveys in the Surkhab district. (Site 451).
- C. L. Griesbach, ABC—topographical surveys in the north, north-west, and west of Bamiyan. (Sites 100, 171, 249, 276, 279, 322, 414, 415, 493, 534, 645, 668, 777, 833, 862).
- Hira Singh, ABC—topographical surveys in the north-west. (Sites 331, 1023, 1033).
- Imam Sharif, ABC—topographical survey in the north-west. (Site 1051).
- P. J. Maitland, ABC—topographical surveys in the north. (Sites 68, 75, 99, 213, 214, 294, 296, 314, 316, 325, 407, 427, 454, 465, 496, 541, 542, 550, 556, 568, 569, 572, 604, 609, 628, 629, 657, 681, 753, 760, 776, 800, 846, 915, 932, 934, 944, 952, 977, 1018, 1076, 1094, 1095, 1113, 1138, 1149, 1155, 1226, 1244).
- W. Peacocke, ABC—topographical surveys in the north, north-west, and centre. (Sites 9, 41, 298, 439, 466, 552, 628, 952, 1049, 1076, 1099, 1139, 1150, 1207, 1242, 1243).

- Shahzada Taimus, ABC—topographical survey of the Hindu Kush passes. (Site 616).
- M. G. Talbot and P. J. Maitland, ABC survey of Takht-i Rustam. (Site 1135).
- C. E. Yate, ABC—topographical surveys in the north and north-west. (Sites 35, 99, 541, 542, 850, 890, 1043, 1134, 1216).

1887
- Akbar Khan and Ata Muhammad, ABC—topographical survey in the Hazarajat. (Site 284).

1898/99
- O. Olufsen, Danish Army—expedition into the Pamirs. (Sites 448, 873, 1261).

1901
- Aurel Stein, ASI—survey through the Pamirs. (Sites 524, 533, 678).

1903/05
- G. P. Tate, SAC—surveys in Seistan. (Sites 144, 190, 201, 225, 363, 376, 383, 394, 479, 558, 561, 714, 715, 788, 792, 810, 824, 842, 857, 861, 871, 883, 958, 1006, 1044, 1147, 1238, 1264, 1269).

1922
- Alfred Foucher, DAFA—survey of Bamiyan and survey of the ancient route from Balkh to Jalalabad. (Sites 33, 100, 105, 178, 519, 705).

1923
- S. Flury and Yves Godard, DAFA—architectural and epigraphic studies at Ghazni. (Site 358).
- Alfred Foucher, DAFA—survey of Kuh-i Daman area, and of Begram and Takht-i Rustam. (Sites 122, 435, 491, 606, 884, 1135, 1197).
- Alfred Foucher and André Godard, DAFA—sondages at Tepe Kalan, Hadda, and architectural study of Nandarra stupa. (Sites 404, 761).
- Yves Godard, DAFA—survey of Bamiyan. (Sites 100, 508).

1924
- Alfred Foucher, DAFA—excavations at Balkh (Site 99), and survey of the Balkh area. (Sites 63, 74, 496, 753, 1018).
- André Godard and Joseph Hackin, DAFA—investigation of Dukhtar-i Nushirwan. (Sites 305, 493, 885).
- Joseph Hackin, DAFA—survey of Bamiyan and excavations at Begram and Paitava. (Sites 100, 122, 790).

1925
- J. Barthoux, DAFA—excavations at Begram. (Site 122).
- Alfred Foucher, DAFA—excavations at Balkh and surveys in Kuh-i Daman and Laghman. (Sites 99, 211, 247).

1926
- J. Barthoux, DAFA—excavations at Hadda. (Sites 404, 815).
- AlfredFoucher, DAFA—survey of Bamiyan. (Site 100).

1927
- J. Barthoux, DAFA—excavations at Hadda. (Site 404).

1928
- J. Barthoux, DAFA—excavations at Hadda. (Site 404).

1930
- J. Barthoux, DAFA—excavations at Hadda. (Site 165).
- J. Carl and J. Hackin, DAFA—excavations at Begram and survey of Kakrak. (Sites 100, 508).

1933
- J. Carl, DAFA—excavations at Nijrau and Tepe Maranjan. (Sites 773, 1173).

1934
- J. Carl, DAFA—excavations at Khair Khana. (Site 546).
- Joseph Hackin, DAFA—excavations at Shahr-i Banu. (Site 1034).

1935
- Robert Byron, American Institute of Iranian Art—survey of Timurid monuments. (Sites 99, 346, 428).
- J. Carl, DAFA—excavations at Saka. (Site 972).
- Eric Schroeder, American Institute of Iranian Art—survey of Daulatabad minaret. (Site 2053).

1936
- Roman Ghirshman, DAFA—excavations at Nad-i 'Ali. (Site 752).
- Joseph Hackin, DAFA—excavations at Begram and survey of Funduqistan. (Sites 122, 332).
- Joseph Hackin and Jacques Meunié, DAFA—survey in Seistan. (Sites 164, 190, 201, 363, 638, 648, 715, 788, 792, 810, 839, 842, 861, 871, 883, 983, 1006, 1044, 1264).
- Jacques Meunié, DAFA—excavations at Shotorak. (Site 1088).
- Eric Schroeder and Donald Wilber, American Institute of Iranian Art—survey of the Herat monuments. (Site 428).

1937
- J. Carl, DAFA—excavations at Funduqistan. (Site 332).
- Joseph Hackin, DAFA—excavations at Begram, Qunduz Bala Hisar, and Tepe Ahingaran. (Sites 122, 931, 1160).
- Jacques Meunié, DAFA—excavations at Shotorak. (Site 1088).
- Eric Schroeder and Donald Wilber, American Institute of Iranian Art—survey of the Herat monuments. (Sites 346, 428).

1938
- Evert Barger, ASI—survey in the north and north-east. (Sites 150, 314, 325, 437, 776, 789, 800, 930, 931, 1037, 1244).
- J. Carl, DAFA—sondages at Deh Warda (Zakar Tepe) and Shahr-i Banu. (Sites 290, 1034).
- Joseph Hackin, DAFA—excavations at Begram. (Site 122).

1939
- Joseph Hackin, DAFA—excavations at Begram. (Site 122).
- Jacques Meunié, DAFA—excavations at Qul-i Nadir. (Site 928).

1940
- Joseph Hackin, DAFA—excavations at Begram. (Site 122).

1941
- Roman Ghirshman, DAFA—excavations at Begram. (Site 122).

1942
- Roman Ghirshman, DAFA—excavations at Begram and Sadiqabad. (Sites 122, 963).
- R. Stuckert—architectural survey of the Herat Friday Mosque. (Site 428).

1943
- R. Stuckert—architectural survey of the Herat Friday Mosque. (Site 428).

1946
- Ahmad Ali Kohzad, HSA—survey of Ghur and the central route. (Sites 15, 27, 39, 114, 188, 195, 255, 433, 485, 537, 566, 612, 683, 704, 742, 864, 875, 1081, 1103, 1130, 1144, 1185, 1234, 1239).

- Jacques Meunié, DAFA—excavations at Begram. (Site 122).
- R. E. M. Wheeler, ASI—reconnaissance, mainly in the north. (Sites 25, 29, 49, 99, 150, 169, 178, 194, 325, 437, 494, 522, 707, 744, 776, 800, 919, 931, 1055, 1056, 1227, 1232).

1947
- Daniel Schlumberger, DAFA—excavations at Balkh. (Site 99).

1948
- Marc Le Berre, DAFA—sondages at Kama Dakka and Mir Zakah (Sites 518, 728), and survey in the Balkh-Aqcha-Daula-tabad area. (Sites 8, 14, 42, 49, 51, 60, 62, 150, 152, 174, 271, 316, 325; 382, 397, 413, 437, 520, 550, 568, 593, 605, 690, 692, 708, 766, 770, 771, 800, 814, 919, 920, 924, 935, 954, 978, 1054, 1055, 1164, 1170, 1175, 1183, 1188, 1219, 1227, 1245, 1250).
- Daniel Schlumberger, DAFA—excavations at Balkh. (Site 99).

1949
- Beatrice De Cardi, Council for British Archaeology—survey in the south and west. (Sites 108, 149, 274, 454, 507, 810, 1017, 1098, 1157, 1165).
- Walter A. Fairservis Jr, AMNH—survey in Seistan. (Sites 584, 1156).
- Daniel Schlumberger, DAFA—excavations at Lashkari Bazar-Bust. (Sites 149, 685).

1950
- Louis Dupree, AMNH—excavations at Shamshir Ghar. (Site 1069).
- Walter A. Fairservis Jr, AMNH—surveys in Seistan and Kandahar. (Sites 108, 167, 262, 264, 360, 368, 506, 558, 672, 684, 798, 810, 824, 836, 842, 976, 979, 1041, 1044, 1070, 1097, 1136, 1166).
- Daniel Schlumberger, DAFA—excavations at Lashkari Bazar-Bust. (Sites 149, 685).

1951
- F. R. Allchin and K. de B. Codrington—survey in Bamiyan-Surkhab area and excavations at Shahr-i Zuhak. (Sites 1004, 1042, 1052, 1139, 1199).
- Jean-Marie Casal, DAFA—excavations at Mundigak (Site 743) and survey in the Kandahar area. (Sites 23, 55, 73, 180, 522, 578, 744, 754, 798, 962, 968, 1048, 1109, 1248, 1249).
- Louis Dupree, AMNH—excavations at Deh Morasi Ghundai. (Site 287).
- Walter A. Fairservis Jr, AMNH—sondages at Said Qal'a Tepe (Site 968) and survey in Seistan. (Sites 2, 3, 108, 145, 147, 206, 270, 335, 369, 551, 559, 721, 823, 831, 876, 900, 957, 991, 1006, 1158, 1177, 1178, 1266).
- Daniel Schlumberger, DAFA—excavations at Lashkari Bazar-Bust. (Sites 149, 685).

1952
- Jean-Marie Casal, DAFA—excavations at Mundigak. (Site 743).
- Roman Ghirshman and Richard N. Frye—survey of Tang-i Azau. (Site 1144).
- Marc Le Berre and Jean-Claude Gardin, DAFA—survey in the north-west and west. (Sites 13, 84, 157, 212, 232, 235, 318, 328, 340, 354, 395, 507, 573, 576, 603, 610, 697, 724, 764, 781, 794, 802, 813, 841, 852, 856, 859, 874, 895, 961, 992, 1030, 1046, 1057, 1115, 1259).

- Daniel Schlumberger, DAFA—survey of Shakh Tepe and excavations at Surkh Kotal. (Sites 1065, 1123).

1953
- A. D. H. Bivar, SOAS—reconnaissance in Uruzgan. (Sites 320, 498, 1029, 1221).
- Schuyler B. Cammann, University Museum Pennsylvania—excavations at Tepe Ahingaran. (Site 1160).
- Jean-Marie Casal, DAFA—excavations at Mundigak and Shakh Tepe. (Sites 743, 1065).
- Daniel Schlumberger, DAFA—excavations at Surkh Kotal. (Site 1123).
- Rodney S. Young, University Museum Pennsylvania—excavations of south wall of Balkh. (Site 99).

1954
- Jean-Marie Casal, DAFA—excavations at Mundigak. (Site 743).
- Carleton S. Coon, University Museum Pennsylvania—excavations at Kara Kamar. (Site 526).
- Daniel Schlumberger, DAFA—excavations at Surkh Kotal. (Site 1123).

1955
- Jean-Marie Casal, DAFA—excavations at Mundigak. (Site 743).
- Klaus Fischer, DAAD—surveys, mainly in the north-east. (Sites 54, 79, 86, 148, 208, 218, 260, 302, 313, 350, 400, 440, 442, 447, 454, 497, 522, 553, 583, 659, 818, 930, 931, 941, 942, 944, 960, 988, 1013, 1014, 1065, 1073, 1076, 1091, 1118, 1139, 1160, 1165, 1176).
- Marc Le Berre, DAFA—investigations of Balkh city walls. (Site 99).
- Daniel Schlumberger, DAFA—excavations at Surkh Kotal. (Site 1123).

1956
- P. Bell, R. Evans, and L. Holland, Oxford University—expedition to Tang-i Azau. (Site 1144).
- Alessio Bombaci and Umberto Scerrato, IsMEO—excavations at Ghazni. (Site 358).
- Jean-Marie Casal, DAFA—excavations at Mundigak. (Site 743).
- Marc Le Berre, DAFA—investigations of Balkh city walls. (Site 99).
- André Maricq and Marc Le Berre, DAFA—survey of Jam. (Site 468).
- T. N. Ramachandra and Y. D. Sharma, ASI—reconnaissance around the circular route. (Sites 29, 178, 285, 388, 437, 454, 507, 548, 628, 745, 794, 841, 874, 887, 925, 941, 975, 1004, 1056, 1098, 1109, 1163, 1165, 1189, 1232).
- Daniel Schlumberger, DAFA—excavations at Surkh Kotal. (Site 1123).

1957
- Alessio Bombaci and Umberto Scerrato, IsMEO—excavations at Ghazni and survey of Band-i Sultan. (Sites 103, 358).
- Jean-Marie Casal, DAFA—excavations at Mundigak. (Site 743).
- K. Lindberg—speleological survey. (Sites 319, 327, 477, 523, 747, 1069).
- Daniel Schlumberger, DAFA—excavations at Surkh Kotal. (Site 1123).

1958
- Alessio Bombaci and Umberto Scerrato, IsMEO—excavations at Ghazni. (Site 358).
- Jean-Marie Casal, DAFA—excavations at Mundigak. (Site 743).
- K. Lindberg—speleological survey. (Sites see 1957).
- Umberto Scerrato, IsMEO—survey and sondages in Jaghatu area. (Sites 71, 461).
- Daniel Schlumberger, DAFA—excavations at Surkh Kotal. (Site 1123).

1959
- D. Adamesteanu, IsMEO—excavations at Tepe Sardar. (Site 1180).
- Alessio Bombaci and Umberto Scerrato, IsMEO—excavations at Ghazni. (Site 358).
- Louis Dupree and Bruce Howe, AUFS—survey for Stone Age sites in the north. (Sites 46, 138, 240, 242, 422, 1151).
- Jan Fischer, John Lonsdale, David Owen, and Bill Purver, Cambridge University—survey in Jam area. (Sites 468, 1144).
- Klaus Fischer, DAAD—survey in Kunar. (Sites 154, 453, 706, 713, 763, 827, 880) and in various other places. (Sites—see under 1955).
- Daniel Schlumberger, DAFA—excavations at Surkh Kotal. (Site 1123).

1960
- D. Adamesteanu, IsMEO—excavations at Tepe Sardar. (Site 1180).
- Alessio Bombaci and Umberto Scerrato, IsMEO—excavations at Ghazni. (Site 358).
- Klaus Fischer, DAAD—surveys in the north-east, east, and south-east (Sites 29, 67, 79, 131, 307, 315, 337, 345, 356, 444, 467, 479, 512, 587, 649, 695, 705, 798, 821, 832, 842, 940, 1059, 1073, 1181, 1189; see also under 1955), and in Seistan (Sites 52, 142, 143, 144, 146, 159, 164, 184, 200, 219, 228, 293, 318, 347, 375, 399, 417, 482, 507, 639, 646, 684, 688, 734, 778, 811, 822, 962, 990, 1085, 1114, 1133, 1200).
- Klaus Fischer and Louis Dupree—survey and sondages in Shahrak area. (Sites 781, 820).
- M. Hayashi and M. Sahara, Kyoto University—survey in the north. (Sites 21, 46, 49, 63, 81, 99, 166, 169, 173, 178, 191, 194, 316, 329, 407, 437, 447, 467, 526, 550, 567, 591, 628, 689, 753, 776, 791, 800, 868, 925, 931, 941, 975, 993, 1034, 1055, 1139, 1175, 1179, 1189).
- Marc Le Berre, DAFA—architectural study of Chisht and excavations at Danistama. (Sites 212, 231).
- Seiichi Mizuno and Koji Nishikawa, Kyoto University—survey of Takht-i Rustam. (Site 1135).
- Daniel Schlumberger, DAFA—excavations at Surkh Kotal. (Site 1123).

1961
- Alessio Bombaci and Umberto Scerrato, IsMEO—excavations at Ghazni. (Site 358).
- Andrea Bruno, IsMEO—architectural studies at Jam. (Site 468).
- Andrea Bruno and A. D'Amico, IsMEO—restoration of shrine of Abdur Razzaq at Ghazni. (Site 358).

- Louis Dupree and Klaus Fischer—sondages in Shahrak area. (Sites 781, 1031).
- Klaus Fischer, DAAD—surveys in various places. (Sites—see under 1955 and 1960).
- S. M. Puglisi, IsMEO—excavations at Tepe Sardar. (Site 1180).
- Daniel Schlumberger, DAFA—excavations at Surkh Kotal. (Site 1123).

1962
- A. D. H. Bivar, SOAS—reconnaissance in Luman area. (Sites 125, 955, 1184).
- Alessio Bombaci and Umberto Scerrato, IsMEO—excavations at Ghazni. (Site 358).
- Andrea Bruno, IsMEO—architectural studies at Jam. (Site 468).
- Andrea Bruno and A. D'Amico, IsMEO—restoration of the shrine of Abdur Razzaq at Ghazni. (Site 358).
- Bruno Dagens, DAFA—survey of Fuladi. (Site 330).
- Louis Dupree, AMNH—excavations at Aq Kupruk. (Site 46).
- M. Hayashi and M. Sahara, Kyoto University—survey of Hazar Sum. (Site 425).
- Marc Le Berre, DAFA—sondage at Khisht Tepe. (Site 569).
- Alexandre Lézine, UNESCO—restoration of Guldarra stupa and survey of monuments in Herat. (Sites 389, 428).
- Seiichi Mizuno, Kyoto University—survey of Buddhist monuments in Jalalabad and Kabul areas. (Sites 34, 122, 326, 504, 1087, 1116, 1124, 1237).
- S. M. Puglisi, IsMEO—excavations at Hazar Sum. (Site 425).
- Daniel Schlumberger, DAFA—excavations at Surkh Kotal. (Site 1123).
- Maurizio Taddei, IsMEO—survey of Gudul-i Ahangaran. (Site 385).

1963
- Paul Bernard and Charles Kieffer, DAFA—excavations at Kuhna Masjid. (Site 630).
- Alessio Bombaci and Umberto Scerrato, IsMEO—excavations at Ghazni. (Site 358).
- Andrea Bruno and A. D'Amico, IsMEO—restoration of the shrine of Abdur Razzaq at Ghazni. (Site 358).
- Gérard Fussman and Marc Le Berre, DAFA—excavations at Guldarra monastery and survey of Musa-i Logar area. (Sites 277, 357, 389, 545, 749, 921, 922).
- Marc Le Berre, DAFA—Shakh Tepe excavations. (Site 1065).
- Alexandre Lézine, UNESCO—restoration of Guldarra stupa. (Site 389).
- Seiichi Mizuno and Nakao Odani, Kyoto University—excavations at Durman Tepe, Qunduz Bala Hisar, and survey in the Qunduz area. (Sites 20, 309, 564, 931, 1131).
- Daniel Schlumberger, DAFA—excavations at Surkh Kotal. (Site 1123).
- G. W. Thompson, Oxford University—survey, mainly in Badakhshan. (Sites 273, 449, 1001, 1072).

1964
- Alessio Bombaci and Umberto Scerrato, IsMEO—excavations at Ghazni. (Site 358).
- Andrea Bruno and A. D'Amico, IsMEO—restoration of the shrine of Abdur Razzaq at Ghazni. (Site 358).
- Louis Dupree, AMNH excavations at Āq Kupruk. (Site 46).
- Gérard Fussman, CNRS—survey in Wardak. (Sites 621, 1229).

- Gérard Fussman and Marc Le Berre, DAFA—excavations at Guldarra monastery, survey of Kandahar Old City (Sites 389, 522) and survey in Musa-i Logar (Sites—see under 1963).
- Erkin Hansen, Kabul Museum/UNESCO—restoration of the Ghurid Portal in Herat. (Site 428).
- Takayasu Higuchi and Shoshin Kuwayama, Kyoto University—excavations at Chaqalaq Tepe and Durman Tepe. (Sites 172, 309).
- Alexandre Lézine, UNESCO—restoration of Guldarra stupa. (Site 389).
- Daniel Schlumberger, DAFA—survey of Ai Khanoum. (Site 18).

1965
- Paul Bernard, DAFA—excavations at Ai Khanoum. (Site 18).
- Andrea Bruno and A. D'Amico, IsMEO—restoration of the shrine of Abdur Razzaq at Ghazni. (Site 358).
- Klaus Fischer, DAAD—surveys, mostly in Seistan. (Sites 78, 301, 558, 563, 722, 733, 740, 792, 844, 883, 894, 966, 1120, 1174, 1193, 1247, 1264; see also under 1955 and 1960).
- Takayasu Higuchi and Shoshin Kuwayama, Kyoto University—excavations at Chaqalaq Tepe and Durman Tepe. (Sites 172, 309).
- L. Leshnik, Heidelberg University—survey and sondages in Ghur. (Site 15).
- Seiichi Mizuno, Kyoto University—excavations at Lalma (Site 673) and survey of Buddhist sites in Jalalabad, Kabul, and Kuh-i Daman areas. (Sites 30, 106, 121, 127, 155, 163, 283, 370, 389, 426, 469, 471, 622, 667, 727, 761, 806, 847, 855, 986, 1087, 1102, 1116, 1125, 1169, 1197, 1237).
- Shahibye Mustamandi, AIA—excavations at Tepe Shutur, Hadda. (Site 404).
- S. M. Puglisi, IsMEO—excavations at Darra-i Kalan. (Site 244).

1966
- Paul Bernard, DAFA—excavations at Ai Khanoum. (Site 18).
- Paul Bernard and Marc Le Berre, DAFA—excavations at Shahr-i Zuhak. (Site 1052).
- Andrea Bruno and A. D'Amico, IsMEO—restoration of the shrine of Abdur Razzaq at Ghazni. (Site 358).
- Louis Dupree, AMNH—excavations at Darra-i Kur. (Site 245).
- Klaus Fischer, DAAD—surveys in the south-east (Sites 73, 168, 170, 192, 217, 368, 384, 636, 744, 746, 769, 805, 807, 809, 817, 907, 1048, 1109, 1211, 1248), in the north (Sites—see under 1960), and in Seistan (Sites—see under 1955, 1960, 1965).
- Lisa Golombek, ROM—survey at Gazurgah. (Site 346).
- Lisa Golombek and Deborah Salter—survey of Haji Piyada. (Site 410).
- Norman Hammond, Cambridge University—survey along the Helmand. (Sites 24, 77, 91, 101, 197, 227, 251, 253, 297, 311, 359, 396, 411, 429, 521, 527, 539, 560, 595, 608, 662, 687, 701, 709, 849, 863, 898, 901, 938, 964, 1068, 1111, 1163, 1228, 1252, 1260).
- Charles C. Kolb, AMNH—sondage at Hazar Gusfand. (Site 422).
- L. Leshnik, Heidelberg University—survey in the north. (Site 155).
- Seiichi Mizuno, Kyoto University—excavations at Lalma. (Site 673).
- Shahibye Mustamandi, AIA—excavations at Tepe Shutur, Hadda (Site 404), and at Kuh-i Muri (Site 622).

- Umberto Scerrato, IsMEO—survey in Jaghatu area. (Site 303).
- Rauf Wardak, Kabul Museum—sondages at Khush Tepe. (Site 582).

1967
- Paul Bernard, DAFA—excavations at Ai Khanoum. (Site 18).
- Gérard Fussman, CNRS—survey in Wardak. (Site 1229).
- Takayasu Higuchi and Shoshin Kuwayama, Kyoto University—excavations at Chaqalaq Tepe. (Site 172).
- Shahibye Mustamandi, AIA—excavations at Tepe Shutur, Hadda, and sondage at Mir Bacha Kot. (Sites 404, 723).
- Galina A. Pugachenkova, Afghan/Soviet Mission—survey of Timurid monuments in the Herat area. (Sites 278, 349, 428, 634, 661, 1263).
- Maurizio Taddei, IsMEO—excavations at Tepe Sardar. (Site 1180).

1968
- Paul Bernard, DAFA—excavations at Ai Khanoum. (Site 18).
- George F. Dales, University Museum Pennsylvania—excavations at Nad-i 'Ali (Site 752) and survey in southern Seistan (Sites 229, 1006, 1147).
- Klaus Fischer, Bonn University—survey in Seistan (Sites 190, 312, 834, 871, 889, 1073; see also under 1955, 1960, 1965) and in the north (Sites—see under 1960).
- Shahibye Mustamandi, AIA—excavations at Tepe Shutur, Hadda, and excavations at Wazirabad. (Sites 404, 1232).
- Galina A. Pugachenkova, Afghan/Soviet Mission—survey of Timurid monuments in the Herat area. (Sites—see under 1967).
- Maurizio Taddei, IsMEO—excavations at Tepe Sardar. (Site 1180).

1969
- Paul Bernard, DAFA—excavations at Ai Khanoum. (Site 18).
- George F. Dales, University Museum Pennsylvania—survey and sondages in southern Seistan. (Sites 335, 383, 393; see also under 1968).
- Richard S. Davis, Louis Dupree, and Lawrence H. Lattmann, AMNH—survey of Kuk Jar. (Site 635).
- Louis Dupree, AMNH—sondages at Ghar-i Morda Gusfand, and Gharluli. (Sites 352, 355).
- Klaus Fischer, Bonn University—survey in Seistan (Sites 341, 486, 601, 607, 889, 983; see also under 1960, 1965).
- Gérard Fussman, CNRS—survey in Wardak. (Site 1229).
- Philippe Gouin, DAFA—survey of Tashqurghan area. (Sites 65, 141, 213, 289, 290, 628, 745, 915, 1022, 1034, 1035, 1036, 1056, 1061, 1062, 1063, 1101, 1152, 1181, 1212, 1213, 1240).
- Kotera, Nagoya University—survey of the Bamiyan caves. (Site 100).
- Irina T. Kruglikova and Shahibye Mustamandi, Afghan/Soviet Mission—excavations at Dashli, Dilbarjin, and Emshi Tepe, and survey at Daulatabad. (Sites 256, 257, 295, 314, 1191, 2053).
- Shahibye Mustamandi, AIA—excavations at Tepe Shutur, Hadda. (Site 404).
- Galina A. Pugachenkova, Afghan/Soviet Mission—survey of Timurid monuments in the Herat area. (Sites—see 1967).
- Viktor I. Sarianidi, Afghan/Soviet Mission—excavations at Tilla Tepe. (Site 1192).
- R. Sengupta, Afghan/Indian Mission—preservation of 38 m Buddha and associated shrines and frescos at Bamiyan. (Site 100).

- Maurizio Taddei, IsMEO—excavations at Tepe Sardar. (Site 1180).
- A. V. Vinogradov, Afghan/Soviet Mission—survey of Stone Age sites in the north. (Sites 181, 452, 473, 540, 589, 590, 609, 905, 906, 912, 982).

1970
- Paul Bernard, DAFA—excavations at Ai Khanoum. (Site 18).
- Tim Brett *et al.*, Bristol University—survey of fortifications in east central Afghanistan. (Sites 124, 189, 556, 1004, 1042, 1052).
- Louis Dupree, AMNH—excavations at Ghar-i Morda Gusfand and survey for Stone Age sites in Gurziwan. (Sites 352, 401, 777, 1258).
- Klaus Fischer, Bonn University—survey in Seistan. (Sites 190, 201, 300, 478, 648, 719, 808, 866, 1073; see also under 1960, 1965, 1969).
- Philippe Gouin, DAFA—sondages at Burat Tepe. (Site 141).
- Takayasu Higuchi and Shoshin Kuwayama, Kyoto University—excavations at Tepe Skandar. (Site 1185).
- Robert Kostka—photogrammetrical survey of the 53 m Buddha at Bamiyan. (Site 100).
- Irina T. Kruglikova, Afghan/Soviet Mission—survey of Achaemenid wall in Balkh-Jauzjan. (Site 520).
- Irina T. Kruglikova and Shahibye Mustamandi, Afghan/Soviet Mission—excavations at Dilbarjin and Emshi Tepe. (Sites 295, 314).
- Shahibye Mustamandi, AIA—excavations at Tepe Shutur, Hadda. (Site 404).
- Viktor I. Sarianidi and Zemaryalai Tarzi, Afghan/Soviet Mission—excavations at Tilla Tepe. (Site 1192).
- R. Sengupta, Afghan/Indian Mission—preservation of 38 m Buddha at Bamiyan. (Site 100).
- Maurizio Taddei, IsMEO—excavations at Tepe Sardar. (Site 1180).
- Yoshiyuki Ushikawa, Kyoto University—photogrammetrical survey of Kurrindar stupa. (Site 651).
- White, AMNH—survey of Tepe Shahidan. (Site 1181).

1970/71
- Jim G. Shaffer, AMNH—excavations at Sa'id Qal'a Tepe. (Site 968).

1971
- Paul Bernard, DAFA—excavations at Ai Khanoum. (Site 18).
- Klaus Fischer, Bonn University—survey in Seistan. (Site 390; see also under 1969).
- Irina T. Kruglikova, Afghan/Soviet Mission—excavations at Altin 10 and Dilbarjin. (Sites 37, 295).
- C. B. M. McBurney, Cambridge University—survey and sondages at Stone Age sites in the north. (Sites 46, 526, 613).
- Shahibye Mustamandi, AIA—excavations at Tepe Shutur, Hadda. (Site 404).
- Viktor I. Sarianidi and Zemaryalai Tarzi, Afghan/Soviet Mission—excavations at Tilla Tepe. (Site 1192).
- R. Sengupta, Afghan/Indian Mission—preservation of 38 m Buddha at Bamiyan. (Site 100).
- Maurizio Taddei, IsMEO—excavations at Tepe Sardar. (Site 1180).
- William Trousdale, Smithsonian Institution—survey in Seistan. (Sites 554, 597, 881, 1006, 1107).

- Giorgio Vercellin, Venice University—survey in Ghur. (Site 468).

1971/72
- George F. Dales, University Museum Pennsylvania—survey and sondages in southern Seistan. (Sites—see under 1968 and 1969).

1972
- Paul Bernard, DAFA—excavations at Ai Khanoum. (Site 18).
- Klaus Fischer, Bonn University—survey in Seistan. (Sites 390, 607, 983).
- Gérard Fussman, CNRS—survey in Wardak. (Site 1229).
- Philippe Gouin, DAFA—sondages at Burat Tepe. (Site 141).
- Takayasu Higuchi and Shoshin Kuwayama, Kyoto University—excavations at Tepe Skandar. (Site 1185).
- Irina T. Kruglikova, Afghan/Soviet Mission—excavations at Dilbarjin. (Site 295).
- Shahibye Mustamindi, AIA—excavations at Tepe Shutur, Hadda. (Site 404).
- Galina A. Pugachenkova, Afghan/Soviet Mission—survey of ancient fortifications in Balkh and Jauzjan (Sites 459, 642, 732, 1198, 1243) and survey of Islamic monuments in the Balkh area (Sites 8, 69, 725).
- Viktor I. Sarianidi and Zemaryalai Tarzi, Afghan/Soviet Mission—excavations at Tilla Tepe. (Site 1192).
- R. Sengupta, Afghan/Soviet Mission—preservation of 38 m Buddha at Bamiyan. (Site 100).
- Maurizio Taddei, IsMEO—excavations at Tepe Sardar. (Site 1180).
- William Trousdale, Smithsonian Institution—survey in Seistan and excavations at Sar-o Tar. (Sites—see under 1971).

1973
- Daniel Balland, CNRS—hydrological survey in the Ghazni area. (Sites 102, 103, 104).
- Paul Bernard, DAFA—excavations at Ai Khanoum. (Site 18).
- Werner Herberg, Berlin University—survey at Jam and in Ghur. (Site 468).
- Irina T. Kruglikova, Afghan/Soviet Mission—excavations at Dilbarjin and Uvlia Tepe. (Sites 295, 1225).
- Shahibye Mustamandi, AIA—excavations at Tepe Shutur, Hadda, (Site 404), and sondages at Pachirwagam (Site 782).
- Galina Pugachenkova, Afghan/Soviet Mission—survey of fortifications in Balkh and Jauzjan and survey of Islamic monuments in the Balkh area. (Sites—see under 1972).
- Viktor I. Sarianidi and Zemaryalai Tarzi, Afghan/Soviet Mission—excavations at Dashli and Tilla Tepe and surveys in the north and north-west. (Sites 43, 44, 53, 256, 257, 258, 259, 323, 324, 430, 641, 666, 1191, 1192).
- R. Sengupta, Afghan/Indian Mission—preservation of the 38 m Buddha at Bamiyan. (Site 100).
- Maurizio Taddei, IsMEO—excavations at Tepe Sardar. (Site 1180).
- William Trousdale, Smithsonian Institution—excavations at Sar-o Tar and survey in Seistan. (Sites—see under 1971).

1974
- AIA—preservation of Haji Piyada. (Site 410).
- Paul Bernard, DAFA—excavations at Ai Khanoum. (Site 18).
- Louis Dupree, AUFS—survey in the Ab-i Istada area. (Sites 272, 345, 481, 762, 1078, 1273).

- Klaus Fischer, Bonn University—survey in Seistan. (Sites 839, 983).
- Jean-Claude Gardin, CNRS—survey in eastern Bactria. (Sites 374, 631, 632, 1205). Takayasu Higuchi and Shoshin Kuwayama, Kyoto University—excavations at Tepe Skandar. (Site 1185).
- Takayasu Higuchi and Akira Miyaji, Kyoto University—survey of caves and frescos at Bamiyan. (Site 100).
- Irina T. Kruglikova and Shahibye Mustamandi, Afghan/Soviet Mission—survey of Altin Dilyar Tepe. (Site 38).
- Marc Le Berre, DAFA—survey of fortifications in the Bamiyan-Surkhab area. (Sites 16, 47, 100, 109, 118, 233, 238, 263, 302, 330, 350, 398, 441, 466, 480, 489, 508, 514, 517, 592, 682, 784, 786, 804, 969, 1014, 1021, 1042, 1049, 1052, 1074, 1075, 1077, 1117, 1139, 1199, 1202, 1256).
- Shahibye Mustamandi, AIA—excavations at Tepe Shutur, Hadda. (Site 404).
- Roberto Orazi, IsMEO—architectural study and preservation of the shrine of Muhammad Shari Khan at Ghazni. (Site 358).
- Galina A. Pugachenkova, Afghan/Soviet Mission—survey of Islamic monuments in the Balkh area (Sites—see under 1972) and excavations at Jiga Tepe (Site 475).
- Viktor I. Sarianidi and Zemaryalai Tarzi, Afghan/Soviet Mission—excavations at Tilla Tepe. (Site 1192).
- R. Sengupta, Afghan/Indian Mission—preservation of 38 m Buddha at Bamian and the shrine of Khwaja Abu Nasr Parsa at Balkh. (Sites 99, 100).
- Stuart Swiny, BIAS—survey in the west. (Sites 416, 500, 573, 731, 865, 874, 950, 951, 984, 1246).
- Maurizio Taddei, IsMEO—excavations at Tepe Sardar. (Site 1180).
- Maurizio Taddei and Giovanni Verardi, IsMEO—survey in Jaghuri area. (Sites 431, 434, 671, 758, 985, 1025, 1184).
- Zemaryalai Tarzi, AIA—excavations at Tepe Shutur, Hadda. (Site 404).
- William Trousdale, Smithsonian Institution—excavations at Sar-o Tar and surveys in Seistan. (Sites—see under 1971).
- David Whitehouse, BIAS—excavations at Kandahar. (Site 522).
- David Whitehouse and Stuart Swiny, BIAS—survey in Kandahar area. (Sites 55, 56, 73, 85, 180, 956, 967, 988, 1041, 1048, 1097).

1975
- Paul Bernard, DAFA—excavations at Ai Khanoum. (Site 18).
- Jean-Claude Gardin, CNRS—survey in eastern Bactria. (Sites 509, 1089, 1271).
- Karl Gratzl, Robert Kostka, and G. Patzelt—exploration in the Pamirs. (Sites 196, 455, 768, 816, 1126).
- Philip L. Kohl—survey in the north-east. (Sites 29, 50, 59, 64, 107, 175, 315, 342, 371, 400, 582, 583, 650, 765, 860, 942, 1037, 1201).
- Marc Le Berre, DAFA—survey of fortifications in Bamiyan-Surkhab area. (Sites see under 1974).
- Anthony McNicoll, BIAS—excavations at Kandahar. (Site 522).
- Ministry of Information/UNESCO—preservation of monuments in Herat. (Site 428).
- Bernard O'Kane, BIPS—survey of Timurid monuments in the Herat area. (Sites 111,165, 351, 373, 948).

- Galina A. Pugachenkova, Afghan/Soviet Mission—excavations at Jiga Tepe. (Site 475).
- G. K. Rao, BIAS—preservation of Minar-i Chakri. (Site 718).
- Viktor I. Sarianidi and Zemaryalai Tarzi, Afghan/Soviet Mission—excavations at Tilla Tepe. (Site 1192).
- R. Sengupta, Afghan/Indian Mission—preservation of the shrine of Khwaja Abu Nasr Parsa at Balkh and of the 38 m Buddha at Bamiyan. (Sites 99, 100).
- Maurizio Taddei, IsMEO—excavations at Tepe Sardar. (Site 1180).
- Maurizio Taddei and Giovanni Verardi, IsMEO—survey Jaghuri and Muqqur areas. (Sites 97, 117, 168, 434, 623, 758, 1167, 1184).
- Zemaryalai Tarzi, AIA—excavations at Tepe Shutur at Hadda. (Site 404).
- William Trousdale, Smithsonian Institution—survey and excavation at Sar-o Tar. (Site 1006).
- A. V. Vinogradov, Afghan/Soviet Mission—survey of Stone Age sites in the north. (Sites 110, 408, 999, 1056, 1149, 1209).

1976
- Ajan and Furughi, AIA—preservation of the arch at Bust. (Site 149).
- Paul Bernard, DAFA—excavations at Ai Khanoum. (Site 18).
- Louis Dupree and Richard S. Davis—survey of the Dasht-i Nawur. (Site 266).
- Henri-Paul Francfort, DAFA—excavations at Shortughai. (Site 1089).
- Svend Helms, BIAS—excavations at Kandahar. (Site 522).
- Takayasu Higuchi and Shoshin Kuwayama, Kyoto University—excavations at Tepe Skandar. (Site 1185).
- Takayasu Higuchi and Akira Miyaji, Kyoto University—survey of Bamiyan caves and frescos. (Sites 100, 330, 508).
- Philip L. Kohl—survey in Panjshir and Nijrau-Tagau areas. (Sites 161, 281, 686, 773, 903, 1182, 1186, 1187, 1214).
- Ministry of Information/UNESCO—preservation of Herat monuments. (Site 428).
- Galina A. Pugachenkova, Afghan/Soviet Mission—excavations at Jiga Tepe. (Site 475).
- G. K. Rao, BIAS—preservation of the Minar-i Chakri. (Site 718).
- Viktor I. Sarianidi and Zemaryalai Tarzi, Afghan/Soviet Mission—excavations at Tilla Tepe. (Site 1192).
- Maurizio Taddei, IsMEO—excavations at Tepe Sardar. (Site 1180).
- Maurizio Taddei and Giovanni Verardi, IsMEO—survey Jaghuri, Muqqur, and Ab-i Istada areas. (Sites 125, 292, 343, 345, 353, 769, 902, 985, 1053, 1066, 1096, 1110, 1190).
- Zemaryalai Tarzi, AIA—excavations at Tepe Shutur, Hadda. (Site 404).
- William Trousdale, Smithsonian Institution—survey and excavations at Sar-o Tar. (Site 1006).
- A. V. Vinogradov, Afghan/Soviet Mission—survey of Stone Age sites in the north. (Sites 202, 203, 204, 910, 939, 965, 1012, 1101).

1977
- AIA—repair of the minarets at Ghazni. (Site 358).
- Ajan and Furughi, AIA—preservation of the arch at Bust. (Site 149).

- Paul Bernard, DAFA—excavations at Ai Khanoum. (Site 18).
- Warwick Ball—survey in Ghur and Herat area. (Sites 84, 95, 177, 267, 683, 742, 767, 787, 970, 987).
- T. Berthoud, R. Besenval, J. P. Carbonel, F. Cesbron, and J. Liszak-Hours, CNRS—geological survey of ancient mines. (Sites 19, 234, 372, 438, 696, 729, 780, 1003, 1058, 1084, 1255).
- Henri-Paul Francfort, DAFA—excavations at Dasht-i Qal'a and Shortughai. (Sites 268, 269, 1089).
- Jean-Claude Gardin, CNRS—survey in eastern Bactria. (Sites 54, 61, 89; 94, 115, 139, 162, 182, 209, 288, 307, 308, 321, 421, 440, 450, 487, 510, 511, 512, 513, 579, 580, 583, 611, 633, 643, 738, 741, 772, 799, 904, 909, 911, 917, 933, 936, 959, 1008, 1032, 1080, 1086, 1092, 1142, 1162, 1217, 1220, 1224, 1233).
- Svend Helms, BIAS—excavations at Kandahar. (Site 522).
- Ministry of Information/UNESCO—preservation of Herat monuments. (Site 428).
- G. K. Rao, BIAS—preservation of Guldarra, stupa. (Site 389).
- Viktor I. Sarianidi and Zemaryalai Tarzi, Afghan/Soviet Mission—excavations at Tilla Tepe. (Site 1192).
- Maurizio Taddei, IsMEO—excavations at Tepe Sardar. (Site 1180).
- Zemaryalai Tarzi, AIA—excavations at Tepe Shutur, Hadda. (Site 404).

1978
- AIA—repair of the minarets at Ghazni. (Site 358).
- Paul Bernard, DAFA—excavations at Ai Khanoum. (Site 18).
- Henri-Paul Francfort, DAFA—excavations at Shortughai. (Site 1089).
- Jean-Claude Gardin, CNRS—survey in eastern Bactria. (Sites 1, 5, 6, 28, 31, 40, 50, 70, 83, 134, 135, 136, 156, 160, 175, 187, 194, 208, 210, 215, 218, 220, 252, 386, 400, 412, 420, 444, 445, 446, 447, 462, 472, 484, 495, 505, 515, 516, 525, 553, 569, 587, 591, 594, 626, 640, 674, 750, 791, 797, 853, 892, 913, 927, 931, 937, 943, 960, 980, 981, 1007, 1019, 1090, 1128, 1132, 1235, 1253).
- Svend Helms, BIAS—excavations at Kandahar. (Site 522).
- Takayasu Higuchi and Shoshin Kuwayama, Kyoto University—excavations at Tepe Skandar. (Site 1185).
- Takayasu Higuchi and Akira Miyaji, Kyoto University—survey of caves and frescos at Bamiyan. (Site 100).
- Jonathan Lee, BIAS—survey in Maimana and Gurziwan areas. (Sites 248, 286, 362, 392, 490, 624, 1129).
- Ministry of Information/UNESCO—preservation of Herat monuments. (Site 428).
- G. K. Rao, BIAS—preservation of Guldarra stupa. (Site 389).
- Viktor I. Sarianidi and Zemaryalai Tarzi, Afghan/Soviet Mission—excavations at Tilla Tepe. (Site 1192).
- Rafi Samizay, Kabul University/UNESCO—survey of monuments in the Herat area. (Sites 66, 111, 212, 278, 346, 349, 373, 428, 532, 585, 634, 661, 947, 1259, 1263).
- Zemaryalai Tarzi, AIA—excavations at Tepe Shutur, Hadda (Site 404).
- Régis de Valence, DAFA—restoration of the shrine of Baba Hatim at Imam Sahib. (Site 439).

1979
- Henri-Paul Francfort, DAFA—excavations at Shortughai. (Site 1089).
- Ministry of Information/UNESCO—preservation of monuments in Herat. (Site 428).

- G. K. Rao, BIAS—preservation of the Guldarra monastery. (Site 389).
- Rafi Samizay, Kabul University/UNESCO—survey of monuments in the Herat area. (Sites—see under 1978).
- Zemaryalai Tarzi, AIA—excavations at Tepe Shutur, Hadda. (Site 404).
- Régis de Valence, DAFA—restoration of the shrine of Baba Hatim at Imam Sahib. (Site 439).

1994
- Jonathan L. Lee—surveys in the north. (Sites 41, 186).

1996
- Jonathan L. Lee—survey in north-west. (Sites 9, 248, 279, 286).

1996(?)
- DACAAR—repairs to roof of Gauhar Shad mausoleum and Pul-i Malan. (Site 428).

1997
- Jonathan L. Lee—reconnaissance in Andkhui. (Site 41).

2000
- Bruno and Akbari, Dept. of Historic Monuments—structural survey and conservation at Jam. (Site 468).

2002
- Lee, Society for South Asian Studies—survey in Bamiyan Province. (Sites 124, 189, 239, 286, 398, 489, 845, 1021, 1039, 2046, 2105, 2116, 2141, 2158, 2251).
- Taddei, IsIAO—survey and conservation work at Ghazni (Site 358).

2003
- Tarzi, French Ministry of Foreign Affairs/National Geographic—excavations at Bamiyan. (Site 100).
- Verardi, IsIAO—limited soundings at Tepe Sardar. (Site 1180).
- Taddei, IsIAO—survey and conservation work at Ghazni. (Site 358).
- Thomas, Pastori, Cucco, IsAIO/UNESCO—excavation and survey at Jam. (Site 468).

2004
- Fouache, Besenval, et al., DAFA—survey of Balkh oasis. (Sites 38, 99).
- Tarzi, French Ministry of Foreign Affairs/National Geographic—excavations at Bamiyan (Site 100).
- Taddei, IsIAO—survey and conservation work at Ghazni. (Site 358).
- Marquis, Adle, et al., DAFA—preservation and study of Haji Piyada. (Site 410).
- Grenet and Lee, DAFA—survey of Rag-i Bibi. (Site 2227).
- Paiman, AIA—excavations at Khana Sangi, Khwaja Safa, and Tepe Narenj. (Sites 555, 2138, 2268).

2005
- Thomas, Pastori, Cucco, IsAIO/UNESCO—excavation and survey at Jam. (Site 468).
- Besenval, Marquis, DAFA—excavations at Tepe Zargārān. (Site 99).
- Besenval, Marquis, and Franke, DAFA and DAI—excavations and architectural studies at Kuhandizh and Herat citadel. (Site 428).
- AKTC—preservation work at Gazurgah and Herat. (Sites 346, 428).

- Tarzi, French Ministry of Foreign Affairs/National Geographic—
  excavations at Bamiyan. (Site 100).
- Franke and Urban, DAI—survey of Herat region. (Sites 185,
  391, 212, 532, 2018, 2056, 2057, 2084, 2103, 2105, 2123,
  2128, 2148, 2173, 2179, 2183, 2221, 2247, 2248, 2255, 2264,
  2266).
- Marquis, Adle, *et al.*, DAFA—preservation and study of Haji
  Piyada. (Site 410).
- Paiman, AIA—excavations at Khana Sangi, Uryakhel, and Tepe
  Narenj. (Sites 555, 1222, 2268).

2006
- Besenval, Marquis, DAFA—excavations at Tepe Zargārān.
  (Site 99).
- Besenval, Marquis, and Franke, DAFA and DAI—excavations
  and architectural studies at Kuhandizh and Herat citadel.
  (Site 428).
- Tarzi, French Ministry of Foreign Affairs/National
  Geographic—excavations at Bamiyan. (Site 100).
- Lee—reconnaissance in north. (Site 186, 818).
- AKTC—preservation work at Gazurgah, Haji Piyada, and
  Herat. (Sites 346, 410).
- Marquis, Adle, *et al.*, DAFA—preservation and study of Haji
  Piyada. (Site 410).
- Paiman, AIA—excavations at Tepe Narenj. (Site 2268).

2007
- Marquis, DAFA—archaeological studies of Kābul Bālā Hisār.
  (Site 483).
- Besenval, Marquis, DAFA—excavations at Tepe Zargārān.
  (Site 99).
- Besenval, Marquis, and Franke, DAFA and DAI—excavations
  and architectural studies at Kuhandizh and Herat citadel. (Site
  428).
- Tarzi, French Ministry of Foreign Affairs/National
  Geographic—excavations at Bamiyan. (Site 100).
- Stevens, UNESCO/Norway Funds-in-Trust—conservation
  work on Gawharshad. (Site 428).
- AKTC—preservation work at Gazurgah, Haji Piyada, and
  Herat. (Sites 346, 410, 428).
- Paiman, AIA—excavations at Tepe Narenj. (Site 2268).

2008
- Stevens, UNESCO/Norway Funds-in-Trust—conservation
  work on Gawharshad. (Site 428).
- Besenval, Marquis, DAFA—excavations at Tepe Zargārān.
  (Site 99).
- Besenval, Marquis, DAFA—excavations at Chashma-i Shafa.
  (Site 186).
- Besenval, Marquis, and Franke, DAFA and DAI—excavations
  and architectural studies at Kuhandizh and Herat citadel. (Site
  428).
- Tarzi, French Ministry of Foreign Affairs/National
  Geographic—excavations at Bamiyan. (Site 100).
- AKTC—preservation work at Gazurgah, Haji Piyada, and
  Herat. (Sites 346, 410, 428).
- Paiman, AIA—excavations at Tepe Narenj. (Site 2268).

2009
- Stevens, UNESCO/Norway Funds-in-Trust—conservation
  work on Gawharshad. (Site 428).
- Besenval, Marquis, and Franke, DAFA and DAI—excavations
  and architectural studies at Kuhandizh and Herat citadel.
  (Site 428).
- AIA—excavations at Ainak. (Site 19).
- AKTC—preservation work at Gazurgah and Herat. (Sites 346,
  428).
- Paiman, AIA—excavations at Tepe Narenj. (Site 2268).

2010
- AIA—excavations at Ainak. (Site 19).
- AKTC—preservation work at Gazurgah and Herat. (Sites 346,
  328).
- Paiman, AIA—excavations at Tepe Narenj. (Site 2268).

2011
- AIA—excavations at Ainak. (Site 19).
- AKTC—conservation of main monuments at Balkh. (Site 99).
- AKTC—preservation work at Gazurgah and Herat. (Sites 346,
  428).
- Paiman, AIA—excavations at Tepe Narenj. (Site 2268).

2012
- AIA—excavations at Ainak. (Site 19).
- AKTC—conservation of main monuments at Balkh. (Site 99).
- AKTC—preservation work at Gazurgah and Herat. (Sites 346,
  428).
- ACHCO—assessment work at Jam. (Site 468).
- Paiman, AIA—excavations at Tepe Narenj. (Site 2268).

2013
- AIA—excavations at Ainak. (Site 19).
- AKTC—conservation of main monuments at Balkh. (Site 99).
- Paiman, AIA—excavations at Tepe Narenj. (Site 2268).

2014
- AIA—excavations at Ainak. (Site 19).
- AKTC—conservation of main monuments at Balkh. (Site 99).
- ACHCO—conservation of Shahzada Abdulla and Abdul
  Qasim mausolea at Herat. (Site 428).
- Paiman, AIA—excavations at Tepe Narenj. (Site 2268).

2015
- ACHCO—conservation assessment at Takht-i Rustam. (Site
  1135).
- ACHCO—conservation of Shahzada Abdulla and Abdul
  Qasim mausolea at Herat. (Site 428).

2016
- ACHCO—conservation assessment at Takht-i Rustam. (Site
  1135).
- ACHCO—conservation of Shahzada Abdulla and Abdul
  Qasim mausolea at Herat. (Site 428).

2017
- Noori, ACHCO and Oriental Institute Chicago—restoration
  work at Tepe Maranjan and Topdarra. (Sites 1173, 1197).

2018
- Noori, ACHCO and Oriental Institute Chicago—restoration
  work at Tepe Maranjan and Topdarra. (Sites 1173, 1197).

APPENDIX 4

Glossary

āb	water, stream	būs	kiss
ābdān	cistern	būt	idol
āhingarān	blacksmiths	buta	bush
ala'	high	būtgāh	temple
alaf	grass	buz	goat
alti	six	chādur	tent, veil
altin	gold	chāh	well
amīrān	princes	chahār	four
aq	white	chahārshanba	Wednesday
āragh, āriq	canal	chai	stream
asb	horse	chakmakh	flint
āsyā	mill	chakri	wheel
bābā	father	chaman	field
bacha	child	chapar	enclosure
bād	wind	chār	four
badām	almond	chāsh	noon
bād-i āysā	windmill	chashma	spring
bād-i sah	windmill	chaupān	shepherds
bādqāq	dry wind	chehel	forty
bāgh	garden	cheheltān	forty heads
bāghak	small garden	chīnī	Chinese
baghal	edge	chirāgh	lamp
bai	beg, chief	chūb	wood
bājgāh	tollhouse	chughūr	deep
bakhsh	part	chūl	desert
bālā	upper, high	chung	depression
banādir	port	da	article
band	dam, mountain range	dāgh	hill, hot
barbara	barbarian	dagh	barren
barkhān	sand dunes	daghal	fake
beg	chief	dahan	mouth
begum	lady	dāman	skirt
bīni	spur	damb	tail, mound
bish	five	dandān	teeth
bīyābān	desert	darāz	long
buland	high	darband	gorge
bulāq	spring	dargāh	threshold, gate
bulut	oak	darra	valley
burj	tower	darwāza	gate

darwīsh	holy man	hauz	cistern
daryā	river	hazār	thousand
darz	crack	hazrāt	exalted
dasht	plain	hisār	fort, citadel
dast	hand	hokūmati	district
daulat	state, wealth	imām	saint
dāwar	judge, ruler	istāda	standing
deh	village	īwān	portal
dīnār	coin	jā	place
dirāz	long	jabal	mount, hill
dīv	demon	jadīd	new
dīwāl, dīwār	wall	jalāb	pendant
dūāb	confluence	jangal	forest
dukhtar	maiden	jangalak	small forest
dūn	lower	jar	ravine, stream
duzd	robber	jarīb	area of land
effendi	gentleman	jūi	canal
falaq	split	jum'a	Friday
fīlkhāna	elephant-house	kadu	marrow
funduq	hazel	kāfir	pagan
gāh	place	kaftār	hyena
gai	ox	kāk	cistern
gala	flock	kaka	slave
gardān	whirling	kalān	large
gardāu	whirlpool	kam	slight, rim
garmāb	hot spring	kamar	cliff
gau	cow	kand	fort, blunt
gaud	depression	kappa	hat
gaza	tamarisk	kārīz	underground canal
ghāl	hole	khair	wealth, goodness
ghār	cave, mountains	khaista	beautiful
ghulām	slave	khāk	dust
ghulāmān	slaves	khām	raw
ghulghula	whirling, bubbling	kham	bent
ghundai, ghundi	mound	khān	lord
gibar	pagan	khāna	place, house
girdi	round	khāniqāh	Islamic monastery
gudār	ford	kharāba	ruins
gūdūl	pit	khawāl	natural cave
gul	flower	khaz'	cutting
gumbaz, gunbad	dome	khazana	hoard, treasure
gūr	tomb	khēl	tribal place
gusfand	sheep	khisht	mud-brick
guzār, guzar	ford, passage	khud	god
hāji	pilgrim	khūja	saint
hāmūn	lake	khumdān	repository

khumri	dove	pahlawān	strong man
khūr	mouth, channel	pai	foot
khurd	small	pā'in	lower
khushk	dry	paisa	money
khwāja	saint	pakhsa	mud (walls)
kiz	maiden	palang	leopard
kot	fort, house	panj	five
kotal	pass	paryāna	ancient
kuchi	nomad	pīr	elder, saint
kuh	mountain	pista	pistachio
kuhna	old	piyāda	pedestrian
kupruk	bridge	pul	bridge
kūshk	palace, kiosk	push	behind
kūt	fort, house	pusht	back
lalma, lalmi	unirrigated cultivation	pūst	hide
lar	meagre	pūza	spur
lār	pass	qabristān	cemetery
lashkar	soldiers	qal'a	fort
lūli	entertainer	qalandari	nomadic
madar	mother	qand	sugar
māhi	fish	qaq	dry
malakh	locust	qara	black
malik	chief	qarāwal	guard
manār	tower	qarya	village
mār	snake	qasr	palace
markaz	centre	qishlāq	winter camp
mashhad	holy	qiz	maiden
masjid	mosque	qizil	red
mazār	grave	quduq	well
mihr	light	qūl	glen, gully
min	thousand	qurghān	tumulus, fort
mingbashi	head of a thousand	rabāt	caravanserai, fort
minār	minaret	rāh	way, road
mīr	chief	rīg, rīgān	sand
nahr	canal	rūd	river
nakhchir	ibex	rūdbār	river system
namak	salt	rustāq	farm
naqshi	decorated	sabz	green, grass
nau	new	safīd	white
nawā	ravine, stream	sahīb	gentleman
nīmrūz	noon	samūch	caves
nūkar	servant	sang, sangi	stone
nukri	silver	sar	head, face
obeh	water	sarai	caravanserai
pā, pai	foot	sardāba	cistern
pādshāh	king	sayad, sayyid	saint

seh	three		tāq	arch
sehshanba	Monday		tāsh	stone
shāh	king		tepe	mound
shāhidān	martyrs		tikar	piece, sherds
shahr	city		tillā	gold
shaikh	chief, saint		tope	stupa
shaila	hollow, valley		toprakkale	earth fort
shākh	branch		tūp	stupa, cannon
shamshir	sword		tūpchi	gunner
shan, shand	gravel		tūr	black
sharīf	noble		ūch	three
shikān	break		ulya	upper
shīr	lion, milk		urta	middle
shish	six		utāq	room
shūr	salty		wairān	ruined
shutur	camel		wakīl	governor
siāh	black		walang	grassy place
sitāra	star		wali	governor
sna	green, blue		wazīr	minister
spīn	white		yakh	ice
sra	red		yan	new
sufla	lower		yangi	new
sūm	caves		yarik	split
surkh	red		yass	mourning
tagau	valley		zaitūn	olive
tāgh	tamarisk		zar	gold
tāj	crown		zard	yellow
takht	platform, throne		zargarān	goldsmith
talā	gold		zindān	prison
tan	head, body		zīrra	cumin
tang	narrow		ziyārat	shrine
tangi	ravine			

APPENDIX 5

Subject Index

SUBJECT BIBLIOGRAPHY

This classification system is based on the 'Afghanistan-Thesaurus' by the Foundation Bibliotheca Afghanica, Bubendorf, Switzerland. This was developed in the 1980s by Afghan and European specialists specifically for Afghan Studies. It has been slightly modified for the present use.

SUBJECT CLASSIFICATION

1.0 General
1.1 Bibliographies
1.41 Gazetteers
1.42 General books on Afghanistan
1.44 Picture books
1.52 Maps and atlases
1.61 General guide books
1.62 Route reports
1.64 Travel, pre-1914
1.65 Travel, 1915–1945
1.66 Travel, 1946–1973
1.67 Travel, 1974–2001
1.68 Travel, 2002–
1.83 Museums, catalogues, and archaeological exhibitions

2.0 Natural Sciences
2.1 Geography
2.2 Geology and mines

4.1 Archaeology
4.11 Excavation reports
4.111 Survey reports
4.112 General works and summaries
4.115 Restoration and conservation
4.116 Destruction and looting
4.12 Prehistory
4.121 Protohistory
4.13 Iron Age/Achaemenid

4.14 Hellenistic
4.15 Kushan
4.16 Gandharan/Buddhist
4.17 Hunnic/Shahi
4.18 Islamic, pre-1221
4.19 Islamic, post-1221

4.2 Numismatics and Epigraphy
4.21 Numismatics—general reports
4.211 Achaemenid numismatics
4.212 Greek numismatics
4.213 Saka, Indo-Parthian, and Roman numismatics
4.214 Kushan numismatics
4.215 Sasanian and Kushano-Sasanian numismatics
4.216 Hunnic numismatics
4.217 Shahi numismatics
4.218 Islamic numismatics, pre-1221
4.219 Islamic numismatics, post-1221
4.23 Glyptic
4.24 Epigraphy—general reports
4.241 Petroglyphs
4.242 Cuneiform
4.243 Greek
4.244 Aramaic and Prakit
4.245 Kharoshthi and Pahlavi
4.246 Bactrian
4.247 Sanskrit
4.248 Hebrew
4.249 Arabic and Persian

BIBLIOGRAPHY

1. General

1.1 Bibliographies
Akram 1947
Arbeitsgemeinschaft Afghanistan and Deutsches Orient-Institut 1968
Ball 1982a
Bleaney, Gallego, and Vogelsang 2006
Creswell 1961
Deydier 1950
Kern Institute 1928–72
Mairs 2011b
McLachlan and Whitaker 1982

Srivastava 1978–9
Srivastava 1980
Stwodah and Modarissi 1978
Wilber 1968

1.41 Gazetteers
Ball 1982a
Ball 1982b
Ball 2008
Gazetteer 1907–14
Gazetteer 1972–80
MacGregor 1871

Provisional Gazetteer of Afghanistan 1975
Qāmūs-i Jughrāfiyyi Afghānistān 1956–60
Shokoohy 1984

1.42 General books on Afghanistan
Ball 2008
Caspani and Cagnacci 1951
Dollot 1937
Dupree 1978
Fouchet 1931
Hamilton 1906
Holdich 1910
Kābul Times 1970
Raverty 1878
Sālnāma 1933/34 (1312)
Sālnāma 1936/37 (1315)
Sālnāma 1937/38 (1316)
Sālnāma 1939/40 (1318)
Sālnāma 1934/35 (1313)

1.44 Picture books
Atkinson 1842b
Auboyer 1968
Cambon and Jarrige 2006
Cambon and Jarrige 2007
Hill and Grabar 1967
Jackson 1842
Kessel 1959
Masson 1833c
Niedemeyer and Diez 1924

1.52 Maps and atlases
Afghanistan 1:100,000 1960
Afghanistan 1:100,000 1967
Afghanistan 1:100,000 1968–1970
Afghanistan, Iran, Pakistan, USSR Quarter Inch 1941–53
Gazetteer 1972–80
Schwartzenberg 1978

1.61 General guidebooks
Afghan 1930
Caspani 1946c
Dupree, N. H. 1967a
Dupree, N. H. 1967b
Dupree, N. H. 1971a
Dupree, N. H. 1977
Ghawwas 1969
Hackin, J. and R. 1934
Kohzad 1950a
Kohzad 1955/56 (1334)
Wolfe 1966

1.62 Route reports
Akbar Khan and Ata Muhammad 1891
Akbar Khan 1891
Amir Khan and Shahzada Taimus 1888a

Amir Khan and Shahzada Taimus 1888b
Amir Khan and Shahzada Taimus 1888c
Amir Khan 1888
Broadfoot 1884
Browne 1879
Campbell 1880
Clifford 1879
Drummon 1888
Griesbach 1888a
Griesbach 1888b
Griffith 1879
Hira Singh 1891
Holdich 1881a
Holdich 1881b
Holdich 1887
Imam Sharif 1888
Imam Sharif 1891a
Imam Sharif 1891b
Leach 1880
Maitland and Drummond 1888
Maitland 1879
Maitland 1888a
Maitland 1888b
Maitland 1891
Maitland 1897
Maitland, Drummond, and Strachey 1889
Merk 1888
Merk 1891
Peacocke 1885a
Peacocke 1887a
Peacocke 1887b
Peacocke 1887c
Raverty 1878
Ridgeway 1888
Sahibdad Khan 1888
Sahibdad Khan 1891a
Sahibdad Khan 1891b
Shahzada Taimus 1888
Shamsuddin Khan 1888

1.64 Travel, pre-1914
Abbott 1884
Ashe 1881
Atkinson 1842a
Bellew 1862
Bellew 1874
Burnes 1834a
Burnes 1843
Conolly 1834
Conolly 1837
Conolly 1841
Court 1836
Eyre 1857
Ferrier 1857
Gardiner 1853

Gerard 1833
Griffith 1847
Grodekoff 1880
Holdich 1901
Honigberger 1852
Jewett 1948
Kennedy 1840
Khanikoff 1861
Lal 1846
Le Mesurier 1880
Lee 1991
MacGregor 1879
MacGregor 1882
Maitland 1888a
Maitland 1888b
Masson 1839
Masson 1840
Masson 1842
Moorcroft and Trebeck 1841
Olufsen 1904
Peacocke 1887
Smith 1876
Tate 1909
Vambery 1864
Vigne 1837
Vigne 1840
Wood 1872
Yate C. E. 1888
Yate, A. C. 1887
Yavorski 1885

1.65 Travel, 1915–1945
Byron 1937
Caspani 1946a
Emanuel 1939
Fox 1943
Jewett 1948
Niedemeyer and Diez 1924
Trinkler 1928

1.66 Travel, 1946–1973
Balsan 1972a
Balsan 1972b
Gardner 1971
Hill 1966
Klimburg 1958
Klimburg 1960
Kohzad 1951–4
Matheson 1961
Stark 1970
Zestovski 1948
Zestovski 1949

1.67 Travel 1974–2001
Wannell 2002

1.68 Travel 2002+
Stewart 2004

1.83 Museums, catalogues, and archaeological exhibitions
Barrett and Pinder-Wilson 1967–8
Bopearachchi, Landes, and Sachs 2003
Cambon and Jarrige 2006
Cambon and Jarrige 2007
Du Colombier 1929
Dupree, N. H., Dupree, L., and Motamedi 1974
Foucher 1929
Franke 2008
Franke and Müller-Wiener 2016
Ghosh 1945
Godard 1925a
Gray 1936
Grousset 1929
Gullini 1960
Gullini 1961
Hamada 1929
Hiebert and Cambon 2008
Jenkins 1968
Kalus 1979
Kohzad 1954
Migeon 1929b
Mizuno 1964
Monod 1966
Monod-Brühl 1939
Motamedi 1972
Rowland and Rice 1971
Rowland 1966a
Royal Academy 1931
Shakur 1946
Tissot and Darbois 2002
Tissot 2006

2 Natural Sciences

2.1 Geography
Anderson 1849
Balland 1976
Belenitski 1945
Bernard and Francfort 1978a
Campbell 1880
Codrington 1944
Donini 1972
Fouache and Besenval 2012
Fussman 1966
Gardin and Gentelle 1976
Gardin and Gentelle 1979
Gentelle 1977
Gentelle 1978
Gentelle 1989
Holdich 1885
Holdich 1886
Kaye 1879

Kieffer 1975
Kohzad 1956b
Koshkaki 1923/24
Le Strange 1905
Lumsden 1885
MacGregor 1871
MacMahon 1897
MacMahon 1906
Markham 1876
Naïmi 1949
Rawlinson 1842
Rawlinson 1872
Rawlinson 1873
Rawlinson 1885
Samizay 1974
Scheibe 1937
Snead 1978
Thomas and Kidd 2017
Thomas et al. 2006

2.2 Geology and mines
Barthoux1933b
Berthoud 1978
Berthoud, Besnenval, Carbonel, Cesbron, and Liszak-Hours
    1977
Courtois 1962–3
De Lapparent and Desparmet 1973
Griesbach 1888a
Griesbach 1888b
Kohzad 1948b
Kulke 1976
Lindberg 1949
Lindberg 1961
Lord 1838
Merkel, Bräutigam, Klein, and Hauptmann 2013
Nasiri 1962–6
Thomalsky, Bräutigam, Karaucak, and Kraus 2013

4.1 Archaeology

4.11 Excavation reports
Annen 2011
Barthoux 1930a
Barthoux 1933a
Bernard and Guillaume 1985
Bernard and Rapin 1980
Bernard 1964
Bernard 1976b
Bernard 1980
Bernard et al. 1973
Bernard et al. 1976
Bernard et al. 1980
Bernard, Besenval, and Jarrige 2002
Bernard, Besenval, and Marquis 2006

Bloch 2015
Bombaci 1959
Buchel 1997
Cambon 1996
Carl and Hackin 1959
Carl 1959a
Carl 1959b
Carl 1959c
Carl 1959d
Casal 1954a
Casal 1954c
Casal 1961
Coon and Coulter 1955
Dales 1977a
Dupree 1951
Dupree 1963
Dupree et al. 1972
Dupree, Lattman, and Davis 1970
Dupree 1958a
Engel 2011
Fischer 1983a
Fischer 1983b
Foucher 1942–7
Francfort and Le Berre 1976
Francfort 1983
Francfort 1984
Francfort 1989
Franke 2015
Fussman and Guillaume 1990
Garczynski 1980
Gardin 1957a
Gardin 1963
Ghirshman 1939
Ghirshman 1946
Grenet, Liger, and de Valence 1980
Guillaume and Rougeulle 1987
Guillaume 1983
Guillaume, Liger, and de Valence 1980
Hackin and Carl 1936
Hackin 1937
Hackin 1939a
Hackin 1954a
Hackin 1954b
Hackin 1959b
Hackin 1959d
Hackin et al. 1954
Helms 1979
Helms 1982
Helms 1997
Higuchi 1974a
Higuchi 1978
Higuchi and Kuwayama 1970
Higuchi, Kuwayama, and Yamada 1971
Jacquet 1836b

Jacquet 1837
Jacquet 1839
Kābul Times 1979b
Kolb 1977
Kruglikova 1973a
Kruglikova 1974
Kruglikova 1977a
Kruglikova 1977d
Kruglikova 1984
Kruglikova 1986
Kruglikova *et al.* 1976
Kruglikova *et al.* 1979
Kruglikova and Sarianidi 1971b
Kruglikova and Sarianidi 1971c
Kuwayama 1972b
Kuwayama 1974a
Kuwayama 1978
Kuwayama 1980
Kuwayama and Momono 1976
Le Berre and Schlumberger 1964
Le Berre 1965
Le Berre 1970
Lecuyot 2013
Leriche 1986
Leshnik 1967
McNicoll and Ball 1996
McNicoll 1978
Marquis 2013
Masson 1841
Massoudi 2011
Matson 1957
Meunié 1942
Meunié 1954
Meunié 1959c
Meunié1959a
Meunié1959b
Mustamandi 1968a
Mizuno and Fujita 1968
Mizuno and Odani 1968
Mizuno 1968
Mustamandi 1969b
Mustamandi 1969–70
Mustamandi 1971
Mustamandi 1973
Mustamandi 1974b
Mustamandi, S. and Mustamandi, M. 1967/68a
Mustamandi, S., and Mustamandi, M. 1967/68b
Mustamandi, S., and Mustamandi, M. 1969
Paiman and Alram 2010
Paiman and Alram 2013
Paiman 2005
Paiman 2008
Pugachenkova 1979b
Puglisi 1963

Rainey 1953
Rapin 1992
Sarianidi 1972a
Sarianidi 1974b
Sarianidi 1976
Sarianidi 1979b
Sarianidi 1984
Sarianidi 1985
Sarianidi 1989
Schlumberger 1946
Schlumberger 1948
Schlumberger 1949c
Schlumberger 1949d
Schlumberger 1952c
Schlumberger 1954d
Schlumberger 1955d
Schlumberger 1957b
Schlumberger 1961b
Schlumberger 1964c
Schlumberger 1964d
Schlumberger 1978
Schlumberger, Le Berre, and Fussman 1983
Schlumberger and Sourdel-Thomine 1978
Shaffer 1978a
Shaffer, Callender, and Rodriguez 1973
Shaffer and Hoffman 1971
Sikandarpūr 1980
Sourdel-Thomine 1978
Taddei and Verardi 1978
Taddei and Verardi 1985
Taddei 1969a
Tarzi 1976a
Tarzi 1977d
Tarzi 2003
Tarzi 2012
Tarzi, N. 2006
Thomas 2004a
Thomas, Pastori, and Cucco 2005
Thoraval 1980
Veuve 1987
Veuve, Liger, and de Valence 1980
Whitehouse 1976
Whitehouse 1978
Young 1954
Young 1955

4.111 Survey Reports
Aalund 1990
Amiri 1973
Amiri 1979
Azizi 1980
Baker and Allchin 1991
Bākhtar 1966
Barger 1938

Barger 1939a
Barger 1939b
Barger 1944
Barger and Wright 1941
Bernard and Francfort 1978a
Brett 1970
Caspani 1947b
Coon 1957
Dales 1972
Davis 1974
Davis and Dupree 1977
De Cardi 1950
de la Vaissière and Marquis 2013
De Laessöe, Talbot, and Simpson 1886
Dupree 1960
Dupree 1976
Dupree and Davis 1976
Dupree and Howe 1963
Fairservis 1952
Fairservis 1961
Fairservis 1971
Fischer 1958b
Fischer 1960
Fischer 1961a
Fischer 1961b
Fischer 1961d
Fischer 1964
Fischer 1967a
Fischer 1969
Fischer 1969–70
Fischer 1970b
Fischer 1971a
Fischer 1971b
Fischer 1971c
Fischer 1973b
Fischer 1973c
Fischer 1973d
Fischer and Mauelshagen 1984
Fischer, Lonsdale, Owen, and Purver 1959
Fischer, Mauelshagen, and Thewalt 1976
Fischer, Mauelshagen, and Tonnessen 1976
Fischer, Morgenstern, and Thewalt 1974–76
Foucher 1942-7
Franke and Urban 2006
Fussman 1966
Fussman 1974b
Fussman 1974c
Fussman, Murad, and Olivier 2008
Gaibov, Košalenko, and Trebeleva 2010
Gardin 1959
Gardin 1977
Gardin 1979
Gardin 1980
Gardin 1981

Gardin 1995
Gardin 1998
Gardin and Gentelle 1976
Gardin and Lyonnet 1978–79
Gentelle 1977
Gentelle 1978
Gentelle 1989
Godard Godard, and Hackin 1928
Gouin 1973a
Grenet, Lee, and Pinder-Wilson 1980
Hackin and Carl 1933
Hackin 1959a
Hackin 1959c
Hammond 1970
Hayashi and Sahara 1962
Herberg 1973
Holdich 1887
Kalb 1973
Kluyver 2000
Knobloch 1981
Kohl 1978
Kohzad 1941–54
Kohzad 1950b
Kruglikova and Mustamandi 1970
Kruglikova and Sarianidi 1971b
Kruglikova and Sarianidi 1976
Kruglikova 1973b
Kruglikova 1984
Kyoto University Archaeological Mission 2003
Le Berre 1987
Lee and Sims-Williams 2003
Lee 1980
Lee 1982
Lee 2006
Lyonnet 1997
Maricq and Wiet 1959
Marquis 2013
McBurney 1972
McMahon 1906
Masson 1833a
Masson 1842
Mizuno 1962
Mizuno 1967
Mizuno 1971
Mizuno and Higuchi 1967
Mizuno and Nishikawa 1962
Mock 2011
Mock 2016
Mouchet and Blanc 1972
Muroga 1972
Pugachenkova 1970
Pugachenkova 1976b
Puglisi 1962
Ramachandran and Sharma 1956

Sarianidi 1977b
Sarianidi 1977c
Schroeder 1936
Shakur 1947
Simpson 1879–80
Stein 1904
Stein 1928
Swinnerton 1879
Taddei 1974b
Taddei 1975
Taddei 1976
Talbot, Maitland, and Simpson 1886
Tarzi 2003
Tate 1910
Thomas and Kidd 2017
Thomas, Kidd, Nikolovski, and Zipfel 2008
Thompson 1964
Trousdale 1976a
Trousdale 1976b
Verardi and Paparatti 2004
Verardi 1977a
Verardi 1977c
Verardi 2007
Vinogradov 1979
Wheeler 1947
Wilber 1937
Woodburn 2009

4.112 General works and summaries

Alessio, Bachechi, and Cortesi 1967
Allchin 1957
Allchin and Hammond 1978
Alram and Klimburg-Salter 1999
Alram, Klimburg-Salter, Inaba, and Pfisterer 2010
Altheim and Rehork 1969
Aruz and Fino 2012
Asimov and Bosworth 1998
Auboyer 1938
Auboyer 1960
Auboyer 1968
Ball 2008
Ball and Harrow 2002
Baumer 2012
Baumer 2014
Bendezu-Sarmiento 2015
Besenval and Rassouli 2010
Bivar 1988
Bopearachchi 2015
Bopearachchi and Boissac 2005
Bopearachchi, Landes, and Sachs 2003
Bosch 1958
Bosworth 1971
Bussagli 1962a
Cambon and Jarrige 2006

Cambon and Jarrige 2007
Cassar and Noshadi 2015
Coningham and Young 2015
Courtois 1961
Deshayes 1977
Dupree, L. 1958a
Dupree, N. H. 1974
Dupree, N. H. 1977
Errington and Cribb 1992
Errington and Curtis 2007
Fergusson 1876
Filigenzi and Giunta 2009
Fleming 1978
Foucher 1928
Foucher 1942–7
Francfort 1976
Francfort 1979a
Francfort *et al.* 2014
Franke 2008
Franke 2015
Frifelt and Sorenson 1989
Frumkin 1957
Fussman 1996
Gail 1998
Gardin 1982
Geoffroy-Schneiter 2001
Gilles 2000
Gorshenina and Rapin 1991
Grenet 1979
Grenet 1981
Grenet 1984
Grenet 1998
Gullini 1960
Habibi 1968
Hackin 1932b
Hackin 1933
Hackin 1934
Hackin 1938a
Hackin 1938b
Hackin 1938c
Hammond 1973
Härtel 1981
Hillenbrand 1984
Invernizzi 1995
Jarrige 1992
Jodidio 2017
Knobloch 2002
Kohl 1982
Kohl 1984
Kohl 2007
Kohzad 1953b
Kohzad 1954
Kohzad 1955c
Kohzad, M. N. 1959

Kouremenos, Chandrasekaran, and Rossi 2011
Kruglikova 1976
Kruglikova 1979
Leriche 1973
Ligabue and Salvatore 1989
Mairs 2011b
Mairs 2014a
Mandelshtam 1954
Masson and Sarianidi 1969
Michaud and Barry 1996
Motamedi, A. H. 1967
Motamedi, H. 1975c
Motamedi, H. 1976
O'Kane 1987
Olivier-Utard 1997
Petersen 1996
Possehl 1993
Prinsep 1858
Pugachenkova 1963
Rowland and Rice 1971
Schimmel 1984
Schlumberger 1947a
Schlumberger 1949b
Schwartzenberg 1978
Sidky 2000
Sidqi 1952
Simpson 2012
Sims-Williams 2002
Srivastava 1980
Staviskij 1986
Taddei 1972b
Taddei 1979
Talbot Rice 1965
Trousdale 1975
Van Krieken-Pieters 2006
Van Lohuizen-de Leeuw and Ubaghs 1974
Vogel 1939
Vogelsang 2002
Wightman 2007
Yoshikawa 1944
Zaryab 1974b

4.115 Restoration and conservation

Abassi 2016
Abbasi 2015
Aga Khan Trust for Culture 2006
Bihdād 1981
Bouchenaki 2015
Bruno 1962
Bruno 1976
Bruno 1979
Butcher 1956
Cassar and Noshadi 2015
de Valence 1979
de Valence 1983
Deshpande 1974
Deshpande 1975b
Firūzi 1979
Furughi 1981
Galdieri 1978
Gazzola and Perrin 1971
Golombek 2016
Hansen 1971
Hansen 1974
Jawād 1979
Jawād 1980
Jodidio 2017
Kabul Times 1975
Kabul Times 1976a
Kabul Times 1976b
Kabul Times 1977a
Kabul Times 1977b
Kabul Times 1979a
Lal 1973
Le Berre 1973
Le Berre 1978
Lézine 1964
Lin and de Leon Wheeler 2011
Najimi 1988
Orazi 1977
Petzet 2009
Petzet 2015
Rao, Pinder-Wilson, and Ball 1985
Rau 1979
Samizay 1981
Sengupta 1971
Sengupta 1972
Sengupta 1973
Sengupta 1976
Stevens 2015
Suzuki and Aoki 2004
Suzuki and Aoki 2005
Taniguchi 2007
Thapar 1979
Tirard-Collet 1998
UNESCO 1980
Zander 1972

4.116 Destruction and looting

Ambers, Cartright, et al. 2014
Bopearachchi 2002
Flood 2002a
Lauricella, Cannon, Branting, and Hammer 2017
Lewis 2000
Margotinni 2009
Passmore et al. 2012

Thomas and Gascoigne 2006
Thomas 2004b

4.12 Prehistory
Allchin 1953
Allchin and Allchin 1982
Angel 1972
Bābak 1980
Boulanger, Davis, and Glascock 2012
Chakrabarti 1990
Coon 1957
Coon and Coulter 1955
Coon and Ralph 1955
Dales 1973a
Davis 1969–70
Davis 1974
Davis 1978
Davis and Dupree 1977
Dupree 1960
Dupree 1964
Dupree 1967
Dupree 1968a
Dupree 1968b
Dupree 1969
Dupree 1972
Dupree 1975
Dupree 1976
Dupree *et al.* 1972
Dupree and Davis 1972
Dupree and Davis 1976
Dupree and Howe 1963
Dupree, Lattman, and Davis 1970
Gupta 1979
Hiebert 1994
Jacobsen 1979
Kohl 1977
Kohl 1978b
Kohl 1982
Kohl 1984
Kohl, Biscione, and Ingraham 1982
Lyonnet 1981
McBurney 1972
Marshak 1972
Maxwell-Hyslop 1982
Micheli 2009
Micheli 2013
Perkins 1972
Pottier 1980
Pottier 1984
Puglisi 1963
Sarianidi 1977c
Shaffer 1976
Solem 1972

Srivastava 1979b
Vinogradov 1979
Zāhir 1980

4.121 Protohistory
Allchin 1995
Amiet 1977
Bernard and Francfort 1979
Besenval and Francfort 1994
Biscione and Tosi 1979
Biscione 1977
Caley 1972a
Caley 1972b
Casal 1952
Casal 1954a
Casal 1954b
Casal 1955a
Casal 1955b
Casal 1956
Casal 1957
Casal 1961
Casal 1964b
Casal 1965a
Casal 1969
Chowdhury 1963
Dales 1965
Dales 1968
Dales 1971
Dales 1972
Dales 1973a
Dales 1973b
Dales 1974
Dales 1977b
Dales 1977c
Dales 1985
Dales and Flam 1969
Davis-Kimball 2000
Deshayes 1977
Dupree 1963
Dupree 1981
Dupree *et al.* 1972
Dupree and Kolb 1972
Dupree, Gouin, and Omer 1971
Fairservis 1952
Fairservis 1953
Falkner 1954–6
Francfort 1979b
Francfort 1981a
Francfort 1981b
Francfort 1983
Francfort 1984
Francfort 2015
Francfort and Pottier 1978

Gardin 1981
Gardin 1995
Gouin 1969
Gouin 1973a
Gouin 1974
Gupta 1979
Herrman 1970
Jacobsen 1979
Jettmar 1978
Kohl 1984
Libby 1953
Lyonnet 1977
Matson 1963
Meadow 1973
Mendez 1966
Motamedi, A. A. 1975
Motamedi, A. A. 1979
Motamedi, A. A. 1980
Noorzai 1979
Pollack 1977b
Poulain 1966
Qadriyān 1980
Sankalia 1980
Sarianidi 1968
Sarianidi 1971
Sarianidi 1972b
Sarianidi 1974a
Sarianidi 1976
Sarianidi 1977a
Sarianidi 1977b
Sarianidi 1977c
Sarianidi 1979b
Shaffer 1971
Shaffer 1974
Shaffer 1976
Shaffer 1978a
Shaffer 1978b
Srivastava 1978–9
Srivastava 1979b
Thornton 1963
Tosi 1977
Tosi 1979
Tosi and Wardak 1972

4.13 Iron Age/Achaemenid
Azizi 1969/70
Bernard and Francfort 1979
Bernard 1974c
Casal 1961
Cattenat and Gardin 1976
Dales 1977a
Francfort 1975
Gardin 1981
Gardin 1995

Ghirshman 1939
Grenet 2002b
Kruglikova 1977c
Mac Dowall and Taddei 1978a
Mairs 2014b
Pichikyan and Judelson 1998
Pugachenkova 1976b
Sarianidi 1972a
Sarianidi 1976
Sarianidi 1977a
Sarianidi 1977b
Sarianidi 1977c

4.14 Hellenistic
Balika 1976
Bernard 1966
Bernard 1967a
Bernard 1967b
Bernard 1968a
Bernard 1968b
Bernard 1969
Bernard 1970a
Bernard 1970b
Bernard 1971a
Bernard 1971b
Bernard 1972a
Bernard 1972b
Bernard 1973a
Bernard 1973b
Bernard 1973c
Bernard 1973d
Bernard 1973e
Bernard 1973f
Bernard 1974a
Bernard 1974b
Bernard 1974c
Bernard 1975a
Bernard 1976a
Bernard 1976b
Bernard 1977a
Bernard 1977b
Bernard 1978b
Bernard 1978c
Bernard 1979a
Bernard 1979b
Bernard 1980a
Bernard 1981
Bernard 1982a
Bernard 1982b
Bernard 1982c
Bernard 1999
Bernard 2003
Bernard and Le Berre 1973
Bernard and Liger 1976

Bernard, Gouin, and Le Berre 1973
Bernard, Le Berre, and Stucki 1973
Berthoud 1978
Boardman 1992
Boardman 1994
Boardman 2012
Bopearachchi 2001
Bopearachchi 2003
Bopearachchi 2005
Bopearachchi 2007
Buchel 1997
Buhler 1958b
Carl 1959b
Caspani 1946a
Colledge 1987
Daffinà 1967
De Lapparent and Desparmet 1973
Foucher 1939b
Francfort 1973
Francfort 1977
Francfort and Liger 1976
Garczynski 1980
Gardin 1970
Gardin 1971
Gardin 1973
Gardin 1975
Gardin and Lyonnet 1976
Gouin 1973b
Grenet 1980b
Grenet 1982
Grenet 1983a
Guillaume 1979
Guillaume, Liger, and de Valence 1980
Holt 2012b
Humayun 1973
Janin 1978
Kouremenos, Chandrasekaran, and Rossi 2011
Kruglikova 1973a
Kruglikova and Sarianidi 1971a
Kuwayama 1969
Lane Fox 1980
Lawn 1974
Lecuyot 2007
Leriche 1974a
Leriche 1974b
Leriche 1976
Leriche and Thoraval 1979
Leriche, Rougeulle, and Ghassouli 1980
Lerner 2011
Lerner 2003–4
Lerner 2010
Liger 1979
Mac Dowall and Taddei 1978a
Mairs 2008

Mairs 2011a
Mairs 2011b
Mairs 2013
Mairs 2014a
Mairs 2015
Martinez-Sève 2010
Martinez-Sève 2014
Martinez-Sève 2015
Mustamandi 1968c
Nāsir 1971
Pollack 1977a
Pollack 1977c
Pugachenkova 1974a
Pugachenkova 1974b
Rapin 1979
Rapin 2003
Rohr 1980
Schlumberger 1965
Schlumberger 1967
Schlumberger 1970
Schlumberger and Bernard 1965
Sedov 1984
Shenkar 2011
Sidky 2000
Staviski 1973
Sultan 1978
Thoraval 1980
Veuve 1982
Veuve and Liger 1976
Veuve and Liger 1980
Veuve, Liger, and de Valence 1978
Wheeler 1978
Wolski 1982

4.15 Saka and Kushan

Adriani 1955
Agrawala 1970
Agrawala 1976
Ali 1964
Ambers, Cartright, *et al.* 2014
Auboyer 1948
Auboyer 1953
Auboyer 1954
Auboyer 1955–6
Auboyer 1971
Azimi 1979
Azizi 1976
Ball 1997
Barnett 1968
Basham 1968
Bernard 1987
Bernard and Francfort 1979
Bertrand 1958
Boardman 1992

Boardman 1994
Boardman 2003a
Boardman 2003b
Boardman 2012
Bopearachchi 2000b
Brill 1972a
Brill 1972b
Brown 2003
Buri 1976
Buri 1979
Bussagli 1949
Bussagli 1955–6
Bussagli 1962c
Bussagli 1968
Canepa 2015
Carl 1959a
Carl 1959c
Carter 2006
Chakrabarti 1981
Coarelli 1961
Coarelli 1962
Coarelli 1963
Courtois 1959
Davidson 1971
Davidson 1972
de la Vaissière, Marquis, and Bendezu-Sarmiento 2015
Delacour 1993
Desbordes, Rapin, and Cambon 2003
Dobbins 1968a
Dobbins 1968b
Dolgorukov 1974
Dussubieux and Gratuze 1991
Dussubieux, Gratuze, and Bernard 2003
Elisséeff 1954
Errington 2017a
Errington 2017b
Foucher 1939a
Foucher 1954
Francfort 2012
Gafurov 1974
Gangoly 1937–8
Gerard 1834
Ghirshman 1943–5
Ghirshman 1946
Ghirshman 1953
Ghirshman 1957
Gill 1991
Göbl 1964
Grenet 1983b
Grenet 2005
Grenet, Lee, Martinez, and Ory 2007
Hackin 1926
Hackin 1937
Hackin 1939/40

Hackin 1939a
Hackin 1939b
Hackin 1940a
Hackin 1940b
Hackin 1940c
Hackin 1946
Hackin 1950a
Hackin 1951
Hackin 1954a
Hackin 1954b
Hackin 1959b
Hackin *et al.* 1954
Hallade 1962a
Hamelin 1952
Harper 1981
Iourkevich 1974
Irwin 1979
Jacquet 1836b
Jacquet 1837
Jacquet 1839
Jettmar 1959–60
Kato 1979
Katsuno 1959
Kieffer 1961
Kieffer 1962
Kohzad 1938/39
Kohzad 1952/53
Kohzad 1953c
Kohzad 1953d
Kohzad 1953e
Kohzad 1954/55
Kohzad 1956a
Kruglikova 1974
Kruglikova 1976
Kruglikova 1977a
Kruglikova 1977b
Kruglikova 1977d
Kruglikova 1978
Kruglikova 1979
Kruglikova and Sarianidi 1971b
Kumar 1973
Kurz 1954a
Kurz 1954b
Kuwayama 1969
Kuwayama 1991
Kuwayama 1997
Kuwayama 2010
Lantier 1951
Lazard, Grenet, and de Lamberterie 1984
Le May 1943
Lee and Grenet 1998
Leidy 2012
Lo Muzio 1999
Lyonnet 1998

Mac Dowall and Taddei 1978b
Mairs 2012
Maricq 1968
Mehendale 1996
Mehendale 2012
Menninger 1996
Meunié 1954
Meunié 1959a
Meunié 1959b
Motamedi, H. 1971a
Mukherjee 1967
Mustamandi 1969a
Mustamandi 1972
Nehru 2004
Odani 2005
Omar 1949
Picard 1956
Pugachenkova 1974a
Pugachenkova 1976b
Pugachenkova 1979a
Pulatov 1974
Rogers 1952
Rosen Stone 2008
Rosenfield 1967
Roshan 1962
Rowland 1964a
Sarianidi 1979a
Sarianidi 1985
Sarianidi 1989
Schaeffer 1942
Schippmann 1971
Schlumberger 1952b
Schlumberger 1952c
Schlumberger 1953a
Schlumberger 1953b
Schlumberger 1954a
Schlumberger 1954b
Schlumberger 1954c
Schlumberger 1954d
Schlumberger 1955a
Schlumberger 1955c
Schlumberger 1955d
Schlumberger 1957a
Schlumberger 1959
Schlumberger 1960a
Schlumberger 1960b
Schlumberger 1961a
Schlumberger 1961b
Schlumberger 1964a
Schlumberger 1964d
Schlumberger 1970
Schlumberger 1967
Sidqi 1975
Simpson 2011a

Sivaramurti 1971
Sokolovsky 1979
Srivastava 1979c
Staviski 1977
Staviskij 1986
Stern 1954
Stwodah 1980
Sultan 1978
Takahama 1981
Tarzi 1977b
Tarzi 1999–2000
Tarzi 2000
Time 1979
Tucci 1939
Van Lohuizen de Leeuw 1949
Wheeler 1949
Wheeler 1955
Whitehouse 1989a
Whitehouse 1989b
Whitehouse 1991
Whitehouse 2012
Zafar 1979
Zeymal 1999
Zhang 2011
Zhelninskaya, Berlin, Druzhina, and Buri 1979

4.16 Gandharan/Buddhist
Ali 1961
Allchin, Allchin, Kreitman, and Errington 1997
Anand 1971a
Anand 1971b
Annen 2011
Antonini 1979a
Antonini 1979b
Asian Art 2005
Auboyer 1969
Azizi 1969/70
Azizi 1981
Bachhofer 1925
Bachhofer 1929
Bachhofer 1931a
Bachhofer 1931b
Bachhofer 1932
Ball 1976
Barthoux 1928
Barthoux 1929
Barthoux 1930a
Barthoux 1930b
Barthoux 1930c
Barthoux 1933a
Bernard 1964
Bernard and Jullien 1982
Bivar 1954b
Bivar 1971

Boardman 1994
Breshna 1972
Brown 2003
Bruno 1972
Buhler 1958a
Buhot 1927
Bulliet 1976
Burnes 1833
Burnes 1934b
Bussagli 1953a
Bussagli 1953b
Bussagli 1956–7
Bussagli 1962b
Bussagli 1962c
Bussagli 1963
Bussagli 1968
Cambon 1996
Carl 1959d
Carl and Hackin 1959
Carter 1997
Caspani 1945
Caspani 1947a
Caspani 1948
Cnningham 1841
Combaz 1935
Compareti 2008
Coomaraswamy 1926–7
Courtois 1962–3
Cribb 2017
Dagens 1964a
Dagens 1964b
Dagens, Le Berre, and Schlumberger 1964
Dallapiccola 1980
De Marco 1983
Deshpande 1975a
Deydier 1949–50
Deydier 1950
Dobbins 1970
Dorneich 1968
Du Colombier 1929
Duccoeur 2012
Dupree, N. H. 1967b
Dupree, N. H. 1971b
Errington 2017a
Errington 2017b
Fabri 1931
Faticoni 2014
Filigenzi 2009a
Filigenzi 2009b
Fischer 1956
Fischer 1957
Fischer 1958a
Fischer 1959a
Fischer 1959b

Fischer 1961c
Fischer 1966
Fischer 1967b
Fischer 1974a
Fischer 1976
Fischer 1980
Fischer 1987
Foucher 1906–22
Foucher 1924
Foucher 1929
Franz 1977–8
Franz 1978
Frye 1946a
Fujita 1866a
Fujita 1966b
Fujita 1971
Fussman 1974a
Fussman and Le Berre 1976
Fussman, Murad, and Ollivier 2008
Gaulier, Jera-Bezard, and Mailard 1976
Geoffroy-Schneiter 2001
Gettens 1938
Godard, Godard, and Hackin 1928
Goshal 1928
Gray 1936
Green 2017
Grenet 1980a
Grenet 1994
Grenet, Lee, and Pinder-Wilson 1980
Grousset 1929
Grousset 1930
Gullini 1971
Hackin 1928a
Hackin 1928b
Hackin 1932a
Hackin 1935a
Hackin 1959a
Hackin, and Bruhl 1933
Hackin and Carl 1933
Hackin, J., and R. 1934
Hallade 1962a
Hallade 1962b
Hallade 1964–5
Hallade 1968
Hallade and Hinz 1978
Hamada 1929
Hayden 1910
Higuchi 1969
Higuchi 1972
Higuchi 1974b
Higuchi 1976
Higuchi and Kuwayama 1970
Iwade and Kubudera 2012
Jongeward, Errington, Salomon, and Baums 2012

Kabul Times 1978
Kamāl 1979
Khairzada 2015
Klimburg-Salter 1989
Klimburg-Salter 1993
Klimburg-Salter 2006
Klimburg-Salter 2008
Kohzad 1944/45a
Kohzad 1955/56
Kohzad 1955a
Kohzad 1958/59
Kohzad 1950a
Kostka 1974
Kurita 2003
Kuwayama 1973
Kuwayama 1974b
Kyoto University Archaeological Mission 2003
Lal 1971
Leshnik 1967
Lévêque 1974
Lézine 1962
Lézine 1964
Mac Dowall and Taddei 1978b
Maeda 2006
Makino 1957
Masson 1833b
Masson 1834b
Masson 1836d
Matsumoto 1929
Meunié 1943–5
Meunié 1959c
Migeon 1929a
Migeon 1929b
Miyaji 1976a
Miyaji 1976b
Miyaji 1978
Miyaji 1980
Miyaji 2012
Mizuno 1962
Mizuno 1967
Mizuno 1968
Mizuno 1971
Mizuno and Fujita 1968
Mizuno and Higuchi 1967
Mizuno and Nishikawa 1962
Mizuno and Nishikawa 1967
Mizuno and Odani 1968
Morgenstern 1935
Motamedi, A. A. 1978
Motamedi, H. 1975a
Motamedi, H. 1975b
Motamedi, H. 1977
Motamedi, H. 1978b
Motamedi, H. 1980

Mustamandi 1968a
Mustamandi 1968b
Mustamandi 1969b
Mustamandi 1971
Mustamandi 1973
Mustamandi 1974a
Mustamandi 1974b
Mustamandi 1979–70
Mustamandi, S., and M. 1967/68a
Mustamandi, S., and M. 1967/68b
Mustamandi, S., and M. 1969
Narain 1991
Nehru 1989
Okamoto 1935
Omland 2006
Pandit 1927
Pandit 1929
Peter 1963
Pigou 1841
Plaeschke 1971
Prinsep 1838
Quagliotti 2012
Rhie 1976
Rowland 1936
Rowland 1938
Rowland 1946
Rowland 1947
Rowland 1953
Rowland 1961
Rowland 1964
Rowland 1966b
Rowland 1971
Rowland 1972
Rowland 1974
Rowland and Coomaraswamy 1938
Sadakata 1971
Scerrato 1960
Schlumberger 1971
Seckel 1964
Shaffer and Hoffman 1971
Shaffer and Hoffman 1976
Shahrani 1973
Sharma 2011
Shoten 2006a
Shoten 2006b
Simpson 1879–80
Simpson 1879a
Simpson 1881
Simpson 1882
Simpson 1893
Soper 1949–50
Stadtner 2000
Strzygowski 1930–2
Swinnerton 1879

Taddei 1974c
Taddei 1979b
Talbot, Maitland, and Simpson 1886
Tanabe 1973
Tarzi 1973
Tarzi 1976/77
Tarzi 1976a
Tarzi 1976b
Tarzi 1977a
Tarzi 1977c
Tarzi 2004
Tissot 1976
Tissot 1980
Tissot 2003
Trebeck 1834
Tsuchiya 2000
Tucci 1968
Ushikawa 1972
Verardi 1975
Verardi 1977a
Verardi 1977b
Verardi 1984
Veuve 1974
Yoshikawa 1941
Yoshikawa 1949
Yoshikawa 1964
Yoshikawa 1976
Zafar 1973
Zaryab 1974a
Zaryab 1976
Zwalf 1996

4.17 Hunnic-Shahi
Adamesteanu 1960
Agrawala 1968
Antonini 1979a
Antonini 1979b
Asian Art 2005
Baker and Allchin 1991
Ball 1984
Barrett 1957
Bernard and Grenet 1981
Casal 1954c
Caspani 1946b
Castaldi 1963
Dhavalikar 1971
Dorneich 1999
Duccoeur 2012
Dupree 1956
Dupree 1957
Dupree 1958a
Dupree 1958b
Edelberg 1957
Edelberg 1960

Filigenzi 2009a
Filigenzi 2009b
Fischer 1959a
Fischer 1960
Fischer 1961c
Fischer 1964
Fischer 1966
Fischer 1971b
Fischer 1972
Flood 2007
Frye 1946a
Frye 1946c
Fussman 1974b
Ghirshman 1948
Gingnoux 2003
Goetz 1957
Grenet 2002a
Habibi 1972
Hackin 1935c
Hackin 1936a
Hackin 1936b
Hackin 1950
Hackin 1959d
Hackin 1940d
Hackin and Carl 1936
Hackin and Rowland 1971
Hallade 1962b
Henkl 1952
Higuchi 1974a
Holdich 1896
Iwade and Kubudera 2013
Klimburg-Salter 1989
Klimburg-Salter 1993
Klimburg-Salter 2006
Klimburg-Salter 2008
Klimburg-Salter 2010
Kohzad 1944//45
Kohzad 1946/47
Kohzad 1949b
Kohzad 1953a
Kohzad 1955/56–56/57
Kohzad 1955b
Kuwayama 1972a
Kuwayama 1974a
Kuwayama 1976
Kuwayama 1978
Kuwayama 1980
Kuwayama 1991
Kuwayama 19972b
Kuwayama and Momono 1976
Le Berre 1987
Mac Dowall and Taddei 1978b
Maeda 2007
Maeda 2015

Marguier 2012
Matson 1958
Momii 2007
Morgan 2012
Motamedi, H. 1971b
Paiman 2010
Paiman and Alram 2013
Petech 1964
Rahman 1979
Scerrato 1967
Schlumberger 1955b
Schlumberger 1964c
Sharqi 1980
Srivastava 1979a
Taddei 1967
Taddei 1968
Taddei 1969a
Taddei 1969b
Taddei 1970a
Taddei 1970c
Taddei 1971
Taddei 1972a
Taddei 1973
Taddei 1974a
Taddei 1978
Taddei 1999
Taddei 1970b
Taddei and Verardi 1978
Taddei and Verardi 1981a
Taddei and Verardi 1981b
Tarzi 1975
Tarzi 1978
Van Lohuizen de Leeuw 1959
Verardi 1977b
Verardi 1984
Verardi 2010

4.18 Islamic, pre-1221
Abassi 2015
Achak 1970
Adamesteanu 1960
Adamesteanu 1960
Adle 2011
Adle 2015a
Adle 2015b
Allegranzi 2014
Allegranzi 2015
Amiri 1973
Amiri 1979
Anand 1970
Aziz 1964
Balland 1976
Bihdād 1981
Bivar 1966

Boissier 1963
Bombaci 1957
Bombaci 1959
Bombaci 1961
Bombaci 1962
Bruno 1962
Bruno 1963
Bruno 1979
Casal, G 1978
Casimir and Glatzer 1971a
Casimir and Glatzer 1971b
Crane and Trousdale 1972
Creswell 1927
Davary 1975
Davary 1978
Desai 1975
Diez 1923
Diez 1936
Diez 1950
Donini 1972
Dupree 1956
Dupree 1957
Dupree 1958b
Ettinghausen and Michaud 1976
Fairservis 1950
Fischer 1966
Fischer 1969–70
Fischer 1970a
Fischer 1971a
Fischer 1971b
Fischer 1972
Fischer 1973a
Fischer 1973e
Fischer 1974a
Fischer 1974b
Fischer 1976
Fischer 1978a
Fischer 1978c
Flury 1918
Flury 1925
Francfort 1978
Furughi 1981
Galdieri 1978
Gardin 1957b
Gardin 1963
Ghūriyāni 1971
Glatzer 1973
Glatzer 1980
Gnoli 1967
Godard 1925a
Godard 1951
Godard and Godard 1936
Golombek 1969b
Golombek 1977

Golombek 2016
Habibi 1977
Habibi 1980
Herberg 1973
Herberg 1978
Herberg and Davary 1976
Herrman 1965
Hill and Grabar 1967
Hill 1966
Husain Shah 1954
Husain Shah 1962
Hutt 1974
Hutt 1977
Jalali 1972
Janata 1971
Kästner 1968
Kieffer 1960b
Klimburg 1960
Klimburg 1963
Kohzad 1948a
Kohzad 1949a
Kohzad 1951
Kohzad 1953
Kohzad 1957
Kohzad, M. N. 1949
Le Berre 1970
Le Berre 1978
Le Berre 1981
Le Strange 1905
Lee 1980
Leshnik 1968
Mandersloot 1959
Maricq and Wiet 1959
Maricq 1959
Matson 1958
Mayer 1956
Melikian-Chirvani 1968
Melikian-Chirvani 1969a
Melikian-Chirvani 1970
Melikian-Chirvani 1972
Melikian-Chirvani 1974
Melikian-Chirvani 1975a
Melikian-Chirvani 1975b
Melikian-Chirvani 1977
Moline 1975
Motamedi, H. 1972
Motamedi, H. 1978a
Naïmi 1949
Otto-Dorn 1964
Pinder-Wilson 1980
Pinder-Wilson 2001
Pope 1935
Pope 1938
Pugachenkova 1968a

Pugachenkova 1975
Pugachenkova 1978
Rafat 1980
Rahīq 1980
Rawlinson 1843
Reuther 1973
Rogers 1973
Samizay 1981
Scarcia and Taddei 1973
Scerrato 1959
Scerrato 1961
Scerrato 1962a
Scerrato 1971a
Scerrato 1971b
Schlumberger 1949a
Schlumberger 1949e
Schlumberger 1950
Schlumberger 1951
Schlumberger 1952a
Schlumberger 1978
Schlumberger and Gardin 1978
Schlumberger and Sourdel-Thomine 1978
Schroeder 1936
Schroeder 1938
Sīstānī 1967
Sourdel and Sourdel 1968
Sourdel-Thomine 1953
Sourdel-Thomine 1956
Sourdel-Thomine 1959
Sourdel-Thomine 1960
Sourdel-Thomine 1978
Sourdel-Thomine 1971
Sourdel-Thomine and Spuler 1973
Taddei 1967
Taddei 1979a
Trousdale 1964
Trousdale 1965a
Vercellin 1972
Vercellin 1976a
Vercellin 1976b
Vincent 1979
Whitehouse 1976
Zhwandun 1974

4.19 Islamic, post-1221

Aalund 1990
Abassi 2016
Afghān 1930
Allen 1983
Anand 1970
Azad 2013
Ball 1981
Behrens and Klinkott 1973
Belenitski 1945

Bruno 1976
Butcher 1956
Byron 1935a
Byron 1935b
Byron 1938
Caroe 1973
Chaghatai 1970
Crowe 1978
English 1973
Erffa 1946
Fischer 1970a
Fischer 1971a
Fischer 1971b
Fischer 1973a
Fischer 1974b
Fischer 1978b
Fischer 1978c
Fischer 1983a
Fischer 1983b
Fischer, Mauelshagen, and Tonnessen 1976
Franke 2008
Franke and Müller-Wienr 2016
Frye 1946b
Frye 1948
Gardin 1957a
Gaube 1977
Ghawwās 1969
Ghawwās 1974
Golombek 1969a
Golombek 1983
Golombek and Wilber 1988
Grube 1974
Hariri 1939
Herawi 1968
Herawi 1970
Hill and Grabar 1967
Hillenbrand 1984
Hoag 1968
Hoag 1972
Itemadi 1946
Itemadi 1953
Jawād 1979
Jawād 1980
Khanikoff 1860
Klimburg 1963
Klinkott 1982
Lal 1834
Le Strange 1905
Lee 1996
Lee 1998
Lentz 1996
Lézine 1963–64
McChesney 1991a
McChesney 1991b

Melikian-Chirvani 1969b
Melikian-Chirvani 1982b
Michaud and Barry 1996
Mukhtarov 1980
Mustamandi 1967
Nāhiz 1978
Najimi 1982
Najimi 1988
O'Kane 1984b
O'Kane 1985
O'Kane 1987
O'Kane 2000
O'Kane 2002
O'Kane 2009
O'Kane 2011
Orazi 1977
Pope 1938
Pugachenkova 1968a
Pugachenkova 1968b
Pugachenkova 1969
Pugachenkova 1969–70
Pugachenkova 1970
Pugachenkova 1976a
Pugachenkova 1979c
Pugachenkova and Khakimov 1972
Rafat 1980
Rahīq 1980
Reha 1980
Royal Academy 1931
Sālik 1979
Samizay 1981
Schimmel 1984
Schroeder 1936
Seljuki 1962/63
Seljuki 1967a
Shokoohy 1983
Stuckert 1980
Subtelny 1997
Wāla 1980
Wilber 1937
Wolfe 1966
Woodburn 2009
Yate 1887

4.2 Numismatic and Epigraphy

4.21 Numismatics—general reports
Alram and Klimburg-Salter 1999
Alram, Klimburg-Salter, Inaba, and Pfisterer 2010
Bopearachchi 1991a
Bopearachchi 1999a
Bopearachchi 2015
Codrington 1904
Curiel and Schlumberger 1953

Errington 2001
Errington 2017a
Errington 2017b
Fussman and Guillaume 1990
Hackin 1935b
Hoernle 1889
Kritt 2015
Mac Dowall 1978
Mac Dowall 1979
Mac Dowall and Ibrahim 1978
Masson 1834a
Masson 1836a
Masson 1836c
Rapson 1904
Tate 1904
Wilson 1841

4.211 Achaemenid numismatics
Bivar 1954c
Bivar 1982
Hulin 1954
Schlumberger 1953c

4.211 Greek, Graeco-Bactrian, and Indo-Greek numismatics
Audouin and Bernard 1973
Audouin and Bernard 1974
Bernard 1975b
Bernard 1979c
Bernard and Guillaume 1980
Bernard and Guillaume 1985
Bernard and Rapin 1980
Bivar 1951
Bivar 1954c
Bivar 1954d
Bivar 1955a
Bivar 1965
Bivar 1972
Bopearachchi 1991b
Bopearachchi 2000a
Cunningham 1840
Cunningham 1842
Cunningham 1846
Curiel and Fussman 1965
Curiel and Schlumberger 1953
Guillaume 1991
Haughton 1948
Hay 1840
Holt 1999
Holt 2012a
Holt 2012b
Jenkins 1959
Le Rider 1973
Lerner J. D. 2011

Mac Dowall 2005
Mac Dowall and Wilson 1960
Narain 1957
Narain 1968
Petito-Biehler 1975
Prinsep 1836a
Rapin 1979
Schlumberger 1953
Torrens 1840
Whitehead 1923
Whitehead 1940–50

4.213 Saka, Indo-Parthian, and Roman numismatics
Avdall 1836
Bivar 1981a
Bivar 1981b
Bopearachchi 2013
Cunningham 1854
Cunningham 1879
Cunningham 1890
Curiel and Schlumberger 1953
Hoernle 1879
Jacquet 1836a
Jenkins 1955
Kohzad 1947/48
Mac Dowall 1965
Prinsep 1836b
Scerrato 1962b
Simpson 1879b

4.214 Kushan numismatics
Bopearachchi 1999b
Bopearachchi 2008
Bopearachchi 2013
Cunningham 1889
Cunningham 1892
Koshalenko and Sarianidi 1992
Mac Dowall 1968a
Mac Dowall 1968c
Mac Dowall 1974
Narain 1968
Vainberg and Kruglikova 1976

4.215 Sasanian and Kushano-Sasanian numismatics
Bivar 1983
Curiel 1953
Curiel and Gyselen 1983
Mochiri 1983
Nikitin 1995

4.216 Hunnic numismatics
Alram 2000
Alram and Pfisterer 2010
Cunningham 1894
Ghirshman 1948

Göbl 1961
Göbl 1967
Paiman and Alram 2010
Vondrovec 2007
Vondrovec 2008

4.217 Shahi numismatics
Ghose 1952
Mac Dowall 1968b
Rahman 1979

4.218 Islamic numismatics, pre-1221
Bivar 1968
Bivar 1975
Gardin 1963
Kalus 1979
Sourdel 1963–64

4.23 Glyptic
Bivar 1955b
Chapman 1841
Conolly 1840
Lerner 2009
Tate 1904
Torrens 1842

4.24 Epigraphy—general reports
Alram and Klimburg-Salter 1999
Alram, Klimburg-Salter, Inaba, and Pfisterer 2010
Bernard, Grenet, and Rapin 1980
Buddruss and Davary 1980
Davary 1977
Davary 1981
Davary 2003
Fussman 1994
Habibi 1971

4.241 Petroglyphs
Agresti 1970
Bivar 1971
Bourgeois 1971
Castaldi 1963
Dor 1976
Gratzl, Kostka, and Patzeli 1976
Mock 2011
Mock 2016
Trousdale 1965b

4.242 Cuneiform
Fisher and Stolper 2015
Hulin 1954
Torrens 1842
Trousdale 1968

4.243 Greek
Alsdorf 1960
Altheim and Stiehl 1959b
Altheim 1959–61

Benveniste 1964
Bernard and Rougemont 2003
Bernard, Pinault, and Rougemont 2004
Clarysse and Thompson 2007
Eggermont and Hoftijzer 1962
Fraser 1979
Fraser 1982
Fussman 1980
Gallavotti 1959a
Gallavotti 1959b
Grenet 1996
Kosambi 1959
Lerner 2011
Mairs 2015
Norman 1972
Perkins and Braidwood 1947
Rapin 1983
Rapin 1996
Rea, Senior, and Hollis 1994
Robert 1968
Rougemont 2012a
Rougemont 2012b
Scerrato 1958a
Scerrato 1958b
Scerrato, Pugliese Carratelli, and Garbini 1964
Scerrato, Pugliese Carratelli, and levi Della Vida 1958
Schlumberger 1947b
Schlumberger 1964b
Schlumberger and Benveniste 1967
Schlumberger, Robert, Dupont-Sommer, and Benveniste 1958
Zucker 1959

4.244 Aramaic and Prakit
Ahang 1969–70
Alsdorf 1960
Altheim 1947
Altheim 1959–61
Altheim and Stiehl 1958
Altheim and Stiehl 1959a
Altheim and Stiehl 1959b
Altheim and Stiehl 1959c
Benveniste and Dupont-Sommer 1966
Bernard, Grenet, and Rapin 1980
Birkeland 1938
Bogolyubov 1973
Bourgeois 1971
Caillat 1966
Davary and Humbach 1974
Dupont-Sommer 1966
Dupont-Sommer 1970
Eggermont and Hoftijzer 1962
Henkelman, Wouter, and Folmer 2016
Henning 1949
Humbach 1971

Humbach 1973
Itō 1977
Kosambi 1959
Mairs 2016
Naveh and Shaked 2012
Scerrato 1958a
Scerrato, Pugliese Carratelli, and Garbini 1964
Scerrato, Pugliese Carratelli, and Levi Della Vida 1958
Schlumberger, Robert, Dupont-Sommer, and Benveniste 1958
Shaked 1969
Shaked 2003
Zucker 1959

4.245 Kharoshthi and Pahlavi
Ahang 1968
Allon 2001
Allon and Salomon 2000
Bayley 1861
Bivar 1976
Deydier 1949–50
Dowson 1863
Fussman 1969
Fussman 1970
Fussman 1974c
Grierson 1913
Hultzsch 1919
Humbach 1968b
Konow 1929
Konow 1935
Konow 1938
Lüders 1909
Masson 1836b
Mitra 1861
Pargita 1921
Pargiter 1912
Pargiter 1914
Salomon 1999
Senart 1890
Senart 1894
Senart 1914
Shakur 1946
Thomas, E. 1863
Thomas, F. W. 1915

4.246 Bactrian
Ahang 1968
Altheim and Stiehl 1957
Benveniste 1961
Bivar 1963
Bivar 1976
Bivar 1954a
Brandenstein 1961
Curiel 1954
Davary and Humbach 1976

Davary 2012
Falk 2001
Falk 2009
Fussman 1977
Fussman 1994
Fussman 1998
Gershevitch 1963
Gershevitch 1966
Gershevitch 1967
Gershevitch 1979
Gershevitch 1980
Göbl 1965
Göbl 1966
Habibi 1963/64a
Habibi 1963/64b
Habibi 1969/70b
Habibi 1974
Hansen 1964
Harmatta 1964
Harmatta 1965
Henning 1956
Henning 1960
Henning 1965
Humbach 1960
Humbach 1961a
Humbach 1961b
Humbach 1962
Humbach 1963
Humbach 1966–7
Humbach 1967
Humbach 1968a
Kieffer 1960a
Kosambi 1968
Lee and Sims-Williams 2003
Livshits 1976
Livshits 1979
Livshits and Kruglikova 1979
Mac Dowall 2002
Maricq 1958
Mayrhofer 1962
Mekarska 1974
Mukherjee 1964
Rahman 1979
Rezakhani 2010
Sims-Williams 1973
Sims-Williams 1991
Sims-Williams 1998
Sims-Williams 1998
Sims-Williams 1999
Sims-Williams 2000
Sims-Williams 2000/2012
Sims-Williams 2001
Sims-Williams 2002b
Sims-Williams 2005

Sims-Williams 2007a
Sims-Williams 2007b
Sims-Williams 2008
Sims-Williams 2010
Sims-Williams 2012a
Sims-Williams 2012b
Sims-Williams 2015
Sims-Williams and Cribb 1996
Sims-Williams and de Blois 1998
Sims-Williams and Falk 2014

4.247 Sanskrit
Braavig 2000–2
de la Vaissière 2007
Falk 2001
Kohzad 1944/45b
Levi 1932
Melzer 2006
Pauly 1967
Rahman 1979
Sircar 1963
Taddei 1970b
Tucci 1958
Vogel 1911
Vorobieva-Desyatovskaya 1976
Yamada 1972

4.248 Hebrew
Asmussen 1973
Bruno 1963
Dupont-Sommer 1946
Fischel 1949
Frye 1954
Gnoli 1962
Gnoli 1963
Gnoli 1964
Henning 1957
Hunter 2009a
Hunter 2009b
Hunter 2010
Lintz 2015

Rapp 1965
Rapp 1967
Rapp 1971
Rapp 1973
Rapp 1974/75
Shaked 1982
Shaked 2010
Stern 1949

4.249 Arabic and Persian
Allegranzi 2015
Attar 1976
Bivar 1977
Bombaci 1966
Combe, Sauvaget, and Wiet 1936
Combe, Sauvaget, and Wiet 1954
Crane and Trousdale 1972
Flury 1918
Flury 1925
Giunta 2003
Giunta 2012
Godard 1936
Habibi 1969–70a
Herawi 1970
Horowitz 1913
Lal 1834
Riza and Humayun 1977
Riza 1967
Sauvaget 1946
Scarcia 1963
Scarcia 1966
Schneider 1984
Seljuki 1967a
Seljuki 1967b
Seljuki 1973
Sourdel-Thomine 1956
Sourdel-Thomine 1978
Yate 1887
Yate 1926

GENERAL BIBLIOGRAPHY

(Numbers in parentheses at the end of entries refer to sites in the catalogue.)

Abbreviations

AA	*Arts Asiatiques*
AAH	*Acta Antiqua Academiae Scientiarum Hungaricae*
ABC	Afghan Boundary Commission
ABIA	*Annual Bibliography of Indian Archaeology*
AJA	*American Journal of Archaeology*
AMI	Archälogische Mitteilungen aus Iran
Annali	Instituto Orientale di Dapoli. Annali
BAI	*Bulletin of the Asia Institute*
BAIPAA	*Bulletin of the American Institute for Persian Art and Archaeology*
BEFEO	*Bulletin de l'Ecole Française d'Extrême Orient*
BSOAS	*Bulletin of the School for Oriental and African Studies*
CAC I	Michael Alram and Deborah E. Klimburg-Salter (eds), *Coins, Art and Chronology: Essays on the Pre-Islamic History of the Indo-Iranian Borderlands*. Vienna, 1999.
CAC II	Michael Alram, Deborah Klimburg-Salter, Minoru Inaba, and Matthias Pfisterer (eds), *Art and Chronology, II. The First Millennium* C.E. *in the Indo-Iranian Borderlands*. Vienna, 2010.
CRAI	*Comptes-rendus de l'Acadêmie des Inscriptions et Belles-lettres*
EI	*Encyclopaedia of Islam*
EW	*East and West*
FAKh	*Fouilles d'Aï Khanoum*
ILN	*Illustrated London News*
JA	*Journal Asiatique*
JASB	*Journal of the Asiatic Society of Bengal*
JISOA	*Journal of the Indian School of Oriental Art*
JNSI	*Journal of the Numismatic Society of India*
JRAS	*Journal of the Royal Asiatic Society*
JRCAS	*Journal of the Royal Central Asian Society*
JRGS	*Journal of the Royal Geographical Society*
JRIBA	*Journal of the Royal Institute of British Architects*
MDAFA	*Mémoires de la Délégation Archéologique Française en Afghanistan*
NC	*Numismatic Chronicle*
OAZ	*Ostasiatische Zeitschrift*
PASB	*Proceedings of the Asiatic Society of Bengal*
PRGS	*Proceedings of the Royal Geographical Society*
RAA	*Revue des Arts Asiatiques*
RCHIA	*Recent Cultural Heritage Issues in Afghanistan*
REI	*Revue des Etudes Islamiques*
RGS	Royal Geographical Society
SAA	*South Asian Archaeology*
SRAA	*Silk Road Art and Archaeology*
TRIBA	*Transactions of the Royal Institute of British Architects*
ZDMG	*Zeitschrift der Deutschen Morgenländischen Gesellschaft*

Aalund, Flemming. 1978. 'The Road to Paradise Goes through Herat'. In *Islamic Cairo: Architectural Conservation and Urban Development of the Historic Centre*. Ed. Michael Meinecke, 87–90. Cairo. (428)

Aalund, Flemming. 1990. *Draft Up-dated Inventory of Historic Monuments, Herat Province, Afghanistan*. Report prepared for the Government of Afghanistan by UNESCO. Paris. (66, 111, 212, 278, 428, 634)

Abassi, Abdul Ahad. 2015. 'Minarets and Mughal Gardens: Projects Undertaken and Supported by DoHM for the Preservation of Historical Monuments, 2002–2012'. In *Keeping History Alive: Safeguarding Cultural Heritage in Post-Conflict Afghanistan*. Ed. Brendan Cassar and Sara Noshadi, 216–20. Paris and Kabul. (212)

Abassi, A. Ahad, ed. 2016. *Conservation at Kuhandiz, Herat*. Afghan Cultural Heritage Consulting Organization. Kabul. (428)

Abbot, James. 1884. *Narrative of a Journey from Heraut to Khiva, Moscow and St. Petersburg*. 2 vols. London. (1206)

Achak, Bayazit. 1970. 'Shāh-i Mashhad'. *Āryānā*, 28/6: 56–62. (1023)

Adamesteanu, D. 1960. 'Notes sur le site archéologique de Ghazni'. *Afghanistan*, 15/1: 21–30. (358, 1171, 1180)

Adle, Chahryar. 2011. 'La mosquée Hâji Pijâda/Noh Gonbad à Balkh, en Bactriane. Afghanistan. Un chef-d'oeuvre construit en 178–179/794–795 par Fazl le Barmacide?'. *CRAI* 155/1. Reprinted in L. Golombek et al., *The Nine Domes of the Universe*, 201–61. Bergamo, 2016. (410)

Adle, Chahryar. 2015a. 'Trois mosquées du debut de l'ère islamique au Grand Khorassan: Bastam, Noh-Gonbadan/Haji-Piyadah de Balkh et Zuzan d'après des investigations archéologiques'. In *Greater Khorasan: History, Geography, Archaeology and Material Culture*. Ed. Rocco Rante, 89–114. Berlin. (410)

Adle, Chahryar. 2015b. 'Noh Gonbadân Hâji Piyâda Mosque, and Architectural Chef-d'oeuvre in Balkh Considered as a Potential World Heritage Landscape'. In *Keeping History Alive: Safeguarding Cultural Heritage in Post-Conflict Afghanistan*. Ed. Brendan Cassar and Sara Noshadi, 120–33. Kabul and Paris. (410)

Adriani, Achille. 1955. 'Segnalazioni alessandriae: Le scoperte di Begram e l'arte alessandrina'. *Archaeologia Classica*, 7: 124–38. (122)

Afghān, Khalil. 1930. *Asār-i Herāt*. Kabul. (428, 468, 819)

Afghanistan 1:100,000. 1960. Stereo-topographic survey of 1958. Maps 117F, 118D–F, 122F, 123B, 123D–F, 124A–F, 211D–F, 212C, 212E, 213C–F, 214C, 214E–F, 215E–F, 216C–F, 217A–F, 218B, 218D–E, 219A–F, 220A–F, 221A–D, 222A–D, 223A–B, 224A–D, 313F, 314C–F, 315C–F, 319A–B, 320A–B, 321A, 402C–F, 403C–F, 404A–F, 405A–D, 406A–B, 407F, 408A–F, 410A, 413 B, 414A–B, 415A–B.

Afghanistan 1:100,000. 1967. Ministry of Mines, Fairchild Aerial Surveys, surveyed 1957–9. Maps 221E–F, 222E–F, 223C–F, 224E, 405E–F, 406C–F, 410B–F, 411A–F, 418A–F, 419B, 419D, 419F, 420A–F, 424A–F, 501A–F, 511A–F, 512A, 512C, 512E, 513A–F, 516A–F, 517C, 519A–F, 521A–F, 522A, 522C, 522E, 601B, 601D, 602A–D, 602F, 603A–F, 606A–F, 608B, 608D–F, 609A–F, 612A–F, 614A–B, 614D, 615A–D, 606A–D, 617A–D, 618A–C, 701A–F, 702A–E, 703A–B, 704A, 707C, 707E, 713A.

Afghanistan 1:100,000. 1968–1970. Prepared by the US Army Topographic Command. TV), Washington, DC. Maps 1285, 1384–7, 1481–2, 1484, 1486–7, 1581, 1585–7, 1687–8, 1787, 1880, 1888, 1978, 1980, 2081, 2177–8, 2181–2, 2279, 2281–2, 2380, 2382, 2480–1, 2483, 2485, 2487, 2581–8, 2682–3, 2685–7, 2781, 2786–7, 2886–8.

Afghanistan, Iran, Pakistan, U.S.S.R. Quarter Inch. 1941–53. War Office, London. Maps H/41/A–R, H/42/A–D, H/42/G, H/42/M, I/41/A–X, I/42/A–Q, I/42/S–V, J/41/Q–R, J/41/V–X, J/42/K–L, J/42/M–X, J/43/M–P, J/43/S–U.

Aga Khan Trust for Culture. 2006. *Afghanistan Newsletter*, 3 (Sept.–Oct.): 2. (428)

Agrawala, R. C. 1968. 'Ūrdhvaretas Gaṇeśa from Afghanistan'. *EW* 18: 167–8. (337, 1064)

Agrawala, R. C. 1970. *Human Figurines on Pottery Handles from India and Allied Problems*. Ahmedabad. (99, 122)

Agrawala, R.C. 1976. 'A Newly Discovered Sherd from Sonkh and the Kinnarī Pot from Begram'. *EW* 26: 341–2. (122)

Agresti, Henri. 1970. 'Rock Drawings in Afghanistan'. *Field Research Projects: Occasional Paper, 14*. Miami. (236, 670)

Ahang, Mohammad Kazem, ed. 1968. 'Inscriptions Discovered in the Kushanides and Khurushty Languages'. *Afghanistan*, 20/4: 103. (265)

Ahang, Mohammed Kazem, ed. 1969–70. 'Archaeological News: Four Readable Ashokan Era Edicts Found'. *Afghanistan*, 22/3–4: 148–50. (1067)

Akbar Khan. 1891. 'Journey from Kirman along the Main Road from Herat to Kabul through the Dai Zangi Country and Besud, and Finally to Bamian'. In ABC IV. Ed. P. J. Maitland, 414–27. (570)

Akbar Khan, and Ata Muhammad. 1891. 'Journey from Band-i-Amir Ziarat, north of the Koh-i-Baba, across the Hazarajat to Ghazni'. In ABC IV. edited. P. J. Maitland, 428–50. (284)

Akram, M. 1947. *Bibliographie analytique de l'Afghanistan: Ouvrages parus hors de l'Afghanistan*. Paris.

Alessio, M., F. Bachechi, and C. Cortesi. 1967. 'University of Rome Carbon-14 Dates'. *Radio Carbon*, 9: 360. (244)

Ali, Mohammed. 1961. 'Bamiyan: Symbol of Indo-Afghan Cultural Unity'. *Afghanistan*, 16/2: 1–8. (100)

Ali, Mohammed. 1964. 'The Graeco-Buddhist Art of Gandhara'. *Afghanistan*, 19/2: 20–5. (1123, 1160)

Allchin, Bridget, ed. 1984. *South Asian Archaeology 1981*. Cambridge.

Allchin, Bridget, and Raymond Allchin. 1982. *The Rise of Civilization in India and Pakistan*. Cambridge. (743)

Allchin, F. R. 1953. 'A Flake-Tool from the Oxus'. *Proceedings of the Prehistoric Society*, NS 19: 227. (1251)

Allchin, F. R. 1957. 'The Culture Sequence of Bactria'. *Antiquity*, 31: 131–41. Reprinted in *Afghanistan*, 15/1 (1960): 1–20. (99, 122, 526, 931, 1052, 1160, 1251)

Allchin, F. R. 1995. *The Archaeology of Early Historic South Asia: The Emergence of Cities and States*. Cambridge. (522)

Allchin, F. R., and N. Hammond, eds. 1978. *The Archaeology of Afghanistan from the Earliest Times to the Timurid Period*. London.

Allchin, Raymond, and Bridget Allchin, eds. 1997. *South Asian Archaeology, 1995*. New Delhi.

Allchin, Raymond, and Bridget Allchin. 2012. *From the Oxus to Mysore in 1951. The Start of a Great Partnership in Indian Scholarship*. Kilkerran. (1004, 1042)

Allchin, Raymond, Bridget Allchin, Neil Kreitman, and Elizabeth Errington, eds. 1997. *Gandharan Art in Context: East–West Exchanges at the Crossroads of Asia*. Delhi.

Allchin. See also Baker.

Allegranzi, Viola. 2014. 'Royal Architecture Portrayed in the Tarīḫ-i Masʿūdī and Archaeological Evidence from Ghazni'. *Annali dell'Istituto Orientale di Napoli*, 74: 95–120. (358)

Allegranzi, Viola. 2015. 'The Use of Persian in Monumental Epigraphy from Ghazni (Eleventh–Twelfth Centuries)'. *Eurasian Studies*, 13: 23–41. (358)

Allen, Terry. 1981. *A Catalogue of the Toponyms and Monuments of Timurid Herat.* Studies in Islamic Architecture, 1. Cambridge, MA.

Allen, Terry. 1983. *Timurid Herat.* Tubingen.

Allen, Terry. 1988. 'Notes on Bust'. *Iran*, 26: 55–68. (149, 685)

Allen, Terry. 1989. 'Notes on Bust'. *Iran*, 27: 57–66. (149, 685)

Allen, Terry. 1990. 'Notes on Bust'. *Iran*, 28: 23–30. (149, 685)

Allon, M. 2001. *Three Gāndhārī Ekottarikāgama-Type Sūtras: British Library Kharoṣṭhī Fragments 12 and 14.* Seattle. (404)

Allon, M., and R. Salomon. 2000. 'Kharoṣṭhī Fragments of a Gāndhārī Mahāparinirvānasutra'. In *Manuscripts in the Schøyen Collection*, I. *Buddhist Manuscripts*, 1. Ed. J. Braavig, 243–73. (100)

Alram, Michael. 2000. 'A Hoard of Copper Drachms from the Kāpiśa-Kabul Region'. *SRAA* 6: 129–50. (483)

Alram, Michael, and Deborah E. Klimburg-Salter, eds. 1999. *Coins, Art, and Chronology: Essays on the Pre-Islamic History of the Indo-Iranian Borderlands.* Vienna.

Alram, Michael, and Matthias Pfisterer. 2010. 'Alkhan and Hephthalite Coinage'. *CAC* II. 13–38. Vienna. (1142)

Alsdorf, Ludwig. 1960. 'Zu den Aśoka-Inschriften'. In *Indolen Tagung 1959.* Ed. E. Waldschmidt, 58–66. Göttingen. (522)

Altheim, Franz. 1947. *Weltgeschichte Asiens im Griechischen Zeitalter.* Halle. Pages 25–40 on the Darunta inscription reprinted as: 'Eine neue Aśoka-Inschrift'. In *Festschrift Otto Eissfeldt.* Halle an der Saale, 29–46. (250)

Altheim, Franz. 1959–61. *Geschichte der Hunnen.* 5 vols. Berlin. (522)

Altheim, Franz, and Joachim Rehork, eds. 1969. *Der Hellenismus in Mittelasien.* Darmstadt.

Altheim, Franz, and Ruth Stiehl. 1957. 'Alexander the Great and the Avesta'. *EW* 8: 123–36. (1123)

Altheim, Franz, and Ruth Stiehl. 1958. 'The Aramaic Version of the Kandahar Bilingual Inscription of Aśoka'. *EW* 9: 192–8. (522)

Altheim, Franz, and Ruth Stiehl. 1959a. 'Zwei neue Inschriften: Die Aramäische Fassung der Aśoka-Bilinguis von Kandahar'. *AAH* 7: 107–26. (522)

Altheim, Franz, and Ruth Stiehl. 1959b. 'The Greek-Aramaic Bilingual Inscription of Kandahar and its Philological Importance'. *EW* 10/4: 243–60. (522)

Altheim, Franz, and Ruth Stiehl. 1959c. *Die aramäische Sprache unter den Achämeniden.* Frankfurt am Main.

Reprinted in *Der Hellenismus in Mittelasian.* Ed. F. Altheim and J. Rehork: 418–31. Darmstadt, 1969. (522)

Ambers, J., and C. R. Cartwright et al. 2014. *Looted, Recovered, Returned: Antiquities from Afghanistan.* Oxford. (122)

Amiet, Pierre. 1977. 'Bactriane proto-historique'. *Syria*, 54: 89–121. (257)

Amiet, Pierre. 1978. 'Antiquités de Bactriane'. *La Revue du Louvre et des Musées de France*, 28/3: 153–64. (257)

Amir Khan. 1888. 'Report on Journey from Yakatal by the Dara Yusuf to Bamian, and on to Hajigak and Irak Kotals'. ABC V. *Miscellaneous Reports.* Ed. J. West Ridgeway et al., 157–84. Simla. (171, 570, 660, 739, 854, 867, 923, 1040, 1100, 1121)

Amir Khan, and Shahzada Taimus. 1888a. 'Report on Route from Girishk to Herat'. ABC V. *Miscellaneous Reports.* Ed. J. West Ridgeway et al., 125–38. Simla. (13, 293)

Amir Khan, and Shahzada Taimus. 1888b. 'Report on Journey through Gurziwan and the Country South of Maimana'. ABC V. *Miscellaneous Reports.* Ed. J. West Ridgeway et al., 231–41. Simla. (45, 414)

Amir Khan, and Shahzada Taimus. 1888c. 'Report on Reconnaissance from Maimana up the Darzab Road to Sar-i-Pul, etc'. ABC V. *Miscellaneous Reports.* Ed. J. West Ridgeway et al., 242–56. Simla. (720, 897, 926, 1015)

Amiri, Ghulam Rahman. 1973. 'Shahr-i Ghulghula (the City of Screams) of Tar-o-Sar'. *Afghanistan*, 26/2: 79–90. (1006)

Amiri, Ghulam Rahman. 1979. 'Da Sār-u Tār da ghulghuli'. *Bāstān Shināsi Afghānistān*, 1/1: 5–9. (1006)

Amirsoleimani, S. 2005. 'Clothing in the Early Ghaznavid Courts: Hierarchy and Mystification'. *St.Ir.* 32: 213–42. (685)

Anand, Mulk Raj. 1970. 'The Development of Islamic Architecture in Afghanistan'. *Mārg*, 24/1: 19–45. (99, 149, 212, 346, 358, 410, 428, 468, 2053)

Anand, Mulk Raj. 1971a. 'The Buddha as Cosmos'. *Mārg*, 24, 2: 2–4. (100)

Anand, Mulk Raj. 1971b. 'The Development of the Standing Buddha Sculpture from Moti Mardhan to Bamiyan'. *Mārg*, 24/2: 11–16. (100)

Anderson, W. 1849. 'Notes on the Geography of Western Afghanistan'. *JASB* 18: 553–87. (373)

Angel, J. I. 1972. 'A Middle Palaeolithic Temporal Bone from Darra-i-Kur, Afghanistan'. In *Prehistoric Research in Afghanistan.* Ed. Louis Dupree et al., 54–6. Philadelphia. Reprinted in *Afghanistan*, 26/2 (1975): 20–4. (245)

Annen, Susanne, et al. 2011. *Mes Aynak: Recent Discoveries along the Silk Road.* Kabul.

Antonini, Chiara Silva. 1979a. 'A short note on the pottery from Tapa Sardar'. *South Asian Archaeology 1977.* Ed. M. Taddei, 847–64. Naples. (1180)

Antonini, Chiara Silva. 1979b. 'Note su un area sacra di Tapa Sardār'. *Annali*, 39: 480–90.

Antonini, Chiara Silva. 1979c. 'The Sacred Area 64 at Tapa Sardār'. Paper presented at the 2nd International Congress of Kushan Studies, Kabul. (1180)

Antonini, Chiara Silva. 1981. 'Wall Paintings from Tapa Sardār'. *South Asian Archaeology 1979*. Ed. H. Härtel. Berlin.

Arbeitsgemeinschaft Afghanistan and Deutsches Orient-Institut 1968. *Bibliographie der Afghanistan-Literatur 1945–1967*. Teil 1. Literatur in Europäischen Sprachen. Teil 2. Literatur in Orientalischen Sprachen und Ergänzungen in Europäischen Spratchen. Hamburg.

Arbeitsgemeinschaft Afghanistan. 1981. *Neue Forschungen in Afghanistan*. Hamburg.

Artusi, S. 2009. 'Architectural Decoration from the Palace of Mas'ūd III in Ghazni: Brickwork and Brickwork with Stucco, a Preliminary Analaysis'. *The IsIAO Italian Archaeological Mission in Afghanistan 1957–2007: Fifty Years of Research in the Heart of Eurasia*. Ed. Anna Filigenzi and Roberta Giunta, 117–29. Rome. (358)

Aruz, Joan, and Elisabetta Valtz Fino, eds. 2012. *Afghanistan: Forging Civilizations along the Silk Road*. New York.

Ashe, W. 1881. *Personal Records of the Kandahar Campaign*. London. (962, 988, 2004)

Asian Art. 2005. 'Bamiyan Dating in Afghanistan'. *Asian Art* (Feb.): 1. (100)

Asimov, A. S., and C. E. Bosworth, eds. 1998. *History of Civilizations in Central Asia, IV. The Age of Achievement: AD 750 to the End of the Fifteenth Century*. Paris.

Asmussen, J. P. 1973. *Studies in Judeo-Persian Literature*. Leiden.

Atkinson, James. 1842a. *The Expedition into Afghanistan*. London. (358, 522)

Atkinson, James. 1842b. *Sketches in Afghanistan*. London. (358)

Attar, Muhammad Ali. 1976 (1355). *Barkhi az Katībahā wa sang-i nawishtahā-i Herāt*. Kabul. (346, 428, 1259)

Auboyer, Jeannine. 1938. 'French Excavations in Indo-China and Afghanistan: 1935–37'. *Harvard Journal of Asiatic Studies*, 3: 213–22. (122, 332, 1088)

Auboyer, Jeannine. 1948. 'Ancient Indian Ivories from Begram, Afghanistan'. *JISOA* 16: 34–46. (122)

Auboyer, Jeannine. 1953. 'An Old Indian Swing'. *Mārg*, 6/4: 45. (122)

Auboyer, Jeannine. 1954. 'La vie privée dans l'Inde ancienne d'après les ivoires de Begram'. In J. Hackin et al., 'Nouvelles recherches archéologiques à Begram'. *MDAFA* 11: 59–82. (122)

Auboyer, Jeannine. 1955–6. 'Rencontre de trois civilisations au cœur de l'Asie: Grèce, Inde et Chine'. *Antiquity and Survival*, 2/6: 447–57. (122)

Auboyer, Jeannine. 1960. 'Les travaux archéologiques français en Afghanistan, dans l'Inde et au Cambodge au cours des dernières années'. In *Indologen-Tagung 1959*. Ed. Ernst Waldschmidt, 122–38. Göttingen. (743, 1123)

Auboyer, Jeannine. 1968. *L'Afghanistan et son art*. Prague. (100, 122, 332, 337, 350, 358, 404, 1052, 1088, 1123)

Auboyer, Jeannine. 1969. 'Les Bouddhas-colosses de Bamiyan'. *Revue d'Art*, 179: 28–35. (100)

Auboyer, Jeannine. 1971. 'Private Life in Ancient India as Seen from the Ivory Sculptures of Begram'. *Mārg*, 24/3: 49–54. (122)

Audouin, R., and Paul Bernard. 1973. 'Trésor de monnaies Indiennes et Indo-Grecques d'Aï Khanoum. Afghanistan. I: Les monnaies indiennes'. *Revue Numismatique*, 6th ser. 15: 238–89. (18)

Audouin, R., and Paul Bernard. 1974. 'Trésor de monnaies Indiennes et Indo-Grecques d'Aï Khanoum. Afghanistan. II: Les monnaies Indo-Grecques'. *Revue Numismatique*, 6th ser. 16: 6–41. (18)

Avdall, Johannes. 1836. 'Note on Some of the Indo-Scythic Coins Found by Mr. C. Masson at Beghrām, in the Kohistān of Kābul'. *JASB* 5: 266–8. (122)

Azad, Arezou. 2013. *Sacred Landscape in Medieval Afghanistan: Revisiting the Fadā'il Balkh*. Oxford. (99)

Azimi, Habīb. 1979. 'Tilla Tappa'. *Bāstān Shināsi Afghānistān*, 1/1: 24–8. (1192)

Aziz, Abdul. 1964. 'Two Days in Ghazni'. *Afghanistan*, 19/3: 39–48. (358)

Azizi, Nasir Muhammad. 1969/70a (1348). 'Sahnahāyi mītiūlūzi wa muzahabi dar ārt-i grīkūbūdik-i Tappa-i Shutur-i Hadda'. *Aryānā*, 27/5: 20–5. (404)

Azizi, Nasir Muhammad. 1969/70b (1348). 'Ayā dar mujassamahā-yi shīwān Kāpīsā asar-i hunar-i hakhāminishi mūjawad ast'. *Aryānā*, 28/1: 21–31. (122)

Azizi, Nasir Muhammad. 1976. *Tārīkh-i impirātūri-yī Kūshānihā*. Kabul. (122, 1123)

Azizi, Nasir Muhammad. 1980 (1359). 'Sīāsat-i iqtisādi-yi zarā'ati wa sīstīm-i kānālā zastūn dar simān-i kushānī'. *Tahqiqāt-i Kūshānī*, 3/2: 33–41. (18)

Azizi, Nasir Muhammad. 1981. 'Mukhtasari dar maurad-i tārīkhcha-i tarz wa shīwa-i mi'marī-yi hunarī-yi Tappa-i Shutur-i Hadda'. *Bāstān Shināsi Afghānistān*, 4/2: 3–25. (404)

Bābak, M. 1980. 'Kasfiyāt-i tāza-i sāhāt-i māqabl al-tārikh dar Dasht-i Nāar-i Ghazni'. *Bāstān Shināsi Afghānistān*, 2/2: 9–14. (266)

Bachhofer, Ludwig. 1925. *Zur Datierung der Gandhara-Plastik*. Munich. (127)

Bachhofer, Ludwig. 1929. *Early Indian Sculpture*. 2 vols. Paris. Translation of *Die Frühindische Plastik*. 2 vols. Munich. (127, 404)

Bachhofer, Ludwig. 1931a. 'Zur Plastik von Hadda'. *Ostasiatische Zeitschrift*, 7: 106–11. (404)

Bachhofer, Ludwig. 1931b. 'Plastik der Kushāna'. Panthéon. 8: 355–9, 502–6. (12, 404)

Bachhofer, Ludwig. 1932. 'Eine Sammlung Nordwestindischen Stückplastik'. Panthéon, 10: 348–51. (404)

Baker, P. H. B., and F. R. Allchin. 1991. Shahr-i Zohak and the History of the Bamiyan Valley, Afghanistan. Oxford. (1052)

Bāktar, Mustarab. 1966 (1345). 'Mulahazāt-i dū istād-i bāstān shinās-i almāni'. Aryānā, 24/5–6: 282–7. (153)

Balīka, Aziz. 1976. 'Aī Khānum'. Zhwandūn, 27/45: 8–11. (18)

Ball, Warwick. 1976. 'Two Aspects of Iranian Buddhism'. BAI 1–4: 103–63. (100)

Ball, Warwick. 1981. 'The Remains of a Monumental Timurid Garden outside Herat'. EW 32: 79–82. (84, 428)

Ball, Warwick. 1982. 'Project for an Archaeological Gazetteer of Afghanistan'. Afghan Studies, 3–4: 89–93. (801, 875, 879)

Ball, Warwick. 1984. 'The So-Called Minars of Kabul'. St. Ir. 13/1: 117–27. (536, 718, 1124, 1223)

Ball, Warwick. 1990. 'Some Notes on the Masjid-i Sangi at Larwand in Central Afghanistan'. South Asian Studies, 6: 105–10. (267, 683)

Ball, Warwick. 1997. 'Kandahar, the Saka and India'. South Asian Archaeology, 1995: 439–50. Cambridge. (522)

Ball, Warwick. 2002. 'The Towers of Ghur: A Ghurid "Maginot Line"?' In Cairo to Kabul: Afghan and Islamic Studies Presented to Ralph Pinder-Wilson. Ed. Warwick Ball and Leonard Harrow, 21–45. London. (39, 267, 433, 468, 683, 742, 751, 767, 775, 787, 970, 987, 1130, 1234, 1236, 1239, 1257)

Ball, Warwick. 2008. The Monuments of Afghanistan: History, Archaeology and Architecture. London. (18, 39, 41, 46, 98, 99, 100, 122, 127, 149, 155, 179, 189, 190, 201, 212, 229, 231, 245, 256, 257, 265, 266, 295, 300, 305, 332, 335, 337, 346, 349, 358, 362, 375, 389, 390, 404, 417, 428, 468, 483, 520, 522, 532, 546, 557, 558, 565, 569, 597, 601, 607, 622, 627, 630, 634, 648, 661, 667, 683, 685, 716, 718, 728, 743, 752, 761, 776, 778, 790, 792, 810, 824, 836, 839, 842, 863, 871, 875, 930, 931, 944, 1000, 1001, 1004, 1006, 1023, 1039, 1087, 1088, 1089, 1123, 1135, 1147, 1180, 1185, 1192, 1197, 1229, 1239, 1245, 1263, 1270, 2053, 2227, 2261)

Ball, Warwick. 2017. 'The Sasanian Empire and the East: A Summary of the Evidence and its Implications for Rome'. In Sasanian Persia: Between Rome and the Steppes of Eurasia. Ed. Eberhard Sauer, 151–78. Edinburgh. (362, 389, 522, 1000, 2227)

Ball, Warwick, and Leonard Harrow, eds. 2002. Cairo to Kabul: Afghan and Islamic Studies Presented to Ralph Pinder-Wilson. London.

Ball, Warwick, with the collaboration of Jean-Claude Gardin. 1982. Archaeological Gazetteer of Afghanistan. 2 vols. Paris.

Ball, Warwick. See also McNicoll.

Ball, Warwick. See also Rao.

Balland, Daniel. 1976. 'Passée et present d'une politique des barrages dans la region de Ghazni'. St.Ir. 5/2: 239–53. (102, 103, 104)

Balsan, François. 1972a. Au Registan inexploré: Sud-Afghan. Paris. (699, 848)

Balsan, François. 1972b. 'Exploring the Registan Desert'. Asian Affairs, 59: 153–6. (699, 848)

Barger, Evert. 1938. 'The Results of the Recent Archaeological Expedition to Swat and Afghanistan, in Relation to the Present Position of Indian Studies in This Country'. Journal of the Royal Society of Arts, 87/4490: 102–24. (931, 1037)

Barger, Evert. 1939a. 'Exploration of Ancient Sites in Northern Afghanistan'. Geographical Journal, 93/5: 377–98. (789, 930, 931, 1037, 1160)

Barger, Evert. 1939b. 'Opening up a Rich New Field of Archaeological Research in Central Asia'. ILN (24 Apr.): 682–3. (930, 931, 1037)

Barger, Evert. 1944. 'Some Problems of Central Asian Exploration'. Geographical Journal, 103: 1–18. (1160)

Barger, E., and P. Wright. 1941. 'Excavations in Swat and Explorations in the Oxus Territories of Afghanistan: A Detailed Report of the 1938 Expedition'. Memoirs of the Archaeological Survey of India, 64. Delhi. (150, 314, 325, 437, 776, 789, 800, 892, 930, 931, 1037, 1244)

Barmes. See Higuchi.

Barnett, R. D. 1968. 'The Art of Bactria and the Treasure of the Oxus'. Iranica Antiqua, 8: 34–53. (1123)

Barrett, Douglas. 1957. 'Sculptures of the Shahi Period'. Oriental Art, NS 3/2: 54–9. (546)

Barrett, Douglas, and Ralph Pinder-Wilson. 1967–8. Ancient Art from Afghanistan. London. (122, 404, 1168)

Barthélémy, F. 2004. 'Dans les montagnes afghans: Une étrange chasse au rhinoceros'. Le Monde, 2 (6 Nov.): 62–5. (2227)

Barthoux, J. 1928. 'Bagh-Gaï'. RAA 5/2: 77–81. (404)

Barthoux, J. 1929. 'Les fouilles de Hadda. Afghanistan'. Gazette des Beaux-Arts, 1: 121–32. (404)

Barthoux, J. 1930a. 'Les fouilles de Hadda. III: Figures et figurines'. MDAFA 6. Paris. (404)

Barthoux, J. 1930b. 'Recent Explorations by the French Mission in Afghanistan'. ABIA 1928: 6–13. (404)

Barthoux, J. 1930c. 'Griechisch-indische Kunst in Afghanistan'. Atlantis (Mar.): 181–91. (404)

Barthoux, J. 1933a. Les Fouilles de Hadda, I. Stupas et sites. Texte et dessins. MDAFA 4. Paris. (165, 404, 815)

Barthoux, J. 1933b. 'Lapis-lazuli et rubis balais des cipolins afghans'. CRAI 196: 1131–4. (1001)

Basham, A. L., ed. 1968. Papers on the Date of Kanishka. Leiden.

Bassetti, M. 2009. 'The Lithic Industry of Hazar Sum: A Brief Geological Note'. In The IsIAO Italian Archaeological Mission in Afghanistan 1957–2007: Fifty Years *of Research in the Heart of Eurasia.* Ed. Anna Filigenzi and Roberta Giunta, 19–21. Rome. (425)

Baumer, Christoph. 2012. *The History of Central Asia*, I. *The Age of the Steppe Warriors.* London. (1192)

Baumer, Christoph. 2014. *The History of Central Asia*, II. *The Age of the Silk Roads.* London. (19, 1021, 2141, 2268)

Bayley, E. C. 1861. 'Notes on Bāba R. L. Mitra's Paper on the Translation of a Bactrian Inscription from Wardak'. *JASB* 30: 347–8. (1229)

Behrens, H., and M. Klinkott. 1973. 'Das Ivan-Hofhaus in Afghanisch-Sistan'. *AMI* 6: 230–52. (201, 390, 778)

Belenitski, A. M. 1945. 'Istoricheskaya Topografiya Gerata XVv'. In *Alisher Navoi-Sbornik Statei.* Ed. A. K. Borovkov, 175–202. Moscow. (428)

Bellew, Henry Walter. 1862. *Journal of a Political Mission to Afghanistan in 1857.* London. (358, 522, 1048, 1193)

Bellew, Henry Walter. 1874. *From the Indus to the Tigris.* London. (58, 77, 96, 101, 149, 224, 299, 361, 405, 502, 522, 527, 544, 581, 586, 608, 619, 638, 684, 687, 702, 709, 721, 736, 796, 810, 842, 863, 898, 901, 979, 1260)

Benava, Abdul Rauf.1953. 'Panjawi'. *Afghanistan*, 8, 3: 23–26. (798, 1067, 1069)

Bendezu-Sarmiento, Julio, and Philippe Marquis. 2015. 'A Short History of Nearly a Century of Scientific Research in Afghanistan (1922–2015)'. In *Keeping History Alive: Safeguarding Cultural Heritage in Post-Conflict Afghanistan.* Ed. Brendan Cassar and Sara Noshadi, 104–12. Paris and Kabul. (186)

Beneviste, Emile. 1961. 'Inscriptions de Bactriane'. *JA* 249: 113–52. (1123)

Benveniste, Emile. 1964. 'Edits d'Aśoka en traduction grecque'. *JA* 252: 137–57. (522)

Beneviste, Emile, and A. Dupont-Sommer. 1966. 'Une inscription Indo-Araméenne d'Aśoka provenant de Kandahar, Afghanistan'. *JA 254*: 437–65. (522)

Bernard, Paul. 1964. 'Fouilles de Kohna Masjid'. *CRAI* 212–21. (630)

Bernard, Paul. 1966. 'Première campagne de fouilles d'Aï Khanoum'. *CRAI* 127–33. (18)

Bernard, Paul. 1967a. 'Deuxième campagne de fouilles d'Aï Khanoum'. *CRAI* 306–24. (18)

Bernard, Paul. 1967b. 'Aï Khanum on the Oxus: A Hellenistic City in Central Asia'. *Proceedings of the British Academy*, 53: 71–95. (18)

Bernard, Paul. 1968a. 'Troisième campagne de fouilles à Aï Khanoum en Bactriane'. *CRAI* 263–79. (18)

Bernard, Paul. 1968b. 'Chapiteaux corinthiens hellénistiques d'Asie Centrale découverts à Aï Khanoum'. *Syria*, 45: 111–51. (18)

Bernard, Paul. 1969a. 'Colonnes gréco-bactriennes d'Aï Khanoum'. *Actes de 5è Congrès d'art et d'archéologie de l'Iran tenu à Téhéran en 1967*, 517–23. Tehran.

Bernard, Paul. 1969b. 'Quatrième campagne de fouilles à Aï Khanoum, Bactriane'. *CRAI* 313–55. (18)

Bernard, Paul. 1970a. 'Campagne de fouilles 1969 en Afghanistan'. *CRAI* 301–49. (18)

Bernard, Paul. 1970b. 'Sièges et lits en ivoire d'époque hellénistique en Asie Centrale'. *Syria*, 47: 327–43. (18)

Bernard, Paul. 1971a. 'Influences orientales dans l'archéologie gréco-bactrienne d'Aï Khanoum'. *Annales Archéologiques Arabes Syriennes*, 21/1–2: 165–9. (18)

Bernard, Paul. 1971b. 'La campagne de fouilles de 1970 à Aï Khanoum'. *CRAI* 385–452. (18)

Bernard, Paul. 1972a. 'Fouilles d'Aï Khanoum, campagne de 1971'. *CRAI* 605–32. Reprinted in *Afghanistan*, 26/2 (1973): 51–78. (18)

Bernard, Paul. 1972b. 'Colonnes gréco-bactriennes d'Aï Khanoum, Afghanistan'. In *The Memorial Volume of the Vth International Congress of Iranian Art and Archaeology 1.* Ed. A. Tajvidi and M. Y. Kiani, 239–50. (18)

Bernard, Paul. 1973a. 'Campagne de fouilles à Aï Khanoum, Afghanistan 1972'. *CRAI* 605–32. (18)

Bernard, Paul. 1973b. 'Fouilles d'Aï Khanoum. I: Généralités'. In *Aï Khanoum*, I. MDAFA 21. Ed. Paul Bernard et al., 1–5. Paris. (18)

Bernard, Paul. 1973c. 'Fouilles d'Aï Khanoum. II: Matériaux et techniques de construction'. In *Aï Khanoum*, I. MDAFA 21. Ed. Paul Bernard et al., 7–15. Paris.

Bernard, Paul. 1973d. 'Fouilles d'Aï Khanoum. VI: Résumé chronologique'. In *Aï Khanoum*, I. MDAFA 21. Ed. Paul Bernard et al., 104–11. Paris. (18)

Bernard, Paul. 1973e. 'Fouilles d'Aï Khanoum. IX: La statuaire'. In *Aï Khanoum*, I. MDAFA 21. Ed. Paul Bernard et al., 189–93. Paris. (18)

Bernard, Paul. 1973f. 'Aï Khanoum'. *Enciclopedia dell'Arte Antica*, suppl.: 21–4. (18)

Bernard, Paul. 1974a. 'Fouilles d'Aï Khanoum, Afghanistan, campagnes de 1972 et 1973'. *CRAI* 280–308. (18)

Bernard, Paul. 1974b. 'Aux confines de l'orient barbare, Aï Khanoum, ville coloniale grecque'. *Les Dossiers de l'Archéologie*, 5: 99–114. (18)

Bernard, Paul. 1974c. 'Les noms anciens de Qandahar'. *St. Ir.* 3: 171–85. Reprinted in *Afghanistan*, 28/1 (1975): 1–15, and in *Afghanistan*, 33/1 (1980): 49–63. (522)

Bernard, Paul. 1975a. 'Fouilles d'Aï Khanoum, campagne de 1974'. *CRAI* 167–97. Reprinted in *Afghanistan*, 28/4 (1976): 43–73. (18)

Bernard, Paul. 1975b. 'Trésor d'Aï Khanoum: Note sur la signification historique de la trouvaille'. *Rev.Num.* 6th ser. 17: 23–57. (18)

Bernard, Paul. 1976a. 'Campagne de fouilles de 1975 à Aï Khanoum'. *CRAI* 287–322. (18)

Bernard, Paul. 1976b. 'Les traditions orientales dans l'architecture gréco-bactrienne'. In *Le plateau iranien et l'Asie Centrale des origines à la conquête islamique.* Colloques internationaux du C.N.R.S. 567. Ed. J. Deshayes, 263–6. Paris. (18)

Bernard, Paul. 1977b. 'Aï Khanoum: Une cite hellénistique en Afghanistan'. *Encyclopaedia Universalis*. Reprinted in *Afghanistan Archaeological Review*, 4/2 (1981): 20–23. (18)

Bernard, Paul. 1978b. 'Aï Khanoum'. *Afghanistan*, 31/2: 15–32. (18)

Bernard, Paul. 1978c. 'Campagne de fouilles 1976–1977 à Aï Khanoum, Afghanistan'. *CRAI* 421–63. Reprinted in *Afghanistan Archaeological Review*, 4/2 (1981): 34–66. (18)

Bernard, Paul. 1979a. 'Rapport préliminaire sur la campagne de fouilles de l'automne à Aï Khanoum'. *Afghanistan Archaeological Review*, 1/1: 1–6. (18)

Bernard, Paul. 1979b. 'Aï Khanoum: Cité Gréco-Bactrienne'. In *Journées Archéologiques*. Ed. F. Grenet. (18)

Bernard, Paul. 1979c. 'Pratiques financiers grecques dans la Bactriane hellénisée'. *Bulletin de la Société Française de Numismatique*, 34/5: 517–20. (18)

Bernard, Paul. 1980a. 'Campagne de fouilles 1978 à Aï Khanoum, Afghanistan'. *CRAI* 435–59. (18)

Bernard, Paul. 1981. 'Problèmes d'histoire coloniale grecque à travers l'urbanisme d'une cité hellénistique d'Asie Centrale'. *150 Jahre Deutsches Archäologisches Institut 1829–1979*, 108–20. Mainz.

Bernard, Paul. 1982b. 'Aï Khanoum, une ancienne cité grecque d'Asie Centrale'. *Pour la Science*, 53 (Mar.): 88–97. (18)

Bernard, Paul. 1982a. 'An Ancient Greek City in Central Asia'. *Ancient Cities* (Jan.): 66–75. (18)

Bernard, Paul. 1982b. 'An Ancient Greek City in Central Asia'. *Scientific American*, 246/1: 148–59. (18)

Bernard, Paul. 1987. 'Les nomades conquérants de l'empire gréco-bactrien: Réflexions sur leur identité ethnique et culturelle'. *CRAI* 131/4: 758–68.

Bernard, Paul. 1999. 'Greek Geography and Literary Fiction from Bactria to India: The Case of the Aornoi and Taxila'. *CAC* I. 52–98. Vienna. (1152)

Bernard, Paul. 2003. 'Aï Khanoum, une ancienne cité grecque d'Asie Centrale'. In *De l'Indus à l'Oxus*. Ed. O. Bopearachchi et al., 110–14. Lattes. (18)

Bernard, Paul, and Henri-Paul Francfort. 1978a. *Etudes de géographie historique sur la plaine d'Aï Khanoum, Afghanistan*. Paris. (18, 237, 569, 892, 1001)

Bernard, Paul, and Henri-Paul Francfort. 1979. 'Nouvelles découvertes dans la Bactriane Afghane'. *Annali*, 39 (NS 29): 119–48. (37, 256, 295)

Bernard, Paul, and Frantz Grenet. 1981. 'Découverte d'une statue du dieu solaire Surya dans la région de Caboul'. *St.Ir.* 10/1: 127–46. (483)

Bernard, Paul, and Olivier Guillaume. 1980. 'Monnaies inédites de la Bactriane grecque à Aï Khanoum, Afghanistan'. *Rev.Num.* 22: 9–32.

Bernard, Paul, and Olivier Guillaume. 1985. *Fouilles d'Aï Khanoum IV: Les monnaies hors trésors. Questions d'histoire gréco-bactrienne*. MDAFA 28. Paris.

Bernard, Paul, and Ch. P. Jullien. 1982. 'Haltères votives de lutteurs dans le Gandhara'. *St.Ir.* 11: 33–48.

Bernard, Paul, and Claude Rapin. 1980. 'Campagne de fouilles 1978 à Aï Khanoum. III. Le palais. La trésorerie'. *BEFEO* 68: 10–38. (18)

Bernard, Paul, and Georges Rougemont. 2003. 'Une nouvelle inscription Grecque de l'Afghanistan'. *CRAI* 147/3: 1159–61. (522)

Bernard, Paul, and Marc Le Berre. 1973. 'Fouilles d'Aï Khanoum. III: Architecture. Le quartier administrative: l'ensemble Nord'. In *Aï Khanoum, I*. MDAFA 21. Ed. Paul Bernard et al., 17–61. Paris. (18)

Bernard, Paul, and Jean-Claude Liger. 1976. 'Fouilles d'Aï Khanoum: Campagne de 1974. I. Le quartier administrative'. *BEFEO* 63: 6–25. (18)

Bernard, Paul, et al. 1973. *Fouilles d'Aï Khanoum, I (Campagnes 1966, 1967, 1968)*. MDAFA 21. Paris. (18)

Bernard, Paul, et al. 1976. 'Fouilles d'Aï Khanoum: Campagne de 1974'. *BEFEO* 63: 5–51. (18)

Bernard, Paul, et al. 1980. 'Campagne de fouilles 1978 à Aï Khanoum, Afghanistan'. *BEFEO* 68: 1–103. (18)

Bernard, Paul, Roland Besenval, and Jean-François Jarrige. 2002. 'Carnet de route en images d'un voyage sur les sites archéologiques de la Bactriane afghane (mai 2002)'. *CRAI* 146/4: 1385–1428. (18, 99, 100, 410, 944, 1123)

Bernard, Paul, Roland Besenval, and Philippe Marquis. 2006. 'Du "mirage bactrien" aux réalités archéologiques: Nouvelles fouilles de la Délégation archéologique française en Afghanistan (DAFA) à Bactres. 2004–2005'. *CRAI* 150/2: 1175–1248. (99)

Bernard, Paul, Philippe Gouin, and Marc Le Berre. 1973. 'Fouilles d'Aï Khanoum. IV: Architecture. Le quartier administrative: l'ensemble Sud'. In *Aï Khanoum, I*. MDAFA 21. Ed. Paul Bernard et al., 63–83. Paris. (18)

Bernard, Paul, Frantz Grenet, and Claude Rapin. 1980. 'Discovery of an Inscription in an Unknown Language at Aï-Khanum'. *Afghanistan*, 33/1: 45–8. (18)

Bernard, Paul, Marc Le Berre, and R. Stucki. 1973. 'Fouilles d'Aï Khanoum. V: Architecture. Le téménos de Kinéas'. In *Aï Khanoum, I*. MDAFA 21. Ed. Paul Bernard et al., 85–102. Paris. (18)

Bernard, Paul, Georges-Jean Pinault, and Georges Rougemont. 2004. 'Deux nouvelles inscriptions grecques de l'Asie centrale'. *Journal des Savants* 227–356. (522)

Bernardini, M. 1994. 'I giardini di Samarcanda e Herat'. In *Il giardino islamico: architettura, natura, paesaggio*. Ed. A. Petruccioli, 237–48. Milan. Translated as 'Die Gärten von Samarkand und Herat'. In *Der islamische Garten: Architektur, Natur, Landschaft*. Ed. A. Petruccioli, 237–48. Stuttgart.

Bertholet, A. 1930. *L'Asie Ancienne Centrale et Sud-Orientale d'après Ptolomée*. Paris.

Berthoud, T. 1978. 'Analyse de quelques fragments et matériaux archéologiques provenant d'une zone d'ateliers d'Ai Khanum—Afghanistan'. Unpublished manuscript in the DAFA library, Kabul. (18)

Berthoud, T., R. Besenval, J.-P. Carbonel, F. Cesbron, and J. Liszak-Hours. 1977. *Les anciennes mines d'Afghanistan*. Recherche Coopérative sur Programme No. 442. Paris. (19, 57, 234, 372, 438, 696, 729, 780, 1003, 1058, 1084, 1255)

Bertrand, Gabrielle. 1958. 'The Ruins of Surkh Kotal'. *Afghanistan*, 13/1: 7–9. Translated as 'Ma'bad-i Zardusht dar Surkh Kūtal'. *Aryānā*, 16/3. 1337: 50–3. (1123)

Besenval, R., and H.-P. Francfort. 1994. 'The Nad-i Ali "Surkh Dagh": A Bronze Age Monumental Platform in Central Asia?'. In *From Sumer to Meluhha: Contributions to the Archaeology of South and West Asia in Memory of George F. Dales, Jr.* Wisconsin Archaeological Reports, 3. Ed. J. M. Kenoyer, 3–14. Madison, WI. (24, 608, 752, 849, 1260)

Besenval, R., and N. Rassouli. 2010. 'Les travaux de l'Insitut Afghane d'Archéologie et de la Délégation Archéologique de France en Afghanistan'. *Afghanistan Archaeological Review*, 1–27. (99, 186)

Bihdād, Akbar. 1981. 'Maqbara-i Bābā Hātim wa tarmīm-i ān'. *Bāstān Shināsi Afghānistān*, 4/1: 137–50. (439)

Birkeland, Harris. 1938. 'Eine aramäische Inschrift aus Afghanistan'. *Acta Orientalia*, 16: 222–3. (250)

Biscione, Raffaele. 1977. 'The Crisis of Central Asia Urbanization in II Millennium BC and Villages as an Alternative System'. In *Le plateau iranien et l'Asie Centrale des origins à la conquête islamique*. Colloques internationaux du CNRS 567. Ed. J. Deshayes, 113–27. Paris. (256, 257, 323, 430, 1191)

Biscione, Raffaele, and Maurizio Tosi. 1979. *Protostoria degli Stati Turanici: Aspetti dell'evoluzione urbana e forme d'insediamento nel poplamento dell'Asia centrale nell'età del Bronzo. 2500–1000 a.c. alla luce dei dati archeologici*. Suppl. Annali. 39. Naples.

Bivar, A. D. H. 1951. 'The Bactra Coinage of Euthydemus and Demetrius'. *NC* 6th ser. 11: 22–39.

Bivar, A. D. H. 1954a. 'The Inscriptions of Uruzgan'. *JRAS* 117–18. Reprinted in *Afghanistan*, 12/4 (1958): 1–4. (320, 498, 499, 677, 1029, 1221)

Bivar, A. D. H. 1954b. 'Fire-Altars of the Sassanian Period at Balkh'. *Journal of the Warburg and Courtauld Institute*, 17/1–2: 182–3.

Bivar, A. D. H. 1954c. 'The Chaman Huzuri Hoard: Countermarked Greek Flans as the Prototypes of the Indian Punch-Marked Coinage'. *NC* 6th ser. 14: 163–72. (483)

Bivar, A. D. H. 1954d. 'The Qunduz Treasure'. *Spinks Numismatic Circular* (May). (99, 569)

Bivar, A. D. H. 1955a. 'Bactrian Treasure of Qunduz'. *Numistmatic Notes and Monographs of the Numismatic Society of India*, 3, and in *JNSI* 17: 37–52. (569)

Bivar, A. D. H. 1955b. 'Notes on Kushan Cursive Seal Impressions'. *NC* 6th ser. 15: 203–10.

Bivar, A. D. H. 1963. 'The Kanishka Dating from Surkh Kotal'. *BSOAS*. 26: 498–502. (1123)

Bivar, A. D. H. 1965. 'Indo-Bactrian Problems'. *NC* 7th ser. 5: 69–108. (337, 728)

Bivar, A. D. H. 1966. 'Seljuqid *ziyarats* of Sar-i Pul, Afghanistan'. *BSOAS* 29: 57–63. Reprinted in *Afghanistan*, 27/3 (1974): 46–64. (668, 1000)

Bivar, A. D. H. 1968. 'Fresh Evidence on the "Sijistan Barbarous" Series of Arab-Sasanian Dirhems'. *JNSI* 30: 152–7. (49, 685)

Bivar, A. D. H. 1971. 'Petroglyphs and Buddhist Remains of Jāghūrī District, Afghanistan'. In *Iran and Islam*. Ed. C. E. Bosworth, 79–89. (125, 955, 1184)

Bivar, A. D. H. 1972. 'The Sequence of Menander's Drachmae'. *Afghanistan*, 24/2: 33–52. (569, 723, 728)

Bivar, A. D. H. 1975. 'A Mongol Invasion Hoard from Eastern Afghanistan'. *Afghanistan*, 28/1: 16–28. (693)

Bivar, A. D. H. 1976. 'The Kusana Trilingual'. *BSOAS* 39: 333–40. (265)

Bivar, A. D. H. 1977. 'The Inscription of Sālār Khalīl in Afghanistan'. *JRAS* 145–9. (439)

Bivar, A. D. H. 1981a. 'Gondophares and the Shāhnāma'. *St.Ir.* 16. In *In Memoriam Roman Ghirshman*. Ed. Louis vanden Berghe. Ghent: 141–50.

Bivar, A. D. H. 1981b. 'The 'Vikrama' Era, the Indravarma Casket, and the coming of the Indo-Scythians, forerunners of the Afghans'. In *Hommages et Opera Minora*, VII. *Monumentum Georg Morgenstierne I*. Acta Iranica 21: 47–58.

Bivar, A. D. H. 1982. 'Bent Bars and Straight Bars: An Appendix to the Mir Zakah Hoard'. *St.Ir.* 11: 49–60. (728)

Bivar, A. D. H. 1983. Preface to Mochiri 1983.

Bivar, A. D. H. 1986. 'Naghar and Īryāb: Two Little Known Islamic Sites on the North-West Frontier of Afghanistan and Pakistan'. *Iran*, 24: 131–8. (2052)

Bivar, A. D. H. 1988. 'The Indus Lands'. In *Persia, Greece and the Western Mediterranean c. 525 to 479 BC. Cambridge Ancient History*, 2nd edn, IV. Ed. John Boardman et al., 194–210. Cambridge.

Blair, Sheila. 1992. *The Monumental Inscriptions from Early Islamic Iran and Transoxiana*. Leiden. (358, 1000)

Bleaney, C. H., M. A. Gallego, and Willem Vogelsang. 2005. *Afghanistan: A Bibliography*. Leiden.

Bloch, Hannah. 2015. 'Rescuing Mes Aynak'. *National Geographic* (Sept.): 110–20. (19)

Bloom, J. 1989. *Minaret: Symbol of Islam*. Oxford Studies in Islamic Art, 7. Oxford.

Bloom, J., and S. Blair. 2009. *Grove Encyclopaedia of Islamic Art*. Oxford.

Boardman, John. 1992. 'The Iranian and Nomad Contributions: And "Greek" Art in Asia'. In *The Crossroads of Asia: Transformation in Image and Symbol in the Art of Ancient Afghanistan and Pakistan*. Ed. Elizabeth Errington and Joe Cribb, 35–8. Cambridge. (122, 428)

Boardman, John. 1994. *The Diffusion of Classical Art in Antiquity.* London.

Boardman, John. 2003a. 'Three Monsters at Tillya Tepe'. *Ancient Civilizations from Scythia to Siberia,* 9/1: 133–46. (1192)

Boardman, John. 2003b. 'The Tillya Tepe Gold: A Closer Look'. *Ancient West and East,* 2/2: 348–74.

Boardman, John. 2012. 'Tillya Tepe: Echoes of Greece and China'. In *Afghanistan: Forging Civilizations along the Silk Road.* Ed. Joan Aruz and Elisabetta Valtz Fino, 102–11. New York. (1192)

Bogolyubov, M. N. 1973. 'Arameyskaya zakonodatel'naya nadpis' Asoki iz Afganistana'. *Voprosy Yazykoznaniya,* 3: 71–7. (1067)

Bombaci, Alessio. 1957. 'Ghazni'. *EW* 8: 247–59. (358)

Bombaci, Alessio. 1959. 'Summary Report on the Italian Archaeological Mission in Afghanistan. (1) Introduction to the Excavations at Ghazni'. *EW* 10/1–2: 3–22, and *Afghanistan,* 14/4: 1–23. (179, 358)

Bombaci, Alessio. 1961. 'Les Turcs et l'art Ghaznavide'. *First International Congress of Turkish Arts,* 65–70. Ankara. (358, 685)

Bombaci, Alessio. 1962. 'Ghaznevid Art'. *Encyclopaedia of World Art,* VI. 399–412. New York. (358, 685)

Bombaci, Alessio. 1966. *The Kufic Inscription in Persian Verses in the Court of the Royal Palace of Masud III at Ghazni.* Rome. (358)

Bopearachchi, Osmund. 1991. *Les Données numismatiques et las datation du Bazar de Begram.* Lyon.

Bopearachchi, Osmund. 1991. *Monnaies gréco-bactriennes et indo-grecques: Catalogue raisonné.* Paris.

Bopearachchi, Osmund. 1999a. 'Afghanistan 1993: Le dépôt de Mir Zakah. Le plus grand trésor du monde, son destin et son intérêt'. *Dossiers de l'archéologie,* 248: 36–43.

Bopearachchi, Osmund. 1999b. 'Recent Coin Hoard Evidence on Pre-Kushana Chronology'. *CAC* I. 99–149. Vienna.

Bopearachchi, Osmund. 2000a. 'Two Unreported Coins from the Second Mir Zakah Deposit'. *Oriental Numismatic Society Newsletter,* 165: 15–16. Reprinted in Bopearachchi 2015: I. 38–41. (728)

Bopearachchi, Osmund. 2000b. 'Gilded Silver Statue of a Modest Venus from Begram'. *SRAA* 6: 75–81. Reprinted in Bopearachchi 2015: II. 15–25. (122)

Bopearachchi, Osmund. 2001. 'A Faience Head of a Graeco-Bactrian King from Ai Khanum'. *BAI* 12: 23–30. Reprinted in Bopearachchi 2015: II. 3–14. (18)

Bopearachchi, Osmund. 2002. 'The Destruction of Afghanistan's Cultural Heritage'. *IIAS Newsletter,* 27: 13–14. (18, 728)

Bopearachchi, Osmund. 2003. 'Les successeurs d'Alexandre le Grand en Asie Centrale et en Inde: Les Gréco-Bactriens'. In *De l'Indus à l'Oxus.* Ed. O. Bopearachchi et al., 81–108. Lattes. (728)

Bopearachchi, Osmund. 2005. 'Greek Realms in Afghanistan: New Data'. *Actes d'une journée d'étude, UNESCO* (11 Mar.): 49–69. Reprinted in Bopearachchi 2015: I. 60–81. (42)

Bopearachchi, Osmund. 2007. 'Acroliths from Bactria and Gandhāra'. In *On the Cusp of an Era: Art in the Pre-Kushana World.* Ed. D. Meth-Srinivasan. Leiden. Reprinted in Bopearachchi 2015: I. 63–79. (18)

Bopearachchi, Osmund. 2008. 'Les premiers souverains kouchans: Chronologie et iconographie monétaire'. *Journal des Savants* (Jan.–June): 3–56. Reprinted and translated as 'The First Kushan Sovereigns: Chronology and Monetary Iconography', in *From Bactria to Taprobane: Selected Works of Osmund Bopearachchi.* 2 vols. II. 110–61: I. New Delhi, 2015. (122, 944)

Bopearachchi, Osmund. 2013. 'Begram Stūpa Deposit: Further Study on the Origin of Kushan Gold'. In *Re-Visiting Early India: Essays in Honour of D. C. Sircar.* Ed. S. Ghish, S. Ray Bandyopadhyay, S. Basu Majumdar, and S. Pal, 27–36. Kolkata. Reprinted in Bopearachchi 2015: I. 600–13. (122)

Bopearachchi, Osmund. 2015. *From Bactria to Taprobane: Selected Works of Osmund Bopearachchi.* 2 vols. New Delhi.

Bopearachchi, Osmund, and Marie-Françoise Boussac, eds. 2005. *Afghanistan, ancien carrefour entre l'Est et l'Ouest.* Turnhout.

Bopearachchi, Osmund, Christian Landes, and Christine Sachs, eds. 2003. *De l'Indus à l'Oxus: Archéologie de l'Asie central. Catalogue de l'exposition.* Lattes.

Bosch, F. D. K. ed. 1958. 'Two Important Sites in Afghanistan'. *ABIA* 16: 87–151. (743, 1123)

Bossier, Jacques. 1963. 'Etude chiminique de la céramique de Lashkari Bazar'. In *Lashkari Bazar II.* MDAFA 18. Ed. J.-C. Gardin, 145–9. Paris. (685)

Bosworth, C. E., ed. 1971. *Iran and Islam: In Memory of the Late Vladimir Minorsky.* Edinburgh.

Bosworth, C. E. See also Asimov.

Bouchenaki, Mounir. 2015. 'Safeguarding the Buddha Statues in Bamiyan and Sustainable Protection of Afghan Heritage'. In *Keeping History Alive: Safeguarding Cultural Heritage in Post-Conflict Afghanistan.* Ed. Brendan Cassar and Sara Noshadi, 232–7. Paris and Kabul. (100)

Boulanger, Matthew, T. Richard, S. Davis, and Michael D. Glascock. 2012. 'Preliminary Characterization and Regional Comparison of the Dasht-i Nawur Obsidian Source near Ghazni, Afghanistan'. *Journal of Archaeological Science,* 39: 2320–8. (266)

Bourgeois, J., and D. Bourgeois. 1971. 'Les inscriptions et dessins rupestres de la vallée du Laghmān'. *Afghanistan,* 24/2–3: 52–9. (1067)

Braavig, J., ed. 2000–2. *Buddhist Manuscripts: Manuscripts in the Schøyen Collection,* I–III. Oslo.

Brandenberg, Dietrich. 1977. *Herat.* Graz. (428)

Brandenstein, Wilhelm. 1961. 'Kusanisch'. *Indo-Iranian Journal*, 5/4: 233–6. (1123)

Brentjes, B. 1981. 'Archäologie Afghanistans'. *Das Altertum*, 27: 133–46.

Brentjes, B. 1983. 'Das Grabmal des Muhammad Boššaro – ein Vorläufer timuridischer baukunst'. In *Ibn Haldun und seine Zeit*. Ed. D. Sturm, 17–23. Halle.

Brentjes, B. 1989. 'Incised Bones and a Ceremonial Belt: Finds from Kurgan-Tepe and Tillia-Tepe'. *BAI* 3: 39–44.

Breshna, A. F. 1972. 'A Glance at the History of Fine Arts in Afghanistan'. *Afghanistan*, 25/3: 11–21. (100)

Brett, Tim, et al. 1970. *Afghan Expedition 1970*. Bristol. (124, 189, 556, 1004, 1042, 1052)

Brill, Robert H. 1972a. 'A Laboratory Study of a Fragment of Painted Glass from Begram'. *Afghanistan*, 25/2: 75–81. (122)

Brill, Robert H. 1972b. 'Report on Chemical Analysis of Some Glasses from Afghanistan'. In *Prehistoric Research in Afghanistan*. Ed. L. Dupree et al., 51–3. Philadelphia. Reprinted in *Afghanistan*, 26/3 (1973): 84–9. (46, 422)

Broadfoot, J. S. 1884. 'Reports on Parts of the Ghilzi Country, and on Some of the Tribes in the Neighbourhood of Ghazni; and on the Route from Ghazni to Dera Ismail Khan by the Ghwalari Pass'. *RGS Supplementary Papers*, 341–400. (102, 103)

Brown, Robert L. 2003. 'The Walking Tilya Tepe Buddha: A Lost Prototype'. *BAI* 14: 77–87. (1192)

Browne, L. F. 1879. 'Notes on Route from Kandahar to Girishk'. *Reports on Afghanistan 1879*. Bound vol. in British Library, Shelf-mark no. I.S.164. (96)

Bruno, Andrea. 1962. 'The Planned and Executed Restoration of Some Monuments of Archaeological and Artistic Interest in Afghanistan'. *EW* 13: 99–186. (35, 100, 358, 468, 1000)

Bruno, Andrea. 1963. 'Notes on the Discovery of Hebrew Inscriptions in the Vicinity of the Minaret of Jām'. *EW* 14: 206–208. (468)

Bruno, Andrea. 1976. *The Citadel and Minarets of Herat, Afghanistan*. Turin. (428)

Bruno, Andrea. 1979. 'The Minaret of Jam: A UNESCO Project to Restore an Historic Afghan Monument'. *UNESCO Courier*, 20 (Oct.): 32–4. (468)

Bruno, Andrea. 1983. 'Le minaret de Jam, Afghanistan'. *Monumentum*, 26/3: 189–200. (468)

Bruno, Andrea. 2003. 'The Minaret of Jam, Afghanistan'. *World Heritage Review*, 29: 4–15. (468)

Buchel, L. 1977. 'Squelettes d'Aï Khanoum, Afghanistan: Etude anthropologique'. *Bulletin d'Anthropologie Basse Normandie*, 1: 2–11. (18)

Buddruss, G., and G. Djelani Davary. 1980. 'Dari-Inschriften aus dem Wakhan'. *Afghanistan Journal*, 7: 109–10.

Bühler, Jean. 1958a. 'Les grandes Bouddhas taillés dans la montagne de Bamiyan'. *Afghanistan*,13/2: 23–6. (100)

Buhler, Jean. 1958b. 'Balkh, la plus vieille ville du monde'. *Afghanistan*, 13/3: 8–11. (99)

Buhot, Jean. 1927. 'Les antiquités bouddhiques de Bamiyan'. *RAA* 4/3: 133–45, and *RAA* 4/4: 204–11. (100, 305)

Bulliet, Richard W. 1976. 'Naw Bahār and the Survival of Iranian Buddhism'. *Iran*, 14: 140–5. (99)

Buri, V. P. 1976. 'Tekhnika zhivopisi'. In *Drevnyaya Baktriya*, I. Ed. I. T. Kruglikova, 111–24. Moscow. (295)

Buri, V. P. 1979. 'Tekhnika rospisei pomeshcheniya 16'. In *Drevnyaya Baktriya*, II. Ed. I. T. Kruglikova, 146–65. Moscow. (295)

Burnes, Alexander. 1833. 'On the Colossal Idols of Bamiyan'. *JASB* 11: 561–4. (100)

Burnes, Alexander. 1834a. *Travels into Bukhara*. 3 vols. London. (99, 100, 163)

Burnes, Alexander. 1834b. 'Note sur les idoles colossales à Bamiyan'. *JA* 14: 470–5. (100)

Burnes, Alexander. 1843. *Cabool: A Personal Narrative of a Journey To, and Residence in that City*. London. (565, 718, 1124)

Bussagli, Mario. 1949. 'Brevi note sui Kūsana'. *Atti della Accademia Nazionale de Lincei Serie*, 8/4: 7–10: 446–53. (122)

Bussagli, Mario. 1953a. 'L'irrigidimento formale nei bassorilievi del Gandhara in rapporto all'estetica indiana'. *Archaeologia Classica*, 15/1: 67–83. (122, 404)

Bussagli, Mario. 1953b. 'L'influsso classico e iranico sull'arte dell'Asia Centrale'. *Rivista dell'Instituto Nazionale d'Archaeologia e storia dell'Arte*, NS 11: 171–262. (100, 305, 332, 404, 508)

Bussagli, Mario. 1955–6. 'Un particulare aspette religioso della regalita presso I Kusana'. *Studi e Materiali di Storia delle Religioni*, 24–5. (122)

Bussagli, Mario. 1956–7. 'Osservazioni sulla persistenze delle forme ellenistiche nell'arte del Gandhara'. *Rivista dell'Instituto Nazionale di Archeologia e Storia dell'Arte*, 5–6: 149–247. (122, 404, 790, 1088, 1123)

Bussagli, Mario. 1962a. 'Afghanistan'. *Encyclopaedia of World Art*. I. 32–47. New York. (100, 122, 404, 428, 930, 1123, 1135, 1160)

Bussagli, Mario. 1962b. 'Gandhara'. *Enclyclopaedia of World Art*, VI. 18–37. New York. (404)

Bussagli, Mario. 1962c. 'Cusana et Serica'. *Rivista degli Studi Orientali*, 37: 79–103. (1009)

Bussagli, Mario. 1963. *La peinture de l'Asie Centrale*. Geneva. (100)

Bussagli, Mario. 1968. 'The Problem of Kanishka as Seen by the Art Historian'. In *Papers on the Date of Kanishka*. Ed. A. L. Basham, 39–56. Leiden. (127, 1088, 1123)

Butcher, G. M. 1956. 'Architectural Restoration in Afghanistan'. *Geographical Magazine*, 29/2: 73–6. (428)

Byron, Robert. 1935a. 'The Shrine of Khwaja Abu Nasr Parsa at Balkh'. *BAIPAA* 4/1: 12–14. (99)

Byron, Robert. 1935b. 'Timurid Monuments in Afghanistan'. In *IIIè Congrès international d'art et d'archéologie iraniens*, 34–8. Leningrad. (358, 346, 428)

Byron, Robert. 1937. *The Road to Oxiana*. London. (99, 346, 358, 428, 870)

Byron, Robert. 1938. 'Timurid Architecture: General Trends'. In *A Survey of Persian Art*. Ed. A. U. Pope, 1119–43. Oxford. (99, 346, 428, 716).

Caillat, Colette. 1966. 'La sequence *shyty* dans les inscriptions indo-araméennes d'Aśoka'. *JA* 254: 467–70. (250, 522)

Caley, Earle R. 1972a. 'Results of an Examination of Corroded Metal from the 1962 Excavations at Snake Cave, Afghanistan'. In *Prehistoric Research in Afghanistan*. Ed. Louis Dupree et al., 43. Philadelphia. (46)

Caley, Earle R. 1972b. 'Chemical Examination of Metal Artefacts from Afghanistan'. In *Prehistoric Research in Afghanistan*. Ed. Louis Dupree et al., 44–50. Philadelphia. Reprinted in *Afghanistan*, 27/2 (1974): 1–17. (46, 245, 422)

Cambon, P. 1996. 'Fouilles anciennes en Afghanistan. 1924–1925, Païtava, Karratcha'. *AA* 51: 13–28. (790, 2111)

Cambon, Pierre. 2003. 'The Role of the Guimet Museum in the Study and Preservation of Afghan Heritage'. *Museum International*, 55 (3–4): 54–61.

Cambon, Pierre, and Jean-François Jarrige, eds. 2006. *Afghanistan, les trésors retrouvés: Collections du musée national de Kaboul*. Paris. (18, 99, 122, 582, 1123, 1173, 1192)

Cambon, Pierre, and Jean-François Jarrige. 2007. *Hidden Afghanistan*. Amsterdam. (18, 99, 122, 582, 1123, 1173, 1192)

Campbell, W. M. 1880. 'Shorawak Plain and the Toba Plateau'. *PRGS* 2: 620–6. (76)

Canepa, Matthew P. 2015. 'Dynastic Sanctuaries and the Transformation of Iranian Kingship between Alexander and Islam'. *Persian Kingship and Architecture: Strategies of Power in Iran from the Achaemenids to the Pahlavis*. Ed. Sussan Babaie and Gregor Talinn, 65–118. London. (1123)

Carl, J. 1959a. 'Le fortin du Saka et le monastère de Guldara'. *MDAFA* 8: 13–18. (389, 773, 922, 972)

Carl, J. 1959b. 'Fouilles dans le site de Shahr-i-Banu et sondages au Zakar-Tepé'. *MDAFA* 8: 59–81. (290, 628, 1034)

Carl, J. 1959c. 'Le bazaar de Begram'. *MDAFA* 8: 85–102. (122)

Carl, J. 1959d. 'Le Tépé Kalān du Koh-i Pahlavān'. *MDAFA* 8: 128–33. (1088)

Carl, J., and Joseph Hackin. 1959. 'Le monastère bouddhique de Tèpè Marandjān'. *MDAFA* 8: 7–12. (1173)

Caroe, Olaf. 1973. 'The Gauhar Shad Musalla Mosque in Herat'. *Asian Affairs*, 60: 295–8. (428)

Carter, Martha L. 1997. 'A Reappraisal of the Bīmarān Reliquary'. In *Gandharan Art in Context*. Ed. R. Allchin et al., 71–93. Delhi. (127)

Carter, Martha L. 2006. 'Notes on Kuṣāṇa Chronology in the Bactrian Era'. *Journal of Inner Asian Art and Archaeology*, 1: 81–8.

Casal, Geneviève. 1978. 'Description des peintures de la grande sale d'audience du château du sud à Lashkari Bazar'. In *Lashkari Bazar IA*. MDAFA 18. Ed. D. Schlumberger, 100–8. Paris. (685)

Casal, Jean-Marie. 1952. 'Mundigak: Un site de l'âge du bronze en Afghanistan'. *CRAI* 382–88, and *Afghanistan*, 7/4: 41–8. (743)

Casal, Jean-Marie. 1954a. 'Quatre campagnes de fouilles à Mundigak'. *AA* 1/3: 163–78. (743)

Casal, Jean-Marie. 1954b. 'Fouilles de Mundigak. Afghanistan'. *CRAI* 284–5. (743)

Casal, Jean-Marie. 1954c. 'Tumuli du Turkestan Afghan'. Unpublished report in the DAFA library, Kabul. (1065)

Casal, Jean-Marie. 1955a. 'Nouvelles recherches à Mundigak'. *Afghanistan*, 10/3: 19–24. (743)

Casal, Jean-Marie. 1955b. 'The Afghanistan of 5000 Years Ago: Excavating the Huge Bronze Age Mound of Mundigak Abandoned 3000 Years Ago'. *ILN* (7 May): 832–4. (743)

Casal, Jean-Marie. 1956. 'L'Afghanistan et les problèmes de l'archéologie'. *Artibus Asiae*, 19: 213–20. (743)

Casal, Jean-Marie. 1957. 'Mundigak as a Link between Pakistan and Iran in Prehistory'. *Journal of the Asiatic Society of Pakistan*, 2: 3–12. (743)

Casal, Jean-Marie. 1961. *Fouilles de Mundigak*. 2 vols. MDAFA 17. Paris. (743)

Casal, Jean-Marie. 1964a. 'Monument de Mundigak'. *Afghanistan*, 19/3: 9–12. (743)

Casal, Jean-Marie. 1964b. 'Mundigak'. In *Afuganistan Kodai Bijutsu: Ancient Art of Afghanistan*. Ed. Seiichi Mizuno, 202–7. Tokyo. (743)

Casal, Jean-Marie. 1969. *La civilisation de l'Inde et ses enigmas*. Paris. (743)

Casimir, Michael, and Bernt Glatzer. 1971a. 'Kurzmitteilung über eine bisher unbekannte ghoridischer Moschee in Badghis, Afghanistan'. *Arabische Paläographie*, 11: 191–6, and in *Zentralasiatische Studien*, 5: 191–7. (1023)

Casimir, Michael, and Bernt Glatzer. 1971b. 'Shah-i Māshad, a Recently Discovered Madrasah of the Ghurid Period in Garghistan, Afghanistan'. *EW* 21: 53–68. (1023)

Caspani, P. E. 1945. 'The Cave of the Shadow of the Buddha at Nagaraha'. *JASB* 49–52. (855)

Caspani, P. E. 1946a. 'Lahore-Delhi'. *Afghanistan*, 1/1: 41–2. (453, 705)

Caspani, P. E. 1946b. 'Les murs de Kaboul'. *Afghanistan*, 1/2: 33–6. Translated as 'Dīwārhā-yi qadīm-i Kābul'. *Āryānā*, 32/3 (1353): 32–5. (483)

Caspani, P. E. 1946c. 'La promenade Archéologique de Kaboul'. *Afghanistan*, 1/4: 35–43. (483, 718, 1087, 1173)

Caspani, P. E. 1947a. 'The Nau-Bahar of Balkh'. *Afghanistan*, 2/1: 39–43. (99)

Caspani, P. E. 1947b. 'Terres de pique-niques et d'archéologie'. *Afghanistan*, 2/2: 45–50. (92, 198, 254, 366, 571, 598, 600, 665, 1222)

Caspani, P. E. 1948. 'A propos d'une supposée sculpture sur roche dans la region de Mazar-é Charif'. *Afghanistan*, 3/1: 20–4. (1000, 1051)

Caspani, P. E., and E. Cagnacci. 1951. *Afghanistan Crocevia dell'Asia*. Milan. (29, 42, 98, 169, 194, 291, 318, 337, 428, 435, 522, 565, 628, 651, 761, 764, 765, 971, 1099, 1134, 1185, 1229, 1232, 1254)

Cassar, Brendan, and Sara Noshadi, eds. 2015. *Keeping History Alive: Safeguarding Cultural Heritage in Post-Conflict Afghanistan*. Paris and Kabul.

Castaldi, Editta. 1963. 'Italian Archaeological Mission in Afghanistan: Preliminary Report on the Researches at Hazār Sum, Samangan'. *EW* 14: 183–205. (425)

Cattenat, Annette, and Jean-Claude Gardin. 1976. 'Diffusion comparée de quelques genres de poteries caractérisques de l'époque achéménide sur le plateau iranien et en Asie Centrale'. In *Le plateau iranien et l'Asie Centrale des origins à la conquête islamique. Colloques internationaux du C.N.R.S. 567*. Ed. J. Deshayes, 225–48. Paris. Reprinted in *Afghanistan Archaeological Review*, 2/2 (1980): 1–24. (99, 743, 752, 1192)

Chaghatai, M. A. 1970. 'A Fugitive Architect'. *Afghanistan*, 23/1: 24–8. (346)

Chakrabarti, Dilip K. 1990. *The External Trade of the Indus Civilization*. Delhi. (1089)

Chakrabarti, Kanchan. 1981. *Society, Religion and Art of the Kushana India: A Historico-Symbiosis*. Calcutta.

Chapman, J. S. 1841. 'Notes on the Gems Found at Beghram'. *JASB* 10: 613–14. (122)

Chowdhury, K. A. 1963. 'Plant Remains from Deh Morasi Ghundai, Afghanistan'. In *Deh Morasi Ghundai*. Ed. Louis Dupree, 126–31. New York. (287)

Civil and Military Gazette. 1874. Lahore. (863, 1006)

Clarysse, Willy, and Dorothy J. Thompson. 2007. 'Two Greek Texts on Skin from Hellenistic Bactria'. *Zeitschrift für Papyrologie und Epigraphik*, 59: 273–9. (99, 2280)

Clifford, C. 1879. 'Notes on the Arghastan Valley and its villages, and the villages in the valley of the Arghastan Lora'. *Reports on Afghanistan 1879*. Bound vol. in British Library, Shelf-mark I.S.164. (694)

Coarelli, Filippo. 1961. 'Nuovi elementi per la chronologia di Begram: Cinque recipienti bronzei in forma di busto'. *Archaeologia Classica*, 13: 168–79. (122)

Coarelli, Filippo. 1962. 'The Painted Cups of Begram and the Ambrosian Iliad'. *EW* 13: 317–35. (122)

Coarelli, Filippo. 1963. 'Su alcuni vetri dipinti scoperti nella Germania Indipendente e sul commercio Allesandrino in Occidente vei primi due seculi dell'Impero'. *Archaeologia Classica*, 15: 61–85. (122)

Codrington, K. de B. 1944. 'A Geographical Introduction to the History of Central Asia'. *JRGS* 27–40 and 73–91. (1052)

Codrington, O. 1904. 'Note on Mussalman Coins Collected by Mr G. P. Tate in Seistan'. *JRAS* 681–6. (1006)

Colledge, Malcolm. 1987. 'Greek and Non-Greek Interaction in Art and Architecture'. In *Hellenism in the East: The Interaction of Greek and Non-Greek Civilizations from Syria to Central Asia After Alexander*. Ed. Amélie Kuhrt and Susan Sherwin-White, 134–62. London. (18)

Combaz, G. 1935. 'L'évolution du stupa en Asie. Contributions nouvelles et vue d'ensemble'. *Mélanges Chinois et Bouddhiques*, 3: 93–144. (404)

Combe, E. J. Sauvaget, and G. Wiet. 1936. *Répertoire chronologique d'epigraphie arabe*, VII. Cairo. (1106)

Combe, E. J. Sauvaget, and G. Wiet. 1954. *Répertoire chronologique d'epigraphie arabe*, XIV. Cairo. (428)

Compareti, Mateo. 2008. 'The Painting of the "Hunter-King" at Kakrak: Royal Figure or Divine Being?'. *Annali di ca' Foscari*, 47/3: 131–47. (508)

Coningham, Robin, and Ruth Young. 2015. *The Archaeology of South Asia: From the Indus to Asoka, c.6500 BCE–200 CE*. Cambridge. (522)

Connolly, Arthur. 1834. *Journey to the North of India*. 2 vols. London. (346, 428)

Connolly, E. B. 1841. 'Journal Kept While Travelling in Seistan'. *JASB* 10: 319–41. (684, 841)

Conolly, E. B. 1840. 'Note on Discoveries of Gems from Kandahar'. *JASB* (9: 97–107. (522, 752)

Coomaraswamy, Ananda K. 1926–7. 'The Origin of the Buddha Image'. *Art Bulletin*, 9/4: 287–330. (127)

Coon, Carleton S. 1957. *Seven Caves*. New York. (526, 1005)

Coon, C. S., and H. W. Coulter. 1955. 'Excavation of the Kara Kamar Rock Shelter'. *Afghanistan*, 10 (1): 12–16. (526)

Coon, C. S., and E. K. Ralph. 1955. 'Radiocarbon Dates for Kara Kamar, Afghanistan'. *Science*, 122: 921–2. (526)

Court, Alexandre. 1836. 'Conjectures on the March of Alexander'. *JASB* 5: 387–95. (522, 1048)

Court, Alexandre. 1837. 'Conjectures sur la marche d'Alexandre'. *JA* 4: 359–96. (33, 118, 365)

Courtois, J. C. 1961. 'Summary of the History of Archaeological Research in Afghanistan'. *Afghanistan*, 16/2: 18–29. (100, 122, 148, 169, 358, 404, 944, 1123)

Courtois, Liliane. 1959. 'Note sur le cruchon N° 72 de Begram-Capici, conservé au musée de Kabul'. *AA* 6/2: 135–40. Reprinted in *Afghanistan*, 16/2 (1961): 8–12. (122)

Courtois, Liliane. 1962–3. 'Examen minéralogique de quelques roches de monuments grécobouddhiques'. *AA* 9/1–2: 107–13. (404, 790, 1088)

Crane, Howard. 1979. 'Helmand-Sistan Project: An Anonymous Tomb in Bust'. *EW* 29: 241–6. (149)

Crane, Howard, and William Trousdale. 1972. 'Carved Decorative and Inscribed Bricks from Bust'. *Afghanistan*, 28/2: 25–47, and *EW* 22: 215–26. (149)

Creswell, K. A. C. 1927. 'The Evolution of the Minaret'. *Burlington Magazine*, 48: 134–40, 252–8, and 290–8. (1106)

Creswell, K. A. C. 1961. *A Bibliography of the Architecture, Arts and Crafts of Islam.* Cairo.

Cribb, Joe. 2017. 'Dating the Bimaran Casket: Its Conflicted Role in the Chronology of Gandharan Art'. *Gandhāran Studies* 10: 57–91. (127)

Cribb, Joe. See also Errington.

Cribb, Joe. See also Sims-Williams.

Crowe, Yolande. 1978. 'Central Asia and Afghanistan'. In *Architecture of the Islamic World: Key Monuments of Islamic Architecture.* Ed. George Michel, 258–63. London.

Cucco, I. See Thomas.

Cunningham, A. 1854. 'Coins of Indian Buddhist Satraps, with Greek Inscriptions'. *JASB* 23: 679–714. (127)

Cunningham, A. 1879. 'Notes on the Gold Coins Found in the Ahin Posh Tope'. *Proceedings of the Asiatic Society of Bengal* 205–12. (17)

Cunningham, A. 1889. 'Coins of the Tochari, Kushāns, or Yue-ti'. *NC* 3rd ser. 9: 268–311. (17)

Cunningham, A. 1890. 'Coins of the Sakas'. *NC* 3rd ser. 10: 103–72. (122, 522)

Cunningham, A. 1892. 'Coins of the Kushāns, or Great Yue-ti'. *NC* 3rd ser. 12: 40–82 and 98–159. (17)

Cunningham, A. 1894. 'Coins of the Later Indo-Scythians: Ephthalites or White Huns'. *NC* 3rd ser. 14: 243–93. (404)

Cunningham, Alexander. 1840. 'Notes on Captain Hay's Bactrian Coins'. *JASB* 9: 531–45. (100)

Cunningham, Alexander. 1841. 'A Sketch of the Second Silver Plate Found at Badakhshan'. *JASB* 10: 570–2. (650)

Cunningham, Alexander. 1842. 'Second Notice of Some New Bactrian Coins'. *JASB* 11: 130–7. (100)

Cunningham, Alexander. 1846. 'An Attempt to Explain Some of the Monograms Found upon the Greek Coins of Ariana and India'. *NC* 8: 175–97. (122, 435, 522, 774)

Curiel, Raoul. 1953. 'Le trésor du Tépé Maranjan'. In *Trésors monétaires d'Afghanistan.* MDAFA 14. Ed. R. Curiel and D. Schlumberger, 101–31. Paris. (122, 404, 1173)

Curiel, Raoul. 1954. 'Inscriptions de Surkh Kotal'. *JA* 242: 189–97. (1123)

Curiel, Raoul, and Gérard Fussman. 1965. *Le Trésor Monétaire de Qunduz.* MDAFA 20. Paris. (569)

Curiel, Raoul, and R. Gyselen. 1983. *Une collection de monnaies de cuivre sasanides tardives et arabo-sasanides.* St.Ir. 2. Paris.

Curiel, Raoul, and Daniel Schlumberger. 1953. 'Le trésor de Mir Zakah'. In *Trésors monétaires d'Afghanistan.* MDAFA 14: 65–98. Paris. (728)

Daffinà, Paolo. 1967. *L'immigrazione dei Sakā nella Drangiana.* IsMEO Reports and Memoirs, 9. Rome. (522)

Dagens, Bruno. 1964a. 'Fragments de sculpture inédits'. In *Monuments préislamiques d'Afghanistan.* MDAFA 19. Ed. B. Dagens et al., 9–13. Paris. (169, 404, 689, 790, 1160, 1185)

Dagens, Bruno. 1964b. 'Monastères rupestres de la vallée de Foladi'. In *Monuments préislamiques d'Afghanistan.* MDAFA 19. Ed. B. Dagens et al., 41–60. Paris. (330)

Dagens, Bruno, Marc Le Berre, and Daniel Schlumberger. 1964. *Monuments préislamiques d'Afghanistan.* MDAFA 19. Paris.

Dales, George F. 1965. 'A Suggested Chronology for Afghanistan, Baluchistan and the Indus Valley'. In *Chronologies in Old World Archaeology.* Ed. R. W. Ehrich, 257–84. Chicago. (46, 743)

Dales, George F. 1968. 'The South Asia Section'. *Expedition,* 11/1: 38–45. (752)

Dales, George F. 1971. 'Early Human Contacts from the Persian Gulf through Baluchistan and Southern Afghanistan'. In *Food, Fiber and the Arid Lands.* Ed. W. G. McGinnies et al., 145–70. Tucson, AZ. (287, 335, 743)

Dales, George F. 1972. 'Prehistoric Research in Southern Afghan Seistan'. *Afghanistan,* 24/4: 14–40. (229, 335, 383, 393, 1147)

Dales, George F. 1973a. 'Recent Pre- and Proto-Historic Research in Pakistan and Afghanistan'. In *Radio-Carbon and Indian Archaeology.* Ed. D. P. Agrawal and A. Ghosh, 118–30. Bombay. (46, 287, 582, 968)

Dales, George F. 1973b. 'Archaeological and Radiocarbon Chronologies for Protohistoric South Asia. In *South Asian Archaeology.* Ed. N. Hammond, 157–69. London. (287, 743)

Dales, George F. 1974. 'Turkmenistan, Afghanistan und Pakistan. In *Fruhe Stüfen der Kunst.* Ed. Machteld J. Mellink and Jan Filip, 166–82. Berlin. (287, 743)

Dales, George F. 1974. *The Earliest Art of Turkestan, Afghanistan and Pakistan: The Art of Early Near East and South Asia.* Propylaen Kunstgeschichte 13. Berlin.

Dales, George F. 1977a. *New Excavations at Nad-i Alī, Sorkh Dagh, Afghanistan.* Berkeley, CA. (752)

Dales, George F. 1977b. 'Shifting Trade Patterns between the Iranian Plateau and the Indus Valley in the Third Millenium BC'. In *Le plateau iranien et l'Asie Centrale des origins à la conquête islamique.* Colloques internationaux du CNRS 567. Ed. J. Deshayes, 67–78. Paris. (743)

Dales, George F. 1977c. 'Hissar IIIc Stone Objects in Afghan Sistan'. In *Mountains and Lowlands.* Ed. Louis D. Levine and T. Cuyler Young, Jr, 17–28. Malibu, CA. (229, 383)

Dales, George F. 1985. 'Stone Sculptures from the Protohistoric Helmand Civilization, Afghanistan'. In *Orientalia Iosephi Tucci Memoriae Dicata.* Ed. G. Gnoli and L. Lanciotti. Serie Orientale Roma, 56/1: 219–24. Rome. (743)

Dales, George F., and L. Flam. 1969. 'On Tracking Woolly Kullis and the Like'. *Expedition,* 12/1: 15–23. (335, 383, 1147)

Dallapiccola, A., ed. 1980. *The Stupa: Its Religious, Historical and Architectural Significance.* Sudasien Institut. Heidelberg.

Darbois, Dominique. See Tissot.

Davary, Ghulam Djelani. 1975. 'Die Ruinstadt Bost am Helmand'. *Acta Iranica,* 2nd ser. 4: 201–8. Reprinted in *Afghanistan,* 28/4 (1976): 29–42. (149)

Davary, Ghulam Djelani. 1977. 'A List of the Inscriptions of the Pre-Islamic Period from Afghanistan'. *Studien zur Indologie und Iranistik,* 3: 11–22. (18, 71, 122, 127, 163, 250, 265, 295, 320, 337, 389, 404, 464, 522, 630, 675, 776, 1067, 1123, 1185, 1221, 1229)

Davary, Ghulam Djelani. 1978. 'Jam and Feroz-koh: A New Study'. *Afghanistan,* 30/4: 69–91. (468)

Davary, Ghulam Djelani. 1981. 'Epigraphische Forschungen in Afghanistan'. *St.Ir.* 10: 53–60. (250, 1067)

Davary, Ghulam Djelani. 2003. 'Découvertes en Afghanistan'. *Archéologia,* 403: 50–8.

Davary, Ghulam Djelani. 2012. 'Die bakrische Inschrift Tangi Safedak aus Yakaolang'. In *Autour de Bāmiyān: De la Bactriane hellénisée à l'Inde bouddhique.* Ed. G. Duccoeur, 253–77. Paris. (2261)

Davary, Ghulam Djelani. See also Buddruss, G.

Davary, Ghulam Djelani, and Helmut Humbach. 1974. 'Ein weitere aramäoiranische Inschrift der Periode des Aśoka aus Afghanistan'. *Abhandlungen der Akademie der Wissenchaften und der Literatur in Mainz,* 1: 1–16. Reprinted in *Aghanistan,* 28/1 (1975): 41–54. (1967)

Davary, Ghulam Djelani, and Helmut Humbach. 1976. *Die baktrische Inschrift IDN 1 von Dasht-e Nawur: Afghanistan.* Wiesbaden. (265, 1067)

Davidson, J. Le Roy. 1971. 'Begram Ivories and Indian Stones'. *Mārg,* 24/3: 31–45. (122)

Davidson, J. Le Roy. 1972. 'Begram Ivories and Early Indian Sculpture'. In *Aspects of Indian Art.* Ed. P. Pal, 1–14. Leiden. (122)

Davis, Richard S. 1969–70. 'Prehistoric Investigation in Northern Afghanistan'. *Afghanistan,* 22/3–4: 75–90. (352, 355, 635)

Davis, Richard S. 1974. *The Late Palaeolithic of Northern Afghanistan.* Ann Arbor, MI. (46, 244, 526, 635)

Davis, Richard S. 1978. 'The Palaeolithic'. In *The Archaeology of Afghanistan.* Ed. F. R. Allchin and N. Hammond, 37–40. London. (46, 244, 266, 352, 425, 526, 635, 1101)

Davis, Richard S., and Louis Dupree. 1977. 'Prehistoric Survey in Central Afghanistan'. *Journal of Field Archaeology,* 4/2: 139–48. (266)

Davis-Kimball, J., et al. 2000. *Kurgans, Ritual Sites and Settlements, Eurasian Bronze and Iron Age.* Oxford.

De Cardi, Beatrice. 1950. 'On the Borders of Pakistan: Recent Exploration'. *Art and Letters,* 24/2: 52–7. (108, 962, 1098)

de la Vaissière, Étienne. 2007. 'A Note on the Schoyen Copper Scroll: Bactrian or Indian?' *BAI* 27: 127–30. (1142)

de la Vaissière, Étienne, and Philippe Marquis. 2013. 'Nouvelles recherches sur le paysage monumental de Bactres'. *CRAI* 157/3: 1155–71.

de la Vaissière, Étienne, Philippe Marquis, and Julio Bendezu-Sarmiento. 2015. 'A Kushan Military Camp near Bactra'. *Kushan Histories: Literary Sources and Selected Papers from a Symposium at Berlin, December 5th to 7th, 2013.* Ed. H. Falk, 241–54. Bremen. (520, 814, 2281)

De Laessöe, F. M., G. Talbot, and W. Simpson. 1886. 'Discovery of Caves on the Murghab'. *JRAS* NS 18: 92–102. (477)

De Lapparent, A. F., and R. Desparmet. 1973. 'Fouilles d'Aï Khanoum. XIII: Observations sur la géologie du site'. In *MDAFA* 21. Ed. Paul Bernard et al., 239–46. Paris. (18)

De Marco, Giuseppe. 1983. *I "Kusana" nella vita del Buddha: Per una analisi del rapporto tra potere politico e religione nell'antico Gandhara.* Annali Suppl. 34. Naples.

De Menasce, J. 1972. *A propos d'une inscription araméenne d'Aśoka.* Israel Oriental Studies 2. London. (522)

de Valence, Régis. 1979. 'La restauration du mausolée islamique de Baba Hatim'. In *Journées archéologiques.* Ed. Frantz Grenet. (439)

de Valence, Régis. 1983. *La restauration du mausolée de Baba Hatim en Afghanistan.* ADPF. Paris. (440)

Deckers, K. See Thomas, D. J.

Delacour, C. 1993. 'Redécouvrir les verres de la trésor de Begram'. *AA* 48: 53–71. (122)

Desai, Z. A. 1975. 'Cultural Relations between Afghanistan and India during the Medieval Period'. *Afghanistan,* 28/3: 9–17. (468, 685)

Desbordes, Christelle, Claude Rapin, and Pierre Cambon. 2003 'Bagram-Kapiçi, carrefour commercial dans l'Empire Kouchan'. In *De l'Indus à l'Oxus,* 307–12. Ed. O. Bopearachchi et al. Lattes. (122)

Deshayes, Jean, ed. 1977a. *Le Plateau iranien et l'Asie Centrale des origins à la conquête islamique.* Colloques Internationaux du CNRS 567. Paris.

Deshayes, Jean. 1977b. 'A propos des terrasses hautes de la fin du IIIe millénaire en Iran et en Asie Centrale'. In *Le plateau iranien et l'Asie Centrale des origins à la conquête islamique.* Colloques internationaux du CNRS 567. Ed. J. Deshayes, 95–112. Paris. (383, 582, 743)

Deshpande, M. N., ed. 1974. *Expedition Outside India: Preservation of Buddhist Shrines at Bamiyan, Afghanistan.* Indian Archaeology 1970–71, 103. (100)

Deshpande, M. N. 1975a. 'Cultural Relations between Afghanistan and India with Special Reference to Archaeological Findings in the Two Countries'. *Afghanistan,* 28/2: 48–55. (100, 122, 245, 305, 404, 522, 546, 743, 1180)

Deshpande, M. N. 1975b. 'Preservation of Buddhist Shrines at Bamiyan, Afghanistan'. *Indian Archaeology,* 1971–2: 125–6. (100)

Deydier, H. 1949–50. 'L'inscription du bas-relief de Kā-picī-Begram et la chronologie de l'art du Gandhara'. *Oriental Art*, 11/3: 110–15. (122)

Deydier, H. 1950. *Contribution à l'étude de l'art du Gandhara*. Paris. (99, 100, 122, 322, 404, 546, 790, 1160)

Dhavalikar, M. K. 1971. 'A Note on Two Ganeśa Statues from Afghanistan'. *EW* 21: 331–6. (1064)

Diez, Ernst. 1923. *Persien. Islamische Baukunst in Churasan*. Hagen-Munich. (358, 1106)

Diez, Ernst. 1936. 'Manara'. *Encyclopaedia of Islam*, 1st edn., III. 226–31. Leiden. (358)

Diez, Ernst. 1950. 'Die Siegestürme in Ghazna als Weltbilder'. *Kunst des Orients*, 1: 37–44. (358)

Djindjian, F. See Hardy-Guilbert, C.

Dobbins, K. Walton. 1968a. 'Two Gandharan Reliquaries'. *EW* 18: 151–61. (127)

Dobbins, K. Walton. 1968b. 'Gandhara Buddha Images with Inscribed Dates'. *EW* 18: 281–8. (122)

Dobbins, K. Walton. 1970. 'Eros of Gandhara'. *Journal of the Oriental Society of Australia*, 7/1–2: 23–36. (1123)

Dobbs, H. R. C. 1904. 'Diary of a Political Agent on Deputation from Mashhad Mission'. Unpublished manuscript in Curzon Reports on Afghanistan, vol. 8. India Office Library and Records, 186–7. (2142)

Dolgorukov, V. S. 1974. 'Le chantier de fouilles C-VI'. Unpublished manuscript in the Afghan Institute of Archaeology, Kabul. (295)

Dollot, René. 1937. *L'Afghanistan*. Paris. (546, 972, 1006, 1173)

Donini, G. 1972. 'L'orografia del Ghūr secondo Jūzjāni (sec. XIII)'. *Annali di Ca'Foscari*, 11/3. Serie Orientale 3: 191–5. (468)

Dor, R. 1976. 'Lithoglyphes du Wakhan et du Pamir'. *Afghanistan Journal*, 3/4: 122–9. (88, 737, 953)

Dorneich, Christof M. 1968. *Minar-i Tschakari: Illustrierte Studien zur Geschichte und Kunstgeschichte der beiden buddhistischen Säulen bei Kabul*. Stuttgart. (718, 1124)

Dorneich, Christof M. 1999. *Minar-i Chakari: Afghanistan's Lost and Unsolved Architectural Riddle of Great Antiquity*. Peshawar. (718)

Dowson, J. 1863. 'On a Newly-Discovered Bactrian Pali Inscription; and on Other Inscriptions in the Bactrian Pali Character'. *JRAS* 1st ser. 20: 221–68. (127, 404, 1229)

Drummond, F. H. R. 1888. 'Report on the Road from Dahan-i-Kaian in the Surkhab Valley, across the Hindu Kush by the Chahardar Pass, to Siah Gird in Ghorband'. *ABC* V. Ed. J. West Ridgeway et al., 335–43. Simla. (451, 994)

Du Colombier, P. 1929. 'Griechisch-buddhistische Plastik im Museum Guimet'. *Cicerone*, 21: 404–6. (404)

Duccoeur, Guillaume, ed. 2012. *Autour de Bāmiyān: De la Bactriane hellénisée à l'Inde bouddhique*. Paris. (100)

Dupont-Sommer, André. 1946. 'Une inscription hébraïque d'Afghanistan'. *CRAI* 252–7. (373)

Dupont-Sommer, André. 1966. 'Une nouvelle inscription araméenne d'Aśoka'. *CRAI* 440–51. (522)

Dupont-Sommer, André. 1970. 'Une nouvelle inscription araméenne d'Aśoka trouvée dans la vallée du Laghman, Afghanistan'. *CRAI* 158–73. (1067)

Dupont-Sommer, André. 1980. 'Essénisme et Bouddhisme'. *CRAI* 698–715. (1067)

Dupree, Louis. 1951. 'Preliminary Field Report on Excavation at Shamshir Ghar, Kuh-i Duzd and Deh Morasi Ghundai'. *Afghanistan*, 6/2: 22–31; 6/3: 30–5. (287, 1069)

Dupree, Louis. 1956. 'Shamshir Ghar. A Historic Cave Site in Kandahar Province. Afghanistan'. *AA* 3/3: 195–206, and *Orientalistische Literaturzeitung*, 51/7–8: 294–6. (1069)

Dupree, Louis. 1957. 'Shamshir Ghar: A Cave in Afghanistan'. *Archaeology*, 10/2: 108–16. (1067)

Dupree, Louis. 1958a. *Shamshir Ghar: Historic Cave Site in Kandahar Province, Afghanistan*. Anthropological Papers of the American Museum of Natural History, 46/2. New York. (780, 1069)

Dupree, Louis. 1958b. 'Shamshir Ghar, a Historic Cave Site in Kandahar Province, Afghanistan'. *Afghanistan*, 13/2: 27–32. (1067, 1069)

Dupree, Louis. 1960. 'An Archaeological Survey in North Afghanistan'. *Afghanistan*, 10/3: 13–15. (46, 242)

Dupree, Louis. 1963. *Deh Morasi Ghundai: A Chalcholithic Site in South Central Afghanistan*. Anthropological Papers of the American Museum of Natural History, 50/2. New York. (287)

Dupree, Louis. 1964. 'Prehistoric Surveys and Excavations in Afghanistan: 1959–1960 and 1961–1963'. *Science*, 146/3644: 638–40. (46, 1031)

Dupree, Louis. 1967. 'The Prehistoric Period of Afghanistan'. *Afghanistan*, 20/3: 8–27. (46, 245, 422, 526)

Dupree, Louis. 1968a. 'The Oldest Sculptured Head?'. *Afghanistan*, 21/2: 49–50, and *Natural History*, 77/5: 26. (46, 245)

Dupree, Louis. 1968b. 'Prehistoric Excavations in Afghanistan'. *American Philosophical Society Yearbook 1967*, 504–8. (46, 245)

Dupree, Louis. 1969. 'Recent Research in Afghanistan'. *Explorers Journal*, 47/2: 84–93. (245)

Dupree, Louis. 1972. 'Tentative Conclusions and Tentative Chronological Charts'. In *Prehistoric Research in Afghanistan*. Ed. Louis Dupree et al., 74–82. Philadelphia. (46, 245)

Dupree, Louis. 1973. *Afghanistan*. Princeton. (18, 46, 245, 287, 522, 546, 743, 1123)

Dupree, Louis. 1975. 'New Palaeolithic Localities near Dasht-i-Nawur'. *Afghanistan Journal*, 2/3: 105–7. (266)

Dupree, Louis. 1976. 'Results of a Survey for Palaeolithic Sites in the Dasht-i Nawur'. *Afghanistan*, 29/2: 55–63. (266)

Dupree, Louis. 1981. 'Notes on Shortugai: An Harappan Site in Northern Afghanistan'. In *Indus Civilisation. New Perspectives*. Ed. A. H. Dani, 103–11. Islamabad. (345, 582, 1069, 1089)

Dupree, Louis, and Richard S. Davis. 1972. 'The Lithic and Bone Specimens from Aq Kupruk and Darra-i-Kur'. In *Prehistoric Research in Afghanistan*. Louis Dupree et al., 14–32. Philadelphia. Reprinted in *Afghanistan*, 26/4: 52–74; 27/1: 35–54. 1974). (46, 245)

Dupree, Louis, and Richard S. Davis. 1976. 'New Prehistoric Localities in the Dasht-i Nawur'. *Afghanistan*, 29/3: 13–17. (266)

Dupree, Louis, and Klaus Fischer. 1961. 'Preliminary Report on the Discovery of a Prehistoric Valley in Central Afghanistan'. In *International Conference on Asian Archaeology: Summary of Papers*. New Delhi, 32–3. (820, 1031)

Dupree, Louis, and Bruce Howe. 1963. 'Results of an Archaeological Survey for Stone Age Sites in North Afghanistan'. *Afghanistan*, 18/2: 1–15. (46, 138, 240, 242, 245, 422, 1151)

Dupree, Louis, and C. C. Kolb. 1972. 'Ceramics from Aq Kupruk, Darra-i-Kur, and Hazar Gusfand'. In *Prehistoric Research in Afghanistan*. Ed. Louis Dupree et al., 33–42. Philadelphia. Reprinted in *Afghanistan*, 27/4 (1975): 47–69. (46, 245, 422)

Dupree, Louis, Lawrence H. Lattman, and Richard S. Davis. 1970. 'Ghar-i-Mordeh Gusfand (Cave of the Dead Sheep): A New Mousterian Locality in North Afghanistan'. *Science*, 167: 1610–12, and *Afghanistan*, 23/3: 60–4. (352)

Dupree, Louis, Philippe Gouin, and N. Omer. 1971. 'The Khosh Tapa Hoard from Northern Afghanistan'. *Archaeology*, 24: 28–34, and *Afghanistan*, 24/1: 44–54. (582)

Dupree, Louis, et al. 1972. *Prehistoric Research in Afghanistan, 1959–1966*. Transactions of the American Philosophical Society, 62/4. Philadelphia. (46, 245)

Dupree, Nancy Hatch. 1967a. *The Road to Balkh*. Kabul. (46, 99, 240, 242, 425, 526, 569, 716, 1123, 1135)

Dupree, Nancy Hatch. 1967b. *The Valley of Bamiyan*. Kabul. (100, 508, 1004, 1042, 1052)

Dupree, Nancy Hatch. 1971a. *An Historical Guide to Kabul*. Kabul. (122, 389, 418, 483, 972, 1137, 1173, 1180)

Dupree, Nancy Hatch. 1971b. 'The Colossal Buddhas and the Monastic Grottos'. *Mārg*, 24/2: 17–24. (100)

Dupree, Nancy Hatch. 1974. 'Archaeology and the Arts in the Creation of a National Consciousness'. In *Afghanistan in the 1970s*. Ed. L. Albert and L. Dupree, 208–38. New York.

Dupree, Nancy Hatch. 1977. *An Historical Guide to Afghanistan*. 2nd edn. Kabul. (18, 95, 112, 149, 212, 295, 345, 352, 358, 401, 404, 409, 410, 419, 468, 507, 522, 609, 610, 634, 685, 723, 724, 743, 785, 786, 820, 1028, 1065, 1077, 1081, 1112, 1180, 1232)

Dupree, Nancy Hatch, Louis Dupree, and Ahmad Ali Motamedi. 1974. *The National Museum of Afghanistan: An Illustrated Guide*. Kabul. (18, 46, 100, 122, 169, 242, 245, 332, 337, 358, 404, 483, 508, 518, 522, 526, 546, 569, 582, 622, 630, 685, 723, 728, 743, 832, 928, 1042, 1069, 1088, 1123, 1168, 1173)

Durand, Sir Edward. N.d. *Afghan Boundary Commission. Views and Sketches. Parts 1 and 2*. Political and Secret Department, Govt of India, India Office Library [*c*.1885]. (35, 41, 298, 428, 454, 711, 764, 863, 1147)

Dussubieux, Laure, and B. Gratuze. 1991. *Analyses d'objets en verre provenant d'Arikamedu (Inde) et de Begram (Afghanistan) prêtés par le Muséee Guimet*. Orléans. (122)

Dussubieux, Laure, B. Gratuze, Paul Bernard, et al. 2003. 'Nature et origine des objets en verre retrouvées à Begram (Afghanistan) et à Bara (Pakistan)'. In *De l'Indus à l'Oxus*. Ed. O. Bopearachchi et al., 315–33. Lattes. (122)

Edelberg, K. 1957. 'Fragments d'un stūpa dans la vallée du Kunar en Afghanistan'. *AA* 4: 199–207. (154)

Edelberg, K. 1960. 'An Ancient Hindu Temple in Kunar'. *Afghanistan*, 15/3: 11–12. (154)

Eggermont, P. H. L., and J. Hoftijzer. 1962. 'The Moral Edicts of King Aśoka Including the Graeco-Aramaic Inscriptions of the Maurian Period'. *Textus Minores*, 29: 42–5. (522)

Elisséef, V. 1954. 'Les laques chinois de Begram'. In *Nouvelles recherches archéologiques à Begram*. MDAFA 11. Ed. J. Hackin et al., 151–6. Paris. (122)

Emanuel, W. V. 1939. 'Some Impressions of Swat and Afghanistan'. *JRCAS* 26: 195–213. (789, 930)

Engel, Nicolas. 2011. *Mes Aynak*. Kabul. (19)

English, Paul. 1973. 'The Traditional City of Herat, Afghanistan'. In *From Madina to Metropolis: Heritage and Change in the Near Eastern City*. Ed. L. Carl Brown, 73–90. Princeton. (428)

Erffa, H. von. 1946. 'A Tomb Stone of the Timurid Period in the Gardner Museum of Boston'. *Ars Islamica*, 1/ 11–12: 184–90. (428)

Errington, Elizabeth. 2001. 'Charles Masson and Begram'. *Topoi*, 11/1: 357–409. (122)

Errington, Elizabeth. 2017a. *Charles Masson and the Buddhist Sites of Afghanistan: Explorations, Excavations, Collections 1832–1835*. London. (4, 10, 17, 30, 100, 106, 113, 127, 129, 155, 163, 283, 326, 364, 370, 381, 389, 404, 418, 453, 471, 504, 519, 555, 574, 627, 651, 664, 667, 718, 727, 748, 756, 761, 779, 806, 1017, 1087, 1088, 1116, 1125, 1137, 1169, 1173, 1197, 1229)

Errington, Elizabeth. 2017b. *The Charles Masson Archive: British Library, British Museum and Other Documents Relating to the 1832–1838 Masson Collection from Afghanistan*. London. (10, 17, 106, 113, 127, 155, 163, 283, 326, 370, 389, 404, 418, 471, 519, 555, 574, 667, 718, 761, 806, 1017, 1087, 1116, 1125, 1137, 1169, 1173, 1197, 1229)

Errington, Elizabeth. See also Allchin, F. R.

Errington, Elizabeth, and Joe Cribb, eds. 1992. *The Cross-roads of Asia: Transformation in Image and Symbol in the Art of Ancient Afghanistan and Pakistan.* Cambridge. (17, 122, 127, 358, 428)

Errington, Elizabeth, and Vesta Sarkhosh Curtis, ed. 2007. *From Persepolis to the Punjab: Exploring Ancient Iran, Afghanistan and Pakistan.* London.

Ettinghausen, Richard, and Roland and Sabrina Michaud. 1976. 'Islamische Architekturornamente'. *Du Euro-päische Kunstzeitscher*, 426: 12–65. (468)

Eyre, Vincent. 1843. *The Military Operations at Cabul.* London. (100, 718)

Fabri, A. 1931. 'Two Notes on the Indian Headdresses'. *JRAS* 597–601. (100)

Fairservis, Jr, Walter A. 1950. 'Archaeological Research in Afghanistan'. *Transactions of the New York Academy of Science*, 2nd ser. 12/5: 172–4, and *Afghanistan*, 5/4: 31–4. (810)

Fairservis, Jr, Walter A. 1952. *Preliminary Report on the Prehistoric Archaeology of the Afghan-Baluchistan Areas.* American Museum Novitiates, 1587. New York. (108, 287, 335, 968)

Fairservis, Jr, Walter A. 1953. 'Future Archaeological Research in Afghanistan'. *South-Western Journal of Anthropology*, 9/2: 139–46. (287, 752, 968)

Fairservis, Jr, Walter A. 1961. *Archaeological Studies in the Seistan Basin of Southwestern Afghanistan and Eastern Iran.* Anthropological Papers of the American Museum of Natural History, 48/1. New York. (2, 3, 108, 145, 147, 206, 262, 264, 270, 335, 369, 551, 558, 559, 584, 684, 721, 752, 810, 823, 824, 831, 836, 842, 876, 900, 957, 979, 991, 1006, 1044, 1070, 1136, 1147, 1156, 1158, 1166, 1177, 1178, 1266)

Fairservis, Jr, Walter A. 1971. *The Roots of Ancient India.* New York. (46, 108, 167, 287, 360, 368, 506, 672, 743, 798, 968, 976, 1041)

Falk, Harry. 2001. *The Yuga of Sphujiddhvaja. and the Era of the Kushanas.* SRAA. Kamakura 7. (244)

Falk, Harry 2009. 'The Name of Vema Takhtu'. In *Fest-schrift in Honour of Nicholas Sims-Williams.* Ed. Werner Sunderman, Almut Hintze, and François de Blois, 105–16. Wiesbaden. (944)

Falkner, M. 1954–6. 'Neue Entdeckungen in Afghanistan'. *Archiv für Orientforschung*, 17: 478–9. (743)

Faticoni, Barbara. 2014. 'First Notes on a Treasure from Mes Aynak'. In *Central Asia in Antiquity: Interdisciplin-ary Approaches.* Ed. Borja Antela-Bernárdez and Jordi Vidal, 23–36. Oxford. (19)

Fehévári, Géza. 2008. 'The Lions of Ghazni'. *Journal of Inner Asian Art and Archaeology*, 3: 23–8.

Fehérvári, G., and Mehrdad Shokoohy. 1980. 'Archaeo-logical Notes on Lashkari Bazar'. *Wiener Zeitschrift für die Kunde des Morgenlandes*, 72: 83–95. (685)

Fergusson, James. 1876. *History of Indian and Eastern Architecture.* London. (17, 358, 404, 1116)

Ferrier, J. 1857. *Caravan Journeys and Wanderings in Per-sia, Afghanistan, Turkistan, and Baluchistan.* London. (123, 274, 318, 339, 346, 377, 378, 428, 454, 522, 634, 656, 659, 661, 684, 700, 776, 792, 810, 819, 841, 842, 849, 868, 875, 879, 881, 962, 988, 1000, 1046, 1051, 1079, 1107, 1165, 1257, 1259, 1263, 2164)

Filigenzi, Anna. 2009a. 'The Buddhist Site of Tapa Sardar. In *The IsIAO Italian Archaeological Mission in Afghani-stan 1957–2007: Fifty Years of Research in the Heart of Eurasia.* Ed. Anna Filigenzi and Roberta Giunta, 41–57. Rome. (1180)

Filigenzi, A. 2009b. 'Ritual Forms, Cult Objects: Tapa Sardar at the Crossroads of Places and Phases of the Buddhist Ecumene. In *The IsIAO Italian Archaeological Mission in Afghanistan 1957–2007: Fifty Years of Research in the Heart of Eurasia.* Ed. Anna Filigenzi and Roberta Giunta, 59–75. Rome. (1180)

Filigenzi, Anna, and Roberta Giunta, eds. 2009. *The IsIAO Italian Archaeological Mission in Afghanistan 1957–2007: Fifty Years of Research in the Heart of Eurasia.* Rome.

Filigenzi, Anna, and Roberta Giunta. 2015. 'The Italian Archaeological Mission to Afghanistan'. In Cassar and Noshadi 2015: 80–91. (358, 468, 565, 1180)

Firūzi, A. W., ed. 1979. 'Akhbār'. *Bāstān Shināsi Afghāni-stān*, 1/1: 56–8. (439)

Fischel, W. J. 1949. 'Encore un mot à propos de l'inscrip-tion hébraïque d'Afghanistan'. *JA* 237: 299–300. (373)

Fischel, W. J. 1965. 'The Rediscovery of the Medieval Jew-ish community at Firuzkuh in Central Afghanistan'. *Journal of the American Oriental Society*, 85: 148–53.

Fischer, Jan, John Lonsdale, David Owen, and Bill Purver. 1959. 'The Cambridge Afghanistan Expedition 1959: General Report'. Unpublished report in the DAFA library, Kabul. (468, 1144)

Fischer, Klaus. 1956. 'Archaeological Remains of Jainism in West Pakistan and Afghanistan'. *Voice of Ahimsa*, 6/3–4. (100)

Fischer, Klaus. 1957. 'Neue Funde und Forschungen zur indischen Kunst in Arachosien, Baktrien und Gandhara'. *Archäologischer Anzeiger des Deutschen Archäologischen Instituts*, 417–35. (1009)

Fischer, Klaus. 1958a. 'Gandharan Sculptures from Qunduz and Environs'. *Artibus Asiae*, 21/3–4: 231–49. (1091, 1160)

Fischer, Klaus. 1958b. 'Kandahar in Arachosien'. *Wis-senschaftliche Zeitschrift der Martin-Luther-Universität Halle-Wittenberg*, 7: 1151–64. (522)

Fischer, Klaus. 1959a. *Schöpfungen indischer Kunst von den frühesten Bauen und Bildern bis zum mittelalterlichen Tempel.* Cologne. (971, 1009, 1123)

Fischer, Klaus. 1959b. 'Ikonographische Besonderheiten in buddhistischen Reliefs von Kunduz in Baktrien'. In

Akten des 24en Internationalen Orientalisten-Kongresses München Sekt, X. 528–30. Munich. (1160)

Fischer, Klaus. 1960. 'Pre-Islamic Fortification, Habitations and Religious Monuments in the Kunar Valley'. *Afghanistan*, 15/3: 7–10. (154, 453, 706, 821, 827, 880)

Fischer, Klaus. 1961a. 'Preliminary Notes on Some Ancient Remains at Qunduz'. *Afghanistan*, 16/1: 12–26. (29, 194, 208, 400, 442, 444, 553, 930, 931, 942, 1013, 1065, 1091, 1160)

Fischer, Klaus. 1961b. 'Recent Researches in Ancient Seistan'. *Afghanistan*, 16/2: 30–9. (842, 1073)

Fischer, Klaus. 1961c. 'The Westernmost Monuments of Hindu, Jain and Sikh Religion in Afghanistan'. In *International Congress in Asian Archaeology—Delhi, 1961*. Unpublished transcript in the DAFA library, Kabul. (154, 337, 358, 453, 1009, 1069, 1123, 1160)

Fischer, Klaus. 1961d. 'Report on Archaeological Reconnaissances in Afghanistan 1960–1961'. Unpublished report in the DAFA library, Kabul. (781, 818)

Fischer, Klaus. 1962. 'A Jaina Tīrthankara in Afghanistan'. *Voice of Ahimsa*, 12/1.

Fischer, Klaus. 1964. 'Une tête de Durga en marbre de l'Afghanistan oriental'. *AA* 10/1: 35–42. (649, 832, 1059)

Fischer, Klaus. 1966. 'Indo-Iranian Contacts as Revealed by Mud-Brick Architecture from Afghanistan'. *Oriental Art*, 12: 25–31. (143, 208, 302, 350, 440, 479, 844, 1073)

Fischer, Klaus. 1967a. 'Alexandropolis metropolis Arachosias: Zur Lage von Kandahar an landverbindungen Iran und Indien'. *Bonner Jahrbücher*, 67: 129–232. (73, 86, 103, 168, 170, 192, 217, 274, 318, 337, 345, 356, 368, 384, 522, 636, 659, 744, 746, 769, 798, 805, 807, 809, 817, 899, 907, 962, 966, 988, 1048, 1109, 1174, 1193, 1211, 1248)

Fischer, Klaus. 1967b. 'Der spät-sassanidische Feuertempel-Typus im Obergeschloss eines Lehmziegelturmes in Afghanisch-Seistan und die indoislamische Baukunst'. In *Festschrift für Wilhelm Eilers*, 420–8. Wiesbaden. (143)

Fischer, Klaus. 1969. 'Preliminary Remarks on Archaeological Survey in Afghanistan'. *Zentralasiatische Studien*, 3: 327–408. (15, 29, 54, 67, 73, 78, 79, 86, 103, 109, 131, 142, 143, 148, 154, 168, 170, 173, 192, 194, 201, 208, 217, 218, 231, 260, 265, 282, 302, 307, 313, 315, 337, 345, 350, 356, 368, 384, 400, 403, 440, 442, 447, 453, 454, 463, 467, 479, 497, 512, 522, 553, 562, 583, 587, 617, 636, 649, 650, 659, 683, 688, 689, 695, 705, 706, 713, 733, 734, 746, 763, 765, 769, 792, 805, 807, 809, 817, 818, 820, 821, 827, 832, 842, 844, 880, 899, 907, 930, 931, 940, 941, 942, 944, 960, 962, 966, 988, 1009, 1014, 1031, 1048, 1052, 1059, 1065, 1073, 1076, 1091, 1118, 1139, 1160, 1165, 1172, 1174, 1176, 1181, 1189, 1193, 1211, 1247, 1248)

Fischer, Klaus. 1969–70. 'Archaeological Studies in Seistan and Adjacent Areas'. *Afghanistan*, 22/3–4: 91–107. (190, 312, 486, 601, 607, 824, 871, 889, 983, 1073)

Fischer, Klaus. 1970a. 'Interrelations of Islamic Architecture in Afghanistan—The Remains of Afghan-Seistan: Notes on the Evolution of Islamic Architecture in Turan, Iran and India'. *Mārg*, 24/1: 46–56. (146, 201, 390, 479, 601, 607, 839, 842, 844, 889, 983, 1073, 1264)

Fischer, Klaus. 1970b. 'Projects of Archaeological Maps from Afghan-Seistan between 31°20′ to 30°50′N and 62°00′ to 62°10′E'. *Zentralasiatische Studien*, 4: 483–534. (143, 146, 190, 201, 228, 301, 390, 417, 558, 722, 740, 778, 824, 839, 871, 894, 983, 1073, 1120, 1264, 2182)

Fischer, Klaus. 1971a. 'Rapport préliminaire sur la prospection archéologique du Seistan septentrional en Octobre 1970'. *Afghanistan*, 23/4: 37–50. (190, 201, 228, 300, 648, 808, 866)

Fischer, Klaus. 1971b. 'Types of Architectural Remains in the Northern Part of Afghan Seistan'. *Bulletin of the Asia Institute of Pahlavi University*, 2: 40–72. (164, 190, 201, 228, 301, 312, 375, 390, 486, 558, 601, 607, 719, 778, 824, 839, 871, 883, 889, 1120)

Fischer, Klaus. 1971c. 'Historical, Geographical and Philological Studies on Seistan by Bosworth, Daffina and Gnoli in the Light of Recent Archaeological Field Surveys'. *EW* 21: 45–51. (479, 601, 792, 824, 844)

Fischer, Klaus. 1972. 'Ancient Iranian and Medieval Islamic Vaulting Systems in the Mud-Brick Architecture of Afghan Seistan'. In *Sixth International Congress of Iranian Art and Archaeology: Summary of Papers*, 21. Oxford. (201, 301, 390, 889)

Fischer, Klaus. 1973a. 'Nimruz and the Archaeology of Afghanistan'. *Afghanistan*, 26/3: 1–16. (300)

Fischer, Klaus. 1973b. 'Archälogische Landesaufnahme im Norden von Afghanische-Sistan'. *AMI* 6: 213–30. (300, 390, 962)

Fischer, Klaus. 1973c. 'Archaeological Field Surveys in Afghan Seistan 1960–1970'. In *South Asian Archaeology*. Ed. Norman Hammond, 131–55. London. (143, 146, 164, 190, 201, 228, 300, 301, 390, 417, 558, 563, 607, 648, 722, 733, 740, 824, 839, 883, 894, 983, 1073, 1120, 1264, 2182)

Fischer, Klaus. 1973d. 'Archäologische Landesaufnahme im afghanisch Sistan'. In *Indologen-Tagung 1971*. Ed. H. Hartel and V. Moeller, 204–9. Wiesbaden. (607, 824, 889)

Fischer, Klaus. 1973e. 'Archaeological Reconnaissance in Afghan Seistan with Special Reference to Saljuq Art'. *Colloquies on Art in Asia*, 4: 150–5. (607)

Fischer, Klaus. 1974a. *Dächer, Decken und Gewölbe indischer Kultstätten und Nutzbauten*. Wiesbaden. (683, 1052, 1160)

Fischer, Klaus. 1974b. 'Architectue au Seistan islamique'. *Afghanistan*, 17/1: 12–34. (607, 778)

Fischer, Klaus. 1976. *Indischer Baukunst islamischer Zeit*. Baden-Baden. (99, 607)

Fischer, Klaus. 1978a. 'From the Rise of Islam to the Mongol Invasion'. In *The Archaeology of Afghanistan*. Ed.

F. R. Allchin and N. Hammond, 301–55. London. (39, 179, 195, 201, 231, 358, 403, 410, 468, 683, 685, 742, 875, 1236)

Fischer, Klaus. 1978b. 'From the Mongols to the Mughals'. In *The Archaeology of Afghanistan*. Ed. F. R. Allchin and N. Hammond, 357–404. London. (390, 428, 607, 752, 778)

Fischer, Klaus. 1978c. 'Fortified and Open Settlements in Medieval Sistan'. In *Storia della Città: Rivista internazionale di storia urbana e territoriale*, 3: 59–63. Milan. (300, 390, 778, 824)

Fischer, Klaus. 1980. 'Zu erzehlenden Gandhara-Reliefs'. *Beiträge zur Allgemeinen und Vergleichenden Archäologie*, 2. (1160).

Fischer, Klaus. 1983a. 'Überlieferungen volkstümlicher und herrschaftlicher bauformen in Sistan'. *Ethnologie*, 135–46. (839)

Fischer, Klaus. 1983b. 'Archaeological Fieldwork in Afghan Sistan and Current Research on Eastern Iranian Architecture'. In *Forschungsprojekt DFG Mohenjo-daro*. Ed. G. Urban and M. Jansen, 81–9. Aachen. (300, 390)

Fischer, Klaus. 1987. 'Eine Kraftwagenstraßenmarkierung aus der Zeit des Habibillah nach dem Vorbild einer buddhistischen Kultsäule'. In *Festschrift Martin Graßnick aus Anlaß der Vollendung seines 70. Geburtstages Kaiserslautern*, 139–47. (718, 1124)

Fischer, Klaus, and L. Mauelshagen. 1984. 'Archaeological Survey in Afghan Sistan: A Short Review'. In *Symposium international de Tunis sur la photogrammétrie appliqué à l'architecture islamique. Octobre 1984*, 239–51. Tunis.

Fischer, Klaus, Landolf Mauelshagen, and Karl Tonnessen. 1976. 'Photogrammetrische Aufnahme schwer zuganglicher Ruinen im Orient'. *Architektur-Photogrammetrie*, 2: 49–66. (300, 390, 607)

Fischer, Klaus, Dietrich Morgenstern, and Volker Thewalt. 1974–6. *Nimruz: Gelandebegehungen in Sistan 1955–1973 und die Aufnahme von Dewal-i Khodaydad 1970*. 2 vols. Bonn. (52, 142, 143, 144, 146, 159, 164, 184, 190, 200, 201, 219, 274, 293, 300, 301, 318, 341, 347, 375, 390, 399, 457, 478, 479, 482, 486, 507, 522, 597, 601, 607, 639, 646, 648, 659, 684, 688, 734, 740, 752, 778, 808, 811, 822, 824, 839, 866, 889, 894, 962, 983, 990, 1073, 1085, 1115, 1133, 1200, 1247)

Fisher, M. T., and M. W. Stolper. 2015. 'Achaemenid Elamite Administrative Tablets. 3. Fragments from Old Kandahar'. *ARTA* 1/1: 26. (522)

Fleming, David. 1978. 'A Simple Wooden Bipod for Vertical Photography'. *Bulletin of the Institute of Archaeology*, 15: 131–48. (522)

Flood, Finbarr B. 2002a. 'Between Cult and Culture: Bamiyan, Islamic Iconoclasm, and the Museum'. *Art Bulletin*, 84: 641–59. (100)

Flood, Finbarr B. 2002b. 'Between Ghazna and Delhi: Lahore and its Lost Manāra'. In *Cairo to Kabul: Afghan and Islamic Studies Presented to Ralph Pinder-Wilson*. Ed. Warwick Ball and Leonard Harrow, 102–12. London. (358)

Flood, Finbarr B. 2005a. 'Ghurid Monuments and Muslim Identities: Epigraphy and Exegesis in Twelfth-Century Afghanistan'. *Indian Economic and Social History Review*, 42/3: 263–94. (468, 1023)

Flood, Finbarr B. 2005b. 'Revue of Le Minaret Ghouride de Jam by J Sourdel-Thomine'. *Art Bulletin*, 87/3: 536–43. (468)

Flood, Finbarr B. 2007. 'Lost in Translation: Architecture, Taxonomy and the Eastern "Turks"'. *Muqarnas*, 24: 79–116. (358)

Flood, Finbarr B. 2009a. 'Islamic Identities and Islamic Art: Inscribing the Qur'an in Twelfth-Century Afghanistan'. In *Dialogues in Art History, from Mesopotamian to Modern: Readings for a New Century*. Ed. Elizabeth Cropper, 91–118. Studies in the History of Art Series. National Gallery of Art. Washington, DC. (468, 1023)

Flood, Finbarr B. 2009b. 'Masons and Mobility: Indic Elements in Twelfth-Century Afghan Stone-Carving'. In *Fifty Years of Research in the Heart of Eurasia: Istituto Italiano per l'Africa et l'Oriente*. Ed. Anna Filigenzi and Roberta Giunta, 137–60. Rome. (358, 683)

Flury, S. 1918. 'Das Schriftband an der Türe des Mahmud von Ghazna. 998–1030'. *Der Islam*, 8: 214–27. (358)

Flury, S. 1925. 'Le décor épigraphique des monuments de Ghazna'. *Syria*, 6: 61–90. (358)

Fouache, Eric, Roland Besenval, et al. 2012. 'Palaeochannels of the Balkh River, Northern Afghanistan and Human Occupation since the Bronze Age Period'. *Journal of Archaeological Science*, 39: 3415–27. (38)

Foucher, Alfred. 1906–22. *L'art gréco-bouddhique du Gandhara*. 3 vols. Paris.

Foucher, Alfred. 1924. 'Notes sur les antiquités bouddhiques de Haïbak'. *JA* 205/1: 139–54. (1135)

Foucher, Alfred. 1928. 'The French Archaeological Delegation in Afghanistan: October, 1922–November, 1925'. *Indian Art and Letters* NS 2: 21–7. (99, 100, 122, 404)

Foucher, Alfred. 1929. 'Buste provenant de Hadda (Afghanistan) au Musée Guimet'. *Monuments Piot*, 30: 101–10. (404)

Foucher, Alfred. 1939a. 'Deux jātaka sur ivoire, provenant des fouilles de Joseph et Ria Hackin au Bēgrām de Kāpici. Afghanistan'. In *India Antiqua: A Volume of Oriental Studies Presented to J. P. Vogel*, 124–30. Leiden. (122)

Foucher, Alfred. 1939b. 'La Nicée d'Afghanistan'. *CRAI* 435–47. (122, 705)

Foucher, Alfred. 1942–7. *La vielle route de l'Inde de Bactres à Taxila*. 2 vols. MDAFA 1. Paris. (17, 33, 63, 74, 99, 100, 105, 122, 178, 191, 211, 217, 247, 250, 305, 404, 435, 464, 483, 491, 493, 496, 519, 548, 606, 651, 705, 718, 753, 761, 773, 840, 884, 885, 1016, 1018, 1042, 1052, 1087, 1135, 1146, 1185, 1197, 2138, 2180)

Foucher, Alfred. 1954. 'Deux jātaka sur ivoire'. In *Nouvelles recherches archéologiques à Begram*. MDAFA. Ed. J. Hackin et al., 83–7. Paris. (122)

Fouchet, Maurice 1931. *Notes sur l'Afghanistan: Œuvres posthumes*. Paris. (99, 100)

Fox, E. J. 1943. *Travels in Afghanistan: 1937–1938*. New York. (39, 454, 801, 1001)

Francfort, Henri-Paul. 1973. 'Le motif ornamental des cœurs emboîtés dans l'art de l'Asie Centrale'. *Afghanistan*, 26/3: 95–8. (18)

Francfort, Henri-Paul. 1975. 'Un cachet achéménide d'Afghanistan'. *JA* 263: 219–22.

Francfort, Henri-Paul. 1976a. 'Les fortifications en Asie centrale des Achéménides aux Kouchans'. Unpublished thesis, University of Paris. (18, 99, 122, 295, 314, 892, 1034, 1123)

Francfort, Henri-Paul. 1976b. 'Le modèles gréco-bactriens de quelques reliquaries et palette à fard gréco-bouddiques'. *AA* 32: 91–8.

Francfort, Henri-Paul. 1977. 'Le plan des maisons gréco-bactriennes et le problème des structures de type "megaron" en Asie Centrale et Iran'. In *Le plateau iranien et l'Asie Centrale des origins à la conquête islamique*. Colloques internationaux du C.N.R.S., 567. Ed. J. Deshayes, 267–80. Paris. (18)

Francfort, Henri-Paul. 1978. 'Zulm-Andijarag: Métripole de la plaine à l'époque pré-mongole'. In *Etudes de géographie historique sur la plaine d'Aï Khanoum*. Ed. Paul Bernard and Henri-Paul Francfort, 27–38. Paris. (1271).

Francfort, Henri-Paul. 1979a. *Les fortifications en Asie Centrale de l'âge du bronze à l'époque kouchane*. Paris. (18, 38, 99, 122, 189, 256, 257, 295, 314, 459, 630, 641, 642, 666, 732, 892, 1034, 1052, 1123, 1198)

Francfort, Henri-Paul. 1979b. 'La prospection archéologique de la Bactriane orientale et la fouille de Shortugai'. *Journées archéologiques*. Ed. Frantz Grenet. Paris. (1089)

Francfort, Henri-Paul. 1981a. 'Shortughaï, an Indus Valley Settlement on the River Oxus'. *Archaeology*. (1089)

Francfort, Henri-Paul. 1981b. 'The Late Periods of Shortughaï and the Problem of the Bishkent Culture: Middle and Late Bronze Age in Bactria'. *South Asian Archaeology 1979*. Ed. H. Härtel, 191–202. Berlin. (1089)

Francfort, Henri-Paul. 1983. 'Excavations at Shortughaï in Northeast Afghanistan'. *AJA* 87/4: 518–19.

Francfort, Henri-Paul. 1984a. *Fouilles d'Aï Khanoum III: Le sanctuaire du temple à niches indentées*. MDAFA 27. Paris. (18)

Francfort, Henri-Paul. 1984b. 'The Early Periods of Shortughaï and the Dashly Culture'. *South Asian Archaeology 1981*. Ed. B. and F. R. Allchin, 170–5. Cambridge.

Francfort, Henri-Paul. 1989. *Fouilles de Shortughaï. Recherches sur l'Asie Centrale Protohistorique. Mémoires de la Mission Archéologique Française en Asie Centrale*, II. Paris. (1089)

Francfort, Henri-Paul. 2012. 'Tillya Tepe and its Connections with the Eurasian Steppes'. In *Afghanistan. Forging Civilizations along the Silk Road*. Ed. Joan Aruz and Elisabetta Valtz Fino, 88–101. New York. (1192)

Francfort, Henri-Paul. 2015. 'Une idole protohistorique d'Aï Khanoum hellénistique (Bactriane, Afghanistan)'. In *De Samarcande à Istanbul: Etapes orientales*. Ed. V. Schiltz, II. 41–51. Paris. (18)

Francfort, Henri-Paul, and Jean-Claude Liger. 1976. 'Fouilles d'Aï Khanoum: Campagne de 1974. II. L'hérôon au caveau de Pierre'. *BEFEO* 63: 25–39. (18)

Francfort, Henri-Paul, and Marie-Helène Pottier. 1978. 'Sondage préliminaire sur l'éstablissement protohistorique harappéen et post-harappéen de Shortugaï. Afghanistan du N.-E'. *AA* 34: 29–79. (1089)

Francfort, Henri-Paul, Frantz Grenet, Guy Lecuyot, Bertille Lyonnet, Laurianne Martinez, and Claude Rapin. 2014. *Il y a 50 ans… la découverte d'Aï Khanoum*. Paris. (18)

Franke, Ute. 2008a. 'Baluchistan and the Borderlands'. *Encyclopaedia of Archaeology*. Ed. Deborah M. Pearsall, 651–70. New York. (743)

Franke, Ute, ed. 2008b. *National Museum Herat—Areia Antiqua through Time*. Berlin. (212, 391, 428, 532, 794, 2087)

Franke, Ute. 2015a. 'Ancient Herat and its Cultural Heritage: New Evidence from Recent Research'. In *Keeping History Alive: Safeguarding Cultural Heritage in Post-Conflict Afghanistan*. Ed. Brendan Cassar and Sara Noshadi, 92–103. Paris and Kabul. (428)

Franke, Ute. 2015b. 'Ancient Herat Revisited: New Data from Recent Archaeological Fieldwork'. In *Greater Khorasan*. Ed. Rocco Rante, 63–241. Berlin. (212, 428, 794)

Franke, Ute, and Martina Müller-Wiener, eds. 2016. *Ancient Herat. Research Reports of the German-Afghan Archaeological Mission to Herat, Afghanistan*, III. *Herat through Time: The Collections of the Herat Museum and Archive*. Staatliche Museen zu Berlin—Preußischer Kulturbesitz. Berlin. (391, 428)

Franke, Ute, and Thomas Urban. 2006. *Areia Antiqua—Ancient Herat: Summary of the Work Carried out by the DAI-Mission in Collaboration with the Institute of Archaeology, Ministry of Information and Culture, Afghanistan*. Berlin. (185, 794, 2018, 2047, 2056, 2057, 2084, 2103, 2105, 2123, 2128, 2148, 2173, 2179, 2183, 2209, 2221, 2247, 2248, 2255, 2264, 2266)

Franz, H. Gerhard. 1977–8. 'Der buddhistische Stupa in Afghanistan'. *Afghanistan Journal*, 4/4: 131–43; 5/1: 26–38. (389, 404, 673, 761, 1087)

Franz, H. Gerhard. 1978. 'Das Chakri Minar als buddhistische Kultsäule'. *Afghanistan Journal*, 5/3: 96–101. (718)

Fraser, P. M. 1979. 'The Son of Aristonax at Kandahar'. *Afghan Studies*, 2: 9–23. (522)

Fraser, P. M. 1982. 'Palamedes at Baġlan'. *Afghan Studies*, 3–4: 77–8. (1123)

Frifelt, Karen, and Per Sorenson, eds. 1989. *South Asian Archaeology 1985*. Honolulu.

Frumkin, G. 1957. 'Afghanistan, carrefour des civilisations'. *Journal de Genève*, 6–7 July. (100, 122, 332, 404)

Frye, Richard N. 1946a. 'Notes on the History of Architecture in Afghanistan'. *Ars Islamica*, 21–2: 200–2. (718, 1052, 1237)

Frye, Richard N. 1946b. 'The Cultural Traditions of Afghanistan'. *Gazette des Beaux-Arts*, 29: 65–72. (428, 716)

Frye, Richard N. 1946c. 'Observations on Architecture in Afghanistan'. *Gazette des Beaux-Arts*, 29: 129–38. Reprinted in R. N. Frye, *Islamic Iran and Central Asia: 7th–12th Centuries*, 129–38. London, 1979. (1052)

Frye, Richard N. 1948. 'Two Timurid Monuments in Herat'. *Artibus Asiae*, 11: 206–12. (346, 428)

Frye, Richard N. 1954. 'An Epigraphical Journey into Afghanistan'. *Archaeology*, 7/2: 114–18. (1144, 1259)

Fujita, Kunio. 1966a. 'Hadda Shatsudo no joshinzō (A Goddess Figure from Hadda)'. *Kobijutsu*, 13: 95–7. Summary in H. Motamedi 1975c: 279–80. (404)

Fujita, Kunio. 1966b. 'Hadda no Iseki' (The Hadda Site). *Geijutsu Shinchō*. 197: 134–41. Summary in H. Motamedi 1975c: 280–1. (404, 673)

Fujita, Kunio. 1971. 'Afuganistan ni okeru Kushan-chô Bukkyô bijutsu ni kansuru ni san no mondai' (Some Problems Concerning Kushan Buddhist Art in Afghanistan). *Tokyo Kuritsu Hakubutsukan Kiyō. Tokyo National Museum Bulletin*, 7: 59–133. Summary in H. Motamedi 1975c: 236–8. (309, 673)

Furughi, Bābā Murād. 1981. 'Tarmīm chāh-i Qal'a-i Bust'. *Bāstān Shināsi Afghānistān*, 4/2: 136. (149)

Fussman, Gérard. 1966. 'Notes sur la topographie de l'ancienne Kandahar'. *AA* 13: 33–57. (522, 536)

Fussman, Gérard. 1969. 'Une inscription Kharoshthī à Hadda'. *BEFEO* 56: 5–9. (404)

Fussman, Gérard. 1970. 'Inscriptions Kharoshthī du Musée de Caboul'. *BEFEO* 57: 43–56. (122, 464)

Fussman, Gérard. 1974a. 'Nouvelle découverte à Bamiyan'. *Afghanistan*, 27/2: 57–78. (100)

Fussman, Gérard. 1974b. 'Ruines de la Vallée de Wardak'. *AA* 30: 65–130. (621, 1229)

Fussman, Gérard. 1974c. 'Documents épigraphiques Kouchans'. *BEFEO* 61: 1–77. (265, 266, 317, 621, 630, 877, 930, 1045, 1140)

Fussman, Gérard. 1977. 'Le renouveau iranien dans l'empire Kouchan'. In *Le plateau iranien et l'Asie Centrale, des origins à la conquête islamique*. Colloques internationaux du CNRS 567. Ed. J. Deshayes, 313–32. Paris. (1123)

Fussman, Gérard. 1980. 'Nouvelles inscriptions Saka: Ere d'Eucratide, ère d'Azès, ère, Vikrama, ère de Kaniska'. *BEFEO* 67: 1–43. (18)

Fussman, Gérard. 1994. 'DAŠT-E NĀWOR'. *Encyclopaedia Iranica*, 7/1: 96. (265, 266)

Fussman, Gérard. 1996. 'Southern Bactria and Northern India before Islam: A Review of Archaeological Reports'. *Journal of the American Oriental Society*, 116/2: 243–59. (18, 631)

Fussman, Gérard. 1998. 'L'inscription de Rabatak et l'origine de l'ére saka'. *Journal Asiatique*, 286/2: 571–651. (944)

Fussman, Gérard, and Olivier Guillaume. 1990. *Surkh Kotal en Bactriane*, II. *Les monnaies. Les Petits objets*. MDAFA 32. Paris. (1123)

Fussman, Gérard, and Marc Le Berre. 1976. *Monuments bouddhiques de la région de Caboul*, I. *Le monastère de Gul Dara*. MDAFA 22. Paris. (19, 277, 357, 389, 545, 749, 921, 922, 1173)

Fussman, Gérard, Baba Murad, and Éric Olivier. 2008. *Monuments Bouddhiques de la région de Caboul/Kabul Buddhist Monuments*, II. Paris. (388, 389, 435, 458, 483, 519, 606, 622, 647, 651, 718, 723, 790, 884, 928, 972, 1016, 1087, 1088, 1124, 1173, 1197, 1222, 1223, 1237, 2111, 2138, 2275)

Gafurov, B. G., ed. 1974. *Central Asia in the Kushan Period*. 2 vols. Moscow.

Gaibov, Vassif A., Gennadij A. Košalenko, and Galina V. Trebeleva. 2010. 'Archaeological Gazetteer of Afghanistan, Addenda, I, Herat Oasis'. *Parthica*, 12: 107–16. (13, 354, 454, 634, 781, 841, 874, 895, 908, 984, 1060, 1079, 1165, 1206, 1259, 1263, 2003, 2048, 2049, 2050, 2086, 2132, 2140, 2162, 2223, 2228, 2262)

Gail, Adalbert J., ed. 1998. *South Asian Archaeology 1991*. Berlin.

Galdieri, Eugenio. 1978. *A Few Conservation Problems Concerning Several Islamic Monuments in Ghazni (Afghanistan). Technical Report and Notes on a Plan of Action*. Rome. (358)

Gallavotti, Carlo. 1959a. 'The Greek Version of the Kandahar Bilingual Inscription of Aśoka'. *EW* 10: 185–91. (522)

Gallavotti, Carlo. 1959b. 'Il Manifesto di Aśoka nell'Afghanistan'. *Rivista di Cultura Classica e Medievale*, 1: 113–26. (522)

Gangoly, O. C. 1937–8. 'The Antiquity of the Buddha-Image: The Cult of the Buddha'. *Ostasiatische Zeitschrift*, NS 14/2–3: 41–59. (127)

Garczynski, Paul. 1980. 'Campagne de fouilles 1978 à Aï Khanoum. IV. Le palais. La cour dorique'. *BEFEO* 68: 39–43. (18)

Gardin, Jean-Claude. 1957a. *Céramiques de Bactres*. MDAFA 15. Paris. (99)

Gardin, Jean-Claude. 1957b. 'Potieres de Bamiyan'. *Ars Orientalis*, 2: 227–45. (1042)

Gardin, Jean-Claude. 1959. 'Tessons de poterie musulmane provenant du Seistan afghan'. In *Diverses recherches archéologiques en Afghanistan: 1933–1940*. MDAFA 8. Ed. J. Hackin et al., 29–38. Paris. (752, 792, 1006)

Gardin, Jean-Claude. 1963. *Lashkari Bazar II: Les trouv-ailles. Céramiques et monnaies de Lashkari Bazar et de Bust.* MDAFA 18. Paris. (149, 685)

Gardin, Jean-Claude. 1970. 'Campagne de fouilles de 1969 en Afghanistan: La céramique'. *CRAI* 247-9. (18)

Gardin, Jean-Claude. 1971. 'La campagne de fouilles de 1970 à Aï Khanoum (Afghanistan). VI. Céramique'. *CRAI* 447-52. (18)

Gardin, Jean-Claude. 1973. 'Fouilles d'Aï Khanoum. VIII. Les céramiques'. In *Aï Khanoum*, I. MDAFA 21. Ed. Paul Bernard et al., 121-88. Paris. (18)

Gardin, Jean-Claude. 1975. 'Campagne de fouilles 1974 à Aï Khanoum. IV. Céramique'. *CRAI* 193-5. (18)

Gardin, Jean-Claude. 1977. 'New Aspects of Old World Archeology: A Case Study in Northern Afghanistan'. Working paper for the George Grant MacCurdy Lectureship, Apr. Unpublished paper in the British Institute of Afghan Studies library, Kabul. (18)

Gardin, Jean-Claude. 1980. 'L'archéologie du paysage bactrien'. *CRAI* 480-501. (18, 54, 421, 536, 553, 580, 594, 931, 959, 1142, 2078)

Gardin, Jean-Claude. 1981. 'The Development of Eastern Bactria in Pre-Classical Times'. *Puratáttva*, 10 (1978-9): 8-13.

Gardin, Jean-Claude. 1982. 'Vers une géographie archéologique de l'Afghanistan'. *St.Ir.* 11: 97-110. (622, 633, 931, 2059, 2217)

Gardin, Jean-Claude. 1995. 'Fortified Sites of Eastern Bactria (Afghanistan) in Pre-Hellenistic Times'. In *The Land of the Gryphons: Papers on Central Asian Archaeology in Antiquity.* Ed. Antonio Invernizzi, 83-105. Florence. (209, 288, 487, 495, 510, 525, 594, 611, 631, 633, 931, 933, 936, 937, 1220)

Gardin, Jean-Claude. 1998. *Prospections archéologiques en Bactriane Orientale (1974-1978). Sous la direction de Jean-Claude Gardin, III. Description des sites et notes de synthèse.* Paris. (1, 5, 6, 28, 31, 40, 43, 50, 54, 61, 70, 83, 89, 94, 115, 134, 135, 136, 139, 156, 160, 162, 175, 182, 187, 194, 208, 209, 210, 218, 220, 252, 260, 268, 269, 288, 307, 308, 321, 374, 386, 400, 412, 420, 421, 440, 444, 445, 446, 446, 447, 450, 462, 472, 484, 487, 495, 505, 509, 510, 511, 512, 513, 515, 516, 525, 553, 569, 579, 580, 583, 587, 591, 594, 611, 626, 632, 633, 640, 643, 643, 674, 738, 741, 750, 772, 791, 797, 799, 853, 892, 904, 909, 911, 913, 917, 927, 931, 933, 936, 937, 943, 959, 960, 969, 980, 981, 1007, 1008, 1009, 1019, 1032, 1080, 1086, 1089, 1090, 1092, 1093, 1128, 1132, 1142, 1143, 1162, 1205, 1217, 1220, 1224, 1233, 1235, 1253, 1271)

Gardin, Jean-Claude, and Pierre Gentelle. 1976. 'Irrigation et peuplement dans la plaine d'Aï Khanoum de l'époque achéménide à l'époque musulmane'. *BEFEO* 63: 59-99. (18)

Gardin, Jean-Claude, and Pierre Gentelle. 1979. 'L'exploitation du sol en Bactriane Antique'. *BEFEO* 66: 1-29.

Translated as: 'Zar'at dar Bakhtar-i bastān'. *Bāstān Shināsi Afghānistān*, 3/1: 78-83. (18, 1089)

Gardin, Jean-Claude, and Bertille Lyonnet. 1976. 'Fouilles d'Aï Khanoum: Campagne de 1974. IV. La céramique'. *BEFEO* 63: 45-51. (18)

Gardin, Jean-Claude, and Bertille Lyonnet. 1978-9. 'La prospection archéologique de la Bactriane orientale. 1974-1978: Premiers resultats'. *Mesopotamia*, 13-14: 99-154. (1, 5, 6, 18, 26, 28, 31, 40, 50, 54, 61, 70, 83, 89, 94, 115, 134, 135, 136, 139, 156, 160, 162, 175, 182, 187, 194, 208, 209, 210, 215, 218, 220, 252, 268, 269, 288, 307, 308, 321, 374, 386, 400, 412, 420, 421, 440, 444, 445, 446, 447, 450, 462, 472, 484, 487, 495, 505, 509, 510, 511, 512, 513, 515, 516, 525, 553, 569, 579, 580, 583, 587, 588, 591, 594, 611, 626, 631, 632, 633, 640, 643, 674, 738, 741, 750, 772, 791, 797, 799, 853, 892, 904, 931, 1086, 1090, 1092, 1093, 1128, 1132, 1142, 1143, 1162, 1205, 1217, 1224, 1233, 1235, 1253, 1271)

Gardiner, A. 1853. 'Description of Mohzarkhala in the Kohistan of the Western Hazara', ed. M. P. Edgeworth. *JASB* 22: 383-7. (223)

Gardner, N. M. 1971. 'Journeys in Afghanistan, July and August 1971. Part One: Wakhan and Munjan'. Unpublished report in the Map Room of the RGS, London. (449, 1072, 1230)

Gascoigne, A. L. 2010. 'Pottery from Jām: A Medieval Ceramic Corpus from Afghanistan'. *Iran*, 48: 107-51. (468)

Gaube, Heinz. 1977. 'Innenstadt und Vorstadt Kontinuität und Wandel im Stadtbild von Herat zwischen dem 10 und dem 15 Jahrhundert'. In *Beiträge zur Geographie orientalischer Städte und Märkte.* Ed. G. Schweizer, 213-40. Wiesbaden. (428)

Gaulier, Simone, Robert Jera-Bezard, and Monique Maillard. 1976. *Buddhism in Afghanistan and Central Asia.* Iconography of Religions, 23/14. Leiden. (100, 332, 404, 790, 1088)

Gazetteer 1907-14. *Gazetteer of Afghanistan.* Compiled in the Division of the Chief of Staff, India. Part 1. *Badakhshan.* 5th edn. Simla, 1914. Part II. *Afghan Turkistan.* 4th edn. Calcutta, 1907. (35) Part III. *Herat.* 4th edn. Calcutta, 1910. Part IV. *Kabul.* 4th edn. Calcutta, 1910. (158, 189, 466, 602, 691, 1029, 1039) Part V. *Kandahar.* 4th edn. Calcutta, 1908. (1270) Part VI. *Farah.* Calcutta, 1908.

Gazetteer 1972-80. *Historical and Political Gazetteer of Afghanistan*, ed. Ludwig W. Adamec. Graz. Reprints of Gazetteer 1907-14. I. *Badakhshan Province and Northeastern Afghanistan.* 1972. (315, 432, 448, 524, 640, 650, 846, 873, 891, 1011) II. *Farah and Southwestern Afghanistan.* 1973. (58, 77, 225, 230, 293, 318, 377, 436, 454, 476, 527, 652, 702, 709, 736, 841, 842, 849, 863, 878, 898, 901, 979, 1047, 1115, 1147, 1195, 1260) III. *Herat and Northwestern Afghanistan.* 1975. (7, 13, 22, 193, 207, 216, 331,

427, 454, 541, 599, 610, 614, 654, 676, 724, 764, 802, 820, 843, 850, 869, 875, 890, 908, 947, 952, 1023, 1119, 1159, 1165, 1196, 2070, 2075, 2114, 2132, 2203, 2229, 2240) IV. *Mazar-I Sharif and North-Central Afghanistan*. 1979. (9, 41, 48, 93, 205, 213, 249, 279, 296, 298, 322, 331, 398, 415, 439, 465, 496, 552, 569, 640, 645, 657, 697, 757, 776, 777, 834, 837, 918, 944, 1018, 1038, 1040, 1049, 1051, 1076, 1094, 1099, 1139, 1149, 1150, 1207, 1212, 1241, 1242, 1243, 2074, 2130) V. *Kandahar and South-Central Afghanistan*. 1980. (76, 96, 280, 367, 368, 694, 698, 1193)

Gazzola, P., and J. B. Perrin. 1971. *Afghanistan: Protection et mise en valeur de la vallée de Bamiyan*. Paris. (100)

Gentelle, Pierre. 1977. 'Quelques observations sur l'extension de deux techniques d'irrigation sur le plateau iranien et en Asie Centrale'. In *Le plateau iranien et l'Asie Centrale des origins à la conquête islamique*. Colloques Internationaux du CNRS 567. Ed. Jean Deshayes. 249–62. Paris. (18)

Gentelle, Pierre. 1978. *Etude géographique de la plaine d'Aï Khanoum et de son irrigation depuis les temps antiques*. Paris. (18, 269)

Gentelle, Pierre. 1989. *Prospections archéologiques en Bactriane Orientale (1974–1978). Sous la direction de Jean-Claude Gardin, I. Données paléogéographiques et fondements de l'irrigation*. Paris. (18, 54, 440, 553, 931, 1089, 1142)

Geoffroy-Schneiter, Bérénice. 2001. *Gandhara: La mémoire de l'Afghanistan*. (English edn: *Gandhara: The Memory of Afghanistan*). Paris. (100, 122, 332, 404, 508)

Gerard, A. 1833. 'Continuation of the Route of Lieut. A. Burnes and Dr. Gerard, from Peshawar to Bokhara'. *JASB* 2: 1–22. (100)

Gerard, J. G. 1834. 'Memoir on the Topes and Antiquities of Afghanistan'. *JASB* 3: 321–9. Reprinted in *Essays on Indian Antiquities*. Ed. J. Prinsep, 109–12. London, 1858. (761)

Gershevitch, Ilya. 1963. 'Review of Humbach 1960'. *BSOAS* 26: 193–6. (1123)

Gershevitch, Ilya. 1966. 'The Well of Baghlan'. *Asia Major,* NS 12/1: 90–109. (1123)

Gershevitch, Ilya. 1967. 'Bactrian Inscriptions and Manuscripts'. *Indogermanische Forschungen,* 72/1–2: 27–57. (1123)

Gershevitch, Ilya. 1979. 'Nokonzok's Well'. *Afghan Studies,* 2: 55–64. (1123)

Gershevitch, Ilya. 1980. 'Chāh-i Baghlān'. *Tahqiqāt-i Kūshānī,* 3/2: 176–85. (1123)

Gettens, Rutherford J. 1938. 'The Materials in the Wall-Paintings of Bāmiyān, Afghanistan'. *Technical Studies,* 6: 186–93. (100)

Getty, Alice. 1928. *The Gods of Northern Buddhism*. Oxford.

Ghawwās, Muhammad Ghulam. 1969. *Rāhnāmāyi Harāt*. Herat. (212, 346, 351, 373, 428, 634, 947, 1259, 1263)

Ghawwās, Muhammad Ghulam. 1974. 'Qarya-i Zīyarat-gāh'. *Herat,* 'Aqrab: 5–8; Qus: 5–8. (1263)

Ghirshman, Roman. 1939. 'Fouilles de Nad-i Ali dans le Seistan Afghan'. *RAA* 13: 10–20. Reprinted as: 'Recherches préhistoriques dans la partie afghane du Seistan'. *MDAFA* 8 (1959): 39–48. Translated as 'Hafriyāt-i Nād-i 'Ali dar Sīstā-n-i Afghān'. *Sālnāmā-yi Kābul,* 1317 (1938/9): 196–203. (752)

Ghirshman, Roman. 1943–5. 'Fouilles de Begram'. *JA* 134: 59–71. (122)

Ghirshman, Roman. 1946. *Bégram: Recherches archéologiques et historiques sur les Kouchans*. MDAFA 12. Cairo. (122)

Ghirshman, Roman. 1948. *Les Chionites-Hephthalites*. MDAFA 13. Cairo. (332, 483, 963)

Ghirshman, Roman. 1953. 'Die französische archäologische Forchung in Iran and Afghanistan (1940-1951)'. *Saeculum,* 4: 115–23. (122)

Ghirshman, Roman. 1957. 'Le problème de la chronologie des Kouchans'. *Cahiers d'Histoire Mondiale,* 3/3: 689–720. (122)

Ghose, Ajit. 1952. 'A Unique Gold Coin of the Hindu Kings of Kabul'. *NC* 6th ser. 12: 133–5. (483)

Ghosh, D. 1945. 'Exhibition of Afghanistan Antiquities at the Calcutta University'. *Journal of the Greater India Society,* 12: 144–6. (404)

Ghūriyāni, Muhammad Azam. 1971. 'Dar justjū-i asar-i tārīkhī Fūshanj'. *Herāt,* Hūt: 25–6; Dalw: 36–7; Hadi: 35–6; Mīzān: 39–40; 'Aqrab: 27–8; Qūs: 28–9. (1259)

Gignoux, Philippe. 2003 'Le christianisme à Hérat'. In *De l'Indus à l'Oxus*. Ed. O. Bopearachchi et al., 397–401. Lattes. (428)

Gill, S. 1991. 'Procédés narratives dans les ivoires de Begram'. *Topoi,* 11: 515–35. (522)

Gilles, R. 2000. 'L'Afghanistan: Cinquante ans d'archéologie vingt ans de guerre'. *Archéologia,* 365: 16–31. (100, 468)

Giunta, Roberta. 2001. 'The Tomb of Muhammad al-Harawi (447/1055) at Gazni (Afghanistan) and Some New Observations on the Tomb of Mahmud the Gaznavid'. *EW* 51, 1–2: 109–26. (358)

Giunta, Roberta. 2003. *Les inscriptions funéraires de Gazni*. Naples. (358)

Giunta, Roberta. 2005. 'Islamic Gazni an IsAIO Archaeological Project in Afghanistan: A Preliminary Report'. *EW* 55/1–4: 473–84. (358)

Giunta, Roberta. 2009. 'Islamic Ghazni: Excavations, Surveys and New Research Objectives'. In *The IsIAO Italian Archaeological Mission in Afghanistan 1957–2007: Fifty Years of Research in the Heart of Eurasia*. Ed. Anna Filigenzi and Roberta Giunta, 89–104. Rome. (358)

Giunta, Roberta. 2010. 'The Renewal of the Activities of the Italian Archaeological Mission in Afghanistan: The Emerging Retrieval of Documents and Finds of Islamic

Epoch in Ghazni'. In *Proceedings of the 6th International Congress of Archaeology of the Ancient Near East.* Ed. P. Matthiae et al., 75–89. Wiesbaden. (358)

Giunta, Roberta. 2012. 'New Epigraphic Data from the Excavations of the Ghaznavid Palace of Mas'ūd III at Ghazni (Afghanistan)'. *South Asian Archaeology 2007, II. Historic Periods,* 123–32. Oxford. (358)

Giunta, Roberta. See also Filigenzi, Anna.

Glatzer, Bernt. 1973. 'The Madrasah of Shah-i Mashhad in Badghis'. *Afghanistan,* 25/4: 46–68. (1023)

Glatzer, Bernt. 1980. 'Das Mausoleum und die Moschee des Ghoriden Ghiyath ud-Din in Herat'. *Afghanistan Journal,* 7: 6–22. (428)

Gnoli, Gherardo. 1962. 'Jewish Inscriptions in Afghanistan'. *EW* 13: 311–12. (468)

Gnoli, Gherardo. 1963a. 'The Tyche'. *EW* 14: 36.

Gnoli, Gherardo. 1963b. 'Further Information Concerning Judaeo-Persian Documents of Afghanistan'. *EW* 14: 209–10. (468)

Gnoli, Gherardo. 1964. *Le inscrizioni giudeo-persiane del Gur (Afghanistan).* Serie Orientale Roma, 30. Rome. (468)

Gnoli, Gherardo. 1967. *Ricerche storiche sul Sistan antico.* Rome. (149, 752, 824)

Gnoli, Gherardo. 1983. *Iranian Studies.* Orientalia Romana. Essays and Lectures, 5—Serie Orientale Roma, 52. Rome.

Gnoli, Gherardo. 2009. 'Some Notes on the Religious Significance of the Rabatak Inscription'. In *Festschrift in Honour of Nicholas Sims-Williams.* Ed. Werner Sunderman, Almut Hintze, and François de Blois, 141–59. Wiesbaden. (944)

Gnoli, Gherardo. 2009. 'Some Notes on the Religious Significance of the Rabatak Inscription'. In *Festschrift in Honour of Nicholas Sims-Williams.* Ed. Werner Sunderman, Almut Hintze, and François de Blois, 141–59. Wiesbaden. (944)

Göbl, Robert. 1961. 'Bericht über die Numismatischen Haphtaliten und Kidariten Forschungen auf dem Gebiet der Sasaniden, Kushān'. In *Congresso Internazionale del Numismatica,* I. 193–207. Rome.

Göbl, Robert. 1964. 'Zwei neue Termini für ein zentrales Datum der Alten Geschichte Mittelasiens, das Jahr 1 des Kushankönigs Kaniska'. *Anzeiger der phil.-hist. Klasse der Österreichischen Akademie der Wissenschaften,* 101/20: 137–51. (1123)

Göbl, Robert. 1965. *Die drei Versionen der Kaniska-Inschrift von Surkh Kotal.* Vienna. (1123)

Göbl, Robert. 1966. 'Vašiska I, ein bisher unbekannter König der späteren Kušan'. *Österreichischen Akademie der Wissenschaft,* 11: 283–300. (1123)

Göbl, Robert. 1967. *Dokumente zur Geschichte der iranischen Hunnen in Baktrien und Indien.* 3 vols. Wiesbaden. (332, 337, 1173)

Godard, André. 1925a. *Exposition des récentes découvertes et des récents travaux archéologiques en Afghanistan et en Chine.* Paris. (100, 358, 404, 761)

Godard, André. 1925b. 'Ghazni'. *Syria,* 6: 58–60. (358)

Godard, André. 1951. 'L'origine de la Mosquée et du Caravansérail à quatre iwans'. *Ars Islamica,* 15–16: 1–9. (1042)

Godard, André, Yves Godard, and Joseph Hackin. 1928. *Les antiquités bouddhiques de Bāmiyān.* MDAFA 2. Paris. Translated as: *Asār-i 'atīq-i Bāmiyān.* Kabul, 1936/7. (100, 305)

Godard, Yves. 1936. 'L'inscription de Mas'ūd III à Ghazna'. *Arthār-é-Īrān* 1/notes: 367–9. (358)

Goetz, Hermann. 1957. 'Late Gupta Sculpture in Afghanistan: The "Scoretti Marble" and Cognate Sculptures'. *AA* 4/1: 11–19. (337, 546)

Golombek, Lisa. 1969a. *The Timurid Shrine at Gazurgah.* Toronto. (346)

Golombek, Lisa. 1969b. 'Abbasid Mosque at Balkh'. *Oriental Art,* 15: 173–89. Reprinted in L. Golombek et al., *The Nine Domes of the Universe,* 173–89. Bergamo, 2016. (410)

Golombek, Lisa. 1977. 'Mazār-i Sharīf: A Case of Mistaken Identity?' In *Studies in Memory of Gaston Wiet.* Ed. M. Rosen-Ayalon, 335–43. Jerusalem. (716)

Golombek, Lisa. 1983. 'The Resilience of the Friday Mosque: The Case of Herat'. *Muqarnas,* 1: 95–102. (428)

Golombek, Lisa, and Donald Wilber. 1988. *The Timurid Architecture of Iran and Turan.* 2 vols. Princeton. (69, 99, 111, 278, 358, 373, 428, 532, 634, 661, 716, 725, 781, 1263).

Golombek, Lisa, et al. 2016. *The Nine Domes of the Universe: The Ancient Noh Gonbad Mosque. The Study and Conservation of an Early Islamic Monument at Balkh.* Bergamo. (410)

Gorshenina, S., and C. Rapin. 1991. *De Kaboul à Samarcande: Les archéologues en Asie centrale.* Paris.

Goshal, Upendra Nath. 1928. *Ancient Indian Culture in Afghanistan. Greater India Society Bulletin,* 5. (100)

Gouin, Philippe. 1969. 'Figurines de terre cuite de l'Afghanistan et du Waziristan'. *AA* 14: 37–52. (287, 743)

Gouin, Philippe. 1973a. 'Prospection Archéologique à Tash Qurghan'. *Afghanistan,* 25/4: 75–95. (141, 1101)

Gouin, Philippe. 1973b. 'Fouilles d'Aï Khanoum. X: Les petits objets'. In *Aï Khanoum,* I. MDAFA 21. Ed. Paul Bernard et al., 195–201. Paris. (18)

Gouin, Philippe. 1974. 'Céramiques protohistoriques d'Asie Centrale Méridionale. 2e–1er millénaires)'. Unpublished thesis, University of Paris. (65, 141, 256, 289, 290, 745, 1034, 1035, 1036, 1056, 1061, 1062, 1063, 1152, 1181, 1212, 1213, 1240)

Gratuze. See Dussubieux.

Gratzl, Karl, Robert Kostka, and G. Patzelt. 1976. 'Petroglyphen im Wardak und im Grossen Pamir'. In *Grosser Pamir.* Ed. Roger Senarclens De Grancy and Robert Kostka, 311–41. Graz. (196, 455, 678, 816, 1126)

Gray, Basil. 1935. 'Stucco Figurines from Hadda'. *British Museum Quarterly*, 10/1: 7. (404)

Green, Nile. 2017. 'The Afghan Discovery of Buddha: Civilizational History and the Nationalizing of Afghan History'. *International Journal of Middle Eastern Studies*, 49/1: 47–70. (100, 122, 1123)

Grenet, Frantz. 1980b. (1359). 'Kashf-i qabristān-i zardūshtī dar Aī Khānoum'. *Tahqiqāt-i Kūshānī*, 3/2: 103–10. Translation of: 'Une nécropole zoroastrienne à Aï Khanoum?' Paper presented at the 2nd International Congress of Kushan Studies, Kabul 1978. (18)

Grenet, Frantz. 1982. 'Trois documents religieux de Bactriane Afghane'. *St.Ir.* 11: 155–62. (99, 295)

Grenet, Frantz. 1983a. 'L'onomastique iranienne à d'Aï Khanoum'. *Bulletin de Correspondance Hellénique*, 107/1: 373–81. (18)

Grenet, Frantz. 1983b. 'Un plat sasanide d'Ardašīr (379–383) au bazaar de Kabul'. *St.Ir.* 12/2: 195–205.

Grenet, Frantz. 1984. *Les pratiques funéraires dans l'Asie Central sédentaire de la conquête grecque à l'islamisation.* Paris. (18, 332, 362)

Grenet, Frantz. 1994. 'Bāmiyān and the Mihr Yašt'. *BAI* 7: 87–94. (100)

Grenet, Frantz. 1996 'Asaggôrnois, Askisaggorago, Sangchârak'. *Topoi*, 6: 470–4. (2237)

Grenet, Frantz. 1998. *Cultes et monuments religieux dans l'Asie centrale préislamique.* Paris.

Grenet, Frantz. 2002a. 'Regional Interaction in Central Asia and Northwest India in the Kidarite and Hephthalite Periods'. In *Indo-Iranian Languages and Peoples.* Ed. N. Sims-Williams, 203–24. London. (846)

Grenet, Frantz. 2002b. 'Zoroastre au Badakhshan'. *St.Ir.* 30: 193–214. (981)

Grenet, Frantz. 2005. 'Découverte d'un relief sassanide dans le Nord de l'Afghanistan. Note d'information'. *CRAI* 149/1: 115–34. (2227)

Grenet, Frantz, Jonathan Lee, Philippe Martinez, and François Ory. 2007. 'The Sasanian Relief at Rag-i Bibi (Northern Afghanistan)'. In *After Alexander: Central Asia Before Islam.* Ed. Joe Cribb and Georgina Herrmann, 243–67. Oxford. (2227)

Grenet, Frantz, Jonathan Lee, and Ralph Pinder-Wilson. 1980. 'Les monuments anciens du Gorzivân (Afghanistan du nord-ouest)'. *St.Ir.* 9/1: 69–98. Reprinted in *Afghanistan Archaeological Review*, 3/1: 1–35. (362)

Grenet, Frantz, Jean-Claude Liger, and Régis de Valence. 1980. 'Compagne de fouilles 1978 à Aï Khanoum. VII. L'arsenal'. *BEFEO* 68: 51–63. (18)

Grierson, George A. 1913. 'On the Phonetics of the Wardak Vase'. *JRAS* 141–3. (1229)

Griesbach, C. C. 1888a. 'Notes on the Country between Tirpul and the Doshakh Range'. ABC V. Ed. J. West Ridgeway et al., 78–80. Simla. (373, 543)

Griesbach, C. C. 1888b. 'Report on Journey from Chaharshamba through Maimana, Belchirag, and the Hill Country South of Belchirag'. ABC V. Ed. J. West Ridgeway et al., 185–215. Simla. (45, 100, 171, 249, 276, 279, 322, 414, 415, 493, 534, 645, 668, 777, 833, 862)

Griesbach, C. L. 1885a. 'Notes on the Country between Tirpul and the Doshakh Range' (Enclosure No. 8, dated 14 May 1885. Political and Secret Letters from India, vol. 44. India Office). (610, 764)

Griesbach, C. L. 1885b. 'Notes on the Road to Herat via the Band-i Baba and the Band-i Zurmat' (Enclosure No. 23E, dated 20 Apr 1885. Political and Secret Letters from India, vol. 44. India Office). (346, 373)

Griffith, H. H. 1879. 'Report on the Fort of Khelat-i-Ghilzai'. *Reports on Afghanistan 1879.* Bound vol. in British Library, Shelf-mark I.S.164. (899)

Griffith, W. 1847. *Journals of Travels in Assam, Burma, Bootan, Afghanistan and the Neighbouring Countries.* Arranged by J. M. Clelland. London. (100, 1042, 1052)

Grodekoff, N. 1880. *Ride from Samarcand to Herat, through Balkh and the Uzbek States of Afghan Turkestan.* Translated by Charles Marvin. London. (35, 98, 126, 697, 818, 890, 1099, 1134)

Grötzbach. 1976. *Aktuelle Probleme der regionalentwicklung und Städtgeographie Afghanistan.* Meisenheim am Glan. (42)

Grötzbach. 1979. *Stäte und Bazare in Afghanistan: Eine Städtgeographische Untersuchung.* Tübingen. (697)

Grousset, René. 1929. 'La nouvelle sale grécobouddhique du Musée Guimet'. *Revue de l'Art*, 55: 135–9. (404)

Grousset, René. 1930. 'The Afghanistan Discoveries and their Historical Significance'. *Formes* (May): 12–14. (100, 305, 404)

Grube, Ernst. 1974. 'Notes on the Decorative Art of the Timurid Period'. In *Gururājamañjarikā: Studi in onore di Guiseppe Tucci*, I. 233–79. Naples. (428)

Guillaume, Olivier. 1979. 'Le grand propylene sur rue d'Aï Khanoum'. Unpublished thesis, Université de Lyon. (18)

Guillaume, Olivier. 1983. *Fouilles d'Aï Khanoum, II. Les propylées de la rue principale.* MDAFA 26. Paris. (18)

Guillaume, Olivier. 1991. *Graeco-Bactrian and Indian Coins from Afghanistan.* Delhi. (569, 728)

Guillaume, Olivier, and Axelle Rougeulle. 1987. *Fouilles d'Aï Khanoum VII. Les petits objets.* MDAFA 31. Paris. (18)

Guillaume, Olivier, Jean-Claude Liger, and Régis de Valence. 1980. 'Campagne de fouilles 1978 à Aï Khanoum. II. Propylées sur la route principale'. *BEFEO* 68: 7–9. (18)

Gullini, Giorgio, ed. 1960. *Attivita archeologia italiana in Asia: Mostra de resultati delle missioni in Pakistan e in Afghanistan (1956–1959).* Turin and Rome. (358, 1180)

Gullini, Giorgio. 1961a. 'Problemi di archeologia e d'arte dell' Afghanistan preislamico'. In *L'Afghanistan dalla preistoria all'Islam.* Ed. G. Gullini, 23–57. Turin. (100, 122, 404)

Gullini, Giorgio, ed. 1961b. *L'Afghanistan dalla preistoria all'Islam: Capalavori del Museo di Kabul.* Turin. (100, 122, 332, 358, 404, 743, 1088)

Gupta, S. P. 1979. *Archaeology of Soviet Central Asia and the Indian Borderlands,* I. *Prehistory;* II. *Protohistory.* New Delhi. (46, 256, 257, 425, 743)

Haase, Claus-Peter, and Ute Franke. 2016. 'The Cenotaph from the Mazar Khoja Muhammad Ghazi in Fushanj'. In *Ancient Herat. Research Reports of the German-Afghan Archaeological Mission to Herat, Afghanistan,* III. *Herat through Time.* Ed. U. Franke and M. Müller-Wiener, 373–89. Berlin. (1259)

Habibi, Abdulhayy. 1971. *Tārikh-i khatt wa nawishtahā-i kuan-i Afghānistān az asr-i qabl al-tārīkh ta kanūm.* Kabul. (71, 100, 127, 247, 250, 265, 346, 349, 358, 404, 428, 522, 1067, 1221, 1229)

Habibi, Abdulhayy. 1963/64a (1342). *Zabān-i dū hazār sāla-i Afghānistān yā mādar-i Dāri. tahlīl-i katība-i Surkh Kūtal-i Baghlān).* (Kabul). Translated as: 'The Mother of the Dari Language'. *Afghanistan,* 21/3 (1968): 1–10; 22/1 (1969): 1–5; 22/2: 55–63; 22/3–4 (1969–70): 28–33; 23/1: 1–5; 23/2: 1–7; 23/3: 1–8; 23/4 (1971): 1–8; 24/1: 1–10; 24/2–3: 1–9; 25/1 (1972): 1–8; 25/2: 1–3; 25/4; 1973: 1–10. (1123)

Habibi, Abdulhayy. 1963/64b (1342). 'Zabān-i darī-yi dū hazār sāl qabl; muhimtarīn sanadi qadīm zabān ahd-i kūshānān kashf shud'. *Āryānā,* 21/3: 1–8; 21/4: 1–6; 21/5: 58–70. (1123)

Habibi, Abdulhayy. 1968. 'Afghanistan's Importance from the Viewpoint of the History and Archaeology of Central Asia'. *Afghanistan,* 20/4: 1–19. (522, 1123)

Habibi, Abdulhayy. 1969–70a. 'On the Mode of Efflorescence of the Calligraphic Styles of the Timurid Period as Artistic Manifestations on Buildings and on Books'. *Afghanistan,* 22/3–4: 1–14. (428)

Habibi, Abdulhayy. 1969–70b (1348). 'Haft Katība-yi Qadīm-i tukhāri-yi Sanskrit wa 'arabi dar Uruzgān wa Jaghatū wa Tūchi'. *Āryānā,* 27/2: 1–53. (71, 265, 320, 1221)

Habibi, Abdulhayy. 1972. 'The Temple of Sunagir, Zoon or Zoor'. *Afghanistan,* 25/1: 73–7. (291)

Habibi, Abdulhayy. 1974. 'Word Dividers in Greek Script of the Kushan Period of Afghanistan'. In *Central Asia in the Kushan Period,* I. Ed. B. G. Gafurov, 322–7. Moscow. (71, 1123, 1221)

Habibi, Abdulhayy. 1977. 'Nukāt-i nau dar tārikh-i hunar wa dānish-i Khurāsān'. *Honar va Mardom,* 6: 213–30. (1023)

Habibi, Abdulhayy. 1977. *Tārikh-i khatt wa nawishtahā-i Afghānistān az asr-i qabl al-tārīkh ta kanūn.* Kabul. (71, 100, 127, 247, 250, 265, 346, 349, 358, 404, 428, 522, 1067, 1221, 1229)

Habibi, Abdulhayy. 1980. 'The City of Firuzkuh: Where was it?' *Afghanistan,* 33/1: 34–44. (468)

Hackin, Joseph. 1926. 'Sculptures Gréco-bouddhiques de Kāpisa'. *Monument Piot,* 28: 35–44. (790)

Hackin, Joseph. 1928a. 'The Colossal Buddhas at Bāmiyān; their First Influence on Buddhist Sculpture'. *Eastern Art,* 1: 108–16. (100)

Hackin, Joseph. 1928b. 'Les fouilles de Hadda (Afghanistan)'. *RAA* 5/2: 66–76. (122, 404)

Hackin, Joseph. 1931. *Recherches Archéologiques en Asie Centrale.* Paris.

Hackin, Joseph. 1932a. *Bāmiyān.* Tokyo. (100, 508)

Hackin, Joseph. 1932b. 'Les dernières découvertes d'Afghanistan (1930)'. *Études d'orientalisme Linossier,* 287–91. (100, 508)

Hackin, Joseph. 1933. *L'œuvre de la Délégation Archéologique Française en Afghanistan (1922–1932).* Archéologie bouddhique. Tokyo. (100, 122, 305, 404, 508, 790, 1243)

Hackin, Joseph. 1934. 'Explorations at Bamiyan by the French Archaeological Mission in Afghanistan (Mission Hackin-Carl)'. *ABIA* 1932/8: 16–18. (100, 508)

Hackin, Joseph. 1935a. 'The Eastward Extension of Sassanian Motives'. *BAIPAA* 4: 5–6. (100)

Hackin, Joseph. 1935b. 'Réparation des monnaies anciennes en Afghanistan'. *JA* 226: 287–92. Translated as: 'Dasta Bandi-yi maskūkāt-i qadīm dar Afghānistān'. *Āryānā,* 2/5 (1323): 37–41. (358, 378, 1000, 1034)

Hackin, Joseph. 1935c. 'Influences sassanides dans l'art brahmanique: Fouilles de la Délégation Archéologique Française en Afghanistan'. In *IIIè Congrès international d'art et d'archéologie iraniens,.* 89–90. Leningrad. (546)

Hackin, Joseph. 1936a. 'Archaeological Explorations of the Neck of the Khair Khaneh (near Kabul)'. *Journal of the Greater India Society,* 3/1: 23–35. (546)

Hackin, Joseph. 1936b. 'Au sujet de quelques statues bouddhiques récemment mises au jour en Afghanistan'. *RAA* 10/3: 130–1. (332)

Hackin, Joseph. 1937. *L'art bouddhique de la Bactriane et l'origine de l'art gréco-bouddhique.* Kabul. (1160)

Hackin, Joseph. 1938a. 'The Work of the French Archaeological Mission in Afghanistan, September 1936 to August 1937'. *Indian Art and Letters,* 12: 41–9. (122, 332, 1088)

Hackin, Joseph. 1938b. 'Die Arbeiten der franzöischen archäologischeischen Delegation in Afghanistan'. *OAZ* 14: 221–6. (122, 332)

Hackin, Joseph. 1938c. 'Les travaux de la Délégation Archéologique Française en Afghanistan'. *RAA* 12/1: 2–11. (122, 332, 1088)

Hackin, Joseph. 1939/40. 'Les fouilles de Begram. 1939'. *Sālnāmā-yi Kābul* 1–10. (122)

Hackin, Joseph. 1939a. *Recherches archéologiques à Begram.* 2 vols. MDAFA 9. Paris. (122)

Hackin, Joseph. 1939b. 'Deux verres peints d'origine syrienne, mis au jour (chantier R.10) à Begram (Afghanistan):

Fouilles de la DAFA'. In *Mélanges syriens offerts à M.R. Dussaud*, 941–5. Paris. (122)

Hackin, Joseph. 1940a. *Recherches archéologiques à Begram* (1939). Kabul. (122)

Hackin, Joseph. 1940b. 'The 1939 Dig at Begram'. *Asia* (Oct.): 525–6 and (Nov.): 608–610. (122)

Hackin, Joseph. 1940c. 'A New Campaign of Excavations at Begram (Afghanistan), 1939'. *Journal of the United Provinces Historical Society*, 13/1: 1–7. (122)

Hackin, Joseph. 1946. 'Incised and Carved Ivory Plaques from Begram, Afghanistan'. *Bulletin of the Iranian Institute*, 6/1–4: 20–1. (122)

Hackin, Joseph. 1950a. 'L'art bouddhique de la Bactriane et les origines de l'art Gréco-Bouddhique'. *Afghanistan*, 5/1: 1–9. (1160)

Hackin, Joseph. 1950b. 'The Buddhist Monastery of Fondukistan'. *Afghanistan*, 5/2: 19–35. (332)

Hackin, Joseph. 1951. 'Les fouilles de Begram'. *Afghanistan*, 6/4: 1–10. (122)

Hackin, Joseph. 1954a. '*Les fouilles de Begram* (1939)'. *MDAFA* 11: 11–16. (122)

Hackin, Joseph. 1954b. 'Catalogue descriptif des objets découverts à Begram rédigé en cours de fouille'. *MDAFA* 11: 157–314. (122)

Hackin, Joseph. 1959a. 'Recherches archéologiques à Bāmiyān en 1933'. In *Diverses recherches archéologiques en Afghanistan*. MDAFA 8. Ed. J. Hackin et al., 23–8. Paris. (201, 638, 752, 792, 810, 839, 842, 871, 1006)

Hackin, Joseph. 1959b. 'Fouilles de Kunduz 1936'. *MDAFA* 8: 19–22. (1160)

Hackin, Joseph. 1959d. 'Le monastère bouddhique de Fondukistan: Fouilles de J. Carl, 1937'. *MDAFA* 8: 49–58. (332)

Hackin, Joseph. 1959c. 'Recherches archéologiques dans la partie afghane du Seistan'. In *Diverses rechereches archéologiques en Afghanistan*. MDAFA 8. Ed. J. Hackin et al., 23–8. Paris. (201, 638, 752, 792, 810, 839, 842, 871, 1006)

Hackin, Joseph, et al. 1954. *Nouvelles recherches archéologiques à Begram*. 2 vols. MDAFA 11. Paris. (122)

Hackin, Joseph, and O. Bruhl. 1933. 'Derniers travaux de la Délégation Archéologique de France en Afghanistan'. *RAA* 8: 116–9. (100, 122)

Hackin, Joseph, and J. Carl. 1933. *Nouvelles recherches archéologiques à Bāmiyān*. MDAFA 3. Paris. (100, 508)

Hackin, Joseph, and J. Carl. 1936. *Recherches archéologiques au col de Khair Khana près de Kabul*. MDAFA 7. Paris. (546)

Hackin, Joseph and Ria. 1934. *Le site archéologique de Bāmiyān*. Paris. Translated as: *Rahnāma-yi Bāmiyān*. Kābul. 5/1–8 (1315): 20–6, 74–8, 79–86, 105–12, 138–41; and as: Bamian. Führer zu der buddhistischen Höhlenklostern und Kolossalstatuen. Paris 1939. (100, 508, 1004, 1052)

Hackin, Joseph, and B. Rowland. 1971. 'Fondukistan'. *Mārg*, 24, 2: 45–9. (332)

Hald, K. See Thomas, D. C.

Hallade, Madeleine. 1962a. 'Bactrian Art'. *Encyclopaedia of World Art*, II. 199–205. New York. (99, 305, 1123, 1135, 1160)

Hallade, Madeleine. 1962b. 'Indo-Iranian Art'. *Enclyclopaedia of World Art*, VII. 1–18. New York. (100, 332)

Hallade, Madeleine. 1964–5. 'The Ornamental Veil or Scarf'. *EW* 15: 36–48. (404, 1088)

Hallade, Madeleine. 1968. *The Gandhara Style and the Evolution of Buddhist Art*. Paris. (100, 122, 332, 404, 1088)

Hallade, Madeleine, and Hans Hinz. 1968. *Gandharan Art of North India*. New York. (100, 122, 332, 404, 790, 1088)

Hamada, Seiryō. 1929. 'Afuganistan no Buttō' (Two Buddha Heads from Afghanistan). *Bukkyo Bijutsu*, 14: 83–90. Summary in H. Motamedi 1975c: 277–8. (404)

Hambly, Gavin, ed. 1969. *Central Asia*. London.

Hamelin, Pierre. 1952. 'Sur quelques verreries de Begram'. *Cahiers Byrsa*, 2: 11–36. (122)

Hamilton, Angus. 1906. *Afghanistan*. London. (98, 428, 850, 711)

Hammond, Norman. 1970. 'An Archaeological Reconnaissance in the Helmand Valley, South Afghanistan'. *EW* 20: 437–59. Reprinted in *Afghanistan*. 28/4 (1976): 74–98; 29/2 (1976): 1–17. (24, 77, 91, 101, 197, 227, 251, 253, 297, 311, 359, 396, 411, 429, 521, 527, 539, 560, 595, 608, 662, 687, 701, 709, 849, 863, 898, 901, 938, 964, 1068, 1111, 1163, 1228, 1252, 1260, 2081)

Hammond, Norman, ed. 1973. *South Asian Archaeology*. Park Ridge, NJ.

Hansen, Erik. 1964. 'Les monuments historiques et nous'. *Afghanistan*, 19/4: 20–3. (99)

Hansen, Erik. 1971. *Afghanistan: Conservation et restauration des monuments historiques*. Paris. (428)

Hansen, Erik, Abdul Wasay Najimi, and Claus Christensen. 2015. *The Ghurid Portal of the Friday Mosque of Herat, Afghanistan*. Aarhus. (428)

Hansen, Olaf. 1964. 'Zur Sprache der Inschrift von Surh Kotal'. *Indo-Iranica: Melanges presentes à Georg Morgenstierne à l'occasion de son soixante-dixième anniversaire*. Wiesbaden: 89–94. (1123)

Hansman, John. 1981. 'The Measure of Hecatompylos'. *JRAS* 1: 3–9. (522)

Hardy-Guilbert, C., and F. Djindjian. 1980. 'Organisation des décors de stuc sur l'arc de la mosque de Bust (en Afghanistan)'. *Dossiers de l'Archéologie*, 42: 88–93. (149)

Hariri, Ralph. 1939. 'Metalwork after the Early Islamic Period'. In *A Survey of Persian Art*. Ed. A. U. Pope, 2466–2529. Oxford. (428)

Harmatta, J. 1964. 'The Great Bactrian Inscription'. *AAH* 12: 373–471. (1123)

Harmatta, J. 1965. 'Minor Bactrian Inscriptions'. *AAH* 13: 149–205. (1123)

Harper, P. 1981. *Silver Vessels of the Sasanian Period*, I. *Royal Imagery*. New York.

Harrow, Leonard. See Ball, Warwick.

Härtel, Herbert, ed. 1981. *South Asian Archaeology 1979*. Berlin.

Haughton, H. L. 1948. 'Some Coins of Eucratides and Apollodotos from Afghanistan'. *NC* 6th ser. 8: 103. (176)

Hay, William. 1840. 'Account of Coins Found at Bameean'. *JASB* 9: 68–70. (100)

Hayashi, M., and M. Sahara. 1962. 'Archaeological Sites of Northern Afghanistan'. In *Haibāk and Kashmir-Smast*. Ed. Seiichi Mizuno, 106–9. Kyoto. (5, 21, 41, 46, 49, 63, 81, 99, 166, 169, 173, 178, 191, 194, 316, 329, 407, 425, 437, 447, 467, 526, 550, 567, 591, 628, 689, 707, 753, 776, 791, 800, 868, 925, 931, 941, 975, 993, 1034, 1055, 1135, 1139, 1160, 1175, 1179, 1189, 1218, 2276)

Hayden, H. H. 1910. 'Notes on Some Monuments in Afghanistan'. *Memoirs of the Asiatic Society of Bengal*, 2/10: 341–6. (718)

Helms, Svend W. 1979. 'Old Kandahar Excavations 1976: Preliminary Report'. *Afghan Studies*, 2: 1–8. (522)

Helms, Svend W. 1982. 'Excavations at the City and the Famous Fortress of Kandahar, the Foremost Place in All of Asia'. *Af.St.* 3–4: 1–24. (522)

Helms, Svend W. 1983. 'Kandahar of the Arab Conquest'. *World Archaeology*, 14/3: 342–54. (522)

Helms, Svend W. 1997. *Excavations at Old Kandahar in Afghanistan 1976–1978*. Oxford. (522)

Henkelman, Wouter F. M., and Margaretha L. Folmer. 2016. 'Your Tally is Full! On Wooden Credit Records in and after the Achaemenid Empire'. In *Silver, Money and Credit: A Tribute to Robartus J. van der Spek on the Occasion of his 65th Birthday*. Ed. Kristen Kleber and Reinhard Pirngruber, 133–225. Leiden. (99)

Henkl, Rolf. 1952. 'The Clay Images from Fondoukistan'. *Journal of the Asiatic Society* (Calcutta), 18: 179–83. (332)

Henning, W. B. 1949. 'The Aramaic Inscription of Aśoka Found in Lampāka'. *BSOAS* 13: 80–8. Reprinted in *Acta Iranica*. 15/1877: 331–40. (250)

Henning, W. B. 1956. 'Surkh Kotal'. *BSOAS* 18: 366–7. (1123)

Henning, W. B. 1957. 'The Inscriptions of Tang-i Azao'. *BSOAS* 20, *Studies in Honour of Ralph Turner*, 335–42. (1144)

Henning, W. B. 1960. 'The Bactrian Inscription'. *BSOAS* 23: 47–55. (1123)

Henning, W. B. 1965. 'Surkh Kotal und Kaniska'. *ZDMG* 115: 75–87. (1123)

Herawi, Mayel. 1968. 'The Patron Artists of Bernabad'. *Afghanistan*, 21/1: 77–80. (111)

Herawi, Mayel. 1970. 'Az Shākhārhā-yi hunar-i Afghānistān'. *Āryānā*, 28/2: 32–4, and *Honar va Mardom*, 93: 50–2. (349)

Herberg, Werner. 1973. 'Bericht über die dritte Landreise ins Innere von Afghanistan'. *Mainzer Afghanica II:*

Jahrbuch der Vereinigen Freunde der Universität Mainz, 79–84. (468)

Herberg, Werner. 1978. 'Das Land Ghor in Afghanistan: Auf der Suche nach einem verschollenen Imperium'. *Die Waage*, 17/5: 216–20. (468, 683, 1023)

Herberg, Werner. 1979. *Mittelalterliche Wehrbauten in der Afghanischen Provinz Ghor*. Thesis dissertation, Technical University, Berlin.

Herberg, Werner. 1982. 'Die Wehrbauten von Ghor. Afghanistan: Zusammenfassende Dokumentation der Bestandsaufnahmen von 1975, 1977 und 1978'. *Die Welt des Islam*, 22/1/4: 67–84.

Herberg, Werner, and Ghulam Djelani Davary. 1976. 'Topographische Feldarbeiten in Ghor: Bericht über Forschungsarbeiten zum Problem Jam-Ferozkoh'. *Afghanistan Journal*, 3/2: 57–69. (468)

Hermann, Georgina. 1965. 'A Golden Tower in the Hindu Kush: The Minaret of Djām'. *The Connoisseur*, 159: 230–1. (468)

Herrman, Georgina. 1970. 'Lapis Lazuli: The Early Phases of its Trade'. *Iraq*, 30: 21–57. (1001)

Hiebert, Fredrik T. 1994. *Origins of the Bronze Age Oasis Civilization in Central Asia*. Cambridge, MA.

Hiebert, Fredrik T., and Pierre Cambon, eds. 2008. *Afghanistan: Hidden Treasures from the National Museum, Kabul*. Washington, DC.

Higuchi, Takayasu. 1969. 'Saiiki Bukkyō Bijutsu ni okeru Okusasuryûha' (The Oxus School in the Central Asian Buddhist Art). *Bukkyô Geijutsu*, 71: 42–62. Summary in H. Motamedi 1975c: 234–5. (931)

Higuchi, Takayasu. 1972. 'Excavations of Ancient Tepes in the Northern District of the Hindu Kush'. In *The Memorial Volume of the Vth International Congress of Iranian Art and Archaeology*, II. Ed. A. Tajvidi and M. Y. Kiani, 322–4. Tehran. (172, 309)

Higuchi, Takayasu. 1974a. *Kyoto University Archaeological Survey in Afghanistan. Excavations at Tapa Skandar: Second Interim Report*. Kyoto. (1185)

Higuchi, Takayasu. 1974b. 'Kyoto University Mission's Work in the Kushan Area'. In *Central Asia in the Kushan Period*, I. Ed. B. G. Gafurov, 117–9. Moscow. (172, 309)

Higuchi, Takayasu. 1976. 'Bamiyan and its Surroundings'. In *Bamiyan. Crossroads of Culture*. Ed. A. Miyaji, 27–30. Tokyo. (100)

Higuchi, Takayasu, ed. 1978. *Japan-Afghanistan Joint Archaeological Survey in 1976*. Kyoto.

Higuchi, Takayasu, ed. 1980. *Japan-Afghanistan Joint Archaeological Survey in 1978*. Kyoto.

Higuchi, Takayasu, ed. 1983–4. *Bāmiyān. Art and Archaeological Researches on the Buddhist Cave Temples in Afghanistan 1970–1978*, I. Plates. *Murals*; II. Plates. *Construction of Caves*; III. *Text*; IV. *Summary. Plan*. Kyoto. (In Japanese). (100)

Higuchi, Takayasu, and G. Barnes. 1995. 'Bamiyan: Buddhist Cave Temples in Afghanistan'. *World Archaeology*, 27/2: 282–302. (100)

Higuchi, Takayasu and Shoshin Kuwayama. 1970. *Chaqalaq Tepe, Fortified Village in North Afghanistan Excavated in 1964–67*. Ed. Seiichi Mizuno. Kyoto. (172)

Higuchi, Takayasu, Shoshin Kuwayama, and Meiji Yamada. 1971. 'Kyoto Chūō Ajia Gakujutsu Chōsatai 1970 nendo no chōsa' (The Report of the Kyoto University Archaeological Mission to Central Asia for the Year 1970). *Shirin*. 54/3: 139–74. (1185)

Hill, Derek. 1966. 'Journey to Jam'. *Apollo*, NS 84: 390–6. (212, 468, 634)

Hill, Derek, and Oleg Grabar. 1967. *Islamic Architecture and its Decoration AD 800–1500*. 2nd edn. London. (142, 149, 212, 346, 358, 428, 638, 2053)

Hillenbrand, Robert. 1984. *Islamic Architecture: Style, Function, and Meaning*. Edinburgh. (358, 685)

Hillenbrand, Robert. 2000. 'The Architecture of the Ghaznavids and Ghurids'. In *Studies in Honour of Clifford Edmund Bosworth*, II. *The Sultan's Turret: Studies in Persian and Turkish Culture*. Ed. C. Hillenbrand, 124–206. Leiden. (69, 149, 212, 231, 248, 358, 428, 439, 468, 607, 638, 683, 685, 1000, 1023, 1042, 2053)

Hillenbrand, Robert. 2002 'The Ghurid Tomb at Herat'. In *Cairo to Kabul: Afghan and Islamic Studies Presented to Ralph Pinder-Wilson*. Ed. Warwick Ball and Leonard Harrow, 123–43. London. (428)

Hira Singh. 1891. 'Journey into the Firozkohi Country'. ABC V. Ed. P. J. Maitland, 142–60. Simla. (331, 1023, 1033)

Hoag, John D. 1968. 'The Tomb of Ulugh Beg and Abdu Razzaq at Ghazni: A Model for the Taj Mahal'. *Journal of the Society of Architectural Historians*, 27: 234–48. (358)

Hoag, John D. 1972. The Tomb of Ulugh Beg and Abdu Razzaq at Ghazni, a prototype for the Taj Mahal'. In *The Memorial Volume of the Vth International Congress of Iranian Art and Archaeology*, II. Ed. A. Tajvidi and M. Y. Kiani, 102–7. Tehran. (358)

Hoernle, A. F. R. 1879. 'Gold Coins from Jalalabad'. *JASB* 122–38. (17)

Hoernle, A. J. R. 1889. 'Catalogue of the Central Asiatic Coins, Collected by Captain A. F. De Laessoe, in the Indian Museum, Calcutta'. *JASB*, suppl. for no. 4: 1–9.

Holdich, Thomas H. 1881a. 'Notes on the Route from Kabul through the Laghman Valley'. *General Report on the Operations of the Survey of India, 1879–80*. Appendix, 18–21. Calcutta. (250, 618, 761, 817)

Holdich, Thomas H. 1881b. 'Notes on the Logar Valley'. *General Report on the Operations of the Survey of India, 1879–80*. Appendix, 21–3. Calcutta. (519, 718, 1223)

Holdich, Thomas H. 1885a. 'Afghan Boundary Commission: Geographical Notes'. *PRGS* 7: 39–43, 160–6, 273–92. (752, 842, 863, 1196)

Holdich, Thomas H. 1885b. 'Report on the Herat Defences'. Enclosure No. 5, dated 28 May 1885. Political and Secret Letters from India, vol. 44: 1–9, 102. India Office. (428)

Holdich, Thomas H. 1886. *Geographical Results of the Afghan Boundary Commission*. India Office Political Dept. Memorandum 76. London. (99, 207, 331, 408, 468, 552, 569, 1033, 1051, 1099, 1149, 1257)

Holdich, Thomas H. 1887. *Report on Survey Operations in Western and North-Western Afghanistan, in 1884, 1885, 1886*. India Office Political Dept. Memorandum 77. London. (188, 207, 298, 331, 408, 425, 468, 541, 552, 569, 589, 628, 752, 842, 846, 863, 875, 890, 1033, 1051, 1099, 1134, 1135, 1149, 1236, 1239, 2253)

Holdich, Thomas H. 1896. 'The Origin of the Kāfirs of the Hindu Kush'. *Geographical Journal*, 7: 42–9. (154)

Holdich, Thomas H. 1901. *The Indian Borderland*. London. (154)

Holdich, Thomas H. 1910. *The Gates of India*. London. (154, 189, 274, 378, 556, 962, 988, 1039)

Holt, Frank L. 1999. *Thundering Zeus: The Making of Hellenistic Bactria*. Berkeley, CA.

Holt, Frank L. 2012a. *Lost World of the Golden King: In Search of Ancient Afghanistan*. Berkeley, CA. (569)

Holt, Frank L. 2012b, 'When did the Greeks Abandon Aï Khanoum?'. *Anabasis. Studia Classica et Orientalia*, 3: 161–72. (18)

Honigberger, John Martin. 1852. *Thirty-Five Years in the East*. London. (1087)

Horowitz, J. 1913. 'The Inscription on "Buddha's Bowl" at Qandahār'. *Archaeological Survey of India, Annual Reports, Years 1909–1910*, 142–5. (522)

Hulin, P. 1954. 'The Signs on the Kabul Silver Piece'. *NC* 6th ser. 14: 174–6. (483)

Hultzsch, E. 1919. 'Zur Inschrift der Wardak-Vase'. *ZDMG* 73: 224–8. (1229)

Humayun, G. S. 1973. 'On Ay Khanum'. *Afghanistan*, 25. 3: 96–103. (18)

Humbach, Helmut. 1960. *Die Kaniska Inschrift von Surkh-Kotal*. Wiesbaden. (1123)

Humbach, Helmut. 1961a. *Kusan und Hephthaliten*. Münchener Studien zur Sprachwissenschaft. Munich. (1123)

Humbach, Helmut. 1961b. 'Die Götternamen der Kusan-Münzen'. *ZDMG* 111/3: 475–9. (1123)

Humbach, Helmut. 1962. 'Die neugenfunden Versionen der Kaniska-Inschrift von Surkh-Kotal'. *Wiener Zeitschrift für die Kunde Süd-und Ostasiens und Archiv für Indischer Philosophie*, 6: 40–3. (1123)

Humbach, Helmut. 1963. 'Baktrische Phantasmagorie'. Unpublished manuscript in the DAFA library. Kabul. (1123)

Humbach, Helmut. 1966–7. *Baktrische Sprachdenkmäler*. 2 vols. Wiesbaden. (71, 320, 1123, 1221)

Humbach, Helmut. 1967. 'Two Inscriptions in Graeco-Bactrian Cursive Script from Afghanistan'. *EW* 17: 25–6. (71, 461)

Humbach, Helmut. 1968a. 'The Kanishka Inscription from Surkh Kotal Discovered by Dr Maricq'. In *Papers on the Date of Kanishka*. Ed. A. L. Basham, 121–2. Leiden. (1123)

Humbach, Helmut. 1968b. 'Die Inschrift des Ksatrapa Tiruvharna'. *Indo-Iranian Journal*, 11/1: 29–33. (464)

Humbach, Helmut. 1971. 'Indien und Ostiran zur Zeit des Aśoka'. *AAH* 19/1–2: 53–8. (522, 1067)

Humbach, Helmut. 1973. 'Die Aramäische Aśoka-Inschrift von Laghman-Fluss'. In *Indolen-Tagung 1971*. Ed. H. Härtel and V. Moeller, 161–9. Wiesbaden. (1067)

Hunter, Edward. 1959. *The Past Present: A Year in Afghanistan*. London.

Hunter, Erica C. D. 2009a. 'Men Only: Hebrew-Script Tombstones from Jam, Afghanistan'. *AIA Newsletter*, 45: 11–14. (428)

Hunter, Erica C. D. 2009b. 'A Jewish Inscription from Jām, Afghanistan'. In *Festschrift in Honour of Nicholas Sims-Williams*. edited. Werner Sunderman, Almut Hintze, and François de Blois, 191–6. Wiesbaden. (428)

Hunter, Erica C. D. 2010. 'Hebrew-Script Tombstones from Jam, Afghanistan'. *Journal of Jewish Studies*, 41/1: 72–87. (428)

Husain Shah, Mia. 1954. 'Merve Rud'. *Afghanistan*, 9/3: 8–17; 9/4: 10–25. (98, 711)

Husain Shah, Mia. 1962. 'Panjwayee-Fanjiwai'. *Afghanistan*, 17/3: 23–7. (798)

Hutt, Antony. 1974. 'The Development of the Minaret in Iran under the Saljūqs'. Unpublished thesis, University of London. (212, 428, 468)

Hutt, Antony. 1977. 'The Central Asian Origin of the Eastern Minaret Form'. *Asian Affairs*, 64: 157–62. (358)

Imam Sharif. 1888. 'Report on journey from Shibarghan, through the districts of Sar-i-Pul and Sangcharak'. ABC V. *Miscellaneous Reports*. Ed. J. West Ridgeway et al., 216–30. Simla. (1051)

Imam Sharif. 1891a. 'First Journey in the Taimani Country'. ABC IV. Edited by P. J. Maitland, 205–11. Simla. (188, 207, 1236, 1257)

Imam Sharif. 1891b. 'Second Journey in the Taimani Country'. ABC IV. Ed. P. J. Maitland, 212–20. (875, 1239)

Invernizzi, A., ed. 1995. *In the Land of the Gryphons: Papers on Central Asian Archaeology in Antiquity*. Florence.

Iourkevitch, E. A. 1974. 'Histoire de l'exploration des monuments Kushans d'Afghanistan'. *Afghanistan*, 27/1: 77–88; 27/2: 46–56. (122, 404)

Irwin, J. 1979. 'The Stūpa and the Cosmic Axis: The Archaeological Evidence'. In *South Asian Archaeology*. Ed. M. Taddei, 799–846. Naples. (1116)

Itemadi, Sarwar Goya. 1946. 'Le dome vert, ou le Mausolée des princes Timurides'. *Afghanistan*, 1/1: 15–19. (428)

Itemadi, Sarwar Goya. 1953. 'The General Mosque at Herat'. *Afghanistan*, 8/2: 40–50. (428)

Itō, Gikyō. 1977. 'A New Interpretation of Aśokan Inscriptions, Taxila and Kandahar I'. *St.Ir.* 6/2: 151–61. (522)

Itō, Gikyō. 1979. 'Aśokan Inscriptions, Laghmān I and II'. *St. Ir.* 9: 175–84. (250, 1067)

Iwade, Mayu, and Shigeru Kubudera. 2013. *Structure, Design and Technique of the Bamiyan Buddhist Caves*. RCHIA 5. London. (100)

Jackson, Keith A. 1842. *Views in Afghanistan, etc. from Sketches Taken during the Campaign of the Army of the Indus*. London. (358).

Jacobsen, J. 1979. 'Recent Developments in South Asian Prehistory and Protohistory'. *Annual Review of Anthropology*, 8: 468–502.

Jacquet, E. 1836a. 'Notice de la collection de médailles bactriennes et indo-scythiques rapportées par M. le general Allard'. *JA* 1: 122–90. (122)

Jacquet, E. 1836b. 'Notice sur les découvertes archéologiques faites par Martin Honigberger dans l'Afghanistan'. *JA* 2: 234–77. (99, 389, 1016, 1087, 1197, 1237)

Jacquet, E. 1837. 'Notice sur les découvertes archéologiques faites dans l'Afghanistan par M. Honigberger'. *JA* 3: 401–40. (100, 106, 122, 155, 1042, 1116, 1124)

Jacquet, E. 1839. 'Mémoire sur les découvertes archéologiques faites dans l'Afghanistan par M. le Dr Honigberger'. *JA* 7: 385–404. (155, 404, 519, 847, 1087)

Jalali, Ghulam Jilani. 1972 (1351). *Ghazna wa Ghaznawian*. Kabul. (358)

Janata, Alfred. 1971. 'On the Origin of the Firuzkuhis in Western Afghanistan'. *Archiv für Völkerkunde*, 25: 57–65. (468, 683, 1239)

Janin, Louis. 1978. 'Un cadran solaire grec à Aï Khanoum, Afghanistan'. *L'Astronomie* (Sept.): 357–62. (18)

Jarrige, Catherine, ed. 1992. *South Asian Archaeology: 1989*. Paris.

Jarrige, Jean-François. See Cambon, Pierre.

Jawād, Said. 1979. 'Qal'a Ikhtiyāruddīn'. *Herāt-i Bāstān*, 1/1: 13–19. (428)

Jawād, Said. 1980. 'Guzārish-i kār-i tarmīm-i Qal'a-i Ikhtiyāruddin'. *Herāt-i Bāstān*, 1/2: 41–6. (428)

Jenkins, G. K. 1955. 'Indo-Scythic Mints'. *JNSI* 17/2: 1–26. (1108)

Jenkins, G. K. 1959. 'The Apollodotus Question: Another View'. *JNSI* 21/1: 20–33. (176, 728)

Jenkins, G. K. 1968. 'Some Recent Indo-Greek Accessions of the British Museum'. *JNSI* 30: 23–7. (569)

Jettmar, Karl. 1959–60. 'Zum Heiligtum von Surkh-Kotal'. *Central Asiatic Journal*, 5/3: 198–205. (1123)

Jettmar, Karl. 1978. 'Auf den Spuren der Indoiraner? Bronzezeitfunde sowjetischer Archäologen in Nordwest-Afghanistan'. *Afghanistan Journal*, 5/3: 87–95. (257)

Jewett, A. C. 1948. *An American Engineer in Afghanistan*. edited Marjorie Jewett Bell. Minneapolis. (458)

Jodidio, Philip, ed. 2017. *Afghanistan: Preserving Historic Heritage*. Munich. (99, 346, 410, 428, 2094)

Jongeward, David, Elizabeth Errington, Richard Salomon, and Stefan Baums. 2012. *Gandharan Buddhist Reliquaries*. Seattle and London. (17, 106, 127, 155, 283, 326, 389, 404, 519, 667, 761, 773, 806, 855, 928, 1087, 1116, 1125, 1197, 1229)

Kabul Times. 1970. *Annual*. Kabul. (875, 879, 893, 2069)

Kabul Times. 1975. 'Ministry of Information and Culture. Year End Report. Part 4'. *Kabul Times* (12 May): 2. (99, 410, 718)

Kabul Times. 1976a. 'Information and Culture Ministry's Year-End Report. Part II'. *Kabul Times* (27 Apr.): 3–4. (149, 346, 428)

Kabul Times. 1976b. 'Repair of Hajipiyadah Historic Mosque Begins'. *Kabul Times* (6 Nov.): 1. (410)

Kabul Times. 1977a. 'Second Phase of Ghazni Monuments Repair Begins'. *Kabul Times* (7 July): 1. (358)

Kabul Times. 1977b. 'Work on Wells, Qalai Bost Begins'. *Kabul Times* (11 Aug.): 1. (149)

Kabul Times. 1978. 'Kham-i-Zargar'. *Kabul Times* (21 Jan.): 3. (622)

Kabul Times. 1979a. 'Repair of Magnificent Monuments of Herat'. *Kabul Times* (10–12 Feb.). (111, 212, 278, 346, 373, 428, 634, 661, 819, 1023, 1196, 1259)

Kabul Times. 1979b. 'Excavations on Tapai Shutur, Tope Kalan Carried out'. *Kabul Times* (17 Apr.): 4. (404)

Kalb, P. 1973. 'Rote Glättstreifen-Keramik in Afghanistan'. *AMI* 6: 265–71. (962)

Kalus, L. 1979. 'La collection des monnaies islamiques du Musée de Kaboul'. *Afghanistan Journal*, 6/2: 50–3, and *Afghanistan*, 32/3: 1–9. (173)

Kamāl, Zamri. 1979. 'Azamat-i Bāmiyān dar chahra'i paikarahā-i ān'. *Bāstān Shināsi Afghānistān*, 1/1: 49–55. (100)

Kästner, Hermann. 1968. 'Ruinen aler Wehranlagen westlich Shahrak in der Provinz Ghōr, Afghanistan'. *Central Asiatic Journal*, 12/3: 269–79. (717, 759, 793)

Kato, Kyuzo. 1979. 'A Great Discovery on the Ancient Silk Route'. *Afghanistan*, 32/3: 41–8. (1192)

Katsuno, Yutaka. 1959. 'Suruhu Kotal no Shinden' (Temple of Surkh Kotal). *Kodaigaku. Palaeologia*, 8/1: 54–68. Summary in H. Motamedi 1975c: 245–74. (1123)

Kaye, E. 1879. 'The Mountain Passes Leading to the Valley of Bamiān'. *Indian Antiquary*, 8: 254–6. (100)

Kennedy, R. H. 1840. *Narrative of the Campaign of the Army of the Indus in Sind and Kauboul, in 1838–39*. 2 vols. London. (358, 522, 1048)

Kern Institute. 1928–72. *Annual Bibliography of Indian Archaeology 1926–1966*, I–XXI. Leiden.

Kervran, Monique. 1999. 'La mosquée des "neuf coupoles" à Balkh'. *Dossiers d'Archéologie*, 247: 35. (410)

Kessel, Joseph. 1959. *Afghanistan*. London. (358)

Khairzada, Khair Mohammed. 2015. 'Recent Archaeological Discoveries at Mes Aynak, Logar Province'. In *Keeping History Alive: Safeguarding Cultural Heritage in Post-Conflict Afghanistan*. Ed. Brendan Cassar and Sara Noshadi, 114–19. Paris and Kabul. (19)

Khan, F. 1964. *The Indus Valley and Early Iran*. Karachi.

Khanikoff, Nicholas de. 1860. 'Lettre à M. Reinaud'. *JA* 15: 537–43. (428)

Khanikoff, Nicolas de. 1861. 'Mémoire sur la partie Méridionale de l'Asie centrale (Khorasan, Afghanistan, midi de la Perse)'. *Recueil de voyages et de mémoires publiés par la Société de Géographie*, 7: 239–451. (1106)

Kieffer, Charles M. 1960a. 'La grande découverte épigraphique de Sorkh-Kotal et la langue de la Bactriane'. *Afghanistan*, 15/2: 1–50. (1123)

Kieffer, Charles M. 1960b. 'Le minaret de Ghiyath al-Din à Firuzkuh'. *Afghanistan*, 15/4: 16–60. (468)

Kieffer, Charles M. 1961. 'L'art Kouchan: La situation parmi les descendants non-méditerranéens de l'art grec'. *Afghanistan*, 16/2: 40–51. (1123)

Kieffer, Charles M. 1962. 'Kusana Art and the Historic Effigies of Mat (India) and Surkh Kotal (Afghanistan)'. *Mārg*, 15/2: 43–8. (1123)

Kieffer, Charles M. 1975. 'Wardak, toponyme et ethnique d'Afghanistan'. *Acta Iranica*, 2nd ser. 4: 475–83. (132)

King, G. R. D. 1989. 'The Nine Bay Domed Mosque in Islam'. *Sonderdruck aus den Madrider Mitteilungen*, 30: 332–90. (410)

Klimburg, Max. 1958. 'Short Preliminary Report on our Expedition to the Ghorat in October 1958'. *Afghanistan*, 14/4: 16–19. (683, 751, 1236, 1239)

Klimburg, Max. 1960. 'Blick auf Ghor'. *Du, Kulturelle Monatsschrift*, 20: 40–50. (183, 212, 403, 468, 683, 742, 775, 875, 1236, 1239, 1257)

Klimburg, Max. 1963. 'Die islamische Kunst in Afghanistan'. *Bustan*, 4/3: 32–5. (179, 358, 428, 468, 683)

Klimburg-Salter, Deborah. 1989. *The Kingdom of Bāmiyān. Buddhist Art and Culture of the Hindu Kush*. Naples and Rome. (100)

Klimburg-Salter, Deborah. 1993. 'Dokhtar-i-Noshirwan (Nigar) Reconsidered'. *Muqarnas*, 10: 355–68. (305)

Klimburg-Salter, Deborah. 2006. 'Mahākāśyapa and the Art of Bāmiyān'. In *South Asian Archaeology 2001*, II. *Historical Archaeology and Art History*. Ed. Catherine Jarrige and Vincent Lefèvre, 535–49. Paris. (100)

Klimburg-Salter, Deborah. 2008. 'Buddhist Painting in the Hindu Kush ca. VIth to Xth Centuries'. In *L'Islamisation de l'Asie Centrale: Processus locaux d'acculturation du VIe au XIe siècles*. Ed. Étienne de la Vaissière, 131–59. Leuven. (100)

Klimburg-Salter, Deborah. 2010. 'Corridors of Communication across Afghanistan 7th to 10th Centuries'. In *Paysages de centre de l'Afghanistan: Paysages naturels, paysages culturels*. Ed. Véra Marigo, 173–86. Paris. (100)

Klimburg-Salter, Deborah. See also Alram, Michael.

Klinkott, M. 1976. 'Hüdenhäuser in Afghanistan'. *Architectura*, 8, 104–12.

Klinkott, M. 1982. *Islamische Baukunst in Afghanisch-Sīstān: Mit einem geschichlichen Überblick von Alexander der Grossen bis zur Zeit der Safawiden-Dynastie*. Berlin. (190, 201, 300, 318, 390, 482, 861)

Kluyver, Robert. 2000. 'Fortresses of the Hazarajat: Report on Sites Visited in Saighan, Yakawlang, Band-e Amir and Chaghcheran Districts'. Unpublished report in the Bibliotheca Afghanica, Bubendorf, Switzerland. (15, 118, 189, 845)

Knobloch, Edgar. 1981, 'Survey of Archaeology and Architecture in Afghanistan. Part 1: The South—Ghazni, Kandahar and Sistan'. *Afghanistan Journal*, 8: 3–20.

Knobloch, Edgar. 2002. *The Archaeology and Architecture of Afghanistan*. Stroud, UK.

Kodera M., K. Maeda, and A. Miyaji. 1971. *Bamiyan*. Nagoya. (In Japanese). (100)

Kohl, Philip L. 1979. 'The World Economy of Western Asia in the 3rd Millennium B.C'. *South Asian Archaeology 1977*. Naples.

Kohl, Philip L. 1978a. 'Archaeological Reconnaissances in Eastern Afghanistan, 1975–1976'. *Annali dell'Instituto Orientale di Napoli*, 38, N.S. 28: 63–74. (29, 50, 59, 64, 107, 175, 281, 315, 342, 371, 400, 474, 476, 582, 583, 650, 686, 765, 780, 860, 942, 1037, 1201, 1214)

Kohl, Philip L. 1978b. 'The Balance of Trade in Southwestern Asia in the 3rd Millennium BC'. *Current Anthropology*, 19/3: 463–75. (29, 50, 59, 64, 107, 315, 342, 371, 400, 474, 476)

Kohl, Philip L. 1982. *The Bronze Age Civilization of Central Asia: Recent Soviet Discoveries*. New York.

Kohl, Philip L. 1984a. *Central Asia: Palaeolithic Beginnings to the Iron Age*. Paris. (257)

Kohl, Philip L. 1984b. *L'Asie central des origins à l'âge du Fer*. Paris. (256, 323, 430, 641, 1191)

Kohl, Philip L. 2007. *The Making of Bronze Age Eurasia*. Cambridge. (257)

Kohl, Philip L., R. Biscione, and M. L. Ingraham. 1982. 'Implications of Recent Evidence for the Prehistory of Northeastern Iran and Southwestern Turkmenistan'. *St. Ir.* 16: 185–204.

Kohzad, Ahmad Ali. 1935b. 'Recherches archéologiques en Afghanistan'. *Afghanistan*, 8/2: 1–11. (99, 100, 122, 404, 963, 1088)

Kohzad, Ahmad Ali. 1938–9 (1317). 'Bagrām'. *Kābul*, 8/6: 77–83, 80–6, 58–63, 85–9, 66–70, 73–8. (122)

Kohzad, Ahmad Ali. 1944–5a (1323). 'Qadīmtarī-i ma'bad-i Bāmiyān'. *Aryānā*, 2/6: 20–6. Translated and reprinted as: 'The Most Ancient Temple in Bāmiyān'. *Afghanistan*, 8/2 (1953): 12–17. (100)

Kohzad, Ahmad Ali. 1944–5b. 'Kashf-i mitūn-i qadīma-i Sānskrit dar Bāmiyān'. *Aryānā*, 2/7: 1–7. (100)

Kohzad, Ahmad Ali. 1944–5c (1323). 'Butkada-i Sakāwand'. *Aryānā*, 3/2: 13–18. (971)

Kohzad, Ahmad Ali. 1946–7 (1325). 'Ma'bad-i Sūryā yā ma'bad-i āftāb parasti Kūtal-i Khairkhāna'. *Aryānā*, 5/2: 1–6. (546)

Kohzad, Ahmad Ali. 1947–8 (1326). 'Kashf-i maskūkāt az Mīr Zaka-i Gardīz'. *Aryānā*, 5/7: 23–31; 5/8: 1–7. (728)

Kohzad, Ahmad Ali. 1948a. 'Les travaux sur metal de l'époque Ghaznévide'. *Afghanistan*, 13/3: 24–32. (358)

Kohzad, Ahmad Ali. 1948b. 'Le lapis-lazuli et son role dans les relations de l'Ariana avec les pays de l'Asie occidentale'. *Afghanistan*, 3/4: 1–2. (1001)

Kohzad, Ahmad Ali. 1949a. 'Lashkargah (Camp militaire)'. *Afghanistan*, 4/1: 30–5. (685)

Kohzad, Ahmad Ali. 1949b. 'Marenjan Hill'. *Afghanistan*, 4/4: 24–6. (1173)

Kohzad, Ahmad Ali. 1950a. *A Short Guide to Bāmiyān*. Kabul. (100, 1042)

Kohzad, Ahmad Ali. 1950b. 'The Tour of the American Archaeological Mission in Afghan Seistan'. *Afghanistan*, 5/1: 29–32. (752)

Kohzad, Ahmad Ali. 1951. 'Uniformes et armes des Gardes des Sultans de Ghazna'. *Afghanistan*, 6/1: 48–53. (685)

Kohzad, Ahmad Ali. 1951–4. 'Along the Koh-i-Baba and Hari Rud'. *Afghanistan*, 6/1: 1016; 6/2: 1–21: 7/1: 50–5; 8/4: 54–65; 9/1: 20–43; 9/2: 1–21. (15, 27, 39, 114, 188, 189, 195, 212, 255, 433, 468, 485, 537, 566, 612, 653, 683, 704, 742, 767, 803, 864, 875, 989, 1033, 1039, 1081, 1103, 1130, 1144, 1234, 1239)

Kohzad, Ahmad Ali. 1952–3 (1331). 'Hifrayāt dar Surkh Kūtal yā Chashma Shīr dar Ghūri'. *Aryānā*, 10/6: 16–20. (1123)

Kohzad, Ahmad Ali. 1953a. 'Le temple de Sakawand'. *Afghanistan*, 8/1: 34–42. (971)

Kohzad, Ahmad Ali. 1953b. 'Recherches archéologiques en Afghanistan'. *Afghanistan*, 8/2: 1–11. (99, 100, 122, 404, 963, 1088)

Kohzad, Ahmad Ali. 1953c. 'Gardien de la ville de Capici'. *Afghanistan*, 8/2: 18–31. (122)

Kohzad, Ahmad Ali. 1953d. 'Les capitals de l'empire afghan koushanide au temps de Kanischka'. *Afghanistan*, 8/2: 22–30. (122)

Kohzad, Ahmad Ali. 1953e. 'Recherches archéologiques à Sorkh Kotal'. *Afghanistan*, 8/2: 51–7. (122)

Kohzad, Ahmad Ali. 1954. 'Recherches archéologiques et monuments anciens en Afghanistan—le Musée de Kaboul'. *Afghanistan*, 9/4: 1–18.

Kohzad, Ahmad Ali. 1954–5 (1333). 'Atishkada-Ii Surkh Kūtal dar Kūshānshahr'. *Aryānā*, 12/8: 1–8. (1123)

Kohzad, Ahmad Ali. 1955a. 'Bāmiyān'. *Afghanistan*, 10/3: 1–6. (100)

Kohzad, Ahmad Ali, ed. 1955b. 'Deh Kundi'. *Afghanistan*, 10/4: cover plate. (223)

Kohzad, Ahmad Ali. 1955c. *L'Afghanistan antico e moderno*. Rome. (100, 122, 332, 404, 428)

Kohzad, Ahmad Ali. 1955–6 (1334). 'Rāhnāmā-yi Bamiyān'. *Aryānā*, 13/4–7: 1–8, 1–12, 9–20. (100, 1042)

Kohzad, Ahmad Ali. 1955–6/1956–7 (1334–5). 'Bālā hisār-i Kābul wa pīsh āmadhā-yi tārīkhi'. *Aryānā*, 13/9–12: 14, 1–9. (483)

Kohzad, Ahmad Ali. 1956a. 'Begram in the Light of the Recent Work'. *EW* 7/3: 244–6. (122)

Kohzad, Ahmad Ali. 1956b. 'Geographical and Historical Sketches of Some Localities'. *EW* 7/2: 128–37.

Kohzad, Ahmad Ali. 1957. 'Firoz Koh'. *Afghanistan*, 12/4: 31–4. (468)

Kohzad, Ahmad Ali. 1958–9 (1337). 'Cham Kalā'. *Aryānā*, 16/2: 45–8. (169)

Kohzad, Mohammad Nabi. 1949. 'Trois jours à Lashkari Bazar'. *Afghanistan*, 4/3: 60–2. (685)

Kohzad, Mohammad Nabi. 1953. 'Un ouvrage afghan sur Lashkargah'. *Afghanistan*, 8/3: 57–9. (685)

Kohzad, Mohammad Nabi. 1959. 'Tourist Sites of Afghanistan'. *Afghanistan*, 14/3: 1–7. (178, 875, 882, 974)

Kolb, Charles C. 1977. 'Imitation of Arretine Pottery in Northern Afghanistan'. *Current Anthropology* 18/3: 536–8. (46)

Konow, Sten. 1929. 'Kharoshthī Inscriptions'. In *Corpus Inscriptionum Indicarum*, vol. 2, part 1. Oxford. (127, 404, 1229)

Konow, Sten. 1935. 'Kharoshthī Inscription on a Bagram Bas-Relief'. *Epigraphia Indica*, 22: 11–14. (122)

Konow, Sten. 1938. 'Kabul Museum Stone Inscription of the Year 83'. *Acta Orientalia*, 16: 234–40. (464)

Kosambi, D. D. 1959. 'Miscellanea: Notes on the Kandahar Edict of Aśoka'. *Journal of the Economic and Social History of the Orient*, 2: 204–6. (522)

Kosambi, D. D. 1968. 'Kanishka and the Saka Era'. In *Papers on the Date of Kanishka*. Ed. A. L. Basham, 123–5. Leiden. (1123)

Koshelenko, G. A., and V. I. Sarianidi. 1992. 'Les monnaies de la nécropole de Tilia-Tepe (Afghanistan)'. *St.Ir.* 21: 21–32. (1192)

Koshkaki, Mawlawi Borhān al-din Khān. 1923–4 (1302). *Rāhnāmā-yi Qataghan wa Badakhshān*. Kabul. Translated by Marguerite Reut as: *Qataghan et Badakhshān: Description du pays d'après l'inspection d'un minister afghan en 1922*. Paris, 1979. (18)

Kostka, Robert 1974. 'Die stereophotogrammetrische Aufnahme des Grossen Buddha in Bamiyan'. *Afghanistan Journal*, 1/3: 65–74. (100)

Kouremenos, Anna, Sujatha Chandrasekaran, and Roberto Rossi. 2011. *From Pella to Gandhara: Hybridisation and Identity in the Art and Architecture of the Hellenistic East*. Oxford.

Kraus, W. 1975. *Afghanistan: Natur, Geschichte und Kultur*. Tübingen.

Kreitman, Neil. See Allchin.

Kritt, Brian. 2015. *New Discoveries in Bactrian Numismatics*. Classical Numismatic Studies, 8. Lancaster, PA. (18)

Kruglikova, Irina T. 1973a. 'Gorodishche Emshitepe v severnom Afganistane'. *Kratkie soobshcheniya Instituta arkheologii Akademii Nauk SSSR*, 136: 104–13. (314)

Kruglikova, Irina T. 1973b. 'Le rapport des travaux de l'expédition archéologique soviéto-afghane en 1973'. Unpublished report in the Afghan Institute of Archaeology, Kabul. (295, 323, 641, 1225)

Kruglikova, Irina T. 1974. *Dilberdzhin I (1970–1972)*. Moscow. (295, 520)

Kruglikova, Irina T. 1976. 'Nastennie rospisi Dilberdzhina'. In *Drevnyaya Baktriya 1*. Ed. I. T. Kruglikova et al., 87–110. Moscow. (295)

Kruglikova, Irina T. 1977a. *Dilberdzhin 2 (1970–1973)*. Moscow. (295)

Kruglikova, Irina T. 1977b. 'Sovetsko-Afganskaya ekspeditsiya'. In *Arkheologicheskiye Otkrytiya 1976 Goda*, 389–90. Moscow. (295)

Kruglikova, Irina T. 1977c. 'Joint Afghan-Soviet Archaeological Expedition'. *Kabul Times* (18 Apr.): 2. (37)

Kruglikova, Irina T. 1977d. 'Les fouilles de la mission archéologique soviéto-afghane sur le site gréco-kushan de Dilberdjin en Bactriane'. *CRAI* 407–27. (295, 475)

Kruglikova, Irina T. 1978. 'Delberjin'. *Afghanistan*, 31/1: 32–42. (295)

Kruglikova, Irina T. 1979. 'Nastenniye rospisi v pomeshchenii 16 severo-vostochnogo kultovogo kompleska Dilberdzhina'. In *Drevnyaya Baktriya 2*. Ed. I. T. Kruglikova et al., 120–45. Moscow. (295)

Kruglikova, Irina T. 1984. *Drevnyaya Baktriya 3*. Moscow.

Kruglikova, Irina T. 1986. *Del'berdzhin*. Moscow. (295)

Kruglikova, Irina T. et al. 1976. *Drevnyaya Baktriya 1*. Moscow.

Kruglikova, Irina T. et al. 1979. *Drevnyaya Baktriya 2*. Moscow.

Kruglikova, Irina T., and Shahibye Mustamandi. 1970. 'Résultats preliminaries des travaux de l'expédition archéologique afghano-soviétique en 1969'. *Afghanistan*, 23/1: 84–97. (314, 609, 1191, 1192)

Kruglikova, Irina T., and Viktor I. Sarianidi. 1971a. 'Arkheologicheskiye issledovoniya v Severnom Afganistane'. *Arkeologicheskiye Otkrytiya*, 1970: 457–9. (314)

Kruglikova, Irina T., and Viktor I. Sarianidi. 1971b. 'La Bactriane ancienne dans l'optique de nouvelles recherches archéologiques'. In *Kushan Culture and History*, II. Ed. Fahima Ayubi, 9–42. Kabul. (256, 257, 295, 314)

Kruglikova, Irina T., and Viktor I. Sarianidi. 1971c. 'Sovetskiye arkheologi v Afganistane'. *Vestnik Akademii Nauk*, 9. (1192)

Kruglikova, Irina T., and Viktor I. Sarianidi. 1976. 'Pyat let rabot Sovietsko-Afghanskoy arkheologicheskoy ekspeditsii'. In *Drevnyaya Baktriya 1*. Ed. I. T. Kruglikova, 3–21. Moscow. (37, 38, 256, 295, 314, 666)

Kulke, Holger. 1976. 'Die Lapis-lazuli-Lagerstätte Sare Sang. Badakhshan: Geologie, Entstehung, Kulturgeschichte und Bergbau'. *Afghanistan Journal*, 3/2: 43–56. (1001)

Kumar, Baldev. 1973. *The Early Kusanas*. Delhi. (1123)

Kurita, I. 2003. *Gandharan Art*. Tokyo.

Kurz, Otto. 1954a. 'Le rinceau d'acanthe de la plaque d'ivoire n° 329 (fouilles 1937)'. In *Nouvelles recherches archéologiques à Begram*. MDAFA 11. Ed. J. Hackin et al. Paris. (122)

Kurz, Otto. 1954b. 'Begram et l'occident gréco-romain'. In *Nouvelles recherches archéologiques à Begram*. MDAFA 11. Ed. J. Hackin et al., 89–150. Paris. (122)

Kuwayama, Shoshin. 1969. 'Chūso to tsubo to Hindukushi' (Pillar Bases, Vases and the Hindu Kush). *Space Design*, 96–102. Summary in H. Motamedi 1975c: 235–236. (18, 172, 309, 1088, 1123)

Kuwayama, Shoshin. 1972a. 'Dairiseki Hindū-zō wa Hindu Ōchō no monoka' (Brahmanical Marble Sculptures of Turki Shahis). *Tōhō Gakuhō*, 43: 1–54. Summary in H. Motamedi 1975c: 263–7. (337, 546, 832, 1180, 1185)

Kuwayama, Shoshin. 1972b. 'The First Excavation at Tape Skandar'. In *Archaeological Survey of Kyoto University in Afghanistan 1970*. Ed. Takayasu Higuchi, 5–14. Kyoto. (1185)

Kuwayama, Shoshin. 1973. 'Hadda Saikin no Hakkutsu ni kansuru Mondai' (Problems on the Recent Excavations at Hadda). *Tōhō Gakuhō Kyoto*, 14: 335–7. Summary in H. Motamedi 1975c: 282–4. (404)

Kuwayama, Shoshin. 1974a. 'Excavations at Tapa Skandar: Second Interim Report'. In *Kyoto University Archaeological Survey in Afghanistan 1972*. Ed. Takayasu Higuchi, 5–13. Kyoto. (1185)

Kuwayama, Shoshin. 1974b. 'Kapisi Begram III: Renewing its Dating'. *Orient*, 10: 57–78. Summary in H. Motamedi 1975c: 259–62. (122, 172, 630)

Kuwayama, Shoshin. 1976. 'The Turki Shahis and Relevant Brahmanical Sculptures in Afghanistan'. *EW* 26: 375–407. (100, 122, 332, 337, 358, 546, 723, 832, 1064, 1185)

Kuwayama, Shoshin. 1978. 'The Fourth Excavation at Tapa Skandar'. In *Japan-Afghanistan Joint Archaeological Survey in 1976*. Ed. Takayasu Higuchi, 5–12. Kyoto. (1185)

Kuwayama, Shoshin. 1980. 'The Fifth Excavation at Tepe Skandar'. In *Japan-Afghanistan Joint Archaeological Survey in 1978*. Ed. Takayasu Higuchi, 5–15. Kyoto. (1185)

Kuwayama, Shoshin. 1991. 'L'inscription du Gaṇeśa de Gardez et la chronologie des Turki-Ṣāhis'. *JA* 279/3–4: 267–87. (1173, 1180, 1185)

Kuwayama, Shoshin. 1991. 'The Horizon of Begram III and Beyond: A Chronological Interpretation of the Evidence for Monuments in the Kāpiśī-Kabul-Ghazni Region'. *EW* 41/1–4: 79–120. (122, 546, 1088, 1229)

Kuwayama, Shoshin. 1997. 'A Hidden Import from Imperial Rome Manifest in Stupas'. In *Gandharan Art in Context*. Ed. R. Allchin et al., 119–71. Delhi. (326)

Kuwayama, Shoshin. 2010. 'Between Begram II and III—a Blank Period in History'. *CAC* II. 283–97. Vienna. (122, 630, 1185)

Kuwayama, Shoshin, and Shinko Momono. 1976. 'The Third Excavation at Tape Skandar'. In *Japan-Afghanistan Joint Archaeological Survey in 1974*. Ed. Takayasu Higuchi, 5–15. Kyoto. (1185)

Kyoto University Archaeological Mission. 2003. *Bāmiyān Cultural Heritage over the Centuries*. Kyoto. (100)

Lal, B. B. 1971. 'Bamiyan: Past and Present'. *Mārg*, 24/2: 5. (100)

Lal, B. B., ed. 1973. 'Preservation of Buddhist Shrines at Bamiyan, Afghanistan'. *Indian Archaeology* (1969–70): 108. (100)

Lal, B. B., and S. P. Gupta, eds. 1982. *Frontiers of the Indus Civilization: Sir Mortimer Wheeler Commemoration Volume*. New Delhi.

Lal, Mohan. 1834. 'A Brief Description of Herat'. *JASB* 3: 9–18. (346, 428, 819)

Lal, Mohan. 1846. *Travels in the Punjab, Afghanistan and Turkistan to Balk, Bokhara and Herat*. London. (100, 373, 418, 519, 520, 522, 655, 716, 724, 841, 847, 1020, 1052, 1079)

Lands. See Bopearachchi.

Lane Fox, Robin. 1980. *The Search for Alexander*. London

Lansdell, H. 1887. *Through Central Asia; with a Map and an Appendix on the Diplomacy and Delimitation of the Russo-Afghan Frontier*. London.

Lantier, Raymond. 1951. 'Begram ou Cologne?'. *Revue Archéologique*, 38: 66. (122)

Lauricella, Anthony, Joshua Cannon, Scott Branting, and Emily Hammer. 2017. 'Semi-Automated Detection of Looting in Afghanistan Using Multispectral Imagery and Principal Component Analysis'. *Antiquity*, 91/359: 1344–55. (18)

Lawn, Barbara. 1974. 'University of Pennsylvania Radiocarbon Dates XVII'. *Radiocarbon*, 16/2: 219–37. (18)

Lazard, Gilbert, Frantz Grenet, and Charles de Lambert-erie. 1984. 'Notes bactriennes'. *St.Ir.* 13/2: 199–232. (1123)

Le Berre, Marc. 1965. 'Prospection à Khisht Tépé (3–9 janvier 1962)'. In *Le Trésor monétaire de Qunduz*. MDAFA 20. Ed. Raoul Curiel and Gérard Fussman, 83–5. Paris. (569, 892)

Le Berre, Marc. 1970. 'Le monument de Danestama en Afghanistan'. *REI* 38: 45–53. (231)

Le Berre, Marc. 1973. 'Le monastère bouddhique et le stupa de Gul Dara: Rapport préliminaire en vue de la reprise des travaux de restauration du stupa et de la restauration partielle du monastère'. Unpublished report in the British Institute of Afghan Studies library, Kabul. (389)

Le Berre, Marc. 1978. 'La depose des peintures murales et des panneaux de stuc et de briques taillées provenant de la sale d'audience'. In *Lashkari Bazar IA*. MDAFA 18. Ed. Daniel Schlumberger, 109–10. Paris. (685)

Le Berre, Marc. 1987. *Monuments pré-islamiques de l'Hindukush central*. MDAFA 21. Paris. (16, 100, 109, 118, 233, 238, 263, 286, 302, 330, 346, 441, 466, 480, 489, 508, 514, 517, 592, 682, 784, 786, 969, 1004, 1014, 1021, 1049, 1052, 1074, 1075, 1077, 1117, 1199, 1202, 2146)

Le Berre, Marc, and Daniel Schlumberger. 1964. 'Remparts de Bactres'. In *Monuments préislamiques d'Afghanistan.* MDAFA 19. Ed. Bruno Dagens, Marc Le Berre, and Daniel Schlumberger, 61–105. Paris. (99)

Le May, Reginald. 1943. 'The Bimaran Casket'. *Burlington Magazine*, 82/482: 116–23. (127)

Le Mesurier, A. 1880. *Kandahar in 1879.* London. (522)

Le Rider, G. 1973. 'Fouilles d'Aï Khanoum. XI. Les monnaies'. In *Aï Khanoum, I.* MDAFA 21. Ed. Paul Bernard et al., 203–5. Paris. (18)

Le Strange, Guy. 1905. *The Lands of the Eastern Caliphate.* Cambridge. (15, 41, 98, 99, 142, 149, 212, 291, 318, 358, 428, 482, 483, 486, 522, 532, 601, 628, 697, 711, 716, 764, 798, 819, 1000, 1001, 1006, 1042, 1076, 1079, 1259)

Leach, E. P. 1880. 'Report on Survey Operations'. *General Report of the Operations of the Survey of India 1878–79.* Calcutta. (17, 158, 404, 488)

Lecuyot, Guy. 2007 'Ai Khanum Reconstructed'. In *After Alexander: Central Asia Before Islam.* Ed. Joe Cribb and Georgina Herrmann, 155–62. Oxford. (18)

Lecuyot, Guy, ed. 2013. *Fouilles d'Aï Khanoum IX. L'habitat.* MDAFA 34. Paris. (18)

Lee, Jonathan L. 1980. 'L'exploration de la région: Le site Islamique de Darra-i Shākh et le réseau fortifié'. *St.Ir.* 9/1: 71–81. (243, 248, 348, 362, 624, 893, 1129)

Lee, Jonathan L. 1982. 'Ferrier's Journey from Sar-i Pul to Daulatyār'. *EW* 32/1–4: 99–113. (362, 1000, 1051)

Lee, Jonathan L. 1996. *The Ancient Supremacy.* Leiden. (41, 42, 697, 2164)

Lee, Jonathan L. 1998. '*The New Year's Festival and the Shrine of 'Ali ibn Abi Talib at Mazar-i Sharif, Afghanistan'.* Unpublished Ph.D. thesis, University of Leeds. (716)

Lee, Jonathan L. 2006. 'Monuments of Bamiyan Province, Afghanistan'. *Iran*, 44: 229–52. (124, 189, 239, 286, 398, 489, 845, 862, 1021, 1039, 2045, 2046, 2116, 2141, 2145, 2158, 2251)

Lee, Jonathan L., ed. 1991, *The Journals of Edward Sterling in Persia and Afghanistan 1828–1829.* Naples. (98)

Lee, Jonathan L., and Frantz Grenet. 1998. 'New Light on the Sasanid Painting at Ghulbiyan, Faryab Province, Afghanistan'. *South Asian Studies*, 14: 75–85. (362)

Lee, Jonathan L., and Nicholas Sims-Williams. 2003. 'The Antiquities and Inscriptions of Tang-i Safedak'. *SRAA* 9: 159–84. (2261)

Lee, Jonathan L. See also Grenet, Frantz.

Leidy, Denise Patry. 2012. 'Links, Missing and Otherwise: Tillya Tepe and East Asia'. In *Afghanistan. Forging Civilizations along the Silk Road.* Ed. Joan Aruz and Elisabetta Valtz Fino, 112–21. New York. (1192)

Lentz, T. 1996. 'Memory and Ideology in the Timurid Garden'. In *Mughal Gardens: Sources, Places, Representations, and Prospects.* Ed. J. L. Westcoat and J.-Wolschke-Bulmahn. 30–57. Washington, DC.

Leriche, Pierre. 1973. 'L'Asie Centrale dans l'antiquité'. *Revue des Etudes Anciennes*, 75/304: 280–310. (18, 743)

Leriche, Pierre. 1974a. 'Création de l'art gréco-iranien'. *Les Dossiers de l'Archéologie*, 5: 84–98. (18)

Leriche, Pierre. 1974b. 'Aï Khanoum, un rempart hellénistique en Asie centrale'. *Revue Archéologique*, 231–70. (18, 295)

Leriche, Pierre. 1976. 'La fouille du rempart d'Aï Khanoum: Signification historique'. In *Actes du XXIXe Congrès international des Orientalistes Paris, Juillet 1973. Asie Centrale*, 43–8. Paris. (18)

Leriche, Pierre. 1986. *Fouilles d'Aï Khanoum V: Les remparts et les monuments associés.* MDAFA 29. Paris. (18)

Leriche, Pierre, and Joël Thoraval. 1979. 'La fontaine du rempart de l'Oxus à Aï Khanoum'. *Syria*, 56: 171–205. (18)

Leriche, Pierre, Axelle Rougeulle, and Nader Ghassouli. 1980. 'Campagne de fouilles 1978 à Aï Khanoum. VIII. Recherches sur les fortifications de la ville haute et de la citadelle sudest'. *BEFEO* 68: 64–75. (18)

Lerner, Jeffrey D. 2003–4. 'Correcting the Early History of Ây Kânom'. *AMI* 35–6: 373–410. (18)

Lerner, Jeffrey D. 2010. 'Revising the Chronologies of the Hellenistic Colonies of Samarkand-Marakanda (Afrasiab II–III) and Aï Khanoum (Northeastern Afghanistan)'. *Anabasis: Studia Classica et Orientalis,* 1: 58–79. (18)

Lerner, Jeffrey D. 2011. 'A Reappraisal of the Economic Inscriptions and Coin Finds from Aï Khanoum'. *Anabasis: Studia Classica et Orientalis*, 2: 103–47. (18)

Lerner, Judith A. 2009. 'Animal Headresses on the Sealings of the Bactrian Documents'. In *Festschrift in Honour of Nicholas Sims-Williams.* Ed. Werner Sunderman, Almut Hintze, and François de Blois, 215–26. Wiesbaden. (2230)

Leshnik, L. S. 1967. 'Kushano-Sasanian Ceramics from Central Afghanistan: A Preliminary Note'. *Berliner Jahrbuch für Frügeschichte*, 7: 311–34. (15)

Leshnik, L. S. 1968. 'Ghor, Firuzkuh and the Minar-i Jam'. *Central Asiatic Journal*, 12: 36–49. (468)

Lévêque, Pierre. 1974. 'A la suite d'Alexandre: L'unité indienne et l'art gréco-bouddhique'. *Les Dossiers de l'Archéologie*, 5: 115–35. (404)

Levi, Peter. 1972. *The Light Garden of the Angel King.* London. (86, 149, 169, 313, 337, 817, 860, 1117, 2109, 2160, 2245)

Levi, S. 1932. 'Notes sur les manuscrits sanscrits provenant de Bāmiyān (Afghanistan) et de Gilgit (Cachemire)'. *JA* 1–45. (100)

Lewis, J. 2000. 'Pillage d'une culture: Le patrimoine afghan en peril'. *Archéologia*, 365: 32–41. (718)

Lézine, A. 1962. 'Monuments historiques de l'Afghanistan: Stupas des environs de Kabul'. *Afghanistan*, 17/4: 39–47. (389, 1087, 1197)

Lézine, A. 1963–4. 'Hérat: Notes de voyage'. *Bulletin d'Etudes Orientales*, 18: 127–45. Reprinted in *Afghanistan*, 33/2 (1980): 68–91; 33/3: 88–100. (428)

Lézine, A. 1964. 'Trois stupas de la region de Caboul'. *Artibus Asiae*, 27: 5–24. (389, 1087, 1197)

Libby, W. F. 1953. *Chicago Radiocarbon Dates*, IV. Chicago. (743)

Ligabue, Giancarlo, and Sandro Salvatore, eds. 1989. *Bactria: An Ancient Civilization from the Sands of Afghanistan*. Venice. (256)

Liger, Jean-Claude. 1979. 'La physionomie urbaine d'une cite hellénistique en Asie Centrale'. Unpublished thesis, Université de Paris. (18)

Lin, Roland, and Aurora de Leon Wheeler, eds. 2011. *Final Report of the 8th UNESCO Expert Working Group Meeting for the Preservation of the Cultural Landscape and Archaeological Remains of the Bamiyan Valley, Afghanistan*. Paris. (100)

Lindberg, K. 1949. 'Observations au sujet de quelques grottes asiatiques'. *Afghanistan*, 4/3: 39–44. (198, 327)

Lindberg, K. 1961. 'Recherches biospéléoligiques en Afghanistan'. *Lunds Universitets Arsskrift*, NF Avd. 2, 57/1: 179–222. (319, 327, 477, 523, 747, 1069)

Lintz, Ulrike-Christiane. 2015, 'Judaeo-Persian Tombstone Inscriptions from Djām, Central Afghanistan'. In *The Silk Road: Interwoven History*. Ed. Mariko N. Walter and James P. Ito-Adler, 132–77. Cambridge, MA. (468, 1144)

Livshits, V. A. 1976. 'Nadpisi iz Dilberdzhina'. In *Drevnyaya Baktriya* 1. Ed. I. T. Kruglikova, 163–9. Moscow. (295)

Livshits, V. A. 1979. 'Dva ostraka iz Dilberdzhina'. In *Drevnyaya Baktriya* 2. Ed. I. T. Kruglikova, 95–7. Moscow. (295)

Livshits, V. A., and Irina T. Kruglikova. 1979. 'Fragmenti bakriyskoy monumentalnoy nadpisi iz Dilberdzhina'. In *Drevnyaya Baktriya* 2. Ed. I. T. Kruglikova, 98–112. Moscow. (295)

Lo Muzio, C. 1999. 'The Dioscuri at Dilberjin: Northern Afghanistan: Reviewing their Chronology and Significance'. *St.Ir.* 28: 41–71. (295)

Lord, M. B. 1838a. *The Uzbek State of Kundooz*. Simla.

Lord, M. B. 1838b. 'Some Account of a Visit to the Plain of Koh-i-Daman, the Mining District of Ghorband, and the Pass of the Hindu Kush'. *JASB* 6: 521–38. (327)

Lüders, H. 1909. 'The Mānikiāla Inscription'. *JRAS* 645–66. (1229)

Lumsden, Peter. 1885. 'Countries and Tribes Bordering the Koh-i-Baba Range'. *PRGS* 7: 561–77. (711)

Lyonnet, Bertille. 1977. *Découverte de sites de l'âge du bronze dans le NE de l'Afghanistan: Leurs rapports avec la civilizations de l'Indus*. Annali dell'Instituto Orientale di Napoli. Naples. (237, 1089)

Lyonnet, Bertille. 1981. 'Établissements chalcolithiques dans le Nord-Est de l'Afghanistan: Leur rapports avec les civilisations du basin de l'Indus'. *Paléorient*, 7/2: 57–74. (579, 633, 799, 1142, 1220)

Lyonnet, Bertille. 1997. *Prospections archéologiques en Bactriane Orientale. 1974–1978. Sous la direction de Jean-Claude Gardin, II. Céramique et peuplement du Chalcolithique à la Conquête Arabe*. Paris. (1, 5, 6, 28, 31, 40, 43, 50, 54, 61, 70, 83, 89, 94, 115, 134, 135, 136, 139, 156, 160, 162, 175, 182, 194, 208, 209, 210, 218, 220, 252, 260, 268, 269, 288, 307, 308, 321, 374, 386, 400, 412, 421, 440, 444, 445, 446, 446, 447, 450, 462, 472, 487, 495, 505, 509, 510, 511, 512, 513, 515, 516, 525, 569, 579, 580, 583, 591, 594, 611, 626, 632, 633, 640, 643, 643, 674, 738, 741, 750, 772, 791, 797, 799, 853, 892, 904, 909, 911, 917, 927, 931, 933, 936, 937, 943, 959, 969, 980, 981, 1007, 1008, 1009, 1019, 1032, 1080, 1086, 1089, 1090, 1092, 1093, 1128, 1132, 1143, 1162, 1205, 1217, 1220, 1224, 1233, 1235, 1253, 1271)

Lyonnet, Bertille. 1998: 'Les Grecs, les nomades et l'indépendence de la Sogdiane, d'après l'occupation comparée d'Aï Khanoum et de Marakanda au cours des derniers siècles avant notre ère'. *BAI* 12: 141–59. (18)

McBurney, C. B. M. 1972. 'Report of an Archaeological Survey in Northern Afghanistan, July–August 1971'. *Afghanistan*, 25/2: 22–32. Reprinted in *Afghanistan Archaeological Review*, 4/2 (1981): 12–14. (46, 526, 613)

McChesney, R. D. 1991a. 'Architecture and Narrative: The Khwaja. Abu Nasr Parsa Shrine. Part 1: Constructing the Complex and its Meaning, 1469–1696'. *Muqarnas*, 18: 94–119. (99)

McChesney, R. D. 1991b. *Waqf in Central Asia*. Princeton. (41, 716)

McChesney, R. D. 2002. 'Architecture and Narrative: The Khwaja. Abu Nasr Parsa Shrine. Part 2: Representing the Complex in Word and Image, 1696–1998'. *Muqarnas*, 19: 78–108. (99)

Mac Dowall, David W. 1965. 'The Dynasty of the Later Indo-Parthians'. *NC* 7th ser. 5: 137–48. (728)

Mac Dowall, David W. 1968a. 'Soter Megas, the King of Kings, the Kushāna'. *JNSI* 30: 28–48. (122)

Mac Dowall, David W. 1968b. 'The Shahis of Kabul and Gandhara'. *NC* 7th ser. 8: 189–224. (483)

Mac Dowall, David W. 1968c. 'Numismatic Evidence for the Date of Kanishka'. In *Papers on the Date of Kanishka*. Ed. A. L. Basham, 134–49. Leiden. (17)

Mac Dowall, David W. 1974. 'Implications for Kushan Chronology of the Numismatic Context of the Nameless King'. In *Central Asia in the Kushan Period*, I. Ed. B. G. Gafurov, 246–64. Moscow. (122, 728)

Mac Dowall, David W. 1978. 'Excavations at Kandahar: Coin Finds'. *Afghan Studies*, 1: 50–1. (522)

Mac Dowall, David W. 1979. 'Pre-Islamic Coins in the Herat Museum'. *Afghan Studies*, 2: 45–54. (428)

Mac Dowall, David W. 2002. 'The Rabatak Inscription and the Nameless Kushan King'. In *Cairo to Kabul: Afghan and Islamic Studies Presented to Ralph Pinder-Wilson*. Ed. Warwick Ball and Leonard Harrow, 163–9. London. (944)

Mac Dowall, David W. 2005. 'The Early Indo-Greek Currency in Arachosia'. In *South Asian Archaeology 2003*.

edited. Ute Franke-Vogt and Hans-Joachim Weisshaar, 241–5. Aachen. (522)

Mac Dowall, David W., and M. Ibrahim. 1978. 'Pre-Islamic Coins in the Kandahar Museum'. *Afghan Studies*, 1: 67–77. (522)

Mac Dowall, David W., and Maurizio Taddei. 1978a. 'The Early Historic Period: Achaemenids and Greeks'. In *The Archaeology of Afghanistan*. Ed. F. R. Allchin and N. Hammond, 187–232. London. (18, 37, 127, 250, 464, 483, 522, 728, 782, 1067, 1108)

Mac Dowall, David W., and Maurizio Taddei. 1978b. 'The Pre-Muslim Period'. In *The Archaeology of Afghanistan*. Ed. F. R. Allchin and N. Hammond, 233–99. London. (17, 71, 155, 265, 295, 332, 389, 461, 464, 522, 675, 971, 1052, 1087, 1123, 1180)

Mac Dowall, David W., and N. G. Wilson. 1960. 'Apolloditi Reges Indorum'. *NC* 6th ser. 20: 221–8. (122, 176, 728)

MacGregor, C. M. 1871. *Central Asia Part II: A Contribution Towards the Better Knowledge of the Topography, Ethnology, Resources and History of Afghanistan*. Calcutta.

MacGregor, C. M. 1879. *Narrative of a Journey through the Province of Khorassan and on the N.W. Frontier of Afghanistan in 1875*. 2 vols. London. (373, 454, 1165)

MacGregor, C. M. 1882. *Wanderings in Baluchistan*. London. (383, 2031)

McLachlan, K. S., and W. Whittaker, eds. 1982. *Bibliography of Afghanistan*. Wisbech.

MacMahon, A. H. 1897. 'The Southern Borderland of Afghanistan'. *Geographical Journal*, 9: 393–415. (383)

MacMahon, A. H. 1906. 'Recent Survey and Exploration in Seistan'. *Geographical Journal*, 28/3–4: 209–18 and 333–52. (190, 335, 752, 842, 1006, 1147)

McNicoll, Anthony. 1978. 'Excavations at Kandahar 1975: Second Interim Report'. *Afghan Studies*, 1: 41–66. (522)

McNicoll, Anthony, Warwick Ball, et al. 1996. *Excavations at Kandahar 1974 and 1975*. Oxford. (55, 522)

Maeda, Kosaku. 2006. 'The Mural Paintings of the Buddhas of Bamiyan: Description and Conservation Operations'. In *Art and Archaeology of Afghanistan: Its Fall and Survival*. Ed. J. Van Krieken-Pieters, 127–44. Leiden. (100)

Maeda, Kosaku. 2007. 'Mural Painting along the Silk Road'. In *Mural Painting of the Silk Road. Cultural Exchanges between East and West*. Ed. Kazuya Yamauchi, Yoko Taniguchi, and Tomoko Uno, 20–6. London. (100)

Maeda, Kosaku. 2015. 'The Recent Discovery of Tang Dynasty Artefacts in Bamiyan, Afghanistan'. In *Keeping History Alive: Safeguarding Cultural Heritage in Post-Conflict Afghanistan*. Ed. Brendan Cassar and Sara Noshadi, 244–8. Paris and Kabul. (1042)

Mairs, Rachel. 2008. 'Greek Identity and the Settler Community in Hellenistic Bactria and Arachosia'. *Migrations and Identities*, 1/1: 19–43. (18, 522)

Mairs, Rachel. 2011a. 'The Places in between: Model and Metaphor in the Archaeology of Hellenistic Arachosia'. In *From Pella to Gandhara: Hybridisation and Identity in the Art and Architecture of the Hellenistic East*. edited. Anna Kouremenos, Sujatha Chandrasekaran, and Roberto Rossi. 177–89. Oxford. (522)

Mairs, Rachel. 2011b. *The Archaeology of the Hellenistic Far East: A Survey*. Oxford. (18, 522)

Mairs, Rachel. 2012. 'Glassware from Roman Egypt at Begram (Afghanistan) and the Red Sea Trade'. *British Museum Studies in Ancient Egypt and the Sudan*, 18: 2–14. (122)

Mairs, Rachel. 2013. 'The "Temple with Indented Niches" at Ai Khanoum: Ethnic and Civic Identity on Hellenistic Bactria'. In *Cults, Creeds and Identities in the Greek City after the Classical Age*. edited. Richard Alston, Onno M. van Nijf, and Christina G. Williamson, 85–117. Leuven. (18)

Mairs, Rachel. 2014a. *The Hellenistic Far East. Archaeology, Language, and Identity in Greek Central Asia*. Oakland, CA. (18, 522)

Mairs, Rachel. 2014b. 'Ai Khanoum and the Achaemenids'. *AMI* 46. (18)

Mairs, Rachel. 2015. 'Heroes and Philosophers? Greek Personal Names and their Bearers in Hellenistic Bactria'. In *The Silk Road: Interwoven History*. Ed. Mariko N. Walter and James P. Ito-Adler, 71–100. Cambridge, MA. (18)

Mairs, Rachel. 2016. 'New Discoveries of Documentary Texts from Bactria: Political and Cultural Change, Administrative Continuity'. In *Proceedings of the 27th International Congress of Papyrology Warsaw, 29 July–3 August 2013*. Ed. Thomās Derdā, Ādām Łājtār and Jākub Urbānik, 2037–71. Warsaw. (99)

Maitland, P. J. 1879. 'Report of Reconnaissance from Sadat Killa in a Westerly Direction'. *Reports on Afghanistan 1879*. Bound volume in British Library, Shelf-mark I. S. 164. (680, 886, 1071, 1262)

Maitland, P. J. 1885. 'Note on the Defences of Herat'. (Enclosure No. 3, dated 6 Sept. 1885. Political and Secret Letters from India, vol. 44, pp. 1–8, 102. India Office.) (428)

Maitland, P. J. 1887a. 'The Robat-i Surkh Pass'. ABC III. 448–50.

Maitland, P. J. 1887b. 'The Batun, Boton or Botan Pass'. ABC III. 470–5.

Maitland, P. J. 1887c. 'The Kush Robat, or Ardewan Pass'. ABC III. 476–82. (216, 427, 661, 946, 951, 2213)

Maitland, P. J. 1887d. 'The Baba Pass'. ABC III. 483–7.

Maitland, P. J. 1888a. *Records of the Intelligence Party, Afghan Boundary Commission, I. Diary of Major Maitland*. Simla. (15, 58, 98, 100, 177, 189, 193, 195, 197, 212, 235, 346, 391, 394, 427, 428, 436, 454, 482, 508, 527, 556, 610, 634, 654, 656, 661, 687, 704, 711, 733, 752, 764, 781,

792, 796, 819, 820, 824, 843, 844, 845, 849, 866, 867, 869, 871, 908, 946, 947, 951, 961, 974, 984, 1017, 1031, 1038, 1042, 1052, 1144, 1159, 1165, 1196, 1206, 1252, 1259, 1263, 2007, 2017, 2019, 2022, 2025, 2027, 2036, 2037, 2041, 2042, 2058, 2071, 2072, 2073, 2088, 2090, 2093, 2118, 2119, 2147, 2149, 2150, 2152, 2153, 2156, 2165, 2172, 2188, 2190, 2191, 2192, 2193, 2195, 2199, 2200, 2202, 2208, 2210, 2214, 2215, 2225, 2231, 2233, 2234, 2240, 2243, 2289)

Maitland, P. J. 1888b. *Records of the Intelligence Party, Afghan Boundary Commission*, II. *Diary of Major Maitland.* Simla. (35, 38, 47, 68, 75, 99, 137, 153, 178, 186, 199, 213, 214, 286, 294, 296, 314, 315, 316, 325, 398, 407, 408, 415, 424, 425, 465, 489, 492, 493, 496, 541, 542, 550, 568, 569, 572, 596, 604, 609, 628, 629, 640, 642, 657, 666, 681, 697, 707, 708, 753, 760, 768, 776, 800, 833, 835, 846, 862, 872, 890, 892, 915, 918, 932, 934, 944, 945, 952, 977, 1011, 1018, 1021, 1038, 1043, 1076, 1082, 1094, 1095, 1113, 1135, 1138, 1149, 1153, 1155, 1212, 1226, 1244)

Maitland, P. J. 1888c. *Afghan Boundary Commission Routes. Daolat Yar Series. Comprising Routes from Daolat Yar to Strategic Front Maimana—Mazar-i Sharif.* Simla. (1263, 2021, 2044, 2151, 2252)

Maitland, P. J. 1891. *Records of the Intelligence Party, Afghan Boundary Commission*, IV. *Reports on Tribes.* Simla.

Maitland, P. J., and F. H. R. Drummond. 1888. *Afghan Boundary Commission Routes. Herat Series. All Roads from Herat into Khorasan, Russian Territory, and Afghan Turkistan.* Simla. (541, 610, 826, 949, 951, 952, 984, 1017, 1106, 1159, 1206, 2018, 2038, 2108, 2112, 2115, 2132, 2135, 2137, 2147, 2159, 2177, 2178, 2181, 2189, 2196, 2199, 2201, 2203, 2211, 2214, 2215, 2231, 2235, 2240, 2274, 2278)

Maitland, P. J., F. H. R. Drummond, and R. J. Strachey. 1889. *Afghan Boundary Commission Routes. Helmand Series. Comprising All the Roads from the Advanced British Bases at Kandahar and Nushki to the Helmand, and there to Herat.* Simla. (482, 865, 1268, 2000, 2040, 2070, 2083, 2126, 2185, 2220, 2271)

Makino, Masami. 1957. 'Diffuse Talks on Buddhist Arts in Afghanistan'. *Afghanistan,* 12/3: 16–18. (100)

Mandelshtam, A. M. 1954. 'O nekotorikh rezultatakh rabot frantsuzkoy arkheologicheskoy missii v Afganistane'. *Sovetskaya Arkheologiya,* 21: 415–29. (99, 100, 122, 1123)

Mandersloot, G., and Josephine Powell. 1972. 'Die Moschee Nouh Goumbad: Ein kürzlich entdecktes früh-islamisches Bauwerk in Afghanistan'. *Du,* 32/11: 842–50. (410)

Margotinni, C., ed. 2009. *The Destruction of the Giant Buddha Statues in Bamiyan, Central Afghanistan.* UNESCO Special Publication. Paris. (100)

Marguier, Arnaud. 2012. 'La céramique de Bāmiyān: Un court aperçu'. In *Auteur de Bāmiyān: De la Bactriane hellénisée à l'Inde bouddhique.* Ed. G. Duccoeur, 243–52. Paris. (100)

Maricq, André. 1958. 'Inscriptions de Surkh Kotal (Baghlān): La grande inscription de Kaniška et l'éteo-tokharien, l'ancienne langue de la Bactriane'. *JA* 266: 345–440. (1123)

Maricq, André. 1959. 'The Mystery of the Great Minaret: The Remarkable and Isolated 12th-Century Tower of Jham Discovered in Unexplored Afghanistan'. *ILN* (10 Jan.): 56–8. (468, 658)

Maricq, André. 1968. 'La date de Kaniska'. In *Papers on the Date of Knishka.* Ed. A. L. Basham, 157–78. Leiden. (122)

Maricq, André, and Gaston Wiet. 1959. *Le Minaret de Djam: La découverte de la capitale des sultans ghorides (XII–XIII siècles).* MDAFA 16. Paris. (12, 123, 189, 212, 468, 658, 1000)

Markham, C. R. 1876. 'Afghan Geography'. *PRGS* 20: 241–8. (306, 379, 703, 851, 1104)

Marquis, Philippe. 2013. 'Les activités récentes de la Délégation archeologique française en Afghanistan (DAFA)'. *Cahiers d'Asie centrale,* 21/22: 93–8. (19, 524)

Marshack, A. 1972. 'Aq Kupruk: Art and Symbol'. In *Prehistoric Research in Afghanistan.* Ed. Louis Dupree et al., 66–72. Philadelphia. Reprinted in *Afghanistan,* 27/3 (1974): 20–32. (46)

Martinez-Sève, Laurianne. 2010. 'A propos du temple aux niches indentèes d'Aï Khanoum: Quelques observations'. In *Paysage et religion Gréce antique.* Ed. Pierre Carlier and Charlotte Lerouge-Cohen, 195–207. Paris. (18)

Martinez-Sève, Laurianne. 2014. 'The Spatial Organization of Ai Khanoum, a Greek City in Afghanistan'. *AJA* 118/2: 267–83. (18)

Martinez-Sève, Laurianne. 2015. 'Ai Khanoum and Greek Domination in Central Asia'. *Electrum,* 22: 17–46. (18)

Masson, Charles. 1833a. 'The Caves of Jellālābād and Kābul'. Unpublished. manuscript in the India Office Library, London. (10, 87, 163, 326, 404, 418, 523, 555, 1137, 1169, 1173)

Masson, Charles. 1833b. 'Caves of Bamiyan'. Unpublished manuscript in the India Office Library, London. (100)

Masson, Charles. 1833c. 'Sketches of Baluchistan and Afghanistan'. Unpublished manuscript in the India Office Library, London. (358, 718, 1042, 1048, 1193)

Masson, Charles. 1834a. 'Memoir on the Ancient Coins Found at Beghram, in the Kohistān of Kaboul'. *JASB* 3: 152–75. Reprinted in Prinsep 1858: 80–81. (122).

Masson, Charles. 1834b. 'Extracts from Mr Masson's Letter to Dr Gerard, on the Excavation of Topes'. *JASB* 3: 329–32. (761)

Masson, Charles. 1836a. 'Second Memoir on the Ancient Coins Found at Beghram, in the Kohistān of Kabul'. *JASB* 5: 1–28. Reprinted in Prinsep 1858: 344–8. (122, 327, 332, 620, 651, 774, 798, 838, 1088, 1154)

Masson, Charles. 1836b. 'Note on an Inscription at Bamian'. *JASB* 5: 188. (100)

Masson, Charles. 1836c. 'Third Memoir on the Ancient Coins Discovered at the Site Called Beghram in the Kohistān of Kabul'. *JASB* 5: 537–47. Reprinted in Prinsep 1858: 348–51. (122)

Masson, Charles. 1836d. 'Notes on the Antiquities of Bamian'. *JASB* 5: 707–20. (100, 1052)

Masson, Charles. 1839. 'Narrative of an Excursion into the Hazaureh Country of Bisut, and the Districts of Bamian and Seghan'. *Proceedings of the Bombay Geographical Society*, 2 (May): 34–122. (47, 118, 140, 221, 456, 739, 786, 1042, 1121, 1194, 1202, 1215)

Masson, Charles. 1840. 'Papers on Afghanistan, Containing the Narrative of Journeys Performed in That and the Adjacent Countries between 1827 and 1830'. *Proceedings of the Bombay Geographical Society*, 5 (Sept.–Nov.). (10, 113, 116, 163, 380, 402, 406, 523, 549, 735, 1148)

Masson, Charles. 1841. 'Memoir on the Buildings Called Topes'. In *Ariana Antiqua*. Ed. H. H. Wilson, 55–118. London. (17, 30, 106, 121, 127, 133, 155, 261, 283, 310, 326, 334, 364, 370, 389, 404, 418, 426, 469, 471, 519, 574, 620, 651, 664, 667, 718, 727, 756, 761, 773, 806, 847, 855, 1016, 1087, 1088, 1102, 1116, 1124, 1125, 1169, 1197, 1229, 1237, 1273)

Masson, Charles. 1842. *Narrative of Various Journeys in Balochistan, Afghanistan and the Panjab*. 3 vols. London. (4, 10, 32, 33, 47, 87, 90, 100, 113, 116, 118, 119, 122, 123, 129, 140, 151, 155, 163, 176, 198, 211, 221, 230, 246, 319, 327, 344, 358, 365, 380, 402, 404, 406, 418, 435, 453, 456, 458, 460, 483, 488, 503, 517, 522, 523, 528, 529, 530, 531, 549, 555, 575, 588, 615, 620, 627, 644, 647, 651, 710, 735, 739, 748, 773, 774, 779, 786, 795, 838, 840, 907, 995, 1027, 1029, 1042, 1048, 1052, 1087, 1088, 1121, 1122, 1137, 1148, 1154, 1174, 1185, 1193, 1194, 1197, 1202, 1215, 1229, 1254, 2239)

Masson, V. M. 1976. 'The Art of Altin-depe'. In *To Illustrate the Monuments: Essays on Archaeology presented to Stuart Piggot*. Ed. J. V. S. Megaw. London.

Masson, V., and V. Sarianidi. 1969. 'Afghanistan in the Ancient East'. *Afghanistan*, 22/2: 7–19. (46, 245, 287, 526, 743, 968)

Massoudi, O. K., ed. 2011. *Mes Aynak: New Excavations in Afghanistan*. Kabul.

Matheson, Sylvia. 1961. *Time off to Dig*. London. (743)

Matson, Frederick R. 1957. 'Area 15 — Western Asia'. *Cowa Survey*, 1. (99, 1160)

Matson, Frederick R. 1958. 'A Technological Look at the Shamshir Ghar Potsherds'. In *Shamsir Ghar*. Ed. L. Dupree, 294–8. New York. (1069)

Matson, Frederick R. 1963. 'Notes on the Manufacture of Pottery at Deh Morasi Ghundai'. In *Deh Morasi Ghundai*. Ed. Louis Dupree, 121–3. New York. (287)

Matsumoto, Yeiichi. 1929. 'Development of the Characteristics of the Buddhist Pictures in Central Asia in its Relation to the Far East. Parts 1–3'. *Kokka*, 465/2; 466/1; 466/2. (100)

Mauelshagen. See Fischer.

Maxwell-Hyslop, R. 1982. 'The Khosh Tapa-Fullol Hoard'. *Afghan Studies*, 3–4: 25–38. (582)

Mayer, L. A. 1956. *Islamic Architects and their Works*. Geneva. (1106)

Mayrhofer, Manfred. 1962. 'Das Bemühen die Surkh-Kotal-Inschrift'. *ZDMG* 112: 325–44. (1123)

Meadow, R. H. 1973. 'A Chronolgy for the Indo-Iranian Borderlands and Southern Baluchistan 4000–2000 BC'. In *Radio-Carbon and Indian Archaeology*. Ed. D. P. Agrawal and A. Ghosh, 190–204. Bombay. (287, 743)

Mehendale, Sanjyot. 1996. 'Begram: Along Ancient Central Asian and Indian Trade Routes'. *Cahiers d'Asie Centrale*, 1/2: 47–64. (122)

Mehendale, Sanjyot. 2012. 'The Begram Carvings: Itinerancy and the Problem of "Indian" Art'. In *Afghanistan: Forging Civilizations along the Silk Road*. Ed. Joan Aruz and Elisabetta Valtz Fino, 65–77. New York. (122)

Mekarska, Barbara. 1974. 'An Attempt at the Reconstruction of the Bactrian Language System'. *Folio Orientalia*, 15: 149–65. (1123)

Melikian-Chirvani, Asadoulla Souren. 1968. 'Remarques preliminaires sur un mausolée ghaznévide'. *AA* 17: 59–92. (439)

Melikian-Chirvani, Asadoulla Souren. 1969a. 'La plus ancienne mosquée de Balkh'. *AA* 20: 3–20. (410)

Melikian-Chirvani, Asadoulla Souren. 1969b. 'Un basin iranien de l'an 1375'. *Gazette des Beaux Arts*, 73: 5–18. (428)

Melikian-Chirvani, Asadoulla Souren. 1970. 'Eastern Iranian Architecture: Apropos of the Ghurid Parts of the Great Mosque of Herat'. *BSOAS* 33: 322–7. (428)

Melikian-Chirvani, Asadoulla Souren. 1972. 'Baba Hatem: Un chef d'œuvre inconnu d'époque ghaznévide en Afghanistan'. In *The Memorial Volume of the Vth International Congress of Iranian Art and Archaeology*, II. Ed. A. Tajvidi and M.Y. Kiani, 108–24. Tehran. (439)

Melikian-Chirvani, Asadoulla Souren. 1974. 'L'évocation littéraire du bouddhisme dans l'Iran musulman'. *Le Monde Iranien et l'Islam*, 2: 1–72. (178, 1243)

Melikian-Chirvani, Asadoulla Souren. 1975a. 'The White Bronzes of Early Islamic Iran'. *Metropolitan Museum Journal*, 1974/9: 123–51. (1208)

Melikian-Chirvani, Asadoulla Souren. 1975b. 'Les bronzes du Khorāssān 3, bronzes inédits du Xè et Xiè siècles'. *St. Ir.* 14/2: 187–205. (697)

Melikian-Chirvani, Asadoulla Souren. 1977a. 'Les bronzes de Khorâssân V'. *St.Ir.* 6/2: 185–210.

Melikian-Chirvani, Asadoulla Souren. 1977b. 'Un chef-d'œuvre inconnu dans une Vallée afghane'. *Connaissance des Arts*, 308: 76–9. (179)

Melikian-Chirvani, Asadoulla Souren. 1979. 'Les bronzes de Khorâssân VI et VII'. *St.Ir* 8: 7–32, 223–43.

Melikian-Chirvani, Asadoulla Souren. 1982a. 'Le rhyton selon les sources persanes: Essai sur la continuité culturelle iranienne de l'Antiquité à l'Islam'. *St.Ir.* 11: 263–92.

Melikian-Chirvani, Asadoulla Souren. 1982b. *Islamic Metalwork from the Iranian World, 8th–18th Centuries.* Victoria and Albert Museum Catalogues. London.

Melzer, G. 2006. 'A Copper Scroll Inscription from the Time of the Alchon Huns'. In *Manuscripts Schøyen Collection: Buddhist Manuscripts.* Ed. Lore Sander and J. Braavig, 251–314. Oslo. (1142)

Mendez, Christiane. 1966. 'Etude anthropologique des squelettes de Mundigak (Afghanistan)'. *BEFEO* 53/1: 101–17. (743)

Menninger, Michael. 1996. *Untersuchungen zu den Gläsern und Gipsabgüssen aus dem Fund von Begram/Afghanistan.* Würzburg. (122)

Merk, C. S. 1888. 'Report on the Country from Chaharburjak on the Helmand, through the South of Seistan'. ABC V. Ed. J. West Ridgeway et al., 25–36. Simla. (147, 206, 376, 829, 830, 858, 888, 1147)

Merk, C. S. 1891. 'Diary of a Journey from the Herat Valley to Farsi and Back'. ABC IV. Ed. P. J. Maitland, 221–33. Simla. (7)

Merkel, Stephen, Bernt Bräutigam, Sabine Klein, and Andreas Hauptmann. 2013. 'The Analysis of Slag from the Panjhīr Mining Region, Afghanistan: An Investigation of (Medieval) Silver Production Technology'. *AMI* 45: 231–49. (686)

Meunié, Jacques. 1942. *Shotorak.* MDAFA 10. Paris. (1088)

Meunié, Jacques. 1943–5. 'Le couvert des otages de Kanishka au Kāpiça'. *JA* 134: 151–62. (928, 1088)

Meunié, Jacques. 1954. 'Begram, chantier 2, 1939'. In *Nouvelles recherches archéologiques à Bégram.* MDAFA 11. Ed. J. Hackin et al., 7–9. Paris. (122)

Meunié, Jacques. 1959a. 'Begram – fouille de 1938'. In *Diverses recherches archéologiques en Afghanistan. 1933–1940.* MDAFA 8. Ed. J. Hackin et al., 103–6. Paris. (122)

Meunié, Jacques. 1959b. 'Une entrée de la ville à Begram'. In *Diverses recherches archéologiques en Afghanistan.* MDAFA 8. Ed. J. Hackin et al., 107–13. Paris. (122)

Meunié, Jacques. 1959c. 'Qol-i-Nāder, une petite fondation bouddhique au Kapiça'. In *Diverses recherches archéologiques en Afghanistan.* MDAFA 8. Ed. J. Hackin et al., 115–27. Paris. (928)

Michaud, Roland and Sabrina, and Michael Barry. 1996. *Colour and Symbolism in Islamic Architecture: Eight Centuries of the Tile-Maker's Art.* London. (99, 346, 428, 468, 716)

Micheli, Roberto. 2009. 'Prehistory of Afghanistan: The Italian Contribution and Research Perspectives'. In *The*

IsIAO Italian Archaeological Mission in Afghanistan 1957–2007: Fifty Years of Research in the Heart of Eurasia. Ed. Anna Filigenzi and Roberta Giunta. 1–17. Rome. (425)

Micheli, Roberto. 2013. 'The Lithic Industry from Hazar Sum. Samangan, Afghanistan: New Perspectives and Old Data'. In *South Asian Archaeology 2007,* I. *Prehistoric Periods.* Ed. Dennys Frenez and Maurizio Tosi, 193–200. Oxford. (425)

Migeon, Gaston K. 1929a. 'Excavations at Hadda'. *Eastern Art,* 1/4: 219–25. (404)

Migeon, Gaston. K. 1929b. 'Exposition des fouilles de Hadda au Musée Guimet'. *Revue Archéologique,* 29 (Apr.–June): 366–8. (404)

Mitchiner, M. 1976–7. *Indo-Greek and Indo-Scythian Coinage.* 9 vols. London.

Mitra, Rājendralāla. 1861. 'Translation of a Bactrian Inscription from Wardak in Afghanistan'. *JASB* 30: 337–47. (1229)

Miyaji, Akira. 1976a. 'The Art of Bamiyan'. In *Bamiyan Crossroads of Culture.* Ed. A. Miyaji, 23–6. Asian Cultural Centre for UNESCO. Tokyo. (100)

Miyaji, Akira. 1976b. 'Wall Paintings of Bamiyan: A Stylistic Analysis'. In *Japan-Afghanistan Joint Archaeological Survey in 1974.* Ed. T. Higuchi, 17–31. Kyoto. (100)

Miyaji, Akira. 1978. 'The Parinirvāna Scenes of Bamiyan: An Iconographical Analysis'. In *Japan-Afghanistan Joint Archaeological Survey in 1976.* Ed. T. Higuchi, 13–22. Kyoto. (100, 622, 1088)

Miyaji, Akira. 1980. 'The Wall Paintings of Bamiyan Caves (Continued): Stylistic Analysis'. In *Japan-Afghanistan Joint Archaeological Survey in 1978.* Ed. T. Higuchi, 16–26. Kyoto. (100)

Miyaji, Akira. 2012. 'Le schéma iconographique des peintures murales des plafonds des grottes de Bāmiyān'. In *Auteur de Bāmiyān: De la Bactriane hellénisée à l'Inde bouddhique.* Ed. G. Duccoeur, 209–39. Paris. (100)

Mizuno, Seiichi. 1962. 'Hindūkushi Nanboko no Bukkyō Iseki' (Buddhist Sites on Both Sides of the Hindu Kush Mountains). In *Bunmei no Jūjiro: A Cross Road of Civilizations,* 131–43. Summary in H. Motamedi 1975c: 232. (99, 100, 404, 425, 931, 1135)

Mizuno, Seiichi, ed. 1962. *Haibāk and Kashmir-Smast.* Kyoto. (407)

Mizuno, Seiichi, ed. 1964. *Afuganisutan Kodai Bijutsu (The Ancient Art of Afghanistan).* Tokyo. (332, 358, 518, 546, 790, 1088)

Mizuno, Seiichi, ed. 1967. *Hazār Sum and Fīl-Khāna: Cave Sites in Afghanistan Surveyed in 1962.* Kyoto. (326, 425)

Mizuno, Seiichi, ed. 1968. *Durman Tepe and Lalma: Buddhist Sites in Afghanistan Surveyed in 1963–1965.* Kyoto.

Mizuno, Seiichi, ed. 1971. *Basawal and Jalalabad-Kabul: Buddhist Cave-Temples and Topes in South-East*

Afghanistan Surveyed Mainly in 1965. Kyoto. (17, 30, 34, 106, 121, 122, 127, 155, 163, 283, 326, 370, 388, 389, 426, 469, 471, 504, 622, 667, 718, 727, 761, 806, 847, 855, 986, 1026, 1087, 1102, 1116, 1124, 1125, 1169, 1197, 1237)

Mizuno, Seiichi, and Kunio Fujita. 1968. 'Lalma Temple Site'. In *Durman Tepe and Lalma*. Ed. Seiichi Mizuno, 109–12. Kyoto. (673)

Mizuno, Seiichi, and Takayasu Higuchi. 1967. 'Hazār Sum and Fīl Khāna'. In *Hazār Sum and Fīl-Khāna: Cave Sites in Afghanistan Surveyed in 1962*. Ed. S. Mizuno, 59–67. Kyoto. (425)

Mizuno, Seiichi, and Kojo Nishikawa. 1962. 'Haibāk Caves'. In *Haibāk and Kashmir-Smast*. Ed. Seiichi Mizuno, 87–96. Kyoto. (1135)

Mizuno, Seiichi, and Kojo Nishikawa. 1967. 'Fīl Khāna'. In *Hazār Sum and Fīl Khāna*. Ed. Seiichi Mizuno, 68–77. Kyoto. (326)

Mizuno, Seiichi, and Nakao Odani. 1968. 'Durman Tepe'. In *Durman Tepe and Lalma*. Ed. Seiichi Mizuno, 93–108. Kyoto. (20, 309, 564, 931, 1131)

Mochiri, M. I. 1983. *Etude de numismatique iranienne sous les sassanides et arabe-sassanides*, II. Leiden.

Mock, John. 2011. 'Shrine Traditions of Wakhan Afghanistan'. *Journal of Persianate Studies*, 4: 117–45. (524, 557, 873)

Mock, John. 2016. 'Tibetans in Wakhan: New Information on Inscriptions and Rock Art'. *Revue d'Etudes Tibétaines*, 36 (Oct.): 121–41. (524)

Moline, J. 1975. 'The Minaret of Jām. Afghanistan'. *Kunst des Orients*, 9: 131–48. (468)

Momii, Motomitsu, and Hiromitsu Seki. 2007. 'Displaced Cultural Properties: Non-Invasive Study on Mural Painting Fragments from Bamiyan'. In *Mural Painting of the Silk Road: Cultural Exchanges between East and West*. Ed. Kazuya Yamauchi, Yoko Taniguchi, and Tomoko Uno, 93–100. London. (100)

Monod, Odette. 1966. *Guide du Musée Guimet*. Paris. (100, 122, 332, 404, 508, 743, 1088)

Monod-Brühl, Odette. 1939. *Guide-Catalogue du Musée Guimet*. Paris. (100, 122, 332, 404, 508, 743, 1088)

Moorcroft, William, and George Trebeck. 1841. *Travels in the Himalayan Provinces of Hindustan and the Panjab; in Ladakh and Kasmir; in Peshawar, Kabul, Kunduz, and Bokhara*. Ed. H. H. Wilson. 2 vols. London. (99, 100, 163, 425, 628, 761, 1042, 1135, 2171)

Morgan, Llewelyn. 2012. *The Buddhas of Bamiyan*. London. (100)

Morgenstern, Laure. 1935. 'La peinture murale dans l'art iranien'. In *IIIe Congrès international d'art et d'archéologie iraniens*, 140–5. Leningrad. (305)

Motamedi, Ahmad Ali. 1967. 'Archaeology in Afghanistan'. *Afghanistan*, 30/3: 28–34. (108, 820, 1042, 1160)

Motamedi, Ahmad Ali. 1975. 'Prehistoric Afghanistan'. *Afghanistan*, 28/1: 85–93. (743)

Motamedi, Ahmad Ali. 1978. 'Mujasama-i tari rātnā'. *Tahqiqāt-i Kūshānī*, 1: 27–31. (404)

Motamedi, Ahmad Ali. 1979. 'Bronze Age Sites in North-East Afghanistan'. *Afghanistan*, 32/3: 49–55. (1089)

Motamedi, Ahmad Ali. 1980. 'Some Notes on the Excavation at Shortughai'. *Afghanistan*, 32/4: 53–6. (1089)

Motamedi, Haruko. 1971a. 'Two New Outstanding Kushan Statues'. *Afghanistan*, 23/4: 20–3. (790, 1088)

Motamedi, Haruko. 1971b. 'The Buddhic Monastery of Fondukistan'. *Afghanistan*, 24/1: 18–22. (332)

Motamedi, Haruko. 1972. 'The Museum of Islamic Art in Ghazni'. *Afghanistan*, 24/4: 11–13. (358)

Motamedi, Haruko. 1975a. 'The Influence of the Buddhist Art of Afghanistan on the Buddhist Art of Japan'. *Afghanistan*, 27/4: 32–5. Translated as: 'Ta'sīr-i hunar-i Būdda'i-yi Afghānistān bar hunar-i Būdda-yi Jāpān'. *Aryānā*, 33/2 (1354): 70–74. (404)

Motamedi, Haruko. 1975b. 'Paintings from Bamiyan'. *Afghanistan*, 28/2: 8–13, and *Kabul Times* (15 July): 3. (508)

Motamedi, Haruko. 1975c. 'Contribution of Japanese Scholars to the Study of Art and Archaeology of Afghanistan'. *Memoirs of the Research Department of the Toyo Bunko*, 33: 219–84. Reprinted in *Afghanistan*, 31/3: 62–72; 31/4: 10–22; 31/1: 50–62; 32/2: 26–44 (1978–9). (172, 309, 326, 673)

Motamedi, Haruko. 1976. 'Archaeological Surveys of Kyoto University in Afghanistan'. *Afghanistan*, 29/3: 56–62. (100, 330, 508, 1185)

Motamedi, Haruko. 1977. 'The Footprints of Buddha at the Kābul Museum'. *Afghanistan*, 30/1: 78–88. (518)

Motamedi, Haruko. 1978a. 'Ghazni and its Culture'. *Afghanistan*, 31/1: 59–65. (358)

Motamedi, Haruko. 1978b. 'A General View on Hadda Art and History'. *Afghanistan*, 31/2: 69–90. (404)

Motamedi, Haruko. 1980. 'Bamiyan and its Culture. Part 1'. *Afghanistan*, 33/2: 27–32. (100)

Mouchet, Jacqueline, and Jean-Charles Blanc. 1972. 'Khandud, village de la Vallée du Wakhan'. *Afghanistan*, 25/2: 57–70. (72, 557, 1204)

Mukherjee, Bratindra Nath. 1964. 'The Dates of the Three Versions of the Surkh-Kotal Inscription Referring to the Year 31'. *Indian Studies Past and Present*, 5/3: 273–4. (1123)

Mukherjee, Bratindra Nath. 1967. *The Kushāna Genealogy*. Calcutta. (1123)

Mukhtarov, A. 1980. *Pozdnesrednevekoviy Balkh. (Material kistoricheskoy topografii goroda b XVI–XVII vv)*. Dushanbe. (69, 99, 410, 725)

Muroga, Teruko. 1972. 'Chemical Analysis on Some Archaeological Samples Especially from Iran and Afghanistan'. In *The Memorial Volume of the 5th International Congress on Iranian Art and Archaeology 1*. Ed. A. Tajvidi and M. Y. Kiani, 137–41. Tehran. (628)

Mustamandi, Shahibye. 1967. 'A Building by the Name of Gowharshad in Kohsan of Herat'. *Afghanistan,* 20/4: 65–6. (634)

Mustamandi, Shahibye. 1968a. 'A Preliminary Report on the Excavation of Tapa-i Shotur in Hadda'. *Afghanistan,* 21/1: 58–69. (404)

Mustamandi, Shahibye. 1968b. 'The Fish Porch'. *Afghanistan,* 21/2: 68–80, and as: 'Riwāq-i Mahīhā'. *Aryānā,* 26/5: 6–9. (404)

Mustamandi, Shahibye. 1968c. 'Greco-Bactrian Art'. *Afghanistan,* 21/3: 67–74, and as: 'Art-i Grīku Bāktar'. *Aryānā,* 26/6: 8–11. (122, 1123)

Mustamandi, Shahibye. 1969a. 'Kushanids' Art'. *Afghanistan,* 22/1: 78–84. (1123)

Mustamandi, Shahibye. 1969b. 'La fouille de Hadda'. *CRAI* 119–28. (404)

Mustamandi, Shahibye. 1969–70. 'Recent Excavation of Hadda Tapa-i Shotor 1345–1347 (1966–1968)'. *Afghanistan,* 22/2: 64–72; 22/3–4: 34–51. Translation of: 'Hafriyāt-i jadīd-i Hadda; Tapa Shutur'. *Aryānā,* 27/3: 13–18; 27/4: 19–38; 27/5: 24–50; 27/6: 74–78; 28/1: 67–78; 28/2: 94–6; 28/3: 43–60; 28/4: 78–84 (1348/49). (404)

Mustamandi, Shahibye. 1971. 'Preliminary Report on Hadda's Fifth Excavation Period'. In *Kushan Culture and History,* II. Ed. Fahima Ayubi, 43–50. Kabul. Also *Afghanistan,* 24/2–3: 128–137. (404)

Mustamandi, Shahibye. 1972. 'Le motif d'aigle à une ou deux têtes dans l'art Kouchan'. *Afghanistan,* 25/1: 9–16. (127, 1123)

Mustamandi, Shahibye. 1973. 'Preliminary Report on the Sixth and Seventh Excavation Expeditions in Tapa-Shutur, Hadda'. *Afghanistan,* 26/1: 52–62. (404)

Mustamandi, Shahibye. 1974a. 'The Herakle of Hadda'. *Afghanistan,* 26/4: 75–7. (404)

Mustamandi, Shahibye. 1974b. 'Les nouvelles fouilles de Hadda'. In *Central Asia in the Kushan Period,* I. Ed. B. G. Gafurov, 107–12. Moscow. (404)

Mustamandi, Shahibye. 1997. 'The Impact of Hellenised Bactria on Gandharan Art'. In *Gandharan Art in Context.* Ed. R. Allchin et al., 17–27. Delhi. (18, 122, 404, 1009)

Mustamandi, Shahibye and Mary. 1967–8a (1346). 'Rāpūr-i hafriyāt-i Bāstānshināsi Afghān dar Hadda'. *Aryānā,* 25/5–6: 5–12. (404)

Mustamandi, Shahibye and Mary. 1967–8b (1346). 'Kāwishhā-yi Hay'at-i Bāstānshināsi Afghan dar Kāpisā'. *Aryānā,* 26/1: 31–43. Translated as: 'The excavation of the Afghan Archaeological Mission in Kapisa'. *Afghanistan,* 20/4: 67–79. (622)

Mustamandi, Shahibye and Mary. 1969. 'Nouvelles Fouilles à Hadda (1966–1967) par l'Institut Afghan d'Archéologie'. *AA* 19: 15–36. Reprinted as: *Nouvelles Fouilles à Hadda.* Kabul, 1970. (404)

Nāhiz, Nasir. 1978. 'Qal'a-i tārīkhī-yi Ikhtīyāruddīn'. *Herāt,* 2–3: 14–15. (428)

Naïmi, Ali Ahmad. 1949. 'Un regard sur Ghor. Préambule: la géographe, l'histoire et les sites historiques'. *Afghanistan,* 4/4: 1–23. (683, 875, 1257)

Najimi, Abdul Wasay. 1982. 'The Cistern of Char-Suq (a Safavid Building in Herat, Built After 1634 AD)'. *Afghanistan Journal,* 9: 38–41.

Najimi, Abdul Wasay. 1988. *Herat: The Islamic City—A Study in Urban Conservation.* London. (428)

Najimi, Abdul Wassay. 2015. 'The Ghurid Madrasa and Mausoleum of Shah-i Mashhad, Ghur, Afghanistan'. *Iran,* 53: 143–69. (1023)

Narain, A. K. 1957. 'Apollodotus and his Coins'. *JNSI* 19/2: 121–34. (176, 728)

Narain, A. K. 1968. 'The Date of Kanishka'. In *Papers on the Date of Kanishka.* Ed. A. L. Basham, 206–39. Leiden. (17, 122, 1123)

Narain, R. B. 1991. *Buddhist Remains in Afghanistan.* Varanasi. (404)

Nāsir, Ghulām Sarwar. 1971. 'Ai Khānum'. *Ma'ruf-i Kultūr-i Milli,* 10: 8–13. (18)

Nasiri, A. 1962–3. 'The Lapis Lazuli in Afghanistan'. *Afghanistan,* 17/4: 48–56; 18/1: 51–6; 18/2: 23–8. (1001)

Naveh, Joseph, and Shaul Shaked. 2012. *Aramaic Documents from Ancient Bactria (Fourth Century BCE) from the Khalili Collections.* London. (99)

Nehru, Lolita. 1989. *The Origins of the Gandhāran Style.* Delhi.

Nehru, Lolita. 2004. 'A Fresh Look at the Bone and Ivory Carvings from Begram'. *SRAA* 10: 97–150. (122)

Niedemeyer, Oskar von, and Ernst Diez. 1924. *Afghanistan.* Leipzig. (41, 99, 100, 149, 212, 346, 358, 428, 483, 634, 697, 716, 764, 819, 1087, 1124, 1263)

Nikitin, A. B. 1995. 'The Sasanian Šahrab of Balkh'. *Ancient Civilizations from Scythia to Siberia,* 1/3: 365–8. (475)

Noorzai, Gul Mohammad. 1979. 'The Historical Link between Mundigak and the Indus Valley Civilization'. *Afghanistan,* 31/4: 23–8. (743)

Norman, K. R. 1972. 'Notes on the Greek Version of Aśoka's Twelfth and Thirteenth Rock Edicts'. *JRAS* 2: 111–18. (522)

O'Kane, Bernard. 1984a. 'Salğūk Minarets: Some New Data'. *Annales Islamologiques,* 20: 61–84. (752)

O'Kane, Bernard. 1984b. 'Timurid Stucco Decoration'. *Annales Islamologiques,* 20: 85–101. (428)

O'Kane, Bernard. 1985. 'The Tomb of Muhammad Ġāzī at Fūsaṅg'. *Annales Islamologiques,* 21: 113–28. (1259)

O'Kane, Bernard. 1987. *Timurid Architecture in Khurasan.* Costa Mesa. (66, 349, 373, 428, 634, 661, 725, 781, 1192, 1263, 2076)

O'Kane, Bernard. 2000. 'The Uzbek Architecture of Afghanistan'. *Cahiers d'Asie Centrale,* 8: 122–60. (99, 716)

O'Kane, Bernard. 2002. 'The Timurid Bazaar and the Origin of the Domed *Tim*'. In *Essays in Honor of George Scanlon.* Ed. Jill Edwards, 17–28. Cairo.

O'Kane, Bernard. 2006. 'The Nine-Bay Plan in Islamic Architecture: Its Origin, Development and Meaning'. In *Studies in Honor of Arthur Upham Pope*. Survey of Persian Art, 18. Ed. Abbas Daneshvari, 189–244. Costa Mesa. (410)

O'Kane, Bernard. 2009. *The Appearance of Persian on Islamic Art*. Biennial Ehsan Yarshater Lecture series, 4. New York. (428)

O'Kane, Bernard. 2011. 'The Development of Iranian Cuerda Seca Tiles and the Transfer of Tilework Technology'. In *And Diverse are their Hues*. Ed. Sheila Blair and Jonathan Bloom, 174–203. New Haven. (428)

Odani, Nakao. 2005. 'Re-examining the Finds at the Basawal Caves'. In *Art et archéologie des monastères gréco-bouddhiques du Nord-Ouest de l'Inde et de l'Asie Centrale*. Ed. Zemaryalaï Tarzi and Denyse Villancourt, 113–21. Paris. (100)

Okamoto, Kan'ei. 1935. 'Afuganistan no Bukkyō Geijutsu—Hadda ni okeru Girisha Geijutsu ni tsuite' (Buddhist Art in Afghanistan—On the Influence of Greek Art at Hadda). *Rekishi Kōron*, 4/11: 62–9. Summary in H. Motamedi, 1975c: 278–9. (404)

Olivier-Utard, Françoise. 1997. *Politique et archéologie: Histoire de la Délégation archéologique française en Afghanistan (1922–1982)*. Paris. (Revised edn, 2003.)

Olufsen, O. 1904. *Through the Unknown Pamirs*. London. (448, 678, 873, 1261)

Omar, Ghulam. 1949. 'Commentaire sur les resultants des dernières fouilles archéologiques français en Afghanistan'. *Afghanistan*, 4/1: 19–25. (122)

Omland, Atle. 2006. 'Claiming Gandhara: Legitimizing Ownership of Buddhist Manuscripts in the Schøyen Collection, Norway'. In *Art and Archaeology of Afghanistan: Its Fall and Survival*. Ed. J. Van Krieken-Pieters, 227–64. Leiden. (100)

Orazi, Roberto. 1977. 'The Mausoleum of Muhammad Sharīf Khān near Ghazni: Architectural Survey with a View to Restoration'. *EW* 27: 255–76. (358)

Otto-Dorn, K. 1964. *Kunst des Islam*. Baden-Baden. (358, 685)

Owen, David. 1960. 'Heart of the Ghorid Empire'. *Geographical Magazine* (Nov): 400–7. (468)

Paiman, Zafar. 2005. 'Découvertes à Kaboul: La renaissance de l'archéologie afghane'. *Archéologia*, 419: 24–39. (555, 1222, 2138, 2268)

Paiman, Zafar. 2008. 'Kaboul, foyer d'art bouddhique'. *Archéologia*, 461: 58. (1173, 2268)

Paiman, Zafar. 2010. 'Kaboul. Les Bouddhas colorés des monastères'. *Archéologia*, 473: 52–8. (19)

Paiman, Zafar, and Michael Alram. 2010. 'Tepe Narenj: A Royal Monastery on the High Ground of Kabul, with a Commentary on the Coinage'. *Journal of Inner Asian Art and Archaeology*, 5: 33–58.

Paiman, Zafar, and Michael Alram. 2013. *The Tepe Narenj Buddhist Monastery at Kabul: Buddhist Art during the First Muslim Raids Against the Town*. Collège de France. Publications de l'Institut de Civilisation Indienne Paris, 82. Paris. (2268)

Pandit, Ranjit S. 1927. 'Buddhist Remains in Afghanistan'. *Modern Review*, 41: 131–41. (100, 127, 404, 718, 761, 1016)

Pandit, Ranjit S. 1929. 'Greek Artists in Buddhist Afghanistan'. *Modern Review*, 45: 674–82. (404)

Pargiter, F. E. 1912. 'The Inscriptions on the Wardak Vase'. *JRAS* 1060–2. (1229)

Pargiter, F. E. 1914. 'The Phonetics of the Wardak Vase: Inscription on the Wardak Vase: Two Corrections'. *JRAS* 126–9. (1229)

Pargiter, F. E. 1921. 'The Inscriptions on the Bimaran Vase'. *Epigraphia Indica*, 16: 97–100. (127)

Parlato, Sandro. 1979. 'A Brāhmī Inscription on a Mud-Plaster Floor at Tapa Sardâr, Ghazni'. *EW* 29: 265–9. (1180)

Passmore, Emma, Janet Ambers, Catherine Higgitt, Clare Ward, Barbara Wills, St John Simpson, and Caroline Cartwright. 2012. 'Hidden, Looted, Saved: The Scientific Research and Conservation of a Group of Begram Ivories from the National Museum of Afghanistan'. *British Museum Technical Research Bulletin*, 6: 33–46. (122)

Pastori. See Thomas, David.

Pauly, Bernard. 1967. 'Fragments Sanscrits d'Afghanistan (fouilles de la D.A.F.A.)'. *JA* 255: 273–83. (100, 1042)

Peacocke, W. 1885a. *Afghan Boundary Commission. Notes by Captain Peacocke, R.E. on the Route of the Afghan Boundary Commission from Khwaja Ali to Kuhsan*. Simla.

Peacocke, W. 1885b. 'Report on the Defences of Herat'. (Enclosure No. 5, dated 28 May 1885. Political and Secret Letters from India, vol. 44, pp. 10–20. India Office.) (428)

Peacocke, W. 1887a. *Records of the Intelligence Party, Afghan Boundary Commission*, III. *Diary of Captain Peacocke and Reports on Passes North of the Herat Valley*. Simla. (9, 99, 193, 197, 428, 454, 819, 1206, 1263)

Peacocke, W. 1887b. 'The Baba Surkh Pass'. ABC III. 488–92. (391, 2176, 2225, 2274)

Peacocke, W. 1887c. 'The Robat-i Surkh Pass'. ABC III. 451–4. (2213)

Perkins, Ann, and Robert J. Braidwood. 1947. 'Archaeological News: Afghanistan'. *AJA* 51: 201, pl. 41. (776)

Perkins, Jr, D. 1972. 'The Fauna of the Aq Kupruk Caves: A Brief Note'. In *Prehistoric Research in Afghanistan*. Ed. Louis Dupree et al., 73. Philadelphia. (46)

Petech, A. 1964. 'Note su Kapisi e Zabul'. *Rivista degli studi Orientali*, 39/4: 287–94. (337)

Peter, Prince of Greece and Denmark. 1963. 'The Rope of Bamyan'. *Folk* (Copenhagen) 5: 265–7. (100)

Petersen, A. 1996. *Dictionary of Islamic Architecture*. London.

Petitot-Biehler, C.-Y. 1975. 'Le Trésor de monnaies gréco-bactriannes trouvées à Aï Khanoum en 1973'. *Revue Numismatique*, 6th ser. 17: 58–69. (18)

Petzet, Michael 2015. 'Preserving the Fragments of the Buddha's [sic] of Bamiyan and their Future Presentation'. In *Keeping History Alive: Safeguarding Cultural Heritage in Post-Conflict Afghanistan*. Ed. Brendan Cassar and Sara Noshadi, 238–43. Paris and Kabul. (100)

Petzet, Michael, ed. 2009. *The Giant Buddhas of Bamiyan: Safeguarding the Remains*. Berlin. (100)

Picard, C. 1956. 'A Surkh Kotal en Bactriane'. *Revue Archéloogique*, 67: 106–7. (1123)

Pichikyan, I. R., and Kathy Judelson. 1998. 'Rebirth of the Oxus Treasure from the Miho Museum Collection'. *Ancient Civilizations from Scythia to Siberia*, 4: 306–83. (728)

Pigou, Lieut. 1841. 'On the Topes of Darounta and the Caves at Bahrabad'. *JASB* 10: 381–6. (106, 761)

Pinder-Wilson, Ralph. 1980. 'Le mihrab décoré de Darra-i Shākh/Gorzivan'. *St.Ir.* 9/1: 90–8. (248)

Pinder-Wilson, Ralph. 2001. 'Ghaznavid and Ghurid Minarets'. *Iran*, 39: 155–86. (358, 468, 607, 752, 1106)

Pinder-Wilson. See also Grenet.

Pinder-Wilson. See also Rao.

Pioneer. 1885. 7 Jan., 3 Apr., 17 June, 22 July. Allahabad. (391, 661, 764, 908, 1083, 1265)

Pioneer. 1886. 5 Jan., 3 July. Allahabad. (890, 952, 1206)

Plaeschke, Herbert. 1961. 'Zur Stilentwicklung und Verwendung des Buddhabildes in der Gandharaschule'. *Wissenschaft Zeitschrift der Martin-Luther-Universität*, 10 (Feb.): 139–48. (790, 1088)

Pollack, Leyla B. 1977a. 'The Cybele Medallion from Ai Khanum'. *Afghanistan*, 30/1: 12–20. (18)

Pollack, Leyla B. 1977b. 'The Animal Style of the Pottery of Mundigak'. *Afghanistan*, 30/2: 92–6; 30. 4: 64–67. (743)

Pollack, Leyla B. 1977c. 'The Heroon at Ai Khanum'. *Afghanistan*, 30/3: 73–9. (18)

Pope, Arthur Upham. 1935. 'The Mosque at Qal'a-i Bist'. *BAIPAA* 4/1: 7–11. (149)

Pope, Arthur Upham. 1938. 'Architectural Ornament'. In *A Survey of Persian Art*. Ed. A. U. Pope et al., 1258–1364. Oxford. (358)

Possehl, Gregory L., ed. 1993. *South Asian Archaeology Studies*. Oxford.

Pottier, M.-H. 1980. 'Un cachet en argent de Bactriane'. *Iranica Antiqua*, 15: 167–74.

Pottier, M.-H. 1984. *Matériel funéraire de la Bactriane méridionale de l'âge du bronze*. Paris.

Pottier, M.-H. See also Francfort, H.-P.

Poulain, Thérèse. 1966. 'Fouilles de Mundigak: Etude de la faune'. *BEFEO* 53/1: 119–35. (743)

Prinsep, James. 1836a. 'New Varieties of Bactrian Coins'. *JASB* 5: 548–54. (122)

Prinsep, James. 1836b. 'New Varieties of the Mithraic or Indo-Scythic Series of Coins and their Imitations'. *JASB* 5: 639–57. (122)

Prinsep, James. 1838. 'Coins and Relics from Bactria'. *JASB* 7: 1047–52. (650)

Prinsep, James. 1858. *Essays on Indian Antiquities, Historic, Numismatic, and Palaeographic*. Ed. Edward Thomas. London. (122, 127, 1229)

Provisional Gazetteer of Afghanistan. 1975. 3 vols. Afghan Demographic Studies, Central Statistics Office, Prime Ministry. Kabul.

Pugachenkova, Galina A. 1963. *Iskusstvo Afganistana: Tri etyuda*. Moscow. (99, 100, 122, 149, 212, 332, 346, 348, 358, 404, 428, 468, 483, 685, 716, 718, 1042, 1088, 1123, 1173, 2053)

Pugachenkova, Galina A. 1968a. 'Les monuments peu connus de l'architecture médiévale de l'Afghanistan'. *Afghanistan*, 21/1: 17–52. Reprinted in L. Golombek et al., *The Nine Domes of the Universe*, 171–81. Bergamo, 2016. (410, 634)

Pugachenkova, Galina A. 1968b. 'Stranitsa iz istorii timuridskoy kultury'. *Narody Azii i Afriki*, 4: 129–35. (634)

Pugachenkova, Galina A. 1969. 'Tri pozdnetimuridskikh pamyatnika v zyaratgokho bliz Gerata'. *Uzbekistana izhtimoii fanlar*, 8–9: 30–42. (1263)

Pugachenkova, Galina A. 1969–70. 'The Architecture of Central Asia in the Time of the Timurids'. *Afghanistan*, 22/3–4: 15–27. (428)

Pugachenkova, Galina A. 1970. 'A l'étude des monuments timurides de l'Afghanistan'. *Afghanistan*, 23/3: 24–49. (99, 278, 349, 358, 428, 634, 661, 1263)

Pugachenkova, Galina A. 1974a. 'L'art bactrien de l'époque Kouchane'. *Afghanistan*, 27/2: 18–33. (18, 295, 1034, 1123)

Pugachenkova, Galina A. 1974b. 'O kultakh Baktrii v svete arkheologii'. *Doklad I Soobshcheniya*, 3: 124–35. (18)

Pugachenkova, Galina A. 1975. 'Dva neizvestnikh pamyatnika srednesvekovoy arkhitekturi Severnogo Afganistana'. *Stroytelstvo I Arkhitektura Uzbekistana*, 5: 28–32. (8, 69, 2053)

Pugachenkova, Galina A. 1976a. *Zodchestvo Tsentralnoi Asii XV bek*. Tashkent. (99, 278, 349, 428, 1263)

Pugachenkova, Galina A. 1976b. 'K poznaniyo antichnoy I rannesred-nevekovoy arkhitektury Severnogo Afganistana'. In *Drevnyaya Baktriya* 1. Ed. I. T. Kruglikova, 125–62. Moscow. (99, 295, 459, 520, 642, 732, 1198, 1243)

Pugachenkova, Galina A. 1978. 'Little-Known Monuments of the Balkh Area'. *Art and Archaeology Research Papers*, 13: 31–40. (6, 8, 69, 725)

Pugachenkova, Galina A. 1979a. *Iskusstvo Baktrii epokhi Kushan*. Moscow. (18, 99, 295, 1123)

Pugachenkova, Galina A. 1979b. 'Zhiga-tepe. Raskopi 1974 g'. In *Drevnyaya Baktriya* 2. Ed. I. T. Kruglikova, 63–94. Moscow. (475)

Pugachenkova, Galina A. 1979c. 'Mi'māri-yi Asyā-i miyāna-i qran-i "15"'. *Herāt-i Bāstān*, 1/1: 54–77. (428, 1263)

Pugachenkova, Galina A. 1982. 'Sur la typologie de l'architecture monumentale des anciens pays de l'Asie'. *St.Ir.* 17: 21–42.

Pugachenkova, Galina A., and Z. A. Khakimov. 1972. 'Khanaka Sheikha Saddredina—maloizvestnyj pamyatnik timuridskogo vremeni v Afganistane'. *Narody Azii i Afriki*, 2: 140–4. (1263)

Puglisi, S. M. 1962. 'Italian Mission Activities in Samangan Area'. *Afghanistan*, 17/4: 26–31. (425)

Puglisi, S. M. 1963. 'Preliminary Report on the Researches at Hazar Sum (Samangan)'. *EW* 14: 3–12. (425)

Pulatov, U. 1974. 'Chantier des fouilles C-IV'. Unpublished report in the Afghan Institute of Archaeology, Kabul. (295)

Qadrīyān, Abdulsamad. 1980. 'Shūrtūghai yā gahwāra-i madaniyyat-i qabl al-tārīkh-i Takhār-i zamīn'. *Bāstān Shināsi Afghānistān*, 2/2: 5–8. (1089)

Qāmūs-i Jughrāfāyyi Afghānistān. 1956–60. 4 vols. *Aryānā*. Dairat al-Ma'rif. Kabul.

Quagliotti, Anna Maria. 2012 'La grotte A de Tape Shotor (Hadda)'. In *Auteur de Bāmiyān: De la Bactriane hellénisée à l'Inde bouddhique*. Ed. G. Duccoeur, 346–62. Paris. (404)

Rafat, M. Shah. 1980. 'Master Mohammad Saied Mashal, Torch of the Art School of Behzad'. *Herāt-i Bāstān*, 1/2: 1–5. (683, 747, 783, 803, 974, 1024, 1119, 1236)

Rahīq, Habīb. 1980a. 'Khāniqāh-i Chisht'. *Herāt-i Bāstān*, 1/1: 23–7. (212)

Rahīq, Habīb. 1980b. 'Madāras-i Herāt'. *Herāt-i Bāstān*, 1/2: 1–11. (428)

Rahman, A., Frantz Grenet, and Nicholas Sims-Williams. 2006. 'A Hunnish Kushan-shah'. *Journal of Inner Asian Art and Archaeology*, 1: 125–31.

Rahman, Abdur. 1979. *The Last Two Dynasties of the Shahis: An Analysis of their History, Archaeology, Coinage, Palaeography*. Islamabad. (71, 320, 332, 337, 1221)

Rainey, Froelich. 1953. 'Afghanistan'. *University Museum Bulletin* (Pennsylvania), 17/4: 40–56. (1160)

Ramachandran, T. N., and Y. D. Sharma. 1956. *Archaeological Reconnaissance in Afghanistan: Preliminary Report of the India Archaeological Delegation*. New Delhi. (18, 29, 122, 155, 178, 274, 285, 287, 293, 332, 337, 388, 428, 437, 454, 507, 522, 526, 546, 548, 569, 628, 663, 697, 698, 728, 745, 776, 794, 800, 841, 874, 887, 925, 941, 962, 975, 1004, 1009, 1048, 1064, 1065, 1079, 1098, 1109, 1135, 1144, 1160, 1163, 1165, 1189, 1193, 1232)

Rao, G. K. 1979. 'The Preservation of Some Historical Monuments in the Kabul Area'. *Afghanistan Archaeological Review*, 1/1: 17–18. (389, 718)

Rao, G. K., R. Pinder-Wilson, and W. Ball. 1985. 'The Stupa and Monastery at Guldarra: Report on the British Institute's Preservation Programme'. *South Asian Studies*, 1: 79–88. (389)

Rapin, C. 1983. 'Les inscriptions économiques de la trésorie hellénistique d'Aï Khanoum (Afghanistan)'. *Bulletin de Correspondance Hellénique*, 107/1: 315–71. (18)

Rapin, Claude. 1979. 'Aï Khanoum (Afghanistan): A Trésorerie hellénistique'. Unpublished thesis, Université de Lausanne. (18)

Rapin, Claude. 1992. *Fouilles d'Aï Khanoum VIII. La Trésorie du palais hellénistique d'Aï Khanoum*. MDAFA 33. Paris. (18)

Rapin, Claude. 1996. 'Nouvelles observations sur le parchemin greco-bactrien d'Asangorna'. *Topoi*, 6: 458–69. (2237)

Rapin, Claude, et al. 2003. 'Le nom antique d' Aï Khanoum et de son fleuve'. In *De l'Indus à l'Oxus*. Ed. O. Bopearachchi et al., 115–25. Lattes. (18)

Rapin. See also Gorshenina.

Rapp, Eugen Ludwig. 1965. 'On the Jewish Inscription from Afghansitan'. *EW* 15: 194–200. (373)

Rapp, Eugen Ludwig. 1967. 'The Date of the Judaeo-Persian Inscriptions of Tang-i Azao in Central Afghanistan'. *EW* 17: 51–8. (1144)

Rapp, Eugen Ludwig. 1971. 'Die persisch-hebräischen Inschriften Afghanistans aus dem 11. bis 13. Jahrhundert. Mainzer Beiträge zur Geschichte der Ghuriden-Hauptstadt Ferozkoh mit der Erstausgabe der datierten Herbergschen Neufunde'. *Jahrbuch der Vereinigen Freunde der Universität Mainz*, 20: 74–118. (468)

Rapp, Eugen Ludwig. 1973. 'Neue Persisch-hebräische Inschriften Afghanistans aus dem Mittelalter, eine Gesamtübersicht. Mainzer Afghanica II'. *Jahrbuch der Vereinigen Freunde der Universität Mainz*, 22: 52–66. (468, 522, 1144)

Rapp, Eugen Ludwig. 1974–5. 'Mainzer Afghanica III'. *Jahrbuch der Vereinigen Freunde der Universität Mainz*, 23–4: 115–20. (468)

Rapson, E. J. 1904. 'Note on Ancient Coins Collected in Seistan by Mr G. P. Tate of the Seistan Boundary Commission'. *JRAS* 673–80. (1006)

Raverty, Henry George. 1878. *Notes on Afghanistan and Baluchistan*. London. (128, 226, 304, 336, 337, 406, 460, 483, 523, 535, 549, 971, 1270, 1275)

Rawlinson, Henry C. 1842. 'Comparative Geography of Afghanistan'. *JRGS* 12: 112–14. (1211)

Rawlinson, Henry C. 1872. 'Monograph on the Oxus'. *JRGS* 42: 482–513. (18, 99)

Rawlinson, Henry C. 1873. 'Notes on Seistan'. *JRGS* 43: 272–95. (486)

Rawlinson, Henry C. 1885. 'Countries and Tribes Bordering the Koh-i-Baba Range. Discussion'. *PRGS* 7: 577–83. (711)

Rawlinson, J. A. 1843. 'Documents Relating to the Gates of Somnath'. *JASB* 134: 73–8. (358)

Rea, J., R. J. C. Senior, and A. S. Hollis. 1994. 'A Tax Receipt from Hellenistic Bactria'. *Zeitschrift für Papyrologie und Epigraphik*, 104: 261–80. (2237)

Reha, Said Azim. 1980. 'Gazurgāh wa ābadāt-i tārīkhi ān'. *Herāt-i Bāstān*, 1/2: 21–7. (346)

Reuther, Hans. 1973. 'Die Lehmziegelwölbungen von Gol-i Safed: Versuch einer Typologie'. *AMI* 6: 253–63. (390)

Rezakhani, Khodadad. 2010. 'Balkh and the Sasanians: The Economy and Society of Northern Afghanistan as Reflected in the Bactrian Economic Documents'. In *Ancient and Middle Iranian Studies: Proceedings of the 6th European Conference of Iranian Studies, held in Vienna, 18–22 September 2007*. Ed. Maria Macuch, Dieter Weber, and Desmond Durkin-Meisterernst, 191–203. Wiesbaden. (2230)

Rhie, Marylin M. 1976. 'Some Aspects of the Relation of 5th Century Chinese Buddha Images with Sculptures from N. India, Pakistan, Afghanistan and Central Asia'. *EW* 26: 439–61. (1088)

Ridgeway, J. West, et al. 1888. *Records of the Intelligence Party, Afghan Boundary Commission,. V. Miscellaneous Reports.* Simla.

Riza, S. M., and Sarwar Humayun. 1977 (1356). *Riyaz ul-Alwah.* Kabul. (358)

Riza, Shaikh Muhammad. 1967. *Riaz ul-Alwah of Ghazna.* Kabul. (358)

Robert, L. 1968. 'De Delphes à l'Oxus, inscriptions grecques nouvelles de la Bactriane'. *CRAI* 416–67. Reprinted in *Afghanistan*, 22/3–4 (1969–70): 108–129, and as: 'Fouilles d'Aï Khanoum. VII: Les inscriptions'. In *Aï Khanoum. I.* MDAFA 21. Ed. Paul Bernard et al., 207–37. Paris, 1973. (18)

Robertson, George Scott. 1896. *The Kafirs of the Hindu Kush.* London.

Rogers, Michael. 1973. 'The 11th Century: A Turning Point in the Architecture of the Masriq?' In *Islamic Civilization 950–1150*. Ed. D. S. Richards, 211–49. Oxford. (358)

Rogers, Millard. 1952. 'An Ivory Sārdāla from Begram'. *Artibus Asiae*, 15: 5–9. (122)

Rohr, René R.-J. 1980. 'A Unique Greek Sundial Recently Discovered in Central Asia'. *Journal of the Royal Astronomical Society*, 74(5): 271–8. (18)

Rosen Stone, E. 2008. 'Some Begram Ivories and the South Indian Narrative Tradition: New Evidence'. *Journal of Inner Asian Art and Archaeology*, 3/3: 45–59.

Rosenfield, J. M. 1967. *The Dynastic Art of the Kushans.* Berkeley and Los Angeles. (404, 1088, 1123)

Roshan, Mohammad K., ed. 1962. 'Bagram: The Centre of an Ancient Culture. Afghanistan'. *Ariana*, 1/9 (Apr.–May): 39–50. (122)

Rougemont, Georges. 2012a. 'Hellenism in Central Asia and the North-West of the Indo-Pakistan Sub-Continent: The Epigraphic Evidence'. *Ancient Civilizations from Scythia to Siberia*, 18: 175–82. (18, 522)

Rougemont, Georges. 2012b. *Inscriptions grecques d'Iran et d'Asie centrale.* Corpus Inscriptionum Iranicarum, 2. Inscriptions of the Seleucid and Parthian Periods and of Eastern Iran and Central Asia, 1. Inscriptions in Non-Iranian Languages. London. (18, 314, 475, 522, 776, 1123, 1192, 2237, 2280)

Rougeulle. See Guillaume.

Rowland, Jr, Benjamin. 1936. 'A Revised Chronology of Gandhara Sculpture'. *Art Bulletin*, 17: 387–400. (127, 404)

Rowland, Jr, Benjamin. 1938. 'Buddha and the Sun God. Zalmoxis'. *Revue des Etudes Religieuses*, 1: 69–84. (100, 508)

Rowland, Jr, Benjamin. 1946. 'The Dating of the Sasanian Paintings at Bamiyan and Dukhtar-i Nushirvan'. *Bulletin of the Iranian Institute*, 6: 35–42. (100, 305)

Rowland, Jr, Benjamin. 1947. 'The Colossal Buddhas at Bamiyan'. *Journal of the India Society of Oriental Art*, 15: 62–73. (100)

Rowland, Jr, Benjamin. 1953. *The Art and Architecture of India: Buddhist, Hindu, Jain.* Baltimore. (100, 127, 404)

Rowland, Jr, Benjamin. 1961. 'The Bejewelled Buddha in Afghanistan'. *Artibus Asiae*, 24: 20–4. (100, 332)

Rowland, Jr, Benjamin. 1964a. 'Begram'. In *Afuganistan Kodai Bijutsu: Ancient Art of Afghanistan*. Ed. S. Mizuno, 208–14. Tokyo. (122)

Rowland, Jr, Benjamin. 1964b. 'Hadda'. In *Afuganistan Kodai Bijutsu: Ancient Art of Afghanistan*. Ed. S. Mizuno, 222–6. Tokyo. (404)

Rowland, Jr, Benjamin. 1966a. *Ancient Art from Afghanistan: Treasures of the Kabul Museum.* New York. Translated as *Hunar-i Qadīm-i Afghānistān.* Kabul, 1967–8. (100, 122, 169, 332, 358, 404, 743, 790, 1088, 1168)

Rowland, Jr, Benjamin. 1966b. 'The Tyche of Hadda'. *Oriental Art*, 12/3: 1–7. (404)

Rowland, Jr, Benjamin. 1971. 'The Wall Paintings of Bamiyan'. *Mārg*, 24/2: 25–43. (100)

Rowland, Jr, Benjamin. 1972. 'Iranian Elements in the Art of Afghanistan and Central Asia: The Formation of a Central Asian Style'. In *The Memorial Volume of the Vth International Congress of Iranian Art and Archaeology 1*. Ed. A. Tajvidi and M. Y. Kiani, 379–82. Tehran. (100, 508)

Rowland, Jr, Benjamin. 1974. *The Art of Central Asia.* New York. Translation of *Zentralasien.* Baden-Baden. (100, 332, 1123)

Rowland, Jr, Benjamin, and A. K. Coomaraswamy. 1938. *The Wall-Paintings of India, Central Asia and Ceylon.* Boston. (100)

Rowland, Jr, Benjamin, and Frances Mortimer Rice. 1971. *Art of Afghanistan: Objects from the Kabul Museum.* London. (100, 122, 332, 358, 404, 483, 508, 518, 546, 569, 685, 697, 743, 790, 1042, 1088, 1160, 1168, 1173)

Royal Academy. 1931. *Catalogue of the International Exhibition of Persian Art, 7th January to 28th February.* London. (428)

Rugiadi, Martina. 2006. 'A Carved Wooden Door from Jam—Preliminary Remarks'. *Iran*, 64: 363–5. (468)

Rugiadi, Martina. 2009. 'Documenting Marbles of the Islamic Period from the Area of Ghazni: The Italian

Contribution (1957–2007)'. In *The IsIAO Italian Arch-aeological Mission in Afghanistan 1957–2007: Fifty Years of Research in the Heart of Eurasia.* Ed. Anna Filigenzi and Roberta Giunta, 105–15. Rome. (358)

Rugiadi, Martina. 2010. 'Marble from the Palace of Mas'ūd III at Ghazni'. In *South Asian Archaeology 2007*, II. *Historic Periods*, 297–306. Oxford. (358)

Rugiadi, Martina. 2012. *Decorazione Architettonica in Marmo da Ġaznī (Afghanistan)*. Bologna. (358)

Sachs. See Bopearachchi.

Sadakata, Akira. 1971. 'Nagarahāra oyobi Hadda no Buk-kyō'. (Buddhism at Nagarahāra and Hadda). *Tōkai Daigaku Kiyō. Bungakubu*, 15: 131–47. Summary in H. Motamedi 1975c: 281–2. (404)

Sahibdad Khan. 1888. 'Report on Road from Rui to Ak Kupruk, Thence up the River to Sar-i-Pul (Balkh Ao), and Back to Homakai (or Omakai)'. ABC V. *Miscellaneous Reports.* Ed. J. West Ridgeway et al., 139–56. Simla. (93, 241, 249, 547, 834, 1231)

Sahibdad Khan. 1891a. 'Journey from Herat through Tai-mani Country and the Pusht-i-Rud to Girishk'. ABC IV. Ed. P. J. Maitland, 234–52. Simla. (679, 742, 974, 1047, 1127, 1236, 1268)

Sahibdad Khan. 1891b. 'Note on the Pusht-i-Rud District'. In ABC IV. Ed. P. J. Maitland, 253–70. Simla. (274, 1047, 1267, 2291)

Sālik, Shakib. 1979. 'Ma'rufi wa tārīkhcha'i mukhtasar-i masjid-i jāmi Herāt'. *Bāstān Shināsi Afghānistān*, 1/1: 29–32. (428)

Sālnāma. 1933/4 (1312). *Sālnāma-yi Majala-yi Kābul.* Kabul. (546, 773, 1168, 1173)

Sālnāma. 1934/5 (1313). *Sālnāma-yi Majala-yi Kābul.* Kabul. (483, 522)

Sālnāma. 1936/7 (1315). *Sālnāma-yi Majala-yi Kābul.* Kabul. (428, 716)

Sālnāma. 1937/8 (1316). *Sālnāma-yi Majala-yi Kābul.* Kabul. (164, 1006, 1076)

Sālnāma. 1939/40 (1318). *Sālnāma-yi Majala-yi Kābul.* Kabul. (428)

Salomon, Richard. 1999. *Ancient Buddhist Scrolls from Gandhāra: The British Library Kharoṣṭhī Fragments.* London and Seattle. (404)

Samizay, M. Rafi. 1974. *Urban Growth and Residential Prototypes in Kabul, Afghanistan.* Cambridge, MA. (428, 483)

Samizay, M. Rafi. 1981. *Islamic Architecture in Herat: A Study Towards Conservation.* Kabul. (66, 111, 212, 278, 346, 349, 373, 428, 468, 532, 585, 634, 661, 947, 1023, 1259, 1263, 2076)

Sankalia, H. D. 1980. 'Mundigak'. *Bāstān Shināsi Afghāni-stān*, 2/2: 41–4. (743)

Sarianidi, Viktor I. 1968. 'O velikom lazuritovom puti na Drevnem Vostoke'. *Kratkiye Soobshcheniya*, 114: 3–9. (743)

Sarianidi, Viktor I. 1971. 'North Afghanistan in the Bronze Period'. *Afghanistan*, 24/2–3: 26–38. (256, 257)

Sarianidi, Viktor I. 1972a. *Raskopki Tillyatepe v severnom Afganistane*, I. Moscow. (1192)

Sarianidi, Viktor I. 1972b. 'Izucheniye pamyatnikov epokhi bronzi I rannego zheleza v severnom Afganistane'. *Kratkiye Soobshcheniya*, 132. Reprinted in *Afghanistan Archaeological Review*, 4/2 (1981): 1–7. (257)

Sarianidi, Viktor I. 1974a. 'Baktriya v epokhu bronzii'. *Sovietskaya Arkheologiya*, 4: 49–71. (256, 257)

Sarianidi, Viktor I. 1974b. 'Compte rendu des travaux de l'équipe de recherches préhistoriques de l'Expédition afghano-soviétique, effectués dans l'oasis de Dachly en 1974'. Unpublished manuscript in the Afghan Institute of Archaeology, Kabul. (257)

Sarianidi, Viktor I. 1976. 'Issledovaniye pamyatnikov dash-linskogo oazisa'. In *Drevnyaya Baktriya*, I. Ed. G. I. Kruglikova, 21–86. Moscow. (256, 257)

Sarianidi, Viktor I. 1977a. 'Ancient Horasan and Bactria'. In *Le plateau iranien et l'Asie Centrale des origins à la conquête islamique.* Colloques Internationaux du CNRS 567. Ed. J. Deshayes, 129–41. Paris. (256, 257)

Sarianidi, Viktor I. 1977b. 'Bactrian Centre of Ancient Art'. *Mesopotamia*, 12: 97–110. (36, 37, 43, 44, 257, 666)

Sarianidi, Viktor I. 1977c. *Drevnie zemledeltsy Afganis-tana.* Moscow. (37, 53, 256, 257, 258, 259, 323, 324, 430, 641, 666, 1056, 1101, 1149, 1191, 1192, 1209)

Sarianidi, Viktor I. 1978. 'Ancient Bactria: New Aspects of an Old Problem'. *Journal of Central Asia* (Islamabad), 1/1: 76–7.

Sarianidi, Viktor I. 1979a. 'Die Schätze Kushchanen-Könige'. *Afghanistan Journal*, 6/4: 121–32. (1192)

Sarianidi, Viktor I. 1979b. 'New Finds in Bactria and Indo-Iranian Connections'. In *South Asian Archaeology.* Ed. M. Taddei, 643–59. Naples. (256, 257)

Sarianidi, Viktor I. 1979c. 'Ob odnay gruppe kultovikh izde-liy baktrii'. *Sovietskaya Arkheologiya*, 1979/3: 262–5.

Sarianidi, Viktor I. 1979d. 'Bactrian Centre of Art'. *Meso-potamia*, 12: 97–110.

Sarianidi, Viktor I. 1980. 'The Treasure of Golden Hill'. *AJA* 84/2: 125–32. (1192)

Sarianidi, Viktor I. 1981. 'Zerkala drevnei baktrii'. *Soviets-kaya Arkheologiya*, 1981/1: 288–93. (99)

Sarianidi, Viktor I. 1984. *Bakria skvoz mglu vekov.* Moscow.

Sarianidi, Viktor I. 1985. *Bactrian Gold: From the Excava-tions of the Tillya-Tepe Necropolis in Northern Afghani-stan.* Leningrad. (1192)

Sarianidi, Viktor I. 1989. *Khram I nekropol Tillyatepe.* Moscow. (1192)

Sarianidi. See also Koshelenko.

Sarkhosh Curtis. See Errington.

Saunders. c.1880s. 'Report on Herat'. Unpublished papers in the India Office Library and Records P/V 679. (428)

Sauvaget, Jean. 1946. 'Glanes épigraphiques'. *REI* 15: 17–29. (428)

Scarcia, Gianroberto, and Marizio Taddei. 1973. 'The Masjid-i Sangī of Larvand'. *EW* 23: 89–108. (291, 683)

Scarcia, Gianroberto. 1963. 'A Preliminary Report on a Persian Legal Document of 470–1078 Found at Bamiyan'. *EW* 14: 73–85. (100)

Scarcia, Gianroberto. 1966. 'An Edition of the Persian Legal Document from Bamiyan'. *EW* 16: 290–5. (100)

Scerrato, Umberto. 1958a. 'An Inscription of Aśoka Discovered in Afghanistan: the Bilingual Greek-Aramaic of Kandahar'. *EW* 9: 4–6. (522)

Scerrato, Umberto. 1958b. 'Notizie sull'edito bilingue Greco-aramaico di Aśoka scoperto in Afghanistan'. *Archeologia Classica*, 10: 262–6. (522, 726)

Scerrato, Umberto. 1959. 'Summary Report on the Italian Archaeological Mission to Afghanistan. II. The Two First Excavation Campaigns at Ghazni. 1957–8'. *EW* 10/1–2: 23–56. (358)

Scerrato, Umberto. 1960. 'A Short Note on Some Recently Discovered Buddhist Grottoes near Bamiyan, Afghanistan'. *EW* 11: 94–120. (275)

Scerrato, Umberto. 1961. 'Problemi di storia e d'arte dell'Afghanistan Islamico'. In *L'Afghanistan dalla preistoria all'Islam*. Ed. G. Gullini, 59–77. Turin. (358)

Scerrato, Umberto. 1962a. 'Islamic Glazed Tiles with Moulded Decoration from Ghazni'. *EW* 13: 263–87. (358)

Scerrato, Umberto. 1962b. 'On a Silver Coin of Traianus Decius from Afghanistan'. *EW* 13: 17–23. (122)

Scerrato, Umberto. 1967. 'A Note on Some Pre-Muslim Antiquities of Ğagatū'. *EW* 17: 11–24. (71, 103, 303, 337, 461)

Scerrato, Umberto. 1971a. 'Oggetti Metallici di Eta Islamica in Afghanistan. IV. Su un tipo di amuleto del XII secolo'. *Annali*, 31: 288–310. (122, 358)

Scerrato, Umberto. 1971b. 'Oggetti metallica di Eta Islamica in Afghanistan. III. Staffe ghaznavidi'. *Annali*, 31, NS 21: 457–66. (358)

Scerrato, Umberto. 1980. 'Due tombe ad incinerazione del Museo di Kandahar'. *Annali*, 40/4: 627–50. (522, 726)

Scerrato, Umberto, G. Pugliese Carratelli, and G. Garbini. 1958. *Un editto bilingue Greco-aramaico di Aśoka*. Serie Orientale Roma, 21. Rome. (522)

Scerrato, Umberto, G. Pugliese Carratelli, and G. Garbini. 1964. *A Bilingual Greco-Aramaic Edict by Aśoka: The First Greek Inscription Discovered in Afghanistan*. Serie Orientale Roma, 19. Rome. (522)

Schaeffer, C. F. A. 1942. 'French Archaeological Excavations in Syria between the Two Wars'. *Journal of the Royal Central Asian Society*, 29: 184–94. (122)

Schiebe, V. ed. 1937. *Deutsche im Hindukusch: Bericht der Deutschen Hindukusch Expedition 1935 der Deutschen Forschungs-gemeinschaft*. Berlin. (154)

Schimmel, Annemarie. 1970. *Islamic Calligraphy*. Leiden.

Schimmel, Annemarie. 1984. *Calligraphy and Islamic Culture*. New York.

Schippmann, Klaus. 1971. *Die iranischen Feuerheiligtümer*. Berlin. (1123)

Schlumberger, Daniel. 1946. 'Rapport sur une mission en Afghanistan'. *CRAI* 169–77. (99)

Schlumberger, Daniel. 1947a. 'L'exploration archéologique de l'Afghanistan'. *Afghanistan*, 2/4: 1–23. (122, 404, 546)

Schlumberger, Daniel. 1947b. 'Communication à la séance du 14 Mars 1947'. *CRAI* 241–3. (776)

Schlumberger, Daniel. 1948. 'La prospection archéologique de Bactres (printemps 1947)'. *Afghanistan*, 3/1: 40–51. (99)

Schlumberger, Daniel. 1949a. 'Les fouilles de Lashkari Bazar: Recherches archéologiques sur l'époque ghaznévide'. *Afghanistan*, 4/2: 34–44. (685)

Schlumberger, Daniel. 1949b. 'Archaeology in Afghanistan: Work of the French Archaeological Delegation'. *Archaeology*, 2: 11–6. (99, 122, 404, 518, 728)

Schlumberger, Daniel. 1949c. 'Une residence présummée Ghaznévide découverte en Afghanistan'. In *Actes du XXIè Congrès International des Orientalistes, Paris. 1948*, 331–2. Paris. (99, 685)

Schlumberger, Daniel. 1949d. 'La prospection archéologique de Bactres (printemps 1947). Rapport sommaire'. *Syria*, 26/3–4: 173–90. (99)

Schlumberger, Daniel. 1950. 'Les fouilles de Lashkari Bazar: Les resultats de la deuxième et de la troisième campagne'. *Afghanistan*, 5/4: 46–56. (685)

Schlumberger, Daniel. 1951. 'The Great Palace of Mahmud in Afghanistan: Carvings and Decorations from a Unique Spectacular Building of the Ghaznavid Era, the Palace of Lashkari Bazar'. *ILN* (16 June): 972–3. (685)

Schlumberger, Daniel. 1952a. 'La grande mosquée de Lashkari Bazar'. *Afghanistan*, 7/1: 1–4. (685)

Schlumberger, Daniel. 1952b. 'Note sur les antiquités de Sar-i Tchechmé en Bactriane'. *CRAI* 225–7. (1123)

Schlumberger, Daniel. 1952d. 'Le palais ghaznévide de Lashkari Bazar'. *Syria*, 19: 251–70. (685)

Schlumberger, Daniel. 1953a. 'Surkh Kotal: A Late Hellenistic Temple in Bactria'. *Archaeology*, 6/4: 232–8. Reprinted in *Afghanistan*, 19/2 (1954): 41–7. Translated as: 'Ma'bad-i Surkh Kūtal dar Bākhtar'. *Aryānā*, 11/11 (1932): 1–6. (1123)

Schlumberger, Daniel. 1953b. 'La découverte en Bactriane d'un temple presumé d'époque kouchane'. *CRAI* 30–3. (1123)

Schlumberger, Daniel. 1953c. 'L'argent grec dans l'empire achéménide'. In *Trésors monétaires d'Afghanistan*. MDAFA 14. Ed. R. Curiel and D. Schlumberger, 1–64. Paris. (483)

Schlumberger, Daniel. 1954a. 'Surkh Kotal: Un site archéologique d'époque kouchane en Bactriane'. *Afghanistan*,

9/1: 44–54. Translated as: 'Surkh Kūtal, āmda-i bāstāni asr-i Kūshānī dar Bākhtar'. *Aryānā*, 12/7 (1333): 1–13. (1123)

Schlumberger, Daniel. 1954b. 'Surkh Kotal: Un sanctuaire du feu d'époque kouchane en Bactriane'. *AA* 1/2: 132–8. (1123)

Schlumberger, Daniel. 1954c. 'Note sur la deuxième campagne des fouilles de Surkh Kotal en Bactriane'. *CRAI* 107–8. (1123)

Schlumberger, Daniel. 1955a. 'Surkh Kotal in Bactria'. *Archaeology*, 8/2: 82–7. (1123)

Schlumberger, Daniel. 1955b. 'Le marbre Scoretti'. *AA* 2/2: 112–19. (337)

Schlumberger, Daniel. 1955c. 'Note sur la troisième campagne des fouilles de Surkh Kotal en Bactriane'. *CRAI* 64–71. (1123)

Schlumberger, Daniel. 1957a. 'Les fouilles de Surkh Kotal en Bactriane (IVe, Ve, VIe campagnes)'. *CRAI* 176–81. (1123)

Schlumberger, Daniel. 1957b. 'La Délégation archéologique à Bactres (1947)'. In *Céramiques de Bactres*. MDAFA 15. Ed. J.-C. Gardin, 9–13. Paris. (99, 518)

Schlumberger, Daniel. 1959. 'Surkh Kotal'. *Antiquity,* 33/130: 81–6. (1123)

Schlumberger, Daniel. 1960a. 'Les fouilles de Surkh Kotal et l'histoire de l'Afghanistan'. *Afghanistan*, 15/3: 26–47. Translated as: 'Hafriyāt-i Surkh Kūtal wa tārikh-i qadīm-i Afghānistān'. *Aryānā*, 18/8 (1339): 1–16.

Schlumberger, Daniel. 1960b. 'Descendants non-Méditerranéens de l'art grec'. *Syria*, 37: 131–66 and 254–318. Reprinted and translated as: 'Nachkommen der griechischen Kunst ausserhalb des Mittelmeerraums'. In *Der Hellenismus in Mittelasien*. Ed. F. Altheim and J. Rehork, 281–404. Darmstadt. (1123)

Schlumberger, Daniel. 1961a. 'Art parthe, art gréco-bouddhique, art gréco-romain'. *Archaeologia Classica*, 3: 9–16. (1123)

Schlumberger, Daniel. 1961b. 'The Excavations at Surkh Kotal and the Problem of Hellenism in Bactria and India'. *Proceedings of the British Academy*, 47: 77–95. (1123)

Schlumberger, Daniel. 1964a. 'Surkh Kotal'. In *Afuganistan Kodai Bijutsu: Ancient Art of Afghanistan*. Ed. S. Mizuno, 215–21. Tokyo. (1123)

Schlumberger, Daniel. 1964b. 'Une nouvelle inscription grecque d'Açoka'. *CRAI* 126–40. Translated and reprinted as: 'Eine neue riechische Aśoka-inschrift'. In *Der Hellenismus in Mittelasien*. Ed. F. Altheim and J. Rehork, 406–17. Darmstadt. (522)

Schlumberger, Daniel. 1964c. 'La nécropole de Shakh Tépé, près de Qunduz'. *CRAI* 207–11. (1065)

Schlumberger, Daniel. 1964d. 'Le temple de Surkh Kotal en Bactriane, IV'. *JA* 252: 303–26. (1123)

Schlumberger, Daniel. 1965a. 'Aï Khanoum, une ville hellénistique en Afghanistan'. *CRAI* 36–46. (18)

Schlumberger, Daniel. 1965b. 'Ai Khanoum'. *Bull. Corr. Hell.* 89: 590–657.

Schlumberger, Daniel. 1967. 'L'Hellénisme en Afghanistan'. *Afghanistan*, 20/3: 66–78. (18, 522)

Schlumberger, Daniel. 1970. *L'Orient hellénisé*. Paris. (18)

Schlumberger, Daniel. 1971. 'Le rhyton de Kohna Masjid'. *AA* 24: 3–7. (630)

Schlumberger, Daniel. 1978. *Lashkari Bazar: Une residence royale ghaznévide et ghuride, IA. L'architecture*. MDAFA 18. Paris. (149, 685)

Schlumberger, Daniel, and Émile Benveniste. 1967. 'New Greek Inscription of Aśoka at Kandahar'. *Epigraphia Indica*, 37/5: 193–200. (522)

Schlumberger, Daniel, and Paul Bernard. 1965. 'Aï Khanoum'. *Bulletin de Correspondance Hellénique*, 89/2: 590–657. (18)

Schlumberger, Daniel, L. Robert, A. Dupont-Sommer, and É. Benveniste. 1958. 'Une bilingue gréco-araméenne d'Aśoka'. *JA* 246: 1–48. (522)

Schlumberger, Daniel, and Jean-Claude Gardin. 1978. 'Tableau chronologique pour l'histoire du site de Bust-Lashkari Bazar'. In *Lashkari Bazar*, IA. MDAFA 18. Ed. D. Schlumberger, 97–8. Paris. (149, 685)

Schlumberger, Daniel, Marc le Berre, and Gérard Fussman. 1983. *Surkh Kotal en Bactriane, I. Les temples: Architecture, sculpture, inscriptions*. 2 vols. MDAFA 25. Paris. (1123)

Schlumberger, Daniel, and Janine Sourdel-Thomine. 1978. *Lashkari Bazar: Une residence royale ghaznévide et ghuride. Planches*. MDAFA 18. Paris. (149, 685)

Schneider, M. 1984. 'Remarques au sujet d'une inscription du mausolée dit de Baba Hatim'. *St. Ir.* 13: 165–7.

Schroeder, Eric. 1936. 'Preliminary Note on Work in Persia and Afghanistan, April–December, 1935'. *BAIPAA* 4/3: 130–5. (428, 2053)

Schroeder, Eric. 1938. 'The Seljuq Period'. In *A Survey of Persian Art*. Ed. A. U. Pope et al., 981–1045. (149, 358, 752)

Schwartzenberg, J. E., ed. 1978. *A Historical Atlas to South Asia*. Chicago. (743)

Seckel, Dietrich. 1964. *The Art of Buddhism*. New York. (100, 127)

Sedov, A. V. 1984. 'Keramichekie kompleksi ai-khanum skogo tipa na Pravoberezhe Amudari'. *Sovietskaya Arkheologiya*, 3: 171–80. (18)

Seljuki, Fikri. 1962/3 (1341). *Gāzurgāh*. Kabul. (346)

Seljuki, Fikri. 1967a. *Mazirat-i Herat*. Kabul. (111, 212, 346, 351, 373, 428, 947, 948)

Seljuki, Fikri. 1967b. 'The Complete Copy of the Ancient Inscription of the Ghiassuddine Grand Mosque in Herat'. *Afghanistan*, 20/3: 78–80. (428)

Seljuki, Fikri. 1973. 'The Gravestone of Gawhar Shad'. *Afghanistan*, 25/4: 29–31. (428)

Senart, M. E. 1890. 'Notes d'épigraphie indienne. V'. *JA* 4: 504–18. (127, 1229)

Senart, M. E. 1914. 'L'inscription du vase de Wardak'. *JA* 4: 569–85. (1229)

Sengupta, S. 1971. 'The Preservation Work'. *Marg*, 24/2: 44. (100)

Sengupta, S. 1972. *The Buddha in Afghanistan: India's Aid to Bring Bamiyan Back to Life*. New Delhi. (100)

Sengupta, S. 1973. 'India Helps Afghanistan in Preserving her Heritage'. *Afghanistan*, 26/3: 23–34. (100)

Sengupta, S. 1976. 'Preservation and Conservation of Bamiyan'. In *Bamiyan: Crossroads of Culture*. Ed. Akira Miyaji, 9–15. Tokyo. (100)

Shaffer, Jim G. 1971. 'Preliminary Field Report on Excavations at Said Qala Tepe'. *Afghanistan*, 24/2–3: 89–127. (968)

Shaffer, Jim G. 1974. 'The Prehistory of Baluchistan: Some Interpretive Problems'. *Arctic Anthropology Supplement*, 11: 224–35. (287, 743, 968)

Shaffer, Jim G. 1976a. 'Kinship and Burial among Kushano-Sasanians: A Preliminary Assessment'. *EW* 26/1–2: 133–52. (968)

Shaffer, Jim G. 1976b. 'Neolithic-Bronze Age Afghanistan: Recent Developments'. *Afghanistan*, 29/3: 73–83. (46, 245, 256, 968)

Shaffer, Jim G. 1978a. *Prehistoric Baluchistan*. Delhi. (968)

Shaffer, Jim G. 1978b. 'The Later Prehistoric Periods'. In *The Archaeology of Afghanistan*. Ed. F. R. Allchin and N. Hammond, 71–86. London. (46, 245, 256, 257, 287, 743, 968)

Shaffer, Jim G., C. A. Callender, and Ralph J. Rodriguez. 1973. 'A Proposal to National Science Foundation for Support of Research on Prehistoric Cultural Development and Interaction in South Central Afghanistan'. Cleveland. Unpublished paper in the British Institute of Afghan Studies, Kabul. (968)

Shaffer, Jim G., and Michael A. Hoffman. 1971. 'The Kushano-Sasanian Cemetery of Said Qala Tepe'. *Afghanistan*, 24/2–3: 138–66. (968)

Shah, M. H. 1982. 'Al-Rukhaj in Hudud-al-Alam'. *Afghanistan*, 35/3: 1–10. (798)

Shahrani, Enayatullah. 1973. 'The History of Fine Arts in Afghanistan'. *Afghanistan*, 26/3: 17–22. (100, 404)

Shahzada Taimus. 1888. 'Report on Road from the Ghori Valley, via Narin, Andarab, and the Khawak Pass to Charikar'. In ABC V. *Miscellaneous Reports*. Ed. J. West Ridgeway et al., 303–34. Simla. (616, 765)

Shaked, Shaul. 1969. 'Notes on the New Aśoka Inscription from Kandahar'. *JRAS* 101/2: 118–22. (522)

Shaked, Shaul, ed. 1982. *Irano-Judaica: Studies Relating to Jewish Contacts with Persian Culture throughout the Ages*. Jerusalem.

Shaked, Shaul. 2003. 'De Khulmi à Nikhšapaya: Les données des nouveaux documents araméens de Bactres sur la toponymie de la région (IVe siècle av. n. è.)'. *CRAI* 147/4: 1517–35. (99)

Shaked, Shaul. 2010. 'A Note on Hebrew-Script Tombstones from Jām, Afghanistan'. *Journal of Jewish Studies*, 61: 305–7. (468)

Shaked, Shaul. 2016. 'Jews in Khorasan before the Mongol Invasion.' *Iran Namag*, 1/2: 4–16. (468)

Shakur, M. A. 1946. *A Handbook to the Inscriptions Gallery in the Peshawar Museum*. Peshawar. (675)

Shakur, M. A. 1947. *A Dash through the Herat of Afghanistan Being Personal Narrative of an Archaeological Tour with the Indian Cultural Mission*. Peshawar. (25, 29, 49, 99, 122, 150, 169, 178, 194, 325, 404, 437, 494, 522, 631, 707, 716, 744, 776, 800, 919, 1055, 1056, 1160, 1185, 1193, 1227, 1232)

Shamsuddin Khan. 1888. 'Report on Journey from Zindajan to Herat, and Thence to Kushk, Kala Nao and Bala Murghab'. In ABC V. *Miscellaneous Reports*. Ed. J. West Ridgeway et al., 112–24. Simla. (610)

Sharma, Nirmala. 2011. *Bamiyan, Hārītī and Kindred Iconics*. New Delhi. (100)

Sharqi, Asaf. 1980. 'Kūtal-i Khair Khāna yā ma'bad-i Sūryā'. *Bāstān Shināsi Afghānistān*, 3/1: 98–9. (546)

Shenkar, Michael. 2011 'Temple Architecture in the Iranian World in the Hellenistic Period'. In *From Pella to Gandhara: Hybridisation and Identity in the Art and Architecture of the Hellenistic East*. Ed. Anna Kouremenos, Sujatha Chandrasekaran, and Roberto Rossi, 117–35. Oxford. (18, 295)

Shokoohy, Mehrdad. 1983. 'The Monuments of the Kuhandiž of Herat, Afghanistan'. *JRAS* 1: 7–31. (428)

Shokoohy, Mehrdad. 1984. 'Review of Gazetteer'. *BSOAS* 47/3: 571–2.

Shokoohy, Mehrdad. 1989. 'The Shrine of Imam-i Kalan in Sar-i Pul, Afghanistan'. *BSOAS* 52/2: 306–14.

Shokoohy. See also Fehérvári.

Shoten, Akashi. 2006a. *Radiocarbon Dating of the Bamiyan Mural Paintings*. RCHIA 2. Tokyo. (100)

Shoten, Akashi. 2006b. *Study of the Afghanistan's Displaced Cultural Properties, Materials and Techniques of the Bamiyan Mural Paintings*. RCHIA 3. Tokyo. (100)

Sidky, H. 2000. *The Greek Kingdom of Bactria: From Alexander to Eucratides the Great*. Lanham, MD.

Sidqi, Osman. 1952. 'Les villes d'Ariana'. *Afghanistan*, 7/1: 5–21; 7/2: 29–44; 7/3: 33–44. Reprinted as: *Shahrhā-yi Aryānā*. Kabul, 1975–6. (1004, 1033, 1079)

Sidqi, Osman. 1975. 'Afghan Culture, History: Religious and Cultural Movement'. *Kabul Times* (18 Nov.): 3–4. (1123)

Sikandarpūr, Said Akbar. 1980. 'Tahqiqāt-i bāstān shināsi dar Shahr-i Kuhna-i Kandahār'. *Bāstān Shināsi Afghānistān*, 2/2: 47–52. (522)

Simpson, St John. 2011a. *The Begram Hoard: Ivories from Afghanistan*. London. (122)

Simpson, St John. 2011b. 'Ancient Afghanistan Revealed'. *Current World Archaeology*, 46: 16–24.

Simpson, St John. 2012. *Afghanistan: A Cultural History*. London.

Simpson, William. 1879a. 'Buddhist Remains in the Jallalabad Valley'. *Indian Antiquary*, 8: 227–30. (17, 326, 364, 404, 756)

Simpson, William. 1879b. 'Coins from the Ahin Posh Tepe near Jalalabad'. *JASB* 77–9. (17)

Simpson, William. 1879–80. 'Buddhist Architecture of the Jelalabad Valley'. *TRIBA* 36–64. (17, 158, 326, 364, 381, 404, 423, 453, 456, 627, 756, 761)

Simpson, William. 1881. 'On the Identification of Nagarahāra with Reference to the Travels of Hiouen-Thsang'. *JRAS* NS 13: 183–207. (17, 283, 326, 364, 381, 404, 464, 627, 756, 761, 806, 812, 1169)

Simpson, William. 1882. 'The Buddhist Caves of Afghanistan'. *JRAS* NS 14: 319–31. (163, 226, 326, 404)

Simpson, William. 1893. 'The Classical Influence in the Architecture of the Indus Region and Afghanistan'. *JRIBA* 3rd series, 93–115. (100, 404, 453, 627)

Sims-Williams, Nicholas. 1973. 'A Note on Bactrian Syntax'. *Indogermanische Forschungen*, 78: 95–9. (1123)

Sims-Williams, Nicholas. 1998a. 'A Bactrian Deed of Manumission'. *SRAA* 5: 191–215. (2230)

Sims-Williams, Nicholas. 1998b. 'Further Notes on the Bactrian Inscription of Rabatak, with an Appendix on the Names of Kujula Kadphises and Vima Taktu in Chinese'. In *Proceedings of the Third European Conference of Iranian Studies Part 1: Old and Middle Iranian Studies*. Ed. Nicholas Sims-Williams, 79–93. Wiesbaden. (944)

Sims-Williams, Nicholas. 1999. 'From the Kushan-Shahs to the Arabs: New Bactrian Documents Dated in the Era of the Tochi Inscriptions'. *CAC* I. 243–58. Vienna. (2230)

Sims-Williams, Nicholas. 2000. 'Four Bactrian Economic Documents'. *BAI* 11: 3–16. (2230)

Sims-Williams, Nicholas. 2001. *Bactrian Documents from Northern Afghanistan: Legal and Economic Documents*. Studies in the Khalili Collection of Islamic Art. Oxford. (2230)

Sims-Williams, Nicholas. 2002a. *Indo-Iranian Languages and Peoples*. London.

Sims-Williams, Nicholas. 2002b. 'New Documents in Ancient Bactrian Reveal Afghanistan's Past'. *IIAS Newsletter*, 27 (Mar.): 12–13. (2230)

Sims-Williams, Nicholas. 2005. 'Bactrian Legal Documents from 7th- and 8th-Century Guzgan'. *BAI* 15: 9–30. (609, 1000)

Sims-Williams, Nicholas. 2007a. *Bactrian Documents from Northern Afghanistan*, II. *Letters and Buddhist Texts*. London. (609)

Sims-Williams, Nicholas. 2007b. 'A Bactrian Quarrel'. *BAI* 17: 9–16.

Sims-Williams, Nicholas. 2008. 'The Bactrian Inscription of Rabatak: A New Reading'. *BAI* 18: 53–68. (265, 944)

Sims-Williams, Nicholas. 2010. 'Two Late Bactrian Documents'. In *Coins, Art and Chronology*, II. 203–11. Vienna. (2261)

Sims-Williams, Nicholas. 2012a. *Bactrian Documents from Northern Afghanistan*, I. *Legal and Economic Documents*. 2nd edn. London. (2230)

Sims-Williams, Nicholas. 2012b. *Bactrian Documents from Northern Afghanistan*, III. *Plates*. London. (609)

Sims-Williams, Nicholas. 2012c. 'Bactrian Historical Inscriptions of the Kushan Period'. *Silk Road*, 10: 76–80. (1123)

Sims-Williams, Nicholas. 2015. 'A Bactrian Document from Southern Afghanistan?' *BAI* NS 25: 39–53. (784)

Sims-Williams, Nicholas, and Joe Cribb. 1996. 'A New Bactrian Inscription of Kanishka the Great'. *SRAA* 4: 75–142. (265, 944)

Sims-Williams, Nicholas, and François de Blois. 1998. 'The Bactrian Calendar'. *BAI* 10: 149–65. (2230)

Sims-Williams, Nicholas, and Harry Falk. 2014. 'Kushan Dynasty II. Inscriptions of the Kushans'. In *Encyclopædia Iranica*, online edn, available at <http://www.iranicaonline.org/articles/kushan-02-inscriptions>. Accessed Dec. 2014. (944)

Sims-Williams. See also Lee.

Sims-Williams. See also Rahman.

Sircar, D. C. 1963. 'Three Early Medieval Inscriptions: (1) Kabul Inscription of Shāhi Khingāla'. *Epigraphia Indica*, 5/1: 44–7. (337)

Sīstāni, Muhammad Azam. 1967 (1345). 'Sār-u Tār yā Hisār-i Tāq'. *Āryānā*, 25/1: 37–46. (1006)

Sivaramamurti, C. 1971. 'Begram Ivories: The Tradition of the Mastercraftsman'. *Mārg*, 24/4: 9–14. (122)

Smith, Euan. 1876. 'The Perso-Afghan Mission, 1871–72'. In *Eastern Persia: An Account of the Journeys of the Persian Boundary Commission, 1870–71–72*. Ed. F. J. Goldsmid, 225–394. London. (225, 394, 482, 638, 684, 752, 796, 810, 842, 1195)

Snead, Rodman E. 1978. 'Geomorphic History of the Mundigak Valley'. *Afghanistan Journal*, 5/2: 59–69. (743)

Snellgrove. David L., ed. 1978. *The Image of the Buddha*. New Delhi.

Sokolovsky, V. M. 1979. 'Rekonstruktsiya dvukh skulpturikh izobrazheniy iz Dilberdzhina (raskop X)'. In *Drevnyaya Bektriya*, 2. Ed. I. T. Kruglikova et al., 113–19. Moscow. (295)

Solem, Alan. 1972. 'Mollusks from Prehistoric Sites in Afghanistan'. In *Prehistoric Research in Afghanistan*. Ed. Louis Dupree et al., 57–65. Philadelphia. (46)

Soper, A. C. 1949–50. 'Aspects of Light Symbolism in Gandharan Sculpture'. *Artibus Asiae*, 12: 252–83; 12: 314–30; 13: 63–85. (100, 1088)

Sorenson. See Frifelt.

Sourdel, Dominique. 1963–4. 'Un trésor de dinars gaznavides et saljūqides découvert en Afghanistan'. *BEFEO* 18: 197–219. (173)

Sourdel, Dominique, and Janine Sourdel. 1968. *La civilisation de l'Islam classique*. Paris. (212, 358, 468, 685)

Sourdel-Thomine, Janine. 1953. 'Deux minarets Seljoukides en Afghanistan'. *Syria*, 30: 108–36. (358, 1106, 2053)

Sourdel-Thomine, Janine. 1956. 'Stèles arabes de Bust (Afghanistan)'. *Arabica*, 3: 285–306. (149)

Sourdel-Thomine, Janine. 1959. 'Les décors de stuc dans l'est iranien à l'époque saljūqide'. In *Akten des vierundzwanzigsten international Orientalisten-Kongresses. München 1957*, 342–4. Munich. (685)

Sourdel-Thomine, Janine. 1960. 'L'art gūride l'Afghanistan, à propos d'un livre recent'. *Arabica*, 7: 273–80. (468, 685)

Sourdel-Thomine, Janine. 1971. 'Le mausolée de Baba Hatim en Afghanistan'. *REI* 39/2: 293–320. (439)

Sourdel-Thomine, Janine. 1978. *Lashkari Bazar: Une residence royale ghaznévide et ghuride, IB. Le décor non figurative et les inscriptions*. MDAFA 18. Paris. (149, 685)

Sourdel-Thomine, Janine. 1981, 'A propos du cénotaphe de Mahmūd à Ghazna (Afghanistan)'. In *Essays in Islamic Art and Architecture in Honor of K. Otto-Dorn*. Ed. Abbas Daneshvari, 127–35. Malibu, CA. (358)

Sourdel-Thomine, Janine. 2004. *Le minaret Ghouride de Jam: Un chef d'oeuvre du XIIe siecle*. Mémoires de l'Académie des inscriptions et belles-lettres, 29. Paris. (468)

Sourdel-Thomine, Janine, and Bertold Spuler. 1973. *Die Kunst des Islam*. Berlin. (346, 358, 685)

Srivastava, V. C. 1979a. 'A Note on a Ganesá Image from Afghanistan'. *Afghanistan*, 32/1: 41–9.

Srivastava, V. C. 1979b. 'Economy and Society in Prehistoric Afghanistan'. *Afghanistan*, 32/2: 54–9. (46, 256, 323, 430, 609, 1101, 1191)

Srivastava, V. C. 1979c (1358). 'The Kushan Archaeology in Afghanistan'. *Tahqiqāt-i Kūshānī*, 2/1: 107–19. (122, 295, 404, 1123, 1181, 1192)

Srivastava, V. C. 1980. 'Historiographical Bibliography of Historical Archaeology in Afghanistan'. *Afghanistan*, 32/4: 27–50.

Srivastava, V.C. 1978–9. 'Historical Bibliography of Protohistoric Research in Afghanistan'. *Afghanistan*, 31/2: 50–68; 31/3: 41–6; 31/4: 69–96.

Stadtner, David. 2000. 'Two Fifth-Century Bodhisattvas from Afghanistan'. *South Asian Studies*, 16: 37–44. (337, 546, 1180)

Stark, Freya. 1970. *The Minaret of Jam: An Excursion in Afghanistan*. London. (468)

Staviski, Boris J. 1973. 'The Capitals of Ancient Bactria'. *EW* 23: 265–78. Translated as: 'Da qadīm bāktar sar sitūni'. *Bāstān Shinasi Afghānistān*, 4/2 (1981): 114–24. (18, 169, 1123)

Staviski, Boris J. 1977. *Kushanskaya Baktriya: Problemy, istorii i kultury*. Moscow. (18, 99)

Staviskij, Boris J. 1986. *La Bactriane sous les Kushans: Problèmes d'histoire et de culture*. Paris.

Stein, Aurel. 1904. *Serindia*. London. (524, 533, 557, 678)

Stein, Aurel. 1928. *Innermost Asia*. 4 vols. Oxford. (644, 752, 824, 979, 1006, 1136)

Stern, Philippe. 1954. 'Les ivories et os découverts à Begram: Leur place dans l'évolution de l'art de l'Inde'. In *Nouvelles recherches archéologiques à Begram*. MDAFA 11. Ed. J. Hackin et al., 17–54. Paris. (122)

Stern, S. M. 1949. 'A propos de l'inscription juive d'Afghanistan'. *JA* 237: 47–9. (373)

Stevens, Tarcia. 2015. 'Safeguarding the Gawharshad Mausoleum: The Conservation of a Timurid Monument in Herat'. In *Keeping History Alive: Safeguarding Cultural Heritage in Post-Conflict Afghanistan*. Ed. Brendan Cassar and Sara Noshadi, 184–93. Paris and Kabul. (428)

Stewart, Rory. 2004. *The Places in Between*. London. (112, 468, 2033, 2075)

Strzygowski, J. 1930–2. 'Griechischer Iranismus in buddhistischer Bildnerei'. *AA* 4/2–3: 118–26; 4/4: 185–91; 5/1: 5–9. (404)

Stuckert, R. 1980. 'Der Baubestand der Masjid-al-Jami in Herat 1942–43'. *Afghanistan Journal*, 7/1: 3–5. (428)

Stuckert. R. 1994. *Erinnerungen an Afghanistan, 1940–1946*. Liestal. (41, 42, 186, 716, 818)

Stwodah, Mohammad Ibrahim. 1980 (1359). 'Library Condition in the Kushan Civilization (A Preliminary Historical Research)'. *Tahqiqāt-i Kūshānī*, 3/2: 1–8. (100, 404)

Stwodah, Mohammad Ibrahim, and A. Z. Modarissi. 1978. *Kūshānān kitābshināsi-yi tūsifi*. Kabul.

Subtelny, M. E. 1997. 'Agriculture and the Timurid chahārbāgh: The Evidence from a Medieval Persian Agricultural Manual'. In *Gardens in the Time of the Great Muslim Empires: Theory and Design*. Ed. A. Petruccioli, 120–8. Leiden.

Sultan, S. O. 1978. 'Hellenistic Influence in Afghanistan'. *Kushan International Research Center*, 1: 11–22. (18, 99, 100, 122, 404, 1123)

Suzuki, Norio, and Shigeo Aoki. 2004. *Protecting the World Heritage Site of Bamiyan: Key Issues for the Establishment of a Comprehensive Management Plan*. Tokyo. (100, 330, 1042, 2125, 2282)

Suzuki, Norio, and Shigeo Aoki, eds. 2005. *Preserving Bamiyan*. RCHIA 1. Tokyo. (100)

Swinnerton, C. 1879. 'Ancient Remains in Afghanistan'. *The Indian Antiquary*, 8: 198–200. (1, 17, 380, 404, 761)

Taddei, Maurizio. 1967. 'IsMEO Activities'. *EW* 17: 344–5. (358, 1180)

Taddei, Maurizio. 1968. 'IsMEO Activities'. *EW* 18: 443–8. (385, 1180)

Taddei, Maurizio. 1969a. 'Tapa Sardār: First Preliminary Report'. *EW* 19: 109–24. (1180)

Taddei, Maurizio. 1969b. 'IsMEO Activities'. *EW* 19: 544–9. (470, 1180)

Taddei, Maurizio. 1970a. 'Results of a New Excavation in Tapa-i Sardar'. *Afghanistan*, 23/3: 85–7. (1180)

Taddei, Maurizio. 1970b. 'Inscribed Clay Tablets and Miniature Stūpas from Ghazni'. *EW* 20: 70–86. Reprinted in *Afghanistan*, 26/2: 21–50. (385)

Taddei, Maurizio. 1970c. 'IsMEO Activities'. *EW* 20: 508–17. (1180)

Taddei, Maurizio. 1971. 'IsMEO Activities'. *EW* 21: 42. (1180)

Taddei, Maurizio. 1972a. 'IsMEO Activities: Archaeological Mission in Afghanistan'. *EW* 22: 379–84. (1180)

Taddei, Maurizio. 1972b. 'Problemi di storia dell'arte e ricerca archeologica. II'. *Veltro, rivista della civiltà italiana*, 16: 549–61. (18, 332, 404, 1180)

Taddei, Maurizio. 1973. 'The Mahisamardini Image from Tapa Sardar, Ghazni, Afghanistan'. In *South Asian Archaeology*. Ed. N. Hammond, 203–13. London. (1180)

Taddei, Maurizio. 1974a. 'A Note on the Parinirvāna Buddha at Tapa Sardar'. In *South Asian Archaeology 1973*. Ed. J. E. Van Lohuizen-de Leeuw and J. M. M. Ubaghs, 111–15. Leiden. (1180)

Taddei, Maurizio. 1974b. 'Archaeological Mission in Afghanistan'. *EW* 24: 478. (434, 1025, 1180)

Taddei, Maurizio. 1974c. 'Appunti sull'iconografia di alcune manifestazioni luminose dei Buddha'. In *Gururājamanjarikā: Studi in onore de Guiseppe Tucci*, II. 435–49. Naples. (1088)

Taddei, Maurizio. 1975. 'Archaeological Mission in Afghanistan'. *EW* 25: 544–6. (117, 303, 431, 434, 671, 758, 985, 1180, 1184)

Taddei, Maurizio. 1976. 'Archaeological Mission in Afghanistan'. *EW* 26: 599–601. (292, 345, 769, 902, 1066, 1110, 1180, 1190)

Taddei, Maurizio. 1978a. 'Il santuario buddhistica di Tapa Sardâr'. *Un decennio di scoperte archeologiche*, I. 575–89. Rome. (434, 985, 1180)

Taddei, Maurizio. 1978b. 'Il santuario buddhistico di Tapa Sardar, Afghanistan'. *La ricerca scientifica*, 100: 575–89. (434, 985, 1180)

Taddei, Maurizio. 1979a. 'A Note on the Barrow Cemetery at Kandahar'. In *South Asian Archaeology*. Ed. M. Taddei, 909–16. Naples. (522)

Taddei, Maurizio. 1979b. 'Meditation on Death in Gandharan Art'. Paper presented at the 2nd International Congress of Kushan Studies, Kabul. (404)

Taddei, Maurizio, ed. 1979c. *South Asian Archaeology 1977: Papers from the Fourth International Conference of the association of South Asian Archaeologists in Western Europe*. 2 vols. Naples.

Taddei, Maurizio. 1999. 'Chronological Problems Connected with Buddhist Unbaked-Clay Sculpture'. *CAC* I. 391–7. Vienna. (1180)

Taddei, Maurizio, and Giovanni Verardi. 1978. 'Tapa Sardâr: Second Preliminary Report'. *EW* 28: 33–136. (1180)

Taddei, Maurizio, and Giovanni Verardi. 1981a. 'Buddhistische Plastik in Tepe Sardar be Ghazna'. *Das Altertum*, 27/3: 167–76.

Taddei, Maurizio, and Giovanni Verardi. 1981b. 'Tapa-Sardâru no bukkyô chôkuko'. *Bukkyô Geijutsu*, 138: 11–22.

Taddei, Maurizio, and Giovanni Verardi. 1985. 'La missione Archeologica Italiana in Afghanistan 1976–1979'. In *Scavi ee ricerche Archeologiche degli anni 1976–1979*, 273–301. Rome.

Takahama, Shu. 1981. 'An Ordos Plaque from Bactria'. *Bull. of the Anc. Orient Mus.* (Tokyo), 111: 63–8.

Talbot Rice, Tamara. 1965. *Ancient Arts of Central Asia*. London. (100, 122, 305, 332, 508, 930, 1123, 1173)

Talbot, M. G., P. J. Maitland, and W. Simpson. 1886. 'The Rock-Cut Caves and Statues of Bāmiyān'. *JRAS* 18: 323–50. (100, 189, 239, 425, 485, 845, 997, 1039, 1135, 1144)

Tanabe, Katsumi. 1973. 'Kapisi-koku shutsodo no Bukkyō chōkuku no seisaku nendai ni tsuite' (On the Date of the Buddhist Sculptures excavated in Kapisa). *Orient*, 15/2: 87–121. Summary in H. Motamedi 1975c: 258–9. (122)

Tanabe, Katsumi. 2008. *Gandharan Art from the Hirayama Collection*. Tokyo. (2230)

Taniguchi, Yoko. 2007. 'Issues of Conservation for the Bamiyan Buddhist Paintings'. In *Mural Painting of the Silk Road: Cultural Exchanges between East and West*. Ed. Kazuya Yamauchi, Yoko Taniguchi, and Tomoko Uno, 144–51. London. (100)

Tarzi, Nadia. 2006. 'Tarzi on Tarzi: Afghanistan's Plight and the Search for the Third Buddha'. In *Art and Archaeology of Afghanistan: Its Fall and Survival*. Ed. J. Van Krieken-Pieters, 145–54. Leiden. (100)

Tarzi, Zemaryalai. 1973. 'Les vases d'abondance de la grotte I de Bamiyan'. *Afghanistan*, 26/2: 15–20. (100)

Tarzi, Zemaryalai. 1975. 'Fondukistan Excavations'. *Afghanistan*, 28/2: 1–7. (332)

Tarzi, Zemaryalai. 1976a. 'Hadda à la lumière des trois dernières campagnes de fouilles de Tapa-é Shotor (1974–1976)'. *CRAI* 381–410. Translated as: 'Hadda After the Last Three Seasons of Excavation at Tepe Shotor (1974–1976)'. *Afghanistan*, 32/2 (1979): 60–89. (404)

Tarzi, Zemaryalai. 1976b. 'Discovery of the First Buddhist Meditation Grotto in Afghanistan'. *Āryānā* (Autumn): 22–4. (404)

Tarzi, Zemaryalai. 1976–7. 'Three Significant Niches: Explanatory Notes on Hadda'. *Āryānā* (Winter–Spring): 27–9. (404)

Tarzi, Zemaryalai. 1977a. *L'architecture et le décor rupestre des grottes de Bamiyan*, I. *Texte*; II. *Planches*. Paris. (100, 330, 508)

Tarzi, Zemaryalai. 1977b. 'The Treasure of Begram'. *Āryānā* (Summer): 27–9. (122)

Tarzi, Zemaryalai. 1977c. 'Shotorak: Another Treasure'. *Āryānā* (Autumn): 28–9. (1088)

Tarzi, Zemaryalai. 1977d. 'The Old City of Kandahar'. *Aryana. Afghanistan Republic)* (Winter): 22–3. Reprinted in *Kabul Times* (7 Mar. 1978): 3. (522)

Tarzi, Zemaryalai. 1978. 'Yak prublim-i saka shinãsi iftali'. *Tahqiqãt-i Kūshānī*, 1: 10–26. (100)

Tarzi, Zemaryalaï. 2000. 'Mise au point sur quelques schistes "gréco-bouddhiques" d'Afghanistan'. *SRAA* 6: 83–96. (154, 773)

Tarzi, Zemaryalai. 2003. 'Bamiyan: Professor Tarzi's Survey and Excavation Archaeological Mission, 2003'. *The Silk Road* (Newsletter of the Silk Road Foundation), 1/2: 37–9. (100)

Tarzi, Zemaryalai. 2004. *Bamiyan, la valle des grand Bouddhas*. Paris. (100)

Tarzi, Zemaryalaï. 2012. 'Les fouilles strasbourgeoises de la mission Z. Tarzi à Bāmiyān (2002–2008)'. In *Auteur de Bāmiyān: De la Bactriane hellénisée à l'Inde bouddhique*. Ed. G. Duccoeur, 27–207. Paris. (100, 508)

Tate, G. P. 1904. 'Coins and Seals Collected in Seistan, 1903–4'. *JRAS* 663–72. (190, 486, 1006)

Tate, G. P. 1909. *The Frontiers of Baluchistan*. London. (225, 383, 700, 721, 752, 792, 842, 849, 857, 881, 1006, 1147)

Tate, G. P. 1910. *Seistan: A Memoir on the History, Topography, Ruins and People of the Country*. Calcutta. (144, 190, 197, 201, 225, 229, 363, 376, 383, 394, 443, 479, 558, 561, 607, 638, 656, 684, 714, 715, 752, 788, 792, 824, 836, 842, 844, 858, 861, 871, 883, 896, 1006, 1010, 1044, 1147, 1238, 1264, 1269, 2061, 2182)

Thapar, B. K., ed. 1979. 'Preservation of Buddhist Shrines at Bamiyan, Afghanistan'. *Indian Archaeology* (1973–4): 84–5. (100)

Thomalsky, Judith, Bernt Bräutigam, Mehmet Karaucak, and Steffen Kraus. 2013. 'Early Mining and Metal Production in Afghanistan: The First Year of Investigations'. *AMI* 45: 199–230. (19, 256, 335, 686, 743, 1089)

Thomas, David C. 2004a. 'Excavations at Jam, Afghanistan'. *EW* 54: 87–119. (468)

Thomas, David C. 2004b. 'Looting, Heritage Management and Archaeological Strategies at Jam, Afghanistan'. *Culture without Context*, 14: 16–20. (468)

Thomas, David C. 2007. 'Firuzkuh: The Summer Capital of the Ghurids'. In *Cities in the Pre-Modern Islamic World*. Ed. A. K. Bennison and A. L. Gascoigne, 115–44. London. (468)

Thomas, David C. 2015. 'Google Earth™ @ Ghazni'. In *Asian Horizons: Giuseppe Tucci's Buddhist, Indian, Himalayan and Central Asian Studies*. Ed. A. A. di Castro and D. Templeman, 495–528. Melbourne. (71, 102, 103, 104, 303, 356, 358, 385, 461, 470, 636, 805, 907, 1140, 1171, 1180)

Thomas, David C., et al. 2006. 'Environmental Evidence from the Minaret of Jam Archaeological Project, Afghanistan'. *Iran*, 64: 253–76. (468)

Thomas, David C., and Alison L. Gascoigne. 2006. 'Recent Archaeological Investigations of Looting around the Minaret of Jam, Ghur Province'. In *Art and Archaeology of Afghanistan: Its Fall and Survival*. Ed. J. Van Krieken-Pieters, 155–67. Leiden. (468)

Thomas, David C., and Fiona J. Kidd. 2017. 'On the Margins: Enduring Pre-Modern Water Management Strategies in and around the Registan Desert, Afghanistan'. *Journal of Field Archaeology*, 42/1: 29–42. (848)

Thomas, David C., Fiona J. Kidd, Suzanna Nikolovski, and Claudia Zipfel. 2008. 'The Archaeological Sites of Afghanistan in Google Earth'. *AARG News* (The newsletter of the Aerial Archaeology Research Group), 37: 20–30. (848)

Thomas, David C., G. Pastori, and I. Cucco. 2005. 'Excavations at Jam, Afghanistan'. *EW* 87–119. (468)

Thomas, David C., Ustād Sayid 'Umar, Faisal Ahmad, and David Smith. 2014. 'The Rediscovery of the "Lost" Minaret of Qal'a-i Zārmurgh, Sāghar, Afghanistan'. *Iran*, 52: 133–42. (974)

Thomas, Edward. 1863. 'The Bactrian Alphabet'. *NC* NS 3: 225–35. (127, 404, 1229)

Thomas, F. W. 1915. 'A Kharoshthī Inscription'. *JRAS* 91–6. (404).

Thompson, G. W. 1964. *The Oxford University Expedition to Afghanistan*. Oxford. (73, 273, 338, 449, 1001, 1072)

Thoraval, Joël. 1980. 'Campagne de fouilles 1978 à Aï Khanoum. V. Le palais: sondages sur la cour sud'. *BEFEO* 68: 44–5. (18)

Thornton, Charles. 1963. 'Identification of Certain Stones Found in Various Levels'. In *Deh Morasi Ghundai*. Ed. Louis Dupree, 124–5. New York. (287)

Time. 1979. 'Gleaming Trove of Afghan Gold: Uncovering a Dark Epoch in Ancient Melting Pot's Past'. (2 July): 46–7. Reprinted in *Afghanistan*, 32/2: 10–20. (1192)

Tirard-Collet, O. 1998. 'After the War: The Condition of Historical Buildings and Monuments in Herat, Afghanistan'. *Iran*, 36: 123–38. (428)

Tissot, Francine. 1976. 'In Search of Alexander'. *Orientations*, 7/2: 30–9. (404)

Tissot, Francine. 1980 (1359). 'Maujūdit-i kūchīhā-yi kūshānā dar Gandhāra'. *Tahqiqāt-i Kūshānī*, 3/2: 42–7. (1088)

Tissot, Francine. 2006. *Catalogue of the National Museum of Afghanistan 1931–1985*. Paris. (18, 46, 100, 122, 154, 169, 172, 256, 295, 332, 358, 404, 483, 508, 518, 522, 546, 555, 582, 622, 630, 685, 689, 697, 723, 743, 773, 790, 832, 928, 1069, 1088, 1123, 1160, 1168, 1173, 1185, 2138)

Tissot, Francine, et al. 2003. 'Le Bouddhisme en Afghanistan'. In *De l'Indus à l'Oxus*. Ed. O. Bopearachchi et al., 281–304. Lattes. (404)

Tissot, Francine, and Dominique Darbois. 2002. *Kaboul. Le Passé Confisqué. Trésors du musée de Kaboul 1931–1965*. Paris. (100, 122, 332, 404, 508, 518, 790, 1088, 1123, 1168, 1173)

Torrens, H. 1840. 'Note on Bameean Coins'. *JASB* 9: 70–5. (100)

Torrens, H. 1842. 'On a Cylindar and Certain Gems, Collected in the Neighbourhood of Herat, by Major Pottinger'. *JASB* 11: 316–21. (428)

Tosi, Maurizio. 1974a. 'The Lapis Trade across the Iranian Plateau in the 3rd Millennium'. *Gururajamanjarika: Studi in Onore di Giuseppe Tucci*, 3–22. Naples.

Tosi, Maurizio. 1974b. 'The North-Eastern Frontier of the Ancient Near East'. *Mesopotamia*, 8–9: 21–77.

Tosi, Maurizio. 1977. 'The Archaeological Evidence for Protostate Structures in Eastern Iran and Central Asia at the End of the 3rd Millenium BC'. In *Le plateau iranien et l'Asie Centrale des origins à la conquête islamique*. Colloques Internationaux du CNRS 567. Ed. J. Deshayes, 45–65. Paris. (743)

Tosi, Maurizio. 1979. 'The Proto-Urban Cultures of Eastern Iran and the Indus Civilization'. In *South Asian Archaeology*. Ed. M. Taddei, 149–72. Naples. (743)

Tosi, Maurizio, and Rauf Wardak. 1972. 'The Fullol Hoard: A New Find from Bronze Age Afghanistan'. *EW* 22: 9–17. Reprinted in *Afghanistan*, 26/1 (1973): 13–33. (582)

Trebeck, George. 1834. 'The Topes near Jelalabad'. *JASB* 3: 574–6. (283)

Trinkler, Emil. 1928. *Through the Herat of Afghanistan*. London. (195, 428)

Trousdale, William. 1964. 'A Chinese Handle-Bearing Mirror from Northern Afghanistan'. *Afghanistan*, 19/4: 27–38. (400)

Trousdale, William. 1965a. 'The Minaret of Jam, a Ghorid Monument in Afghanistan'. *Archaeology*, 18/2: 102–8. (468)

Trousdale, William. 1965b. 'Rock-Engravings from the Tang-i Tizao in Central Afghanistan'. *EW* 15/3–4: 201–10. (1145)

Trousdale, William. 1968. 'An Achaemenian Stone Weight from Afghanistan'. *EW* 18: 277–80. (149)

Trousdale, William. 1975. *The Long Sword and Scabbard Slide in Asia*. Washington, DC. (100, 404, 546, 1088, 1123)

Trousdale, William. 1976a. 'The Helmand-Sistan Project in South-Western Afghanistan'. In *Actes du XXIX Congrès international des Orientalistes, Paris, Juillet 1973*. Asie Centrale, 57–61. Paris. (554, 597, 881, 1006, 1107)

Trousdale, William. 1976b. 'The Homeland of Rustam'. *Afghanistan*, 29/2: 64–71. (1006)

Tsuchiya, Haruka. 2000. 'An Iconographic Study of the Buddhist Art of Shotorak, Paitāva and Kham Zargar'. *SRAA* 6: 97–114. (622, 790, 1088)

Tucci, Giuseppe. 1958. 'Preliminary Report on an Archaeological Survey in Swat'. *EW* 9: 277–80. (337)

Tucci, Giuseppe. 1968. 'The Syncretic Image of Mazar-i Sharif'. *EW* 18: 293–4. (1009)

Tucci, Guiseppe. 1939. 'Nuove scoperte archeologiche nell'Afghanistan e l'arte del Gandhara'. *Asiatica* (Bolletino dell'IsMEO), 18/6: 497–503. (122)

UNESCO. 1980. 'Mīnār-i Jām'. *Bāstān Shināsi Afghānistān*, 2/2: 53–4. (468)

Urban. See Franke.

Ushikawa, Yoshiyuki. 1972. 'Photogrammetrical Survey'. In *Archaeological Survey of Kyoto University in Afghanistan 1970*. Ed. T. Higuchi, 23. Kyoto. (100, 651)

Vainberg, B. I., and Irina T. Kruglikova. 1976. 'Monetiye nakhodki iz raskopok Dilberdzhina'. In *Drevnyaya Baktriya*, 1. Ed. I. T. Kruglikova, 172–82. Moscow. (295)

Vambery, Arminius. 1864. *Travels in Central Asia*. London. (99, 235, 346, 610)

Van Krieken-Pieters, Juliette, ed. 2006. *Art and Archaeology of Afghanistan: Its Fall and Survival*. Leiden.

Van Lohuizen-de Leeuw, J. E. 1949. *The Scythian Period*. Leiden. (127, 404, 1088)

Van Lohuizen-de Leeuw, J. E. 1959. 'An Ancient Hindu Temple in Eastern Afghanistan'. *Oriental Art*, NS 5: 61–9. (154)

Van Lohuizen-de Leeuw, J. E., and J. M. M. Ubaghs, eds. 1974. *South Asian Archaeology 1973*. Leiden.

Ventrone, G. 1996. 'Un ricordo "special"'. In *Un ricordo che non si spegne*, 563–7. Naples.

Verardi, Giovanni. 1975. 'Notes on Afghan Archaeology, I. A Gandharan Relief from Qarabāgh-i Ghazni'. *EW* 25: 287–90. Reprinted in *Afghanistan*, 30/1 (1977): 57–66. (470)

Verardi, Giovanni. 1977a. 'Report on a Visit to Some Rock-Cut Monasteries in the Province of Ghazni'. *EW* 27: 129–50. (97, 117, 125, 168, 343, 353, 431, 434, 501, 623, 671, 758, 902, 907, 985, 1025, 1053, 1066, 1096, 1140, 1167, 1184, 1190)

Verardi, Giovanni. 1977b. 'Notes on Afghan Archaeology, II. Ganeśa Seated on Lion: A New Shāhi Marble'. *EW* 27: 277–83.

Verardi, Giovanni. 1977c. 'Buddhist Cave Complex at Homay Qala'. In *South Asian Archaeology*. Ed. J. E. Van Lohuizen-de Leeuw, 119–26. Leiden. (71, 434, 461, 1203)

Verardi, Giovanni. 1981. 'Un 'ipotesi sulla decorazione di una grotta del Jâghûri'. *Annali*, 41: 263–70.

Verardi, Giovanni. 1984. 'Gandharan Imagery at Tapa Sardar'. *South Asian Archaeology 1981*. Ed. B. and F. R. Allchin. New Delhi. (1180)

Verardi, Giovanni. 2007. 'The Archaeological Perspective'. In *Afghanistan: How Much of the Past in the New Future*. Ed. Giandomenico Picco and Antonio Luigi Palmisano. 221–54. Gorizia. (565)

Verardi, Giovanni. 2010. 'Issues in the Excavation, Chronology and Monuments of Tapa Sardar'. *CAC* II. 341–55. Vienna. (1180)

Verardi, Giovanni, and Elio Paparatti. 2004. *Buddhist Caves of Jāghūri and Qarabāgh-e Ghaznī Afghanistan*. Rome. (71, 97, 117, 125, 265, 292, 343, 353, 434, 746, 758, 902, 907, 985, 1025, 1066, 1096, 1110, 1180, 1184, 1190, 2242)

Vercellin, Giorgio. 1972. 'Appunti su Firuzkuh e Shahr-e Dāvar'. *Annali di Ca' Foscari*, 14/3 (Serie Orientale, 16): 375–84. (291, 1047)

Vercellin, Giorgio. 1974. 'Šindand: Le vicende di un toponimo afghano'. *Annali di Ca' Foscari*, 13/3 (Serie Orientale, 5): 99–107. (1079)

Vercellin, Giorgio. 1976a. 'Sulla voce "Fīrūzkūh" in E.I.'. *Rivista degli Studi Orientali*, 50/3–4: 319–28. (468)

Vercellin, Giorgio. 1976b. 'The Identification of Firuzkuh: A Conclusive Proof'. *EW* 26: 337–40. (468)

Vercellin, Giorgio. 1976c. 'Firuz, Firuzkuh, Firuzkuhi'. *Annali di Ca' Foscari*, 15/3 (Serie Orientale, 7): 75–85.

Vercellin, Giorgio. 1980. 'Un santuario timuride mancato'. *Atti del III Convegno Internazionale sull'Arte e sull Civiltà Islamica*, 43–50. Venice.

Veuve, Serge. 1974. 'La céramique de Kohna Masdjid (Afghanistan)'. Unpublished thesis, University of Bordeaux. (630)

Veuve, Serge. 1982. 'Cadrans solaire gréco-bactriens à Aï Khanoum (Afghanistan)'. *Bull. de Corr. Hellénique*, 106/2: 23–51. (18)

Veuve, Serge. 1987. *Fouilles d'Aï Khanoum VI. Le Gymnase. Architecture, céramique, sculpture*. MDAFA 30. Paris. (18)

Veuve, Serge, and Jean-Claude Liger. 1976. 'Fouilles d'Aï Khanoum: Campagne de 1974. III. Le gymnase'. *BEFEO* 63: 40–5. (18)

Veuve, Serge, and Jean-Claude Liger. 1980. 'Campagne de fouilles 1978 à Aï Khanoum. I. Le gymnase'. *BEFEO* 68: 5–6. (18)

Veuve, Serge, Jean-Claude Liger, and Régis de Valence. 1980. 'Campagne de fouilles 1978 à Aï Khanoum. VI. Bâtiment public en vordure de la route principale'. *BEFEO* 68: 46–50. (18)

Vidale, M. 2017. *Treasures from the Oxus: The Art and Civilization of Central Asia*. London and New York. (582)

Vigne, G. T. 1837. 'Some Account of the Valley of Kashmir, Ghazni, and Kabul'. *JASB* 6: 766–77. (103, 122, 358)

Vigne, G. T. 1840. *A Personal Narrative of a Visit to Ghuzni, Kabul, and Afghanistan*. London. (103, 358, 418, 1229, 1270)

Vincent, Robert K. 1979. 'The Lost Kingdom of Tamerlane'. *Sunday Times Magazine* (18 Nov.): 52–61. (1006)

Vinogradov, A. V. 1979. 'Issledovaniya pamyatnikov kammenogo veka v Severnom Afganistane'. In *Drevnyaya Baktriya*, 2. Ed. I. T. Kruglikova, 7–62. Moscow. (110, 181, 202, 203, 204, 408, 452, 473, 540, 589, 590, 609, 905, 906, 910, 912, 939, 965, 982, 999, 1012, 1056, 1101, 1149, 1209)

Vogel, J. P. 1911. *Antiquities of Chamba State*. Memoirs of the Archaeological Survey of India, 36. Calcutta. (464)

Vogel, J. P. 1939. 'Explorations by the French Mission in Afghanistan'. *ABIA* 1937/12: 30–4. (122, 332)

Vogelsang, W. J. 1992. *The Rise and Organisation of the Achaemenid Empire: The Eastern Iranian Evidence*. Leiden. (522, 752)

Vogelsang, Willem. 2002. *The Afghans*. Oxford.

Vogelsang. See also Bleaney.

Vondrovec, Klaus. 2007. 'Coins from Gharwal (Afghanistan)'. *BAI* 17: 159–75. (2077)

Vondrovec, Klaus. 2008. 'Numismatic Evidence of the Alchon Huns Reconsidered'. *Beiträge zur Ur- und Frühgeschichte Mitteleuropas*, 50: 25–56. (1142)

Vorobieva-Desyatovskaya, M. I. 1976. 'Nadpis brakhmi iz Dilberdzhina'. In *Drevnyaya Baktriya*, 2. Ed. I. T. Kruglikova, 170–1. Moscow. (295)

Wāla, Farīd. 1980. 'Dīg-i buzurg-i Masjid-i Jāma'. *Herāt-i Bāstān*, 1/2: 47–9. (428)

Wannell, Bruce. 2002 'Echoes in a Landscape: Western Afghanistan in 1989'. In *Cairo to Kabul: Afghan and Islamic Studies Presented to Ralph Pinder-Wilson*. Ed. Warwick Ball and Leonard Harrow, 236–47. London. (349, 683, 742, 775, 947, 961, 987, 1023, 1033, 1144, 1239, 2064)

Wheeler, R. E. Mortimer. 1947. 'Archaeology in Afghanistan'. *Antiquity*, 21/82: 57–65. Reprint of: *Report of the Indian Cultural Mission to Afghanistan, 1946*. ASI Reports. Delhi. (29, 42, 99, 483, 522, 707, 744, 776, 800, 930, 931, 1056, 1160)

Wheeler, R. E. Mortimer. 1949. 'Romano-Buddhist Art: An Old Problem Restated'. *Antiquity*, 23: 4–19. (122, 404)

Wheeler, R. E. Mortimer. 1951. 'Roman Contact with India, Pakistan and Afghanistan'. In *Aspects of Archaeology: Essays Presented to O. G. S. Crawford*. Ed. W. F. Grimes, 354–81. London.

Wheeler, R. E. Mortimer. 1954. *Archaeology from the Earth*. Oxford. (99)

Wheeler, R. E. Mortimer. 1955. *Rome Beyond the Imperial Frontiers*. London. (122)

Wheeler, R. E. Mortimer. 1963. 'Gandharan Art: A Note on the Present Position'. *Le rayonnement des civilisations grecques et romaines sur les cultures périphériques. 8ème Congrès Int. d'Archéol. Classique*. Paris.

Wheeler, R. E. Mortimer. 1968. *Flames over Persepolis*. London. (18, 122, 522)

Whitehead, R. B. 1923. 'Notes on Indo-Greek Numismatics'. *NC* 5th ser. 3: 294–43. (483)

Whitehead, R. B. 1940–50. 'Notes on the Indo-Greeks'. *NC* 5th ser. 20: 89–122; 6th ser. 7: 29–51; 10: 206–32. (122)

Whitehouse, David. 1976. 'The Barrow Cemetery at Kandahar'. *Annali dell'Instituto Orientale di Napoli*, 36: 473–88. (522)

Whitehouse, David. 1978. 'Excavations at Kandahar 1974: First Interim Report'. *Afghan Studies*, 1: 9–39. (522, 988, 1048)

Whitehouse, David. 1989a. 'Begram Reconsidered'. *Kölner Jahrbuch für Vor- und Frühgeschichte*, 22: 151–7. (122)

Whitehouse, David. 1989b. 'Begram, the Periplus and Gandharan Art'. *Journal of Roman Archaeology*, 2: 93–100. (122)

Whitehouse, David. 1991. 'Begram: The Glass'. *Topoi*, 11: 437–49. (122)

Whitehouse, David. 2012. 'The Glass from Begram'. In *Afghanistan: Forging Civilizations along the Silk Road*. Ed. Joan Aruz and Elisabetta Valtz Fino, 54–63. New York. (122)

Wier. 1893. 'Journey with and after the Afghan Boundary Commission'. Unpublished papers in the India Office Library and Records. (428)

Wightman, G. J. 2007. *Sacred Spaces: Religious Architecture in the Ancient World*. Leuven. (18, 389, 1123)

Wilber, Donald N. 1937. 'The Institute's Survey of Persian Architecture: Preliminary Report on the Eighth Season of the Survey'. *BAIPAA* 5/2: 109–36. (346, 428)

Wilber, Donald N. 1968. *Annotated Bibliography of Afghanistan*. 3rd edn. New Haven.

Wilber. See also Golombek.

Wilson, H. H. 1841. *Ariana Antiqua: A Descriptive Account of the Antiquities and Coins of Afghanistan*. London. (121, 122, 127, 471, 855, 1116, 1125)

Wolfe, Nancy Hatch. 1966. *Herat: A Pictorial Guide*. Kabul. (66, 346, 428, 819, 1263)

Wolski, J. 1982. 'Le problème de la fondation de l'état gréco-bactrien'. *St.Ir.* 17: 131–46.

Wood, John. 1872. *Journey to the Source of the Oxus*. London. (18, 315, 531, 650, 730, 931, 1001, 1052, 1261)

Woodburn, C. W. 2009. *The Bala Hissar of Kabul: Revealing a Fortress-Palace in Afghanistan*. The Institution of Royal Engineers Professional Paper, 1. Chatham, Kent. (483)

Yamada, Meiji. 1972. 'Skandar Inscription of the Umā Maheśvara Image'. In *Archaeological Survey of Kyoto University in Afghanistan 1970*. Ed. T. Higuchi, 15–22. Kyoto. (1064, 1185)

Yate, A. C. 1887. *England and Russia Face to Face: Travels with the Afghan Boundary Commission*. Edinburgh and London. (98, 391, 394, 482, 610, 634, 684, 711, 752, 842, 863, 870, 908, 1006, 1060, 1083, 1196, 1265)

Yate, C. E. 1885. 'Letter to Sir West Ridgway'. (Enclosure No. 4 dated 5 Aug. 1885. Political and Secret Letters from India, vol. 46: 2–16, 102.) (428)

Yate, C. E. 1887. 'Notes on the City of Hirat'. *JASB* 56: 84–106. (98, 346, 428)

Yate, C. E. 1888. *Northern Afghanistan, or Letters from the Afghan Boundary Commission*. Edinburgh and London. (35, 41, 63, 99, 191, 279, 298, 322, 327, 346, 391, 428, 454, 541, 542, 589, 628, 634, 711, 716, 764, 776, 819, 850, 890, 947, 949, 1018, 1043, 1099, 1134, 1135, 1147, 1165, 1206, 1216, 2253)

Yate, C. E. 1900. *Khorasan and Sistan*. London. (318, 383, 393, 841, 874, 1046, 1079, 1115, 1147)

Yate, C. E. 1926. 'Inscriptions Formerly in the Musalla of Herat'. *JRAS* 290–4. (428)

Yavorski, J. L. 1885. *Journey of the Russian Embassy through Afghanistan and the Khanate of Bukhara in 1878–1879*. 2 vols. Calcutta. Abridged and translated by E. R. Elles and W. E. Gowan from *Puteshestvije Russkago Posolstva po Afganistanu i Bukharskomu Khanstvu v 1878–1898*. St Petersburg, 1882. (21, 100, 118, 493, 628, 739, 833, 862, 867, 918, 1038, 1042, 1052)

Yoshikawa, Itsuji. 1941. 'Art and Archaeology in Afghanistan'. *Bulletin of Eastern Art* (Tokyo), 16: 3–19. Summary in H. Motamedi 1975c: 225–6. (100, 122, 404)

Yoshikawa, Itsuji. 1944. 'Afghanistan ni okeru Furansukoko Hakendan no Hakkutsu Jigyō' (French Archaeological Delegation to Afghanistan; its Excavations and Achievements). *Nichifutsu Bunka*, 10: 100–41. Summary in H. Motamedi 1975c: 227–30. (100, 122, 332, 404, 546, 1088)

Yoshikawa, Itsuji. 1949. 'Shotoraku no Hakkutsu' (Excavations at Shotorak). *Bukkyo Geijutsu*, 5: 68–78. Summary in H. Motamedi 1975c: 262. (1088)

Yoshikawa, Itsuji. 1964. 'Bamiyan'. In *Afuganistan Kodai Bijutsu: Ancient Art of Afghanistan*. Ed. S. Mizuno, 227–34. Tokyo. (100)

Yoshikawa, Itsuji. 1976. 'Memories of Bamiyan'. In *Bamiyan: Crossroads of Culture*. Ed. A. Miyaji, 31–5. Tokyo. (100)

Young, Rodney S. 1954. 'Afghanistan Reconnaissance'. *Archaeology*, 7/1: 51–2. (99, 1160)

Young, Rodney S. 1955. 'The South Wall of Balkh-Bactra'. *AJA* 59: 11–34. (99)

Zafar, Mahila Fazel, ed. 1973. 'News. Ancient Finds in the Hills of Pachirwagan'. *Afghanistan*, 26/2: 101. (782)

Zafar, Mahila Fazel, ed. 1979. 'News. Unique Golden Relics Unearthed in Tela Tapa'. *Afghanistan*, 31/4: 99–104. (1192)

Zāhir. 1980. 'Tahqiqāt wa bararasi-yi mukhtasar-i asr-i kuhan-i sangi dar Afghānistān'. *Bāstān Shināsi Afghānistān*, 3/1: 30–5. (46, 244, 245, 266, 352, 526, 635, 1101)

Zander, Giuseppe. 1972. 'L'IsMEO e i restauri di monumenti. II Veltro'. *Rivista della civilta italiana*, 16: 563–78. (100, 358, 468)

Zaryab, Azam Rahnaward, ed. 1974a. 'New Excavations Reveal More Cultural Riches in Afghanistan'. *Āryānā. Afghanistan Republic*, 4 (July): 62–3. (404)

Zaryab, Azam Rahnaward, ed. 1974b. 'Seven Groups of Experts Study Afghanistan's Past'. *Āryānā. Afghanistan Republic*, Special Issue: 10–12. (295, 323, 1006, 1180, 1185)

Zaryab, Azam Rahnaward, ed. 1976. 'Bamiyan, and Where is the Sleeping Buddha?' *Āryānā. Afghanistan Republic* (Summer): 30–3. (100)

Zestovski, P. I. 1948. 'Esquisses architecturales de l'Afghanistan: Vallée de Bamiyan'. *Afghanistan*, 3/2: 39–62. (100, 508, 786, 1052)

Zestovski, P. I. 1949. 'Esquisses d'architecture afghane: Herat-Kaboul-Herat'. *Afghanistan*, 4/3: 1–25. (428)

Zeymal, E. 1999. 'Tillya-Tepe within the Context of the Kuchan Chronology'. *CAC* I. 239–44. Vienna. (1192)

Zhang, Liangren. 2011. 'Chinese Lacquerwares from Begram: Date and Provenance'. *International Journal of Asian Studies*, 8/1: 1–24. (122)

Zhelninskaya, Z. M., T. I. Berlin, L. G. Druzhina, and V.P. Buri. 1979. 'Analizi krasok nastennikh rospisei Dilberdzhina'. In *Drevnyaya Baktriya*, 2. Ed. I. T. Kruglikova et al., 166–72. Moscow. (295)

Zhwandun. 1974. 'The Haji-i-Peyada Mosque: A Treasure in the "Mother of Cities"'. *Āryānā. Afghanistan Republic*, 1/2 (Jan.): 51–4. (410)

Zucker, F. 1959. 'Mitteilung über eine Kürlich Gefundene Griechisch-Aramäische Bilingue des Königs Aśoka'. *AAH* 7: 103–6. (522)

Zwalf, W. 1996. *A Catalogue of the Gandhāra Sculpture in the British Museum*. 2 vols. London.